Lecture Notes in Computer Science 11620

Commenced Publication in 1973
Founding and Former Series Editors:
Gerhard Goos, Juris Hartmanis, and Jan van Leeuwen

Editorial Board Members

David Hutchison
  Lancaster University, Lancaster, UK
Takeo Kanade
  Carnegie Mellon University, Pittsburgh, PA, USA
Josef Kittler
  University of Surrey, Guildford, UK
Jon M. Kleinberg
  Cornell University, Ithaca, NY, USA
Friedemann Mattern
  ETH Zurich, Zurich, Switzerland
John C. Mitchell
  Stanford University, Stanford, CA, USA
Moni Naor
  Weizmann Institute of Science, Rehovot, Israel
C. Pandu Rangan
  Indian Institute of Technology Madras, Chennai, India
Bernhard Steffen
  TU Dortmund University, Dortmund, Germany
Demetri Terzopoulos
  University of California, Los Angeles, CA, USA
Doug Tygar
  University of California, Berkeley, CA, USA

More information about this series at http://www.springer.com/series/7407

Sanjay Misra · Osvaldo Gervasi ·
Beniamino Murgante · Elena Stankova ·
Vladimir Korkhov · Carmelo Torre ·
Ana Maria A. C. Rocha ·
David Taniar · Bernady O. Apduhan ·
Eufemia Tarantino (Eds.)

Computational Science and Its Applications – ICCSA 2019

19th International Conference
Saint Petersburg, Russia, July 1–4, 2019
Proceedings, Part II

 Springer

Editors
Sanjay Misra (iD)
Covenant University
Ota, Nigeria

Beniamino Murgante (iD)
University of Basilicata
Potenza, Italy

Vladimir Korkhov (iD)
Saint Petersburg State University
Saint Petersburg, Russia

Ana Maria A. C. Rocha (iD)
University of Minho
Braga, Portugal

Bernady O. Apduhan
Kyushu Sangyo University
Fukuoka, Japan

Osvaldo Gervasi (iD)
University of Perugia
Perugia, Italy

Elena Stankova (iD)
Saint Petersburg State University
Saint Petersburg, Russia

Carmelo Torre (iD)
Polytechnic University of Bari
Bari, Italy

David Taniar (iD)
Monash University
Clayton, VIC, Australia

Eufemia Tarantino (iD)
Polytechnic University of Bari
Bari, Italy

ISSN 0302-9743   ISSN 1611-3349 (electronic)
Lecture Notes in Computer Science
ISBN 978-3-030-24295-4   ISBN 978-3-030-24296-1 (eBook)
https://doi.org/10.1007/978-3-030-24296-1

LNCS Sublibrary: SL1 – Theoretical Computer Science and General Issues

This Springer imprint is published by the registered company Springer Nature Switzerland AG
The registered company address is: Gewerbestrasse 11, 6330 Cham, Switzerland

Preface

These six volumes (LNCS volumes 11619–11624) consist of the peer-reviewed papers from the 2019 International Conference on Computational Science and Its Applications (ICCSA 2019) held in St. Petersburg, Russia during July 1–4, 2019, in collaboration with the St. Petersburg University, St. Petersburg, Russia.

ICCSA 2019 was a successful event in the International Conferences on Computational Science and Its Applications (ICCSA) series, previously held in Melbourne, Australia (2018), Trieste, Italy (2017), Beijing, China (2016), Banff, Canada (2015), Guimaraes, Portugal (2014), Ho Chi Minh City, Vietnam (2013), Salvador, Brazil (2012), Santander, Spain (2011), Fukuoka, Japan (2010), Suwon, South Korea (2009), Perugia, Italy (2008), Kuala Lumpur, Malaysia (2007), Glasgow, UK (2006), Singapore (2005), Assisi, Italy (2004), Montreal, Canada (2003), and (as ICCS) Amsterdam, The Netherlands (2002) and San Francisco, USA (2001).

Computational science is a main pillar of most of the current research, industrial and commercial activities, and plays a unique role in exploiting ICT innovative technologies. The ICCSA conference series have been providing a venue to researchers and industry practitioners to discuss new ideas, to share complex problems and their solutions, and to shape new trends in computational science.

Apart from the general track, ICCSA 2019 also included 33 workshops, in various areas of computational sciences, ranging from computational science technologies, to specific areas of computational sciences, such as software engineering, security, artificial intelligence, and blockchain technologies. We accepted 64 papers distributed in the five general tracks, 259 in workshops and ten short papers. We would like to show our appreciations to the workshop chairs and co-chairs.

The success of the ICCSA conference series, in general, and ICCSA 2019, in particular, is due to the support of many people: authors, presenters, participants, keynote speakers, workshop chairs, Organizing Committee members, student volunteers, Program Committee members, Advisory Committee members, international liaison chairs, reviewers and people in other various roles. We would like to thank them all.

We also thank our publisher, Springer, for accepting to publish the proceedings, for sponsoring part of the best papers awards and for their kind assistance and cooperation during the editing process.

We cordially invite you to visit the ICCSA website http://www.iccsa.org where you can find all relevant information about this interesting and exciting event.

July 2019

Osvaldo Gervasi
Beniamino Murgante
Sanjay Misra

Welcome to St. Petersburg

Welcome to St. Petersburg, the Venice of the North, the city of three revolutions, creation of czar Peter the Great, the most European city in Russia. ICCSA 2019 was hosted by St. Petersburg State University, during July 1–4, 2019.

St. Petersburg is the second largest city in Russia after Moscow. It is the former capital of Russia and has a lot of attractions related to this role in the past: imperial palaces and parks both in the city center and suburbs, respectable buildings of nobles and state institutions, multitude of rivers and canals with more than 300 bridges of various forms and sizes. Extraordinary history and rich cultural traditions of both imperial Russia and the Soviet Union attracted and inspired many examples of world's greatest architecture, literature, music, and visual art, some of which can be found in the famous Hermitage and State Russian Museum located in the heart of the city. Late June and early July is the season of white nights where the sun sets only for a few hours, and the nighttime is covered with mysterious twilight.

What to do in the city:

- Enjoy the white nights, see the open bridges during the night and cargo ships passing by from Ladoga Lake to the Gulf of Finland and back. Dvortsovy bridge is open at about 1am. Be sure to stay on the correct side of the river when the bridges open!
- Visit Hermitage (Winter palace) and State Russian Museum to see great examples of international and Russian art, and the Kunstkammer, the oldest museum of St. Petersburg founded by Peter the Great.
- Travel to St. Petersburg suburbs Peterhof and Tsarskoe Selo to see imperial palaces and splendid parks, famous Peterhof fountains.
- Eat Russian food: borsch (beetroot soup), pelmeni and vareniki (meat and sweet dumplings), bliny (pancakes), vinegret (beetroot salad), drink kvas and maybe some vodka.
- Walk around and inside the Peter and Paul Fortress, the place where the city began in 1703.
- Visit the Mariinsky Theater for famous Russian ballet and opera.
- Have a boat tour along the Neva River and canals to look at the city from the water.
- Walk along Nevsky Prospect, the main street of the city.
- Climb St. Isaac's Cathedral colonnade to enjoy great city views.
- Go down to the Metro, the city's underground train network with some Soviet-style museum-like stations.
- Pay a visit to the recently renovated Summer Garden, the oldest park of St. Petersburg.
- Visit a new modern open space on the New Holland Island to see modern art exhibitions, performances and just to relax and enjoy sitting on the grass with an ice cream or lemonade during a hot summer day.

St. Petersburg State University is the oldest university in Russia, an actively developing, world-class center of research and education. The university dates back to 1724, when Peter the Great founded the Academy of Sciences and Arts as well as the first Academic University and the university preparatory school in Russia. At present there are over 5,000 academic staff members and more than 30,000 students, receiving education in more than 400 educational programs at 25 faculties and institutes.

The venue of ICCSA is the Faculty of Economics located on Tavricheskaya Street, other faculties and university buildings are distributed all over the city with the main campus located on Vasilievsky Island and the natural science faculties (Mathematics and Mechanics, Applied Mathematics and Control Processes, Physics, Chemistry) located on the campus about 40 kilometers away from the city center in Peterhof.

Elena Stankova
Vladimir Korkhov
Nataliia Kulabukhova

Organization

ICCSA 2019 was organized by St. Petersburg University (Russia), University of Perugia (Italy), University of Basilicata (Italy), Monash University (Australia), Kyushu Sangyo University (Japan), University of Minho, (Portugal).

Honorary General Chairs

Antonio Laganà	University of Perugia, Italy
Norio Shiratori	Tohoku University, Japan
Kenneth C. J. Tan	Sardina Systems, Estonia

General Chairs

Osvaldo Gervasi	University of Perugia, Italy
Elena Stankova	St. Petersburg University, Russia
Bernady O. Apduhan	Kyushu Sangyo University, Japan

Program Committee Chairs

Beniamino Murgante	University of Basilicata, Italy
David Taniar	Monash University, Australia
Vladimir Korkov	St. Petersburg University, Russia
Ana Maria A. C. Rocha	University of Minho, Portugal

International Advisory Committee

Jemal Abawajy	Deakin University, Australia
Dharma P. Agarwal	University of Cincinnati, USA
Rajkumar Buyya	Melbourne University, Australia
Claudia Bauzer Medeiros	University of Campinas, Brazil
Manfred M. Fisher	Vienna University of Economics and Business, Austria
Marina L. Gavrilova	University of Calgary, Canada
Yee Leung	Chinese University of Hong Kong, SAR China

International Liaison Chairs

Ana Carla P. Bitencourt	Universidade Federal do Reconcavo da Bahia, Brazil
Giuseppe Borruso	University of Trieste, Italy
Alfredo Cuzzocrea	ICAR-CNR and University of Calabria, Italy
Maria Irene Falcão	University of Minho, Portugal
Robert C. H. Hsu	Chung Hua University, Taiwan
Tai-Hoon Kim	Hannam University, South Korea
Sanjay Misra	Covenant University, Nigeria

Takashi Naka   Kyushu Sangyo University, Japan
Rafael D. C. Santos   National Institute for Space Research, Brazil
Maribel Yasmina Santos   University of Minho, Portugal

Workshop and Session Organizing Chairs

Beniamino Murgante   University of Basilicata, Italy
Sanjay Misra   Covenant University, Nigeria
Jorge Gustavo Rocha   University of Minho, Portugal

Award Chair

Wenny Rahayu   La Trobe University, Australia

Publicity Committee Chairs

Elmer Dadios   De La Salle University, Philippines
Hong Quang Nguyen   International University (VNU-HCM), Vietnam
Daisuke Takahashi   Tsukuba University, Japan
Shangwang Wang   Beijing University of Posts and Telecommunications,
                                China

Workshop Organizers

Advanced Transport Tools and Methods (A2TM 2019)

Massimiliano Petri   University of Pisa, Italy
Antonio Pratelli   University of Pisa, Italy

Advanced Computational Approaches in Fractals, Wavelet, Entropy and Data Mining Applications (AAFTWTETDT 2019)

Yeliz Karaca   University of Massachusetts Medical School, USA
Yu-Dong Zhang   University of Leicester, UK
Majaz Moonis   University of Massachusettes Medical School, USA

Advances in Artificial Intelligence Learning Technologies: Blended Learning, STEM, Computational Thinking and Coding (AAILT 2019)

Alfredo Milani   University of Perugia, Italy
Sergio Tasso   University of Perugia, Italy
Valentina Poggioni   University of Perugia, Italy

Affective Computing and Emotion Recognition (ACER-EMORE 2019)

Alfredo Milani   University of Perugia, Italy
Valentina Franzoni   University of Perugia, Italy
Giulio Biondi   University of Florence, Itay

Advances in Information Systems and Technologies for Emergency Management, Risk Assessment and Mitigation Based on the Resilience Concepts (ASTER 2019)

Maurizio Pollino	ENEA, Italy
Marco Vona	University of Basilicata, Italy
Beniamino Murgante	University of Basilicata, Italy

Blockchain and Distributed Ledgers: Technologies and Application (BDLTA 2019)

Vladimir Korkhov	St. Petersburg State University, Russia
Elena Stankova	St. Petersburg State University, Russia

Bio and Neuro-inspired Computing and Applications (BIONCA 2019)

Nadia Nedjah	State University of Rio de Janeiro, Brazil
Luiza de Macedo Mourell	State University of Rio de Janeiro, Brazil

Computer Aided Modeling, Simulation, and Analysis (CAMSA 2018)

Jie Shen	University of Michigan, USA
Hao Chen	Shanghai University of Engineering Science, China
Youguo He	Jiangsu University, China

Computational and Applied Statistics (CAS 2019)

Ana Cristina Braga	University of Minho, Portugal

Computational Mathematics, Statistics, and Information Management (CMSIM 2019)

M. Filomena Teodoro	Portuguese Naval Academy and Lisbon University, Portugal

Computational Optimization and Applications (COA 2019)

Ana Maria Rocha	University of Minho, Portugal
Humberto Rocha	University of Coimbra, Portugal

Computational Astrochemistry (CompAstro 2019)

Marzio Rosi	University of Perugia, Italy
Dimitrios Skouteris	Master-up, Perugia, Italy
Fanny Vazart	Université Grenoble Alpes, France
Albert Rimola	Universitat Autònoma de Barcelona, Spain

Cities, Technologies, and Planning (CTP 2019)

Beniamino Murgante	University of Basilicata, Italy
Giuseppe Borruso	University of Trieste, Italy

Econometrics and Multidimensional Evaluation in the Urban Environment (EMEUE 2019)

Carmelo M. Torre	Polytechnic of Bari, Italy
Pierluigi Morano	Polytechnic of Bari, Italy
Maria Cerreta	University of Naples Federico II, Italy
Paola Perchinunno	University of Bari, Italy
Francesco Tajani	University of Rome La Sapienza, Italy

Future Computing System Technologies and Applications (FISTA 2019)

Bernady O. Apduhan	Kyushu Sangyo University, Japan
Rafael Santos	National Institute for Space Research, Brazil

Geographical Analysis, Urban Modeling, Spatial Statistics (GEO-AND-MOD 2019)

Beniamino Murgante	University of Basilicata, Italy
Giuseppe Borruso	University of Trieste, Italy
Hartmut Asche	University of Potsdam, Germany

Geomatics for Resource Monitoring and Control (GRMC 2019)

Eufemia Tarantino	Polytechnic of Bari, Italy
Rosa Lasaponara	Italian Research Council, IMAA-CNR, Italy
Benedetto Figorito	ARPA Puglia, Italy
Umberto Fratino	Polytechnic of Bari, Italy

International Symposium on Software Quality (ISSQ 2019)

Sanjay Misra	Covenant University, Nigeria

Land Use Monitoring for Sustainability (LUMS 2019)

Carmelo M. Torre	Polytechnic of Bari, Italy
Alessandro Bonifazi	Polytechnic of Bari, Italy
Pasquale Balena	Polytechnic of Bari, Italy
Beniamino Murgante	University of Basilicata, Italy
Eric Gielen	Polytechnic University of Valencia, Spain

Machine Learning for Space and Earth Observation Data (ML-SEOD 2019)

Rafael Santos	Brazilian National Institute for Space Research, Brazil
Karine Reis Ferreira	National Institute for Space Research, Brazil

Mobile-Computing, Sensing, and Actuation in Cyber Physical Systems (MSA4CPS 2019)

Saad Qaisar	National University of Sciences and Technology, Pakistan
Moonseong Kim	Seoul Theological University, South Korea

Quantum Chemical Modeling of Solids with Computers: From Plane Waves to Local Structures (QuaCheSol 2019)

Andrei Tchougréeff	Russia Academy of Sciences, Russia
Richard Dronskowski	RWTH Aachen University, Germany
Taku Onishi	Mie University and Tromsoe University, Japan

Scientific Computing Infrastructure (SCI 2019)

Vladimir Korkhov	St. Petersburg State University, Russia
Elena Stankova	St. Petersburg State University, Russia
Nataliia Kulabukhova	St. Petersburg State University, Russia

Computational Studies for Energy and Comfort in Building (SECoB 2019)

Senhorinha Teixeira	University of Minho, Portugal
Angela Silva	Viana do Castelo Polytechnic Institute, Portugal
Ana Maria Rocha	University of Minho, Portugal

Software Engineering Processes and Applications (SEPA 2019)

Sanjay Misra	Covenant University, Nigeria

Smart Factory Convergence (SFC 2019)

Jongpil Jeong	Sungkyunkwan University, South Korea

Smart City and Water. Resource and Risk (Smart_Water 2019)

Giuseppe Borruso	University of Trieste, Italy
Ginevra Balletto	University of Cagliari, Italy
Gianfranco Becciu	Polytechnic University of Milan, Italy
Chiara Garau	University of Cagliari, Italy
Beniamino Murgante	University of Basilicata, Italy
Francesco Viola	University of Cagliari, Italy

Sustainability Performance Assessment: Models, Approaches, and Applications Toward Interdisciplinary and Integrated Solutions (SPA 2019)

Francesco Scorza	University of Basilicata, Italy
Valentin Grecu	Lucia Blaga University on Sibiu, Romania
Jolanta Dvarioniene	Kaunas University, Lithuania
Sabrina Lai	University of Cagliari, Italy

Theoretical and Computational Chemistry and Its Applications (TCCMA 2019)

Noelia Faginas Lago	University of Perugia, Italy
Andrea Lombardi	University of Perugia, Italy

Tools and Techniques in Software Development Processes (TTSDP 2019)

Sanjay Misra	Covenant University, Nigeria

Virtual Reality and Applications (VRA 2019)

Osvaldo Gervasi	University of Perugia, Italy
Sergio Tasso	University of Perugia, Italy

Collective, Massive and Evolutionary Systems (WCES 2019)

Alfredo Milani	University of Perugia, Italy
Valentina Franzoni	University of Rome La Sapienza, Italy
Rajdeep Niyogi	Indian Institute of Technology at Roorkee, India
Stefano Marcugini	University of Perugia, Italy

Parallel and Distributed Data Mining (WPDM 2019)

Massimo Cafaro	University of Salento, Italy
Italo Epicoco	University of Salento, Italy
Marco Pulimeno	University of Salento, Italy
Giovanni Aloisio	University of Salento, Italy

Program Committee

Kenneth Adamson	University of Ulster, UK
Vera Afreixo	University of Aveiro, Portugal
Filipe Alvelos	University of Minho, Portugal
Remadevi Arjun	National Institute of Technology Karnataka, India
Hartmut Asche	University of Potsdam, Germany
Ginevra Balletto	University of Cagliari, Italy
Michela Bertolotto	University College Dublin, Ireland
Sandro Bimonte	CEMAGREF, TSCF, France
Rod Blais	University of Calgary, Canada
Ivan Blečić	University of Sassari, Italy
Giuseppe Borruso	University of Trieste, Italy
Ana Cristina Braga	University of Minho, Portugal
Massimo Cafaro	University of Salento, Italy
Yves Caniou	Lyon University, France
José A. Cardoso e Cunha	Universidade Nova de Lisboa, Portugal
Leocadio G. Casado	University of Almeria, Spain
Carlo Cattani	University of Salerno, Italy
Mete Celik	Erciyes University, Turkey
Hyunseung Choo	Sungkyunkwan University, South Korea
Min Young Chung	Sungkyunkwan University, South Korea
Florbela Maria da Cruz Domingues Correia	Polytechnic Institute of Viana do Castelo, Portugal
Gilberto Corso Pereira	Federal University of Bahia, Brazil
Alessandro Costantini	INFN, Italy
Carla Dal Sasso Freitas	Universidade Federal do Rio Grande do Sul, Brazil
Pradesh Debba	The Council for Scientific and Industrial Research (CSIR), South Africa
Hendrik Decker	Instituto Tecnológico de Informática, Spain

Jongchan Lee	Kunsan National University, South Korea
Chendong Li	University of Connecticut, USA
Gang Li	Deakin University, Australia
Fang Liu	AMES Laboratories, USA
Xin Liu	University of Calgary, Canada
Andrea Lombardi	University of Perugia, Italy
Savino Longo	University of Bari, Italy
Tinghuai Ma	NanJing University of Information Science and Technology, China
Ernesto Marcheggiani	Katholieke Universiteit Leuven, Belgium
Antonino Marvuglia	Research Centre Henri Tudor, Luxembourg
Nicola Masini	National Research Council, Italy
Eric Medvet	University of Trieste, Italy
Nirvana Meratnia	University of Twente, The Netherlands
Noelia Faginas Lago	University of Perugia, Italy
Giuseppe Modica	University of Reggio Calabria, Italy
Josè Luis Montaña	University of Cantabria, Spain
Maria Filipa Mourão	IP from Viana do Castelo, Portugal
Louiza de Macedo Mourelle	State University of Rio de Janeiro, Brazil
Nadia Nedjah	State University of Rio de Janeiro, Brazil
Laszlo Neumann	University of Girona, Spain
Kok-Leong Ong	Deakin University, Australia
Belen Palop	Universidad de Valladolid, Spain
Marcin Paprzycki	Polish Academy of Sciences, Poland
Eric Pardede	La Trobe University, Australia
Kwangjin Park	Wonkwang University, South Korea
Ana Isabel Pereira	Polytechnic Institute of Bragança, Portugal
Massimiliano Petri	University of Pisa, Italy
Maurizio Pollino	Italian National Agency for New Technologies, Energy and Sustainable Economic Development, Italy
Alenka Poplin	University of Hamburg, Germany
Vidyasagar Potdar	Curtin University of Technology, Australia
David C. Prosperi	Florida Atlantic University, USA
Wenny Rahayu	La Trobe University, Australia
Jerzy Respondek	Silesian University of Technology Poland
Humberto Rocha	INESC-Coimbra, Portugal
Jon Rokne	University of Calgary, Canada
Octavio Roncero	CSIC, Spain
Maytham Safar	Kuwait University, Kuwait
Chiara Saracino	A.O. Ospedale Niguarda Ca' Granda - Milano, Italy
Haiduke Sarafian	The Pennsylvania State University, USA
Francesco Scorza	University of Basilicata, Italy
Marco Paulo Seabra dos Reis	University of Coimbra, Portugal
Jie Shen	University of Michigan, USA

Qi Shi	Liverpool John Moores University, UK
Dale Shires	U.S. Army Research Laboratory, USA
Inês Soares	University of Coimbra, Portugal
Elena Stankova	St. Petersburg University, Russia
Takuo Suganuma	Tohoku University, Japan
Eufemia Tarantino	Polytechnic of Bari, Italy
Sergio Tasso	University of Perugia, Italy
Ana Paula Teixeira	University of Trás-os-Montes and Alto Douro, Portugal
Senhorinha Teixeira	University of Minho, Portugal
M. Filomena Teodoro	Portuguese Naval Academy and University of Lisbon, Portugal
Parimala Thulasiraman	University of Manitoba, Canada
Carmelo Torre	Polytechnic of Bari, Italy
Javier Martinez Torres	Centro Universitario de la Defensa Zaragoza, Spain
Giuseppe A. Trunfio	University of Sassari, Italy
Pablo Vanegas	University of Cuenca, Equador
Marco Vizzari	University of Perugia, Italy
Varun Vohra	Merck Inc., USA
Koichi Wada	University of Tsukuba, Japan
Krzysztof Walkowiak	Wroclaw University of Technology, Poland
Zequn Wang	Intelligent Automation Inc., USA
Robert Weibel	University of Zurich, Switzerland
Frank Westad	Norwegian University of Science and Technology, Norway
Roland Wismüller	Universität Siegen, Germany
Mudasser Wyne	SOET National University, USA
Chung-Huang Yang	National Kaohsiung Normal University, Taiwan
Xin-She Yang	National Physical Laboratory, UK
Salim Zabir	France Telecom Japan Co., Japan
Haifeng Zhao	University of California, Davis, USA
Fabiana Zollo	University of Venice Cà Foscari, Italy
Albert Y. Zomaya	University of Sydney, Australia

Additional Reviewers

Adewumi Oluwasegun	Covenant University, Nigeria
Afreixo Vera	University of Aveiro, Portugal
Agrawal Akshat	International Institute of Information Technology Bangalore, India
Aguilar Antonio	University of Barcelona, Spain
Ahmad Rashid	Microwave and Antenna Lab, School of Engineering, South Korea
Ahmed Waseem	Federal University of Technology, Nigeria
Alamri Sultan	Taibah University, Medina, Saudi Arabia
Alfa Abraham	Kogi State College of Education, Nigeria
Alvelos Filipe	University of Minho, Portugal

Amato Federico	University of Basilicata, Italy
Amin Benatia Mohamed	Groupe Cesi, Francia
Andrianov Serge	Institute for Informatics of Tatarstan Academy of Sciences, Russia
Apduhan Bernady	Kyushu Sangyo University, Japan
Aquilanti Vincenzo	University of Perugia, Italy
Arjun Remadevi	National Institute of Technology Karnataka, India
Arogundade Oluwasefunmi	Federal University of Agriculture, Nigeria
Ascenzi Daniela	University of Trento, Italy
Ayeni Foluso	Southern University and A&M College, USA
Azubuike Ezenwoke	Covenant University, Nigeria
Balacco Gabriella	Polytechnic of Bari, Italy
Balena Pasquale	Polytechnic of Bari, Italy
Balletto Ginevra	University of Cagliari, Italy
Barrile Vincenzo	Mediterranean University of Reggio Calabria, Italy
Bartolomei Massimiliano	Spanish National Research Council, Spain
Behera Ranjan Kumar	Indian Institute of Technology Patna, India
Biondi Giulio	University of Florence, Italy
Bist Ankur Singh	KIET Ghaziabad, India
Blecic Ivan	University of Cagliari, Italy
Bogdanov Alexander	St. Petersburg State University, Russia
Borgogno Mondino Enrico Corrado	University of Turin, Italy
Borruso Giuseppe	University of Trieste, Italy
Bostenaru Maria	Ion Mincu University of Architecture and Urbanism, Romania
Braga Ana Cristina	University of Minho, Portugal
Cafaro Massimo	University of Salento, Italy
Capolupo Alessandra	University of Naples Federico II, Italy
Carvalho-Silva Valter	Universidade Estadual de Goiás, Brazil
Cerreta Maria	University Federico II of Naples, Italy
Chan Sheung Wai	Hong Kong Baptist Hospital, SAR China
Cho Chulhee	Seoul Guarantee Insurance Company Ltd., South Korea
Choi Jae-Young	Sungkyunkwan University, South Korea
Correia Anacleto	Base Naval de Lisboa, Portugal
Correia Elisete	University of Trás-Os-Montes e Alto Douro, Portugal
Correia Florbela Maria da Cruz Domingues	Instituto Politécnico de Viana do Castelo, Portugal
Costa e Silva Eliana	Polytechnic of Porto, Portugal
Costa Lino	Universidade do Minho, Portugal
Costantini Alessandro	Istituto Nazionale di Fisica Nucleare, Italy
Crawford Broderick	Pontificia Universidad Católica de Valparaíso, Chile
Cutini Valerio	University of Pisa, Italy
D'Acierno Luca	University of Naples Federico II, Italy
Danese Maria	Italian National Research Council, Italy
Dantas Coutinho Nayara	University of Perugia, Italy
Degtyarev Alexander	St. Petersburg State University, Russia

Dereli Dursun Ahu	UNSW Sydney, Australia
Devai Frank	London South Bank University, UK
Di Bari Gabriele	University of Florence, Italy
Dias Joana	University of Coimbra, Portugal
Diaz Diana	National University of Colombia, Colombia
Elfadaly Abdelaziz	University of Basilicata, Italy
Enriquez Palma Pedro Alberto	Universidad de la Rioja, Spain
Epicoco Italo	University of Salento, Italy
Esposito Giuseppina	Sapienza University of Rome, Italy
Faginas-Lago M. Noelia	University of Perugia, Italy
Fajardo Jorge	Universidad Politécnica Salesiana (UPS), Ecuador
Falcinelli Stefano	University of Perugia, Italy
Farina Alessandro	University of Pisa, Italy
Fattoruso Grazia	ENEA, Italy
Fernandes Florbela	Escola Superior de Tecnologia e Gestão de Bragancca, Portugal
Fernandes Paula	Escola Superior de Tecnologia e Gestão, Portugal
Fernández Ledesma Javier Darío	Universidad Pontificia Bolivariana, Bolivia
Ferreira Ana C.	University of Lisbon, Portugal
Ferrão Maria	Universidade da Beira Interior, Portugal
Figueiredo Manuel Carlos	Universidade do Minho, Portugal
Florez Hector	Universidad Distrital Francisco Jose de Caldas, Colombia
Franzoni Valentina	University of Perugia, Italy
Freitau Adelaide de Fátima Baptista Valente	University of Aveiro, Portugal
Friday Agbo	University of Eastern Finland, Finland
Frunzete Madalin	Polytechnic University of Bucharest, Romania
Fusco Giovanni	Laboratoire ESPACE, CNRS, France
Gabrani Goldie	Bml Munjal University, India
Gankevich Ivan	St. Petersburg State University, Russia
Garau Chiara	University of Cagliari, Italy
Garcia Ernesto	University of the Basque Country, Spain
Gavrilova Marina	University of Calgary, Canada
Gervasi Osvaldo	University of Perugia, Italy
Gilner Ewa	Silesian University of Technology, Poland
Gioia Andrea	University of Bari, Italy
Giorgi Giacomo	University of Perugia, Italy
Gonçalves Arminda Manuela	University of Minho, Portugal
Gorbachev Yuriy	Geolink Technologies, Russia
Gotoh Yusuke	Kyoto University, Japan
Goyal Rinkaj	Guru Gobind Singh Indraprastha University, India
Gümgüm Sevin	Izmir Economy University, Turkey

Gülen Kemal Güven	Istanbul Ticaret University, Turkey
Hegedus Peter	University of Szeged, Hungary
Hendrix Eligius M. T.	University of Malaga, Spain
Iacobellis Vito	Polytechnic of Bari, Italy
Iakushkin Oleg	St. Petersburg State University, Russia
Kadry Seifedine	Beirut Arab University, Lebanon
Kim JeongAh	George Fox University, USA
Kim Moonseong	Korean Intellectual Property Office, South Korea
Kolingerova Ivana	University of West Bohemia, Czech Republic
Koo Jahwan	Sungkyunkwan University, South Korea
Korkhov Vladimir	St. Petersburg State University, Russia
Kulabukhova Nataliia	St. Peterburg State University, Russia
Ladu Mara	University of Cagliari, Italy
Laganà Antonio	Master-up srl, Italy
Leon Marcelo	Universidad Estatal Peninsula de Santa Elena – UPSE, Ecuador
Lima Rui	University of Minho, Portugal
Lombardi Andrea	University of Perugia, Italy
Longo Savino	University of Bari, Italy
Maciel de Castro Jessica	Universidade Federal da Paraíba, Brazil
Magni Riccardo	Pragma Engineering S.r.L., Italy
Mandanici Emanuele	University of Bologna, Italy
Mangiameli Michele	University of Catania, Italy
Marcellini Moreno	Ecole normale supérieure de Lyon, France
Marghany Maged	Universiti Teknologi Malaysia, Malaysia
Marques Jorge	Universidade de Coimbra, Portugal
Martellozzo Federico	University of Florence, Italy
Mengoni Paolo	University of Florence, Italy
Migliore Marco	University of Cassino e del Lazio Meridionale, Italy
Milani Alfredo	University of Perugia, Italy
Milesi Alessandra	Istituto Auxologico Italiano, Italy
Mishra Biswajeeban	University of Szeged, Hungary
Molaei Qelichi Mohamad	University of Tehran, Iran
Monteiro Vitor	University of Minho, Portugal
Moraes João Luís Cardoso	University of Porto, Portugal
Moura Ricardo	Universidade Nova de Lisboa, Portugal
Mourao Maria	Universidade do Minho, Portugal
Murgante Beniamino	University of Basilicata, Italy
Natário Isabel Cristina Maciel	Universidade Nova de Lisboa, Portugal
Nedjah Nadia	Rio de Janeiro State University, Brazil
Nocera Silvio	University of Naples Federico II, Italy
Odun-Ayo Isaac	Covenant University, Nigeria
Okewu Emmanuel	University of Lagos, Nigeria
Oliveira Irene	University of Trás-Os-Montes e Alto Douro, Portugal
Oluranti Jonathan	Covenant University, Nigeria

Osho Oluwafemi	Federal University of Technology Minna, Nigeria
Ozturk Savas	The Scientific and Technological Research Council of Turkey, Turkey
Panetta J. B.	University of Georgia, USA
Pardede Eric	La Trobe University, Australia
Perchinunno Paola	University of Bari, Italy
Pereira Ana	Instituto Politécnico de Bragança, Portugal
Peschechera Giuseppe	University of Bari, Italy
Petri Massimiliano	University of Pisa, Italy
Petrovic Marjana	University of Zagreb, Croatia
Pham Quoc Trung	Ho Chi Minh City University of Technology, Vietnam
Pinto Telmo	University of Minho, Portugal
Plekhanov Evgeny	Russian Academy of Economics, Russia
Poggioni Valentina	University of Perugia, Italy
Polidoro Maria João	University of Lisbon, Portugal
Pollino Maurizio	ENEA, Italy
Popoola Segun	Covenant University, Nigeria
Pratelli Antonio	University of Pisa, Italy
Pulimeno Marco	University of Salento, Italy
Rasool Hamid	National University of Sciences and Technology, Pakistan
Reis Marco	Universidade de Coimbra, Portugal
Respondek Jerzy	Silesian University of Technology, Poland
Riaz Nida	National University of Sciences and Technology, Pakistan
Rimola Albert	Autonomous University of Barcelona, Spain
Rocha Ana Maria	University of Minho, Portugal
Rocha Humberto	University of Coimbra, Portugal
Rosi Marzio	University of Perugia, Italy
Santos Rafael	National Institute for Space Research, Brazil
Santucci Valentino	University Stranieri of Perugia, Italy
Saponaro Mirko	Polytechnic of Bari, Italy
Sarafian Haiduke	Pennsylvania State University, USA
Scorza Francesco	University of Basilicata, Italy
Sedova Olya	St. Petersburg State University, Russia
Semanjski Ivana	Ghent University, Belgium
Sharma Jeetu	Mody University of Science and Technology, India
Sharma Purnima	University of Lucknow, India
Shchegoleva Nadezhda	Petersburg State Electrotechnical University, Russia
Shen Jie	University of Michigan, USA
Shoaib Muhammad	Sungkyunkwan University, South Korea
Shou Huahao	Zhejiang University of Technology, China
Silva-Fortes Carina	ESTeSL-IPL, Portugal
Silva Ângela Maria	Escola Superior de Ciências Empresariais, Portugal
Singh Upasana	The University of Manchester, UK
Singh V. B.	University of Delhi, India

Skouteris Dimitrios	Master-up, Perugia, Italy
Soares Inês	INESCC and IPATIMUP, Portugal
Soares Michel	Universidade Federal de Sergipe, Brazil
Sosnin Petr	Ulyanovsk State Technical University, Russia
Sousa Ines	University of Minho, Portugal
Stankova Elena	St. Petersburg State University, Russia
Stritih Uros	University of Ljubljana, Slovenia
Tanaka Kazuaki	Kyushu Institute of Technology, Japan
Tarantino Eufemia	Polytechnic of Bari, Italy
Tasso Sergio	University of Perugia, Italy
Teixeira Senhorinha	University of Minho, Portugal
Tengku Adil	La Trobe University, Australia
Teodoro M. Filomena	Lisbon University, Portugal
Torre Carmelo Maria	Polytechnic of Bari, Italy
Totaro Vincenzo	Polytechnic of Bari, Italy
Tripathi Aprna	GLA University, India
Vancsics Béla	University of Szeged, Hungary
Vasyunin Dmitry	University of Amsterdam, The Netherlands
Vig Rekha	The Northcap University, India
Walkowiak Krzysztof	Wroclaw University of Technology, Poland
Wanderley Fernando	New University of Lisbon, Portugal
Wang Chao	University of Science and Technology of China, China
Westad Frank	CAMO Software AS, USA
Yamazaki Takeshi	University of Tokyo, Japan
Zahra Noore	University of Guilan, India
Zollo Fabiana	University of Venice Ca' Foscari, Italy
Zullo Francesco	University of L'Aquila, Italy
Žemlička Michal	Charles University in Prague, Czech Republic
Živković Ljiljana	Republic Agency for Spatial Planning, Serbia

Sponsoring Organizations

ICCSA 2019 would not have been possible without tremendous support of many organizations and institutions, for which all organizers and participants of ICCSA 2019 express their sincere gratitude:

Springer Nature Switzerland AG, Germany
(http://www.springer.com)

St. Petersburg University, Russia
(http://english.spbu.ru/)

University of Perugia, Italy
(http://www.unipg.it)

University of Basilicata, Italy
(http://www.unibas.it)

Monash University, Australia
(http://monash.edu)

Kyushu Sangyo University, Japan
(www.kyusan-u.ac.jp)

Universidade do Minho, Portugal
(http://www.uminho.pt)

Contents – Part II

**Advances in Artificial Intelligence Learning Technologies:
Blended Learning, STEM, Computational Thinking
and Coding (AAILT 2019)**

Affective Computing and Emotion Recognition (ACER-EMORE 2019)

xxviiiContents – Part II

Bio and Neuro inspired Computing and Applications (BIONCA 2019)

Computer Aided Modeling, Simulation, and Analysis (CAMSA 2018)

Short Papers

Short Papers

Expert System for Urban Multimodal Mobility Estimation Based on Information from Public Mobile Network

Krešimir Vidović[1] , Sadko Mandžuka[2](✉) ,
and Marko Šoštarić[2]

[1] Ericsson Nikola Tesla, 10000 Zagreb, Croatia
kresimir.vidovic@ericsson.com
[2] Faculty of Transport and Traffic Science, University of Zagreb,
10000 Zagreb, Croatia
sadko.mandzuka@gmail.com

Abstract. Paper present new approach of urban multimodal mobility (UMM) estimation using anonymized data from public mobile network (PMN). The data set is derived from Call Data Records database, and urban multimodal mobility indicators were defined and relativized. Usage of indicators relativized values ensures that they can be applied for mobility estimation in all urban environment regardless of their physical differences, with existing public mobile network as single prerequisite. Travel mode classification is based on Adaptive Neuro Fuzzy Inference System (ANFIS) and trained using set of rules that were determined using method of surveying experts in domain of urban mobility. Accurate estimate creates a foundation for improvement of existing end creation of new services in urban mobility. Also, this approach has potential through implementation within advanced applications of Intelligent Transport Systems with the goal to improve travel modal shift, passenger comfort, efficiency of urban transport etc.

Keywords: Urban mobility · Multimodality · ANFIS ·
Mobile communication network · Call detail record

1 Introduction

Fostering multimodal transport is one of the key enablers for solving mobility issues in cities resulting in easing the movement of people and goods. This paper presents an approach in which the urban multimodal mobility indicators (UMMI) can be derived from non-location services related data being logged in public mobile network (PMN). Authors will elaborate on potential of usage of anonymized data from mobile network operators' databases with the goal of estimating urban multimodal mobility (UMM) by utilizing three base and one derived indicator. Additional data set, information about availability of transport modes will be used as well. This approach has a potential of creation of multimodal mobility estimation methodology applicable for all urban environments, since PMN, as (besides digital map) only required data source, exists in all urban environments. It is possible to apply this methodology through advanced

S. Misra et al. (Eds.): ICCSA 2019, LNCS 11620, pp. 3–11, 2019.
https://doi.org/10.1007/978-3-030-24296-1_1

applications within Intelligent Transport Systems (ITS), where similar applications, like driver and passenger information systems, traffic management, incident management systems, urban public transport management and similar, already exists [1–3].

2 PMN Generated Data in Urban Mobility Research

Recent developments have strengthened capabilities to understand and process telecom related big data sets and produce new data insights and can offer advanced data analytics that exclusively utilizes anonymized telecom network's data sets. The technology has evolved and user habits have changed. Mobile phone penetration in 2008 was 59,4%, and in 2018 it was 105% (4,9 billion users). More than 54% of those users own a smartphone (2,5 billion), and 85% of users are using mobile internet [4]. Therefore, increase in mobile phone penetration, together with increased number of smartphone share, enlarged number of mobile internet users and possibilities of precise user location determination in 3G and 4G networks have created the basis for efficient use of such data types in traffic engineering. Extreme computing performance and telecom knowledge makes it possible to understand telecom data, process millions of data records and produce new data insights. Scientific community has recognized telecom big data sets as quality data source for transport engineering which is evident from numerous scientific and professional bibliographies in this area. Authors have, in general, proven that this data type is representative, reliable and have been using them for various applications, like monitoring traffic flows, urban planning, travel mode detection, origin-destination matrix determination, public transport capacity evaluation and optimization, traffic volume determination, transport planning, traffic anomalies identification, mobility analysis etc., just to name few [5–14].

3 Spatial Decomposition

The telecommunication domain consists of a telecommunication network with the corresponding elements. It is a contextual, information world in which a CDR record is generated. In the context of the telecommunication network architecture in the contextual (information world), the physical locations of individual elements are not important, but how they are interrelated and what are their interrelated relationships. The transport network and the entities in the transport system are primarily related to the physical world, i.e. the traffic infrastructure (roads, tunnels, bridges). Traffic Engineering studies that part, or where the entity on the network is located and where it is and how it goes. The telecommunications system belongs to the contextual, information domain, while the traffic system belongs to the physical, material domain. When data from a CDR record is added to the information on the position of base stations in the space, the first step in transition from the contextual, information world into physics has been made, in which mobility as such takes place. Therefore, it is necessary to make that transition using the appropriate procedure (Fig. 1). Each base station has the appropriate coverage area, and its size and shape depend on several parameters. Base cell coverage limits are not isolated so that overlaps of coverage area occur, especially in urban, densely populated areas. The surface area covering the base station therefore needs to be approximated to decompose the space in such a way that the exact surface area in the space, using the appropriate methodology, is assigned to the appropriate base station.

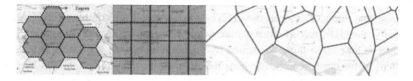

Fig. 1. Spatial decomposition (hexagonal, raster, Voronoi)

The space can be commonly divided into hexagonal cells, raster fields or Voronoi cells. Voronoi cells represent a special kind of decomposition on discrete sets of objects in space. Discrete sets of space points are defined by distance, where the position of the base station is taken as the center of the cell and includes all points that are closer to the center of that cell than the center of any other cell. Points that are equally distanced from both centers represent the boundary of the cell. Voronoi cells give a better, more realistic and high-quality image distribution over hexagonal cells and raster fields, and therefore will be used in this paper.

4   Multimodal Mobility Indicators and Calculation Methodology

In this paper, we have identified and defined three base indicators of urban mobility, and one derived from them. Number of trips refers to the number of movements between certain urban areas and presents a sum of all the recorded movements of users between certain urban areas within an appropriate timeframe. Second indicator is travel time indicator. The travel time indicator refers to the duration of each trip in the observed time frame. Value of indicators travel time can be made relative by calculating the contribution of each trip in relation to the longest trip, and the value of travel time for each trip is normalized with respect to a trip that has lasted longest during the typical day. In this case, the longest trip is the one in which the distance travelled is the largest, and that in fact the origin and destination remain within the same coverage area. Indicator "distance" is used as an approximation of the distance travelled. It refers to the distance the user has travelled between individual urban areas, i.e. the distance between the source and the destination of the trip. The length of travel or the distance travelled differs between the different urban agglomerations, as it may depend on the number of inhabitants, the density of housing, the surface of the city and the attractiveness of the attraction. Value of indicator distance can be relativized by calculating the contribution of each travel in relation to the maximum recorded travel, with the value of the distance travelled each trip is being normalized with respect to the longest journey in a typical day. In this case, the longest trip is the one in which the distance travelled is the largest, and that in fact the origin and destination remain within the same coverage area. Calculation methodology is described in following parts of paper. After filtration of unneeded data, it contains temporary ID of users, the time of start of the telecommunications activities and geographical location of the base station. Prior to indicator calculation process, several assumptions and terms need to be defined and describer. The trip is the movement of the user between the two base station of the PMN (corresponding urban areas) where he has achieved telecommunication activity registered in the CDR record. Authors are aware that real origin and destination of trip might differentiate from those identified by telecommunication activities. This will be the subject of further researches, where the relationship among migrations identified from telecommunication activities and migrations that really occurred will be analyzed. False motion or false travel is a user's trip identified by changing the base station, which did not actually happen, or there was no physical user location change. This occurs due to the operation of PMN and the tendency to optimize the operation of some of base stations by transferring excess users on the other base station coverage area at that time less load (Load balancing). Time threshold is used to filter records on the "false" movements and is 10 min < x < 60 min, which means it eliminates all trips that have lasted for less than 10 or more than 60 min. Spatial threshold is used to filter the records of the "false" movements which eliminate all trips shorter than 1 km. Speed threshold is eliminating all trips that, due to speed indicator values, assume that they are not realistic or are the result of an error. (average speed > 100 km/h). Application of these filters might also affect some real migrations, which might affect estimation in smaller or medium size cities. These issues will be addressed in further research, where the signaling data will be utilized and fused with CDR data. User position is more precisely determined, by using trilateration method, and therefore, previously mentioned uncertainties, like false movements, will be mitigated. Additionally, that methodology also solves the problem of capturing only segment of trip in which the user has performed telecommunication activities, since signaling occurs even without telecommunication activities, since the only prerequisite is that the mobile terminal is switched on.

Therefore, the input data file is transformed into a table. Base stations are then identified and are stored in the corresponding table. A variable ID location is being introduced, containing the unique ID for the same pair of LAT, LONG, it is matched and is added to the table of base stations. Following steps include determination of Euclidean distance between each pair of base stations identified in previous steps. The values are stored in the table for each pair of base stations end are calculated using Haversine formula. Then, the process continues for identifying all location changes for each trip, for each user, in each individual data set, and calculating the value of time difference between the change of state (Δt). In the next step, the travel time indicator is defined as the difference in time between the recorded start of telecommunication activities at the source base station and recorded start of telecommunication activities at the destination base station for each trip. Then, in following step the travel speed is being calculated for each trip as the quotient of Euclidean distance value and time changes. It is presented in km/h. Next step is the calculation of the values of the indicators using analyzed input data. Origin destination matrix contains number of trips between all pairs of base stations among which the trips occurred within a certain time.

Indicator of the number of trips between individual base station pairs is calculated using the relation (1):

$$A(i,j) = \sum Trip\_ID(i,j) \tag{1}$$

where, the $A(i, j)$ represents the total number of recorded trips between individual pairs of base stations (Origin-Destination Matrix), $Trip\_ID(i, j)$ represents trip between two base stations in the appropriate time frame, where all assumptions are met. The matrix (or the table) of travel time contains the time values of average travel time between all pairs of base stations and is calculated as the average of all recorded travel times between same pairs of base stations within a predefined time. Indicator travel time (B) is calculated using the expression (2):

$$\bar{B}(i,j) = \frac{\sum B(i,j)}{n} \tag{2}$$

Where $\bar{B}(i,j)$ represents the average value of all travel times between base stations in a predefined time frame, B(i,j) represents the value of the travel time for each trip in the time frame, and n represents the number of registered trips between base station pairs within the time frame. Following indicator is matrix of distances and it contains distances between all pairs of base stations among which the trips occurred within a certain time. Also, it is important to note that the Euclidean distance between base station pairs is the same regardless of the direction of travel.

Indicator travel speed is calculated using expression (3):

$$D1(i,j) = \frac{C(i,j)}{B(i,j)} \tag{3}$$

Where D1(i, j) stands for the travel speed for each trip in the time frame, C(i, j) stands Euclidean distance between base station pairs and B(i, j) stands for the duration of each travel trip in a time frame. The result of the previous step are values stored in four matrices for each time frame; in the matrix of number of trips (Origin Destination Matrix), travel time matrix and distance matrix, and travel speed. To ensure that the model is applicable to all urban areas, regardless of their size, the data obtained should be normalized, i.e. the data should be kept in the interval [0, 1]. Normalization is performed so that the value of the indicator in a given time interval is normalized with the highest value of the individual indicator for all eight-time intervals. The purpose of the normalization conducted in this way is to include in the calculation and the extent to which each indicator participates in the overall mobility of urban agglomeration in each individual frame, i.e. to identify its maximum. This will result in a more credible calculation of the UMM estimation for each time frame.

5 Design of ANFIS Based Expert System

Following the process of calculation of urban mobility indicators, next step includes determination of relationship between the values of the UMMI and the value of the multimodal mobility estimation. This paper utilizes so called expert knowledge gathering method for this purpose. Expert knowledge is what qualified individuals know as a result of their technical practices, training, and experience. It may include recalled facts or evidence, inferences made by the expert based on "hard facts" in response to new or undocumented situations, and integration of disparate sources in conceptual models to address system-level issues. Experts are usually identified based on qualifications, training, experience, professional memberships, and peer recognition. Therefore, selected experts will be presented with a set of questions (survey). The question arises from an expert's opinion ("knowledge gathering") on how and to what extent the combination of values of indicators affects the UMM, in the context of mode identification. Survey questions include all permutations of the value of indicators included in the UMM estimation, enriched with several modal options (walking, car, public transport) The expert answers to the question by giving the appropriate value of the multimodal mobility estimate based on their own knowledge and experience in each issue. The scenarios are formed used following principle:

If <value of number of trips indicator> & <value of travel time indicator> & <value of distance travel indicator> & <value of speed indicator>, travel mode is <travel mode> and multimodal mobility is <mobility estimation> .

Through the questionnaires, experts then point to the value of the offered scale for which the mobility estimate can be ranked in different categories.

Upon completion of the survey process, the responses of all the experts participating were evaluated and processed and were used in further steps in the multimodal mobility estimation process. Analysis of the data will be performed for checking the consistency of the response. In order to establish an expert system for multimodal mobility estimation, a method of fuzzy logic, or an adaptive neuro-fuzzy inference system (ANFIS), will be used. ANFIS process overview is presented in Fig. 2. Training process begins by obtaining training data set and checking data set. Training data consist of two vectors, first is input and second is output vector. Those vectors are used to train the ANFIS system. Training data set is used to determine parameters for membership function and threshold value for the error between the actual and desired

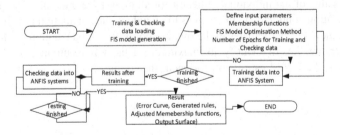

Fig. 2. ANFIS training process, based on [15]

output is determined. Consequent parameters are found using least square method, and when the error becomes less than defined threshold value, process will terminate.

ANFIS training learning rules use hybrid learning, combining the gradient descent and the least squares method. Training begins by creating a set of training data to be able to train the Neuro-Fuzzy system. The data set used as the input must be in a matrix form. First four columns represent input data with values of urban mobility indicators, as presented to the experts, and the last column in the matrix is the output, value of mobility estimation, generated by processing responses from survey data. Initial membership functions for al input variables are created (for four mobility indicators), and the parameter of membership function is determined. Input and output variables for fuzzy interference system are presented at Fig. 3. Following the initial membership functions creation, system training begins. When the training process is finished the final membership functions and training error from the training data set are produced. To identify the most appropriate system, system must be trained with a variety of settings for items such as data set sample, epoch number, membership function type and number, and number of inputs to achieve the best performance. The checking data is then used in conjunction with the training data set for accuracy enhancement.

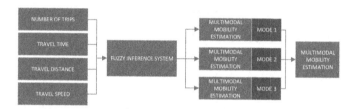

Fig. 3. Input and output variables to fuzzy interference system

Preliminary training result (without multimodality analysis) was network with 78 nodes, 108 linear parameters, 36 nonlinear parameters. In this simulation 654 data pairs used for model training, Fig. 4.

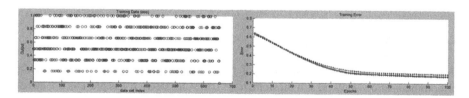

Fig. 4. Characteristics of preliminary training results (distribution of training data and dynamics of training error)

Analysis of model prediction results by comparing the results of models derived from the data set for learning, the data set for validation and the data set for model verification, Fig. 5. The average error check of the model was 0.1907. The process of validation was carried out for each Fuzzy Inference System (total of 32 proposed candidates). The result of this process is ANFIS based expert system for urban mobility estimation based on user's telecommunication activities in PMN. Therefore, based on values of UMMI, identified and calculated from data from PMN, and rules gathered from surveying experts, using ANFIS method, expert system was formed that is capable of categorizing user migration according to travel mode (based on indicator speed) and evaluate UMM. UMM is separately calculated for each identified transport mode and is stored in multimodal mobility estimation matrix for each defined mode. So, in this case, it will result in three matrixes that will contain multimodal mobility estimation values for each base station pair. In case that user have combined different transportation modes during the trip, this trip will be divided by segments based on identified mode, and those segments will be addressed as independent trips.

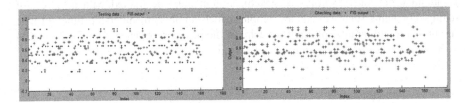

Fig. 5. Testing data and checking data

To determine the extent to which each mode of transport affects total multimodal mobility, it is necessary to determine the share of different modes represented by the number of trips in the total number of trips. Therefore, after the identification of travel mode, it will be possible to identify how much each mod participates in migrations between the appropriate pair of urban areas. The identified value will then be used to relativize the share of each individual travel mode in total multimodal mobility. At the end, multimodal mobility estimation value between the two pairs of base stations (equivalent urban areas) will be calculated as the sum of multiple values of urban mobility estimates for each mode of travel and the relative value of the representation of each mode of travel.

6   Conclusion

This paper demonstrated the potential of the data derived from the public mobile telecommunications networks in the domain of UMM research. It has presented a novel approach in which the data derived from the CDR database from public telecommunication networks can be used in area of smart mobility. Paper has described mobile network topology and addressed issues regarding spatial decomposition and propose solution to get an accurate multimodal mobility estimate. Paper has presented a methodology for modelling four UMMI (number of trips, distance, travel time and speed), and has proposed an approach in which the relativized values of UMMI can be used in all urban environments, regardless of its size, population or local characteristics. This paper has proven that the urban mobility of inhabitants within an urban environment can in a specific time frame be described with an urban mobility indicator based on information about recorded telecommunication activities of users in a PMN.

References

1. Vidović, K., Mandžuka, S., Brčić, D: Estimation of urban mobility using public mobile network. In: Proceedings of 59th International Symposium, ELMAR-2017. Faculty of Electrical Engineering and Computing, Zadar, Zagreb, p. 21–24 (2017)
2. Škorput, P., Mandžuka, S., Jelušić, N.: Real-time detection of road traffic incidents. Promet - Traffic Transp. **22**(4), 273–283 (2010)
3. Mandžuka, S., Kljaić, Z., Škorput, P.: The use of mobile communication in traffic incident management process. J. Green Eng. **1**(4), 413–429 (2011)
4. GSMA: The Mobile Economy Global (2018). https://bit.ly/2oTFrsl. Accessed 29 Jan 2019
5. Zhang, D., Zhao, J., Zhang, F.: UrbanCPS: a cyber-physical system based on multi-source big infrastructure data for heterogeneous model integration. In: Proceedings of the ACM/IEEE Sixth International Conference on Cyber-Physical Systems, ICCPS 2015, pp. 238–247 (2015)
6. González, M.C., Hidalgo, C.A., Barabási, C.A.: Understanding individual human mobility patterns. Nature **453**, 779–782 (2008)
7. Gillis, D., Semanjski, I., Lauwers, D.: How to monitor sustainable mobility in cities? Literature review in the frame of creating a set of sustainable mobility indicators. Sustainability **8**(1), 1–30 (2016)
8. Qiu, Y., Tatem, A.J.: Data-mining cellphone-based trajectory data for collective human mobility pattern analysis. World Wide Web Internet Web Inf. Syst. **2009**, 2–3 (2009)
9. Calabrese, F., Diao, M., Lorenzo, G., Ferreira, J., Ratti, C.: Understanding individual mobility patterns from urban sensing data: a mobile phone trace example. Transp. Res. Part C **26**, 301–313 (2013)
10. Diana, M., Pirra, M.: A comparative assessment of synthetic indices to measure multimodality behaviours. Transp. A Transp. Sci. **12**(9), 771–793 (2016)
11. Qu, Y., Gong, H., Wang, P.: Transportation mode split with mobile phone data. In: Proceedings of the IEEE Conference on Intelligent Transportation Systems, ITSC, vol. 2015, October, pp. 285–289 (2015)
12. Bachir, D., Khodabandelou, G., Gauthier, V., El Yacoubi, M., Vachon, E.: Combining Bayesian inference and clustering for transport mode detection from sparse and noisy geolocation data. In: Brefeld, U., et al. (eds.) ECML PKDD 2018. LNCS (LNAI), vol. 11053, pp. 569–584. Springer, Cham (2019). https://doi.org/10.1007/978-3-030-10997-4_35
13. Biljecki, F., Ledoux, H., Van Oosterom, P.: Transportation mode-based segmentation and classification of movement trajectories. Int. J. Geogr. Inf. Sci. **27**(2), 385–407 (2013)
14. Williams, N.E., Thomas, T.A., Dunbar, M., Eagle, N., Dobra, A.: Measures of human mobility using mobile phone records enhanced with GIS data. PLoS ONE **10**(7), 1–16 (2015)
15. Jang, J.S.R.: ANFIS: adaptive-network-based fuzzy inference system. IEEE Trans. Syst. Man Cybern. **23**(3), 665–685 (1993)

Asymtotic Distribution of the Bootstrap Parameter Estimator for the AR(p) Model

Bambang Suprihatin$^{(\boxtimes)}$, Endro Setyo Cahyono, and Novi Rustiana Dewi

Sriwijaya University, Indralaya, Indonesia
bambangs@unsri.ac.id

Abstract. This paper is the generalization of our two previous researches about asymptotic distribution of the bootstrap parameter estimator for the AR(1) and AR(2) models. We investigate the asymptotic distribution of the bootstrap parameter estimator of pth order autoregressive or AR(p) model by applying the delta method. The asymptotic distribution is the crucial property in inference of statistics. We conclude that the bootstrap parameter estimator of the AR(p) model is asymptotically converges in distribution to the p–variate normal distribution.

Keywords: Autocovariance function · Limiting distribution · Measurable function · Residuals bootstrap

1 Introduction

Consider the following stationary second order autoregressive AR(p) process:

$$X_t = \theta_1 X_{t-1} + \theta_2 X_{t-2} + \cdots + \theta_p X_{t-p} \epsilon_t, \tag{1}$$

where ϵ_t is a zero mean white noise process with constant variance σ^2. Let the vector $\widehat{\boldsymbol{\theta}} = (\widehat{\theta}_1, \widehat{\theta}_2, \ldots, \widehat{\theta}_p)^T$ is the estimator of the parameter vector $\boldsymbol{\theta} = (\theta_1, \theta_2, \ldots, \theta_p)^T$ of (1) and $\widehat{\boldsymbol{\theta}}^*$ be the bootstrap version of $\widehat{\boldsymbol{\theta}}$. Studying of estimation of the unknown parameter involves: (i) what estimator should be used? (ii) having chosen a particular estimator, is this consistent? (iii) how accurate is the chosen estimator? (iv) what is the asymptotic behavior of such estimator? (v) what is the method used in proving the asymptotic properties?

Bootstrap is a general methodology for answering the second and third questions, while the delta method is one of tools used to answer the last two questions. Consistency theory is needed to ensure that the estimator is consistent to the actual parameter as desired, and thereof the asymptotic behavior of such estimator will be studied.

The consistency theories of parameter of autoregressive model have studied in [1,3,4], and for bootstrap version of the same topic, see *e.g.* [5–8,10]. They deal with the bootstrap approximation in various senses (*e.g.*, consistency

© Springer Nature Switzerland AG 2019
S. Misra et al. (Eds.): ICCSA 2019, LNCS 11620, pp. 12–22, 2019.
https://doi.org/10.1007/978-3-030-24296-1_2

of estimator, simulation results, limiting distribution, applying of Edgeworth expansions, etc.), and they reported that the bootstrap works usually very well. The accuracy of the bootstrapping method for autoregressive model studied in [2,9]. They showed that the parameter estimates of the autoregressive model can be bootstrapped with accuracy that outperforms the normal approximation. The asymptotic result for the AR(1) model has been exhibited in [11]. We concluded that the bootstrap parameter estimator for the AR(1) model converges in distribution to the normal distribution. A good perform of the bootstrap estimator is applied to study the asymptotic distribution of $\widehat{\theta}^*$ using the delta method. We describe the asymptotic distribution of the autocovariance function and investigate the bootstrap limiting distribution of $\widehat{\theta}^*$. Section 2 reviews the asymptotic distribution of estimator of mean and autocovariance function for the autoregressive model. Section 3 describes the bootstrap and delta method. Section 4 deals with the main result, i.e. the asymptotic distribution of $\widehat{\theta}^*$ by applying the delta method. Section 5 briefly describes the conclusions of the paper.

2   Estimator of Mean and Autocovariance for the Autoregressive Model

Suppose we have the observed values $X_1, X_2, \ldots, X_n$ from the stationary AR(p) process. Mean and autocovariance are two important statistics in investigating the consistency properties of the estimator $\widehat{\theta} = (\widehat{\theta}_1, \widehat{\theta}_2, \ldots, \widehat{\theta}_p)^T$ for the parameter θ of the AR(p) model. A natural estimators for parameters mean, covariance and correlation function are

$$\widehat{\mu}_n = \overline{X}_n = \frac{1}{n} \sum_{t=1}^{n} X_t, \ \widehat{\gamma}_n(h) = \frac{1}{n} \sum_{t=1}^{n-h} (X_{t+h} - \overline{X}_n)(X_t - \overline{X}_n),$$

and $\widehat{\rho}_n(h) = \widehat{\gamma}_n/\widehat{\gamma}_n(0)$ respectively. These all three estimators are consistent (see, e.g. [3,13]). The following theorem describes the property of the estimator $\overline{X}_n$, is stated in [3].

Theorem 1. *If $\{X_t\}$ is stationary process with mean μ and autocovariance function $\gamma(\cdot)$, then as $n \to \infty$,*

$$Var(\overline{X}_n) = E(\overline{X}_n - \mu)^2 \to 0 \quad \text{if } \gamma(n) \to 0,$$

and

$$nE(\overline{X}_n - \mu)^2 \to \sum_{j=-\infty}^{\infty} \gamma(h) \quad \text{if } \sum_{j=-\infty}^{\infty} |\gamma(h)| < \infty.$$

It is not a loss of generality to assume that $\mu_X = 0$. Under some conditions (see, e.g., [13]), the sample autocovariance function can be written as

$$\widehat{\gamma}_n(h) = \frac{1}{n} \sum_{t=1}^{n-h} X_{t+h} X_t + O_p(1/n). \tag{2}$$

The asymptotic behavior of the sequence $\sqrt{n}\left(\widehat{\gamma}_n(h) - \gamma_X(h)\right)$ depends only on $n^{-1}\sum_{t=1}^{n-h} X_{t+h}X_t$. Note that a change of $n - h$ by n or vice versa, is asymptotically negligible, so that, for simplicity of notation, to study the behavior of (2) we can equivalently study the average

$$\widetilde{\gamma}_n(h) = \frac{1}{n}\sum_{t=1}^{n} X_{t+h}X_t. \tag{3}$$

Both (2) and (3) are unbiased estimators of $E(X_{t+h}X_t) = \gamma_X(h)$, under the condition that $\mu_X = 0$. Their asymptotic distribution then can be derived by applying a central limit theorem to the averages $\overline{Y}_n$ of the variables $Y_t = X_{t+h}X_t$. As in [13], the autocovariance function of the series Y_t can be written as

$$V_{h,h} = \kappa_4(\varepsilon)\gamma_X(h)^2 + \sum_g \gamma_X(g)^2 + \sum_g \gamma_X(g+h)\gamma_X(g-h), \tag{4}$$

where $\kappa_4(\varepsilon) = E(\varepsilon_1^4) - 3\left(E(\varepsilon_1^2)\right)^2$, the fourth cumulant of ε_t. The following theorem is due to [13] that gives the asymptotic distribution of the sequence $\sqrt{n}\left(\widehat{\gamma}_n(h) - \gamma_X(h)\right)$.

Theorem 2. *If $X_t = \mu + \sum_{j=-\infty}^{\infty} \psi_j\varepsilon_{t-j}$ holds for an i.i.d. sequence ε_t with mean zero and $E(\varepsilon_t^4) < \infty$ and numbers ψ_j with $\sum_j |\psi_j| < \infty$, then*

$$\sqrt{n}\left(\widehat{\gamma}_n(h) - \gamma_X(h)\right) \to_d N(0, V_{h,h}).$$

3   Bootstrap and Delta Method

Let $X_1, X_2, \ldots, X_n$ be a random sample of size n from a population with common distribution F, and let $T(X_1, X_2, \ldots, X_n; F)$ be the specified random variable or statistic of interest, possibly depending upon the unknown distribution F. Let F_n denote the empirical distribution function of the random sample $X_1, X_2, \ldots, X_n$, i.e., the distribution putting probability $1/n$ at each of the points $X_1, X_2, \ldots, X_n$. A bootstrap sample is defined to be a random sample of size n drawn from F_n, say $X^* = X_1^*, X_2^*, \ldots, X_n^*$. The bootstrap sample at first bootstrapping is usually denoted by X^{*1}. In general, the bootstrap sample at Bth bootstrapping is denoted by X^{*B}. The bootstrap data set $X^{*b} = X_1^{*b}, X_2^{*b}, \ldots, X_n^{*b}$, $b = 1, 2, \ldots, B$ consists of members of the original data set $X_1, X_2, \ldots, X_n$, some appearing zero times, some appearing once, some appearing twice, etc. The bootstrap method is to approximate the distribution of $T(X_1, X_2, \ldots, X_n; F)$ under F by that of $T(X_1^*, X_2^*, \ldots, X_n^*; F_n)$ under F_n.

Let a functional T is defined as $T(X_1, X_2, \ldots, X_n; F) = \sqrt{n}(\widehat{\boldsymbol{\theta}} - \boldsymbol{\theta})$, where $\widehat{\boldsymbol{\theta}}$ is the estimator for the coefficient $\boldsymbol{\theta}$ of a stationary AR(p) model. The bootstrap version of T is $T(X_1^*, X_2^*, \ldots, X_n^*; F_n) = \sqrt{n}(\widehat{\boldsymbol{\theta}}^* - \widehat{\boldsymbol{\theta}})$, where $\widehat{\boldsymbol{\theta}}^*$ is a bootstrap version of $\widehat{\theta}$ computed from sample bootstrap $X_1^*, X_2^*, \ldots, X_n^*$. The residuals bootstrapping procedure for the time series data to obtain $X_1^*, X_2^*, \ldots, X_n^*$ was proposed in [6]. In bootstrap view, the key of bootstrap terminology says that the population is to the sample as the sample is to the bootstrap samples. Therefore, when we want to investigate the asymptotic distribution of bootstrap estimator $\widehat{\theta}^*$, we investigate the distribution of $\sqrt{n}(\widehat{\theta}^* - \widehat{\theta})$ contrast to the distribution of $\sqrt{n}(\widehat{\theta} - \theta)$. Thus, the bootstrap is a device for estimating $P_F(\sqrt{n}(\widehat{\theta} - \theta) \leq x)$ by $P_{F_n}(\sqrt{n}(\widehat{\theta}^* - \widehat{\theta}) \leq x)$. We propose the delta method in estimating for such distribution.

The delta method consists of using a Taylor expansion to approximate a random vector of the form $\phi(T_n)$ by the polynomial $\phi(\theta) + \phi'(\theta)(T_n - \theta) + \cdots$ in $T_n - \theta$. This method is useful to deduce the limit law of $\phi(T_n) - \phi(\theta)$ from that of $T_n - \theta$, which is guaranteed by the following theorem, as stated in [12].

Theorem 3. *Let $\phi : \mathbf{D}_\phi \subset \mathbf{R}^k \to \mathbf{R}^m$ be a map defined on a subset of $\mathbf{R}^k$ and differentiable at θ. Let T_n be random vector taking their values in the domain of ϕ. If $r_n(T_n - \theta) \to_d T$ for numbers $r_n \to \infty$, then $r_n(\phi(T_n) - \phi(\theta)) \to_d \phi'_\theta(T)$. Moreover, $\left| r_n(\phi(T_n) - \phi(\theta)) - \phi'_\theta(r_n(T_n - \theta)) \right| \to_p 0$.*

Assume that $\widehat{\theta}_n$ is a statistic, and that ϕ is a given differentiable map. The bootstrap estimator for the distribution of $\phi(\widehat{\theta}_n) - \phi(\theta)$ is $\phi(\widehat{\theta}_n^*) - \phi(\widehat{\theta}_n)$. If the bootstrap is consistent for estimating the distribution of $\sqrt{n}(\widehat{\theta}_n - \theta)$, then it is also consistent for estimating the distribution of $\sqrt{n}(\phi(\widehat{\theta}_n) - \phi(\theta))$, as given in the following theorem. The theorem is due to [12].

Theorem 4 (Delta Method For Bootstrap). *Let $\phi : \mathbf{R}^k \to \mathbf{R}^m$ be a measurable map defined and continuously differentiable in a neighborhood of θ. Let $\widehat{\theta}_n$ be random vector taking their values in the domain of ϕ that converge almost surely to θ. If $\sqrt{n}(\widehat{\theta}_n - \theta) \to_d T$, and $\sqrt{n}(\widehat{\theta}_n^* - \widehat{\theta}_n) \to_d T$ conditionally almost surely, then both $\sqrt{n}(\phi(\widehat{\theta}_n) - \phi(\theta)) \to_d \phi'_\theta(T)$ and $\sqrt{n}(\phi(\widehat{\theta}_n^*) - \phi(\widehat{\theta}_n)) \to_d \phi'_\theta(T)$ conditionally almost surely.*

4   Main Result

We now address our main result, which is summarized in the following theorem.

Theorem 5. *Let $\widehat{\theta} = (\widehat{\theta}_1, \widehat{\theta}_2, \ldots, \widehat{\theta}_p)^T$ be the estimator of $\theta = (\theta_1, \theta_2, \ldots, \theta_p)^T$ of the stationary AR(p) process, and $\widehat{\theta}^* = (\widehat{\theta}_1^*, \widehat{\theta}_2^*, \ldots, \widehat{\theta}_p^*)^T$ would be the bootstrap version of $\widehat{\theta}$. The sequence of random variables $\sqrt{n}(\widehat{\theta}^* - \widehat{\theta})$ converges in distribution to the normal distribution with mean $\mathbf{0}$ and covariance matrix as defined in (11).*

Proof. The model of an AR(p) process is:

$$X_t = \theta_1 X_{t-1} + \theta_2 X_{t-2} + \cdots + \theta_p X_{t-p} + \varepsilon_t. \tag{5}$$

The Yule-Walker equation for (5) as follows:

$$\widehat{M} \begin{pmatrix} \widehat{\theta}_1 \\ \widehat{\theta}_2 \\ \vdots \\ \widehat{\theta}_p \end{pmatrix} = \begin{pmatrix} \sum_{t=2}^{n} X_t X_{t-1} \\ \sum_{t=3}^{n} X_t X_{t-2} \\ \vdots \\ \sum_{t=p+1}^{n} X_t X_{t-p} \end{pmatrix},$$

with

$$\widehat{M} = \begin{pmatrix} \sum_{t=1}^{n} X_t^2 & \sum_{t=2}^{n} X_t X_{t-1} & \cdots & \sum_{t=p}^{n} X_t X_{t-p+1} \\ \sum_{t=2}^{n} X_t X_{t-1} & \sum_{t=1}^{n} X_t^2 & \cdots & \sum_{t=p-1}^{n} X_t X_{t-p+2} \\ \vdots & \vdots & \ddots & \vdots \\ \sum_{t=p}^{n} X_t X_{t-p+1} & \sum_{t=p-1}^{n} X_{t-p+2} & \cdots & \sum_{t=1}^{n} X_{t^2} \end{pmatrix}.$$

From the Yule-Walker equation, by applying the moment method we obtain

$$\begin{pmatrix} \widehat{\theta}_1 \\ \widehat{\theta}_2 \\ \vdots \\ \widehat{\theta}_p \end{pmatrix} = \widehat{M}^{-1} \begin{pmatrix} \sum_{t=2}^{n} X_t X_{t-1} \\ \sum_{t=3}^{n} X_t X_{t-2} \\ \vdots \\ \sum_{t=p+1}^{n} X_t X_{t-p} \end{pmatrix}. \tag{6}$$

From (6), the vector of estimator $\widehat{\boldsymbol{\theta}} = \left(\widehat{\theta}_1, \widehat{\theta}_2, \ldots, \widehat{\theta}_p\right)^T$ can be expressed as a measurable function $\phi = \left(\phi_1, \phi_2, \ldots, \phi_p\right)^T : \mathbf{R}^{p+1} \to \mathbf{R}^p$, with

$$\widehat{\theta}_i \equiv \phi_i \left(\sum_{t=1}^{n} X_t^2, \sum_{t=2}^{n} X_t X_{t-1}, \ldots, \sum_{t=p+1}^{n} X_t X_{t-p} \right).$$

For each function $\phi_i : \mathbf{R}^{p+1} \to \mathbf{R}$, $i = 1, 2, \ldots, p$ can be described from the system (6) and be written as $\phi_i \equiv \phi_i(u_1, u_2, \ldots, u_{p+1})$. The function ϕ_i is differentiable and its derivative matrix is

$$\phi_i' = \left(\frac{\partial \phi_i}{\partial u_1} \ \frac{\partial \phi_i}{\partial u_2} \ \cdots \ \frac{\partial \phi_i}{\partial u_{p+1}} \right).$$

By using Theorem 3, we obtain

$$\sqrt{n}\left(\phi\left(\tfrac{1}{n}\sum_{t=1}^{n}X_t^2,\ldots,\tfrac{1}{n}\sum_{t=p+1}^{n}X_{t-p}X_t\right)-\phi\left(\gamma_X(0),\ldots,\gamma_X(p)\right)\right)$$

$$=\phi'_{(\gamma_X(0),\gamma_X(1),\ldots,\gamma_X(p))}\begin{pmatrix}\sqrt{n}\left(\tfrac{1}{n}\sum_{t=1}^{n}X_t^2-\gamma_X(0)\right)\\\sqrt{n}\left(\tfrac{1}{n}\sum_{t=2}^{n}X_{t-1}X_t-\gamma_X(1)\right)\\\vdots\\\sqrt{n}\left(\tfrac{1}{n}\sum_{t=p+1}^{n}X_{t-p}X_t-\gamma_X(p)\right)\end{pmatrix}+\mathbf{o}_p(1)$$

$$=\begin{pmatrix}\phi'_{1(\gamma_X(0),\gamma_X(1),\ldots,\gamma_X(p))}\\\phi'_{2(\gamma_X(0),\gamma_X(1),\ldots,\gamma_X(p))}\\\vdots\\\phi'_{p(\gamma_X(0),\gamma_X(1),\ldots,\gamma_X(p))}\end{pmatrix}\begin{pmatrix}\sqrt{n}\left(\tfrac{1}{n}\sum_{t=1}^{n}X_t^2-\gamma_X(0)\right)\\\sqrt{n}\left(\tfrac{1}{n}\sum_{t=2}^{n}X_{t-1}X_t-\gamma_X(1)\right)\\\vdots\\\sqrt{n}\left(\tfrac{1}{n}\sum_{t=p+1}^{n}X_{t-p}X_t-\gamma_X(p)\right)\end{pmatrix}+\mathbf{o}_p(1)$$

$$=\begin{pmatrix}A_{11}&A_{12}&\ldots&A_{1(p+1)}\\A_{21}&A_{22}&\ldots&A_{2(p+1)}\\\vdots&\vdots&\ddots&\vdots\\A_{p1}&A_{p2}&\ldots&A_{p(p+1)}\end{pmatrix}\begin{pmatrix}\sqrt{n}\left(\tfrac{1}{n}\sum_{t=1}^{n}X_t^2-\gamma_X(0)\right)\\\sqrt{n}\left(\tfrac{1}{n}\sum_{t=2}^{n}X_{t-1}X_t-\gamma_X(1)\right)\\\vdots\\\sqrt{n}\left(\tfrac{1}{n}\sum_{t=p+1}^{n}X_{t-p}X_t-\gamma_X(p)\right)\end{pmatrix}+\mathbf{o}_p(1),$$

where A_{ij}, $i=1,2,\ldots,p$, $j=1,2,\ldots,p+1$ are the constants depend on $\gamma_X(0),\gamma_X(1),\ldots,\gamma_X(p)$. Precisely, for every $i=1,2,\ldots,p$, it holds

$$A_{ij}=\frac{\partial\phi_i}{\partial u_j}\Bigg|_{(\gamma_X(0),\gamma_X(1),\ldots,\gamma_X(p))}\,,\qquad j=1,2,\ldots,p+1. \tag{7}$$

According Theorem 2, the limiting distribution for $\left(\tfrac{1}{n}\sum_{t=1}^{n}X_t^2,\right.$ $\left.\tfrac{1}{n}\sum_{t=2}^{n}X_tX_{t-1},\ldots,\tfrac{1}{n}\sum_{t=p+1}^{n}X_tX_{t-p}\right)^T$ is

$$\sqrt{n}\left(\begin{pmatrix}\tfrac{1}{n}\sum_{t=1}^{n}X_t^2\\\tfrac{1}{n}\sum_{t=2}^{n}X_tX_{t-1}\\\vdots\\\tfrac{1}{n}\sum_{t=p+1}^{n}X_tX_{t-p}\end{pmatrix}-\begin{pmatrix}\gamma_X(0)\\\gamma_X(1)\\\vdots\\\gamma_X(p)\end{pmatrix}\right)$$

$$\to_d N_{p+1}\left(\begin{pmatrix}0\\0\\\vdots\\0\end{pmatrix},\begin{pmatrix}V_{0,0}&V_{0,1}&\cdots&V_{0,p}\\V_{1,0}&V_{1,1}&\cdots&V_{1,p}\\\vdots&\vdots&\ddots&\vdots\\V_{p,0}&V_{p,1}&\cdots&V_{p,p}\end{pmatrix}\right). \tag{8}$$

By Theorem 3, if $(Z_1, Z_2, \ldots, Z_{p+1})^T$ having multivariate normal distribution as in (8), then

$$
\begin{pmatrix} A_{11} & A_{12} & \cdots & A_{1(p+1)} \\ A_{21} & A_{22} & \cdots & A_{2(p+1)} \\ \vdots & \vdots & \ddots & \vdots \\ A_{p1} & A_{p2} & \cdots & A_{p(p+1)} \end{pmatrix}
\begin{pmatrix} \sqrt{n}\left(\frac{1}{n}\sum_{t=1}^n X_t^2 - \gamma_X(0)\right) \\ \sqrt{n}\left(\frac{1}{n}\sum_{t=2}^n X_{t-1}X_t - \gamma_X(1)\right) \\ \vdots \\ \sqrt{n}\left(\frac{1}{n}\sum_{t=p+1}^n X_{t-p}X_t - \gamma_X(p)\right) \end{pmatrix}
$$

$$
\rightarrow_d
\begin{pmatrix} A_{11} & A_{12} & \cdots & A_{1(p+1)} \\ A_{21} & A_{22} & \cdots & A_{2(p+1)} \\ \vdots & \vdots & \ddots & \vdots \\ A_{p1} & A_{p2} & \cdots & A_{p(p+1)} \end{pmatrix}
\begin{pmatrix} Z_1 \\ Z_2 \\ \vdots \\ Z_{p+1} \end{pmatrix}
$$

$$
\sim N_p\left(\begin{pmatrix} 0 \\ 0 \\ \vdots \\ 0 \end{pmatrix}, \begin{pmatrix} \tau_1^2 & \tau_{12} & \cdots & \tau_{1p} \\ \tau_{21} & \tau_2^2 & \cdots & \tau_{2p} \\ \vdots & \vdots & \ddots & \vdots \\ \tau_{p1} & \tau_{p2} & \cdots & \tau_p^2 \end{pmatrix} \right),
$$

with

$$
\tau_i^2 = Var(A_{i1}Z_1 + A_{i2}Z_2 + \cdots + A_{i(p+1)}Z_{p+1})
$$

$$
= \sum_{j=1}^{p+1} A_{ij}^2 Var(Z_j) + 2 \sum_{1 \le k < j \le p+1} A_{ik}A_{ij}Cov(Z_k, Z_j)
$$

$$
= \sum_{j=1}^{p+1} A_{ij}^2 V_{j-1,j-1} + 2 \sum_{1 \le k < j \le p+1} A_{ik}A_{ij}V_{k-1,j-1}
$$

$$
\tau_{ik} = Cov(A_{i1}Z_1 + \cdots + A_{i(p+1)}Z_{p+1}, A_{k1}Z_1 + \cdots + A_{k(p+1)}Z_{p+1}),
$$

for every $i \ne k$, $i, k = 1, 2, \ldots, p$. Thus, according Theorem 3 can be concluded that

$$
\sqrt{n}\left(\widehat{\theta} - \theta\right) = \sqrt{n}\left(\phi\left(\sum_{t=1}^n X_t^2, \ldots, \sum_{t=p+1}^n X_{t-p}X_t\right) - \phi(\gamma_X(0), \ldots, \gamma_X(p))\right)
$$

$$
\rightarrow_d N_p\left(\begin{pmatrix} 0 \\ 0 \\ \vdots \\ 0 \end{pmatrix}, \begin{pmatrix} \tau_1^2 & \tau_{12} & \cdots & \tau_{1p} \\ \tau_{21} & \tau_2^2 & \cdots & \tau_{2p} \\ \vdots & \vdots & \ddots & \vdots \\ \tau_{p1} & \tau_{p2} & \cdots & \tau_p^2 \end{pmatrix} \right).
$$

Furthermore, analog with the asymptotic distribution for the random vector $\sqrt{n}\left(\widehat{\theta} - \theta\right)$, we do the same for the random vector $\sqrt{n}\left(\widehat{\theta}^* - \widehat{\theta}\right)$, with $\widehat{\theta}^*$ is the bootstrap version of $\widehat{\theta}$. Let $T(X_1, X_2, \ldots, X_n; F)$ be a statistic. Let $\widehat{F}_n$ be the emphirical distribution function of $X_1, X_2, \ldots, X_n$, *i.e.* the distribution taking probability of $1/n$ for each $X_1, X_2, \ldots, X_n$. Bootstrap sample $X_1^*, X_2^*, \ldots, X_n^*$ can be obtained by using the residuals bootstrap. The function T is defined as the random variable

$$T(X_1, X_2, \ldots, X_n; F) = \sqrt{n}\big(\widehat{\boldsymbol{\theta}} - \boldsymbol{\theta}\big),$$

with $\widehat{\boldsymbol{\theta}} = \big(\widehat{\theta}_1, \widehat{\theta}_2, \ldots, \widehat{\theta}_p\big)^T$ is the estimator for the coefficient $\boldsymbol{\theta}$ of AR(p) model. The bootstrap version of T is

$$T(X_1^*, X_2^*, \ldots, X_n^*; \widehat{F}_n) = \sqrt{n}\big(\widehat{\boldsymbol{\theta}}^* - \widehat{\boldsymbol{\theta}}\big),$$

with $\widehat{\boldsymbol{\theta}}^*$ is the bootstrap version of $\widehat{\boldsymbol{\theta}}$ which is computed using bootstrap sample $X_1^*, X_2^*, \ldots, X_n^*$. Bootstrap method is a tool for estimating the distribution $P_F\big(\sqrt{n}(\widehat{\theta}_i - \theta_i) \leq x\big)$ using distribution $P_{\widehat{F}_n}\big(\sqrt{n}(\widehat{\theta}_i^* - \widehat{\theta}_i) \leq x\big)$.

The stationary of an autoregressive process $\{X_t\}$ infer that X_t can be expressed as linear process and the residuals bootstrap yielding the sequence of i.i.d. $\{\varepsilon_t^*\}$, hence the Theorem 2 can be applied. According Theorem 2, the multivariate central limit of $\Big(\frac{1}{n}\sum_{t=1}^n X_t^{*2}, \frac{1}{n}\sum_{t=2}^n X_t^* X_{t-1}^*, \ldots, \frac{1}{n}\sum_{t=p+1}^n X_t^* X_{t-p}^*\Big)^T$ is

$$\sqrt{n}\left(\begin{pmatrix} \frac{1}{n}\sum_{t=1}^n X_t^{*2} \\ \frac{1}{n}\sum_{t=2}^n X_t^* X_{t-1}^* \\ \vdots \\ \frac{1}{n}\sum_{t=p+1}^n X_t^* X_{t-p}^* \end{pmatrix} - \begin{pmatrix} \widehat{\gamma}_X(0) \\ \widehat{\gamma}_X(1) \\ \vdots \\ \widehat{\gamma}_X(p) \end{pmatrix}\right)$$

$$\to_d N_{p+1}\left(\begin{pmatrix} 0 \\ 0 \\ \vdots \\ 0 \end{pmatrix}, \begin{pmatrix} V_{0,0}^* & V_{0,1}^* & \cdots & V_{0,p}^* \\ V_{1,0}^* & V_{1,1}^* & \cdots & V_{1,p}^* \\ \vdots & \vdots & \ddots & \vdots \\ V_{p,0}^* & V_{p,1}^* & \cdots & V_{p,p}^* \end{pmatrix}\right). \tag{9}$$

By applying the *plug-in* principle on the estimator $\widehat{\boldsymbol{\theta}}$, we obtain the bootstrap estimator $\widehat{\boldsymbol{\theta}}^*$. As in the previous process, the estimator $\widehat{\boldsymbol{\theta}}^* = \big(\widehat{\theta}_1^*, \widehat{\theta}_2^*, \ldots, \widehat{\theta}_p^*\big)^T$ can be expressed as a measurable functional $\boldsymbol{\phi} = (\phi_1, \phi_2, \ldots, \phi_p)^T : \mathbf{R}^{p+1} \to \mathbf{R}^p$. Each component of estimator $\widehat{\theta}_i^*, i = 1, 2, \ldots, p$ can be expressed as a measurable function $\phi_i : \mathbf{R}^{p+1} \to \mathbf{R}$,

$$\widehat{\theta}_i^* \equiv \phi_i\left(\sum_{t=1}^n X_t^{*2}, \sum_{t=2}^n X_t^* X_{t-1}^*, \ldots, \sum_{t=p+1}^n X_t^* X_{t-p}^*\right).$$

The function ϕ_i for every $i = 1, 2, \ldots, p$ can be determined from the system (6) and be written as $\phi_i \equiv \phi_i(u_1, u_2, \ldots, u_{p+1})$. The function ϕ_i is differentiable and its derivative matrix is

$$\phi_i' = \left(\frac{\partial \phi_i}{\partial u_1} \ \frac{\partial \phi_i}{\partial u_2} \ \cdots \ \frac{\partial \phi_i}{\partial u_{p+1}} \right).$$

By applying Theorems 3 and 4, we obtain

$$\sqrt{n}\left(\phi\left(\tfrac{1}{n}\sum_{t=1}^n X_t^{2*}, \ldots, \tfrac{1}{n}\sum_{t=p+1}^n X_{t-p}^* X_t^* \right) - \phi\left(\widehat{\gamma}_X(0), \ldots, \widehat{\gamma}_X(p) \right) \right)$$

$$= \phi_{(\widehat{\gamma}_X(0),\widehat{\gamma}_X(1),\ldots,\widehat{\gamma}_X(p))}' \begin{pmatrix} \sqrt{n}\left(\tfrac{1}{n}\sum_{t=1}^n X_t^{2*} - \widehat{\gamma}_X(0) \right) \\ \sqrt{n}\left(\tfrac{1}{n}\sum_{t=2}^n X_{t-1}^* X_t^* - \widehat{\gamma}_X(1) \right) \\ \vdots \\ \sqrt{n}\left(\tfrac{1}{n}\sum_{t=p+1}^n X_{t-p}^* X_t^* - \widehat{\gamma}_X(p) \right) \end{pmatrix} + o_p(1)$$

$$= \begin{pmatrix} \phi_{1(\widehat{\gamma}_X(0),\widehat{\gamma}_X(1),\ldots,\widehat{\gamma}_X(p))}' \\ \phi_{2(\widehat{\gamma}_X(0),\widehat{\gamma}_X(1),\ldots,\widehat{\gamma}_X(p))}' \\ \vdots \\ \phi_{p(\widehat{\gamma}_X(0),\widehat{\gamma}_X(1),\ldots,\widehat{\gamma}_X(p))}' \end{pmatrix} \begin{pmatrix} \sqrt{n}\left(\tfrac{1}{n}\sum_{t=1}^n X_t^{2*} - \widehat{\gamma}_X(0) \right) \\ \sqrt{n}\left(\tfrac{1}{n}\sum_{t=2}^n X_{t-1}^* X_t^* - \widehat{\gamma}_X(1) \right) \\ \vdots \\ \sqrt{n}\left(\tfrac{1}{n}\sum_{t=p+1}^n X_{t-p}^* X_t^* - \widehat{\gamma}_X(p) \right) \end{pmatrix} + o_p(1)$$

$$= \begin{pmatrix} B_{11} & B_{12} & \cdots & B_{1(p+1)} \\ B_{21} & B_{22} & \cdots & B_{2(p+1)} \\ \vdots & \vdots & \ddots & \vdots \\ B_{p1} & B_{p2} & \cdots & B_{p(p+1)} \end{pmatrix} \begin{pmatrix} \sqrt{n}\left(\tfrac{1}{n}\sum_{t=1}^n X_t^{2*} - \widehat{\gamma}_X(0) \right) \\ \sqrt{n}\left(\tfrac{1}{n}\sum_{t=2}^n X_{t-1}^* X_t^* - \widehat{\gamma}_X(1) \right) \\ \vdots \\ \sqrt{n}\left(\tfrac{1}{n}\sum_{t=p+1}^n X_{t-p}^* X_t^* - \widehat{\gamma}_X(p) \right) \end{pmatrix} + o_p(1),$$

where B_{ij}, $i = 1, 2, \ldots, p$, $j = 1, 2, \ldots, p+1$ are constants depend on $\widehat{\gamma}_X(0), \widehat{\gamma}_X(1), \ldots, \widehat{\gamma}_X(p)$. More precisely, for every $i = 1, 2, \ldots, p$,

$$B_{ij} = \frac{\partial \phi_i}{\partial u_j}\bigg|_{(\widehat{\gamma}_X(0),\widehat{\gamma}_X(1),\ldots,\widehat{\gamma}_X(p))}, \qquad j = 1, 2, \ldots, p+1. \tag{10}$$

If $(W_1, W_2, \ldots, W_{p+1})^T$ having multivariate normal distribution as in (9), then by Theorem 4, we obtain

$$
\begin{pmatrix}
B_{11} & B_{12} & \cdots & B_{1(p+1)} \\
B_{21} & B_{22} & \cdots & B_{2(p+1)} \\
\vdots & \vdots & \ddots & \vdots \\
B_{p1} & B_{p2} & \cdots & B_{p(p+1)}
\end{pmatrix}
\begin{pmatrix}
\sqrt{n}\left(\frac{1}{n}\sum_{t=1}^{n} X_t^{2*} - \widehat{\gamma}_X(0)\right) \\
\sqrt{n}\left(\frac{1}{n}\sum_{t=2}^{n} X_{t-1}^* X_t^* - \widehat{\gamma}_X(1)\right) \\
\vdots \\
\sqrt{n}\left(\frac{1}{n}\sum_{t=p+1}^{n} X_{t-p}^* X_t^* - \widehat{\gamma}_X(p)\right)
\end{pmatrix}
$$

$$
\rightarrow_d
\begin{pmatrix}
B_{11} & B_{12} & \cdots & B_{1(p+1)} \\
B_{21} & B_{22} & \cdots & B_{2(p+1)} \\
\vdots & \vdots & \ddots & \vdots \\
B_{p1} & B_{p2} & \cdots & B_{p(p+1)}
\end{pmatrix}
\begin{pmatrix}
W_1 \\
W_2 \\
\vdots \\
W_{p+1}
\end{pmatrix}
$$

$$
\sim N_p \left(
\begin{pmatrix} 0 \\ 0 \\ \vdots \\ 0 \end{pmatrix},
\begin{pmatrix}
\tau_1^{2*} & \tau_{12}^* & \cdots & \tau_{1p}^* \\
\tau_{21}^* & \tau_2^{2*} & \cdots & \tau_{2p}^* \\
\vdots & \vdots & \ddots & \vdots \\
\tau_{p1}^* & \tau_{p2}^* & \cdots & \tau_p^{2*}
\end{pmatrix}
\right),
\tag{11}
$$

where

$$
\tau_i^{2*} = Var(B_{i1}W_1 + B_{i2}W_2 + \cdots + B_{i(p+1)}W_{p+1})
$$

$$
= \sum_{j=1}^{p+1} B_{ij}^2 Var(W_j) + 2 \sum_{1 \leq k < j \leq p+1} B_{ik}B_{ij} Cov(W_k, W_j)
$$

$$
= \sum_{j=1}^{p+1} B_{ij}^2 V_{j-1,j-1}^* + 2 \sum_{1 \leq k < j \leq p+1} B_{ik}B_{ij} V_{k-1,j-1}^*
$$

$$
\tau_{ik}^* = Cov(B_{i1}W_1 + \cdots + B_{i(p+1)}B_{p+1}, B_{k1}W_1 + \cdots + B_{k(p+1)}W_{p+1}),
$$

for every $i \neq k$, $i, k = 1, 2, \ldots, p$. Hence, by Theorem 4 we conclude that

$$
\sqrt{n}\left(\widehat{\theta}^* - \widehat{\theta}\right) = \sqrt{n}\left(\phi\left(\sum_{t=1}^{n} X_t^{2*}, \ldots, \sum_{t=p+1}^{n} X_{t-p}^* X_t^*\right) - \phi\left(\widehat{\gamma}_X(0), \ldots, \widehat{\gamma}_X(p)\right)\right)
$$

$$
\rightarrow_d N_p \left(
\begin{pmatrix} 0 \\ 0 \\ \vdots \\ 0 \end{pmatrix},
\begin{pmatrix}
\tau_1^{2*} & \tau_{12}^* & \cdots & \tau_{1p}^* \\
\tau_{21}^* & \tau_2^{2*} & \cdots & \tau_{2p}^* \\
\vdots & \vdots & \ddots & \vdots \\
\tau_{p1}^* & \tau_{p2}^* & \cdots & \tau_p^{2*}
\end{pmatrix}
\right),
$$

completing the proof.

5 Conclusions

We conclude that the bootstrap parameter estimators of the $AR(p)$ model are asymptotic and converge in distribution to the p–variate normal distribution.

References

1. Bibi, A., Aknounche, A.: Yule-Walker type estimators in periodic bilinear model: strong consistency and asymptotic normality. J. Stat. Methods Appl. **19**, 1–30 (2010)
2. Bose, A.: Edgeworth correction by bootstrap in autoregressions. Ann. Statist. **16**, 1709–1722 (1988)
3. Brockwell, P.J., Davis, R.A.: Time Series: Theory and Methods. Springer, New York (1991)
4. Brouste, A., Cai, C., Kleptsyna, M.: Asymptotic properties of the MLE for the autoregressive process coefficients under stationary Gaussian noise. Math. Methods Statist. **23**, 103–115 (2014)
5. Efron, B., Tibshirani, R.: An Introduction to the Bootstrap. Chapman & Hall, New York (1993)
6. Freedman, D.A.: On bootstrapping two-stage least-squares estimates in stationary linear models. Ann. Statist. **12**, 827–842 (1984)
7. Hardle, W., Horowitz, J., Kreiss, J.P.: Bootstrap methods for time series. Int. Stat. Rev. **71**, 435–459 (2003)
8. Politis, D.N.: The impact of bootstrap methods on time series analysis. Stat. Sci. **18**, 219–230 (2003)
9. Sahinler, S., Topuz, D.: Bootstrap and jackknife resampling algorithms for estimation of regression parameters. J. Appl. Quant. Methods **2**, 188–199 (2007)
10. Singh, K.: On the asymptotic accuracy of Efron's bootstrap. Ann. Statist. **9**, 1187–1195 (1981)
11. Suprihatin, B., Guritno, S., Haryatmi, S.: Asymptotic distribution of the bootstrap parameter estimator for AR(1) process. Model Assist. Statist. Appl. **10**, 53–61 (2015)
12. Van der Vaart, A.W.: Asymptotic Statistics. Cambridge University Press, Cambridge (2000)
13. Van der Vaart, A.W.: Lecture Notes on Time Series. Vrije Universiteit, Amsterdam (2012)

Weighted Coefficients to Measure Agreement Among Several Sets of Ranks Emphasizing Top and Bottom Ranks at the Same Time

Sandra M. Aleixo[1(✉)] and Júlia Teles[2]

[1] CEAUL and Department of Mathematics,
ISEL – Instituto Superior de Engenharia de Lisboa,
IPL – Instituto Politécnico de Lisboa, Lisbon, Portugal
sandra.aleixo@adm.isel.pt
[2] CIPER and Mathematics Unit, Faculdade de Motricidade Humana,
Universidade de Lisboa, Lisbon, Portugal
jteles@fmh.ulisboa.pt

Abstract. In this paper, two new weighted coefficients of agreement to measure the concordance among several (more than two) sets of ranks, putting more weight in the lower and upper ranks simultaneously, are presented. These new coefficients, the signed Klotz and the signed Mood, generalize the correspondent rank-order coefficients to measure the agreement between two sets of ranks previously proposed by the authors [1]. Under the null hypothesis of no agreement or no association among the rankings, the asymptotic distribution of these new coefficients was derived. To illustrate the worth of these measures, an example is presented to compare them with the Kendall's coefficient and the van der Waerden correlation coefficient.

Keywords: Rank-order correlation · Weighted coefficients ·
Concordance measures · Signed Klotz coefficient ·
Signed Mood coefficient · van der Waerden coefficient

1 Introduction

Concordance coefficients are widely used in several applied fields. The choice for a specific parametric or nonparametric measure depends on the type of data and the purpose of agreement evaluation. The intraclass correlation coefficients [2,3] and Kendall's coefficient of concordance W [4] are examples of these two types of measures. The nonparametric measures of agreement allow to evaluate the degree of agreement or concordance among several sets of ranks. Despite in most of these measures all ranks have the same weight when evaluating agreement, several studies focus on the evaluation of agreement among the upper (respectively, lower) ranks, neglecting the disagreement in the lower (respectively, upper) ranks. In these cases, weighted rank concordance coefficients are

ⓒ Springer Nature Switzerland AG 2019
S. Misra et al. (Eds.): ICCSA 2019, LNCS 11620, pp. 23–33, 2019.
https://doi.org/10.1007/978-3-030-24296-1_3

the appropriate choice [5]. Iman and Conover [6] proposed the top-down concordance, which weighted the lower and upper ranks differently. However, in some situations, may be important that coefficients give more weight to the lower and upper ranks simultaneously. In the case of two sets of ranks, several measures have been proposed, namely the van der Waerden correlation coefficient [7] and the new weighted rank correlations coefficients sensitive to agreement on top and bottom rankings [8].

There are several situations where n objects are ranked by more than two independent observers and in which the interest is focused on agreement on the top rankings. Kendall's coefficient of concordance [4] assigns equal weights to all rankings and thus can not be used for this purpose. In 2014, Coolen-Maturi introduced a new coefficient of concordance which was more sensitive to agreement on the top rankings [9].

In this paper, other weighted coefficients of agreement to measure the concordance among $m > 2$ sets of ranks, putting more weight in the lower and upper ranks simultaneously, are presented. These new coefficients generalize the rank-order coefficients to measure the agreement between two sets of ranks ($m = 2$) putting more weight in the extreme ranks, previously proposed by the authors [1].

The remainder of paper is organized in five sections. Weighted coefficients to measure the concordance among several sets of ranks putting emphasis on the extremes ranks are shown in Sect. 2. In Sect. 3, distribution of the generalized weighted agreement coefficients is derived. In Sect. 4, an illustrative example is presented and in Sect. 5 some future work is mentioned.

2   Weighted Coefficients to Measure the Concordance Among Several Sets of Ranks Putting Emphasis on the Extremes Ranks

Suppose that there are n subjects to be ranked by $m > 2$ independent observers or judges or in m moments, producing m sets of ranks.

Let R_{ij} represents the rank assigned to the jth subject by the ith observer, for $i = 1, 2, \ldots, m$ and $j = 1, 2, \ldots, n$. After obtaining the m sets of ranks for the n subjects, the corresponding scores were calculated.

Consider that S_{ij} denotes a generic score, associated to the rank that was awarded by the ith observer to the jth subject, for $i = 1, 2, \ldots, m$ and $j = 1, 2, \ldots, n$. The score S_{ij} can be the van der Waerden score $W_{ij} = \Phi^{-1}\left(\frac{R_{ij}}{n+1}\right)$ [10], the signed Klotz score $SK_{ij} = sign\left(R_{ij} - \frac{n+1}{2}\right)\left(\Phi^{-1}\left(\frac{R_{ij}}{n+1}\right)\right)^2$, or the signed Mood score $SM_{ij} = sign\left(R_{ij} - \frac{n+1}{2}\right)\left(R_{ij} - \frac{n+1}{2}\right)^2$ [1]. In Table 1, it can be observed the structure of the scores for the m observers.

Note that, for any score among those three, we have $\sum_{j=1}^{n} S_{1j} = \sum_{j=1}^{n} S_{2j} = \cdots = \sum_{j=1}^{n} S_{mj} = 0$. In fact, in the case of van der Waerden and signed Klotz scores, one has: (i) if n odd then $\Phi^{-1}\left(\frac{k}{n+1}\right) = -\Phi^{-1}\left(\frac{n+1-k}{n+1}\right)$,

Table 1. Scores corresponding to the m sets of ranks

Observers/judges	Subjects						Total
	1	2	$\ldots$	j	$\ldots$	n	
1	S_{11}	S_{12}	$\ldots$	S_{1j}	$\ldots$	S_{1n}	$S_{1\bullet} = \sum_{j=1}^{n} S_{1j} = 0$
2	S_{21}	S_{22}	$\ldots$	S_{2j}	$\ldots$	S_{2n}	$S_{2\bullet} = \sum_{j=1}^{n} S_{2j} = 0$
$\vdots$	$\vdots$	$\vdots$	$\ddots$	$\vdots$	$\ddots$	$\vdots$	$\vdots$
i	S_{i1}	S_{i2}	$\ldots$	S_{ij}	$\ldots$	S_{in}	$S_{i\bullet} = \sum_{j=1}^{n} S_{ij} = 0$
$\vdots$	$\vdots$	$\vdots$	$\ddots$	$\vdots$	$\ddots$	$\vdots$	$\vdots$
m	S_{m1}	S_{m2}	$\ldots$	S_{mj}	$\ldots$	S_{mn}	$S_{m\bullet} = \sum_{j=1}^{n} S_{mj} = 0$
Total	$S_{\bullet 1}$	$S_{\bullet 2}$	$\ldots$	$S_{\bullet j}$	$\ldots$	$S_{\bullet n}$	$S_{\bullet\bullet} = 0$

for $k = 1, 2, \ldots, \lfloor \frac{n}{2} \rfloor$, and $\Phi^{-1}\left(\frac{(n+1)/2}{n+1}\right) = \Phi^{-1}\left(\frac{1}{2}\right) = 0$; (ii) if n even then $\Phi^{-1}\left(\frac{k}{n+1}\right) = -\Phi^{-1}\left(\frac{n+1-k}{n+1}\right)$, for $k = 1, 2, \ldots, \frac{n}{2}$. For the signed Mood scores, notice that: (i) if n odd then $\left(k - \frac{n+1}{2}\right)^2 = \left(n+1-k-\frac{n+1}{2}\right)^2$, for $k = 1, 2, \ldots, \lfloor \frac{n}{2} \rfloor$; (ii) if n even then $\left(k - \frac{n+1}{2}\right)^2 = \left(n+1-k-\frac{n+1}{2}\right)^2$, for $k = 1, 2, \ldots, \frac{n}{2}$.

Moreover, $\sum_{j=1}^{n} S_{1j}^2 = \sum_{j=1}^{n} S_{2j}^2 = \cdots = \sum_{j=1}^{n} S_{mj}^2$ is a non null constant, denoted by C_S, that depends on the sample size n. Therefore, in [1] the authors had defined the rank-order correlation coefficient between the two sets of rankings assigned to the n subjects by the observers/judges i and k as follows

$$R_S^{ik} = \frac{\sum_{j=1}^{n} S_{ij} S_{kj}}{\sum_{j=1}^{n} S_{ij}^2} = \frac{1}{C_S} \sum_{j=1}^{n} S_{ij} S_{kj},$$

which take values in the interval $[-1, 1]$.

In this work, the idea to build two new weighted coefficients of agreement is similar to the one used on the construction of Kendall's coefficient of concordance W [4,11]. This coefficient is based on the ratio between the variance of the sums of scores awarded to subjects, denoted by S_{SS}^2, and the maximum value that this variance can attain considering the values of m and n. So, the weighted coefficients of agreement to measure the concordance among m sets of ranks, giving more weight to the extremes ones, can be defined by

$$A_S = \frac{S_{SS}^2}{\max S_{SS}^2}$$

with

$$S_{SS}^2 = \frac{1}{n-1} \sum_{j=1}^{n} \left(S_{\bullet j} - \overline{S}_{\bullet \bullet}\right)^2 = \frac{1}{n-1} \sum_{j=1}^{n} S_{\bullet j}^2,$$

attending that $\overline{S}_{\bullet \bullet} = \sum_{j=1}^{n} S_{\bullet j}/n = S_{\bullet \bullet}/n = 0$.

Therefore

$$A_S = \frac{\dfrac{1}{n-1} \sum_{j=1}^{n} S_{\bullet j}^2}{\max \left(\dfrac{1}{n-1} \sum_{j=1}^{n} S_{\bullet j}^2 \right)} = \frac{\sum_{j=1}^{n} S_{\bullet j}^2}{\max \sum_{j=1}^{n} S_{\bullet j}^2}$$

$$= \frac{\sum_{j=1}^{n} \left(\sum_{i=1}^{m} S_{ij} \right)^2}{\max \sum_{j=1}^{n} S_{\bullet j}^2}.$$

When all the observers agree on the ranks assigned to the n subjects, the rank R_{ij} is equal to j, for $i = 1, 2, \ldots, m$ and, consequently, all the m scores S_{ij} are equal. So, in this case, the sum of the scores assigned to the jth subject, for $j = 1, 2, \ldots, n$, is given by mS_{ij}. So, one has

$$\max S_{SS}^2 = \max \sum_{j=1}^{n} S_{\bullet j}^2 = \sum_{j=1}^{n} (mS_{ij})^2$$

$$= m^2 \sum_{j=1}^{n} S_{ij}^2 = m^2 \, C_S.$$

Thus, the weighted coefficients to measure the concordance among m sets of ranks, putting emphasis on the extremes ones, are given by

$$A_S = \frac{\sum_{j=1}^{n} \left(\sum_{i=1}^{m} S_{ij} \right)^2}{m^2 \, C_S}. \tag{1}$$

These coefficients take values in the interval $[0, 1]$.

It is possible to verify that there is a relationship between the weighted coefficients A_S and the average $\overline{R}_S$ of the weighted rank-order correlation coefficients between the $\binom{m}{2}$ possible pairs of ranks (i, k), for $i, k = 1, 2, \ldots, m$. In fact, one has

$$
\begin{aligned}
\overline{R}_S &= \frac{1}{\binom{m}{2}} \sum_{i<k} R_S^{ik} \\
&= \frac{2}{m(m-1)} \sum_{i<k} \left[\frac{1}{C_S} \sum_{j=1}^{n} S_{ij} S_{kj} \right] \\
&= \frac{1}{m(m-1)C_S} \sum_{j=1}^{n} \left[2 \sum_{i<k} S_{ij} S_{kj} \right] \\
&= \frac{1}{m(m-1)C_S} \sum_{j=1}^{n} \left[\left(\sum_{i=1}^{m} S_{ij} \right)^2 - \sum_{i=1}^{m} S_{ij}^2 \right] \\
&= \frac{1}{m(m-1)C_S} \left[\sum_{j=1}^{n} \left(\sum_{i=1}^{m} S_{ij} \right)^2 - \sum_{i=1}^{m} \sum_{j=1}^{n} S_{ij}^2 \right] \\
&= \frac{1}{m(m-1)C_S} \left[\sum_{j=1}^{n} \left(\sum_{i=1}^{m} S_{ij} \right)^2 - m \, C_S \right].
\end{aligned}
$$

Attending to (1) it follows that

$$
\sum_{j=1}^{n} \left(\sum_{i=1}^{m} S_{ij} \right)^2 = m^2 \, C_S \, A_S, \tag{2}
$$

so $\overline{R}_S$ can be written as follows

$$
\overline{R}_S = \frac{1}{m(m-1)C_S} \left(m^2 \, C_S \, A_S - m \, C_S \right) = \frac{m \, A_S - 1}{m - 1}.
$$

This allow us to conclude that each one of the weighted agreement coefficients A_S can be obtained from the average $\overline{R}_S$ of the weighted rank-order correlation coefficients between the $\binom{m}{2}$ possible pairs of ranks (i, k), for $i, k = 1, 2, \ldots, m$, that is

$$
A_S = \frac{(m-1)\overline{R}_S + 1}{m}.
$$

3 Distribution of the Generalized Weighted Agreement Coefficients

For small values of n and m, it is possible to obtain the exact quantiles for the generalized weighted agreement coefficients A_S, considering all possible permutations $(n!)^m$ of rankings. This is very demanding computationally and it becomes impossible for larger values of n and m. However, to slightly larger values n and m, it is still possible to obtain approximate quantiles using Monte Carlo simulation. For larger values of n and m, it can be presented the asymptotic distribution of A_S, under the null hypotheses of no agreement or no association between the rankings, i.e., under the hypotheses of random assignment of ranks by all observers/judges.

Theorem 1: Under the null hypotheses of no agreement or no association among the rankings, the statistic $m(n-1)A_S$ has an asymptotic Chi-Square distribution with $(n-1)$ degrees of freedom, as $m \to \infty$.

Proof 1: In p. 173 of [7] is postulated the following Theorem: considering the number of observations in each block fixed and denoted by n, and the scores $a(1), \ldots, a(n)$ also fixed and arbitrary but not constants, and the number of blocks m tending to ∞, the statistic

$$Q_m = \frac{n-1}{m} \left(\sum_{j=1}^{n} (a(j) - \bar{a})^2 \right)^{-1} \sum_{j=1}^{n} \left(\sum_{i=1}^{m} a(R_{ij}) - m \, \bar{a} \right)^2$$

has asymptotically a Chi-Square distribution with $(n-1)$ degrees of freedom.

For the three scores considered in this work, denoted by S_{ij}, we get: $\bar{a} = \overline{S}_{\bullet\bullet} = 0$; $a(j) = S_j$ which is the score correspondent to the rank $R_{ij} = j$ (recall that when all the observers agree on the ranks assigned to the n subjects, the m scores S_{ij} are equal and denoted by S_j); $a(R_{ij}) = S_{ij}$. Therefore,

$$Q_m = \frac{n-1}{m} \left(\sum_{j=1}^{n} a(j)^2 \right)^{-1} \sum_{j=1}^{n} \left(\sum_{i=1}^{m} a(R_{ij}) \right)^2$$

$$= \frac{n-1}{m} \left(\sum_{j=1}^{n} S_j^2 \right)^{-1} \sum_{j=1}^{n} \left(\sum_{i=1}^{m} S_{ij} \right)^2 .$$

So, considering $C_S = \sum_{j=1}^{n} S_j^2 = \sum_{j=1}^{n} S_{ij}^2$ and (1), it comes

$$Q_m = \frac{n-1}{m} C_S^{-1} \left(m^2 C_S A_S \right) = m(n-1)A_S,$$

leading to what is intended to demonstrate. □

In the case of many ties among the assigned ranks within judges, these tied observations are replaced by the average of the corresponding ranks that the observations would have if they were not tied. In this case, the usual F statistic for the two-way analysis of variance over the set of ranks can be used, as this statistics corrects for ties. This statistic has an approximate F distribution with $(n-1)$ and $(m-1)(n-1)$ degrees of freedom, as was shown by Iman and

Davenport for the case of Friedman statistics [12]. Similarly to what was done by these authors, we can state the following

Proposition 1: Considering the weighted coefficients A_S, the statistic F is given by $(m-1)A_S/(1-A_S)$, which has an asymptotic F distribution with $(n-1)$ and $(m-1)(n-1)$ degrees of freedom.

Proof 2: To deduce the statistic F, the usual one for the two-way analysis of variance over the set of ranks or, more precisely, over the set of scores obtained from ranks, the total variability in the data (SS_T) is partitioned into three components: the between subjects sum of squares (SS_{BS}), the between judges sum of squares (SS_{BJ}) and the error sum of squares (SS_E). In this case, the F statistic is the quotient between two ratios, the between subjects mean square $(MS_{BS} = SS_{BS}/(n-1))$ and the error mean square $(MS_E = SS_E/((m-1)(n-1))$, being $(n-1)$ and $(m-1)(n-1)$ the degrees of freedom of SS_{BJ} and SS_E, respectively.

In our case, the total sum of squares is given by

$$SS_T = \sum_{i=1}^{m}\sum_{j=1}^{n}\left(S_{ij} - \overline{S}_{\bullet\bullet}\right)^2 = \sum_{i=1}^{m}\sum_{j=1}^{n} S_{ij}^2;$$

the between subjects sum of squares is

$$SS_{BS} = \sum_{i=1}^{m}\sum_{j=1}^{n}\left(\overline{S}_{\bullet j} - \overline{S}_{\bullet\bullet}\right)^2 = \sum_{i=1}^{m}\sum_{j=1}^{n}\overline{S}_{\bullet j}^2$$

$$= \sum_{i=1}^{m}\sum_{j=1}^{n}\left(\frac{S_{\bullet j}}{m}\right)^2 = \frac{1}{m^2}\sum_{i=1}^{m}\sum_{j=1}^{n} S_{\bullet j}^2$$

$$= \frac{m}{m^2}\sum_{j=1}^{n} S_{\bullet j}^2 = \frac{1}{m}\sum_{j=1}^{n}\left(\sum_{i=1}^{m} S_{ij}\right)^2$$

$$= \frac{1}{m}m^2 C_S A_S \quad \text{attending to (2)}$$

$$= m C_S A_S; \tag{3}$$

the between judges sum of squares is

$$SS_{BJ} = \sum_{i=1}^{m}\sum_{j=1}^{n}\left(\overline{S}_{i\bullet} - \overline{S}_{\bullet\bullet}\right)^2 = 0;$$

and finally, the error sum of squares is

$$SS_E = \sum_{i=1}^{m}\sum_{j=1}^{n}\left(S_{ij} - \overline{S}_{\bullet j}\right)^2$$

$$= \sum_{i=1}^{m}\sum_{j=1}^{n} S_{ij}^2 - 2\sum_{i=1}^{m}\sum_{j=1}^{n} S_{ij}\overline{S}_{\bullet j} + \sum_{i=1}^{m}\sum_{j=1}^{n}\overline{S}_{\bullet j}^2$$

$$= \sum_{i=1}^{m}\sum_{j=1}^{n} S_{ij}^2 - 2\sum_{j=1}^{n} S_{\bullet j}\frac{S_{\bullet j}}{m} + \sum_{i=1}^{m}\sum_{j=1}^{n}\left(\frac{S_{\bullet j}}{m}\right)^2$$

$$= \sum_{i=1}^{m}\sum_{j=1}^{n} S_{ij}^2 - \frac{2}{m}\sum_{j=1}^{n} S_{\bullet j}^2 + \frac{m}{m^2}\sum_{j=1}^{n} S_{\bullet j}^2$$

$$= \sum_{i=1}^{m}\sum_{j=1}^{n} S_{ij}^2 - \frac{1}{m}\sum_{j=1}^{n} S_{\bullet j}^2$$

$$= \sum_{i=1}^{m} C_S - \frac{1}{m}\sum_{j=1}^{n}\left(\sum_{i=1}^{m} S_{ij}\right)^2$$

$$= mC_S - \frac{1}{m}m^2 C_S A_S \quad \text{attending to (2)}$$

$$= mC_S\left(1 - A_S\right). \tag{4}$$

Considering (3) and (4), it is proved that

$$F = \frac{MS_{BS}}{MS_E} = \frac{\dfrac{SS_{BS}}{n-1}}{\dfrac{SS_E}{(m-1)(n-1)}} = \frac{(m-1)mC_S A_S}{mC_S(1-A_S)}$$

$$= \frac{(m-1)A_S}{1-A_S} \overset{\circ}{\sim} F(n-1,(m-1)(n-1)). \qquad \square$$

4   Example

In this example, we are going to consider three judges and twenty subjects to show the usefulness of the new weighted coefficients. The four top and bottom ranks are in total agreement, while the remaining ranks were obtained through a permutation of the numbers 5 to 16.

The three sets of ranks $\{(R_{1j}, R_{2j}, R_{3j}), j = 1, \ldots, 20\}$ are listed in Table 2 and displayed in Fig. 1. In Table 2, the correspondents van der Waerden, signed Klotz and signed Mood scores are also shown.

The Kendall's coefficient, the van der Waerden correlation coefficient, the signed Klotz and the signed Mood coefficients were calculated for these data. The 95% bootstrap confidence intervals were estimated by the percentile method, based on $100,000$ samples [13]. The results, obtained using the package *bootstrap* [14] of R software, are displayed in Table 3.

Table 2. Sets of ranks (R_{1j}, R_{2j}, R_{3j}), $j = 1, \ldots, 20$, and the corresponding van der Waerden (W_{1j}, W_{2j}, W_{3j}), signed Klotz $(SK_{1j}, SK_{2j}, SK_{3j})$ and signed Mood scores $(SM_{1j}, SM_{2j}, SM_{3j})$.

R_{1j}	R_{2j}	R_{3j}	W_{1j}	W_{2j}	W_{3j}	SK_{1j}	SK_{2j}	SK_{3j}	SM_{1j}	SM_{2j}	SM_{3j}
1	1	1	−1.668	−1.668	−1.668	−2.784	−2.784	−2.784	−90.250	−90.250	−90.250
2	2	2	−1.309	−1.309	−1.309	−1.714	−1.714	−1.714	−72.250	−72.250	−72.250
3	3	3	−1.068	−1.068	−1.068	−1.140	−1.140	−1.140	−56.250	−56.250	−56.250
4	4	4	−0.876	−0.876	−0.876	−0.768	−0.768	−0.768	−42.250	−42.250	−42.250
5	16	9	−0.712	0.712	−0.180	−0.508	0.508	−0.032	−30.250	30.250	−2.250
6	15	15	−0.566	0.566	0.566	−0.320	0.320	0.320	−20.250	20.250	20.250
7	14	5	−0.431	0.431	−0.712	−0.186	0.186	−0.508	−12.250	12.250	−30.250
8	13	7	−0.303	0.303	−0.431	−0.092	0.092	−0.186	−6.250	6.250	−12.250
9	12	12	−0.180	0.180	0.180	−0.032	0.032	0.032	−2.250	2.250	2.250
10	11	16	−0.060	0.060	0.712	−0.004	0.004	0.508	−0.250	0.250	30.250
11	10	10	0.060	−0.060	−0.060	0.004	−0.004	−0.004	0.250	−0.250	−0.250
12	9	14	0.180	−0.180	0.431	0.032	−0.032	0.186	2.250	−2.250	12.250
13	8	6	0.303	−0.303	−0.566	0.092	−0.092	−0.320	6.250	−6.250	−20.250
14	7	11	0.431	−0.431	0.060	0.186	−0.186	0.004	12.250	−12.250	0.250
15	6	13	0.566	−0.566	0.303	0.320	−0.320	0.092	20.250	−20.250	6.250
16	5	8	0.712	−0.712	−0.303	0.508	−0.508	−0.092	30.250	−30.250	−6.250
17	17	17	0.876	0.876	0.876	0.768	0.768	0.768	42.250	42.250	42.250
18	18	18	1.068	1.068	1.068	1.140	1.140	1.140	56.250	56.250	56.250
19	19	19	1.309	1.309	1.309	1.714	1.714	1.714	72.250	72.250	72.250
20	20	20	1.668	1.668	1.668	2.784	2.784	2.784	90.250	90.250	90.250

Table 3. Rank-order correlation coefficients and 95% bootstrap confidence intervals.

Coefficient	Correlation	95% C.I.
Kendall's coefficient	0.809	$(0.594, 0.923)$
van der Waerden	0.866	$(0.672, 0.950)$
Signed Klotz	0.972	$(0.886, 0.992)$
Signed Mood	0.932	$(0.802, 0.979)$

The Kendall's coefficient, that assigns equal weights to all rankings, takes the value 0.809, whereas the other three coefficients that put more weight simultaneously on top and bottom ranks reach higher values, in particular the new coefficients proposed by the authors, the signed Klotz and the signed Mood coefficients. The greater value corresponds to the signed Klotz coefficient, which achieve the value 0.972.

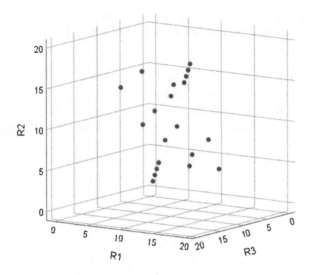

Fig. 1. 3D Scatter plot of the 20 pairs of three sets of ranks.

5   Future Work

In the continuity of this work, we intend to carry out a Monte Carlo simulation study to compare the performance of the new coefficients with other weighted coefficients that also emphasized the top and bottom ranks at the same time, but also with the Kendall's coefficient, that assigns equal weights to all rankings.

It would also be interesting to apply these new coefficients to real data in order to evaluate their performance against the usual coefficients.

Acknowledgments. Research was partially sponsored by national funds through the Fundação Nacional para a Ciência e Tecnologia, Portugal – FCT, under the projects PEst-OE/SAU/UI0447/2011 and UID/MAT/00006/2019.
Conflict of Interest: None declared.

References

1. Aleixo, S.M., Teles, J.: Weighting lower and upper ranks simultaneously through rank-order correlation coefficients. In: Gervasi, O., et al. (eds.) ICCSA 2018. LNCS, vol. 10961, pp. 318–334. Springer, Cham (2018). https://doi.org/10.1007/978-3-319-95165-2_23
2. Müller, R., Büttner, P.: A critical discussion of intraclass correlation coefficients. Stat. Med. **13**, 2465–2476 (1994)
3. McGraw, K.O., Wong, S.P.: Forming inferences about some intraclass correlation coefficients. Psychol. Methods **1**(1), 30–46 (1996)
4. Kendall, M.G., Babington-Smith, B.: The problem of m rankings. Ann. Math. Stat. **10**, 275–287 (1939)

5. Teles, J.: Concordance coefficients to measure the agreement among several sets of ranks. J. Appl. Stat. **39**, 1749–1764 (2012)

6. Iman, R.L., Conover, W.J.: A measure of top-down correlation. Technometrics **29**, 351–357 (1993)

7. Hájek, J., Šidák, Z.: Theory of Rank Tests. Academic Press, New York (1972)

8. Coolen-Maturi, T.: New weighted rank correlation coefficients sensitive to agreement on top and bottom rankings. J. Appl. Stat. **43**(12), 2261–2279 (2016)

9. Coolen-Maturi, T.: A new weighted rank coefficient of concordance. J. Appl. Stat. **41**(8), 1721–1745 (2014)

10. van der Waerden, B.L.: Order tests for the two-sample problem and their power. In: Proceedings of the Koninklijke Nederlandse Akademie van Wetenschappen, Series A, vol. 55, pp. 453–458 (1952)

11. Wallis, W.A.: The correlation ratio for ranked data. J. Am. Stat. Assoc. **34**, 533–538 (1939)

12. Iman, R.L., Davenport, J.M.: Approximations of the critical region of the Friedman statistic. Commun. Statist. - Theor. Metheds A **9**(6), 571–595 (1980)

13. Efron, B., Tibshirani, R.J.: An Introduction to the Bootstrap. Chapman and Hall, New York (1993)

14. S original, from StatLib and by R. Tibshirani; R port by F. Leisch: bootstrap: Functions for the Book "An Introduction to the Bootstrap". R package version 2015.2 (2015). http://CRAN.R-project.org/package=bootstrap

Metrics to Rank Illegal Buildings

Paolino Di Felice[✉]

Department of Industrial and Information Engineering and Economics,
University of L'Aquila, 67100 L'Aquila, Italy
paolino.difelice@univaq.it

Abstract. The problem of illegal buildings (IBs) is becoming dramatic in developing countries due to the population explosion, but, at the same time, it is still an unsolved issue also in several states usually called *advanced* (e.g., Italy). To protect the environment and, hence, people, authorities must respond to the challenge of IBs by demolishing them. However, in countries where the phenomenon is extended, it is indispensable provide land managers with IT tools that guide them in defining an order of intervention towards demolition. Through remote sensing methods, we can identify suspicious buildings with a good approximation, but they are all ex-aequo. The research described in this work proposes three *metrics* to rank the IBs located close to rivers. The ranking may be used as the IBs demolition order.

Keywords: Illegal building · Flood · Metric · Exposure · Ranking

1 Introduction

Italy is the country of contradictions. Magical and populous cities are located close to important rivers. Florence is a well-known example. It is crossed by the Arno river. In November 1966, Florence was overwhelmed by a violent flood. The balance: 17 victims, enormous damage to the city and its artistic heritage (Fig. 1).

Thousands of volumes, including precious manuscripts or rare printed works, were covered with mud in the Central National Library's. One of the most important pictorial works of all time, the Crucifix of Cimabue (preserved in the Basilica of Santa Croce) despite restoration, is lost up to 80%. Countless were the damages to the Uffizi.

To prevent the recurrence of mournings caused by events such as the one just mentioned, in Italy laws have been promulgated such as the Decree Law n.42 of January 2004. The art.142, of this DL, fixes in 150 m the width of the so-called *Band of Respect (BofR)* around rivers, that is the band of land where is forbidden to build. The prohibition applies to both sides of rivers and obviously concerns new constructions.

Research supported by an internal grant of the University of L'Aquila.

S. Misra et al. (Eds.): ICCSA 2019, LNCS 11620, pp. 34–43, 2019.
https://doi.org/10.1007/978-3-030-24296-1_4

Fig. 1. Two images about the flood of Florence (1966).

The ongoing research summarized in this paper proposes metrics on which to base the creation of a GIS software easy to be used by public administrations to combat the scourge of IBs that particularly afflicts developing countries, but which does not spare countries like Italy where this problem extends to all its regions. The very recent report by LegAmbiente [1] provides a detailed picture of this bad custom of Italians. Fighting this phenomenon is important for:

- hinder the destruction of the landscape, the primary source of revenue for Italy thanks to tourism;
- to punish those who violate the law;
- protect people's lives. In 2018, different Italian regions (Liguria and Sicily above all) suffered very severe episodes with damage to buildings and many victims. For example, at the beginning of November 2018, the wave of bad weather caused a massacre in Sicily with at least 12 victims.

The present study pursues the following objectives: (a) takes a census of IBs in the BofR of rivers, (b) relates the unauthorized urbanization to the flood danger to which people living in those IBs are exposed. The scope of the present contribution is the brown area of Fig. 2.

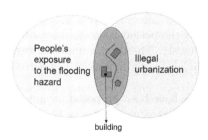

Fig. 2. The paper's scope (Color figure online)

The paper is structured as follows. Next section: (a) focuses on the relevance of the problem addressed by the research; (b) introduces definitions and notations that will be used throughout the paper; (c) formalizes the metrics proposed to rank IBs; (d) introduces the reference software architecture on which we plan to implement those metrics and the tables of the underlying geographical database. Conclusions and a look to the future work end the paper.

2   Materials and Methods

2.1   Relevance of the Problem

Kundzewicz et al. [10] pointed out that in the near future in Europe the risk of flooding will increase. To limit the mourning events caused by this danger it will be fundamental: (a) to make urban planning that takes into account this increased danger – a suggestion that has also emerged from other studies (e.g., [8]); (b) to increase the severity of intervention against building abuses, in particular to discourage buildings in river basins. Below, we focus on points (a) and (b), in sequence.

Many published studies have investigated the impact of urbanization on flood events (e.g., [2,3,7,8,11–13]). According to the findings in the study by Agbola et al. [2], besides prolonged rainfalls and river overflows, there are *anthropogenic factors* of flooding. Uncontrolled building construction is a relevant factor because such constructions obstruct the free flow of water (and, as a consequence, they are at high risk of being flooded). Reporting about the 26 August 2011 flood in Ibadan (Nigeria), Agbola et al. [2] say that in the city there were 600 buildings close to the riverbanks.

The remainder of this section focuses on the phenomenon of IBs. In recent decades, municipalities and governments in all parts of the world are struggling against IBs. The problem of IBs is becoming dramatic in developing countries due to the population explosion, but, unfortunately, it is still an unsolved issue also in States usually called *advanced* (as Italy).

In 2007, LegAmbiente, an Italian non-Governmental Organization, published the results of a nation-wide study [5]. In the report, it is mentioned that 402,676 IBs were built in Italy from 1994 to 2003. In 2018, LegAmbiente, published the results of another study [1]. The data refer to the registered violations (i.e., the infringements for which a demolition sentence was issued) in *all* the Italian regions. The report covers the period 2005 - (June) 2018. In 2004 in Italy there was the last building amnesty. The total number of registered infringements is 57,432. A big value. Obviously the figures of the actual violations are greater the official ones.

So far, several methods have been proposed for automatic building detection from high-resolution remote sensing images [4,15,16]. Moreover, there are few papers specifically focused on IBs detection (e.g., [9,14,17,18]) Soon, most of them will be available as plug-in of GIS software on the marketplace. Hence, this is the easiest and fastest way to produce cyclically up-to-date datasets about the study area of interest to keep updated also the underlying geographic database.

Today, many urban planning departments all over the world use IT software systems to detect illegal buildings; for example Yang et al. [17] describe the architecture of one of them. A relevant part of those systems is the spatial database storing city maps in the vector data format. Our proposal can also be seen as an extension of those systems, since it operates on data stored into the spatial DB.

In order to protect the environment and, hence, people, authorities must respond to the challenge of IBs by demolishing them. However, where the phenomenon of construction against the law is extended, it is essential to help land manager with IT tools that guide them in prioritizing demolitions. Using the remote sensing methods just mentioned, we arrive at the identification of the suspicious buildings with a good approximation (even if rarely with 100% accuracy), but all them remain ex-aequo. Returning to the land managers the ranking of IBs overcomes this shortcoming.

2.2   Notations

Hereinafter we use the following notations:

GeoArea is the portion of land of interest for the study, (e.g., a municipality, a region, or a state). *GeoArea* is defined as the pair $\langle description, geometry\ of\ the\ boundary\ of\ GeoArea \rangle$, where *description* is a string.

$\mathcal{C} = c_g (g = 1, 2, ..., card(\mathcal{C}))$ where c_g is a contour line, that is a curve whose points have the same elevation with respect to the sea level. A generic contour line is defined as the tuple $\langle ID, elevation, geometry \rangle$.

$\mathcal{R}(Rivers) = r_k (k = 1, ..., card(\mathcal{R}))|r_k$ is a *river* that crosses the *GeoArea*}. The generic river is described by the tuple $\langle ID, name, geometry \rangle$. $RiverBuffer(r_j)$ denotes the buffer around river r_j, of width m.

$\mathcal{B} = b_i (i = 1, 2, ..., card(\mathcal{B}))$ where b_i denotes a building in the *GeoArea*. Each building in $\mathcal{B}$ is defined by the tuple $\langle ID, name, position, geom, elevation, exp_i \rangle$, being ID an identifying code, *position* the geographic coordinates of the centroid of b_i, and *elevation* the value of the building's higt. exp_i is a positive numeric value denoting the degree of (spatial) exposure of b_i to the flood hazard. Next sub-section introduces three alternative metrics to compute the value of parameter exp_i. $BuildingBuffer(b_i)$ denotes a circular area centered on building b_i. Hereinafter, this geometry is used as a surrogate of the building footprint (parameter *geom*) that it is not necessarily available for any *GeoArea* in the world. The concepts introduced are general, therefore it is trivial to adapt the equations to the lucky case where the *geom* of buildings is made available.

2.3   Metrics

Figure 3 shows six different geometric configurations of a generic building (b_i), described by its centroid (the purple dot) and its buffer (radious of 25 m), and a generic river, described by the line (blue) and its buffer (width of 150 m). Moving from right to left, the six cases show the geometric configurations that give rise to IBs, with a violation that becomes gradually more severe.

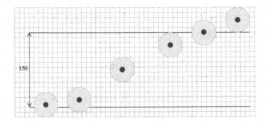

Fig. 3. The seven geometric configurations of IBs (Color figure online)

In the following, first, it is shown *how* to detect IBs inside the *GeoArea*, (that is buildings that intersect the *BofR* of some river); then, three metrics are introduced. The metrics allow to rank the severity of the violations according to different criteria.

Step 1: Census of IBs. The buildings (b_i) that violate the law are those for which it happens that there is a non-zero intersection between $BuildingBuffer(b_i)$ and $RiverBuffer(r_j)$.

Step 2: Ranking of IBs. The (dimensionless) parameter P (Eq. 1) measures the extent of the penetration of building b_i (modeled by its buffer) into the *BofR* of the generic river, whose width is established by the law. $P = 0$ denotes the absence of violation, while any other value of P in the range $(0,1]$ denotes the opposite; therefore, the IB "at hand" is to be added to the list of those to be demolished.

$$P = \frac{Area(BuildingBuffer(b_i) \cap RiverBuffer(r_j))}{Area(BuildingBuffer(b_i))} \qquad (1)$$

The three metrics attribute to each IB a value that measures their degree of exposure at the risk of flooding, following prolonged periods of rain. For this reason it is correct to state that the such metrics pursue the purpose of suggesting to land managers the priority of demolition in order to prevent, hopefully, casualties. In the following the letter S denotes the score attributed to the generic IB (b_i). S takes decimal values greater than zero. S corresponds to the exp_i parameter of Sect. 2.2

Metric S1 (Eq. 2)
Geography teaches that rivers can have tributaries. For buildings that are near the points where two waterways merge, it can happen that their geometry overlaps the *BofR* of both waterways. Therefore, for the same building we can have more values for P. Metric $S1$ is defined as in Eq. 2.

$$S1 = max\{P_k\}, \text{for } k \in [1, 2, ..., n] \qquad (2)$$

being n the number of intersections building-rivers.

Metric S2 (Eq. 3)

The value of metric $S2$ is given by Eq. 3, where d denotes the Euclidean distance between the boundary of the building (or the $BuildingBuffer(b_i)$, when the geometry of b_i is not known) and the geometry that models the river.

$$S2 = max\{P_k/d_k\}, \text{for } k \in [1, 2, ..., n] \tag{3}$$

Table 1 shows the value of metric $S2$ for the configurations of Fig. 3 (moving from left to right). If d is less than 1m, then d is set to 1 to avoid *division by zero*.

Table 1. Values of metric $S2$

P	1	1	1	1	0.5	0
d	0..1	10	50	100	125	150
$S2$	1	0.1	0.02	0.01	0.004	0

The values in Table 1 show that $S2$ fluctuates from the maximum value 1 (if $0 \le d \le 1$) to the minimum value 0 (if $d = 150$, that is, if the buffer of b_i touches, from the outside, the boundary of the river buffer).

Metric S3 (Eq. 5)

Metric $S2$ is simple to understand and to calculate, but it has a fragility: it ignores the territory elevation inside the *GeoArea*. $S3$ overcomes this limit. Figure 4 shows four different configurations of hypothetical IBs, in pairs of two. In each couple, what changes is the relative altimetric position between the building and the river. Below, we comment the two pairs of geometric scenes, in sequence.

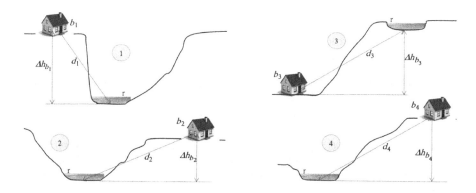

Fig. 4. Four IBs

Figure 4 *(left)* – Buildings b_1 and b_2 satisfy the following: $d_1 < d_2$ (their Euclidean distance from the river bed), while $\Delta h_{b_2} < \Delta h_{b_1}$ (the elevation difference, in meters, above the sea level, between the centroid of building b_i and the geometry of the river bed, at the point of minimum distance between those two geometries).[1] With respect to the flood risk due to the river (r_j), building b_2 is more exposed than b_1 as the barrier separating it from the river is lower than the barrier separating b_1 from the river. Δh_{b_1} and Δh_{b_2} are both positive.

Figure 4 *(right)* – Buildings b_3 and b_4 satisfy the following: the values of d_3 and d_4 and the values of Δh_{b_3} and Δh_{b_4} are comparable. The values of d_1 and d_4 are comparable too, while $\Delta h_{b_3} < \Delta h_{b_1}$. With respect to the flood risk due to the river (r_j), building b_3 is more exposed than b_4 since does not exist any protective barrier in case of river flooding, unlike what is observed for building b_4. Finally, Δh_{b_3} and Δh_{b_4} have a discordant sign; negative and positive, in order. In summary, the ranking that correctly reflects the degree of exposure to the flooding danger of the four IBs of Fig. 1 is: b_3, b_2, b_4, and b_1. Metric $S3$ (Eq. 5) returns the expected result, if applied to the configurations of Fig. 4.

$$S_3 = max \left\{ \frac{P_k \times H_k}{d_k} \right\}, \ k \in [1, 2, ..., n] \tag{5}$$

where

$$H_k = \begin{cases} |\Delta h_{b_i}| \ , \ \text{if } \Delta h_{b_i} < 0 \\ 1/\Delta h_{b_i} \ , \ \text{if } \Delta h_{b_i} > 0. \end{cases} \tag{6}$$

Equation 5 corrects the values of metric $S2$ by taking into account the height difference between the centroid of building b_i and the geometry of the river bed, at the point of minimum distance between the two geometries. In fact, Eq. 5 amplifies the value of metric $S2$ when the IB is located below the river, while reducing it in the opposite case. For the remaining case, the value of $S3$ is identical to that of $S2$. The final effect on the ranking is that the buildings below the level of the river raise towards the "top" positions, while the buildings above the level of the river slide in the "queue".

2.4   A GIS Technological Setting for the Implementation of the Proposal

Figure 5 shows the reference software architecture to implement the method summarized in the previous section. The architecture can be interpreted at two different levels: one *abstract*, the other *concrete*. The abstract level highlights

---

[1] The elevation of point Q is its height above the sea level; while the elevation variation of building b_i (described by its centroid) with respect to a river (described by the point, belonging to the river geometry, most close to b_i) is the value, taken with sign, of the difference given by the equation:

$$\Delta h_{b_i} = h_{b_i} - h_{r_j}. \tag{4}$$

the basic element of the solution, namely the *Spatial DataBase Management System* (SDBMS). It is on top of a *Geographic DataBase* (Geo-DB) where to store the input data of the problem as well as the ranking about the IBs in the *GeoArea*. The concrete level, vice versa, details a software technology that might be chosen, i.e., PostgreSQL/PostGIS.

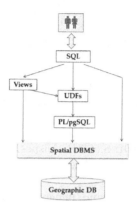

Fig. 5. The proposed reference software architecture

Table 2 shows the mapping of the theoretical concepts into database entities.
   The four tables of the Geo-DB are shown below. The underlined attribute denotes, as usual, the *primary key* of the table it belongs to. Columns P, S1, S2 and S3 store the value of the exp_i parameter (Sect. 2.2).

- GeoArea(<u>id</u>, geom)
- ContourLines(<u>id</u>, elevation, geom)
- Rivers(<u>id</u>, name, geom)
- Buildings(<u>id</u>, name, centroid, geom, elevation, P, S1, S2, S3).

Within the setting of Fig. 5 the computation of the proposed metrics takes place by writing SQL spatial queries. To keep the queries easy, it is helpful to make recourse to *views* and PL/pgSQL *User Defined Functions* (Fig. 5).

Table 2. Entity mapping

Definition	Entity
GeoArea	GeoArea
$\mathcal{C}$	ContourLines
$\mathcal{R}$	Rivers
Buildings	Buildings

3   Discussion and Future Work

This paper formalised the main ideas of an ongoing research was final goal is to implement a software that fed with datasets about the *GeoArea*, the contour lines of the territory delimited by the *GeoArea*, the rivers crossing the *GeoArea*, and the buildings in the *GeoArea*, outputs the IBs (if any) as a ranked list. State government and local stakeholders fighting against the infringement of the urbanization planning rules are looking for an IT tool like this because it offers to them a numerical criteria on which a demolition strategy might be based. In countries like Italy the demolition of IBs is the unique way to discourage future infringements of the law.

Metric $S3$ can be used either alone or as part of a set of criteria selected for computing a "robust" ranking about IBs to be demolished, in the well-known general framework of "multicriteria problems". A similar approach has been adopted, recently, by Forte et al. [6]. Their proposal was inspired by a preliminary version of the DDL S.580-B (Disposizioni in materia di criteri per l'esecuzione di procedure di demolizione di manufatti abusivi) approved by the Italian Parliament on March 2018.

Unauthorized building is a rapid phenomenon. There are many cases of dwellings built in a few days. It is, therefore, unrealistic to assume that there are up to date data available from institutional sites. But, because the IT tool we plan to develop becomes really effective, it is necessary that the set B is updated frequently (let say every three months). A way of obtaining updated data about land use consists of the following steps: (a) acquisition of satellite raster data; (b) their processing through some of the known methods for automatic building detection (of high-resolution remote sensing images); (c) transformation of the raster into a vector (the set B) by using a GIS software (for instance, QGIS). Use this dataset to update the *buildings* table of the Geo-DB. It is also opportune stimulate the citizen participatory sensing (by means of awareness campaigns) to report suspicious cases via social media (Twitter on all).

The future work will take place in four steps: (a) creation of the Geo-DB of Sect. 2.4 and tables loading with the input data of the problem; (b) implementation of the proposed metrics, as SQL queries; (c) sperimentation of the method on a case study concerning the Abruzzo region (Centre of Italy); (d) validation of the results through checks on the field.

References

1. Biffi, L., et al.: Abbatti l'abuso. I numeri delle (mancate) demolizioni nei comuni italiani. Palermo, Sept. 2018. www.legambiente.it. (in Italian)
2. Agbola, B.S., et al.: The August 2011 flood in Ibadan, Nigeria: anthropogenic causes and consequences. Int. J. Disaster Risk Sci. **3**(4), 20–217 (2012). https://doi.org/10.1007/s13753-012-0021-3
3. Chen, X., et al.: Analyzing the effect of urbanization on flood characteristics at catchment levels. In: Proceedings of IAHS, vol. 370, pp. 33–38 (2015). prociahs.net/370/33/2015/. https://doi.org/10.5194/piahs-370-33-2015

4. Dong, Y., et al.: Extraction of buildings from multiple-view aerial images using a feature-level-fusion strategy. Remote Sens. **10**(12), 1947 (2018). https://doi.org/10.3390/rs10121947

5. Fiorillo, A., et al. (eds.): 2007 Urban ecosystem. Legambiente (2007). (in Italian). http://www.legambiente.it/contenuti/dossier/ecosistema-urbano-2007

6. Forte, F., Granata, M.F., Nesticò, A.: A prioritisation model aiding for the solution of illegal buildings problem. In: Gervasi, O., et al. (eds.) ICCSA 2016. LNCS, vol. 9786, pp. 193–206. Springer, Cham (2016). https://doi.org/10.1007/978-3-319-42085-1_15

7. Hollis, G.E.: The effects of urbanization on floods of different recurrence intervals. Water Resour. Res. **11**(3), 431–435 (1975)

8. Huang, G.: A revisit to impact of urbanization on flooding. In: Huang, G., Shen, Z. (eds.) Urban Planning and Water-related Disaster Management. Strategies for Sustainability. Springer, Cham (2019). https://doi.org/10.1007/978-3-319-90173-2_4

9. Karathanassi, V., Iossifidis, C., Rokos, D.: Remote sensing methods and techniques as a tool for the implementation of environmental legislation. The Greek Forest Law case study. Int. J. Remote Sens. **24**(1), 39–51 (2003). https://doi.org/10.1080/01431160305004

10. Kundzewicz, Z.W., et al.: Assessing river flood risk and adaptation in Europe - review of projections for the future. Mitig. Adapt. Strat. Glob. Change **15**, 641–656 (2010). https://doi.org/10.1007/s11027-010-9213-6

11. Li, G.F., et al.: Impact assessment of urbanization on flood risk in the Yangtze River Delta. Stoch. Environ. Res. Risk Assess. **27**, 1683–1693 (2013). https://doi.org/10.1007/s00477-013-0706-1

12. Mukherjee, D.: Effect of urbanization on flood - a review with recent flood in Chennai (India). Int. J. Eng. Sci. Res. Technol. **5**(7), 1–5 (2016)

13. Nirupama, N., Simonovic, S.P.: Increase of flood risk due to urbanisation: a canadian example. Nat. Hazards **40**, 25–41 (2007). https://doi.org/10.1007/s11069-006-0003-0

14. Prathap, G. Afanasyev, I.: Deep learning approach for building detection in satellite multispectral imagery. In: International Conference on Intelligent Systems (IS) (2018)

15. Shetty, A.R., Krishna Mohan, B.: Building extraction in high spatial resolution images using deep learning techniques. In: Gervasi, O., et al. (eds.) ICCSA 2018. LNCS, vol. 10962, pp. 327–338. Springer, Cham (2018). https://doi.org/10.1007/978-3-319-95168-3_22

16. Singhal, S., Radhika, S.: Automatic detection of buildings from aerial images using color invariant features and canny edge detection. Int. J. Eng. Trends Technology (IJETT) **11**(8), 393–396 (2014)

17. Yang, L., et al.: Research of illegal building monitoring system construction with 3S integration technology. In: 2nd International Conference on Information Science and Engineering, pp. 3908–3911 (2010)

18. Zhu, D., Fan, J.: IBMDCH: illegal building monitoring in digital city based on HPC. In: Proceedings of SPIE 7145, Geoinformatics 2008 and Joint Conference on GIS and Built Environment: Monitoring and Assessment of Natural Resources and Environments, p. 71451A, 3 November 2008. https://doi.org/10.1117/12.813024

Fog Based IIoT Architecture Based on Big Data Analytics for 5G-networked Smart Factory

Yohan Han, Byungjun Park, and Jongpil Jeong[✉]

Department of Smart Factory Convergence, Sungkyunkwan University,
Suwon, Gyeonggi-do 16419, Republic of Korea
{coco0416,jpjeong}@skku.edu

Abstract. Industrial IoT data analysis is an essential means of obtaining important information in efficient smart factory operation. IoT devices connected to Smart Factory produce large amount of data from variety of mechanical facilities that actually operate. Because the collected data can be analyzed in real time, optimizing plant operations can be optimized, predicting maintenance schedules for mechanical facilities or quickly replacing equipment with faulty ones. In addition, various information needed for efficient operation can be obtained, such as improving the quality of the products produced. Using 5G wireless network and fog node and cloud computing, this paper introduces a new platform that supports efficient analysis of big data collected in smart factories. Leveraging various resources of 5G wireless network, it provides an optimized environment for collecting IoT data such as size, speed, delay and variety. It also provides big data analytic services through fog nodes and cloud computing and addresses various requirements for data collection, processing, analysis and management. This paper describes the requirements and design components of the proposed platform. Introduce case studies using data sets obtained from smart factories to validate the platform and provide meaningful results. The experimental results clearly show the benefits and practicalities of the platform.

Keywords: Industrial IoT · 5G-networked Smart Factory · Big data ·
Fog computing · Cloud computing

1 Introduction

Many countries around the world are building smart factories as part of their manufacturing innovations. Due to advances in telecommunications networks, Internet of Things, and smart factory are generating large amounts of data from various devices connected to the IoT system. The collected data plays an important role in improving the quality of the products produced, reducing costs, and ensuring efficient operation and management of mechanical equipment. In this

© Springer Nature Switzerland AG 2019
S. Misra et al. (Eds.): ICCSA 2019, LNCS 11620, pp. 44–52, 2019.
https://doi.org/10.1007/978-3-030-24296-1_5

paper, we propose a new platform by combining IoT and big data analysis technology with 5G network, fog node and cloud. The proposed platform quickly processes large amounts of data generated by smart factories and provides reliable analysis and results. On this platform, the 5G wireless network handles large amounts of data collection and massive traffic, storing data on fog nodes and core networks, while fog computing provides fast analytics close to real-time of the collected data. Also, fog computing is highly resource efficient as it has virtual machine technology that can continuously process new IoT data. The 5G wireless network plays a critical role in handling big data due to ubiquitous coverage as well as storage and computing capabilities within the network. A 5G wireless network consisting of a wireless access network and a core network segment can transmit data to data storage on fog computing nodes. Thus, a 5G wireless network can serve as a bridge between data sources and fog computing. Cloud computing offers a variety of benefits, such as Infrastructure as a Service (IaaS), Platform as a Service (PaaS), Software as a Service (SaaS). To accommodate large amounts of data, network capacity must be greatly increased. To meet speed and diversity, the 5G wireless network provides differentiated networking by integrating appropriate network resources to meet various service requirements in terms of latency, security and reliability. The main contributions of this paper are as follows. 5G Wireless Network, Fog Node and Cloud Computing will present platforms for big data analysis at IoT Smart Factory.

The composition of this paper is as follows: Sect. 2 describes the related work. Section 3 introduces the requirements and components of the proposed platform. Section 4 introduces open challenges for 5G smart factory issues. Finally, Sect. 5 presents the conclusions of the study and gives directions to future work.

2   Related Work

Due to the development of Internet of Things, the number of devices connected to the device is expected to reach about 50 billion by 2020, with around 20% in the industrial sector to be connected to the IoT [1]. Based on the architecture of IoT, industrial sites can be monitored and large amounts of data can be collected and processed in real time. Until now, mobile telecommunication technologies have developed rapidly. The key meaning of 5G is to expand the benefits of mobile technology in new applications, to work together in an optimal way, connecting, controlling, exchanging and deploying everything, and to overcome the limitations of space and time to create new business modes. 5G communication network has made tremendous strides in many respects, including a 1,000x increase in communication capacity and less than 1ms in end to end delays [2]. [3]'s study focused on predictive analysis of data access that should be stored on cloud systems. The author of [4] has developed a new gateway system that automatically integrates and configures new IoT data for seamless analysis in cloud systems. [5]'s study proposes a system that supports various IoT protocols for data collection and analysis. [6] presents a real-time data analysis engine that facilitates data processing near the information source. The proposed analysis engine ensures that data is processed before it is offloaded. [7]'s study develops mechanisms to predict this problem and the latency of cloud-fog-IoT continuum systems. For real-time analysis of IoT data in an uncontrolled environment, the work presented in [8] proposes universal IoT frame work that integrates wireless hub nodes to support analysis reliability and ensure real-time data collection. [9]'s study proposed a system for performing data analysis in a distributed manner. Use fog computing, IoT devices, edges, and central servers. The main approach is to optimize the decision-making of the analysis so that all IoT devices are treated fairly and satisfied. The results of this work show a promising solution that increases utilization of fog and cloud computing systems. To facilitate the intelligence of edge networks that provide a strong analysis of the IoT system, [10]'s work explained a new approach to dynamically automating the transition between central cloud systems and edges, taking into account the various conditions and requirements of the application. In this paper, the requirements and components of the platform architecture for IoT big data analysis platform for smart factories are presented.

3   Industrial IoT Platform for Smart Factory

Smart factories are spreading rapidly around the world, and are becoming a remarkable business opportunity in a variety of industrial environments. Smart factories supported by IoT generate a lot of useful data. This chapter describes the requirements necessary to collect, process, analyze and manage IoT big data using 5G wireless networks and fog nodes and cloud computing, and presents the components of the proposed platform.

3.1   Design Requirements

Designing innovative platforms suitable for handling large amounts of data generated by smart factories requires the following requirements

Resource Distribution. Large amounts of data generated by smart factories require cost-effective and resource-efficient analysis of large amounts of data that are close to physical systems. Delay times should be short because they are processed and analyzed almost in real time. Therefore, resource proximity helps overcome the high latency associated with provisioning cloud-based services. This requires an optimized scheduling mechanism and appropriately allocates resources between fog nodes and cloud computing.

Extensible Tools. Smart Factory Data Streams require a very high level of processing and analysis. These data streams are received from high volumes, from various sources, and the data is changed by different environments. Thus, these data require scalable tools to process and analyze in a variety of environments. These data also require additional cleaning and preprocessing to reduce the size of the data and better extract meaningful data.

Integration. Data collected from different devices in smart factories are not structured and cannot be processed using existing tools. Thus, IoT data from smart factories should deal with additional dedicated integration mechanisms in the integrated system. Automated adaptive data collection methods should be developed to integrate various data transfer speeds and volumes and accommodate diverse data source and application requirements.

Visualization. Another requirement for dealing with IoT big data in smart factories is related to data through visualization. This requirement is quite important because each application relies on recognized representations of data after processing and analysis to visualize and make decisions. Application-specific data visualization provides expertise by providing meaningful results based on data quality. The following topics describe the components required for the proposed platform.

3.2   Components of Industrial IoT Platform

Figure 1 shows the structure of the proposed platform. It consists of a 5G wireless network and of fog nodes and cloud computing, and the components of the platform support continued integration, processing and analysis of smart factory data. Fog computing extends the main function of cloud computing to network edges close to the physical location of smart factories, speeding up data processing that is only available within a specific time limit. Data collected from smart factories are generally delivered to smart factory IoT gateways from various sources. Data acquisition is usually performed by certain IoT protocols, such as MQTT, which communicate with smart factory devices and IoT gateways. The IoT gateway acts as an agent to mediate between smart factories and cloud systems. IoT gateway also provides local processing and storage functions, including automatic control and filtering of data streams. During this communication process, the task of acquiring data will go through a step until the data is stored in the cloud where further processing may be performed. The following are the details of the platform components.

Smart Factory Components. Figure 2 shows the components of the Smart Factory. The components of smart factories are generally classified into three layers: cyber physical, connectivity and context aware. The cyber physical layer consists of smart metering system, smart renewable system, smart sensor system, and smart energy management system. These elements are responsible for all actual operation of the plant and are installed within the factory. This interacts with the outside world through the connectivity layer and, as mentioned earlier in this section, uses multiple communication protocols to enable these devices to communicate with the cloud system through the IoT gateway. The connectivity layer is responsible for inbound and outbound communications at smart factories, and is communicated to administrators through mobile or Web applications. The context aware layer provides the intelligence of smart

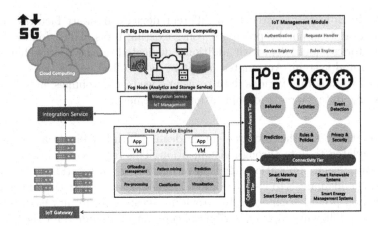

Fig. 1. IoT big data analytics with fog computing architecture.

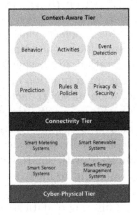

Fig. 2. Smart factory components.

factories, behavior, activity, event detection, prediction, rules policies and privacy security are performed by fog nodes, cloud computing systems and reported to smart factory applications.

IoT Management Service. IoT management service is a broker-based subsystem that processes IoT service requests from smart factory applications with cloud systems. Ensure that the approval rules are consistent with pre-configured policies in the rule engine and play an important role in providing certification services for these requests. Services that require access to smart factory-related data should be registered as IoT management brokers before using data from cloud systems. IoT management service is operated regardless of protocol and is responsible for maintaining continuity and flexibility of the entire IoT ecosystem.

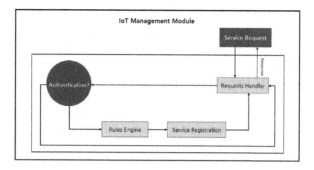

Fig. 3. The IoT big data management module.

Figure 3 shows the operation of the IoT management service. In this illustration, all services are first authenticated and registered before accessing the data. Integrated services ensure security as external applications cannot access the analytical engine directly. It also adds data visualization by enabling data to be used for a variety of user-specific applications, including mobile and desktop applications. Another key benefit is to provide interoperability for various channel technologies (Wi-Fi, Bluetooth, ZigBee and LPWAN) and data transfer protocols M2M, MQT and CoAP.

5G Wireless Network. 5G Wireless Network builds infrastructure such as various small cell base stations to support vast amounts of traffic and diverse services. With such a built-in wireless network, users can easily connect mobile devices and inaccessible devices, simplify line layout, and reduce costs. In addition, the 5G wireless network overcomes the limitations of existing communication technologies, providing an optimized environment for collecting IoT data such as high transmission speed, high coverage, low latency, large numbers of connections, high reliability and high security. Figure 4 shows the industrial 5G connectivity network architecture in a smart factory.

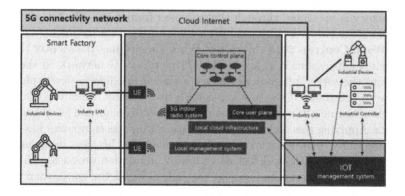

Fig. 4. 5G-networked Smart Factory Architecture.

Fog Computing Nodes. The fog computing nodes provide additional resources and computing services to support a variety of time-sensitive applications in smart factories. The Fog compute nodes provide a means to accelerate the analysis of collected data while increasing the responsiveness of the cloud infrastructure. Figure 1 shows the main functions of the fog computing nodes on the platform. It consists of several functions such as data preprocessing, pattern mining, classification, prediction and visualization. These functions are responsible for rapid analysis of smart factory data collected through the IoT system, and the aggregated results are transmitted directly to the cloud or service applications. The fog computing node performs all short-term analysis at the edge of the cloud system. The data that arrives at the fog compute node is not structured and there is no predefined model. Errors, duplication, and specificities are eliminated during the cleaning/preprocessing process to ensure consistency. In the pre-processing phase, all IoT data streams are filtered, analyzed and converted into an integrated data structure to perform further analysis. At this stage, raw data containing millions of data records is converted to predefined resolutions for each device.

Cloud Systems. In the proposed platform, cloud systems serve as key services for applications that include historical data analysis, extended storage capabilities, and core smart factory management infrastructure. Cloud services include smart factory device tracking, configuration, analysis, reporting, authentication and authentication services. These features provide value-added services that allow users to control and manage smart factories using mobile and Web applications and interact with third-party suppliers. Cloud systems also use large data mining resources such as Map Reduce, Spark, Storm, and others to deliver large-scale computing capabilities. Cloud systems use back-end computing to gain business insight and update fog computing nodes for new operational rules.

4   Open Challenges for 5G Smart Factory

In this paper, IoT data analysis for manufacturing equipment and devices of smart factory is presented through the proposed framework. SK Telecom introduced the 5G network artificial intelligence machine vision technology through Mobile World Congress 2019 (MWC19). When the product passes over the conveyor belt, high-resolution camera takes 24 pictures 5G network to the cloud server, and the server's high-performance artificial intelligence reads photos in real time to determine if the product is defective. Finally, when the results are sent to the machine, the robot arm distinguishes between normal parts and defective parts. Applying this technology to realistic auto parts companies has proven that productivity per worker is up to twice as much. In this case, deep runs have yielded meaningful data on defect detection in production products, which can help improve productivity and quality through defect detection in smart factories. In addition, a number of open issues are discussed in this section.

Balancing Between Communications, Caching and Computing. 5G wireless networks provide heterogeneous communications, calculations and caching resources. It is very important to efficiently utilize these heterogeneous resources to support heterogeneous big data applications. For example, additional computational resources may be exchanged to reduce communication loads. In addition, intermediate or final results of the calculations may need to be stored as valuable resources. Storing all of these data can be costly to store, but deleting the data may require recalculation as needed. In-depth research is needed to uncover tradeoff relationships between these heterogeneous resources to provide guidance on resource provisioning to efficiently handle big data.

Integrating Fog Computing. Implementing mobile fog computing can efficiently store and preprocess data collected from different sources. Due to the uneven distribution of data load in both space and time zones, collaborative fog computing is a useful solution for storing and processing large amounts of data in a cost-effective manner. While distributed storage systems can be co-configured by different cache, distributed fog computing can provide parallel computing capabilities for data processing.

Custom Networking for IoT Data. Network slicing has the potential to efficiently support various data services/use cases by establishing service-oriented networking in physical network infrastructure. End-to-end networking solutions can be customized in terms of virtual topology, resource provisioning, and built-in capabilities to meet service requirements such as delays. In addition, multiple slices should be well coordinated to efficiently utilize networking resources and meet their respective requirements. In addition, network slicing should adapt to the dynamics of network conditions and service requests.

Security and Personal Information. In smart factories, collection data can find information for efficient operation, but it also raises concerns about security and privacy. In order to obtain meaningful information from insights from data analysis, the data collected must be trusted and reliable. Prevent any deformation or deterioration of data that occurs during processing and analysis. In addition, only authorized entities can access data to protect data from unreliable entities. In addition, data mining for user data can violate user personal information such as location and habits information. Security and privacy issues must be addressed well for the proliferation of big data collection and analysis technologies at industrial sites.

5   Conclusion

This paper presented a smart factory IoT big data analysis platform using 5G wireless network, fog node and cloud computing. Leveraging various resources of 5G wireless network, it provides an optimized environment for collecting IoT data such as size, speed and variety. Through fog nodes and cloud computing, it will address a variety of requirements needed for efficient big data analysis such as data collection, processing, analysis and management. In addition, a platform for processing data collected from fog nodes and cloud computing is presented, and the analyzed results can be utilized in a variety of ways. In addition, the proposed frame work was applied to provide examples and effects on the technology to detect defects through 5G network artificial intelligence machine vision technology in the manufacturing process. In the future, we will conduct various and ongoing research activities in this field to efficiently collect, process and analyze big data in smart factories.

Acknowledgements. This research was supported by Basic Science Research Program through the National Research Foundation of Korea(NRF) funded by the Ministry of Education (NRF-2017R1A6A3A11035613).

References

1. Palattella, M.R., et al.: IoT in the 5G era: enablers, architecture, and business models. IEEE J. Sel. Areas Commun. **34**(3), 510–527 (2016)
2. Agiwal, M., et al.: Next generation 5G wireless networks: a comprehensive survey. IEEE Commun. Surv. Tutor. **18**(3), 1617–1655 (2016)
3. Cai, H., et al.: IoT-based big data storage systems in cloud computing: perspectives and challenges. IEEE Internet Things J. **4**(1), 75–87 (2017)
4. Kang, B., et al.: Internet of everything: a large-scale autonomic IoT gateway. IEEE Trans. Multi-Scale Comput. Syst. **3**(3), 206–214 (2017)
5. Lohokare, J., et al.: An IoT ecosystem for the implementation of scalable wireless home automation systems at smart city level. In: TENCON 2017–2017 IEEE Region 10 Conference, pp. 1503–1508 (2017)
6. Mehdipour, F., et al.: FOG-Engine: towards big data analytics in the fog. In: 2016 IEEE 14th International Conference on Dependable, Autonomic and Secure Computing, 14th International Conference on Pervasive Intelligence and Computing, pp. 640–646 (2016)
7. Li, J., et al.: Latency estimation for fog-based internet of things. In: 2017 27th International Telecommunication Networks and Applications Conference, pp. 1–6 (2017)
8. Hou, L., et al.: Internet of things cloud: architecture and implementation. IEEE Commun. Mag. **54**(15), 32–39 (2016)
9. Hong, H.J., et al.: Supporting IoT analytics in a fog computing platform. In: International Conference on Cloud Computing Technology and Science, pp. 138–145 (2017)
10. Patel, P., et al.: On using the intelligent edge for IoT analytics. IEEE Intell. Syst. **32**(5), 64–69 (2017)

Design and Analysis of OpenStack Cloud Smart Factory Platform for Manufacturing Big Data Applications

Dae Jun Ahn and Jongpil Jeong[✉]

Department of Smart Factory Convergence, Sunkyunkwan University,
Suwon, Gyeonggi-do 16419, Republic of Korea
{djahn92,jpjeong}@skku.edu

Abstract. In building an open source cloud platform, you can configure the OpenStack cloud architecture to implement services with capabilities for smart factories. In addition, we study the limitations, speed, and security analysis of existing cloud. In addition, we confirm that the data that accumulates when smart factory data is generated becomes unstructured data, and solves the problem with the prototype and various types of open source cloud to overcome this problem. The Smart Factory is composed of users in various environments in connection with all tasks such as distribution, production, and research, as well as the manufacturing environment. We design a smart factory cloud that integrates these environments. When storing files of various types, it is possible to store secure data by encrypting and decrypting various types of files and the like. In addition, for the convenience of cloud users, all data can be stored, edited and modified on any local PC connected to the cloud. Finally, open source-based cloud computing optimized for big data environments for smart factories can be configured.

Keywords: Smart Factory · BigData · OpenSource ·
OpenStack Cloud · Local cloud disk

1 Introduction

The world is working on various forms of cloud-related research for new types of manufacturing. In addition, the idea of a smart factory that can communicate all the machines in forming a new type of manufacturing industry has emerged. The concept of smart factories is emerging as an extended method of operating factories technologically by integrating ICT (Information Communication Technology) technology into manufacturing industries. At this time, IoT (Internet of Things) is a key factor connecting all the machines. However, in a small-sized company, a smart factory is configured according to a manufacturing environment, and a general company that manages actual data needs to centrally manage all data. At this time, there is a need for a new type of cloud that can be used both by the Smart Factory and the general company.

© Springer Nature Switzerland AG 2019
S. Misra et al. (Eds.): ICCSA 2019, LNCS 11620, pp. 53–61, 2019.
https://doi.org/10.1007/978-3-030-24296-1_6

In order to apply the cloud that can overcome this point, we can build a new type of cloud through this study using open source. By building a cloud of data, which is a core data store for the smart factory, the real-time analysis can be done through the dashboard environment to predict. The objectives and goals of this paper are as follows. Data is exchanged and created through a connection between the actual manufacturing environment and general companies. Most of the documents used at this time are stored in files such as Doc, xlsx, and CSV. In this paper, we propose a method to apply the cloud environment to the smart factory and apply architecture that can be applied to the smart factory environment through researching a new type of cloud. This paper is a total of five sections. Section 1 describes the research background and purpose necessary for carrying out the research and describes the necessary explanations and specific goals for the paper. Section 2 introduces the concepts and broader insensibility that are necessary to construct the cloud of the key core of this paper. Section 3 introduces the data collection process and cloud construction method to implement the network architecture necessary for configuring the smart factory cloud, and to apply a new type of cloud by combining open source. Section 4 shows the Smart Factory environment test bed configuration with cloud component selection using open source. Finally, we discuss the conclusions of the ideas proposed in Sect. 5 and future research projects.

2   Related Work

OpenStack provides virtualization computing technology, data storage technology, and a network where various software can communicate. Using this technology, data used between different machines can be stored in the cloud storage using OpenStack technology. One of the biggest advantages of OpenStack is that it can be deployed as a reassembly to meet the needs of servers. Figure 1 shows the types of cloud platforms and cloud ecosystem used to apply the cloud. OpenStack solutions used in the form of Infrastructure as a Service IaaS (Infrastructure as a Service) have been researched in recent years and continue to be resolved through the open source community. OpenStack is also a reliable cloud networking platform developed by NASA [1]. This will allow you to build a cloud for smart factories that can accommodate these environments. At this time, as shown in Fig. 1, data can be stored using Swift (Object Storage) which can configure storage among the services of OpenStack. The proxy node stores data through object storage (swift), and is stored in a cluster form through the connected storage node, so that smart factory data can be stored and utilized [2]. As the connectivity of IoT comes up, we propose a cloud mechanism to collect sensor data and implement necessary functions in the cloud through Openstack services through architecture implementation. Devices such as various communication modules and open hardware, such as Arduino, enable all objects and equipment in everyday life to communicate at low cost.

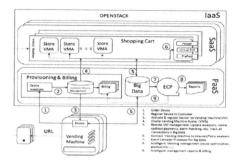

Fig. 1. High Level end to end system design applied to vending machines [3].

In addition, as shown in Fig. 1, it is possible to provide an OpenCart type service which is an open hardware type. It is implemented as an Openstack based integrated platform for this configuration. Once the service is built in the Open-Cart format, the VM can be built in the integrated OpenStack and the service can be implemented in conjunction with the device. In other words, the user can purchase the integrated environment in which the user can connect the device and store and serve the big data as a vending machine, receive the service after connection, easily integrate the data between the users or the manufacturing, You can make it possible. In addition, research on the manufacturing cloud for the Smart Factory has created a new concept called CM (Cloud Manufacturing) system through research on data interoperability (Morgan and O'Donnell 2017) as shown in Fig. 2.

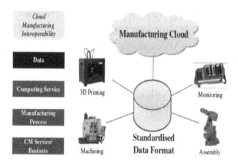

Fig. 2. Data Interoperability [4].

The CM must be able to communicate with the standardized data format through communication, all hardware and software must be able to communicate within the system, and the resources of the cloud should be described and managed and presented to the user. In addition, a data model is designed based on an ontology, and a cloud that can be used as a central data format is constructed. [4]. Each layer is divided into a physical layer, control layer, application layer, etc.

[5]. At this time, the proxy performs both roles of encryption/decryption and can perform this role when a security key is requested to a user receiving data. [6]. Once the role of the cloud server is defined in the Smart Factory, a database of IIoT data generated between the fats is constructed [7] and load balancing for resource allocation through networking as well as proxy nodes is additionally needed as follows. [8] In addition, an integrated architectural design of these elements is needed. In order to apply Smart Factory, we need to implement a unified architecture like [9–11], and it is necessary to study how to store big data from the network type design [12, 13].

3   OpenStack Cloud Smart Factory Platform Design Study

The architecture of Keystone is shown in Fig. Token Backed manages Tokens for each user, and Catalog Backed manages URLs accessible to all services of OpenStack. In this paper, we create and manage Token URL that can manage Swift that manages Smart Factory DB and Storage Data in Swift. Policy backed integrates and manages accounts of newly created users and existing registered users, and integrates and manages user authentication through Identity Backed. In addition, the user information is confirmed through the API information, the policy and the authority used in the cloud are given, and the function of storing, deleting and modifying the ID is performed. The algorithms used to implement Swift and Unified Architecture can be represented as follows, and the Open Source type data can be defined in accordance with the operation flow chart. As shown in Fig. 3, there are 7 types of data authentication procedure through Keystone in Smart Factory environment applied OpenStack Cloud. The procedure is as follows. (1) Perform a request to transfer smart factory data. (2) Generation of authentication key through keystone. (3) API call request to Proxy Server via Token. (4) Account data and first data check through Token key. (5) Swift Data Check to provide data to the Web. (6) The Dashboard enables data transmission and confirmation, and data download and upload functions are provided. (7) It becomes possible to manufacture a Smart Factory cloud by

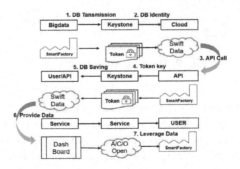

Fig. 3. OpenStack Cloud Keystone authentication procedure diagram

applying A/C/O data. Through the above 7 types, Swift Data can be configured to be able to transmit and store data through Keystone authentication key and various servers. You can also design and demonstrate the algorithm through the source code for these procedures as shown below. As it is based on open source, we can change the source according to the Smart Factory environment through the following source code algorithm, then apply it after encoding, and explain the Python source which is the core of each source.

Data: ID/PW Login
Result: OpenStack Keystone Token;
while *Token* **do**
$\quad$ Value;
$\quad$ **if** *Account/Object/Container* **then**
$\quad\quad$ Policy-0;
$\quad\quad$ Timestamp : 1501164819, X-ID : TXD7VEXE607;
$\quad\quad$ Main = Proxy-server, A/C/O Server;
$\quad\quad$ Token Identity;
$\quad$ **else**
$\quad\quad$ Hash Token with path Identity;
$\quad$ **end**
$\quad$ Identity Reload;
end

Algorithm 1. OpenStack Token ID/PW Identity

Algorithm 1 shows the source and contents of Swift and Keystone. Through the ID/PW, the keystone applies the token value to acquire and apply various login information to the user. Then check the association with the data in Swift's Account through the Hash value.

Data: OpenStack Server
Result: A/C/O Server, Hash$_p$ath;
while *Server.py* **do**
$\quad$ Util.py,Ring.py;
$\quad$ **if** *Transfer Storage Value* **then**
$\quad\quad$ Server.py;
$\quad\quad$ Util.py;
$\quad\quad$ ring.py;
$\quad\quad$ ring data with identity;
$\quad$ **else**
$\quad\quad$ Hash Ring with path Identity;
$\quad$ **end**
$\quad$ Server Data Open;
end

Algorithm 2. OpenStack Server data wiht Identity

Algorithm 2 shows the source and contents of Server and Storage data. This procedure is transmitted through the Swift Proxy Server, and the information is checked on the Main Servers to prepare to transmit the data. Through the API, the Proxy receives input to provide the data. After this procedure is performed, the data is retrieved according to the Token value in the next Fig. 4. When the token is confirmed, it checks the path through the hash value and provides data corresponding to the post-operation state of the source which confirms whether the cloud user is proper policy. At this point, Ring performs the role of transporting the list in A/C/O Swift Storage. Algorithms can be used to identify and modify various key sources and apply them to smart factories according to the situation.

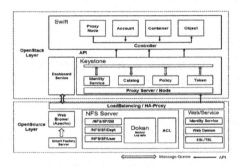

Fig. 4. Openstack base Open Cloud Architecture

In OpenStack Layer, Proxy Node and A/C/O, which are the components of Swift mentioned above, call API through the controller and provide data. OpenSource Layer should build an open source environment to build optimized services for OpenStack Layer resources and the web. The NFS server provides this, and when requesting data with the data path, it is possible to request a key for receiving data through the web service environment through Dokan. In addition, HA-Proxy, in LoadBalancing, should be used to block the load on the server and to configure the server for smooth interoperation between the client and the server. By selecting components according to the environment of the server, a fast and encrypted network environment can be constructed in accordance with the smart factory environment to utilize the services.

4 Designed Big Data Application Cloud TEST BED and ANALYSIS

The plant complex is composed of dozens of sensors for manufacturing automobile parts. Through the technology research institute, integrated management of manufacturing environment through CAD, ERP and MES systems is being carried out. In order to build a smart factory environment by integrating the data of the Smart Factory cloud environment, there is an example of data loss, which

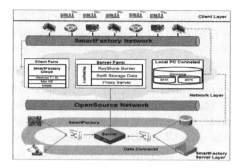

Fig. 5. Smart Factory cloud integration diagram

is not possible to centralize the integrated management data of the manufacturing environment. The Client Layer has completed the router connection for connecting each client user and the manufacturing factory to operate the Smart Factory and the firewall settings for allowing the server IP access shown in Fig. 5. In the Network Layer, we configured an environment that can connect with the local PC, ERP, and manufacturing environment used by the client in order to verify the data through keystone authentication. This paper evaluates and compares the performance of smart factory clouds using the following formulas and Tables 1.

Table 1. Smart Factory cloud speed and measurement related table.

Devision	Explanation
W	Workfow Speed
C	Server Load
Idle	Authentication speed of authentication server
D	Check the amount of data capacity
N	Network speed
A	API Call Check Speed
P	Proxy Node Count (EA)

Equation (1) is a formula for calculating the work speed of Workflow, and C is a formula for checking the load on the server.

$$C = C_w + C_n \tag{1}$$

Equation (2) is a formula for calculating the operation speed of the section that is authenticated in KeyStone Sever. It can check the network speed amount by checking the token value generation interval through Idle.

$$Idle = A_n + P_w \tag{2}$$

By calculating W, it is possible to check the time taken in the interval to transmit and store the final data after the whole process of the cloud is finished.

$$W = N \times Idle_n + C_n + P_w \tag{3}$$

In Eq. (3), the network speed is related to the speed of authenticating the Keystone Token. Since the load of the server is allocated according to the generation of the proxy node, the entire Workflow can be calculated by the formula as shown in the formula. The Cloud Disk environment for the Smart Factory is constructed to enhance user's convenience and real-time data from the factory is converted to excel data and Text file from parts such as quality management and production management, And additional features allow the stored data to be transferred to the analytics environment and dashboard for the Smart Factory.

5   Conclusion

Smart Factory A new type of open source-based cloud computing architecture for big data applications will be used to collect, analyze and utilize the data used in smart factory operations. Unlike conventional cloud computing, a computing device can be located at the edge of a device close to a terminal device rather than being located in a distant center. With the emergence of a new data storage method, the amount of information is increasing exponentially. Today, it is a computing method that attempts to jump to a new level by abandoning existing data processing methods. Research on cloud systems has been increasing among various processing methods for processing data generated in smart factory operations. In future research, we will build a tested environment by constructing an architecture that integrates various types of cloud proposed in this paper. In addition, through the study of the open source base which all users can develop, it is aimed to construct various network platforms that can be used in the Smart Factory and to configure the network to connect various types of Smart Factory.

Acknowledgment. This research was supported by the MSIT (Ministry of Science and ICT), Korea, under the ITRC (Information Technology Research Center) support program (IITP-2019-2018-0-01417) supervised by the IITP (Institute for Information & communications Technology Promotion). This work has supported by the Gyeonggi Techno Park grant funded by the Gyeonggi-Do government (No. Y181802).

References

1. Sefraoui, O., Aissaoui, M., Eleuldj, M.: OpenStack: toward an open-source solution for cloud computing. Int. J. Comput. Appl. **55**, 38–42 (2012)
2. Ruan, M., et al.: On the synchronization bottleneck of OpenStack Swift-like cloud storage systems. IEEE Trans. Parallel Distrib. Syst. **29**, 2059–2074 (2018)
3. Solano, A., Dormido, R., Duro, N., Sanchez, J.M.: A self-provisioning mechanism in OpenStack for IoT devices. Sensors (Basel) **16**, 1306 (2016)

4. Wang, X.V., Wang, L., Gördes, R.: Interoperability in cloud manufacturing: a case study on private cloud structure for SMEs. Int. J. Comput. Integr. Manuf., 1–12 (2017)
5. Wan, J., Tang, S., Shu, Z., Li, D., Wang, S.: Software-defined industrial internet of things in the context of industry 4.0. IEEE Sens. J. **16**, 7373–7380 (2016)
6. Chekired, D.A., Khoukhi, L., Mouftah, H.T.: Industrial IoT data scheduling based on hierarchical fog computing: a key for enabling smart factory. IEEE Trans. Ind. Inform. **14**, 4590–4602 (2018)
7. Sookhak, M., Yu, F.R., Khan, M.K., Xiang, Y., Buyya, R.: Attribute-based data access control in mobile cloud computing: taxonomy and open issues. Future Gener. Comput. Syst. **72**, 273–287 (2017)
8. Fu, J.-S., Liu, Y., Zhang, Z.-J., Chao, H.-C., Bhargava, B.K.: Secure data storage and searching for industrial IoT by integrating fog computing and cloud computing. IEEE Trans. Ind. Inform. **14**, 4519–4528 (2018)
9. Pereira, R.I.S., Dupont, I.M., Carvalho, P.C.M., Jucab, S.C.S.: IoT embedded Linux system based on Raspberry Pi applied to real-time cloud monitoring of a decentralized photovoltaic plant. Measurement **114**, 286–297 (2018)
10. Li, D., Tang, H., Wang, S., Liu, C.: A big data enabled load-balancing control for smart manufacturing of Industry 4.0. Cluster Comput. **20**, 1855–1864 (2017)
11. Ahn, D.J., Jeong, J.: A PMIPv6-based user mobility pattern scheme for SDN-defined smart factory networking. Procedia Comput. Sci. **134**, 235–242 (2018)
12. Ahn, D.J., Jeong, J., Lee, S.: A novel cloud-fog computing network architecture for big-data applications in smart factory environments. In: Gervasi, O., et al. (eds.) ICCSA 2018. LNCS, vol. 10964, pp. 520–530. Springer, Cham (2018). https://doi.org/10.1007/978-3-319-95174-4_41
13. Chi, Y., Li, G., Chen, Y., Fan, X.: Design and implementation of OpenStack cloud platform identity management scheme. In: 2018 International Conference on Computer, pp. 1–5(2018)

Towards a Resident Static Analysis

Maxim Menshikov[✉] [iD]

Saint Petersburg State University, 7-9, Universitetskaya nab,
St. Petersburg 199034, Russian Federation
info@menshikov.org

Abstract. The software engineering industry is moving from run-once tools to resident servers. This is well seen in the compiler industry, which accelerated the development of Language Server protocols used in Integrated Development Environments. Static analysis can also benefit from it. In our static analyzer framework, we experimented with making the analysis resident. The implementation comprises the mediator serving user's requests and analyzer units doing static analysis, saving the results to shared or local databases. Thus, the resident analyzer is an adaptation of a software-as-a-service model to the field. In the paper, we present the stages the analyzer goes through, including controlled compilation, data fetching, preliminary and on-demand analysis, show their corner cases. The model was tested in two scenarios. For a single query, the resident analyzer is acting 6–40% worse than a standalone version with a defined analysis plan, which is expected due to memory usage optimization. In a failover scenario, the rescheduling avoids data loss at the cost of increased computation time. These effects shape the differences between models and their applications.

Keywords: Resident server · Static analysis · Architecture · Software-as-a-service

1 Introduction

The industrial software is moving towards a service model. The compilers are evolving into compiler servers powered by Language Server Protocols, which are used by a variety of IDEs, linters, and analyzers. Static analyzers like Coverity [2], SonarQube/SonarCloud[1] are making such model available through the cloud, via continuous integration services. During the evolution of our static analysis framework, briefly mentioned in [8], we observed the need to bring the analyzer to an interactive level as spanning a new analyzer instance every time is resource-consuming. When checking tools available commercially, we noticed that essentially no analyzer performs deep analysis in real time, with all the architecture available on demand.

---

[1] https://sonarcloud.io.

© Springer Nature Switzerland AG 2019
S. Misra et al. (Eds.): ICCSA 2019, LNCS 11620, pp. 62–71, 2019.
https://doi.org/10.1007/978-3-030-24296-1_7

This paper summarizes the author's approach to making an analyzer resident.

Goal. Turn the static analysis framework into a resident service. The main contribution of the paper is a model for performing such an analysis type.

Motivation. The need to add interactivity to analysis, enable querying of program properties, and the essence of building it the proper way.

Novelty. According to the observations described in Sect. 2, the idea to keep analysis resident as opposed to IDE-bound or standalone model is new (at least authors are not aware of the analogs), therefore the architecture is novel.

Methodology. We employ engineering methods widespread in the industry. The main contribution is a result of task decomposition combined with the distributed technology stack and a critical view on the analyzer's workflow.

The paper is organized as follows. In Sect. 2 we review existing solutions. In Sects. 3 and 4 we propose and describe our approach. The implementation of the approach is evaluated in Sect. 5 and discussed in Sect. 6.

2   Related Work

SonarQube [3] is close to the idea. We observe a few substantial differences from our idea: the project is focused on non-interactive problem search (although SonarLint can be used for real-time feedback). Also, the SonarQube saves results of analysis rather than semantic data, which is particularly useful for tackling memory issues, but ultimately prohibits advanced queries.

Language Server Protocol [1] is Microsoft's effort to unite Integrated Development Environments with compilers and development tools. It sparked a number of tools and servers, such as Clangd[2], Rust Language Server[3] and a number of other utilities. It is mainly created for IDEs, so a server is relatively short-lived. Our project is aimed at a longer lifetime.

GrammaTech has announced a Static Analysis Server Protocol[4], which is not yet backed by a specification. It aims at supporting the Static Analysis Result Interchange Format (SARIF).

ReSharper [6] is a tool developed by JetBrains acting as a Visual Studio extension for a deeper analysis of C++/C# source codes. Visual Studio historically had several limitations, such as the 32-bit constraint. This induced major performance and memory issues, which were overcome by moving the tool out of process[5]. ReSharper is proprietary, so it is hard to judge about its internal

---

[2] https://clang.llvm.org/extra/clangd.html.

[3] https://github.com/rust-lang/rls.

[4] https://resources.grammatech.com/blog-3/static-analysis-results-a-format-and-a-protocol-sarif-sasp.

[5] https://blog.jetbrains.com/dotnet/2018/05/29/taking-resharper-process-resharper-performance-series.

architecture, however, an opensource intercommunication protocol[6] used in the tool is worth investigation.

Overall, no solution allows queries on the source code while keeping the semantic data cached.

3   Proposed Method

The approach is a direct evolution of a Semantic Virtual Machine framework [8]. However, hypervisor-based load distribution and virtual machine code execution model don't really handle user's requests. With this paper, we are placing the hypervisor at the level of individual executors. Before discussing technical details, let's compare different models.

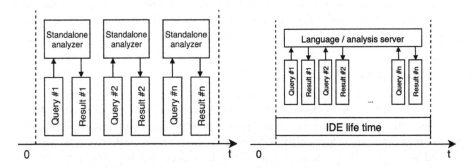

Fig. 1. Standalone model example

Fig. 2. Language/analysis server model example

Analyzer Life Cycle. A static analyzer may run in multiple ways. The first model is *standalone* (Fig. 1). The standalone model implies invoking analysis again for each query. This is redundant because queries are usually run on more

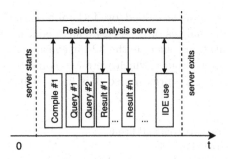

Fig. 3. Resident server model example

---

[6] https://github.com/JetBrains/rd.

or less the same code base, and sophisticated incremental analysis algorithm is required to make it effective. *Language/analysis server*-like model (Fig. 2) involves running analyzer supplementary to client-side application or IDE. A tool runs in the background, caches results and semantic data. It is bound to IDE and therefore other applications may not be able to take advantage of it. *Resident server* (Fig. 3) can run supplementary, ideologically similar to Software-as-a-Service (SaaS) [5]. This offers a performance improvement for a series of interactive queries made within a long time frame (e.g. within a week).

Load Distribution. The solution is aimed at a distribution of user requests. For small programs, the need for this is not obvious, but as the program grows, the more variables and functions spawn more interconnections. The state space explodes, increasing the memory and CPU requirements. Another problem is the questionable stability of a single analyzer: it is usually not hard to crash or invoke undesired behavior by passing invalid input. The only possible solution is to offload the requests to various units and collect their findings in one place.

Mediator. A *mediator* is put atop of hierarchy. From the end user's point of view, it is simply a server of a client/server architecture. The difference is caused by increased complexity. The mediator *potentially* can execute simple queries, but if query goes beyond a general knowledge of a program structure, the query is sent to units with more specific knowledge of the domain.

Consider the following examples in the pseudo query language.

Query 1:
```
in resource (type = function, name = X), verify \result = 0
```

This query is specific to a single function, it is sent to a unit containing its intermediate representation.

Query 2:
```
in resource (type = function), verify \valid(\result)
```

Whenever the request covers the unit's zone of responsibility, the unit is invoked. This particular request may potentially invoke all units.

Failover. If a unit fails—due to crash, host shutdown or Out Of Memory condition—the engine tries to restore it, and if it is unsuccessful, a job to a different unit is scheduled. In that case, there is a high probability that analyzer would have to verify an apparently missing part of the code and invalidate global database cache. There are simple guarantees of integrity. If a source file is changed, the Invalidation Request must be passed to Mediator, and then the database and all its dependencies (even in other units) are invalidated. Each unit contains a workspace version number, and databases still contain previous versions until all units swap to this version. Thus *the constant changes of many source files with inherent cross-invalidation do not correspond to a primary use case for the model.*

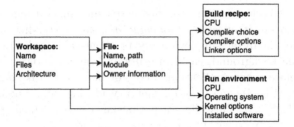

Fig. 4. Workspace schema

The critical part of the failover mechanism is similar to the well-known Google's MapReduce [4] pattern, which adds up the confidence that the model is tested on high-load servers.

Communication Format. The communication message format selection is a debatable question because its choice depends on the environment. Among possible alternatives, we see JSON-RPC—which is free-form and human-readable. It fits the position of the frontend message format. For internal inter-unit/mediator messaging, the Protocol Buffers[7] are our choice.

4   Operating Modes

The whole operation can be divided into 5 core phases. They relate to the creation of workspace, the retrieval of compilation information or sources, analysis of different kinds.

4.1   Workspace Creation

Each workspace is created on a per-request basis. The client submits a Workspace Creation request and obtains a Workspace ID. During this early exchange, the parties use Diffie-Hellman exchange to generate session keys. As a workspace is a permanent entity, unlike a relatively short-lived session, the user might set a secret to access it in the future.

The internals of the workspace and its relations to other entities are presented in Fig. 4. The user is obliged to fill the target environment data as static analyzers depend on it.

4.2   Controlled Compilation

When the analysis server is running for the first time, it might not know anything about the project being analyzed. The client-side agent has to collect the compilation information. A typical approach to solve this problem is to run

---

[7] https://developers.google.com/protocol-buffers.

agent hand-to-hand to original compiler[8] [2] (or rather *instead* of a compiler) and propagate its arguments.

Our approach is based on it as well, except that gathered arguments are not analyzed on the client and are passed to the server *as is*. The process can be divided into the following phases:

1. Obtaining a build recipe comprising target CPU, compiler options and linker flags.
2. Retrieving owner information from the code repository.
3. Creating a dependency graph between files and modules.
4. Saving the retrieved data to a workspace.

4.3 Data Fetching

The data is obtainable by a variety of ways:

1. If the analyzer is running on the same machine as the user, it can be read as is.
2. The file can be passed by an encrypted channel along with compilation request.
3. The file can be obtained from FTP, taken by SSH, or transparently fetched using NFS.

The client and server must negotiate the ways to deliver information. If the user didn't set up any means, the only reasonable way is using an encrypted channel to pass the whole file. However, as data can be sensitive, the system administrator is obliged to set up methods to avoid a possible data leak channel.

4.4 Preliminary Analysis

Once data is fetched, it can finally be analyzed. In the case of our project, the analysis converts the code to intermediate representation [8], obtains function summaries and saves them up in a database. The stage is triggered automatically after fetching data. The ways to analyze code are detailed sufficiently in other research papers aiming specifically at static analysis.

4.5 Analysis on Demand

This stage is triggered by the user's query. The incoming request contains a file name(s) if selected, and the query expression. The analyzer may either perform a query on one file or the whole workspace (thus requiring a mediator to select a unit to solve the query). The request life cycle is presented in Fig. 5.

---

[8] Clang Analyzer Scan Build: https://clang-analyzer.llvm.org/scan-build.html.

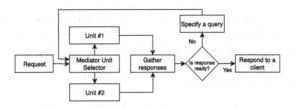

Fig. 5. Request life cycle

5   Evaluation

The proposed method was evaluated as a part of author's Equid analyzer project
[7]. It is not easy to do a quantitative evaluation as differences from other models
are rather qualitative, however, we are able to measure the time taken for specific
parts of a run.

We conducted two experiments on the analyzer, comparing a standalone
version with resident analyzer:

1. Check the full time for performing queries. For that test, the workspace had
   been already propagated, but not sent to the analyzer. We used a 300KLOC
   proprietary project and an Intel Core i7-7700HQ-based computer with 16 GB
   RAM, NVMe SSD and Ubuntu 18.04. The analyzer was instrumented to
   measure the time required. The formula for query time T is as follows:

$$T = T_w + \sum_{i=1}^{N} \cdot (T_{c_i} + T_{f_i} + T_{p_i}) + \sum_{j=1}^{M} T_{q_j}$$

   where T_w, T_c, T_f, T_p, T_q are times to perform workspace creation, controlled
   compilation, fetching, preliminary analysis and analysis on demand, respectively. N designates a number of files in the workspace, M is a number of
   files required for a query to succeed. This formula doesn't take operations like
   dependency check, minor intercommunication periods into account because
   otherwise, the formula would be unreadable. For the standalone version, we
   assume that whole bringup is required for all tests. For the resident version, we
   assume that bringup is required only once, therefore this part is not included
   in a calculation.

   (a) Query #1: check that the return value of all functions is always initialized.
       Summaries can be used, but the initialization check is more consuming.
   (b) Query #2: check if there are functions with the constant return value.
       The summaries are used, therefore the check is cheap.
   (c) Query #3: verify that all functions calling **mutex lock** also call **mutex
       unlock** afterward (no matter how it is called in the target operating sys-
       tem). This check is flow-sensitive and requires a deeper look into Virtual
       Machine codes, but the analyzer preserves metadata and therefore is able
       to filter out functions not using mutexes at all.

Table 1. Time required for queries in case of standalone and resident analyzers

Test	Time (ms)			Difference (%)
	Standalone (1)	w/o bringup (2)	Resident (3)	(2) − (3)
Initial bringup	12536	0	12682	−
Query #1	14854	2318	2772	−19.5
Query #2	12673	137	194	−41.6
Query #3	15742	3206	3430	−6.9

Table 2. Time required for queries in failover case

Test	No failure case (ms)	Rescheduling case (ms)	
		Shared database	Local database
Query #1	2318	3709	14515
Query #2	137	210	10273
Query #3	3206	3857	13929

Success criteria: resident analyzer is faster or at most twice slower than a standalone version on the evaluation without a bringup stage.

The results are presented in Table 1. Initial bringup is more or less on par (around 1% difference), but standalone version queries are definitely more expensive than queries to a resident analyzer. For the visibility, we subtracted a bringup stage from standalone version results. In this case, resident analyzer acts 6.9–41.6% worse, but as the algorithms are the same for both cases, it is a direct result of query scheduling.

2. Check the time needed to reschedule the execution which failed in the middle of operation (around 50% of corresponding query time). "No failure" case is measured for a shared database. A few nodes of similar processing power (the same CPU as in the previous test) were used, connected by 1 gbps Ethernet using a star topology.

Success Criteria: the execution continues after the failure and is taking no more than twice a time of a regular case.

Saving to a shared database in these tests is 1% slower than to a local one, so a separate measure is not provided. "Rescheduling" is a case when *all operating nodes fail* (4 nodes are running among 8 available) and the execution is transitioned to other nodes. The overview is provided in Table 2. It is observed that rescheduled execution is taking 20%–60% of the original time depending on the non-determinable stage of the nodes. Complete rescheduling in case of local database is taking a bringup time minus supposed T_w, T_c, so a federation of separate analysis units doesn't pass the test.

6   Discussion

The results presented in a previous section hint that the model is good enough for its use cases. The best part is that a new execution mechanism handles real-time queries much better compared to a standalone scheme. Comparison-wise, it would be the same as IDE-bound server, thus, in general, the model equals the *language server* approach with a distribution.

The validity of the described method relies on static analyzer implementation. Our tool supports load distribution natively, so the method naturally extends it. The schema is not "drop-in" for all analyzers, in some architectures, the performance penalties will overweigh the benefits of having the analysis resident.

Some of the details must be finalized by the community. A common Analysis Server Protocol defining request models, query format and result representation should take more uncovered industrial applications into account. Therefore the described communication way is not a final solution, but rather an invitation to start the discussion.

7   Conclusion

We presented a model of a resident static analyzer, comprising a mediator and analysis engines. The mediator is backed by a workspace database containing build recipes and target environment details. Each analysis engine uses a local database and has access to a common database. That makes it possible to serve real-time user requests. The model was tested quantitatively and acted with a 6.9–41.6% slowdown compared to a standalone analyzer with a predefined analysis plan, which is expected as the latter is meant to be random for the resident analyzer. The failover mechanism helped avoid data loss on analyzer unit failure at the cost of additional computation time. These results are important for an analyzer project which is meant to stay at the background and respond to queries.

References

1. Language Server Protocol. https://microsoft.github.io/language-server-protocol
2. Bessey, A., et al.: A few billion lines of code later: using static analysis to find bugs in the real world. Commun. ACM **53**(2), 66–75 (2010)
3. Campbell, G., Papapetrou, P.P.: SonarQube in action. Manning Publications Co., Shelter Island (2013)
4. Dean, J., Ghemawat, S.: MapReduce: A flexible data processing tool. Commun. ACM **53**(1), 72–77 (2010)
5. Dubey, A., Wagle, D.: Delivering software as a service. McKinsey Q. **6**(2007), 2007 (2007)
6. Gasior, L.: ReSharper Essentials. Community Experience Distilled. Packt Publishing, Birmingham (2014)

7. Menshchikov, M.: Hybrid system of static analysis with proof-based verification of invariants. Master's thesis, Saint Petersburg State University (2018)
8. Menshchikov, M.: Scalable semantic virtual machine framework for language-agnostic static analysis. In: Distributed Computing and Grid-technologies in Science and Education, pp. 213–217 (2018)

Distributed Shortest Paths on Power Law Networks in the Generalized Linear Preference Model: An Experimental Study

Mattia D'Emidio and Daniele Frigioni[(✉)]

Department of Information Engineering, Computer Science and Mathematics,
University of L'Aquila, Via Vetoio, L'Aquila 67100,
Italy
{mattia.demidio,daniele.frigioni}@univaq.it

Abstract. The problem of computing, in a distributed fashion, the shortest paths of a dynamic graph is a core functionality of modern communication networks. Distance vector algorithms are widely adopted solutions for this problem when scalability and reliability are key issues or when nodes have limited hardware resources, as they result very competitive in terms of memory and computational requirements. In this paper, we first discuss some recent distance vector solutions, and then present the results of an ongoing experimental study, conducted on a prominent category of networks, namely *generalized linear preference* power-law networks, to rank the performance of such solutions.

1 Introduction

The efficient distributed computation of the shortest paths of a graph whose topology dynamically changes over time is a core functionality of many modern and emergent digital infrastructures, as, for example, communication networks. For this reason, the problem has been widely investigated in past decades and many solutions have been proposed, which can be classified into two categories, namely *distance vector* and *link state* algorithms [12,13,15].

On one hand, distance vector algorithms, as for example the *Distributed Bellman-Ford* (DBF) method [17] are characterized by a *local* nature, in the sense that a generic node interacts only with its neighbors and stores minimal information about the global status of the network. In more details, each node typically maintains only a *routing table* containing, for each other node of the network, the *distance*, i.e. the weight of a shortest path, and the *next hop*, i.e. the next node on the same shortest path. The computation of the routing table is performed by solving very simple equations (see [4] and references therein), thus making distance vector algorithms very competitive solutions from the computational complexity point of view. However, in dynamic scenarios they can suffer from the well-known *looping* and *count-to-infinity* phenomena, that can heavily

© Springer Nature Switzerland AG 2019
S. Misra et al. (Eds.): ICCSA 2019, LNCS 11620, pp. 72–81, 2019.
https://doi.org/10.1007/978-3-030-24296-1_8

affect their performance in terms of communication resources (a.k.a. *message complexity*), tough quite efficient countermeasures are known (see, e.g. [12]).

On the other hand, link state algorithms, as for example the *Open Shortest Path First* (OSPF) protocol [15], are characterized by a *global* nature, as they require each node to store the entire network topology. Shortest paths are usually computed by running a centralized algorithm, as for example the classic Dijkstra's algorithm. This results in a usage of memory which is quadratic in the number of nodes of the network. On the positive side, link state approaches do not incur in looping and count-to-infinity phenomena, thus being more competitive than distance vector algorithms in terms of message complexity. However, this is counterbalanced in dynamic scenarios, where they perform quite poorly in this sense, since each node needs to receive and store up-to-date information on the entire network topology after any change [15,17].

In the last years, there has been a renewed interest in devising efficient and light-weight distance vector shortest path algorithms for large-scale networks (see, e.g., [4–11,18]), when scalability and reliability are key issues or when the computational resources of the nodes of the network are limited. The most important distance vector algorithm in the literature is considered DUAL (*Diffuse Update ALgorithm*) [12], which is part of CISCO's *Enhanced Interior Gateway Routing Protocol* (EIGRP). DUAL is more complex than DBF since it uses, besides the routing table, several auxiliary data structures to guarantee freedom from looping and count-to-infinity. Another loop-free distance vector algorithm that is worth to be mentioned is *Loop Free Routing* (LFR), which has been more recently proposed in [6]. LFR has the same message complexity of DUAL but it uses an amount of data structures per node which is always smaller than that of DUAL. From the experimental point of view, LFR has been shown in [6] to be very effective in practice. In [10], a general technique, named *Distributed Computation Pruning* (DCP) has been proposed in order to overcome some of the main limitations of distance vector algorithms, e.g. high number of messages sent and poor convergence. DCP can be applied to any distance vector algorithm to boost its performance, and it has been designed to be effective on networks following a power-law node degree distribution, also referred as *power-law networks*. Such class of networks is of particular practical relevance, since it includes some of the most important modern network applications, as the Internet and social networks. In [10] the effectiveness of DCP has been shown via an experimental study conducted on: (i) IPv4 topology datasets of the *Cooperative Association for Internet Data Analysis* (CAIDA) [14]; (ii) synthetic power-law topologies generated by the *Barabási-Albert* algorithm [1].

In this paper, we show the results of an ongoing experimental study whose purpose is to assess the performance of DUAL, LFR and their combinations with DCP on a practically relevant class of power-law networks, namely the artificial instances obtained by the Generalized Linear Preference (GLP) model [3]. The GLP framework has been shown to model very well the Internet, and parts of it. In particular, GLP predicts the structure of real-world communication networks better than the *Barabási-Albert* model. This is due to the fact that GLP adds more flexibility in specifying how nodes connect to other nodes. Our experimental study gives strong evidences that combining DUAL and LFR with DCP, and running them on GLP topologies, allows: (i) a huge reduction in the utilization of communication resources (measured in terms of number of messages sent) with respect to the case without DCP; (ii) a significant improvement in terms of memory requirements with respect to the case without DCP.

2 Background

We consider the classic distributed scenario where we have a network made of processors that are connected through communication channels and exchange data using a message passing model, in which: each processor can send messages only to processors it is connected with; messages are delivered to their destination within a finite delay; there is no shared memory among the processors; the system is *asynchronous*, that is a sender of a message does not wait for the receiver to be ready to receive the message. The message is delivered within a finite time.

Graph Notation. We represent a network by an undirected weighted connected graph $G = (V, E, w)$, where V is a finite set of n nodes, one for each processor, E is a finite set of m edges, one for each communication channel, and w is a weight function $w : E \rightarrow \mathbb{R}^+$. Given a graph $G = (V, E, w)$, we denote by: (v, u) an edge of E that connects nodes $v, u \in V$, and by $w(v, u)$ its weight, respectively; $N(v) = \{u \in V : (v, u) \in E\}$ the set of neighbors of a node $v \in V$; $deg(v) = |N(v)|$ the degree of v, for each $v \in V$; $\{u, \ldots, v\}$ a generic path in G between nodes u and v and, given a path P, $w(P)$ is its *weight*, i.e. the sum of the weights associated to its edges. A path $P = \{u, \ldots, v\}$ is called a *shortest path* if and only if P is a path having minimum weight among all possible paths between u and v in G. Given two nodes $u, v \in V$, we denote by $d(u, v)$ the topological *distance* between u and v, i.e. the weight of a *shortest path* between u and v. Finally, we call $via(u, v)$ the *via* from u to v, i.e. the set of neighbors of u that belong to a shortest path from u to v. More formally, $via(u, v) \equiv \{z \in N(u) \mid d(u, v) = w(u, z) + d(z, v)\}$. We concentrate on the realistic case of *dynamic networks* that vary over time due to change operations occurring on the edges.

Distance Vector Algorithms. Most of distance vector algorithms share a set of common features which can be summarized as follows. Let be given a weighted graph $G = (V, E, w)$, and a generic node v of G executing a distance vector algorithm. Node v knows the identity of any other node of G, as well as the identity of its neighbors and the weights of its adjacent edges. It maintains a routing table that has n entries, one for each $s \in V$, which consists of at least two fields: (1) the *estimated distance* $D_v[v, s]$ towards s, i.e. an estimation of $d(v, s)$; (2) the *estimated via* $VIA_v[s]$ towards s, i.e. an estimation of $via(v, s)$. Node v requests data to neighbors, regarding estimated distances, and receives the corresponding replies from them, through a dedicated exchange of messages. v propagates a variation, occurring on the distance or on the via, to the rest of the network by sending out to its neighbors a dedicated notification message; a node that receives this kind of message executes a corresponding routine. It is well known that a distance vector algorithm can be designed to be free of looping or count-to-infinity by incorporating suitable sufficient conditions in the routing table update procedures [12].

Power-Law Networks. A *power-law network*, in the most general meaning, is a network where the distribution of the nodes' degree follows a power-law trend, thus having many nodes with low degree and few (core) nodes with very high degree (see e.g. [1]). Such class of networks is very important in practice, since it includes many of the currently implemented communication infrastructures, like the Internet, some social networks, and so on. For this reason, many methods to generate artificial topologies exhibiting a power-law behaviour have been proposed in the literature. Among them, the most prominent are the Barabási-Albert (BA) model [1] and the Generalized Linear Preference (GLP) model [3].

3   Distributed Computation Pruning

The DCP technique of [10] is not an algorithm by itself, instead it is a general technique that can be applied on top of a distance vector algorithm with the aim of improving its performance. Given a generic distance vector algorithm A, the combination of DCP with A induces a new algorithm, denoted by A-DCP.

In the following, we report some definitions given in [10] that are useful to capture the typical structure of a power-law network. Given a graph $G = (V, E, w)$, nodes, edges and paths in G can be classified as follows. A node $v \in V$ is *central* if $deg(v) \geq 3$ and *non-central* otherwise. A non-central node v can be either *semi-peripheral*, if $deg(v) = 2$, or *peripheral*, if $deg(v) = 1$. Given a path $P = \{v_0, v_1, \ldots, v_j\}$ of G, P is *central* if v_i is central, for each $0 \leq i \leq j$. Any edge belonging to a central path is called *central edge*. P is *peripheral* if v_0 is central, v_j is peripheral, and all v_i, for each $1 \leq i \leq j - 1$, are semi-peripheral. Any edge belonging to a peripheral path, accordingly, is called *peripheral edge*. P is *semi-peripheral* if v_0 and v_j are two distinct central nodes, and all v_i are semi-peripheral nodes, for each $1 \leq i \leq j - 1$. If $v_0 \equiv v_j$ then P is called a *semi-peripheral cycle* Each edge belonging to such a path is called *cyclic edge* and each node $u \neq v_0$ in P is called *cyclic node*.

Description. DCP has been designed to reduce the communication overhead of distance vector algorithms in power-law networks. This can be done since nodes with small degree often do not provide any useful information for the distributed computation of shortest paths. in fact, there are many topological situations in which these nodes neither perform, nor be involved in any kind of distributed computation, since their shortest paths depend on those of higher degree nodes.

In particular, DCP forces the distributed computation to be carried out by the central nodes only (which are few in power-law networks). Non-central nodes, which are instead the great majority, play a passive role and receive updates about routing information from the central nodes, without taking part to any kind of distributed computation and by performing few trivial operation to update their routing data. Hence, it is clear that the larger is the set of non-central nodes of the network, the bigger is the improvement in the pruning of the distributed computation of shortest paths and, consequently, the improvement in the global number of messages sent by A-DCP with respect to A.

The main difference in the behaviour of A, when combined with DCP, resides in the fact that in a A every node performs the same code thus having the same behaviour, while in A-DCP, central and non-central nodes are forced to have different behaviours. In particular, central nodes detect (and handle) changes concerning all kinds of edges, while peripheral, semi-peripheral, and cyclic nodes detect changes concerning only peripheral, semi-peripheral, and cyclic edges.

Practical Effectiveness of DCP. In [10] DCP has been combined with both DUAL and LFR by obtaining algorithms denoted as DUAL-DCP and LFR-DCP, and an extensive experimental study has been performed to assess the effectiveness of DCP. In these experiments the power-law networks of the *CAIDA IPv4 topology dataset* [14], and the random power-law networks generated by the *Barabási-Albert* (BA) algorithm [1] were used, subject to randomly generated sequences of updates. The results of [10] have shown that the combinations of DUAL and LFR with DCP provide a huge improvement in the number of messages sent. In particular, in CAIDA instances the ratio between the number of messages sent by DUAL-DCP and those sent by DUAL is within 0.03 and 0.16 which means that DUAL-DCP sends a number of messages which is between 3% and 16% that of DUAL. The ratio between the number of messages sent by LFR-DCP and those sent by LFR is within 0.10 and 0.26. Similar results are obtained on *Barabási-Albert* instances.

4   Generalized Linear Preference Model

The Generalized Linear Preference (GLP) model has been introduced in [2], and it is a variant of the Barabási–Albert (BA) model [1]. A BA topology is generated by iteratively adding one node at a time, starting from a connected graph with at least two nodes. A newly added node is connected to any other existing nodes with a probability that is proportional to the degree of the existing nodes. In detail, let $P(i)$ denote the probability that a new node will be connected to node i, the *linear preference* connectivity rule of the BA model is defined as follows:

$$P(i) = \frac{deg(i)}{\sum_j deg(j)} \tag{1}$$

As a result of the above connectivity mechanism, the power-law graphs generated by the BA algorithm have average node degree approximately equal to 3 and a number of nodes with degree smaller than 3 approximately equal to $7/10n$, where n is the number of nodes of the graph. In [3] it has been shown that in the real Internet, new Autonomous Systems (AS) have a much stronger preference to connect to high degree ASs than predicted by the linear preference model. This behaviour is better captured by the GLP model which adds more flexibility than the BA one in specifying how nodes connect to other nodes. In detail, the GLP model reflects the fact that the evolution of the AS graph is mostly due to two operations, the addition of new nodes and the addition of new links between existing nodes. It starts with n_0 nodes connected through $n_0 - 1$ links. At each time-step, one of the following two operations is performed: (1) with probability $p \in [0,1]$, $k < n_0$ new links are added between existing nodes; (2) with probability $1 - p$, a new node is added and connected to k existing nodes. If $P(i)$ denotes the probability that a new node is connected to node i, the *generalized linear preference* connectivity rule is defined as follows:

$$P(i) = \frac{deg(i) - \beta}{\sum_j (deg(j) - \beta)} \tag{2}$$

where $\beta \in (-\infty, 1)$ is a tunable parameter that can be adjusted such that nodes have a stronger preference of being connected to high degree nodes than predicted by Eq. (1). In particular, it indicates the preference for a new node (edge) connecting to high degree nodes. The smaller the value of β is, the less preference is given to high degree nodes. As a result of Eq. (2), Power-law graphs generated by the GLP model have average node degree of 4.8 and a number of nodes with degree smaller than 3 that is on average around $8/10n$.

5   Evaluation of DCP on GLP Networks

In this section we present the results of our new experimental study of algorithms DUAL, LFR, DUAL-DCP, and LFR-DCP on GLP networks. Our experiments have been performed on a workstation equipped with a Quad-core 3.60 GHz Intel Xeon X5687 processor, with 12 MB of internal cache and 24 GB of main memory, and consist of simulations within the OMNeT++ 4.0p1 environment [16]. All software has been written in C++ and compiled with GNU g++ compiler v.4.8 under Linux (Kernel 2.6.32).

Executed Tests. We implemented the GLP algorithm and first generated a large connected graph, having 16 031 nodes, by fixing β to 0.6447, since this choice has been shown to allow the generation of networks that are similar to real-world ones [3]. Since DUAL has high memory requirements, we were unable to perform tests on such large graph. Therefore, we randomly extracted different subgraphs of smaller sizes, by performing pruned Breadth First Searches rooted at different randomly chosen nodes. Finally, we generated a set of different experimental settings similarly to what was done in [10], where each setting consists of a n-node subgraph of the above graph, denoted as G_{GLP-n}, and a set of k edge updates, with k assuming values in $\{5, 10, \ldots, 30\}$. Edge weights are non-negative real numbers randomly chosen in $[1, 1\,000\,000]$ and an edge update consists of multiplying the weight of a random selected edge by a percentage value randomly chosen in $[50\%, 150\%]$. For each test configuration (a graph and a fixed value of k) we performed 5 different experiments (for a total amount of 30 runs), measured performance metrics of interest, and computed average values for each

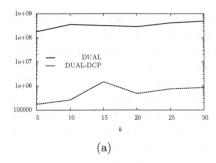
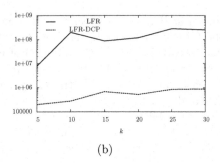

(a)   (b)

Fig. 1. (a) Number of messages sent by DUAL and DUAL-DCP on $G_{GLP-8000}$. (b) Number of messages sent by LFR and LFR-DCP on $G_{GLP-8000}$.

metric. We ran simulations on GLP instances with $n \in \{1200, 5000, 8000\}$. The results of our experiments on the different instances are similar, hence we report only those on $G_{GLP-8000}$, having 8000 nodes, 19158 edges, average node degree equal to 4.8, around 58% of peripheral nodes, and around 22% of semi-peripheral nodes.

Analysis. A summary of our results is shown in Fig. 1, where we report in (a) the average number of messages sent by DUAL and DUAL-DCP, and in (b) that of LFR and LFR-DCP, respectively, on $G_{GLP-8000}$, per test.

Our data suggest that the use of DCP provides a huge improvement in the global number of messages sent. In more details, in the tests of Fig. 1(a) the ratio between the number of messages sent by DUAL-DCP and those sent by DUAL is within $73 \cdot 10^{-5}$ and $457 \cdot 10^{-5}$ while in the tests of Fig. 1(b) the ratio between the number of messages sent by LFR-DCP and those sent by LFR is within $138 \cdot 10^{-5}$ and $2555 \cdot 10^{-5}$. The improvement provided by DCP in GLP graphs is by far more significant than that provided in case of BA graphs in [10]. In fact, the ratio between the number of messages sent by DUAL-DCP (LFR-DCP, respectively) and those sent by DUAL (LFR, respectively) is always larger than 10^{-2}. Since the GLP model is known to better predict real-world network infrastructures with respect to the BA one, this provides even more evidences of the effectiveness of DCP in real-world network instances.

Notice that the very good performance of DCP in this case is probably due to the topological structure of GLP graphs, which have more central nodes than BA ones. This results in a much more effective pruning of both DUAL and LFR with respect to what happens in BA instances. Notice also that this behaviour is more evident for LFR-DCP as LFR includes two sub-routines, the LOCAL-COMPUTATION and the GLOBAL-COMPUTATION, which worst case message complexity depends on the number of central nodes (see [6]), while DUAL uses a single sub-routine, the DIFFUSE-COMPUTATION, which worst case message complexity depends on the same parameter (see [12]).

By the two diagrams of Fig. 1, it is clear that LFR outperforms DUAL on $G_{GLP-8000}$. This is due to the fact that GLP graphs have been shown to model very accurately real world topologies where LFR is very effective in terms of

Table 1. Space occupancy per node of the algorithms on $G_{GLP-8000}$.

Algorithm	MAX		AVG	
	Bytes	Ratio	Bytes	Ratio
DUAL	38 888 000	1	359 580	1
DUAL-DCP	8 163 826	0.21	327 366	0.91
LFR	241 115	1	192 069	1
LFR-DCP	354 212	1.47	348 636	1.82

number of messages sent. This consideration also explains why the reduction in the number of messages sent induced by DCP is less emphasized for LFR.

To conclude our analysis, we consider the space occupancy. Note that, when DCP is combined with DUAL, a subset of nodes of the network can avoid to maintain some data structures of DUAL, as either the information stored in them can be inferred, or it is not needed due to the pruning mechanism of DCP. For instance, each node of the network executing DUAL-DCP does not need to store the data structure of DUAL that implements the finite state machine with respect to non-central nodes, as no distributed computation can be initiated for this kind of nodes. Similar observations can be done with respect to LFR, since also here some of the nodes of the network can avoid to maintain some of the data structures used by the algorithm, which can be either inferred or it is not needed at all due to the pruning mechanism of DCP.

To support the above considerations we provide measurements on the space occupancy per node in Table 1, where we report the maximum and the average space occupancy per node (in Bytes) of each algorithm on $G_{GLP-8000}$. We also report the ratio between the space occupancy per node of the algorithms integrating DCP and that of the original algorithms, for each test instance. Since the space occupancy per node of LFR and LFR-DCP depends on the number of weight change operations, we report median values for each of the algorithms.

Our experiments show that the use of DCP induces a clear improvement also in the space requirements per node. In particular, DUAL-DCP requires a maximum space occupancy per node which is 0.29 times that of DUAL. This behaviour is confirmed also in the average case, where DUAL-DCP requires 0.91 times the average space occupancy per node of DUAL. On the contrary, our data show that the average space occupancy per node of LFR-DCP is slightly larger than that of LFR and that the use of DCP induces an overhead in the average space occupancy per node which is equal to 82%. This is due to the fact that the space occupancy of LFR is quite low by itself and that, in this case, the space occupancy overhead due to the data structures of DCP (see [10]) is larger than the space occupancy reduction induced by the use of DCP.

6   Conclusions

In conclusion, our experiments show that in the case of GLP networks, the DCP technique is very effective when combined with some prominent distance vector algorithms in terms of improving the usage of communication resources.

The study of new techniques, which take advantage of the structural properties of real-world networks, deserves further investigation. In particular, it would be interesting to evaluate how DCP scales to bigger a/o more dynamic networks, and also to develop techniques for shortest paths distributed algorithms to be efficient in other practically interesting scenarios.

References

1. Albert, R., Barabási, A.-L.: Emergence of scaling in random networks. Science **286**, 509–512 (1999)
2. Albert, R., Jeong, H., Barabási, A.-L.: Error and attack tolerance of complex networks. Nature **406**, 378–381 (2000)
3. Bu, T., Towsley, D.: On distinguishing between internet power law topology generators. In: Proceedings IEEE INFOCOM, pp. 638–647 (2002)
4. Cicerone, S., D'Angelo, G., Di Stefano, G., Frigioni, D., Maurizio, V.: Engineering a new algorithm for distributed shortest paths on dynamic networks. Algorithmica **66**(1), 51–86 (2013)
5. D'Angelo, G., D'Emidio, M., Frigioni, D.: Fully dynamic update of arc-flags. Networks **63**(3), 243–259 (2014)
6. D'Angelo, G., D'Emidio, M., Frigioni, D.: A loop-free shortest-path routing algorithm for dynamic networks. Theor. Comput. Sci. **516**, 1–19 (2014)
7. D'Angelo, G., D'Emidio, M., Frigioni, D.: Distance queries in large-scale fully dynamic complex networks. In: Mäkinen, V., Puglisi, S.J., Salmela, L. (eds.) IWOCA 2016. LNCS, vol. 9843, pp. 109–121. Springer, Cham (2016). https://doi.org/10.1007/978-3-319-44543-4_9
8. D'Angelo, G., D'Emidio, M., Frigioni, D.: Fully dynamic 2-hop cover labeling. J. Exp. Algorithmics **24**(1), 1.6:1–1.6:36 (2019)
9. D'Angelo, G., D'Emidio, M., Frigioni, D., Maurizio, V.: A speed-up technique for distributed shortest paths computation. In: Murgante, B., Gervasi, O., Iglesias, A., Taniar, D., Apduhan, B.O. (eds.) ICCSA 2011. LNCS, vol. 6783, pp. 578–593. Springer, Heidelberg (2011). https://doi.org/10.1007/978-3-642-21887-3_44
10. D'Angelo, G., D'Emidio, M., Frigioni, D., Romano, D.: Enhancing the computation of distributed shortest paths on power-law networks in dynamic scenarios. Theory Comput.Syst. **57**(2), 444–477 (2015)
11. Elkin, M.: Distributed exact shortest paths in sublinear time. In: Proceedings of 49th Annual Symposium on Theory of Computing (STOC 2017), pp. 757–770. ACM (2017)
12. Garcia-Lunes-Aceves, J.J.: Loop-free routing using diffusing computations. IEEE/ACM Trans. Netw. **1**(1), 130–141 (1993)
13. Humblet, P.A.: Another adaptive distributed shortest path algorithm. IEEE Trans. Commun. **39**(6), 995–1002 (1991)
14. Hyun, Y., et al.: The CAIDA IPv4 routed/24 topology dataset. http://www.caida.org/data/active/ipv4_routed_24_topology_dataset.xml

15. Moy, J.T.: OSPF: Anatomy of an Internet Routing Protocol. Addison-Wesley, Boston (1998)
16. OMNeT++. Discrete event simulation environment. http://www.omnetpp.org
17. Rosen, E.C.: The updating protocol of ARPANET'S new routing algorithm. Comput. Netw. **4**, 11–19 (1980)
18. Ray, S., Guérin, R., Kwong, K., Sofia, R.: Always acyclic distributed path computation. IEEE/ACM Trans. Netw. **18**(1), 307–319 (2010)

Financial Feasibility Assessment of Public Property Assets Valorization: A Case Study in Rome (Italy)

Francesco Tajani[1], Carmelo Maria Torre[2(✉)], and Felicia Di Liddo[1]

[1] Department of Architecture and Design, "Sapienza" University of Rome,
00196 Rome, Italy
francesco.tajani@uniromal.it
[2] Department of Civil Engineering Sciences and Architecture,
Polytechnic University of Bari, 70125 Bari, Italy
carmelomaria.torre@poliba.it

Abstract. In the present research the financial feasibility assessment of a public-private partnership initiative concerning the valorization of a public property located in the city of Rome (Italy) has been examined. The development of the assessment, which has provided for the implementation of the Discounted Cash-Flow Analysis, has been anticipated by a preliminary phase in which the public and private parties involved in the initiative have been identified, the respective roles have been defined and the costs and the revenues generated by the intervention have been assessed. The work highlights the significant support that, in the initial phases of the definition of an investment in public-private partnership, may result from the disaggregation of the different subjects and by the explanation of their roles in the initiative. The functions mix considered in the valorization process and the different management modalities allow the private investor to transfer the risks of the intervention to subjects most competent in the market sector in which they will be involved. The performance indicators obtained for the case study have pointed out the financial sustainability of the investment for the private operator and therefore the feasibility of a project able to generate significant positive impacts on the local community.

Keywords: Public-Private partnerships · Discounted Cash-Flow Analysis · Financial sustainability · Public property assets valorization

1 Introduction

In the current economic situation, characterized by a persistent scarcity of public resources, the Public-Private Partnership (PPP) constitutes a fundamental tool able to bridge the gap between the limited amount of funding and the need for valorization of public property assets [1, 5, 14].

The progressive involvement of the private investor in the public assets regeneration has been highlighting how this form of collaboration currently represents an effective procedure for the functional reconversion of collective interest properties, considering the current contraction of the public spending capacity. It is therefore

S. Misra et al. (Eds.): ICCSA 2019, LNCS 11620, pp. 82–93, 2019.
https://doi.org/10.1007/978-3-030-24296-1_9

evident that the PPP techniques could be a valid alternative for financing public initiatives, able to give an immediate response to the contingent needs of modernization and improvement of the public architectural and cultural property assets [6].

Furthermore, the use of cooperation procedures between Public Administrations and private investors favors the inclusion of appropriate organizational skills in the transformation and management of the public property assets. From this perspective, the PPP is currently an interesting solution not only to the financial deficit that characterizes the public funds, but also to the frequent lack of entrepreneurial skills in the public sector, which, in this way, entrusts to third parties (private) the realization of activities that are able, on the one hand, to revitalize abandoned assets through appropriate functional re-uses, on the other hand, to satisfy the community needs of collective interest new spaces [2, 7].

The relationships that are established between the different subjects involved in the PPP initiatives are often multiple, and mainly depend on the complexity of the investment. The participation of a private investor, individual or - more frequently - in a corporate form, in a process of recovery and transformation of a public property, presupposes the satisfaction of the financial criterion of the initiative, i.e. its capacity to remunerate the capital initially invested and to generate an adequate profit for the private investor: it is evident that the private entrepreneur will invest his capital and take the risks of the initiative if the feasibility assessment of the initiative attests that the revenues will be higher than the transformation and management costs [9].

Within the wide range of PPP operational tools, in Italy the "enhancement concession" allows the development of public property assets, through the transfer to private operators of the right to use public properties for economic purposes for a fixed period of time, in exchange for their requalification, functional reconversion and ordinary and extra-ordinary maintenance (article 3-bis of Decree Law No. 351/2001, amended and supplemented by Law 228/2012). Taking into account the numerous positive impacts that these modalities of valorization are able to generate, a rigorous and targeted planning action to be carried out on the urban territory, an appropriate assessment of the PPP procedures and a selection of the feasible initiatives are key priority steps.

2   Aim

The topic of the present research concerns the framework outlined. In particular, the assessment of the financial feasibility of a PPP initiative, concerning the re-functionalization of a public property located in the city of Rome (Italy) through the "enhancement concession" procedure has been developed.

The assessment of the convenience for the private parties involved in the valorization process presupposes the preliminary definition of the roles played by each subject that takes part in the initiative and the relationships established between the different figures involved [13]. In view of an effective synergy between the Public Administration and the private investors [12, 14, 15], it is fundamental to clarify the different positions of each subject in order, first of all, to modulate the structure of the financing sources for the success of the initiative and of the respective revenues and, then, to carry out an assessment of the convenience in the use of the PPP tool. The analysis of the case study highlights the multiplicity and the consequent "cascade" system of the subjects involved in urban regeneration initiatives through PPP procedures [3, 4, 10].

The paper is structured as follows. In Sect. 3 the case study, related to the initiative for the valorization of the former Police Station located in the Ostiense district of Rome, has been described; the roles assumed by each subject involved in the initiative have been specified, the cost (investment and management) and the revenue items necessary for the development of a Discounted Cash-Flow Analysis have been identified, in order to assess the financial sustainability of the initiative for the private subject; therefore, the financial assessment of the initiative has carried out, by determining the relative performance indicators. In Sect. 4, comments on the results obtained and the conclusions of the work have been discussed.

3   Case Study

3.1   Current Use

The case study concerns a hypothesis of enhancement concession of the public complex of the former Police Station, located in the Ostiense district of Rome (Italy).

The building, built in 1918, is a former military warehouse included in the *'Plan of Alienation and Valorization of Military Buildings of the City of Rome'*, approved by the Municipality (public property owner) in 2010, as a building no longer used for the original functions and convertible to new uses. Currently, the entire urban area in which the building is located has significant critical issues, caused by the widespread degradation that characterizes this area of the Ostiense district: presence of illegal and illicitly occupied structures, lack of parking spaces and green areas, high noise pollution index generated from the proximity of the site to the railway and from the high and continuous flow of road transport means, being the property located at the intersection of two important road axes (Ostiense street and Porto Fluviale street). Furthermore, the building has been illegally occupied since 2003 and it is in an advanced state of degradation.

3.2   Description of the Enhancement Initiative

The project proposed provides for, on the one hand, the recovery and redevelopment of the existing property and, on the other hand, the construction of a building adjacent to the existing one, to be used as a hydroponic greenhouse for the production and the sale of vegetables.

With reference to the building to be renovated, on the ground floor, spaces for restaurants, rooms for training activities and language courses and a conference room have been planned. At the first and second levels, residential units of different sizes to be used for short-term lease (e.g. bed & breakfast) and offices have been expected.

In the Figs. 1 and 2 the existing building project plans with an indication of the functions provided for in each space have been reported.

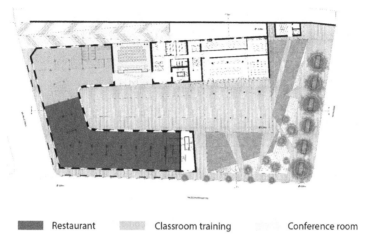

Restaurant   Classroom training   Conference room

Fig. 1. The existing building project plan (ground floor)

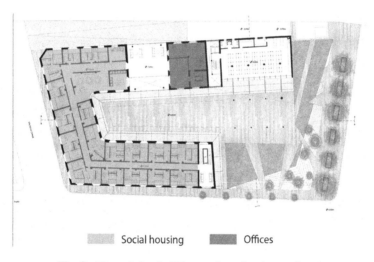

Social housing   Offices

Fig. 2. The existing building project plan (upper floors)

The new building is placed in continuity with the volume of the existing one and it will be the site of a hydroponic greenhouse. In particular, the new construction will be composed of three levels: at the first floor the spaces for crops produced retail will be located, whereas at the next levels the structures for growing vegetables will be put. An underground car park will be on the new building basement. Figure 3 shows the project plan of the new building with the identification of the proposed functions. The rehabilitation of the external public space with the creation of a square in front of the greenhouse building completes the proposed transformation project (Fig. 4).

Each intended use identified in the valorization initiative of the former Police Station takes into account the main needs identified in the urban reference area.

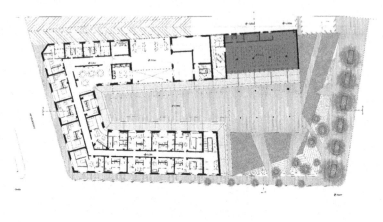

Hydroponic greenhouse

Fig. 3. The new building project plan

Fig. 4. Overall view of the project

The valorization project effects on the Ostiense district entire urban system involve several sectors: *(i) economic*, through the construction of the hydroponic greenhouse, generating important opportunities related to the offer of new employment [4], *(ii) social*, through the redevelopment of an area currently in a state of degradation [3, 12], *(iii) ecological-environmental*, through the production of controlled and quality food, without requiring the exploitation of large agricultural land [8, 11, 13].

3.3   The Subjects Involved in the Enhancement Initiative

The hypothesis assumed in the present research is that the Municipality of Rome, current owner of the building in disuse, chooses, within the range of PPP operational tools, the procedure of "enhancement concession" for the property redevelopment and the structural and functional modernization process for the entire urban district [10, 16, 17].

In particular, it is assumed that the buildings restructuring and construction interventions are carried out by a private investor (*main* subject), in exchange for the temporary use of the building for a period of twenty years. At the end of the concession period, the availability of the property will come back to the public subject, as well as the acquisition of any transformation, improvement, addition and accession realized by the private entrepreneur.

The *main* subject bears the costs *(i)* of modernization and new construction and *(ii)* related to the hydroponic greenhouse management. In addition, the *main* subject will lease the restaurant (subject A), the rooms for language courses and training activities (subject B), the offices (subject C), the conference room (subject D), the housing (subject E) and garages (subject F). Furthermore, the subject B and D do not represent two "fixed" figures, as it is assumed that both the classrooms and the conference room are rented to different subjects who pay a fee for the temporary use of spaces limited to specific activity duration. In the same way, the subject C (the offices lessee subject) and E (the residences lessee subject) synthetically identify the different entities to which the corresponding surfaces will be leased. Figure 5 summarizes the cascade structure of the subjects involved in the redevelopment initiative carried out through the enhancement concession procedure. In Fig. 6 a schematic graph of the subdivision of the costs and the revenues related to each private subject involved in the initiative has been proposed. It should be noted that in the diagram the arrows "->" represent payments, i.e. costs (C) for the relative private subject, whereas the arrows "<-" express earnings, i.e. operating revenues (R) for the relative investor. The leases (L) paid by each lessee subject, for simplicity of representation, are represented by the "incoming" arrows only for the *main* subject.

3.4   Financial Feasibility Assessment of the Initiative for the Private Investor (Main Subject)

The verification of the financial convenience of a PPP initiative has been performed from the exclusive point of view of the "first" private investor, i.e. the *main* subject, in individual or corporate-consortium form. This assessment has been carried out through the development of a Discounted Cash-Flow Analysis (DCFA).

The project feasibility conditions have been verified in terms of Net Present Value (NPV), Internal Rate of Return (IRR) and Revenues/Costs Ratio (R/C). The *main* subject availability to accept the mechanism of cooperation with the Public Administration will depends on the intervention private convenience and, therefore, on the initiative's ability to repay the initial monetary outlay, to remunerate the management costs and to generate a financial surplus.

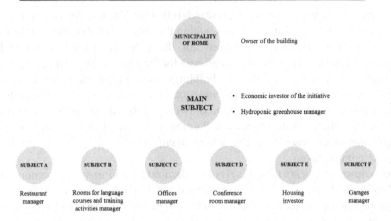

Fig. 5. Subjects involved in the valorization initiative analyzed

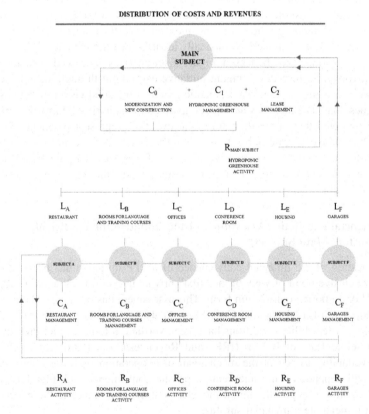

Fig. 6. Cost and revenue items related to each private figure involved in the valorization initiative

3.5   Costs

The costs of the initiative concern *(i)* the *investment* for the restructuring and modernization of the existing building (building and outdoor area) and for the construction of the new building (C_0 in Fig. 6), *(ii)* the *management*, direct for the hydroponic greenhouse (C_1 in Fig. 6), and indirect for the intended uses leased to third parties (C_2 in Fig. 6).

3.6   Investment Costs

Table 1 shows the investment costs, relating to the renovation of the existing building, the construction of the new building, the redevelopment of the outdoor area, the technical costs and the general expenses deriving from them.

Table 1. Investment costs for the main subject

Investment costs	
Renovation of the existing building	3,681,703.32 €
Construction of the new building	1,620,879.22 €
Redevelopment of the outdoor area	139,200.00 €
Technical costs	326,506.95 €
General expenses	163,253.48 €
Total	**5,931,542.986 €**

The analysis of the construction costs has been developed taking into account the price lists of public and private works, currently used in the Lazio Region, and validated through formal surveys carried out among the construction companies operating in the city of Rome. Technical expenses and general expenses are determined as a percentage, respectively equal to +6% and +3% of the construction costs.

3.7   Operating Costs

Assuming that the economic subject of the initiative (*main* subject) will be the direct manager of the hydroponic greenhouse, whereas the management of the remaining areas will be given to third parties (restaurant, classrooms for training, conference room, offices, housing and garages), in exchange for a monetary fee equal to the established rent, the operative costs of the *main* subject are related to the operating phase of the hydroponic greenhouse and to the expenses concerning the leasing of the areas assigned to the different subjects (Table 2).

Table 2. Operating costs for the main subject

Operating costs	
Hydroponic greenhouse	105,270.27 €/year
Existing building (taxes for the lease contracts registration, insurance installments, etc.)	122,099.65 €/year
Total	**227,369.92 €/year**

The direct management of the greenhouse costs - the only activity to remain in full management of the *main* subject - involves the costs of cleaning the building, the costs of wages, electricity and the purchase costs of products for planting and growth of crops, and they amount to a total of 105,270.27 €/year.

The costs related to the annual management of the leased spaces concern the taxes for the lease contracts registration (1% of the annual rents), the vacancy costs (2% of the annual rents), the extra-ordinary expenses (0.75% of the construction costs), the insurance installments (0.10% of the estimated construction costs), the one-off rental commission paid to real estate agents (10% of the rents).

3.8   Revenues

The revenues will come from *(i)* the lease of the existing building spaces, intended to the restaurant, the residences, the offices, the conference room and the training rooms; *(ii)* the lease of the basement of the new building used as a garage; *(iii)* the management of the hydroponic greenhouse.

Table 3 shows the annual revenues estimated during the analysis period, coinciding with the period of the enhancement concession (twenty years). In particular, it should be noted that the rental incomes have been valued starting from the market rents for the homogeneous area of the city of Rome where the building complex is located and relative to each intended use. The annual revenues from hydroponic greenhouse management derive from the sale of crops produced through the hydroponic system. In particular, these revenues have been quantified assuming an average selling price of the products, whereas the total annual production quantity has been determined on the basis of the area for the greenhouse: for each crop, the average annual price at source, the average annual production in greenhouses, the number of plants per m^2, the expected quantity of each cultivated variety (per m^2) and the planned quantity to be produced per kg have been firstly estimated; then, for each crop the production cycles in the year have been evaluated and the revenues for each greenhouse product have been assessed [16, 17].

Table 3. Revenues for the main subject

Revenues	
Lease revenue	
Existing building (restaurant, residences, offices, conference room and training rooms)	593 555 35 6/year
Garages	47,740.99 €/year
Total	**551,396.35 €/year**
Management revenue	
Hydroponic greenhouse	334,725.00 €/year
Total	**886,121.36 e/year**

3.9   Development of the DCFA

The development of the DCFA of the initiative allows to verify the feasibility of the investment from the private economic investor (*main* subject) point of view.

The analysis period has been set in twenty years and it has been divided into three phases: the construction phase (two years) involves the project realization, considering both the existing building renovation and the hydroponic greenhouse building new construction; the development phase (two years), which defines the beginning of the greenhouse production processes. In particular, a first year of the development phase (i.e. the third year of the analysis period), in which revenues are equal to 30% of the annual revenues expected, and a second year (the fourth year of the analysis period) in which the revenues are equal to 70% of the annual revenues expected have been considered; the fully operational phase, in which the greenhouse activity generates 100% of the estimated annual revenues for the private investor (*main* subject).

The situation reflects the ordinary process that characterizes a productive activity: in correspondence of the first years of the analysis period (construction phase), the investment costs have been concentrated; in the following development phase, represented by a shorter or longer time frame, the progressive activity take-off has been highlighted with the consequent revenues growth for the private investor; finally, the full capacity of the investment allows the economic subject to cover the initial capital employed and to obtain a financial surplus. Figure 7 shows the development of the DCFA for the case study analyzed.

	Construction phase		Development phase		Fully operational phase		
	YEAR 1	YEAR 2	YEAR 3	YEAR 4	YEAR 5	....	YEAR 20
Investment costs							
Construction cost	€ 1,779,462.89	€ 1,779,462.89					
Operating costs							
New building + existing			€ 172,230.27	€ 172,230.27	€ 172,230.27	....	€ 172,230.27
Commissions on leasing			€ 55,139.63				
Mortgage payment	€ 206,855.57	€ 206,855.57	€ 206,855.57	€ 206,855.57	€ 206,855.57	....	€ 206,855.57
TOTAL COSTS	€ 1,986,318.47	€ 1,986,318.47	€ 434,225.49	€ 379,085.85	€ 379,085.85	....	€ 379,085.85
TOTAL REVENUES			€ 265,836.40	€ 620,284.94	€ 886,121.35	....	€ 886,121.35
Cash flow	€ - 1,9863,18.47	€ -1,986,318.47	€ -168,389.08	€ 241,199.09	€ 507,035.50	....	€ 507,035.50
Discounted costs	€ 1,873,885.35	€ 1,767,816.36	€ 364,584.09	€ 300,271.50	€ 283,275.00	....	€ 118,200.76
Discounted revenues	€ 0.00	€ 0.00	€ 223,201.37	€ 491,323.77	€ 662,161.42	....	€ 276,296.82
Discounted cash flow	€ -1,873,885.35	€ -1,767,816.36	€ -141,382.72	€ 191,052.27	€ 378,886.421	....	€ 158,096.06

Fig. 7. Development of the DCFA for the case study

Table 4 shows the main performance indicators (NPV, IRR, R/C), considering a discounting rate equal to 6%, that coincides with the acceptability threshold of the investment for the *main* subject, taking into account the risks of the reference market. The results obtained highlight the financial convenience of the initiative for the *main* subject.

Table 4. Performance indicators for the case study

NPV	466,693.52 €
IRR	7.34%
R/C	1.06

4 Conclusions

With reference to the current increasing use of PPP tools for the enhancement of public property assets, in this research the financial assessment of a property valorization initiative of a public building (former Police Station in the Ostiense district of Rome) to be activated through the procedure of the "enhancement concession", has been developed.

The analysis has allowed to identify the different public and private subjects involved in the initiative, specifying the roles of each subject in the PPP mechanism and highlighting the relative costs and revenues [10, 11]. The "cascade" system that triggers among the different operators (Public Administration and private investors) is activated only in the situation in which each individual involved finds a "personal" convenience in taking part in the initiative. The analysis carried out, therefore, has highlighted the significant support that can derive, in the initial phases of definition of a PPP investment, from the disaggregation of the different subjects involved in the project, allowing to explain, to systematize and to clarify the roles of each operator and the related costs to be incurred and the revenues that could be earned.

The implementation of the DCFA and the assessment of the performance indicators have made it possible to verify the capacity of the initiative to adequately offset the risks for the private investor. Furthermore, the combination of functions provided for in the buildings and the different management modalities (direct and indirect) have allowed, on the one hand, to satisfy the financial requirement for the private investor, on the other hand, to transfer a large part of the risks of the initiative to the different operators, that will be more competent for each specific market sector.

Finally, as the new functions respond to the needs of social (e.g. requalification of a territorial area in a state of degradation through the creation of new aggregation spaces) and environmental sustainability (activation of a hydroponic greenhouse, limiting the consumption of agricultural land), further studies may concern the assessment, through a Cost-Benefit Analysis, of the investment convenience for the local communities [12, 13].

References

1. Attardi, R., Cerreta, M., Sannicandro, V., Torre, C.M.: Non-compensatory composite indicators for the evaluation of urban planning policy: the land-use policy efficiency index (LUPEI). Eur. J. Oper. Res. **264**(2), 491–507 (2018)
2. Berto, R., Stival, C.A., Rosato, P.: Enhancing the environmental performance of industrial settlements: an economic evaluation of extensive green roof competitiveness. Build. Environ. **127**, 58–68 (2018)

3. Cosentino, C., Amato, F., Murgante, B.: Population-based simulation of urban growth: the Italian case study. Sustainability **10**(12), 4838 (2018)
4. Del Giudice, V., De Paola, P.: The value of intellectual capital in shipping companies. In: Stanghellini, S., Morano, P., Bottero, M., Oppio, A. (eds.) Appraisal: From Theory to Practice. GET, pp. 231–239. Springer, Cham (2017). https://doi.org/10.1007/978-3-319-49676-4_17
5. Guarini, M.R.: Self-renovation in Rome: Ex Ante, in Itinere and Ex post evaluation. In: Gervasi, O., et al. (eds.) ICCSA 2016. LNCS, vol. 9789, pp. 204–218. Springer, Cham (2016). https://doi.org/10.1007/978-3-319-42089-9_15
6. Pace, R.K., Zhu, S.: The influence of house, seller, and locational factors on the probability of sale. J. Hous. Econ. **43**, 72–82 (2019)
7. Khan, M.M.A., Ibrahim, N.I., Mahbubul, I.M., Ali, H.M., Saidur, R., Al-Sulaiman, F.A.: Evaluation of solar collectors designs with integrated latent heat thermal energy storage: a review. Sol. Energy **166**, 334–350 (2018)
8. Las Casas, G., Scorza, F., Murgante, B.: New urban agenda and open challenges for urban and regional planning. In: Calabrò, F., Della Spina, L., Bevilacqua, C. (eds.) ISHT 2018. SIST, vol. 100, pp. 282–288. Springer, Cham (2019). https://doi.org/10.1007/978-3-319-92099-3_33
9. Montrone, S., Perchinunno, P., Di Giuro, A., Rotondo, F., Torre, C.M.: Identification of "hot spots" of social and housing difficulty in urban areas: scan statistics for housing market and urban planning policies. In: Murgante, B., Borruso, G., Lapucci, A. (eds.) Geocomputation and Urban Planning. Studies in Computational Intelligence, vol. 176, pp. 57–78. Springer, Berlin, Heidelberg (2009). https://doi.org/10.1007/978-3-540-89930-3_4
10. Morano, P., Tajani, F.: Break even analysis for the financial verification of urban regeneration projects. Appl. Mech. Mater. **438**, 1830–1835 (2013)
11. Morano, P., Tajani, F.: Saving soil and financial feasibility. A model to support public-private partnerships in the regeneration of abandoned areas. Land Use Policy **73**, 40–48 (2018)
12. Pontrandolfi, P., Scorza, F.: Making urban regeneration feasible: tools and procedures to integrate urban agenda and UE cohesion regional programs. In: Gervasi, O., et al. (eds.) ICCSA 2017. LNCS, vol. 10409, pp. 564–572. Springer, Cham (2017). https://doi.org/10.1007/978-3-319-62407-5_40
13. Sajid, M.U., Ali, H.M.: Recent advances in application of nanofluids in heat transfer devices: a critical review. Renew. Sustain. Energy Rev. **103**, 556–592 (2019)
14. Sullivan, E., Ward, P.: Sustainable housing applications and policies for low-income self-build and housing rehab. Habitat Int. **36**(2), 312–323 (2012)
15. Tajani, F., Morano, P.: Concession and lease or sale? A model for the enhancement of public properties in disuse or underutilized. WSEAS Trans. Bus. Econ. **11**, 787–800 (2014)
16. http://www.ismea.it/istituto-di-servizi-per-il-mercato-agricolo-alimentare
17. https://www.efsa.europa.eu/it

Modeling an Optimal Control Problem for the Navigation of Mobile Robots in an Ocduded Environment Application to Unmanned Aerial Vehicles

Kahina Louadj[1]([✉])(iD), Philippe Marthon[2], and Abdelkrim Nemra[3]

[1] Laboratoire de Conception et Conduites Systèmes de Production (L2CSP),
Tizi-Ouzou, Algérie
louadj_kahina@yahoo.fr
[2] IRIT-ENSEEIHT, Toulouse, France
Philippe.marthon@enseeiht.fr
[3] Laboratoire Robotique et Productique, Ecole Militaire Polytechnique,
Bordj El Bahri, Algiers, Algérie
karim_nemra@yahoo.fr

Abstract. An optimal control problem of two Unmanned autonomous Vehicles to follow the trajectory and avoid the collision between them. The aim is to minimize energy, the distance between state and desired, and maximize the distance between the two drones. For this study, we used midpoint such discretization method, the simulation results ar given by Bocop software.

Keywords: Navigation · UAV · Trajectory planning

1 Introduction

Today, the emergence of robotics [20,21] led to make robots more autonomous and increasingly easy to drive. A robotic system is defined as an artificial system, equipped with sensors and actuators, designed to act on the outside world. In the beginning, these robots were installed in industries to perform us tasks that are painful, repetitive or impossible for humans. nowadays, we can find robots in different fields: industrial, domestic, medical, military, etc.

UAVs are autonomous or semi-autonomous flying machines capable of flying missions without human presence on board [6,7]. This earned them the name "Unmanned Arial Vehicle: UAV". Today we are witnessing a rise of drones in civil and military aeronautics. The potential application of these flying machines is very high, but there are still a number of difficulties that slow down their expansion. Researchers and designers have been working intensively over the past two decades to try to iron out these difficulties. This concerns the field of mechanical and aerodynamic design as well as the fields of embedded systems and automation. As for classic aircraft cases the design of a drone requires

© Springer Nature Switzerland AG 2019
S. Misra et al. (Eds.): ICCSA 2019, LNCS 11620, pp. 94–102, 2019.
https://doi.org/10.1007/978-3-030-24296-1_10

mastery of previous scientific fields. However, despite some similarities with aircraft, the design of drones raises completely new specific problems. Experiments and publications concerning the resolution of these problems are increasing exponentially.

In some problems, the workspace can be dynamic. the location of obstacles may change over time, making time an important parameter in evaluating the validity of drone movement, as opposed to path planning. Thus, the trajectory planning must respect the dynamic constraints that arise from the environment (mobile obstacles) and from the robotic system considered (its dynamics). We distinguish, essentially, two categories of methods of trajectory planning: methods based on a reference trajectory and those not using them. In fact, for the first category, the planner has a calculated reference trajectory in a model of the environment using a global method.

Optimal control theory has been formulated as an extension of the calculus of variations. Based on the theoretical foundation laid by several generations of mathematicians, optimal control has developed into a well established research area and nds its applications in many scienticelds, ranging from mathematics and engineering to biomedical and management sciences [9–11].

Trajectory planning consists of generating an optimal trajectory between two points in the configuration space [1–3,5]. This trajectory minimizes a particular criterion such as time, energy or distance traveled. The feasibility of the trajectory generated depends on the technique used, the chosen cost function and the different constraints.

Our goal is to find a control of two drones that can follow the trajectory and avoid the collision between the two drones. for this, we use discretization method such as the midpoint method and the simulations are made using the Bocop software [22]. The criterion is to minimize distance between state and state desired, energy and maximize the distance between the two drones [14–19].

The article is organized as follows; In Sect. 1 defines the general problem of navigation and as application is two quadrotor drones. In Sect. 2, the mathematical model of the optimal control problem of the two drones. The results are given by Bocop in Sect. 3 and finished by conclusion.

2   Definition of General Problem of Navigation

In Autonomous Vehicle's, the development of trajectory planners capable of guiding choices towards maximum efficiency is of crucial importance. One of the major problems in robotics lies in the establishment of autonomous robots. By autonomy, we mean that by means of a high level specification of the task to be executed by the robot, it will be able to realize it without any external intervention.

The development of such plans is a complex task that requires a fine and accurate modeling of the work environment and a precise definition of the objectives to be achieved. In general, trajectory planning approaches are classified into two major families: the so-called reactive or non-reference pathways consist of iteratively modifying, over time, a movement initially calculated to best guarantee convergence towards the goal. The trajectory deformation approach allows a mobile robot to navigate safely in a dynamic environment so as to move away from obstacles and satisfy the kinematic constraints of the system [24–26].

The motion planning for a drone evolving in an environment is to determine a sequence of actions allowing it to move between two given configurations while respecting a certain number of constraints and criteria. This sequence of actions is defined by a succession of crossing points belonging to the trajectory of the considered mobile which must respect a certain number of constraints and criteria which generally depend on the nature of the task to be carried out, the nature of the environment and characteristics of the drone itself. This subject has sparked many studies. Anyway, the difficulty of such a problem depends largely on the nature of the environment which can be static ie not changing over time (such as walls, furniture ...), ie dynamic that there are entities (obstacles or other drones), besides the drone that move there. It should be noted, of course, that most real environments are dynamic.

Although the path deformation is to distance every moment the path followed by the robot of the current position of the obstacles, the trajectory deformation aims to anticipate their movements by removing this trajectory of the forecast model from the future movements of moving objects. In fact, the trajectory followed decomposes itself into a path followed by the drone and a law of speed (kinematics). Thus a trajectory tells us, at every moment, the position of the drone on its way. Mathematically, a trajectory is described by a parametric curve which represents the path to be covered in time. It is important to note here that when it comes to a dynamic environment, a motion planner is required to predict trajectory deformations to avoid possible collisions. To this end, the planner can distort the path he intends to follow, as well as modify his speed to avoid an obstacle: to avoid an animal crossing a road, a driver may brake or change his path [24–26].

In our case, Given n moving vehicles in an environment cluttered with fixed and moving obstacles, find the controls and trajectories of these vehicles to avoid collision and to complete their route in minimal time (safety and efficiency).

An admissible movement that the drone must perform between the initial position and a given end position. Depending on the nature of the environment, including the obstacles, we distinguish:

- **Path Planning:** Representing the simplest motion planning case in which the drone moves in an environment populated by static obstacles. Thus, we limit ourselves to the geometrical aspect of the problem which amounts to calculating a continuous sequence of configurations without collision between two given configurations.
- **Trajectory Planning:** In some problems, the workspace can be dynamic. The location of obstacles may change over time, making the temporal dimension an important parameter in evaluating the validity of the movement of the drone. Thus, the trajectory planning becomes unavoidable as soon as the problem requires taking into account the dynamic constraints of the robotic

system that are those concerning the environment or those that describe the dynamics of the drone.

We are interested in the decision of the navigation of the drone namely the planning of movement for a drone for which the taking into account of cinematic constraints this primordial, coupled with the need to consider its own geometry and without forgetting the good mastery of the environment in which it evolves.

3   Application to the Case of Two Quad-Rotor Drones

A quad-rotor is an aerial vehicle which rotates by producing differentials in thrust between it's for motors. The following section presents the mathematical model of the quad-rotor [6,7].

The motion of the quad-rotor can be divided into two subsystems, rotational subsystem (roll, pitch and yaw) and translation subsystem (altitude and x and y position). The mathematical model of the two quad-rotor can be written in a state space representation as follows

$$
\begin{cases}
\dot{x}_{1i} = \dot{\varphi} = x_{2i}, \\
\dot{x}_{2i} = \ddot{\varphi} = a_1 x_{4i} x_{6i} + a_2 x_{4i} \Omega + b_1 u_{1i}, \\
\dot{x}_{3i} = \dot{\theta} = x_{4i}, \\
\dot{x}_{4i} = \ddot{\theta} = a_3 x_{2i} x_{6i} + a_4 x_{2i} \Omega + b_2 u_{2i}, \\
\dot{x}_{5i} = \dot{\psi} = x_{6i}, \\
\dot{x}_{6i} = \ddot{\psi} = a_5 x_{2i} x_{4i} + b_3 u_{3i}, \\
\dot{x}_{7i} = \dot{z} = x_8, \\
\dot{x}_{8i} = \ddot{z} = \dfrac{u_{4i}}{m}(cosx_{1i} sinx_{3i} cosx_{5i} + sinx_{1i} sinx_{5i}), \\
\dot{x}_{9i} = \dot{x} = x_{10i}, \\
\dot{x}_{10i} = \ddot{x} = \dfrac{u_{4i}}{m}(cosx_{1i} sinx_{3i} sinx_{5i} - sinx_{1i} cosx_{5i}), \\
\dot{x}_{11i} = \dot{y} = x_{12i}, \\
\dot{x}_{12i} = \ddot{y} = \dfrac{cosx_{1i} cosx_{3i}}{m} u_{4i} - g, \\
-\pi/2 \le x_{1i} \le \pi/2, -\pi/2 \le x_{3i} \le \pi/2, \\
-\pi \le x_{5i} \le \pi, x_k i(0) = 0, k = \overline{1,12}, i = \overline{1,2} \\
-20 \le u_{ji} \le 20, \ j = \overline{1,4}, \ 0 \le u_{4i} \le 20.
\end{cases}
\tag{1}
$$

Where $g(m/s^2)$: gravity acceleration; $I_x, I_y, I_z(kg/m^2)$: roll, pitch and yaw inertia moments respectively, $J_r(kg/m^2)$: the rotor inertia; $m(kg)$: mass; $x, y, z(m)$: longitudinal, lateral and vertical motions respectively; $\phi, \theta, \psi(rad)$: roll, pitch and yaw angles, respectively; $w_k(rad/s)$: rotor angular velocity, where, k equal to 1, 2, 3 and 4; $d(m)$: the distance between the quad-rotor center of mass and the propeller rotation axis; $u_1, u_2, u_3(N.m)$: aerodynamical roll, pitch and yaw moments respectively; $u_4(N)$: lift force.

With $\Omega = w_1 - w_2 + w_3 - w_4$, $a_1 = \dfrac{I_y - I_z}{I_x}$, $a_2 = \dfrac{-J_r}{I_x}$, $a_3 = \dfrac{I_z - I_x}{I_y}$,

$a_4 = \dfrac{J_r}{I_y}$, $a_5 = \dfrac{I_x - I_y}{I_z}$, $b_1 = \dfrac{d}{I_x}$, $b_2 = \dfrac{d}{I_y}$, $b_3 = \dfrac{d}{I_z}$.

One of the main objectives of this paper is to find control which ensures the convergence of positions $\{x, y, z\}$, to their desired trajectories respectively $\{x_d, y_d, z_d\}$, while maintaining stability of roll and pitch angle $\{\psi, \phi, \theta\}$ in final time.

Then, the criterion is formulated as follows:

$$
J = \int_0^{t_f} \rho_1 [\sum_{i=1}^{2} (x_{7i} - x_{di})^2 + (x_{9i} - y_{di})^2
$$
$$
+ (x_{11i} - z_{di})^2] - \rho_2 [(x_{71} - x_{72})^2 + (x_{91} - x_{92})^2
$$
$$
+ (x_{111} - x_{112})^2] + (1 - (\rho_1 + \rho_2))(\sum_{i=1}^{2} (u_{1i}^2 + u_{2i}^2 + u_{3i}^2 + u_{4i}^2)dt \rightarrow min \quad (2)
$$

where $t_f(second)$: final time; $\{x_d, y_d, z_d\}$: desired trajectory of $\{x, y, z\}$.

4   Results Simulation

$\omega = 340; d = 0.23; \ m = 0.6; \ I_x = I_y = 7.5e - 3, \ I_z = 1.3e - 2; \ J_r = 6e - 5; \ g = 9.8$.

The red line is the delimiter of $x_1, \ x_3, \ x_5$ respectively. And the blue line is the trajectories.

The results given by Bocop software are presented in Figs. 1, 2, 3, 4, 5, 6, 7 and 8. And Figs. 9, 10, is the criterion for $\rho = 1e - 9$. Else, the optimal solution is ensured in 100 iterations with 3.69 s. And $J = 7.2963$. The results are compatible with desired state, and satisfies the objective of this problem's.

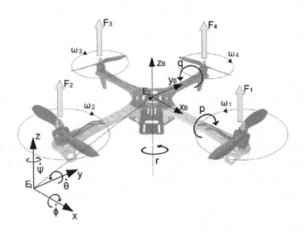

Fig. 1. Quad-rotor

(a) (b)

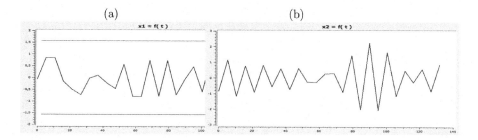

Fig. 2. Trajectory state of x_1 and x_2 respectively.

(a) (b)

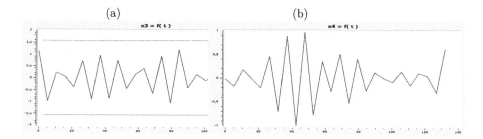

Fig. 3. Trajectory state of x_3 and x_4 respectively.

(a) (b)

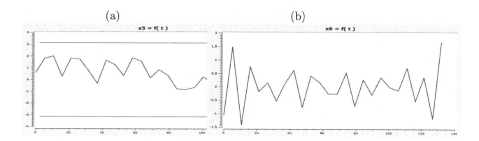

Fig. 4. Trajectory state of x_5 and x_6 respectively.

(a) (b)

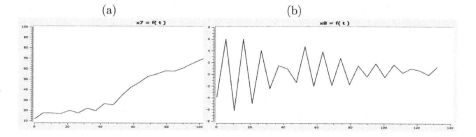

Fig. 5. Trajectory state of x_7 and x_8 respectively.

(a)   (b)

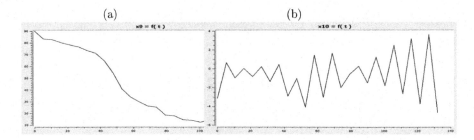

Fig. 6. Trajectory state of x_9 and x_{10} respectively.

(a)   (b)

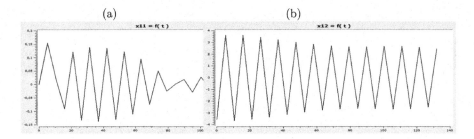

Fig. 7. Trajectory state of x_{11} and x_{12} respectively.

(a)   (b)

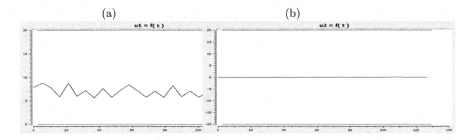

Fig. 8. Control u_1 and u_2 respectively.

(a)   (b)

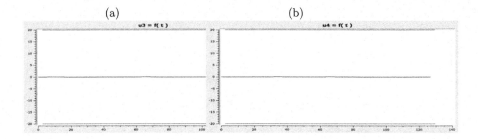

Fig. 9. Control of u_3 and u_4 respectively.

5   Conclusion

In this work, we are Modeling an optimal control problem for the navigation of mobile robots in an occluded environment Application to unmanned aerial vehicles. And we have solved this problem using discretization method with Bocop software. An optimal control problem of unmanned aerial vehicle to minimize the energy and distance between the state and desired trajectory, and maximize the distance between the two quadrotor in free final time. The results are adequate for our purpose in the computational time is 3.69 s in 100 iterations with Bocop software. The convergence is fast and the computational time is small.

References

1. Slotine, J.-J.E., Li, W.: Applied Nonlinear Control. Prentice Hall, Englewood Cliffs (1991)
2. Wise, K.A., Sedwick, J.L., Eberhardt, R.L.: Nonlinear control of missiles McDonnell Douglas Aerospace Report MDC 93B0484, October 1993
3. Ehrler, D., Vadali, S.R.: Examination of the optimal nonlinear regulator problem. In: Proceedings of the AIAA Guidance, Navigation, and Control Conference, Minneapolis, MN (1988)
4. Beard, R., et al.: Autonomous vehicle technologies for small fixed-wing UAVs. AIAA J. Aerosp. Comput. Inf. Commun. **2**, 92–108 (2005)
5. Guo, W., Gao, X., Xiao, Q., Multiple UAV cooperative path planning based on dynamic Bayesian network. In: Control and Decision Conference (CCDC), pp. 2401–2405, July 2008
6. Mechirgui, M.: Commande Optimale minimisant la consommation d'énergie d'un Drone, Relai de communication, Maîtrise en Génie Eléctrique, Montréal, Le 15 Octobre 2014
7. Boudjellal, A.A., Boudjema, F.: Commande par Backstepping basée sur un Observateur Mode Glissant pour un Drone de type Quadri-rotor. In: ICEE2013 (2013)
8. Hull, D.G.: Optimal Control Theory for Applications. Springer, Heidelberg (2003). https://doi.org/10.1007/978-1-4757-4180-3
9. Trelat, E.: Contrôle optimal: théorie et applications, Vuibert, collection Mathématiques Concrètes (2005)
10. Sethi, S.P., Thompsonn, G.L.: Optimal Control Theory, Applications to Management Science and Economics, 2nd edn. Kluwer Academic Publishers, Dordrecht (2000)
11. Zaslavski, A.J.: Structure of Approximate Solutions of Optimal Control Problems. Springer, Heidelberg (2013)
12. Akulenko, L.D.: Problems and Methods of Optimal Control. Springer, Heidelberg (1994)
13. Pytlak, R.: Numerical Methods for Optimal Control Problems With State Constraints. Springer, Heidelberg (1999)
14. Demim, F., Louadj, K., Aidene, M., Nemra, A.: Solution of an optimal control problem with vector control using relaxation method. Autom. Control Syst. Eng. J. **16**(2) (2016). ISSN 1687–4811
15. Louadj, K., Aidene, M.: Optimization of a problem of optimal control with free initial state. Appl. Math. Sci. **4**(5), 201–216 (2010)

16. Louadj, K., Aidene, M.: Adaptive method for solving optimal control problem with state and control variables. Math. Probl. Eng. **2012**, 15 (2012)
17. Louadj, K., Aidene, M.: Direct method for resolution of optimal control problem with free initial condition. Int. J. Differ. Equ. **2012**, 18 (2012). Article ID 173634
18. Louadj, K., Aidene, M.: A problem of optimal control with free initial state. In: Proceedings du Congres National de Mathematiques Appliquees et Industrielles, SMAI 2011, Orleans du 23rd May to au 27th, pp. 184–190 (2011)
19. Titouche, S., Spiteri, P., Messine, F., Aidene, M.: Optimal control of a large thermic. J. Control Syst. **25**, 50–58 (2015)
20. Geisert, M., Mansard, N.: Trajectory generation for Quadrotor based systems using numerical optimal control. In: IEEE International Conference on Robotics and Automation (ICRA) Stockholm, Sweden, 16–21 May 2016
21. Fethi, D., Nemra, A., Louadj, K., Hamerlain, M.: Simultaneous localization, mapping, and path planning for unmanned vehicle using optimal control. Adv. Mech. Eng. **10**(1), 1–25 (2018)
22. Bonnans, F., Martinon, P., Grélard, V.: Bocop - a collection of examples. Research report RR-8053, INRIA (2012)
23. Louadj, K., Demim, F., Nemra, A., Marthon, P.: An optimal control problem of unmanned aerial vehicle. In: International an Conference on Control, Decision and Information Technologies (CoDIT 2018), Thessaloniki, 10 April 2018–13 April 2018 (2018)
24. Jalel, S.: Optimisation de la navigation robotique. Thesis, Toulouse University (INP) (2016)
25. Atyabi, A., Powers, D.: Review of classical and heuristic based navigation and path planning approaches. Int. J. Adv. Comput. Technol. **5**(14), 1–14 (2013)
26. Jalel S., Marthon, P., Hamouda, A.: Optimum path planning for mobile robots is static environments using graph modelling and NURBS Curves. In: WSEAS International Conference on Signal Processing, Robotics and Automation, 20–22 February 2013, Cambridge, UK, pp. 216–221 (2013)

Advanced Transport Tools and Methods
(A2TM 2019)

The Effectiveness of Strategies to Reduce External Costs from Commuting in Central Europe

Silvio Nocera[✉] and Francesco Bruzzone

IUAV, University of Venice, Santa Croce, 191 – I, 30135 Venice, Italy
nocera@iuav.it

Abstract. Transportation is a major source of both primary pollution and greenhouse gas emissions, and has been hence frequently the object of past analyses at several levels. This paper examines the outcomes of numerous previous strategies that dealt with one or more of the multiple dimensions of commuting (green technologies, transport management, urban planning and behavior changes etc.) to check their results, and to introduce the first outcomes of the European project SMART-COMMUTING. The core of the paper is the accurate description of such strategies, including the estimation of the emission ranges under different modal scenarios in the different locations. The discussion regards on the other hand their efficiency to reduce the external costs of commuting, with the aim of offering transport planners, stakeholders and policy makers a way of substantiating their future strategies about commuting.

Keywords: Transport external costs · Smart commuting · Emission reduction

1 Introduction

The transport sector is responsible for around 65% of global oil consumption and for around 25% of global Greenhouse Gas emissions [1–4]. Furthermore, road transportation accounts for between half and three-quarters of total emissions from the transport sector (depending on the study area), and its impact could be even greater in urban areas [5]. Considered the increasing urbanization trend [6] and taken into account that the worldwide number of automobiles is forecasted to triple by 2050 [7], effects such as air pollution, noise pollution, congestion and accidents are destined to increase. It is therefore evident that a strategy to tackle the tendency towards increasing energy consumption and emissions is needed.

Both academic and political institutions have in fact started to extensively address the transportation emission issue and have come up with several different goals, strategies and policy options to reduce GHG emissions from the transport sector. Strategies include mobility management, which reduces traffic volumes through a variety of measures, clean vehicle strategies, which reduces energy consumption and emissions per kilometer through technical improvements [8], and others which focus on land use planning and more in general on the built environment [3]. Commuting, thanks to its regular pattern, its close connection with congestion problems, and its

© Springer Nature Switzerland AG 2019
S. Misra et al. (Eds.): ICCSA 2019, LNCS 11620, pp. 105–119, 2019.
https://doi.org/10.1007/978-3-030-24296-1_11

association with people's choices about locations of work and housing, has long been an important target of transport policy and urban planning [9].

The European Commission has as well developed an Energy, Climate and Environment strategy, and has included the reduction of GHG emissions from the transport sector as part of its targets and strategies, reiterating its commitment to low-carbon transport in 2011 [10] and thus launching several different projects, among which Smart Commuting, part of the Interreg Central Europe program. The Smart Commuting Project aims at improving mobility planning capability in participating functional urban areas with the goal of cooperating in the development of a low-carbon strategy to lower CO_2 emissions from the transport sector. Smart Commuting presents a transnational strategy containing different measures, among which the different project partners (municipalities) choose those which best match their needs and whose outcomes are best effective for the accomplishment of the project's goals [11].

This paper will first present the outcomes of several studied or implemented strategies, which dealt with the multiple dimensions of commuting (mobility management, technology improvements, land use planning, behavioral changes, etc.), and will then include the measures identified by Smart Commuting project's transnational strategy into possible external costs and GHG emission mitigations strategies, to estimate their effectiveness at lowering emissions and more in general external costs of commuting in different geographical contexts.

2 Commuting External Costs

Passenger transportation generates a number of negative externalities on the physical and social environment in which it takes place. It is well known that very often the most convenient transport option for individuals is by far not the best option for society, in terms of environmental sustainability as well as in terms of economic expenditure. According to Move [12] and Liew and Chu [13], external costs are generated by individuals, but borne by either the agency (government) or society. The external cost is the difference between total and private (internal) costs reflecting all costs occurring due to the provision and use of transport infrastructure, such as wear and tear costs of infrastructure, capital costs, congestion costs, accidents costs, environmental costs.

Various cities have started informing citizens about how much their choice to commute or move using motorized transport costs to society. The City of Vancouver (Canada), for example, has published and promoted some independent studies, which show how for an individual 1$ expenditure on buses society pays 1,50$, whereas for an individual 1$ expenditure on car transport society pays 9,20$. Active transportation on the contrary requires much smaller societal investments (lower than 0,10$ for each 1$ individually spent). Such figures are pretty much confirmed by Glazebrook [14] whose report stated that the "out-of-pocket" cost for car users in Sydney (Australia) was only about one-sixth of the total cost. If faced with full costs, motorists transport mode selection would therefore be different in many cases [13]. The external costs of transportation and of urban passenger transport specifically are studied by many different authors and institutions: congestion, air pollution, accidents and noise are the main externalities on which all scholars and reports agree (among others [12, 15–19]). Besides the four cited external cost categories, others which are often considered in recent works are: climate change costs, costs of up- and downstream processes and marginal infrastructure costs. Maibach et al. [16] also include costs for nature and landscape preservation and rehabilitation, for soil and water pollution, and for energy dependency. Liew and Chu [13] interestingly include among external costs the category "government subsidies", both addressed to public and private transport.

Generally speaking, though, internalization and/or reduction of external costs of urban transport are themes which are not yet mastered by the general public despite their great impact on everyday life and on government expenditure. Scientific literature and governance and research institutions, on the contrary, have studied the topic extensively and have defined, estimated and evaluated both major external costs and their internalization or reduction strategies. It is however surprising to note that literature seems not to have concentrated on the specific aspect of the external costs generated by commuting, while the distinction between passenger and freight transport has been made. Commuting "rush-hours", in facts, are the moments in which transport infrastructure and services are mostly exploited and in which their residual capacity is put at risk. This aspect is well stressed by the general press (e.g. Business Insider [20]) but seems not to be part of scientific literature yet.

Rather than on internalization strategies, this paper concentrates on the reduction of external costs of commuting by acting on the factors which combined contribute to causing such costs (such as environmental quality, congestion, modal share, social equity and others). Reduction strategies and internalization strategies are clearly related as lowering or removing cost-causing factors erases the necessity to internalize such costs. It is however not completely true that externalities reduction strategies and cost internalization strategies always pursue the same objectives: whereas modal shift towards public transit is often considered a success for the first goal [21–24] – we will discuss this point further in this paper - for the second it might result in the intensification of some of the cost factors (typically, subsidies) even while soothing other negative effects such as for example congestion and air pollution.

3   External Cost Reductions Strategies: A Literature Review

Different authors have studied policy instruments aiming at reducing transport emissions in order to understand their effectiveness and/or have come up with strategies and instruments which could serve to achieve political and institutional strategies (such as emission reduction goals), or to tackle increasingly relevant issues such as congestion and pollution. In this section, we will review some examples of policy and strategies classification, simulation and outcomes, with the aim to identify a proper framework in which to place Smart Commuting Project's measures so to estimate their effectiveness in lowering GHG emissions.

Available research concentrates on three different types of mitigation options: some studies investigated the impact of urban design on emissions with varied results, but giving as a general assumption that urban planning policies by themselves yield modest emission reductions. Other studies investigated the impact of using alternative technologies such as low carbon fuels, hybrid and electric vehicles, while incorporating life-cycle emissions. Travel demand management policies are the third relevant literature sector [25]. Scenario analysis has moreover been used to integrate the economic, technological and transportation demand changes that affect GHG emissions, thus combining the three abovementioned sectors [1]. In those cases, authors underline how acting through comprehensive strategies is more effective compared to concentrating on one sector only (either the built environment, vehicle technology or transport demand management). Hickman et al. [26], for instance, found that in the Oxfordshire area low emission vehicles and alternative fuels could reduce CO_2 emissions by 37,4% compared to a BAU scenario with a 2030 horizon, while the inclusion of other policy packages (such as driver education, different freight management and slower speed driving) could result in a 48,3% reduction over the same BAU level.

Regarding the planning sector, there is an ongoing debate on whether the most effective urban form to reduce emissions is a polycentric or a monocentric approach. While most authors agree on the fact that a compact city is more efficient compared to a sprawl situation, the mono-, dual-, or polycentrism of a city appears to respond differently to different study approaches and – above all – to different geographical contexts [3, 5, 9, 27–31]. Some of the authors also mention that urban development strategies should consider social geography and socioeconomic aspects, since they strongly affect people's commuting habits and choices [9, 32].

The debate on the effectiveness of the other two possible strategies, that is cleaner vehicle strategies and travel demand management strategies, has been carried on by most authors as either a comparison between scenarios ascribable to the two groups or as an integrated approach between policies from both strategies, seeking for the most effective combination. Still, some articles are available where the purpose is to establish whether cleaner vehicles strategies or travel demand management strategies are most effective (for instance [33]).

Findings related to cleaner technology implementation are not very homogeneous. Most authors agree when saying that cleaner vehicle technology by itself is not sufficient to achieve emissions reductions coherent with politically declared local and national targets, but while in some cases the role acknowledged to technology resulted in satisfying emission reduction gains [1, 34] in most cases it is only regarded as part of a much broader strategy and its standalone impacts are evaluated as not very significant (among others [8, 35]). It must moreover be noted that converting existing vehicle fleets to cleaner technologies (in developed countries) or using cleaner technologies for expanding vehicle fleets (in rising economies) does not tackle primary issues such as congestion and travel time, which will rather stay like they are or grow worse as a business-as-usual scenario, even with green vehicles substantially developing.

Some authors give evidence of the relevance of the role of active transportation. As part of an integrated strategy, walking and cycling – having a zero-emission level – are often keys to obtaining predetermined goals [1, 3, 34, 35] and are included in most of the articles on the topic of lowering emissions. Some other authors, however, given their particular contexts of study, assign to active transportation an even more relevant role in cutting emissions and identify the shift towards active transportation as being one of the most effective possibilities [36, 37].

After discussing in general terms the scholars' attitude and research orientations with regard to urban transport emission and energy consumption reductions, with a specific focus on commuting patterns, in the next section of this work we will try to identify an appropriate way to classify Smart Commuting project's measures and strategies so to evaluate their effectiveness. For this purpose, the works of Nakamura and Hayashi [38], (which refers to the CUTE project [39]), and the ones published by the German Agency for Technical Cooperation (*Deutsche Gesellschaft für Technische Zusammenarbeit* GTZ, [40–42]) provide a good classification framework, which when adapted reveals itself to be suitable to the various cities partner of Smart Commuting project as well to the different measures and strategies which are part of the project itself. GTZ in their works summarized the possible strategies towards a more sustainable urban transport system as AVOID (reducing unnecessary travel demand), SHIFT (shifting transport to low-carbon modes) or IMPROVE (improving intensity of transit-oriented emissions) strategies. Instruments are instead classified by Nakamura and Hayashi [38] as being related to technology, regulation, information or economy. The authors provided an overview of trends and effects of low-carbon measures for urban transport, in order to understand their feasibility and effectiveness and their affinity to CUTE project's strategies. The authors' conclusions indicate that cities pursuing AVOID and SHIFT strategies seem to prefer – them being more effective – first stage instruments, whereas more developed context aiming at IMPROVE strategies concentrate on later-stage strategies. They also underline how no generic strategy is valid for all cities: specific policy packages should be designed.

Starting from the instruments classification presented by Nakamura and Hayashi and integrating it with other available literature and with GTZ's results, we can divide Smart Commuting project's measures in five different categories: planning instruments, regulatory/governance instruments, economic instruments, information/ict instruments, vehicle/hardware technology instruments. Table 1 shows the categories to which each measure of Smart Commuting belongs.

We can then trace back every proposed measure of Smart Commuting project to a more general category of instruments (often referred to as "policy packages" in literature). This is because the specific effects and impacts of such policy packages have been to some extent discussed by scholars and it is therefore easier to investigate them with reference to Smart Commuting project's context. Sticking to policy instruments categories described by Hickman et al. [35] and Litman [33], measures part of Smart Commuting project can be more specifically framed into the following policy packages, as detailed in Table 2: 1-Public transport development, 2-Active commuting incentive, 3-Urban and strategic planning, 4-Ride-sharing growth and incentive, 5-Information Communication Technologies, 6-Behavioral interventions/education, 7- Technology advancements.

Table 1. Synthesis of the measures which are part of smart commuting project and allocation into measure categories

	Planning instruments	Regulatory and governance instruments	Economic instruments	Information and ICT instruments	Vehicle and hardware technology improvements
Incentive app for cycling				X	
Bike park roof	X				
Bus/tram stop roof and benches	X				
Pedestrian-friendly access to bus/tram stops	X				
Backside exit of railway stations	X				
New stations/stops	X				
Non profit car sharing		X		X	
Bike sharing (fixed station)	X	X		X	
Car pooling		X		X	
Electric vehicle charging spots	X				
Mutual learning		X		X	
Awareness raise in clean/active mobility				X	
Mobility education				X	
Participatory processes for strategy-building				X	
Mobility service points	X			X	
Mobility information portal				X	
Bike parks at schools	X				
Bike repair corners	X				
Teleworking incentives		X			
Companies' mobility plans	X			X	
Coordination between transit and workers' shifts	X	X			
Companies' employees car pooling				X	
Electric vehicle incentives			X		X
Workplaces relocations (closer to transit stops)	X		X		

Table 2. Allocation of measures into policy packages which are useful for a more clear discussion of their effectiveness

	1- Public transport development	2- Active commuting incentive	3- Urban and strategic planning	4- Ride share growth and incentive	5- Information communication technologies	6- Behavioral interventions and education	7- Technology advancements
Incentive app for cycling					X		
Bike park roof		X					
Bus/tram stop roof and benches	X						
Pedestrian-friendly access to bus/tram stops	X						
Backside exit of railway stations	X						
New stations/stops	X						
Non profit car sharing				X			
Bike sharing (fixed station)		X					
Car pooling				X			
Electric vehicle charging spots							X
Mutual learning						X	
Awareness raise in clean/active mobility						X	
Mobility education						X	
Participatory processes for strategy-building			X				
Mobility service points			X				
Mobility information portal					X		
Bike parks at schools		X					
Bike repair corners		X					
Teleworking incentives					X		
Companies' mobility plans			X				
Coordination between transit and workers' shifts	X						
Companies' employees car pooling				X			
Electric Vehicle incentives							X
Workplaces relocations (closer to transit stops)			X				

4   The Effectiveness of Smart Commuting Project's Externality Reduction Strategies

According with the above-mentioned policy packages, this paragraph describes which measures Smart Commuting project has identified for each package and brings evidences of how such measure could be effective at reducing impacts and external costs from commuting, particularly focusing on the geographical contexts of Smart Commuting project's partner cities.

Regarding policy package "1- Public transport development", the measures proposed by Smart Commuting project are: installation of shelters, benches and information displays at transit stops; access improvement to transit stops (for the elderly and the impaired especially); new exit for train stations (to improve accessibility); additional stop/station for transit services (to increase the number of potential users); fostering coordination between transit schedules and workers' shift hours; fostering coordination between transit service and school buses service. All of these measures have to do with accessibility and attractiveness of the public transit system, either strictly or in a broader sense; which is, improving accessibility through inclusion of disadvantages categories among potential users and by widening the basin of potential users; and improving attractiveness through stops and stations improvements (weather shelters, real-time information screens and seating) [11].

The identified and described measures are effective in reducing emissions and congestion from the transport sector in urban areas and specifically in the contexts of Smart Commuting Projects' partners, which are all mid- or small sized European cities, since – as it is highlighted in the project's Deliverable D.T1.2.1 "Transnational strategy to change commuting models in the FUAs" [11] - the provision of additional transport facilities within a certain radius from homes and job location strongly affects the willingness of people to make use of such facilities and to cover on foot the distance to reach them. All reviewed authors, when discussing transit as a modal choice, agreed that accessibility in terms of walking time and quality of the walking itinerary has a decisive role. There is some discussion on the exact distances and times that people are willing to walk as they are strongly affected by a variety of factors, including culture, climate, and other context-specific aspects. Cervero [43] finds that for distances over circa 1 km walking is not considered as an option to access transit by the majority of users. As Smart Commuting project's Deliverable D.T1.2.1 [11] underlines, in an unfriendly walking environment such distance is much lower. Taking into account 600 meters (10-minute walk) as a maximum accessibility radius for transportation facilities, it is evident how the provision of additional stops and stations in urban and peri-urban areas can effectively increase the number of potential transit users. Chien and Qin [44] also underline how the correct localization of transit stops can help in reducing the cost of providing transport service, thus tackling another of the external costs of commuting identified by scholars. Litman [45], moreover, values waiting areas improvements in terms of users' willingness to pay, finding that the improvement of users' waiting experience could lead to a 3,3% additional fare (incl. the installation of ticket vending machines, otherwise 2,4%).

Policy package two is centered on incentivizing and encouraging active commuting. The measures proposed by Smart Commuting project are the installation of shelters for bike parks, the implementation of a fixed-stall bike sharing system, the provision of bike parking facilities at schools, and the diffusion of bike repair corners. The diffusion of active transportation is by far the most effective strategy towards the reduction of emissions, congestion and externalities from transportation in general, including health costs and accidents costs ([9, 26, 34, 36, 37, 46] and others). Lindsay et al. [46] for example found that shifting to biking just 5% of New Zealand's annual vehicle kilometers would result in a total yearly saving of 200 millions NZ dollars. The issue, however, is that not every trip can be done by bike or on foot or that anyways not all users are willing to do so. The provision of a bike sharing system and other bike-incentive facilities, in the context of European mid-sized cities, can be effective in increasing the modal shift of biking. It must though be researched whether new bikers will be subtracted from private transportation or from public transit, which would still be effective but would consistently reduce the potentiality of the shift towards active modes. Mrkajic et al. [47] studied the provision of bike parking infrastructure at a university facility in Novi Sad, using EFC's [48] data to estimate emissions. They found that bike parking provision was effective in shifting students' commute to biking and estimated yearly CO_2 emissions savings as 1845,9kgs. Buehler [49] used chi-square tests and found that significantly more individuals commute by bike if employers provide cyclist showers, bike lockers, and bike parking. He also found that the share of bike commuters is greater in the urban core, at higher population densities, and in areas with more bike paths and lanes. Lastly, he stated that in the area of Washington, DC (USA) more individuals commute by bike during the warmer summer months. This is also found by other studies which deal with areas with rough winter climate (e.g. [37]) but could not be an issue of relevance in some of the cities which are part of Smart Commuting project, given the different environmental conditions.

Regarding policy package three, which focuses on urban and strategic planning, the measures proposed by Smart Commuting project are: the provision of mobility service points, the preparation of companies' mobility plans, the promotion of participatory processes among citizens for strategy building, incentives for workplaces relocations to gain higher public transit accessibility. Despite the four measures being very different from each other, they are all converging on the need of strategic location of attractors and on the need to plan public transit and urban development with an orientation towards operations sustainability. The idea here is again to increase transit availability and accessibility, through economic support for relocating workplaces at more acceptable and incentivizing distances from public transit facilities and through the facilitation of mobility usage thanks to the concentration of all mobility-related offers and services at strategic locations. Moreover, the project aims at involving the general public in mobility planning (public and private) so that strategies can be shared and can be perceived as part of everyone's identity. It is however hard to quantify benefits from measures such as those, given that they surely contribute to a general performance enhancement.

Policy package four insists on growth and incentive of ride sharing, proposing the implementation of a no-profit car sharing system (suitable for mid-sized towns) and the promotion of car pooling and of co-workers ride sharing (also through a specific online platform). The potential of car sharing and car pooling in terms of motorization rate reduction is noticeable. According to Baptista et al. [50] one car-sharing vehicle takes the place of approximately six privately owned cars, leading to various advantages among which: lower consumption of physical and economic resources, contribution to the reduction of energy and environmental impacts, direct benefits from the changes on vehicle ownership and usage patterns, also meaning less congestion and less space usage. Privately operated free-floating car sharing, however, only works in densely populated cities. Such systems are not applicable to peripheral residential locations, where a significant fraction of long-distance commuters originates (see e.g. [51]). This is also true for concepts where sharing is a question of private coordination, such as peer-to-peer car sharing or ridesharing among coworkers or cohabitants [52]. Public input for car sharing in mid-sized cities is fundamental to grant the system's effectiveness and sustainability and could remedy to its natural economic characteristic of being suitable to high-density contexts only. A web platform for ride-sharing and car pooling could moreover allow this type of transport choice to broaden its appeal, making it able to compete with one of the greatest advantages of private car usage: immediate access to door-to-door transportation [53]. Literature shows that given that in the western world the vast majority of car trips are done by single individuals, with an average vehicle occupancy of just 1.3 [11, 54]. Ride-sharing could significantly contribute to traffic volume reduction, even when considering constraints such as people's unwillingness to sharing their commute with strangers and therefore limiting ride-sharing to friends, colleagues, or friends of friends [54]. In the context of Smart Commuting Project's partner cities, ride-sharing between co-workers or between acquaintances could produce relevant benefits.

Regarding policy package five (Information Communication Technologies), the measures proposed by Smart Commuting project are: the launch of a mobile app for cyclists (with an incentive mechanism), the creation of a comprehensive mobility service web portal, incentives to tele-working practices. Again, the measures are different from each other but all fall under the common "ICT" hat. In fact, this policy package inevitably has relations with many of the proposed measures as information communication technologies are gaining an increasingly relevant role in everyday commuting patterns and actions, from the choice of the best itinerary to better usage of travel time and economic resources, independently from the usage of private, public or shared means of transport. Mobility-as-a-service is becoming a commonly known concept. The integration – from a policy perspective as well as from a customer-oriented perspective – of all transport and mobility options has been proven to be a fundamental step towards the increase of attractiveness of alternatives to private motorized transport [55]. In this discourse fit some efforts which have been done to fully include private and shared bike mobility within cities' mobility offer, both in terms of infrastructure and service. There are several examples of private or public institutions which have launched mobile applications or other programs to pay commuters for biking to work [56]. According to policy makers, this is still more convenient than having society to pay for external costs generated by less optimal modal choices, as discussed previously in this paper. The success of such efforts have not yet been clearly discussed, also given that initiatives are in most cases relatively recent. There is however a discussion on whether paying commuters to bike to work can be effective in shifting users from more impacting modes. According to some sources, in fact, users willing to participate in this sort of programs already bike to work or use other low-impact modes. It was demonstrated that unless the program is accompanied by other policy measures, such as the reduction of parking space and the increase of parking price, the shift from private motorized transport to biking is hardly obtainable [57]. Tele-working is another impact-reducing option which has been available by the large-scale diffusion of technology. Tele-working introduction for existing businesses has not been discussed widely in terms of emission reduction potential. Smart commuting [11] hints that considering a single worker and a five-days working week, one day of tele-working corresponds to a weekly 20% emission reduction. This is true from an individual perspective but not generally accurate if the worker – for example – uses for its commute a transit vehicle which rides anyways. Even when broadening the horizon and considering a whole working population with mixed commuting habits, though, it has been demonstrated that the option to telecommute is vital in keeping environmental impacts under control [37].

Mutual-learning practices among administrations and policy makers, awareness raise in clean and active mobility and related health gains, mobility education in schools are all measures recognized as significant by the project Smart Commuting and are grouped together in policy package six, which deals with behavioral and educational interventions. Vertical and horizontal coordination among stakeholders is often indicated as an effective strategy to improve conditions and performances, not only in the transport sector but more broadly in the field of planning and policy making. On topics related to climate change, emissions and environment, public awareness is not ideal as they are not yet – or have not been until recently – part of the daily debate. It is therefore important to foster awareness about individual, societal and environmental benefits from active mobility and from the various commuting alternatives to private cars. All reviewed authors agree on the fact that behavioral change has a very relevant if not prevailing impact on the success of emissions containment strategies, regardless if hinged on travel-demand-management or on the provision of new transport services and infrastructures. Education and awareness raise, together with the provision of valid and valuable alternatives, are the first steps to ensure success of the mental and modal shift towards cleaner transport practices.

Finally, policy package seven deals with the topic of technology advancements. The measures proposed by Smart Commuting project are: installation of electric vehicles charging spots, incentives to the diffusion of electric vehicles. Scientific discussion on benefits from Electric Vehicle implementation strategies is abundant. It is generally agreed that for developed economies – such as European ones – the shift towards electric vehicles is cost-effective [58] and scope-effective, meaning that it contributes significantly to overall emissions reduction achievements. This is mainly because developed economies have cleaner and more efficient energy procurement strategies and higher technology levels [35, 38], in addition to higher expenditure capacity to procure electric vehicles, currently expensive. Public input to foster a widespread EV charging grid, plus incentives to acquire public and private EVs, would therefore be likely to produce relevant advantages in the contexts of Smart Commuting Project's Functional Urban Areas. Impacts, though, can only be estimated when relating measures to their local and national energy market and policies.

5 Conclusion

The scientific community is very active on the topic of the limitation of the negative impacts from the transport sector and, even though a specific focus on commuting is only sometimes to be found, it is acknowledged that the movement of fixed-schedule workers and students has a great impact on the mobility system since it constitutes one of the parts of its highest stress peaks, especially in terms of congestion and space-related issues.

This paper has identified some of the best strategies aiming at reducing externalities from commuting, also highlighting how and when they have proven to be effective - even with a relatively small resource investment. It has also been seen, though, that integrated strategies, in which demand-management measures are flanked by the insertion of greener technologies, appear to be generally much more successful in terms of final outcomes.

The discussion in this paper was on the Smart Commuting project, that proposes a variety of measures which can be promisingly effective in tackling transport externalities, and that have specifically been tailored for each single partner for solving local issues. It must however be underlined that an effort to integrate such measures into broader local, regional and national strategies is still needed to comment on the effective potential of the single measures: a first focus on Smart Commuting project's partner cities, located in mid-Europe, seems to confirm the well-known result that great achievements can be obtained by an increased integration between public transit, private and shared motorized transportation, and active transportation. The first outcomes of the project seem to confirm this to a considerable extent. Still, though, more incisive measures, the integration of IT systems, and an input for broader strategies seem to be desirable to grant higher effectiveness of the cities' efforts in reducing impacts and externalities of commuting.

Mapping the responsiveness of each commuting measure against potential externalities represents an important avenue for future research within and outside the Smart Commuting project, aiming at helping policy makers to integrate their knowledge surrounding expectations about the outcome of each measure, thus making better decisions for the sake of the community.

Acknowledgement. This research has been partially funded through the Interreg Central Europe Programme (2014–2020), Priority Low carbon Cities and Regions, under Project Smart Commuting.

References

1. Al-Rijleh, M.K., Alam, A., Foti, R., Gurian, P.L., Spatari, S., Hatzopoulou, M.: Strategies to achieve deep reductions in metropolitan transportation GHG emissions: the case of Philadelphia. Transp. Plann. Technol. **41**, 797–815 (2018)
2. Long, S., Klungboonkrong, P., Chindaprasirt, P.: Impacts of urban transit system development on modal shift and greenhouse gas emission reduction: a KhonKaen, Thailand case study. Eng. Appl. Sci. Res. **45**(1), 8–16 (2018)

3. Zahabi, S.A.H., Miranda-Moreno, L., Patterson, Z., Barla, P., Harding, C.: Transport greenhouse gas emissions and its relationship with urban form, transit accessibility and emerging green technologies: a montreal case study. Soc. Behav. Sci. **54**, 966–978 (2012)
4. Zeng, Y., Tan, X., Gu, B., Wang, Y., Baoguang, X.: Greenhouse gas emissions of motor vehicles in Chinese cities and the implications for China's mitigation targets. Appl. Energy **184**, 1016–1025 (2016)
5. Chow, A.S.Y.: Spatial-modal scenarios of greenhouse gas emissions from commuting in Hong Kong. J. Transp. Geogr. **54**, 205–213 (2016)
6. Savelsbergh, M.W.P.M., van Woensel, T.: City logistics: challenges and opportunities. Transp. Sci. **50**(2), 579–590 (2016)
7. IEA/OECD: Transport, Energy and CO_2: moving towards sustainability (2009)
8. Liu, X., Ma, S., Tian, J., Jia, N., Li, G.: A system dynamics approach to scenario analysis for urban passenger transport energy consumption and CO_2 emissions: a case study of Beijing. Energy Policy **85**, 253–270 (2015)
9. Garcia-Sierra, M., van den Bergh, J.C.J.M.: Policy mix to reduce greenhouse gas emissions of commuting: a study for Barcelona, Spain. Travel Behav. Soc. **1**, 113–126 (2014)
10. Luè, A., et al.: Future priorities for a climate-friendly transport: a European strategic research agenda towards 2030. Int. J. Sustain. Transp. **10**(3), 236–246 (2016)
11. Lemmerer, H., Nocera, S., Shibayama, T., Tonin, S.: Transnational strategy to change commuting models in the FUAs. Deliverable D.T1.2.1 of SMART COMMUTING, Co-funded by Interreg Central Europe (2018)
12. Ricardo, AEA.: Update of the Handbook on External Costs of Transport (2014)
13. Liew, N., Chu J.: How much is your daily commute? Developing a working model to estimate the total travel cost. In: Australasian Transport Research Fortum 2016 Proceedings (2016)
14. Glazebrook, G.: Taking the con out of convenience: the true cost of transport modes in Sydney. Urban Policy and Res. **27**(1), 5–24 (2009)
15. Mayeres, I., et al.: The External Costs of Transportation. Final report. Sustainable Mobility Programme, Federal Office for Scientific, Technical and Cultural Affairs, State of Belgium, Prime Minister's Services (2001)
16. Maibach, M., et al.: In: Handbook on Estimation of External Cost in the Transport Sector. Version 1.0. CE Delft (2007)
17. Danish Ministry of Transport: External Costs of Transport. 1st Report – Review of European Studies (2004)
18. Gibbons, E., O'Mahony, M.: External cost internalization of urban transport: a case study of Dublin. J. Environ. Manag. **64**, 401–410 (2002)
19. European Environmental Agency. https://www.eea.europa.eu/data-and-maps/figures/marginal-external-costs-of-freight-transport-minimum-and-maximum-values-per-transport-mode-euro-10-vehicle-km-for-road-freight-euro-vehicle-km-for-other-modes. Consulted 09 January 2019
20. Business Insider. https://www.businessinsider.com/traffic-jams-commuting-world-cities-pictures-2018-1?IR=T#paris-france-10. Consulted 09 January 2019
21. Nocera, S.: Un approccio operativo per la valutazione della qualità nei servizi di trasporto pubblico/an operational approach for quality evaluation in public transport services. Ingegneria Ferroviaria **65–4**, 363–383 (2010)
22. Nocera, S.: The key role of quality assessment in public transport policy. Traffic Eng. Control **52–9**, 394–398 (2011)
23. Eboli, L., Forciniti, C., Mazzulla, G.: Spatial variation of the perceived transit service quality at rail stations. Transp. Res. Part A: Policy and Pract. **114**, 67–83 (2018)

24. Calvo, F., Eboli, L., Forciniti, C., Mazzulla, G.: Factors influencing trip generation on metro system in Madrid (Spain). Transp. Res. Part D: Transp. Environ. **67**, 156–172 (2019)
25. Libardo, A., Nocera, S.: Transportation elasticity for the analysis of Italian transportation demand on a regional scale. Traffic Eng. Control **49–5**, 187–192 (2008)
26. Hickman, R., Ashiru, O., Banister, D.: Transport and climate change: simulating the options for carbon reduction in London. Transp. Policy Paper **17**, 110–125 (2012)
27. Cirilli, A., Veneri, P.: Spatial structure and carbon dioxide (CO_2) emissions due to commuting: an analysis of Italian urban areas. Reg. Stud. **48**(12), 1993–2005 (2014)
28. Li, X., Mou, Y., Wang, H., Yin, C., He, Q.: How does polycentric urban form affect urban commuting Quantitative measurement using geographical big data of 100 cities in China. Sustainability **10**, 4556 (2018)
29. Schwanen, T., Mieleman, F.M., Dijst, M.: Travel behaviour in Dutch monocentric and policentric urban systems. J. Transp. Geogr. **9**, 173–186 (2011)
30. Wang, M., Madden, M., Liu, X.: Exploring the relationship between urban forms and CO_2 emissions in 104 Chinese cities. Am. Soc. Civ. Eng. **143**, 1–8 (2017)
31. Yang, L., Wang, Y., Bai, Q., Han, S.: Urban form and travel patterns by commuters: comparative case study of Wuhan and Xi'an. Am. Soc. Civil Eng., China (2017)
32. Modarres, A.: Commuting and energy consumption: toward an equitable transportation policy. J. Transp. Geogr. **33**, 240–249 (2013)
33. Litman, T.: Comprehensive evaluation of transport energy conservation and emission reduction policies. Transp. Res. Part A Policy and Pract. **47**, 153–166 (2012). Victoria Transport Policy Institute
34. Harwatt, H., Tight, M., Timms, P.: Personal transport emissions within London: exploring policy scenarios and carbon reductions up to 2050. Int. J. Sustain. Transp. **5**(5), 270–288 (2011)
35. Hickman, R., Ashiru, O., Banister, D.: Transitions to low carbon transport futures: strategic conversations from London and Delhi. J. Transp. Geogr. **19**, 1553–1562 (2011)
36. Lopes Toledo, A.L., Lèbre La Rovere, E.: Urban mobility and greenhouse gas emissions: status public policies and scenarios in a developing economy City Natal Brazil. Sustainability **10**, 3995 (2018)
37. Mathez, A., Manaugh, K., Chakour, V., El-Geneidy, A., Hatzopoulou, M.: How can we alter our carbon footprint? Estimating GHG emissions based on travel survey information. Transportation **40**(1), 131–149 (2013)
38. Nakamura, K., Hayashi, Y.: Strategies and instruments for low-carbon urban transport: an international review on trends and effects. Transp. Policy **29**, 264–274 (2013)
39. World Conference on Transport Research Society and Institute for Transport Policy Studies: Urban Transport and the Environment. An International Perspective. Emerald Group Publishing Limited (2004)
40. Dalkmann, H, Brannigan, C.: Transport and Climate Change. Module 5e. Deutsche Gesellschaft fuer Technische Zusammenarbeit (GTZ) GmbH (2007)
41. Bongardt, D., Breithaupt, M., Creutzing, F.: Beyond the Fossil City: Towards low Carbon Transport and Green Growth. Sustainable Urban Transport Technical Document #6. Deutsche Gesellschaft fuer Technische Zusammenarbeit (GTZ) GmbH (2011)
42. Strompen, F., Litman, T., Bongardt, D.: Reducing Carbon Emissions through Transport Demand Management Strategies. A review of international examples. Deutsche Gesellschaft fuer Technische Zusammenarbeit (GTZ) GmbH and Beijing Transportation Research Center (2012)
43. Cervero, R.: Walk-and-ride: factors influencing pedestrian access to transit. J. Public Transp. **3**(4), 1–23 (2001)

44. Chien, S.I., Qin, Z.: Optimization of bus stops locations for improving transit accessibility. Transp. Plann. Technol. **27**(3), 221–227 (2004)
45. Litman, T.: Valuing transit service quality improvements. J. Public Transp. **11**(2), 43–63 (2008)
46. Lindsay, G., Macmillan, A., Woodward, A.: Moving urban trips from cars to bicycles: impact on health and emissions. Aust. and N.Z. J. Public Health **35**, 54–60 (2010)
47. Mrkajic, V., Vukelic, D., Mihajlov, A.: Reduction of CO_2 emissions and non-environmental co-benefits of bicycle infrastructure provision: the case of the University of Novi Sad, Serbia. Renew. Sustain. Energy Rev. **49**, 232–242 (2015)
48. Blondel, B., Mispelon, C., Ferguson, J.: Cycle more often to cool down the planet. Quantifying CO_2 savings of cycling. European Cyclists' Federation ASBL (2011)
49. Buehler, R.: Determinants of bicycle commuting in the Washington, DC region: the role of bicycle parking, cyclist showers, and free car parking at work. Transp. Res. Part D **17**, 525–531 (2012)
50. Baptista, P., Melo, S., Rolim, C.: Energy, environmental and mobility impacts of car-sharing systems. Empirical results from Lisbon. Portugal. Soc. Behav. Sci. **111**, 28–37 (2014)
51. Firnkorn, J., Mueller, M.: Selling mobility instead of cars: new business strategies of automakers and the impact on private vehicle holding. Bus. Strategy Environ. **21**, 264–280 (2012)
52. Steiniger, K.W., Bachner, G.: Extending car-sharing to serve commuters: an implementation in Austria. Ecol. Econ. **101**, 64–66 (2014)
53. Agatz, N., Erera, A., Savelsbergh, M., Wang, X.: Optimization for dynamic ride-sharing: a review. Eur. J. Oper. Res. **233**, 295–303 (2012)
54. Cici, B., Markopoulou, A., Frias-Martinez, E., Laotaris, N.: Assessing the potential of ride-sharing using mobile and social data: a tale of four cities. In: Proceedings of the 2014 ACM International Joint Conference on Pervasive and Ubiquitous Computing, 201–211 (2014)
55. European Platform on Mobility Management. http://www.epomm.eu/newsletter/v2/content/2017/1217_2/doc/eupdate_it.pdf. Consulted 02 July 2019
56. Various News Agencies. https://www.reuters.com/article/us-france-bicycles/france-experiments-with-paying-people-to-cycle-to-work-idUSKBN0ED1O120140602. https://www.fastcompany.com/3069271/this-app-lets-your-company-pay-you-to-bike-to-work. https://www.theguardian.com/world/2018/mar/07/new-zealand-cycle-cash-10-a-day-employees-work-company; all visited 18 January 2019
57. CityLab: https://www.citylab.com/transportation/2015/03/the-problem-with-paying-people-to-bike-to-work/388099/, visited 18 January 2019
58. Hartgen, D.T., Fields, M.G., Scott, M., San Jose, E.: Impacts of Transportation Policies on Greenhouse Gas Emissions in U.S. Regions. Policy Study, 387 (2011)

Effects of Rolling Stock Unavailability on the Implementation of Energy-Saving Policies: A Metro System Application

Marilisa Botte[1]([✉]) [iD], Luca D'Acierno[1] [iD], and Mariano Gallo[2] [iD]

[1] Department of Civil, Architectural and Environmental Engineering,
Federico II University of Naples, 80125 Naples, Italy
{marilisa.botte,luca.dacierno}@unina.it
[2] Department of Engineering, University of Sannio, 82100 Benevento, Italy
gallo@unisannio.it

Abstract. The recent world policies have shown the necessity of implementing suitable strategies, especially in urban contexts, in order to promote more sustainable transportation systems. In this context, the rail-based systems allow to achieve sustainable goals according to a threefold effect: reduction in externalities (such as congestion, accidents, air and noise pollution), increase in efficiency (in terms of operational cost per real/potential carried passenger), and delocalization of energy production centres (large industrial plants out of population centres producing with optimal yields). Positive environmental aspects of the rail and metro systems may be further amplified by implementing *Energy-Saving Strategies (ESSs)* based on the adoption of suitable driving profiles and/or the installation of onboard/wayside recovery devices. In this context, we investigate the effects of rolling-stock unavailability (for breakdowns, maintenance or under-sized fleet) on the effectiveness of ESSs within a multi-objective framework which combines the reduction in energy consumption with a passenger-oriented perspective. A real metro line in the south of Italy has been analysed as case-study in order to show the feasibility of the proposed approach.

Keywords: Rail-based public transport · Energy-Saving Strategies · Passenger-oriented approach

1 Introduction

The relevance of promoting the adoption of rail-based systems lies in the advantages they offer, both in terms of sustainability and efficiency. Indeed, besides a low environmental impact, such transport mode offers lower operational costs per real/potential carried passenger with respect to other transport systems. As pointed out by [1], one of the major cost items in rail operations is the power supply required for rolling stock and, for this reason, the implementation of energy saving measures, aimed at reducing energy consumption, is of great importance.

© Springer Nature Switzerland AG 2019
S. Misra et al. (Eds.): ICCSA 2019, LNCS 11620, pp. 120–132, 2019.
https://doi.org/10.1007/978-3-030-24296-1_12

However, in addition to service providers (i.e. infrastructure operators and/or rail service operators) which aim to minimise operational costs, there are the users which, instead, aim to minimise their total travel times. Therefore, they represent two sides of the same coin, whose needs have to be properly balanced. Moreover, as shown by [2,3], the interaction between rail service and involved passenger flows, occurring at the interface train-platform, needs to be properly modelled for an accurate analysis of rail operations. Hence, travel demand not only represents a perspective to be taken into account but also a factor to be considered in the evaluation of rail systems performance. In light of the above, the strict correlation of rail systems with the energy domain, on one side, and the demand domain, on the other side, appears clear [4].

Nevertheless, also the sub-systems mentioned above (i.e. energy and travel demand) are strictly related to each other. Indeed, as shown by [5,6], the implementation of eco-driving strategies, aimed at reducing energy consumption, implies an increase in user travel times. This happens because, in order to adopt an energy-efficient driving behaviour, speed profiles differ by the so-called *Time Optimal* (*TO*) scenario (in which the convoy operates at maximum performance), with an increase in train running times. Such an increase needs to be properly compensated by exploiting specific reserve times set in the timetable structure, thus minimising passenger inconvenience [7,8]. Also, energy recovery strategies based on the use of regenerative braking can be implemented [9–11]. Different approaches have been proposed in the literature for modelling the implementation of energy-saving measures, namely optimisation [12,13], simulation [14,15] and data-driven [16,17] methods. However, such contributions deal with the adoption of energy-saving strategies in ordinary conditions, without considering failure scenarios.

Given the vulnerability of rail transport to system failure, dispatching and rescheduling issues cover a large part of the rail operational research area. In particular, [18] makes a distinction between online and off-line approaches, and between static and dynamic methods. Online interventions are implemented during rail operations and are characterised by short computational times; while, off-line strategies require greater computational times and are performed in advance (even months before). Moreover, static methods are run only once, without any updates when new information arises; while, adjustments to rescheduling solutions on the basis of further available data can be carried out in the case of dynamic procedures. If the timetabling process is intrinsically a static and off-line procedure [19], the most desirable methodology for addressing a rescheduling problem is characterised by a dynamic structure and an online framework [20–23]. Moreover, further preferable conditions for an accurate evaluation of rescheduling issues are represented by a microscopic modelling of the analysed rail system and the assessment of stochastic factors affecting rail service. Instances of microscopic approaches can be found in [24–26]. While, regarding the type of randomness analysed, it can concern train performance [27,28], running and dwell times [29], arrival and recovery times [30,31], delays [32,33], disruption information [34] and travel demand features [35]. The importance of being able to react to perturbed conditions properly lies in the fact that a certain level of vulnerability to breakdowns characterises each rail system component, such as infrastructure [36,37], signalling and control devices [38,39], and rolling stock [40,41]. For instance, a complete blockage of some rail sections could bring to the interruption of the whole service; while, a failure to the onboard control system could generate only some delays. Unavailability of traction units, instead, could affect the headway between two successive runs or the carrying capacity offered by the line. However, according to the network analysed and the severity of failure addressed, a different solution turns out to be the one which minimises alterations to ordinary service conditions.

In particular, the paper presents a rescheduling methodology which takes into account all three outlined domains (i.e. rail operation, energy and travel demand). Specifically, the implementation of eco-driving speed profiles under rolling-stock disruption conditions is evaluated and a bi-objective framework, combining the reduction in energy consumption with a passenger-oriented perspective, is proposed.

This paper is structured as follows: Sect. 2 focuses on the rolling stock disruption analysis; Sect. 3 shows an application to a real case study of the proposed approach; finally, Sect. 4 provides concluding remarks and future research.

2   Rolling Stock Unavailability Analysis

As widely shown in the literature (see, for instance, [6,8]), in the case of rail or metro systems, there is a strong analytical relationship among the service headway (indicated as H_{serv}), the number of utilised rail convoys (indicated as N_{rc}) and the service cycle time (indicated as CT_{serv}), that is:

$$H_{serv} \cdot N_{rc} = CT_{serv} \tag{1}$$

However, it is worth noting that all terms of Eq. (1) are subject to proper constraints.

For instance, in terms of service headway, although this term may theoretically be equal to any value as long as it is positive (i.e. $H_{serv} \in R^+$), it has to satisfy some network constraints. Indeed, the infrastructure and the signalling system impose a time spacing between two successive convoys along the line. Likewise, the inversion and recovery times at the terminuses and the terminus layouts may require a time spacing between a departing train and the subsequent arriving rail convoy. These time spacing values impose the identification of a minimum headway value, indicated as H_{min}, which has to constrain the service headway value as follows:

$$H_{min} \leq H_{serv} \tag{2}$$

Likewise, in the case of the number of utilised rail convoys (i.e. term N_{rc}), once fixed the cycle time and the service headway, it can be univocally calculated using Eq. (1). However, for physical considerations, it is necessary to impose that N_{rc} has to be a positive integer number (i.e. $N_{rc} \in Z^+$).

Finally, the service cycle time may be defined as the total time that a rail convoy spends for the outward trip (including all stops at stations), for all inversion and recovery operations at the outward terminus, for the subsequent return trip (including all stops at stations) and for all inversion and recovery operations at the return terminus. Hence, each train is in the same condition after an interval equal to the cycle time. However, as shown by [6], besides these physical times (i.e. travel times between two successive stations, dwell times at stations and inversion times at terminuses), it is necessary to consider two further time categories: the buffer and the layover times. The former ones are additional times adopted for recovery delays due to the variability of travel, dwell and inversion times. The latter ones express the time spent at the red signal of the initial stations waiting for the departure time according to the planned timetable.

These three constraints mentioned above provide further implications in terms of the feasibility of operational schemes. Indeed, for instance, once fixed service headway H_{serv}, since N_{rc} has to belong to Z^+, it implies that layover times in the cycle time cannot be arbitrary, but have to be fixed so to satisfy Eq. (1). Likewise, the value of the layover times (conditional to the terminus layouts) may affect the inversion time and, therefore, the minimum headway H_{min} which, in turn, affects value H_{serv} by means of Eq. (2). Finally, the sum of layover times and buffer times cannot exceed term H_{serv}, since they represent train stop times.

However, D'Acierno et al. [6] have shown a procedure for determining the feasible operational schemes which satisfy all abovementioned constraints.

In order to increase the sustainability of rail and metro systems, as widely shown in Sect. 1, many authors have proposed the adoption of numerous Energy Saving Strategies (ESSs) where some of them are based on the definition of proper driving speed profiles. As already mentioned, an eco-driving behaviour requires lower energy consumptions but implies higher travel times. In this context, D'Acierno and Botte [8] proposed a bi-level optimisation model for determining the optimal compromise between energy reductions and travel time increases by preserving service headway in a passenger-oriented perspective. In particular, their proposal consisted of adopting layover times as reserve time for compensating travel time increases.

Our contribution represents an advance of the research provided by [6] and [8], since it concerns the analysis of eco-driving strategies within a disruption framework. Specifically, the failure analysed is related to a rolling stock unavailability condition. In order to evaluate breakdown effects, preliminary, it is necessary to identify two kinds of passenger convoy configurations:

- traditional rail convoys consisting of locomotives hauling passenger carriages;
- railcars consisting of self-propelled passenger vehicles which may travel also coupled in multiple units.

Indeed, in the first case, whether the unavailability concerns some passenger carriages, it is possible to preserve the number of rail convoys N_{rc} and, therefore, the service headway H_{serv} according to Eq. (1). Obviously, some (or all) rail convoys will be shorter with a lower passenger capacity. By an optimisation perspective, shorter rail convoys will require lower energy consumptions but, in some cases, passengers could not be able to board the first arriving train, increasing their waiting time.

On the contrary, whether the unavailability concerns some locomotives, it is not possible to preserve the number of convoys N_{rc} and, therefore, it is necessary to adopt lower service frequencies (i.e. higher service headways according to Eq. 1), which imply a reduction in service carrying capacity, being calculated as:

$$Cap_{serv} = \frac{Cap_{conv}}{H_{serv}} \tag{3}$$

where Cap_{serv} is the service capacity and Cap_{conv} is the convoy capacity. Obviously, the higher the service headway, the higher the waiting time of passengers. Moreover, also in this case, the reduction in carrying capacity may imply the impossibility, for some passengers, to board the first arriving train by further increasing their waiting time. However, this last negative effect could be smoothed by increasing (if possible) the length of working trains by adding to them the passenger cars of the broken convoys. Finally, in terms of energy consumption, the reduced number of rail convoys and the higher value of service headway require a lower amount of energy consumption.

In the second configuration (i.e. when rail convoys consist in railcars), the unavailability of rolling stock may generate three possible rescheduling service schemes:

a. the number of rail convoys N_{rc} is preserved, the service headway H_{serv} is preserved and the length of some (or all) rail convoys is reduced;
b. the number of rail convoys N_{rc} is reduced, the service headway H_{serv} is increased (according to Eq. 1) and the length of all rail convoys is preserved;
c. the number of rail convoys N_{rc} is increased, the service headway H_{serv} is reduced (according to Eq. 1) and the length of some (or all) rail convoys is reduced.

The feasibility of each of the three abovementioned configurations is related to the initial number of railcars, train composition (i.e. the number of railcars for any convoy) and the failure severity (i.e. the number of unavailable railcars). However, in this case, by an optimisation perspective, it is not possible to state a priori which of the three abovementioned functional scheme is the optimal one, since:

– shorter rail convoy provides a lower train capacity and, therefore, some passengers could be not able to board the first arriving train and forced to wait for a subsequent rail convoy;
– the increase in service headway imposes an increase in passenger waiting times and, vice versa, the reduction in service headway implies a reduction in passenger waiting times;

– in a railcar configuration, the amount of required energy depends on the total
  number of railcars riding jointly on the network and, therefore, unavailability
  conditions ensure the reduction in energy consumptions with respect to the
  condition of full availability.

Thus, in this paper, we propose to analyse the rolling stock unavailability
in the case of convoys based on the railcar configuration in order to verify the
feasibility of the abovementioned service schemes and the related implications
in the case of implementation of ESSs.

3   Application to a Real Metro Line

In order to show the effects of rolling stock failures in the case of *Energy Saving
Strategy (ESS)* implementation, we have applied the proposed analysis method
in the case of a real metro line: Line 1 of the Naples metro system in Italy. Main
details of the line and its service can be found in [6]. However, the service is
performed by railcars which may be coupled up to 3 multiple units.

The line was inaugurated in 1993 with an initial length of about 4 km. Over
the years, it has been progressively extended up to the current length of 18 km.
Obviously, the higher the line length, the higher the cycle time since travel times
increase. Hence, according to Eq. (1), to preserve the service headway H_{serv}, it
is necessary to adopt a higher number of rail convoys N_{rc}.

In 1993, the initial fleet consisted of 45 railcars, named as '*Unit of Trac-
tions (UoT)*', which allowed to provide 15 triple-header rail convoys. Now, after
23 years, in the absence of fleet renewal, due to maintenance reasons, we may
assume that the service is performed by using 8 double-header convoys (i.e. 16
traction units) per day with a service headway equal to 10 min. This condition
represents the scenario 1 (i.e. the ordinary condition) in the following application.

Our analysis consists in considering that, during an average working-day, a
failure occurs by implying the breakdown of a double-header convoy so that
the working number of traction units becomes 14. Hence, assuming that all
rail convoys should have the same number of railcars for operational uniformity
issues, we can consider two possible operational schemes:

– Scenario 2 with 7 rail convoys consisting in double-header convoys (i.e. service
  scheme *b*, with a reduced number of rail convoy, an increased service headway
  and a fixed train length);
– Scenario 3 with 14 rail convoys consisting in single-header convoys (i.e. service
  scheme *c*, with an increased number of rail convoy, a reduced service headway
  and a reduced train length).

Hence, having fixed the service cycle time CT_{serv}, using the approach proposed by [6], we are able to identify two corresponding service frequencies and
related operational parameters as shown in Table 1. In particular, Scenario 2,
based on rescheduling service scheme *b*, provides a service headway higher than

Table 1. Service parameters in the analysed scenarios.

Analysed scenario [#]	Total traction units [#]	Number of units per convoy [#]	Total number of convoys [#]	Service headway [min]	Total layover time [min]
1	16	2	8	10.0	3.8
2	14	2	7	11.0	0.8
3	14	1	14	5.5	0.8

Scenario 1 (i.e. 11.0 min); likewise, Scenario 3, based on rescheduling service scheme c, provides a service headway lower than Scenario 1 (i.e. 5.5 min).

However, by performing the optimisation procedure proposed by [8] (based on the use of OPENTRACK® micro-simulation software [42] and an ad-hoc optimisation tool) for implementing the ESSs, we obtained results described in Tables 2, 3, 4, 5 and 6. Moreover, it is necessary to highlight that, since the reduction in transportation service generally provides a reduction in travel demand, it is necessary to calculate travel times and objective function values in terms of average values per carried passenger and not as a total value. Likewise, variations in train compositions (i.e. double-header vs single-header convoys) require the estimation of service performance indicators such as the daily distance in terms of railcars and not only in terms of rail convoys.

In particular, Table 2 shows that the reduced number of working railcars implies a reduction in the daily round runs (from 95 to 87) in the case of Scenario 2. However, although the adoption of single-header convoys (i.e. Scenario 3) allows increasing the number of daily round runs (from 95 to 173), in terms of daily distance (expressed in terms of railcar-km), as well as in terms of operational costs, both rescheduling scenarios provide similar results.

Table 2. Operational parameters in the analysed scenarios.

Analysed scenario [#]	Daily round runs [#]	Daily distances [convoy-km]	Daily distances [railcar-km]	Daily operational cost [€]
1	95	3,151	6,301	114,491
2	87	2,885	5,771	104,850
3	173	5,737	5,737	104,247

Table 3 shows that rescheduling scenarios requiring lower layover times (as shown in Table 1) allow to increase the service duration by a total of 12 min (6 min per direction). Hence, although they represent scenarios in disruption conditions (i.e. with a lower availability in railcars), as shown in Table 6, it is possible to attract slightly higher demand values (i.e. +0.18%).

Table 3. Daily service duration in the analysed scenarios.

Analysed scenario [#]	First run/Last run in the outward trip [hh:mm]	First run/Last run in the return trip [hh:mm]
1	06:00/21:40	06:43/22:23
2	06:00/21:46	06:39/22:25
3	06:00/21:46	06:40/22:26

Table 4. Speed limit effects in the analysed scenarios.

Analysed scenario [#]	Speed limit in the outward trip [km/h]	Speed limit in the return trip [km/h]	Travel time increase in the outward trip [min]	Travel time increase in the return trip [min]
1	47	76	3.5	0.0
2	77	61	0.0	0.7
3	66	65	0.4	0.3

Table 5. Energy parameters in the analysed scenarios.

Analysed scenario [#]	Consumed energy in the outward trip [kWh/convoy]	Consumed energy in the return trip [kWh/convoy]	Daily consumed energy [kWh]	Daily consumption in Time Optimal condition [kWh]
1	139.3	257.0	37,648	42,029
2	184.9	241.6	37,109	38,489
3	86.2	124.5	36,454	38,268

Table 6. Travel demand parameters in the analysed scenarios.

Analysed scenario [#]	Number of carried passengers [#]	Average passenger travel time [min/pax]	Average passenger waiting time [min/pax]	Average objective function value [€/pax]
1	202,062	13.7	8.9	3.03
2	202,431	13.2	18.5	4.99
3	202,431	13.2	15.9	4.44

Table 4 shows that both rescheduling scenarios (i.e. Scenario 2 and 3) provide similar reductions in travel time increases (i.e. 0.7 min as the sum of values related to the outward and the return trips), even if distributed differently between the outward and the return trip.

Table 5 provides the required mechanical energies. In particular, in *Time Optimal* condition, a railcar (i.e. a single-header convoy) requires 92.5 kWh and 128.7 kWh, respectively, in the outward and the return trip. Obviously, in the case of double-header convoys, these values become 184.9 kWh and 257.5 kWh. However, the implementation of ESSs provides a reduction in energy consumption equal to 10.4% in the case of Scenario 1 (ordinary condition) which has to decrease to 3.6% and 4.7% in the case of rescheduling scenarios (i.e. Scenario 2 and 3) for compensating waiting time increases (respectively, +157% in the Scenario 2 and +121% in the Scenario 3), as shown by Table 6.

Finally, in terms of optimal intervention strategy, Table 6 highlights that the adoption of shorter trains with a higher service frequency (i.e. Scenario 3) allows reducing the waiting time increase (from 18.5 min to 15.9 min) and the corresponding objective function value (from 4.99 € to 4.44 €).

4   Conclusions and Research Prospects

The adoption of *Energy Saving Strategies* (*ESSs*) based on the definition of proper driving speed profiles allows reducing energy consumptions by increasing travel times. Hence, it is necessary to identify an optimal compromise between a reduction in energy consumption and a worsening in transportation system performance, to avoid negative effects on passengers.

In this context, we have investigated the effects of rolling stock unavailability on the definition of ESSs. Indeed, in case of breakdown related to rolling stock, since the ordinary service (in terms of headway, number of convoys and train length) may be unfeasible, it is necessary to reschedule rail operations according to the residual working fleet. Obviously, the new feasible service configurations may have different optimal conditions in terms of ESS implementation.

To confirm these statements, we have analysed a breakdown condition in the case of a metro line whose fleet is based on railcars. In particular, we have simulated a disruption which implies the reduction of available convoys by identifying two possible feasible alternatives: a decrease in service frequency by preserving train lengths and a decrease in train length by increasing service frequencies. Both solutions were able to provide similar performance in terms of service capacities (difference lower than 0.57%), carried passengers (same value), daily consumed energy (difference equal to 1.76%), increase in cycle time (difference equal to 1 second) and average travel time (difference equal to 0.3%). However, due to different convoy capacities, the solution based on single-header convoys was able to provide an increase in the objective function (which represents the total cost of the system per carried passenger) equal to 65.4% with respect to the ordinary condition; while, in the case of double-header convoys, the objective function increase was equal to 85.7% (i.e. a difference in objective function increase equal to 20.3%).

These results show that, although many indicators may assume similar values, slight differences weighted on the passenger flows of a metro system may provide significant global differences. Hence, it is necessary to have suitable analytical tools for estimating these differences in order to identify the optimal scenario in terms of reductions of negative impacts on passengers.

As research perspective, we propose to analyse different breakdown severities by adopting different initial scenarios, both in terms of service performance (i.e. different initial service frequencies) and in terms of network complexity (i.e. different rail networks such as regional or national railways). Finally, we propose to investigate the effects of mitigation strategies based on the adoption of heterogeneous fleet compositions (such as some double-header convoys alternated with single-header convoys).

References

1. Caprara, A., Kroon, L., Monaci, M., Peeters, M., Toth, P.: Passenger railway optimization. Handbooks Oper. Res. Manag. Sci. **14**, 129–187 (2007). https://doi.org/10.1016/S0927-0507(06)14003-7
2. D'Acierno, L., Botte, M., Montella, B.: Assumptions and simulation of passenger behaviour on rail platforms. Int. J. Transp. Dev. Integr. **2**(2), 123–135 (2018). https://doi.org/10.2495/TDI-V2-N2-123-135
3. D'Acierno, L., Botte, M., Placido, A., Caropreso, C., Montella, B.: Methodology-for determining dwell times consistent with passenger flows in the case ofmetro services. Urban Rail Transit **3**(2), 73–89 (2017). https://doi.org/10.1007/s40864-017-0062-4
4. Botte, M., D'Acierno, L.: Dispatching and rescheduling tasks and theirinteractions with travel demand and the energy domain: models and algorithms. Urban Rail Transit **4**(4), 163–197 (2018). https://doi.org/10.1007/s40864-018-0090-8
5. D'Acierno, L., Botte, M.: An analytical approach for determining reserve timeson metro systems. In: Proceedings of the 17th IEEE International Conferenceon Environment and Electrical Engineering (IEEE EEEIC 2017) and 1ndIndustrial and Commercial Power Systems Europe (I&CPS 2017). Milan, Italy (2017). https://doi.org/10.0.4.85/EEEIC.2017.7977519
6. D'Acierno, L., Botte, M., Gallo, M., Montella, B.: Defining reserve times for metro systems: an analytical approach. J. Adv. Transp. **2018**, 1–15 (2018). https://doi.org/10.1155/2018/5983250
7. D'Acierno, L., Botte, M.: Passengers' satisfaction in the case of energy-saving strategies: a rail system application. In: Proceedings of the 18th IEEE International Conference on Environment and Electrical Engineering (IEEE EEEIC 2018) and 2nd Industrial and Commercial Power Systems Europe (I&CPS 2018). Palermo, Italy (2018). https://doi.org/10.1109/EEEIC.2018.8494575
8. D'Acierno, L., Botte, M.: A passenger-oriented optimization model for implementing energy-saving strategies in railway contexts. Energies **11**(11), 1–25 (2018). https://doi.org/10.3390/en11112946
9. Gonzalez-Gil, A., Palacin, R., Batty, P.: Sustainable urban rail systems: strategies and technologies for optimal management of regenerative braking energy. Energy Convers. Manage. **75**, 374–388 (2013). https://doi.org/10.1016/j.enconman.2013.06.039

10. Ghavihaa, N., Campilloa, J., Bohlinb, M., Dahlquista, E.: Review of application of energy storage devices in railway transportation. Energy Procedia **105**, 4561–4568 (2017). https://doi.org/10.1016/j.egypro.2017.03.980

11. Song, R., Yuan, T., Yang, J., He, H.: Simulation of braking energy recovery for the metro vehicles based on the traction experiment system. Simulation **93**, 1099–1112 (2017). https://doi.org/10.1177/0037549717726146

12. Yan, X., Cai, B., Ning, B., ShangGuan, W.: Online distributed cooperative model predictive control of energy-saving trajectory planning for multiple high-speed train movements. Transp. Res. Part C **69**, 60–78 (2016). https://doi.org/10.1016/j.trc.2016.05.019

13. Huang, Y., Ma, X., Su, S., Tang, T.: Optimization of train operation in multiple interstations with multi-population genetic algorithm. Energies **8**, 14311–14329 (2015). https://doi.org/10.3390/en81212433

14. De Martinis, V., Weidmann, U.: Definition of energy-efficient speed profiles within rail traffic by means of supply design models. Res. Transp. Econ. **54**, 41–50 (2015). https://doi.org/10.1016/j.retrec.2015.10.024

15. Sicre, C., Cucala, A., Fernandez, A., Lukaszewicz, P.: Modeling and optimizing energy-efficient manual driving on high-speed lines. IEEJ Trans. Electr. Electron. Eng. **7**, 633–640 (2012). https://doi.org/10.1002/tee.21782

16. Zhao, N., Roberts, C., Hillmansen, S., Tian, Z., Weston, P., Chen, L.: An integrated metro operation optimization to minimize energy consumption. Transp. Res. Part C **75**, 168–182 (2017). https://doi.org/10.1016/j.trc.2016.12.013

17. De Martinis, V., Corman, F.: Data-driven perspectives for energy efficient operations in railway systems: current practices and future opportunities. Transp. Res. Part C **95**, 679–697 (2018). https://doi.org/10.1016/j.trc.2018.08.008

18. Corman, F., Meng, L.: A review of online dynamic models and algorithms for railway traffic management. IEEE Trans. Intell. Transp. Syst. **16**(3), 1274–1284 (2015). https://doi.org/10.1109/TITS.2014.2358392

19. Goverde, R.: Punctuality of Railway Operations and Timetable Stability Analysis. Delft University of Technology, Delft, The Netherlands (2005)

20. Caimi, G., Fuchsberger, M., Laumanns, M., Lüthi, M.: A model predictive control approach for discrete-time rescheduling in complex, central railway station areas. Comput. Oper. Res. **39**(11), 2578–2593 (2012). https://doi.org/10.1016/j.cor.2012.01.003

21. Mazzarello, M., Ottaviani, E.: A traffic management system for real-time traffic optimization in railways. Transp. Res. Part B **41**(2), 246–274 (2007). https://doi.org/10.1016/j.trb.2006.02.005

22. Quaglietta, E., Corman, F., Goverde, R.: Stability analysis of railway dispatching plans in a stochastic and dynamic environment. J. Rail Transp. Plann. Manag. **3**(4), 137–149 (2013). https://doi.org/10.1016/j.jrtpm.2013.10.009

23. Törnquist, J.: Railway traffic disturbance management-an experimental analysis of disturbance complexity, management objectives and limitations in planning horizon. Transp. Res. Part A **41**(3), 249–266 (2007). https://doi.org/10.1016/j.tra.2006.05.003

24. Corman, F., D'Ariano, A., Pacciarelli, D., Pranzo, M.: Bi-objective conflict detection and resolution in railway traffic management. Transp. Res. Part C **20**(1), 79–94 (2012). https://doi.org/10.1016/j.trc.2010.09.009

25. D'Ariano, A., Pacciarelli, D., Samà, M., Corman, F.: Microscopic delay management: Minimizing train delays and passenger travel times during real-time railway

traffic control. In: Proceedings of the 5th IEEE International Conference on Models and Technologies for Intelligent Transportation Systems (IEEE MT-ITS 2017). Naples, Italy (2017). https://doi.org/10.1109/MTITS.2017.8005686

26. Xu, P., Corman, F., Peng, Q., Luan, X.: A timetable rescheduling approach and transition phases for high speed railway traffic during disruptions. Transp. Res. Rec. **2607**(1), 82–92 (2017). https://doi.org/10.3141/2607-11

27. Botte, M., D'Acierno, L., Montella, B., Placido, A.: A stochastic approach for assessing intervention strategies in the case of metro system failures. In: Proceedings of 2015 AEIT Annual Conference (AEIT 2015). Naples, Italy (2015). https://doi.org/10.1109/AEIT.2015.7415258

28. D'Acierno, L., Placido, A., Botte, M., Gallo, M., Montella, B.: Defining robust recovery solutions for preserving service quality during rail/metro systems failure. Int. J. Supply Oper. Manag. **3**(3), 1351–1372 (2016). https://doi.org/10.22034/2016.3.01

29. Larsen, R., Pranzo, M., D'Ariano, A., Corman, F., Pacciarelli, D.: Susceptibility of optimal train schedules to stochastic disturbances of process times. Flex. Serv. Manuf. J. **26**, 466–489 (2014). https://doi.org/10.1007/s10696-013-9172-9

30. Davydov, B., Chebotarev, V., Kablukova, K.: Stochastic model for the real-time train rescheduling. Int. J. Transp. Dev. Integr. **1**(3), 307–317 (2017). https://doi.org/10.2495/TDI-V1-N3-307-317

31. Li, X., Shou, B., Ralescu, D.: Train rescheduling with stochastic recovery time: a new track-backup approach. IEEE Trans. Syst. Man Cybern. Syst. **44**(9), 1216–1233 (2014). https://doi.org/10.1109/TSMC.2014.2301140

32. Kecman, P., Corman, F., Meng, L.: Train delay evolution as a stochastic process. In: Proceedings of the 6th International Conference on Railway Operations Modelling and Analysis (RailTokyo 2015). Narashino, Japan (2015)

33. Kecman, P., Corman, F., Peterson, A., Joborn, M.: Stochastic prediction of train delays in real-time using bayesian networks. In: Proceedings of Conference on Advanced Systems in Public Transport (CASPT 2015). Rotterdam, The Netherlands (2015). https://doi.org/10.3929/ethz-b-000175478

34. Meng, L., Zhou, X.: Robust single-track train dispatching model under a dynamic and stochastic environment: a scenario-based rolling horizon approach. Transp. Res. Part B **45**(7), 1080–1102 (2011). https://doi.org/10.1016/j.trb.2011.05.001

35. Yin, J., Tang, T., Yang, L., Gao, Z., Ran, B.: Energy-efficient metro train rescheduling with uncertain time-variant passenger demands: an approximate dynamic programming approach. Transp. Res. Part B **91**, 178–210 (2016). https://doi.org/10.1016/j.trb.2016.05.009

36. Louwerse, I., Huisman, D.: Adjusting a railway timetable in case of partial or complete blockades. Eur. J. Oper. Res. **235**, 583–593 (2014). https://doi.org/10.1016/j.ejor.2013.12.020

37. Zhan, S., Kroon, L., Veelenturf, L., Wagenaar, J.: Real-time high-speed train rescheduling in case of a complete blockage. Transp. Res. Part B **78**, 182–201 (2015). https://doi.org/10.1016/j.trb.2015.04.001

38. Durmus, M., Takai, S., Söylemez, M.: Fault diagnosis in fixed-block railway signaling systems: a discrete event systems approach. IEEJ Trans. Electr. Electron. Eng. **9**(5), 523–531 (2014). https://doi.org/10.1002/tee.22001

39. D'Acierno, L., Placido, A., Botte, M., Gallo, M., Montella, B.: A methodological approach for managing rail disruptions with different perspectives. Int. J. Math. Models Meth. Appl. Sci. **10**, 80–86 (2016). http://naun.org/cms.action?id=12152

40. Hao, W., Meng, L., Veelenturf, L., Long, S., Corman, F., Niu, X.: Optimal reassignment of passengers to trains following a broken train. In: Proceedings of the 2018 IEEE International Conference on Intelligent Rail Transport (IEEE ICIRT 2018). Marina Bay Sands, Singapore (2018). https://doi.org/10.1109/ICIRT.2018.8641524
41. Botte, M., Puca, D., Montella, B., D'Acierno, L.: An innovative methodology for managing service disruptions on regional rail lines. In: Proceedings of the 10th International Conference Environmental Engineering (ICEE 2017). Vilnius, Lithuania (2017). https://doi.org/10.3846/enviro.2017.134
42. Nash, A., Huerlimann, D.: Railroad simulation using opentrack. Comput. Railways **9**, 45–54 (2004). https://doi.org/10.2495/CR040051

Latent Classes Exploring the Sense of Passengers Well-Being in the Terminal: Evidence from a Peripheral Airport

Maria Grazia Bellizzi[(✉)] [iD], Laura Eboli [iD],
and Gabriella Mazzulla [iD]

University of Calabria, 87036 Rende, CS, Italy
{mariagrazia.bellizzi, laura.eboli,
gabriella.mazzulla}@unical.it

Abstract. This paper aims to explore the sense of passengers well-being in the terminal of an airport. The proposed methodology is performed into two stages: firstly, we use a basic latent class modeling approach in order to identify the latent classes representing air passengers' attitude towards the different provided service quality aspects, and detecting the sense of passengers well-being in the terminal; then, we introduce covariates in order to better explore latent class memberships as a function of socio-economic characteristics, travel habits and flight features. Evidences from a peripheral airport placed in the south of Italy were used for testing the proposed methodology and for obtaining practical issues. Specifically, we found that three latent classes of air passengers can be identified, namely no-sensitive passengers, cleanliness-sensitive and information-sensitive passengers. We found also that among the socio-economic characteristics, gender does not very influence very much class memberships, whereas age and level of education strongly affect class population shares. At the same time, travel purposes, country and arrival time before the flight showed a certain influence in predicting passengers class memberships.

Keywords: Latent class analysis · Air transport service quality · Passenger well-being

1 Introduction

Airport facilities and services are the first experiences that a passenger receives upon arrival. Therefore, measuring the sense of passengers well-being in the terminal by using passengers' evaluation about the service is essential to understand the needs of customers. In this manner, the different needs of the actors involved in the overall airport system should be satisfied: to optimize resource allocation for improving terminal infrastructures and services, and to have high-quality services for passengers. In order to better understand passengers' needs and expectations, a deep analysis for exploring the differences among people or groups of air transport users is of a certain importance; it was not very explored in previous works especially regarding peripheral airport with less importance to national and international level.

© Springer Nature Switzerland AG 2019
S. Misra et al. (Eds.): ICCSA 2019, LNCS 11620, pp. 133–147, 2019.
https://doi.org/10.1007/978-3-030-24296-1_13

Literature studies, where differences in perceptions of service quality among different groups of users were analyzed, were proposed by Bezerra and Gomez [1, 2], Pantouvakis and Renzi [3], and Bellizzi et al. [4]. Bezerra and Gomez [1, 2] considered personal characteristics of the passengers like parameters of models as a way to divide the sample of users to calibrate different models. Specifically, in Bezerra and Gomes [1] nationality, gender, trip purpose and mobility condition presented no significant effect; however, they found that the earlier the passenger arrives at the airport, the more likely he/she is to present a higher overall satisfaction. On the other hand, Bezerra and Gomes [2] discovered differences of perceptions between international and domestic passengers for service aspects such as availability and quality of stores, cleanliness of airport facilities, and wayfinding. Pantouvakis and Renzi [3] explore only the potential differences concerning resident versus visiting nationalities perceptions of airport service quality. They considered three groups of respondents: Italian passengers, English speaking travelers, and airport users from other nationalities. They found that Italian air travelers displayed significantly lower scores in their perceptions of the service quality offered by their homeland's airport industry regarding all the dimensions. Also Bellizzi et al. [4] found significant differences between Italian passengers and passengers from other countries; specifically, their results showed that announcements, staff and noise are very important for Italians, whereas baggage control and the aspect concerning display are more relevant for the foreign passengers. They also discovered that people travelling for leisure retain as most important aspects related to comfort, while people travelling for purposes linked to work or study give priority to technical aspects such as modal integration and information. Other interesting findings regarded people arriving more than two hours early, who give more importance to terminal cleanliness.

The aim of this paper is to contribute to the literature review by introducing covariates in order to better explore latent class memberships as a function of socio-economic characteristics, travel habits and flight features. The remainder of the paper is structured into 6 sections. The next section introduces the adopted methodology. Section 3 describes the case study in terms of airport characteristics, sample data and air passengers' evaluation. Section 4 explains the estimation results (Subsect. 4.1), with latent class memberships presented in Subsect. 4.2. The paper ends with a discussion of the main findings and a concluding section where some directions for future study are given.

2 Methodology

The proposed methodology performs into two stages: (1) to use a basic latent class modeling approach in order to identify the latent classes representing air passengers' attitude towards the different provided service quality aspects, and detecting the sense of passengers well-being in the terminal; (2) to introduce covariates in order to better explore latent class memberships as a function of socio-economic characteristics, travel habits and flight features. Latent class analysis is a statistical technique for the analysis of multivariate categorical data like observed data taking the form of a series of categorical responses [5]. In our study, individual-level voting data are analyzed for identifying and characterizing clusters of similar cases. Latent class analysis is a useful tool for accomplishing these goals. The latent class model seeks to stratify a number of observed variables by an unobserved latent unordered categorical variable that eliminates all confounding between the observed variables. The unobserved latent variable is nominal, namely the membership of a class. Conditional upon values of this latent variable, responses to all of the observed variables are assumed to be statistically independent: the model probabilistically groups each observation into a latent class, which in turn produces expectations about how that observation will respond on each observed variable [5]. Although the model does not automatically determine the number of latent classes in a given data set, it offers a variety of parsimony and goodness of fit statistics that the researcher may use in order to make a theoretically and empirically sound assessment. An extension of this basic model permits the inclusion of covariates to predict latent class membership. While in the basic model every observation has the same probability of belonging to each latent class prior to observing the responses to the observed variables, in the more general latent class regression model these prior probabilities vary by individual as a function of some sets of independent concomitant variables [5]. For estimating latent class models and latent class regression models, poLCA user-friendly package in R software was used [6, 7].

3   Case Study

3.1   Airport Characteristics

The international airport of Lamezia Terme was chosen as a case study, that is a peripheral airport placed in the Calabria region, south of Italy. Lamezia Terme is the most important airport in the region, connecting Calabrian citizen with the Italian hubs of Roma Fiumicino and Milano Malpensa, and directly with various national and international airports. In 2018, about 40 airlines provided flights from/to the airport, mainly low-cost airlines providing connections with the cities in the northern Italy (Milan, Turin, Venice, Genoa, Bologna, Bergamo, Pisa, Treviso) or in all the European countries (Hamburg, Brussels, Bucharest, Budapest, Cologne, Krakow, Düsseldorf, Frankfurt, London, Madrid, Prague, Warsaw, Vienna, Zurich). The airport infrastructures and all the activities of private operators working in the airport are managed by the S.A.CAL. (Società Aeroportuale Calabrese). During 2017, Lamezia Terme registered more than 2,500,000 passengers and about 22,000 flights between landings and take-offs [8].

3.2   Sample Data

The data supporting this study were collected by S.A.CAL. through Customer Satisfaction Surveys during the period from January 2015 to December 2016. Face-to-face interviews were addressed to the departing passengers. An amount of 2,087 interviews were collected but, after a preliminary selection of valid data, a sample of 1,873 records was obtained.

Each interviewed passenger had to evaluate the service aspects expressing a rating through a 5-level verbal scale ranging from "very poor", "poor" and "fair" to "good" and "excellent". In Table 1, sample socio-economic characteristics are reported joined with travel habits and flight characteristics.

Table 1. Sample socio-economic and flight characteristics, and travel habits.

Sample characteristics		n.	%
Gender	Male	884	47.2
	Female	989	52.8
Age	Less than 30	248	17.3
	Between 30 and 40	444	31.0
	Between 40 and 50	303	21.1
	Between 50 and 60	249	17.4
	More than 60	189	13.2
Level of education	Junior high school diploma	135	12.1
	High school diploma	539	47.9
	Bachelor or Master degree	450	40.0
Country	Italy	1133	60.5
	Other Europe Countries	541	28.9
	Extra Europe Countries	199	10.6
Flight destination	Italy	895	47.8
	Other European Countries	765	40.8
	Extra European Countries	213	11.4
Trip purpose	Work/business	291	15.5
	Holiday	1389	74.2
	Study	22	1.2
	Medical care	74	4.0
	Other	97	5.2
Travelling alone	Yes	125	6.7
	No	1748	93.3
Mode for reaching the airport	Car as driver (16.0%),	300	16.0
	Car as passenger (46.8%),	876	46.8
	Taxi (3.7%),	70	3.7
	Rental car (15.5%),	290	15.5
	Rental bus (7.3%),	137	7.3
	Bus (5.8%),	108	5.8
	Bus shuttle (4.9%)	39	2.1
	Other	53	2.8
Time of arrival	Less than 1 h before the flight	152	8.1
	From 1 to 2 h before the flight	912	48.7
	More than 2 h before the flight	809	43.2

The sample is made up of more females (53%) than males; about 70% of users are under 50, half of them with a High School diploma. The major part of the sample comes from Italy (60%), but about 30% of the passengers is going towards other European Countries. Domestic flights account for 48% of the total flights. A strong tourist vocation of the airport is highlighted by the high percentage of users who travel for holiday (74%).

Regarding travel habits, we can observe that most of the interviewed passengers travel with other people (93.3%), and arrive at the airport by car (82%), especially by a car driven by someone (47%). Almost half of the sample arrives at the airport from one to two hours before the departure time of the flight, 43% of users arrive more than two hours early, and the remaining part of passengers less than one hour before.

3.3 Air Passengers' Evaluation

In Table 2, statistics about the judgements expressed by the passengers about each analyzed service aspects were reported.

Table 2. Judgements about each airport service quality aspect.

V	Service quality aspect	Non-positive judgements		Positive judgements	
		n.	%	n.	%
V1	Road signposting	296	16.8	1469	83.2
V2	Flight information	127	7.3	1616	92.7
V3	Terminal signposting	131	7.2	1683	92.8
V4	Infopoint and security staff	87	5.0	1655	95.0
V5	Information accessibility	76	4.5	1626	95.5
V6	Personal security	86	4.9	1682	95.1
V7	Cleanliness of terminal	244	13.6	1547	86.4
V8	Cleanliness of toilets	322	22.5	1107	77.5
V9	Terminal air conditioning	343	19.3	1437	80.7
V10	Terminal comfort	245	13.7	1537	86.3

For the attribute "cleanliness of toilets" we have a relevant lack of information (23.7% of non-response data) because the toilets are not used by all the passengers during their staying in the airport. For all the attributes, we can note that positive judgements are largely chosen by the passengers, although certain aspects were less satisfactory for the passengers; as an example, "cleanliness of the toilets" shows 22.5% of non-positive judgements, "cleanliness of terminal" shows a percentage of 13.6%, and "terminal air conditioning" show a percentage of non-positive judgements closed to 19%. The service quality aspects with the highest percentage of positive judgements are "information accessibility" (95.5%), "personal security" (95.1%), and "Infopoint and security staff" (95.0%); in our opinion, the perception of the passengers can relate to the geographical favorable position of the airport and the size of the terminal.

4 Latent Class Memberships

4.1 Basic Latent Class Modeling

The proposed methodology is oriented to use a basic latent class modeling approach in order to identify the latent classes representing air passengers' attitude towards the different provided service quality aspects, and detecting the sense of passengers well-being in the terminal.

This approach allows to estimate a class population share on the basis of the judgements expressed by the air passengers about the analyzed service quality aspects in the terminal. Each service aspect is represented by a dichotomous variable assuming a value equal to 1 when the judgement expressed by the passenger is non-positive ("very poor", "poor", or "fair") and equal to 2 when the judgement is positive ("good" or "excellent"). The aim of this analysis is examining how subjects might be divided into groups depending upon the consistency of their judgements.

A three-class basic latent class model was estimated, where Fig. 1 represents a screen capture of the model results. Each group of red bars represents the conditional probabilities, by latent class, that passengers rated positively each of the ten service quality aspect (labeled V1 through V10). Taller bars correspond to conditional probabilities closer to 1 of a positive judgement. The three estimated latent classes clearly correspond to a pair of classes (the first and the third one) that are consistently rated positive (class population share 79%) or quite non-positive (class population share 14%), plus an intermediate class representing only 7% of the population. In the second class, only the variables V7 and V8 tend to have non-positive judgements whereas the other service aspects tend to have positive judgements. On the contrary, in the third class service aspects from V1 to V5 tend to have a non-positive judgement whereas service aspects from V6 to V10 tend to have positive judgements.

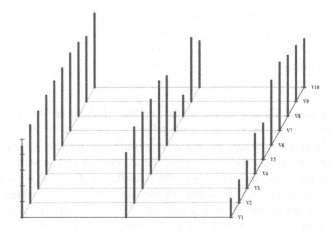

Fig. 1. Estimation of the three-class basic latent class model.

In order to choose the optimal number of latent classes, a number of goodness of fit statistics were performed. Specifically, both the minimum Akaike information criterion, or AIC [9], and Bayesian information criterion, or BIC [10], indicate that the three-class model is most parsimonious: the AIC is 10321 and the BIC is 10498. When a two-class model was performed AIC resulted equal to 10816 and BIC 10932 (about 500 units more than the previous values in both cases); in addition, in this case the predicted class memberships reached more than 90% of share for the first class. On the contrary, when a four-class model was performed we obtained quite lower value for AIC and BIC (10225 and 10463 respectively) but, conversely, the third and fourth classes registered low class population shares (4% in both cases) by maintaining the same class population share in the first class (79%). Definitively, as suggested by some authors [11, 12], the four-class model is over-specified containing very small groups of passengers; therefore, the three-class model was selected.

By following the statistical results of the basic latent class model, we can conclude that air passengers using Lamezia Terme terminal facilities can be subdivided into three classes, where: (1) the first class represents passengers with a strong sense of well-being in the terminal, and with attitude to express positive judgements towards all the service quality aspects (so-called "no sensitive passengers"); (2) the second class represents passengers with a soft sense of well-being in the terminal, and with attitude to express positive judgements towards all the service quality aspects except for cleanliness (so-called "cleanliness-sensitive passengers"); (3) the third class represents passengers with a weak sense of well-being in the terminal, and with attitude to express non-positive judgements towards the service quality aspects linked to the information (so-called "information-sensitive passengers").

4.2   Exploring Latent Class Memberships with Covariates

The above introduced latent classes were deeply explored with the aim to explain air passengers' membership as a function of socio-economic characteristics, travel habits and flight features. For this aim, a number of covariates were introduced, as reported in Table 3.

Firstly, we analyzed trip purposes and age interactions, by distinguishing among traveling for holiday and for other purposes (see Fig. 2). By examining the estimated class-conditional response probabilities, it seems confirmed that the model finds that the three groups indeed separate as expected, with 80–90% of passengers belonging to the first class, 10–20% to the second one, and 0–10% to the third class.

As we can note, no-sensitive passengers have a probability of latent class membership invariant with the age when they travel for holiday, whereas the probability tends to increase with the age when they travel for other purposes. Passengers cleanliness-sensitive seem to be also not changing with the age when they travel for holiday, whereas they tend to become less sensitive when traveling for other purposes.

On the contrary, information-sensitive passengers, when travelling for holiday, tend to become more sensitive towards these aspects when they are aged.

Concerning the interactions between trip purposes and education level, it can be noted that passengers with higher education levels traveling for holiday are more sensitive towards both cleanliness and information.

Table 3. Covariates

Covariate	Item	Value
Gender	Male	1
	Female	2
Age	Less than 30	1
	Between 30 and 40	2
	Between 40 and 50	3
	Between 50 and 60	4
	More than 60	5
Level of education	Junior high school diploma	1
	High school diploma	2
	Bachelor or Master degree	3
Country	Italy	1
	Other Countries	2
Trip purpose	Holiday	1
	Other purposes	2
Time of arrival	Less than 1 h before the flight	1
	From 1 to 2 h before the flight	2
	More than 2 h before the flight	3

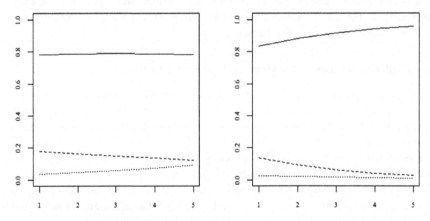

Fig. 2. Predicted probabilities of latent class memberships for "holiday as trip purpose" (on the left side), and "other trip purposes" (on the right side) and age [less than 30 (1), between 30 and 40 (2) betwccn 40 and 50 (3), between 50 and 60 (4), more than 60 (5)] [*continuous line represents the first latent class, dashed line the second one, and dotted line represents the third latent class*].

As you can see from Fig. 3, the probability of belonging to the first latent class tends to decrease whereas the probabilities of belonging to both the second and the third classes increases. The same tendency can be noted for passengers traveling for holiday when their arrival time at the terminal increases (see Fig. 4).

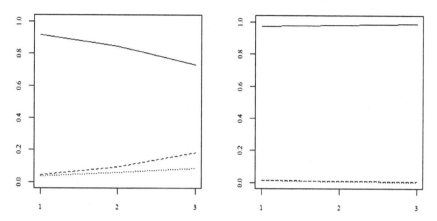

Fig. 3. Predicted probabilities of latent class memberships for "holiday as trip purpose" (on the left side), and "other trip purposes" (on the right side) and education level [Junior high school diploma (1), High school diploma (2) and Bachelor or Master degree (3)] [*continuous line represents the first latent class, dashed line the second one, and dotted line represents the third latent class*].

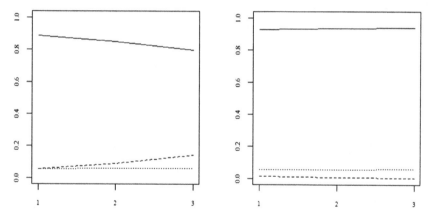

Fig. 4. Predicted probabilities of latent class memberships for "holiday as trip purpose" (on the left side), and "other trip purposes" (on the right side) and arrival time before the flight [less than 1 h (1), from 1 to 2 h (2) and more than 2 h (3)] [*continuous line represents the first latent class, dashed line the second one, and dotted line represents the third latent class*].

In Fig. 5 the interactions between gender and age are shown. In this case, it emerges that there is not difference in the attitude between male and female, and the passengers tend to become less sensitive towards all service quality aspects when their age increases; definitely, aged passengers are less exigent and with a higher sense of well-being in the terminal.

Relevant differences emerge between males and females when the interactions with passengers' education level are analysed (Fig. 6).

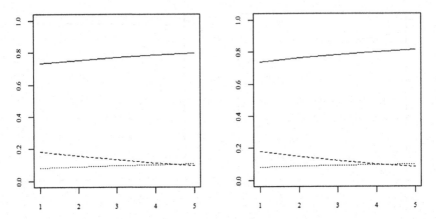

Fig. 5. Predicted probabilities of latent class memberships for "male" (on the left side), and "female" (on the right side) and age [less than 30 (1), between 30 and 40 (2) between 40 and 50 (3), between 50 and 60 (4), more than 60 (5)] [*continuous line represents the first latent class, dashed line the second one, and dotted line represents the third latent class*].

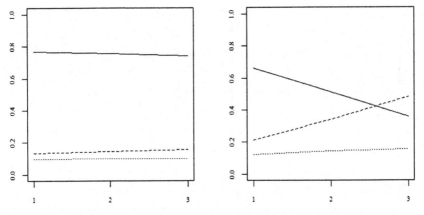

Fig. 6. Predicted probabilities of latent class memberships for "male" (on the left side), and "female" (on the right side) and education level [Junior high school diploma (1), High school diploma (2) and Bachelor or Master degree (3)] [*continuous line represents the first latent class, dashed line the second one, and dotted line represents the third latent class*].

In this case, male passengers with different education levels have the same probabilities of latent class memberships. Differently, female passengers are not very information-sensitive but their membership to the first latent class drastically decreases when their level of education increases and the sensitiveness towards cleanliness strongly increases.

Gender differences are highlighted also by Fig. 7, where predicted probabilities of latent class memberships are shown as a function of the arrival time at the terminal. In this case, females arriving more than 2 h before the flight become more sensitive towards cleanliness and their sense of well-being decreases.

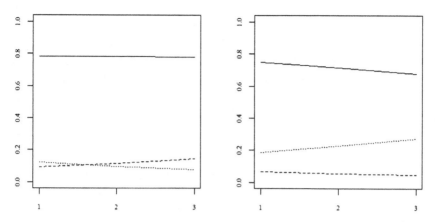

Fig. 7. Predicted probabilities of latent class memberships for "male" (on the left side), and "female" (on the right side) and arrival time before the flight [less than 1 h (1), from 1 to 2 h (2) and more than 2 h (3)] [*continuous line represents the first latent class, dashed line the second one, and dotted line represents the third latent class*].

Lastly, differences between Italian passengers and passengers from other countries were analysed (Figs. 8, 9 and 10). Generally, passengers from countries different from Italy are more sensitive towards all the service quality aspects, because latent class memberships show lower probabilities, but the probabilities to belong to each latent class are quite invariant with age. Conversely, aged Italian passengers become less cleanliness-sensitive and tend to increase their sense of well-being in the terminal.

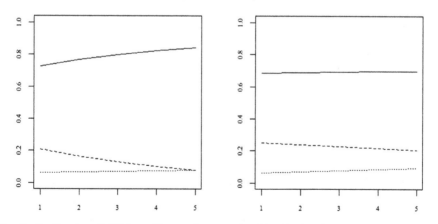

Fig. 8. Predicted probabilities of latent class memberships for "Italian travelers" (on the left side), and "travelers from other Countries" (on the right side) and age [less than 30 (1), between 30 and 40 (2) between 40 and 50 (3), between 50 and 60 (4), more than 60 (5)] [*continuous line represents the first latent class, dashed line the second one, and dotted line represents the third latent class*].

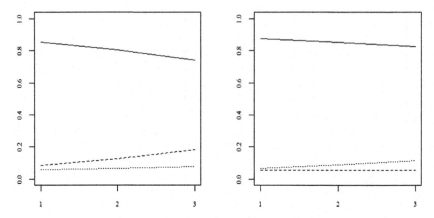

Fig. 9. Predicted probabilities of latent class memberships for "Italian travelers" (on the left side), and "travelers from other Countries" (on the right side) and education level [Junior high school diploma (1), High school diploma (2) and Bachelor or Master degree (3)] [*continuous line represents the first latent class, dashed line the second one, and dotted line represents the third latent class*].

Similar attitudes can be noted from Fig. 9, where the interactions with nationality and education level are shown. However, in this case passengers from countries different from Italy have a higher probability to belong to the first latent class (more than 80%), showing an attitude to have a good sense of well-being. Differently from Fig. 8, Italian passengers with higher levels of education increase their sensitiveness to quality aspects, especially those linked to cleanliness.

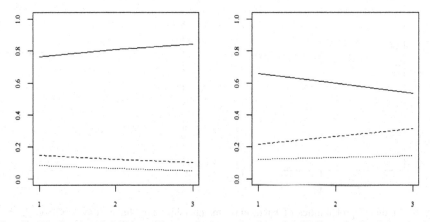

Fig. 10. Predicted probabilities of latent class memberships for "Italian travelers" (on the left side), and "travelers from other Countries" (on the right side) and arrival time before the flight [less than 1 h (1), from 1 to 2 h (2) and more than 2 h (3)] [*continuous line represents the first latent class, dashed line the second one, and dotted line represents the third latent class*].

Finally, attitudes quite different can be noted by comparing Italian travelers with travelers from other countries when arrival time before the flight is considered (Fig. 10). In this case, Italian passengers are very inclined to a good sense of well-being, whereas non Italian passengers are more exigent and become more sensitive, especially towards cleanliness and especially when arrival time increases.

5   Discussion of the Results

The influence of age over the class memberships is clear: aged passengers tend to be less exigent (increasing the probability to belong to no-sensitive class of passengers) and less sensitive towards terminal cleanliness (decreasing the probability to belong to cleanliness-sensitive class of passengers). This behavior was observed also in studies investigating on bus service quality; in fact, some authors verified that young people are more exigent than aged passengers [13, 14]. This evidence is particularly relevant when passengers travel for purposes different from holiday and for Italian passengers. Also Bellizzi et al. [4] registered that people travelling for work or study retain as less important aspects related to comfort. Instead, concerning the perceptions of the Italian passengers, Pantouvakis and Renzi [3] discovered that the opinions of Italian passengers regarding airport's physical environment and facilities, are less positive than those of the other passengers.

Differently from age, education level contributes to have more exigent passengers, decreasing the probability to belong to no-sensitive class of passengers; at the same time, sensitiveness towards terminal cleanliness and information increases. The emerging results is highlighted especially for female, Italian passengers and holiday travels. From the literature analyzing bus service quality, analogous findings emerges; Allen et al. [13, 14] verified that females are more demanding than males in travelling by a public transport mode concerning the need of time, security level, comfort and cleanliness, and so on.

Lastly, we consider the influence of arrival time over the latent class memberships. We can note that when arrival time before the flight increase air passengers reduced their sense of well-being in the terminal, probably due to their longer stay at the airport. In this case, the probability to belong to the no-sensitive class decreases and conversely the probabilities to belong to the cleanliness and information-sensitive classes increases, by proving a higher passengers' sensitiveness. These attitudes are particularly evident for female, passengers traveling for holiday and from countries different from Italy. Concordant findings were discovered by Bellizzi et al. [4] who found that people arriving more than two hours early give a certain importance to terminal cleanliness. On the contrary, Bezerra and Gomes [1] found that the earlier the passenger arrives at the airport, the more likely he/she is to present a higher overall satisfaction. They interpret this evidence by considering that the fact that passenger's level of stress is related to the amount of time available for complying with the required checkpoints.

6 Conclusion

In this paper, the sense of passengers well-being in the terminal of the Lamezia Terme international airport, a peripheral airport placed in the south of Italy, was explored. Experimental evidences showed that the sense of passengers well-being in the terminal can be explored by three latent classes, and specifically: (1) a first class representing passengers with attitude to express positive judgements towards all the service quality aspects (no-sensitive passengers); (2) a second class representing passengers with attitude to express positive judgements towards all the service quality aspects except for the aspect linked to the cleanliness (cleanliness-sensitive passengers); (3) a third class representing passengers with attitude to express non-positive judgements towards the service quality aspects linked to the information (information-sensitive passengers).

Also, a deeper analysis of the interactions among socio-economic characteristics, travel habits and flight features allowed some interesting issues to be discovered. We found that among the socio-economic characteristics, gender is not always very influencing class memberships, whereas age and level of education strongly affect class population shares. At the same time, travel purposes, country and arrival time before the flight showed a certain influence in predicting passengers class memberships.

The obtained results have practical implications because allow the agency managing airport infrastructures and services to better understand the needs and attitudes of air passengers. In turn, these issues can be used for improving the quality levels of the provided services and for suggesting customized services for each class of passengers using the terminal, by taking into account especially the sensitiveness towards cleanliness and information of certain class of users'.

References

1. Bezerra, G.C.L., Gomes, C.F.: The effects of service quality dimensions and passenger characteristics on passenger's overall satisfaction with an airport. J. Air Transp. Manag. **44**, 77–81 (2015)
2. Bezerra, G.C.L., Gomes, C.F.: Measuring airport service quality: a multidimensional approach. J. Air Transp. Manag. **53**, 85–93 (2016)
3. Pantouvakis, A., Renzi, M.F.: Exploring different nationality perceptions of airport service quality. J. Air Transp. Manag. **52**, 90–98 (2016)
4. Bellizzi, M.G., Eboli, L., Forciniti, C., Mazzulla, G.: Air transport passengers' satisfaction: an ordered logit model. Transp. Res. Procedia **33**, 147–154 (2018)
5. Linzer, D.A., Lewis, J.B.: poLCA. An R package for polytomous variable latent class analysis. J. Stat. Softw. **42**(10), 1–29 (2011)
6. Linzer, D.A., Lewis, J.: poLCA. Polytomous Variable Latent Class Analysis. R package version 1.3 (2011). http://CRAN.R-project.org/package=poLCA
7. R Development Core Team R: A Language and Environment for Statistical Computing. R Foundation for Statistical Computing, Vienna, Austria (2010). http://www.R-project.org
8. S.A.CAL: Calabrian Airport Company: Service Charter Guide, Lamezia Terme (2018)
9. Akaike, H.: Information theory and an extension of the maximum likelihood principle. In: Petrov, B., Csake, F. (eds.) Second International Symposium on Information Theory, pp. 267–281. Akademiai Kiado, Budapest (1973)

10. Schwartz, G.: Estimating the dimension of a model. Ann. Stat. **6**, 461–464 (1978)
11. Greene, W.H.: Heterogeneity. Latent Class Models. New York University (2014)
12. Hensher, D.A., Rose, J.M., Greene, W.H.: Applied Choice Analysis, 2nd edn. Cambridge University Press, New York (2015)
13. Allen, J., Eboli, L., Mazzulla, G., de Dios Ortúzar, J.: Effect of critical incidents on public transport satisfaction and loyalty: an Ordinal Probit SEM-MIMIC approach. Transportation (2018). https://doi.org/10.1007/s11116-018-9921-4
14. Allen, J., Eboli, L., Forciniti, C., Mazzulla, G., de Dios Ortúzar, J.: The role of critical incidents and involvement in transit satisfaction and loyalty. Transp. Policy **75**, 57–69 (2019)

Some Features of Formatting the Arrival Time Distribution

Vladimir Chebotarev[1], Boris Davydov[2], Kseniya Kablukova[1(✉)],
and Vadim Gopkalo[2]

[1] CC FEB RAS, Kim Yu Chen Street 65, 680000 Khabarovsk, Russia
vladimir.ch@ccfebras.ru, kseniya0407@mail.ru
[2] FESTU, Seryshev Street 47, 680021 Khabarovsk, Russia
dbi@rambler.ru, vng@yandex.ru

Abstract. The paper discusses the basic stochastic two-train and multi-train models. These models describe the process of running and arrival time distributions formation. It is shown that the distribution of arrival times is determined by the cumulative effect of several independent factors. We investigate the process of occurring the asymmetric output probability density function. The main reason of distribution skewness is a train interaction. The study takes the real world data into account. In considered model the departure deviation and running time are input random variables. The types of input distributions are selected by using statistical data. The results of theoretical analysis are confirmed by statistical data obtained on the main railway lines of Russia.

Keywords: Stochastic model · Bimodal probability distribution ·
Arrival deviation · Deformation of the probability density function

1 Introduction

Stochastic models of train traffic are used to predict the situation progress in the presence of random disturbances. Traffic modeling allows you to detect intertrain conflicts and to consider their further distribution along the railway network. Most common are problems in which the cumulative value of delay all the trains is determined. This indicator reflects the result of appearing the set of knock-on delays in a wide spatial and temporal horizon. Obviously, with such a mapping of a complex multi-conflict situation, it is almost impossible to assess the impact of each individual deviation from the schedule.

In another group of papers, the process of delay propagation is studied, which is observed in a limited space-time zone when a single disturbance occurs. These researches are focused on solving local problems of train operational dispatching. When selecting a particular adjustment, the set of delays that appear in a restricted (local) area is a result of modeling. Such an adjustment is chosen as optimal, which reduces the number or duration of non-scheduled delays.

© Springer Nature Switzerland AG 2019
S. Misra et al. (Eds.): ICCSA 2019, LNCS 11620, pp. 148–161, 2019.
https://doi.org/10.1007/978-3-030-24296-1_14

There is a gap between two approaches described. Models of the first group do not provide effective solutions to local problems. At the same time, the delay propagation process in the local area, which is considered in present article, doesn't allow to reflect some important points that must be taken into account when traffic macro-modeling is made at railway network. Many studies don't take into account the process of changing the scattering behavior of train arrival times under the influence of destabilizing factors. Ignoring this process leads to significant errors in deviations predicting from the schedule.

It should be subjected to comparative analyzing the results of delay calculations based on different imitating models of their propagation along the train chain. This will allow us to estimate the scale of the difficulties encountered in train delays predicting. The present paper attempts to perform the analysis of modeling results obtained from using some common scenarios which cause the process of delays propagation.

2   Literature Review

Modeling the process of random delays occurrence and their propagation along the train chain makes it possible to assign rational traffic adjustments and predict their likely consequences. In one of the first papers considering this problem, an analytical method was proposed for delay determining by convolving the distributions of the initial (at the site entry) and newly arising deviations [1]. The analysis carried out is limited since the assumption of a uniform law of the secondary delays distribution is used. In reality, this assumption is not confirmed.

A productive approach is one in which the expected values of operating times are obtained from statistics of previous periods. Situational-heuristic method (SEMN) is used to determine these quantities, that allows you to take into account the peculiarity of train traffic conditions in the scheduled period while a prognosis being created [2]. A similar approach is used in the paper [3] in which modeling is performed using average values of train processing time. It should be noted that there are attempts to derive some average train schedule based on the emerging situation. Such attempts are fraught with conservation of technological problems that exist on the site.

One of the fundamental papers is devoted to the problem of traffic stochastic modeling under consideration [4]. The authors describes a model of delay formation in a train set traffic using a probabilistic approach. Total run time of the train is considered as a sum of random intervals of movement along the elements of the section when analyzing the process of delay propagation. The paper [5] shows that calculation of the arrival time distribution at the terminal station is based on repeated use of convoluting the distributions of random variables characterizing each of the travel elements.

Below mentioned papers use this approach to analyze the process of delay propagation along the train chain. The authors of the study [6] solve the problem of interacting the two trains in a flow that have different speeds and are influenced by random impacts. The result of analysis is used to model the train traffic in a dense heterogeneous train flow. This idea develops in the papers [5,7,8]. The paper [7] represents trains traffic in a form occupying an intermediate position between the macro-models and models with very detailed description of the process, i.e. micro-models. Approximation method is proposed for exact representation of delay distributions. Cumulative distribution is calculated from the sequence of activities which is determined by a stochastic event-graph.

Most fully the problem of predicting the random delay appearance and propagation across the large railway network is considered in [8]. Scattering of arrival moments is treated as a random variable generated with joint accounting the departure times and the running intervals. The main subject of research is the process of adjusting the schedule at transfer stations in the presence of multiple delays. The model operates with discrete distributions of travel, dwell times and deviations from the schedule. The authors use a simplified description of input random variables so that they receive a small computing time.

The proposed approach was further developed in the study [5] which attempts to take the realistic distribution of operation time into account and choose the appropriate approximation. The approach proposed uses a probabilistic operational graph which considers transfer operation and conflict situations. The authors argue that mesoscopic modelling of traffic is the purposeful approach to compute the delay propagation. The purpose of the study is to reduce computing time. The authors apply the phase-type approximation function which is analytically converted to cdf. Such representation simplifies the data processing when searching the output distribution. The model created is a logically incomplete. The authors consider only station and crossing as the operating points where conflicts can occur.

The general characteristics of the schedule which is realized under conditions of random disturbances are considered to be its robustness and stability. Timetable robustness is understood as its ability to absorb small current deviations [9,10]. The compensatory mechanism begins to fail with increasing the intensity of traffic which leads to the multiplication of delays. A characteristic that shows the ability to eliminate the disturbances that occur is defined as timetable stability [11] and it correlates with the time interval that is needed to restore the normative traffic.

The results obtained in these papers do not allow analytically combining the results of calculating the probability distributions of unscheduled deviations after each regular operation. These distributions are obtained using various stochastic models.

3   Stochastic Model of Arrival Deviation Formation

Consider the following two-train model. Trains with numbers 1 and 2 depart one by one from a certain station and move in the same direction. Planned trajectories of their movement are the same, only the moments of departure are different. It is assumed that the condition of compliance with the minimum safe inter-train interval is fulfilled. When departing and in the process of movement trains are influenced by random factors that lead to scattering of departure times and travel times. To describe the movement of a train with the number i $(i = 1, 2)$ we introduce the following notations:

δ_i is the deviation from the scheduled departure time,

$F(t) = \mathbf{P}(\delta_i \leq t)$ is the distribution function of the random deviation δ_i, $i = 1, 2$, of the departure moments from the schedule; it is assumed that the variables δ_1 and δ_2 are equally distributed;

$f(t)$ is the density function of δ_1,

ρ_i is the travel time between stations,

$$L_i(t) = \mathbf{P}(\rho_i < t), \tag{1}$$

$l_i(t)$ is the density function of ρ_i;

d_i is the departure time of the i-th train according to schedule;

a_i is the arrival time of the i-th train according to schedule;

ξ_i is the random deviation of the i-th train from the scheduled arrival time; then $a_i + \xi_i$ is actual arrival time of the i-th train;

$U_i(t) = P(\xi_i < t)$, $u_i(t)$ is the density function of ξ_i;

t_0 is the minimum permissible time interval between trains;

$s_0 = s_0(v) = v \cdot t_0$ is the minimum safe distance between trains, corresponding to an arbitrary speed v.

Figure 1 shows the formation of the arrival times $a_j + \xi_j$, $j = 1, 2$.

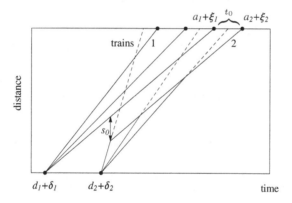

Fig. 1. The formation of the arrival times $a_j + \xi_j$, $j = 1, 2$.

Now we deduce formula

$$U_2(t) = \int_0^\infty F(t - d_1 + a_2 - t_0 - y) l_1(y)\, dy. \tag{2}$$

We have (see Fig. 1) $a_1 + \xi_1 - (d_1 + \delta_1) = \rho_1$, consequently, $a_1 + \xi_1 = \rho_1 + \delta_1 + d_1$. Next, since $a_2 + \xi_2 = a_1 + \xi_1 + t_0$, then

$$\xi_2 = \rho_1 + \delta_1 + d_1 - a_2 + t_0.$$

Hence,
$$U_2(t) = \mathbf{P}(\xi_2 < t) = \mathbf{P}(\rho_1 + \delta_1 < t - d_1 + a_2 - t_0). \tag{3}$$

Assume that ρ_1 and δ_1 are independent. Then (2) follows from (3).

Note that in [12] a different formula was deduced, although similar to (2). The difference is that in [12] the constant s_0 is taken as a given technological constant, but not t_0.

By (2) the density function of ξ_2 has the following form:
$$u_2(t) = \int_0^\infty f(t - d_1 + a_2 - t_0 - y) l_1(y)\,dy. \tag{4}$$

According to the collected statistics, the train travel time often obeys some bimodal distribution law. Studies show that in the case of relatively free traffic, the graph of the density function of the time travel has a longer right branch.

In [13] is shown that such distribution is well approximated by the gamma distribution. It can be assumed that the influence of several (in particular, two) factors on the train traffic is of a similar nature. Take the travel time density function $\tilde{l}(t)$ as a mixture of two gamma densities $\tilde{l}_1(t)$ and $\tilde{l}_2(t)$:
$$\tilde{l}(t) = \tilde{l}(t, p) = p\tilde{l}_1(t) + (1 - p)\tilde{l}_2(t), \quad 0 \le p \le 1, \tag{5}$$

where
$$\tilde{l}_1(t) = I(t > b_1)\frac{e^{-(t-b_1)/\beta}(t - b_1)^{\alpha-1}}{\Gamma(\alpha)\beta^\alpha}, \quad \tilde{l}_2(t) = \tilde{l}_1(t - b_2), \tag{6}$$

$\alpha > 0$, $\beta > 0$. Note that hereinafter, all the density functions with the *tilde* icon refer to the case when travel time density is a mixture of gamma distributions (5).

The parameters $b_1, b_2 > 0$ set the shift of the initial gamma densities $\tilde{l}_1(t)$ and $\tilde{l}_2(t)$ along the horizontal axis to the right, because travel time is a strictly positive random variable. In this case, it is necessary to ensure that the support of the density function $\tilde{l}(t)$ lies only on the positive semi-axis, and it is significantly separated from zero.

The bimodality of the density $\tilde{l}(t)$ is determined by the influence of two random destabilizing factors. To simulate the degree of influence of each of them, we use the weighted (probabilistic) parameter p, $0 \le p \le 1$. The more p, the stronger the first factor influences (the multiplier p before $\tilde{l}_1(t)$ in (5)) and the weaker the influence of the second factor, and vice versa.

Let us set the actual form and parameters of the input distributions in (4). Suppose that the departure deviation δ_1 obeys the exponential distribution law with a density function
$$f(t) = I(t > 0)\lambda e^{-\lambda t}, \quad \lambda > 0. \tag{7}$$

Let $\lambda = 0.3$. Such a value of the parameter λ corresponds to reality, because in this case, the mean departure deviation $\mathbf{E}\delta_1 = 1/\lambda \approx 3.3$ min.

Next, we set $\alpha = 16$, $\beta = 0.25$, $b_1 = 6$, $b_2 = 3$. The symbols $\tilde{\rho}_1$ and $\tilde{\rho}_2$ denote random variables with densities $\tilde{l}_1(t)$ and $\tilde{l}_2(t)$, respectively. By using the properties of the gamma distribution, we get $\mathbf{E}\tilde{\rho}_1 = \alpha\beta + b_1 = 10$ min (under influence of factor 1) and $\mathbf{E}\tilde{\rho}_2 = \alpha\beta + b_1 + b_2 = 13$ min (under influence of factor 2). The standard deviation for both random variables is one: $\sqrt{\mathbf{D}\tilde{\rho}_1} = \sqrt{\alpha\beta^2} = 1$ min.

The following parameters are determined by the normative schedule:

$$d_1 = 0 \, \text{min}, \quad a_2 = 15 \, \text{min}, \quad t_0 = 3 \, \text{min}. \tag{8}$$

By varying the parameter p, let us see the behavior of the density function $\tilde{l}(t) = \tilde{l}(t, p)$ from (5) and its impact to the corresponding density $\tilde{u}_2(t)$, defined by (4). The results of the calculation are collected in Table 1.

When the parameter p is close to zero (see Table 1, $p = 0.1$), the first factor has a negligible effect on the travel time, the influence of the second factor prevails. Due to its impact, the mean travel time increases, which is accompanied by a higher right-hand vertex of the density graph $\tilde{l}(t)$ compared to the left. In this case, the advance of the train traffic schedule is practically not observed because the graph of the density function $\tilde{u}_2(t)$ is concentrated on the positive semi-axis.

As the parameter p increases, the degree of each factor impact changes: the mean travel time gradually decreases, the bimodal density $\tilde{l}(t)$ (see Table 1, $p = 0.3$) is changed by the unimodal one (see Table 1, $p = 0.8$). The deformation of the density $\tilde{l}(t)$ entails the deformation of the density $\tilde{u}_2(t)$. This leads to increase in the probability to advance the train traffic schedule, namely the support of the density function $\tilde{u}_2(t)$ "captures" a segment of the negative semi-axis.

Thus, the choice of the parameter p allows adjusting the degree of influence of each factor depending on the specific situation. In this case the following rule which is in good agreement with reality is observed: the smaller the value of the mean travel time, the smaller the mean of the delay. In addition, in this case negative arrival deviations are more often observed, that is an advance of the schedule.

4   An Example of the Joint Influence of Random Factors on the Arrival Deviation Distribution

One of the independent factors that are involved in the formation of travel time as a random variable is the mutual influence of trains. A stochastic model that reflects this influence was proposed in [6]. The paper studies the case when a faster train catches up with a slow leading train in the middle of the section, and later both trains move with a fixed time interval t_0 (see the diagram in Fig. 2). In the simulation, it is assumed that the train speed fluctuates, as it is subject to random influences. Obviously, the scattering rate can be considered as one of the factors that we considered in Sect. 3 in constructing a model for the formation of arrival deviations. Thus, the multimodality of the run time is determined by the presence of two random variables, namely, the departure time and train speed. In the following, we will assume that slow trains, which move in a flow, belong to type 1, fast – to type 2.

Table 1. The behavior of the functions $\tilde{l}(t,p)$ and $\tilde{u}_2(t)$ for different values of the weight parameter p.

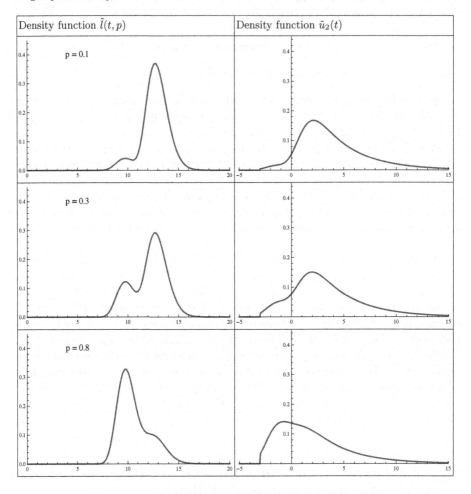

In Sect. 3, we considered the first important particular case of the proposed model, when train travel time obeys a mixture of two gamma distributions (5). As already mentioned, the multimodality of the run time density can be determined not only by the influence of several random factors, but also by the presence in the flow on one track the trains of different types. The train type is determined by its speed [6].

The article [6] deals with the general case of finding the distribution of the actual travel time on open tracks that takes $K > 0$ types of trains into consideration. Each of these types is characterized by values of free running time on a section F_n, where n denotes a train number in the flow. The cumulative

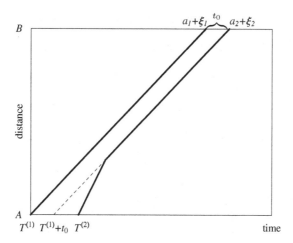

Fig. 2. Train interaction scenario: fast train catches up with slow one.

distribution function of F_n (provided that train n is of type k, i.e. $Q_n = k$) is determined as follows:

$$V_k(t) = \mathbf{P}(F_n \le t | Q_n = k). \tag{9}$$

Random variable R_n denotes actual travel time of the train n. Suppose that the number of types $K = 2$. Let p be a probability that train n is of type 1. Further, we use a formula (16) from the article [6] with new notation. The cumulative distribution function of the actual travel time of the train type j, $j = 1, 2$, is determined as follows for $t \ge 0$:

$$\hat{L}_j(t) \equiv \hat{L}_j(t, p) = \lim_{n \to \infty} \mathbf{P}(R_n \le t | Q_n = j)$$
$$= V_j(t) \exp\left(-\hat{\lambda} \int_t^\infty \left(1 - p V_1(x) - (1 - p) V_2(x)\right) dx \right), \tag{10}$$

where $\hat{\lambda}^{-1}$ denotes the mean departure intertrain interval provided that it has an exponential distribution with the parameter $\hat{\lambda} > 0$.

The parameter $\hat{\lambda}$ can be found from the following relation:

$$\hat{\lambda}^{-1} = \mathbf{E}H - t_0, \tag{11}$$

where $\mathbf{E}H$ denotes an average intertrain interval by the train flow (in minutes).

Denote a probability density function of the train travel time (train has a type j, $j = 1, 2$) as

$$\hat{l}_j(y) \equiv \hat{l}_j(y, p) = \hat{L}'_j(y) = \exp\left\{ -\hat{\lambda} \int_y^\infty \left(1 - p V_1(x) - (1 - p) V_2(x)\right) dx \right\}$$
$$\times \left(v_j(y) + \hat{\lambda} V_j(y) \left(1 - p V_1(y) - (1 - p) V_2(y)\right) \right), \tag{12}$$

where $v_j(y) = V'_j(y)$.

Consider a mixture of densities

$$\hat{l}(y) \equiv \hat{l}(y,p) = p\hat{l}_1(y,p) + (1-p)\hat{l}_2(y,p), \tag{13}$$

with $0 \le p \le 1$. The probability density function $\hat{l}(y)$ is used for simulation of arrival deviations with the following types of input distributions:

$$V_1(y) = \frac{I(y > b_1)}{\Gamma(\alpha_1)} \int_0^{(y-b_1)/\beta_1} x^{\alpha_1 - 1} e^{-x} \, dx, \tag{14}$$

$$V_2(y) = \frac{I(y > b_2)}{\Gamma(\alpha_2)} \int_0^{(y-b_2)/\beta_2} x^{\alpha_2 - 1} e^{-x} \, dx, \tag{15}$$

$$v_1(y) = \frac{dV_1(y)}{dy} = I(y > b_1) \frac{e^{-(y-b_1)/\beta_1}(y - b_1)^{\alpha_1 - 1}}{\Gamma(\alpha_1)\beta_1^{\alpha_1}}, \tag{16}$$

$$v_2(y) = \frac{dV_2(y)}{dy} = I(y > b_2) \frac{e^{-(y-b_2)/\beta_2}(y - b_2)^{\alpha_2 - 1}}{\Gamma(\alpha_2)\beta_2^{\alpha_2}}, \tag{17}$$

where $\Gamma(\cdot)$ implies the Euler gamma-function.

According to (14)–(17), a free running time of the train type j, $j = 1, 2$, obeys a gamma-law with the parameters $\alpha_j > 0$, $\beta_j > 0$ and shift $b_j > 0$.

Note that hereinafter, all density functions with the *cover* icon refer to the case when density of the travel time is based on the paper [6].

We assume the parameter $\hat{\lambda} = 0.5$. This value describes the situation when $\mathbf{E}H = 5$ min, $t_0 = 3$ min (see (11)).

Let us set the real parameters of the input distributions $v_1(y)$ and $v_2(y)$ estimated on the basis of statistical data:

$$\alpha_1 = 16, \quad \beta_1 = 0.25, \quad b_1 = 10,$$
$$\alpha_2 = 9, \quad \beta_2 = 1/3, \quad b_2 = 7.$$

In this scenario, train type 1 characterizes slow trains with the mean travel time $\alpha_1\beta_1 + b_1 = 14$ min, type 2 – fast trains with the mean $\alpha_2\beta_2 + b_2 = 10$ min. Dispersions of both distributions are equal to 1: $\alpha_1\beta_1^2 = \alpha_2\beta_2^2 = 1$ min^2.

We explore how the behavior of a density $\hat{l}(t) = \hat{l}(t,p)$ changes being determined by the equality (13), as well as a density $\hat{u}_2(t)$ defined by the equality (4), by changing the parameter p. In Table 2, parameter p is fixed. The thinner and bold lines correspond to the graphs of $\hat{l}_1(t)$ and $\hat{l}_2(t)$ respectively, the boldest line represents the graph of $\hat{l}(t)$ (for all left sided figures). In the left column of Table 2, the graphs of densities $\hat{l}_1(t)$ and $\hat{l}_2(t)$ defined by the equality (12) with $j = 1, 2$, and their mixtures $\hat{l}(t,p) = p\hat{l}_1(t) + (1-p)\hat{l}_2(t)$ are depicted. Corresponding densities $\hat{u}_2(t)$ are shown at the right column.

The Table 2 reflects the form of densities $\hat{l}(t)$ and $\hat{u}_2(t)$ changes with the growth of the parameter p. This fact can be explained as follows. If value of p is close to 1 then slow trains (with a density $\hat{l}_1(t)$) prevail in the common flow. Therefore, the function $\hat{l}(t)$ is close to unimodal density $\hat{l}_1(t)$. Then $\hat{u}_2(t)$ is also unimodal (see Table 2, $p = 0.8$). At the same time, the number of fast trains

Table 2. Behavior of the travel time density function $\hat{l}(t,p)$ and arrival deviation density function $\hat{u}_2(t)$ with a different ratio of slow and fast trains.

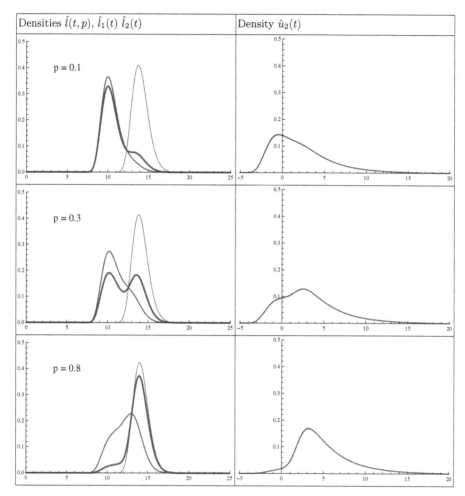

which are influenced by slow ones is less than the number of slow trains. As a result, the frequency of delays is small.

If the parameter p is close to zero (but not equal to 0) then the share of fast trains in the flow is greater than the share of slow ones. If there is a delay of a preceding train, the knock-on effect of secondary delays will be observed more often. Hence, the density $\hat{l}(t)$ is close to the density $\hat{l}_2(t)$, which is unimodal in the scenario under consideration. Then $\hat{u}_2(t)$ is also unimodal (see Table 2, $p = 0.1$).

If $p = 0.3$, then the density $\hat{l}(t)$ takes into account the properties of both densities $\hat{l}_1(t)$ and $\hat{l}_2(t)$, which leads to the bimodality of $\hat{l}(t)$. This in turn leads to a deformation of $\hat{u}_2(t)$ whose form can be bimodal or close to bimodal (see Table 2, $p = 0.3$).

The density form of fast train actual travel times $\hat{l}_2(t)$ varies as the parameter p changes. The less p, the more fast trains in the common flow and the more correct (symmetric) form of the graph $\hat{l}_2(t)$ is observed. Note the support of function $\hat{l}_2(t)$ for $p = 0$ is the "narrowest" since there is no impact of slow train traffic. Increasing the parameter p entails support expansion of $\hat{l}_2(t)$ and a gradual change in the skewness from positive (for $p \to 0$) to negative (for $p \to 1$). Negative asymmetry is acquired due to the fact that fast trains are forced to adjust to slow ones reducing its speed. Consequently, the support of $\hat{l}_2(t)$ completely "absorbs" the support of $\hat{l}_1(t)$ and running times of fast trains begin to coincide with running times of slow ones.

5   Validation of the Model by Using Statistical Data

This section is devoted to the analysis of research results by means of real statistical data of travel time and arrival deviations. The observed features are discussed taking into account the results of a theoretical analysis conducted in Sects. 3 and 4.

We explore the statistics collected for the trains of the suburban radial railway line Moscow-Tver. It turned out that bimodal travel time densities are not uncommon, but appear quite often. Table 3 contains the examples of histograms plotted from samples of travel time and arrival deviations distributions in the morning and evening rush hours. Note that for the convenience of displaying in travel time histograms, the vertical axis intersects the horizontal one not at the origin, but at the point $(18, 0)$ or $(5, 0)$.

The given examples show that the appearance of a bimodal travel time distribution leads to a rise in the left tail of the arrival deviation density, that is, it creates a left-sided asymmetry. If the influence of random factors on the train traffic is comparable, then it leads to the presence of two modes in the output density function. Thus, the nature of the histograms constructed on the basis of experimental data agrees well with the result of theoretical constructions for both special cases of the travel time distribution (5) and (13), which are given in Sects. 3 and 4 of this article.

The histograms of the travel time given in Table 3 are fairly well approximated by a mixture of gamma distributions (5) with an approximately same degree of each factor influence on the travel time. In Tables 1, 2 this variant corresponds to the figures, which illustrate the densities of the considered random variables in the case when the weight parameter p is equal to 0.3. For example, the following calculated parameters of the resulting arrival deviation density $\tilde{u}_2(t)$ are characterize morning peak hours:

$$p = 0.3, \quad \alpha = 16, \quad \beta = 0.25, \quad b_1 = 17.5, \quad b_2 = 2.5, \quad \lambda = 1, \quad (18)$$

the parameters of the arrival deviation density $\hat{u}_2(t)$:

$$p = 0.3, \ \alpha_1 = 16, \ \beta_1 = 0.25, \ b_1 = 21,$$

$$\alpha_2 = 9, \ \beta_2 = 1/3, \ b_2 = 19, \ \hat{\lambda} = 0.5, \ \lambda = 1. \quad (19)$$

Moreover, the normative parameters for a given track are following:

$$d_1 = 0 \, \text{min}, \quad a_2 = 27 \, \text{min}, \quad t_0 = 3 \, \text{min}. \quad (20)$$

Table 4 contains a histogram of arrival deviations for morning rush hours from Table 3 with two approximating density curves: (i) graph of the density

Table 3. Histograms of the travel time and arrival deviation distribution.

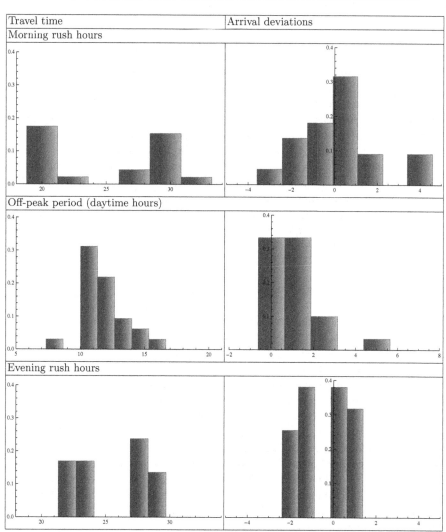

Table 4. Agreement of $\tilde{u}_2(t)$ and $\hat{u}_2(t)$ with statistical data.

Histogram and $\tilde{u}_2(t)$	Histogram and $\hat{u}_2(t)$

$\tilde{u}_2(t)$ with the parameters from (18), (20) (left sided), (ii) graph of the density of $\hat{u}_2(t)$ with the parameters from (19), (20) (right sided). Parameters correspond to the considered scenario. From the figures in Table 4 it can be seen that the theoretical density from (4) in both cases is consistent with the experimental data, but in the first case (left) the agreement is better. It should be noted that the degree of agreement can be increased by using the "cutting" of the density $u_2(t)$ ($\tilde{u}_2(t)$ or $\hat{u}_2(t)$) into the finite segment (the histogram support).

Results similar to passenger train traffic were obtained when considering statistical data on the freight train traffic through Trans-Siberian main line. The analysis shows that during periods of increase the train flow intensity, the number of sections in which a bimodal distribution of travel time is observed reaches 20%. Accordingly, the shape of the arrival deviations density curve becomes symmetrical or has left-sided skewness.

6   Conclusions and Future Research

The stochastic model of the arrival deviation formation considered in this paper allows us to substantiate the assumption that the presence of independent influencing factors leads to a change in the shape and symmetry of arrival deviation distribution. The flexibility of the model is that the resulting analytical formula allows using arbitrary theoretical distributions that adequately reflect the influence of these factors in various real-world scenarios.

Experimental data collected on Russian railways show that, in practice, bimodal travel time density is not uncommon and is observed quite often. Such nature of the travel time distribution also causes the deformation of the output arrival deviation distribution that is often observed in reality, that is, it acquires a negative skewness. The factor causing the bimodality of travel time density is often determined by mutual influence of the trains in flow due to the difference in their speeds. This fact allows us to build a more adequate train traffic model and increase the accuracy of delay prediction.

Subsequently, the authors plan to carry out an in-depth analysis of the arrival deviation formation process and apply the regularities identified in this research to a number of existing stochastic models of train traffic.

References

1. Muhlhans, E.: Berechnung der Verspatungsentwicklung bei Zugfahrten/ Eisenbahntechn. Rundschau ETR **39**(7/8), 465–468 (1990)
2. Shapkin, I.N., Yusipov, R.A., Kozhanov, E.M.: Simulation of train functioning on the basis of multivariate regulation of technological operations. Bull. VNIIZhT **4**, 30–36 (2006). (in Russian)
3. Karetnikov, A.D., Vorobyev, N.A.: Schedule of train traffic. Transport, Moscow, 301 p. (1979). (in Russian)
4. Carey, M., Kwiecinski, A.: Stochastic approximation to the effects of headways on knock-on delays of trains. Transp. Res. Part B **28**(4), 251–267 (1994)
5. Buker, T., Seybold, B.: Stochastic modelling of delay propagation in large networks. J. Rail Transp. Plan. Manag. **2**(12), 34–50 (2012)
6. Boucherie, R.J., Huisman, T.: Running times on railway sections with heterogeneous train traffic. Transp. Res. Part B Methodol. **35**(3), 271–292 (2001)
7. Meester, L.E., Muns, S.: Stochastic delay propagation in railway networks and phase-type distributions. Transp. Res. Part B **41**, 218–230 (2007)
8. Berger, A., Gebhardt, A., Muller-Hannemann, M., Ostrowski, M.: Stochastic delay prediction in large train networks. In: Proceedings of the 11th Workshop on Algorithmic Approaches for Transportation Modelling, Optimization, and Systems (ATMOS 2011), Saarbrucken, Germany, 8 September 2011, pp. 100–111 (2011)
9. Salido, M.A.: Robustness in railway transportation scheduling. In: Salido, M.A., Barber, F., Ingolotti, L. (eds.) 7th World Congress on Intelligent Control and Automation (WCICA 2008), Chongqing, China, pp. 2833–2837 (2008)
10. Al-Ibrahim, A.: Dynamic delay management at railways. A semi-Markovian decision approach. Ph.D. thesis, Universiteit van Amsterdam, 335 p. (2010)
11. Goverde, R.M.P.: Punctuality of railway operations and time-table stability analysis. Ph.D. thesis, Technical University of Delft, 165 p. (2005)
12. Chebotarev, V., Davydov, B., Kablukova, K.: Random delays forming in the dense train flow. In: World Conference on Transport Research (WCTR 2019), Mumbai, 26–31 May 2019, 13 p. (2019, in Publication)
13. Chebotarev, V., Davydov, B., Kablukova, K.: Probabilistic model of delay propagation along the train flow. In: Kostogryzov, A. (ed.) Probabilistic Modeling in System Engineering, IntechOpen, pp. 171–193 (2018)

Basic Framework for Adjusting the Freight Train Schedule

Boris Davydov[1] ⓘ, Vyacheclav Esaulov[2], Vadim Gopkalo[1(✉)] ⓘ,
and Kseniya Kablukova[3]

[1] Far Eastern State Transport University,
Khabarovsk 680000, Russian Federation
vng@yandex.ru
[2] JST Russian Railways, Far Eastern Branch,
Khabarovsk 680000, Russian Federation
[3] Computer Center FEB RAS, Khabarovsk 680000, Russian Federation

Abstract. Robustness of the train schedule is ensured by use of time margins. The features of each particular section and disturbing factors are not sufficiently taken into account when a master train schedule is created. The paper studies the methodology of effective scheduling the freight train traffic according to the criteria of economic efficiency and punctuality. The methods are proposed for group and individual traffic adjustments. Statistical characteristics of freight train traffic on the main railway line are investigated. The framework of finding margins to the departure headways based on statistical analysis is described. This improvement aimed increasing the punctuality and economic efficiency of freight traffic. The theoretical conclusions are confirmed by statistical data obtained on the Russian railways.

Keywords: Railway traffic · Freight train flow · Dispatching · Schedule · Time margins · Optimization

1 Introduction

Train traffic is subject to disturbing influences which causes schedule deviation as a result. These deviations weaken by adjusting the train flow dynamics which is made by traffic manager effort. For example, dispatching in the passenger segment solves the task to exclude (or decrease) train delays quantity and duration. This provides high level of passenger train punctuality including on time arrivals at intermediate stations. On the other hand, freight train traffic does not imply exact moments of services arriving and departing from the small stations. There is an large additional time which is included in the schedule to provide the freight train on time arrival just on the destination station. Time margins usually added to line sections run time without necessary argumentations. Besides that, features of specific train flow as intensity, daylight or dark hours and others are not taken during the operational planning process into account. So we can see punctuality degradation leads to wasting an infrastructure capacity and to economic losses as a result. Obviously it needs create the methodology for the schedule adjusting which reflects the real situation on the rail line sections.

© Springer Nature Switzerland AG 2019
S. Misra et al. (Eds.): ICCSA 2019, LNCS 11620, pp. 162–176, 2019.
https://doi.org/10.1007/978-3-030-24296-1_15

A stochastic model for the train traffic process [1] is the basis for an effective approach determining the freight train schedule parameters. The model is grounded at the statistical historical data analysis. Besides, it takes the weather conditions and the clear visibility distance into account. This information uses for prediction the probabilistic process of schedule deviations and intertrain conflicts appearance in a future.

On this basis, the main parameters of the schedule are determined, such as travel time at the each line section and departure intervals from technical stations. Timetable of train traffic at the rail link is formed by coordinating the schedule fragments created for all the sections.

This paper examines the methodological issues of operational rescheduling the freight train traffic, taking the criteria of punctuality and economic efficiency of their travel into account. Section 3 analyzes the criteria for operational decisions developing that are used to solve the optimization problem when determining adjustments to the movement of freight trains. Methods are proposed for group and individual traffic control (see Sect. 4). There is described the methodology of finding and processing an experimental data about train traffic in the Sect. 5. The regularities of formation the main indicators of actually executed schedule with the existence of random perturbations are discussed in Sect. 6. The results of the analysis obtained are used to justify the adjustments to the parameters of the schedule (see Sect. 7). There are summarizes the results of the study and outlines the direction for further work in the final section.

2 Literature Review

The problem of providing high quality of operational adjusting train flow finds a wide scale of discussions amid researchers (look at, e.g., 4). Nowadays, admitted that the main point of increasing the quality is a dynamic change of schedule according to the real situation. A case of providing adaptive adjusting in the passenger segment seems was researched in the [2]. At the beginning of 2000th was offered a concept of dynamic adjusting passenger trains flow by European scientists (Railway Dynamic Traffic Management- RDTM) [3]. Further the concept RDTM were designed computer's models for using this principles in complex [4–6].

Extremely fast increasing of railways freight traffic in Russia in 1970th sunk the common productivity of the main lines. This factor was the reason for new interest to the problem of adaptive adjusting. One of the firsts Klimanov [7] estimates in details circle of assignments in the field of operational changes for freight schedule. The problems of optimization train traffic by the adaptive adjusting in Russia were researched by scientists [9–12]. Besides in Europe this kind of problems were researched (see, e.g., review [13]). However, there were not tools for changes freight schedule according to the changed conditions. Taking attention on last articles we have to note [14, 15]. There is a classic way of building optimal schedule in [14]. There is a multiagent way of building optimal schedule in [15]. The particular example of using online adjusting for solving the task automatic change the schedule immediately before the maintenance gap in [16].

The key question in operational adjusting is a complex of full using the infrastructure ability and robustness train traffic, another words is a complex of the «physical top» and the «economy optimal» [17].

There are deterministic and stochastic models, described in [18, 19], for building train schedule. The first group of models allows building optimal schedule and fixing it in real time in case of dominance accurate factors. Anyway, often effectiveness of prediction operational situation would be increase by using stochastic models matched the historical information about train traffic.

Main items of the deterministic analysis of the dynamic operational situations were illuminated in [20–22]. Looking for schedule solves for minimizing delays managing by making discrete models and using methods of line soft programming [23]. The absence of taking attention on the random disturbing factors is the main flaw in modeling.

This flaw amends in significant rate by using stochastic describing of train traffic. In one of the firsts paper in this field analytical method for finding delays by integrate initial delays (on the segment's gate) and further delays was proposed [24]. The model of forming delay while following several trains one after another by using probability approach [25] consider full moving time on the line as a sum of random moving intervals segmentally.

The adjusting middle level model of freight traffic [26] took gathered segment and terminal stations as the basic units. The deep of planning is 12–24 h periods. Micro level deep of operational planning decreases time to 3 h. The simplest segment of adjusting traffic considered the dispatch part of line.

The changes freight traffic have an economy ground just with a decision support system for modeling cases and choosing optimal way of adjusting (look at the review [27]). There is only idea of estimating the results of decisions for improving train traffic by the analysis of the current losses in the [28]. There are limit articles (e.g. [29]) shows the main role energy losses in forming variable part of current losses.

There are some gaps in last researches in the field of management of train flow on main lines and measures of getting optimal traffic controllers decisions. This article gives principally new methodology for solving described difficulties.

3   Criteria for Determining the Operational Decisions

The process of making effective adjustments to a disrupted schedule requires adequate criteria for optimality. There are some important differences between criteria used in passenger and freight segment. Submit the model for creating economy result, oriented mainly on the freight segment, for the reason of proving measures using in modern traffic adjusting.

Train manager solve optimization task in taking adjusting decisions. There are two main measures supporting decisions. First one for the local income - improve rates of using line traffic ability. Second one for general economy result of working whole railways direction.

As were underlined, there are some differences between criteria used in passenger and freight segment. The quality for passenger trains defines by comparing fulfilled and actual schedule using summarize delays for gathered trains. Many papers estimate passenger segment by special term such as train operating reliability [30].

The punctuality in freight segment has a different meaning. There are just some points for dismiss conflicts between trains. Significant additional time in the schedule allows you to rebuild speed ways and changes the order of freight trains in the process of disturbing liquidation.

Nowadays line speed and number of followed trains are the most popular measures for characterize effectiveness of railways infrastructure. Obviously, effectiveness of these measures in the local scale does not enough. Quality of operational adjusting has to be estimated by the rate of using train operating productivity and cost-effective operating mainly. Gather of adjusting decisions which gives the top of income in the process of following freight traffic should be the result of solving optimization task.

Increasing railroad traffic denies renew specific measures for operate adjusting, e.g., there are common income on a vehicle via solving task of increasing trains weight and route distance [31].

Every adjusting decision follows the local change of the loss measure on a quantity ΔE_i. This quantity includes currant traffic losses and penalty losses in case of unpunctuality. In case of submit the optimal schedule decision there is a criteria of summarize the losses on the road line: $\sum_i \Delta E_i \rightarrow \min$.

According to [166], the simple model of traffic losses has a view:

$$E = E_r + T \sum e_i + W_r e_w,$$

where E_r the component defined by the length of mileage for a vehicle

$T = L/v$ – the traffic time for a train on the line segment L;

$e_i^{вp}$ – the unitary loss rate for i-time measure;

$e^{зэ}$, $W^{эквб}$ – the pay rate and the volume of energy power.

As a rule, traffic adjusting follows some changes of traffic time on the ΔT and rebuilds the loss measure on a quantity:

$$\Delta E = \Delta T \sum e_i + \Delta W e_p$$

As an analysis shows, according to the cost rate the power component dominates in the traffic process for Russian railways.

The irrational traffic adjusting can decrease the common income R in the economic result. Particularly, decreasing of the number of trains were followed is a reason of losses. So looking for the optimal decisions has to be based on the model reflected income *in* a traffic process. The clear approach to the economic estimation the freight traffic quality described in [32]. Shown that income P for using a thread of timetable is a difference between the traffic rate R_{map} and the summarize loss C for guiding the train on the route:

$$P = R_{map} - C$$

The objective function used for building the optimal scheme of guiding trains in common case is reaching the top of the **local economic result**: $\sum_i P_i \rightarrow$ max

In a process of building income and loss element of the economy measure using the processed approach distinguished the business processes and fragmentized it on parts (sub processes or elements), further is coming economic estimation of every single parts [33].

The economic model reflected the process of discrete coordinating trains in the space «coordinate – time - cost». The route of changing the object condition is a points gather. Every point reflected income in the moment of finished traffic or technic stopped on the station.

The changing of income in a traffic process on the route shows on the chart (see Fig. 1). Items on the time scale matched the moments of the train operation beginning and finishing. The elements of chart AB, $A'B'$, CD, $C'D'$ matched the operations of following train on the open tracks. The elements BC, $B'C'$ are characterizing changing of economy result on the technic stations.

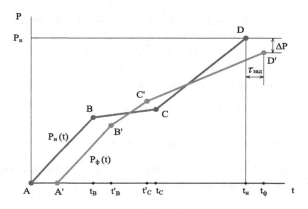

Fig. 1. Example of dynamic changing of economic result

The way ABCD shows the dynamic of income in case of guiding train in schedule. In case of delay (point A') the line of account income $P_\phi(t)$ is situated under planned income line $P_{_H}(t)$. The forcing service of train follows some improving of situation as we can see the point C' is getting above the point C. However on the segment CD the conditions do not give the opportunity for realizing the staff traffic. The train arrives on the destination station with delay $\tau_{зад}$ and economy result decreased on the quantity ΔP relatively of norm.

The choice of effective adjusting decision submitting according to the expression (relatively constant components were excluded):

$$\Delta P = (\Delta R_i - \Delta R_k) - (\Delta E_i - \Delta E_k)$$

4 Group and Sighting Adjustments of Train Traffic

There is an absence of strict demand to the local punctuality, as a specific of freight trains managing gives a relative freedom in traffic adjusting which is aimed to disturbances liquidation. There are two significantly distinguished ways of on-line managing such as group and individual (sighting) adjustment of train traffic. The first one is oriented to prevent gathered conflicts. The second one suggests using an implicit technique which purposefully increases departure headways to create additional time reserve. This reserve can be used for improving the common economic result due to decreasing the threat of intertrain conflict happening.

The sighting adjustment of traffic does not suggest changing the headways and the speed trajectories for all trains. This kind of adjustment represents the schedule correction just for single train for the reason of solving two next tasks. The first one is realized the optimal speed profile of the train approach to the potential conflict point which allows you to dismiss unplanned delay and (or) save the economic losses. The second task is to provide minimal influence to other trains of the same or reverse moving in case of crossing occur. Needs to create a prediction model and solve the local optimization problem for the reason of planning and realizing the on-line traffic adjustments.

The group adjustment suggests choosing so regulation mode for the whole train flow as the goal of decreasing the number of unscheduled delays and energy losses. This kind of traffic adjustments creates by schedule correcting on the determined period of time with duration from one to few hours. The group adjusting of traffic shows especial effectiveness in case of decreasing the train flow intensity.

The group adjusting is in definition the schedule time segments for using intensive or economic mode of managing. The economic mode suggests increasing the departure headways and (or) additional traffic time for trains included in the package.

There are three blocks of adaptation technology used in Traffic Control Centers. The first one is definition of schedule segments in which would be used intensive or economic traffic mode. The separation problem is based on the data described real train run and delay forming at the stations.

The second block suggests finding the order of departing freight trains from the terminal stations with taking attention on the commercial or technical priority. There are two ways of solving the problem. The first one includes prediction economic result for every variant of train departure sequence. The second one considers scenario of forced train waiting on the terminal stations because of random deviations in case of different sequence of depart. The same approach has place in case of looking for the optimal regulation in the telecommunication package net [34].

The adjusting block III provides the assignment a trajectory of motion optimized according to the criteria of a local economic result or energy consumption to each individual train or group of trains. This solves the optimization problem which is similar to the problem of minimizing delays in the flow of passenger services. In this case the freight train has new parameters of technology elements (stops, traffic times).

Usually the system of organizing freight traffic uses the parallel schedule (the Fig. 2). The main operational schedule changes on the limit period of time are increasing the travel time (item c) or intertrains (item) or the sequence of trains following.

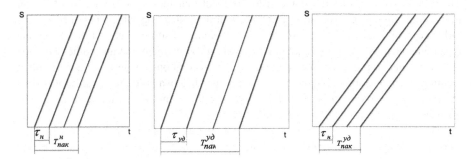

Fig. 2. The ways of organizing the package of trains on the railroad section (a) by schedule; (b) by rareschedule; (c) with increasing traffic time

There is a package of trains «N». The package sends on the section of line from the initial station «A» and fills the time segment $T_{pac} = (N - 1)T_s$, where T_s is a departure headway. In real conditions there are periods of time characterized by decreasing of intensity of train flow. In this very periods of time there is an opportunity of increasing interval between trains to the T'_s. In this case the line of time filled by package of trains becomes wider to the T'_{pac} (Fig. 2b). Increasing of headways prevents distributing further delays in case of short deviation of train from the traffic way. Decreasing the number of unscheduled delays comes dismissing of energy losses.

In the period of decreasing of intensity of trains flow the additional time would be used for organizing energy saving regime. Obviously there is way of organizing the package of trains with appointing for all trains increased travel time (Fig. 2c). The additional traffic time distributed on elementary sections of line in the way providing the top of energy economy and current losses in conclusion. The appointing increased travel time comes energy economy by using the optimal running regimes.

5   Methodology of Analysis Fulfilled Traffic Schedule

In case of creating effective traffic schedule needs to use the traffic parameters close to the real situation. Traditionally the count of the parameters builds on the base of so called pulled count. The reserves of traffic time included in schedule are often unproved. There are sink of punctuality and decreasing of railroad line productivity as a result.

The short-term infrastructure limits, the technic broke, the weather influence and the human factor have the random influences on an accomplishing of the schedule. The human factor shows by different reaction of train team on the same factors and situations and depends on the personal experience, skills and personal features. For the reason of increasing the quality of schedule needs to use the historic information about real train traffic. The information creates the base of stochastic model for using in definition the trains traffic time.

The main feature of suggesting methodology of correcting the train traffic time and intervals between trains is using the statistic data got to distinguished scenarios. There are some gathered scenarios researched in analysis process.

– trains moving in conditions of day and night;
– trains moving in conditions of short of wide intervals;
– trains moving in conditions of appearance of difficulties and absence of difficulties: infrastructure maintenance works, short-term speed limits and so on;
– train moving in conditions of normal weather and spoiled weather.

Obviously has to account some combinations of scenarios in further detailed analysis.

On the first step researched the statistic data about fluent train traffic on the railroad line. There were the statistic data about fluent train traffic in periods of absence of infrastructure maintenance working, technics broke and other negative factors. In the statistic gather were included trains without influence of trains moved in front of.

There were investigated that in January, 2018, in the period of minimal infrastructure maintenance closing on the segment of main line «O – Kh» (360 km by length) were followed 105 trains of odd direction and 50 trains of even direction in a fluent traffic conditions. By another hand, were investigated that in June, 2018, in the period of huge number of infrastructure maintenance works on this segment were fixed 24 trains of odd direction and 4 trains of even direction in a fluent traffic conditions.

In conclusion, absence of negative disturbing factors does not guarantee punctuality in freight segment (Table 1).

Table 1. The figures of accomplishing the freight train schedule

The number of trains on line segment O-Kh:	Periods, 2018	
	January	July
Followed fluently (in even direction)	50	4
Arrived on time (in even direction)	0	0
Followed fluently (in odd direction)	105	24
Arrived on time (in odd direction)	7	1

There were fulfilled the factor analysis of data gathering for the reason of distinguishing influences that come to delays. The trains were gathered in groups on different features characterized the main kinds of influences. In particular, separating was fulfilled by traffic direction (odd/even), time of daylight (day/night), intervals between trains in the moments of depart.

The next step is in building the bar chart of common traffic time on segment of line, defines statistic figures (value of mathematical expectation, standard deviation) and creates of approximation function. The approximation quality is estimated by using probability theories [35]. The probability of increasing the scheduled traffic time is fond by standard methodology by path of integrating matched segment of distribution density of noted figure.

The probability model of analysis the historic data allows to define the additional time to the schedule with account the different scenarios of train traffic situations. It has immediate practical significance especially in time of automatic timetable forming.

6   Regularities of Forming the Schedule Features When Random Disturbances Occur

There is a need to pay attention to the statistical characteristics of train run time in order to correctly determine the train schedule parameters and to adjust them online. The statistical features are various in different periods and those differences depend on the real traffic conditions. Obviously, firstly has to be researched the cases when there are no any negative factors on the rail line such as temporary speed limits, broken infrastructure or damaged rolling stock.

There were taken the historical information about real train traffic on the East region of Transsiberian main rail line. This area is characterized mainly by freight train traffic. There are heavy haul services, in the main, runs in the east direction (in the "even" direction). The overlong trains flow is observed in the west direction (the odd direction). Such a train includes until 100 freight cars. The historical data taken from the information system ASOUP which operated at the JSC «RZD» for some periods of the 2018 that characterized by different traffic conditions. According to historical data about trains that followed without delays

There were analyzed the four sets of the run time random value on the section K-O of the Eastern rail region. The first two samples collected for the odd train traffic direction that traveled in January, 2018. One of this sample matches to day time period, another – to night period. The volume of the first set includes n = 55 samples, the second set is n = 50. The second two sets gathered for "even" trains traveled in July, 2018. Here also one of the samples matches to day time, another – to night period. The volume of the third sample is n = 16, of the fourth sample – n = 8.

Let's check the following statistic hypothesis for every data samples: they were taken for gamma distribution with the density

$$l(t; \alpha_1, \beta) = I(t > 0) \exp(-t/\beta) \frac{t^{\alpha_1 - 1}}{\Gamma(\alpha_1) \beta^{\alpha_1}} \tag{1}$$

with matched parameters $\alpha_1 > 0$, $\beta > 0$.

In literature we can notice the gamma distributions with other parameters and with other form (e.g. [36], p. 170)

We use the Kolmogorov criteria for approximating functions verification. The critical meaning defines by the formula $\lambda_n(\alpha) \approx \frac{\lambda_\alpha}{\sqrt{n}}$, where α is a level of criteria's significance, λ_α is a root of an equation

$$1 - K(\lambda) = \alpha, \tag{2}$$

$K(\lambda)$ - the Kolmogorov function, n- the sample's volume.

Take $\alpha = 0.1$. The root $\lambda_\alpha = 1.224$ in Eq. (2) is known ([37], p. 157, $\lambda = 1.2$). We can also find it by computer.

Let's describe the way of solving for the first sample in details.

The sample 1: The "odd" trains, January, 2018, the day period of time, n = 55. The conclusions of the Kolmogorov criteria based on the statistic's meaning $D_n = \sup_x |F_n(x) - F(x)|$, where $F_n(x)$ - the observational disturbance function, $F(x)$ - the hypothetical disturbance function. For the reason of finding the meaning D_n by the sample, we have to find the parameters of hypothetical disturbance (1). The random figure of common traffic time sights as ρ. As known [100, p. 170]:

$$E\rho = \alpha_1\beta, \quad D\rho = \alpha_1\beta^2. \tag{3}$$

We finds by sample: sample average $\bar{\rho} = \frac{1}{55}\sum_{j=1}^{55} \rho_j = 367.3\ldots$ and sample mean-square deviation $s_0 = \sqrt{\frac{1}{54}\sum_{j=1}^{55}(\rho_j - \bar{\rho})^2} = 14.3$. Solving the system of equations by taken (3) $\bar{\rho}$ instead $E\rho$, and s_0^2 instead $D\rho$:

$$\bar{\rho} = \alpha_1\beta, \quad s_0^2 = \alpha_1\beta^2 \tag{4}$$

relatively α_1 и β we have found the meanings of accurate estimations of the parameters $\alpha_1 \approx 659.8$ and $\beta \approx 0.56$.

For the reason of counting the statistic of D_n has to build the set of variate values for the observational disturbance function and formula of the hypothetical disturbance function $L(x) = \int_{-\infty}^{x} l(t; \alpha_1, \beta)\, dt$, of matched condensation (1). As a result there is a $D_n = 0.088$. There is an approximate critical meaning of the criteria for this sample $\frac{\lambda_\alpha}{\sqrt{n}} = \frac{1.224}{\sqrt{55}} = 0.165\ldots$ so the conclusion is:

the checking statistic hypothesis does not controversies the sample data by the Kolmogorov criteria with level of significance 0,1, because the meaning of the statistic more less than the meaning of critical meaning.

Although there is a comparison of observational and hypothetical disturbance functions in the Kolmogorov criteria, we will show on the Fig. 3 and further the bar chart and hypothetical condensation.

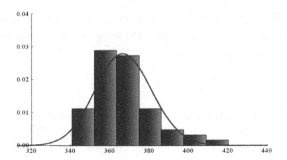

Fig. 3. The disturbances of common train traffic for the odd trains were followed in January, 2018, in day period of time.

The sample 2: The odd trains, January, 2018, the night period of time, n = 50. The approximate meaning of the sample criteria is $\frac{\lambda_\alpha}{\sqrt{n}} = \frac{1.224}{\sqrt{50}} = 0.173\ldots$ So the meaning of $\overline{p} = 370.1$ and $s_0 = 18.6$. We have got the $\alpha_1 \approx 395.9$, $\beta \approx 0.93$ by solving the system of Eq. (4). Afterwards the $D_n \approx 0.094$. As $D_n < \frac{\lambda_\alpha}{\sqrt{n}}$, we have taken the same conclusion as for the first sample with only one distinguish that the hypothetical disturbance has the other parameters. The bar chart and hypothetical condensation are shown on the Fig. 4.

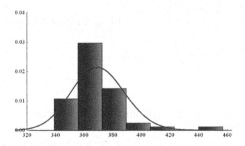

Fig. 4. The disturbances of common train traffic for the odd trains were followed in January, 2018, in night period of time.

The sample 3: The odd trains, June, 2018, the day period of time, n = 16. The approximate meaning of the sample criteria is $\frac{\lambda_\alpha}{\sqrt{n}} = \frac{1.224}{\sqrt{16}} = 0.306$. So the meaning of $\overline{p} = 366.2$, $s_0 = 16.4$. We have got the $\alpha_1 \approx 498.6$, $\beta = 0.734$ by solving the system of Eq. (4). Afterwards the $D_n \approx 0.132$. As $D_n < \frac{\lambda_\alpha}{\sqrt{n}}$, we have taken the same conclusion as for the last samples with only one distinguish that the hypothetical disturbance has the other parameters. The bar chart and hypothetical condensation are shown on the Fig. 5.

The sample 4: The odd trains, June, 2018, the night period of time, n = 8. The approximate meaning of the sample criteria is $\frac{\lambda_\alpha}{\sqrt{n}} = \frac{1.224}{\sqrt{8}} = 0.4327\ldots$ So the meaning of $\overline{p} = 379.4$, $s_0 = 15.5$. We have got the $\alpha_1 \approx 599.14$, $\beta = 0.63$ by solving the system

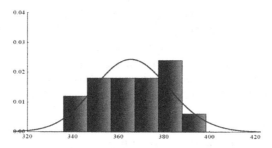

Fig. 5. The disturbances of common train traffic for the odd trains were followed in July, 2018, in day period of time.

of Eq. (4). Afterwards the $D_n = 0.295$. As $D_n < \frac{\lambda_\alpha}{\sqrt{n}}$, we have taken the same conclusion as for the last samples with only one distinguish that the hypothetical disturbance has the other parameters. The bar chart and hypothetical condensation are shown on the Fig. 6.

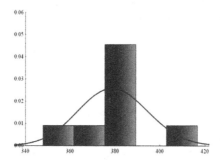

Fig. 6. The disturbances of common train traffic for the odd trains were followed in July, 2018, in night period of time.

7   The Grounding of Train Schedules Adjustments

In a process of planning and building the train schedule has to create the grounded parameters for the reason to fulfill the demands of accurate accomplishment of this schedule. First of all the parameters include the departure headway and the section run time. There is a methodology in this very article for ground the reliable figure of section run time at the determined headway interval.

There is a statistic approach in the base of the methodology. According to this approach creates the probability of fulfill the section run time in different disturbing conditions for the trains flow like speed limits, weather, excess of stations capacity and so on.

On the next step has to select the trains which followed the line in the same conditions. There is a main gather of trains characterized by absence of intensive negative factors for grounding the basic section run time. There is absence of trains delays while move as a particular feature of conflict free following.

Further has to build the bar chart and find the parameters of function approximate the distribution of run time figures. After forming the probability P_{rp} of accomplishing this parameter find the meaning of ground run time which get into the main schedule. This parameter will provide the necessary level of punctuality in arriving trains on the technic stations.

There is an example of a count the run time for the main schedule for the segment of Transsiberian main rail line shown in the paper.

8   Conclusions

The analysis of characteristics of probability distributions of run time and arrive delays of trains create the opportunity of grounding the schedule's demands. There is a high level of punctuality in condition of following the demands. Besides, the analysis of distribution shape helps to recognize the main factors which lead delays while adjusting the trains flow. There are most frequent negative influences as initial delays and unplanned stoppings which lead the further delays in the intensive traffic. There is also incorrect realization of technique processes on the line stations as a reason of happening unscheduled delays before the entrance signals.

References

1. Chebotarev, V., Davydov, B., Godyaev, A.: Stochastic traffic models for the adaptive train dispatching. In: Proceedings of the First International Scientific Conference "Intelligent Information Technologies for Industry" (IITI 2016). Advances in Intelligent Systems and Computing, vol. 451, pp. 323–333 (2016). https://doi.org/10.1007/978-3-319-33816-3_32
2. Karetnikov, A.D.: In: Karetnikov, A.D., Vorob'ev, N.A. (eds.) Grafik dvizheniya poezdov, Transport, 301 (1979)
3. Schaafsma, A.: Dynamisch Railverkeersmanagement, besturings-concept voor railverkeer op basis van het Lagenmodel Verkeer en Vervoer: PhD thesis-Delft, The Netherlands, p. 165 (2001)
4. D'Ariano, A., Pranzo, M., Hansen, I.: Conflict resolution and train speed coordination for solving real-time timetable perturbations. IEEE Trans. Intell. Transp. Syst. 8(2), 208–222 (2007)
5. Quan, L., Dessouky, M., Leachman, R.C.: Modeling train movements through complex rail networks. ACM Trans. Model. Comput. Simul. 14, 32–76 (2004)
6. Baranov, L.A., Erofeev, E.V., Melyoshin, I.S., CHin', L.M.: Optimizaciya upravleniya dvizheniem poezdov: pod red. MIIT, 164 s. (2011)
7. Klimanov, V.S.: Voprosy operativnogo regulirovaniya poezdopotokov na napravlenii: diss... kand. tekh. nauk: 05 12 08. Klimanov Vladimir Sergeevich. 213 s (1982)
8. Nikiforov, B.D., Tishkin, E.M., Makarov, V.M., V.S.Klimanov: Upravlenie poezdnoj rabotoj na napravlenii: ZHeleznodorozhnyj transport, vol. 2, S.17–24 (1982)
9. Levin, D.Y.: Teoriya operativnogo upravleniya perevozochnym processom: monografiya: GOU «Uchebno-metodicheskij centr po obrazovaniyu na zheleznodorozhnom tr-te», 625 s (2008)

10. SHapkin, I.N., YUsipov, R.A., Kozhanov, E.M.: Modelirovanie poezdnoj raboty na osnove mnogo-faktornogo normirovaniya tekhnologicheskih operacij: Vestnik VNIIZHT, vol. 4, S.30–36 (2004)

11. Mohon'ko, V.P., Isakov, V.S., Kurenkov, P.V.: Situacionnoe upravlenie perevozochnym processom: Transport: nauka, tekhnika, upravlenie, vol. 11, S. 14–16 (2004)

12. Ivnickij, V.A., Poplavskij, A.A.: Problema perekhoda k informacionno-upravlyayushchemu rezhimu v sisteme operativnoj organizacii perevozochnogo processa: Vestnik VNIIZHT, vol. 1, S.15–21 (2007)

13. Cordeau, J.-F., Toth, P., Vigo, D.: A survey of optimization models for train routing and scheduling. Transp. Sci. **32**(4), 380–404 (1998)

14. Jamili, A., et al.: Solving a periodic single-track train timetabling problem by an efficient hybrid algorithm. Eng. Appl. Artif. Intell. **25**, 793–800 (2014)

15. Abramov, A.A., Skobelev, P.O., Belousov, A.A., Eremin, A.S., Belov, M.V.: Mul'tiagent-nye tekhnologii adaptivnogo postroeniya grafika dvizheniya poezdov: Intellektual'nye sistemy upravleniya na zheleznodorozhnom transporte, Trudy vtoroj nauchno-tekhnicheskoj konferencii, ISUZHT-2013, Moskva, S.27–29 (2013)

16. Umanskij, V.I.: Ob organizacii propuska poezdov v period tekhno-logicheskih «okon»: ZHeleznodorozhnyj transport, vol. 9, S.21–24 (2009)

17. Abril, M., Barber, F., Ingolotti, L., Salido, M.A., Tormos, P., Lova, A.: An assessment of railway capacity. Transp. Res., Part E: Logistics and Transp. Rev. **44**(5), 774–806 (2008)

18. Cacchiani, V., Huisman, D., Kidd, M., Kroon, L., Toth, P., Veelenturf, L., Wagenaar, J.: Overview of recovery models and algorithms for real-time railway rescheduling. Transp. Res. Part B **63**, 15–37 (2014)

19. Törnquist, J.: Computer-based decision support for railway traffic scheduling and dispatching: a review of models and algorithms. In: 5th Workshop on Algorithmic Approaches for Transportation Modelling, Optimization, and Systems (ATMOS 2005), Palma de Mallorca, Spain, pp. 114–127 (2015)

20. Sotnikov, E.A., SHapkin, I.N.: EHkspluatacionnaya rabota na zheleznyh dorogah mira: ZHeleznodorozhnyj transport, vol. 2, S.72–77 (2009)

21. Kecman, P., Goverde, M., Van den Boom, A.: A model-pre-dictive control framework for railway traffic management. In: Proceedings of the 3th International Seminar on Railway Operations Modelling and Analysis, pp. 57–72 (2011)

22. Lazarev, A.A., Musatova, E.G., Gafarov, E.R., Kvarackheliya, A.G.: Teoriya raspisanij. Zadachi zheleznodorozhnogo planirovaniya: FGBU nauki Institut problem upravleniya im. V. A. Trapeznikova RAN, 287 s (2012)

23. Huisman, D., Kroon, L., Lentink, R., Vromans, M.: Operations research in passenger railway transportation: research paper. Erasmus Research Institute of Management (ERIM), ERS-2005-023-LIS. p. 46 (2005)

24. Muhlhans, E.: Berechnung der Verspatungsentwicklung bei Zug- fahrten: Eisenbahntechn. Rundschau ETR, 39(7/8), 465–468 (1990)

25. Carey, M., Kwiecinski, A.: Stochastic approximation to the effects of headways on knock-on delays of trains. Transp. Res. Part B **28**(4), 251–267 (1994)

26. Goverde, R.M.P.: Punctuality of Railway Operations and Timetable Stability Analysis: PhD thesis - Technical University of Delft, 165 p (2005)

27. Mazzarello, M., Ottaviani, E.: A traffic management system for real-time traffic optimazation in railways. Transp. Res. Part B **41**(2), 246–274 (2007)

28. Mes, M., van der Heijden, A., van Harten, N.: Comparison of agent-based scheduling to look-ahead heuristics for real-time transportation problems. Eur. J. Oper. Res. **181**(1), 59–75 (2007)

29. Davydov, B.I., Kotlyarova, E.V., Davydov, B.I.: EHkonomicheskoe obosnovanie racional'noj skorosti dvizheniya poezdov: EHkonomika zheleznyh dorog, vol. 4, S.17–23 (2008)
30. Kovalev, A.P.: Ocenka nadezhnosti grafika i skorosti dvizheniya pas-sazhirskih poezdov: ZHeleznod. transport, vol. 5, S.42–45 (2006)
31. Mazo, L.A., Mikul'skij, A.A.: Pokazateli ispol'zovaniya perevozochnyh resursov [Tekst]: Mir transporta, vol. 2, S. 66–73 (2008)
32. Gapanenok, V.I., ZHabrov, S.S., Popov, Y.V.: EHkonomika grafika: ZHeleznodorozhnyj transport, vol. 5, S. 24–28 (2006)
33. Karchik, V.G., Pershin, I.V., YUrkova, E.A.: Processnyj podhod k rabote uchastkovoj stancii [Tekst]: EHkonomika zheleznyh dorog, vol. 11. – S. 24–39 (2009)
34. Bent, R., Van Hentenryck, P.: The value of consensus in online stochastic scheduling [Text]. In: Proceedings of the ICAPS, pp. 219–226 (2004)
35. Ventcel' E.S., Ovcharov, L.A., Vysshaya shkola, M.: Teoriya veroyatnostej i ee inzhenernye prilozheniya, 480 s (2000)
36. Borovkov A.A.: Teoriya veroyatnostej: Ucheb. posobie dlya vuzov. – 2-e izd., pererab. i dop.: Nauka, 432 s (1986)
37. Ventcel', E.S.: Teoriya veroyatnostej: Nauka, 576 s (1969)

SaveMyBike – A Complete Platform to Promote Sustainable Mobility

Massimiliano Petri[✉] and Antonio Pratelli

Department of Civil and Industrial Engineering, University of Pisa, Pisa, Italy
{m.petri,a.pratelli}@ing.unipi.it

Abstract. Bicycle theft is a prevalent problem in every country around the world and its part of everyday life, especially in urban areas. At the same time, the return of stolen bicycles to their owners is generally very low. This phenomenon decreases bike use in our cities, and population feels it in depth. In Europe, only 14% of SUMP has done the biennial monitoring plan due to the difficulty to recover data: another need of our urban areas is the continuous monitoring of mobility behaviour useful to verify mobility measures impacts. So, the SaveMyBike platform joins a private bike antitheft and identification service with a mobility rewarding system (including all sustainable transport modes) called "Good-Go" to collect great amounts of anonymised data to analyse mobility patterns and to make mobility measures evaluation and to incentive sustainable mobility.

Keywords: Bicycle · Sustainable mobility · Rewarding · Incentive · Big data · Monitoring

1 The Actual State of Art

In this first part, the state of the art of each feature linked to the SaveMyBike platform is described underlining its actual development level and the main problems. In the following second part, the platform is described in detail, while the third section presents the experimental results obtained from the prototypical application to the city of Livorno. The paper ends with some conclusions outlining and addressing to possible future developments.

1.1 Urban Transport Planning Needs

The recent report on the "User' need analysis on SUMP take-up" [1] submitted to European Commission from Civitas SUMPS-UP project analyzes the current status of SUMP take-up in 328 European Cities indicating drivers, barriers and support needs. One of the main extracted feature is the need of tools to facilitate the biennial SUMP monitoring measure (as recommended from the European SUMP guidelines [2] and from the Italian Transport and Infrastructure Ministerial Decree [3]); this because only 14% of the surveyed cities have a monitoring plan implemented (in Italy no sump has implemented it). Moreover, medium-small cities often do not have adequate resources to implement a suitable ITS system to monitor systematically mobility behavior.

© Springer Nature Switzerland AG 2019
S. Misra et al. (Eds.): ICCSA 2019, LNCS 11620, pp. 177–190, 2019.
https://doi.org/10.1007/978-3-030-24296-1_16

So they do not have enough data to implement all the indices that many European Projects describe in detail to evaluate the impact of their mobility measures [4, 5]. For this reason, SaveMyBike arises, monitoring at low cost a significant population sample in its daily trips as a possible supplier of decision support elements and urban mobility monitoring. Therefore, SaveMyBike is a basic element for many urban areas in order to encourage cycling and plan the whole sphere of mobility.

Traffic emissions in our cities do not decrease as required by European strategic policies [6–8], that is why it is important to highlight sustainable mobility. While the autonomous vehicles market is going to be implemented, thanks to the interests of the car companies, the transition to the 'cycle towns' seems a step back. Recent 'defeats' of the most innovative cycling systems (see the free-floating bike sharing, abandoned due to vandalism and low profitability in some important European companies), show how the possible improvements in the cycle area are still wide. SaveMyBike introduces a new incentive system for private bicycles, able to open new roads for cycle mobility, such as bike-sharing peer-to-peer (a field not yet experienced in reality). In addition, it combines the GOOD_GO system, an innovative rewarding system capable of encouraging sustainable mobility in general.

1.2 Mobility Rewarding System

A detailed description of the state of art regarding the mobility rewarding platforms and systems has been already analyzed in a previous paper [9] but here we want to underline the main problems of these incentive systems. They are mainly experiments often temporally limited to the period of application of European projects. These last coped with individual subsystems of SaveMyBike, in cities such as Berlin ("Green Jobs" with bike discovery), Massarosa and Bari (monetary incentive to use bike), Bologna (with the App "Bella Mossa", today no longer active), Trento/Rovereto (with the "Play&Go" system, the only one with a minimum level of longevity), Singapore (awards) and a few others (see the Deliverable D1.1.2 of the SaveMyBike project at www.savemybike.eu). The main problem is to create a system for a continuous time plan, due to the following:

- problems in the incentives financing;
- problems in the citizen involvement and loyalty

The first problems arise where monetary rewards have adopted, in a wrong way following the rewarding psychology:

In fact, the image of an individual that has communicated to others is an element of important incentive, as it leads the citizen to appear as a person of high social standing.

Often the use of monetary prizes goes against this principle because the citizen loses the social purpose to the more venal economic one. In addition, the virtuous behavior of acquaintances and colleagues can influence individuals and therefore, once again, the use of social networks to spread virtuous behavior acquires a high importance.

Furthermore, Ampt [10] highlights how the communication of one's own virtuous behavior to others involves a mental process of strengthening one's commitment to sustainability.

Prizes that coincide with a person's wishes and stimuli can help to break the habit and create new patterns of behavior. Every time we receive a prize, the new model has reinforced. When we celebrate a behavioral change with prizes, we are recognizing successes, motivating ourselves to continue and increasing self-esteem.

This last part is the fulcrum to keep the changes in time, as self-esteem gives us the courage to keep going and trying. As can be seen, the psychological analysis of the prizes goes well beyond their monetary value. Compared to the monetary prizes, with the presents the participants are more satisfied and motivated, although, when asked, most people say they prefer to receive money.

1.3 Bike Antitheft and Recovery System

Bike-sharing in general is profitable only in metropolitan areas and not in medium-small cities where the use of private bicycles prevails. The use of private bikes could increase if one finds the way to reduce the number of the thefts linked to them.

The phenomenon of theft has become a worldwide phenomenon that has not yet found effective solutions. The European Cyclist Federation said that every year there are 20,000 bikes stolen in London's streets. In Berlin there are 85 bikes stolen per day, which accumulates into a total value of 160 million Euros in stolen bikes across the whole Germany. The Netherlands' Central Bureau of Statistics estimates that 630,000 thefts reported to the police in only 30% while a survey of cyclists in Montreal showed a percentage of returned 2.4%. There are also anti-theft systems certified but, to date they only delay the theft but do not prevent it. SaveMyBike tries to develop low-cost systems that can really be used by everyone, studying advanced and differentiated sensors depending on the cost of the bike, including futuristic solutions that allow efficient and low-cost communications (e.g. Lora sensors). At the Italian National level, the ANCMA-National Association of Cycles, Motorcycles and Accessories (branch of ConfIndustria) are developing the BiciAcademy project with the development of a web platform for the registration of the different bike identification systems that will go into operation after summer 2019. SaveMyBike could be among the first identification systems to connect with this national platform and have an official recognition within the National Bicycle Register. There are identification systems such as "SecurMark" that fulfill this need by writing a code on the bicycle frame and protecting it with a label. This system is only limited to this function, moreover it is easily manipulated and requires the close reading of the single bar code.

2 The SaveMyBike Platform

The strength of SaveMyBike consists in joining a set of services for the cycling world with a rewarding multimodal system in a single platform, succeeding in creating a system that adapts to every type of city and that brings benefits to more types of customers. SaveMyBike platform is a new system to accommodate every type of technological development, the interest of citizens, administrations, large companies (which have a Mobility Manager who must monitor home-work travels), schools (monitoring and user rewards) with the "bicibus" and the "pedibus" and for the home-study trips. SaveMyBike also accomplishes the interest of the environmental and cycling associations or other association types and the interest of the activities located in the urban area. The platform is customizable and connectable to other existing platforms in a streamlined way (see Fig. 1).

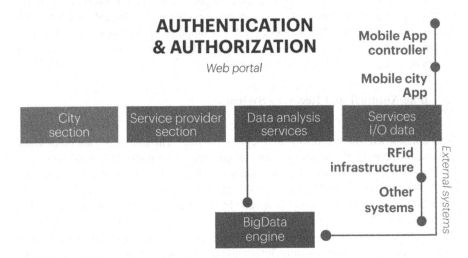

Fig. 1. Scheme of the GOOD_GO platform

In addition, the combination of multiple services, such as the burglar alarm, the description and complaint of the bike, the discovery of the bikes, the reward and the *gamification* [11] of each of its elements, make SaveMyBike an attractive element for most citizens. All this above allows, for the first time, the direct collection of trips data for a statistically significant population sample, proposing itself as a system for collecting user data of particular interest to the Administrations.

In the following paragraphs, the two main parts ("bike" and "rewarding" sections) has described.

2.1   The Bike-Side Platform

SaveMyBike offers an antitheft-identification-recovery system for private bikes providing several sensors offers that vary with the value of the bicycle to be 'protected'. The 'basic version' provides a retrieval/tracing system through additional low-cost tags (about 10 € 0.20/each) RFID UHF external "hidden" legible at the same time simply walking a meter away from the bikes, then with an high efficiency level. To this it add an identification system consisting of a low-cost tag (about 4.0 Euros) RFID HF to be installed inside the bike frame, unmovable and readable by telescopic antennas equally low-cost but invisible, non-intrusive on the structure of the bicycle. Finally, it can be added (this is an ongoing research) a bluetooth device coupled with an accelerometer capable of communicating with the safe area bluetooth reader and able of emitting an acoustic signal during the theft/movement of the bike. It then joins an internal digital identification/digital plate to an external tracing system that also becomes, in its extended version, a system of disincentive to theft.

The system is based on a client-side platform called GOOD_GO with the homonymous App (see Fig. 2) allowing the users' registration, the uploading of their bike characteristics and images, the complaints of theft and the record of notification in case of bike recovery.

Fig. 2. Some screenshots of the GOOD_DO App relative to the bike module

For example, the complaints of theft allows you to build maps of areas at risk of theft to be communicated to citizens or to be 'in safety' through the ex-post installation of video cameras or other technologies. This service is not today present in Europe, but is in the USA with the BIKE INDEX system where you record the bike, alert in case of theft and the community helps to find the bike. As you can see, SaveMyBike becomes, therefore, a system to find the bike also 'participated', where users access the list of stolen bikes and can report the probable finding, also indicating the location and a photo. This is, moreover, an incentive to citizens to customize the bike as much as possible so that others can find it more easily.

In addition to the client side platform, there is a platform to manage sensor installations, allowing the joining of each sensor ID to the its bike and to the owner, the management of installation booking (cancelations, changes, corrections, etc.) and the annual sensor revision service (see Fig. 3). There is the ADMIN section that manages of user types, roles and permissions, the SMD section that allows portable RFid reader loading and assignment to operators (auxiliary, police, sensor installators, etc.), the

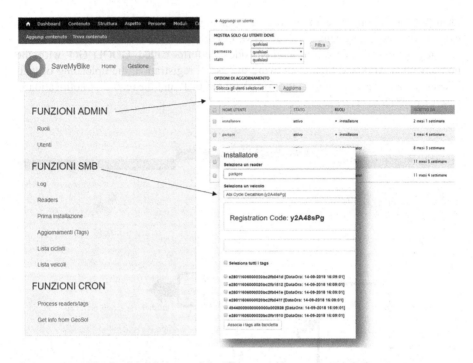

Fig. 3. Some images of the bike sensors management platform

installation of additional tags to already "*sensorized*" bike and manage the user list and "*sensorized*" bike list.

2.2   The Rewarding-Side Platform GOOD_GO

The reward system is integrated in the same GOOD_GO App; it tracks daily trips monitoring the mean speed, the total distance and time, the start and end time of each track, calculating a general individual score about sustainable mobility and the following three indices groups (see Figs. 4 and 5):

- Environmental indices: atmospheric emissions produced and avoided about CO_2, SO_2, NO_x, CO and PM10
- Transport cost indices: transport costs per single mode aggregated or divided by km
- Health indices
  - Calories consumed in the trips
  - Benefit index (reduction of the probability of cardiovascular disease from the HEAT model [12])

The reward platform developed and already working in the prototype, implements welfare policies towards the elderly, or divides the premiums by age group. To date, in Europe there are rewarding systems, such as "Positive Drive", or "Bella Mossa", but they all put the whole population in competition, slowly losing the participation of an

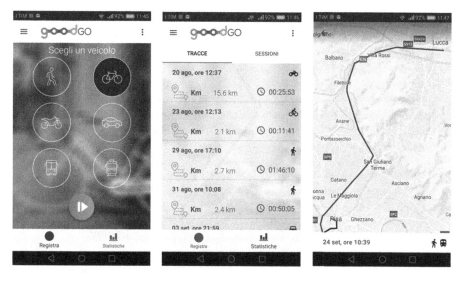

Fig. 4. Some screenshots about the tracking system

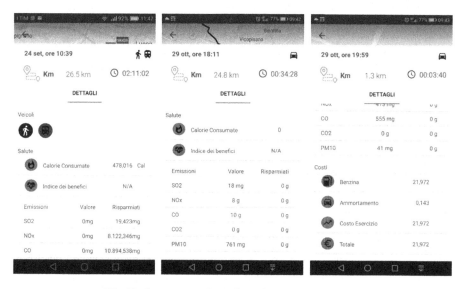

Fig. 5. Some screenshots about the calculated indices

important band of citizens, the elderly. SaveMyBike divide population in three age groups giving a weekly prize to the first classified of each one.

The reward system gives the possibility to involve local businesses, offering them the opportunity to promote their products in this way.

There are other systems connected to the single reward function (e.g., "Positive Drive" developed by the Dutch IJsberg Consultants; "Bella Mossa" developed by the

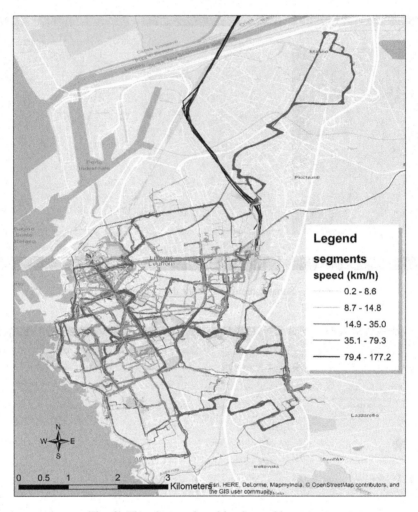

Fig. 6. The trips monitored by the tracking system

English BetterPoints Spitsmijden a Dutch incentive project; "Travel Smart Rewards" a pilot study for Singapore commuters; "TripZoom" developed by the Dutch Locatienet; "TravelWatcher" developed by the Dutch project I-Zone; "Viaggia Play & Go" developed by Smart Community Lab and applied in the Italian cities of Trento and Rovereto and others). Nevertheless, the main problem, to a certain extent, of these systems lies in their low audience of the participants. This last problem has solved by SaveMyBike, which introduces the private bicycles service, a service very felt by citizens that allows them to be loyal to them continuously.

3   The Prototypical Application Results

In the prototypal application period, which runs from September to December 2018 (the system is still active even today) more than 2.158 displacements have been traced (see Fig. 6) with a total number of over 180,000 GPS points. In total, 1,000 citizens were involved with over 300 "sensorized" bicycles.

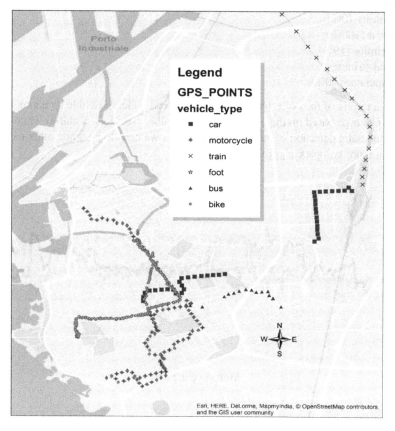

Fig. 7. Some examples of GPS points acquired

For each GPS point acquired (see Fig. 7), the Good_Go App has detected the following attributes (we find an attributes completeness very variable and represented in brackets as percentage):

- Transport mode used (100%);
- Belonging tracks (100%);
- Longitude and latitude (100%);
- Acceleration spatial components X, Y, Z (100%);
- Signal accuracy (100%);

- Timestamp (100%);
- Battery consumption per hour (69%);
- Battery level (69%);
- Device bearing (86%);
- Device roll (86%);
- Device pitch (86%);
- GPS bearing (97%);
- Elevation (100%);
- Humidity (0%);
- Lumen (100%);
- Proximity (19%);
- Speed (67%);
- Temperature (0%)

The analysis of the collected GPS points showed a clear possible detection system for the bike trips based on the only acceleration values (see Figs. 8 and 9) while for the future automatic detection of other transport modes we need to integrate other territorial data in a more complex algorithm [13] (Fig. 10).

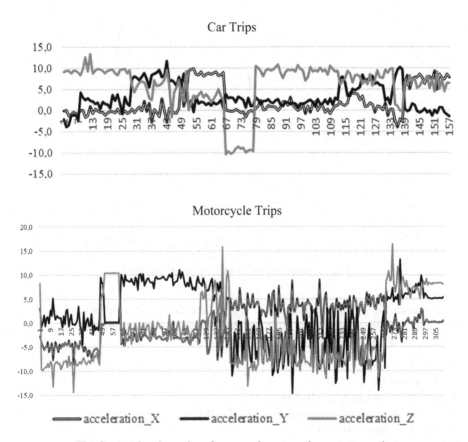

Fig. 8. Acceleration values for car and motorcycle transport modes

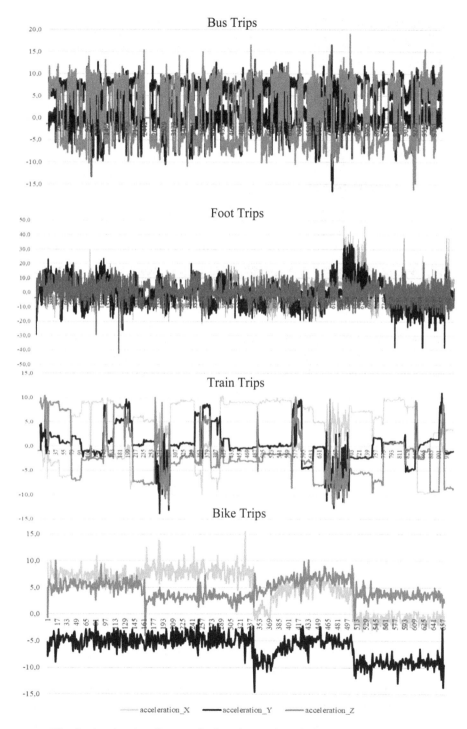

Fig. 9. Acceleration diagrams for bus, foot, train and bicycle transport modes

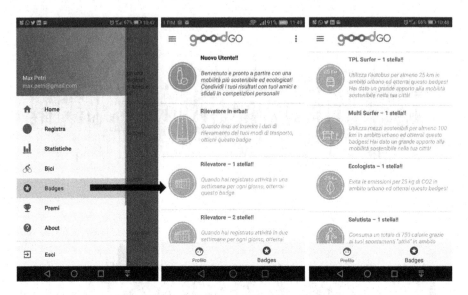

Fig. 10. The "*Gamification*" system with badges

Finally, we talk about the theft complaints acquired from the App Good_Go. In the four months of the prototypical application, among the 300 sensorized bicycles 9 were stolen (with a percentage of 3%). In Fig. 11, we represents some registered theft locations labeled with the bike id, the theft day and time.

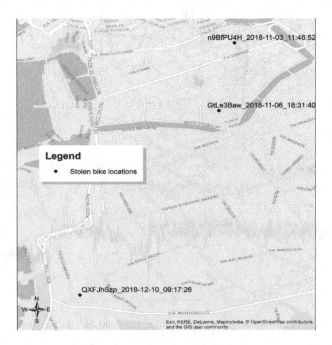

Fig. 11. Some registered bike thefts

4   Conclusions and Future Developments

The actual strength of SaveMyBike lies in its large number of potential users. They can be summarized in citizens and city users, municipal administrations, school of all levels, big companies (where a mobility manager is obligatory), insurances, associations of cyclists/environmentalists, managers of activities connected with the use of the bike (bike renters, hotels providing a bike park and others), bike manufacturers, bicycle sellers/repairers, engineering studies and commercial activities. The prototypical application has shown very good results, with the feasibility confirmation about an automatic transport recognition system, and a big interest from citizens for the whole service. Moreover, the project has seen the emergence of a cooperation system with the people who gave voluntary availability to walk around the city and detect bicycles parked along the roads.

In the future, the SaveMyBike sensors could also allow the communication between bike and autonomous vehicles by preventing accidents and giving more safety for cyclists. A first solution has proposed by the AUTOPILOT project but plans to install a real OBU-On Board Unit on the bikes, in respect to a cost that is not desirable for the final user. In the SaveMyBike project we would like to evaluate a low-cost system based on LORA technology, whose readers have rays of action of 500–800 m which can cover the entire city. This technology can allow the localization of the bicycle parking area and can facilitate data communication [14].

In this way, an autonomous vehicle can, thanks to its OBU, detect the cycle vehicles even without having direct visibility and, therefore, be able to activate actions capable of avoiding dangerous accidents (not possible with actual cameras or laser scanners).

Therefore, the results of the prototypical application and the previous analysis clearly show that now it is time to start the SaveMyBike improvement phase that will engage partners for a unique project in Europe.

References

1. Chinellato, M., et al.: Sumps-Up-Users' needs analysis on SUMP take up, European Programme for Accelerating the Take-up of Sustainable Urban Mobility Plans, Deliverable 1.2 (2017)
2. Rupprecht Consult: Guidelines. Developing and Implementing a Sustainable Urban Mobility Plan, ELTISPlus Project (2014)
3. Italian Transport and Infrasctucture Ministry: Individuazione delle linee guida per i piani urbani di mobilita' sostenibile, ai sensi dell'articolo 3, comma 7, del decreto legislativo 16 dicembre 2016, n. 257. (17A06675) - DECRETO 4 agosto 2017
4. DISTILLATE Project: Improved Indicators for Sustainable Transport and Planning, Deliverable C1 Sustainable Transport Indicators: Selection and Use (2005)
5. Rupprecht Consult: Guidelines. Developing and Implementing a Sustainable Urban Mobility Plan, ELTISPlus Project (2014)

6. European Commission 2007: Sustainable Urban Transport Plans - Preparatory Document in relation to the follow-up of the Thematic Strategy on the Urban Environment, Annex, 25 September 2007. Source. http://ec.europa.eu/environment/urban/pdf/transport/2007_sutp_annex.pdf

7. European Commission, 2009: Action Plan on Urban Mobility COM (2009) 490/5. Source: http://ec.europa.eu/transport/themes/urban/urban_mobility/action_plan_en.htm

8. European Commission 2011: WHITE PAPER. Roadmap to a Single European Transport Area – Towards a competitive and resource efficient transport system. COM (2011) 144 final. Source: http://ec.europa.eu/transport/themes/strategies/2011_white_paper_en.htm

9. Petri, M., Frosolini, M., Pratelli, A., Lupi, M.: ITS to change behaviour: a focus about bike mobility monitoring and incentive—The SaveMyBike system. In: 16th International Conference on Environment and Electrical Engineering (EEEIC). IEEE (2016) https://doi.org/10.1109/eeeic.2016.7555463. ISBN: 978-1-5090-2321-9

10. Ampt, E.: Understanding voluntary travel behaviour change, Paper presented to the XXVI Australian Transport Research Forum, Wellington (2003)

11. Kazhamiakin, R., Pistore, M., Marconi, A., Valetto, G.: Using gamification to incentivize sustainable urban mobility", Conference Paper (2015). www.researchgate.net/publication/281377423

12. World Hearth Organization-Regional Office for Europe: Health economic assessment tool (HEAT) for cycling and walking. Methods and user guide on physical activity, air pollution, injuries and carbon impact assessments. Supported by the Project Physical Activity through Sustainable Transport Approaches (PASTA) (2017)

13. Petri, M., Fusco, G., Pratelli, A.: A new data-driven approach to forecast freight transport demand. In: Murgante, B., et al. (eds.) ICCSA 2014. LNCS, vol. 8582, pp. 401–416. Springer, Cham (2014). https://doi.org/10.1007/978-3-319-09147-1_29

14. Petri, M., Pratelli, A., Nepa, P., Giannecchini, S.: The SaveMyBike Project: ITS Technologies and Rewarding Policies to Improve Sustainable Mobility in Cities. Poster n. 10922, Transportation Research Arena, TRA, Vienna (2018)

Big Data and Policy Making: Between Real Time Management and the Experimental Dimension of Policies

Grazia Concilio[1], Paola Pucci[1($\boxtimes$)], Giovanni Vecchio[2], and Giovanni Lanza[1]

[1] Dastu, Politecnico di Milano, piazza da Vinci 32, 20133 Milan, Italy
{grazia.concilio,paola.pucci,
giovanni.lanza}@polimi.it
[2] CEDEUS, Pontificia Universidad Católica de Chile, Los Navegantes 1963, Providencia, Santiago de Chile, Chile
giovanni.vecchio@uc.cl

Abstract. The paper aims at exploring how big data can support decision making for and about cities at different strategic levels and temporal perspectives. Big data can improve the effectiveness of urban mobility policy, but such contribution heavily needs to consider the multiplicity of big data, as reflected by three elements: the different sources that produce data and the knowledge they provide; the many actors who produce, store, manage and use big data; the different roles that data may play in the different stages of a policy making process. Based on this, the paper presents a sound policy cycle focusing on the experimental dimension of policy making and provides a ground for the assessment of project implications for the 'business of government'. The paper considers specifically mobility policies and, referring to the experience of the Polivisu research project, provides a policy cycle tested in relation to three pilot cases using big (open) data visualizations in a clear mobility policy context: Ghent (Belgium), Issy-les-Moulinaux (France), and Pilsen (Czechia). By considering the cycle of the policy process, the policy making activities the pilots are experiencing, and the data they are processing, the paper shows how the pilot cases are internalizing the policy experimentation opportunity, addressing the further pilots' activities, into a continuous policy adaptation cycle.

Keywords: Policy cycle · Experimental dimension · Pilot cases · Big data · Urban mobility

1 Introduction

Cities are more and more recognized and referred to as environments of data production. The digitalization of an enormous amount of existing services and the development of new smart ones are the evident causes of the city being a data producing engine. Data in fact represents the key ingredient for the services to be properly and effectively produced and supplied [1]: the use of services produce data that, at the

© Springer Nature Switzerland AG 2019
S. Misra et al. (Eds.): ICCSA 2019, LNCS 11620, pp. 191–202, 2019.
https://doi.org/10.1007/978-3-030-24296-1_17

same time, is used as basic resources for the services to be growingly effective and efficient. The more this is true, the more the produced data sets give rise to big-data, that is, "everything captured or recorded digitally by modern information and communications technologies such as networked sensors, 'smart' objects and devices, the web and social media" [2, p. 28].

Big data is both an opportunity and a resource for policy making: the size of information it provides, the epistemological value it assumes and its necessary interactions with other forms of knowledge provide "an important new source of insights into the management, governance and experience of urban life" [2, p. 29], which nonetheless is still object of a huge academic and practice-oriented debate [3–5]. However, the opportunities ICTs provide in supporting urban policy making processes represents a basic component of the discourse on "smart cities" and several public institutions, such as the EU, are devoting efforts to strategically promote their use towards a "smart" urban growth [6, p. 3]. The aim of these efforts is to experiment and establish processes of evidence-based policy making using the most advanced technologies and big data to "find patterns, linkages and relationships that shed fresh light on policy problems" [7].

Based on these premises, the paper aims at exploring how big data can support decision making for and about cities at different strategic levels and temporal perspectives. Drawing on an ongoing research project (Polivisu) in which three pilot cases are using big (open) data visualizations in relation to mobility issues, the paper presents a policy cycle focusing on the experimental dimension of policy making and provides a ground for assessing the project implications for the 'business of government' as far as mobility policies are concerned.

2   Urban Decisions and the Multiplicity of Big Data

The multiplicity intrinsic of big data explains the relevance of the knowledge it provides and its potential contribution to urban decision making, but also raises significant practical issues. Three elements, here explored in relation to urban mobility, are crucial for the multiplicity of big data: its sources, its possible contributions to policy making, and the actors involved in its production, storage, management and usage.

2.1   Big Data and Its Different Sources

Big data improves our ability to understand human mobility in many respects: first, it makes possible to overcome the limitations in the detection of latency typical of traditional data sources; second, it can exploit the pervasiveness guaranteed by the ubiquity of digital devices and mobile phone networks; third, a 'longitudinal perspective' becomes available on the variability in human travel activities [8], thus validly complementing traditional research methods. These conditions depend strongly from the type of sources of big data: whether data is produced voluntarily or not, aggregated or not, anonymous or not, its possible uses in urban planning and in other policy domains changes, and determines different challenges in terms of use and interoperability with other data relevant for evidence-based policy making processes.

Different sources produce three main categories of big data [9, p. 4]: directed, automated and volunteered. *Directed data*, monitoring the movement of individuals or physical objects moved by humans, is generated by traditional forms of surveillance. *Automated data* is produced by automatic digital devices such as mobile phones, capture systems, clickstreams and sensors, but also by image data like aerial and satellite images. *Volunteered data* is generated by users who interact with social media or produce crowdsourced data contributing to a common system, such as OpenStreetMap.

Such multiplicity of sources raises the issue of organizing and structuring the data itself as well as reducing its size by trying to keep the information (signal) alive and by eliminating everything that is not needed for the analysis (noise). This issue is crucial for the policy use of big data: the availability of a large amount of data improves the accuracy and completeness of the measurements to capture phenomena that were previously difficult to investigate, but at the same time increases the level of complexity in the approaches finalized to process, integrate and analyze this data [10]. Central in this sense is also the expediency to improve/validate/integrate big data with existing ones. If the main features characterizing big data are velocity (data that can be obtained in real time), volume (large amount of data) and variety (data coming from different sources), it follows that big data is not 'big' for its size, but for the possibility of being linked to other data from different sources [11]. Data integration would be crucial also to gain new insights on existing and potential policy issues involving multiple actors.

2.2 Big Data and Actors' Expertise

According to Kitchin [9, p. 136], "data are not useful in and of themselves. They only have utility if meaning and value can be extracted from them". The use of big data to face mobility issues is therefore deployed in an environment in which different expertise are involved, from the wide range of actors who have a deep knowledge on software and hardware management, statistics, machine learning and other technical specialists [9, p. 202], to the subjects with the political and managerial competencies required to define a policy problem that the use of big data can contribute to face, design a policy solution to it and mediate between all the actors involved in the process. This last skill is fundamental, considering the crucial role of private companies in relation to big data [12, p. 7].

Four categories of expertise should be involved as actors to work effectively with data in a policy making process [13, pp. 15–21]:

Domain expertise, with a profound knowledge and understanding of the humanities and social science tradition connected to the policy issue. It can guide the process of data selection and help in defining the policy problem;

Data expertise, to select, gather, assess the quality and validity of data and to understand the relation between them and the material objects and dynamics they describe in a digital form;

Analytical expertise, to help obtaining relevant insights from big data through specific technical actions and digital tools for research and analysis purposes;

Project management expertise, relevant to make the whole process and the interactions between different expertise running smoothly.

The multiplicity of big data is thus a challenge for policy makers and has relevant consequences in an operative perspective.

2.3 Big Data and Their Role in Mobility Policy Making

Even if the increasing use of big data in the policy domain poses relevant challenges and is subject to limitations, networked technologies are important drivers of knowledge for mobility and urban practices: from a policy perspective, big data provides a huge amount of information, offering a question-oriented knowledge. Depending on the question or issue faced by the subject using it, big data both supports a real-time knowledge of mobility needs/practices and offers valuable support for 're-scaling' urban policy, contributing to multi-scalar maps of heterogeneous urban phenomena. In both perspectives, big data becomes a valuable tool for (mobility) policy makers: the use of data along the policy making process in fact can contribute to create evidences for developing a broader knowledge of complex issues and for the design of more effective policy.

The contribution of big data changes according to the stages of the policy making process (Fig. 1), which can be considered a recurring sequence of three main cycles: design, implementation, and evaluation [14]. These cycles are strongly interdependent, and this is at the core of the experimental dimension of policy making that our proposal intends to implement. The *policy design* cycle is focused on highlighting the existence

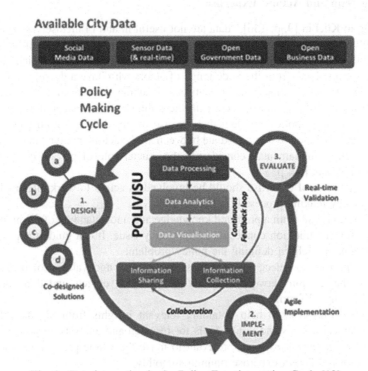

Fig. 1. Data integration in the Policy Experimentation Cycle [18].

of a collective problem, mobilizing a set of goals and objectives in relation to it, and defining policy strategies and actions as attempts to contribute to solving the problem; in this phase, the usage of big data could be relevant to promote forms of problem crowdsourcing [15]. The *policy implementation* cycle gives form to the policy defined in the previous stages, delivering it to the public; data can contribute to putting the policy into practice and reshaping it, if necessary, depending on the reactions of the setting or on the achieved results. In this complex stage, data contributes to manage urban mobility issues in real time; to support private initiatives addressing emerging urban mobility needs [16]; to improve the 'infostructure' of mobility by providing information that is updated, complete and personalized [17]; to involve citizens in the implementation of policy measures; to provide accountable information. Finally, the *policy evaluation* cycle examines the desired and undesired impacts achieved with the implementation of a policy; data can contribute to estimating the obtained outcomes and if the desired changes were obtained.

3   Data Relevance at the Intersection Between Data Production Systems and Policy Making

3.1   Data for Short- and Long-Term Decisions and Reasoning

The three issues discussed in the previous section show how big data introduces unprecedented complexity in policy making, using new technologies but, more importantly, questioning the very basis of the policy making process towards new interpretative models. The growing data availability increasingly affects the way we analyze complex urban problems and make decisions for cities: data are a promising resource for more effective decisions as well as for better interacting with the context where decisions are implemented.

Decisions for and about cities are made at different urban scales, refer to different strategic levels and have different time perspectives, with reciprocal interdependencies that are changing due to the data availability. Here we mainly focus on the interplay between the different steps of decisions in policy making (those introducing the longest time perspective) and those necessary for the daily management of the city (connected to the shortest, real-time perspective), an intersection at which data can play a key role. Short-term management is embedded in the smart sphere of decisions for/about cities: here decisions are less analytic and more routinary. Routines may depend on data-driven learning mechanisms (also using data series) supporting smart systems to recognize situations and apply solutions/decisions that have already proved to work. The decision has a temporary value related to the specific condition detected in a precise moment by the smart system. Opposite to real-time decisions, policy making works in a long-time perspective. Anticipatory is the prevailing mode for reasoning in this case and data-driven models are often adopted as supporting means to deal with the impacts of the policy measures, representing thus a relevant source for exploring decision options mainly having a strategic nature (since they consider recurring issues and aim at more systemic changes) (Fig. 2).

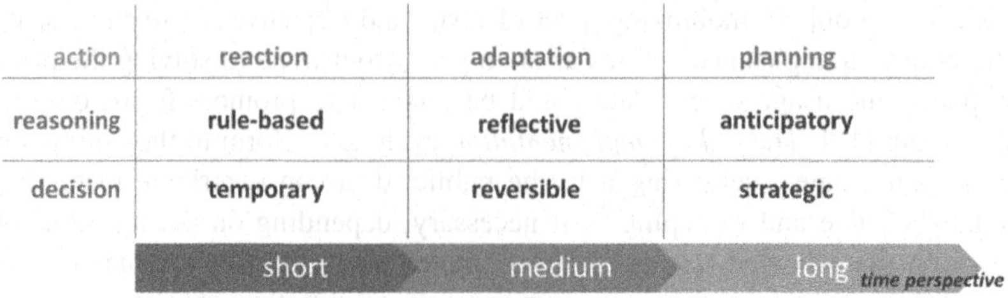

action	reaction	adaptation	planning
reasoning	**rule-based**	reflective	anticipatory
decision	**temporary**	reversible	strategic

short   medium   long *time perspective*

Fig. 2. Decision/reasoning along diverse timeframes

Between short-term and long-term decisions a variety of situations is possible, which may be considered as characterized by decisions having a reversible nature: they are neither strategic in value (like those oriented to long term perspective for systemic changes), nor aiming at dealing with temporary, contingency situations asking decisions which are known as having the same (short) duration of the phenomenon to be managed. For such decisions, reasoning is not (fully) anticipatory and its temporariness allows reflection as embedded in action. Within the three different time-frames, actions are different in nature and show different use and role of data:

- in the *short term*, action (the smart action) is mainly reactive; real time data are used as reference info to interpret situations;
- in the *medium term*, action is mainly adaptive; data series, including current data, are used to detect impacts of the action itself and to improve it along time;
- in the *long term*, action has a planning nature; data series become crucial to detect problems and to develop scenarios for long lasting changes.

3.2 Opportunities for an Experimental Approach to Policy Design

The interdependency between policy design, implementation and evaluation is strictly related to two factors, especially when considering the role (big) data can play. Design and implementation can be clearly and sequentially distinguished when a systematic, impact-oriented analysis is possible at the stage of design as it allows a clear costs and benefits assessment of different action opportunities (see the planning mode of strategy making in [19]).

Comprehensive analyses have the value to drive long range, strategic actions, and consequently show a clear dependency and distinction of the implementation from the design cycle. At the same time, the bigger is the uncertainty (not only related to the possible lack of data, rather also consequent to the high complexity of the problem/phenomenon to be handled), the smaller is the chance to carry out a comprehensive analysis. Therefore, goals and objectives cannot be defined clearly and the policy making shifts from a planning towards an adaptive mode [19]. Inevitably, this shift reduces the distance between design and implementation, transforming policy design into a more experimental activity that uses learning from implementation as food for design within adaptive dynamics (Fig. 3).

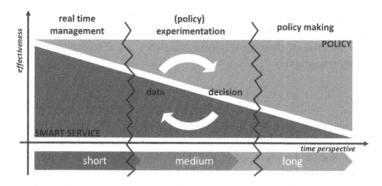

Fig. 3. Real time management vs policy making.

Coherently with the discussion on the time frame perspective adopted in the previous paragraph, it may be clear that a merge between policy design and implementation is consistent with the situation described in the medium term: within an adaptive mode for decisions, policy making can clearly become experimental. Experiments may refer to both the policy strategies and measures. They can reduce the risk of trial-errors approaches while considering the learning in action opportunity to improve, adapt, adjust the policy while making it in order to increase its capacity to affect the context in an evolving manner. Differently from the Mintzberg's considerations [19], the merge between policy design and implementation does not represent a sort of inevitable but not preferred option when a comprehensive analysis is not possible. In the era of (big) data availability, this merge can be looked at as an opportunity to create policies while verifying the policies themselves throughout their interactions with the contexts.

4   The Experimental Dimension at Work in the Polivisu Pilots

The experimental dimension of policy making is at the core of the concept of the Polivisu project. The experimental dimension puts emphasis on the learning dynamics of policy making through a strong relation with iterations cycle. This section reconsiders the elements discussed in the previous sections and observes them in action, discussing three pilot cases that differently face the limits and opportunities related to data sourcing, mobility policy-related data use and collaboration among different actors: these use big (open) data visualizations in a clear mobility policy context, to deal with different transport and mobility issues. The pilot cases are Ghent (Belgium), Issy-les-Moulinaux (France), and Pilsen (Czechia). This process works at two scales. From one side, it relies on small scale experiments, exploiting the real time opportunities offered by big data, in each of the pilot. From the other, it concerns also large-scale experiments as an entire policy cycle taking into account the in-depth throughout monitoring enabled by big data. For each pilot, the next subsections describe the problem to be faced, the imagined solutions, the actions taken, the following steps and a brief discussion on the short- and long-term decisions and reasoning allowed by data as experimented by the pilots.

The three pilots are at their second cycle of development (on four planned ones in the project) and key results are not yet clearly there. Still it is possible to highlight the experimental dimensions they are exploring and they are discussed at the closure of each following paragraphs.

4.1 Ghent

Ghent is the second biggest city in the Flanders with 260.000 inhabitants and it is an industrial and commercial focal point for the region. Moreover, it is an important cultural center due to the presence of the well-known Ghent University. The participation of Ghent in the Polivisu project is related to the increasing number of students and commuters attracted by the local university and other important research centers located within the municipality: around 440.000 city users, not registered as residents, are estimated to reach or reside in Ghent on a daily base. This trend generates wide impacts on many policy domains, including mobility, and is combined with other urban issues, such as uncontrolled increase in housing prices and crisis of commercial activities.

The interest of Ghent in the opportunities provided by the Polivisu toolbox are mainly related to the potential role that big data can play in measuring the extent of the city user population, with a specific focus on students' housing. Big data in fact may help policy makers in adapting city services to changing populations, assessing the impact of policy proposals on previously 'hidden' inhabitants but also estimating the effects determined by students on city services. The process followed by Ghent started in 2016 with an evaluation on local policies that assessed the necessity to use data to understand the extent of the student population. Subsequently, the aim of the following design phase was to find available microscale data sources to build informative and intuitive visualization for the different stages of the policy making process related to student housing. The pilot worked in the implementation phase assessing the availability and quality of data related to student housing to build a visualization tool, defining relevant local stakeholders to collaborate with.

Ghent uses big data to react to an emerging issue, the growing presence of city users and the impact they generate. The city intends to use visualisations as a tool for anticipatory reasoning, contributing to represent the presence of city users before defining evidence-based strategic measures to deal with their growing number. Within this ongoing process, until now an evidence-based policy making process involving the use of (big) data has proved to be challenging due to the difficulties in obtaining information that is privately owned or with different degrees of quality and completeness. For this reason, the main action that has been taken by the pilot is a negotiation that is both internal (across different administrative entities) and external (with communication providers) to facilitate data gathering. In parallel, promoters have started considering data scraping from social media (Twitter and Facebook) as a potential source of information. In future steps, the intention is to increase the amount of data, looking for new ways to find information that were not considered before and could help to produce more insightful visualizations.

At the process level the experimental dimension of the Ghent pilot is related to the exploration of big data as an opportunity to explore the problem at a larger scale within the context of the students' life in the city. The learning will not be limited to the intention to create the evidence for the demonstration of the hypothesis rather also to the understanding of their systemic interaction with urban services and spaces. The level of small experiments is not yet in the focus of this pilot.

4.2   Issy-les-Molinaux

Issy-les-Molinaux is a large town of 70.000 inhabitants in the Ile de France Region, bordering the city of Paris, particularly vital both from the demographic and economic points of view. It hosts a relevant amount of economic activities (tertiary industry) and it is affected by traffic congestion, even if residents have a limited use of car and public transport system is well developed. The main leverage to find innovative solution for mobility and traffic management is the upcoming opening of massive work sites for the construction of Grand Paris Express, a new system of metro lines that will serve Issy and several other municipalities surrounding Paris. In forecast of these massive work that will have a relevant impact on already existing issues of traffic congestion, local authorities had set three main targets to be reached by using big data and visualization: understand in detail traffic trends, evaluate the impact of mobility-related policies and upcoming construction works, help people improve mobility behaviors. The main expected outcome is an easy to use visualization toolkit able to register and to predict mobility behaviors in relation to forecasted road works, useful not only for policy-makers but also for citizens that could rely on real time monitoring and predictions applications to make more sustainable mobility choices.

The pilot worked, in a first step, creating three focus groups involving public and private actors in the definition of a project to be presented to various local stakeholders. In parallel, the pilot worked matching data and policy making by analyzing existing data, defining other valuable digital information not yet available and analyzing the role that data could play in policy making processes. Finally, an effort has been made to stimulate potential users of the toolkit by analyzing existing barriers in the use of data and in data literacy. This preliminary process highlighted challenges related to data availability (public bodies have access to limited resources and need to cooperate with private entities), institutional fragmentation (big data-measurable trends are related to administrative scopes that are wider than the single municipality) and interoperability. In the future steps, the pilot intends to deepen the availability and use of other datasets to provide more relevant visualization prototypes, developing a traffic app and involving other stakeholders in the process so to build a wider set of visualization tools.

In the pilot, the smart actions taken act as answers to local and metropolitan infrastructural and economic changes. The experience of Issy-les-Molinaux intercepts two main decisional timeframes. Real time data are used to guide actions as exploratory reactions to contingent events (roadworks, traffic jams, closures…). These reactions, under the form of data series, are then used to detect the outcomes of the action itself and to understand the impact on travelers' behaviors and may contribute to policy measures promoting modal shift, moving thus the contribution of data to a strategic level. Nonetheless, until now Issy-les-Molinaux is working assessing the role of data to guide decisions that are in-between the short and the medium terms.

This pilot is the one that at most highlights the potentials of an experimental approach to policy making as for the use of big data. One of the most crucial mobility problems in the city is related to parking. The public administration is continuously changing its parking management strategies and actions due to the fast-changing needs in the area also consequent to the coming Grand Paris Express that is pushing new companies to settle in the Issy area. The Polivisu team in Issy-les-Molinaux is aware of the relevance for learning of these frequent and not fully successful attempts and is planning to work with the public administration to consider those attempts as small experiments whose impacts data can feed the tuning or re-shaping of future policy decisions.

4.3 Pilsen

Pilsen is a medium sized city of 170.000 inhabitants, one of the most important industrial centers in the Czech Republic. The city is affected by huge traffic congestion exacerbated by the presence of important productive sites, the weakness of the road network and the lack of diagnostic tools for traffic and road work management. Aware of these issues, the local public administration drafted in 2016/17 a plan for sustainable mobility, promoting relevant strategies such as new bypass roads, reconstruction of important arteries and bridges and a new tram line. In forecast of these interventions, local authorities have considered the opportunity to introduce big data-related tools and visualization in the governance of urban mobility at the implementation stage of the policy cycle, to better plan and coordinate upcoming road works, identify the most congested areas and simulate the impact of new infrastructures on traffic trends.

The pilot aims at developing, with the support of different stakeholders, a web application that will visualize approved road closures and will provide a recalculation of traffic volumes based on real time measurement of the actual mobility trends, allowing a better coordination in presence of contingent and long planned interventions. The tool will be also useful for citizens, who will obtain via the web application all the relevant information related to major traffic problems and the schedule of planned works, towards a minimization of negative impacts of road works in their daily displacements.

The pilot worked promoting a direct cooperation among public and private actors in defining and take a set of relevant actions to test the contribution of big and open data in traffic and infrastructure management, starting with the identification of significant datasets (public open data, police data, sensor recording…). In these first steps, pilot promoters faced relevant challenges related to the multiplicity of actors involved in infrastructure planning and construction, which generates problems of coordination and a limited possibility to know information related to closures in sufficient advance. As for the future, the city of Pilsen intends to furtherly develop the web application by creating a reliable list of planned roadwork and cooperating with the police to guarantee a continuous flow of information from the city sensors.

The experience of Pilsen clearly shows how data use in policy making intercepts multiple decisional dimensions. The smart model for traffic management that has been developed can guide reasoning and decision making at any timeframe (short-, medium- and long-term). However, the model is particularly relevant in a long-time perspective, because it allows to develop anticipatory reasoning on how to implement the local plan for sustainable mobility and to define an experimental path to orient related strategic decisions.

At the opposite side of the Issy-les-Molinaux experience is the Pilsen pilot: its experimental focus is mainly at the process scale and is clearly related to the traffic model they developed by using data collected during the implementation period of the existing Sustainable Urban Mobility Plan (SUMP). This model interiorizes the existing SUMP as a complex experiment and allows to approach the new coming SUMP as a new one.

5   Discussion and Conclusions

Considering the cycle of the policy process (design, implementation, evaluation), the policy making activities the pilots are experiencing, and the data they are processing, the paper shows that it is possible to internalize the policy experimentation opportunity, addressing the further pilots' activities, into a continuous policy adaptation cycle. Further evidence in this sense may derive from the future availability of quantitative and qualitative data referred to later stages of the policy processes developed in each city.

Mapping the pilots' activities clearly shows that:

- the policy making process is not a linear one and each pilot bridges more than one activity related to mobility problems (among those listed by the model). This does not affect the correctness of the model and rather suggests that it is more effective to observe and describe their work at the scale of single activities rather than referring to cycles or steps;
- open and big data processed are mainly used to monitor the current conditions of a setting and provide evidence for making decisions accordingly;
- a clear usage of big data within the policy making cycle emerges only from a limited share of actors, with a focus on the formulation of policy measures;
- one of the pilots has opened new smart city services to the public, and they are now producing the most of the available big data which are not considered for future initiatives regarding policy making by the policy makers and politicians in the city.

The type of action that results from big and open data visualization is not often attributable to a policy, which by its nature affects the medium-long term perspective. In many cases in fact, big data improves the *management* of a policy. This suggests considering the time dimension of a policy cycle distinguishing short, medium and long term, exploring thus the tension between real-time management and the experimental dimension that the use of big data enables.

Acknowledgments.   The authors acknowledge the funding received from the European Union's Horizon 2020 research and innovation programme under grant agreement No 769608 "Policy Development based on Advanced Geospatial Data Analytics and Visualisation". Polivisu Project H2020 -SC6-CO-CREATION-2016-2017.

References

1. Abella, A., Ortiz-de-Urbina-Criado, M., De-Pablos-Heredero, C.: A model for the analysis of data-driven innovation and value generation in smart cities' ecosystems. Cities **64**, 47–53 (2017)
2. Rabari, C., Storper, M.: The digital skin of cities: urban theory and research in the age of the sensored and metered city, ubiquitous computing and big data. Camb. J. Reg. Econ. Soc. **8** (1), 27–42 (2015)
3. Batty, M.: Big data, smart cities and city planning. Dialogues Hum. Geogr. **3**(3), 274–279 (2013)
4. Kitchin, R.: Big Data, new epistemologies and paradigm shifts. Big Data Soc. **1**(1) (2014)
5. Kitchin, R.: The real-time city? Big data and smart urbanism. GeoJournal **79**(1), 1–14 (2014)
6. Caragliu, A., Del Bo, C., Nijkamp, P.: Smart cities in Europe. Research Memoranda VU University Amsterdam, Faculty of Economics, Business Administration and Econometrics, 48 (2009)
7. European Commission: Quality of Public Administration: a Toolbox for Practitioners (2017)
8. Järv, O., Ahas, R., Witlox, F.: Understanding monthly variability in human activity spaces: a twelve-month study using mobile phone call detail records. Transp. Res. Part C Emerg. Technol. **38**, 122–135 (2014)
9. Kitchin, R.: The Data Revolution. Big Data, Open Data, Data Infrastructures and Their Consequences. Sage, Singapore (2014)
10. Einav, L., Levin, J.D.: The Data Revolution and Economic Analysis. NBER Working Paper Series, 19035 (2013)
11. Boyd, D., Crawford, K.: Critical questions for big data. Inf. Commun. Soc. **15**(5), 662–679 (2012)
12. Gantz, J., Reinsel, D.: Extracting value from chaos. IDC IView **1142**, 1–12 (2011)
13. Williford, C., Henry, C.: One culture. Computationally intensive research in the humanities and social science. A report on the experiences of first respondents to the digging into data challenge. Council on Library and Information Resources, 151 (2012)
14. Pucci, P., Vecchio, G., Concilio, G.: Big data and urban mobility: a policy making perspective. Transportation Research Procedia (forthcoming)
15. Brabham, D.C.: Crowdsourcing the public participation process for planning projects. Plan. Theory **8**(3), 242–262 (2009)
16. Vecchio, G., Tricarico, L.: "May the force move you": roles and actors of information sharing devices in urban mobility. Cities **88**, 261–268 (2019)
17. Schwanen, T.: Beyond instrument: smartphone app and sustainable mobility. Eur. J. Transp. Infrastruct. Res. **15**(4), 675–690 (2015)
18. Polivisu: The PoliVisu Policy Making Model (DRAFT) (2018)
19. Mintzberg, H.: Strategy-making in three modes. Calif. Manag. Rev. **16**(2), 44–53 (1973)

Detection of Points of Interest
from Crowdsourced Tourism Data

Ivana Semanjski[1,2](✉) ⓘ, Moustapha Ramachi[3], and Sidharta Gautama[1,2] ⓘ

[1] Department of Industrial Systems Engineering and Product Design,
Ghent University, Technologiepark 903, 9052 Gent-Zwijnaarde, Belgium
{ivana.semanjski,sidharta.gautama}@ugent.be
[2] Industrial Systems Engineering (ISyE), Flanders Make, Ghent University,
9052 Gent-Zwijnaarde, Belgium
[3] Department of Telecommunications and Information Processing, Ghent University,
St-Pietersnieuwstraat 41, 9000 Gent, Belgium
moustapha.ramachi@gmail.com
http://www.FlandersMake.be

Abstract. Availability of the big data on human mobility raised a lot
of expectations regarding the possibility to have a more detailed insights
into daily and seasonal mobility patterns. However, this is not a trivial task and often noisy positioning data pose a great challenge among
researchers and practitioners. In this paper, we tackle the detection of
the Points of Interest (PoI) locations from the mobile sensed tourist data
gathered in Zeeland (Netherlands) region. We consider different clustering approaches to detect individuals and collective PoI locations and find
that OPTICS proved to be the most robust against initial parameters
choices and k-means the most sensitive. K-means also seemed not appropriate to use to extract individual places but it indicates promising to
extract areas of city which are often visited.

Keywords: Human mobility · Positioning data · Tourism ·
Clustering · Points of Interest · K-means · OPTICS · DBSCAN

1   Introduction

Understanding human mobility from the crowdsourced GNSS (Global Navigation Satellite System) data has gathered much attention in the research over the
past decade [10,11,13]. This research is mainly based on the trajectory analysis
[7] called the trajectory data mining. Trajectory data mining is a broad field that
draws from many fields of study to process spatial data. The typical goals of trajectory data mining are evenly broad and can range from predicting movements
to mining points of interest (PoI) and even more complex questions with regard
to the connected mobility in an urban environment [3,14]. However, none of this

Supported by Province of Zeeland, VVV Zeeland and Urban Innovative Actions
program.

S. Misra et al. (Eds.): ICCSA 2019, LNCS 11620, pp. 203–216, 2019.
https://doi.org/10.1007/978-3-030-24296-1_18

is a trivial task as crowdsourced data are often noisy and extracting meaningful insights from them proves to be a challenging task [4,6,9].

In this paper, we will focus on detection of PoI locations from the crowd-sourced positioning data. Our motivation for this is twofold. For one, detection of PoI locations is needed to correctly split the continuous sequence of movement into meaningful trips (travelled path from the trip origin to the trip destination location) or trip segments (parts of the trip made by single trans-port mode). Secondly, correct interpretation of one's PoI locations leads toward activity detection, where activity detection enables assigning a stay point or trip with a semantic meaning. To this day, this remains a topic of much ongoing research. Most of the existing research on activity detection is founded on the rule based approaches and empirical knowledge [5,12]. An example of such an approach would be to detect a work-location when a location is often visited during office hours. The most widely identified trips are home-based-work trips, home-based-other trips, non-home-based-work trips and non-home-based-other trips [5]. Among others, Cao et al. propose a general framework for the mining of semantically meaningful, significant locations, e.g., work and restaurants, from a large collection of GNSS records data. Authors propose a model that bares resemblance to (internet) search engine algorithms. They combine several indi-cators to assess the 'interestingness' (how attractive a page is for a user): (1) number of visits, (2) duration of visits and (3) the distance the users travel to visit locations. By using a propagation model, e.g. if a location is often visited together with a location that is visited for a long duration its significance is related, to assign increased significance. The same logic is applied to the users to determine how authoritative they are. These significant locations and author-itative users are combined in a two-layered graph. Our research departs from the exiting approaches as we focus on the mobile sensed data gathered among tourism population. We examine and discuss transferability of the approaches used for general population towards the specific population analysis needs (in our case tourism). For this we consider different clustering approaches over two datasets: (i) smartphone data of individual's tracks and (ii) group tourism data.

The paper is structured as follows, after the introduction the data collection process and main data characteristics are defined as well as methods used within this research. This is followed with the qualitative data considerations and results section. The paper concludes with the discussion about the results on individual's and group (global) data and main finding.

2   Data and Methods

2.1   Data Properties

The data collection process happen during a five month period in 2017 where a group of 1500 people was surveyed for geospatial data. The participants were a users of a tourism mobile phone application for Zeeland (a region in the Nether-lands) shown on Fig. 1. The initial purpose of the application was to provide tourist information, however during the five month period the users were asked

Fig. 1. Tourism application used for survey

if they wanted to contribute their positioning data and mobility patterns for our research. Data of users who explicitly consent were used in our study.

2.2 Data Structure

The collected data were structured as follows, a *mobile phone record* is defined as a five-tuple $G = (u, t, x, y, s)$, where u is the ID of the user for which G is recorded, t is the timestamp, x and y are the spatial coordinates and s is the velocity as reported by the device sensors. The speed and ID field can be omitted to define a *geospatial point* $p = (x, y, t)$. In the following sections the concept of a (way)point will always refer to this definition of a geospatial point.

Waypoints are aggregated into legs which are in turn also aggregated into trips. A trip leg models a movement performed using a single transport mode. Trips are multimodal and can contain multiple legs. The recording of waypoints starts and stops when the user starts (or stops) moving. Each record of waypoint, trip and trip leg has a unique identifier which can be used to extract cohesive structures (e.g. all waypoints belonging to a trip leg).

2.3 Data Exploration

The total number of users that participated was 1505. The first user started recording on 31/05/2017 and the last one on 08/11/2017. During the survey 2427491 points were recorded, 1061763 or 43% of them were recorded near Zeeland (Fig. 2). These points were aggregated into 124725 trips. It is important to note that not every user participated for the full duration of the survey. The median participation time was 10 days and the average participation time, 26.25 days (Table 1, Fig. 3).

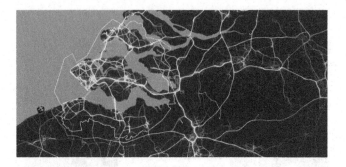

Fig. 2. Users trajectories

Table 1. General summary

Attribute	Recordings
Users	1505
Trips	124725
Distance	2201957
Duration	151612

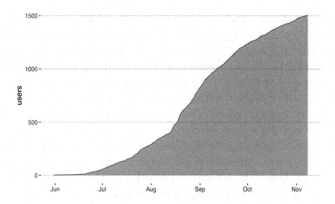

Fig. 3. Evolution of number of participants trough the five months period

Modal Split. To get a basic overview of the modal split, we used commercially preprocessed data on transport mode detection. The results indicate that the users made use of several modes of transport. Most of the legs were performed by car. Car trip legs were also those with the largest travelled distance and the longest trip leg duration of all the modes. Walking and biking complete the top three, the other modes occur significantly less frequent (Fig. 4).

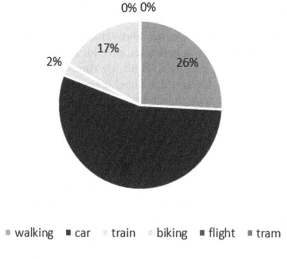

Fig. 4. Modal split

Temporal Data. Each data point has a timestamp associated with it. This information can be used to more precisely categorize interesting locations, as in the above mentioned literature based examples where the timestamps during business hours was used to indicate a work location. In our dataset (Fig. 5), the timestamps form almost a bell curve where the most of the recording occurred during the midday, between 10 a.m. and 2 p.m.

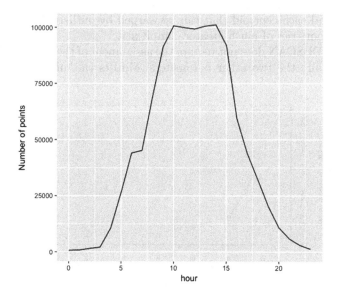

Fig. 5. Absolute number of points per hour of the day

2.4   Methods

To process the data, we first extract individual participants history. After extracting the user history, we aimed to cluster location points into *places*. We do this because a place can be visited multiple times, each time resulting in a slightly different stay point due to introduced measurement errors. To do so, we consider several clustering techniques described in more details bellow.

K-Means. K-means clustering is an iterative non-deterministic approach to cluster n points into k clusters. K-means takes input data with no labels and attempts to form clusters which are *near* to each other. This concept points of being *near* to each other can be quantified by using a distance metric. A common distance metric is the Euclidean distance but for our research we used a distance metric that considers the curvature of the earth. The number of clusters is a parameter that has to be set beforehand. A common way to determine this factor is to plot the sum of squares inside each cluster against the number of clusters. This is a measure for the variance in each cluster. A number of clusters should be chosen so that adding another cluster doesn't give much better modelling of the data. In the graph this will be represented by a reduction in the angle, hence this is called the *elbow criterion* (Fig. 6).

DBSCAN. *Density-based spatial clustering of applications with noise* is similar to k-means in the sense that it produces clusters of points, but unlike k-means the number of cluster does not have to be specified. DBSCAN's biggest advantage is its relative robustness against noise because outliers are not assigned to clusters. The distance metric used in k-means usually results in symmetrical (spherical) clusters around each centroid that can be warped by outliers. DBSCAN allows for cluster geometries of much greater complexity.

Although DBSCAN does not require the assignment of the number of clusters k it does require the two other parameters: MinPts the minimum size of the

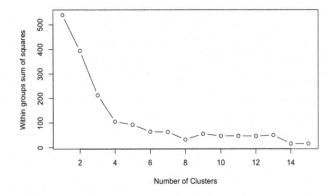

Fig. 6. Illustration of the elbow criterion

clusters (in number of points) and ϵ the maximum distance between neighbours in a cluster. DBSCAN is a popular and widely used algorithm but has known limitations [1]. The most interesting one is that DBSCAN cannot work properly on data sets with significant variations in density due to the fixed initial variables. DBSCAN also has problem of high complexity, in some cases its complexity reaches to $O(n^2)$.

OPTICS. *Ordering points to identify the clustering structure* is a clustering algorithm that overcomes one of the largest drawbacks of DBSCAN. Because of it input parameters DBSCAN naturally results in cluster with similar density. In the context of this research the problem might arise that a select number of high density clusters (e.g. home or a hotel location) are accompanied with several low density clusters (shop, bar etc.). Having this in mind, the DBSCAN would not be able to identify different clusters from Fig. 7.

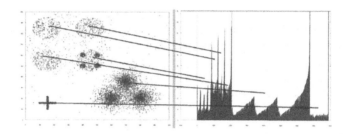

Fig. 7. Clusters with different density [8]

Hence, to improve upon DBSCAN, OPTICS introduces three new concepts:

Directly Density-Reachable. Object p is directly density reachable from object q wrt ϵ and *MinPts* in a set of objects D if:

- $p \subset N_\epsilon$ p is in the ϵ-neighborhood of q
- Card($N_\epsilon \geq$ MinPts Card(N) denotes the cardinality of set N

Density-Reachable. Object p is density reachable from object q wrt ϵ and *MinPts* in a set of objects D if there is a chain of objects $p_1, p_2, ..., p_n$, $p_1 = p$, $p_n = q$ such that $p_i \subset D$ and p_{i+1} is directly density-reachable from p_i.

Density-Connected. Object p is density-connected from object q wrt ϵ and MinPts in a set of objects D if there is a $o \subset D$ such that both p and q are density-reachable from o. Density-connectivity is a symmetric relation, a cluster can now be defined as a set of density-reachable objects. Noise can be defined as a point not in such a cluster. For each point the core-distance is recorded, this can be intuitively described as the smallest possible radius that around a point that will cover *MinPts* points. This value can be used to extract clusters of varying density.

3 Qualitative Data Considerations

The goal of this research is to extract meaningful places that are represented by clusters of points which model a period of time when the user was within a certain context, e.g. at the beach, in shopping etc. To extract these places from the data several qualitative issues have to be taken into consideration. The following section will discuss the main qualitative issues with the raw data. Besides the raw data a benchmark data set was also provided.

3.1 Data Issues

Oversegmentation. Trip recording starts when users starts moving around and ends when the user stops moving. This process is subject to many outsider influences that can distort a correct recording, e.g. slow moving traffic, driving through a tunnel and similar.

Active vs Passive Tracking. Most of the tracking was performed passively, the smartphone of the user was recording its location without user interference. These recordings can be influenced when a user starts using his/her smartphone while being tracked in the background. Holding the phone can introduce noise to the sensor (gyroscope, accelerometers,...) signals.

Measurement Accuracy. A number of different sensors are used to accurately determine the location of the user, all of these used sensors introduce a measurement error. In the context of this paper a wide variety of mobile phones was used, each phone could potentially have dozens of different sensor suppliers each with their own unique error characteristic. We assume that the fused data set selects the most reliable location reading that is available for a given device in a given time moment.

4 Problem Statement

By using the constructed framework the problem statement can be translated to a more precise description. The core problem is the extraction of interesting *places* from passively tracked smartphone data. The *places* that are of interest will be modelled as a cluster of points. These clusters have several features to describe how important they are, e.g. number of visits, number of users who visited this place, etc.

For the purpose of this research, the benchmark data is also available. This benchmark data is a result of an imperfect knowledge extraction process and is provided by the commercial partner who processes the tracking data. Hence, it can not be taken as ground truth, it is however an interesting dataset to compare against. This comparison is especially interesting for places which are relatively easy to detect such as home and can be used as an initial validation.

The extracted places can change whether we take the full dataset into consideration compared to using the data of individual users. The full dataset will extract public places of interest while the individual data results in a mix of public and personal places of interest.

5   Results

The analysis was performed on the aggregate and on a individual basis. The first section will discuss the global results (for aggregated data) and the second will discusses the results for individual users. The scope of the extracted places depends upon the input data, when examining the full dataset the extracted places will be mostly public points of interest. The individual analysis will extract a mix of public and personal places which no other user visits besides the examined user.

5.1   Global Results

DBSCAN. seems very dependant on the initial parameter choice. Figure 8 shows how the number of cluster varies for different choices of epsilon. Low epsilon reduce the ability of DBSCAN to link together far away points which results in many individual clusters, larger epsilon allows for the linking of these clusters into larger clusters. The algorithm was very robust against changes in minpts and shows minimal variations.

K-means. clustering diverged to relatively large clusters. Figure 9 displays the results for a clustering with k = 40, this values can be considered reasonable because of how larger values of k do not drastically improve the compactness of the cluster. The relatively large clusters are too spread out to model a single place.

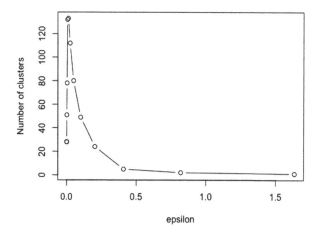

Fig. 8. Impact of varying epsilon

Fig. 9. K-means clustering

OPTICS. To extract clusters from this dataset the contrast parameter xi has so to be set. The silhouette index is relatively robust against changes in xi, the difference in compactness is the maximum and minimum choice of xi is very small (Fig. 10).

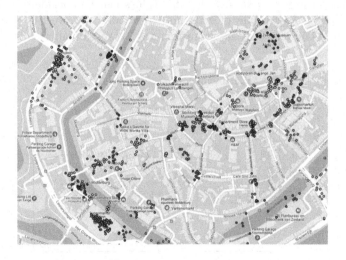

Fig. 10. Outcome of OPTICS algorithm

5.2 Individual Analysis

The home location is often used as an anchor point when analysing the mobility patterns of users. The home location is the most regularly visited location that can be extracted, this greatly reduces the complexity of extracting such a location. In this regard, three different extraction methods were performed and analysed. Each method uses the same algorithm to extract the home location but by feeding it different inputs different outputs are extracted. The following inputs were considered:

- All data points
- The same method as described by [5], the location with the most visits between 7 a.m. and 8 a.m. is labelled as the home location
- Only the beginning and ends of trips

These outputs were compared to the available benchmark data.

Home Detection. The y-axis of Fig. 11 contains every possible tuple of the mentioned data sets, for every tuple the median and average deviation over the top 100 users was calculated. The best median deviation compared to the benchmark is only 4 meters and was obtained by only using the trip data.

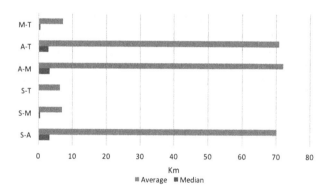

Fig. 11. Average and mean of deviation

OPTICS. does not make use of a predetermined epsilon making it a possible ideal choice to use compared to DBSCAN. The only choice that needs to be made is for the parameter xi. Figure 12 shows how the silhouette index changes for varying xi. Although the optimal value appears to occur for small xi, the silhouette index remains relatively small.

5.3 Places

This section is devoted to the extractions of places. The importance of a place will be derived from its hub score, this is done in the following subsection.

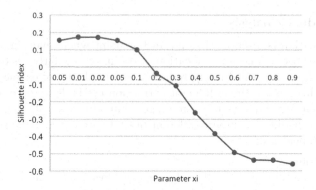

Fig. 12. Analysis of silhouette index

Extraction of Places. When modelling the travel pattern of a user as a graph, it might occur that some location frequently act as the origin of trips (e.g. home location), to find such interesting places a parallel to the internet is drawn. Hub and authoritative scores were developed for use on the world wide web. Hubs were expected to contain catalogues with a large number of outgoing links; authorities get many incoming links from hubs (due to their high quality information). This model can be altered to extract significant locations as they will appear as hubs [2]. Figure 13 represent the hub score for all of the extracted clusters for a single user. The large spike represents the home location. The Home locations naturally act as a hub due to the many trips that originate from this location.

Other clusters demonstrate a hub score significantly less than the home location.

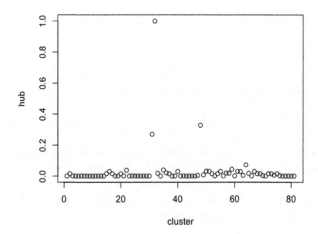

Fig. 13. Hub score

5.4   Discussion

For the global results, various cluster algorithms were compared based on their ability to extract places of interest. The choice of the initial parameters remains of the utmost importance and greatly influences the outcome. OPTICS proved to be the most robust against initial parameters choices and k-means the most sensitive. While the optimal choice for k, in terms of the within cluster sum of squares by cluster, can be easily determined this value still results in very large clusters. It seems that it is not appropriate to use this algorithm to extract individual places but it seems promising to extract areas of city which are often visited. Figure 9 is the outcome of this algorithm with the clusters closely aligning to the aggregated points of interest, e.g. beginning/middle/end of shopping street, main square,... DBSCAN and OPTICS succeeded in pinpointing the many significant places on the map, but are confronted with their own set of issues. OPTICS extracts a very high number of clusters compared to DBSCAN, this can be useful in very dense areas (e.g. main square) but also tends to oversegement in other areas.

For the individual results, the home location is the center most people's life and as such is the easiest to extract. A mapping of the late night location of user to the nearest hotel did not result in interesting insights, the nearest hotel was usually too far away. This can also be the result of an imperfect hotel location database (Open street map data were used). When comparing the densest cluster to the home labels in the benchmark data, which is the most often used label, a very small deviation registered. When limiting the search area to Zeeland the median deviation between the extracted cluster and the benchmark data is only 4 meters. This approach translates less well when comparing the second most dense cluster to the most frequent benchmark label (work). The median deviation rises to 2 km.

The proposed enhanced DBSCAN algorithm did not overcome the limitations of DBSCAN on the examined dataset. The heuristic to optimize the epsilon parameter tended to diverge to unrealistically high values. OPTICS was chosen as the preferred algorithm in this case. The extracted places were modelled in a graph to assign hub and authority scores, these tended to peak for interesting values (e.g. home).

6   Conclusion

We can conclude that tourist data can be used to extract valuable insights into their location history. When compared to a general location history survey, a survey of tourist data is characterized by a relatively short duration of their tourist visit. In many cases the survey will also contain information from their 'normal' life which can introduce noise when extracting tourism related activities. However, we can conclude that although these factors do indeed contribute in a negative manner it's still possible to gather valuable insights. Short tourism surveys can be used to model tourist behaviour on an individual and general basis. This kind of data is especially useful to detect locations which generally attract tourists, such as hotels, local points of interests, etc. One of the key issues when dealing with venue mapping is the lack of a definitive ground truth. The mapping of overnight stays was limited because of the lack of a complete hotel database. In the case of Zeeland the Google maps database appeared to be of a higher quality than the Open Street Map database but was subject to restrictive constraints.

References

1. Ali, T., Asghar, S., Sajid, N.A.: Critical analysis of DBSCAN variations. In: 2010 International Conference on Information and Emerging Technologies, ICIET 2010 (v) (2010). https://doi.org/10.1109/ICIET.2010.5625720
2. Cao, X., Cong, G., Jensen, C.S.: Mining significant semantic locations from GPS data. Proc. VLDB Endow. **3**(1–2), 1009–1020 (2010). https://doi.org/10.14778/1920841.1920968. http://dl.acm.org/citation.cfm?doid=1920841.1920968
3. Ćavar, I., Kavran, Z., Petrović, M.: Hybrid approach for urban roads classification based on GPS tracks and road subsegments data. Promet-Traffic Transp. **23**(4), 289–296 (2011)
4. Ćavar, I., Marković, H., Gold, H.: GPS vehicles tracks data cleansing methodology. In: International Conference on Traffic Science ICTS 2006 (2006)
5. Çolak, S., Alexander, L.P., Alvim, B.G., Mehndiratta, S.R., González, M.C.: Analyzing cell phone location data for urban travel. Transp. Res. Rec. J. Transp. Res. Board **2526**, 126–135 (2015). https://doi.org/10.3141/2526-14. http://trrjournalonline.trb.org/doi/10.3141/2526-14
6. Giannotti, F., Nanni, M., Pedreschi, D., Pinelli, F., Renso, C., Rinzivillo, S., Trasarti, R.: Unveiling the complexity of human mobility by querying and mining massive trajectory data. VLDB J. Int. J. Very Large Data Bases **20**(5), 695–719 (2011)
7. Gonzalez, M.C., Hidalgo, C.A., Barabasi, A.L.: Understanding individual human mobility patterns. Nature **453**(7196), 779 (2008)
8. Iván, G., Grolmusz, V.: Dimension reduction of clustering results in bioinformatics. arXiv preprint arXiv:1309.1892 (2013)
9. Lopez, A.J., Semanjski, I., Gautama, S., Ochoa, D.: Assessment of smartphone positioning data quality in the scope of citizen science contributions. Mob. Inf. Syst. **2017**, 11 pages (2017). Article ID 4043237
10. Semanjski, I., Bellens, R., Gautama, S., Witlox, F.: Integrating big data into a sustainable mobility policy 2.0 planning support system. Sustainability **8**(11), 1142 (2016)
11. Spangenberg, T.: Development of a mobile toolkit to support research on human mobility behavior using GPS trajectories. Inf. Technol. Tour. **14**(4), 317–346 (2014)
12. Wang, Z., He, S.Y., Leung, Y.: Applying mobile phone data to travel behaviour research: a literature review. Travel. Behav. Soc. (2016). https://doi.org/10.1016/j.tbs.2017.02.005
13. Wu, C., Yang, Z., Xu, Y., Zhao, Y., Liu, Y.: Human mobility enhances global positioning accuracy for mobile phone localization. IEEE Trans. Parallel Distrib. Syst. **26**(1), 131–141 (2015)
14. Zheng, Y.: Trajectory Data Mining: An Overview. ACM Trans. Intell. Syst. Technol. **6**(29) (2015). Article, https://doi.org/10.1145/2743025

Cycling for Home-to-School Travel in Palermo: A Method for Assessing the Optimal Allocation of New Cycling Infrastructure

Gabriele D'Orso and Marco Migliore[(✉)]

Dept. of Engineering, University of Palermo,
Viale Delle Scienze Building 8, 90128 Palermo, Italy
{gabriele.dorso,marco.migliore}@unipa.it

Abstract. In order to reduce the number of cars on the road, one of the most incisive actions is to encourage cycling, e.g. through the introduction of bike-sharing systems. In particular, the activation of special bike-sharing programs for school students could lead students to choose this mode of transport to make their own home-school travel. The success of such initiatives is primarily linked to the presence of a continuous and functional cycle network, which can create safe routes to school. It is, therefore, necessary a cycle network design model that allows determining the optimal allocation of new cycle paths, maximizing the number of users and considering technical and economic constraints. As a case study, the city of Palermo has been chosen; in fact, the Go2School project, a bike-sharing initiative aimed at students of four high schools, has been launched in Palermo.

Keywords: Cycling · Active transportation · Safe routes to school · Bike sharing · Network design problem

1 Introduction

Physical activity is recognized as an important element of a healthy lifestyle since it reduces the risk of illness and premature death. The modern lifestyle, with its dependence on the car, sedentary activities, and automation of some activities at home and in the workplace, has led to a worrying increase in obesity, depression and cardiovascular diseases. According to ISTAT data in Italy, the proportion of the population aged 18 and over with excess weight is 45.9% (35.5% overweight, 10.4% obese), while 23 million 85 thousand people (39.2% of the population aged 3 and over) declare that they do not engage in sports or physical activity in their free time.

Adolescents are not immune to the consequences of a sedentary lifestyle, so much so that in Italy 24.7% of people aged between 6 and 17 are overweight or obese. One of the interventions that policymakers can put into place to counteract this problem is to encourage active modes of transport, i.e. pedestrian and cycle mobility, especially for transit between home and school or home and work. Furthermore, more widespread use of these transport modes would benefit pollution reduction and urban mobility. The excessive and often indiscriminate use of the private car in the city has, in fact, had a

© Springer Nature Switzerland AG 2019
S. Misra et al. (Eds.): ICCSA 2019, LNCS 11620, pp. 217–230, 2019.
https://doi.org/10.1007/978-3-030-24296-1_19

series of negative consequences on the liveability of the urban environment, such as congestion, land consumption, noise and atmospheric pollution, and accidents.

As a transport mode, cycling has predictable travel times, continuous availability, easily maintained routes and non-emission of pollutants, and it offers a relaxing and healthy exercise. Therefore, the design of the city has effects on the inactivity of the population - the World Health Organization also affirms it - and having neighborhoods designed for pedestrians and cyclists means putting the citizen in a position to practice physical activity [9, 19]. For many people, in fact, the most acceptable form of physical activity is the one embodied in everyday life, such as walking or cycling, instead of using the car. Therefore, in order to counteract inactivity and decrease the health costs that derive from it, the administrations, which until now have underestimated the problem and have not considered it in their decision-making processes, should make interventions that promote cycling and make it a safe, convenient and attractive way to do our daily errands [8].

The creation of an urban environment suitable for cyclists and pedestrians is, therefore, one of the main objectives of the most recent urban planning approaches, like the Transit Oriented Development (TOD) approach. This urban planning approach, created to counter the phenomenon of urban diffusion, provides for the creation of livable neighborhoods, where there are different activities (shops, schools, restaurants, offices, residences, etc.), designed to guide the transport demand as much as possible towards public transport and active modes (on foot and cycling). The introduction of cycle paths and bike sharing systems in urban areas contributes to reducing the number of private cars circulating, to reducing road congestion and emissions [23], to increasing accessibility, to creating flexible mobility, to improving the health of citizens through exercise, and to supporting multimodal connections and intermodality with public transport, offering a possible solution to the first/last mile problem.

Nowadays urban planners and engineers are starting to pay more attention to the role that walking and cycling have to play in urban mobility. This can be seen in the adoption, by many cities, of Sustainable Urban Mobility Plans, which include pedestrianization, downsizing of roadways in favor of pedestrian and cycling space, limitations of vehicle speeds and introduction of 30 km/h zones, in the creation of safe routes to school and in the construction of new infrastructures dedicated to bicycles and pedestrians. For example, Copenhagen is a model to be followed in the context of incentive policies for the use of bicycles and in the construction of infrastructures such as pedestrian bridges and cycle paths. New attention is also evident in the diffusion and success of many applications for smartphones that seek to encourage walking and promote an active lifestyle through the reward mechanism (e.g. the Empower project, funded by the European Union) [3].

The introduction of bike-sharing programs is certainly one of the most incisive actions to promote and encourage the use of bicycles in the city. The aim of this paper is to implement a methodology that allows determining the optimal location of new cycle paths in order to maximize the demand attracted by a bike-sharing service designed for schools. As a case study, the city of Palermo has been chosen, where the Go2School project is taking place. The project is promoted and implemented by the Municipality of Palermo, AMAT Palermo SpA, the University of Palermo and four public schools (Liceo Scientifico Albert Einstein, Liceo Linguistico Statale Ninni

Cassarà, Istituto Tecnico Vittorio Emanuele III, Istituto Tecnico Commerciale Pio la Torre). It consists of making a special bike-sharing service available to students via subscriptions and bike parking marked with the initiative's logo throughout the territory, as well as new cycle docks and new cycle paths near the schools.

2 Background

The choice for cycling is influenced by several factors [18]. First of all, the quality of the cycling infrastructure is important, since there is a greater propensity to use the bicycle where there is a network that has continuity and cycle paths are well delineated and separated from road traffic. The extension of the cycle network and its quality have a greater impact on the use of bike sharing systems, than the creation of new cycle paths, which also increase the accessibility of the service [22]. The decision to cycle is influenced by the availability of bicycle-parking spaces, changing rooms and showers in the workplace or places of study, the absence of obstacles in cycle lanes, the number of traffic lights, the volume and speed of vehicles that travel the adjacent streets, the number of turning movements and the resulting conflicts. Therefore, these factors are not only linked to accessibility but above all are related to security. For underage students, safety becomes a determining factor in their propensity to make the home-school trips with their own bicycle or taking advantage of a bike sharing service, since they are still subject to the will of their parents, who often view to these transport modes as high risk. The safety of home-school routes must, therefore, be taken into consideration for the success of a bike sharing program. It is important to note that safety is not only referred to the separation of the cycle traffic from other vehicular traffic or to the absence of obstacles on the cycle paths but also to the sense of security that the urban environment transmits, in relation to architectural degradation and crime [21]. The analyses carried out have lead us to determine that the size of the family, the type of school attended by the students, the professional status of the parents, the presence of other people (grandparents, relatives, friends), disposable income (possibility to pay a baby sitter) and the availability of more than one family car, all play a role in the choice of how to get students to school [14].

Mattson e Godavarthy [13] have reviewed the studies that identify the other factors which determine the success of bike sharing programs. These factors include the presence of schools and university campuses, parks and recreational areas, the topography of the territory, the weather (low temperatures, snow, rain, high humidity, and strong winds diminish the propensity to use bike sharing [10]), the proximity of bike parks to railway stations and stops of local public transport as well as the walkability of neighborhoods [7]. Moro et al. [17] have instead identified all those factors that are barriers to the success of a bike-sharing service, classifying them in organizational obstacles, referable to the difficulties of the company that manages the service, regulatory obstacles (lack of regulation and incentive policies) and cultural barriers (resistance of citizens to change their mobility habits).

Even the location and configuration of the new cycle paths becomes a determining factor as it not only influences accessibility but also influences the choice to use the bike sharing service due to the different perception of the safety of the home-school journey. Very often the deliberate choice not to cycle is caused by the configuration of the road, and in particular by the conflict that occurs when a road has different functions and the danger that arises when it is used by different categories of users. Furthermore, the construction of the cycle paths influences the other modes of transport in a more or less decisive way, since the space required for them is often removed from road traffic, reducing the space available for cars and motorcycles. In Europe, many experiences have shown, however, how the redesign of the roads, through a different distribution of spaces, can ensure that the different components of traffic (motorized vehicles, cyclists and pedestrians) can coexist in safety, reducing the severity and number of accidents.

Some scholars have developed models useful for the design of cycling routes. Lin and Yu [12] have developed a bikeway network design model for cycling in urban areas which has the objectives of minimizing cyclists risk, maximizing comfort, maximizing service coverage for residents and minimizing the impact of the bikeway on road traffic, considering at the same time the network continuity, the monetary budget and the bikeway types as constraints. Dondi et al. [4] proposed as a design tool the approach of the Contest Sensitive Design, which involves all stakeholders in the development of the cycle facilities and an interdisciplinary approach in identifying the best design solution.

Caggiani et al. [2] have implemented an urban bikeway network design model, which consists of an objective function that minimizes the inequalities between different groups of users, in terms of accessibility to cycle paths.

3   The Bike-Sharing Service in Palermo

A bike sharing service is currently active in the city of Palermo, which is managed by AMAT Palermo S.p.A., the municipal company that carries out public transport services by bus and tram, and also manages a car-sharing service. Since AMAT is a company linked to the municipal administration, adopting strategies for encouraging shared mobility services in synergy with political action is therefore easier. The implementation of the bike-sharing system, called BiciPA, took place in 2016 through co-financing by the Italian Ministry of the Environment. The service has about 2360 subscribers and in 2018 had a fleet of 400 bicycles, 210 of which are already available for users. BiciPA is a station-based service, so users can pick up and drop bicycles off in 37 bicycle parks located within the municipal area (Fig. 1). 7 new cycle docks are being installed by the company, in order to extend the service to areas and trip attractors not yet served. The annual subscription cost is 25 euros and the rental cost is linked to the time of use. The first 30 min are free, which makes this service desirable for short trips as these are usually home-school trips. Sixty percent of subscribers use the service for less than an hour a day. The service is integrated with the car-sharing system - a unique case in Italy - as it is possible to use both services using the same subscription card, at a cost of 35 euros.

The Go2School program for students is therefore an extension of the current bike-sharing service.

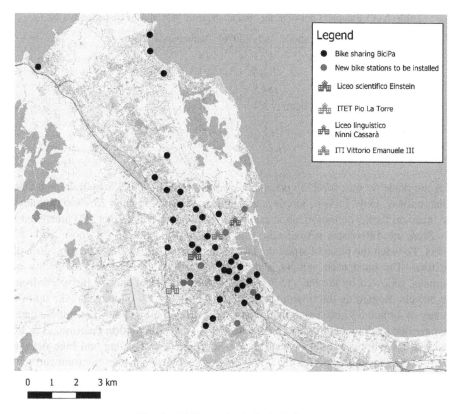

0   1   2   3 km

Fig. 1. BiciPa cycle docks in Palermo.

4   Cycling in Italy and in Palermo

The Go2School initiative is part of a mobility context where car use is dominant over other modes of transport. In Italy, there are about 625 cars per 1000 inhabitants and only one out of two Italians owns a bicycle. Italy is, therefore, very far from other European countries, like Netherlands, which has 481 cars per 1000 inhabitants and 1.2 bikes per inhabitant. Approximately 51% of urban journeys are carried out in Utrecht by bike and around 48% in Amsterdam (Knowledge Institute for Mobility Policy, 2017). A comparison between the modal share in Italy [11] and in Netherlands [20] is presented in Table 1.

In Palermo, cycling mobility suffers even more than in other Italian cities. According to the ISTAT data (2011) of the Municipality of Palermo, 278,954 people commute daily; equal to 42.4% of the resident population. More specifically, 42.1% of daily trips (equal to 117,495 people) are made to reach the place of study, while 57.9% (equal to 161,459 people) are made to reach the workplace.

The most used mode of transport for systematic trips is the private car, both as a driver (33.4% of the total number of journeys) or as a passenger (17.4%). The motorcycle (motorbike, scooter, moped) follows, with 11.9%. An estimated 10.9% of

Table 1. Comparison between the modal share in Italy and in Netherlands (%).

Transport mode	Italy (2016)	Netherlands (2016)
Pedestrian	17.1	18
Bicycle	3.3	27
Car	64.5	47
Bus/tram/metro	4.4	3
Train	0.9	2
Other	8.9	3

trips are made by bus, 0.7% by private bus or school bus and 0.3% by train or by the urban railway. Only 1.4% of journeys are made by bicycle. Finally, 23.7% of journeys are made on foot. The motorization rate is high: there are 57 cars per 100 inhabitants.

There are differences between the trips made by the students and those made by others. To reach the place of study the largest number of trips is made on foot; 36% of the total. The most used vehicle is the private car (as a passenger), for 33.8% of journeys, followed by the bus (15.7%), the motorbike (7.5%) and for just 0.9% from the bicycle. Regarding the time taken to reach school, 57.1% of students take up to a quarter of an hour; 87.6% reach their destination within half an hour. From these data, we note that cycling is a mode of transport that is very little used in Palermo, even by students, for whom it could instead be a valid alternative. Cycling and bike-sharing offer several advantages, such as a low cost, zero impact on the environment, and flexibility.

Furthermore, cycling is faster than other modes of transport for trips of up to 5 km [6]. Moreover, the city of Palermo, because of its topography and favorable climate, has a high potential for increasing the use of the bicycle.

5 The Italian Legislation About Cycling Infrastructure and the Cycle Network in Palermo

In order to illustrate the situation of the cycling infrastructure in Palermo, it is necessary to briefly introduce the current Italian legislation. The M.D. 557/1999 describes the types of cycle paths permitted in Italy. The cycle itineraries, located within the inhabited center or connecting to neighboring towns, can include the following types in descending order with respect to the safety they offer for the cycling users:

- cycle tracks;
- cycle lanes on a reserved lane;
- pedestrian and cycle promiscuous paths;
- vehicular and cycle promiscuous paths.

The cycle path can be realized:

- with a single or double direction cycle track, physically separated from vehicles and pedestrians with some sorts of vertical barrier;

– on a reserved lane in the roadway, with a single direction of travel, located on the right side of the roadway and marked with paint;
– on a reserved lane, obtained from the sidewalk, with a single or double direction, located on the side adjacent to the roadway.

The current cycle network in Palermo extends for about 44 km and consists of cycle tracks, cycle lanes on the sidewalk or cycle lanes in reserved lanes shared with buses (Fig. 2). The latter have the limit not to be well signaled to users, who do not recognize them as lanes for bicycles, and to be, moreover, traveled by buses, which stop and restart and have a different speed from that of bicycles, which increases the risk of accidents.

In 2015 the municipal administration has drawn up the Soft Mobility Plan determining the future cycle network, consisting of cycle paths that are safe, interconnected with other transport modes and accompanied by dedicated services and facilities. The planned network will have a total extension of 144.98 km (Fig. 3).

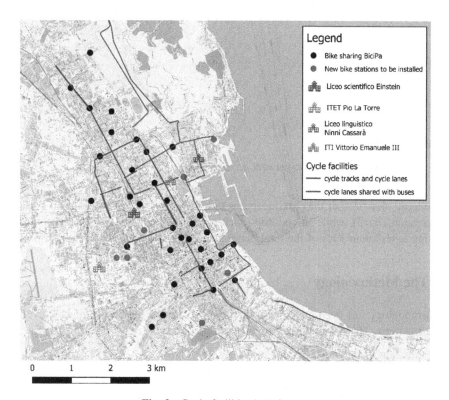

Fig. 2. Cycle facilities in Palermo.

Little has been done compared to the project. In fact, an obstacle in the construction of bicycle lanes is the old fabric of the city, characterized by narrow roads, especially in the old town, and by the on-street parking. The latter is an all-Italian problem,

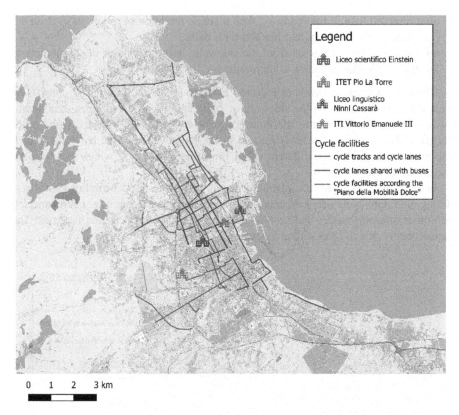

Legend

🏫 Liceo scientifico Einstein

🏫 ITET Pio La Torre

🏫 Liceo linguistico
    Ninni Cassarà

🏫 ITI Vittorio Emanuele III

Cycle facilities

—— cycle tracks and cycle lanes

—— cycle lanes shared with buses

—— cycle facilities according the
    "Piano della Mobilità Dolce"

0   1   2   3 km

Fig. 3. The cycle network according to the Soft Mobility Plan.

considering that 56% of the parking spaces in Italy are on the road (European Parking Association, 2013), while in countries such as the Netherlands and Sweden on-road parking is less than 30% of the total parking space (respectively 28% and 20%).

6   The Methodology

A methodology has been developed for the proposal and the design of new cycling infrastructures. This methodology involves the following steps:

- calibration of a demand model;
- optimization process using an objective function in order to determine the optimal allocation of new cycling infrastructures;
- extension of the methodology to other schools; this is possible only by knowing the origins of home-school travel, i.e. students' residences.

The last step is necessary because the investment in the cycling infrastructure is justified only if there is an adequate demand.

6.1   Calibration of the Demand Model

For the case study of Palermo, the first step of the methodology has been described in a previous work [5]. For the Go2School project, an experimental demand analysis has been carried out, through which the probability that users choose cycling instead of other modal alternatives has been determined. The analysis has started with the administration of a questionnaire to a sample of students from the four schools. The total number of students interviewed is 1131; out of these, 754 are males and 377 are females. The most represented school is ITI Vittorio Emanuele III with 416 students (Table 2). The questionnaire made it possible to investigate the students' mobility habits regarding home-to-school trips and the willingness to cycle. In particular, only 1.8% of students routinely use the bicycle and the absence of cycle paths is the main reason (19%) for which students do not use this mode of transport for their home-to-school trips (Fig. 4).

Table 2. The sample for the Go2School project.

School	Number of interviewed students	Total students	Sampling fraction
ITET Pio La Torre	227	938	24,2%
ITI Vittorio Emanuele III	416	1521	27,4%
L.Linguistico Cassarà	190	606	31,4%
L.Scientifico Einstein	298	834	35,7%
Total	1131	3899	29,0%

The analysis leads to the estimation of the demand potentially attracted by the Go2School bike-sharing service thanks to the knowledge of the O/D paths and the application of a modal choice model. A demand model as the multinomial logit has been used. Through this model it is possible to quantify, for a given scenario, the probability that the user chooses a specific mode of transport and to evaluate the modal share. The user attributes a utility, or in the case of the model in question, a disutility, that is a cost to be faced, to every transport mode, and, since the user is a rational decision maker, he will most likely choose the mode that minimizes his costs.

Five different transport modes have been considered: private cars (as passengers), public transport (urban buses, extra-urban buses, train and tram), pedestrian mobility, motorcycles and bike-sharing.

Starting from the results obtained with this analysis, the methodology provides that the cycle paths need to be built on the road axes in which the desire lines of the potential users are concentrated. If the cycle track overlaps with the desire lines of the user, the probability that cycling will be chosen as a mode of transport will increase since it is more responsive to the needs of the students.

Moreover, the change in the modal choice by the students in favor of the shared bicycle is decidedly interesting, if the possibility of traveling along safe cycle paths is guaranteed. According the model results, in the current situation in which the lacking state of the cycle infrastructure is present, the percentage of students traveling by

Fig. 4. Reasons why students don't ride a bike to school.

bicycle is around 2%, while with the introduction of the new bike-sharing service the percentage would increase enormously, reaching 52%. This result shows that the students could modify their mobility habits in favor of the shared bicycle if an effective bike-sharing service and a safe route to school exist. In the presence of a safe cycling infrastructure, in fact, the user associates a high utility with bike.

6.2 The Optimization Process

Starting from the analysis of some works about optimization problems [1, 15, 16] it was decided to formalize the problem of the cycle network design as an optimization problem considering an objective function for maximizing users' satisfaction subject to constraints. The optimization process takes into account the user satisfaction, the costs associated with investment in new cycling infrastructure and with management, the reduction of negative externalities (i.e. the reduction of atmospheric and acoustic pollution).

In the case in question, the analysis of modal share shows that many students switch from walking or public transport use to cycling; this causes the reduction of negative externalities to be limited. Since investment costs in cycle infrastructure are also limited, it was preferred not to include these factors in the optimization process, as there is a compensation between the investment costs and the benefits due to the reduction of externalities.

The optimal allocation of the new cycle infrastructures can be estimated by maximizing the objective function:

$$Argmax_{(x \in X)} = \sum_{od} d_{od}[ln(e^{V_{car}} + e^{V_{TPL}} + e^{V_{motorbike}} + e^{V_{bike}} + e^{V_{walking}})_{cyclepaths}$$
$$- ln(e^{V_{car}} + e^{V_{TPL}} + e^{V_{motorbike}} + e^{V_{bike}} + e^{V_{walking}})_0]$$

subject to the constraints:

- X = vector of feasible cycle paths in the transport network taking into account the technical constraints
- $\underline{f}^* = \underline{\underline{A}}\,\underline{\underline{P}}\left(\underline{c}\left(\underline{x},\underline{f}^*\right)\right)\underline{d}\left(\underline{x},\underline{f}^*\right)$

where:

- the users' "surplus" is expressed as the product of the total demand d_{od} and the variation in satisfaction between the project scenario and the initial one (without new cycle paths); the satisfaction has been calculated using the *logsum* function (user maximum perceived utility) for each origin-destination *o-d* pair (V_{car}, V_{TPL}, $V_{motorbike}$, V_{bike} and $V_{walking}$ are the car systematic utility function, the local public transport systematic utility function, the motorbike systematic utility function, the bike systematic utility function and the walking systematic utility function);
- the flow on each link of the network must be the solution of the fixed point problem depending from the interaction between the transport supply function and the transport demand function. In the last constraint $\underline{f}^*$ is the equilibrium flow vector, $\underline{x}$ is the cycle paths vector, $\underline{\underline{A}}$ is the incidence link-path matrix, $\underline{\underline{P}}$ is the path choice probability matrix, $\underline{d}$ is the demand vector.

By maximizing the surplus, it is possible to evaluate the cycle path that makes the O-D route safe for cyclists without wasting time for users who continue to move with other modes (in particular for cars and buses for which the travel time depends on the effective road width dedicated to vehicle flow).

The cycle paths set by the Soft Mobility Plan have been the starting point in evaluating possible proposals for the allocation of new cycle paths.

Furthermore, the methodology takes into account the rail and tram transport network. The intermodality between cycling and public transport must, in fact, be absolutely incentivized in order to ensure that urban mobility benefits in terms of reducing the use of private cars. Public transport such as tram, train, and metro allows students to get on the bike on board and becomes points of aggregation of the demand for cycling: students who live at a remarkable distance from the school can take advantage of the rail transport to arrive at the nearest station to the institute, and then continue the trip with the bicycle, owned or shared. In this sense, the method considers, therefore, the possibility that cycling is used for last mile journeys, identifying roads that connect the metro/rail/tram stations to schools as priority roads where to place the new cycle facilities. The new cycle facilities should also be located near the trip attractors and generators, i.e. close to areas of historical and tourist interest, parks, public transport hubs and neighborhoods where residences (origins) are concentrated.

About the technical constraints, the location of the new cycle facilities depends primarily on the topography of the city. Interventions must also comply whit plans and regulations. All roads with a longitudinal slope greater than 5% have been rejected, as they are not suitable for the circulation of bicycles by law (Article 8 of Legislative Decree 557/1999). Another constraint is the type of road: it was discarded as a possible road on which to insert new bike facilities Viale Regione, which is a motorway, as the legislation does not allow it because the excessive difference between the speed of the cars and that of the bicycles increases the risk of accidents.

Through the application of the objective function it is possible to maximize the surplus of users: the public administration can invest where there is high cycling demand, realizing safe routes for students respecting technical constraints.

The process of optimization, applied to only four schools, resulted in the cycle paths in Fig. 5. They connect the schools to the places where the student residences are more concentrated, to the main train or tram stations, to the park and ride parking lots and to the existing bike-sharing docks, thus creating a continuous network.

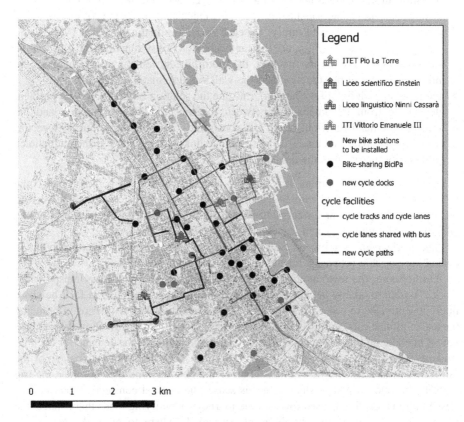

Fig. 5. New cycle paths resulting from the application of the optimization process.

7   Conclusion

One of the actions that policymakers can implement to encourage cycling, especially among young people, is the activation of special bike-sharing programs for schools.

The bike-sharing service succeeds in attracting demand from other modes of transport - first of all cars - not only with an appropriate distribution in the territory of bicycle docks but also with careful planning and placement of new cycling infrastructures. The location of the new cycle paths has to be decided on the basis of a methodology that maximizes the number of students can potentially take advantage of using the bike-sharing service, taking into account the addresses of their homes or the proximity to park and ride parking lots or stations railways for the identification of the streets in which to build new cycling infrastructure.

The methodology proposed here consists, therefore, in an optimization process that allows maximizing the users' "surplus", while taking into account in general investment costs and externalities. Investments, which are in any case limited, should be oriented where the presence of cycle paths can significantly increase the share of users using the bicycle. In terms of externalities, it is obvious that the more bikes there are, the more environmental benefits are obtained; however, externalities are very difficult to assess. In this paper, therefore, a compensatory process between investment costs and gain in terms of reduction of negative externalities has been considered. For the location of the new cycle paths and their design, technical constraints must also be taken into account: there must be a consistency of the interventions with the Sustainable Urban Mobility Plan and the existing regulations concerning the design of the cycle facilities.

The optimization process, which involves the development of an objective function, has been applied to the case study of Palermo, determining where new cycle infrastructure could be needed to ensure that students switch from private car use to cycling.

The method can be applied also to other cities and other contexts if the cycling demand and the constraints are well known. The methodology is, therefore, a valid decision support system for the public administration, as the optimization process indicates where the investments will give the best results.

Further studies, which take investments costs and externalities into account, will need to be performed. Calibrating the modal choice model considering other types of users, such as teachers and school staff, and extending the analysis to other schools will therefore necessary.

References

1. Amoroso, S., Migliore, M., Catalano, M., Galatioto, F.: A demand-based methodology for planning the bus network of a small or medium town. Eur. Transp. - Trasporti Europei **44**, 41–56 (2010)
2. Caggiani, L., Camporeale, R., Binetti, M., Ottomanelli, M.: An urban bikeway network design model for inclusive and equitable transport policies. Transp. Res. Procedia **37**, 59–66 (2019). https://doi.org/10.1016/J.TRPRO.2018.12.166

3. Di Dio, S., La Gennusa, M., Peri, G., Rizzo, G., Vinci, I.: Involving people in the building up of smart and sustainable cities: how to influence commuters' behaviors through a mobile app game. Sustain. Cities Soc. **42**, 325–336 (2018). https://doi.org/10.1016/J.SCS.2018.07. 021

4. Dondi, G., Simone, A., Lantieri, C., Vignali, V.: Bike lane design: the context sensitive approach. Procedia Eng. **21**, 897–906 (2011). https://doi.org/10.1016/j.proeng.2011.11.2092

5. D'Orso, G., et al.: School bike sharing program: will it succeed? (in press)

6. European Commission: Città in bicicletta, pedalando verso l'avvenire (1999)

7. Faghih-Imani, A., Eluru, N., El-Geneidy, A.M., Rabbat, M., Haq, U.: How land-use and urban form impact bicycle flows: evidence from the bicycle-sharing system (BIXI) in Montreal. J. Transp. Geogr. **41**, 306–314 (2014)

8. Forsyth, A., Krizek, K.: Urban design: is there a distinctive view from the bicycle? J. Urban Des. **16**(4), 531–549 (2011). https://doi.org/10.1080/13574809.2011.586239

9. Fulton, J.E., Shisler, J.L., Yore, M.M., Caspersen, C.J.: Active transportation to school: findings from a national survey. Res. Q. Exerc. Sport **76**(3), 352–357 (2005)

10. Gebhart, K., Noland, R.B.: The impact of weather conditions on bikeshare trips in Washington, DC. Transportation **41**(6), 1205 (2014)

11. ISFORT. 13° Rapporto sulla mobilità in Italia (2016)

12. Lin, J.-J., Yu, C.-J.: A bikeway network design model for urban areas. Transportation (Amst). **40**, 45–68 (2013). https://doi.org/10.1007/s11116-012-9409-6

13. Mattson, J., Godavarthy, R.: Bike share in Fargo, North Dakota: keys to success and factors affecting ridership. Sustain. Cities Soc. **34**(July), 174–182 (2017)

14. McDonald, N.C.: Household interactions and children's school travel: the effect of parental work patterns on walking and biking to school. J. Transp. Geogr. **16**(5), 324–331 (2008)

15. Migliore, M., Catalano, M.: Urban public transport optimization by bus ways: a neural network-based methodology. WIT Trans. Built Environ. **96**, 347–356 (2007)

16. Migliore, M., Lo Burgio, A., Di Giovanna, M.: Parking pricing for a sustainable transport system. Transp. Res. Procedia **3**, 403–412 (2014)

17. Moro, S.R., Imhof, A.C., Fettermann, D.C., Cauchick-Miguel, P.A.: Barriers to bicycle sharing systems implementation: analysis of two unsuccessful PSS. Procedia CIRP **73**, 191–196 (2018). https://doi.org/10.1016/J.PROCIR.2018.03.312

18. Muhs, C.D., Clifton, K.J.: Do characteristics of walkable environments support bicycling? Toward a definition of bicycle-supported development. J. Transp. Land Use **2**, 147–188 (2015)

19. Schofield, G., Schofield, L., Mummery, K.: Active transportation: an important part of adolescent physical activity. Youth Stud. Aust. **24**(1), 43–47 (2005)

20. Statistics Netherlands (CBS). Netherlands Travel Survey (OViN) (2016)

21. Stewart, O., Vernez Moudon, A., Claybrooke, C.: Common ground: eight factors that influence walking and biking to school. Transp. Policy **24**, 240–248 (2012)

22. Wang, J., Lindsey, G.: Do new bike share stations increase member use: a quasi-experimental study. Transp. Res. Part A Policy Pract. **121**, 1–11 (2019). https://doi.org/10.1016/J.TRA.2019.01.004

23. Zhang, Y., Mi, Z.: Environmental benefits of bike sharing: a big data-based analysis. Appl. Energy **220**, 296–301 (2018)

A Land Use and Transport Interaction Model for the Greater Florence Metropolitan Area

Massimiliano Petri[1](✉) ⓘ, Antonio Pratelli[1], Guglielmo Barè[2],
and Leonardo Piccini[3]

[1] Department of Civil and Industrial Engineering, University of Pisa, Pisa, Italy
{m.petri,a.pratelli}@ing.unipi.it
[2] Citilabs, Lodz, Poland
gbare@citilabs.com
[3] IRPET-Regional Institute for Economic Planning of Tuscany, Florence, Italy
leonardo.piccini@irpet.it

Abstract. The paper presents the first results of the LUTI model built to analyse territorial impact of future project in the area around Florence, starting from the province of Pistoia, and arriving to Florence throw Prato province. The works is made of two main steps: the first one is the collection, homogenization and comparison of actual most important planned measures at different scale, from the single involved municipalities to the Tuscany Regional Plan.

The second main step is the construction of a LUTI model to evaluate different evolution scenario joining complementary infrastructure and territorial evolution measures. The obtained results show the importance of the LUTI model to support territorial planning at a multidisciplinary level.

Keywords: Land use · Transport model · Big data · LUTI model · Florence metropolitan area

1 Introduction

Recent studies on the status of mobility at urban level, both at Italian national level [1] and at European level [2] show that actually there are not so satisfactory level of sustainability in our mobility relative to the objective of the general Environmental policies and objectives [3–5].

One of the causes of this phenomenon is the almost total absence of interdisciplinary in the daily practice of territorial and urban planning. Planning sectoriality leads to solutions that are not able to optimize the city and territory system, but it only provides partial solutions that answer the single problem (energy, transport, commerce, etc.) but do not read the city as a whole, a *"unicum"* body.

A clear and explanatory example of this phenomenon was the occasion of an analysis for the City of Cascina (Tuscany, Italy). It is an example of rare multidisciplinary approach regarding the impact of the measures of its Urban Planning

© Springer Nature Switzerland AG 2019
S. Misra et al. (Eds.): ICCSA 2019, LNCS 11620, pp. 231–246, 2019.
https://doi.org/10.1007/978-3-030-24296-1_20

Regulation on mobility, joining two sectors, which often and erroneously are very different[1].

The obtained results show that the urban planning already carried out is not compatible with the existing road infrastructures and with the flows generated by the new activities. In fact, these generate an increase in total traffic (daily there are about 125,000 trips in the urban area) between 20 and 44% (with some areas arriving in increments of over 500%) with consequent problems of congestion and the inadequate spaces parking number (actually, the parking supply is about 1,000 places).

This paper starts from the above necessary premise and describes a strategic and interdisciplinary planning case, carried out thanks to the sensitivity of the IRPET, Regional Institute for Economic Planning of Tuscany, highlighting all the innovative and interdisciplinary analysis.

In the first part of the paper, there is a general introduction about LUTI models, in the second part both the specific software program, and its embedded LUTI Model have introduced. The crucial and innovative research aspects have described in brief, while in the third part of the paper the study area jointly with the update project forecasts have presented. Finally, some results are discussed (the study is yet in progress for scenarios definition and simulation phase) of the first simulation scenarios implemented, emphasizing the multidisciplinary decision support provided by these applied models.

2 The Land Use and Transport Interaction Models

The models integrating urban development/land-use and the transport field are mainly divided between top-down models and bottom-up ones. Nevertheless, in the current literature, there are numerous classifications based on the purpose of the models, on their structure, on the analytical approach (own top-down versus bottom-up), on the general methodology, on the mathematical approach (optimization against simulation), on the analysis sectors, on the analyzed time horizons, on the data requested and other [6–9].

Taking four of the main criteria mentioned above and better detailed below, it is possible to make the following first attempt classification:

Criterion 1: Does the system allow interaction within the various elements that compose it (users, services, housing, etc. ..)?
Criterion 2: Do models capture emerging properties (bottom-up vs top-down)?
Criterion 3: Does the model consider time explicitly (static vs. dynamic)?
Criterion 4: Are spatial information explicitly considered?

Starting, in order of presentation, from these four criteria, can be sketched the following classification tree (see Fig. 1).

---

[1] For instance, also the new Tuscany Regional Urban Planning law on territorial governance, L. R.41/2018, does not never mention the word 'mobility'.

Reading the same from bottom to top it has found that the only models that do not consider the relationships between the internal elements of the system are the localization optimization models. These, starting from a series of possible localizations, following purely mathematical maximization principles under different kind of constraints (they are the models deriving from the theories of Operational Research), identify the best solution. These last have often used at the commercial level to locate the warehouse with respect to a network of sales points or to locate a sales point with respect to an existing network, trying to maximize the new customers reached and minimize the cannibalism effect.

All the other models can be considered as interaction models, where the LUTI models specifically consider the interaction between population, land-use/distribution of activities/gravitation of the individual areas and existing transport services.

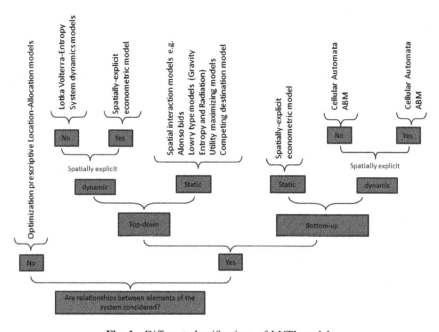

Fig. 1. Different classifications of LUTI models

Another differentiation is the type of model, or if the same captures emerging behaviors, in which case the analyst is faced to bottom-up models or does not have this ability and then it has talked about top-down models.

The most famous static top-down models are spatial interaction models deriving from Lowry's theory that predict travel flows between different zones, assuming the achievement of an equilibrium but without directly explaining the concept of time and considering variables such as population density, travel costs and job offers as invariants.

The top-down dynamic models work on successive simulations where a step represents the previous temporal situation that supplies the input data to the next step.

In this case the equilibrium can or cannot be reached (see the example in the following figure of the dynamic top-down model elaborated by Lombardo and Petri [10, 11] on the basis of the dynamic formulation of Wilson's spatial interaction model [12]) where the system dynamics is given by the following non-linear differential equation:

$$\frac{dS_j}{dt} = \varepsilon \left[\sum_i (R_i \cdot A_i \cdot S_j^\alpha \cdot e^{-\beta d_{ij}} \cdot fc_j) - B_j \cdot S_j \right] \tag{1}$$

$$A_i = \left(\sum_j S_j^\alpha \cdot e^{-\beta d_{ij}} \right)^{-1}$$

where:

S_j is the number of employees in the services; the considered typology includes services with a users basin which exceed the local size (municipalities), for example high schools, ipermarkets, sanitary services, etc.;

R_i is the number of users living in zone i;

d_{ij} is the time distance between cell i and j (calculated with the Floyd algorithm);

α is a measure of users scale-economies;

β is a measure of users predisposition to travel;

B_j is the total cost of management and installation of services;

A_i is a normalization factor;

fc_j is a scale factor.

These models can implicitly insert the spatial aspect, and then we talk about models such as the Lotka-Volterra, or models of the prey-predator type, or models that are called double constraint gravitational models (case of calculation of the simple flows) or with a single constraint in origin (for typical applications of the geo-marketing field) or in destination (for typical urban planning applications). In the case of explicit representation of the geographical component, we speak of spatial econometric models based on dynamic systems estimating their parameters on elements such as distance from the CBU, accessibility to areas and more.

On the other hand, there are bottom-up type models, i.e. models whose dynamics derive from the interaction between the individual elements of the system (also called microsimulation models). These models are of the cellular automata type or MAS-based agent-based models. The only static models are those with cellular automata or MAS where the individual cells/elements interact on the basis of pre-established rules that do not change during the simulation and that lead to predict the changes in distribution of land use.

These models have had different developments over time with bottom-up microsimulations representing the latest recent developments. We started in the mid-70s (Lowry's theory dates back to 1964 with the Model of Metropolis) with top-down models of the gravitational family, then we switched to the aggregate econometric type models that were the precursors of the models of microsimulation that apply theories of random utility at the individual level.

Focusing now on the LUTI models, these can be both top-down and bottom-up but they are usually dynamic, as they must explicitly insert internal dynamics and processes of change of different speeds [13]:

- Very slow changes: changes in the network and land use;
- Slow changes: variation in the distribution of assets and residences;
- Fast changes: changes in employees and the population;
- Very fast changes: changes to freight and passenger journeys

In the territorial area all these activities and changes interact, each with its own times, as shown in Table 1. The distribution of land uses (residential, industrial, commercial areas) determines the locations of human activities such as residence, work, shopping, study or recreational activities. The geographical distribution of activities requires travel to cover the distances necessary to move. The distribution of the transport infrastructure provides the accessibility levels and this distribution of accessibility in the space contributes to being a datum for future locations of activities and changes in land use. Then a cycle has activated and its center is precisely the use of the land.

Many of these (excluding the CUFM model) use the theory of Discrete Choice Models and involve behaviors of territorial actors such as investors, families, companies or travelers. The following table shows the main features of some of these models.

Table 1. Urban subsystems represented in land-use transport models and their temporal dimension (source: [14])

Models	Very slow		Slow		Fast		Immediate	
	Networks	Land use	Work-places	Housing	Employ-ment	Popula-tion	Goods transport	Travel
BOYCE	+				+	+		+
CUFM	(+)	+	+	+	+	+		(+)
DELTA	(+)	+	+	+	+	+		(+)
ILUTE	+	+	+	+	+	+	+	+
IMREL	+	+	+	+	+	+		+
IRPUD	+	+	+	+	+	+		+
ITLUP	+	+			+	+		+
KIM	+				+	+	+	+
LILT	+	+	+	+	+	+		+
MEPLAN	+	+	+	+	+	+	+	+
METROSIM	+	+	+	+	+	+		+
MUSSA	(+)			+	+	+		(+)
PECAS	+	+	+	+	+	+	+	+
POLIS	(+)	+			+	+		(+)
RURBAN	(+)	+			+	+		(+)
STASA	+	+	+	+	+	+	+	+
TLUMIP	+	+	+	+	+	+	+	+
TRANUS	+	+	+	+	+	+	+	+
TRESIS	+	+	+	+	+	+		+
URBANSIM	(+)	+	+	+	+	+		(+)

(+) provided by linked transport model

3 The Choice of the LUTI Model

The problem is the choice of the LUTI model compatible with the data and time available for the study.

The IRPET Institute needed results within a few months and had no functioning and updated transport model. This has led to the need to find a model integrating the transport part with the land use model and that does not require a long calibration time (so, for example, it can't be used the Austrian MARS model). On the other hand, IRPET wanted to use a model capable of providing simulations of dynamics not only for the employees or factories localization, but also for the evolution of the land use value (e.g., the dynamics of property values).

Therefore, the final choice has been the Cube Land Framework of Citilabs, a commercial software already used in many areas in the world (Milan, Montgomery-Alabama, Bakersfield-California, Metropolitan Council of the Twin Cities and others).

Cube Land models can be estimated by using disaggregated as well as aggregated data also if the forecasting process is represented by using an aggregate approach because it deal with zones, demand clusters and supply groups.

As input data, it requires:

- Control totals of households and jobs by type;
- Transportation accessibility measures by zone (to be defined by the modeler and calculated in the transport model of Cube);
- Any other relevant data and/or policies by zone (restrictions that certain land use types cannot be attributed to certain zones, subsidies and taxes)

As output data it gives:

- Households and jobs by type in each zone;
- Land uses by category in each zone;
- Locations (socio-economic information): number of Households/Firms (by cluster) in each zone and each real estate type
- Updated endogenous measures (e.g. average income)
- Supply (land uses by category): number of occupied real estates (by type) in each zone
- Economic measures: relative rental values for each real estate type (of land uses) by zone

Cube Land is a land-use forecasting model based on the Bid-Rent Theory [15, 16]. Bid Rent Theory says that the closer a property is to the center of the district, the more desirable it is. The further out a piece of land is, the smaller its value. The amount that the competing land users are willing to pay for these properties is called the bid rent. Following this theory Cube Land allocates aggregation of households and firms to real estate in each zone.

The Land Use algorithms have based on the MUSSA Land Use model developed by the Laboratory of Transport and Land Use Modelling (LABTUS) of the Faculty of Physical and Mathematical Sciences, University of Chile. The original model is been developed in 2000 for studies of land-use and transportation policy and in year 2006 it has been integrated into Cube™ suite. We do not want here to describe MUSSA model [17–20] in detail but only to introduce its main features.

MUSSA models land use changes by simulation of the real-estate market solving the classical location problem that is to say simulating the expected location of agents (residents and firms) in the urban area. Agents' behaviour is probabilistic while there are internal interactions that makes the equilibrium research a complex and nonlinear problem. In fact, the model assumes a final land use equilibrium state with a Microeconomic approach the system need to reach equilibrium between suppliers (developers) and consumers (households and firms). The calculation complexity is due to each agent location choice that depends on all other agents' choices with an internal endogenous dynamic. The system, also allows the explicit representation of the set of physical constraints (e.g. land availability) and planning regulations that supply must comply with (taxes, fares and others).

MUSSA has developed initially to build land use scenarios as inputs for the transportation model of the Santiago del Chile area. In this case study it has been used to forecast residential and non-residential location and, then, to estimate the transport demand required by the strategic transport equilibrium model in Santiago (previously, land use scenarios were estimated by using historical trends, linear growth rates, information of recent real estate projects, spatial capacity constraints, etc.). Thereafter, this model has also been used to detect relocation processes originated by transport projects (as we will see in the next paragraph, this is one of the project presents of our study area).

4   The Study Area and the Urbanistic Forecasts

The study area includes the whole Florence city urban area and the metropolitan area linking Florence to the city of Prato and Pistoia, the so-called "Piana Fiorentina". The main feature of this Area, which covers a surface of approximately 681 km², consists of the presence of a high tourist attractive city, i.e. Florence.

Moreover, there are several industrial locations, such as Pistoia tree nursery sector and industrial area of Prato, as well as a number of medium-sized urban centers (Signa, Lastra a Signa, Scandicci and other centers) gravitating towards Florence Area (see Fig. 2). In addition, the road network contains the E35 motorway linking Florence and surroundings to Northern Italy, mainly with Milan and Bologna, and to the South with Rome; while the A11 motorway, which connects Florence with the coastal area of Versilia, i.e. with cities of Viareggio and Forte dei Marmi. Finally, the regional road S. G.C. Fi-Pi-Li, links Florence Area with West cities of Pisa and Livorno [21].

4.1   The Collection of Project Forecasts

The first step, preliminary to each modeling activity, was the collection of data relating to the projects planned in the aforementioned area, searching from the regional Mobility plan up to the urbanistic forecasts of the single municipality.

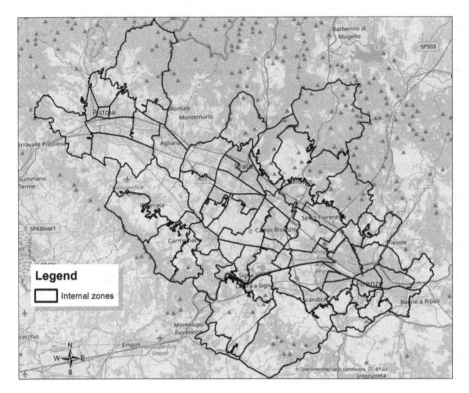

Fig. 2. The study area

The main road infrastructure projects are the four tramway lines completion, three new roads to avoid crossing flows in urban centers and four new roads including the one near Peretola Airport (dues to main airport runway direction change).

The greatest data collection work was the gathering and homogenization of the urbanistic forecasts (surfaces foreseen for each land use type) in the thirteen Municipalities involved. Results involved about 2.6 km^2 of which 49% of new residential settlements, 29% of new commercial areas and 22% of future productive/industrial areas. The new residential areas widely distributed, with the exception of the municipalities in the province of Pistoia while commercial areas are concentrated near Calenzano and Campi Bisenzio and the industrial/productive settlements are mainly in the area of Osmannoro in the North-West of Florence and in the South-West of Prato (see Fig. 3).

4.2   The Multimodal Transport Model

The multimodal transport model is based on a daily temporal step for an average winter school day. The area was divided into internal zones (71 zones, see Fig. 2), local outdoor areas, corresponding to the neighboring municipalities within the Florence province and areas outside the province itself. The private network transport supply was inherited from the existing graph of the Tuscany Region model, introducing some

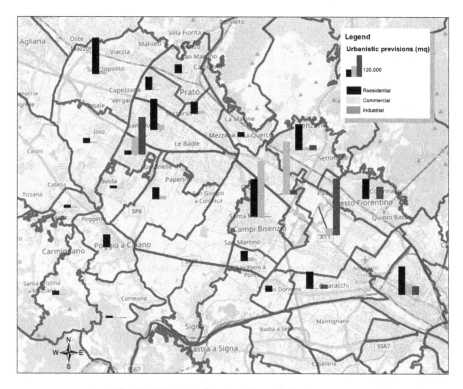

Fig. 3. Urbanistic forecasts for each land use type

further details in correspondence with future project areas. Furthermore, for the road cost functions calibration, the data of car insurance Black Box were asked at the CNR (Italian National Research Center), data consisting of GPS tracking points that is real big data, data on which extensive research has already been done [22–24] and which, after verifying the statistical significance of the data, allow us to calculate the average vehicles speed on the single street links.

Daily schedule public transport program where collected, both of rail service and for bus one and over 400 lines with frequency scheme and their mileage rates were loaded in the model.

Now the generation and distribution model step has built within Cube Voyager™, and both the generation and distribution steps have calibrated. The greatest difficulty has encountered in the generation step, because there were areas with similar characteristics at the level of employees and population but with different ability to generate/attract movements. The final calibration of the generation phase reported an RSquare index of 0.59 with a trend per zone as shown in Fig. 4. After, the distribution phase has calibrated, reaching in this case an RSquare value of 0.89 and verifying the same for distance bands equal to five kilometers (see Fig. 5). At the level of the modal split model, the model used in the city of Florence was inherited. The assignment phase finally has produced the cost matrices that are one of the inputs of the land use model and represent the interaction between the latter and the transport theory.

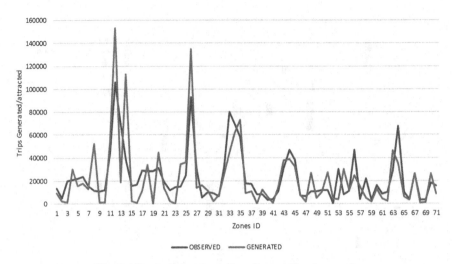

Fig. 4. Graph of the generation phase calibration results

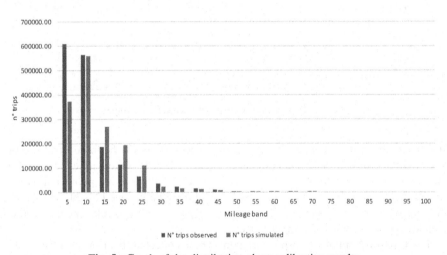

Fig. 5. Graph of the distribution phase calibration results

4.3   The Land Use Model

The Land Use model implement two main markets, namely the housing market and that of economic activities. For each market, a series of agents have introduced competing for the occupation of the territory and localization choice.

In relation to the residential market, the agents identified, quantified at household level for each zone, are:

- Household with head without work - Agent 1 (divided between students and unemployed);
- Household with head without work - agent 2 (retired);

- Low-income households;
- Middle-income households;
- High-income households.

In relation to the business sector, the following agents have introduced:

- Activities of the large-scale retail trade;
- Minor commercial activities (<20,000 km² surface);
- Tertiary sector activities;
- Productive/Industrial activities

The data collected, about accessibility (time to reach all other zones with private or public modes or time to be reached in a passive viewpoint), land values, employees, population, school system and others, allowed us to calibrate the Land Use model Bid Rent Functions based on two Discrete Choice Models (Login Multinomial model), one relating to the residential market and the other relating to economic activities one. Biogeme™ software [25] has used to calibrate the above models. The following are the utility functions generated by the aforementioned model for the two markets:

- Residential Market (Likelihood ratio test: 225.025, Adjusted rho-square: 0.179)
    Utility (Students/Unemployed) = −0.00765 * Private active Accessibility Index + 5.87 * N° Household (Stud/Unempl.)
    Utility (Retired) = −0.000914 * Private active Accessibility Index + 5.87 * N° Household (Retired)
    Utility (Low Income Hous.) = −0.0104 * Private active Accessibility Index + 7.13 * N° Household (Low Income Hous.)
    Utility (Medium Income Hous.) = −0.00592 * Private active Accessibility Index + 6.67 * N° Household (Medium Income Hous.)
    Utility (High Income Hous.) = −0.0223 * Private active Accessibility Index + 12.6 * N° Household (High Income Hous.)
- Activities Market (Likelihood ratio test: 237.581, Adjusted rho-square: 0.271)
    Utility (Minor Commercial Act.) = −1.48 * av1 −0.0113 * Private active Accessibility Index + 8.65 * Minor Commercial Act. Percentage
    Utility (Large-scale Retail Trade Act.) = −2.55 * av2 −0.00626 * Private active Accessibility Index + 18 * Large-scale Retail Trade Act. Percentage
    Utility (Tertiary Sector Act.) = 2.44 * av3 −0.0172 * Private active Accessibility Index −3.84 * Tertiary Sector Act. Percentage
    Utility (Productive Act.) = 1.60 * av4 −0.0103 * Private active Accessibility Index −2.18 * Productive Act. Percentage

The previous equations show some important features: High Income Households, in the Residential Market, are the agents most sensitive to proximity to other agents of the same type. Moreover, these last give greater weight to accessibility while accessibility is important for all residential agents excluding retired people. With attention focused on the Activities Market, it is clear that Large-scale Retail Trade activities are the most sensitive to proximity to similar agents, but they give low importance to accessibility index; commercial activities, in general, search to localize near other commercial ones while for Tertiary and Productive Sectors there is a negative weight to the presence of other similar activities.

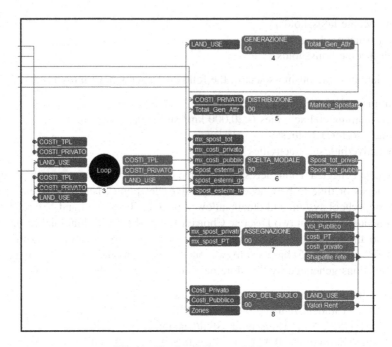

Fig. 6. The Land-Use model loop

These equations have introduced in the model inside the Land-Use equilibrium loop (see Fig. 6).

5   Results and Future Researches

The first simulated scenario regards the complete functionality of the tramway lines, including some extensions not yet present but planned. The introduction of an easy access system to the Florence CBU highlighted two very interesting phenomena, one relating to the population residences distribution and the other to the activity market.

In relation to the first one, given the increase of real estate values of the center, a phenomenon of migration towards external areas was highlighted; areas at lower costs, made closer by the tramway, became of interest for low-income households against an increase of population in the center for high-income households (see Fig. 7). Probably, this interest for the center underline their attempt to invest in its space and in the value that this area comes to have, buying homes to rent to foreigners and tourists. In practice, it can be hypothesized the origin of the classical Gentrification dynamic, given the tourist rents high profitability. This would lead to the loss of identity of the central inhabited areas, certainly a phenomenon to be avoided by housing policies aimed at encouraging population to remain in the city center. Another phenomenon emerged, relating to the activity sector, is due to the increase in the land value in the peripheral areas made more accessible by the tramway. The model shows a replacement phenomenon between tertiary and industrial activities: in fact the former tend to move to

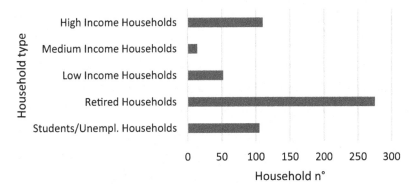

Fig. 7. Number of households divided for type changing their residential location

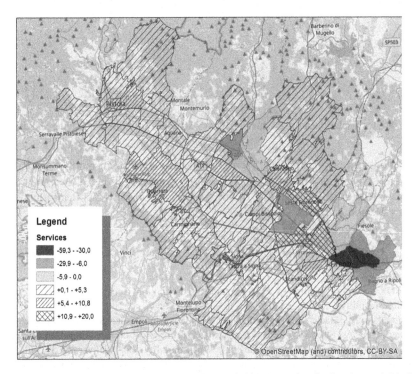

Fig. 8. The replacement of Tertiary/Services activities (negative for leaving activities)

the new areas made accessible by the tramway where the population will increase while the industrial activities tend to move to areas where land value does not change, areas not affected by the tramway presence (see Figs. 8 and 9).

As a result, the model in this first scenario shows very interesting and useful land-use dynamics able to change the residences and activities distribution in the study area and to influence the territory gravitational power with a deep impact on the flows

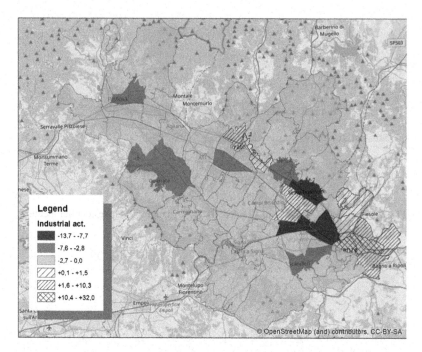

Fig. 9. The replacement of Productive Sectors activities (negative for leaving activities)

distribution with respect to a static territorial scenario, typical of purely transportation models. The analysis of further scenarios, for example, the one related to the City Urbanistic Plan forecasts (see Fig. 6) will add other decision support information for Tuscany Region and IRPET Institute.

References

1. ISFORT-Superior Institute of Teaching and Researching on Transport, 2018: 15° Report on Italian mobility
2. Chinellato, M., Staelens, P., Wennberg, H., Sundberg, R., Bohler, S., Brand, L., Adams, R., Dragutescu, A.: Sumps-Up-Users' needs analysis on SUMP take up. European programme for accelerating the take-up of sustainable urban mobility plans, deliverable 1, 2 (2017)
3. European Commission 2007: Sustainable Urban Transport Plans - Preparatory Document in relation to the follow-up of the Thematic Strategy on the Urban Environment, Annex, 25 September 2007, Source. http://ec.europa.eu/environment/urban/pdf/transport/2007_sutp_annex.pdf
4. European Commission 2009: Action Plan on Urban Mobility COM, 490/5 (2009). Source. http://ec.europa.eu/transport/themes/urban/urban_mobility/action_plan_en.htm
5. European Commission 2011: WHITE PAPER. Roadmap to a Single European Transport Area – Towards a competitive and resource efficient transport system. COM (2011). 144 final. Source: http://ec.europa.eu/transport/themes/strategies/2011_white_paper_en.htm

6. Oliva Garcia, C.R., Feijòo, C., Aggarwal, S.: D2.3 Review of Urban Models: Use in Urban Policy, European project Insight (2014)
7. Ransford, A.A., Silva, E.: Land use-transport interaction modeling: a review of the literature and future research directions. J. Transp. Land Use (2014)
8. Iacono, M., Levinson D., El-Genheidi A.: Models of transportation and land use change: a guide to the territory (2010)
9. Rosenbaum, A.S., Koenig, B.E.: Evaluation of Modeling Tools for Assessing lan use policies and strategies, Office of Mobile Sources U.S. Environmental Protection Agency (1997)
10. Lombardo, S., Petri, M.: The simulation of spatial change: what relation between knowledge and modeling? A proposal and its application. In: Albeverio, S., Andrey, D., Giordano, P., Vancheri, A. (eds.) The Dynamics of Complex Urban Systems. An Interdisciplinary Approach. Springer, Heidelberg (2007). https://doi.org/10.1007/978-3-7908-1937-3_16
11. Lapucci, A., Lombardo, S., Petri, M., Rotonda, M.: A participative multi agent system for urban sustainable mobility. In: Murgante, B., Borruso, G., Lapucci, A. (eds.) Geocomputation and Urban Planning a cura di Borruso. Murgante e Lapucci. Springer, Heidelberg (2009). https://doi.org/10.1007/978-3-540-89930-3_15. ISBN 978-3-540-89929-7
12. Wilson, A.G., Bennett, R.J.: Mathematical Methods in Human Geography and Planning. John Wiley and Sons, Chichester (1985)
13. Waddell, P.: Building an integrated model: some guidance. In: Presented at, TRB workshop 162 on integrated land use-transport models, Washington, D.C. (2005)
14. Wegener, M.: Overview OD land-use transport models. In: Hensher, D.A., Button, K. (eds.) Transport Geography and Spatial Systems, Handbook 5 of the Handbook in Transport, pp. 127–146. Pergamon/Elsevier Science, Kidlington (2004)
15. Alonso, W.: Location and Land Use, Towards a General Theory of Land Use. Harward University Press, Cambridge (1964). ISBM 9780674730854
16. Ross, S., Morgan, J., Heelas, R.: Essential AS Geography, Nelson Thornes Ltd (2000). ISBN-10: 0748751750
17. Martínez, F., Donoso, P.: MUSSA: a behavioural land use equilibrium model with location externalities, planning regulations and pricing policies, University of Chile (2006)
18. Martínez, F., Aguila, F., Hurtubia, R.: The constrained multinomial logit: A semi-compensatory choice model. University of Chile, Santiago, Chile (2009)
19. Martínez, F.J.: MUSSA: A Land Use Model for Santiago City. Transportation Research Record 1552: Transportation Planning and Land Use at State, Regional and Local Levels, pp. 126–134 (1996)
20. Martínez, F.J.: The bid-choice land use model: an integrated economic framework. Environ. Plann. A. **24**, 871–885 (1992)
21. Pratelli, A., Petri, M., Ierpi, M., Di Matteo, M.: Integration of Bluetooth, vechicle count data and transport model results by means of Datamining Techniques. The application to the regional highway S.G.C.Fi-Pi-Li linking Florence to Leghorn and Pisa. In: 2017 IEEE 16th International Conference on Environment and Electrical Engineering (EEEIC), 12–15 June 2018. Palermo (2018)
22. Petri, M., Frosolini, M, Pratelli, A., Lupi, M.: ITS to change behaviour: a focus about bike mobility monitoring and incentive—The SaveMyBike system. In: IEEE 16th International Conference on Environment and Electrical Engineering (EEEIC) (2016). https://doi.org/10.1109/eeeic.2016.7555463. ISBN: 978-1-5090-2321-9
23. Petri, M., Fusco, G., Pratelli, A.: A new data-driven approach to forecast freight transport demand. In: Murgante, B., et al. (eds.) ICCSA 2014. LNCS, vol. 8582, pp. 401–416. Springer, Cham (2014). https://doi.org/10.1007/978-3-319-09147-1_29

24. Petri, M., Pratelli, A., Fusco, G.: Data mining and big freight transport database analysis and forecasting capabilities. Trans. Marit. Sci. **5**(2), 99–110 (2016)
25. Bierlaire, M.: BIOGEME: a free package for the estimation of discrete choice models. In: Proceedings of the 3rd Swiss Transportation Research Conference. Ascona, Switzerland (2003)

Advanced Computational Approaches in FracTals, WaveleT, EnTropy and DaTa mining applications (AAFTWTETDT 2019)

Computational Methods for OCT Images Analyze Provided Within Diabetic Retinopathy

Daniela Moraru[1]($\boxtimes$), Sanziana Istrate[2], Cecilia Eniceicu[3],
and Paul E. Sterian[1,4]

[1] Academic Center for Optical Engineering and Photonics,
Politehnica University, Bucharest, Romania
`moraru.danuta@gmail.com`
[2] Ophthalmology Department, "Carol Davila" University of Medicine
and Pharmacy, Bucharest, Romania
[3] Ophthalmology Department, University Emergency Hospital Bucharest,
Bucharest, Romania
[4] Academy of Romanian Scientists, Bucharest, Romania

Abstract. The paper aims to evaluate the variability of the retinal macular thickness to the glycaemic level in non-proliferative diabetic retinopathy by measuring the retinal thickness using the spectral domain optical-coherence tomography (SD-OCT), during daytime, for patients with diabetic retinopathy (DR) or without diabetes mellitus (DM). The evaluation was carried out using the ImageJ software as a processed method of OCT images from the analysed patients and the Origin 6.0 software as an analytical method of OCT macular thickness data. The paper demonstrated that not only the age of the patients but also the time of the day are significant factors that influence diabetic retinopathy. In addition, the paper also highlights the possibility of controlling retinopathy through differential correction of the glycaemic index at the time the specific medication is provided.

Keywords: Optical coherence tomography · Diabetes mellitus ·
Diabetic retinopathy · Macular retinal thickness · ImageJ

1 Introduction

In the first part of this paper, are shown some aspects regarding Optical Coherence Tomography (OCT) from both theoretical and biomedical point of view. Also the paper contains some information about Diabetes Mellitus (DM) and Diabetic Retinopathy (DR) as important elements in understanding the study field of interest. In the second part are presented the method we used in data collecting: patients characteristics, instruments, timetable, investigation type. In the same time, we included in this paper the way we used ImageJ in making supplementary distances measurements, as OCT offered directly. The paper is continuing with results presentation, using graphics for comparison between OCT data and ImageJ data, for all foveolar zones. This paper is ending with conclusions regarding obtained results.

© Springer Nature Switzerland AG 2019
S. Misra et al. (Eds.): ICCSA 2019, LNCS 11620, pp. 249–256, 2019.
https://doi.org/10.1007/978-3-030-24296-1_21

This paper compares overall data provided automatically by OCT device for retinal macular thickness with data provided by individual measurements of retinal layers thickness. More than that the comparisons are made for all three macular sectorial zones, in order to provide a more detailed analyses of variability of these thicknesses with glycaemic level.

Optical Coherence Tomography (OCT) is a broadband lower coherence interferometric imaging technique which measures the backscattering light from the sample to reconstruct the depth-resolved structures. Depending on the implementation scheme, OCT can be categorized into time-domain OCT (TD-OCT) and Fourier-domain OCT (FD-OCT). FD-OCT can be realized by different configurations of light sources and detectors, such as point-scanning spectral domain OCT (SD-OCT), and point-scanning and full-field swept source OCT (SS-OCT). The collected data is equivalent, or equivalent under a Fourier transform along the axial/wavenumber axis [1].

Other specialized papers as [2, 14]: indicate the following OCT methods frequency domain (FD-OCT), time domain (TD-OCT) and spectral domain (SD-OCT). The last one could be of two types: based on a spectrometer (SB-OCT) or having laser with controlled frequency (SS-OCT). The swept-source version proves to be the fastest OCT methods who offers enough clarity of in vivo images. For both spectral-domain methods it is a limitation for coherence length for interference who is decreasing with increasing the emitting spectral length. The advantage of this method consists in N times greater sensitivity (N being the number of spectral windows in OCT) and in superiority regarding acquisition data rates (a much better signal/noise ratio).

The intensity of the light incident upon the detector (1) is given by recombination of the light in both arms of the interferometer:

$$\langle I \rangle = \langle I_r \rangle + \langle I_s \rangle + 2Re\left[\langle \Psi_r^*(t, z_r) \cdot \Psi_s(t, z_s)\rangle\right] \tag{1}$$

where $\Psi(t, z)$ is the light-amplitude field vector, subscripts r and s denote the reference and the sample arms, respectively, z_r and z_s are the optical path lengths (see Fig. 1), and the angle brackets denote ensemble averaging.

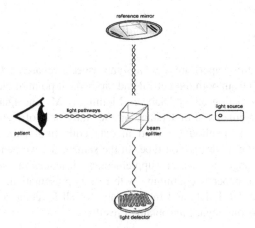

Fig. 1. Functioning principle of OCT based on interferometer

The source spectral density $S(\omega)$ is assumed to be Gaussian (2):

$$\left\{ \propto exp\left[-(\omega - \omega_0)^2 \Omega^2 \right] \right\} \tag{2}$$

with

$$\text{FWHM} = 2\Omega\sqrt{ln2}\,\text{rad/s} \tag{3}$$

Optical Coherence Tomography is used as a non-invasive and in-time imaging method of in vivo tissues, where the new technological methods of the microsurgery and nanotechnology are present [3, 4]. This investigation method is very valuable for medical fields, because it has the capacity to deliver tissues images with high depth resolution, histologic visible. OCT is of interest to ophthalmology, to dermatology, to dentine imaging or, using catheter, to internal organs.

Diabetes Mellitus (DM) has become one of the most prevalent health worldwide problems during last years. Type 2 of DM as the most common form of DM typically occurs in adult patients; meanwhile Type 1 diabetes typically occurs in young patients.

If in 2013 the estimated number was 382 million people suffering from DM and 415 million in 2015, this number could rise to 592 million in 2035, or 642 million in 2040 [5]. In recognition with this estimation, at European level was developed a strategy based mainly on prevention and control of this chronic disease (arisen from The Joint Action on Chronic Diseases and Promoting Healthy Ageing Across the Life Cycle). [6] The earlier DM is detected the better for patients in avoiding visual loss.

Retinal thickness is calculated by the software of the OCT machine which measures automatically the retinal layers, creating retinal maps that can be compared with the normative database, allowing monitoring of the evolution and treatment in time. Optical coherence tomography can show other characteristics of diabetic retinopathy, like hard exudates from the outer plexiform layer, visualized as hyper-reflective areas, can detect intra-retinal and sub-retinal fluid, visualized as hypo reflective spaces, can even detect subclinical macular edema [7–10]. Through OCT, loss or destruction of other retinal layers can be demonstrated, for example, photoreceptor layer or retinal nerve fibre layer, which helps with the differential diagnosis of decreased vision in a diabetic patient. It is useful in the diagnosis of vitreoretinal interface, epiretinal membrane and vitreomacular traction [11, 12].

2 Methods

The present study was conducted according to an ethical Committee regulation and all patients signed an informed consent.

This study [12] is based on OCT images resulted from investigation of 24 patients with diabetic retinopathy (DR) and 19 patients without diabetes mellitus (DM) as control group. The patients had variable GI values during daytime, at 9.00, 12.00, 15.00

and 18.00 o'clock. The exclusion criteria from the study group consisted in other ocular pathologies than DR, media opacities and score below 7/10. Some works [13, 15] recommended 4 to 7/10 score for a better SD-OCT scanning and over 8/10 score for a high quality.

Our study is based on both OCT images (taken with Cirrus™ HD-OCT model, produced by Carl Zeiss Meditec, Inc., class II, acc. 21 CFR 886.1570) and ImageJ measurement within images provided by OCT for probes from 24 patients with diabetic retinopathy, and 19 patients without diabetes mellitus in the control group, for one or both eyes. Glycaemia level was measured with Beurer GL 42/dl glucometer, and the systemic blood pressure with Beurer BM 44 electronic device.

Cirrus™ HD-OCT model is a computing device which takes and analyses cross-sectional tomograms of anterior and posterior ocular structures (including cornea, retina, optic nerve head layers, macula and optic disc). We used Macular Cube 512 × 128 images acquisition type. On these images we delimitated three relevant zones (central, para-foveolar and peri-foveolar) for our research (see Fig. 2). These are also provided with retinal thickness values by Cirrus™ HD-OCT model computing device (see Fig. 2).

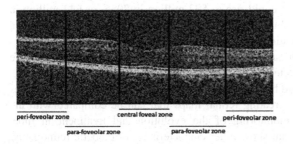
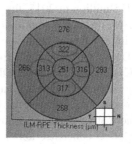

Fig. 2. Zone delimitation on macula cube image type and retinal thickness values provided by OCT device

Particularly we used ImageJ to make distance measurements only on ISel (photoreceptor inner segment ellipsoid) layer (see Fig. 3), as some authors [13, 15] indicate them to be the retinal layers with major influence on eye sight. ImageJ is an open source Java image processing program who can acquire, display, edit, enhance, analyse and animate images. It can be used to measure area, mean, centroid, perimeter, etc. of user defined regions of interest. For a better precision we made three different distance measurements for each zone (marked with black vertical lines). For para-foveolar and peri-foveolar zones, we considered only nasal and temporal sectors.

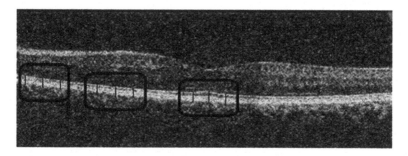

Fig. 3. Areas delimitation for ImageJ measurements

3 Results and Discussions

In our previous articles [7, 12] we established that it's a correlation between daily variation glycaemic level and retinal thickness, both from OCT perspective and ImageJ measurements. Those works were made only for small parts of foveola. This time we realized an overview on all collected data and, in the same time, a complete comparison between values offered by both distance evaluation method.

Comparing data from Fig. 4 we concluded that diabetic retinopathy has two major influences regarding retinal thickness by itself and its variation with glycaemic index. On one hand, patients with DR have a thicker retina for smaller GI and thinner for bigger GI, than retinal thickness for patients without DM. On the other hand, all foveolar zones (central, para-foveolar and peri-foveolar) are affected in thickness by GI daily variation for patients with DR, presenting a significant decreasing with GI increasing, especially for central and para-foveolar zones. In the same time, for patients without DM, GI variation has almost none influence on retinal thickness, in according with OCT delivered data. It seems that for the first group, retina has a pronounced inertia in establishing basic thickness after an increasing of glycaemia.

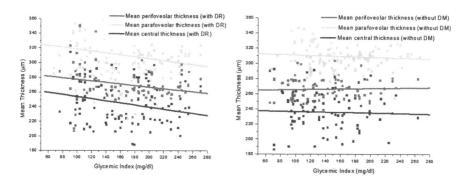

Fig. 4. Retinal thickness variation with GI for patients with DR and without DM

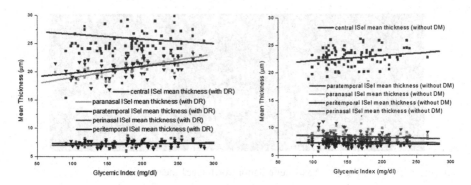

Fig. 5. ISel thickness variation with GI for patients with DR and without DM

From ImageJ measurements we have got graphics from Fig. 5. There is a consistent difference between main value for ISel thickness in para-foveolar zones for patients with DR and without DM.

For patients without DM we obtained almost the same lack of variation as OCT data provided, except central zone where is present a slowly increasing of layer thickness with GI increasing. For patients with diabetic retinopathy measurements have shown instead a consistent increasing of layer thickness in para-foveolar sectors and, in the same time, a considerable decreasing in central zone.

For patients having DR we found a slowly decrease in retinal thickness with increasing of GI, but for ISel we found a consistent increasing of this layer thickness with GI increasing, more obvious for para-foveolar zone, than peri-foveolar zone.

For patients without DM there are small differences between variations at retinal thickness level and variation at ISel thickness level, both for para and peri-foveolar zones.

Another perspective on collected data is the dependence of the retinal thickness by age and moment of the day. Figure 6 illustrates how mean retinal thickness for para-foveolar and peri-foveolar zones is decreasing with age, for both patients with DR and without DM. Only for the central zone, the variations are opposite, being a sensitive increasing for patients with DR.

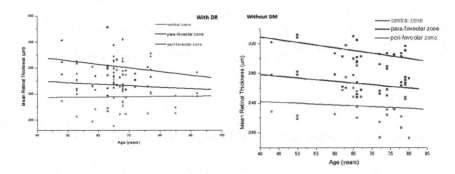

Fig. 6. Mean retinal thickness variation with age for patients with DR and without DM

Figure 7 contains the dependence of central retinal thickness during daytime for both study groups and for different age groups. For patients having DR there is no a significant variation of retinal thickness during daytime for any of age groups. Instead, for the youngest patients (40–60 years old) without diabetes mellitus, there is a consistent thickness increasing during daytime.

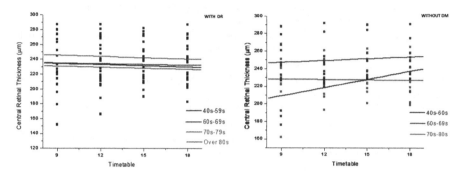

Fig. 7. Central retinal thickness variation with daytime for patients with DR and without DM

4 Conclusions

This study level revealed that glycaemic index daily variation has influence on retinal thickness, but more important for patients having diabetic retinopathy than for those who do not have diabetes mellitus.

Data obtained with ImageJ measurements are almost the same with those resulted from OCT measurements. The biggest difference appeared for para-foveolar sectors, for patients with DR, where the variation in ISel thickness is inversed comparing with variation of retinal thickness. One hypothesis could consist in considering the relevance of energy transformations which are taking place at photoreceptors cells level. The results however correlate with data from literature where the increased retinal thickness in DM is due to the capillary exudations in moments with high glycaemic levels. Probably for retina affected by diabetes tissue rebuilding process is slower and not too efficient.

Our collected data and their interpretations show that this kind of study should be made again, mostly for patients aged between 35 and 60 years old, which retinal thickness variability seems to be partial or totally reversible.

Acknowledgements. All authors have equal contribution to this paper.

The authors declare no financial interest.

References

1. De Boer, J.F., Milner, T.E., Van Gemert, M.J.C., Nelson, S.J.: Two-dimensional birefringence imaging in biological tissue by polarization-sensitive optical coherence tomography. Opt. Lett. **22**(12), 933–936 (1997)
2. Balasubramanian, M., Bowd, C., Vizzeri, G., Weinreb, R.N., Zangwill, L.M.: Effect of image quality on tissue thickness measurements obtained with spectral-domain optical coherence tomography. Opt. Express **17**(5), 4019 (2009)
3. Iliescu, F.S., et al.: Continuous separation of white blood cell from blood in a microfluidic device. UPB Sci. Bull. Ser. A **71**(4), 21–30 (2009)
4. Lazar, B., et al.: Simulating delayed pulses in organic materials. In: Gavrilova, M., et al. (eds.) ICCSA 2006. LNCS, vol. 3980, pp. 779–784. Springer, Heidelberg (2006). https://doi.org/10.1007/11751540_84
5. Kumar, B., Gupta, S.K., Saxena, R., Srivastava, S.: Current trends in the pharmacotherapy of diabetic retinopathy. J. Postgrad. Med. **58**(2), 132 (2012)
6. Richardson, E., Zaletel, J., Nolte, E.: National Diabetes Plans in Europe. World Health Organization 2016 (2016)
7. Moraru, D., et al.: Incursion in a contrast sensitivity changes related to non-proliferative diabetic retinopathy. In: 20th International Conference, Bulgaria, 26–30 June 2018
8. Cunha-Vaz, J., Coscas, G.: Diagnosis of macular edema. Ophthalmologica **224**(Suppl 1), 2–7 (2010)
9. Drexler, W., et al.: Ultrahigh-resolution ophthalmic optical coherence tomography. Nat. Med. **7**(4), 502–507 (2001)
10. Wojtkowski, M., et al.: Ophthalmic imaging by spectral optical coherence tomography. Am. J. Ophthalmol. **138**(3), 412–419 (2004)
11. Sikorski, B.L., et al.: The diagnostic function of OCT in diabetic maculopathy. Mediators Inflamm. 434–560 (2013)
12. Moraru, D., Spulber, C., Istrate, S., Eniceicu, C.: A brief study about the influences of glycemia variations in a non-proliferative diabetic retinopathy. Ann. Acad. Rom. Sci. Ser. Sci. Technol. Inf. **11**(2), 23–34 (2018). ISSN 2066-8562
13. Saxena, S., et al.: Photoreceptor inner segment ellipsoid band integrity on SD-OCT. Clin. Ophthalmol. Dove Press J. **8**, 2507–2522 (2014)
14. Sterian, A.R., et al.: A new possibility of experimental characterization of a time of flight telemetric system. Rom. Rep. Phys. **64**(3), 891–904 (2012)
15. Scoles, D., et al.: Assessing photoreceptor structure associated with ellipsoid zone disruptions visualized with optical coherence tomography. Retina (Philadelphia Pa.) **36**(1), 91 (2016)

Multifractal Analysis with L2 Norm Denoising Technique: Modelling of MS Subgroups Classification

Yeliz Karaca[1](✉), Majaz Moonis[2], and Yu-Dong Zhang[3]

[1] University of Massachusetts Medical School, Worcester, MA 01655, USA
yeliz.karaca@ieee.org, yeliz.karaca@umassmemorial.org
[2] Department of Neurology and Psychiatry, University of Massachusetts
Medical School, Worcester, MA 01655, USA
majaz.moonis@umassmemorial.org
[3] Department of Informatics, University of Leicester, Leicester LE1 7RH, UK
yudongzhang@ieee.org

Abstract. Multifractal methods are employed to recognize the significant attributes through the removal of the noise in any dataset. Being a useful and sensitive technological tool, magnetic resonance imaging (MRI) is employed for the diagnosis of chronic diseases of the central nervous system, one of which is Multiple Sclerosis disease (MS). MS subgroups (Primary Progressive MS (PPMS), Relapsing Remitting MS (RRMS) and Secondary Progressive MS (SPMS)) were examined in this study. The dataset is based on the Expanded Disability Status Scale (EDSS) and MRI that belong to 139 individuals in total, 120 of whom have one of the MS subgroups, and 19 are healthy individuals. The stages of the study are as follows: (i) L2 Norm Denoising, which is a multifractal method was applied on the MS dataset, namely the MS dataset. From this application, the new dataset was formed. (ii) The new dataset (MS_L2 Norm dataset) which is comprised of the significant attributes was obtained as a result of the application in (i). (iii) K-means clustering algorithm was applied on both the MS dataset and MS_L2 Norm dataset for the classification of the MS subgroups. (iv) The classification accuracy rate for the K-means clustering algorithm in relation to the MS dataset and MS_L2 Norm dataset was compared both for patients with MS subgroups and healthy individuals. For the first time, through this study, the K-means classification has been performed by using multifractal denoising methods for the aforementioned dataset. The results of our study show that K-means algorithm and classification yielded more accurate results for the MS_L2 Norm dataset compared to the MS dataset in terms of classification. Overall, this study has aimed to bridge a gap in the literature.

Keywords: Multifractal Denoising method · K-means algorithm · MS subgroup · Clustering · MRI

© Springer Nature Switzerland AG 2019
S. Misra et al. (Eds.): ICCSA 2019, LNCS 11620, pp. 257–269, 2019.
https://doi.org/10.1007/978-3-030-24296-1_22

1 Introduction

Being common in nature, multifractal systems are a generalization of a fractal system where a single exponent, or the fractal dimension, proves is to be insufficient to describe its dynamics, thus, in a continuous spectrum of exponents is required [1]. Multifractal analysis employs the basis of mathematics to examine datasets, frequently accompanied by other fractal analysis methods. Besides being applied in various practical situations, multifractal analysis techniques are implemented for interpreting medical images, in finance sector, bioinformatics and areas concerning natural sciences. The multifractal denoising algorithm is utilized as a technique adapted to complex images and signals. This technique serves for improvement in the data in question [2,3].

Multifractal methods are employed neuroscience. Accordingly, they are used for the neurological disorders' identification and classification. One disease is Multiple Sclerosis (MS), a condition that involves the spinal cord and/or the brain, causing various symptoms. In addition, inflammatory lesions are detected in different regions of the Central Nervous System [4–7]. Some of the most frequently diagnosed MS subgroups are Relapsing-Remitting MS (RRMS), Secondary Progressive MS (SPMS), Primary Progressive MS (PPMS), Relapsing Progressive MS (RPMS), Benign MS, Spinal form of MS, CIS as well as RIS [5].

In this present study, the data from three MS subgroups were examined. These subgroups are RRMS, SPMS and PPMS. RRMS subgroup resembles the benign type and following seizures, a total recovery may be observed [6–9]. The research reports that more than eight in every ten diagnosed MS patients belong to the "Relapsing Remitting" subgroup. In another subgroup, Secondary Progressive MS (SPMS), the onset resembles the one in "Relapsing Remitting" subgroup. Following the early period of an average of 5–6 years, the disorder progresses. It is observed that there is less chance of recovery and more of disability [6–10]. Besides this, RRMS may evolve into SPMS in some patients. Thirdly, Primary Progressive MS (PPMS) may be a slow or rapid progression staring from the very beginning, and generally it does not show any improvement [5–10].

For the classification of MS, in recent years, early diagnosis has critical so that the disease can be taken under control early and treatment process can be initiated as early as possible. Concerning the MS subgroups' diagnosis and classification are examined, several studies can be cited. There are a number of studies concerning the use of linear models formed. A study by Karaca et al. [7] utilized linear model and obtained a 100% accuracy for the distinction of MS patients and healthy individuals. The accuracy rate for the classification of RRMS and SPMS/PPMS patients and RRMS/SPMS patients was 94% and 78.94%, respectively. For the determination and classification of MS subgroups, deep learning methods are also useful. In this regard, the study by [11] employed Support Vector Machines and Deep Learning to the classification of the 3 subgroups of MS, namely RRMS, PPMS and SPMS. Their results show that Deep Learning generated a more comprehensive system in the classification. Furthermore, the accuracy rate of Deep Learning algorithm is higher compared with the accuracy obtained by multiclass SVM algorithm kernel types. Based on deep learning, this study aims to develop a convolutional neural network system that is improved. With the Convex Combination of Infinite Kernels model applied in their study, [6] realized the development of a clinical decision support system for the classification of the diagnostics of the patients. The study results demonstrate that the proposed model classifies MS subgroups' diagnosis level with a higher accuracy rate than the single kernel, artificial neural network and the other machine learning methods.

There are several studies on FCM and k-NN algorithms. To illustrate, [12] proposed a new clustering method using the k nearest neighbours and a density method based on k-nearest neighbours (k-NN) for the completion of the clustering process. The results of their experiments on the human face image data and synthetic data indicated that the algorithm at stake proved to be effective for the aim of their study. Another study by [13] worked on lung cancer, which aimed at identifying the pulmonary nodules in the lung computed tomography (CT) images by employing a hybrid intelligent approach. The authors utilized a type-II fuzzy algorithm and subsequently, a new segmentation algorithm based on fuzzy c-means clustering named as modified spatial kernelized fuzzy c-means (MSFCM) clustering. The researchers used three classifiers, including k-nearest neighbours (k-NN), Support Vector Machine (SVM) and Multilayer Perceptron (MLP) for the actual diagnosis and to determine if the nodule candidate is cancerous or healthy. The results obtained verified the potential useful performance of the proposed hybrid approach. Another relevant study was conducted by [14]. They proposed Computer-aided design (CAD) system, using the cascading of Fuzzy C-Means (FCM) and region-growing (RG) algorithm named FCMRG. As a result of their experiments, the classification accuracy was found out to be of 98.2% for the Mammographic Image Analysis Society (MIAS) dataset and the accuracy rate was found to be 95.8% for the Digital Database for Screening Mammography (DDSM). One more study that can be cited within this scope was conducted by [15] in which an algorithm for tumor delineation in positron emission tomography (PET) was presented. A local active contour algorithm was used to achieve segmentation, and k-nearest neighbour (k-NN) classification method was utilized for the integration and optimization. The approach proposed by the authors considered the delineation of cancers afflicting various body parts such as neck, brain, lung and head. The novel aspect of their approach is related to a novel form of energy. The results of their investigation demonstrate that it is possible to use the proposed method in clinical settings through the attainment of a reasonable level of accuracy in real-life instances.

There has been a major interest in the handling of medical data by means of fractal and multifractal techniques over the recent years. In the studies [16–19], the importance of fractal and multifractal techniques for data analysis in medicine has been highlighted. Apart from these, They [1] have studies with the datasets comprised of MS patients' Magnetic resonance imaging (MRIs). In one of their studies, Brownian motion Hölder regularity functions (polynomial, periodic (sine), exponential) for 2D image were applied to the dataset.

They performed an MS classification based on the multifractal method by the Self-Organizing Map (SOM) algorithm. As a result, a cluster analysis was obtained by identifying pixels from the afflicted regions revealed MRIs through the multifractal methods. Regarding the multifractal fractals, the study by [20] is concerned with the ANN fractal. The MS dataset examined in that study was comprised of MRI's of the patients diagnosed to have one of the MS subgroups is to identify the homogenous and self-similar pixels. For this purpose, Diffusion Limited Aggregation (DLA) was applied to the MRI's. The results show that by means of the application of ANN algorithms, identification of the most significant pixels was possible with the DLA. The study concerning stroke dataset by [21] highlights the significance of multifractal denoising techniques. By using K-means and FCM clustering algorithms. The results demonstrate that the 2D mBd technique is the most accurate feature descriptor in terms of classification accuracy rates.

The approach we adopted in this study focuses on identifying the significant attributes based on the MRI's and EDSS scores of MS patients by applying L2 norm multifractal denoising technique, which is one of the multifractal techniques. The MS dataset includes 139 individuals (76 RRMS, 38 SPMS, 6 PPMS, 19 Healthy). For the detection of the significant attributes in the dataset, the following steps were followed. First, L2 Norm Denoising was applied on the MS dataset. Then, the new dataset (MS_L2 Norm dataset) including the significant attributes was obtained through the application in the first step. Afterwards, K-means clustering algorithm was applied both the MS dataset and MS_L2 Norm dataset to classify the MS subgroups. Finally, the classification accuracy rate for the K-means clustering algorithm based on the MS dataset and MS_L2 Norm dataset was compared for patients with the MS subgroups and healthy individuals. When compared with other relevant studies in the literature, [16–21], in this present study of ours, K-means classification has been conducted by utilizing the multifractal denoising methods for our dataset. The results of the study reveal that the K-Means algorithm yielded more accurate results in terms of classification for the MS_L2 Norm dataset compared to the MS dataset.

The paper is organized as follows: Sect. 2 is concerned with Data and Methods. Section 3 is on Experimental Results and Discussion. Finally, the Conclusion summarizes the experimental results of our study.

2   Data and Methods

2.1   Patient Details

In this study, MRI's of the individuals with subgroups of MS, namely RRMS, SPMS, PPMS, aged between 18 and 65, with the definite clinical MS according to McDonald criteria [6]. The patients were tracked at Hacettepe University (Ankara, Turkey), Faculty of Medicine, Department of Neurology and Radiology and also the EDSS scores of these patients related to those years have been included.

Magnetic Resonance Imaging

Magnetic Resonance Imaging is a significant tool used particularly in medicine for the imaging of the internal structure of living things. With a high level of magnetism, living tissues are monitored through reflection method. The image is formed based on the intensity of the hydrogen atoms and their movements. All the images form in the digital medium and MR is much different from the other imaging methods.

In the present study, MRI is used for displaying soft tissues in the spinal cord and the brain. The MRI data have been taken from the three regions of the brain (upper cervical region, upper brainstem and also corpus callosum–periventricular region). MRI from the 120 patients diagnosed with the subgroups of MS (76 patients who have RRMS, 38 patients who have SPMS and 6 patients who have PPMS) and 19 healthy individuals have been analysed in three different years.

Expanded Disability Status Scale

Expanded Disability Status Scale (EDSS) is based on the measurements regarding the central nervous system. The scale measures the degree of impairment, for instance, temporary numbness or visual impairment of the face and the fingers [6–10] (for further details on EDSS, the readers may resort to reference numbered [22].

The MS dataset in this study has a dimension of (139×228), and consists of the number of lesion diameters and EDSS scores obtained from the MR images of 120 MS patients with the aforementioned subgroups as well as 19 healthy individuals.

2.2 Methods

The method used in our study is based on the steps specified below:

(i) As a multifractal method, L2 Norm Denoising was applied on the MS dataset which is based on MRI and EDSS. From this application, the new dataset was generated.

(ii) The new dataset named the MS_L2 Norm dataset which includes the significant attributes was obtained.

(iii) K-means clustering algorithm was applied both on the MS dataset and MS_L2 Norm dataset for the classification of the MS subgroups.

(iv) The classification accuracy rate for the K-Means clustering algorithm in relation to the MS dataset and MS_L2 Norm dataset was compared both for patients with MS subgroups and healthy individuals.

For the calculations and figures, Matlab and FracLab [23] environment were utilized.

2.2.1 Analysis Related to the Hölder Regularity

Structural details for the MS data can be identified and classified using fractal dimension approaches [18]. Fractional Brownian motion with the Gaussian process yields zero mean, and covariance function equals to number (1) [23].

$$\text{cov}\{B_H(s), B_H(t)\} = \frac{1}{2}\left\{|s|^{2H} + |t|^{2H} - |s-t|^{2H}\right\} \tag{1}$$

W denotes the Wiener process that resembles the signal. It also has intervals with the steady increments [21,23–25]. The Hurst base (H) has significance for signal continuity and also for the signal dependency properties [22–25]. Instead of Hurst exponent as $0 < H(t) < 1$, t can be denoted by Hölder function $H(t)$. Therefore, Hölder function replaces the stochastic integral by the integral that has an upper bound of t taken in the mean square sense. For Multi-fractional Brownian Motion, the increments are not stationary, and the signal resembles itself [22–28].

The Hölder exponent offers information on the most significant parts of the singular and irregular signals for the 2-D analysis. In that way, the Hölder base measures the variations in characterization in different areas of the signal processor. Represented by a signal $X(t)$, for a positive measurement, the Hölder exponent specifies the singularity force at $t = t(0)$ [21]. (detailed definition of the Hölder exponent and the related equations thereof can be found at [22,27–29].

In which H refers to the Hurst exponent, $H - a/2$ and $a \in (0,1)$ [20]. Fractional Brownian motion is stated in line with (2) by a stochastic integral.

$$B_H(t) = \frac{1}{\Gamma(H+1/2)} \times \left\{\int_{-\infty}^{0}\left[(t-s)^{H-\left(\frac{1}{2}\right)} - (-s)(t-s)^{H-\left(\frac{1}{2}\right)}\right]\right\}dW(s)$$
$$+ \int_{\infty}^{0}\left[(t-s)^{H-\left(\frac{1}{2}\right)}dW(s)\right] \tag{2}$$

2.2.2 Multifractal Analysis

Multifractal analysis is performed statistically via analysing a huge deviation. This paper concentrates on this method that requires to examine an amount that is coined as the large deviation multifractal data [21,22], [28]. This information can be put expressed as: think about a stochastic procedure. It is accepted not losing any generality that $T = [0,1]$. $N_n^{\epsilon}(\alpha)\#\{s : \alpha - \varepsilon \leq \alpha_n^s \leq \alpha + \varepsilon\}$ where α_n^s is the coarse-grained Hölder exponent which refers to dyadic interval $I_n^s = [s2^{-n}, (s+1)2^{-n}]$ that is shown as follows based on [6]:

$$\alpha_n^s = \frac{\log|Y_n^s|}{-\log n} \tag{3}$$

One can see that Y_n^s is some number that calculates the variation of X in the interval I_n^s. $Y_n^s := X((s+1)2^{-n}) - X(s2^{-n})$, resulting in the most basic forms of analytical calculations. One can also have a different way of doing it. One needs to take Y_n^s to be the wavelet coefficient $x_{n,s}$. Referencing the information of X without citation to the selected analysing wavelet may not look logical. Large deviation data $f_g(\alpha)$ are described conforming to (7) [22,26,27].

$$f_g(\alpha) = \lim_{\varepsilon \to 0} \limsup_{n \to \infty} \frac{\log N_n^{\varepsilon}(\alpha)}{\log n} \tag{4}$$

It is quite clear that whatever the choice of Y_n^s, f_g ranges in $\Re^+ \cup \{-\infty\}$ at all times [26].

2.2.3   L2 Norm Multifractal Denoising Technique

Regularization serves as a significant method in machine learning so that we can avoid overfitting. It contributes a *regularization term* that helps us to avoid the coefficients to fit in such a flawless way to overfit in mathematical terms [25–27].

While applying machine learning, we could encounter an option of the unknown. L2-norm yields non-sparse coefficients. L2 regularization on least squares as (8) [28–32].

$$w^* = \arg\min_{w} \left(\sum_{j} (t(x_j) - \sum_{i} w_i h_i(x_j)) \right)^2 + \lambda \sum_{i=1}^{k} w_i^2 \tag{5}$$

L2-norm loss function is recognised as least squares error (LSE) as well. What it means is essentially keeping the total number of the square of the differences of the target value (y_i) and the estimated values $f(x_i)$ as (9) to the minimum.

$$S = \sum_{i=1}^{n} ((y_i - f(x_i))^2 \tag{6}$$

In this current study, multifractal denoising (L2 Norm) technique is applied to MS dataset's (139 × 228) attributes which belong to MS Subgroups and Healthy control group. MS dataset $(\hat{X})$ was applied on FracLab program to regularity-based enhancement $(\hat{X})$ from multifractal L2-Norm denoising technique. Regularity-based enhancement of MS_L2 Norm dataset has been clustered to K-means algorithm. As a result, the most correct clustering has been accomplished for MS Subgroups and Healthy.

2.2.4   K-Means Algorithm

$X = (x_1, x_2, \ldots, x_n)$ nd-dimensional data should be clustered into a set of K clusters, $C = \{c_k, k = 1, \ldots, K\}$. This algorithm aims at finding groups in the data, with the number of groups which the variable k represents. The working of the algorithm is in a repetitive manner so as to assign each data point to one of k groups depending on the features that are presented. The clustering of the data points are done depending on the feature similarity. With μ_k being the mean of cluster c_k, the squared error between μ_k and the points in cluster c_k can be defined based on (10) [21,22,33–35]

$$J(c_k) = \sum_{x_i \in c_k} \|x_i - \mu_k\|^2 \tag{7}$$

K-means is to keep the total of the squared error over all K clusters to the minimum conforming to (11).

$$J(C) = \sum_{k=1}^{K} \sum_{x_i \in c_k} \|x_i - \mu_k\|^2 \tag{8}$$

K-means is inserted with a primary partition with K groups, it also allocates patterns to groups so that it makes it possible to decrease the squared error. The squared error always declines with a rise in the number of clusters K (with $J(C) = 0$ when $K = n$, it could be minimized only at a fixed number of clusters [31]. Below are the major steps for the K-means algorithm [21, 22] (Fig. 1):

Algorithm: K-means
Input:
The dataset with n number of samples
$X = (x_1, x_2, ..., x_n)$
Method:
1. From the $C < X$ dataset, c number of cluster centres are selected.
2. **while** (it is also possible that the cluster centres do not change below a certain threshold level)
3. The distances to all cluster centres are calculated for each sample in the dataset.
4. According to the following relation, the distance of each sample to the cluster centre is calculated.
Output:
Information on clustering of the n number of samples in the whole dataset

Fig. 1. K-means algorithm general structure

MS dataset $X = (x_1, x_2, \ldots, x_{139 \times 228})$ and MS_L2 Norm dataset $\hat{X} = (\hat{x}_1, \hat{x}_2, \ldots, \hat{x}_{139 \times 228})$ were applied to K-means algorithm to be able to cluster MS subgroups (RRMS, SPMS, and PPMS) and Healthy.

3   Experimental Results and Discussion

In this study, the application has been conducted based on the two datasets. The steps regarding the application of the K-means algorithm to the MS dataset are as presented in Fig. 2. In this study, for the clustering procedure of RRMS, SPMS, PPMS, Healthy, K-means algorithm was applied onto the MS dataset (see Fig. 2(a)). The clustering was performed for the classification of MS subgroups, which are RRMS, SPMS, PPMS, as well as of the Healthy individuals (the details are provided below in Fig. 2(a) (iii).

L2 Norm Denoising technique was applied onto the MS dataset. The steps are presented in Fig. 2(b). The new dataset was generated from this application. The new dataset was named the MS_L2 Norm dataset and it includes the significant

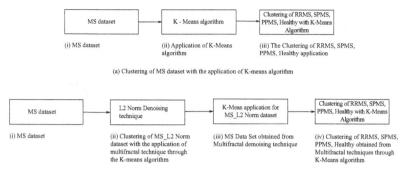

(a) Clustering of MS dataset with the application of K-means algorithm

(b) Clustering of MS_L2 Norm dataset with the application of multifractal technique through the K-means algorithm

Fig. 2. The Procedural Steps with the K-means Algorithm Applications (a) on the MS dataset (b) on the MS_L2 Norm dataset.

attributes obtained. K-means clustering algorithm was applied both on the MS dataset and MS_L2 Norm dataset to classify MS subgroups (see Fig. 2(b) (iii)). As the final step, the classification accuracy rate for the K-means clustering algorithm regarding to the MS dataset and MS_L2 Norm dataset was compared, and this comparison was conducted both for the patients with MS subgroups and the healthy individuals (see Fig. 2(b) (iv)).

3.1 The Application of the K-Means Algorithm

The K-means algorithm applied on the MS dataset and MS_L2 Norm dataset are shown in Table 1, with the parameters used and which has yielded the most accurate result.

Table 1. Parameters for the K-means clustering algorithm

Parameters	Parameters value
K clusters	4
Maximum number of iterations	1000

As regards the most accurate results yielded by the K-means clustering algorithm with 1000 iterations, Fig. 3(a) provides the results for the MS dataset, and Fig. 3(b) indicates the results for the MS_L2 Norm dataset. Computation for classification is terminated at the 1000th iteration as there is no change in centroid values compared to the previous iteration. Figure 3(a) shows the MS dataset (139×228), with the application of the K-means algorithm, which yielded the best total sum of distance for the centroid values $(J\ (C))$ did not change after 0.7 (for 1000 iterations). Figure 3(b) provide the MS_L2 Norm dataset (139×228), with the application of the K-means algorithm, which yielded the best total

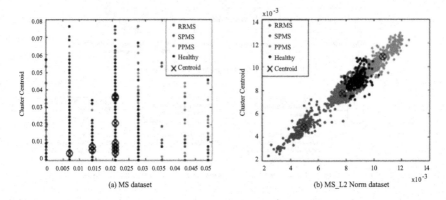

Fig. 3. The Analyses for clustering the K-means Algorithm based on the (a) MS dataset (b) MS_L2 Norm dataset.

sum of distance account for it did not change after 0.1 value. The iteration is terminated here (1000th iteration) since there is no change in the classification calculation after 1000 iterations from the previous iteration. According to the computed best total sum of distance result (see Fig. 3), the K-means clustering performance of the MS_L2 Norm dataset proved to be more accurate than of the MS dataset.

3.2 The Results of the K-Means Algorithm

The results of the classification accuracy rates have been obtained by means of the K-means algorithm application onto the MS dataset and the MS_L2 Norm dataset (see Fig. 2).

In this study, the K-means algorithm was applied on the MS dataset and MS_L2 Norm dataset for the classification the three MS subgroups (RRMS, SPMS, PPMS) and Healthy individuals. The results of the application are presented below in Table 2.

Table 2. Clustering results of the K-means algorithm

MS subgroups	MS dataset (%)	MS_L2 Norm dataset (%)
RRMS	68.9	88
SPMS	67.7	78.4
PPMS	78	86
Healthy	85	89.6

4   Conclusion

The principle contribution of this study is to classify the subgroups of MS through K-means algorithm by selecting and identifying the significant and efficient attributes from the MS dataset by L2 Norm Denoising technique, which is one of the multifractal methods. For the MS dataset, MRI and EDSS scores of the MS patients have been made use of. When compared with other works in the literature [16–21], our study, for the first time, has performed a medical classification for the three subgroups of (Primary Progressive MS (PPMS), Relapsing Remitting MS (RRMS) and Secondary Progressive MS (SPMS). Secondly, on mathematical scale, these particular methods have also been used for the first time in this study for the MS dataset. The study utilized the following steps to get the accuracy performance results for classification: Firstly, L2 Norm Denoising was applied on the MS dataset. From this application, the new dataset was formed. Next, the new dataset, named MS_L2 Norm dataset, which includes the significant attributes was obtained. Afterwards, K-means algorithm was applied on both of the datasets for the classification of the MS subgroups. And finally, the classification accuracy rate for the K-means algorithm as regards the MS dataset and MS_L2 Norm dataset was compared both for MS patients and healthy individuals. Through this study, the K-means classification has been performed by using multifractal denoising methods for the relevant dataset for the first time. The results of our study show that K-means algorithm and classification yielded more accurate results for the MS_L2 Norm dataset compared to the MS dataset with regard to classification. It has also been demonstrated that L2 Norm Denoising technique as one of the multifractal methods play an important role for the classification of the disease and identifying the significant attributes in the dataset. The classification of the MS subgroups also assists medical doctors in their diagnostic processes for early diagnosis and accurate prediction.

References

1. Karaca, Y., Cattani, C.: Clustering multiple sclerosis subgroups with multifractal methods and self-organizing map algorithm. Fractals **25**(04), 1740001 (2017)
2. Kantelhardt, J.W., Zschiegner, S.A., Koscielny-Bunde, E., Havlin, S., Bunde, A., Stanley, H.E.: Multifractal detrended fluctuation analysis of nonstationary time series. Phys. Stat. Mech. Appl. **316**(1–4), 87–114 (2002)
3. Lutton, E., Grenier, P., Vehel, J.L.: An interactive EA for multifractal bayesian denoising. In: Rothlauf, F., Branke, J., Cagnoni, S., Corne, D.W., Drechsler, R., Jin, Y., Machado, P., Marchiori, E., Romero, J., Smith, G.D., Squillero, G. (eds.) EvoWorkshops 2005. LNCS, vol. 3449, pp. 274–283. Springer, Heidelberg (2005). https://doi.org/10.1007/978-3-540-32003-6_28
4. Dangeti, S.V.: Denoising techniques-a comparison (2003)
5. Poser, C.M., et al.: New diagnostic criteria for multiple sclerosis: guidelines for research protocols. Ann. Neurol. **13**(3), 227–231 (1983)

6. Karaca, Y., Zhang, Y.D., Cattani, C., Ayan, U.: The differential diagnosis of multiple sclerosis using convex combination of infinite kernels. CNS Neurol. Disord.-Drug Targets (Former. Curr. Drug Targets-CNS Neurol. Disord.) **16**(1), 36–43 (2017)
7. Karaca, Y., Onur, O., Karabudak, R.: Linear modeling of multiple sclerosis and its subgroubs. Turk. J. Neurol. **21**, 7 (2015)
8. Kurtzke, J.F.: Rating neurologic impairment in multiple sclerosis: an expanded disability status scale (EDSS). Neurology **33**(11), 1444 (1983)
9. Savci, S., Inal-Ince, D., Arikan, H., Guclu-Gunduz, A., Cetisli-Korkmaz, N., Armutlu, K., Karabudak, R.: Six-minute walk distance as a measure of functional exercise capacity in multiple sclerosis. Disabil. Rehabil. **27**(22), 1365–1371 (2005)
10. McDonald, W.I., Compston, A., Edan, G., Goodkin, D., Hartung, H.P., Lublin, F.D., Sandberg-Wollheim, M.: Recommended diagnostic criteria for multiple sclerosis: guidelines from the International Panel on the diagnosis of multiple sclerosis. Ann. Neurol. **50**(1), 121–127 (2001)
11. Karaca, Y., Cattani, C., Moonis, M.: Comparison of deep learning and support vector machine learning for subgroups of multiple sclerosis. In: Gervasi, O., Murgante, B., Misra, S., Borruso, G., Torre, C.M., Rocha, A.M.A.C., Taniar, D., Apduhan, B.O., Stankova, E., Cuzzocrea, A. (eds.) ICCSA 2017. LNCS, vol. 10405, pp. 142–153. Springer, Cham (2017). https://doi.org/10.1007/978-3-319-62395-5_11
12. Zhang, Y.D., Pan, C., Sun, J., Tang, C.: Multiple sclerosis identification by convolutional neural network with dropout and parametric ReLU. J. Comput. Sci. **28**, 1–10 (2018)
13. Shi, B., Han, L., Yan, H.: Adaptive clustering algorithm based on kNN and density. Pattern Recognit. Lett. **104**, 37–44 (2018)
14. Farahani, F.V., Ahmadi, A., Zarandi, M.H.F.: Hybrid intelligent approach for diagnosis of the lung nodule from CT images using spatial kernelized fuzzy c-means and ensemble learning. Math. Comput. Simul. **149**, 48–68 (2018)
15. Comelli, A., et al.: K-nearest neighbor driving active contours to delineate biological tumor volumes. Eng. Appl. Artif. Intell. **81**, 133–144 (2019)
16. Georgieva-Tsaneva, G., Tcheshmedjiev, K.: Denoising of electrocardiogram data with methods of wavelet transform. In: International Conference on Computer Systems and Technologies, pp. 9–16 (2013)
17. Doubal, F.N., MacGillivray, T.J., Patton, N., Dhillon, B., Dennis, M.S., Wardlaw, J.M.: Fractal analysis of retinal vessels suggests that a distinct vasculopathy causes lacunar stroke. Neurology **74**(14), 1102–1107 (2010)
18. Shanmugavadivu, P., Sivakumar, V.: Fractal dimension based texture analysis of digital images. Procedia Eng. **38**, 2981–2986 (2012)
19. Ahammer, H., DeVaney, T.T.: The influence of edge detection algorithms on the estimation of the fractal dimension of binary digital images. Chaos Interdiscip. J. Nonlinear Sci. **14**(1), 183–188 (2004)
20. Karaca, Y., Cattani, C., Karabudak, R.: ANN classification of MS subgroups with diffusion limited aggregation. In: Gervasi, O., Murgante, B., Misra, S., Stankova, E., Torre, C.M., Rocha, A.M.A.C., Taniar, D., Apduhan, B.O., Tarantino, E., Ryu, Y. (eds.) ICCSA 2018. LNCS, vol. 10961, pp. 121–136. Springer, Cham (2018). https://doi.org/10.1007/978-3-319-95165-2_9
21. Karaca, Y., Cattani, C., Moonis, M., Bayrak, Ş.: Stroke subtype clustering by multifractal bayesian denoising with fuzzy means and-means algorithms. Complexity (2018)
22. Karaca, Y., Cattani, C.: Computational Methods for Data Analysis. Walter de Gruyter GmbH & Co KG (2018)

23. Véhel, J. L., Legrand, P.: Signal and image processing with FracLab. In: Thinking in Patterns, pp. 321–322 (2004)
24. Zhang, Y.D., et al.: Fractal dimension estimation for developing pathological brain detection system based on Minkowski-Bouligand method. IEEE Access **4**, 5937–5947 (2016)
25. Esteban, F.J., et al.: Fractal dimension and white matter changes in multiple sclerosis. Neuroimage **36**(3), 543–549 (2007)
26. Birenbaum, A., Greenspan, H.: Multi-view longitudinal CNN for multiple sclerosis lesion segmentation. Eng. Appl. Artif. Intell. **65**, 111–118 (2017)
27. Khayati, R., Vafadust, M., Towhidkhah, F., Nabavi, M.: Fully automatic segmentation of multiple sclerosis lesions in brain MR FLAIR images using adaptive mixtures method and Markov random field model. Comput. Biol. Med. **38**(3), 379–390 (2008)
28. Franchi, B., Lanconelli, E.: Hölder regularity theorem for a class of linear nonuniformly elliptic operators with measurable coefficients. Annalidella ScuolaNormale Superiore di Pisa-Classe di Scienze **10**(4), 523–541 (1983)
29. Carey, W.K., Chuang, D.B., Hemami, S.S.: Regularity-preserving image interpolation. IEEE Trans. Image Process. **8**(9), 1293–1297 (1999)
30. Aizenman, M., Burchard, A.: Hölder regularity and dimension bounds for random curves. Duke Math. **99U**(3), 419–453 (1999)
31. Misawa, M.: Local Hölder regularity of gradients for evolutional p-Laplacian systems. Annali di Matematica Pura ed Applicata **181**(4), 389–405 (2002)
32. Pu, Y., et al.: Fractional partial differential equation denoising models for texture image. Sci. China Inf. Sci. **57**(7), 1–19 (2014)
33. Yau, A.C., Tai, X., Ng, M.K.: Compression and denoising using l 0-norm. Comput. Optim. Appl. **50**(2), 425–444 (2011)
34. Hartigan, J.A., Wong, M.A.: Algorithm AS 136: A K-Means clustering algorithm. J. R. Stat. Soc. Ser. C (Appl. Stat.) **28**(1), 100–108 (1979)
35. Han, J., Pei, J., Kamber, M.: Data Mining: Concepts and Techniques. Elsevier, Amsterdam (2011)

A Comparison of Two Hölder Regularity Functions to Forecast Stock Indices by ANN Algorithms

Yeliz Karaca[1]($\boxtimes$) and Carlo Cattani[2,3]

[1] University of Massachusetts Medical School, Worcester, MA 01655, USA
yeliz.karaca@ieee.org, yeliz.karaca@umassmemorial.org
[2] Engineering School (DEIM), University of Tuscia, Viterbo, VT 01100, Italy
cattani@unitus.it
[3] Ton Duc Thang University, Ho Chi Minh City, Vietnam

Abstract. This study is concerned with local Hölder exponent as a function regularity measure for time series regarding Finance data. The study examines 12 attributes in the Micro, Small and Medium Enterprises (MSME) data for 6 regions (2004–2018). The study has two different approaches. Firstly, (i) multi fractal methods and Brownian motion Hölder regularity functions were used for the identification of the significant and self-similar attributes in the Finance dataset. The steps are: (a) polynomial functions were applied on the Finance dataset and p_finance dataset was obtained. (b) exponential functions were applied and e_Finance dataset was obtained. Secondly, (ii) Artificial Neural Network (ANN) algorithms ((Feed Forward Back Propagation (FFBP) and Cascade Forward Back Propagation (CFBP)) were applied on both datasets in a and b. Finally, (iii) classification accuracy rates as per the outcomes obtained from the second stage by the ANN algorithms were compared. Our study has been conducted for the first time in the literature since with the ANN algorithms' application, it revealed how the most significant attributes are identified in the Finance dataset by Hölder functions (polynomial as well as exponential).

Keywords: Singularity · Hölder regularity · Finance data · Multifractals · ANN

1 Introduction

Feature selection aims to choose a minimal feature subset from a problem area while an appropriately high accuracy is retained for the representation of the original data, which is an essential method with regard to data preprocessing [1,2]. The main principle of fractal analysis is to seek a pattern which is not dependent on scale. A multifractal system is a generalization of a fractal system where a single exponent (the fractal dimension) would not suffice to perform the description of its dynamics. Rather, a continuous spectrum of exponents, namely

© Springer Nature Switzerland AG 2019
S. Misra et al. (Eds.): ICCSA 2019, LNCS 11620, pp. 270–284, 2019.
https://doi.org/10.1007/978-3-030-24296-1_23

singularity spectrum, is required (3). Multifractal Brownian Motion Synthesis 2D method is capable of determining the number of selected features. Therefore, it can be appropriately used for the solution of financial data set [4–6].

The Finance dataset of this study is one that was generated by International Finance Corporation (IFC) that carries out its works so as to develop solutions for bridging the Finance gap about the Micro, Small and Medium Enterprises MSME. IFC operates in more than 100 countries and 6 regions [7]. The data of the study is concerned with 6 regions (Europe and Central Asia, Latin America and the Caribbean, Middle East and North Africa, South Asia, East Asia and the Pacific and Sub-Saharan Africa). The MSME data was taken covering (2004–2018) [8].

In recent years, conventional theoretical approaches need to be expanded further since they explain the problems under ideal and ordinary circumstances. For this reason, alternative theories are required so that the complicated nature of financial markets can be analyzed and explained better taking into consideration the actual financial conditions.

There are various recent studies which use fractal and multifractal methods for Finance data. Their aim is to yield the most accurate results for future prediction. The study by Mulligan et al. [9] is concerned with the examination of maritime equity price series through the use of five self-affine fractal analysis techniques to explore the price series fractal properties by employing Hurst exponent, Mandelbrot-Lévy characteristic exponent, and fractal dimension. Another study by Mulligan [10] shows Hurst exponent signatures from time series of aggregate price indices for the US. The long-term study presented the fractal examination of the interplay between market prices along with added interest based on how those markets react to external shocks. Another study by the same author [11] examined capacity utilization rates and the index of industrial production for multifractality from 1972 to 2012. The study's Hurst signature analysis of capacity utilization allowed the examination as to whether capacity utilization stems from the Cantillon effects of monetary expansion or the organic changes in supply and demand. Concerning the use of Hölder, several other studies may be cited. For instance, Bianchi et al. [12] used Hurst-Hölder exponent for the quantification of the pointwise degree of efficiency or inefficiency, introducing-efficiency notion. Their analysis concerned four stock indexes that represented Asia, Europe as well as the U.S. Garcin's study [13] is also concerned with Hurst exponents to enhance the existing literature on the estimation of time-dependent Hurst exponents. The author proposed a smooth estimate which was obtained by variational calculus, which is said to be a method more accurate globally and easier compared to other non-parametric estimation techniques. In addition, Hurst Exponents used in the study allowed the forecasts that are reliant upon the estimated multifractional Brownian motion.

Regarding the use of artificial neural network algorithms on financial data, we may cite other studies. One study by Lin et al. [14] presents the use of a new recurrent neural network-echo state network (ESN) for the prediction of the next closing price in stock markets. Along with ESN, the Hurst exponent was also applied to determine adaptively the initial transient and select sub-series which have the greatest predictability during training. Their results showed that ESN performed better than the other conventional neural networks in majority of the cases. The paper by Karaca et al. [15] examined the link between Turkey's international trade balance and economic growth, covering a period from 1960 to 2015. Artificial Neural Network methods, Feed Forward Back Propagation and Cascade Forward Back Propagation algorithms were used and classification was made as per international trade volume parameters. Accordingly, factors which influenced the development of economy as well as international trade in Turkey were classified.

The MSME Finance dataset handled in this study has been obtained from one formed by IFC based on 6 regions. The timeframe of the analysis is between the years of 2004 and 2018. In addition, 12 attributes were dealt with during the application, which are date, region, Mortgage Outstanding, Mortgage Outstanding USD($), Microloans Outstanding, Microloans Outstanding USD($), SME Loans Outstanding, SME Loans Outstanding USD ($), Micro Loans to Women-owned Firms Outstanding, Micro Loans to Women-owned Firms Outstanding ($), SME Loans to Women owned Firms Outstanding, SME Loans to Women owned Firms Outstanding($)). The steps in the study can be summarized as follows: In the first approach, multi fractal methods and Brownian motion Hölder regularity functions were employed to identify the self-similar and significant attributes in the dataset. In the related steps, (a) polynomial functions were applied to the Finance dataset, as a result of which p_finance data set was obtained. (b) exponential functions were applied, and as a result of this application, e_Finance dataset was obtained. In the second approach, FFBP and CFBP algorithms were applied on p_finance dataset and e_Finance dataset, respectively. And in the final step, for these two datasets, classification accuracy rates were compared. Having been conducted for the first time in the literature, our study showed how the most significant attributes are identified in the Finance dataset by the Hölder functions, namely polynomial and exponential, through the application of ANN algorithms, which are FFBP and CFBP. As can be seen from the outcomes of the analyses, two main contributions are at stake for this study. The first one is that Hölder regularity functions were applied on Finance data for the first time in literature, and secondly, significant and self-similar attributes were obtained for the first time as well for this particular dataset.

The organization of the paper is as such: Sect. 2 provides Materials and Methods. Methods of our approach are basic facts on Hölder Regularity, Multifractal Analysis, FFBP and CFBP algorithms. Finally, results and conclusions are presented in Sects. 3 and 4.

2   Materials and Methods

2.1   Material

This study is on the Finance dataset which includes 12 attributes with 6 regions covering the years (2004–2018) (for detailed information of data, see Table 1) (8).

Table 1. Attributes of the Finance dateset

Regions (between 2004-2018)	Attributes	Data Size
	Mortgage Outstanding ($)	
	Microloans Outstanding ($)	
East Asia and the Pacific	Microloans Outstanding ($)	
Europe and Central Asia	SME Loans Outstanding, ($)	
Latin America and the Caribbean	SME Loans Outstanding ($)	79x12
Middle East and North Africa	Micro Loans to Women owned Firms Outstanding ($)	
South Asia	...	
Sub-Saharan Africa	Micro Loans to Women owned Firms Outstanding ($)	
	SME Loans Women owned Firms Outstanding ($)	
	SME Loans Women owned Firms Outstanding ($)	

2.2   Methods

Our aim is to classify the financial data set through the Multifractal Brownian Motion Synthesis 2D multifractal analysis. Our method is based on the following procedures:

(i) Multifractal methods and Brownian motion Hölder regularity functions were used for the identification of the self-similar and significant attributes in the dataset. As the steps, (a) polynomial functions were applied to the Finance dataset, and p_finance data set was obtained. (b) exponential functions were applied, and we obtained the e_Finance dataset.

(ii) Two of the ANN algorithms, FFBP and CFBP, were applied on the p_finance dataset and e_Finance dataset, respectively.

(iii) Classification accuracy rates were compared with respect to these two datasets. Having been conducted for the first time in the literature, our study demonstrated how the most significant attributes are identified in the Finance dataset by the Hölder functions (polynomial as well as exponential functions) through ANN algorithms application. Eventually, Hölder regularity functions were applied on Finance data, and significant as well as self-similar attributes were obtained for the particular Finance dataset.

The results of the analyses were obtained by the FracLab [16] and Matlab environment.

2.2.1   2D Multifractal Brownian Motion Analysis

Since financial market behaviors are regarded as complicated systems, the status of the market movements can be explained with fractal structures which are capable of providing significant input related to the long-term memory of market behavior as the parts show complete similarity with the whole. Alternative theories are required so fractal analysis and fractal dimension approaches can be one alternative for risk assessment apart from conventional risk measure methods while addressing Finance data.

With Fractional Brownian motion Gauss process $\{B_H(t)\}$ zero mean and covariance function correspond to Eq. (1) [17,18].

$$cov\left\{B_H(s), B_H(t)\right\} = \frac{1}{2}\left\{|s|^{2H} + |t|^{2H} - |s-t|^{2H}\right\} \tag{1}$$

H Hurst exponent, $H = \alpha/2$ and $\alpha \in (0,1)$ [18,20]. Fractional Brownian motion is denoted according to Eq. (2) with stochastic integral.

$$B_H(t) = \frac{1}{\Gamma(H+(1/2))} \times \left\{ \int_{-\infty}^{0} \left[(t-s)^{H-\left(\frac{1}{2}\right)} - (-s)(t-s)^{H-\left(\frac{1}{2}\right)}\right]\right\} dW(s) + \int_{-\infty}^{0} \left[(t-s)^{H-\left(\frac{1}{2}\right)} dW(s)\right] \tag{2}$$

W denotes the Wiener process that resembles itself in the signal and shows stable increases [18,19,21]. Hurst exponent (H) is significant both for the continuity of the signal and the dependency features of the signal [20]. Hurst exponent can denoted the Hölder function: $H(t)$ and $0 < H(t) < 1, \forall t$. Thus, stochastic integral is replaced by Hölder function. The upper limit of integral of integral of t is taken as mean square. For the Multifractional Brownian Motion, increases are not stable and signals from then on resemble themselves [18,21,22]. Hölder exponent gives information about the most important parts of the signals which are irregular and singular for 2-D analysis. Therefore, Hölder exponent measures the characterization variations in various domains of signal processing. For a positive measurement, represented by $X(t)$, for a signal, Hölder exponent characterizes the singularity power in $t = t(0)$ [18,19,21]. Further details about Hölder Regularity and Hölder Exponent can be obtained from references [18–22].

2.2.2   Artificial Neural Networks

Artificial neural networks (ANNs), which are computational models inspired by the working of the human brain, include a large number of connected nodes. Each node carries out a simple mathematical operation which determines the output of each node along with a set of parameters that are particular for that node. It is possible to learn and calculate very complex functions by connecting these nodes together and setting their parameters in a careful manner. having paved the way for many recent advances in artificial intelligence, artificial neural networks include image recognition, voice recognition, as well as robotics [18].

2.2.3   Feed Forward Back Propagation Algorithm

Feed Forward Neural Networks are one of the artificial neural networks in which the connections between units do not establish a cycle. Feedforward neural networks are the first type of artificial neural network devised and invented, being much simpler than their counterpart, namely the recurrent neural networks. The reason why they are named *feedforward* is that information travels only in forward direction in the network (with no loops). The course is first through the input nodes, subsequently through the hidden nodes (if they are present), and eventually through the output nodes [18].

When the m-dimensional input examples of the network structure are entered into the dataset, $x_i = [x_1, x_2, ..., x_m]^T$ is formed (see Fig. 3). Likewise, $d_k = [d_1, d_2, ..., d_n]^T$ denotes the n-dimensional output examples that are desired. If x_i values are the output values of the neurons in the i layer, the total input that will reach a neuron in j layer is calculated. The output of the neuron in the hidden layer is as shown by Eq. 2:

$$y_j = f_j(net_j), \; j = 1, 2, ..., J \tag{3}$$

Here, f_j is the transfer function of feedback. The total input that will correspond to the k neuron in the output layer is as shown in Eq. 3 [18, 23, 24].

$$net_k = \sum_{j=1}^{J} w_{kj} . \gamma_j \tag{4}$$

The non-linear output of a k neuron in the output layer is as provided in Eq. 4.

$$o_k = f_k(net_k), \; k = 1, 2, ..., n \tag{5}$$

The output obtained from the network is compared with the actual output and e_k error is calculated according to Eq. 5 [18, 23, 24]

$$e_k = (d_k - o_k) \tag{6}$$

Here, d_k corresponds to the target (desired) value of any k neuron in the output layer and ok shows what is obtained from the network (the actual one). One point that should be born in mind is that such a comparison is applicable only for the network's output layer. Hence, it will hold a privileged position in the identification of the weights for the connections that are related to the output layer. Total mean square is calculated according to Eq. 6 for each of the examples [18, 23, 24].

$$E = \frac{1}{2} \sum_{k} (d_k - o_k)^2 \tag{7}$$

In our study, Hölder regularity functions (polinomial and exponential functions) were applied on the Finance dataset. The application of polinomial functions yielded the p_Finance dataset and the application of exponential functions yielded the e_Finance dataset. For these two datasets, x inputs were taken as (8x8) for the classification to be performed for the p_Finance dataset and e_Finance dataset by the FFBP algorithm.

2.2.4 Cascade Forward Back Propagation Algorithm

Cascade Forward Back Propagation (CFBP) algorithm resembles the FFBP algorithm. Yet, there is one difference regarding the connection between the neurons in the input layer, intermediate layer and in the output layer [27]. Cells which track one another are connected with the training performed in this way, andit is possible to apply the training process in two or more levels [25,26].

The algorithmic flow regarding training process is indicated as follows [25–27]:

Step 1: The initial values of the weightings are assigned, for each (x_k, d_k) data pattern x_k inputs are propagated forward through the neural network layers as shown in Eq. 7.

$$p_k = f_j \left(w_j a_{j-1} - b_j \right), \; j = 1, \ldots, J \tag{8}$$

Results and sensitivities are calculated in line with Eq. 10.

$$\delta_j = f_j (d_j - w_{j+1})^T \delta^{j+1}, \; j = J - 1, \ldots, 1 \tag{9}$$

Step 2: Should the error value be more than what has been estimated, weightings (weight and biases) are calculated once again, as indicated in Eqs. 9 and 10.

$$\Delta w^j = -\eta \delta^j (d^{j-1})^T, \; j = 1, \ldots, J \tag{10}$$

$$\Delta b^j = \eta \delta^j, \; j = 1, \ldots, J \tag{11}$$

Step 3: Once the estimated error value is attained, the training process is completed. If the estimated error value has not been attained, Step 2 is required to be reiterated. In our study, Hölder regularity functions (polinomial and exponential functions) were applied on the Finance dataset. The application of polinomial functions yielded the p_Finance dataset and the application of exponential functions yielded the e_Finance dataset. For these two datasets, x inputs were taken as (8x8) for the classification to be performed for the p_Finance dataset and e_Finance dataset by the CFBP algorithm.

3   Experimental Results and Discussion

Our aim is to make the classification of the Finance dataset by the Hölder exponent multifractal analysis [18]. Our method is based on the following steps:

I. Multifractal Brownian Motion Synthesis 2D is applied to the Finance dataset (see Fig. 1 (i)).
II. Brownian Motion Hölder regularity (polynomial, exponential) for analysis is applied to the data so that significant and self-similar attributes in the dataset can be identified (see Fig. 1(ii)).
III. Accuracy rates regarding classification as per the outcomes which were obtained from the application of the ANN algorithms (FFBP and CFBP) were compared. (see Fig. 1 (iii)).

Figure 1 provides a visual depiction of the steps applied to the Finance dataset (79x12) as specified in (i–iii).

The explanation for the steps is demonstrated in Fig. 1 and the steps for application on the Finance dataset (in Table 1).

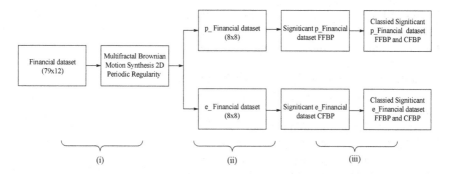

Fig. 1. Classifying the finance dataset with the application of multifractal brownian motion synthesis 2D by the (a) FFBP algorithm (b) CFBP algorithm.

3.1 Application of the FFBP and CFBP to the P_Finance Dataset

(I) Multifractal Brownian Motion Synthesis 2D is applied to the Finance dataset (see Fig. 1(i)).

Step (i): Application of Multifractal Brownian Motion Synthesis 2D to the Finance dataset:

In the Multifractal Brownian Motion Synthesis 2D, first the fractal dimension ($D = [x_1, x_2, ..., x_{79}]$) of the original Finance dataset is calculated. Then, the features which lead to the minimum change of current finance dataset's fractal dimension is dropped sequentially up till the remainder features' number is the upper bound of the fractal dimension D. The new Hölder exponent dataset generated is, $D^{new}(D^{new} = [x_1^{new}, x_2^{new}, ..., x_8^{new}])$.

(II) Brownian Motion Hölder regularity (polynomial) for analysis is applied to the data so that significant and self-similar attributes in the dataset can be identified (see Fig. 1(ii)) [18–20], .

Step (ii): Application of the Multifractal Brownian Motion Synthesis 2D to the data is presented in Fig. 2 below.

The steps of Fig. 2 are provided in detail with the following steps applied.

Step (1): Makes the estimation of the Hölder function, of the input Finance dataset, employing a least square regression [18–20]. The alpha and beta parameters are real values in (0,1) that describe the neighbourhood of each point where the exponent is computed. The Hölder exponent is estimated by using a neighbourhood of points for each point.

Step (2–5): The Averaging estimation utilizes a specific number of neighbours to make the computation of an average of oscillations [18–20]. Averaging enables to get more robust results. Yet, the estimation becomes smoother as the number of points increases. In the average, the gamma and delta parameters are real values in (0:1) that describe the neighbourhood of each point used for computing the average.

Algorithm 1. Application of the Multifractal Brownian Motion Synthesis 2D to the data

Input: Training set including m number of samples

$D = [x_1, x_2, \ldots, x_{79}] (x_i \in R^d)$

Output: The new Hölder exponent dataset generated is

$D^{new} (D^{new} = [x_1^{new}, x_2^{new}, \ldots, x_8^{new}])$ (m > n)

Method:

(1) **while** (stopping condition is false)

(2)   **for each** input vector $[x_1, x_2, \ldots, x_{79}]$

(3)   //n = 8 and the neighborhood is defined by the set of points

V for exponential regularity $V(i) = (0.1 + 0.8 \times x \times y)$

(4)   (Eq.1)

(5)   }

Fig. 2. Application of the multifractal brownian motion synthesis 2D to the finance dataset to obtain polynomial regularity.

If (8, 256) is the size of the data x, then $n=8$. The neighbourhood size is defined by. If (8, 256) is the size of the data$x$, $n= 8$ and the neighbourhood is defined by the set of points V as: //exponential regularity $V(i) = (0.1 + 0.8 \times x \times y)$

$D^{new} = [x_1^{new}, x_2^{new}, \ldots, x_8^{new}]$ is the new Finance dataset generated (p_Finance dataset).

(III) FFBP and CFBP algorithms were applied on the data obtained (p_finance data)

Accuracy rates regarding classification as per the outcomes which were obtained from the application of the ANN algorithms (FFBP and CFBP) were compared. see Fig. 1(iii)) for p_Finance Data.

Step (iii): The singled out Finance dataset is finally classified by using the FFBP and CFBP algorithms.

The details of Multifractals analysis with the FFBP algorithm (**Algorithm 2**) and its steps regarding its application can be found in Reference [18].

Figure 3 provides and explains the steps of the CFBP Algorithm [18–20]:

Step (1): $\delta_j = f_j (d_j - w_{j+1})^T \delta^{j+1}, \ j = J - 1, \ldots, 1$

Step (2): If the error value is more than the estimated one, then weightings (weight and biases) are calculated as per Eqs. 9 and 10.

Step (3): $\Delta w^j = -\eta \delta^j (d^{j-1})^T, \ j = 1, \ldots, J$

Step (4): $\Delta b^j = \eta \delta^j, \ j = 1, \ldots, J$

Step (5): When the estimated error value is attained, the training process is brought to a termination. If this value is not attained, then step 2. is reiterated.

Algorithm 3. Multifractals Analysis with the CFBP Algorithm
Input: New training set that includes n number of samples obtained
(from Fig. 3) ($D^{new} = [x_1^{new}, x_2^{new}, \ldots, x_8^{new}])(x_i \in R^d$)
Output:
label data that corresponds to m number of samples ($Y = [Regions]$)
Method:
(1) $\qquad \delta_j = f_j(d_j - w_{j+1})^T \delta^{j+1}, \ j = J-1, \ldots, 1$
(2) Should the error value be higher than what is estimated, weightings
(weight and biases) are calculated again according to Equation 9 and 10.
(3) $\qquad \Delta w^j = -\eta \delta^j (d^{j-1})^T, \ j = 1, \ldots, J$
(4) $\qquad \Delta b^j = \eta \delta^j, j = 1, \ldots, J$
(5) When the estimated error value is achieved, the training process
comes to a termination. If this value is not attanined, step 2 is required
to be reiterated.

Fig. 3. The application of the CFBP algorithm on the p_Finance dataset [18–20].

3.2 Accuracy Rates Obtained from the FFBP and CFBP Algorithm Classification of E_Finance Dataset

The application of the Exponential Regularity Function on the Finance dataset
and its classification by the FFBP Algorithm and CFBP Algorithm.
(I) Application of Multifractal Brownian Motion Synthesis 2D to the Finance dataset: (see Fig. 1(i)).

Step (i): Application to Finance dataset Multifractal Brownian Motion Synthesis 2D to Finance dataset (e_Finance dataset):
Multifractal Brownian Motion Synthesis 2D can be explained as such: firstly,
the fractal dimension $D(D = [x_1, x_2, \ldots, x_{79}])$ of the original Finance dataset
is calculated. Subsequently, the features that lead to the minimum change of
current Finance dataset's fractal dimension is dropped in a sequential manner
up until the number of remainder features is the upper bound of the fractal
dimension D. The new Hölder Exponential dataset generated is, $D^{new}(D^{new} = [x_1^{new}, x_2^{new}, \ldots, x_8^{new}])$.
(II) Brownian Motion Hölder regularity (exponential) [20–22] for analysis is applied to the data so that significant and self-similar attributes in the dataset can be identified (see Fig. 1(ii)).

Step (ii): Application of the Multifractal Brownian Motion Synthesis 2D on the new dataset (e_Finance dataset) can be seen from Fig. 4.

The steps of Fig. 4 are provided in detail with the following steps applied.
Step (1): Performs the estimation of the Hölder function, H of the input Finance
dataset , by using a least square regression. The alpha and beta parameters are
real values in (0,1) that illustrate the neighbourhood of each point in which the
exponent is calculated. For each point, the estimation of Hölder exponent is done
through using a neighbourhood of points.

Algorithm 4. Application of Multifractal Brownian Motion Synthesis 2D to the data

Input: Training set that includes m number of samples
$D = [x_1, x_2, \ldots, x_8] \ (x_i \in R^d)$
Output: The new Hölder exponent dataset generated is
$D^{new} \ (D^{new} = [x_1^{new}, x_2^{new}, \ldots, x_8^{new}]) \ (m > n)$
Method:
(1) **while** (stopping condition is false) {
(2)   **for each** input vector $[x_1, x_2, \ldots, x_{228}]$
(3)   //n = 8 and the neighborhood is defined by the set of points V for logistic regularity
(4) $V(i) = 0.3 + \frac{0.3}{1 + \exp(-100 \times x - 0.7)}$ (Eq.2)
(5)   }

Fig. 4. Application of the multifractal brownian motion synthesis 2D to the finance dataset to obtain exponential regularity [18–20].

Step (2–5): The Averaging estimation employs a specific number of neighbours to calculate an average of oscillations. Averaging enables to get more robust results, yet as the number of points goes up, the estimation becomes smoother. In the average, the gamma and delta parameters are real values in (0:1) that illustrate the neighbourhood of each point used to make the computation of the average.

If (8,256) is the size of the data x, thus $n=8$. The size of the neighbourhood is defined by $2 \times m + 1$

If (8,256) is the size of the data x, $n= 8$ and the neighbourhood is defined by the set of points V as:
$V(i) = 0.3 + \frac{0.3}{1 + \exp(-100 \times x - 0.7)}$

$D^{new} = [x_1^{new}, x_2^{new}, \ldots, x_8^{new}]$ is the new Finance dataset generated (e_Finance dataset).
The related procedural steps are explained below:

(III) Accuracy rates regarding classification as per the outcomes which were obtained from the application of the ANN algorithms (FFBP and CFBP) were compared. (see Fig. 1(iii)) for e_Finance data).

Step (iii): The singled out e_Finance dataset is finally classified by using the FFBP and CFBP algorithms.
The details of Multifractals analysis with the FFBP algorithm (**Algorithm 5**) and its steps regarding its application can be found in Reference [18].

As a result of the application of Exponential regularity function on the Finance dataset, e_Finance dataset was obtained. For the classification of the e_Finance dataset CFBP algorithm was used. The steps for the CFBP algorithm are provided below:

Algorithm 6. Multifractals Analysis with the CFBP Algorithm
Input: New training set that includes then number of samples obtained
(Fig. 5) ($D^{new} = [x_1^{new}, x_2^{new}, \ldots, x_8^{new}]$) ($x_i \in R^d$)
Output:
label data that corresponds to the m number of samples ($Y = [Regions]$)
Method:
(1) $\delta_j = f_j(d_j - w_{j+1})^T \delta^{j+1}$, $j = J - 1, \ldots, 1$
(2) Should the error value be higher than what is estimated, weightings
(weight and biases) are calculated again according to Equation 9 and 10.
(3) $\Delta w^j = -\eta \delta^j (d^{j-1})^T$, $j = 1, \ldots, J$
(4)
(5) $\Delta b^j = \eta \delta^j$, $j = 1, \ldots, J$
(6) When the estimated error value is attained, the training process
is terminated. If this value is not achieved, step 2 needs to be reiterated.

Fig. 5. The Application of the CFBP algorithm on the e_Finance dataset [18–20].

Figure 5 provides and explains the steps of the CFBP Algorithm [18–20]:

Step (1): $\delta_j = f_j(d_j - w_{j+1})^T \delta^{j+1}$, $j = J - 1, \ldots, 1$
Step (2): Should the error value be higher than what is estimated, weightings
(weight and biases) are calculated again in line with Eqs. 9 and 10.
Step (3): $\Delta w^j = -\eta \delta^j (d^{j-1})^T$, $j = 1, \ldots, J$
Step (4): $\Delta b^j = \eta \delta^j$, $j = 1, \ldots, J$
Step (5): When the estimated error value is attained, the training process is
brought to a termination. If this value is not attained, then step 2. is reiterated.
Step (6): The condition could postulate a fixed number of iterations (i.e. execu-
tions of Step 2) or learning rate achieving a satisfactorily small value.

3.3   Accuracy Rates Obtained from the FFBP and CFBP Algorithm Classification of p_finance Dataset and e_Finance Dataset

Multifractal Brownian Motion Synthesis 2D functions in Finance dataset is provided below with the classification results obtained (Table 2 and Fig. 6).

For the classification of the e_Finance dataset and p_Finance dataset by the
FFBP and CFBP algorithms, which are two of the ANN algorithms, the confusion matrix results are provided below:

Table 2 presents the accuracy rate results obtained as a result of the application of the FFBP and CFBP algorithms on the p_Finance dataset and e_Finance
dataset.

As can be seen from Table 2, for both Polynomial (p_Finance dataset) and
Exponential functions (e_Finance dataset), the application of the FFBP algorithm yielded higher accuracy rates in terms of classification compared to that
of the CFBP algorithm.

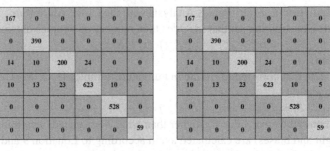

(a) for the FFBP application on p_Finance dataset

(b) for the CFBP application on p_Finance dataset

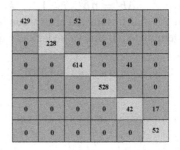

(c) for the FFBP application on e_Finance dataset

(d) for the CFBP application on e_Finance dataset

Fig. 6. Confusion matrix (a) for the FFBP application on p_Finance data (b) for the CFBP application on p_Finance data (c) for the FFBP application on e_Finance data (d) for the CFBP application on e_Finance data.

Table 2. Accuracy rates obtained from the FFBP and CFBP algorithm classification of p_Finance dataset and e_Finance dataset

Algorithms	p_Finance dataset (%)	e_Finance dataset (%)
FFBP	85.30%	82.02%
CFBP	80.30%	81.60%

4   Conclusion

Mainly concerned with local Hölder exponent as a function regularity measure for time series regarding Finance data, this study examined the financial data of Micro, Small and Medium Enterprises in six different regions. The timeframe of the study covers the years from 2004 to 2018. 2D multifractal Brownian Motion analysis was applied on the Finance data. This is the first contribution of the paper which yielded higher accuracy rates for Finance data when compared to other studies in the literature. For the highest level of accuracy rates, polynomial and exponential functions of Hölder functions were applied on the Finance dataset separately. As a second contribution, FFBP and CFBP algorithms, two of the ANN algorithms, were applied on the new datasets (namely e_Finance dataset and p_Finance dataset) which were obtained as a result of the polynomial and exponential functions. For the first time, significant attributes were identified by the Hölder functions. Accordingly, the study has attempted to contribute to the literature by performing multifractal data processing on the Finance data as regards the Micro, Small and Medium Enterprises in six different regions along with the classification of the financial developments concerning the regions. To analyze the complicated nature of financial markets more accurately, conventional theoretical approaches need to be expanded and alternative theories are needed by taking into account the actual financial conditions. Based on this, this study has provided a framework with regard to the economic development of countries and their financial markets. It has also brought to the fore the significance of fractals in financial analyses and related predictions for the future.

References

1. Parveen, A.N., Inbarani, H.H., Kumar, E.S.: Performance analysis of unsupervised Feature selection methods. In: 2012 International Conference on Computing, Communication and Applications, pp. 1–7. IEEE (2012)
2. Kumar, P.S., Lopez, D.: A review on feature selection methodsfor high dimensional. Int. J. Eng. Technol. (IJET) **8**, 0975–4024 (2016)
3. Zunino, L., Tabak, B.M., Figliola, A., Pérez, D.G., Garavaglia, M., Rosso, O.A.: A multifractal approach for stock market inefficiency. Physical A: Stat. Mech. Appl. **387**(26), 6558–6566 (2008)
4. Mensi, W., Hamdi, A., Yoon, S.M.: Modelling multifractality and efficiency of GCC stock markets using the MF-DFA approach: a comparative analysis of global regional and islamic markets. Physical A. Stat. Mech. Appl. **503**, 1107–1116 (2018)
5. Rak, R., Grech, D.: Quantitative approach to multifractality induced by correlations and broad distribution of data. Physical A. Stat. Mech. Appl. **508**, 48–66 (2018)
6. Li, J.: An analytical model for multifractal systems. J. Appl. Math. Phys. **4**(07), 1192 (2016)
7. McCourtie, S.D.: Micro, small, and medium enterprise (MSME) Finance. The World Bank (2013)
8. https://finances.worldbank.org/widgets/2ppx-k958
9. Mulligan, R.F.: Fractal analysis of highly volatile markets: an application to technology equities. Q. Rev. Econ. Financ. **44**(1), 155–179 (2004)
10. Mulligan, R.F.: Multifractality of sectoral price indices: hurst signature analysis of Cantillon effects in disequilibrium factor markets. Physica A. Stat. Mech. Appl. **403**, 252–264 (2014)
11. Mulligan, R.F.: The multifractal character of capacity utilization over the business cycle: an application of Hurst signature analysis. Q. Rev. Econ. Financ. **63**, 147–152 (2017)
12. Bianchi, S., Pianese, A.: Time-varying hurst-hölder exponents and the dynamics of (in) efficiency in stock markets. Chaos, Solitons & Fractals **109**, 64–75 (2018)
13. Garcin, M.: Estimation of time-dependent Hurst exponents with variational smoothing and application to forecasting foreign exchange rates. Physical A: Stat. Mech. Appl. **483**, 462–479 (2017)

14. Lin, X., Yang, Z., Song, Y.: Short-term stock price prediction based on echo state networks. Expert Syst. Appl. **36**(3), 7313–7317 (2009)
15. Karaca, Y., Bayrak, Ş., Yetkin, E.F.: The classification of Turkish economic growth by artificial neural network algorithms, 115–126 (2017)
16. FracLab. https://project.inria.fr/fraclab/
17. Enriquez, N.: A simple construction of the fractional brownian motion. Stochast. Process. Appl. **109**(2), 203–223 (2004)
18. Karaca, Y., Cattani, C.: Computational Methods for Data Analysis. Walter de Gruyter GmbH Co KG, Berlin (2018)
19. Misawa, M.: Local hölderregularity of gradients fore volitional p-Laplaciansystems. Annalidi Matematica Puraed Applicata **181**(4), 389–405 (2002)
20. Karaca, Y., Cattani, C.: Clustering multiple sclerosis subgroups with multifractal methods and self-organizing map algorithm. Fractals **25**(04), 1740001 (2017)
21. Véhel, J.L., Legrand, P.: Signal and Image processingwith Frac Lab. Thinking in Patterns, 321–322 (2004)
22. Franchi, B., Lanconelli, E.: Hölderregularity theorem for a class of linearnon uniformlyel lipticoperators with measurable coefficients. Annalidella Scuola Normale SuperiorediPisa-Classedi Scienze **10**(4), 523–541 (1983)
23. Karaca, Y., Cattani, C., Karabudak, R.: ANN classification of MS subgroups with diffusion limited aggregation. In: Gervasi, O., et al. (eds.) ICCSA 2018. LNCS, vol. 10961, pp. 121–136. Springer, Cham (2018). https://doi.org/10.1007/978-3-319-95165-2_9
24. Karaca, Y., Moonis, M., Zhang, Y.D., Gezgez, C.: Mobile cloud computing based stroke healthcare system. Int. J. Inf. Manag. **45**, 250–261 (2019)
25. Warsito, B., Santoso, R., Yasin, H.: Cascade Forward Neural Network for Time Series Prediction. In: Journal of Physics: Conference Series, 1025(1) 012097. IOP Publishing (2018)
26. Abdul-Kadir, N.A., Sudirman, R., Mahmood, N.H., Ahmad, A.H.: Applications of cascade-forward neural networks for nasal, lateral and trill Arabic phonemes. In: 2012 8th International Conference on Information Science and Digital Content Technology (ICIDT2012), 3, 495–499. IEEE (2012)
27. Karaca, Y.: Case study on artificial neural networks and applications. Appl. Math. Sci. **10**(45), 2225–2237 (2016)

Advances in Artificial Intelligence Learning Technologies: Blended Learning, STEM, Computational Thinking and Coding (AAILT 2019)

Hahai: Computational Thinking in Primary Schools

Sergio Tasso[1]([✉]), Osvaldo Gervasi[1], Anna Locchi[2], and Flavio Sabbatini[1]

[1] Department Mathematics and Computer Science, University of Perugia,
Via Luigi Vanvitelli, 1, 06123 Perugia, Italy
{sergio.tasso,osvaldo.gervasi}@unipg.it, flaviosabbatini96@gmail.com
[2] Giovanni Cena Primary School of Perugia, ICPg4, Via Dalmazio Birago, 6,
06124 Perugia, Italy
annalocchi@gmail.com

Abstract. Nowadays, society needs to keep up with the development of new technologies; the children of the new generation are seen as "digital natives", although they are not necessarily able to use digital devices to their fullest potential.

The "Hahai project" introduces the application of digital devices within the educational approach throughout the Hahai app. The aim of the project is to introduce digital skills and computational thinking through "Digital Storytelling" in primary schools; with the aim of developing problem-solving and the creative approach. Furthermore, these skills are extremely valuable in modern society and for the future.

This paper explores the ideas behind the creation of the project, the development of the app, the testing in first-grade classes of primary school, the statistics obtained from the latter and the final conclusions.

Keywords: Computational thinking · Advanced teaching · Digital storytelling · Apps

1 Introduction

This document aims to identify a possible solution to what is now needed in society: being able to manage the continuous development of technologies in all the areas of the said society. The new generation, hence children considered *"digital natives"*, are familiar with the use of digital devices often before being introduced in school. But the problem is their lack of awareness of the devices they use easily. Empowering them is becoming a formative social necessity.

The definition of "digital natives" is just an incorrect term assigned by society to those born in the new millennium [1]. However, although children's digital literacy seems to be an advantage, it could be an issue: parents and teachers often rely on technology and leave the "digital native" without support.

Statistical data shows that, paradoxically, children are the first to be exposed to danger: they do not have the necessary skills required in the *Digital Age.*

© Springer Nature Switzerland AG 2019
S. Misra et al. (Eds.): ICCSA 2019, LNCS 11620, pp. 287–298, 2019.
https://doi.org/10.1007/978-3-030-24296-1_24

The *AICA* [2] collected statistical data and showed that the gained skills create a wrong awareness of skills that aren't present and that are incomplete.

The ICILS (Computer International and Information Literacy Study) shows that 17% of eighth-grade students do not reach the minimum level of digital knowledge and only 2% of students have full skills in the subject. The worst thing is that 84% believe to have "good"/"great" digital knowledge, but practical tests show that 49% achieved "bad"/"terrible" results.

Young people, without formal education and training, cannot gain the digital skills they need on their own.

Unfortunately, digital devices and smartphone applications are considered by digital natives as a hobby and not as something they will have to live with.

School, as an educational establishment, has the responsibility to instruct young children about digital literacy. Nevertheless, it is necessary that competent adults develop the tools to accommodate users of different ages and abilities; thereby improving the educational approach.

The app called **Hahai** that has been developed and tested is a perfect example that meets this need. The application has become a real scholastic project; it can integrate digital devices into the normal educational approach.

Related work is described in the paper according to the following scheme:

- Section 2: How the problem is experienced by society, the life skills of new generations and innovative solutions;
- Section 3: The design of the Hahai project and the app development;
- Section 4: The testing carried out at the Giovanni Cena primary school of Perugia, Italy and the final report that includes statistics and views;
- Section 5: Conclusions and future developments.

2   Global Society and Technology

2.1   Life Skills

The development of technologies in all areas of society cannot be ignored. In fact, some research estimates that by 2026, 90% of the population will have a device connected to the Internet, including children. Many studies showed how digital devices integrated into everyday life, so the *Department of Mental Health of the World Health Organization* has drawn up a list of skills needed for life, called *Life skills*.

They can be summarized in seven competencies:

- critical and analytical thinking;
- creative and alternative thinking;
- cooperation;
- intercultural relations;
- effective communication;
- digital skills;
- self-awareness or initiative.

To let the digital devices have a positive impact on the digital natives' approach to the future, it is necessary to spread a digital education that makes them aware of the dangers of the Internet: cyberbullying, explicit material, data theft.

Responsibility and Education of Society. In the Digital Age, schools cannot ignore digital change; they must control and promote it in the right direction. School is the biggest promoter of innovation, and therefore also of digital content, and it is with this in mind that in recent years *National Plans* have been promulgated to promote the development of digital skills in students of all ages, aware that school activities cannot exclude the use of technology.

Defining the student required skills is difficult. First of all, the needs of the twenty-first century, which include new knowledge and skills, have to be satisfied. Schools must try to introduce logical and *computational thinking* and then allow students to learn modern technologies.

The *World Economic Forum* realized research [3] and determined that the *digital skills* on which world education must invest resources are eight:

- *Digital Identity*: Awareness of your online presence and guaranteeing your online reputation.
- *Digital Use*: The ability to use different devices and systems.
- *Digital Safety*: It is necessary to recognize and avoid the risks associated with the use of digital technologies.
- *Digital Security*: Learn how to protect personal data and devices appropriately and achieve the ability to predict and recognize the dangers of hacking, scams, or malware.
- *Digital Emotional Intelligence*: Understanding and knowing how to approach to communicate with others through a device.
- *Digital Communication*: The ability to communicate and collaborate through the use of digital devices and media.
- *Digital Literacy*: Learn how to research and share data, considering the source and testing credibility.
- *Digital Rights*: Know the rights of freedom of expression, privacy and the intellectual property of one's own creations.

Unfortunately, adults are *"digital immigrants"* and they are not always able to support digital natives in the careful access of digital systems. For this reason, many educational organizations have started special courses. These courses teach the new generation to use digital devices.

2.2   Computational Thinking

Computational thinking [4] is a skill often associated with the figure of the computer scientist because of its ability to be able to break up big problems into small problems connected between them. This is a skill that everyone has, and it is considered as the *fourth basic skill* besides reading, writing, and mathematics. When human beings are solving problems, designing systems, or following any other behavior based on the concepts used in computer science, we are referring to computational thinking.

Computational thinking improves a child's analytical skills. This ability allows you to find an algorithmic procedure that grants to solve a hard problem through the decomposition and reduction of the problem in smaller sections. Computational thinking is not necessarily related to computer and mathematical fields, but it is a way of thinking to deal with everyday life, study, or work.

The global society needs to have citizens who make their own choices with critical thinking. The new generation will need to be able to identify problem-solving methods. Digital skills can improve this learning process because they are based on two fundamental scenarios: *problem-solving* and *creative approach*.

Problem-Solving. In this scenario, the student has to solve logic problems of increasing difficulty. Computational thinking will be introduced gradually. In the beginning, it starts with a few instructions and then increases the difficulties. The child will need new ways of thinking. Visual programming blocks (coding at school [5]) is the most used model in schools.

Creative Approach. This scenario focuses on creativity: students implement a project without receiving specific input. In this way, students will face computational thinking concepts and they will be more interested in learning how to carry out their projects. The learning process will be less structured: it will happen by trial and error and free associations.

2.3 Solution: Hahai Project

Hahai is developed for children who are learning to read and write. This project combines the concepts of problem-solving and creative approach, also introduces digital devices in the learning process. The children play, have fun and learn by creating stories, and they can do this in collective or in small groups. Digital storytelling is an excellent solution that can be used in this age group and **Hahai** is suitable for its ease of use.

3   The Hahai Project and Development

3.1   Requirements Analysis

First development phase: A brainstorming session was carried out with the teachers of the *Giovanni Cena* primary school (*Perugia, Italy*). In this phase, the requirements analysis was written and **Hahai** was designed. It has designated goals and functions: the focus of the app is *digital storytelling*.

Hahai allows you to create digital stories about *literature* and *mathematics*. *"Storytelling activity"* is a different activity, and it tells these stories. The stories comprise a sequence of images and sounds made with children's drawings and voices [6–8]. In the *Letters* topic, it is possible to create new topics other subjects (e.g. *religion, foreign languages*).

3.2   Wireframe and Graphic Design

After performing the requirements analysis, the application's *navigation map* was designed (*wireframe project*, Fig. 1) to summarize its composition.

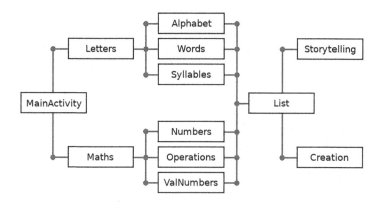

Fig. 1. *Hahai navigation map*

The activities link to each other in the same way you visit the app. The secondary functions required by the app were written next to the wireframe project. Once the wireframe project was approved, the code development was the next phase.

Activities Design. Hahai is developed in *Kotlin programming language* and this app is multilingual: currently, the languages available are English, Italian, and Spanish. **Hahai** recognizes the language set on the device and translates all activities content and views. In the future, with a patch, other foreign languages will be added simply by updating the *translation table*.

The following figures show some layouts of the app (Figs. 2 and 3).

The hardest class to create was *Creation activity* (Fig. 3, a) since it was necessary to manage each task. In the *Creation layout*, the *"Add Drawing"* and *"Add Audio"* buttons show a pop-up where the user can add the file: images and sounds can be *picked* from the storage or *captured* on the spot. A compressed copy will be added to the internal storage, and its *URI* will be stored in an array. This array will be saved in the database when finished creating the story. The bottom buttons manage the narration scenes, and the left views are a preview of the scenes.

The *Storytelling activity* (Fig. 3, b) finds the story in the database and creates arrays of images and sounds. The *ImagePagerAdapter* view will show the images, while the buttons will start/stop the sounds.

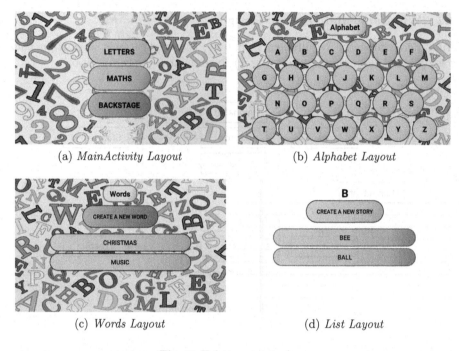

(a) *MainActivity Layout*　　　　(b) *Alphabet Layout*

(c) *Words Layout*　　　　(d) *List Layout*

Fig. 2. *Hahai user interface*

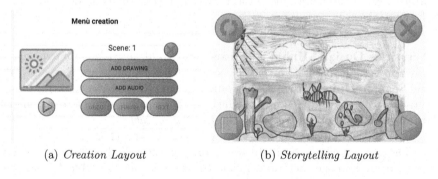

(a) *Creation Layout*　　　　(b) *Storytelling Layout*

Fig. 3. *Creation and Storytelling activities*

4   Testing Phase

4.1   Official Testing in First-Grade Classes

The app was tested on a group of first-grade elementary students composed of 31 children. The testing was carried out in the first month of school, in September and October. Hahai would have improved reading, writing, and mathematics by creating digitized stories as if it were a new game.

Motivations of the Test. As already written, the development of technologies changed people's lives, and in particular that of the new generation. This test aims to integrate digital devices in the school environment to teach children the importance of technological tools.

Test Methods. Starting from the topic, the children invented the story. They chose the characters and the setting of the story. The teacher wrote the story in a notebook and drew a preview of each scene on the blackboard. The children in groups drew the scenes on paper. Once that is done, the students recorded the lines, and the teacher prepared the digital material to build the story on **Hahai**. Everyone worked together to build the story through the interactive multimedia whiteboard. Digital storytelling caught everyone's attention, and the children enjoyed commenting on the quality of the story. Vote chose the title of the story.

Children are intrigued by digital technology. In this regard, **Hahai** shows the potential of using digital devices in teaching methods. Digital natives are familiar with the use of digital devices, but using them in class to teach lessons is new.

In this lesson, the children gained the approach to computational thinking. They have learned to analyze the problem and find the algorithmic procedure to solve it. The students collaborated and realized something creative and instructive. They respected each other's opinions and showed a spirit of initiative.

4.2   Final Report

The teachers gave their views about testing before getting statistics from children. The focus group showed that it is important to introduce digital technologies in schools. The teachers said that the new generations will need to know how to use fully digital technologies. To achieve this goal, it is good to start with the first-grades of primary school. **Hahai** offers easy-to-use digital storytelling, both for teachers and children. Learning from very young people to handle these devices will allow the new generation to be more skilled. Digital devices are an enhancement of the teaching methods and increase children's open-mindedness.

In the last testing phase, the children filled out a questionnaire related to these special lessons. This activity showed the abilities of children to reconstruct the stages to invent a story. The final part of the form required students' opinions and gave a vote to the experience. This questionnaire has become a great tool from which to get statistics.

Statistics. The questionnaire comprised seven questions of varying complexity. The first question required the stages to invent a story with **Hahai** (Fig. 4). Half of the children correctly showed the logical sequences, but the difficulty of connecting seven phases emerged. The children reacted by focusing on the details for them more operative and engaging, ignoring aspects in which the adult did the work.

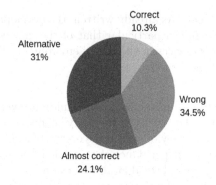

Fig. 4. Correct sequence of progress chart

The other questions required responding with the favorite stage, with the most difficult stage and the most boring stage (Figs. 5 and 6).

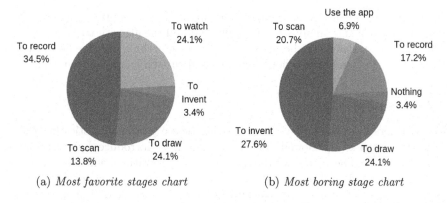

(a) *Most favorite stages chart*   (b) *Most boring stage chart*

Fig. 5. Questionnaire results

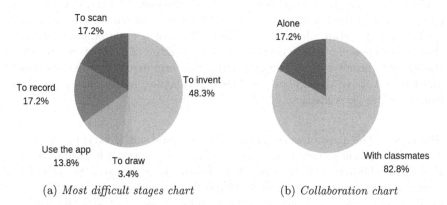

(a) *Most difficult stages chart*   (b) *Collaboration chart*

Fig. 6. Questionnaire results

The stages where the children were most involved turned out to be the favorites.

The answers to the most boring stages were those that occur every day: inventing, drawing. The fact of building the story together has created difficulties: the children will gain group collaboration over time.

In conclusion, the results of the tests ran in the primary school show that the experience was particularly constructive (Fig. 7); the activity of storytelling was positive and pleasant.

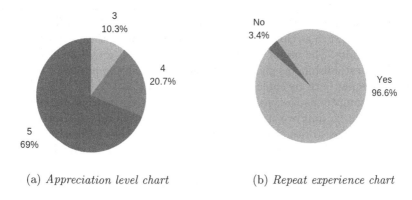

(a) *Appreciation level chart*   (b) *Repeat experience chart*

Fig. 7. Results of the questionnaire

5 Conclusions and Future Developments

5.1 Conclusions

The digital revolution and the use of the Internet have become an integral part of people's lives. As a consequence, the population is affected by a sudden change, which brings to instability and uncertainty because of the fear of changing the everyday routine. Continuous adjustment to new technologies can be positive once people become aware of the changes.

Nowadays revolutions such as the "digital and technological revolution", the globalization, the socio-economic, the cultural and the migratory, influence the society. Individuals can react and handle the above-mentioned revolutions and changes being conscious, mentally flexible, and hence avoid exclusion.

The school system and the family have a major role and the responsibility to educate and guide the new generation, so-called "digital natives", to familiarize with technology in the scholastic environment and use it constructively. As already mentioned, digital natives are born with the ability to use technological devices, although they have to be taught how to do it positively and effectively. It is the duty of competent adults to intervene and neutralize what could become the problem of the third millennium.

Technology and digital literacy are slowly spreading in the scholastic environment, thus the **Hahai** application is an appropriate tool to introduce in schools. The children were enthusiastic and effectively learned in a playful and functional way.

Teachers involved stated their satisfaction towards the effectiveness of the app to improve the strategies of reading, writing, and mathematics.

5.2   Future Developments

Computer scientists have played a major role in developing products on commission; given that it is a different task to implement an application for a specific target audience, such as children and young adults, during their learning journey to become adults. The use of this tool in a single school would be inconvenient. Educational establishments should have the aim of sharing positive online innovative strategies, both technological and disciplinary.

It is presumptuous to consider the app completed; it would be effective to share it online to improve its growth and receive feedback. By setting up an online server, the stories will be uploaded to an online database and can be viewed by any device that uses it. This update would create a global comparison network [9–13, 20].

An app for education is successful if the family uses it in their spare time. In this way, it can become an effective tool for playing with parents who could easily see the stories made by their child.

An interesting and useful addition could be the creation of a website with the same features of the application, in order to make it accessible to different devices and not restricted exclusively to Android devices [14–19].

5.3   Technology as a Tool for Training

The results of this research highlightwhat could prevent the development and diffusion of technologies within the school system. The percentage of teachers willing to use digital devices as teaching tools is very low: 10% of the teachers try to use these devices, an additional 10/15% use them to show films, download course material or as a recreational tool, and the remaining 75/80% does not use them. The low usage of digital devices by teachers could be justified as a lack of knowledge and awareness on the subject. Therefore, they often can not use digital devices; hence, they would find it difficult to change their teaching methods. It could be recommended to act in this matter and offer compulsory training courses for teachers to update them continuously on the development of digital devices.

References

1. Digital Natives: illiteracy that you don't expect. https://www.punto-informatico. it/nativi-digitali-analfabetismo. Accessed Oct 2018

2. Report of the Italian Association for Informatics and Automatic Calculation. http://ecdl.org/media/position_paper_italian.pdf. Accessed Oct 2018

3. World Economic Forum. https://www.weforum.org/reports/world-economic-forum-annual-meeting-2016-mastering-the-fourth-industrial-revolution. Accessed Sept 2018

4. D'Apolito, A.: Thesis aims: La programmazione visuale per lo sviluppo del pensiero computazione nei bambini. University of Perugia, Italy (2017)

5. Coding@School. http://www.indire.it/progetto/coding-a-scuola/. Last accessed Sept 2018

6. Franzoni, V., Leung, C.H.C., Li, Y., Mengoni, P., Milani, A.: Set similarity measures for images based on collective knowledge. In: Gervasi, O., et al. (eds.) ICCSA 2015. LNCS, vol. 9155, pp. 408–417. Springer, Cham (2015). https://doi.org/10.1007/978-3-319-21404-7_30

7. Franzoni, V., Milani, A., Pallottelli, S., Leung, C.H.C., Li, Y.: Context-based image semantic similarity. In: 2015 12th International Conference on Fuzzy Systems and Knowledge Discovery, FSKD 2015, art. no. 7382127, pp. 1280–1284 (2016). https://doi.org/10.1109/FSKD.2015.7382127

8. Chiancone, A., Franzoni, V., Niyogi, R., Milani, A.: Improving link ranking quality by quasi-common neighbourhood. In: Proceedings - 15th International Conference on Computational Science and Its Applications, ICCSA 2015, art. no. 7166159, pp. 21–26 (2015). https://doi.org/10.1109/ICCSA.2015.19

9. Tasso, S., Pallottelli, S., Bastianini, R., Lagana, A.: Federation of distributed and collaborative repositories and its application on science learning objects. In: Murgante, B., Gervasi, O., Iglesias, A., Taniar, D., Apduhan, B.O. (eds.) ICCSA 2011. LNCS, vol. 6784, pp. 466–478. Springer, Heidelberg (2011). https://doi.org/10.1007/978-3-642-21931-3_36

10. Tasso, S., Pallottelli, S., Ferroni, M., Bastianini, R., Laganà, A.: Taxonomy management in a federation of distributed repositories: a chemistry use case. In: Murgante, B., et al. (eds.) ICCSA 2012. LNCS, vol. 7333, pp. 358–370. Springer, Heidelberg (2012). https://doi.org/10.1007/978-3-642-31125-3_28

11. Tasso, S., Pallottelli, S., Rui, M., Laganá, A.: Learning objects efficient handling in a federation of science distributed repositories. In: Murgante, B., et al. (eds.) ICCSA 2014. LNCS, vol. 8579, pp. 615–626. Springer, Cham (2014). https://doi.org/10.1007/978-3-319-09144-0_42

12. Pallottelli, S., Tasso, S., Rui, M., Laganà, A., Kozaris, I.: Exchange of learning objects between a learning management system and a federation of science distributed repositories. In: Gervasi, O., et al. (eds.) ICCSA 2015. LNCS, vol. 9156, pp. 371–383. Springer, Cham (2015). https://doi.org/10.1007/978-3-319-21407-8_27

13. Franzoni, V., Tasso, S., Pallottelli, S., Perri, D.: Sharing linkable learning objects with the use of metadata and a taxonomy assistant for categorization. In: Misra, S. et al. (eds.): ICCSA 2019, LNCS, vol. 11620, pp. 336–348. Springer, Cham (2019)

14. Franzoni, V., Mencacci, M., Mengoni, P., Milani, A.: Semantic heuristic search in collaborative networks: measures and contexts. In: Proceedings - 2014 IEEE/WIC/ACM International Joint Conference on Web Intelligence and Intelligent Agent Technology - Workshops, WI-IAT 2014, vol. 1, pp. 187–217 (2014). https://doi.org/10.1109/WI-IAT.2014.27

15. Franzoni, V., Milani, A., Nardi, D., Vallverdú, J.: Emotional machines: the next revolution. Web Intell. **17**(1), 1–7 (2019). https://doi.org/10.3233/WEB-190395

16. Franzoni, V., Milani, A.: A pheromone-like model for semantic context extraction from collaborative networks. In: Proceedings - 2015 IEEE/WIC/ACM International Joint Conference on Web Intelligence and Intelligent Agent Technology. WI-IAT 2015, 2016-January, art. no. 7396860, pp. 540–547 (2016). https://doi.org/10.1109/WI-IAT.2015.21
17. Franzoni, V., Milani, A., Biondi, G.: SEMO: a semantic model for emotion recognition in web objects. In: Proceedings - 2017 IEEE/WIC/ACM International Conference on Web Intelligence. WI 2017, pp. 953–958 (2017). https://doi.org/10.1145/3106426.3109417
18. Franzoni, V., Li, Y., Mengoni, P.: A path-based model for emotion abstraction on Facebook using sentiment analysis and taxonomy knowledge. In: Proceedings - 2017 IEEE/WIC/ACM International Conference on Web Intelligence. WI 2017, pp. 947–952 (2017). https://doi.org/10.1145/3106426.3109420
19. Franzoni, V., Milani, A.: A semantic comparison of clustering algorithms for the evaluation of web-based similarity measures. In: Gervasi, O., et al. (eds.) ICCSA 2016. LNCS, vol. 9790, pp. 438–452. Springer, Cham (2016). https://doi.org/10.1007/978-3-319-42092-9_34
20. Tasso, S., Pallottelli, S., Gervasi, O., Sabbatini, F., Franzoni, V., Laganà, A.: Cloud and local servers for a federation of molecular science learning object repositories. In: Misra, S. et al. (eds.): ICCSA 2019, LNCS, vol. 11624, pp. 359–373. Springer, Cham (2019)

An Image-Based Encoding to Record and Track Immersive VR Sessions

Bruno Fanini[1,2]([⊠]) [iD] and Luigi Cinque[2] [iD]

[1] CNR ITABC (Institute for Technologies Applied to Cultural Heritage),
Area della Ricerca Roma 1, Via Salaria Km. 29,300, 00015 Rome, Italy
[2] Department of Computer Science, Sapienza University, Via Salaria 113, Rome, Italy
{fanini,cinque}@di.uniroma1.it

Abstract. Capturing and tracking immersive VR sessions performed through HMDs in public spaces, may offer valuable insights on users propensities and spatial affordances. Large collected records can be exploited to analyze or fine-tune locomotion models for time-constrained experiences. The transmission or streaming of such data over the web to analysts or professionals in distance learning field although, can be challenging due to network bandwidth or involve computationally intensive decoding routines. This work investigates compact encoding models to volumetrically absorb user states and propensities during running VR sessions, using image-based encoding approaches. We focus on quantization methods and data layouts to smoothly record immersive sessions and how they compare to standard approaches in terms of storage and spatio-temporal accuracy. Qualitative and quantitative results obtained from public exhibits are presented in order to validate the encoding model.

Keywords: Immersive VR · Visual analytics · Encoding models · Saliency

1 Introduction

Recent consumer head-mounted displays (HMDs) are often employed in public or shared spaces to create engaging and educational immersive experiences with high sense of presence. During a limited amount of time, several users (casual visitors, students, etc.) explore and perform interactions within the 3D virtual environment. An in-depth investigation of spatial affordances, user propensities and saliency for a given immersive virtual environment (IVE) can be useful to improve the overall immersive experience. Capturing, recording and visualizing entire VR sessions can in fact provide valuable insights. For instance within IVEs for education, the ongoing data collection as students interact with the 3D space can be useful for learning assessment [18]. In distance learning technologies and education, such data may support the remote validation of IVEs consumed by students through an HMD and supports the remote analysis of their behaviors and interactions performed in the 3D space. Furthermore, improving or enhancing an IVE often present huge efforts in terms of 3D modeling

© Springer Nature Switzerland AG 2019
S. Misra et al. (Eds.): ICCSA 2019, LNCS 11620, pp. 299–310, 2019.
https://doi.org/10.1007/978-3-030-24296-1_25

and/or optimization tasks: unexpected elements may capture users' attention, depending on locomotion models used and spatial/temporal constraints. From the analyst perspective, in order to understand user sessions from quantitative and qualitative perspectives, collecting per-user fine-grained data is generally a strong requirement. When directly mapped to the original 3D scene, recorded data (e.g. user locomotion) may provide easier interpretation for spatial analysis, when supported by usable UIs. Furthermore, remotely located analysts may be interested into inspection, visualization and analysis of user sessions while the VR application (desktop or WebVR[1] application) is still running. The transmission or streaming of collected data over the web to analysts, teachers or other professionals although, can be challenging due to network bandwidth or involve computationally intensive decoding routines. The whole history of a single user session may contain huge amount of information (locomotion, gaze, orientation, etc.) thus potentially preventing interactive data transport online.

Contribution - Within this work, we investigate an image-based encoding model that offers flexible runtime accessories to volumetrically absorb user states of VR sessions over time. Captured spatial attributes are encoded into compact image-based layouts providing (a) lightweight transmission over the web; (b) minimal computation for encoding/decoding routines; (c) direct manipulation on GPU and (d) offline 2D image processing. We apply the encoding model to previously recorded locomotion data (CSV) during a public event and evaluate obtained results in terms of accuracy, also performing comparisons with raw binary formats and different bit-depths for encoded image.

2   Related Work

Visual Analytics [23] is a proven approach to directly perceive patterns and extract knowledge from massive and dynamic information streams, offering analysts, teachers or other professionals tools to detect the expected and discover the unexpected. Interactive installations in public or shared spaces allow to collect large amounts of data related to users sessions and visually analyze them [1]. Data mining methods are often applied to tourist activities discovering landmark preferences from photo mappings [13] while classical clustering methods [12] can be used to offline analyze spatial behaviors. VR locomotion plays a central role [5] within 3D virtual environments users are free to explore. Understanding users spatial preferences may support or validate the effectiveness of interaction model used for temporally constrained sessions (e.g. public exhibits, shared spaces, virtual classrooms, etc.).

Saliency in VR. There is recently a growing interest in researching virtual environment saliency for immersive VR, although most of these works focus on 360 or omnidirectional visual content from fixed viewpoints. [19] analyzes for instance how people explore virtual environments from a fixed viewpoint (360) collecting and visualizing gaze data. [21] investigates a model to obtain fixation locations and maps from head direction, offering a good approximation when eye

---

[1] https://webvr.info/.

tracking data is not available. Regarding visual attention analysis [14] introduced an efficient metric and visualization method for similarity measures between a director's cut and users scan-paths using color-coded maps.

Image-based encoding can be used to transport spatial data in a compact manner (e.g. coordinates, vectors, etc.) through common 2D images. Regarding image formats for the web, PNG format [22], offers a network-friendly, patent-free, lossless compression scheme that is cross-platform. Previous research employed PNG format for instance as externalized mesh container [7,15] to efficiently transmit geometry data over the network and decoded by client browsers. Previous encoding models in literature also investigated "geometry images" [10] as 2D arrays used to quantize and store spatial information ($< x, y, z >$) as RGB values.

3   Encoding Model

This section describes image-based encoding and layout to capture and store immersive VR sessions. We highlight advantages in terms of model compactness and its lightweight transport over networked scenarios towards remote professionals. Within a previous research [8] we describe user state s as a collection of state attributes (s_a, where a is the attribute we are dealing with). For instance s_p represent user HMD location inside the virtual scene ($< x, y, z >$), s_o represent HMD orientation (for instance as quaternion $< x, y, z, w >$), etc. Each casual visitor performs different interactions within a limited amount of time during the public exhibit, thus we define the session operator S:

$$S_a(u, t) \rightarrow s_a \qquad (1)$$

where u represents the user ID and s_a the state attribute at given time $t \in \mathbb{R}$. Regarding immersive user sessions, we are particularly interested in tracking specific state attributes over time, like location (s_p), HMD view direction (s_d), focus (s_f) or more advanced data. For instance, $S_p(u, t)$ captures user u locomotion or $S_f(u, t)$ can be exploited for tracking visual attention.

3.1   Session Volumes

Session volumes (or *Quantized User Session Volume* - QUSV [8]) are AABB[2] accessories deployed to observe a portion of the virtual space, "absorbing" immersive sessions. The role of a single volume V in a virtual space is to track user states within its volumetric extents and record them as session signals: the model allows to encode them as stream of RGB(A)[3] values and to store them as common images. In order to map spatial attributes (e.g. s_p, s_f) into RGB values, a volume V is uniformly subdivided into several voxels: each attribute is thus *quantized* depending on QUSV extents (Fig. 1).

---

[2] Axis-Aligned Bounding Box.
[3] Red, Green, Blue, Alpha channels.

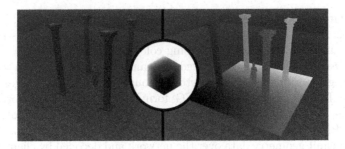

Fig. 1. A session volume arranged in a sample 3D scene (color-coded).

Considering a normalized 3D location ($< x, y, z >$) inside the volume, a direct mapping into a $< R, G, B >$ color using 8 bit per-channel storage allows V to address 256^3 (16.777.216) different voxels. The extents of V have obviously a huge impact on each voxel size, and thus on location quantization. The flexibility of such volumes is to observe limited spatial extents with the purpose of capturing and encoding specific user behaviors. The model allows to deploy multiple volumes in the same virtual environment, each observing different extents and encoding state attributes, offering great scalability and customization.

3.2 Image-Based Encoding and Layout

For a single user u, we can define the encoding of $S_a(u, t)$ for spatial attributes within a given volume as a 1-dimensional stream of RGB(A) values. Given a fixed temporal step increment, each pixel of the 1D stream thus encodes a specific voxel within V boundaries at given time t. V location and extents are indeed crucial for the client application (analyst), in order to decode the signal and retrieve spatial values. The stream can be stored as an image, and common 2D image processing can be optionally employed to perform further data manipulation. This includes for instance: channel isolation (e.g. blue to analyze height variation), temporal compression through resampling methods, common image compression algorithms, and much more. The proposed data layout also allows fast encoding/decoding and direct manipulation on GPU. For instance automatic interpolation of spatial attributes is obtained by common texture filters. From a storage perspective, data compression is furthermore facilitated by PNG format, due to likely continuous RGB data on neighboring pixels [15] (e.g. locomotion data).

Multiple 1D signals can be stacked (see Fig. 2, B) to create image atlases called *QSA* [8]: the volume is thus able to encode the whole $S_a(u, t)$ for a given state attribute a for all recorded users in a single, compact image. Such session atlases allow interactive manipulation on GPU and offline 2D image processing. For instance a QSA tracking a spatial attribute, can be shrinked along the x-axis (time) using nearest-neighbor algorithm for a coherent (but lossy) data reduction (see Fig. 2, C). Such basic 2D operations can be employed to maintain

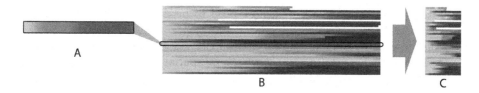

Fig. 2. QSA layout.

an approximation of original record (fetched texels are interpolated on the GPU) or compress old datasets.

3.3 Saliency

Spatial attributes (user location, focus, etc.) recorded during the whole session can be exploited also to compute salient voxels in a given V, providing *volumetric* data on users propensities. Persistence (over time) and other contributing factors (see for instance [1] regarding focus) allow observed voxels in V to be ranked, offering analysts dataset to discover user behaviors in specific parts of the scene. Such data can be encoded as well, to provide a lightweight data transport over the network towards remote analysts.

Fig. 3. A sample saliency table with length $=$ k.

The approach of saliency tables (σ) is to maintain a running record of *VOIs* (voxels of interest) inside a session volume, keeping them sorted depending on a rank value (see Fig. 3). The same color-coding method described in Sect. 3.2 is employed to produce a single image, extended with alpha channel to encode rank. The algorithm is based on [16] with an hash-table to compute frequency counts while keeping a constant memory footprint (k, the size of table) and a running record approach. This results in an evolving "fingerprint" of the tracked spatial attribute (e.g. user location) for V. Once the saliency table is encoded as image, the sorted layout allows GPU routines to partially evaluate it by discarding right-most values (lower rank). Within unconstrained (or partially constrained) VR locomotion models, σ_p can be useful for analysts to study explorative behaviors, selectively improve 3D scene detail or support creation of locomotion graphs [11]. Furthermore, there are several advantages of encoded saliency tables:

– they are ultra-compact (see results in Sect. 5), suitable for networked contexts and remote analytics

- sorted layout for σ allows rightmost pixel to be discarded still maintaining good overall approximation
- multiple σ (e.g. different spatial attributes) can be stacked vertically (like QSA layout in Sect. 3.2) to transport several spatial propensities for a volume, using a single lightweight image.

4   Architecture Overview

We describe the general architecture of our framework, employed within public exhibits or events involving large amounts of casual visitors. We describe three main components: (1) VR application; (2) session encoding node and (3) visual inspection node (for analysts) - see Fig. 4. Depending on public space conditions (e.g. absence of internet connection, etc.) some of these components may physically rely on the same machine - for instance the VR application and encoding node.

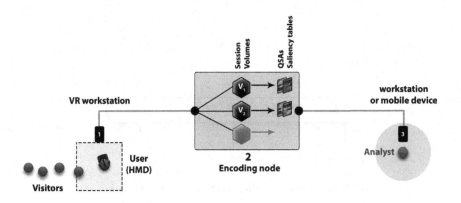

Fig. 4. Architecture of proposed framework.

Casual visitors of the public expo use the VR workstation (1) to explore or interact with a 3D scene: a single session begins when user wear the HMD and user state is being anonymously recorded. The user state is sent to the encoding node (2) including multiple state attributes, for instance: timestamp; virtual location (3D scene coordinates); HMD orientation and view direction; focus (3D coordinates); physical location (local 3D coordinates inside tracked area); etc.

Incoming user states are received by (2) and encoded (see Sect. 3) into multiple QSA and saliency tables as lightweight images. Such operation uses minimal computation for each volume $(V_1, V_2, ... V_k)$, specifically $O(k \cdot h)$ where k is the number of session volumes deployed into the 3D scene and h the number of different state attributes to track $(a_1, a_2, ... a_h)$. Generally h is quite small, since we are interested in a few state attributes (e.g. location, orientation, focus), while number of volumes (k) is highly dependent on analysis requirements and 3D scene complexity (a single volume can be sufficient to understand user propensities in a specific portion of the virtual environment).

The third component (3) is the inspection node, where a visual analyst can remotely inspect produced datasets (lightweight images) using a desktop application (or web-application). Through the definitions of $(V_1, V_2, ...V_k)$ including extents and positions, the application is able to *decode* loaded QSAs and saliency tables for visual analysis.

An implementation of the architecture has been already realized as part of an open-source project[4] [2,4,17] leveraging on node.js ecosystem [6,20] HTML5 websockets and open-source WebGL libraries for the responsive Front-End. Next section will present encoding results interactively inspected and visualized through the implemented web-based architecture.

5 Results

We present in this section different results obtained by applying proposed encoding model to an existing CSV dataset, recorded during a previous public event ("TourismA" 2018 in Florence, Italy). We focused on locomotion data ($S_p(u, t)$), comparing obtained output to common storage models (ASCII, binary) in terms of accuracy, quantization and data storage. We also compare different formats and compression for QSAs and saliency tables generated images.

For original CSV dataset (ASCII), a timestep of 0.1 s was used to record user states: from previous experiences, this is generally a good interval to capture spatial attributes (like location in the virtual environment) during the VR session. For encoded QSA (see Sect. 3.2) this means each pixel of the image atlas represent $\frac{1}{10}$ s (10 contiguous pixels on x-axis represent one second). The 3D scene we considered is an old virtual environment - employed by CNR ITABC in several past projects [3,9] - due to its extents and size.

In order to test and compare meaningful sessions, we first filtered original locomotion data CSV, using a few acceptance policies suitable for this specific virtual environment:

- *Session duration*: discard very short sessions (< 20 s)
- *Session radius*: compute a bounding sphere for each user locomotion data, if radius $r > 5.0$ m, accept the session
- *Variance*: compute user location variance (s^2) for each dimension. If $max(s_x^2, s_y^2, s_z^2) > 5$, accept the session.

From filtered CSV dataset, we performed different tests to assess storage and accuracy, using standard binary encoding and image-based encoding (presented model). We used a session volume V_1 with extents (50.28 m × 76.46 m × 10.0 m): due to voxel quantization, this results in a location error for each dimension of $\epsilon_x = \pm 9$ cm, $\epsilon_y = \pm 14.9$ cm and $\epsilon_z = \pm 1.9$ cm. A second volume V_2 (25.27 m × 12.85 m × 8.28 m) was deployed to capture finer users locomotion on the temple

---

[4] http://osiris.itabc.cnr.it/scenebaker/index.php/projects/aton/.

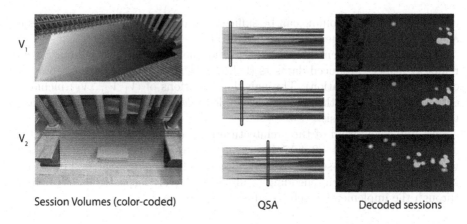

Session Volumes (color-coded)   QSA   Decoded sessions

Fig. 5. The two volumes V_1 and V_2 (left, color-coded). Encoded QSA for V_1 and real-time decoding of HMD locomotion data on the GPU (WebGL) through a temporal slider.

stairs with quantization error of $\epsilon_x = \pm 4.9\,\mathrm{cm}$, $\epsilon_y = \pm 2.5\,\mathrm{cm}$ and $\epsilon_z = \pm 1.6\,\mathrm{cm}$ (Fig. 5).

We compare a part of original recorded locomotion dataset size (CSV, 2,86 Mb) with uncompressed binary (double precision and single byte) and QSA (PNG format, bit depth 8, lossless). As shown in Fig. 6, uncompressed binary encoding (double and single byte precision) offer smaller storage, as expected. Proposed encoding model applied to locomotion data using lossless PNG (bit-depth 8) results in very compact QSA (20,1 Kb) storing all users sessions as described. We also evaluate different bit depths for QSA with increasing error during HMD location decoding. From a macroscopic visual inspection of user sessions, 6 bit-depth still maintains a good approximation compared to original 8-bit encoded HMD location, while 4 bit-depth shows major quantization errors

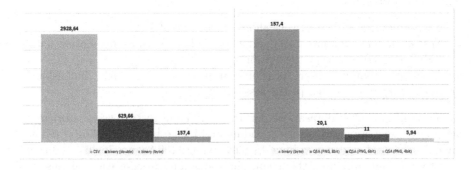

Fig. 6. Left: storage comparison (Kb) between original CSV dataset and binary (double and byte precision). Right: comparison between binary (byte) and proposed image-based encoding (QSA) using different bit depths (8, 6 and 4)

(see Fig. 7). Saliency tables for locomotion data (σ_p) were also evaluated: in this case, the adopted policy to rank voxels was persistence over time. Obtained 1D encoded image (lossless PNG format, bit-depth 8) using a table size of 1024 voxels, resulted in $2,86\,Kb$, thus providing a very comfortable data transport over the network.

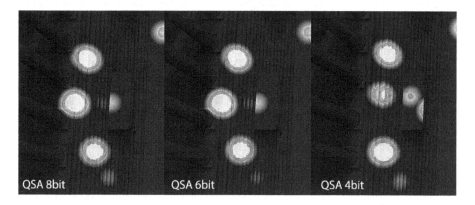

Fig. 7. Comparison between QSAs decoded at runtime using different PNG bit depths (8, 6 and 4)

Figure 8 shows interactive evaluation of σ_p on the GPU through the WebGL Front-End: due to the ranked approach, most salient locations (2%, top left) are related to user starting location as expected, progressively increasing on stairs and entrance of main temple (50% and 80%). The radius (in this case 20 m) also allows to visually understand which parts of the model potentially require

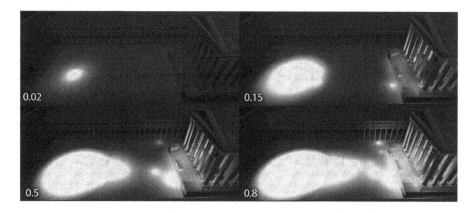

Fig. 8. Interactive evaluation and decoding of saliency table (location persistence over time) on the GPU, using radius of 20 m.

higher detail, supporting selective 3D scene improvements (geometry, texturing, etc.) for immersive VR exploration.

6 Conclusions and Future Developments

We proposed and described an image-based encoding model to volumetrically capture VR sessions during public exhibits or online experiences, producing compact and lightweight data layouts for remote and interactive visual inspection. Within networked scenarios, the model can be particularly useful for analysts, teachers and other professionals to support the remote analysis of spatial affordances and behaviors of users (casual visitors, students, etc.) consuming immersive virtual environments (IVEs) through HMDs.

Session Volumes allow to absorb user attributes and propensities, arranged and deployed at runtime. They are able to encode spatial attributes into special image atlases (*QSA*) allowing to record HMD attributes of several users over time into compact images. Due to the simple RGB mapping and layout, encoding/decoding routines use small computational resources, allowing direct manipulation on GPU and offline intervention through common 2D image processing. We show advantages of proposed solution in terms of scalability and customization, observing only specific portions of the 3D scene and how volume extents impact on accuracy and voxel quantization.

The model has accuracy limitations when encoding HMD spatial attributes due to *voxelization* of the session volume (quantization) introducing controlled error on location decoding (see Sect. 3.1). Such spatial quantization highly depends on bit-depth used for QSA image format (see Fig. 7) and volume extents. On the other hand this issue can be solved or mitigated by arranging multiple smaller session volumes for fine-grained capture, resulting in more accurate decoding. Regarding duration, texture size may limit recording: for instance using a 0.1 s capture interval and a 4096 image width for QSA, the maximum duration we are able to encode for each user is around 6 min. This can be easily solved by using paging techniques [8] thus addressing prolonged immersive sessions. We already employed the model to capture other spatial attributes like focus ($S_f(u, t)$) to visually understand users attention over time and to explore volumetric saliency in a 3D scene. We foresee advantages of encoding model also for the observation of physical motions inside the tracked area and its usage during the session, for instance HMD local motions or VR controllers. Consumer 6DOF headsets allow to track areas of a few meters: for instance a $3\,\text{m} \times 3\,\text{m}$ physical space with session volume attached would result in small quantization errors ($\pm 5\,\text{mm}$) to record spatial attributes.

Acknowledgements. Authors would like to thank D. Ferdani (CNR ITABC) for providing parts of old 3D assets used during Keys2Rome project (http://keys2rome. eu/) and all people involved in VR installation during "TourismA 2018" event.

References

1. Agus, M., Marton, F., Bettio, F., Gobbetti, E.: Interactive 3d exploration of a virtual sculpture collection: an analysis of user behavior in museum setting. In: Proceedings of the 13th Eurographics Workshop on Graphics and Cultural Heritage (2016)
2. Antal, A., et al.: A complete workflow from the data collection on the field to the deployment of a virtual museum: the case of virtual sarmizegetusa (2016)
3. Antonaci, A., Pagano, A.: Technology enhanced visit to museums. a case study: keys to Rome. In: Proceedings of the INTED 2015, Madrid, Spain, pp. 2–4 (2015)
4. Barsanti, S.G., Fanini, B., et al.: The WINCKELMANN300 project: dissemination of culture with virtual reality at the Capitoline Museum in Rome. Int. Arch. Photogramm. Remote Sens. Spat. Inf. Sci. **42**(2) (2018)
5. Boletsis, C.: The new era of virtual reality locomotion: a systematic literature review of techniques and a proposed typology. Multimodal Technol. Interact. **1**(4), 24 (2017)
6. Cantelon, M., Harter, M., Holowaychuk, T., Rajlich, N.: Node.js in Action. Manning Greenwich (2014)
7. Dworak, D., Pietruszka, M.: Fast encoding of huge 3D data sets in lossless PNG format. In: Zgrzywa, A., Choroś, K., Siemiński, A. (eds.) New Research in Multimedia and Internet Systems. AISC, vol. 314, pp. 15–24. Springer, Cham (2015). https://doi.org/10.1007/978-3-319-10383-9_2
8. Fanini, B., Cinque, L.: Encoding VR sessions: image-based techniques to record and inspect immersive experiences. In: 3rd Digital Heritage International Congress (DH2018) held Jointly with 24th International Conference on Virtual Systems & Multimedia (VSMM 2018). IEEE (2019, in press)
9. Fanini, B., d'Annibale, E., Demetrescu, E., Ferdani, D., Pagano, A.: Engaging and shared gesture-based interaction for museums the case study of K2R international expo in Rome. In: 2015 Digital Heritage, vol. 1, pp. 263–270. IEEE (2015)
10. Gu, X., Gortler, S.J., Hoppe, H.: Geometry images. ACM Trans. Graph. (TOG) **21**(3), 355–361 (2002)
11. Habgood, M.J., Moore, D., Wilson, D., Alapont, S.: Rapid, continuous movement between nodes as an accessible virtual reality locomotion technique. In: 2018 IEEE Conference on Virtual Reality and 3D User Interfaces (VR), pp. 371–378. IEEE (2018)
12. Jain, A.K.: Data clustering: 50 years beyond k-means. Pattern Recognit. Lett. **31**(8), 651–666 (2010)
13. Jankowski, P., Andrienko, N., Andrienko, G., Kisilevich, S.: Discovering landmark preferences and movement patterns from photo postings. Trans. GIS **14**(6), 833–852 (2010)
14. Knorr, S., Ozcinar, C., Fearghail, C.O., Smolic, A.: Director's cut-a combined dataset for visual A ention analysis in cinematic VR content (2018)
15. Limper, M., et al.: Fast, progressive loading of binary-encoded declarative-3d web content. IEEE Comput. Graph. Appl. **33**(5), 26–36 (2013)
16. Manku, G.S., Motwani, R.: Approximate frequency counts over data streams. In: VLDB 2002: Proceedings of the 28th International Conference on Very Large Databases, pp. 346–357. Elsevier (2002)
17. Meghini, C., Scopigno, R., Richards, J., Fanini, B., et al.: ARIADNE: a research infrastructure for archaeology. J. Comput. Cult. Herit. (JOCCH) **10**(3), 18 (2017)

18. Shute, V., Rahimi, S., Emihovich, B.: Assessment for learning in immersive environ-
    ments. In: Liu, D., Dede, C., Huang, R., Richards, J. (eds.) Virtual, Augmented,
    and Mixed Realities in Education. SCI, pp. 71–87. Springer, Singapore (2017).
    https://doi.org/10.1007/978-981-10-5490-7_5
19. Sitzmann, V., et al.: Saliency in VR: how do people explore virtual environments?
    IEEE Trans. Vis. Comput. Graph. **24**(4), 1633–1642 (2018)
20. Tilkov, S., Vinoski, S.: Node.js: using JavaScript to build high-performance network
    programs. IEEE Internet Comput. **14**(6), 80–83 (2010)
21. Upenik, E., Ebrahimi, T.: A simple method to obtain visual attention data in head
    mounted virtual reality. In: 2017 IEEE International Conference on Multimedia &
    Expo Workshops (ICMEW), pp. 73–78. IEEE (2017)
22. Wiggins, R.H., Davidson, H.C., Harnsberger, H.R., Lauman, J.R., Goede, P.A.:
    Image file formats: past, present, and future. Radiographics **21**(3), 789–798 (2001)
23. Wong, P.C., Thomas, J.: Visual analytics. IEEE Comput. Graph. Appl. **5**, 20–21
    (2004)

Leveraging Reinforcement Learning Techniques for Effective Policy Adoption and Validation

Nikki Lijing Kuang[1] and Clement H. C. Leung[2(✉)]

[1] Department of Computer Science and Engineering, University of California,
San Diego, La Jolla, CA, USA
llkuang@ucsd.edu
[2] School of Science and Engineering, Chinese University of Hong Kong,
Shenzhen, China
clementleung@cuhk.edu.cn

Abstract. Rewards and punishments in different forms are pervasive and present in a wide variety of decision-making scenarios. By observing the outcome of a sufficient number of repeated trials, one would gradually learn the value and usefulness of a particular policy or strategy. However, in a given environment, the outcomes resulting from different trials are subject to chance influence and variations. In learning about the usefulness of a given policy, significant costs are involved in systematically undertaking the sequential trials; therefore, in most learning episodes, one would wish to keep the cost within bounds by adopting learning stopping rules. In this paper, we examine the deployment of different stopping strategies in given learning environments which vary from highly stringent for mission critical operations to highly tolerant for non-mission critical operations, and emphasis is placed on the former with particular application to aviation safety. In policy evaluation, two sequential phases of learning are identified, and we describe the outcomes variations using a probabilistic model, with closed-form expressions obtained for the key measures of performance. Decision rules that map the trial observations to policy choices are also formulated. In addition, simulation experiments are performed, which corroborate the validity of the theoretical results.

Keywords: Autonomous agent · Aviation safety · Decision rules ·
Multi-agent · Reinforcement learning · Stopping rules

1 Introduction

In order to determine the feasibility or optimality of a given course of action, it is necessary to observe and monitor the outcomes of repeated trials. Repetition is necessary in order to ensure reliability and ongoing effectiveness particularly in an environment which is subject to chance influence and where complete information on all the underlying factors are not available. This is especially vital for mission critical operations, such as aviation safety, where ongoing validation or monitoring of a given policy is essential, but is also relevant for non-mission critical activities [18, 19, 21].

© Springer Nature Switzerland AG 2019
S. Misra et al. (Eds.): ICCSA 2019, LNCS 11620, pp. 311–322, 2019.
https://doi.org/10.1007/978-3-030-24296-1_26

In most practical situations, such trials cannot be performed in parallel but have to be undertaken in a sequential manner. In the context of reinforcement learning, each outcome can be classified as a reward or punishment. However, the cost of carrying out such learning trials can be significant and such sequential validation can have varying degrees of stringency. In this study, the stochastic structure of the environment is explicitly modeled, and the performance measures of the associated validation costs are analyzed.

In trialing or learning a given course of action, the observed rewards and punishments are usually probabilistic. For instance, when one is experimenting a new route between an originating point A and a destination B, an increase of the journey duration by a given amount may be viewed as a punishment, whereas a reduction in the duration of the same may be viewed as a reward, and having thus learned, say, the acceptability of the new route, one would adopt the new route as a policy for traveling between A and B.

Thus, through repeated trials resulting in outcomes of either reward or punishment, one establishes the feasibility of the new policy and completes the learning phase. Subsequent to the learning phase, the new policy, if learned successfully (i.e. when the rewards to punishments ratio is sufficiently high) is adopted from that point onwards without it being questioned or evaluated afterwards. In this particular example, the learning is primarily done during the pre-adoption phase. In some situations, however, even after the policy is adopted, ongoing validation and monitoring is still carried out and this is especially necessary for safety-critical and mission-critical operations. If in the course of ongoing monitoring, there is an overwhelming number of punishments observed, then the adoption of the policy may be called into question, and termination of the policy may be necessary.

In this paper, we study such learning reinforcement scenarios of stochastically receiving rewards and punishments for both the pre-adoption phase as well as the post-adoption phase. To be concrete, we shall use a scenario of aviation safety, as we believe this scenario is sufficiently general and of particular relevance and currency to present day concerns. Despite this, we wish to point out that many other everyday learning situations are similar to this; examples include trialing a new machine translation algorithm, learning the effectiveness of a new advertising channel, and route discovery in self-drive vehicles.

An autonomous agent in reinforcement learning learns through the interaction with the environment to maximize its rewards, while minimizing or avoiding punishments. In most practical situations, the underlying environment is non-stationary and noisy [1, 4, 6, 20, 22], and the next state results from taking the same policy may not result in the same outcome every time but appears to be stochastic [2, 7]. In [3]. Brafman and Tennenholtz introduces a model-based reinforcement learning algorithm R-Max to deal with stochastic games [5]. Such stochastic elements can notably increase the complexity in multi-agent systems and multi-agent tasks, where agents learn to cooperate and compete simultaneously [6, 10]. As other agents adapt and actively adjust their policies, the best policy for each agent would evolve dynamically, giving rise to non-stationarity [8, 9]. In these studies, the cost of a trial to receive either a reward or punishment can be seen to be significant, and ideally, one would like to arrive at the correct conclusion by incurring minimum cost. In reinforce learning algorithms, we are always in the hope to rapidly converge to an optimal policy with least volumes of data, calculations, learning iterations, and minimal degree of complexity [11, 12]. To do so, one should explicitly define the stopping rules for specifying the conditions under which learning should terminate and a conclusion drawn as to whether the learning has been successful or not based on the observations so far.

Establishing stopping rules, is an active research topic in reinforcement learning, which is closely linked to the problems of optimal policies and policy convergence [13]. Conventional approaches mainly aim for relatively small-scale problems with finite states and actions. The stopping rules involved are well-defined for each category of algorithms, such as utilizing Bellman Equation in Q-learning [14]. To deal with continuous action spaces or state spaces, new algorithms, such as the Cacla algorithm [15] and CMA-ES algorithm [16], are developed with specific stopping rules. Some stopping rules for stochastic reinforcement learning under different assumptions have been proposed and studied in [23, 24]. Still, most studies on stopping rules are procedure-oriented and do not have a unified measurement where comparison may be facilitated.

In our study here, in addition to learning from the observations in the pre-adoption and post-adoption phases, we also focus in the stopping criteria, so that what has been observed and learned can form the basis of policy decision making. The next section provides a representation of the stochastic learning environment, and establishes stopping rules for the different phases. An analysis of these rules is given in Sect. 3. Assessment of the learning cost and the rewards ratio, along with experimental evaluation is given in Sect. 4, and the final conclusions are drawn in Sect. 5.

2 The Learning Environment and Stopping Rules

We assume that trials are systematically carried out in a sequential manner. Due to the presence of a multiplicity unknown factors and hidden variables, indicating an environment about which we have incomplete information, the outcome from different trials will be subject to probabilistic influences. As mentioned earlier, we shall employ the aviation safety learning situations to develop the main ideas. The reason for using this situation is twofold:

i. it has a high degree of generality that is able to subsume a variety of learning situations as special cases, and
ii. it has a particular relevance and interest to current concerns of airlines, aircraft manufacturers, and passengers.

We shall divide the learning reinforcement of a policy into two distinct phases:

i. the pre-adoption phase, which we shall refer to as Phase I, and
ii. the post-adoption phase, which we shall refer to as Phase II.

The former phase is concerned with learning the acceptability of the policy through systematic trials, while the latter is concerned with the continued validity of the policy subsequent to adoption, and in this case, whether the policy should under some circumstances be discontinued. An especially relevant example is whether a particular aircraft model recently introduced should continue to be in service or should it be discontinued, at least temporarily, for the safety and well-being of its passengers, perhaps following some serious incidents.

Here, we are dealing with a sequence of independent learning trials, each of which either results in a reward or punishment. In our particular aviation example, typically for each trial a set of indicators are logged and a final score is computed which forms the basis of a decision on either a pass (reward) or failure (punishment) for the trial is attained. We let p and q, with $p + q = 1$, denote the probabilities of receiving a reward or punishment respectively for a given trial. For example, if $p >> q$, then the decision should be that of adopting the policy. In general the requirements for Phase I is much more stringent for Phase II, and the cost of different decision rules will be analyzed in the next section.

Let us consider the following two stopping rules.

Rule I: *In the course of undertaking the learning trials, an agent concludes the learning process when m consecutive rewards are obtained.*

Rule II: *In the course of undertaking the learning trials, an agent concludes the learning process when m total rewards are obtained.*

Rule I is a somewhat stringent stopping rule but is particular applicable for mission critical operations where a high degree of reliability is required. It is also more widely used for the proper learning phase (Phase I) than for the validation phase after learning (Phase II). Rule II is a less stringent stopping rule and is often used for the validation phase. In some applications, such as finding an optimal route from A to B for a self-driving vehicle, it is mostly sufficient just to use Rule II for Phase I learning, and usually no need for Phase II evaluation.

In addition, there is a significant difference between the objective of Phase I, and that of Phase II. While the objective of Phase I is to aim to adopt the policy by accumulating a sufficient number of rewards, the aim of Phase II, on the other hand, is to look for alerts that may lead to a discontinuation of the policy. As we shall see, the analysis in Phase II requires the application of the Reflection Principle [17], by interchanging the probabilities p and q, as well as interchanging the rewards and punishments. Such reversal of roles leads to a variation of Rule I and Rule II, which we shall call Rule IR, and Rule IIR respectively, with the suffix R signifying reflection.

Rule IR: *In the course of undertaking the validation trials, an agent concludes the learning process when m' consecutive punishments are received.*

Rule IIR: *In the course of undertaking the validation trials, an agent concludes the learning process when m' total punishments are received.*

As we shall see in the next section, the use of Rule I for Phase I means that acceptance of the policy is more stringent than that when Rule II is used. On the other hand, the use of IIR in Phase II also signifies a more stringent requirement since rejection of the policy is easier than that of using Rule IR (Table 1).

Table 1. The typical learning scenarios for different types of applications for the two phases.

	Phase I (learning)	Phase II (validation)
Mission critical systems	Rule I	Rule IIR
Intermediate level 2	Rule I	Rule IR
Intermediate level 1	Rule II	Rule IIR
Non-mission critical systems	Rule II	IR

3   Analysis of the Performance of the Stopping Rules

Rule I above is concerned with collecting a given number of consecutive reinforcements or rewards, so that we shall first establish the probability of occurrence of such an event for the first time. Let bn be the probability that m consecutive rewards occurs at trial n, with n $\geq$ m, not necessarily for the first time, and we denote by $B(z)$ be the corresponding probability generating function. From [17], this probability generating function can be obtained as

$$B(z) = \frac{1 - z + qp^m z^{m+1}}{(1-z)(1 - p^m z^m)}. \tag{1}$$

Since we need to obtain the corresponding generating function for the probability that the associated event occurs for the first time, we need to consider the relationship between the two events. We shall use the random variable X to denote the number of trials preceding and including the receiving of the first set of m consecutive rewards. Thus X is the stopping time for Rule I, measured in terms of the number of trials, and we let a_n be the probability

$$a_n = \Pr[X = n], n = m, m+1, \ldots. \tag{2}$$

We denote by $A(z)$ the probability generating function for the event that the accumulation of m rewards occurs for the first time. It can be shown in [17] that the generating function $A(z)$ is related to $B(z)$ by

$$A(z) = \frac{B(z) - 1}{B(z)}. \tag{3}$$

From this, we obtain, after simplification,

$$A(z) = \frac{p^m z^m}{1 - q^m \sum_{k=0}^{m-1} p^k z^k}. \tag{4}$$

From this, the mean and variance of X can be readily obtained after simplification,

$$E[X] = A'^{(1)} = \frac{1 - p^m}{qp^m}, \tag{5}$$

$$\mathrm{Var}[X] = A''(1) + A'(1) - A'(1)^2 = \frac{1}{q^2 p^{2m}} - \frac{2m+1}{qp^m} - \frac{p}{q^2}, \tag{6}$$

where the apostrophe indicates derivative.

Next, we examine Rule II, and let the random variable Y be the number of observations preceding and including the first reward; thus

$$\Pr[Y = k] = pq^{k-1}, k = 0, 1, 2, 3, \ldots \tag{7}$$

The probability generating function for a random variable W which excludes the reward itself has been obtained in [23] and is given by

$$\frac{p}{(1 - qz)}.$$

The random variables W and Y are related by $Y = W + 1$, and since the generating function of 1 is z, we have, for the probability generating function of Y,

$$\frac{pz}{(1 - qz)}. \tag{8}$$

Since after the occurrence of the first reward, the process probabilistically repeats itself again, so that we have for the number of trials to the mth reward, bearing in mind that under Rule II, the rewards need not occur consecutively

$$Z = \sum_{k=1}^{m} Y_k, \tag{9}$$

where each Y_k has the same distributional characteristics as Y. Consequently, the probability generating function of $F(z)$ corresponding to Z may be obtained

$$F(z) = [\frac{pz}{(1 - qz)}]^m \tag{10}$$

From this, the mean and variance of Z can be readily obtained by differentiation,

$$E[Z] = \frac{m}{p}, \tag{11}$$

$$\mathrm{Var}[Z] = \frac{mq}{p^2}. \tag{12}$$

It is not hard to see that $E(X) \geq E(Z)$, since achieving m consecutive rewards necessarily implies achieving at least m total non-consecutive rewards, with equality holding iff $m = 1$, since in this case, there is no difference between the two situations.

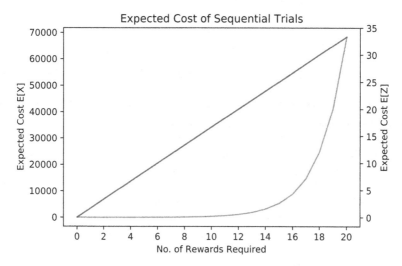

Fig. 1. Cost comparison of Rules I and II ($p = 0.6$).

Figure 1 compares the average cost of sequential trials of the two rules. Here, the left vertical axis is used for $E(X)$, while, the right vertical axis is used for $E(Z)$. We see that the stringency of Rule I is manifested in a steep climb in the number of trials as m increases, as opposed to a relatively moderate increase in Rule II.

4   Learning Cost Evaluation and Experimentation

The number of trials carried out to complete the learning episode is often a costly process. Let h be the numerical representation of cost associated with a single trial, and we can standardize on h as the cost unit so that and without loss of generality we can set $h = 1$. Having specified m, a minimum observation cost of mh must therefore be incurred. What is uncertain is the number of punishments obtained in the process, and ideally to achieve minimum cost, this number should be small. Such average trialing cost are given by Eqs. (5) and (11). Simulation experiments are carried out to compare the actual average learning cost with theoretical predictions, and these are given in Table 2. Table 3 gives the corresponding comparisons of the standard deviation from Eqs. (6) and (12).

The mean number of trials required in order to accumulate m rewards has a direct bearing on the adoption of the given policy. The learning overhead, or cost ratio, is given by the ratio of the average total number of trials to the number of required rewards m. For Rule I, this is given by

$$r_1(m) = \frac{1 - p^m}{mqp^m}, \tag{13}$$

and for Rule II, this is given by,

$$r_2(m) = \frac{1}{p}. \tag{14}$$

Clearly, the decision for adoption or successful validation will tend to be positive for small r_1 and r_2, but tends towards negative when r_1 and r_2 are large. Thus, decision rules can be established by linking them to the cost thresholds h_1 and h_2, whereby, for example, adoption decision is made whenever $r_1 < h_1$.

As indicated earlier, for some situations, only Phase I learning is necessary and Phase II is not required. However, in the case of our aviation scenario, as indicated in the previous section, both Phase I and Phase II are necessary, with Rule I used for Phase I, and Rule IIR used for Phase II. In this case, assuming we have learned the usefulness of the given policy, say, to put the particular aircraft in service, Rule IIR would instead look for punishments that may cause termination of the service to safeguard the safety and well-being of its passengers. We note that Rule IIR represents a stricter criterion with a stronger propensity to termination, since discontinuation would be harder if one uses Rule IR instead: we may decide to discontinue the service if there is an accumulation of m' punishments, not necessarily consecutive. From (11), the mean number of observations $E[Z']$ relating to Rule IIR for Phase II is, by the Reflection Principle,

$$E[Z'] = \frac{m'}{q}. \tag{15}$$

Similarly, from (5), the mean number of observations $E[X']$ relating to Rule IR for Phase II is, again by the Reflection Principle,

$$E[X'] = \frac{1 - q^m}{pq^m}. \tag{16}$$

The associated cost ratios are summarized in Table 2 below.

Simulation experiments are performed to gauge the accuracy of the above results. These are shown in Table 3 below. It compares the average values and the standard deviations, with the latter corresponding to the square roots of the variances determined above. For a given combination of parameters, 100,000 trial episodes are performed; the expected values and standard deviations are calculated based on these 100,000 episodes. The error percentages are computed as follows:

$$Err = \frac{|\text{theoretical prediction} - \text{empirical measurement}|}{\text{empirical measurements}} \times 100\%.$$

Table 2. Cost ratios for the two phases.

	Phase I	Phase II
Mission critical systems	$(1 - p^m)/(mqp^m)$	$1/q$
Intermediate level 2	$(1 - p^m)/(mqp^m)$	$\left(1 - q^{m'}\right)/\left(m'pq^{m'}\right)$
Intermediate level 1	$1/p$	$1/q$
Non-mission critical systems	$1/p$	$(1 - q^{m'})/(m'pq^{m'})$

Table 3. Comparison of the average trialing costs and the standard deviations.

m	p	$E[X]$ (th)	$E[X]$ (expt)	Err (%)	$E[Z]$ (th)	$E[Z]$ (expt)	Err (%)	std. $[X]$ (th)	std. $[X]$ (expt)	Err (%)	std. $[Z]$ (th)	std. $[Z]$ (expt)	Err (%)
3	0.6	9.07	9.05	0.247	5.0	4.99	0.200	7.01	7.01	0.018	1.83	1.81	0.863
	0.75	5.48	5.47	0.018	4.0	4.00	0.000	3.40	3.38	0.307	1.15	1.15	0.006
	0.9	3.71	3.72	0.129	3.33	3.33	0.100	1.46	1.46	0.584	0.61	0.61	0.355
5	0.6	29.65	29.77	0.397	8.33	8.35	0.199	26.00	26.16	0.599	2.36	2.36	0.142
	0.75	12.86	12.84	0.121	6.67	6.66	0.100	9.31	9.31	0.035	1.49	1.49	0.142
	0.9	6.94	6.93	0.031	5.56	5.56	0.080	3.24	3.23	0.469	0.79	0.78	0.253
7	0.6	86.81	87.02	0.242	11.67	11.67	0.029	81.44	81.91	0.673	2.79	2.79	0.292
	0.75	25.97	25.85	0.461	9.33	9.34	0.071	20.89	20.84	0.226	1.76	1.77	0.355
	0.9	10.91	10.91	0.057	7.77	7.78	0.029	5.79	5.80	0.142	0.93	0.93	0.405
10	0.6	410.95	412.69	0.422	16.67	16.67	0.019	402.81	405.22	0.597	3.33	3.34	0.181
	0.75	67.03	67.05	0.030	13.33	13.33	0.025	59.51	59.37	0.244	2.11	2.10	0.334
	0.9	18.68	18.67	0.037	11.11	11.11	0.010	7.01	7.01	0.018	1.83	1.81	0.863

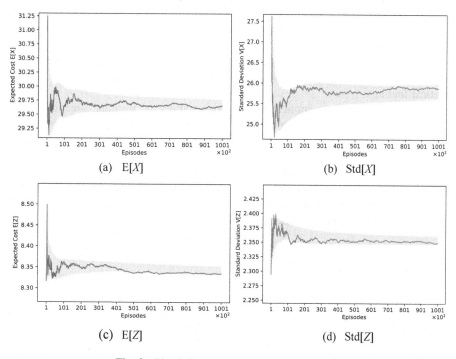

(a) $E[X]$

(b) Std$[X]$

(c) $E[Z]$

(d) Std$[Z]$

Fig. 2. Simulation results with $p = 0.6$, $m = 5$.

We see that the agreement is quite acceptable in all cases, with error below 1%. Figure 2, plots the experimental data for the case $p = 0.6$, $m = 5$. We see that some significant transient fluctuations are evident in the first 200 episodes, but gradually settles to an equilibrium after around 400 episodes. While some fluctuations are still present thereafter, they eventually converge to the values as predicted by the theory. Although we have not shown the behavior for other parameter settings, they behave in much the same way as those shown in Fig. 2.

5 Summary and Conclusion

In this paper, we have studied the practical situation of learning the usefulness of a given policy for adoption by repeated sequential trials, each can result in a reward or a punishment. The entire evaluation process may be divided into two distinct phases, one for assessing initial acceptability, and one for assessing ongoing feasibility. Due to a large number of unknown factors and incomplete information, the outcome of each trial is subject to probabilistic variations and cannot be predicted exactly.

Such learning process requires suitable stopping criteria in order for the results of the observations to be consolidated and learned. Here, the probabilistic influence of the learning environment is explicitly modeled, where the outcome of each observational trial is taken to be independent and identically distributed. Four operational stopping rules, applicable to varying levels of mission-critical requirements, are established that are applicable to the two phases of learning reinforcement.

The performance of these rules are analyzed, and closed-form expressions of key measures of interest are given. In particular, cost ratios are obtained for the two phases of learning for system operations exhibiting different characteristics, and decision rules linking the trial outcomes to policy choices are developed. Experimentations have also been carried out, and the experimental results exhibit good agreements with the theoretical findings.

The present study is applicable to a wide variety of learning situations in an unknown environment based on rewards and punishments. The proposed method is useful in helping to arrive at sound operational decisions, and the associated costs of systematic evaluation has been calculated. While here we have adopted an independent, identically distributed set of random variables for the outcomes, future studies may relax on this assumption and examine situations where the outcomes are Markov dependent or where the underlying random variables are not identically distributed; doing so should be able to further enhance the usefulness of these results.

References

1. Ziebart, B.D., Maas, A.L., A. Bagnell, J., Dey, A.K.: Maximum entropy inverse reinforcement learning. In Proceedings of the Twenty-Third AAAI Conference on Artificial Intelligence (AAAI 08), vol. 8, pp. 1433–1438 (2008)
2. Kaelbling, L.P., Littman, M.L., Moore, A.W.: Reinforcement learning: a survey. J. Artif. Intell. Res. **4**, 237–285 (1996)

3. Kearns, M., Singh, S.: Near-optimal reinforcement learning in polynomial time. In: International Conference on Machine Learning (1998)
4. Santana, H., Ramalho, G., Corruble, V., Ratitch, B.: Multi-agent patrolling with reinforcement learning. In: Proceedings of the Third International Joint Conference on Autonomous Agents and Multiagent Systems, vol. 3, pp. 1122–1129. IEEE Computer Society (2004)
5. Brafman, R.I., Tennenholtz, M.: R-max-a general polynomial time algorithm for near-optimal reinforcement learning. J. Mach. Learn. Res. **3**, 213–231 (2002)
6. Panait, L., Luke, S.: Cooperative multi-agent learning: the state of the art. Auton. Agents Multi-Agent Syst. **11**(3), 387–434 (2005)
7. Ipek, E., Mutlu, O., Martínez, J.F., Caruana, R.: Self-optimizing memory controllers: a reinforcement learning approach. In: ACM SIGARCH Computer Architecture News, vol. 36, no. 3. IEEE Computer Society (2008)
8. Busoniu, L., Babuska, R., De Schutter, B.: A comprehensive survey of multiagent reinforcement learning. IEEE Trans. Syst. Man Cybern. Part C Appl. Rev. **38**(22), 156–172 (2008)
9. Albrecht, S.V., Stone, P.: Autonomous agents modelling other agents: a comprehensive survey and open problems. Artif. Intell. **258**, 66–95 (2018)
10. Tampuu, A., et al.: Multiagent cooperation and competition with deep reinforcement learning. PLoS ONE **12**(4), e0172395 (2017)
11. Moore, A.W., Atkeson, C.G.: Prioritized sweeping: Reinforcement learning with less data and less time. Mach. Learn. **13**(1), 103–130 (1993)
12. Brochu, E., Cora, V.M., De Freitas, N.: A tutorial on Bayesian optimization of expensive cost functions, with application to active user modeling and hierarchical reinforcement learning. arXiv preprint arXiv:1012.2599 (2010)
13. Wei, Q., Lewis, F.L., Sun, Q., Yan, P., Song, R.: Discrete-time deterministic Q-learning: a novel convergence analysis. IEEE Trans. Cybern. **47**(5), 1224–1237 (2017)
14. Watkins, C.J., Dayan, P.: Q-learning. Mach. Learn. **8**(3–4), 279–292 (1992)
15. Van Hasselt, H., Wiering, M.A.: Using continuous action spaces to solve discrete problems. In: Proceedings of the International Joint Conference on Neural Networks (IJCNN 09), pp. 1149–1156. IEEE (2009)
16. Hansen, N., Müller, S.D., Koumoutsakos, P.: Reducing the time complexity of the derandomized evolution strategy with covariance matrix adaptation (CMA-ES). Evol. Comput. **11**(1), 1–18 (2003)
17. Feller, W.: An Introduction to Probability Theory and its Applications, vol. 1, 3rd edn. Wiley, Hoboken (2008)
18. Rodrigues, C., Cusick, S: Commercial Aviation Safety, 5th edn. (2012)
19. Deng, J., Leung, C.H.C.: Dynamic time warping for music retrieval using time series modeling of musical emotions. IEEE Trans. Affect. Comput. **6**(2), 137–151 (2015)
20. Zhang, H.L., Leung, C.H.C., Raikundalia, G.K.: Topological analysis of AOCD-based agent networks and experimental results. J. Comput. Syst. Sci. **74**, 255–278 (2008)
21. Azzam, I., Leung, C.H.C., Horwood, J.: Implicit concept-based image indexing and retrieval. In: Proceedings of the IEEE International Conference on Multi-media Modeling, Brisbane, Australia, pp. 354–359 (2004)
22. Zhang, H.L., Leung, C.H.C., Raikundalia, G.K.: Classification of intelligent agent network topologies and a new topological description language for agent networks. In: Shi, Z., Shimohara, K., Feng, D. (eds.) IIP 2006. IIFIP, vol. 228, pp. 21–31. Springer, Boston, MA (2006). https://doi.org/10.1007/978-0-387-44641-7_3

23. Kuang, N.L.J., Leung, C.H.C., Sung, V.: Stochastic reinforcement learning. In: Proceedings of the IEEE International Conference on Artificial Intelligence and Knowledge Engineering, California, USA, pp. 244–248 (2018)

24. Kuang, N.L.J., Leung, C.H.C.: Performance dynamics and termination errors in reinforcement learning – a unifying perspective. In: Proceedings of the IEEE International Conference on Artificial Intelligence and Knowledge Engineering, California, USA, pp. 129–133 (2018)

Impact of Time Granularity on Histories Binary Correlation Analysis

Paolo Mengoni[1(✉)], Alfredo Milani[1], and Yuanxi Li[2]

[1] Department of Mathematics and Computer Science,
University of Perugia, Perugia, Italy
`paolo.mengoni@dmi.unipg.it, alfredo.milani@unipg.it`
[2] Department of Computer Science, Hong Kong Baptist University,
Kowloon Tong, Hong Kong
`csyxli@comp.hkbu.edu.hk`

Abstract. Activities taken by students within a Virtual Learning Environment (VLE) can be represented by using binary student histories. Virtual Learning Environments allow educators to track most of the students' individual activities that can be used to elicit the students social communities. In this work, we analyse the impact of granularity in the social community elicitation. Granularity can be seen as the resolution of the student history vectors where each time slot is directly dependent from this value. Indeed, the higher is the resolution of the students histories the more precise is the representation of their actions within the VLE. When comparing the histories using various similarity measures to elicit the students' groups, we find the optimal granularity and demonstrate that there is a resolution limit where the similarity measures will not help to distinguish the social communities.

Keywords: Data analysis · Learning analytics · Cluster analysis · Community elicitation

1 Introduction

By using the Virtual Learning Environments (VLE) educators gained the ability to track and analyse the online activities of students. In this scenario, courses can be delivered by teachers by using various mixtures of online and offline activities.

Learning Designs (LD) can be improved by knowing the students' communities. This can help also to identify situations potentially at risk, which will need the teacher intervention, e.g. when there can be risk of exam failure and/or more serious cases of dropping from studies. In online courses, such as MOOCs or SPOCs, all the student's activities can be analysed, including the student's communications. In the blended learning scenario the major part of communications among the students take place using side channels, such as social networking and instant messaging applications, that are out of the control scope of the teacher and don't leave traces to be analysed.

© Springer Nature Switzerland AG 2019
S. Misra et al. (Eds.): ICCSA 2019, LNCS 11620, pp. 323–335, 2019.
https://doi.org/10.1007/978-3-030-24296-1_27

Using the Histories Binary Correlation Analysis (HBCA) [35], we demonstrated in previous work that is possible to discover the latent social communities of students. This methodology makes use of information about the students' activities within a VLE to create the students' history vectors. The similarity between student's histories is the used to gain knowledge about the social interactions of students and their communities.

Similarity measures used to compare student's histories are highly dependant on how the features are extracted from the raw data. One of the parameters that impacts the creation of student's history vectors is the *granularity* of observations. For low granularity values (i.e. at high resolution) the histories are more accurate in representing the exact timing of the activities, while for high granularity values (i.e. at low resolution) more activities are grouped together as on single value of the history vector. The scope of this work is to analyse this parameter impact on the quality of social communities elicited by using the HBCA approach.

This paper is organised as follows. In Sect. 2 we review the related work in Community Detection in networks. In Sect. 3 we present the History Binary Correlation Analysis to find communities of students in VLE. In Sect. 4 we introduce the experimental setting and methodology. In Sect. 5 we discuss the experimental results. Finally, in Sect. 6, we draw conclusion and present future works.

2   Related Work

Nodes of a network that are similar considering specific characteristics can be grouped in communities, whose connections can be used to determine the community structure.

Different classes of problems related to communities have been studied in literature, mainly to find solutions for community search and community detection. The former class of algorithms tries to identify the community to which belongs a given node [46]. The latter tries to identify the all the communities included in a given network [30].

Starting from a given set of partitions, the strategies to elicit the various communities in a network make use of various approaches, and also their combinations, that merge, split and change the assignment of elements from the starting communities. The survey in "Community detection in graphs" [14] includes an extensive review of the methodologies used to find solutions for the community detection class of problems, that exploit various characteristics of the network and its elements.

Network partitioning and clustering are examples of traditional methods used for community detection. Network partitioning is in general a NP-Hard problem that can be solved with some approximate algorithms. It requires that the number of partitions as a parameter and uses features of the network edges to find the communities [28]. Clustering algorithms [1,11,20,21] make use of distance measures [8,19,22,23,34] to group together different nodes of the network. Different community discovery strategies have been developed, such as spectral [13], partitional [32] and hierarchical [26].

To assess the quality of the elicited community and as heuristic to find approximate solutions to the community detection problem in literature is widely used the Q modularity value, in origin used in Girvan-Newman divisive algorithm [24] as stopping criterion. The modularity maximization optimisation problem has been therefore solved by using greedy [5], simulated annealing [25], evolutionary computation [2,44], probabilistic graphical models [3] and other heuristic methods [6].

The interactions of the students with the VLE have been studied in our previous works [35,36] to elicit the students' communities. Monitoring tools, such as SNAPP [4,10] and Dynamical Morphing Interfaces [16], have been developed to understand the social interactions between the students. SNAPP is a tool that uses discussion forum threads to elicit the social network of the students, while Dynamic Morphing Interfaces are used by the instructors to asses the quality and study behaviour of the students. In other works, such as Khosravi et al. [29], the connections between the engagement of the student with the VLE and their learning outcomes have been investigated. Clustering methodologies, that exploit the learning outcomes and study behaviour similarities, have been used to elicit the groups of students.

3   Methodology

In previous works [35,36] we developed a framework to discover the communities of students, basing on the information of the actions they take in Virtual Learning Environments (VLE). The History Binary Correlation Analysis (HBCA) [35] uses the eLearning system logs' information that is related to student's actions. The timing of activities within the VLE is used to model the students' histories and elicit their communities [9]. Clustering is then applied to the students histories to find similar user behaviour and group the students in distinct communities [17]. HBCA approach elicits various groups of students by maximising the similarities of the ones grouped together. The first step of the approach is to retrieve the students' histories, then it proceeds by evaluating pairwise student histories' similarity and use this information to assign the cluster labelling.

3.1   Student Histories

Student histories are summarised by using granularity parameter that refers to the continuity of observation. Different types of granularity can be referred as *continuous* (i.e. CCTV cameras), *Periodic* (i.e. cellular line polling), and *event* (i.e. system logs). Granularity can be transformed from event to periodic using *bucketing* technique. Activities are grouped together in single buckets when they are within a certain γ time threshold. In the histories a binary value is recorded to represent the presence of interaction in that bucket. The number of buckets of each history-summarised vector is proportional to the length of the period and the granularity γ parameter.

3.2 Histories Pairwise Similarity

A student's similarity matrix is build basing on the comparison of the history binary summarised vectors using various binary similarity measures.

Similarity measures. To determine the similarity of the history summarised vectors a wide spectrum of binary similarity measures have been tested to emphasise the different aspects of the co-occurrence of interactions [18,31]. The comparison is made bucket by bucket to set the values of the parameters represented in the contingency table shown in Table 1.

Table 1. Contingency table for pairwise vector comparison.

	Vector 1 Element Feature F present	Vector 2 Element Feature F absent
Vector 1 Element Feature F present	a	b
Vector 2 Element Feature F absent	c	d

Among all the various binary similarity measures, for our experiments we considered the following, representative of different presence and absence of parameters in the computation:

Cooccurence. This simple statistic measure takes in account only of the presence of features in both sets.

$$Cooccurrence = a \tag{1}$$

Jaccard Similarity Measure. Introduced by Paul Jaccard at the start of 20th century [27], this measure is also known as the similarity ratio. It does not use the features' absence parameter in the computation.

$$Jaccard = \frac{a}{a+b+c} \tag{2}$$

Russell and Rao (RR) Similarity Measure. This similarity measure, introduced in 1940 by Russell and Rao [43], considers at the denominator the information about the absence of a features in the two sets.

$$RR = \frac{a}{a+b+c+d} \tag{3}$$

Simple Matching (SM) Similarity Measure. Known also as the Rand Index [40], this measure is the ratio of the number of matches to the total number of characteristics.

$$SM = \frac{a+d}{a+b+c+d} \tag{4}$$

Dice Similarity Measure. Dice similarity measure [12], also known as Czekanowski or Sorenson, is similar to the Jaccard index, but give more emphasis to the presence of common features between the compared sets.

$$Dice = \frac{2a}{2a + b + c} \tag{5}$$

Sokal and Sneath (SS1) Similarity Measure n. 1. In their work, Sokal and Sneath [45], presented various similarity measures. This measure enhances the concurrent presence and absence of features in the two sets.

$$SS1 = \frac{2\,(a + d)}{2\,(a + d) + b + c + d} \tag{6}$$

Ochiai Similarity Measure. Also known as Fowlkes-Mallows index [15], the Ochiai similarity measure [39] is the binary form of the cosine vector similarity.

$$Ochiai = \sqrt{\frac{a}{a + b} \cdot \frac{a}{a + c}} \tag{7}$$

3.3   Cluster Detection

The different history summarised vectors similarity matrices are used to group the students in different clusters. The approach is general and independent on the clustering algorithm. The different labels assigned to the students by the clustering algorithms are used to determine the students' groupings.

Agglomerative. The hierarchical clustering class of algorithms include bottom up approaches to merge the elements in different clusters. The agglomerative technique starts from clusters containing single elements and proceeds to cluster the most similar ones, e.g. the ones that minimise the sum of the square differences between the clusters distances.

Gaussian Mixture. The Gaussian Mixture, also called Expectation-Maximization (EM), is a statistical iterative algorithm for cluster detection. EM iterations switches between expectation (E) computation and maximisation (M) step. The latter step computes the parameters that maximise the expected likelihood. The algorithm stops when the E step does not increase the likelihood anymore.

K-Means. K-Means clustering is used to partition n elements in k clusters where the distance between the elements is minimal considering a specific distance. Although the problem is, in general, NP-hard some approximations exist that make use of heuristics to converge to a local optimum.

Spectral. Spectral clustering is used to reduce the dimensionality of the problem and then cluster in lower dimensions. The algorithm makes use of the spectum (i.e. the set of eigenvalues) of the similarity matrix to reduce the dimensionality. This matrix can be used in combination with all the previously mentioned clustering algorithms to detect the clusters of elements.

4   Experiments

4.1   Dataset

For this study we use a dataset containing anonimised students' activity logs from University of Perugia Moodle eLearning system. The students' activities have been anonymised by using peusonymisation techniques, extensively studied to manage containing medical data [37,38]. Pseudonymisation balances the need of privacy, by replacement of identifiers with pseudonyms, and the reversibility of the process under strict conditions.

Data from the course "Ingegneria del Software" (Software Engineering), taught with blended learning mode (i.e. with online and offline activities). Among all the various online and offline activities, the most important one for our study is the group project that the students were required to complete for successfully complete the course.

In the dataset are recorded all the students' actions and their timings taken with regards of the content available on the Virtual Learning Environment.

4.2   Ground Truth

As introduced in previous section, the students were required to develop a group project and submit to the instructor the related grouping information. This group composition information is then used to compare the performance of the different clustering algorithms as we can assume that students that work together to develop the project were studying together the course material.

4.3   Granularity

Students' histories are extracted from the dataset described in 4.1 and summarised at various granularity levels.

Similarly to the session time that each student spend while interacting with the VLE, granularity used for bucketing the time slots can not be clearly determined. In sessions, the starting action of each session can be easily identified. On the other hand, the end of session is difficult to be determined as the students tend to close the web browser instead of using logout function. In literature there is no agreement on how long it should be the threshold for session expiry. Early works suggest 30 min for web browsing sessions [7], while later works context-based and user-based thresholds have been suggested [33].

In this work, we will explore the impact of granularity parameter γ used to extract the student histories (previously described in Sect. 3.1). Different time slot lengths, starting from 1 h and its multiples and fractions, have been considered. Higher granularity values imply lower resolution when summarising the students actions, while lower granularity values will imply an higher resolution and detail of the students' histories.

All the combinations of measures and clustering algorithms, introduced in Sects. 3.2 and 3.3, have been tested to elicit the groups of students. In total, 28 combination of measure and clustering were experimented for each granularity setting.

4.4   Evaluation Criteria

The qualitative evaluation of the cluster label assignments have been conducted, with respect of the ground truth as defined in Sect. 4.2. Qualitative assessment of the cluster labelling have been conducted by using the following measures:

Homogeneity. High homogeneity is reached if the clusters contain only elements of a single class in the ground truth assignment [42].

Completeness. High completeness values are achieved if all the elements of a single class in the ground truth are assigned to the same cluster [42].

V-measure. Is a measures that balances the satisfaction of both homogeneity and completeness [41], by computing the harmonic mean of the previously cited scores [42].

5   Experiment Results Discussion

To identify the impact of granularity in community elicitation using HBCA approach, we select to use various preset levels representative of the continuous nature of time of actions. We decided to use some values that can be connected to some human activities. The granularity values, expressed in seconds, that we experimented are: 60, 300, 600, 900, 1800, 3600, 7200, 14400, 28800, and 86400. All the granularity levels have been experimented in combination with each measure and clustering algorithm introduced in previous sections, totalling to 280 combinations.

The best results for each clustering algorithm and similarity measure are summarised in Table 2. Agglomerative clustering is performing at best, in terms of V-measure score, when combined with the Jaccard similarity measure at 900 s of granularity. Gaussian Mixture best performance is obtained in combination with the Dice similarity measure at 600 s of granularity. For KMeans clustering the best measure is Ochiai at 900 s of granularity. Finally, Spectral clustering is performing at best when combined with the Dice similarity measure at 1800 s of granularity.

In Fig. 1 are reported detailed scores for each combination of clustering algorithm and similarity measure score, grouped by granularity value. From this figure we can see that with granularity set at 60 and 300 s some measures (specifically RR, SM, and SS1) cannot give enough information to the clustering algorithms to discriminate the communities of students. Moreover, we can see obtain the best results at 600 and 900 s of granularity. Starting from 1800 s the scores are generally dropping in terms of V-measure value and flattening to a score ≈ 0.5.

As shown in Fig. 2 the best results are, in general, obtained when setting the granularity between 600 and 900 s. At this resolutions the time slots in the history summarised vectors are bucketing the interactions between 10 and 15 min, representing the length of the online study session of students. For measures that take in account the absence of activities d (such as RR, SM, SS1), from this figure we can also see that the V-measure score increases with the increasing of granularity. Moreover, V-measure score of Gaussian Mixture combined with this set of measures, at high resolution (i.e. low granularity), is not able to distinguish the different cluster. The very low number of clusters leads to high completeness scores and extremely low homogeneity scores that result in low V-measure scores.

Table 2. V-measure best results for each clustering algorithm and similarity measure combination

	Measure						
	Cooccurrence	Dice	Jaccard	Ochiai	RR	SM	SS1
Agglomerative	0.493	0.654	**0.663**	0.655	0.493	0.496	0.508
Gaussian mixture	0.490	**0.664**	0.640	0.615	0.490	0.519	0.492
KMeans	0.509	0.572	0.582	**0.594**	0.509	0.497	0.523
Spectral	0.430	**0.635**	0.632	0.634	0.563	0.521	0.530

Dice similarity measure has, in general, the best performance followed by from Ochiai and Jaccard measures. For these measures, the best granularity setting can be found at 600 and 900 s, where the various clustering algorithms find communities that are close to the ground truth grouping of students.

It has been confirmed, as in previous works, that the common trait of the best performing measures is that the concurrent absence of interactions is not taken in account. The presence of interactions has very sparse values in the history summarised vectors when compared with the absence of interactions. From the results, we can find that the low resolution vectors (i.e. high granularity values), that are less sparse and with less number of slots when compared to the high resolution ones, help these similarity measures to lower the gap from the best ones given the same granularity setting.

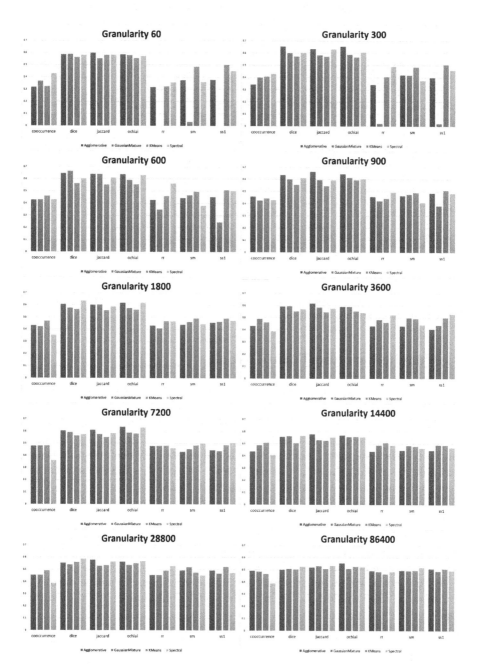

Fig. 1. V-measure score evaluation: comparison of clustering and similarity measures for each granularity level.

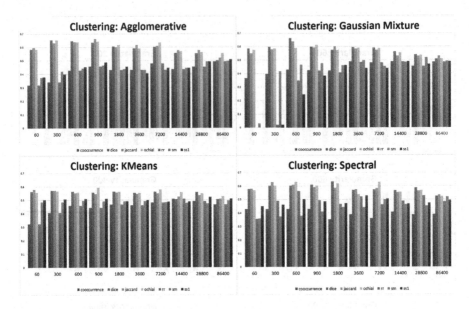

Fig. 2. V-measure score evaluation: comparison of measures at different granularity levels for each clustering algorithm.

6   Conclusions and Future Works

In this work we analysed the impact of granularity when defining the students' history summarised vectors to be used in conjunction with History Binary Correlation Analysis. Different granularity settings lead to different behaviours of similarity measures. In general higher resolution (i.e. lower granularity) histories, until a certain level, help to improve the social community elicitation. Measures that take in account the simultaneous absence of activities have less impact on their performance when lowering the granularity value.

From the experiments, we found that the best granularity values are of 600 and 900 s. With these settings, the best performing similarity measures (specifically Dice, Ochiai, and Jaccard) obtain the best values in terms of V-measure score. This means that the social communities elicited from the approach are close to the ground truth grouping of students.

Future works will include the analysis of student groups' evolution during the course using time windows to evaluate the social communities evolution during time.

References

1. Akarsh, S., Kishor, A., Niyogi, R., Milani, A., Mengoni, P.: Social cooperation in autonomous agents to avoid the tragedy of the commons. Int. J. Agric. Environ. Inf. Syst. **8**(2), 1–19 (2017). https://doi.org/10.4018/IJAEIS.2017040101

2. Baioletti, M., Milani, A., Santucci, V.: A new precedence-based ant colony optimization for permutation problems. In: Shi, Y., et al. (eds.) SEAL 2017. LNCS, vol. 10593, pp. 960–971. Springer, Cham (2017). https://doi.org/10.1007/978-3-319-68759-9_79

3. Baioletti, M., Milani, A., Santucci, V.: Learning bayesian networks with algebraic differential evolution. In: Auger, A., Fonseca, C.M., Lourenço, N., Machado, P., Paquete, L., Whitley, D. (eds.) PPSN 2018. LNCS, vol. 11102, pp. 436–448. Springer, Cham (2018). https://doi.org/10.1007/978-3-319-99259-4_35

4. Bakharia, A., Dawson, S.: SNAPP. In: Proceedings of the 1st International Conference on Learning Analytics and Knowledge - LAK 2011, p. 168. ACM Press, New York, USA (2011). https://doi.org/10.1145/2090116.2090144

5. Blondel, V.D., Guillaume, J.L., Lambiotte, R., Lefebvre, E.: Fast unfolding of communities in large networks. J. Stat. Mech.: Theory Exp. **2008**(10), 10008 (2008). https://doi.org/10.1088/1742-5468/2008/10/P10008

6. Castellano, C., Cecconi, F., Loreto, V., Parisi, D., Radicchi, F.: Self-contained algorithms to detect communities in networks. Eur. Phys. J. B **38**, 311–319 (2004). https://doi.org/10.1140/epjb/e2004-00123-0

7. Catledge, L.D., Pitkow, J.E.: Characterizing browsing strategies in the World-Wide web. Comput. Netw. ISDN Syst. (1995). https://doi.org/10.1016/0169-7552(95)00043-7

8. Chan, S.W., Franzoni, V., Mengoni, P., Milani, A.: Context-based image semantic similarity for prosthetic knowledge. In: 2018 IEEE First International Conference on Artificial Intelligence and Knowledge Engineering (AIKE), pp. 254–258. September 2018. https://doi.org/10.1109/AIKE.2018.00057

9. Chiancone, A., Franzoni, V., Niyogi, R., Milani, A.: Improving link ranking quality by quasi-common neighbourhood, pp. 21–26. IEEE Press (2015). https://doi.org/10.1109/ICCSA.2015.19

10. Dawson, S., Bakharia, A., Heathcote, E.: SNAPP : realising the affordances of real-time SNA within networked learning environments. In: Proceedings of the 7th International Conference on Networked Learning, pp. 125–133 (2010)

11. Deng, J.J., Leung, C.H.C., Mengoni, P., Li, Y.: Emotion recognition from human behaviors using attention model. In: 2018 IEEE First International Conference on Artificial Intelligence and Knowledge Engineering (AIKE), pp. 249–253. September 2018. https://doi.org/10.1109/AIKE.2018.00056

12. Dice, L.R.: Measures of the amount of ecologic association between species. Ecology **26**(3), 297–302 (1945). https://doi.org/10.2307/1932409

13. Donath, W.E., Hoffman, A.J.: Lower bounds for the partitioning of graphs. IBM J. Res. Dev. (1973). https://doi.org/10.1147/rd.175.0420

14. Fortunato, S.: Community detection in graphs (2010). https://doi.org/10.1016/j.physrep.2009.11.002

15. Fowlkes, E.B., Mallows, C.L.: A method for comparing two hierarchical clusterings. J. Am. Stat. Assoc. **78**(383), 553–569 (1983). https://doi.org/10.1080/01621459.1983.10478008

16. Franzoni, V., Mengoni, P., Milani, A.: Dimensional morphing interface for dynamic learning evaluation. In: 2018 22nd International Conference Information Visualisation (IV), pp. 332–337. July 2018. https://doi.org/10.1109/iV.2018.00063

17. Franzoni, V., Milani, A.: Pming distance: a collaborative semantic proximity measure. vol. 2, pp. 442–449. IEEE Press (2012). https://doi.org/10.1109/WI-IAT.2012.226

18. Franzoni, V., Milani, A., Pallottelli, S., Leung, C., Li, Y.: Context-based image semantic similarity, pp. 1280–1284. IEEE Press (2016). https://doi.org/10.1109/FSKD.2015.7382127

19. Franzoni, V., Leung, C.H.C., Li, Y., Mengoni, P., Milani, A.: Set similarity measures for images based on collective knowledge. In: Gervasi, O., et al. (eds.) ICCSA 2015. LNCS, vol. 9155, pp. 408–417. Springer, Cham (2015). https://doi.org/10.1007/978-3-319-21404-7_30

20. Franzoni, V., Li, Y., Mengoni, P.: A path-based model for emotion abstraction on facebook using sentiment analysis and taxonomy knowledge. Proceedings of the International Conference on Web Intelligence - WI 2017, pp. 947–952 (2017). https://doi.org/10.1145/3106426.3109420

21. Franzoni, V., Li, Y., Mengoni, P., Milani, A.: Clustering facebook for biased context extraction. In: LNCS, vol. 10404, pp. 717–729 (2017). https://doi.org/10.1007/978-3-319-62392-4_52

22. Franzoni, V., Mencacci, M., Mengoni, P., Milani, A.: Heuristics for semantic path search in wikipedia. In: Murgante, B., et al. (eds.) ICCSA 2014. LNCS, vol. 8584, pp. 327–340. Springer, Cham (2014). https://doi.org/10.1007/978-3-319-09153-2_25

23. Franzoni, V., Mencacci, M., Mengoni, P., Milani, A.: Semantic heuristic search in collaborative networks: measures and contexts. In: 2014 IEEE/WIC/ACM WI-IAT, vol. 1, pp. 141–148. IEEE, August 2014. https://doi.org/10.1109/WI-IAT.2014.27

24. Girvan, M., Newman, M.E.J.: Community structure in social and biological networks. Proc. Nat. Acad. Sci. 99(12), 7821–7826 (2002). https://doi.org/10.1073/pnas.122653799

25. Guimerà, R., Sales-Pardo, M., Amaral, L.A.: Modularity from fluctuations in random graphs and complex networks. Physical Review E - Statistical Physics, Plasmas, Fluids, and Related Interdisciplinary Topics (2004). https://doi.org/10.1103/PhysRevE.70.025101

26. Hastie, T., Tibshirani, R., Friedman, J.: The elements of statistical learning (2009). https://doi.org/10.1007/b94608

27. Jaccard, P.: Étude comparative de la distribution florale dans une portion des Alpes et des Jura. Bulletin del la Société Vaudoise des Sciences Naturelles 37, January 1901, 547–579 (1901). https://doi.org/10.5169/seals-266450

28. Kernighan, B.W., Lin, S.: An efficient heuristic procedure for partitioning graphs. Bell Syst. Tech. J. (1970). https://doi.org/10.1002/j.1538-7305.1970.tb01770.x

29. Khosravi, H., Cooper, K.M.: Using learning analytics to investigate patterns of performance and engagement in large classes. In: Proceedings of the 2017 ACM SIGCSE Technical Symposium on Computer Science Education - SIGCSE 2017, pp. 309–314 (2017). https://doi.org/10.1145/3017680.3017711

30. Lancichinetti, A., Fortunato, S.: Community detection algorithms: a comparative analysis. Phys. Rev. E 80, 1–12 (2009). https://doi.org/10.1103/PhysRevE.80.056117

31. Leung, C.H.C., Li, Y., Milani, A., Franzoni, V.: Collective evolutionary concept distance based query expansion for effective web document retrieval. In: Murgante, B., et al. (eds.) ICCSA 2013. LNCS, vol. 7974, pp. 657–672. Springer, Heidelberg (2013). https://doi.org/10.1007/978-3-642-39649-6_47

32. Macqueen, J.: Some methods for classification and analysis of multivariate observations. Proceedings of the Fifth Berkeley Symposium on Mathematical Statistics and Probability (1967). citeulike-article-id:6083430

33. Mehrzadi, D., Feitelson, D.G.: On extracting session data from activity logs. In: Proceedings of the 5th Annual International Systems and Storage Conference, pp. 3:1–3:7. SYSTOR 2012, ACM, New York, NY, USA (2012). https://doi.org/10. 1145/2367589.2367592

34. Mengoni, P., Milani, A., Li, Y.: Multi-term semantic context elicitation from collaborative networks. In: 2018 IEEE First International Conference on Artificial Intelligence and Knowledge Engineering (AIKE), pp. 234–238. September 2018. https://doi.org/10.1109/AIKE.2018.00053

35. Mengoni, P., Milani, A., Li, Y.: Clustering students interactions in elearning systems for group elicitation. In: Gervasi, O., et al. (eds.) ICCSA 2018. LNCS, vol. 10962, pp. 398–413. Springer, Cham (2018). https://doi.org/10.1007/978-3-319-95168-3_27

36. Mengoni, P., Milani, A., Li, Y.: Community graph elicitation from students interactions in virtual learning environments. In: Gervasi, O., et al. (eds.) ICCSA 2018. LNCS, vol. 10962, pp. 414–425. Springer, Cham (2018). https://doi.org/10.1007/978-3-319-95168-3_28

37. Neubauer, T., Heurix, J.: A methodology for the pseudonymization of medical data. Int. J. Med. Inform. **80**(3), 190–204 (2011)

38. Neubauer, T., Riedl, B.: Improving patients privacy with pseudonymization. Stud. Health Technol. Inform. **136**, 691 (2008)

39. Ochiai, A.: Zoogeographical studies on the soleoid fishes found in Japan and its neighhouring regions-II. Nippon Suisan Gakkaishi **22**(9), 526–530 (1957). https://doi.org/10.2331/suisan.22.526

40. Rand, W.M.: Objective criteria for the evaluation of clustering methods. J. Am. Stat. Assoc. **66**(336), 846–850 (1971). https://doi.org/10.1080/01621459.1971. 10482356

41. Rijsbergen, C.V.: Information retrieval. Information Retrieval, p. 208 (1979)

42. Rosenberg, A., Hirschberg, J.: V-measure: a conditional entropy-based external cluster evaluation measure. In: Proceedings of EMNLP-CoNLL 2007) 1, June 2007, 410–420 (2007). https://doi.org/10.7916/D80V8N84

43. Rusell, P.F., Rao, T.R.: On habitat and association of species of anopheline larvae in south-eastern madras. J. Malaria Inst. India **3**(1), 153–178 (1940)

44. Santucci, V., Milani, A.: Particle swarm optimization in the EDAs framework. In: Gaspar-Cunha, A., Takahashi, R., Schaefer, G., Costa, L. (eds.) Soft Computing in Industrial Applications, pp. 87–96. Springer, Berlin (2011)

45. Sneath, P.H.A., Sokal, R.R.: The principles and practice of numerical taxonomy. Taxon **12**(5), 190 (1963). https://doi.org/10.2307/1217562

46. Sozio, M., Gionis, A.: The community-search problem and how to plan a successful cocktail party. In: Proceedings of the 16th ACM SIGKDD International Conference on Knowledge Discovery and Data Mining - KDD 2010, p. 939 (2010). https://doi. org/10.1145/1835804.1835923

Sharing Linkable Learning Objects with the Use of Metadata and a Taxonomy Assistant for Categorization

Valentina Franzoni[1,2(✉)], Sergio Tasso[1], Simonetta Pallottelli[1], and Damiano Perri[1]

[1] Department of Mathematics and Computer Science, University of Perugia, via Vanvitelli 1, 06123 Perugia, Italy
{valentina.franzoni, sergio.tasso, simonetta.pallottelli}@unipg.it
[2] Department of Computer, Control, and Management Engineering "Antonio Ruberti", Sapienza University of Rome, via Ariosto 25, 00185 Rome, Italy

Abstract. In this work, a re-design of the *Moodledata* module functionalities is presented to share learning objects between e-learning content platforms, e.g., Moodle and G-Lorep, in a linkable object format. The e-learning courses content of the Drupal-based Content Management System G-Lorep for academic learning is exchanged designing an object incorporating metadata to support the reuse and the classification in its context. In such an Artificial Intelligence environment, the exchange of Linkable Learning Objects can be used for dialogue between Learning Systems to obtain information, especially with the use of semantic or structural similarity measures to enhance the existent Taxonomy Assistant for advanced automated classification.

Keywords: E-learning · Moodle · Learning management system · Linked data · Learning object · CMS · LMS · G-Lorep

1 Introduction

In recent years, e-learning systems became part of the Artificial Intelligence revolution, [1] where machines and intelligent systems can interchange information through an Internet connection. Before this concept, the Linked Data Networks already connected information objects, where the World Wide Web became the path through the creation of a global information space comprising linked documents [2–4].

G-Lorep (Grid Learning Object Repository) [5, 6] is a federation of distributed repositories containing Learning Objects (LO)s from various academic sources, developed as a Learning Managing System (LMS) at the *Department of Mathematics and Computer Science* of the *University of Perugia*, where it can boast an excellent operativity of about twenty years. The implementation of G-Lorep involved the *Department of Chemistry, Biology, and Biotechnologies* of the University of Perugia, as well as other European universities, e.g., Genoa and Thessaloniki. G-Lorep is also useful to support the student for the preparation to tests, including specialized ones

© Springer Nature Switzerland AG 2019
S. Misra et al. (Eds.): ICCSA 2019, LNCS 11620, pp. 336–348, 2019.
https://doi.org/10.1007/978-3-030-24296-1_28

such as the EChemTest® e-test, providing increasingly improved LOs, thanks to the cooperative effort of the multidisciplinary team of management members [8].

Regarding sharing LO Metadata (LOM), G-Lorep leverages different Moodle [7] modules, e.g. *Moodledata*, [8] to share a LOM between a Content Management System (CMS) and a Learning Management System, such as G-Lorep (managed by Drupal) and Moodle, where the same design can be applied with different modules to any other CMS and LMS.

2   The G-LOREP-MOODLE Connections

In previous works [3, 10, 11] we integrated the *Moodledata* module into Drupal, allowing the platform manager (i.e., the user with administrator permissions) to search and download files on the Moodle server, and to upload and classify them on Drupal as LOMs.

Regarding the continuous update of Drupal, we achieved two main objectives:

(a) adapt the module to the new versions of Drupal;
(b) extend the module by adding new features:

- Download files from Moodle.
- Create a new Linkable Learning Object (LLO) from the downloaded data.
- Upload the LLO to Drupal in G-Lorep (see Fig. 1).

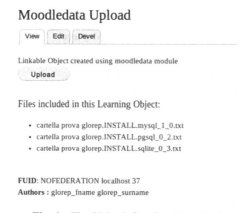

Fig. 1. The Upload-Creation-Download

The module customization, for the *Moodledata* upload, mainly includes three files with extensions "**.module**", "**.install**", "**.info**".

A *README.txt* file provides a brief installation guide for the module, integrated by the online help.

2.1 Design and Environment Setting

As a first step, some features must be set to use the *Moodledata* module. The Drupal side sees two necessary modules for *moodledata* to be installed and set:

- *Collabrep*, to manage the information transmission in the G-Lorep federation.
- *Linkable Object* (LO), to manage the node and check user permissions, where a LO can be defined as a *Learning Object* or a *Software Attachment*.

Such modules can be set in the *Modules* section of Drupal *Administration* settings.

2.2 Setting the Drupal Web-Service

As in the case of download from Moodle to Drupal, [8] also for the case of downloading from Drupal files to be uploaded in Moodle, we need to manage a web service in Drupal. The *Moodledata* menu is used to access the module's features, which contains a short description of the information objects to access. The first is the *Settings* invoice, to set the Moodle access, with the following fields:

- Domain *address* of the Moodle installation.
- *Username*, to access the Moodle account.
- Login *Password*.

A connection to the web-service is attempted upon successful accomplishment of such operations,, and the access token is requested and kept for all the queries of the session. The module is now available to authenticated G-Lorep users.

2.3 G-LOREP *Moodledata* Download and Storage

As easily understandable, the primary functions of the module regard the appropriate managing of the file downloads from G-Lorep.

A file can be searched specifying a string including the full file name or its parts. An *Advanced Search* is available to refine a search combining additional parameters, e.g., course name, file author, and the timestamp of the last editing. The functions are:

1. **Search** (clicking on the *Search button*): files matching the search criteria set are included in a table with the following fields:

   - *select item*: a checkbox for file selection;
   - *course name*: the course containing the file;
   - *filename*: the file name.

2. **Download** (*Download selected items* feature): the selected files are downloaded and stored in a temporary cache in G-Lorep. This intermediate step between download and upload is transparent to the user, for better management of the process in order to prevent and avoid human errors.

3. **Metadata addition**: the most exciting part of this work is the critical update and re-design of the module, replacing the database connection with the use of Moodle web-services to include a metadata exchange. Such semantic addition is to facilitate information retrieval of LLOs, exploited adding automatically content and context-related metadata using the G-Lorep taxonomy. LMSs like Moodle allow to add

courses to categories, such as in a CMS, and this feature perfectly fits the feature of classification metadata exploited through the G-Lorep *Taxonomy Assistant*, which will be presented in Sect. 3.

4. *Save*: the user saves the files shown after a final check. An individual file loaded individually will maintain the name given when loading, while a collection of files will gain the name of both the folder and the file.

In addition to the file name, the other fields in the table are:

- *author*: file author;
- *format*: file type;
- *description*: a string describing the file, or folder given by the Moodle user during loading.
- *last modified*: the last editing timestamp date.

2.4 Moodledata Upload in Moodle

Another primary function of the module provides the possibility to upload to Moodle the Drupal files downloaded in the *moodledata* table. Figure 2 shows the G-Lorep linkable object ready to be shared.

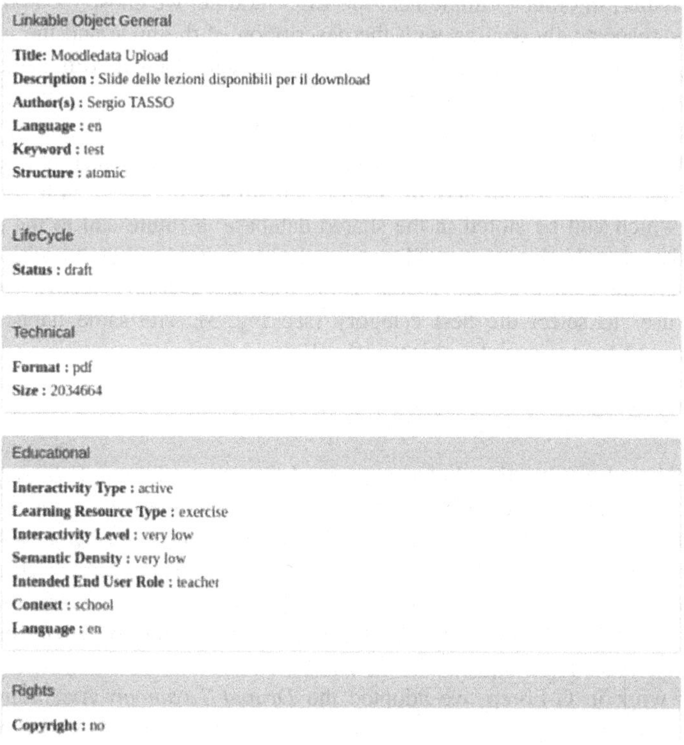

Linkable Object General

Title: Moodledata Upload
Description : Slide delle lezioni disponibili per il download
Author(s) : Sergio TASSO
Language : en
Keyword : test
Structure : atomic

LifeCycle

Status : draft

Technical

Format : pdf
Size : 2034664

Educational

Interactivity Type : active
Learning Resource Type : exercise
Interactivity Level : very low
Semantic Density : very low
Intended End User Role : teacher
Context : school
Language : en

Rights

Copyright : no

Fig. 2. The G-LOREP moodledata object (LLO interface)

The evolution of G-Lorep providing the automation of the upload is a continuous work in progress. The saved LLO, for now, can be uploaded using the import function of Moodle.

It should be noted that additional metadata, e.g., the files list and the taxonomy metadata do not appear in the interface of the LLO (see Fig. 2) because it shows only the editable content. The additional metadata are attached to the Linkable Object and can be visible from the G-Lorep course page, or directly in Moodle after the importing step.

3 G-LOREP Taxonomy Metadata

3.1 Metadata Storage in G-LOREP Through the Drupal API Field

The realization of the LO module makes use of the innovations introduced since the 7.x version of the Drupal CMS by the *Field API*, to customize fields attachable to Drupal entities regarding storage, editing, loading, and view.

To this aim, two data structures are defined:

- *Field*: defines the format of data to attach to the entity.
- *Instance*: allows instantiating the data type.

In particular, in order to implement the LLO module, we chose the *body* and *files* Field APIs, respectively dealing with the description of the node and the information about the files attached to the LLO. The main advantage of Field APIs is the metadata management because Drupal itself takes care of the database management. For instance, about taxonomy metadata, the mentioned fields, stored in the *file_managed* table of the Drupal database, can be attached to the Linkable Object automatically.

The changes are propagated by merely creating the object with the attached metadata, which will be stored in the shared database; a future call to the server that executes the download routine will get all the metadata within the object. At the creation step, the categories are visible to the user and can be selected. An assistant helps the user to select the best category (see Fig. 3). The same happens for the synonyms used for tagging the object [10–12].

3.2 The G-LOREP Taxonomy Assistant

The classification of educational objects (e.g., LLOs) is contributory to the organization of knowledge units in the realm context, allowing efficient reuse and information retrieval through automatic labeling and management. This enhancement is based on appropriate tree classifications (e.g., hierarchies, taxonomies) or graph classifications (e.g., ontologies) linking related entities. Recently, several proposals to manage semantic information through web-based queries shown impressive performances with fewer problems than ontologies [11, 12, 16–29].

In our work in G-Lorep, we adopted the *Drupal Taxonomy Assistant* (TA), [9] where future works will include web-based similarity measures. TA is a module able to

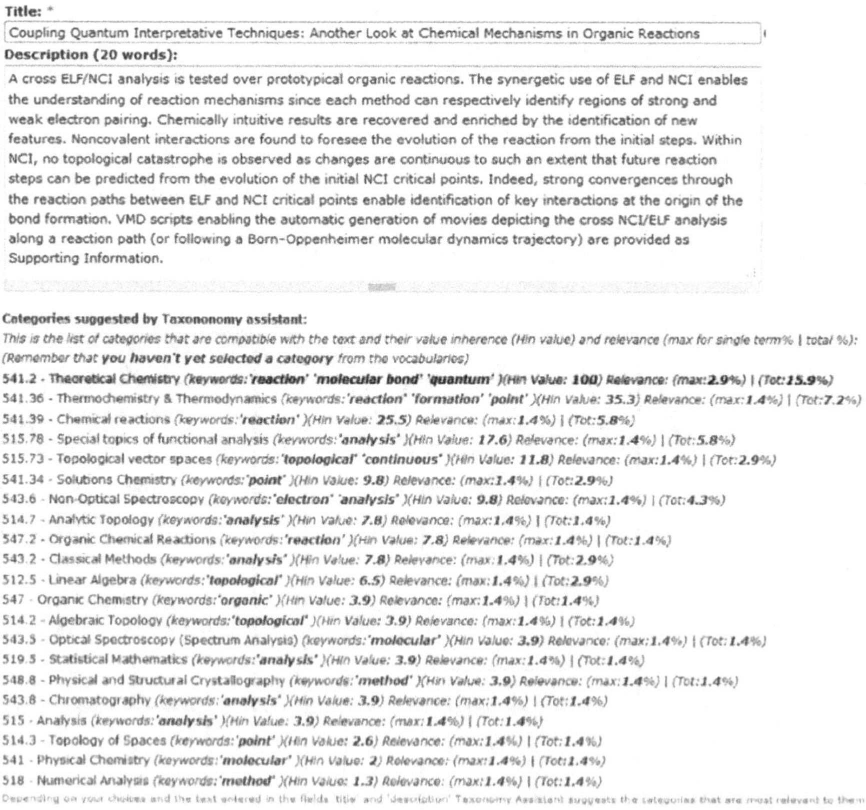

Title: *

Coupling Quantum Interpretative Techniques: Another Look at Chemical Mechanisms in Organic Reactions

Description (20 words):

A cross ELF/NCI analysis is tested over prototypical organic reactions. The synergetic use of ELF and NCI enables the understanding of reaction mechanisms since each method can respectively identify regions of strong and weak electron pairing. Chemically intuitive results are recovered and enriched by the identification of new features. Noncovalent interactions are found to foresee the evolution of the reaction from the initial steps. Within NCI, no topological catastrophe is observed as changes are continuous to such an extent that future reaction steps can be predicted from the evolution of the initial NCI critical points. Indeed, strong convergences through the reaction paths between ELF and NCI critical points enable identification of key interactions at the origin of the bond formation. VMD scripts enabling the automatic generation of movies depicting the cross NCI/ELF analysis along a reaction path (or following a Born-Oppenheimer molecular dynamics trajectory) are provided as Supporting Information.

Categories suggested by Taxonomy assistant:

This is the list of categories that are compatible with the text and their value inherence (Hin value) and relevance (max for single term% | total %):
(Remember that you haven't yet selected a category from the vocabularies)

541.2 - Theoretical Chemistry *(keywords:'reaction' 'molecular bond' 'quantum')(Hin Value: 100) Relevance: (max:2.9%) | (Tot:15.9%)*
541.36 - Thermochemistry & Thermodynamics *(keywords:'reaction' 'formation' 'point')(Hin Value: 35.3) Relevance: (max:1.4%) | (Tot:7.2%)*
541.39 - Chemical reactions *(keywords:'reaction')(Hin Value: 25.5) Relevance: (max:1.4%) | (Tot:5.8%)*
515.78 - Special topics of functional analysis *(keywords:'analysis')(Hin Value: 17.6) Relevance: (max:1.4%) | (Tot:5.8%)*
515.73 - Topological vector spaces *(keywords:'topological' 'continuous')(Hin Value: 11.8) Relevance: (max:1.4%) | (Tot:2.9%)*
541.34 - Solutions Chemistry *(keywords:'point')(Hin Value: 9.8) Relevance: (max:1.4%) | (Tot:2.9%)*
543.6 - Non-Optical Spectroscopy *(keywords:'electron' 'analysis')(Hin Value: 9.8) Relevance: (max:1.4%) | (Tot:4.3%)*
514.7 - Analytic Topology *(keywords:'analysis')(Hin Value: 7.8) Relevance: (max:1.4%) | (Tot:1.4%)*
547.2 - Organic Chemical Reactions *(keywords:'reaction')(Hin Value: 7.8) Relevance: (max:1.4%) | (Tot:1.4%)*
543.2 - Classical Methods *(keywords:'analysis')(Hin Value: 7.8) Relevance: (max:1.4%) | (Tot:2.9%)*
512.5 - Linear Algebra *(keywords:'topological')(Hin Value: 6.5) Relevance: (max:1.4%) | (Tot:2.9%)*
547 - Organic Chemistry *(keywords:'organic')(Hin Value: 3.9) Relevance: (max:1.4%) | (Tot:1.4%)*
514.2 - Algebraic Topology *(keywords:'topological')(Hin Value: 3.9) Relevance: (max:1.4%) | (Tot:1.4%)*
543.5 - Optical Spectroscopy (Spectrum Analysis) *(keywords:'molecular')(Hin Value: 3.9) Relevance: (max:1.4%) | (Tot:1.4%)*
519.5 - Statistical Mathematics *(keywords:'analysis')(Hin Value: 3.9) Relevance: (max:1.4%) | (Tot:1.4%)*
548.8 - Physical and Structural Crystallography *(keywords:'method')(Hin Value: 3.9) Relevance: (max:1.4%) | (Tot:1.4%)*
543.8 - Chromatography *(keywords:'analysis')(Hin Value: 3.9) Relevance: (max:1.4%) | (Tot:1.4%)*
515 - Analysis *(keywords:'analysis')(Hin Value: 3.9) Relevance: (max:1.4%) | (Tot:1.4%)*
514.3 - Topology of Spaces *(keywords:'point')(Hin Value: 2.6) Relevance: (max:1.4%) | (Tot:1.4%)*
541 - Physical Chemistry *(keywords:'molecular')(Hin Value: 2) Relevance: (max:1.4%) | (Tot:1.4%)*
518 - Numerical Analysis *(keywords:'method')(Hin Value: 1.3) Relevance: (max:1.4%) | (Tot:1.4%)*

Depending on your choices and the text entered in the fields 'title' and 'description' Taxonomy Assistant suggests the categories that are most relevant to them.

Fig. 3. User input and categories suggested by the TA

interact with the LLO, via the *Linkable Object* and the *dis_cat* modules. TA analyses the content of the text and the LO description and automatically proposes the best category, then selectable and editable by the user.

The TA algorithm is based on pattern-matching between keywords and the terms of its thesaurus. The editability of the suggested category might introduce human typing mistakes, but its excellent productivity feature is to allow a fast creation of a brand-new thesaurus whenever needed, e.g., when the actual meaning of a word appears in different places with different connotations, and some additions could be implemented in the classification phase. Moreover, in this way the updating phase of the thesaurus is much more comfortable, maintaining it updated as it is used.

In the G-Lorep TA, categories are organized as a forest graph, where each tree epitomizes a science area (e.g., Computer Science, Mathematics, Physics, Chemistry, Biology) filled with sub-categories: the most detailed appear as tree leaves and the most general ones as roots. Such a scheme is compliant with various classification structures, in particular with the *Dewey Decimal Classification* (DDC), [13, 14], which G-LOREP flowchart is sketched in Fig. 4. Out of the input information, the TA builds the classification step applying the following text filtering:

1. lower case conversion;
2. deletion of non-essential characters (e.g., punctuation marks, parentheses, apostrophes);
3. check and deletion of *stopwords*, i.e., words of slight interest, usually not considered particularly meaningful by search engines [15, 16] (e.g., name articles, pronouns, adverbs, and other words whose interest is lowered by frequent usage).

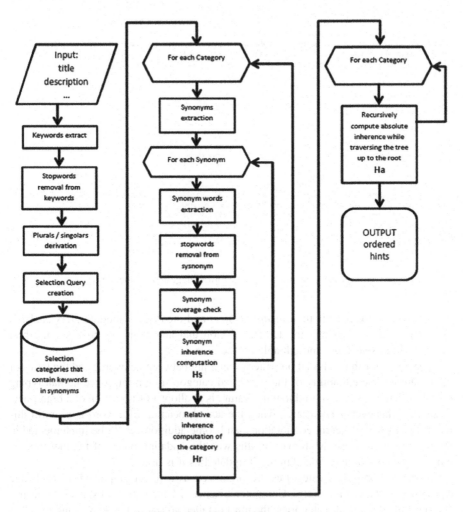

Fig. 4. The TA algorithm scheme

The goal of this filtering process is to obtain a set of keywords, deprived of superfluous terms, for querying the database [9]. In order to increase the likelihood of significant correspondences, a stemming mechanism based on standard syntax guidelines (e.g., for singular/plural extensions) enriches the TA. Each category is then associated with a thesaurus set of terms: synonyms are considered not only as single words but also as sets because they can include expressions [20].

The fraction given by the number X of keywords found in the description of the LO and the total number N of keywords defining the synonym is called *coverage* [21–23].

Coverage is used to compare the user keywords with synonyms sets contained in the taxonomy. For the records obtained from the query, each synonym is also split to subclasses of defined length windows, whose presence in the database is finally counted. The count is taken as a measure of the *inherence*, considered as the **similarity between the synonyms and the user text**, [23–26] expressing the adequacy of a category assignment in the Learning Object context [27–30].

3.3   Synonym Inherence as an Effectiveness Index

The inherence of a synonym H_s with a LO is the extent of pertinence P of the agreed synonym in the description of a LO. Hence, H_s can be taken as an effectiveness measure, with some assumptions:

(a) let the value of H_s be as high as the number N of words composing the synonym;
(b) let the value of H_s for partial coverage depending on the recurrence of a word among those composing the synonym (a coverage of "1 out of 3" must result in a H_s value higher than the one associated with coverage of "1 out of 4").

To give a precise algebraic formulation of H_s we give the following definitions:

- R_i is the number of occurrences of the words in synonym i;
- S_i is the number of words composing synonym i;
- K is the total number of valid keywords;
- $U_i = R_i/S_i$ is the ratio between the number of occurrences of the words R_i found in the synonym i and the number of words S_i found in it;
- $P_i = S_i/K$ is the ratio between the words observed in the synonym i and the total number of considered keywords K (that is called either pertinence or relevance).

The simple formulation of H_s was initially taken to be the power-like formula:

$$H_r = \sum_{i=1}^{\#of\,.Synonyms} R_i^{U_i} U_i P_i \Rightarrow H_r = \frac{1}{k} \sum_{i=1}^{\#of\,.Synonyms} \left(R_i^{\left(\frac{R_i}{S_i}\right)} \frac{R_i^2}{S_i} \right) \tag{1}$$

where the result of (1) will be *1* if there is a "*1 out of N*" coverage, and N for a complete coverage "*N out of N*". The H_s value is the same in both cases. Since such value is in conflict with the (b) requirement, its behaviour can be fixed multiplying the H_s function by U_i:

$$H_S = R_i^{\left(\frac{R_i}{S_i}\right)} \frac{R_i^2}{S_i} \tag{2}$$

3.4 Inherence of Categories

The meaning of repeated partial occurrences in synonyms within a category can be calibrated to obtain the most appropriate efficacy measures:

- *Relative inherence of a category* (H_r): the sum of all the synonym inherences H_s of the category.
- *Absolute inherence of a category* (H_a): the sum of the relative inherences H_r associated with all the categories in the root/node path, weighted by the related level d.

The relative inherence H_r can be expressed as:

$$H_r = \sum_{i=1}^{\#of\,.Synonyms} H_{S_i} \tag{4}$$

Expanding the formula through the substitution of H_s we obtain:

$$H_r = \sum_{i=1}^{\#of\,.Synonyms} R_i^{U_i} U_i P_i \Rightarrow H_r = \frac{1}{k} \sum_{i=1}^{\#of\,.Synonyms} \left(R_i^{\left(\frac{R_i}{S_i}\right)} \frac{R_i^2}{S_i} \right) \tag{5}$$

To obtain an algebraic construction of H_a we express the following positions:

- d is the depth of the node,
- $R_{i,d}$ is the number of matching words in the synonymous i at level d,
- $S_{i,d}$ is the number of words constituting synonym i at level d,
- $U_{i,d} = R_{i,d}/S_{i,d}$ is the ratio between the number of occurrences and the number of words constituting the synonymous i at level d.

We can, finally, work out the absolute inherence of a category obtained by adding the relative inherence value of each ancestor category i lying on the path from the root to the considered category multiplied by the level d to which the category belongs (see Fig. 5):

$$H_a = \sum_{d=1}^{depth} H_{r_d} d \tag{6}$$

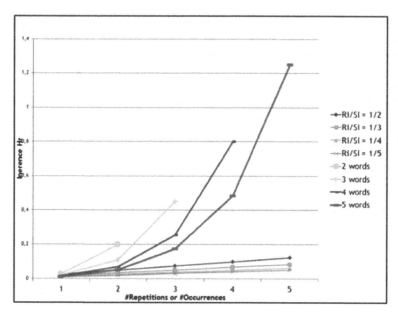

Fig. 5. The H_r values plotted as a function of the number # of repetitions (or occurrences) for different numbers of words composing the synonym

4   Searching LO with a Semantics-Based AI

Recently, Artificial Intelligence (AI) has been introduced to e-learning systems. In our environment, the exchange of Linkable Learning Objects can be used for dialogue between Learning Systems to obtain information, especially with the use of semantic or structural similarity measures to enhance the existent Taxonomy Assistant for advanced automated classification.

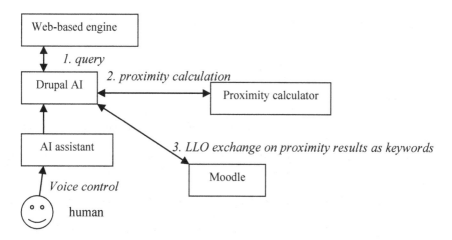

Fig. 6. AI-based LLO exchange

The G-LOREP platform and Moodle, being open-source, are particularly suitable to be enhanced with AI-based tools, e.g., an intelligent assistant to support information exchange. A feasible solution is to develop an assistant based on existing devices, e.g., Google Home, Amazon Alexia, Microsoft Cortana, which offer a set of APIs for voice control.

In such a web-based environment, web-based similarity measures, which rely on search engines (e.g., Google, Bing) to obtain frequency values used for semantic proximity calculation, [27, 31, 32] can be easily integrated into an AI to obtain a set of LLOs to exchange among learning systems. Figure 6 depicts the scheme of an AI-based LLO search and exchange.

5 Conclusions and Future Work

Updating an integrated module on Drupal allows downloading files managed within the G-LOREP federation and share them in the form of Linkable Learning Objects to Moodle or a Linked Data network. The future development of the module will involve a plug-in to automate the procedures for activating the *moodledata* service on the Moodle side.

We also described the use of the Taxonomy assistant (TA) automatically proposing a set of classification elements to the user in the delicate procedure of cataloging an LLO. TA proposes to the user the correct place for a LO in the taxonomy tree. Future activities will address the use of the taxonomy to link the Linkable Object for a Linked Data network. Another improvement will come from the integration in the G-Lorep TA of web-based similarity calculations, such as the *PMING distance* [31, 33] or of other structural or semantic similarity [32] measures to improve the taxonomy prediction [34–36] or the term selection, as proposed and partially explained in [37].

In such an Artificial Intelligence environment, the exchange of Linkable Learning Objects can be used for dialogue between Learning Systems or between a Learning AI and a human user for advanced human-machine communication [29–31, 38, 39].

Acknowledgments. Thanks are due to EGI and IGI and the related COMPCHEM VO for the use of Grid resources. The authors also thank the authors of previous works of the project, cited in this paper.

References

1. Franzoni, V., Milani, A., Nardi, D., Vallverdú, J.: Emotional machines: the next revolution. Web Intell. **17**, 1–7 (2019)
2. Noia, T.D., Ostuni, V.C., Tomeo, P., Sciascio, E.D.: SPrank: semantic path-based ranking for top-n recommendations using linked open data. ACM Trans. Intell. Syst. Technol. **8**, 9:1–9:34 (2016)
3. Bizer, C., Heath, T., Berners-Lee, T.: Linked data - the story so far. Int. J. Semant. Web Inf. Syst. **5**, 1–22 (2009)
4. Heath, T., Bizer, C.: Linked data: evolving the web into a global data space. Synth. Lect. Semant. Web Theory Technol. **1**(1), 1–136 (2011)

5. Pallottelli, S., Tasso, S., Pannacci, N., Costantini, A., Lago, N.F.: Distributed and collaborative learning objects repositories on grid networks. In: Taniar, D., Gervasi, O., Murgante, B., Pardede, E., Apduhan, B.O. (eds.) ICCSA 2010. LNCS, vol. 6019, pp. 29–40. Springer, Heidelberg (2010). https://doi.org/10.1007/978-3-642-12189-0_3
6. Baioletti, M., Milani, A., Poggioni, V., Rossi, F.: Experimental evaluation of pheromone models in ACOPlan. Ann. Math. Artif. Intell. **62**, 197–217 (2011)
7. Marcato, E., Scala, E.: Moodle. In: Handbook of Research on Didactic Strategies and Technologies for Education (2012)
8. Tasso, S., Pallottelli, S., Gervasi, O., Rui, M., Laganà, A.: Sharing learning objects between learning platforms and repositories. In: Gervasi, O., et al. (eds.) ICCSA 2018. LNCS, vol. 10963, pp. 804–816. Springer, Cham (2018). https://doi.org/10.1007/978-3-319-95171-3_62
9. Tasso, S., Pallottelli, S., Ciavi, G., Bastianini, R., Laganà, A.: An efficient taxonomy assistant for a federation of science distributed repositories: a chemistry use case. In: Murgante, B., et al. (eds.) ICCSA 2013. LNCS, vol. 7971, pp. 96–109. Springer, Heidelberg (2013). https://doi.org/10.1007/978-3-642-39637-3_8
10. Tasso, S., Pallottelli, S., Ferroni, M., Bastianini, R., Laganà, A.: taxonomy management in a federation of distributed repositories: a chemistry use case. In: Murgante, B., et al. (eds.) ICCSA 2012. LNCS, vol. 7333, pp. 358–370. Springer, Heidelberg (2012). https://doi.org/10.1007/978-3-642-31125-3_28
11. Tasso, S., Pallottelli, S., Rui, M., Laganá, A.: Learning objects efficient handling in a federation of science distributed repositories. In: Murgante, B., et al. (eds.) ICCSA 2014. LNCS, vol. 8579, pp. 615–626. Springer, Cham (2014). https://doi.org/10.1007/978-3-319-09144-0_42
12. Tasso, S., Pallottelli, S., Bastianini, R., Lagana, A.: Federation of distributed and collaborative repositories and its application on science learning objects. In: Murgante, B., Gervasi, O., Iglesias, A., Taniar, D., Apduhan, B.O. (eds.) ICCSA 2011. LNCS, vol. 6784, pp. 466–478. Springer, Heidelberg (2011). https://doi.org/10.1007/978-3-642-21931-3_36
13. Mitchell, J.S., Vizine-Goetz, D.: Dewey Decimal Classification (DDC). In: Encyclopedia of Library and Information Sciences, 3rd edn. (2016)
14. McClelland, M.: Metadata standards for educational resources. Computer **36**(11), 107–109 (2003)
15. Franzoni, V., Milani, A., Biondi, G.: SEMO: a semantic model for emotion recognition in web objects. In: Proceedings - 2017 IEEE/WIC/ACM International Conference on Web Intelligence, WI 2017 (2017)
16. Franzoni, V., Biondi, G., Milani, A.: A web-based system for emotion vector extraction. In: Gervasi, O., et al. (eds.) ICCSA 2017. LNCS, vol. 10406, pp. 653–668. Springer, Cham (2017). https://doi.org/10.1007/978-3-319-62398-6_46
17. Franzoni, V., Poggioni, V.: Emotional book classification from book blurbs. In: Proceedings - 2017 IEEE/WIC/ACM International Conference on Web Intelligence, WI 2017 (2017)
18. Franzoni, V., Poggioni, V., Zollo, F.: Can we infer book classification by blurbs? In: CEUR Workshop Proceedings (2014)
19. Franzoni, V., Poggioni, V., Zollo, F.: Automated classification of book blurbs according to the emotional tags of the social network Zazie. In: CEUR Workshop Proceedings (2013)
20. Franzoni, V., Leung, C.H.C., Li, Y., Mengoni, P., Milani, A.: set similarity measures for images based on collective knowledge. In: Gervasi, O., et al. (eds.) ICCSA 2015. LNCS, vol. 9155, pp. 408–417. Springer, Cham (2015). https://doi.org/10.1007/978-3-319-21404-7_30
21. Franzoni, V., Milani, A.: A pheromone-like model for semantic context extraction from collaborative networks. In: Proceedings - 2015 IEEE/WIC/ACM International Joint Conference on Web Intelligence and Intelligent Agent Technology, WI-IAT 2015 (2016)

22. Pallottelli, S., Franzoni, V., Milani, A.: Multi-path traces in semantic graphs for latent knowledge elicitation. In: ICNC, pp. 281–288. IEEE (2015)
23. Franzoni, V., Milani, A.: Heuristic semantic walk for concept chaining in collaborative networks. Int. J. Web Inf. Syst. **10**(1), 85–103 (2014)
24. Franzoni, V., Milani, A.: A semantic comparison of clustering algorithms for the evaluation of web-based similarity measures. In: Gervasi, O., et al. (eds.) ICCSA 2016. LNCS, vol. 9790, pp. 438–452. Springer, Cham (2016). https://doi.org/10.1007/978-3-319-42092-9_34
25. Leung, C.H.C., Li, Y., Milani, A., Franzoni, V.: Collective evolutionary concept distance based query expansion for effective web document retrieval. In: Murgante, B., et al. (eds.) ICCSA 2013. LNCS, vol. 7974, pp. 657–672. Springer, Heidelberg (2013). https://doi.org/10.1007/978-3-642-39649-6_47
26. Franzoni, V., Mencacci, M., Mengoni, P., Milani, A.: Heuristics for semantic path search in wikipedia. In: Murgante, B., et al. (eds.) ICCSA 2014. LNCS, vol. 8584, pp. 327–340. Springer, Cham (2014). https://doi.org/10.1007/978-3-319-09153-2_25
27. Franzoni, V., Milani, A., Pallottelli, S., Leung, C.H.C., Li, Y.: Context-based image semantic similarity. In: 2015 12th International Conference on Fuzzy Systems and Knowledge Discovery, FSKD 2015 (2016)
28. Franzoni, V.: Context Extraction by Multi-path Traces in Semantic Networks. In: Rr. {IEEE} Computer Society (2016)
29. Franzoni, V., Milani, A.: Semantic context extraction from collaborative networks. In: Proceedings of the 2015 IEEE 19th International Conference on Computer Supported Cooperative Work in Design, CSCWD 2015 (2015)
30. Franzoni, V., Mencacci, M., Mengoni, P., Milani, A.: Semantic heuristic search in collaborative networks: Measures and contexts. In: Proceedings - 2014 IEEE/WIC/ACM International Joint Conference on Web Intelligence and Intelligent Agent Technology - Workshops, WI-IAT 2014 (2014)
31. Franzoni, V., Milani, A.: PMING distance: a collaborative semantic proximity measure. In: Proceedings - 2012 IEEE/WIC/ACM International Conference on Intelligent Agent Technology, IAT 2012 (2012)
32. Franzoni, V., Milani, A.: Structural and semantic proximity in information networks. In: Gervasi, O., et al. (eds.) ICCSA 2017. LNCS, vol. 10404, pp. 651–666. Springer, Cham (2017). https://doi.org/10.1007/978-3-319-62392-4_47
33. Biondi, G., Franzoni, V., Li, Y., Milani, A.: Web-based similarity for emotion recognition in web objects. In: Proceedings - 9th IEEE/ACM International Conference on Utility and Cloud Computing, UCC 2016 (2016)
34. Chiancone, A., Milani, A., Poggioni, V., Pallottelli, S., Madotto, A., Franzoni, V.: A multistrain bacterial model for link prediction andrea chiancone. In: ICNC, pp. 1075–1079. IEEE (2015)
35. Franzoni, V., Chiancone, A., Milani, A.: A multistrain bacterial diffusion model for link prediction. Int. J. Pattern Recognit Artif Intell. **31**, 1759024 (2017)
36. Chiancone, A., Franzoni, V., Li, Y., Markov, K., Milani, A.: Leveraging zero tail in neighbourhood for link prediction. In: WI-IAT vol. 3, pp. 135–139. IEEE Computer Society (2015)
37. Franzoni, V., Li, Y., Milani, A.: Set semantic similarity for image prosthetic knowledge exchange. In: Misra, S., et al. (eds.): ICCSA 2019, LNCS, vol. 11624, pp. 513–525 (2019)
38. Franzoni, V., Milani, A., Vallverdú, J.: Emotional affordances in human-machine interactive planning and negotiation. In: Proceedings - 2017 IEEE/WIC/ACM International Conference on Web Intelligence, WI 2017 (2017)
39. Brackett, M.A.: The Emotion Revolution: Enhancing Social and Emotional Learning in School: Enhancing Social and Emotional Learning in School (2016)

Affective Computing and Emotion Recognition (ACER-EMORE 2019)

Affective Computing for Enhancing Affective Touch-Based Communication Through Extended Reality

Chutisant Kerdvibulvech[1(✉)] and Sheng-Uei Guan[2]

[1] Graduate School of Communication Arts and Management Innovation,
National Institute of Development Administration,
118 SeriThai Road, Klong-chan, Bangkapi, Bangkok 10240, Thailand
chutisant.ker@nida.ac.th
[2] Department of Computer Science and Software Engineering,
Research Institute of Big Data Analytics, Xi'an Jiaotong-Liverpool University,
Suzhou Industrial Park, Suzhou 215123, People's Republic of China
Steven.Guan@xjtlu.edu.cn

Abstract. Nowadays, affective computing (AC), especially affective touch, plays a significant role in the next generation of human-computer, computer-computer and human-human communications. This is because it allows more senses in human communication to be included simultaneously and interactively, enabling innovative communications both between computers and humans, and between humans and humans. In this paper, we discuss applications and methodologies that researchers, including the author, have recently achieved by utilizing affective computing, affective touch, and extended reality (XR). Our purpose is to review our research work experience and other state-of-the-art results and propose a line of research to use these results in a future work or application. To begin with, we give an overview of extensive works using affective computing and emotion recognition systems for social media. After that, we explore some recent interesting research works about affective touch. Next, augmented reality (AR)-based applications using affective touch communication and affective computing are presented. Then, we review recent virtual reality-based systems using affective touch communication and affective computing. By understanding these approaches for extended reality-based applications with affective touch communication and affective computing presented recently by leading researchers, we believe that it will encourage sustainable advancements regarding human interactions in an integrated cross-disciplinary area.

Keywords: Extended reality · Augmented reality · Virtual reality ·
Force Jacket · Affective computing · Affective touch communication ·
Multimodal communication

© Springer Nature Switzerland AG 2019
S. Misra et al. (Eds.): ICCSA 2019, LNCS 11620, pp. 351–360, 2019.
https://doi.org/10.1007/978-3-030-24296-1_29

1 Background

In this decade of 21st century, there are quick growth of internet as well as emergence and diffusion of smartphones that allow us to effectively deal with a large amount of unstructured data like images, audio and video. Cooking different types of data together is one of the core concepts in extended reality in order to obtain the most realistic or virtualistic user experiences. Recently, extended reality (XR) has become an extremely emerging field in computer science, computational science, and emotion recognition. Extended reality itself refers to the whole spectrum of reality-virtuality continuum, consisting of the core features regarding two majorly immersive technologies named augmented reality (AR) and virtual reality (VR). At the same time, emotion is a mental state and fundamental to human multimodal communication, human experience, and influencing cognition. It is very important for human to communicate. Therefore, affective computing (AC) for recognizing emotional information and human multimodal communication is recently an important research field in computational science, cognitive science, and neurosciences, from human perception of affect to robot perception of affect [1]. This is because it is able to recognize, interpret, and simulate human affects in many uniquely ways, including affective touch communication. At the same time, extended reality is an emerging development referring to all computer-generated environments that mix the real and virtual worlds created by machine and wearables or create an entirely immersive experience for the user interactively. Generally speaking, extended reality includes augmented virtuality (AV), augmented reality, virtual reality, and everything in between real and virtual worlds [2]. In recent years, it has experienced tremendous growth enhancing today's neighboring-fields, including affective computing. In fact, there are recently existing literature reviews on the topic of affective computing [3–5]. For example, Wu et al. [3] surveyed, in 2016, affective computing works in education for understanding the correlation between motivation, emotion, and learning performance. Moreover in 2017, Poria et al. [4] reviewed affective computing methods for unimodal affect analysis, focusing on the use of vision, text, and audio data. They surveyed affect recognition-based techniques for fusing information from various modalities. Also in 2017, recent literature review of the mobile affective computing was done by Politou et al. [5], focusing on affect recognition domain based on mobile-phone gained data. These are mobile-phone usage and mobile-phone embedded sensors. They discussed the exciting research trends towards affective computing on affect recognition from mobile-phone modalities. However, to our best knowledge, most existing literature reviews lack a detailed explanation of state-of-the-art in recent extended reality-based applications enhancing with affective touch communication and affective computing, which this survey aims to contribute and address.

In this paper, we discuss recent methodologies that researchers have presented extended reality-based applications enhancing with affective touch communication and affective computing. The aim of ours is to review our research work experience and other state-of-the-art results and present a way of research to use these results in a future application. This paper is divided into three parts. First, we review existing works of affective computing and emotion recognition systems applying in several related-fields, such as social media and affective touch. Second, we introduce augmented reality-based applications using affective touch communication and affective computing technology. Also, in this main part, virtual reality-based systems that relate to deliberately influence affective touch communication, emotion and affective phenomena are discussed. Finally, we give a proposal for enhancing affective touch-based communication through extended reality.

2   Affective Computing Systems

In this section, it is divided into two subparts. The first subpart is affective computing and emotion recognition systems in social media platforms. The second subpart is about affective touch.

2.1   Affective Computing in Social Media

In recent years, with the rise of social media (e.g., YouTube, Facebook, and Twitter) for online digital marketing and political views, affective touch communication and affective computing works have progressively developed from existing unimodal analysis to more complicated types of multimodal analysis. Therefore, extracting sentiments and emotions from conversations and writings published online in social media is useful for many reasons such as preventing the spread of "false news", sometimes so called "fake news". But it is not easy for recognizing emotions in the context of the text from any social media platforms. According to Kratzwald et al. [6]'s work from ETH Zurich and National Institute of Informatics which was presented recently in 2018, they developed an affect computing system using deep learning technology in social network platforms. They used bidirectional long short-term memory networks (LSTMs) that are able to predict using the data from texts of different lengths, so they can classify news into non-factual and factual for decision support. Thus, by utilizing affective computing and identifying highly polarizing language, their method can help and support people to recognize the spread of "false news" in social media platforms. Furthermore in 2018, Zhao et al. [7] presented a research work for predicting and assuming the individual image emotion perceptions for every viewer in social media platforms. By using rolling multi-task hypergraph learning (RMTHG), they can integrate the elements that possibly influence individual emotion perceptions of images into a learning algorithm for optimization automatically. Their experimental results illustrated that individual emotion classification can be achieved. In addition, Dai et al. [8] proposed an affective computing technique for emotion recognition on vocal social media, focusing on WeChat, based on a LS-SVR (Least Squares SVR) model. They aimed to turn the propagation characteristics of emotions and affective computing into a PAD (Position–Arousal–Dominance) value estimation exercise in three dimensions.

2.2 Affective Touch

Affective touch, especially human affective touch, brings a very great amount of data about distinct emotions in affective computing field. There are recently interesting research works about affective touch. For instance, in 2018, Masson et al. [9] built a space of observed socio-affective touch experiences in many dimensions, called the Socio-Affective Touch Expression Database (SATED). This representational space contained a large range of complicated non-social and social touch interactions. They computed neural similarity values in different eighteen regions of interest (ROI) from following regions: pain, motor, the theory of mind, somatosensory, and vision regions using correlational multivariate pattern analysis algorithms. Pain, the theory of mind, somatosensory, and vision regions represent the socio-affective touch. Next in 2018, Heraz and Clynes [10] studied detection and recognition of various emotions. These emotions included awe, anger, love, desire, laughter, fear, hate, grief, and even no emotion. They then conveyed by affective touch through force-sensitive screens using feature selection and machine learning methods. In this way, they can recognize emotions for precision, calibration, and normalization from the coordinates of person' fingertip touches, number of touches, amount of force, and skin region for affective touch. In addition, affective touch communication can convey uniquely messages-is inexistent in a new form of digital media and interactive digital multimedia applications, as discussed by ours in [11]. According to the concept of touch communication in interactive digital multimedia, an affective tele-touch haptic device was built in 2017 by Cabibihan and Chauhan [12] from Qatar University and National University of Singapore for sending affective touch from a user to another one remotely and entertaining people who are watching movies or films at home. Figure 1 illustrates this overall concept of affective tele-touch haptic device. Therefore, several commands for warmth, tickle, and vibration were transferred remotely to this tele-touch device with a galvanic skin response sensor and a heart rate monitor at the subjects' forearm, while a user is watching emotion-eliciting film. According to our discussion about the research works of affective touch in this section, it is possible to integrate the affective touch into other new technologies such as augmented reality. Therefore, in the next section, we will discuss about extended reality-based applications using affective touch communication and affective computing technology.

Fig. 1. An overall concept of an affective tele-touch haptic device developed by [12] from Qatar University and National University of Singapore in 2017.

Fig. 2. Our integrated system [15] using augmented reality and enhancing affective touch communication for helping and assisting people with disability.

3 Extended Reality Systems with Affective Computing

Since extended reality refers to all real-and-virtual combined environments, including augmented reality and virtual reality, this section is divided into two subparts. The first subpart is augmented reality with affective computing and affective touch. The second subpart is about virtual reality with affective computing and affective touch.

3.1 Augmented Reality with Affective Computing and Affective Touch

Augmented reality is the blending of interactive digital elements to augment the real world, sometimes called physical world. In recent years, there are emerging research works about augmented reality-based applications enhancing with affective computing and affective touch communication. For example, a real-time system was built by Roberts [13] in 2018 utilizing affective computing for proxemic interactions in augmented reality (called it in their paper as mixed reality (MR), a largely synonymous term). Using Magic Leap One as the interface interactively, this augmented reality-based system can be controlled by indicating emotions, which are compatible with affective integrations of tonal analysis and facial micro-expressions. This user interface visualization element of this system can leverage the features of augmented reality by identifying a spatial component to interactive interfaces. Also, in 2017, Datcu and Rothkrantz [14] presented interfaces that can help creating emotional awareness and situational awareness for car driving simulation using augmented reality and affective computing. Their research contribution is to solve some specific problems regarding integration of affective computing and augmented reality for supporting vehicle driving. By using augmented reality, situational awareness can be created. At the same time, by using affective computing, they can build emotional awareness. By integrating these two technologies, it can allow affect-driven remote collaboration for car driving simulation in augmented realty. In addition, in our previous research work [15] in 2016, an integrated application using augmented reality enhancing affective touch communication was built to assist disabled people. By using augmented reality, a cardboard glass, Google Glass-like, was developed to support disabled people with hearing impairment to have a good immersive experience for geometric visualization. As depicted in Fig. 2, by using affective touch communication, a hugging wearable tool, called T.Jacket, was utilized to support people with disability for hugging their loved one from different locations using airbags, 3x Teensy 3.6, computer, arbotiX, serve motor, and air compressor. This affective touch communication can be done by reproducing a touch sense between two people remotely, though artificially. In this case, it is about hug. By combining augmented reality and a wearable jacket for affective touch communication, this can allow disabled people having a new human-computer interaction experience. Nevertheless, this integrated concept is not only limited to utilize in only augmented reality-based applications, but it also can use in virtual reality-based applications. We will discuss this issue in the next subpart.

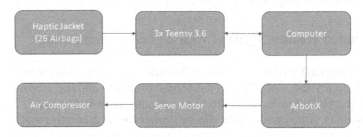

Fig. 3. A technical concept of the Force Jacket developed by Delazio et al. [16] from Disney Research and MIT in 2018 through affective touch

3.2 Virtual Reality with Affective Computing and Affective Touch

While augmented reality is an interactive experience of a real-world environment where the real-world objects are augmented by some immersive information in the virtual world, virtual reality is an interactive experience taking place within a totally immersive virtual world. Similarly to ours [15] in some issues, although presented more recently, Force Jacket was developed by Delazio et al. [16] from Disney Research and MIT in 2018 for the multimodal communication techniques through affective touch using virtual reality technology to help people in communication and entertain people interactively. Figure 3 shows some examples of virtual reality games of the Force Jacket. This pneumatically-actuated jacket was built from an array of airbags and force sensors for haptic experiences. After wearing this jacket, it can directly give force and vibrations energetically to the upper part of body by reproducing an artificial hug, an artificial punch, and an artificial snake moving feeling across the user's body while wearing this pneumatically-actuated jacket. By integrating affective touch communication into virtual reality, it can enhance new immersive experiences and entertain people with virtual reality games.

Also, Ontiveros-Hernández et al. [17] presented insights towards a model using virtual reality and affective computing inducing emotional states in human activities for improving training and learning. This affective computing work was further used to develop the virtual reality-based intelligent tutoring work [18] of Pérez-Ramírez, presented in 2016, using in the classroom classes and camp training. Besides in 2017, Leon [19] proposed an affective distant learning model with the use of online illustrations in a virtual reality world, called avatars, with realistic facial emotional expressions. These expressions are compatible with the emotional state of the real user. Emotional facial expressions of the user are recorded and then analyzed beforehand. The affective user interface was built, and therefore this can utilize avatars as stand-in for users, such as learners and students, remotely by processing emotional facial expression. In addition, Ahmed et al. [20, 21] designed virtual reality-based affective symbiosis, the connection between the human and computer-generated affective virtual information, with biosensors, haptics, and emotive agents. In their virtual reality-based affective symbiosis, people can play an application of air hockey in a virtual world with affective agents. Their game included some features of haptic feedback and psychophysiological measurements. They then gathered the electrocardiography, heart rate variability, electro-dermal activity, and postural data and information for evaluating how these emotional things affected human behavior, physiology, and experience. Furthermore in 2018, Cooney et al. [22] recently identified possible pitfalls of affective computing in emotion visualization. They presented strategies for avoiding pitfalls of affective computing and minimizing the risks when misusing emotion visualization. Because affective computing can improve people's well-being by enabling computers to help making decisions and serving through awareness of people's emotions, by avoiding pitfalls of affective computing, their work can possibly enable emotion visualization to contribute to well-being of people which could solve several related-affective computing issues such as physical or psychological harm, disempowerment and miscommunication. Moreover in 2018, González-Franco et al. [23] from Microsoft Research developed a virtual reality-based system called "uncanny valley" using haptic stimulations. They generated an illusion of spatial touch for human perception of haptic feedback, and then they investigated human response to haptic stimulations of increasing fidelity using virtual reality as a perceptual testbed.

4   Future Directions for Affective Touch-Based Communication

As explained in the previous sections, it is quite clear that affective touch plays an essential role in the future of communications. This is since it allows more senses in human communication to be included simultaneously and interactively, enabling innovative communications both between computers and humans, and between humans and humans. At the same time, research about extended reality grows very quickly, as it effects and impacts on the daily lives of many people. Because of the overlapped areas of the affective touch-based communication and extended reality, we believe that future directions for affective touch-based communication would be indispensably linked to extended reality, especially augmented reality in the next decade. In the point of view of affective computing and emotion recognition, although virtual reality can also be connected to affective touch-based communication, augmented reality can be more profound in our opinion. This is because augmented reality has a more unique capacity to amplify human performance than virtual reality, as suggested similarly by Apple CEO Tim Cook in [24]. A next possible reason is about virtual reality sickness which is about several symptoms of headache, nausea and even sometimes vomiting, when diving in a virtual environment completely and immersively. We also believe that our previous works about augmented reality [2], touch communication [15] and human hand tracking [25] could be more practical when applying in the context of affective computing and emotion recognition. Through this integrated cross-disciplinary context, it could be a big leap in human communication in the next decade to come.

5 Conclusions

Until today, the development of affective computing and extended reality-based applications is not a trivial task for computational scientists, psychologists, and cognitive scientists due to various complexities of artificial emotional intelligence and many challenges in using extended reality. This paper has discussed various state-of-the-art applications and methodologies that researchers, including the author, have recently achieved by utilizing affective computing, affective touch, and extended reality. We have given an overview of extensive works using affective computing and emotion recognition systems for social media. After that, we have explored some recent interesting research works about affective touch. Next, augmented reality-based applications using affective touch communication and affective computing have been proposed. Then, we have discussed recent virtual reality-based systems using affective touch communication and affective computing. We believe that, by perceiving the state-of-the-art concepts and methods for integrated extended reality-based applications with affective touch communication and affective computing achieved by leading researchers around the world, this would possibly advance the interactions that humans would have with modern innovations in an integrated cross-disciplinary area. Also, it will be of great value and good direction to the researchers in these related-fields of affective computing and extended reality.

Acknowledgments. This research presented herein was partially supported by a research grant from the Research Center, NIDA (National Institute of Development Administration).

References

1. Rudovic, O., Lee, J., Dai, M., Schuller, B., Picard, R.W.: Personalized machine learning for robot perception of affect and engagement in autism therapy. Sci. Robot. **3**, eaao6760 (2018)
2. Kerdvibulvech, C.: An innovative real-time mobile augmented reality application in arts. In: De Paolis, L.T., Bourdot, P., Mongelli, A. (eds.) AVR 2017, Part II. LNCS, vol. 10325, pp. 251–260. Springer, Cham (2017). https://doi.org/10.1007/978-3-319-60928-7_22
3. Wu, C.-H., Huang, Y.-M., Hwang, J.-P.: Review of affective computing in education/learning: trends and challenges. Br. J. Educ. Technol. (BJET) **47**(6), 1304–1323 (2016)
4. Poria, S., Cambria, E., Bajpai, R., Hussain, A.: A review of affective computing: from unimodal analysis to multimodal fusion. Inf. Fusion **37**, 98–125 (2017)

5. Politou, E.A., Alepis, E., Patsakis, C.: A survey on mobile affective computing. Comput. Sci. Rev. **25**, 79–100 (2017)
6. Kratzwald, B., Ilic, S., Kraus, M., Feuerriegel, S., Prendinger, H.: Deep learning for affective computing: text-based emotion recognition in decision support. Decis. Support Syst. **115**, 24–35 (2018)
7. Zhao, S., Yao, H., Gao, Y., Ding, G., Chua, T.-S.: Predicting personalized image emotion perceptions in social networks. IEEE Trans. Affect. Comput. **9**(4), 526–540 (2018)
8. Dai, W., Han, D., Dai, Y., Xu, D.: Emotion recognition and affective computing on vocal social media. Inf. Manage. **52**(7), 777–788 (2015)
9. Masson, H.L., Van De Plas, S., Daniels, N., de Beeck, H.P.O.: The multidimensional representational space of observed socio-affective touch experiences. NeuroImage **175**, 297–314 (2018)
10. Heraz, A., Clynes, M.: Recognition of emotions conveyed by touch through force-sensitive screens: observational study of humans and machine learning techniques. J. Med. Internet Res. (JMIR) Ment. Health **5**(3), e10104 (2018)
11. Kerdvibulvech, C.: A study of interactive digital multimedia applications. In: Ho, Y.-S., Sang, J., Ro, Y.M., Kim, J., Wu, F. (eds.) PCM 2015, Part I. LNCS, vol. 9314, pp. 192–199. Springer, Cham (2015). https://doi.org/10.1007/978-3-319-24075-6_19
12. Cabibihan, J.-J., Chauhan, S.S.: Physiological responses to affective tele-touch during induced emotional stimuli. IEEE Trans. Affect. Comput. **8**(1), 108–118 (2017)
13. Roberts, J.: Using affective computing for proxemic interactions in mixed-reality. In: Proceedings of the Symposium on Spatial User Interaction (SUI), p. 176 (2018)
14. Datcu, D., Rothkrantz, L.: Affective computing and augmented reality for car driving simulators. In: Acta Polytechnica CTU Proceedings, vol. 12, pp. 13–23 (2017)
15. Kerdvibulvech, C.: A novel integrated system of visual communication and touch technology for people with disabilities. In: Gervasi, O., et al. (eds.) ICCSA 2016, Part II. LNCS, vol. 9787, pp. 509–518. Springer, Cham (2016). https://doi.org/10.1007/978-3-319-42108-7_39
16. Delazio, A., Nakagaki, K., Klatzky, R.L., Hudson, S.E., Lehman, J.F., Sample, A.P.: Force jacket: pneumatically-actuated jacket for embodied haptic experiences. In: Proceedings of the 2018 CHI Conference on Human Factors in Computing Systems (CHI 2018), Montreal QC, Canada, 21–26 April 2018, Paper No. 320 (2018)
17. Ontiveros-Hernández, N.J., Pérez-Ramírez, M., Hernández, Y.: Virtual reality and affective computing for improving learning. Res. Comput. Sci. **65**, 121–131 (2013)
18. Pérez-Ramírez, M., Ontiveros-Hernández, N.J., Ochoa-Ortíz, C.A., Hernández-Aguilar, J.A., Zayas-Pérez, B.E.: Intelligent tutoring systems based on virtual reality for the electrical domain. Res. Comput. Sci. **122**, 163–174 (2016)
19. Rothkrantz, L.J.M.: An affective distant learning model using avatars as user stand-in. In: CompSysTech, pp. 288–295 (2017)
20. Ahmed, I., Harjunen, V., Jacucci, G., Hoggan, E.E., Ravaja, N., Spapé, M.M.A.: Reach out and touch me: effects of four distinct haptic technologies on affective touch in virtual reality. In: Proceedings of the 18th ACM International Conference on Multimodal Interaction (ICMI 2016), pp. 341–348 (2017). LNCS, vol. 9961, pp. 23–37
21. Ahmed, I., Harjunen, V., Jacucci, G., Ravaja, N., Spapé, Michiel M.: Total immersion: designing for affective symbiosis in a virtual reality game with haptics, biosensors, and emotive agents. In: Gamberini, L., Spagnolli, A., Jacucci, G., Blankertz, B., Freeman, J. (eds.) Symbiotic 2016. LNCS, vol. 9961, pp. 23–37. Springer, Cham (2017). https://doi.org/10.1007/978-3-319-57753-1_3

22. Cooney, M., Pashami, S., Sant'Anna, A., Fan, Y., Nowaczyk, S.: Pitfalls of Affective Computing: how can the automatic visual communication of emotions lead to harm, and what can be done to mitigate such risks. In: Companion Proceedings of the the Web Conference (WWW), Lyon, France, 23–27 April 2018, pp. 1563–1566 (2018)
23. González-Franco, M., Ofek, E., Hinckley, K.: The uncanny valley of haptics. Sci. Robot. **3** (17) (2018)
24. Fitzsimmons, M.: Apple's Tim Cook: AR has the ability to amplify human performance (2018). https://www.techradar.com/news/apples-tim-cook-ar-has-the-ability-to-amplify-human-performance. Accessed 1 Apr 2019
25. Kerdvibulvech, C.: Hand tracking by extending distance transform and hand model in real-time. Pattern Recognit. Image Anal. **25**(3), 437–441 (2015)

Humble Voices in Political Communication: A Speech Analysis Across Two Cultures

Francesca D'Errico[1(✉)], Oliver Niebuhr[2], and Isabella Poggi[1]

[1] Fil.Co.Spe Department, Roma Tre University, Rome, Italy
{francesca.derrico,isabella.poggi}@uniroma3.it
[2] Centre for Industrial Electronics, University of Southern Denmark,
Sonderborg, Denmark
olni@sdu.dk

Abstract. Classical works on affective and persuasive computing have pointed out that technologies whose goal is to influence the user's need to communicate in a charismatic or dominant style, neglecting the potential persuasive strength of other styles, such as a humble style. Humility can be defined as an epistemic and interactional stance aimed at communicating the person's attitude towards an object, topic, or the interlocutor. Previous studies on persuasion in politics conducted multimodal analyses to identify those postures, prosodic features, gaze patterns, and facial expressions that convey humility. In this study, we describe the features of humility associated with a speaker's tone-of-voice, by comparing two pairs of popular politicians from USA (Obama vs Trump) and Italy (Gentiloni vs Salvini) during TV interviews. Results on the acoustic side point out clear differences in the speech characteristics of humble vs. dominant politicians: Gentiloni's and Obama's speech is characterized by short utterances, more hesitations and disfluencies and fewer stressed words. The two speakers' loudness levels are lower, and their voice qualities either more sonorant or even breathier. We discuss our results with respect to their implications for persuasive processes which can be associated not only to the speakers' features but also to the speaker-audience personality-trait matching.

Keywords: Humility · Multimodal communication · Voice · Speech analysis

1 Introduction

Within studies on persuasion, the notion of humility has been neglected since influence over others has been generally viewed as a process where a 'dominant' or a charismatic leader generally uses different maneuverings to show he has more power than his opponent (Fogg 2002; Poggi and D'Errico 2010; D'Errico et al. 2013; Niebuhr and Ochoa 2019). From this point of view, persuasion research has neglected the potential individual differences related to the preference of a dominant vs. humble speaker. In recent studies, in fact, it has emerged that individuals with a low orientation to social dominance, high self-esteem and high level of moral relevance experience much more positive emotions (i.e. joy, enthusiasm) when they listen to communication phrased in a humble rather than a dominant way (D'Errico, forth.). Therefore, in the field of

© Springer Nature Switzerland AG 2019
S. Misra et al. (Eds.): ICCSA 2019, LNCS 11620, pp. 361–374, 2019.
https://doi.org/10.1007/978-3-030-24296-1_30

persuasive technologies (Franzoni et al. 2019) on bodily and linguistic signals that promote a persuasive process in humble communication becomes more and more relevant. In this regard, a definition of humble stance will first be presented by referring to a socio-cognitive model of persuasion in terms of goals and beliefs (Poggi 2007). Subsequently, recent studies on the multimodality of humble communication (D'Errico and Poggi 2017; 2019) will be reviewed, highlighting how the body communicates humility. The last section will present an empirical study focused on the humble speech features as compared with the dominant ones, through advanced speech detection techniques. The speech analysis will also describe potential cultural differences since the audios analysed are selected from two Italian and two American politicians. In particular we present an acoustic analysis by means of the speech-signal processing software PRAAT (Boersma 2001), extracting eleven acoustic prosodic parameters concerning:

(1) Pausing and speaking, measured in the time domain of the signal;
(2) Speech melody, measured in terms of f0 in the spectrum of the acoustic signal and
(3) Tempo and voice.

Furthermore, a second analysis will describe conversation dynamics including four additional parameters like number of disfluencies, overlapping turns, mean duration of overlapping and number of competitive turn taking. Results will be discussed in view of understanding the differences between dominant and humble leaders' voice and its relation to the leaders' charisma.

2   The Humble Stance

In psychological terms, humility is a kind of interactional stance, namely, a way of interacting with others while admitting one's own limitations, showing openness to new ideas and means, giving others a voice, and recognizing their merits (Weidman et al. 2018).

On the opposite side, studies on political persuasion have generally pointed out how a charismatic and trustworthy politician needs to be acknowledged as moral, competent but also dominant. In addition to morality and competence, in fact, the feature of dominance seems to be effective in persuading an audience (Poggi and D'Errico, 2010). Dominance has been defined as a relational construct implying a power comparison (to have "more power than" another); but also the communication of power—the fact of producing signals conveying one's dominance—is very important, because communicating power is a way to maintain it or even to acquire more of it (Castelfranchi 2003). Poggi and D'Errico (2010), in their multimodal analysis of dominance strategies, have shown that politicians sometimes use 'blatant' dominance strategies, clearly characterized by aggressiveness or power display, like using speech acts of criticism or accusation, or speaking aloud; but they can also exploit 'subtle' dominance strategies, that at first sight do not show a clear exhibition of force or power, but are nonetheless more indirect ways to show dominance, like showing a calm strength or ignoring the other.

The preference for the dominant communication in its explicit forms (e.g., discrediting the opponent) is higher when people show adherence to power, security and social dominance orientation (D'Errico and Poggi 2012a; b).

Dominance in some cases plays a role also in political charisma, that set of features of a politician which allow him to influence followers' actions and emotions not by the use of force but through admiration and identification. As shown in recent studies (Signorello et al. 2012; D'Errico et al. 2013), from a perceptual point of view the persuasive strength of charismatic features is correlated with features of dominance.

On the contrary, a humble stance can be defined as a multimodal public act, performed interactively through verbal and bodily communication, by which a person positions oneself with respect to the object of a communicative interaction and also with respect to one's interlocutor. In this sense, a humble stance of a politician can be expressed either by communicating his 'horizontal', 'equal' position toward his interlocutor or by acknowledging one's uncertainty (Vincze et al. 2012), limits and flaws, and thus the consequent possibility of making errors (limit awareness).

According to the qualitative analysis by D'Errico and Poggi (2017) aimed at finding out the features of Humility, the humble stance is a "realistic" approach, an ability to keep one's feet firmly on the ground, in the awareness of being always fallacious and never perfect. Limits awareness implies a feeling/communication of equality to others (Equality feature), not to feel superior to them, not to display any superiority, and if having some power over others, not to take advantage of it (Non-Superiority feature). This stance has behavioral consequences in that the humble person shows being on the same level as others, as well as treating them as equal to oneself (Familiarity), and being empathic to them (Empathy), which implies Care and Attention to the other; hence giving an impression of Altruism, of being oriented to other people more than to objects or to oneself.

The basic feature of Realism entails, from an expressive point of view, not crediting any relevance to any external tinsel or symbolic ornament like status symbols or status tout court (Essentiality), which results in features of Informality and Sincerity, not caring anything but the real substantive value of people.

Such definition of humility from a cognitive perspective shows how the main goal of a humble person is to be "like others", not more and not less, thus for pursuing this goal she does not show nor make appeal to his/her own power, superiority in terms of status, knowledge, merits, contributions, virtues and capabilities. From a communicative point of view s/he considers important "not to put her/himself first" but rather attributes a positive value to a larger dimension of belonging (e.g., others, group, organizations, party) and focuses on the problem rather than on the person who did something. Such horizontal perspective of the humble person focused on others and the group, leads to emphasizing elements of similarity, familiarity, and informality.

3 Charisma and Its Multimodal Communication

In previous works, studies in the psychology of persuasion (D'Errico et al. 2013) and acoustic analysis of voice (Signorello et al. 2012) have investigated the notion of charisma while trying to find out the features of charismatic voice. Charisma, first defined by Weber (1920) as an "extraordinary quality" of a person who is believed to be endowed with superhuman properties, therefore inducing people to acknowledge him as a leader and to develop a cult of him, can be defined, in terms of a socio-cognitive model, as a set of internal features of a person that, when manifested by some external displays – physical traits or behaviors displayed in various modalities – trigger a set of emotions in other people, that induce them to pursue some goals not through coercion but voluntarily and willingly, while feeling involvement, passion, and enthusiasm in what they do together or on behalf of that person. These internal features are displayed in the person's multimodal behavior: his words, gestures, gaze, facial expression, posture, and voice. Inspiring to the cognitive model of persuasion (Poggi 2007), according to D'Errico et al. (2013) the internal features include personal characteristics that endow the person with crucial dimensions of persuasiveness: *emotional intelligence* (the skill of feeling emotions himself, of displaying them to others, and to be empathic with others' emotions) and *emotional induction* (the skill to transmit emotions to others through expressivity and contagion), *benevolence* (an attitude of sociability and inclusiveness: being people-oriented, making followers feel "similar" to him and "together" with him); *competence* (both physical and intellectual capacities: vision, creativity, foresight, and communicative skills), and finally *dominance* (capacity of winning in competitions, not to submit but to dominate).

The external features that display such charismatic internal features of charismatic leaders were analyzed in the words, gestures and postures of Benito Mussolini (Poggi 2017), in the voice of other Italian and French politicians (D'Errico et al. 2013; Signorello et al. 2012), where the parameters of pitch, jitter and shimmer were taken into account, and in the voice of leaders in organizational settings (Niehbur et al. 2016) showing that Steve Jobs's voice, compared to other reference samples, stands out against them in almost all key features of charisma, including melody, loudness, tempo and fluency, thus producing significant quantitative differences in influence potential when addressing customers and investors in his speeches.

While analyzing the change in acoustic parameters of the voice of Umberto Bossi due to a stroke (Signorello et al. 2012), it was found that his charisma did not totally fade away from before to after the stroke, but it changed in type. Three types of charisma were singled out, stemming from different combinations of the charismatic dimensions: an Authoritarian – Threatening one, with prevailing features of dominance and aggressiveness; a Competent-Benevolent one, with the prevalence of skills display and empathy towards followers; and a Proactive-Attractive one, characterized by optimism, orientation to future, and a seductive attitude. Charismatic leaders differ from each other due to their prevailing type of charisma: Mussolini mainly exploits an Authoritarian-Threatening one, with shifts to Proactive-Attractive (Poggi 2017); Bossi shifts from an authoritarian-threatening one before the stroke to a more competent-benevolent in his voice after the stroke. Another study (D'Errico et al. 2013) analyzing the effects of higher or lower pitch and longer or shorter pauses of leaders on the followers found out a cultural difference between Italians and French in the perception of charisma and the interpretation of its signals: both Italians and French appreciate a Proactive-Attractive leader more than a Calm-Benevolent leader, though with slight differences. Both perceive a Calm-Benevolent charisma while listening to short pauses, but the perception differs for pitch. This might mean that they differ in the interpretation of a factor of "human sociability" (a Calm-Benevolent charisma). Italians attribute it more to a high-pitch voice with shorter pauses, whereas the French prefer low-pitch voice and long pauses.

4   The Multimodal Communication of Humble Leadership

D'Errico and Poggi (2017) analysed the multimodal communication of humble leaders. Here the point is to find out the external features in the leader's words, gestures, posture, facial expression that are a cue to the internal features outlined above: equality, non-superiority, empathy, and so on. To this aim, fragments of communication of humble leaders were analysed in terms of an annotation scheme in which, for each body signal (gesture, posture, gaze item) its meaning is annotated, and its underlying humility feature. In the analysis (D'Errico and Poggi 2017), the President of Uruguay José Mujica is described as dressed with a *simple shirt* – a signal of INFORMALITY – *leaning forward* as if communicating a desire to get closer, to create FAMILIARITY with the interlocutor; his *head is lowered* and directed *straight to the camera* but, like gaze

Table 1. Bodily features of humility

Parameter	Signal	Meaning
Head	Bent	Humble
	Leaning forward	Request Or other-oriented
	straight	Authoritative
	Tilted backward	Proud/arrogant
	Head canting	Well-disposed/listening Or Ironic/skeptical
Chin	Downward on chest	Humble, sad, or ashamed
	Downward forward	Request Or other-oriented (Well-disposed towards the other)
	Défault	Authoritative
	Upward	Proud/arrogant
Trunk	Forward relaxed	Humble or modest
	Leaning forward tense	Other oriented/humble
	Erect	Authoritative
	Strutting (straight tense)	Arrogant
	Slouched (backward relaxed)	Careless Or arrogant
Shoulders	Closed forward	Humble or modest
	Bottle shoulders	Sad Or humble
	Horizontal	Self-confident/Authoritative
	Backward	Arrogant Or distant
Gesture amplitude	High	Aggressive (possibly mocking exaggeration
	Défault	Authoritative
	Within shoulder width	Humble

direction, from down upward, *both positioning him in a down-up position, conveys the meaning that he does not judge or command over the potential listener (NON- SUPERI-ORITY). His gaze, by* raised and frowning eyebrows, *expresses worry, hence concern about the interlocutor's future (EMPATHY), while* nose wrinkles tightened lids *and* tightened lips, *that convey anger, communicate the importance of the subject by raising attention.*

Based on such multimodal analysis on several fragments of humble leaders' communication, D'Errico and Poggi (2019) draw a tentative list of correspondences between head, hands, and trunk movements and positions with the features of humility or, to the contrary, with opposite features of superiority or distance (Table 1).

5 The Voice of Humble Politicians Across Two Cultures

The main aims of our work are: 1. to find out the characterizing features of humility in the voice of humble politicians; 2. to test if they are significantly different from features of dominance in dominant-aggressive politicians; 3. to assess possible differences in the external features of humility in two different cultures, American and Italian.

A final aim of our study is to try to disentangle the complex relationship that holds among dominance, humility, and charisma. Is charisma perceived only in dominant leaders, or is there a charismatic humble leadership?

5.1 Comparing American and Italian Dominant and Humble Leaders

To search real cases of political communication by dominant and humble leaders, in a preliminary study we asked participants to list two humble and two dominant American and Italian politicians. Then we chose four politicians (two humble and two dominant) among those most frequently pointed by our participants. In order to explore potential cultural differences we chose two politicians from Italy, Paolo Gentiloni (Prime Minister of the Italian Republic for two years, since 2016 to 2018: the humble one) and Matteo Salvini (Minister in 2018 and 2019; the dominant one), and two from Usa, Barack Obama and Donald Trump, humble and dominant, respectively.

5.2 Method: Speech Material and Analysis

Speech samples of the four politicians were extracted from public YouTube videos. Care was taken that all samples were comparable: all the politicians were interviewed in a well established TV talk show by a male interviewer. Both politician and TV host sit on a chair face-to-face about 2 m away from each other. About 5 min of speech were extracted per politician from the middle of each interview, at a point which was largely free from audience background noise and applause. All turns (i.e. coherent speech contributions like questions or comments) of the talk-show host were removed from the extracted speech sample so that only the respective politician's speech could be analyzed.

The first analysis was conducted on an acoustic basis, using three existing scripts that were written for the PRAAT speech-signal processing software (Boersma 2001) by de Looze and Hirst (2008), de Jong and Wempe (2009), and Xu (2013). Eleven acoustic-prosodic parameters were included in the analysis, covering different characteristics of the tone-of-voice of each politician:

- Pausing and speaking, measured in the time domain of the signal

    (1) number of silent pauses (per minute, min)
    (2) mean duration of silent pauses (milliseconds, ms)
    (3) mean duration of inter-pausal speech units (ms), i.e. everything in between two audible pauses with durations >200 ms, see Walker and Trimboli (1982) and Heldner (2011)

- Speech melody, measured in terms of the fundamental-frequency or f0 in the spectrum of the acoustic signal

    (4) mean pitch level (f0 mean, in Hz),
    (5) mean lower limit of the speaker's pitch range (f0 minimum, in Hz)
    (6) mean upper limit of the speaker's pitch range (f0 maximum, in Hz)
    (7) mean pitch range (f0 min-f0max in number of octaves, semitones, st),
    (8) pitch variability (f0 standard deviation, in Hz),

- Tempo and voice

    (9) net speaking rate (in syllables per second, pauses excluded)
    (10) voice quality in terms of the Hammarberg index (in dB)
    (11) mean dispersion of formants 1–5 (in Hz)

The Hammarberg index is the acoustic-energy difference between two ranges of the speaker's voice spectrum (0–2 kHz and 2–5 kHz). Thus, the index determines how much energy a speaker's voice loses towards higher frequencies (Hammarberg et al. 1980). Louder and more powerful voices have a higher Hammarberg index and softer and thinner voices a lower one. Moreover, the index was found to vary systematically with the perceived emotions and traits of a speaker, with smaller values characterizing angry or urging speakers and/or speakers who sound more thrusting and powerful (Liu and Xu 2014; Nordström et al. 2017). Similarly, the mean dispersion of the first 5 formants is an acoustic correlate of the perceived body size of the speaker. The larger the volume, size, and weight of the speaker's body (i.e. the more imposing and awing the body), the smaller the value of the formant dispersion (Fitch 1997). Xu et al. (2013) found, accordingly, that formant-dispersion values are also related to emotional speech. Angry speakers have a higher formant dispersion than, e.g., happy speakers.

All measurements were taken per inter-pausal speech unit, with PRAAT's default analysis settings. Mean values were formed across all inter-pausal units of a speaker. The total number of inter-pausal units was 78 for Trump, 96 for Obama, 66 for Salvini, and 74 for Gentiloni. Thus, 314 measurements were taken per parameter. The measurements taken per speaker varied between 990 (Salvini) and 1,440 (Obama). The entire acoustic analysis comprised 4,710 individual measurements.

The second analysis concerned the conversation dynamics within the political interviews. It was conducted on an auditory basis by a trained phonetician (2nd author), partly because autonomous computer-based scripts were unable to perform the requested measurements, and partly because the acoustics of the TV recordings made precise acoustic measurements difficult. Note that the auditory analysis was done on the basis of the entire TV interview. It included the following four additional parameters: (12) number of disfluencies, including filled pauses (tokens per min), (13) Number of overlapping turns of politician and TV host (tokens per min), (14) Mean duration of turn overlap (in seconds, s), (15) Number of competitive turn taking events on the part of the politician (tokens per minute). That is, the politician interrupts the moderator and takes his turn or continues talking while the moderator tries to interrupt, cf. Weilhammer and Rabold (2003) for a typology of turn-taking events.

Statistical Analysis

All parameters except for the relative frequencies (i.e. number of tokens per time unit, applies to parameters 1, 12, 13, 15) were statistically analyzed in separate two-way ANOVAs based on the two fixed factors STANCE (humble vs dominant) and COUNTRY (USA vs Italy). As there were only two levels per factor, additional multiple comparisons tests among factor levels were omitted. The relative frequencies were analyzed in terms of individual Chi-squared tests based on a 2×2 contingency tables per parameter.

5.3   Results

Table 2 summarizes the results of the acoustic and auditory analyses of the four politicians. The presentation of the results will start below with the factor STANCE (Sect. 5.3.1), i.e. the differences in interview behavior and tone-of-voice between humble and dominant politicians. The subsequent Sect. 5.3.2 briefly addresses the differences related to the factor COUNTRY. In Sect. 5.3.1, key results of Table 2 are additionally illustrated by figures.

5.3.1   STANCE: Humble vs Dominant Politicians

First, note that all significant differences between humble and dominant politicians were consistent across the two countries, i.e. they apply in the same way to both Italian and American speakers. In terms of the speaking and pausing behavior, this means that the humble politicians Obama and Gentiloni interspersed their turns in the TV interview with more pauses (χ^2 [1] = 26.3, p < 0.001) and longer pauses (F[1,310] = 15.4, p < 0.001) than Trump and Salvini. Trump and Salvini, on the other hand, talked a lot longer before making a (shorter) pause (F[1,310] = 44.6, p < 0.001), see Fig. 1.

With respect to speech melody, the results show that, compared to the humble politicians, the dominant politicians' speeches were characterized by a higher pitch level (F[1,310] = 7.4, p = 0.007). The same applies to the pitch minimum (F [1,310] = 5.6, p = 0.02) and pitch maximum (F[1,310] = 10.9, p = 0.001). In combination, these pitch differences point to a change of the entire pitch register, which seems to be generally shifted upward for dominant as compared to humble politicians, see also Fig. 2. The pitch range stays the same within the higher register of dominant politicians and, thus, does not differ significantly from that of the humble politicians. However, the pitch variability differs and is higher for the dominant politicians (F[1,310] = 32.5, p < 0.001).

Table 2. Results obtained per politician for the 15 acoustic and auditory parameters, organized in 2 × 2 fields representing the factors STANCE (horizontal) and COUNTRY (vertical); IPU = Inter-pausal Unit; N = 78 for Trump, N = 96 for Obama, N = 66 for Salvini, N = 74 for Gentiloni. Light grey 2 × 2 fields indicate significant differences only for the factor STANCE. Dark grey 2 × 2 fields indicate significant differences of both factors STANCE and COUNTRY.

Parameter types	Measures	Politicians (dominant)	Politicians (humble)	Measures	Politicians (dominant)	Politicians (humble)
Type 1 parameters: Speaking & Pausing	Silent pauses/min	Trump 14.7	Obama 21.4	ø silent pause dur. (ms)	Trump 559	Obama 670
		Salvini 10.3	Gentiloni 16.4		Salvini 406	Gentiloni 700
	ø IPU duration (ms)	Trump 3,424	Obama 2,068			
		Salvini 5,250	Gentiloni 2,923			
Type 2 parameters: Speech melody (f0)	ø Pitch level (Hz)	Trump 132	Obama 93	ø Pitch range (octaves)	Trump 1.9	Obama 1.9
		Salvini 140	Gentiloni 122		Salvini 1.7	Gentiloni 2.0
	ø Pitch min (Hz)	Trump 71	Obama 55	ø Pitch variability (sd, Hz)	Trump 30.9	Obama 20.5
		Salvini 81	Gentiloni 70		Salvini 39.7	Gentiloni 23.0
	ø Pitch max (Hz)	Trump 270	Obama 208			
		Salvini 330	Gentiloni 247			
Type 3 parameters: Tempo & Voice	ø Ham.brg. index	Trump 23.2	Obama 16.2	ø Formant dispersion (Hz)	Trump 594	Obama 870
		Salvini 17.6	Gentiloni 14.9		Salvini 768	Gentiloni 852
	ø Net speaking rate (syll/s)	Trump 5.6	Obama 4.4			
		Salvini 5.5	Gentiloni 4.8			
Type 4 parameters: convers. dynamics	Disfl., filled pauses/min	Trump 9.4	Obama 3.6	Turn-overl duration (s)	Trump 2.1	Obama 0.4
		Salvini 7.9	Gentiloni 5.5		Salvini 4.5	Gentiloni 1.7
	Overlapping turns/min	Trump 2.8	Obama 0.4	Comp. turn taking/min	Trump 1.8	Obama 0.2
		Salvini 4.2	Gentiloni 2.2		Salvini 2.6	Gentiloni 0.9

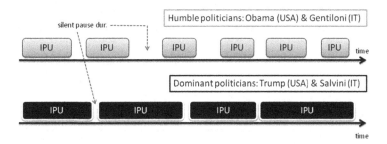

Fig. 1. Illustration of Type-1 parameter results: pausing & speaking

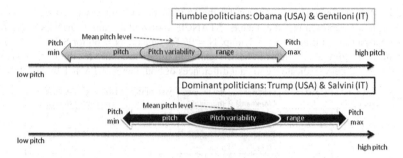

Fig. 2. Illustration of Type-2 parameter results: Speech melody

Regarding the analyzed parameters of tempo and voice, the dominant politicians spoke faster than the humble politicians (F[1,310] = 4.6, p = 0.03). We also found the Hammarberg index to be higher for the dominant than for the humble politicians (F[1,310] = 11.1, p = 0.001). The humble politicians' speech, on the other hand, was characterized by higher formant-dispersion values (F[1,310] = 23.4, p < 0.001).

Finally, the auditory analysis of conversation dynamics within the interviews adds two aspects to the overall results pattern. First, the dominant politicians Trump and Salvini produced significantly more disfluencies and/or used more filled pauses in their speech than the humble politicians Obama and Gentiloni (χ^2 [1] = 5.2, p = 0.02). Second, compared to the humble politicians, the data of their dominant counterparts reflect the strong will to control the conversation, i.e. to take the turn, to keep the turn, and to continue talking when the TV host tries to change the topic or go deeper into a certain argument, see also Fig. 3. Accordingly, overlapping turns (χ^2 [1] = 4.1, p = 0.04) and competitive turn taking (χ^2 [1] = 19.6, p < 0.001) are much more frequent for dominant than for humble politicians, and the duration of overlapping turns is also longer for dominant politicians (F[1,310] = 56.7, p < 0.001). Actually, also the fewer and shorter pauses of dominant politicians, and their preference for repaired over carefully pre-planned speech (larger number of disfluencies) and for filled

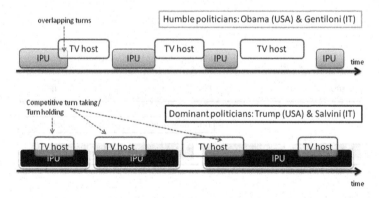

Fig. 3. Illustration of Type-4 parameter results: Conversation dynamics.

over silent pauses can be interpreted as reflecting the will to control the conversation by maximizing talking time and avoiding, by all means, silent intervals that could invite the TV host to start speaking.

5.3.2 COUNTRY: Italy vs USA

Table 2 shows that 66% of the analyzed parameters (i.e. 10 out of 15) also differ significantly as a function of COUNTRY. However, as was stated in Sect. 5.3.1, these differences are only quantitative and not qualitative in nature. That is, Trump (dominant) and Obama (humble) differ from each other in the same way as Salvini (dominant) and Gentiloni (humble), but on either higher or lower parameter levels and, for some parameters, also to a different degree. The latter is the reason for significant interactions STANCE*COUNTRY that emerged (all with $p < 0.001$) in the ANOVAs of three parameters: inter-pausal-unit duration, Hammarberg index, and turn-overlap duration. However, since all interactions are ordinal, we disregard them in the presentation of the results and focus on the main effects only.

For example, besides the differences due to STANCE, the two Italian politicians generally pause less often in their speech (χ^2 [1] = 14.3, $p < 0.001$) and speak in longer inter-pausal units than the two American politicians (F[1,310] = 19.0, $p < 0.001$). The whole speech melody (i.e. pitch register) is also produced at a higher level by the Italian than by the American politicians (pitch level: F[1,310] = 12.8, $p < 0.001$; pitch minimum: F[1,310] = 3.9, $p = 0.04$; pitch maximum: F[1,310] = 9.3, $p = 0.001$). The American politicians have a higher Hammarberg index, though (F [1,310] = 8.8, $p = 0.002$). Finally, our data suggest that political TV interviews in Italy are generally characterized by a higher conversation dynamics than TV interviews in the USA, as we found per minute more competitive turn-taking events (χ^2 [1] = 5.9, $p = 0.01$) and more overlapping turns (χ^2 [1] = 5.2, $p = 0.02$), as well as longer turn overlaps (F[1,310] = 15.6, $p < 0.001$).

5.4   Discussion and Conclusion

According to Simone Weil, 'Humility is primarily a quality of attention' (1991) and despite many other philosophers had woven its praises, within political persuasion studies its persuasive effects have been neglected, focusing mainly on the expression of power. Recently D'Errico and Poggi (2019), starting from the definition of 'humble stance' in communicative terms, observed the bodily signals of humble politicians, showing how a leader's words, gestures, posture, facial expression can be cues of humility features like equality, informality, empathy. The aim of the present study is to explore features of humility associated with a speaker's tone-of-voice, by comparing two pairs of popular politicians from Usa (Obama vs Trump) and Italy (Gentiloni vs Salvini) during TV interviews. From results clear differences emerged between humble and dominant, involving prosodic characteristics from basically all fields of conversation behavior and tone of voice. Mainly three things distinguish the two types of politicians in both countries/cultures: (1) dominant leaders show a higher level of emotionality/expressiveness or arousal in their speech, reflecting here in a higher pitch register and variability as well as in a faster speaking rate; (2) they use a voice quality (Hammarberg & Formant dispersion) that signals urgency (we need to act now!!), power (acoustically larger body size), angriness or righteous indignation (we all know I am right and you/they are not!), and thrusting. (3) dominant politicians also behave dominant/aggressive in a conversation, they talk rather than listen to what others (the TV host) have to say. Humble politicians talk without major interruptions, they rather repair their sentences and start over again (even multiple times) before they dare to stop talking and think before speaking, as the resulting silent pause could be used by the TV host to take the initiative. If the TV host tries to take the initiative they often simply continue talking (a lot louder also), sometimes even shouting the TV host down until he stop stalking.

These tone-of-voice characteristics and conversation behavior were qualitatively the same across the two countries, while from the quantitative point of view: the cultural differences can be reported mainly on Speaking & Pausing (i.e. silent pauses) and Speech melody parameters (i.e. pitch level), while other parameters need to be tested also in other speaking contexts.

More in general, in light of these first results we can discuss which of the parameters identified as characteristic of humble politicians are associated with the ones observed in charismatic leaders. According to these results, there are characteristics of humble politicians which are similar to those analyzed as charismatic (Niebuhr et al. 2019): the shorter IPU durations, the frequent silent pauses, and the higher formant dispersion is what charismatic speakers have in common with humble speakers. From another point of view the faster speaking rate, the larger pitch variation, and the higher levels of mean pitch and the Hammarberg index, for example, is what charismatic (as opposed to non-/less charismatic) speakers share with the dominant speakers. So, in other words, the charismatic speakers combine the urgent, powerful tone-of voice and the high emotionality of dominant speakers, with the smaller acoustic body size, positiveness, and interactional openness of humble speakers. On top come some perhaps charisma-specific parameter settings/changes, such as an extended pitch range and lower rather than higher pitch minima. Altogether, this shows that charismatic speech is based on a separate phonetic-prosodic profile that differs from "dominant" and "humble", but in parts overlaps with these two other profiles. Nevertheless, how strong this overlap actually is (for other parameters not analyzed here, such as emphatic-accent frequency, loudness level and variation, rhyhtmic variability, reduction level in consonant and vowel articulation etc.) still needs to be determined in future studies.

References

Boersma, P.: Praat, a system for doing phonetics by computer. Glot Int. **5**(9/10), 341–345 (2001)

Castelfranchi, C.: Micro-macro constitution of power. ProtoSociology Int. J. Interdiscip. Res. **18–19**, 208–265 (2003)

De Looze, C., Hirst, D.J.: Detecting changes in key and range for the automatic modelling and coding of intonation. In: Speech Prosody 2008, Campinas, Brazil (2008)

De Jong, N.H., Wempe, T.: Praat script to detect syllable nuclei and measure speech rate automatically. Behav. Res. Methods **41**(2), 385–390 (2009)

D'Errico, F., Poggi, I.: Tracking a leader's humility and its emotions from body, face and voice. In: Web Intelligence, vol. 17, no. 1, pp. 63–74. IOS Press (2019)

D'Errico, F., Poggi, I.: "Humble" politicians and their multimodal communication. In: Gervasi, O., et al. (eds.) ICCSA 2017. LNCS, vol. 10406, pp. 705–717. Springer, Cham (2017). https://doi.org/10.1007/978-3-319-62398-6_50

D'Errico, F.: Humility based persuasion: Individual differences in elicited emotions and politician evaluation. (forth.)

D'Errico, F., Signorello, R., Demolin, D., Poggi, I.: The perception of charisma from voice: a cross-cultural study. In: 2013 Humaine Association Conference on Affective Computing and Intelligent Interaction (ACII), pp. 552–557. IEEE (2013)

D'Errico, F., Poggi, I.: Blame the opponent! Effects of multimodal discrediting moves in public debates. Cogn. Comput. **4**(4), 460–476 (2012a)

D'Errico, F., Poggi, I., Vincze, L.: Discrediting signals. A model of social evaluation to study discrediting moves in political debates. J. Multimodal User Interfaces **6**(3–4), 163–178 (2012b)

Fitch, W.T.: Vocal tract length and formant frequency dispersion correlate with body size in rhesus macaques. J. Acoust. Soc. Am. **102**, 1213–1222 (1997)

Fogg, B.J.: Persuasive technology: using computers to change what we think and do. Ubiquity 5 (2002)

Franzoni, V., Milani, A., Nardi, D.: Emotional machines: the next revolution. In: Web Intelligence, vol. 17, no. 1, pp. 1–7. IOS Press (2019)

Hammarberg, B., Fritzell, B., Gauffin, J., Sundberg, J., Wedin, L.: Perceptual and acoustic correlates of abnormal voice qualities. Acta Otolaryngol. **90**, 441–451 (1980)

Heldner, M.: Detection thresholds for gaps, overlaps and nogap-no-overlaps. J. Acoust. Soc. Am. **130**, 508–513 (2011)

Liu, X., Xu, Y.: Body size projection and its relation to emotional speech—evidence from Mandarin Chinese. In: Proceedings of Speech Prosody 2014, Dublin, pp. 974–977 (2014)

Niebuhr, O., Voße, J., Brem, A.: What makes a charismatic speaker? A computer-based acoustic-prosodic analysis of Steve Jobs tone of voice. Comput. Hum. Behav. **64**, 366–382 (2016). https://doi.org/10.1016/j.chb.2016.06.059

Niebuhr, O., Ochoa, S.G.: Do sound segments contribute to sounding charismatic? Evidence from a case study of Steve Jobs' and Mark Zuckerberg's vowel spaces. Int. J. Acoust. Vib. (2019, in press)

Nordström, H., Laukka, P., Thingujam, N.S., Schubert, E., Elfenbein, H.A.: Emotion appraisal dimensions inferred from vocal expressions are consistent across cultures: a comparison between Australia and India. R. Soc. open sci. **4**, 170912 (2017). https://doi.org/10.1098/rsos.170912

Poggi, I.: The "seeds" of charisma: Multimodal rhetoric of Mussolini's discourse. In: Tseronis, A., Forceville, C. (eds.) Multimodal Argumentation and Rhetoric in Media Genres, pp. 263–290. John Benjamins, Amsterdam (2017)

Poggi, I.: Mind, Hands, Face and Body. A Goal and Belief View of Multimodal Communication, pp. 1–432. Weidler (2007)

Poggi, I., D'Errico, F.: Dominance signals in debates. In: Salah, A.A., Gevers, T., Sebe, N., Vinciarelli, A. (eds.) HBU 2010. LNCS, vol. 6219, pp. 163–174. Springer, Heidelberg (2010). https://doi.org/10.1007/978-3-642-14715-9_16

Signorello, R., D'Errico, F., Poggi, I., Demolin, D.: How charisma is perceived from speech. A multidimensional approach. In: Proceedings of IEEE Social Computation, Amsterdam, 3–5 September, pp. 435–440. IEEE Computer Society (2012)

Vincze, L., Poggi, I., D'Errico, F.: Vagueness and dreams: analysis of body signals in vague dream telling. In: Salah, A.A., Ruiz-del-Solar, J., Meriçli, Ç., Oudeyer, P.Y. (eds.) HBU 2012. LNCS, vol. 7559, pp. 77–89. Springer, Heidelberg (2012). https://doi.org/10.1007/978-3-642-34014-7_7

Walker, M.B., Trimboli, C.: Smooth transitions in conversational interactions. J. Soc. Psychol. **117**, 305–306 (1982)

Weber, M.: The Theory of Social and Economic Organization. Oxford University Press, New York, USA (1920)

Weidman, A.C., Cheng, J.T., Tracy, J.L.: The psychological structure of humility. J. Pers. Soc. Psychol. **114**(1), 153 (2018)

Weilhammer, K., Rabold, S.: Durational aspects in turn taking. In: Proceedings of the International Conference of Phonetic Sciences (2003)

Xu, Y.: ProsodyPro — a tool for large-scale systematic prosody analysis. In: Proceedings of Tools and Resources for the Analysis of Speech Prosody (TRASP 2013), Aix-en-Provence, France, pp. 7–10 (2013)

Xu, Y., Lee, A., Wu, W.-L., Liu, X., Birkholz, P.: Human vocal attractiveness as signaled by body size projection. PLoS ONE **8**(4), e623 (2013)

Computer-Generated Speaker Charisma and Its Effects on Human Actions in a Car-Navigation System Experiment - or How Steve Jobs' Tone of Voice Can Take You Anywhere

Oliver Niebuhr[1]([⊠]) [iD] and Jan Michalsky[2] [iD]

[1] Centre for Industrial Electronics, University of Southern Denmark,
Sonderborg, Denmark
oniebuhr@mci.sdu.dk
[2] Chair of Technology Management, University of Erlangen,
Nuremberg, Germany
jan.michalsky@fau.de

Abstract. A particularly persuasive (charismatic) tone of voice has a far reaching influence on people's opinions and actions. However, does this also apply if the charismatic tone of voice is produced by a computer, and if this computer asks people to act against better knowledge? Addressing these questions, an experiment was set up in which 30 locals of Sonderborg/DK were asked to conduct a test drive with a car from the marina to the university campus of the city. The test drive was conducted on the pretext of assessing a newly developed retrofit car navigation system that provides voice instructions only. The locals did not know that the system was only a remote-controlled mock-up that, moreover, started giving its driver wrong instructions after about half of the trip. The instructions got successively falser, until the only option to get to the university campus was to make a complete U-turn. We measured the point at which the drivers aborted the test drive in two conditions. In the first one, the system spoke with the more charismatic tone of voice of Steve Jobs. In the second one, it spoke with the less charismatic tone of voice of Mark Zuckerberg. Results show that drivers followed the navigation system's increasingly worsening instructions significantly longer in the Steve Jobs condition, and that the system received higher quality, trustworthiness, and purchase ratings if it spoke with Steve Jobs' tone of voice. Results are discussed in terms of persuasive technology and implications for charisma/leadership analyses and training.

Keywords: Speaker charisma · Prosody · Tone of voice ·
Text-to-speech-synthesis · Navigation system · Steve jobs · Mark zuckerberg

© Springer Nature Switzerland AG 2019
S. Misra et al. (Eds.): ICCSA 2019, LNCS 11620, pp. 375–390, 2019.
https://doi.org/10.1007/978-3-030-24296-1_31

1 Introduction

1.1 The Importance of Charismatic Speech

Charisma has become a key concept of persuasiveness, influence, and leadership (Grabo et al. 2017; Antonakis and Gardner 2017). Although research on charisma has a long tradition and is firmly rooted in diverse scientific fields, ranging from political sciences through psychology to economics, progress towards reaching an actual understanding has only been made in the past two decades (Antonakis et al. 2016; Niebuhr et al. 2017). While older studies treat charisma as a magical and indescribable property, innate to certain individuals (Weber 1947), it is now clearly defined and operationalized as a competence of "values-based, symbolic, and emotion-laden leader signaling" (Antonakis et al. 2016: 304), a skill that all speakers possess to various, context-specific degrees and that they can train and improve. Most importantly, numerous studies have shown that charisma significantly influences listeners by positively affecting motivation and inspiration (Towler 2003), productivity (Howell and Frost 1989, Antonakis et al. 2011), attention (Towler et al. 2014), trust, and confidence in the speaker's abilities (Davis et al. 2017, Niebuhr and Skarnitzl 2019). These influences are the basis for the ability of speakers to change people's actions, attitudes, and opinions. One potential reason for these extraordinary capabilities of charisma may lie in the finding that charisma can bypass rational thinking and affect a listener's emotions and emotional decisions more directly by inhibiting activity in the medial and dorsolateral areas of the prefrontal cortex of the brain, which contribute to abstract reasoning and rational decision-making (Schjødt et al. 2011). Or, in the words of Soorjoo (2012): The most ancient "reptilian" part of our brain functions as a gatekeeper in all decision-making processes, and charisma signals are like the permit to pass by that gatekeeper.

1.2 Phonetic Exponents of Perceived Speaker Charisma

Advancements in the field of phonetics have contributed greatly to the demystification of charismatic speech. Fox Cabane (2012) already pointed out that "nonverbal modes of communication are hardwired in our brains, much deeper than the more recent language-processing [i.e. word-related] abilities, and they affect us more strongly" (p.17). Phonetic research has refined this statement in showing that it is actually the speaker's tone of voice (rather than body language, the other nonverbal mode) that plays a vital role and represents one if not *the* primary trigger of perceived speaker charisma (Chen et al. 2014, Scherer et al. 2012). Furthermore, phonetic research successively identified the acoustic parameters of charismatic speech and determined how and to what extent they contribute to perceived charisma. Charismatic speakers employ acoustic characteristics such as an enhanced variation in F0 (the acoustic equivalent of perceived pitch), an expanded F0 range, an increased speaking rate, a larger number of silent pauses within and between sentences, fewer and shorter filled pauses (Touati 1993; Strangert and Gustafson 2008; Rosenberg and Hirschberg 2009; D'Errico et al. 2013; Niebuhr et al. 2016a, b, Niebuhr et al. 2018a, b; Niebuhr and Fischer 2019), a strategic placement of empathic accents (Niebuhr 2010, Niebuhr et al.

2016a), as well as a higher level of articulatory precision (Niebuhr and Gonzalez 2019) and a more balanced spectral-energy distribution (Niebuhr et al. 2018b). In conclusion, the phonetics research has – to a large degree – identified the complex constellation of acoustic features that makes a speaker sound more charismatic.

1.3 Using Machines for Understanding Perceived Speaker Charisma

Apart from a few exceptions (e.g., Towler 2003; Antonakis et al. 2011), previous studies mainly tested the influence of acoustic features on the perception of speaker charisma by means of listener ratings (Touati 1993; Strangert and Gustafson 2008; Rosenberg and Hirschberg 2009; D'Errico et al. 2013; Berger et al. 2017; Niebuhr et al. 2018a, b; Jokisch et al. 2018; Niebuhr and Fischer 2019). The first one who, with a focus on tone-of-voice acoustics (i.e. speech prosody), consistently went beyond this rating paradigm was Fischer (2018). She used robots to test people's reactions to differently charismatic voices. These voices (as well as the corresponding sentences that were spoken) were based on computer-generated text-to-speech synthesis (TTS). TTS has the advantage that acoustic parameters, including all listed in 1.2 above, can be very precisely controlled and manipulated, while all other charisma-related factors like the choice of words and the outer appearance of the robot are kept constant. Moreover, robots are, unlike real humans or videos of humans, neutral with respect to aspects like gender, age, attire, and social status. Charismatic voices in robots have been found to affect listeners' opinions and actions in a way similar to that of real charismatic speakers. For example, with respect to actions, the charismatic robots of Fischer (2018) made people fill out longer questionnaires, book certain sightseeing trips, and even choose fruits over sweets as a reward after completing a task.

1.4 The Goal of This Study

In this study we are taking the findings of robots influencing human behavior through vocal charisma one step further. All previous experiments of Fischer and colleagues tested effects of charismatic voices of robots in settings in which listeners had to choose between two equally viable options. By contrast, in this study, we ask whether charisma can influence a listener's choice even if the suggested option is clearly wrong and listeners would have to act against better knowledge. Furthermore, we not only want to ask *whether*, but also *to what degree* a charismatic voice is able to influence listener behavior.

To this end, we designed an experiment which investigates the question how well a (computer-generated) charismatic speaker can make people follow in the very sense of "following", i.e. to obey the instructions of a mock-up car navigation system. The navigation system was fitted with two different tone-of-voice profiles, constituted by a set acoustic features with either a more or a less charismatic parameter setting. These two different tone-of-voice settings are then combined with the same lexical content and the same synthetic TTS voice. Since we are not only interested in *if* but also in *how far* listeners are willing to follow a charismatic voice, we measured the charismatic influence in terms of the duration listeners were following wrong instructions until they aborted the test drive by disobeying the navigation system's instructions.

The parameter settings for the more charismatic condition were derived from the tone-of-voice profile of Steve Jobs, who was an exceptionally charismatic speaker, greatly affecting the opinions of his listeners and enhancing trust in his company (Niebuhr et al. 2016b). The less charismatic tone-of-voice profile was derived from speeches by Mark Zuckerberg, who, unlike Jobs, is as a less charismatic and convincing speaker. These assumptions about the two speakers have already been confirmed for their acoustic profiles by previous perception studies with depersonalized, low-pass-filtered speech (Niebuhr et al. 2018a; Niebuhr and Gonzalez 2019).

In conclusion, this paper investigates whether listeners are more inclined to follow purposefully wrong instructions of a navigation system when fitted with the charismatic acoustic features of Steve Jobs than when fitted with the less charismatic acoustic features of Mark Zuckerberg.

2 Method

2.1 Participants of the Test Drive

A total of 30 participants were included in the experiment, 15 males and 15 females. They were all advanced students on campus Sønderborg of the University of Southern Denmark (SDU) and between 20 and 25 years old (male average 21.5 years; female average 22.3 years). All had a European driver's license for at least 2 years and were well familiar with the city of Sønderborg and the topology of its streets insofar as they had continuously lived in Sønderborg for several years prior to the experiment. Furthermore, all participants were proficient non-native speakers of English (at least level B2 according to university-internal study-entry tests). None of the participants had regular access to an own car with an onboard GPS navigation system (but all had some experience with smart phone navigation apps).

Half of the participants (i.e. 15, 8 males, 7 females) were randomly assigned to Steve Jobs' tone-of-voice condition (SJ), the other half (7 males, 8 females) was assigned to Mark Zuckerberg's tone-of-voice condition (MZ).

2.2 Map and Route of the Test Drive

The route that the participants had to drive in the experiment was designed such that the entire test drive would be at most 15 km long (about 50% of it freeway). Thus, a single experimental test-drive session would not take longer than 15 to 20 min. In addition, the route was created such that the navigation system would give correct instructions for about 1.5 km, in order to familiarize participants with the experimental situation and build up trust in the system. After these initial 1.5 km, the system's route guidance successively led away from the shortest ideal route and the final destination of the test drive. More specifically, there were 4 escalation levels, which are also shown in Fig. 1. Each escalation level was similarly long, i.e. 1.5–2.5 km, and represented by at least two semantically and syntactically similar oral instructions (prompts) of the navigation system.

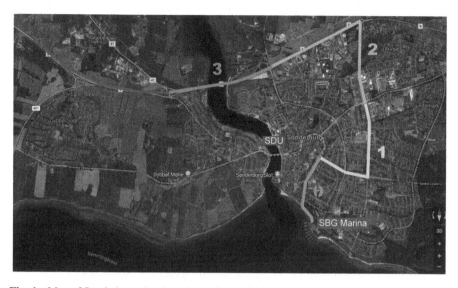

Fig. 1. Map of Sønderborg showing place of departure and destination of the test drive, as well as the ideal route (green) and the stepwise deviations from this route (1–4) demanded by the navigation system. Edited screenshot of Google Maps.

Place of departure was the large parking lot at the Sonderborg Marina (SBG Marina). The test-drive's destination was the large parking lot on the university campus, on the opposite side of the Sonderborg Fjord (SDU). Participants did not know that they would actually never arrive there when following the navigation system's oral instructions. Place of departure and destination were both well known to all participants; and they were close enough together for the correct and ideal (shortest and fastest) route to be obvious to all participants.

The correct and ideal route guidance (escalation level 0) is shown in green in Fig. 1, with a dotted line starting from where the wrong instructions of the navigation system began. Escalation level 1 (yellow) was identifiable by all participants as an obvious detour, but one that still left the door open for many alternative routes that would all lead to the destination with only a little extra time. Escalation level 2 (orange), with its freeway entrance, already meant a substantial detour and extra time and left over only a few alternative routes to the destination. Escalation level 3 (coral) ran past the last freeway exit in front of the fjord bridge, thus leaving over only one possible route guidance to the destination, i.e. the freeway exit immediately after the bridge. Escalation level 4 (red) also ran past this exit and hence led away from very last alternative route to the destination. Thus, except for a U-turn, there was no possibility left anymore for the participants to reach their destination.

An abort of the test drive is defined here as the moment at which the driver no longer followed the instructions of the navigation system and either stopped at the roadside (in order to discuss the subsequent actions with the experimenter) or autonomously took an alternative route to the destination without consulting the experimenter.

If the participant did still not abort the test drive at escalation level 4, then the experimenter aborted the test drive after one more minute by asking the participant to turn around and drive back to the destination (SDU parking lot) without further assistance from the navigation system. After having arrived at the destination, the experimenter asked the participant to fill out a final questionnaire, the discussion of which had then concluded the experimental session. An experimental session took about 30 min, including the participant's briefing and de-briefing.

2.3   Stimuli: Design and Synthesis of Navigation Prompts

The individual stimuli of the navigation system were generated with a free online TTS tool (https://text2speech.us). The TTS voice was "Matthew" and selected for its fluent speech and sonorous voice. "Matthew" also represented American English speech. Thus, the synthetic "Matthew" was in accord with the real speakers SJ and MZ whose prosodic profiles were to be imprinted on the voice in a subsequent step.

Eighteen individual navigation prompts were generated. They corresponded to the prompts of a regular navigation system in length, syntax and instruction content. The navigation prompts were preceded by two supplementary voice prompts, with which the navigation system introduced itself to the driver at the beginning of the experiment and in which it asked the driver to start the navigation by saying "GO". This two-part introduction was about 30 s long.

- TTS: "Hello. I am your new retrofit navigation system. You can install me subsequently in any car radio... even without much cost and effort. Great, right?! Today, I take you from Sonderborg Marina to the University of Southern Denmark on the opposite side of the fjord." Are you ready? I can start right away! Please say "go" to start the navigation.
- Driver (typically after reconfirming eye contact with the experimenter): "Go!"
- TTS: "Thank you, the navigation starts now. I will guide you safely to your destination. Enjoy the trip with me."

The two initial voice prompts were integrated into the experiment for two reasons. First, they were supposed to enhance the driver's trust in the navigation system and embody the system in an acoustic form. Second, the two initial voice prompts were the system's longest coherent stretches of speech in the experiment. Placing them at the beginning of the session allowed the prosodic differences between the SJ and the MZ conditions to be clearly established before the test drive began. Also, the charisma effects of these prosodic differences had a chance to unfold already before driving.

A total of 20 TTS items were generated, including the two initial voice prompts. The total duration of all 20 items (henceforth stimuli) was 1 min and 38 s (or 98 s).

Note that it is a bit unusual to use a male voice for navigation prompts in the car. Voices of navigation systems are usually female (Nass and Yen 2012:7). However, here we had to conduct manipulations of the stimuli based on empirical prosodic profiles of two male speakers. Neither the target values of this manipulation nor their persuasive effects on participants can be transferred 1:1 from men to women (Novák-Tót et al., 2017; Jokisch et al., 2018; Niebuhr et al. Niebuhr et al. 2018a, b). Therefore, we had to use a male voice for the stimuli of the navigation system.

2.4   Stimuli: Creation of Tone-of-Voice Conditions SJ and MZ

After all 20 stimuli had been generated using the free online TTS tool, the two prosodic charisma conditions of the experiment were generated. The manipulation was carried out by means of PSOLA resynthesis in PRAAT (Moulines and Charpentier 1990). As was stated in the Introduction, the acoustic tone-of-voice profiles of SJ and MZ served as a template for the manipulation.

Table 1. Acoustic tone-of-voice profiles (of selected PSOLA-compatible parameters) of SJ and MZ, as determined in a speech-corpus analysis by Niebuhr et al. (2016b).

Acoustic-prosodic parameter	Mean value SJ	Mean value MZ
F0 level (Hz)	221.4	178.3
F0 range (semitones)	23.1	12.1
Speaking rate (syll/s)	4.7	6.1
IPU duration (s)	1.3	1.5
Emphatic-accent frequency (cpm)	5.4	1.2

Five melodic characteristics were manipulated, whose positive correlation with perceived charisma and the persuasive power of a speaker had been attested in previous studies (see 1.2). The five manipulated parameters were: F0 level, F0 range, speaking rate, duration of inter-pausal speech units (IPUs, i.e. how long speakers talk in between two audible breaks), and emphatic-accent frequency (i.e., words whose pitch-accented syllables showed a strong lengthening of either the initial consonant or the syllable nucleus, see Niebuhr 2010). Table 1 shows the mean values obtained for SJ and MZ on these five parameters.

The PSOLA manipulation was performed such that each of the 20 stimuli matched the melody profiles of SJ and MZ in terms of the five mean values. In the case of the emphatic-accent frequency, however, this only applied to the two initial voice prompts. The following 18 navigation prompts were manipulated such that in the SJ condition all of them and in the MZ condition none of them contained an emphatic accent.

Note that the result of the manipulation was not that the navigation system spoke with the actual voices of SJ or MZ. The voice quality was exactly the same (= "Matthew") in both experimental conditions (as was the stimulus wording). Only five aspects of the tone of voice, i.e. the system's speech melody, had been changed.

2.5   Car

The car used for the experiment was a Nissan Qashqai J10 (2014 model) that neither had a built-in navigation system nor a big LCD information screen, see Fig. 2.

2.6   Procedure of the Test Drive

The experiment was conducted in individual experimental sessions per participant. Participants were invited to the experiment on the pretext that they would take part in a

Fig. 2. Pictures of the Nissan Qashqai used for the experimental test drive of all 30 participants.

usability test. At the beginning of each session, the participant was informed that s/he would be supposed to drive with the provided car from Sønderborg Marina to SDU campus Sønderborg, and that the purpose of the short trip would be to test the practicability and usability of a retrofit navigation system, developed by an SDU engineering team in collaboration with Danish industrial partners. The advantage of this innovation would be that it can be installed in any older car radio system without much cost and effort. In consequence, however, the navigation would be fully speech-based, without the visual support of a separate display. To examine if and how well this works was said to be the primary aim of the usability test.

After participants had given their written consent to take part in the experiment, both participant and experimenter got into the car; the participant on the driver's seat and the experimenter in the backseat of the car, opposite the driver's seat.

The participant was told that the experimenter would be on the trip for two reasons; firstly, because the car insurance policy would require his physical presence; and secondly, because the experimenter would take notes on his laptop about how he observes and assesses the test drive. These notes would then be added to the usability ratings that the participant were to make after the test drive by filling out a prepared questionnaire.

That is, the participant was left in the dark for the duration of the entire trip that the navigation system was a mock-up and that individual stimuli (navigation prompts) were triggered in a Wizard-of-Oz fashion (Fischer 2018) at the appropriate time by the experimenter in the back seat. The stimuli were played from the experimenter's laptop at a pre-adjusted loudness level that was kept constant for all 30 participants.

It was stressed to the participant that s/he could abort the experiment (the usability test) at any time. Questions, expressions of uncertainty and other similar comments to the experimenter, however, were not allowed during the trip. The participant was told that, ideally, s/he would behave as if the experimenter were not present at all in the backseat. Upon oral confirmation that this was understood, the trip began with the (Wizard-of-Oz) playback of the first introductory navigation prompt (2.3) by the experimenter.

When the test drive had been aborted either by the participant or by the experimenter after reaching escalation level 4, the participant drove directly to the SDU parking lot. After the car had arrived there and the engine was turned off, the participant was asked to fill out a questionnaire. The questionnaire recorded the personal data of the participant and ended with the following ten questions about the navigation system itself.

(1) How do you rate the quality of the navigation system's speech prompts?
(2) How do you rate the intelligibility of the navigation system's speech prompts?
(3) Were the instructions of the navigation system always clear?
(4) Did the navigation system guide you on the fastest way to your destination? If not, what do you think was the reason for the detour?
    (4a) The navigation system may have attempted to bypass a traffic jam, accident, or road closure,
    (4b) The navigation system is working properly, but the maps or the installation were faulty, or the engineers have made programming errors,
    (4c) The navigation system itself is simply malfunctioning.
(5) How much did you trust the navigation system while driving?
(6) How likely is it that you would buy the navigation system for yourself?
(7) How likely is it that you would recommend the navigation system to your friends and relatives?

The question triplets (1)–(3) and (5)–(7) were answered on the basis of a 7-point Likert scale from 1 'very bad' or 'not at all' to 7 'very good' or 'very much'. Question (4) and its sub-questions were answered by ticking 'yes' or 'no'. Multiple 'yes/no' answers were allowed for (4a–c).

Only after each participant had completed the entire questionnaire, s/he was informed that the navigation system was just a mock-up and actually remotely controlled by the experimenter in the back seat. The participants were told that they did not even take part in a usability test. The real purpose of the experiment had been to test at what point they would abort the test drive and how that would correlate with the navigation system's speech melody, of which there were two variants, i.e. two experimental conditions. No participant indicated that s/he had guessed the actual aim of the experiment.

Note that the experiment was only carried out in between 10.00 in the morning and 14.00 in the afternoon, hence avoiding the rush hours on the streets of Sønderborg.

3 Results

Statistical pilot tests showed that drivers' gender had no separate significant effects on the driving or subsequent rating behaviors. Therefore, we disregarded this factor in the presentation of the results.

Figure 3 shows in percentages how many of the 30 drivers did not or did not abort the test drive at the escalation levels 1–4. Five results are worth being pointed out separately. First, none of the 30 drivers aborted the test drive already at escalation level 0 at which the navigation system still gave the correct instructions. Second, 20% of all drivers in the MZ-condition aborted the test drive already at escalation level 1, i.e. immediately after the navigation system started giving the first wrong instructions (and although there were still many alternative routes left that led to the destination). In the

SJ condition, only 6.7% of all drivers aborted the test drive at this early stage. Third, in the MZ condition the majority of drivers, i.e. 40%, aborted the test drive at escalation level 3 and only a minority of 13.3% continued the test drive until the final escalation level 4. In the SJ condition, these two numbers were equally large, i.e. 26.7%. Fourth, when there was only one possible route guidance left to the destination, i.e. at escalation level 3, a majority 53.3% of all drivers still followed the navigation system's instructions in the SJ condition, as opposed to a minority of only 20% in the MZ condition. Five, and probably most noteworthy, even after escalation level 4 had been reached and no option other than a U-turn was left, more than one quarter of all drivers in the SJ condition, i.e. 26.7%, did not abort the test drive so that the experimenter had to intervene and ask the driver to abort the test drive. In the MZ condition, this only applied to 6.7% of all drivers.

Due to a lack of normally distributed data, conservative Mann-Whitney U tests were conducted to compare the drivers' behavior in the two independent samples represented by the SJ and MZ conditions. Dependent variable was the point in time at which the test drive was aborted. This variable was quantified, in one U test, in terms of

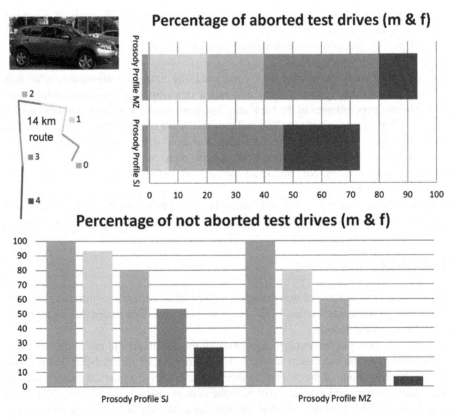

Fig. 3. Summary of test-drive abort/continuation percentages in the SJ and MZ conditions (n = 15).

the abort frequency at the 5 escalation levels and, in another U test, in terms of the chronological number of the navigation prompt (1–20) after which each driver aborted the test drive. The U test on the escalation levels showed a trend towards an overall earlier test-drive abort in the MZ condition (U[15,15] = 72.5, p = 0.100); in the U test on the navigation prompt count, this trend became significant (U[15,15] = 56.0, p = 0.021). We also tried to use the actual driving time as a dependent variable, but it turned out in pilot driving tests that this parameter is too susceptible to random and daytime-related changes in traffic density and traffic-light circuits. Thus, it could not be used for statistical testing.

Figures 4 and 5 show the results of the participants' navigation-system ratings in the questionnaire that concluded the experimental session. Again, Mann-Whitney U tests were used to compare the ratings in the SJ and MZ conditions for the Likert scales summarized in Fig. 4. The yes-no question frequencies in the SJ and MZ conditions were statistically analyzed in terms of an overall Chi-squared test, supplemented by Z-Score Proportion tests for the individual yes-no questions.

It is obvious that the TTS voice "Matthew" was rated better with the SJ manipulation than with the MZ manipulation. Only the clarity of instructions was rated to be similarly good in the SJ and MZ conditions. Besides this exception, the navigation system with SJ's acoustic tone-of-voice charisma profile was rated to have a higher speech quality (U[15,15] = 25.0, p < 0.001) and to be more intelligible (U [15,15] = 32.5, p < 0.001). In addition, compared to the MZ condition, drivers in the SJ condition stated that they had more trust in the navigation system (U[15,15] = 33.0, p < 0.001). There was also a higher willingness of the participants to buy the navigation system for themselves (U[15,15] = 61.0, p = 0.031) and to recommend it to friends and relatives (U[15,15] = 64.5, p = 0.048), if it was based on SJ's rather than by MZ's tone-of-voice profile.

Regarding the yes-no questions, results show that all drivers in both conditions (100%) were aware of the fact that the navigation system had not guided them on the fastest and shortest way to their destination. Besides this general agreement, there is one big difference between the SJ and MZ conditions. In the SJ condition, drivers showed by a large majority of 80.4% the willingness to explain the unexpected route guidance of the navigation system in a positive way, i.e. in terms of an intended avoidance of traffic jams, accidents, or roadblocks. Another large majority of 73.2% was (additionally) of the opinion that, if the unexpected route guidance was not intended, then the failure had been caused by programmers, engineers or faulty maps. Only a minority of 40.2% saw in the unexpected route guidance a failure of the navigation system itself. Exactly the opposite was true for the drivers in the MZ condition. The vast majority, i.e. 73.2%, ascribed the unexpected route guidance to a direct failure of the navigation system. About two thirds of the drivers, i.e. 66.9% also considered blaming programmers, engineers, or the underlying maps for the failure in route guidance. Only a slim majority of 53.6% were willing to see the unexpected route guidance as a clever, intended solution of the navigation system to a traffic problem on the ideal route to the destination.

That is, ratings *de*creased from 'no failure' through 'external failure' to 'system failure' in the SJ condition, whereas they *in*creased in this order in the MZ condition.

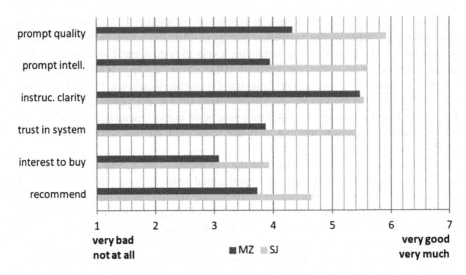

Fig. 4. Mean ratings (from 1 = negative to 7 = positive) on the Likert scales of the concluding questionnaire in the SJ and MZ conditions (n = 15).

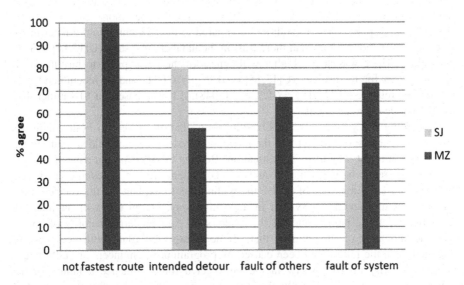

Fig. 5. Percentages of yes/agree answers for the 4 yes-no questions of the concluding questionnaire in the SJ and MZ conditions (n = 15).

This diametrically opposed rating behavior came out significantly in a Chi-squared test ($\chi^2[2]$ = 15.5, p < 0.001). Separate Z-Score Proportion tests showed that it were particularly the differences in 'intended detour' (z[15,15] = 1.7, p = 0.09) and 'fault of system' (z[15,15] = −1.8, p = 0.06) that caused this overall significance.

4   Discussion

The aim of this study was to test if and to what degree the difference between a more and a less charismatic acoustic tone-of-voice profile (represented by melody parameters accessible to PSOLA manipulation and resynthesis) is able to induce a measureable change in listener behavior. We tested this question on the basis of the tone-of-voice profiles of SJ and MZ. The measureable change in behavior was operationalized by a car driver's trust in, and hence his/her obedience to the oral instructions of a mock-up navigation system. That is, the question was if and at what point drivers would abort their test drive with the mock-up car navigation system, and whether this point differs depending on whether the system's oral instructions have SJ's or MZ's acoustic tone-of-voice profile.

The results show that in the less charismatic condition (MZ), participants aborted the test drive after significantly fewer wrong instructions, with 20% disobeying the navigation system already after the first wrong prompt, when numerous alternative routes to the destination were still left. These 20% contrast with only about 7% in the more charismatic condition (SJ). At escalation level 3, when there was only one possible route left, 80% of the participants had already aborted the test drive in the less charismatic MZ condition, while over 50% were still following the navigation system's instructions in the more charismatic SJ condition. Finally, when the experiment entered the final stage at escalation level 4, at which the instructions lead the participants out of the city with the only remaining option being a U-turn, over 25% of the participants in the more charismatic SJ condition were still following the navigation system's instructions. In contrast, only 7% of the participants still obeyed the navigation system at level 4 if it spoke with MZ's less charismatic tone-of-voice profile. Accordingly, the power of melodic (tone-of-voice) charisma manifested itself in the present study in that it made listeners choose to follow wrong instructions against better knowledge much longer when the charisma signal was stronger, i.e. when the acoustic parameters conveying charisma had higher levels.

But why do listeners obey purposefully misleading instructions when presented in a charismatic way? Or, in other words, how does charisma make a voice persuasive? One possibility might be that charisma works through deception. Accordingly, the charismatic voice could have obscured the fact that the navigation system was in fact giving wrong instructions. However, the results of the debriefing questionnaire show that all 30 speakers were aware that the instructions given by the system were deviating from the ideal route, which contradicts this deception hypothesis. As explained above, charisma gets its persuasive quality by making a speaker sound competent and passionate, which, on the part of the listener, strengthens the willingness for an emotional investment in the speakers' goals and visions (Antonakis et al. 2016). Accordingly, another explanation for the behavior observed here is that listeners (drivers in this case) adhere to the message of a charismatic speaker, because the speaker signals trust and confidence in his/her abilities. The results of the debriefing questionnaire show that participants following the more charismatic SJ profile reported a significantly higher overall trust in the system. The participants stated that they were convinced that the deviating instructions were caused by the system intelligently and intentionally leading them around road blockages, accidents, or traffic jams. In contrast, participants in the MZ condition significantly more often attributed the deviating instructions to a failure of the system and an error in the given instructions. These findings support the trust hypothesis.

The remarkable special feature in the present study is that the lower/higher values of confidence and competence and hence the de/increase in trust are not attributed to a real human speaker but to a computer, i.e. a car navigation system. So, listeners project the human social signals of a charismatic voice onto a computer system that uses the voice. This has major implications for any technological hard- or software application out there that involves synthetic speech. Manufacturers will have to be aware that not only the voice itself has an impact on the user (e.g., how sonorant and attractive it is), but also how the charisma-related acoustic tone-of-voice features are employed by the synthetic voice. In the same way as a skilled use of charismatic tone-of-voice features would increase users' trust in the system, the wrong implementation of these features can drastically decrease trust and, thus, have major consequences for consumer satisfaction and product sales rates. This applies in particular, as trust is not the only issues that is at stage in a computer system's tone-of-voice design. As was shown in the present study, the participants of the SJ and MZ conditions also rated the system differently with respect to intelligibility, quality, and their willingness to buy the system and to recommend it to their friends, see also Chebat et al. (2007) for the link between charisma or persuasion and commercial success.

In conclusion, this study has three major implications. First, the acoustic features of a charismatic speech melody identified by previous studies elicit the expected effects even when presented solely on an auditory channel and with all other charisma-related features (like choice of words, voice, and body language) kept constant. Second, expanding on the findings of previous studies, we show that a charismatic tone of voice cannot only influence a listener's behavior towards one of two viable options but even make them choose a illogical option over a viable one. Accordingly, the effects of a charismatic speech melody on human behavior are even stronger than found in previous studies (Fischer 2018). Third, the effects of a charismatic tone of voice are not only applicable to real speakers, but can be transferred to synthetic voices of computer systems, as was suggested by previous research on charismatic robots (Fischer 2018). Thus, the correct implementation of a synthetic voice increases user trust and additionally enhances the overall perceived quality of a product and the willingness to buy and recommend it.

References

Antonakis, J., Bastardoz, N., Jacquart, P., Shamir, B.: Charisma: an ill-defined and ill-measured gift. Annu. Rev. Organ. Psychol. Organ. Behav. **3**(1), 293–319 (2016)

Antonakis, J., Fenley, M., Liechti, S.: Can charisma be taught? Tests of two interventions. Acad. Manag. Learn. Educ. **10**, 374–396 (2011)

Antonakis, J., Gardner, W.L.: Charisma: new frontiers. A special issue dedicated to the memory of Boas Shamir. Leadersh. Q. **28**(4), 471–472 (2017)

Berger, S., Niebuhr, O., Peters, B.: Winning over an audience – a perception-based analysis of prosodic features of charismatic speech (2017). In: Proceedings 43rd Annual Conference of the German Acoustical Society, Kiel, Germany, 1454–1457 (2017)

Chebat, J.C., Hedhli, K.E., Gélinas-Chebat, C., Boivin, R.: Voice and persuasion in a banking telemarketing context. Percept. Mot. Skills **104**, 419–437 (2007)

Chen, L., Feng, G., Joe, J., Leong, C.W., Kitchen, C., Lee, C.M.: Towards automated assessment of public speaking skills using multimodal cues. In: Proceedings of the 16th International Conference on Multimodal Interaction, Istanbul, Turkey, 200–203 (2014)

D'Errico, F., Signorello, R., Demolin, D., Poggi, I.: The perception of charisma from voice. A crosscultural study. In: Proceedings of the Humaine Association Conference on Affective Computing and Intelligent Interaction, Geneva, Switzerland, 552–557 (2013)

Davis, B.C., Hmieleski, K.M., Webb, J.W., Coombs, J.E.: Funders' positive affective reactions to entrepreneurs' crowd-funding pitches: the influence of perceived product creativity and entrepreneurial passion. J. Bus. Ventur. **32**, 90–106 (2017)

Fischer, K.: Talking to robots. In: Elmentaler, M., Niebuhr, O. (eds.) An den Rändern der Sprache. Notes of a lecture series at Kiel University. (2018) https://www.uni-kiel.de/pressemeldungen/index.php?pmid = 2018-084-rv-sprache&pr = 1.KielUniversity

Fox Cabane, O.: The Charisma Myth: How Anyone Can Master the Art and Science of Personal Magnetism. Penguin, New York (2012)

Grabo, A., Spisak, B.R., van Vugt, M.: Charisma as signal: an evolutionary perspective on charismatic leadership. Leadership Q. **28**(4), 473–485 (2017)

Howell, J.M., Frost, P.J.: A laboratory study of charismatic leadership. Organ. Behav. Human Decis. Process. **43**(2), 243–269 (1989)

Jokisch, O., Iaroshenko, V., Maruschke, M., Ding, H.: Influence of age, gender and sample duration on the charisma assessment of German speakers. In: Proceedings 29th Conference on Electronic Speech Signal Process, Ulm, Germany, 1–8 (2018)

Moulines, E., Charpentier, F.: Pitch-synchronous waveform processing tech-niques for text-to-speech synthesis using diphones. Speech Commun. **9**, 453–467 (1990)

Nass, C., Yen, C.: The Man Who Lied to His Laptop: What We Can Learn About Ourselves from Our Machines. Pinguin, London (2012)

Niebuhr, O.: On the phonetics of intensifying emphasis in German. Phonetica **67**, 170–198 (2010)

Niebuhr, O., Brem, A., Novák-Tót, E.: Prosodic constructions of charisma in business speeches – a contrastive acoustic analysis of Steve Jobs and Mark Zuckerberg. In: Proceedings of Speech Prosody, 8, Boston, USA (2016a)

Niebuhr, O., Voße, J., Brem, A.: What makes a charismatic speaker? A computer-based acoustic prosodic analysis of Steve Jobs tone of voice. Comput. Human Behav. **64**, 366–382 (2016b)

Niebuhr, O., Tegtmeier, S., Brem, A.: Advancing research and practice in entrepreneurship through speech analysis – from descriptive rhetorical terms to phonetically informed acoustic charisma metrics. J. Speech Sci. **6**, 3–26 (2017)

Niebuhr, O., Thumm, J., Michalsky, J.: Shapes and timing in charismatic speech – evidence from sounds and melodies. In: Proceedings of Speech Prosody, 9, Poznan, Poland (2018a)

Niebuhr, O., Skarnitzl, R., Tylecková, L.: The acoustic fingerprint of a charismatic voice - initial evidence from correlations between long-term spectral features and listener ratings. In: Proceedings of Speech Prosody, 9, Poznan, Poland, 359–363 (2018b)

Niebuhr, O., Gonzalez, S.: Do sound segments contribute to sound-ing charismatic? Evidence from acoustic vowel space analyses of Steve Jobs and Mark Zuckerberg. International Journal of Acoustics and Vibration 24 (2019)

Niebuhr, O., Skarnitzl, R.: Measuring a speaker's acoustic correlates of pitch - but which? A contrastive analysis based on perceived speaker charisma. In: Proceedings of ICPhS 2019, Melbourne, Australia, 1–5 (2019)

Niebuhr, O., Fischer, K.: Do not hesitate! – unless you do it shortly or nasally: how the phonetics of filled pauses determine their subjective frequency and perceived speaker performance. In: Proceedings 20th International Interspeech Conference, Graz, Austria, 1–5 (2019)

Novák-Tót, E., Niebuhr, O., Chen, A.: A gender bias in the acoustic-melodic features of charismatic speech? In: Proceedings of Interspeech 2018, Stockholm, Sweden, 2248–2252 (2017)

Rosenberg, A., Hirschberg, J.: Charisma perception from text and speech. Speech Commun. **51**, 640–655 (2009)

Scherer, S., Layher, G., Kane, J., Neumann, H., Campbell, N.: An audiovisual political speech analysis incorporating eye-tracking and perception data. In: Proceedings of the 8th International Conference on Language Resources and Evaluation, pp. 1114–1120 (2012)

Schjødt, U., Stodkilde-Jorgensen, H., Geertz, A.W., Lund, T.E., Roepstorff, A.: The power of charisma-perceived charisma inhibits the frontal executive network of believers in intercessory prayer. Soc. Cogn. Affect. Neurosci. **6**, 119–127 (2011)

Soorjoo, M.: Here's the Pitch: How to Pitch Your Business to Anyone, Get Funded, and Win Clients. John Wiley & Sons, Hoboken (2012)

Strangert, E., Gustafson, J.: What makes a good speaker? Subject ratings, acoustic measurements and perceptual evaluations. In: Proceedings of Interspeech 8, Brisbane, Australia, 1688–1691 (2008)

Touati, P.: Prosodic aspects of political rhetoric. Proceedings of the ESCA Workshop on Prosody, Lund, Sweden, 168–171 (1993)

Towler, A.J.: Effects of charismatic influence training on attitudes, behavior, and performance. Pers. Psychol. **56**, 363–381 (2003)

Towler, A., Arman, G., Quesnell, T., Hoffman, L.: How charismatic trainers inspire others to learn through positive affectivity. Comput. Human Behav. **32**, 221–228 (2014)

Weber, M.: The Theory of Social and Economic Organization. The Free Press of Glencoe, New York (1947)

Emotion Recognition for Self-aid in Addiction Treatment, Psychotherapy, and Nonviolent Communication

Valentina Franzoni[1,2(✉)] and Alfredo Milani[1]

[1] Department of Mathematics and Computer Science, University of Perugia, via Vanvitelli 1, 06123 Perugia, Italy
{valentina.franzoni,alfredo.milani}@unipg.it
[2] Department of Computer, Control, and Management Engineering "Antonio Ruberti", Sapienza University of Rome, via Ariosto 25, 00185 Rome, Italy

Abstract. This position paper aims to highlight possible future directions of applications for Affective Computing (AC) and Emotion Recognition (ER) for self-aid applications, as they emerge from the experience of the ACER-EMORE Workshops Series. ER in Artificial Intelligence offers a growing number of problem-solving multidisciplinary opportunities. Most current AC and ER applications are focused on a somewhat controversial enterprise-centered approach, i.e., recognizing user emotions to enable a third-party to achieve its own goals, in areas such as e-commerce, cybersecurity, behavior profiling, user experience. In this work we propose to explore a human-centered research direction, aiming at using AC/ER to enhance user consciousness of emotional states, ultimately supporting the development of self-aid applications. The use of facial ER and text ER to help forms of assistive technologies in the fields of Psychotherapy and Communication is an example of such a human-centered approach.

A general framework for ER in Self-aid is depicted, and some relevant application domains are suggested and discussed: dependencies treatment (DT) (e.g., workaholism, sexaholism); non-violent communication (NVC) for people in leading roles using e-mail or chat communication; empathy learning for parents and teachers in the circle-of-security (COS) caring environment.

Far from being complete and comprehensive, the purpose of this work is to trigger discussions and ideas for feasible studies and applications of ER in self-aid, which we hope to see published in the future editions of our workshops, believing that it may be one of the drops needed in the ocean of a better world.

Keywords: Workaholics · Sexaholics · Non-violent communication · Circle of security · Assistive technologies · NVC · COS

1 Introduction

Among the most studied and efficient technologies for Emotion Recognition (ER) in Affective Computing (AC) and Artificial Intelligence are facial recognition [1] and text analysis. Several models and algorithms have been developed with promising results to

© Springer Nature Switzerland AG 2019
S. Misra et al. (Eds.): ICCSA 2019, LNCS 11620, pp. 391–404, 2019.
https://doi.org/10.1007/978-3-030-24296-1_32

exploit ER in these areas [2–4]. Starting with simple sentiment analysis [5–8] to emotion recognition in texts, [5, 9, 10] following with more sophisticated models of emotion and affect extraction, [11, 12] to future application for intelligent interactive systems [13–15] for daily life support [16–24] or medical assistance, [25–31] emotions and emotional intelligence [32–34] play a crucial role [35]. Crucial is also the application of existent technologies and models, as it is evident from the well-recognized resources cited above, because emotions and affect perception can vary based on culture and other parameters. Crucial is the meaning that we may give to emotions, depending on ethical values and opinions, often vague and not linkable to science decisions.

Finally, emotions analysis can easily be misused for unethical purposes, such as controlling people's emotions to influence their commercial or political choices.

In our vision the research in the ER and AC should be informed by three basic principles:

I. **Ethical goals.** Emotion Recognition deeply involves the user intimate believes and states, sometimes even unknown to the same user which can be unaware of his/her emotional state. Researchers entering in such domains should consider and reflect on their own research goals, in order to avoid creating methods with unclear or no application, or which can easily be misused for different, unethical goals.

II. **Sound and Incremental approach.** New commoners to AC are very easy to contribute to the proliferation of new models, i.e., *reinventing the wheel*: the risk is to create a lot of models and algorithms that reach the same goal starting from the same primary resources, with similar precision, instead of advancing the already existent methods and algorithms. The relevant research contributions from psychology and physiology of human emotions cannot be ignored, and they should represent the starting point and a reference background to understand the difference among affect, moods, emotions, and sentiments [36–38]. One of the aims of this paper is to provide an excellent bibliography to start working in this domain.

III. **Practical and Helping applications.** The third guideline, in our opinion, should be to find practical **applications** to help human beings to live better. This aim is approachable for instance improving management and consciousness of emotions in order to choose the appropriate behavior. E.g., with applications to help who has short availability of funds (i.e. cheap applications, usable from the mass; or applications to help who has ideas but not resources), to invent aids for the weakest (e.g. elders, people with disabilities, people with physical or psychological pathologies), to support helping to diminish pain and providing support for who suffers.

In one sentence, we strongly support a vision of emotion *recognition for self-aid* as an ethical approach to a field of research which is deeply involved with the intimate mental privacy of individuals, which can quickly become controversial or misused. The idea is that applications aiming at self-aid ultimately preserve the individual emotional privacy since the application is playing a prosthetic role for emotional behavior rather than trying to modify or influence it.

Our vision is global and biased: every researcher can find where EM and AC problem-solving need is required in their own culture, state of life, sensibility to the needs of people around them in specific cases.

In Sect. 2 we will depict the general architecture of ER and AC for Self-aid. Sections 3, 4 and 5 three real-life problems are discussed that, in our view, may gain a consistent benefit from application involving Automated Emotion Recognition. In Sects. 6 and 7, two ER techniques for text ER and face ER will be presented as possible tools to support ER based self-aid application. Conclusions will be finally drawn.

2 An Architecture for Emotion Recognition for Self-aid

The scheme we propose shows a general system architecture encompassing a whole class of potential applications focusing on emotion recognition for self-aid. The *user* plays a central role since it is the primary source and object of the system. The role of the system is to support the user without substituting it in decisions which are ultimately under the user's responsibility and choice. The most relevant component is undoubtedly the *ER module* which uses information acquired by sensors for recognizing user emotions and emotions generated by, or embedded, in other human subjects in the application context. Different sources acquire users sensors' information, e.g., text, messages, speech, tone of voice, biometric parameters (e.g., blood pressure, heart pulse rate, myoelectric activity), body tracking and face-tracking videos generated by the user or documenting the user activity. The *AC Reasoning & Modeling* module has the purpose of interpreting the detected emotional input within the *Affective Computing* framework and goals characterizing the application scenario and taking into account the of the particular current context in which the application is used.

Typical goals of this module are:

- *classifying* emotions from sensors data;
- *ranking* the relevance of the detected emotions concerning the application goal and the current context;
- *projecting* the consequence of emotions concerning a specific AC model;
- eventually *triggering* a user emotional feedback in order to call for a *self-aid* action, if the detected emotion appears to affect the application goals.

The *Emotional Status* feedback module is in charge of generating the appropriate emotional affordances [12] to draw the user attention on his/her messages, speech behaviors, gestures or acts which can potentially represent a danger for her/himself or the relationship with a single or many communication partners.

The *contextual info* can vary depending on the application domain. It can represent simple contextual information, like a generic scenario in which the user's emotional behavior takes place or can involve cultural information and may require to analyze the emotional behavior of other human actors, which can be extracted by documents, messages or videos.

In general, because of different reasons, either psychological and perceptive, the user can be unaware of the emotional consequences or their inner status which leaks through their emotions. The idea is that although their emotions are deeply analyzed, users' are not substituted but supported in their decisions. The system has only the role of highlighting the emotional content and consequences of user behavior either respect to themselves or others. In a typical self-aid application, the user feedbacks can range from simple hints, e.g., a danger sign or a meme, to casual explanations, e.g., for instance, a graphic chain of the emotional interaction with other subjects (Fig. 1).

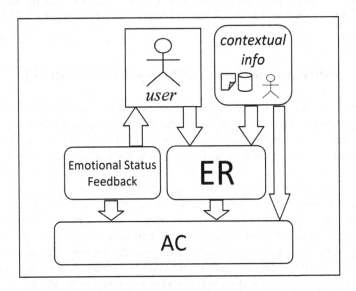

Fig. 1. ER for Self-aid Architecture

3 Self-aid Using ER for Three Real-Life Problems

Considering the ER for self-aid architecture and the three guidelines proposed in the introductory section, we identified three instances of paradigmatic problems which may gain significant added value from the integration of automatic emotion recognition with self-aid components:

A. Self-evaluation in addiction treatment (e.g., *workaholism*, *sexaholism*), where emotional self-evaluation is proved to help to gain and keep sobriety (emotional sobriety helps sobriety) [39–44].

B. Self-support for empathy learning for parents and teachers in a *circle-of-security* (COS) [45–47] caring environment, when they are undergoing therapy to understand their child's emotions better.

C. Self-assessment in *non-violent communication* (NVC) [48–50] for people in leading roles using e-mail or chat communication (e.g., group leaders, professors, managers), often prone to be unconsciously aggressive to their staff.

Problem A represents a class of ER-based self-aid applications, which we can call *one-to-self*, where the ER component supports the user in getting control of his/her own emotions for the betterment of his/her behavior.

Problem B represents the class of **one-to-one** *(or one-to-few)* ER-based applications, where the individual is supported in recognizing and improving the emotional interactions he/she undergoes, with another single individual, or a small community.

Problem C is the class of **one-to-many** *(or one-to-few)* ER-based self-aid applications, where the individual is helped to become aware of the emotional interactions with communication with many other individuals.

In the following sections, we will briefly present the problems and, then, our proposed solutions using text ER and face ER.

4 Addiction Treatment

Many people suffer from dependencies, e.g., *sexaholism* (i.e., the addiction to sex in dependency relationships, or pornographic fantasy), [39] *workaholism* (i.e., the addiction to work and productivity) [41, 42]. Such dependencies have several common traits, and also the treatment can benefit from the same process [44]. Associations exist in these cases to help the addicted with self-evaluation and group help, usually aided with a *12-steps program*, [40] useful not only to exit the dependency, but to keep staying out of it, because in most cases the addiction raises from problems related to the patient history, which cannot be changed, thus the danger to re-fall in the addiction can still be present in all the rest of the life of the ex-addicted.

The 12-steps program was initially created by the association of alcoholics anonymous and then adopted by associations for different dependencies. The process aims to support the personal choice of treatment and recovery, through a progressive mental, spiritual and physical awakening and healing, and includes the following phases:

1. **Admission** of the addiction
2. **Submission** to a Higher Authority (e.g., God)
3. **Restitution**, making amend to any person harmed
4. **Spreading** the message of the 12 steps to help other addicted people

The effectiveness of the program has been proved mainly by experience in all the association helping addicted people who, initially feeling inadequate, driven inward and out of reality, disconnected from others and themselves, and afraid, become confident, autonomous and caring, even if always conscious of needing to be cautious and avoid certain situations in order to stay sober.

During the rest of their life, the recovered addicted should **self-evaluate emotions**, considered the manifestation of future dangerous states which can help to prevent following again in the addiction. Such a method is followed because the addict may fall in situations, especially about relations, [43] which may stir up confusing emotional states leading to be weaker against the temptation of addiction. E.g., any emotional state which leads to self-punishment is dangerous.

Being conscious of emotions helps to react to such states and avoid weakness adequately: *emotional sobriety helps sobriety*. Tools using facial ER to regularly check our facial expression can help in this process, to connect again with ourselves, with others and with the real world.

5 Circle of Security (COS)

The Circle of Security Parenting program (COS-P) is a parent education and psychotherapy intervention developed by Glen Cooper, Kent Hoffman, Robert Marvin, and Bert Powell [48] to shift problematic patterns of attachment-caregiving interactions to a more appropriate developmental pathway.

The COS paradigm [51] describes the aim of the therapy as to:

1. Increase the caregivers **sensitivity** and appropriate responsiveness to the child's signals moving away to explore, and moving back for comfort and soothing.
2. Increase the caregiver's ability to reflect on their own and the child's behavior, **thoughts,** and **feelings** regarding attachment-caregiving interactions.
3. Reflect on experiences in their histories that affect their current **caregiving patterns**. This latter point aims to address the eventually defensive strategies of the caregiver.

The COS-P program is based on filming the interactions within the caregiver/child dyad in a particular situation called *strange situation*, and let the caregiver see the video and reflect on it with the help of a professional psychotherapist, eventually in groups with other caregivers. Professionals classify the dyads based on the interactions as secure, insecure or disorganized, where each class can have further classifications and thus should be treated with the proper therapy.

Such program broadly implies the ability of the caregiver to sense and recognize the child's emotions through the video, supported by the psychotherapist. In this environment, a tool for face-based ER can be useful to support the caregivers in recognizing the child's emotions and their own emotions filmed in the videos of the *strange situation*.

6 Non-violent Communication (NVC)

People in leading roles, e.g., group leaders, professors, managers, often have communication problems when they communicate through emails and chats because such written communication naturally lacks expressivity about emotions. When the staff, employer or student has no sufficient information to understand the tone or mood behind the text, may be due to a wrong interpretation of underlying emotions and see the leader as aggressive. Some words are more emotionally meaningful than others, therefore using synonyms or alternative expressions may help to avoid unconscious aggressivity and the consequent reaction.

Moreover, it is established that a patient relationship with colleagues and superiors leads to a better work environment and higher productivity. Self-assessment about the emotional value of our communication through text can improve people management.

Non-Violent Communication (NVC), developed by the clinical psychologist Marshall Rosenberg in last century, [47] and used in different domains, e.g., work environment and marital relationships, [45, 46] is a specific method for communicating emphatically to avoid any verbal violence. NVC theory supposes all human behavior stems from attempts to meet universal human needs, which are never in conflict. NVC proposes that people identify mutually shared needs, revealed by the words expressing thoughts and by the emotional feelings surrounding such needs, and collaborate to develop strategies and make requests to meet each other's needs, aiming to an interpersonal harmony and social cooperation.

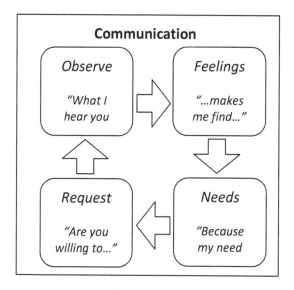

Fig. 2. The NVC Model

The model includes four components (also depicted in Fig. 2):

1. The concrete actions we **observe** that affect our well-being
2. How we **feel about** what we observe
3. The **needs**, values, desires that create our feelings
4. The concrete **actions** we request in order to enrich our lives

NVC is useful not only to choose better words to make requests but also enhance meeting efficiency, bolster teamwork, resolve conflict resolution, because it helps to meet the needs both of the sender and the receiver, in a win-win negotiation approach.

The method, to apply the model in understanding others, better includes questions building for understanding the thought and emotional feelings of the people with whom we are communicating, using particular emotional words to express the understatement. Such questions ask for feedback: if the feedback is positive, the thoughts and feelings are considered well understood; otherwise the questions are repeated with corrections until understatement.

Text ER can help especially for understanding the emotional value of the NVC feedback.

7   Text ER Using the Semantic Emotions Model (SEMO)

The Semantic Emotions Model (SEMO) [38, 52, 53] is based on semantic similarity relations that can be extracted from an emotional ontology, taxonomy or a simple web-based search engine. The main idea is that words with similar meaning often appear together in documents on the Web: Web-based semantic similarity is computable searching for the number of results for each term of a pair, and then the number of results of the search for the pair. These three numbers combined in appropriate formulas (e.g., Normalized Google Distance, [54, 55] Pointwise Mutual Information, [56] PMING distance [57]) give a proximity evaluation between 0 (different) and 1 (equal), in decimal scale. Calculating the semantic proximity between a term/expression and each word [58] expressing the emotions of a model (e.g., Ekman, Plutchick), [11] it is possible to calculate which emotions are carried by the term/expression semantics.

More formally, let the emotion model

$$E_M = \{e_1, \ldots, e_n\} \tag{1}$$

and the Vector Space Model

$$\pi_p(w, E_M) = \big(\pi_p(w, e_1), \ldots, \pi_p(w, e_n)\big) \tag{2}$$

for term w, emotion model E_M and proximity measure p, where each component $\pi_p(w, e_i)$ of the vector represents the proximity between term w and emotion e_i. Then, for sentence s,

$$\pi_p(s, E_M) = \big(\pi_p(s, e_1), \ldots, \pi_p(s, e_n)\big) \tag{3}$$

will be the vector containing the overall emotional content depending on the whole sentence. Each component $\pi_p(s, e_i)$ is calculated considering the single $\pi_p(w, e_i)$ values.

Formally,

$$\pi_p(s, e_i) = AGGR\big(\pi_p(w_1, e_i), \ldots, \pi_p(w_k, e_i)\big) \tag{4}$$

where $AGGR$ can be an aggregation function, e.g., *Max, Average* [56]. In the first case, the *Max* aggregation, the components of the *emotional sentence* vector are obtained by choosing the maximal value for each emotion in words composing the phrase; i.e., it tends to amplify all the emotions. The *Average* aggregation function points out the average emotional content of the phrase.

As a starting phase of the process, the sentence to be analyzed is parsed and preprocessed using NLP techniques; [38] each sentence is decomposed in a set of tokens, from which non-relevant words are removed, including stop-words, ordinal numbers, cardinal numbers and short words, such as articles and prepositions not carrying any emotional value. The set of stop-words is taken from the all-corpora package of the widely used NLTK Python library, [59] while numbers are detected using regular expressions. At the end of this preprocessing phase, each sentence is reduced to an array of potentially emotionally costly words.

The final output of the process is the primary emotion associated with each term of the sentence, which can also be visualized in a radar graph as in Fig. 3.

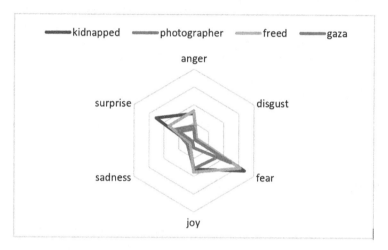

Fig. 3. Visualization in a radar graph of the Ekman emotions associated with the sentence "Kidnapped photographer freed in Gaza"

8 Face ER Using Convolutional Neural Networks (CNN)

The proposed method takes insights from literature about lip reading, [60] and the GUI-based *EmEx* [61] and *EmEx2* [1] software, implemented to recognize in real time emotions of the users whose face is in the camera streaming, but personalized software is easy to develop using the open-source *Caffe* framework [62] for classification, and *OpenCV* libraries [63] for image processing. The classes of recognized emotions are the underlying emotions of the *Ekman* model [37].

After an initial phase of Artificial Intelligence training, feeding the system with a high number of images of the user's facial expressions, each tested image is then processed by the *Convolutional Neural Network* (CNN) [64]. The personal features associated to the emotion expressions of the face of the user are identified, in order to recognize and label the corresponding emotion, giving real-time feedback (visual, with a tag or an emoticon, and sounds).

The two phases of training and test are structured in a similar way, where the training phase is customized on the user's face characteristics (e.g., wrinkles, moles, shapes, [65] imperfections), implying a more complex communication scheme among the layers of the CNN.

The neural network consists of several layers connected. The main level is for the appropriate dataset and tags. A second layer is a *convoluted layer*, where the convolution operations are performed on the image, extracting the specific information of the face. Then, a *pooling layer* reduces the magnitude of the parameters, thus the time needed for computation, and the process continues with convolutional layers.

The layer sequence is crucial to obtain good classification scores: convolutional layers are alternated to normalization layers or pooling layers when it is necessary to improve the quality of the input data making transformations without altering the quality of the image. The *normalization layer* is used to make a linear transformation of the image to improve the readability; the pooling layer is needed to reduce the size of the input data, to speed up the computation. Finally, *inner product layers,* i.e. fully connected layers, alternated with a rectified linear unit layer, quickly train the CNN, ended with the output layer.

During the training phase, the output is represented by the accuracy of the process and the lost information; during the test phase, the output will be the emotion classification.

9   Conclusions

In this position paper, we introduced and motivated, the *ER for Self-aid* paradigm as a theme for emotion recognition research, which can reach, at the same time, the ethical goal of respecting individual emotional privacy and focusing on application improving quality of life. At the basis of a significant number of psychological or interpersonal communications difficulties, there is a correct perception and consciousness of emotions, in either communication directions displaying or reading.

Rather than using emotion analysis for reaching some other goals such as influencing people behavior, we maintain that the focus should be on the prosthetic role of ER.

We have presented a general architecture for ER for Self-aid, and we have identified three classes of applications, *one-to-self, one-to-one* and *one-to-many*, for which we have exemplified useful practical applications respectively in the area of *addiction treatment, circle-of-security,* and *nonviolent communication*. State of the art techniques for ER, like the ones sampled in the last sections without claiming to be complete, show that the goal of developing ER for Self-aid applications is suitable and realistic and we strongly advocate for a research effort in this direction.

Acknowledgments. The authors thank all the researchers who participated to the 2019 edition of the EMORE and ACER workshops, to the previous editions and the special issue Emotional Machines, the Next Revolution (iOS Press, 2019): https://content.iospress.com/articles/web-intelligence/web190395. Thanks are due also to all the researchers who spend their time researching for application to make the life of the weakest easier.

References

1. Gervasi, O., Franzoni, V., Riganelli, M., Tasso, S.: Automating facial emotion recognition. Web Intell. **17**, 17–27 (2019)
2. Calvo, R.A., D'Mello, S.: Affect detection: an interdisciplinary review of models, methods, and their applications. IEEE Trans. Affect. Comput. **1**(1), 18–37 (2010)
3. Medhat, W., Hassan, A., Korashy, H.: Sentiment analysis algorithms and applications: a survey. Ain Shams Eng. J. **5**(4), 1093–1113 (2014)
4. Alm, C.O., Roth, D., Sproat, R.: Emotions from text: machine learning for text-based emotion prediction. In: Proceedings of Human Language Technology Conference and Conference on Empirical Methods in Natural Language Processing (HLT/EMNLP) (2005)
5. Liu, H., Lieberman, H., Selker, T.: A model of textual affect sensing using real-world knowledge. In: Proceedings of the International Conference on Intelligent User Interfaces, pp. 125–132 (2003)
6. Franzoni, V., Li, Y., Mengoni, P.: A path-based model for emotion abstraction on facebook using sentiment analysis and taxonomy knowledge. In: Proceedings - 2017 IEEE/WIC/ACM International Conference on Web Intelligence, WI 2017 (2017)
7. Milani, A., Rajdeep, N., Mangal, N., Mudgal, R.K., Franzoni, V.: Sentiment extraction and classification for the analysis of users' interest in tweets. Int. J. Web Inf. Syst. **14**, 29–40 (2018)
8. Mudgal, R.K., Niyogi, R., Milani, A., Franzoni, V.: Analysis of tweets to find the basis of popularity based on events semantic similarity. Int. J. Web Inf. Syst. **14**(4), 438–452 (2018)
9. Pennebaker, J.W., Mehl, M.R., Niederhoffer, K.G.: Psychological aspects of natural language use: our words. Our Selves. Annu. Rev. Psychol. **54**(1), 547–577 (2002)
10. Thelwall, M., Buckley, K., Paltoglou, G., Cai, D., Kappas, A.: Sentiment in short strength detection informal text. J. Am. Soc. Inf. Sci. Technol. **61**(12), 2544–2558 (2010)
11. Biondi, G., Franzoni, V., Poggioni, V.: A deep learning semantic approach to emotion recognition using the IBM watson bluemix alchemy language. In: Gervasi, O., et al. (eds.) ICCSA 2017. LNCS, vol. 10406, pp. 718–729. Springer, Cham (2017). https://doi.org/10.1007/978-3-319-62398-6_51
12. Franzoni, V., Milani, A., Vallverdú, J.: Emotional affordances in human-machine interactive planning and negotiation. In: Proceedings - 2017 IEEE/WIC/ACM International Conference on Web Intelligence, WI 2017 (2017)
13. Klein, J., Moon, Y., Picard, R.W.: This computer responds to user frustration: theory, design, and results. Interact. Comput. **14**(2), 119–140 (2002)
14. Franzoni, V., Milani, A., Nardi, D., Vallverdú, J.: Emotional machines: the next revolution. Web Intell. **17**, 1–7 (2019)
15. Milani, A., Franzoni, V.: Soft behaviour modelling of user communities. J. Theor. Appl. Inf. Technol. **96**, 217–226 (2018)
16. Dodds, P.S., Harris, K.D., Kloumann, I.M., Bliss, C.A., Danforth, C.M.: Temporal patterns of happiness and information in a global social network: Hedonometrics and Twitter. PLoS ONE **6**(12), e26752 (2011)
17. Dodds, P.S., Danforth, C.M.: Measuring the happiness of large-scale written expression: songs, blogs, and presidents. J. Happiness Stud. **11**(4), 441–456 (2010)
18. Hatch, M.J.: Irony and the social construction of contradiction in the humor of a management team. Organ. Sci. **8**(3), 275–288 (2008)
19. Berlyne, D.E.: Toward a theory of exploratory behavior: II. Arousal potential, perceptual curiosity, and learning. In: Conflict, Arousal, and Curiosity (2006)

20. Bohanek, J.G., Fivush, R., Walker, E.: Memories of positive and negative emotional events. Appl. Cogn. Psychol. **19**(1), 51–66 (2005)
21. Huang, A.H., Yen, D.C., Zhang, X.: Exploring the potential effects of emoticons. Inf. Manag. **45**(7), 466–473 (2008)
22. Lin, K.H.-Y., Yang, C., Chen, H.-H.: What emotions do news articles trigger in their readers? In: WISA 2018: Web Information Systems and Applications, pp. 170–181 (2018)
23. Cheshin, A., Rafaeli, A., Bos, N.: Anger and happiness in virtual teams: Emotional influences of text and behavior on others' affect in the absence of non-verbal cues. Organ. Behav. Hum. Decis. Process. **116**(1), 2–16 (2011)
24. Ringberg, T., Reihlen, M.: Towards a socio-cognitive approach to knowledge transfer. J. Manag. Stud. **45**(5), 912–935 (2008)
25. Rogers, S.N., Gwanne, S., Lowe, D., Humphris, G., Yueh, B., Weymuller, E.A.: The addition of mood and anxiety domains to the University of Washington quality of life scale. Head Neck **24**(6), 521–529 (2002)
26. Needham, I., Abderhalden, C., Halfens, R.J.G., Fischer, J.E., Dassen, T.: Non-somatic effects of patient aggression on nurses: a systematic review. J. Adv. Nurs. **49**(3), 283–296 (2005)
27. Pilgrim, D., Bentall, R.: The medicalisation of misery: a critical realist analysis of the concept of depression (1999)
28. Whitney, J., Murray, J., Gavan, K., Todd, G., Whitaker, W., Treasure, J.: Experience of caring for someone with anorexia nervosa: qualitative study. Br. J. Psychiatry **187**(5), 444–449 (2005)
29. Lieberman, M.A., Goldstein, B.A.: Not all negative emotions are equal: the role of emotional expression in online support groups for women with breast cancer. Psychooncology **15**(2), 160–168 (2006)
30. Looije, R., Neerincx, M.A., Cnossen, F.: Persuasive robotic assistant for health self-management of older adults: design and evaluation of social behaviors. Int. J. Hum Comput Stud. **68**(6), 386–397 (2010)
31. Eriksson, M., Svedlund, M.: "The intruder": spouses' narratives about life with a chronically ill partner. J. Clin. Nurs. **15**(3), 324–333 (2006)
32. Arora, S., Ashrafian, H., Davis, R., Athanasiou, T., Darzi, A., Sevdalis, N.: Emotional intelligence in medicine: a systematic review through the context of the ACGME competencies (2010)
33. Ryan, R.M., Connell, J.P., Plant, R.W.: Emotions in nondirected text learning. Learn. Individ, Differ (1990)
34. Brackett, M.A.: The Emotion Revolution: Enhancing Social and Emotional Learning in School: Enhancing Social and Emotional Learning in School (2016)
35. Beaucousin, V., Lacheret, A., Turbelin, M.R., Morel, M., Mazoyer, B., Tzourio-Mazoyer, N.: FMRI study of emotional speech comprehension. Cereb. Cortex **17**(2), 339–352 (2007)
36. Munezero, M., Montero, C.S., Sutinen, E., Pajunen, J.: Are they different? affect, feeling, emotion, sentiment, and opinion detection in text. IEEE Trans. Affect. Comput. **5**(2), 101–111 (2014)
37. Franzoni, V., Poggioni, V.: Emotional book classification from book blurbs. In: Proceedings - 2017 IEEE/WIC/ACM International Conference on Web Intelligence, WI 2017 (2017)
38. Franzoni, V., Milani, A., Biondi, G.: SEMO: a semantic model for emotion recognition in web objects. In: Proceedings - 2017 IEEE/WIC/ACM International Conference on Web Intelligence, WI 2017 (2017)
39. Efrati, Y., Gola, M.: Compulsive sexual behavior: a twelve-step therapeutic approach. J. Behav. Addict. **7**(2), 445–453 (2018)

40. Volenik, A.: The twelve-step program as a response to contemporary addictive behaviors | Program 12 koraka kao odgovor na moderna ovisnička ponašanja. Obnovljeni Ziv (2014)
41. Bakker, A.B., Schaufeli, W.B., Leiter, M.P., Taris, T.W.: Work engagement: an emerging concept in occupational health psychology. Work Stress 22(3), 187–200 (2008)
42. Schaufeli, W.B., Taris, T.W., Van Rhenen, W.: Workaholism, burnout, and work engagement: three of a kind or three different kinds of employee well-being? Appl. Psychol. 57(2), 173–203 (2008)
43. Bakker, A.B., Demerouti, E., Burke, R.: Workaholism and relationship quality: a spillover-crossover perspective. J. Occup. Health Psychol. 14(1), 23 (2009)
44. McMillan, L.H.W., O'Driscoll, M.P., Marsh, N.V., Brady, E.C.: Understanding workaholism: data synthesis, theoretical critique, and future design strategies. Int. J. Stress Manag. 8(2), 69–91 (2001)
45. Powell, B., Cooper, G., Hoffman, K., Marvin, B.M.: The Circle of Security Intervention: Enhancing Attachment in Early Parent-Child Relationships (2014)
46. Gateway, Child Welfare Information, C.B.: Parent Education to Strengthen Families and Reduce the Risk of Maltreatment ISSUE., Washington, DC (2010)
47. Cassidy, J., et al.: Enhancing maternal sensitivity and attachment security in the infants of women in a jail-diversion program. Attach. Hum. Dev. 12(4), 333–353 (2010). Incarcer. Individ. their Child. viewed from Perspect. Attach. theory. Spec. issue
48. Vazhappilly, J.J., Reyes, M.E.S.: Non-violent communication and marital relationship: efficacy of 'emotion-focused couples' communication program among filipino couples. Psychol. Stud. (Mysore) 62(3), 275–283 (2017)
49. Zimmermann, W.: On promoting non violent communication in Syria. In: Proceedings of the 5th International Disaster and Risk Conference: Integrative Risk Management - The Role of Science, Technology and Practice, IDRC Davos 2014 (2014)
50. Marshall Rosenberg: Words are Windows (or They're Walls) (1998)
51. Marvin, R., Cooper, G., Hoffman, K., Powell, B.: The circle of security project: attachment-based intervention with caregiver–pre-school child dyads. Attach. Hum. Dev. 4(1), 107–124 (2002)
52. Franzoni, V., Biondi, G., Milani, A.: A web-based system for emotion vector extraction. In: Gervasi, O., et al. (eds.) ICCSA 2017. LNCS, vol. 10406, pp. 653–668. Springer, Cham (2017). https://doi.org/10.1007/978-3-319-62398-6_46
53. Biondi, G., Franzoni, V., Li, Y., Milani, A.: Web-based similarity for emotion recognition in web objects. In: Proceedings - 9th IEEE/ACM International Conference on Utility and Cloud Computing, UCC 2016 (2016)
54. Franzoni, V., Milani, A.: Structural and semantic proximity in information networks (2017)
55. Cilibrasi, R.L., Vitanyi, P.M.B.: The google similarity distance. IEEE Trans. Knowl. Data Eng. 19, 370–383 (2007)
56. Franzoni, V., Milani, A., Pallottelli, S., Leung, C.H.C., Li, Y.: Context-based image semantic similarity. In: 2015 12th International Conference on Fuzzy Systems and Knowledge Discovery, FSKD 2015 (2016)
57. Franzoni, V., Milani, A.: PMING distance: a collaborative semantic proximity measure. In: Proceedings - 2012 IEEE/WIC/ACM International Conference on Intelligent Agent Technology, IAT 2012 (2012)
58. Franzoni, V., Leung, C.H.C., Li, Y., Mengoni, P., Milani, A.: Set similarity measures for images based on collective knowledge. In: Gervasi, O., et al. (eds.) ICCSA 2015. LNCS, vol. 9155, pp. 408–417. Springer, Cham (2015). https://doi.org/10.1007/978-3-319-21404-7_30
59. Perkins, J.: Python 3 Text Processing with NLTK 3.0 Cookbook (2014)
60. Alzubi, A., Amira, A., Ramzan, N.: Semantic content-based image retrieval: a comprehensive study. J. Vis. Commun. Image Represent. 32, 20–54 (2015)

61. Riganelli, M., Franzoni, V., Gervasi, O., Tasso, S.: EmEx, a tool for automated emotive face recognition using convolutional neural networks. In: Gervasi, O., et al. (eds.) ICCSA 2017. LNCS, vol. 10406, pp. 692–704. Springer, Cham (2017). https://doi.org/10.1007/978-3-319-62398-6_49

62. Jia, Y., Shelhamer, E., Donahue, J., et al.: Caffe: Convolutional Architecture for Fast Feature Embedding. Arxiv (2014)

63. OpenCV: Open Source Computer Vision Library

64. Krizhevsky, A., Sutskever, I., Hinton, G.E.: ImageNet classification with deep convolutional neural networks. In: ImageNet Classification with Deep Convolutional Neural Networks (2012)

65. Saeed, U., Dugelay, J.-L.: Combining edge detection and region segmentation for lip contour extraction. In: Perales, F.J., Fisher, R.B. (eds.) AMDO 2010. LNCS, vol. 6169, pp. 11–20. Springer, Heidelberg (2010). https://doi.org/10.1007/978-3-642-14061-7_2

Advances in information Systems and Technologies for Emergency management, risk assessment and mitigation based on the Resilience concepts (ASTER 2019)

Risk Analysis: A Focus on Urban Exposure Estimation

Roberto De Lotto, Caterina Pietra, and Elisabetta M. Venco[(✉)]

DICAr, University of Pavia, Via Ferrata 3, 27100 Pavia, Italy
{uplab, elisabettamaria.venco}@unipv.it

Abstract. In risk analysis, extremes natural phenomena become hazardous when they strike human beings, tangible and intangible assets. In urban areas, the exponential growth of population and its density makes cities more exposed to the effects of natural impacts that could become catastrophic and generate high-risk situations. As a result, the current situation makes the population and its economic and social activities highly exposed to the different natural risks. In the last 40 years, the Exposure of built-up area and population to natural hazards doubled: now seismic hazard could affect 2.7 billion, volcanoes eruptions 414 million people and tropical cyclones over 1.6 billion.

Authors consider Exposure as the quantity and quality of the different anthropic elements (population, settlement system, infrastructure network, elements of the environment) of a given territorial area and whose conditions and operation can be damaged, altered or destroyed by natural hazards. Therefore, the exposure assessment of the different urban functions becomes the basis for implementing risk reduction interventions. The presented research defines a methodology to study the location and distribution of population (spatial and temporal dynamic entity), the different urban functions, human assets and their activities. In particular, authors analyze the statistical possibility that human beings are in an area at risk in a well-defined period of time (24 h a day, 7 days a week and 365 a year). It depends on city structure, functions distribution, its widespread elements and through these elements authors estimate Urban Exposure.

Keywords: Urban Exposure · Natural risks · Parameters estimation

1 Introduction

Nowadays, natural hazards have huge social and economic impact in urban areas because urbanization and economic development increase people and assets' concentration in high-risk prone areas. The intensification and diversification of land-uses (especially in low-income and developing countries) lead cities to be exposed to multiple effects of different types of natural hazards. A natural event is a potential threat to human life and property: it become disaster or catastrophe when human beings (and their physical and economic assets) live or work in its path. Consequently, hazards generate risks in relation to population and its physical and economic assets' Exposure [1].

© Springer Nature Switzerland AG 2019
S. Misra et al. (Eds.): ICCSA 2019, LNCS 11620, pp. 407–423, 2019.
https://doi.org/10.1007/978-3-030-24296-1_33

The Atlas of the Human Planet 2017 [2] highlights how the Exposure of built-up area and population to natural hazards doubled in the last 40 years. Seismic hazard accounts for the highest number of people potentially exposed (from 1.4 billion in 1975 to 2.7 billion in 2015). In 2015, 414 million people lived near one of the 220 most dangerous volcanoes. Flood, the most frequent natural disaster, potentially affects more people in Asia (76.9%) and Africa (12.2%). Furthermore, population exposed to tropical cyclones increased from 1 billion in 1975 up to 1.6 billion in 2015 and 45 countries are exposed also to devastating hurricanes. Moreover, in according with that research, the country most at risk to tsunamis is Japan. Finally, sea level surge affects the countries across the tropical region and China has one of the largest increase of population: plus 200 million people from 1990 to 2015.

As many authors define, Exposure means the quantity and quality of the different anthropic elements of a given territorial area whose conditions and operation can be damaged, altered or destroyed by natural hazards [1, 3–8].

In particular, quantity means number of buildings, people or activities; quality means functional/strategic aspects, i.e. existing relationships between physical elements and territorial systems; anthropic elements mean population, settlement system, infrastructure network.

So the dimensions involved are:

- physical dimension, relative to the quantity of goods or persons exposed in the territory;
- functional dimension, relative to the functional role (strategic, economic, historical-cultural heritage) of the physical elements exposed in the territory.

Given the extremely heterogeneous nature and the amount of information and elements to consider, the definition of a general and systematic method is fundamental. For the physical dimension it is possible to identify easily the main characteristics (through classical geographical analysis); for the functional dimension it is not so easy: to understand the functional role of the exposed elements it is necessary to consider, analyze and study the territory itself, its structure and the evolution over time of the relationships existing among each specific part. Therefore, the three macro-categories of elements potentially exposed to risks are:

- Population: resident population and city users (employed, students, users of over-local interest services, tourists)
- Physical elements: housing, cultural/monumental building heritage, strategic and collective interest equipment, mobility and technology networks
- Economic activities: productive and industrial.

The main analysis scales involved are [6]:

- Global scale with statistical information related to the distribution of goods in the considering territory (national/regional/metropolitan/urban level). The use of satellite images and cartographic maps allows the definition of urban density values (m^3/m^2);
- Local scale with databases that provide information at the municipal level (urban blocks and specific buildings). The type and building function (residential,

commercial or tertiary) analysis is fundamental: over time and in space the Exposure values of the related category derives from it. Data (percentage and the gross floor area - GFA of each urban function, number of floors of each building) collection is made through cartographic systems and, if necessary, direct *in-situ* survey. The number of people in a specific urban function derives from the definition of crowding.

In particular, for the population category, it is fundamental using a multi-scale evaluation and considering temporal, spatial, dimensional and functional variables.

2   Exposure

2.1   Urban Exposure at Global Scale

Many cities with a strong emerging economy and rapid urbanization, are protagonists of sprawl phenomena that determine the emergence of areas heavily exposed to risks since they were not properly designed and managed. Some of the effects on Exposure arising from urbanization are found at the micro scale, which means at the neighborhood, block or even a single dwelling level, but most of the times the effects fall on all those areas of new and uncontrolled making.

Urbanization, considered as territorial and social organization, can increase the capacity to react, manage and overcome situations of risk and calamitous events. Indeed, the high building and infrastructure density allows an efficient implementation and faster and more specific operations for the establishment of preventive measures. Services related to the management of emergencies can act more easily and achieve a greater number of users who, together with the public part, contribute increasing the resilience and the ability to overcome the event.

Assuming that the risk appetite of a country or a city depends not only from the magnitude of the disastrous event but also and above all from the elements exposed and from the level of development of the society, the final risk index turns out to be a function of Exposure, vulnerability, adaptability and response capability to the event. "Whether it be an earthquake or a tsunami, a cyclone or floods, the risk of a natural event turning into a disaster always depends only partly on the force of the natural event itself. The living conditions of the people in the regions affected and the options available to respond quickly and to provide assistance are just as significant. [...] Countries that see natural hazards coming, that are preparing for the consequences of climate change and are providing the financial means required will be better prepared for the future" [9].

In WorldRiskReport 2018 [10], urban Exposure map (Fig. 1) shows highs levels in Central America and in the Caribbean areas, in some states on the Pacific coast of South America, in South-East Europe and Asia, in Japan and Oceania. It is important to note that Japan, the Netherlands and Chile "which rank at 5, 13 and 14 respectively in terms of Exposure, show that even a very high Exposure does not necessarily imply a very high risk". African countries and some Asian states are less exposed but more vulnerable because of the low presence of potentially destructive phenomena or of large and numerous conurbations.

Exposure
Exposure of the population to the natural hazards earthquakes, cyclones, floods, droughts, and sea-level rise.

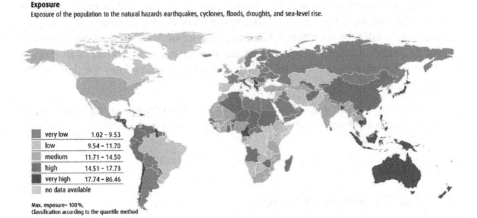

very low	1.02 - 9.53	
low	9.54 - 11.70	
medium	11.71 - 14.50	
high	14.51 - 17.73	
very high	17.74 - 86.46	
no data available		

Max. exposure= 100 %,
Classification according to the quantile method

Fig. 1. World Exposure to natural hazards (WorldRiskReport 2018).

Loss Estimated Method. Among all, in traditional engineering models, the estimation of the expected losses in a site is determined by the following equation [11]:

$$\text{Physical Loss} = \sum\nolimits_{Bk} \left[\left(\sum\nolimits_{Ii} P(I_i|B_k) \right) * \left(\sum d_{rj} P(d_{rj}|I_i, B_k)(d_{rj}|B_k) \right) * V_{Bk} \right] \quad (1)$$

Where:

B_k typology of buildings k;
I_i level of intensity i of the event;
D_{rj} level of the damage expected j;
V_{bk} value of all the buildings of b_k typology;
the sum related to d_{rj} represents the expected damage value for an intensity I_i and for buildings of B_k typology;
the product of this level of damage and the value of all the buildings of b_k typology get the expected loss for the buildings b_k;
the sum respect all the typologies of buildings b_k gives the total expected loss.

It is also interesting the approach for the calculation of Exposure and expected losses that does not use the collected data, but macroscopic indicators: the gross domestic product (GDP) with the underlying assumptions that the number of buildings and artefacts is directly proportional to the social wealth and therefore to the GDP of the region. It follows that the expected physical losses are calculated directly; for a given area or region with a known GDP value [11]:

$$\text{Physical Loss} = \sum I_j \left[P(I_j) \text{MDF}(I_j) \text{GDP g(GDP)} \right] \quad (2)$$

Where:

$p(I_j)$ probability that the event I_j manifests during the next years;
$MDF(I_j)$ damage factor that represents the relation danger-Exposure-loss in case of event of intensity I_j;
$g(GDP)$ function to correlate GDP with the real social prosperity: it is 5 for regions with high-income economies, 4 for regions with medium-income economies and 3 for China, Japan and India.

2.2   Urban Exposure at Local Scale

At urban scale, the Exposure assessment of the different urban functions (residences, commerce, tertiary, strategic services, road, social and economic infrastructures) becomes essential because of the concentration (density) of people.

To achieve this goal, it is essential to study the localization and the distribution in time and place of population (whose characteristics and behaviour during day and year characterize it as a dynamic and non-static entity), different urban functions, assets and human activities in order to know the real quantity of people that can be affected by events in a certain portion of territory (urban block and neighbourhood).

Authors define the Exposure function of each single urban function in relation to the urban block, the municipal territory or the spatial domain considered (trans/interscalarity) [7, 8, 12] as f (people, urban function, population age, hours of functions use, functions m^2):

$$E = \sum \text{age} \left\{ \left[(\text{u.f. m}^2)/(\text{p.d.}) \right]/\text{people} \times \left[(\text{u.f. m}^2)/(\text{tot m}^2) \right] \times C_{age} \times \text{hours/year} \right\}$$

(3)

Where:

u.f. urban function (residential, commercial, tertiary);
p.d. population density; for the residential unit it is considered 50 m^2/habitant, for commercial and tertiary it can be estimated a percentage of the overcrowding index;
age: the population is divided into 3 age groups – children 0–18 years old, adults 19–64 years old and elderly/seniors over 65, already retired;
C_{age}: correction factor based on the population age and on its capacity of not be damaged (i.e. motor skills), calculated by pairwise comparison responding to the question "Which age group is more exposed to risks?";
hours: number of hours of use of an urban function during a year;
m^2: square meters of the single urban function and of the block taken into account;
total number of people: residents and city users of the block taken into account.

Specifically, for the definition of urban Exposure, it is necessary to implement an analysis of urban built-up, through GIS tools, direct surveys and inspections. In particular:

- Definition of building density for urban blocks (it is considered 0–5 m^3/m^2 for low density, 5–10 m^3/m^2 for medium density and > 10 m^3/m^2 for high density) [13, 14];

- Study of the morphology of fabrics (historical, consolidated, open, expansion areas, brownfields, isolated buildings, for mixed activities, for productive activities, for commercial activities, for recreational activities, for services...) [13, 14];
- Definition of areas and percentages of urban functions (residential, commercial, tertiary) for each block;
- Calculation of the crowding index (150 m^3 gross volume/inhabitant[1] for the residences; from the UNI 10339 standard it is considered 0.25 persons/m^2 for the commercial function and 0.1 persons/m^2 for the tertiary)[2] [15].

Once the urban Exposure has been defined, the process goes on with the identification of the types of danger present in the territory through the overlapping of the hazard maps in order to define the most at risk areas and then carry out the evaluation process.

3   Application of the Urban Exposure Function

The urban Exposure calculation function has been analyzed to determine the best possible combinations for block of functions and population in order to reduce Exposure. It is emphasized that to different data on the use of urban functions will correspond different values of Exposure.

Urban settlement areas are characterized by ever-present constitutive elements that determine physical and social form and structure: urban fabrics, collective places and functional mix. Analyzing the city through the study of urban fabrics makes it possible to read the structural conditions of the settlements and the occupation of the land. The following types of fabrics can be found in a small and medium-sized European urban context: historical, consolidated, high density mix, high density mix with production activities, open with medium density, low residential density.

Authors present two case studies that reproduce the situation of a new hypothetical monofunctional residential expansion and an area of functional mix similar to a consolidated context of city center: 10000 m^2 of buildings in a city block 80 × 80 m^3, different functional mixes and crowding indexes. Therefore, they calculate the related Urban Exposure [12].

3.1   Case A

The example presented now considers the 100% residential function and the maximum commercial and tertiary crowding index.

Tables 1 and 2 show the first phase of data entry and the state of affairs to determine urban Exposure at time t = 0. In particular, it reports data concerning areas (m^2)

---

[1] Average value in new buildings according to Italian urban laws.

[2] The productive/industrial sector are not evaluated, since they are no longer present in the urban fabric of most Italian cities, same for the strategic services (i.e. hospitals and schools) because they are regulated by specific and restrictive risk reduction rules.

[3] It is the classical historical cities block deriving from ancient Roman camp grid.

related to the different functions, the urban density, the number of residents in the territory differentiated by families and age classes and the number of users of commercial and tertiary function. Furthermore, for the tertiary and commerce, a preliminary maximum crowding index is used.

Table 1. Data entry: different functions m^2 and indexes.

Areas (U.F.)				Urban Indexes		
Residential R (m^2)	Commercial C (m^2)	Tertiary T (m^2)0	Total (m^2)	R m^2/ inh	C m^2/ inh	T m^2/ inh
10.000	0,00	0,00	10.000	50	4	10
%			%			
100	0	0	100			

Table 2. Data entry: inhabitants.

People							
R (inh)	C (inh)	T (inh)0	Tot inhabitants	Families	Elderly for each family		Children
200	0	0	200	0,25	0,8		0,7

Table 3 shows data referring to the people present in the different urban functions (always taking into account the age class) and the hours of use of these ones during the day compared to the year (it is therefore an average of the presence of people in the urban functions based on work, leisure time, main activity etc.) [16].

Table 4 reports daily hours during which people are not present in the three urban functions studied (they can therefore be in service structures, in open spaces or on means of transportation).

The different combinations tested (summarized in Table 5) show clearly how a homogeneous functional mix within the sector allows to obtain very low Exposure values since the population is not maximal in the residence (it is considerably reduced the Exposure during night hours) and equally distributed throughout the day between the tertiary and commercial sectors (both for work and leisure).

The lowest results are achieved by minimizing the commercial sector: once fixed the square meters of area and the crowding indexes, in the case of 50% residential and 50% tertiary, the overall Exposure is equal to 124 due to the considerable presence of people also in the tertiary (there are 100 people in the residential function and 500 in tertiary). With a functional mix that sees the residential at 60%, the commercial sector at 10% and the tertiary at 30%, the Exposure value reaches its minimum equal to 62.

The last case determines a number of people equal to 120 for the residential function, 250 for the commercial and 300 for the tertiary: the creation of the functional mix with very low values of the commercial reduces the presence of people (for leisure and for work) within the sector. On the other hand, the increase of the residential part makes the Exposure greater at night and so a greater number of people exposed to risk.

Table 3. Project data entry: urban functions times of use.

Residential R					Commercial C						Tertiary T					
Families	Adults for each families	Children	Adults	Elderly	Families	Adults for each families	Children	Adults	Elderly	Families	Adults for each families	Children	Adults	Elderly		
50	100	40	120	40	0	0	0	0	0	0	0	0	0	0		
		14	9,75	16			2	5	2			1	4,5	1		
Hours/year		204.400	427.505	233.600	Hours/year		0	0	0	Hours/year		0	0	0		

Table 4. Project data entry: times of use of urban functions other than Residential, Commercial and Tertiary.

Δ Hours a day			
Children	Adults	Elderly	
4	4,75	5	Hours a day
8760			Hours a year

Table 5. Different mix of urban functions and calculation of urban Exposure for each category of users.

% Resid.	% Comm.	% Tert.	Children	Adults	Elderly	Total
100	0	0	187	146	240	573
0	100	0	333	938	375	1646
0	0	100	67	338	75	480
50	50	0	80	220	92	392
50	0	50	22	76	26	124
0	50	50	64	192	73	328
33	33	33	28	81	32	141
60	10	30	15	27	20	62

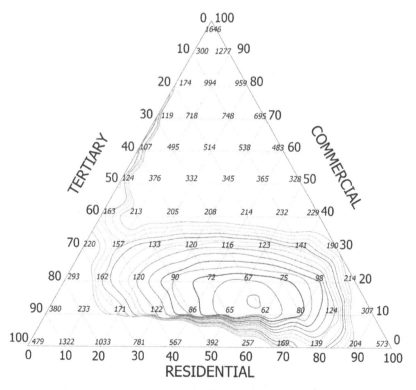

Fig. 2. Graphical representation of urban Exposure in relation to the different urban functions mixes.

From a graphical point of view, the operations described above are represented in Fig. 2.

The graph in Fig. 2 derived by placing the urban functions' percentages (residential, commercial and tertiary) on the sides of the triangle, while the numbers shown inside are the actual Exposure values that are obtained based on the functional mix of reference.

For example, considering 100% residential is obtained a total Exposure of 573; with 50% residential and 50% tertiary, is obtained an Exposure of 124; with 10% residential, 60% commercial and 30% tertiary, the result is a total Exposure of 495; with 60% residential, 30% commercial and 10% tertiary, the result is 141; and so on.

Once the basic grid has been constructed, the different curves representing the Exposure values have been defined (Fig. 3): they are effectively level curves (in this case, they can be called Exposure Curves) because join points with the same Exposure.

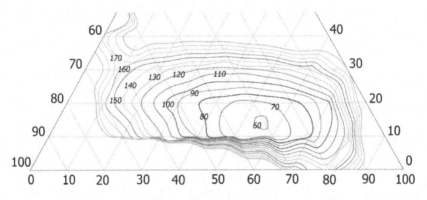

Fig. 3. Graphical representation of urban Exposure in relation to the different urban functions mixes: detail of the Exposure Curves and their value (from 60 to 170).

The last step concerns the identification of the minimum Exposure value (Fig. 4):

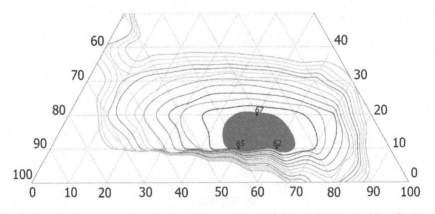

Fig. 4. Graphical representation of urban Exposure in relation to the different urban functions mixes: in evidence, the area with an Exposure value less than or equal to 70.

3.2   Case B

It is presented now the case with the crowding index of the commercial and tertiary function equals to 14 m^2/user[4] (user means both the employee and the person who takes advantage of the function) considering also a functional mix equal to 50% residential and 50% tertiary.

The index of commercial and tertiary use equal to 14 m^2/users determines that a homogeneous functional mix leads to lower Exposure values because the population is not maximized in the residence (thus the Exposure at night is considerably reduced) and, then, equally distributed throughout the day between the tertiary and commercial sectors (both for work and leisure) (Tables 6, 7, 8, 9 and 10).

From a graphical point of view, the operations described above can be represented as follows also with the lowest Exposure values (Fig. 5).

Table 6. Data entry: different functions m^2 and indexes.

Areas (U.F.)				Urban indexes		
Residential R (m^2)	Commercial C (m^2)	Tertiary T (m^2)0	Total (m^2)	R m^2/ inh	C m^2/ inh	T m^2/ inh
5.000	0,00	5.000	10.000	50	14	14
%			%			
50	0	50	100			

Table 7. Data entry: inhabitants.

People						
R (inh)	C (inh)	T (inh)0	Tot inhabitants	Families	Elderly for each family	Children
200	0	0	200	0,25	0,8	0,7

---

[4] In Italy, this value is often used in the analyses carried out by the Municipalities for the average calculation of the users of the specific sector.

Table 8. Project data entry: urban functions times of use.

Residential R

Families	Adults for each families	Children	Adults	Elderly
25	50	20	60	20
		14	9,75	16
Hours/year		102.200	213.525	116.800

Commercial C

Families	Adults for each families	Children	Adults	Elderly
0	0	0	0	0
		2	5	2
Hours/year		0	0	0

Tertiary T

Families	Adults for each families	Children	Adults	Elderly
89	178	71	214	72
		1	4,5	1
Hours/year		25.915	351.730	26.280

Table 9. Project data entry: times of use of urban functions other than Residential, Commercial and Tertiary.

Δ Hours a day			
Children	Adults	Elderly	
4	4,75	5	Hours a day

Table 10. Different mix of urban functions and calculation of urban Exposure for each category of users.

% Resid.	% Comm.	% Tert.	Children	Adults	Elderly	Total
100	0	0	187	146	240	573
0	100	0	95	267	108	470
0	0	100	47	241	54	342
50	50	0	29	60	34	123
50	0	50	19	55	24	98
0	50	50	18	65	20	102
33	33	33	9	26	12	47
60	10	30	22	27	28	77

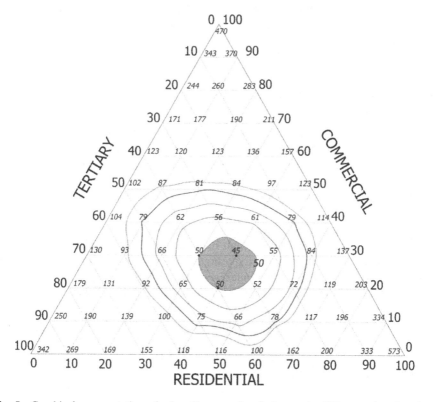

Fig. 5. Graphical representation of urban Exposure in relation to the different urban functions mixes: detail of the Exposure Curves and their value (from 50 to 90) and, in evidence, the area with an Exposure value less than or equal to 50.

4 Discussion

Starting from the simulations described in the previous chapter, in the comparison between the two different examples emerge some interesting comments regarding the urban distribution of functions. As soon as it is an ideal simulation, even if completely similar to real case studies (at least in the European context), the results must be considered as indicators of the directions and purpose of certain existing situations or planning solutions. So, the evaluation of Urban Exposure can be considered also as an instrument to assess different planning scenario.

For the Case A, the minimum Exposure values are around 60. From the point of view of urban and territorial planning, the 3 points highlighted in Fig. 4 are more interesting because they derive from functional mixes that are easily traceable in an existing fabric or just as easily definable when creating new compartments or relocating functions:

- 50% residential, 20% commercial, 30% tertiary → E = 67;
- 50% residential, 10% commercial, 40% tertiary → E = 65;
- 60% residential, 10% commercial, 30% tertiary → E = 62.

For the Case B, the lowest Exposure is equal to or less than 50. In particular, from the point of view of urban and territorial planning, the most interesting Exposure values are the 3 points highlighted in Fig. 5 that derive from functional mixes easily traceable in an existing fabric or equally easily definable when creating new sectors or relocating functions:

- 40% residential, 20% commercial, 40% tertiary → E = 50;
- 40% residential, 30% commercial, 30% tertiary → E = 45;
- 30% residential, 30% commercial, 40% tertiary → E = 50.

Seek the minimum value of the function (3) leads to define a particular point that can hardly be used and therefore is considered not significant: its use, that define such a limiting range of action, does not allow adequate urban development (the 0.1% variation automatically exceeds the set threshold value).

Considering the values obtained from the application of (3), it is clear that the mono-functionalization of the urban area produces Exposure values even 4 times higher than a functional mix. Furthermore, the presence of both a mono-function and maximum crowding indices leads to high Exposure values. In Case A (Fig. 2), in fact, considering 100% of commerce the Exposure reaches a value of 1646. Obviously, as in Case B, the reduction of crowding indexes greatly reduces the Exposure values: there with the 100% of commerce, Exposure reaches a value of 470 (Tables 11 and 12).

Please note that the present analysis starts from statistical data regarding the population, and from objective data regarding the areas (m^2) of the different functions: therefore, the estimation of the population depends on the maximum or average crowding index and on the hours of estimated use of urban functions. It follows that the values can be amplified and purely indicative.

Table 11. Urban Exposure values in Case A.

Exposure highest values				Exposure lowest values			
Case A	%R	%C	%T	Case A	%R	%C	%T
1646	0	100	0	62	60	10	30
1322	10	0	90	65	50	10	40
1277	0	90	10	67	60	10	30
1033	20	0	80	72	40	20	40
994	10	80	10	75	60	20	20

Table 12. Urban Exposure values in Case B.

Exposure highest values				Exposure lowest values			
Case B	%R	%C	%T	Case B	%R	%C	%T
573	100	0	0	45	40	20	40
470	0	100	0	50	40	30	30
370	10	90	0	52	50	20	30
343	0	90	10	55	50	30	20
342	0	0	100	56	30	40	30

5   Conclusion

The presented research outlines that the population is the most important element to be considered. A fundamental next step will be the study of the real-time behaviour of people during the day and related to the different urban functions through specific surveys with questionnaires and the use of satellite data, Big Data, applications and social tools georeferenced or Wi-Fi tools.

From this point of view, interesting is the development of datasets on population distribution (both as forecasts and as realistic and timely analysis) resulting from the intersection of personal data, postal codes, density, flow of students and workers etc. Among all: Gridded Population of the World (GPWv4), Global Rural-Urban Project (GRUMP), LandScan (with attention to day/night variations on 1 km side grids) [17–19], Open WorldPop (estimation of populations with a spatial resolution of 100 mt 100 mt) [20]; GHS-POP (population distribution from GPWv4 data) [21].

Moreover, the presented graphical representation results effective because it allows identifying the area where the urban Exposure has to be maintained or tended: the value will be proportional to the capacity of the urban system to bear economically and socially the changes behind the achievement of the goal. In urban planning, it is not important reach the minimum of the function because it leads to define a particular point that can hardly be used: such a restrictive range of action does not allow an adequate urban development and the definition of advanced strategies to reduce Exposure and then risks.

It is important to underline that the choice to consider a particular index of crowding (or use, considering both workers and users) produces results of quite different Exposure: the consequences can be reflected on the assessments and choices of the decision makers and planners. This is an aspect that decision makers, public administration, experts and citizens' representatives will have to evaluate according to the characteristics of each urban area (cultural and morphological permanencies, economic and productive activities, etc.), population, external contingencies (current natural risk), economic and welfare and the preparation to develop appropriate plans and strategies to respond in advance to the dangers.

Since that, mitigation actions working on Exposure imply removing, reducing and controlling the quantity and quality of the objects exposed in an area subject to risks: at urban/municipal level, therefore, the Exposure analysis must develop by referring to the areas of expansion and the consolidated fabric.

As outlined in the New Urban Agenda [22] (in relation to Sendai Framework) and in the OECD researches [23] (in relation to the better life index), for a shared Disaster Risk Management it is also necessary to define a common line for the Exposure assessment and estimation in order to produce homogeneous, shareable and easily usable results in the different at risk areas and at different urban scales.

References

1. UNISDR (United Nations International Strategy for Disaster Reduction): Terminology: basic terms of disaster risk reduction. International Strategy for Disaster Reduction secretariat, Geneva (2009)
2. Pesaresi, M., et al.: Atlas of the Human Planet 2017: Global Exposure to Natural Hazards, EUR 28556 (2017)
3. IPCC (Intergovernmental Panel on Climate Change): Managing the Risks of Extreme Events and Disasters to Advance Climate Change Adaptation. Cambridge University Press, Cambridge (2012)
4. UN-DESA (Department of economic and social affairs - Population Division): World Urbanization Prospects: The 2014 Revision, Highlights (ST/ESA/SER.A/352). UN-DESA (2014)
5. UN-DESA (Department of economic and social affairs): Risks of exposure and vulnerability to natural disasters at the city level: a global overview. Population Division, Technical paper no. 2015/02. UN-DESA (2015)
6. Gazzola, V.: Valutazione multi scala dell'Esposizione al Rischio. In: Atti della XIX Conferenza Nazionale 2016 SIU. Cambiamenti. Responsabilità e strumenti per l'urbanistica al servizio del paese, Workshop, vol. 4, pp. 582–587. Planum Publisher, Roma-Milano (2016)
7. Venco, E.M.: L'Esposizione nell'analisi del rischio in ambito pianificatorio. In: Atti della XIX Conferenza Nazionale SIU. Cambiamenti. Responsabilità e strumenti per l'urbanistica al servizio del paese, Catania, 16–18 giugno 2016, pp. 641–648. Planum Publisher, Roma-Milano (2017)
8. De Lotto, R., Gazzola, V., Venco, E.M.: Exposure and Risk reduction strategy: the role of Functional Change. In: Margani, G., et al. (eds.) Proceedings of the International Conference on Seismic and Energy Renovation for Sustainable Cities (SER4SC 2018), Catania, Italy, pp. 319–330. EdicomEdizioni, Montefalcone (Go) (2018)

9. Bündnis Entwicklung Hilft (Alliance Development Works), United Nations University – Institute for Environment and Human Security (UNU-EHS): WorldRiskReport 2014. United Nations University EHS Institute and the Alliance Development Works, Berlin (2011–2014)

10. Bündnis Entwicklung Hilft and Ruhr University Bochum – Institute for International Law of Peace and Armed Conflict (IFHV): WorldRiskReport 2018

11. Chen, Q.-F., Chen, Y., Liu, J., Chen, L.: Quick and approximate estimation of earthquake loss based on macroscopic index of exposure and population distribution. Nat. Hazards **15**, 217–229 (1997)

12. De Lotto, R., Gazzola, V., Gossenberg, S., Morelli di Popolo, C., Venco, E.M.: Proposal to reduce natural risks: analytic network process to evaluate efficiency of city planning strategies. In: Gervasi, O., et al. (eds.) ICCSA 2016. LNCS, vol. 9789, pp. 650–664. Springer, Cham (2016). https://doi.org/10.1007/978-3-319-42089-9_46

13. Per, A.F., Mozas, J., Arpa, J.: DBook. Density, Data, Diagrams, Dwellings. A visual analysis of 64 collective housing projects. a+t ediciones, Spain (2007)

14. Mozas, J., Per, A.F: Density: New Collective Housing. a+t ediciones, Spain (2006)

15. UNI 10339:1995 - 30/06/1995 - Impianti aeraulici a fini di benessere. Generalità, classificazione e requisiti. Regole per la richiesta d'offerta, l'offerta, l'ordine e la fornitura

16. ISTAT (Istituto Nazionale di Statistica): Forme, livelli e dinamiche dell'urbanizzazione in Italia. Territorio, letture statistiche. ISTAT (2017)

17. Aubrecht, C., Steinnocher, K., Hollaus, M., Wagner, W.: Interacting earth observation and GIScience for high resolution spatial and functional modelling of urban land use. Comput. Environ. Urban Syst. **33**, 15–25 (2009)

18. Aubrecht, C., Ozceylan, D., Steinnocher, K., Freire, S.: Multi-level geospatial modelling of human exposure patterns and vulnerability indicators. Nat. Hazards **68**, 147–163 (2013)

19. Corbane, C., Gamba, P., Pesaresi, M., Pittore, M., Wieland, M.: Current and innovative methods to define exposure. In: Poljanšek, K., Marín Ferrer, M., De Groeve, T., Clark, I. (eds.) Science for Disaster Risk Management 2017: Knowing Better and Losing Less, EUR 28034 EN, chap. 2.2. Publications Office of the European Union, Luxembourg (2017)

20. Lloyd, C.T., Sorichetta, A., Tatem, A.J.: High resolution global gridded data for use in population studies. Scientific Data 4 (170001) (2017)

21. Pesaresi, M., Melchiorri, M., Siragusa, A., Kemper, T.: Atlas of the Human Planet — Mapping Human Presence on Earth with the Global Human Settlement Layer, EUR 28116 EN. Publications Office of the European Union, Luxembourg (2016)

22. United Nation Habitat III Secretariat. NEW Urban Agenda (2016)

23. OECD. http://www.oecdbetterlifeindex.org/it/#/111111111111. Accessed 16 Feb 2019

SAFE (Safety for Families in Emergency)

A Citizen-Centric Approach for Risk Management

Monica Sebillo[1(✉)], Giuliana Vitiello[1], Michele Grimaldi[1],
and Dimitri Dello Buono[2]

[1] University of Salerno, 84084 Fisciano, SA, Italy
{msebillo,gvitiello,migrimaldi}@unisa.it
[2] IMAA – CNR, 85050 Tito, PZ, Italy
dimitri.dellobuono@imaa.cnr.it

Abstract. In the field of Civil Protection, there is a growing awareness that the involvement of citizens has an immediate impact on decisions and actions to be taken, thanks to the distributed knowledge they hold about their territory. In this paper we describe SAFE (SAfety for Families in Emergency), an information system conceived to improve the certified emergency response procedures which may benefit from user-generated contents deriving from existing intelligent community networks. SAFE design follows the trend of the current research, namely to identify hybrid solutions that let citizens and experts work together to collect and redistribute the information, once properly processed.

Keywords: Volunteered Geographic Information · Citizen-centric design ·
Risk management · Mobile applications · GeoVisual summary

1 Introduction

In the last decade, in the field of Civil Protection, as in other domains, there has been a growing awareness that the involvement of citizens has an immediate impact on decisions and actions to be taken, as they hold distributed knowledge about their own territory. The timeliness of data they provide through a direct participation increases indeed the reliability of information, thus allowing operating on a territory in an efficient and effective way.

Some usages of the so-called Volunteered Geographic Information (VGI) can be found in the field of the *early warning* [1]. *Ushahidi* is the best-known platform that offers local observers an open source software for collecting, visualizing and geolocating information through smartphones and the Internet, thus creating sharable spatio-temporal databases [5].

The rationale behind *Ushahidi* is the concept of social activism entrusted by public responsibility. *Ushahidi* adopts the model known as 'activist mapping', which is the combination of social activism, citizen journalism and geospatial information. It was first used to collect and disseminate on a Google map the eyewitness accounts of violence occurred in Kenya in 2007.

© Springer Nature Switzerland AG 2019
S. Misra et al. (Eds.): ICCSA 2019, LNCS 11620, pp. 424–437, 2019.
https://doi.org/10.1007/978-3-030-24296-1_34

In similar scenarios, citizens play the role of observers, who are geographically distributed on the ground. Moreover, as stated in [1], humans themselves represent a sensor network (of more than 6 billion of components), thanks to their capability of interpreting what they capture by their senses. This is a founding approach for experts and represents the basis from which every action on a territory should start.

Despite this awareness, however, existing methods and tools addressed to support general-purposes monitoring tasks are not satisfactory, yet. They face, indeed, each issue from a unique perspective and, although they represent innovative solutions, they may be limited by the lack of a real involvement of ultimate users by experts and decision makers during the design phase.

The direction that current research is following along this line is then to identify hybrid solutions that let citizens and experts work together to collect and redistribute the information, once properly processed [9, 11].

In this paper we describe SAFE (**SA**fety for **F**amilies in **E**mergency), an information system conceived to pursue this goal, i.e., to improve the certified procedures which, based on the need of a continuous monitoring of a territory, can benefit from the user-generated content deriving from existing intelligent community networks. In SAFE, the involvement of families is relevant to enhance those emergency procedures that are activated in case of an event, such as an earthquake and a landslide. In such cases, the timely communication by citizens allows decision makers to address aids where needed, thus optimizing the available resources.

SAFE is part of a wider initiative, namely *Comune Sicuro*, whose goal is to align the actions performed by Public Administration to the Open Government's ones through methods and tools that enhance the citizens' engagement. In particular, *Comune Sicuro* aims to facilitate and automate most of the tasks in charge of the civil protection professionals, such as the identification of risks on a territory and the planning of needs according to them.

The paper is organized as follows. Section 2 briefly describes the new paradigm underlying *Comune Sicuro*, Civil Protection 2.0. In Sect. 3 the integration of actions performed by citizens with procedures certified by professionals is described. In particular, three goals are presented and the associated results are discussed. Section 4 embeds the obtained results in SAFE and describes both components, SAFE Mobile and SAFE Web. Some conclusions are drawn in Sect. 5.

2 Civil Protection 2.0

The goal of the research we are carrying out is to catch foundation of the systemic process started by the Open Government paradigm, namely transparency, participation and collaboration, and let citizens play a different and more aware role in the evolving scenarios that concern them.

The initiative *Comune Sicuro* stems from a collaboration between the Laboratory of Geographic Information Systems (*LabGIS*) at the Department of Computer Science (University of Salerno) and the research group *geoSDI* at the Institute of Methodologies for Environmental Analysis of the National Council of Research (CNR IMAA).

Research in this domain has been stimulated by the awareness that although each municipality is required to draw up and manage an emergency plan for the possible risks associated with its territory, many of them are defaulting. Reasons are different. Lack of funds to be allocated to that activity, lack of expertise in this field, lack of a continuous monitoring of resources and information, are only some possible causes.

The focus of *Comune Sicuro* is the identification of the risks of a territory, the census of available resources, the planning of the needs according to the risks, the dissemination of the emergency plan to citizens, and the establishment of itself as a geo-social service. In order to reach these goals, *Comune Sicuro* adopts a paradigm that aims to put Civil Protection activities [8] into practice thanks to the use of new methods and tools, including ICT-based solutions. The basic idea is to converge the amount of data managed in the Civil Protection field within a cloud platform to allow a correct and perfect exchange of data and information. The goal is to optimize the available resources management and guarantee the correct involvement and coordination of the various actors present in the various procedures for implementing the municipal plan. To allow that, the project offers a set of features that every day, 24 h a day, makes citizens participate to the execution and management of the procedures.

The whole process scheduled in *Comune Sicuro* starts by acquiring and storing data through an intelligent census based on a Web of data approach [6]. An ontology of the Civil Protection domain is under construction [7]. It allows modelling and validating resources in terms of metadata, state and behavior. Moreover, the ontology can be used also to aggregate subsets of resources to build units to which a composite state and a behavior can be associated. Inference algorithms can be used to derive additional relationships among validated resources. The requirement is to have a system that dynamically generates new cards for the data entry tasks and populates the available dataset, through procedures that are based on an effective territorial knowledge, where instrumental and human resources, rules, behaviors and interactions converge.

A fundamental feature of the whole system, which should be simple and intuitive to use, is the "dynamism of data", meant as a continuous updating of resources and their possible interactions. A high quality standard has also to be guaranteed in order to avoid duplications, inconsistencies, incompleteness and unreliability.

A scenario where the research activities are applied relates in particular to the development of a monitoring and decision support system that allows for activating alert or rescue procedures when events occur that require civil protection actions. Procedures that activate this system are realized by different typologies of users, each operating through a different type of application. End users, citizens, experts and professionals can participate by using mobile applications that are intended to support their *prosumerism* and enable various geo-social processes that in general allow increasing the knowledge of a territory. The following Section describes how SAFE supports this approach towards the collaboration of different actors involved into civil protection actions.

3 Integrating Social Activism and Certified Procedures

The Civil Protection field represents a public sector where the integration of activist mappers and certified data managers could contribute to the enhancement of its efficacy.

Besides the role played by experts and professionals, the citizens' involvement is extremely important. The reason is twofold. Engaging citizens into a decision making process implies to build more efficient solutions because they can contribute to the requirement analysis as active stakeholders, thus focusing attention on real needs. Moreover, contributing to the development of a solution by citizens also guarantees a more convincing adoption of it. These assumptions mean that citizens can acquire awareness about territory and its phenomena and produce collective intelligence.

Researchers from *LabGIS* pursue the goal of designing and developing innovative tools to facilitate citizens' interaction conceived to provide data (the citizen as a producer) and acquire information (the citizen as a consumer) [10].

In order to reach this goal, three specific research topics have been addressed and discussed, namely,

1. diversification of users,
2. visual summary and
3. quantification of risk parameters.

In the following subsections, the results obtained for each topic are discussed and their integration in SAFE is presented.

3.1 The User *Family*

In SAFE, the citizen-centric design and the previous requirements led to the definition of the *Family* (nucleo familiare) user. A *Family* is a sociological unit that represents an aggregation of people belonging to the same core from a fiscal, legal and economic point of view, and sharing the same accommodation. The metadata that characterize a *Family* unit are both quantitative, like the number of components, and qualitative, and in this case, we refer to the components expressed as a hierarchy of family ties between them.

3.2 The Geometaphor *Neighborhood*

As part of SAFE, a fundamental requirement concerns the visualization of data referring to a bound space like a map. In this case, the constraint of a precise geographic reference limits the capability of locating aggregated data in the best position in terms of visualization. The usual visualization techniques may in fact prove ineffective for georeferenced data since these are associated with precise coordinates (geographical or Cartesian) and cannot be arranged in different positions even if contained in areas of respect. On the other hand, leaving the atomic data always visible can lead to misinterpretations of a scenario by a decision maker.

It is then necessary to use a technique that allows both positioning an exact reference for each SAFE user and at the same time visually aggregate users georeferenced in the same space.

The solution proposed in SAFE is a visual summary technique that allows having, under certain conditions, a visual synthesis of data present on a thematism. The idea is based on the Shneiderman mantra [2] and the Keim method [4]. Shneiderman's formulation "first overview, zoom and filter, then details on demand" represents a well-known visualization paradigm, which consists in the visualization, during the supervision phase, of all data contained in the dataset to obtain a complete view of the situation that characterizes a domain of interest. This type of visualization allows the user to have a global vision of information, ensuring a more accurate management.

Keim's formulation "Analyze First - Show the important" states that it is not appropriate to use only visual and interactive methods for displaying large amounts of data. It is reasonable to first apply a series of computational analyzes and then provide an overview of the information that is relevant to the user. In this way, the user can interact with components that represent the synthesis of data without running the risk of losing data that make up the dataset.

By taking account both paradigms, in SAFE a visual geometaphor is introduced that arises as a hybrid solution and adapts to the requirement of georeferencing [3].

The visual geometaphor defines the concept of *Neighborhood* (Vicinato) that visually groups families associated to the same space. This is the case, for example, of families in the same building, then with the same planimetric coordinates, or families present in an area defined by a buffering threshold. Figure 1 shows the components of the *Neighborhood* geometaphor. It consists of a physical component or Geometry, in this case a point geometry, and of a logical component or Icon, expressed as a pair (physical representation and meaning) and a state.

Neighborhood geometaphor		
Geometry		●
Icon	physical representation	 📍
	meaning	aggregation of Family users
	state	• safe • unsafe / danger • unknown

Fig. 1. The *Neighborhood* geometaphor.

As in SAFE the geometaphor is associated with a map, it has been drawn as a usual ballon to which a user navigating a map is accustomed. Its size implicitly includes the concept of one or more *Family* users who are located in a unique spatial reference or in an area defined by a specific threshold. Finally, to manage the state of the geometaphor, its physical representation can be associated with a different well-defined coloration (Fig. 2).

Fig. 2. The *Neighborhood* state representation.

The geometaphor has also a zoom scale associated with it that has an impact on its spatial destruction. This mechanism makes the project scalable and capable of handling large amounts of data in a clear and efficient manner. Figure 3 shows the Family users associated to the geometaphor. They are displayed once the scale value is appropriate for their display.

Spatial operators can be applied to the *Neighborhood* geometaphor, in line with the operations allowed on a point geometry with respect to the geometries present in the other themes. In particular, topological operators (*containment* and *adjacency*), directional operators and metric operators (*distance*) can be applied.

Fig. 3. *Family* users associated to a *Neighborhood* geometaphor.

3.3 Dynamically Quantifying Risk Parameters

The Risk is defined by the formula [12]:

$$R = P \times V \times E,$$

where variables correspond to:

P = Hazard: it is the probability that a phenomenon of a certain intensity occurs in a certain interval of time and in a given area.

V = Vulnerability: the vulnerability of an element (people, buildings, infrastructures, economic activities) is the propensity to suffer damage as a result of the stresses induced by an event of a certain intensity.

E = Exposure or Exposed Value: is the number of units (or "value") of each of the risk elements present in a given area, such as human lives or settlements.

In this formula, the variable E represents the most sensitive data because it is linked to the human component. Usually, when it is processed, the Risk refers to the value obtained from data present in the official registry. However, it is known in literature that this value is the most susceptible to changes, and a value acquired in real time with respect to an estimated or static value can make the difference in emergencies.

In SAFE, it is relevant to make the variables, coming into play during the Risk calculation, visible to the decision maker and at the same time that their values are as realistic as possible. The proposed solution is based on the use of the *Neighborhood* geometaphor and in particular on the value assumed by the component that expresses its state. Then, a value associated with the *quiet* state matches the global value estimated or acquired through the municipal plans. Otherwise, the feedback due to the change of state (*unsafe*, *unknown*) directly influences the calculation of the variable E allowing real-time monitoring of the population distribution. Thus, through SAFE graphical systems for displaying the values of variables updated in real time, the decision maker can have a complete view of all variables involved during rescue operations and make the best decision easier.

4 Acting in *SAFE*

SAFE has been designed as a geo-social application that provides *Family* users with functionality of daily use. As an example, a notification is automatically sent to a mum when the school bus is entering into an area at a given distance from her house (Fig. 4). A citizen can send an alert to a target office in order to report an environmental problem. This daily practice is important because it guarantees that SAFE is used also in case of emergency where stress conditions can complicate the usage of an unfamiliar application.

Figure 5 shows the interface to register the members of a family along with some personal data, such as age, telephone number, possible pathologies and allergies.

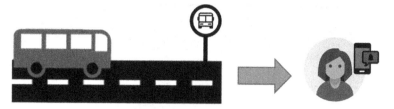

Fig. 4. Geo-social services in SAFE

Fig. 5. Registering family members

Each registered *Family* user is then visualized in a QGIS environment where a map of their geographic distribution is displayed, as shown in Fig. 6. A Python script can be used by the emergency manager to select data about them.

Figure 7 illustrates the architecture of the system, which consists of a Web application, a mobile application and a PostGIS database. Different users interacting with the systems are also displayed, namely a citizen (cittadino), a civil protection professional (operatore protezione civile), and a decision maker (decisore).

In case of an emergency, a decision maker or an emergency manager interacts with the SAFE Web application illustrated in Fig. 8. It shows the environment with a legend (legenda) with two differently-sized geometaphors, namely *Family* (nucleo familiare) and *Neighborhood* (edificio/vicinato), and an icon for the risk areas (aree di rischio). On the right, it also contains both the *Hazard scenario* conceived to define the area of the event and (de)activate an alarm, and the *Exposure scenario* that visually summarizes the global distribution of the *Family* users' state in terms of *safe* (sicuro), *unsafe* (pericolo) and *unknown* (ignoto). Once an alarm is launched, balloons representing both *Family* and *Neighborhood* users are red to indicate that, until SAFE receive feedbacks, citizens are in an *unknown* state.

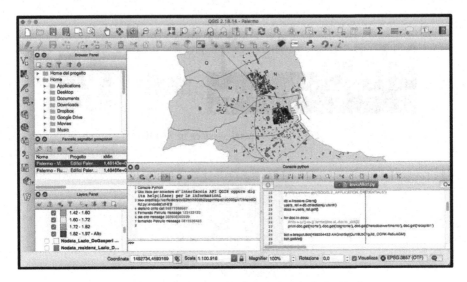

Fig. 6. The environment visualizing the users' distribution

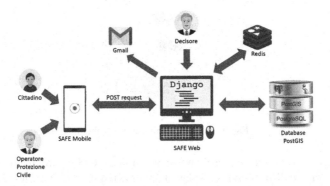

Fig. 7. The SAFE architecture.

From a user point of view, the citizens' involvement is prominent. Once they received an alert on their mobile device, the head of family can communicate the necessary information about the state of each family member. The timeliness of this action makes the difference both in terms of human lives and in terms of optimizing the distribution of rescue interviewees. Figure 9(a) shows the mobile interface through which a citizen is alerted about an occurred event or a possible risk (the detail explains the situation), while Fig. 9(b) illustrates the module the citizen can use to communicate the whole family state, member after member.

As the users' notifications arrive, the color of the balloons can change accordingly. It becomes green when the *Family/Neighborhood* user notifies that each person associated to it is in a *safe* state. Differently, it remains red if even one person is in an *unknown* state, while it becomes yellow if even one person needs aid. Figures 10 show

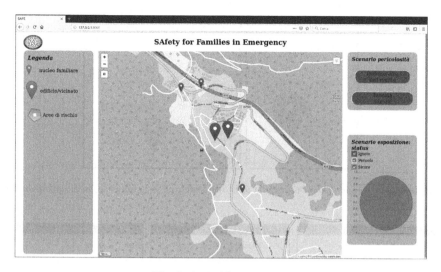

Fig. 8. Launching an alarm.

Fig. 9. (a) An alert sent to a user. (b) The family state communication

a red balloon associated to a *Neighborhood* user. When selected, the former lists the *Family* users associated to it and their state (Fig. 10(a)). The latter displays the state of each person belonging to a selected *Family* user (Fig. 10(b)).

The information that can be derived from the users' notifications also refer to the possibility of optimizing aids distribution. Figures 11(a) ÷ (c) show the interface available for the operators on the field. They can control both their zones of competence (aree di competenza) in general, and scenarios evolving inside them, thus reaching areas where their intervention is extremely important. In particular, Fig. 11(b) lists users who need aids (Soccorsi), while Fig. 11(c) shows the path to reach them.

Fig. 10. (a) A *Neighborhood* user in an *unknown* state. (b) A *Family* user in an *unknown* state

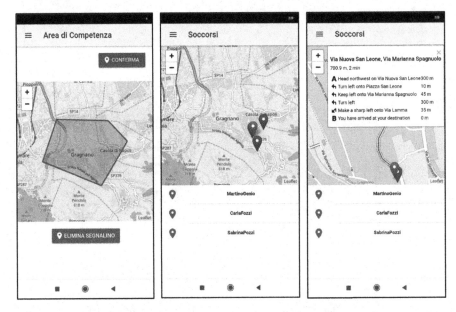

Fig. 11. (a) A zone associated to an operator on the field. (b) Users and operator's position. (c) Details about users.

Finally, as for the Exposure parameter, Fig. 12 shows a detail of the interface, namely the graphic representing the *exposure* scenario in two different moments.

Values associated to them fill in the formula to calculate the risk parameters in real time. This functionality allows performing a real time analysis of risk distribution, as shown in Fig. 13. Besides red balloons that identify the *Family* and the *Neighborhood* users in an *unsafe* location, the environment lists the risk codes that represent the impact levels derived from the risk matrix defined by the basin authority plan (PSAI) *Liri – Garigliano e Volturno* and *Campania Centrale* (Central Campania), Italy.

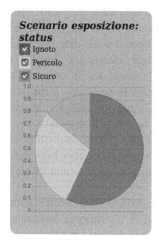
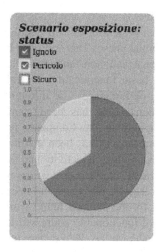

Fig. 12. The evolution of an *exposure* scenario.

Fig. 13. Risk codes and *Family* users located in the high hazard level areas.

5 Final Remarks

SAFE satisfies the initially set objectives. The SAFE Mobile component is a simple and agile tool for citizens who want to contribute to support operations on a territory. The SAFE Web component plays a twofold role. It aims optimizing the available resources management and guaranteeing the correct involvement and coordination of the different actors present in the various procedures for implementing a municipal plan. Moreover, it carries out syntheses of data collected and builds dynamic maps of risk scenarios useful to decision makers for acting on a given area in case of emergency.

SAFE is a very ambitious project and as such it can reach its goal if each user, citizens, professionals and decision makers, participates in the design task from the very initial phase. This approach has been indeed followed while defining both SAFE functional and non-functional requirements. Moreover, during the development of SAFE basic functionality, several events have been simulated in order to test the system performances also through the users' feedbacks. In particular, a memorandum of understanding has been signed by the LabGIS director and a manager of a municipality in the Campania region though which a SAFE prototype for multi-platform devices has been distributed. Currently, the analysis of data collected from users is an ongoing activity and some preliminary investigations have been performed in terms of interface evaluation and comprehensiveness of information displayed for the emergency managers and decision makers.

As for the planned future work, an improvement to SAFE has been scheduled in terms of functionality addressed to the dissemination of information concerning both the behavior to be taken in case of a natural event, and in general the perception of risk itself by people, independently from the role they can play.

Acknowledgments. The authors would like to thank students Vincenzo Nastro, Stefano Cirillo, Marianna Di Gregorio, Fernando Petrulio, Umberto Picariello, Antonio Rapuano and Daniele Vitale for their contribution to the development of the SAFE mobile and the Web components.

References

1. Goodchild, M.F.: Citizens as sensors: the world of volunteered geography. GeoJournal **69**, 211–221 (2007). https://doi.org/10.1007/s10708-007-9111-y
2. Shneiderman, B.: The eyes have it: a task by data type taxonomy for information visualizations. In: Proceedings of the 1996 IEEE Symposium on Visual Languages, pp. 336–343 (1996)
3. Sebillo, M., Tortora, G., Vitiello, G.: The metaphor GIS query language. J. Vis. Lang. Comput. Acad. Press. **11**(4), 439–454 (2000)
4. Keim, D.A., Mansmann, F. Schneidewind, J., Ziegler, H.: Challenges in visual data analysis. In: Proceedings of Information Visualization, (IV 2006), pp. 9–16. IEEE (2006)
5. Ushahidi Project. https://www.ushahidi.com/. Accessed 10 Mar 2019
6. Hitzler, P., Krotzsch, M., Rudolph, S.: Foundations of Semantic Web Technologies. Chapman & HALL/CRC, Boca Raton (2009)
7. Protégé 5.5.0. protege.stanford.edu. Accessed 10 Mar 2019
8. Galanti, E.: Il metodo Augustus. In DPC informa, Periodico informative della Protezione Civile, Giugno (1997)
9. Ginige, A., Paolino, L., Romano, M., Sebillo, M., Tortora, G., Vitiello, G.: Information sharing among disaster responders - an interactive spreadsheet-based collaboration approach. Comput. Support. Coop. Work. (CSCW) **23**(4–6), 547–583 (2014). ISSN: 0925-9724
10. Paolino, L., Romano, M., Sebillo, M., Vitiello, G.: Supporting the on site emergency management through a visualization technique for mobile devices. J. Locat. Based Serv. **4** (03–04), 222–239 (2010). https://doi.org/10.1080/17489725.2010

11. Sebillo, M., Vitiello, G., Paolino, L., Ginige, A.: Training emergency responders through augmented reality mobile interfaces. Multimed. Tools Appl. **75**(16), 9609–9622 (2016). https://doi.org/10.1007/s11042-015-2955-0

12. Varnes, D.J.: IAEG: The principles and practise of landslide hazard zonation. UNESCO Parigi Press (1984)

Blockchain and Distributed Ledgers: Technologies and Application (BDLTA 2019)

Automatic Synthesis of Multilevel Automata Models of Biological Objects

Vasiliy Osipov[1] , Elena Stankova[2] , Alexander Vodyaho[3] ,
Mikhail Lushnov[4] , Yulia Shichkina[3(✉)] ,
and Nataly Zhukova[1]

[1] St. Petersburg Institute for Informatics and Automation of the Russian
Academy of Sciences, St. Petersburg, Russia
osipov_vasiliy@mail.ru, nazhukova@mail.ru
[2] St. Petersburg State University, St. Petersburg, Russia
elenastankova@yandex.ru
[3] St. Petersburg State Electrotechnical University, St. Petersburg, Russia
aivodyaho@mail.ru, strange.y@mail.ru
[4] Almazov National Medical Research Centre, St. Petersburg, Russia
lushnov_ms@almazovcentre.ru

Abstract. In the paper the problem of high computational complexity of synthesis is discussed. Existing models and methods of synthesis don't allow build models of biological objects and systems. The complexity can be significantly reduced due to considering multilevel objects models instead of single level models. The new problem statement for multilevel synthesis is given. To build the models a new method based on inductive and deductive approaches is proposed. To describe the new multilevel models of the objects the theory of automata models is extended to the case of multilevel relatively finite operational automata models. Results of modeling of dynamics of the acid-base state in cavernous sinus of patients with cardiac surgical pathology during the postoperative period in the operating room and in the cardio-resuscitation unit are given.

Keywords: Biological objects · Multilevel automata · Automatic synthesis

1 Introduction

One of the current scientific tasks in the field of biology and medicine is to synthesize models of observed objects [1, 2]. The presence of such models allows predict possible events that refer to past experience, justify and implement targeted actions. The diversity of the observed objects is great. At the physical level they are characterized by the results of their parameters measurements. The time series of measured parameters have temporal, amplitude, frequency, and phase characteristics. At logical levels objects are described by sets of structural properties. There are multiple relations between the elements of the objects that reflect in their descriptions at both levels. From this point of view, the synthesis of observed objects models can be considered as the binding of elements of data about these objects. Known methods of inductive and deductive

© Springer Nature Switzerland AG 2019
S. Misra et al. (Eds.): ICCSA 2019, LNCS 11620, pp. 441–456, 2019.
https://doi.org/10.1007/978-3-030-24296-1_35

synthesis are applicable for such binding [3–16]. Inductive methods of synthesis include methods of agreement, difference, concomitant variations, residues, and others. Using the methods of inductive synthesis, it is possible to move from the time series of the results of parameters measurements to small models of the objects. Deductive synthesis is based on the results of inductive output. It allows synthesize more complex models. For deductive synthesis various implementations of resolution methods, inverse and combined conclusion methods are used.

Despite of the achieved results in the field of automatic synthesis of observed objects models, the following problems remain unsolved. They include reducing the complexity of the synthesis and increasing the efficiency of solving applied problems using the obtained models. Traditional methods of automatic synthesis of such models in many respects do not meet the needs of practice in the field of biology. They require considerable spent of time on obtaining desired solutions. In addition, due to the imperfection of the obtained models, it is impossible to ensure the high efficiency of solving applied problems such as estimating objects state, forecasting events and managing the process of achieving required objects state.

One of the promising approaches to the improvement of such synthesis is an automatic construction of multilevel automata as observed objects models. In the interests of this it is necessary to have appropriate models, methods and algorithms.

2 Problem Description

Let us consider the problem of automatic synthesis of multilevel automata as models of observed objects. As automata structures for formal description of the objects models relatively finite operational automata [17] are used. The generalized structure of the process of models formation (obtaining, pre-processing of information and direct synthesis) is represented in Fig. 1, where RFA 1, ..., N are relatively finite operational automata.

According to the process of models formation, information about observed objects can be obtained by passive or active means of observation. Due to the fact that the data received from objects is generally heterogeneous, it is transformed to a homogeneous form. For this data is represented as a finite set of time series. For each of them time,

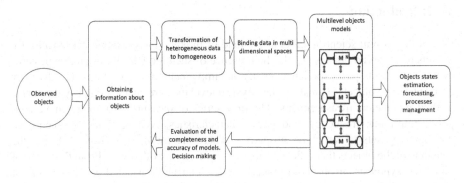

Fig. 1. The structure of the process of obtaining, preprocessing and synthesis of multilevel automata as models of observed objects

frequency or time – frequency representations are formed. The amplitude and phase characteristics of time series are frequency and phase functions. With such a representation, it is possible to talk about spatial and temporal binding, and operate on the lower level with single pulses. Linking can be carried out both within segments of single time series and between different time series or sets of time series.

It is required that, as a result of such linking, multilevel models of the observed objects can be synthesized as multilevel relatively finite operational automata (MRFA). In this regard, it is necessary to develop an appropriate method and algorithms for the synthesis of such models.

3 Features of MRFA and Synthesis Efficiency Criteria

In the interest of developing a method of synthesis of multilevel relatively finite automata as models of observed objects, let's define their features.

Every one-level RFA_r at the r-th moment of time is defined by a set of ten parameters:

$$RFA_r = \{\bar{d}_{a_r}, \bar{d}_{b_r}, \bar{d}_{c_r}, F_r^b, F_r^c, DA(\bar{d}_{b_{r-1}}), DB(\bar{d}_{b_{r-1}}), DC(\bar{d}_{b_{r-1}}), FB(\bar{d}_{b_{r-1}}), FC(\bar{d}_{b_{r-1}})\},$$

where $\bar{d}_{a_r}$ - input vector; $\bar{d}_{b_r}$ - internal state parameter vector; $\bar{d}_{c_r}$ - output state parameter vector. Transition functions F_r^b of the automata from one internal state to another and functions of the outputs F_r^c are defined as:

$$\bar{d}_{b_{r+1}} = F_r^b(\bar{d}_{a_r}, \bar{d}_{b_r}), \quad , \bar{d}_{c_r} = F_r^c(\bar{d}_{a_r}, \bar{d}_{b_r})$$

States $\bar{d}_{b_r}, \bar{d}_{c_r}, \bar{d}_{a_r}$ and functions F_r^b, F_r^c, must satisfy the conditions at the r-th moment of time:

$$\bar{d}_{a_r} \in DA(\bar{d}_{b_{r-1}}), \ \bar{d}_{b_r} \in DB(\bar{d}_{b_{r-1}}), \ \bar{d}_{c_r} \in DC(\bar{d}_{b_{r-1}}),$$
$$F_r^b \in FB(\bar{d}_{b_{r-1}}), \ F_r^c \in FC(\bar{d}_{b_{r-1}}).$$

According to these conditions, the state of the input of the automata at the r-th instant of time is limited to the set $DA(\bar{d}_{b_{r-1}})$ of admissible states defined relatively to the r-1 instant of time. The internal state of the automata at the r-th moment must relate to the set $DB(\bar{d}_{b_{r-1}})$ of its admissible internal states. There are also restrictions on the possible states of the output of the automata. These states should relate to the set $DC(\bar{d}_{b_{r-1}})$. In addition, the transition function F_r^b implemented by the automata at the r-th moment must be included in the set $FB(\bar{d}_{b_{r-1}})$ of admissible functions. The set $FB(\bar{d}_{b_{r-1}})$ of transition functions reflects the system of commands specific of the automata at the r-th moment. Outputs functions F_r^c must belong to the set $FC(\bar{d}_{b_{r-1}})$ of admissible functions.

The transition from automata RFA_r to automata RFA_{r+1} is defined as:

$$F_r^b : RFA_r, \bar{d}_{a_r} \to RFA_{r+1}.$$

Taking this into account, to construct multilevel (hierarchical) relatively finite operational automata as models of observed objects, basic sets of admissible parameters of RFA are selected:

$$HRFA^0 = \{DA^0, DB^0, DC^0, FB^0, FC^0\}.$$

From the elements of these basic sets it is possible to form admissible sets of parameters of higher i-th levels,

$$HRFA^i = \{DA^i, DB^i, DC^i, FB^i, FC^i\}.$$

As a result, multilevel relatively finite automata can be characterized by admissible sets of parameters at different levels of the hierarchy:

$$HRFA^0 \Leftrightarrow HRFA^1 \Leftrightarrow \dots \Leftrightarrow HRFA^i \Leftrightarrow \dots \Leftrightarrow HRFA^K.$$

Considering that in each $HRFA^i = \{DA^i, DB^i, DC^i, FB^i, FC^i\}$ admissible sets change over time, they can be represented as dependent on internal states: $HRFA^i = HRFA^i(\bar{d}_{b_{r-1}^i})$.

In some cases, by expanding the set of internal states of automata to the states of its output, it is possible to obtain automata with a truncated set of the parameters, but with the preservation of properties of the parameters restructuring:

$$HRFA_r = \{\bar{d}_{a_r}, \bar{d}_{b_r}, F_r^b, DA(\bar{d}_{b_{r-1}}), DB(\bar{d}_{b_{r-1}}), FB(\bar{d}_{b_{r-1}})\}.$$

In the logical form the transition functions of automata from one state to another can be represented as $F_r^b(\bar{d}_{a_r}, \bar{d}_{b_r}) \to \bar{d}_{b_{r+1}}$.

The considered automata is a completely reconstructable model. Elements of the upper levels of such model are represented as a set of other interrelated elements of lower levels. From a formal point of view, the transition from one level to another can be reduced to the restructuring of the admissible sets of parameters.

In conditions when the available data are insufficient for the synthesis of automata models, incomplete structures can be constructed. In such models there are parameters of the automata, which are partially defined. The completeness of the description of automata depends on the ratio of the number of its parameters and the number of parameters of the complete automata. It is proposed to determine such completeness Q_r at the r–th instant of time as

$$Q_r = 1 - \frac{1}{c}\sum_{j=1}^{c} q_{jr},$$

$$q_{1r} = \frac{|M_1(DA(d_{b_{r-1}})) - Z_1|}{Z_1}, \quad q_{2r} = \frac{|M_2(DB(d_{b_{r-1}})) - Z_2|}{Z_2}, \quad q_{3r} = \frac{|M_3(DC(d_{b_{r-1}})) - Z_3|}{Z_3}$$

$$q_{4r} = \frac{|M_4(FB(d_{b_{r-1}})) - Z_4|}{Z_4}, \quad q_{5r} = \frac{|M_5(FC(d_{b_{r-1}})) - Z_5|}{Z_5}$$

where $M_1, M_2, \ldots, M_5$ - the capacities of the formed sets of states values and functions of transitions and outputs characterizing automata at the r–th moment; $Z_1, Z_2, \ldots, Z_5$ - admissible values of these capacities; c - a coefficient assigned according to the number of types of automata parameters, c = 5. For complete automata $Q_r = 1$. For automata whose parameters are not defined, the indicator value is zero.

Taking this into account, the models of the observed objects in the form of multilevel relatively finite operational automata with a level of the completeness not lower than the specified are synthesized based on minimizing the time for building models. In some cases when the time for synthesis is limited the construction of an efficient model is possible in trying to achieve the maximum of Q_r.

4 Synthesis Method

To solve the problem of automatic synthesis of MRFA of observed objects considering the results [18, 19] a method based on the combined use of inductive and deductive approaches is proposed. At the first stage, an inductive synthesis of a set of local multilevel automata is carried out, and at the second stage, large structures through deductive synthesis are constructed. Below the new algorithms that form the basis of this method are proposed.

4.1 Algorithm of Inductive Multilevel Synthesis

Recall that according to the above statement of the problem, the initial data for observed objects models synthesis can be sequences of sets of parameters measured values. For the automatic inductive synthesis of MRFA based on the analysis of such sequences, the following steps are proposed:

1. Analysis of sequential sets of parameters values at a given time interval $T = \sum_{j=0}^{N-1} T_j$,

   where T - a temporary pause between adjacent sets of single measurement on this interval.

2. Definition of admissible sets $\{DA^0, DB^0, DC^0, FB^0, FC^0\}$ characterizing the synthesized multilevel relatively finite automata at the zero level. Given that for a zero level $DA^0 = DB^0 = DC^0$, for determining DA^0, DB^0, DC^0 it is enough to find the set of all possible variants of the analyzed sets of single values.

3. Formation of the sets FB^0, FC^0 of admissible functions of transitions and outputs is made in the following way. For example, using the method of least squares, let us carry out the synthesis of private functions connecting adjacent sets of values taking into account previous events. Based on the analysis of these particular functions, it is possible to form sets FB^0, FC^0.

4. Definition of DA^i, DB^i, DC^i for the i-th levels of the hierarchy of synthesized relatively finite automata. To do this, when analyzing sequential sets of values, it is proposed to additionally identify the relative frequencies of the appearance of stable local structures of given scales. Having identified such structures, each of them can be encoded at higher levels of the hierarchy of the automata in its own way, but in other spaces DA^i, DB^i, DC^i defined for the i-th levels of the hierarchy.

5. Formation of FB^i, FC^i. For this purpose, it is proposed to analyze stable combinations of particular transitions functions and outputs at the zero level. These combinations can then be reduced to functions or relatively finite automata FA_s^i of higher levels (Fig. 2). As a result, a multilevel relatively finite automata, as a model of the observed object, is obtained. Note that this automata is relative to the time interval at which events are analyzed. With the receipt of new information about the observed object, the model of the automata may change.

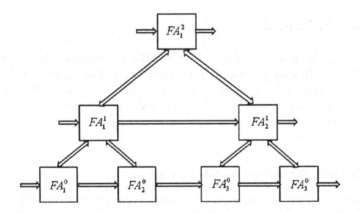

Fig. 2. An example of the structure of three-level relatively finite automata

For the rapid search for stable combinations of possible transition functions for MRFA, special algorithms are applicable.

To assess the completeness of the synthesized multilevel relatively finite automata, the formulas given in the previous section are applicable.

4.2 Algorithm of Deductive Multilevel Synthesis

Deductive synthesis algorithm allows build dynamic models of the observed objects, which reflect changes in objects states in time. To do this, the algorithm links the constructed MRFA into a single dynamic structure. These structures are dynamic models of observed objects.

The presence of levels in the structure of the MRFA allows split the data into groups that form a hierarchy. The peculiarity of the deductive synthesis problem is that the transition from the target state to the final state involves the synthesis of models on many levels.

In the initial formulation of a single-level synthesis, it is assumed that the initial data $\{d_s\}$ and the final result $\{d_w\}$ which is to be achieved are given. Conditions (rules) connecting the initial state with the final state are defined as $F_{zv}(d_{zv_e}; e = \overline{1, E_z}) \rightarrow d_{zv_a}; z = \overline{1, Z}; v = \overline{1, V_z}$. It is necessary to synthesize a process that allows make the transition $\{d_s\} \rightarrow \{d_w\}$. In this case, the desired PRG process can be represented as: $PRG = \{F_{zv}(d_{zv_e}; e = \overline{1, E_z}) \rightarrow d_{zv_a}; \{d_s\}; \{d_w\}; z = \overline{1, Z}; v = \overline{1, V_z}\}$.

If predicates $P_{zv0}(F_{zv0}(\cdot))$, $P_{zv1}(d_{zv1})$, ..., $P_{zva}(d_{zva})$ that take value 1 are defined for the elements, when the variables are defined (true), and 0 otherwise, the conditions of the problem can be written as $\{P_{zv0} \wedge P_{zv1} \wedge, \ldots, P_{ZVE_z} \rightarrow P_{zva} | S_{zv}, M_{zv}, z = \overline{1, Z} : v = \overline{1, V}\}$, where S_{zv} - status of zv - the condition; M_{zv} - the set of numbers of the basic conditions under which the preconditions and post conditions are true and false respectively.

In the new formulation of the synthesis problem the initial data $\{d_s\}$ are divided into data groups $\{d_{w0}\}, \{d_{w1}\}, \ldots, \{d_{wi}\}, \ldots, \{d_{wK}\}$, correlated with the corresponding levels of hierarchy. Conditions $F_{zv}^i(d_{zv_e}^i; e = \overline{1, E_z}) \rightarrow d_{zv_a}^i; z = \overline{1, Z_i}; v = \overline{1, V_{iz}}; i = \overline{1, K}$ connecting the source data with the final result are determined, where $F_{zv}^i(\cdot)$ - functions of z-types and v-types that can be implemented by the process at the i-th level of the hierarchy; $d_{zv_e}^i, d_{zv_e}^i$ - data; K - number of hierarchy levels. At the same time, restrictions are placed on functions and data at the i-th level: $F_{zv}^i(\cdot) \in FB^i$; $d_{si}, d_{zv_e}^i, d_{zv_a}^i, d_{wi} \in D_i; i = \overline{1, K}$, where FB^i, D_i - the set of admissible functions and the set of admissible data at the i-th level. It is required to synthesize a process that allows move from the source data $\{d_s\}$ to result $\{d_w\}$ taking into account the conditions considered.

With such a statement of the problem, it is proposed to carry out the synthesis of models on the base of functions belonging to different levels of the hierarchy. The proposed algorithm for solving the problem can be represented as a sequence of eleven steps:

1. First, $i = K + 1$.
2. $i = i - 1$. Decrease the hierarchy level.
3. If $i < 0$, then the completion of the solution of the problem with achieving a positive or negative result.
4. Appeal to the conditions of the problem at the i-th level.
5. Proof of the existence of a process to move from $\{d_{si}\}$ to $\{d_{wi}\}$ with effectiveness not lower than specified for the i-th level. The proof is based on the rules connecting the initial state to the final one. In all cases, the storage of proved and unproved results at this level of the hierarchy is carried out and added, respectively, to the source data and to the final result at a level lower than the current one.
6. In the absence of such proof, go to step 2.
7. Extract the support process from the results of the proof.
8. If there are no logical conditions in the support process, then go to step 11.

9. Process logical conditions, get subprocesses.
10. Bring the subprocesses together into a general process at the i-th level.
11. Check the ability to reach $\{d_{wi}\}$ using the results of the synthesis process at considered levels. Upon the positive result, the processes synthesized at each level are consolidated into the resulting process. The end of the algorithm. In other cases, go to step 2.

To extract the process from the proof the idea of the reverse conclusion is used. Through the reverse conclusion symmetrically to the direct output, it is possible to build a process that does not contain unnecessary elements.

With this approach, the synthesis of models is reduced to solving a small number $k \leq K$ of simple problems. They are supposed to be solved starting from the top level problem. A low complexity of each problem is determined by a small number of analyzed conditions. When solving a problem at the K-th level, a rough synthesis from large blocks of functions is carried out. In this case, it is not required to strictly prove the possibility of transition from $\{d_{sK}\}$ to $\{d_{wK}\}$. Inconsistencies of $\{d_{wK}\}$ and output of the conclusion at this level are taken into account at corrective synthesis within lower levels of the hierarchy.

In contrast to the known methods, the proposed solution can significantly reduce the time complexity of automatic synthesis. The upper bound of time T_H can be defined as $T_H \approx c \sum_{i=1}^{K} m_i^2 \leq c (\sum_{i=1}^{K} m_i)^2$, where c is a constant coefficient; m_i - the number of conditions of the problem at the i-th level. Notice, that m_i is significantly less than the total number of conditions on which problems of program synthesis are solved by traditional methods. This estimate is valid when the number of conditions for multilevel and single-level synthesis problems is the same. Taking into account that at each top level, one step of output is equivalent to n_i steps at the level "0", it is possible to estimate a lower bound for the time T_L of multilevel program synthesis:

$$T_L \approx c \sum_{i=0}^{K} \frac{m_i^2}{n_i^2} \leq c \sum_{i=0}^{K} m_i^2,$$ where n_i - the number of elements of the i-th level relatively to the base level.

5   Technology of Multilevel Synthesis for Biological Systems

Let's consider specific features of multilevel synthesis of models of biological systems. Such synthesis allows build models of the complex biological systems. The inductive synthesis of biological models is based on processing values of the observed parameters. Let a system is characterized by N parameters which are measured through some time intervals.

Let's define the moments of measurements as reference points and distinguish them with the help of indexes. Taking into account limitation of the period of observation, the number of reference points is limited. As a result of measurements we receive the time series which reflects behavior of the system. The number of elements of each time series is equal to number of reference points. If observed data contain noise, emissions, missed values, then a preprocessing of time series is carried out.

The algorithm of model synthesis may include any number of steps. For the description of technology we will limit the number of steps and we will consider technology of three-step synthesis. On the first step of synthesis functions for calculation of integrated indicators are defined. They are calculated for separate groups of parameters. Groups of parameters are formed from an initial set of parameters. Integrated indicators characterize states of the biological system in fixed moments of time, which correspond to reference points. On the second step of synthesis the integral curves which reflect changes of indicators in time are constructed.

The third step of synthesis assumes creation of the functions providing the joint analysis of the calculated integrated indicators and construction on their basis of the resulting assessment of the biological system state. This assessment is constructed on the basis of the results of comparison of integral curves behavior.

The steps of the process of the inductive synthesis in details are described below.

Creation of integrated indicators for groups of input data (F_0, F_1) for the fixed moment of time t_j:

$$\underbrace{BioM[t_j]}_{\text{static model}} : \underbrace{\left\{ \begin{array}{l} param_1\,[t_i;t_j] \\ param_2\,[t_i;t_j] \\ param_3\,[t_i;t_j] \\ \cdots \\ param_{N-1}\,[t_i;t_j] \\ param_N\,[t_i;t_j] \end{array} \right\}}_{\text{parameters}} \overset{F0}{\Rightarrow} \underbrace{\left\{ \begin{array}{l} gr_1\,(t_j, param\,(\cdot)) \\ gr_2\,(t_j, param\,(\cdot)) \\ \cdots \\ gr_M\,(t_j, param\,(\cdot)) \end{array} \right\}}_{\text{groups of parameters}} \overset{F1}{\Rightarrow} \underbrace{\left\{ \begin{array}{l} ind_1\,(t_j, gr\,1) \\ ind_2\,(t_j, gr\,1) \\ \cdots \\ ind_M\,(t_j, gr\,M) \end{array} \right\}}_{\text{integral indicators}},$$

where $param$ - is a parameter, gr - is a group of parameters, ind - is an integrated indicator calculated for a group of parameters. Creation of integral curves from values of indicators (F_2) and identification of dependences in their behavior (F_3) for time interval $[t_i, t_j]$:

$$\underbrace{BioM[t_i, t_j]}_{\text{dynamic model}} : \underbrace{\left\{ \begin{array}{l} BioM[t_i] \\ BioM[t_{i+1}] \\ \cdots \\ BioM[t_j] \end{array} \right\}}_{\text{static models}} \overset{F2}{\Rightarrow} \underbrace{\left\{ \begin{array}{l} curve_1([t_i, t_j], ind_1\,(\cdot)) \\ curve_2([t_i, t_j], ind_2\,(\cdot)) \\ \cdots \\ curve_M([t_i, t_j], ind_M\,(\cdot)) \end{array} \right\}}_{\text{integral curves}} \overset{F3}{\Rightarrow} \underbrace{\left\{ \begin{array}{l} G_1\,([t_i, t_j],\ curve(\cdot) \\ G_2\,([t_i, t_j],\ curve(\cdot)) \\ \cdots \\ G_L\,([t_i, t_j],\ curve(\cdot)) \end{array} \right\}}_{\text{relations between curves}}$$

where $curve$ - is an integral curve constructed on the base of separate values of indicators; G - dependence in behavior of two or several integrated curves.

Functions F_0, F_1, F_2, F_3 link models elements. So, F_0 links parameters of one group, F_1 - defines linked sequence of transformations which allow pass to integrated indicators, F_2 links separate values of indicators.

Functions $F_0 - F_3$ uniquely define the automata model shown in Fig. 2. In the process of automata model synthesis F_0 is used on the zero level, F_1 is used on the first level, F_2 on the second level, etc. Thus, creation of the functional model of the automata comes down to finding of compliances of elements of automata structural levels and the functions F received as a result of the inductive synthesis: $FA^0 \leftrightarrow F_0$; $FA^1 \leftrightarrow F_1$; $FA^2 \leftrightarrow F_2$; $FA^3 \leftrightarrow F_3$

The state of a biological system Q is defined by a set of links which exist in a system. The structure of links is considered and estimated for some fixed moment of time t_j. In the subsequent and previous periods of time there can be other links which are different from observed at the current moment of time. Also, absolute values of parameters and the counted indicators are dependent on time.

In a system ratios of changes in behavior of integral curves are invariant in time. In behavior of curves the invariance of dependences in behavior of initial parameters is the cornerstone of an invariance of dependences.

Thus, for some k-*th* state of a biological system Q_k are fair the following ratios. The state of a system depends upon time: $Q_k[t_i] \neq Q_k[t_j]$, $i \neq j$. At the same time we assume that the relations between observed parameters are constant: $F[Q_k[t_j]] = F[Q_k[t_i]]$, $\forall\, i, j$. The considered properties of systems are used for assessment of their states on the basis of deductive synthesis.

Deductive synthesis assumes that the goal presents, for example, to estimate an object state in certain moment of time t_w, i.e. $Q[t_w]$ is defined.

As an input we have results of parameters measurements for the previous moments of time t_s: t_w: $s \leq w$. Using built earlier automata model one can proof existence of the transition $FA^3[t_s] \rightarrow FA^3[t_w] = Q[t_w]$.

In the process of transition a number of the intermediate steps can be carried out: $FA^3[t_s] \rightarrow \ldots FA^3[t_k] \rightarrow \ldots \rightarrow FA^3[t_w]$.

In our case the proof at first is carried out on top level (the third level). If it is feasible, then the goal is achieved, and it takes only small number of steps. If a part of links is absent, then for their restitution transition to the second level is carried out and so on. Transitions to lower levels are carried out until links, necessary for the proof, is reestablished or the zero level is reached. In the limiting case when transitions to a zero level are carried out on each step, the sequence of transitions can be defined as:

$$
\rightarrow FA^3[Q] \rightarrow
\left\{
\begin{array}{c}
FA^2[t_s] \rightarrow FA^1[t_s] \rightarrow FA^0[t_s] \rightarrow FA^1[t_s] \rightarrow FA^2[t_s] \\
FA^2[t_j] \rightarrow FA^1[t_j] \rightarrow FA^0[t_j] \rightarrow FA^1[t_j] \rightarrow FA^2[t_j] \\
\ldots \\
FA^2[t_w] \rightarrow FA^1[t_w] \rightarrow FA^0[t_w] \rightarrow FA^1[t_w] \rightarrow FA^2[t_w]
\end{array}
\right\}
$$

$$
\rightarrow FA^3[Q_k[t_w]] \rightarrow
$$

In the given example as a result of the proof it is established that in an instant of time t_w the system is in a state Q_k.

6 Simulation Results for Biological Systems

The considered technology was used to assess the state of patients with c surgical pathology in a cavernous sinus during the postoperative period in the operating room and in the cardio-resuscitation unit. The assessment of the patients' state was carried out at six time control points. The assessment included an analysis of the parameters characterizing the acid-base state (ABS) of the organism. The total number of such parameters was twenty one. These were the following parameters: pH – Acidity, pO2 - Oxygen partial pressure, pCO2 - Carbon dioxide partial pressure, ABE - Excess base, SBE - Lack of reason, cHCO3 - Plasma bicarbonate, cHCO3-st - Bicarbonate (alkali), sO2 - Oxygen boost, ctHb - Reference hemoglobin level, Htc – Hematocrit, K+ - Potassium ion concentration, Na+ - Sodium ion concentration, Ca++ - Calcium ion concentration, Cl− - Chlorine Ion Concentration, Glu - Glucose concentration, Lac - Lactate content, p50 - Hemoglobin affinity for oxygen, mOsm - Blood osmolarity, pH (T) - Acidity corrected for temperature, pO2(T) - Partial oxygen pressure adjusted for temperature, pCO2(T) - Carbon dioxide partial pressure adjusted for temperature.

It is known that when assessing the state of patients by medical specialists, the values of individual measured parameters, the dynamics of their changes are analyzed. However, the focus is on the study of the consistency and synergies of the behavior of various parameters. The behavior of parameters is considered consistent if the ratio of their values is as expected. The expected dependencies are determined by the nature of the parameters. The importance of analyzing coherence and synergy is justified by the fact that the organism is a unified system, within which all processes are connected.

As a consequence, the violation of one process should lead to the violation of other processes. The absence of such cause-effect relationships indicates a violation of one of the main properties of all living organisms - the integrity property. In this case, the organism loses its ability to adapt and ability to self-healing.

The analysis of dependencies of many parameters in dynamics is a complex task that requires in-depth analysis. Some of the modern medical information systems involve the use of separate methods of artificial intelligence, including the methods of Data Mining. However, methods based on direct iteration are not applicable due to the large amount of data being processed, while others can lead to a significant loss of information. In addition, well-known methods do not always allow the formation of capacious structures reflecting the dynamically changing relationships of individual parameters and groups of parameters.

Such problems are successfully solved using the proposed models and methods of multilevel synthesis. They provide the construction of multilevel models describing the state of the organism and changes occurring in it at fixed points in time and relative to the entire time period that is considered.

In the synthesis of patient state models, the features of working with medical data were taken into account through the use of criteria and indicators proposed in specialized medical methods, in particular, by Anokhin [20], Lushnov et al. [21].

Let's consider data on three groups of patients. In the formation of groups, the main diagnosis was taken into account, as well as other characteristics that influence the state of patients. These characteristics are the patient's age, associated diseases and others. For each patient, the values of ABS parameters, measured at six control points, were included in the sample. The measured data contained missing values. To fill them, the KNN (K-Nearest Neighbors) method was applied.

The data prepared in this way were used to synthesize models of patient status. According to the technology, the following steps were performed.

1. Calculation of functionals of biosystems. Search of splitting $R = (R_1, R_2, ..., R_M)$ sets of objects (parameters of ABC) on not crossed classes are sets of the functional subsystem of parameters of ABC: $R_1, R_2, ..., R_M$ ($M = 1$ or $M > 1$), which gives local maximum to F the sum of "internal" correlation links minus some threshold value of correlations characterizing their importance:$F(a, R) = \sum_{S=1}^{M} \sum_{i,j \in R_S} (a_{ij} - a)$

   where a—a threshold of importance of links (at $a_{ij} > a$ the link is stronger between objects i and at $a_{ij} < a$—the link is insignificant), a_{ij}—is an indicator of link between i-th and j-th objects ($a_{ij} = a_{ji}$, a_{ii}—aren't investigated and aren't considered) expression $i, j \in R_S$ means aij element belonging to a set of R_S [22].
2. Construction of integral curves based on calculated values of functionals and thresholds of the essence of links. Formation of a matrix of partitioning into non-intersecting classes of parameters of ABS.
3. Investigation of the consistency of the behavior of functionals, the thresholds of the essence of links and changes in the number of disjoint classes.
4. The formation of dependencies characterizing the state of patients in each group.

Below are the results of a study of data about patients in the first group. The dynamics of system correlation and the corresponding changes in cooperative correlation relationships between many indicators of the acid-base state in this group of patients are given in Fig. 3 and in Tables 1 and 2.

From the Fig. 3 it can be seen that the threshold of essence of links demonstrates substantial stability in the period from the 1st to the 5th point within the limits of 0.45–0.49. However, by the 6th point it rises sharply to a value of 0.654. In this case, the number of partitioning classes increases from 5–7 classes from the 1st to the 5th point to 10 at the 6th point of the study. According to the results of Table 2, the transition from the 5th to the 6th point of the study can be assessed as the most "stressful" of the moments in the system, because at this time there is a "decay" of the set of parameters of the ABS into 10 non-overlapping classes with a sharp increase in the threshold of materiality of the links 1.4 times from a value of 0.462 to 0.654.

Table 1. Indicators of functionals, thresholds of essence of links and the number of classes of splitting ABS cavernous sinus in the 1st group

Point of study	Functional	Thresholds of links	Number of classes
1	35,794	0,457	5
2	32,341	0,455	6
3	24,975	0,432	5
4	27,221	0,488	7
5	39,753	0,462	5
6	21,355	0,654	10

Thus, at the end of the study in group 1 to the 6th point, the system seemed to "crumble" - the number of partitioning classes increased to 10, the threshold of essence

Table 2. Splitting into non-intersecting classes of parameters of ABS in cavernous sinus in the 1st group

	Point_1	Point_2	Point_3	Point_4	Point_5	Point_6
Klass1	pH(T) cHCO3-st SBE ABE pH	pCO2(T) pH(T) mOsm p50 Ca++ Na+ K+ Htc ctHb	pO2(T) pH(T) Lac Cl- Htc ctHb sO2 pO2 pH	pH(T) Glu Htc ctHb cHCO3-st cHCO3 SBE ABE pH	pCO2(T) pH(T) p50 Lac Cl- K+ Htc ctHb cHCO3-	pH(T) cHCO3-st cHCO3 SBE ABE pH
Klass2	pO2(T) sO2 pO2	pO2(T) sO2 pO2	pCO2 (T) p50 pCO2	pO2(T) sO2 pO2	pO2(T) sO2 pO2	pO2(T) sO2 pO2
Klass3	pCO2(T) mOsm p50 Lac Glu Cl- Ca++ Na+ Htc ct	cHCO3-st cHCO3 SBE ABE	K+ cHCO3- st cHCO3 SBE ABE	pCO2(T) p50 Lac pCO2	mOsm Na+	pCO2(T) Cl- pCO2
Klass4	cHCO3	Cl-	mOsm Na+	K+	Ca++	Htc ctHb
Klass5	K+	Glu	Glu Ca++	mOsm Na+	Glu	K+
Klass6		Lac		Ca++		mOsm Na+
Klass7				Cl-		Ca++
Klass8						Glu
Klass9						Lac
Klass10						p50

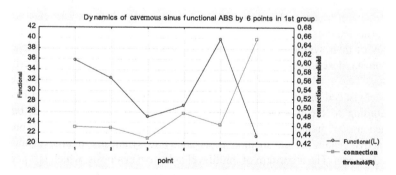

Fig. 3. Dynamics of functionals and thresholds of essence of links between ABS parameters in the cavernous sinus in the 1st group

of links increased to 0.654, and the functional in turn dropped to the minimum value - 21.355 from 39.753, those almost 2 times (1.86). According to the work of Teodorescu et al. [23] here the "critical period" is also observed, since in the period between the 5th and 6th points the ratio of the subsequent value of the functional to the previous one is minimal.

Similar studies were conducted for patients of other two groups. As a result, the following dependencies were identified that determine the state of the patients of the three studied groups.

1. The maximum shifts in the system of ABS parameters in the cavernous sinus of the 1st group of patients occur in the period between the 5th and 6th points of the study.
2. The maximum shifts in the system of ABS parameters in the cavernous sinus of the 2nd group of patients also occur in the period between the 5th and 6th points of the study, but variations in the values of both the significance thresholds of the links and the values of the functionals in the 2nd group are significantly higher than in the first group. In other words, the 2nd group has a more unstable dynamics of ABS parameters.
3. The 3rd group of subjects has relatively the smallest variations of the studied parameters.

When working with data on new patients, the identified dependencies will allow assess the patient's condition and promptly identify deviations from the expected in case of violation of one or several dependencies.

7   Conclusion

In this article the problem of multilevel automatic synthesis of the models of complex objects is discussed. A new problem statement for synthesis is given. The structure of the process of automatic construction of these models, including data acquisition, processing and direct synthesis of the corresponding automata is considered. To formalize the observed objects it is suggested to use relatively finite operational automata. The necessity of transition from single-level automata models to multilevel structures is shown. The features of multilevel relatively finite automata and the criteria for the efficiency of their synthesis are determined. It is proposed to use the completeness of the automata description and the time of its construction as the main criteria of efficiency.

It is envisaged that the synthesis of MRFA of observed objects should be carried out according to the proposed methods and algorithms. A new method, based on combined use of inductive and deductive approaches to the synthesis is proposed. A distinctive feature of the method is its ability to synthesize multilevel models of observed objects. The algorithm of multilevel inductive synthesis, which is a part of the method, allows build automata models on limited time intervals when objects are observed. A new multi-level deductive synthesis algorithm provides linking of the constructed automata models into dynamic structures, that reflect changes in the states of objects over time intervals.

The proposed method makes it possible to significantly reduce the time spent on the synthesis of observed objects models. This is achieved by solving the problem of synthesis on many levels. At each level, its own tasks are formulated and solved. The overall problem is reduced to a small number of simple tasks. Estimates of the complexity of the proposed multilevel synthesis method are obtained.

The results of simulation show that the proposed new solutions for the automatic synthesis of multilevel automata models allow build models of such complicated objects as biological objects.

It is necessary to notice that use of the offered synthesis algorithms of multilevel automata models isn't limited to medical domain. Now authors consider the possibility of use of this approach for creation of models of the complex natural systems for which description automatic models weren't used earlier [24–26]. Results of preliminary researches show that under certain conditions this approach can be useful, especially when multi model approach is used.

The research was supported by Russian Science Foundation (project No. 17-15-01177) and was funded by RFBR and CITMA according to the research project №. 18-57-34001.

References

1. Kotseruba, I., Tsotsos, J.A: Review of 40 years of cognitive architecture research: core cognitive abilities and practical applications. Artif. Intell. Rev. (2018)
2. Goertzel, B., Lian, R., Arel, I., Garis, H., Chen, S.A.: World survey of artificial brain projects, Part II: biologically inspired cognitive architectures. J. Neurocomput. Arch. **74**(1–3), 30–49 (2010)
3. Robinson, J.A.: A machine – oriented logic based on resolution principle. J. ACM **12**, 23–41 (1965)
4. Chang, C., Lee, R.: Symbolic Logic and Mechanical Theorem Proving. Academic, New York (1973)
5. Maslov, SYu.: Teoria deduktivnykh system ieeprimeneniya (Theory of Deductive Systems and Its Applications). Radio I Svyaz', Moscow (1986)
6. Tyugu, E.Kh., Kharf, M.Ya.: Algorithms for structural synthesis of programs. Programmirovanie **4**, 3–13 (1980)
7. Giacomo, G., Patrizi, F., Sardina, S.: Automatic behavior composition synthesis. Artif. Intell. **196**, 106–142 (2013)
8. Kreitz, C.: Program synthesis. In: Bibel, W., Schmitt, P.H. (eds.) Automated Deduction – A Basis for Application, pp. 105–134. Kluwer Publ., Dordrecht (1998)
9. Avellone, A., Ferrari, M., Miglioli, P.: Synthesis of programs in abstract data types. In: Flener, P. (ed.) LOPSTR 1998. LNCS, vol. 1559, pp. 81–100. Springer, Heidelberg (1999). https://doi.org/10.1007/3-540-48958-4_5
10. Srivastava, S., Gulwani, S., Foster, J.S.: Template – based program verification and program synthesis. Int. J. Softw. Tools Technol. Transf. **15**(5), 497–518
11. Tahat, A., Ebnenasir, A.: A hybrid method for the verification and synthesis of parameterized self-stabilizing protocols. In: Proietti, M., Seki, H. (eds.) LOPSTR 2014. LNCS, vol. 8981, pp. 201–218. Springer, Cham (2015). https://doi.org/10.1007/978-3-319-17822-6_12
12. Kant, E.: On the efficient synthesis of efficient programs. Artif. Intell. **20**(3), 253–305 (1983)

13. Bibel, W., et al.: A multi-level approach to program synthesis. In: Fuchs, Norbert E. (ed.) LOPSTR 1997. LNCS, vol. 1463, pp. 1–27. Springer, Heidelberg (1998). https://doi.org/10. 1007/3-540-49674-2_1

14. Fu, P., Komendantskaya, E.: A type-theoretic approach to resolution. In: Falaschi, M. (ed.) LOPSTR 2015. LNCS, vol. 9527, pp. 91–106. Springer, Cham (2015). https://doi.org/10. 1007/978-3-319-27436-2_6

15. Wagner, F., Schmuki, R., Wagner, T., Wolstenholme, P.: Modeling Software with Finite State Machines: A Practical Approach. Auerbach Publications (2006)

16. Osipov, V., Osipova, M.: Space-time signal binding in recurrent neural networks with controlled elements. Neurocomputing **308**, 194–204 (2018)

17. Osipov, VYu.: Automatic synthesis of action programs for intelligent robots. Program. Comput. Softw. **42**(3), 155–160 (2016)

18. Osipov, V., Lushnov, M., Stankova, E., Vodyaho, A., Zukova, N.: Inductive synthesis of the models of biological systems according to clinical trials. In: Gervasi, O., et al. (eds.) ICCSA 2017. LNCS, vol. 10404, pp. 103–115. Springer, Cham (2017). https://doi.org/10.1007/978-3-319-62392-4_8

19. Osipov, V., Zhukova, N., Vodyaho, A., Kalmatsky, A., Mustafin, N.: Towards building of cable TV content-sensitive adaptive monitoring and management systems. Int. J. Comput. Commun. **11**, 75–81 (2017)

20. Anokhin, P.K.: Sketches on physiology of systems of functions. M.: Medicine, 448 p. (1975). (In Russian)

21. Lushnov, A.M., Lushnov, M.S. Medical information systems: multidimensional analysis of medical and ecological data. St. Petersburg, Helicon Plus, 460 p. (2013). (In Russian)

22. Kupershtokh, V.L., Mirkin, B.G., Trofimov of V.A. Summ of intercommunications as index of quality of classification. Automatic equipment and telemechanics 3, 133–141 (1976). (In Russian)

23. Teodorescu, D., Teodorescu, R.: Autoregressive time series analysis via representatives. Biol. Cybern. **51**, 79–86 (1984)

24. Stankova, E.N., Balakshiy, A.V., Petrov, D.A., Shorov, A.V., Korkhov, V.V.: Using technologies of OLAP and machine learning for validation of the numerical models of convective clouds. In: Gervasi, O., et al. (eds.) ICCSA 2016. LNCS, vol. 9788, pp. 463–472. Springer, Cham (2016). https://doi.org/10.1007/978-3-319-42111-7_36

25. Stankova, E.N., Ismailova, E.T., Grechko, I.A.: Algorithm for processing the results of cloud convection simulation using the methods of machine learning. In: Gervasi, O., et al. (eds.) ICCSA 2018. LNCS, vol. 10963, pp. 149–159. Springer, Cham (2018). https://doi.org/10. 1007/978-3-319-95171-3_13

26. Stankova, E.N., Balakshiy, A.V., Petrov, D.A., Korkhov, V.V.: OLAP technology and machine learning as the tools for validation of the numerical models of convective clouds Int. J. Business Intell. Data Min. **14**(1/2), 254–266 (2019). ISSN online 1743-8195 ISSN print 1743-8187 https://doi.org/10.1504/ijbidm.2019.096793

Using Mathematical Models to Describe the Dynamics of the Spread of Traditional and Cryptocurrency Payment Systems

Victor Dostov[1] ⓘ, Pavel Shoust[2(✉)] ⓘ, and Elizaveta Popova[3] ⓘ

[1] Federal State Budgetary Educational Institution of Higher Education "Saint-Petersburg State University", 7-9 Universitetskaya Emb, St Petersburg 199034, Russia
dostov@npaed.ru
[2] Russian Electronic Money and Remittance Association, 5/2 Orlikov Per, Moscow 107078, Russia
shoust@npaed.ru
[3] Saint-Petersburg National Research University of Information Technologies, Mechanics and Optics 49 Kronverkskiy Prospect, St Petersburg 197101, Russia
popova.elizaveta@list.ru

Abstract. As new payment systems emerge, it is important to predict their dynamics and separate payments from speculative transactions. Based on the classification of payment systems as 'one-sided' and 'two-sided' we use mathematical methods to predict their behavior over time. By introducing the fatigue factor and involvement factor, we draw the differential equation that could be used for the analysis of the payment systems' behavior. The analysis shows that any changes in the initial state of the system fade over time; one-time circumstantial changes (such as sudden regulatory change or promotional campaign) have an only temporary effect. Our equations can also be used to identify the prevailing type of transactions (P2P or C2B) in 'mixed' systems. Our model is verified by empirical data from payment card statistics, Web-Money registration rate and can be used to analyze Bitcoin usage as well. Further, research on using the model to explain and predict the competitive effects is also proposed. This is the first attempt at using differential equations for payment system analysis with a model verified by empirical evidence.

Keywords: P2P · B2C · Cryptocurrencies · Payment systems · The dynamics of the spread · Commodization · Payment system · Model · Bass equation · Bitcoin

1 Introduction

According to Summers (1994), a payment system is a set of rules, institutions and technical mechanisms for transferring funds between a sender and a recipient (in case of retail payment systems - from an individual to a legal or physical entity [1, 6]).

Authors are grateful to Dr. Anton Zarubin for drawing our attention to the similarity of our approach to the Bass's approach.

© Springer Nature Switzerland AG 2019
S. Misra et al. (Eds.): ICCSA 2019, LNCS 11620, pp. 457–471, 2019.
https://doi.org/10.1007/978-3-030-24296-1_36

Retail payments are an integral part of the functioning of modern society. Their role—in terms of the value, volume and variety of such payments — has increased particularly in recent decades. According to the World Payments Report [20], the volume of non-cash payments in 2016 grew by 10% per year [18]. The trend is expected to continue in the future, primarily fueled by the growth in the developing economies. At the same time, for almost the entire twentieth century, the market was very technologically uniform—almost exclusively dominated by payment cards (VISA, MasterCard and others) and money transfer systems, both domestic (like postal transfers) and international (Western Union, MoneyGram). Thomas Hugo (2014) in his «Measuring progress toward a cashless society» shows that the last 20 years saw a rapid growth of retail payment systems, both quantitative and (extensively) qualitative [16].

New payment systems continue to emerge. For example, the popularity of distributed ledgers-based payment systems, especially Bitcoin, made researchers wonder about the long-term prospects of such projects [9]. As new virtual currencies might be used for speculation as well as facilitating payments, it is also important to estimate the correlation between these two functions.

This study seeks to answer these questions. The idea is to develop mathematical models that could be used to study both "breakthrough" systems (new payment systems) and traditional solutions in the field of electronic payments.

However, only few research papers so far are dedicated to creating a model that would explain and predict the development of payment systems. The main attention of the researchers is focused on the study of legal [6], technological [4, 8], macroeconomic [16] aspects of the functioning of payment systems. Yet, the analysis and forecasting payment system's development seems to be not only of theoretical but also practical value. The scientific tools that allow to analyze the evolution of such systems can create an empirical basis for decision-making not only in the private sector, but also in the development of national plans for the development of infrastructure and, ultimately, the transition to a cashless society.

Some payment systems are developing incrementally, some are growing rapidly, others leave the market, unable to attract customers. In other words, the market is extremely dynamic—from giants such as International Payment Schemes (IPS) to small crypto-startups [20]. There is an obvious interest in mathematical modeling of their dynamics. However, there are very few papers on this topic. Firstly, such systems are relatively young; secondly, they are quite specific and require special knowledge to understand the principles of their work. Third, unlike the "classical" economy of production and services, their impact on macroeconomic indicators is small, which demotivate "general" economists. A certain incentive for such research was created by the phenomenon of Bitcoin, however, the work usually focuses on deep, although generalized, technical analysis, for example, in the work of Fantazzini et al. [8]. Several papers devoted to systems of gross payments among banks, for example the work of Kopytin [4]. Nevertheless, from the point of the normal economy operation and the interests of the consumer, the importance of retail payment systems is huge and constantly growing. Therefore, we see academic and practical benefits of building a mathematical model of such systems.

In this paper, we assume that in the long term, the behavior of big number of customers that are defined by a wide set of parameters is equivalent to the behavior of a single user, described with a small number of statistically measurable parameters. This hypothesis is confirmed by studies that signal the gradual convergence and simplification of the functionality of payment systems, reducing them to the basic services of money transfer from point "a" to point "b" - called "commodization" [2].

This paper is structured as follows. In the first section, we present the methodology, introduce the concept of the payment systems and their classification, which is relevant for subsequent analysis. We also consider the Bass Models and assess their applicability to the research at hand.

In the second section, we present a model for analyzing the development of payment systems, considering the fatigue and involvement coefficients. In the third section, we test the proposed approach to the available empirical material. In the final part, several conclusions are made regarding the theoretical and practical implications of the use of mathematical apparatus for predicting the growth of financial services. Several proposals for further research are formulated.

The results of this work can be used to predict the behavior of payment systems, payment instruments, cryptocurrencies, etc.

2 Methodology

In this study, "payment system" will be understood as a set of instruments, banking procedures and, typically, interbank funds transfer systems that ensure the circulation of money [23]. We use a holistic approach and consider the payment system as a single actor This means that the internal functioning of the system: internal legal, technological and economic parameters are beyond the interest of the study. In a simplified sense, we consider the payment system as a "black box" - its interaction with the environment can be described by a limited set of parameters. The function of this "black box" is the transfer of funds from the sender to the recipient.

Generally, the research is focused on the qualitative and quantitative influence of external parameters on payment systems.

For further purposes, we use the existing classification of financial services (and retail payment systems as their subset) on C2B and P2P [13]. In C2B (customer to business - hereinafter "one-sided") [21] systems, a limited number of customers make payments to the resource (stores) with infinite capacity. Interaction between customers and stores is carried out through a non-cooperative game (where senders and recipients can not directly determine the actions of each other). A simple example is a credit card payment to a store for some product. P2P payments (person to person - hereinafter "two-sided system") [21] are made between individuals within a closed audience (in this case, the parties can influence each other). Simple examples are international transfers such as Western Union or transfers from card to card, implemented by Sberbank in Russia. The last example shows that the same payment system can serve as P2P and C2B in function. As we will see later, depending on the predominance of one of these areas in the company's behavior of the model vary significantly.

Currently, several approaches to analyzing distribution dynamics of products and services in the market are used. From the methodological point, there are computer-based modeling and differential equation-based approaches. We do not deny the usefulness of computer modeling for cases that cannot be described analytically, but here we suggest further implementation of differential equations. There are two major approaches that lead to formally similar results. The first is the Bass innovations diffusion theory [10], its basic equation takes the following form (1)

$$f(t) = p + [q - p]F(t) - q[F(t)]^2 \tag{1}$$

The Bass Model parameter representing the potential market, which is the ultimate number of purchasers of the product, is constant. Time intervals are numbered sequentially with the first full-time interval (usually a year) of sales at t = 1 in the Srinivasan-Mason form of the Bass Model equations. A time interval is denoted "t". The Bass model coefficient (parameter) of innovation is "P". The Bass model coefficient (parameter) of imitation is "q". The portion (fraction) of the potential market that adopts at time t is f(t). The portion (fraction) of the potential market that has adopted up to and including time t is F(t).

f(t) is the time derivation of F(t), which is expressed

$$f(t) = \frac{d[F(t)]}{dt} \tag{2}$$

The second approach to the market dynamics equations is based on the Furstholz equation [22] borrowed from the simulation of biological systems with limited resource growth; it is often also generalized in the form proposed by Lotka and Volterra [3, 14] which is mathematically similar to Bass model with different modifications.

Since the market of payment systems is quite specific, we will draft equations from scratch and then discuss their relation to the above-mentioned models.

3   C2B Payment Systems

Let's imagine that company X launches a mass retail payment system from scratch for some new audience. An example would be the launch of Diners club credit cards in Russia in 1995 or PayPal e-wallets in the US in 1998. Suppose also that:

1. the behavior of a potential user is random, that is, the user chooses the moment to start using this payment system randomly (while the decision itself, of course, is influenced by user's needs and market supply);
2. the decision is made independently of current users and potential users. In our experience, this behavior is typical for commoditized systems. Thus, for C2B systems, we neglect, unlike the Bass model, the mutual influence of users (or, as Bass defines it, the effect of imitation). As will be shown below, this assumption is confirmed by the empirical data. We will also correlate our model and the Bass model below.

We also introduce the main indicators:

1. the current number of users x;
2. the maximum number of users, for example, the entire audience of a given country N. Therefore, the number of potential users not currently participating in the system is N-x;
3. audience capture rate, which reflects the probability that a given user will start using the service: a > 0 (the reverse time of the decision) within a given period.

Suppose a customer joins the payment system once and continues using it forever. Then the dynamics of the system, expressed in the number of users, is described by the simplest differential equation.

$$\frac{dx}{dt} = a(N - x) \tag{3}$$

with initial condition x (0) = 0. The solution is

$$x = N(1 - e^{-at}) \tag{4}$$

When t is small, the number of users grows linearly, when t is large, audience that has not joined the system decreases exponentially. Two simple but useful modifications can be introduced into Eq. (4) for further consideration.

Firstly, we introduce the fatigue factor b > 0, which describes the probability that an existing user will stop using the system (with the possibility to return). Then Eq. (4) becomes

$$\frac{dx}{dt} = a(N - x) - bx \tag{5}$$

with solution

$$x = \frac{a}{a+b} N \left(1 - e^{-(a+b)t}\right) \tag{6}$$

and audience growth rate

$$\frac{dx}{dt} = ae^{-(a+b)t} \tag{7}$$

Thus, we see that for small t

$$x = aNt \tag{8}$$

and user fatigue obviously does not affect the growth rate. With large t the system adopts a stationary value

$$x = \frac{a}{a+b}N \tag{9}$$

This value is achieved faster, but the volume of system's audience is smaller than if the fatigue factor is not accounted for.

The empirical nature of these equations should be emphasized. The exact definition of 'usage termination' is difficult to determine. It can be assumed that the average user uses a payment system with a frequency $c \gg a$, and the termination is the non-usage of the system for a time, much more than a.

Let's look at the model where the client first joins the system and loses interest in using it after some time (However he/she may start to use it again in future, we do not suppose long-lasting negative experience). Again, in any case, such models remain empirical, although, in our opinion, extremely useful and meaningful for the analysis of the behavior of payment systems.

Secondly, suppose that at time t = 0, there is already some number of clients (x_0). Then (7) takes the form

$$x = \frac{a}{a+b}N\left(1 - \left(1 - \frac{(a+b)\frac{x_0}{N}}{a}\right)e^{-(a+b)t}\right) \tag{10}$$

Thus, the increase in the number of users with a non-zero initial condition is

$$\Delta x = x_0 e^{-(a+b)t} \tag{11}$$

Equation (10) can be rewritten in a simple form

$$x = x_\infty\left(1 - \left(1 - \frac{x_0}{x_\infty}\right)e^{-\frac{t}{T}}\right) \tag{12}$$

$$x_\infty = \left(\frac{a}{a+b}\right)N \tag{13}$$

$$T = \frac{1}{a+b}; \tag{14}$$

or

$$z = \left(1 - (1 - z_0)e^{-\frac{t}{T}}\right) \tag{15}$$

Where $z = \frac{x}{x_\infty}$. Note also that within the framework of this model we can consider the values of

$$\left(\frac{a}{a+b}\right)N < x_0 < N \tag{16}$$

then the value of x (t) will decrease, tending back-exponentially to the stationary one.

Although counterintuitive for non-mathematics, two phenomena are typical for Poisson's processes: the rate of audience growth is defined by the sum of the involvement coefficient and the fatigue coefficient; and changes in initial conditions quickly fade with time. It is also important that the long-term behavior of the system, (9) cannot be inducted from its initial stage (8), does not allow estimation of b, which reduces auditorium at long terms. This explains, partly, the existing hyper-optimism in the assessment of payment startups and their small success rate [7].

There is also another interpretation of the results. The time t = 0 does not have to coincide with the start of the system. Differential equations of this type have no memory and their behavior at t ≫ T is determined only by coefficients a, b and not by the initial value. Thus, if at the time t0 we have drastically changed the number of users of the system and/or the coefficients, then the future behavior of the system will also be described by the formula (10). Therefore, we can say that changes in the coefficients significantly affect the long-term behavior of the C2B system, while one-time promotions that attract a lot of new customers without affecting the coefficients – do not. Similar effects will be shown by external events, such as advertising or regulatory changes (for example, requiring a one-time identification): they may also have a rapid effect on the audience. If these changes have not significantly affected a and b (for example, this identification is very simple and generally available), the effect of this impact will be quickly mitigated at time T.

It is also useful to mark that these equations are quite general. They can be applied not only just for payments, but also for B2C services, for example, in terms of issuing loans and microcredits; in general—to most financial services, where customers are repetitively using a service with an infinite capacity of one of the payment participants group. This may not be true for the C2B systems at the initial stage, when, for example, the number of stores that accept the newly emerged payment instrument is very limited. Analysis of such cases requires further fine-tuning of the model that will be attempted at further stages of our work.

4   P2P Payment Systems

Along with payment systems for goods and services, where the behavior is determined by each user independently, there are payment systems with binary behavior, where the decisions of some users are affected by the decision of others. A simple example is money transfer system or card-to-card system, you need your counterparty to use it as well (of course, it is possible that both sides join the system at the same time, but this is less probable). Then the simplest dynamics of the P2P system will be described by the equation:

$$\frac{dx}{dt} = a(N - x)x \tag{17}$$

with the solution

$$x = \frac{x_0 N e^{aNt}}{x_0(e^{aNt} - 1) + N} \tag{18}$$

At small t the audience grows exponentially

$$x = x_0 e^{aNt} \tag{19}$$

at large t, the number of people who has not joined the system, decreases as

$$x = \frac{N^2}{x_0} e^{-aNt} \tag{20}$$

It is obvious that there is no non-trivial solution at $x_0 = 0$ (at least one client is needed in our assumptions) and, unlike the first model, the dynamics should be more sensitive to the size of the initial audience.

You can also add a fatigue factor b into this equation. In this case, the result is similar to the Ferhulst equation.

$$\frac{dx}{dt} = a(N - x)x - bx \tag{21}$$

which is well studied in relation to, for example, biological models and allows for an analytical, albeit more cumbersome, solution, which, for the sake of clarity, can be described as:

$$x = \frac{K x_0 e^{rt}}{K - x_0 + x_0 e^{rt}} \tag{22}$$

or

$$\frac{x}{K} = \frac{e^{rt}}{\frac{K}{x_0} - 1 + e^{rt}} \tag{23}$$

where

$$K = \frac{(aN - b)}{a} \tag{24}$$

asymptotic stationary solution (21), and

$$r = aN - b \tag{25}$$

Subsequently, we will also need a number of new customers (registrations) R per unit of time

$$R = a(N - x)x = a\left(N - \frac{Kx_0 e^{rt}}{K - x_0 + x_0 e^{rt}}\right)\frac{Kx_0 e^{rt}}{K - x_0 + x_0 e^{rt}} \tag{26}$$

We see that the behavior of such a system is more complex than for the first one. On small time intervals, where $x(t) \ll K$ the system shows fast growth

$$x = x_0 e^{rt} \tag{27}$$

At point $x(t) = \frac{K}{2}$, the function x (t) has an inflection (see Fig. 1) and the growth rate starts to decrease. At large values of t

$$x = K \tag{28}$$

That means there is a limit of users independent of the initial conditions. Thus, the system has either a stage of rapid growth which eventually leads to the period of a stationary value or only a stage where the system moves to a stationary value. This equation also has decreasing solutions at $x_0 > K$. Figure 1 shows the graph of the solution for the 1st type equation (Eq. (6)).

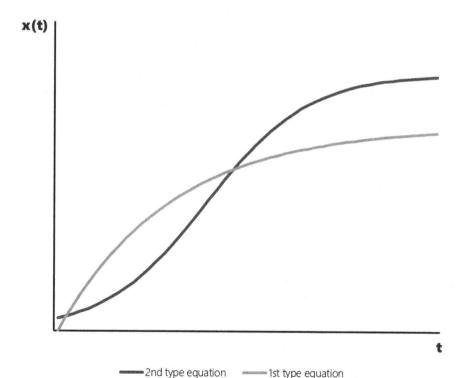

Fig. 1. Graph the solution of the logistic equation.

Similarly, the number of registrations can also behave non-monotonously. At small t it is small

$$R = \left(\frac{r}{K}\right)(N - x_0)x_0, \tag{29}$$

At large t

$$R = a(N - x)x = r(N - K), \tag{30}$$

If $2K > N$, then R reaches an extreme between these values. For small x_0, the extremum is reached at the point

$$t = \frac{1}{r} \ln \frac{KN}{(2K - N)x_0} \tag{31}$$

The lack of the system's memory is relevant here as well. Its behavior is determined by the set of a and b. However, we see that such system is more sensitive to the value of x_0 and advertising or regulatory effects might have more persisting effects.

Practical conclusions can already be drawn from these simple discussions. For example, we have data about system dynamics behavior over a period. After analyzing the second derivative, we can make assumptions about the dominant type of transactions in the system—whether these are P2P or C2B transactions.

We can also analyze the results of the advertising campaign and see whether it has persisting consequences. Finally, if we know about the prevalence of payments (C2B) or transfers (P2P)—we can confidently predict the effects of advertising or the regulatory actions, or changes in the coefficients, and to understand whether the system is at the stage of growth or saturation. It is also possible to emphasize the information from the reverse analysis. In particular, the fatigue coefficient b can indicate the potential of the system to retain clients. This provides additional information for further fine-tuning of marketing strategies and directions of product development.

Analysis of publications on market dynamics inevitably leads to the analogy of the Ferhulst Eq. (21) and subsequent solutions to the Bass equation [10]. While Ferhulst equations and Bass equation are mathematically very similar, there some differences in the interpretation of the parameters.

Bass interprets the appearance of a quadratic multiplier as a consequence of the simulation effect. In P2P payment systems, the nature of this multiplier is more technical – you can't make a transfer if your recipient is not a user of the system. Thus, we can expect that for P2P systems the role of this parameter will be greater than in the diffusion theory of consumer goods and the results will be closer to the empirical data.

We also take into account the fatigue effect, due to which the user can stop using the system at any time, which is absent in the original Bass model.

5   Application to Real-Life Cases

Unfortunately, detailed data on payment systems are usually qualified by companies as confidential and are not publicly available. However, we obtained data sets for some empirical cases.

Let's consider the statistics of the European Central Bank on non-cash payments 2015 [12]. Here we make a raw hypothesis that the number of payments is approximately proportional to the number of active cards. The increase in the number of such operations is well described by the solution of the 1st type: it is a good fit with characteristic T = 15 years (Fig. 2).

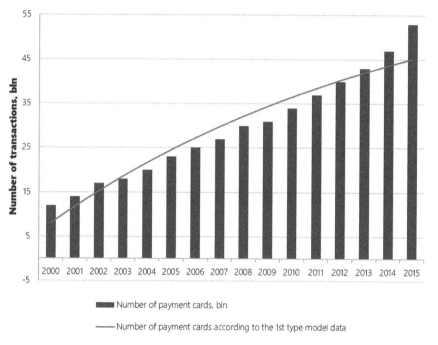

Fig. 2. Card payments in the EU and the 1st model data

According to the Bank of Korea report for 2013, in 2012, for the first time since 2004, when they began to collect statistics, the trend reflecting the number of issued cards per year has turned downward [19]. Here we make a raw hypothesis that the number of issued cards is approximately proportional to the number of active cards. We also see a good fit with characteristics of T = 10 years; n = 180 mln (Fig. 3).

Let us also consider the data of the Central Bank of the Russian Federation on payment cards in use [5] by half-year periods. Model fits well with T = 6 years, N = 390 mln. Application of the model to these cases also supports evident facts that younger markets are growing faster and bigger country has the bigger market capacity (Fig. 4).

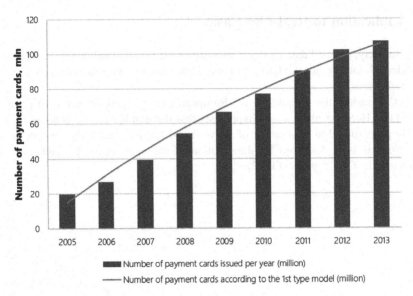

Fig. 3. Number of debit card in South Korea and the 1st model data

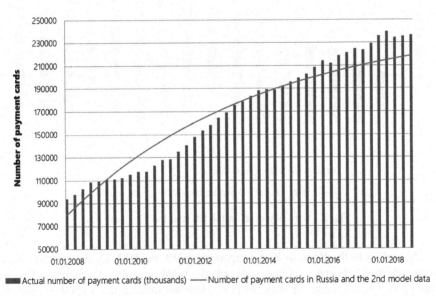

Fig. 4. The number of payment cards in Russia and the 2nd model data

5.1 WebMoney

An example of data from open sources is WebMoney statistics [17]. These statistics provide cumulative data up to 2014. After 2014 the company has only been publishing the data on a particular date. Therefore, we calculated this data for annual values.

The presence of inflection on the chart clearly indicates the predominance of P2P services, although C2B segment is also catered to by the system. As can be seen from the graph, at r = 0.48; K = 21000 (thousands) and N = 25500 (thousands); x_0 = 80. The graph of the formula (24) perfectly describes the empirical data.

If we try to predict the number of registrations for 2019 using the type two equation based on the available data, we will get 2.3 million registrations per year. This equates to 6 301 registrations per day, which is in line with the real-life data (Fig. 5).

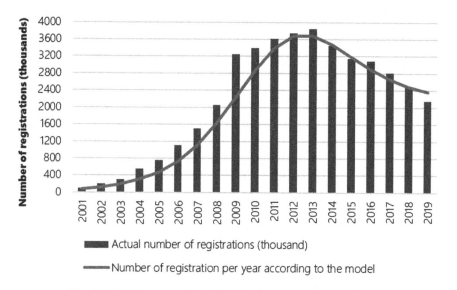

Fig. 5. WebMoney: number of wallets opened per year, thousands

An ambitious goal is to analyze such payment instrument as bitcoin and other cryptocurrencies. P2P transactions dominate in cryptocurrency schemes, so let's apply the equation to the graphs of the number of active Bitcoin [11] and Ethereum [15] wallets (Fig. 6).

As original graphs with factual data are based on the irregular temporal scale to accentuate fluctuations, analytical graphs look grainy as well: this is only a presentation problem. Obviously, the graphic representation of solutions to the (18) is smooth. We can see that the equation of the 2nd type (24) describes the behavior of both cryptocurrencies well for x_0 = 15 000, K = 550 000, r = 0,95 for bitcoin and x_0 = 1 500, K = 320 000 r = 0,5, excluding the around 2017 hype period, when the behavior of the systems was determined not by transactions, but by speculative investments. We can assume that both Bitcoin and Ethereum have reached a steady level and we will not see noticeable growth in their audience unless significant modifications to the business model or functionality are introduced.

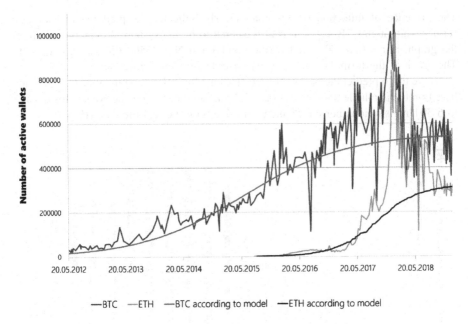

Fig. 6. Bitcoin, Ethereum. Active wallets statistic

6 Summary

This article has demonstrated the effectiveness of simple modeling methods for mass retail payment systems, including such disruptive systems as Bitcoin. The authors demonstrated that the behavior of such systems in the absence of competition can be described by one of two equations types, depending on the nature of the dominant transactions. These equations allow us to estimate the dynamics of the audience, the number of new registrations, to predict the results of advertising and regulatory actions. We have analyzed the behavior of the Bitcoin system and found that, very much like more traditional systems, it is likely to reach a floor limit in the long-run. Interestingly, surges in speculative transactions do not affect the payment functionality dynamics over time. Equations will be useful as a tool for assessing the economic behavior of such systems and as a basis for more detailed research of the financial market. The model describes some cases of early stages of payment systems development and does not include the competition concerns, which will be explored in further research.

References

1. Dostov, V.L., Mamuta, M.V., Shust, P.M.: New in the regulation of retail payment services in the European Union. Money Credit (7), 25–30 (2016). (in Russian)
2. Dostov, V.L., Shust, P.M.: Evolution of the electronic payments industry: problems of quality transition. In: Russian Academy of National Economy and Public Administration under the President of the Russian Federation. Moscow (2017). (in Russian)

3. Kuznetsov, Yu.A., Markova, S.E., Michasova, O.V.: Mathematical modeling of the dynamics of competitive replacement of generations of innovative goods. Math modeling. Optimal control. Bull. Nizhny Novgorod Univ. N.I. Lobachevsky, 2(1), 170–179 (2014). (in Russian)

4. Kopytin, V.Yu.: Modeling of interbank calculations on the basis of mathematical objects. https://bankir.ru/publikacii/20050516/modelirovanie-mejbankovskih-raschetov-na-baze-matematicheskih-obektov-1366664/. Accessed 15 Mar 2019

5. The number of payment cards issued by credit organizations by card types. https://www.cbr.ru/statistics/p_sys/print.aspx?file=sheet013.htm&pid=psrf&sid=ITM_55789. Accessed 12 Mar 2019

6. Payment system: structure, management and control: the lane with ang. In: Summers, B. J. (ed.). IMF. Washington, p. 156 (1994). (in Russian)

7. Sokolov M. Why "flies" only 1% of start-UPS—and that's fine. https://www.forbes.ru/tehnologii/339113-pochemu-vzletaet-tolko-1-startapov-i-eto-normalno. Accessed 15 Mar 2019

8. Fantazzini, D., Nigmatullin, E.M., Sukhanovskaya, V.N., Ivliev, S.V.: Everything you wanted to know about Bitcoin modeling but were afraid to ask. Appl. Econometrics 44, 5–24 (2016). (in Russian)

9. Fantazzini, D., Nigmatullin, E.M., Sukhanovskaya, V.N., Ivliev, S.V.: Everything you wanted to know about Bitcoin modeling but were afraid to ask. Appl. Econometrics 45, 5–28 (2017). (in Russian)

10. The Bass Model. http://bassbasement.org/BassModel/Default.aspx. Accessed 13 Mar 2019

11. Bitcoin Active Addresses historical chart. https://bitinfocharts.com/comparison/bitcoin-activeaddresses.html. Accessed 13 Mar 2019

12. European payments statistics for 2015. https://www.paymentscardsandmobile.com/payments-statistics-2015/. Accessed 13 Mar 2019

13. Four Different Types of Services. https://localfirstbank.com/content/different-types-of-banking-services/. Accessed 10 Mar 2019

14. Gandolfo, G.: The lotka-volterra equations in economics: an Italian precursor. Economia Politica XXIV(3), 343–348 (2007)

15. Helen Partz Ethereum Unique Addresses Break 50 Million, Active Wallet Number Keeps Dropping. https://cointelegraph.com/news/ethereum-unique-addresses-break-50-million-active-wallet-number-keeps-dropping. Accessed 15 Mar 2019

16. Hugo Thomas. Measuring Progress toward a Cashless Society. https://newsroom.mastercard.com/wp-content/uploads/2014/08/MasterCardAdvisors-CashlessSociety-July-20146.pdf. Accessed 15 Mar 2019

17. Statistics by year. https://www.wmtransfer.com/eng/information/statistic/years.shtml. Accessed 12 Mar 2019

18. Top Trends in Payments 2018. https://www.capgemini.com/wp-content/uploads/2017/12/payments-trends_2018.pdf. Accessed 15 Mar 2019

19. Volumes of credit and Debit Cards Approved per year. http://koreabizwire.com/kobiz-stats-volumes-of-credit-and-debit-cards-approved-per-year/7309. Accessed 14 Mar 2019

20. World Payments Report. 2018. https://worldpaymentsreport.com/wp-content/uploads/sites/5/2018/10/World-Payments-Report-2018.pdf. Accessed 16 Mar 2019

21. Laffont, J.-J., Regulation and Development, 440 p. Cambridge University Press (2005)

22. Recherches mathématiques sur la loi d'accroissement de la population, dans Nouveaux Mémoires de l'Académie Royale des Sciences et Belles-Lettres de Bruxelles, N 18, 1–42 (1845)

23. A Glossary of Terms Used in Payments and Settlement Systems. Bank for International Settlements, March 2003

Self-Sovereign Identity for IoT Devices

Nataliia Kulabukhova[✉] [iD], Andrei Ivashchenko, Iurii Tipikin, and Igor Minin

Saint-Petersburg State University, Saint Petersburg, Russia
n.kulabukhova@spbu.ru

Abstract. This work is an overview of different approaches to the self-sovereign identity (SSI) concept. The idea of constructing of a digital passport for each and every person in the world is not unique, but with the growing interest and progress of distributed ledgers, a new way of dealing with existing problems appeared. On the other hand, in our point of view, a lot of development groups are working in parallel on the similar topics, yet it is not clear what is going on inside. In this paper we will try to define the differences and discuss both pros and cons of using such commonly known technologies as Sovrin based upon the Hyperledger Indy technology, Civic, Jolocom, uPort and some others. Besides, we'll tackle the idea of using the SSI for inanimate object and how it can be constructed in this way.

1 Introduction

Obviously, the growing interest in blockchain technology make a lot of people think of its opportunities in variety of areas. One which is the digital identity. During last thirty years the idea of digital identity was defined and presented under different names in the following works [7,11,15]. But in the last ten years it was clarified in the name of self-sovereign identity. For clear understanding lets talk about so-called the self-sovereign identity ecosystem.

Figure 1 shows the most notable players on the field of SSI. All of these projects are focused on the problem, that today people, users of different devices, reveal a lot of private information to the third parties. That means giving the part of personal data which is not needed for some particular purpose. Usually a person does not control what is happening with his data. Third party could reuse it for own profit, manipulate it, etc. Another case is when the whole database of some entity, the company which collects and stores user accounts data on its servers, will be stolen (for example), thus leading to financial or any other personal data related issues for the customers.

To prevent the first problem the concept of self-sovereign identity appeared. As the name tells us, every person must have his or her sovereign data about him or her self, and only he or she has the right to create, use and, what is most important, control it. Besides, as we are talking about the internet communications, in many cases, especially financial and official, you need to be sure that the person you are contacting with is really a person and he or she has, for example,

© Springer Nature Switzerland AG 2019
S. Misra et al. (Eds.): ICCSA 2019, LNCS 11620, pp. 472–484, 2019.
https://doi.org/10.1007/978-3-030-24296-1_37

a right to pay and has enough money for that operation. In the papers authors properly described the concept and the proofs of the cryptography which is used inside.

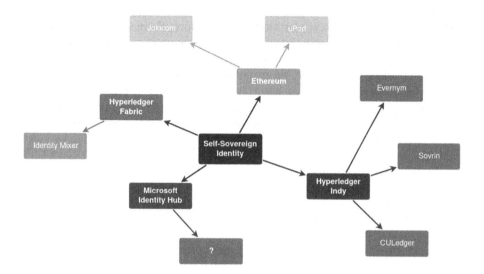

Fig. 1. Overview of the main SSI applications

Practically everything was perfect except two points:

– centralized authority;
– hash tables.

Looking at the centralized authorities which are used in the scheme, it is clear that they play crucial role in decision making. And no one can influence that, or, on the contrary, the authority can be compromised. In both cases it is the key point of the whole scheme.

The concept of distributed ledger is based on the decentralized root of trust which can not be compromised and on which everyone can rely on. Obviously, with the appearance of distributed ledgers came the idea to pass the responsibility of the centralized root of trust to them.

The second problem is the use of hash tables to store and control the key pairs (public keys, private keys) of users. The point is that they are not safe enough, though they have a lot of advantages. Developers were working on the solution for that, and as a result the W3C Community Group is now working on a specification of Decentralized Identifiers (DIDs).

From this specification we can learn that DIDs are a new type of identifiers for verifiable, "self-sovereign" digital identity [2].

2   Overview of SSI Infrastructures

First of all it should be said that SSI concept wasn't based on a blockchain at the beginning, and it was more about a certain protocol, which defines rules of interactions between independent identity agents representing an end user with its identifier. But, as it was already said before, there was a trust issue, in particular there was no way to know whether the counteragent was compromised or not. In example, if someone would be able to substitute government public keys in a storage of an agent, he would be able to make claims on behalf of government identity. So, at that point, a trust store problem was defined.

A fresh view on the matter was given with a popularization of a distributed ledger technology and blockchain in particular, since it was enabling unalterable and secure storage with a state determinated by participants based on a certain consensus rules. Thus, public key placed to the blockchain once can not be substituted, unless 51% attack was performed successfully, and every participant is able to have a full copy of a systems state.

Now, as we know main goals prospectors were trying to achieve, we can take a look on an architecture of self sovereign identity solutions and components in details.

Nevertheless there are plenty of various implementations available, most of them are having almost the same idea in mind, which is shown on Fig. 2

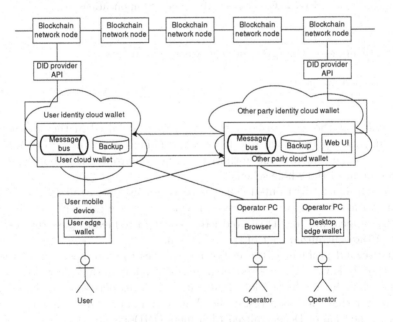

Fig. 2. Generalized scheme of interaction within SSI

Of course, blockchain comes as a basis of solution. Its main purpose is to provide a storage for end user keys and identifiers, or, in other words, to provide a public key infrastructure.

It is worth noting that a particular technology to use should be chosen with very careful consideration. Below you can find few examples (some of them are quite obvious) describing which difficulties can be met during the implementation.

Popular public blockchains, such as Ethereum [3] or Bitcoin [4], could be seen as a good candidates at a first glance. However, there's a simple, yet fundamental issue with them. There is a transaction cost for the creation of DID record, and even if it not quite big, it can bring some hassle to the end user, as he will need to find a way to buy and spend the currency. Also, transaction processing time is a lottery, especially in Ethereum, where you have to gamble on gas amount that should be put as a payment for transaction processing.

Another case could be taken from IOTA [5] snapshot mechanism. Its tangle looks quite interesting, as it allows to perform transactions on a public network really fast and free of charge. But snapshots are allowing full nodes to remove a transaction history that comes before snapshot transaction. As full nodes are storing actual tangle transaction, a public key registry would be simply eliminated.

There are some permissive networks trying to solve particular business case and eliminate conventionalities, such as mining and transaction fees, which are stimulating public participants to stay in the network in exchange to some profit. But, again, a problem of trust appears here, and you can trust the storage only if you trust the organization responsible for it. Indy [6], a particular solution from Hyperledger foundation is aiming exactly to solve this problem with DIDs. It is a public permissive network run by foundation members. In short, "public permissive" means that everyone could read from the ledger, but only ones defined as trusted members can write into it. And, actually Indy has two ledgers. First is responsible to listing all nodes, their keys and addresses, another one handles network members and their roles.

DID provider service comes on top. It is responsible for the definition of interaction rules with a blockchain. In other words, it should define a format for the data that is going to be stored in transaction block. Also DID provider defines an API for routine operations like DID creation, lookup, etc.

Next it comes to the wallet, that is actually a most important part of the system. Here is a list of basic functions it should be able to perform:

- Wallet should store user data and key pairs securely, so that no one else would be able to access them.
- Wallet should be able to find, access and store public keys of another users by their DIDs.
- Wallet should provide a way to encrypt, decrypt, sign and check signature.
- Wallet should be able to receive messages from other wallets.

The last point should be taken with attention. An ability to establish the connection between wallets is important, since pairwise DIDs are generated exactly on connection, so that connection has unique identifiers for parties. However, in most cases user wallet is located on mobile device, like smartphone, that is not able to be permanently online or even have a public endpoint by the nature of cellular networks. So that is where cloud wallet comes into play. It can actually duplicate whole functionality of edge wallet and act like a remote walled with Web UI, but it is not really required to. The main goal of cloud wallet is to provide a public endpoint for the user and accumulate messages until they will be delivered to the edge wallet. So it can just act like an inbox. Also it can be a common case when cloud wallet handles encrypted edge wallet backups.

2.1 Authentication Protocol with DIDs

In respect of last point of basic wallet functions list, we are proposing a protocol for handshake between arbitrary client and server, where are both using wallets/DIDs to identify themselves on a web. Main goal here is to translate an identifier to an actual encrypted key to use it in symmetric traffic encryption process, like TLS/HTTPS protocol does. Suggested steps of such handshake described in the following sequence diagram (Fig. 3). The *Wallets* here could be replaced with generalized Wallet API, then both Client and Server can use it locally or remotely without the need to create an actual transaction to verify opposite side DID on their's hardware. *DLT* stands for Distributed Ledger Technology, which can be any modern ledger system, like Ethereum.

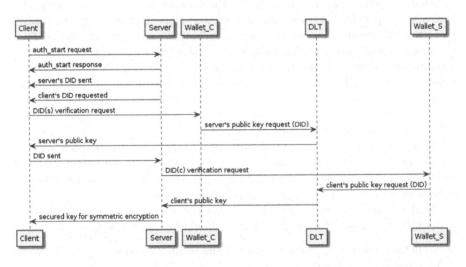

Fig. 3. Authentication protocol with symmetric encryption by DIDs

3 Anonymization Functionality

In the Privacy-ABC concept [13, 18, 20] every user can generate a secret key. However, in comparison with the traditional scheme of public-private key pairs in authentication process, in Privacy-ABC there can be as many public keys for one secret as user wants. These public keys are called pseudonyms. The two very important privacy-related features are based on them. First is untraceability which guarantees that the presentation of credentials can not be linked to their issuance. In other words, that means that given two different pseudonyms, one cannot tell whether they were generated from the same or from different secret keys. Another main feature is unlinkability, which guarantees that the Verifier can not link different presentations of a given user. By generating a different pseudonym for every verifier, users can thus be known under different unlinkable pseudonyms to different sites, yet use the same secret key to authenticate to all of them. In some literature they are called Issuer-unlinkability and Verifier-unlinkability [1].

From the above the following properties of the Privacy-ABC concept can be concluded:

- Pseudonyms;
- Key binding;
- Selective disclosure;
- Predicates over attributes;
- Inspectability.

Today there is two technologies implementing Privacy-ABC concept: Identity Mixer by IBM [7] and U-Prove by Microsoft [8]. In the Table 1 comparison of main features of Identity Mixer and U-Prove is made.

Table 1. Comparison of Identity Mixer and U-Prove main features

Main aspects	Technology	
	Idemix	U-Prove
Signature scheme	Camenisch-Lysyanskaya's signature	Brand's signature
Implementation instantiation	Elliptic curves	Standard subgroup
Untracebility and unlinkability	Has both	Untraceable, but linkable between presentations
Revocation, Inspection	Shared	Shared

In [9] a comparative analysis of the performance of these two technologies was given. From this research we can see that U-Prove is more efficient for Users operations and when the number of attributes in the credentials is big enough. But Identity Mixer has better efficiency in the rest of the cases, also with advanced presentational features.

4   Decentralized Identity Usages in Application Development

When it comes to the actual development and SSI integration into the application, two common problems of authorization and authentication are usually need to be solved, just because from the perspective of developer the concept itself is pushing for it.

On Fig. 4 you can see how a decentralized identity solution can be integrated and used in application with the classic architecture.

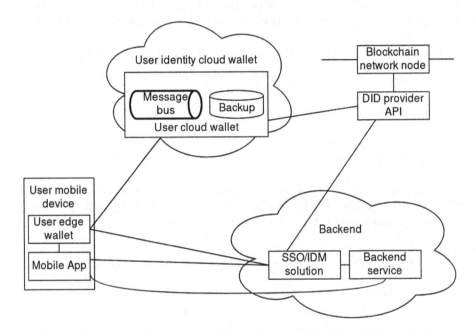

Fig. 4. Integration of DIDs on classic architecture

Taking a closer look on the components, the system has a centralized identity management solution, while the user manipulates with DIDs. Thus, there should be some kind of SSO server that will be able to communicate with SSI infrastructure and transfer claims to IDM [12]. It can be a part of identity management solution, or it can be a separate component.

This approach is similar in some ways with OIDC server intercommunication, where an identity can be shared from one resource to another, and used by target resource server to identify user. You've probably experienced that when you've been using your social account (OAuth), like Facebook or Google one, to login to another website, and it have been asking you to share some data with request originator. Moreover, an implementation of SSI data transfer to IDM can be based on OIDC protocol, so there would be a SSO server responsible to handle logins with SSI.

The main difference of centralized IDM based on OIDC compared to some SSI solution (e.g. Sovrin [14]) is that basically your mobile wallet acts as your very own identity provider, and you are choosing exactly which data you want to share with target resource, if any at all.

At final, user would be able to log into the system with the usage of SSI, and use local identity from centralized IDM to interact with resource. This approach is not completely right from the perspective of decentralized systems, but is capable to easily enable DIDs for variety of infrastructure owners using classic identity management solutions, like corporates, and also shows up a main principle of identity control.

Figure 5 represents a so-called dApp.

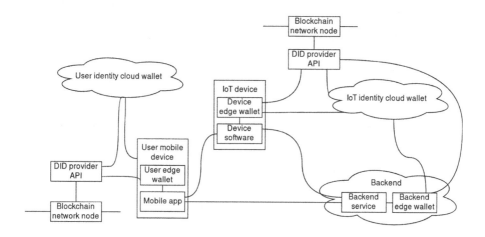

Fig. 5. The general scheme of decentralized application

So far we've been describing authentication and authorization, but another interesting area where SSI/DID solution can be used is a cryptography. These appliances are quite simple and come from basic SSI principles.

Blockchain already contains public key, so we can use it as a basis for public key infrastructure. If we know a DID of machine from the pool where we want to have mutual relationships between nodes, we are able to obtain its public key and check if machine will respond correctly to the message encrypted with that key. Also this is eliminating key exchange phase at connection initialization. Here is where an idea of device identity appears.

Another case aims at a way more global problem with certification authorities. Basically, every operating system has a package of trusted root certificates preinstalled, or such package available for it, and you may not even know or think about it. This certificate set enables a secure communications over the global network. Root authorities should store their certificates securely, issue child certificates and include them to the chain. There is no actual way to know whether authority was compromised or not, you just have to trust it (Explain here how).

5   Digital Identity in Logistic Chains

All we speak about above refers mostly to the human identity. The W3C community asserts that entities means humans or organizations. But will it work with IoT devices? At first glance, the answer is yes. In this paper we are trying to see if it is really suitable for inanimate object and how it will be working in this case (Fig. 6).

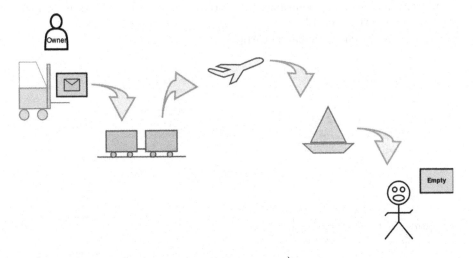

Fig. 6. Logistic chain of some item

Lets suppose we have some kind of "smart box". It can be a huge container traveling on the ship, or just a small post parcel. Each smart box has its identifier, which holds the following static information:

- the identity number;
- the weight;
- the size;
- the owner;
- properties.

At the same time as the box is smart it has some sensors and can dynamically give the information about:

- GPS coordinates;
- temperature;
- humidity;
- shaking;
- etc.

All described above opportunities of the smart box will help the owner to control cargo at each step of the chain. Throughout its journey the box will collect all the information about itself and the goods inside. Besides, if some number of smart boxes are going to join together, they can first make a decision about compatibility of there goods, and only after this check if they will group or not, if impossible.

6   Existing Solutions and Differences

There are a lot of existing SSI solutions, most of which, but not all, are based on distributed technologies and blockchain. Since there are so many of them it might take another paper to cover them so we would only focus on the most popular/famous ones. See Table 2 for some basic comparison.

Table 2. Comparison of existing SSI solutions

Solution	Aspect	
	Protocol	Source
Sovrin	Hyperledger Indy	Open-source
Civic	Ethereum	Closed-source
uPort	Ethereum	Open-source
Jolocom	Ethereum	Open-source
Veres one	Custom	Open-source
Ontology	Custom	Open-source
Remme	Hyperledger Sawtooth	Open-source

As you can see there are a lot of different approaches to the SSI using different technologies. This list is by far not complete. You can see many more solutions on the Decentralized Identity Foundation (DIF) site [28]. All of them are different of course but there are some similarities also. Rather than going through each of the solutions in detail lets just briefly go through them.

The most notable players on the market as of now are Sovrin [13], uPort [22] and Civic [23].

6.1   Source

While Civic might be the most mature project out of all existing ones - it is unfortunately closed-source. In our opinion there's no point of going through closed-source solutions as it is not completely clear what may happen inside. So even though Civic might be the best approach - we will not know until the sources are made public.

As you can see most of the other solutions are actually open-source.

6.2   Protocol

Unfortunately, as already stated above - Ethereum-based SSI solutions have a problem with every transaction being payed for. Which may not be ideal for a lot of scenarios, especially if it is used as some kind of government ID. This way either users will have to pay to use it, or the government will have to sponsor this.

Because of this a lot of consideration should be made before choosing either uPort [22] or Jolocom [24].

Same should be said regarding any of the custom protocols also - as one should investigate them in-depth before relying on them for the future use. For example this is about Veres one [25] and the Ontology [26].

There are also some Bitcoin-based SSI solutions, but clearly, given the Bitcoin architecture and general slowdown with time - using them doesn't seem like the best approach.

6.3   Standards

Another very important topic to consider when choosing SSI solution is standard compliance. The more complaint it is - the less there is a chance to be deprecated. Of course, first of all the solution should use the standard - DID for communications. And DIDs should be complaint with the DID specification [2]. Second - they should be present in the DID method registry [29]. Unfortunately Remme [27] is not present there so it is not clear if they use DIDs at all. Third - ideally public network DIDs should be resolvable by the Universal Resolver [30]. This can serve as an easy check if the DID is actually valid and complaint.

6.4   Our View

From our perspective at this point the best approach is taken by the Sovrin - this blockchain is specifically designed to solve the SSI use case, so it does not suffer from a lot of potential issues with existing blockchains. It is completely open source, with all the documentation available for developers. It is also W3C standard complaint and even works with Universal Resolver. The main downside of the Sovrin is that it is not yet mature enough to be used by everyone though.

7   Conclusion

In this article we have tried to consider the main key points of the SSI technology. Despite the fact that this technology itself has been developing for several decades, with the advent of new concepts, such as distributed ledgers, it has received both further development and new difficulties in application. We have tried to describe the most important problems that modern developers of DIDs and IoT have to face. In the future, we plan to expand the use of the opportunities described here to other cases.

References

1. Camenisch, J., Dubovitskaya, M., Lehmann, A., Neven, G., Paquin, C., Preiss, F.-S.: Concepts and languages for privacy-preserving attribute-based authentication. In: Fischer-Hübner, S., de Leeuw, E., Mitchell, C. (eds.) IDMAN 2013. IAICT, vol. 396, pp. 34–52. Springer, Heidelberg (2013). https://doi.org/10.1007/978-3-642-37282-7_4
2. https://w3c-ccg.github.io/did-spec/
3. https://www.ethereum.org/
4. https://bitcoin.org/en/
5. https://www.iota.org/
6. https://www.hyperledger.org/projects/hyperledger-indy
7. Security Team, Computer Science Dept., IBM Research, Specification of the Identity Mixer Cryptographic Library, p. 49 (2010)
8. https://www.microsoft.com/en-us/research/project/u-prove/
9. Veseli, F., Serna, J.: Evaluation of privacy-ABC technologies - a study on the computational efficiency. In: Habib, S.M.M., Vassileva, J., Mauw, S., Mühlhäuser, M. (eds.) IFIPTM 2016. IAICT, vol. 473, pp. 63–78. Springer, Cham (2016). https://doi.org/10.1007/978-3-319-41354-9_5
10. Sanchez, J.L.C., Bernabe, J.B., Skarmeta, A.F.: Integration of Anonymous Credential Systems in IoT Constrained Environments, p. 11 (2018)
11. Wagner, K., Némethi, B., Renieris, E., Lang, P., Brunet, E., Holst, E.: Self-sovereign Identity. A position paper on blockchain enabled identity and the road ahead, p. 57 (2018)
12. https://github.com/WebOfTrustInfo/rwot4-paris/blob/master/topics-and-advance-readings/dkms-decentralized-key-mgmt-system.md
13. SovrinTM: A Protocol and Token for Self-Sovereign Identity and Decentralized Trust, A White Paper from the Sovrin Foundation, p. 42 (2018). https://sovrin.org/wp-content/uploads/2018/03/Sovrin-Protocol-and-Token-White-Paper.pdf
14. The Sovrin Trust Framework Working Group, Sovrin Provisional Trust Framework, p. 30 (2017). https://sovrin.org/wp-content/uploads/2018/03/Sovrin-Provisional-Trust-Framework-2017-06-28.pdf
15. Brickell, E., Camenisch, J., Chen, L.: Direct Anonymous Attestation, p. 24 (2004)
16. Camenisch, J., Drijvers, M., Lehmann, A.: Anonymous attestation using the strong Diffie Hellman assumption revisited. In: Franz, M., Papadimitratos, P. (eds.) Trust 2016. LNCS, vol. 9824, pp. 1–20. Springer, Cham (2016). https://doi.org/10.1007/978-3-319-45572-3_1
17. Jhttps://ssimeetup.org/
18. Garman, C., Green, M., Miers I.: Decentralized Anonymous Credentials, p. 21 (2013)
19. Fei, C., Lohkamp, J., Rusu, E., Szawan, K., Wagner, K., Wittenberg, N.: Self-Sovereign and Decentralised Identity By Design, Jolocom Technical White Paper, p. 10 (2018)
20. Rannenberg, K., Camenisch, J., Sabouri, A.: Attribute-Based Credentials for Trust, p. 395. Springer, Cham (2015). https://doi.org/10.1007/978-3-319-14439-9
21. Neven, G.: A Quick Introduction to Anonymous Credentials, p. 4 (2008)
22. https://www.uport.me
23. https://www.civic.com/
24. https://jolocom.io/
25. https://veres.one

26. https://ont.io
27. https://remme.io/
28. https://identity.foundation/
29. https://w3c-ccg.github.io/did-method-registry/
30. https://uniresolver.io/

Error Detection in the Decentralized Voting Protocol

Alexander Bogdanov[1,2] , Alexei Uteshev[1,2($\boxtimes$)] , and Valery Khvatov[3]

[1] Faculty of Applied Mathematics, St. Petersburg State University,
7–9 Universitetskaya nab., St. Petersburg 199034, Russia
bogdanov@csa.ru, a.uteshev@spbu.ru
[2] Plekhanov Russian University of Economics,
Stremyanny lane 36, Moscow 117997, Russia
[3] BGX Technologies AG, Hofstrasse 1a, 6300 Zug, Switzerland
valery.khvatov@gmail.com
http://www.apmath.spbu.ru/en/
https://www.rea.ru/en/
http://www.bgx.ai/

Abstract. The decentralized voting protocol based on the Lagrange interpolant construction is analyzed for the potential error detection in the set of shares. We suggest an algorithm for the error locator polynomial construction based on procedure of computation the determinants of the Hankel type generated by the sequence of special symmetric functions of the set of shares.

Keywords: Voting protocol · Homomorphic Secret Sharing · Error correction · Polynomial interpolation

1 Introduction

The decision making problem in a consortium of voters in the lack of the confidence between the members, is of vital importance for variety of applications ranging from elections to blockchain. The growing economic paradigm of the platform economy, represented by Uber, Airbnb, Spotify and other technology startups requires a transition to decentralized information exchange systems. From the point of view of computing and storing information, the central problem is the lack of a single trusted environment between the participants in the information exchange. Last years there has been an intensive development of relevant computational architectures that range from creating systems with zero tolerance levels of trust in each other to regulated pseudo-trusted environments (Private Blockchain). Consortium-based approaches have an intermediate position, allowing to reach a compromise between the necessary level of environmental security and an acceptable performance of information exchange.

Even if the qualified majority of the consortium behaves honestly, some of the unreliable voters and/or vote-counters (administrators) might influence

© Springer Nature Switzerland AG 2019
S. Misra et al. (Eds.): ICCSA 2019, LNCS 11620, pp. 485–494, 2019.
https://doi.org/10.1007/978-3-030-24296-1_38

the voting protocol in order to falsify (compromise) the result. The different approaches for the fault tolerant protocol construction has been developed during past decades; they could be principally distinguished by the attitude to the confidentiality of the voting result by each consortium member. Some of them, concerned with the Byzantine Generals Problem, are focused onto consortiums where all the decisions are assumed to be open at any stage of the vote [1]. This assumption enables the protocol construction based on free distribution of the voting related information between the members. On the contrary, the consortiums where each voter does not know of the others, corresponds only with administrator(s), and wants his vote to be secret, should also be treated as meeting the demands of life.

The voting systems are in demand with the interaction of participants who have real-life relationships with each other, participating in information exchange, but making decisions from different economic backgrounds and interests. The arising task of reaching a consensus within the consortium is the basic for building vertical and horizontal integration of the interacting parties. In the case of vertical integration, interaction occurs along the value chain, when information about the object of economic activity is transmitted along the system, and in the horizontal, the creation of partner ecosystems that complement each other and create new, shared values. Such tasks arise in the real economy in many sectors like building a food chain distribution, energy exchange, trade in digital goods, loyalty systems, etc. When solving problems of exchange, it is necessary to take into account the speed of transactions, their confidentiality, resistance to errors and malicious distortions.

These aspects can be effectively incorporated in protocols which combine secret sharing and decentralized voting. In this regard, the Homomorphic Secret Sharing recently became a topic of intensive investigations [3]. In the present paper we treat such a protocol based on the Lagrange interpolant construction [2] (its brief description is given in Sect. 3).

The problem of our concern is that of potential error detection in some steps of the protocol. In Sect. 4 we treat it first as the one of the (systematic) error occurrence in the data set provided by a polynomial function. It turns out that under some assumptions on relationship between the number of potential errors and the redundancy in the correct values in the data set, the erroneous values can be detected. The algorithm is based on finding zero sets of specially constructed polynomials of the Hankel type.

2   Algebraic Preliminaries: Polynomial Interpolation

The classical univariate polynomial interpolation problem over an infinite field, say $\mathbb{Q}$, is formulated as follows. Given the set of values for the variables x and y

$$\{(x_j, y_j)\}_{j=1}^K \subset \mathbb{Q}^2, \tag{1}$$

with distinct (nodes) $\{x_j\}_{j=1}^K$, find a polynomial $f(x)$ such that $\{f(x_j) = y_j\}_{j=1}^K$. If $\deg f \leq K-1$ then the problem has a unique solution which can be represented in several forms. Set

$$W(x) := \prod_{j=1}^{K}(x - x_j) \, , W_j(x) := \frac{W(x)}{x - x_j} \quad \text{for } j \in \{1, \dots, K\}.$$

Then the polynomial interpolant in Lagrange form is computed as

$$f(x) \equiv \sum_{j=1}^{K} y_j \frac{W_j(x)}{W_j(x_j)} \equiv \sum_{j=1}^{K} y_j \frac{W_j(x)}{W'(x_j)}. \tag{2}$$

Note that formula (2) does not provide one with the explicit representation for the coefficients of the interpolant

$$f(x) \equiv a_0 x^{K-1} + a_1 x^{K-2} + \dots + a_{K-1}. \tag{3}$$

For this aim, a further expansion of $\{W_j(x)\}_{j=1}^{K}$ in the powers of x is needed. This can be organized with the aid of special symmetric functions of the data set (1). The following result can be found in [4].

Theorem 1 (Euler, Lagrange). *For the polynomial $F(x) \in \mathbb{R}[x]$ with the leading coefficient equal to A_0, the following equalities are valid*

$$\sum_{j=1}^{K} \frac{F(x_j)}{W'(x_j)} = \begin{cases} 0 & \text{if } \deg F < K - 1, \\ A_0 & \text{if } \deg F = K - 1. \end{cases} \tag{4}$$

We now generate two sequences from the data set (1)

$$\sigma_\ell = \sum_{j=1}^{K} \frac{x_j^{K+\ell-1}}{W'(x_j)} \quad \text{for } \ell \in \{1, \dots, K\} \tag{5}$$

and

$$\tau_\ell = \sum_{j=1}^{K} y_j \frac{x_j^{\ell}}{W'(x_j)} \quad \text{for } \ell \in \{0, 1, \dots\}. \tag{6}$$

Theorem 2. *The following formulas connect the values (5) and (6) with the coefficients of the interpolant:*

$$\tau_0 = a_0, \quad \tau_\ell = a_0 \sigma_\ell + a_1 \sigma_{\ell-1} + \dots + a_{\ell-1}\sigma_1 + a_\ell \quad \text{for } \ell \in \{1, \dots, K-1\}.$$

Proof. It follows from (4)

$$\tau_\ell = \sum_{j=1}^{K} \frac{y_j x_j^{\ell}}{W'(x_j)} = \sum_{j=1}^{K} \frac{(a_0 x_j^{K-1} + a_1 x_j^{K-2} + \dots + a_\ell x_j^{K-\ell-1} + \dots + a_{K-1})x_j^{\ell}}{W'(x_j)}$$

$$= a_0 \sigma_\ell + a_1 \sigma_{\ell-1} + \dots + a_{\ell-1}\sigma_1 + a_\ell.$$

$\square$

Theorem 2 provides one with the procedure for computation the coefficients of the interpolant (3) recursively starting with that of the highest order of the variable. One can organize an alternative counterpart of this procedure starting the computations with the free term of the interpolant. For instance, one has

$$a_{K-1} = f(0) = (-1)^{K-1} \tau_{-1} \prod_{j=1}^{K} x_j \quad \text{where} \quad \tau_{-1} := \sum_{j=1}^{K} y_j \frac{1}{x_j W'(x_j)} \quad (7)$$

provided that $\{x_j \neq 0\}_{j=1}^{K}$.

The values (6) will be of use in Sect. 4 for the problem of the potential error detection in the data set (1). We will be also in need there of an auxiliary result evidently following from Theorem 1:

Corollary 1. *For the polynomial interpolant generated by the set (1) to be of the degree $k < K - 1$, it is necessary and sufficient that*

$$\tau_0 = 0, \ldots, \tau_{K-k-2} = 0, \tau_{K-k-1} \neq 0. \quad (8)$$

3   Decentralized Voting Protocol

Assume that a consortium consists of $N > 2$ voters and $k > 2$ administrators. Every vote consists of two possible outcomes, either yes or no. In the ideal case, these results are delivered to administrator(s) and counted accordingly. However, in the real life, a particular administrator might corrupt the voting result. The aim is to make a voting scheme involving $k > 2$ administrators in which every particular one receives only a piece (a share) of information from every voter, while the result of the vote can be restored only from the whole collection of the administrators' receipts.

To organize the sharing, let the ℓth administrator generate a <u>nonzero</u> integer x_ℓ and makes it public for the consortium. The obtained k numbers $x_1, \ldots, x_k$ should be <u>distinct</u> (otherwise, some of numbers should be replaced to avoid collisions).

At the same time, let the jth voter generate a polynomial of a degree $\leq k - 1$ with arbitrary integer coefficients, except for the free term which is taken to be equal to $+1$ if he votes yes, and -1 otherwise. This polynomial is kept secret. Thus, the voters hold the system of polynomials

$$f_1(x), \ldots, f_N(x) \quad (9)$$

such that $\{f_1(0), \ldots, f_N(0)\} \subset \{-1, 1\}$ and the polynomial

$$F(x) := \sum_{j=1}^{N} f_j(x)$$

possesses a degree $\deg F \leq k - 1$ and the free term equal to the voting result of the consortium (number of votes yes minus number of votes no).

The next aim is to extract this result, i.e. to compute the polynomial $F(x)$ provided that its summands (9) are still kept secret.

Each voter computes the value of his polynomial at $x_1, \ldots, x_k$ and communicates the obtained values to the corresponding administrators, i.e. the number $f_j(x_\ell)$ is sent off from the jth voter to the ℓth administrator.

Each administrator sums up the received values and makes the result public for the consortium members. Evidently one has

$$\left\{ Y_\ell := \sum_{j=1}^{N} f_j(x_\ell) = F(x_\ell) \right\}_{\ell=1}^{k}, \tag{10}$$

and, therefore, the k values of the polynomial $F(x)$ become available to everybody interested in them. Since $\deg F(x) \le k-1$, the polynomial $F(x)$ is uniquely defined by these values, and the value $F(0)$, computed via (7), yields then the result of the vote.

What prevents the intention to falsify a share by the ℓth administrator? He is not able to definitely match the obtained share $f_j(x_\ell)$ with the voting result $f_j(0)$ and thereby looses motivation to forge the share.

We finally formulate two assumptions that ensure the trustworthy of the voting result.

Assumption 1. The shares $\{Y_\ell\}_{\ell=1}^{k}$ are assumed to be uncorrupted. Even if each administrator does not forge his share, it could be got wrong due to communication failures of the shares $\{f_j(x_\ell)\}$.

Assumption 2. The voters (and their shares $\{f_j(x_\ell)\}$) are assumed to be honest. Otherwise, if the jth one would generate a polynomial $\widetilde{f}_j(x)$ such that $\widetilde{f}_j(0) = +3$ and communicates then the values $\{\widetilde{f}_j(x_\ell)\}_{\ell=1}^{k}$ to the corresponding administrators, the voting result gets $+2$ extra votes yes.

We next intend to discuss whether it is possible to modify the voting scheme for the case where any of these assumptions is violated. For this aim, we rethink the polynomial interpolation problem.

4   Error Detection in the Data Set

If the data set (1) is generated by a polynomial of a degree $k < K - 1$ then it is redundant for computation of this polynomial. Any subset of the data set containing $k + 1$ entries is sufficient for the polynomial restoration. One can establish its true degree on checking the conditions (8).

Suppose now that some of the values $y_1, \ldots, y_K$ originally generated by a polynomial of a degree $k < K - 1$ are corrupted, but we do know neither their amount nor their location. One may then expect that generically the degree of the interpolant formally constructed by (2) would be greater than k, and, therefore, some of the equalities (8) would be violated. This provides one with a sufficient condition for the existence of an error in the data set.

In order to locate the erroneous values, compute the values (6) and compose the following determinant

$$
\mathcal{H}_L(x;\{\tau\}) := \begin{vmatrix} \tau_0 & \tau_1 & \tau_2 & \cdots & \tau_L \\ \tau_1 & \tau_2 & \tau_3 & \cdots & \tau_{L+1} \\ \vdots & \vdots & \vdots & & \vdots \\ \tau_{L-1} & \tau_L & \tau_{L+1} & \cdots & \tau_{2L-1} \\ 1 & x & x^2 & \cdots & x^L \end{vmatrix}_{(L+1)\times(L+1)}
\tag{11}
$$

for $L \in \mathbb{N}$. Expanding (11) by its last row, $\mathcal{H}_L(x;\{\tau\})$ can be represented as a polynomial in x which is sometimes referred to as the Lth **Hankel polynomial** generated by (6).

Example 1. The data set

x	-3	-2	-1	0	1	2	3	4	5
y	19	-2	-7	-8	3	14	37	35	107

is generated by a second order polynomial with the exception of some erroneous values. Construct the polynomials (11) and find out whether their zeros belongs to the set $\{-3, -2, , \ldots, 5\}$ or not.

Solution. Compute the values (6):

$$
\tau_0 = \frac{1}{70}, \; \tau_1 = \frac{53}{1680}, \; \tau_2 = \frac{193}{1680}, \; \tau_3 = \frac{47}{112}, \; \tau_4 = \frac{407}{240}, \; \tau_5 = \frac{11233}{1680}, \ldots
$$

The sequence of polynomials (11) starts as follows

$$
\mathcal{H}_1(x;\{\tau\}) \equiv \frac{1}{70}x - \frac{53}{1680}, \; \mathcal{H}_2(x;\{\tau\}) \equiv \frac{1823}{2822400}x^2 - \frac{6691}{2822400}x + \frac{29}{705600},
$$

and these polynomials do not possess zeros in the desired set. The next polynomial does:

$$
\mathcal{H}_3(x;\{\tau\}) \equiv \frac{33}{313600}(x+2)(x-1)(x-4).
$$

It turns out that the numbers $\{-2, 1, 4\}$ are the values of arguments where the given data set do not coincide with the set $\{(x_j, f(x_j))\}_{j=-3}^{5}$ where $f(x) := 4x^2 + 3x - 8$. Therefore, the polynomial $\mathcal{H}_3(x;\{\tau\})$ is the **error locator** one for the redundant but somewhere erroneous data set generated by $f(x)$. $\square$

We reveal this trick in the proof of the following result where it is assumed that the number of erroneous values in the data set (1) equals E.

Theorem 3. *Let $E \in \{1, 2, \ldots, \lfloor K/2 \rfloor - 1\}$ and $e_1, \ldots, e_E$ be distinct numbers from $\{1, 2, \ldots, K\}$. Let polynomial $f(x)$ be of a degree $k < K - 2E$. Let the data set satisfy the conditions*

(a) $y_j = f(x_j)$ *for* $j \in \{1, \ldots, K\} \setminus \{e_1, \ldots, e_E\}$,
(b) $\widehat{y}_{e_s} := f(x_{e_s}) \neq y_{e_s}$ *for* $s \in \{1, \ldots, E\}$.

Then

$$\mathcal{H}_E(x; \{\tau\}) \equiv \frac{\displaystyle\prod_{s=1}^{E}(y_{e_s} - \widehat{y}_{e_s}) \prod_{1 \le s < t \le E}(x_{e_t} - x_{e_s})^2}{\displaystyle\prod_{s=1}^{E} W'(x_{e_s})} \prod_{s=1}^{E}(x - x_{e_s}). \qquad (12)$$

Proof. Assume, without loss of generality, that $\{e_s = s\}_{s=1}^{E}$. Denote

$$\theta_\ell := \sum_{s=1}^{E} \frac{\varepsilon_s x_s^\ell}{W'(x_s)} \quad \text{where } \varepsilon_j := y_j - \widehat{y}_j \text{ for } j \in \{1, \ldots, E\}, \ell \in \{0, 1, 2, \ldots\}.$$

One has:

$$\tau_\ell = \sum_{s=1}^{E} \frac{\varepsilon_s x_s^\ell}{W'(x_s)} + \sum_{j=1}^{K} \frac{f(x_j)x_j^\ell}{W'(x_j)} \overset{(4)}{=} \theta_\ell \quad \text{for } \ell \in \{0, \ldots, K - k - 2\}.$$

Rewrite the expression for $\mathcal{H}_E(x; \{\tau\})$:

$$\mathcal{H}_E(x; \{\tau\}) \equiv \mathcal{H}_E(x; \{\theta\}) \equiv \begin{vmatrix} \theta_0 & \theta_1 & \ldots & \theta_{E-1} & \theta_E \\ \theta_1 & \theta_2 & \ldots & \theta_E & \theta_{E+1} \\ \vdots & \vdots & \vdots & & \vdots \\ \theta_{E-1} & \theta_E & \ldots & \theta_{2E-2} & \theta_{2E-1} \\ 1 & x & \ldots & x^{E-1} & x^E \end{vmatrix}.$$

The set of zeros of this polynomial coincides with $\{x_1, \ldots, x_E\}$. This follows from the equalities

$$\sum_{s=1}^{E} \frac{\varepsilon_s x_s^{\ell-1}}{W'(x_s)} \mathcal{H}_E(x_s; \{\theta\}) = \begin{vmatrix} \theta_0 & \theta_1 & \ldots & \theta_{E-1} & \theta_E \\ \theta_1 & \theta_2 & \ldots & \theta_E & \theta_{E+1} \\ \vdots & \vdots & \vdots & & \vdots \\ \theta_{E-1} & \theta_E & \ldots & \theta_{2E-2} & \theta_{2E-1} \\ \theta_{\ell-1} & \theta_\ell & \ldots & \theta_{\ell+E-2} & \theta_{\ell+E-1} \end{vmatrix} = 0 \text{ for } \ell \in \{1, \ldots, E\}.$$

These relationships compose the system of E homogeneous linear equations connecting the values $\{\mathcal{H}_E(x_s; \{\theta\})\}_{s=1}^{E}$. The determinant of this system

$$\det\left[\frac{\varepsilon_s x_s^{\ell-1}}{W'(x_s)}\right]_{\ell,s=1}^{E} = \frac{\displaystyle\prod_{s=1}^{E} \varepsilon_s}{\displaystyle\prod_{s=1}^{E} W'(x_s)} \det\left[x_s^{\ell-1}\right]_{\ell,s=1}^{E} = \frac{\displaystyle\prod_{s=1}^{E} \varepsilon_s \prod_{1 \le \ell < t \le E}(x_t - x_\ell)}{\displaystyle\prod_{s=1}^{E} W'(x_s)}$$

$$(13)$$

does not vanish due to the assumption **(b)** of the theorem. Therefore all the values $\{\mathcal{H}_E(x_s;\{\theta\})\}_{s=1}^{E}$ should be equal zero and

$$\mathcal{H}_E(x;\{\tau\}) \equiv C \prod_{s=1}^{E}(x-x_s)$$

for some constant $C \in \mathbb{R}$. It turns out that the expression for the leading coefficient of $\mathcal{H}_E(x;\{\theta\})$ looks similar to (13):

$$\begin{vmatrix} \theta_0 & \theta_1 & \dots & \theta_{E-1} \\ \theta_1 & \theta_2 & \dots & \theta_E \\ \vdots & \vdots & & \vdots \\ \theta_{E-1} & \theta_E & \dots & \theta_{2E-2} \end{vmatrix}$$

$$= \begin{vmatrix} 1 & 1 & \dots & 1 \\ x_1 & x_2 & \dots & x_E \\ \vdots & \vdots & & \vdots \\ x_1^{E-1} & x_2^{E-1} & \dots & x_E^{E-1} \end{vmatrix} \cdot \begin{vmatrix} \dfrac{\varepsilon_1}{W'(x_1)} & 0 & \dots & 0 \\ & \dfrac{\varepsilon_2}{W'(x_2)} & \dots & 0 \\ \vdots & \vdots & \ddots & \vdots \\ 0 & 0 & \dots & \dfrac{\varepsilon_E}{W'(x_E)} \end{vmatrix} \cdot \begin{vmatrix} 1 & x_1 & \dots & x_1^{E-1} \\ 1 & x_2 & \dots & x_2^{E-1} \\ \vdots & \vdots & & \vdots \\ 1 & x_E & \dots & x_E^{E-1} \end{vmatrix}$$

$$= \frac{\displaystyle\prod_{s=1}^{E}\varepsilon_s \prod_{1\le \ell<t\le E}(x_t-x_\ell)^2}{\displaystyle\prod_{s=1}^{E}W'(x_s)}.$$

This concludes the proof of (12). $\square$

We come back now to the problems stated in Sect. 3.

5 Administrators' Faulty Shares

We first treat the case where Assumption 1 from Sect. 3 is violated, i.e. some of the values (10) might be corrupted. Assume that the number of expected errors would not exceed some a priory agreed estimation E small enough compared with the total number of shares. To detect these errors in the framework of the results of Sect. 4, one should organize redundancy in the interpolation problem. This can be performed in two possible ways: either diminishing the degrees of the polynomials $\{f_j(x)\}$ generated by the voters or by increasing the number of administrators. The underlying mathematics for these alternatives is the same, and we restrict ourself with the treatment of the case where the number of administrators is now equal to K and $K > k - 1 \geq \deg f_j(x) - 1$. The error detection protocol performs as follows:

(A) Compute $\tau_0, \ldots, \tau_{K-k-3}$ via (6). If all these numbers vanish, the errors are not detected.

(B) If any of these numbers is nonzero, an error is detected. Compute the sequence of polynomials $\mathcal{H}_1(x; \{\tau\}), \mathcal{H}_2(x; \{\tau\}), \ldots$ via (11). For each nonidentically zero polynomial $\mathcal{H}_L(x; \{\tau\})$ verify if its zero set is a subset of $\{x_1, \ldots, x_K\}$.

(C) Let $\mathcal{H}_E(x; \{\tau\})$ with $E < \lfloor (K - k + 1)/2 \rfloor$ be the first such a polynomial with $x_{e_1}, \ldots, x_{e_E}$ being its zeros. Remove the corresponding erroneous values $\{(x_{e_s}, Y_{e_s})\}_{s=1}^{E}$ from the set $\{(x_\ell, Y_\ell)\}_{\ell=1}^{K}$, and compute the value (7) for the remained subset. Take it as the voting result.

(D) If none of the polynomials $\mathcal{H}_1(x; \{\tau\}), \ldots, \mathcal{H}_{\lfloor (K-k+1)/2 \rfloor - 1}(x; \{\tau\})$ possesses the property from the point (C), the number of erroneous values exceeds the allowable restriction and their location is not possible.

6   Voters' Dishonest Shares

How is it possible to verify the correctness of voters' decisions, namely that the numbers $f_1(0), \ldots, f_N(0)$ belong to the set of acceptable values $\{+1, -1\}$? Collecting together all the shares $\{f_j(x_\ell)\}_{\ell=1}^{k}$ of the number $f_j(0)$ distributed between the administrators, the counting center would be able to restore this number. However, this procedure violates the confidentiality of voting.

The confidentiality would be maintained if the counting center is able to evaluate somehow $f_j^2(0)$ in the lack of the knowledge of $f_j(0)$. At the same time, the knowledge of $f_j^2(0)$ is enough for confirmation of the correctness of the jth voter ballot. Note that the number $f_j^2(0)$ can be made available via interpolation, i.e. via the data set composed of the pairs $(x_j, f_j^2(x_\ell))$ submitted by the administrators. The only problem is that the number of such pairs should increase twice compared with the degrees of the polynomials $f_j(x)$. This results in an additional demand to the redundancy, namely that the number K of administrators and degree $k - 1$ of the exploited polynomials should be connected by the inequality $K \geq 2k - 1$. Under this assumption, any number $f_j^2(0)$ is evaluated via (7).

7   Computational Remarks

1. To avoid the round off errors, all the algorithms are built in $\mathbb{Z}_p$ for sufficiently large prime p. The only specifics of computation in $\mathbb{Z}_p$ is that the division operation by the involved integers should be interpreted as computation of inversion of these integers modulo p.

2. Each Hankel polynomial $\mathcal{H}_L(x; \{\tau\})$ over $\mathbb{Z}_p$ can always be represented with the sequence of coefficients with alternation in signs, i.e.

$$\mathcal{H}_L(x; \{\tau\}) \equiv_p c(x^L - b_1 x^{L-1} + b_2 x^{L-2} - \cdots + (-1)^L b_L)$$

where $\{c, b_1, b_2, \ldots, b_L\} \subset \{1, 2, \ldots, p-1\}$. If the values $\{x_j\}_{j=1}^K$ are positive integers, then the problem of resolving an algebraic equation over $\mathbb{Z}_p$ can be reduced to that of finding positive integer zeros for a polynomial with integer coefficients. The latter is resolved via checking the divisors of b_L.

3. There exists a procedure of computation of the sequence of Hankel polynomials $\{\mathcal{H}_L(x; \{\tau\})\}_{L \in \mathbb{N}}$ which is recursive in the order of these polynomials. Namely, three Hankel polynomials of the consecutive orders are linked by the identity in the form

$$\alpha \mathcal{H}_L(x; \{\tau\}) - (x + \beta)\mathcal{H}_{L-1}(x; \{\tau\}) + 1/\alpha \mathcal{H}_{L-2}(x; \{\tau\}) \equiv 0$$

Here α and β are some constants evaluated via the coefficients of $\mathcal{H}_{L-1}(x; \{\tau\})$ and $\mathcal{H}_{L-2}(x; \{\tau\})$. The related details can be found in [5].

8   Conclusion

The problem of error detection in the set of shares of decentralized voting protocol is resolved with the aid of an alternative solution of the classical polynomial interpolation problem.

In particular, the algorithm can be used to create close economic relationships among enterprise participants, taking advantage of its unique capabilities to form hierarchal (real-life) communications among nodes and guaranteeing security and flexibility in sharing data.

References

1. Lamport, L., Shostak, R., Pease, M.: The Byzantine generals problem. ACM Trans. Program. Lang. Syst. **4**(3), 382–401 (1982)
2. Shamir, A.: How to share a secret. Commun. ACM **22**(11), 612–613 (1979)
3. Boyle, E., Gilboa, N., Ishai, Y.: Breaking the circuit size barrier for secure computation under DDH. In: Robshaw, M., Katz, J. (eds.) CRYPTO 2016. LNCS, vol. 9814, pp. 509–539. Springer, Heidelberg (2016). https://doi.org/10.1007/978-3-662-53018-4_19
4. Pólya, G., Szegö, G.: Problems and Theorems in Analysis II. Springer, Heidelberg (1998). https://doi.org/10.1007/978-3-642-61905-2
5. Uteshev, A.Yu., Baravy, I.: Solution of interpolation problems via the Hankel polynomial construction. arXiv:1603.08752 [cs.SC] (2016)

Cryptography in Blockchain

Nikita Storublevtcev[(✉)]

St. Petersburg State University, Saint Petersburg, Russia
100.rub@mail.ru

Abstract. There is a vast multitude of different hashing and cryptography algorithms out there, and more are developed every year. Blockchain technology, and crypto-currencies specifically, raised many concerns in different institutions. Users want to be sure that their assets are adequately protected by the best available algorithms, but some institutions around the world are opposed to that, or enforce their own standards. Ideally, every platform would allow its users to choose any algorithm they want, but in most situations this is, unfortunately, not the case. In this paper we present a review of the most popular blockchain platforms and the options they provide, and compare their cryptographic strength.

Keywords: Cryptography · Algorithms · Hashing · Blockchain · Digital signature

1 Introduction

1.1 Importance of Cryptography

Every year, cryptography becomes more and more a part of the daily life for many people around the world. The rise of crypto-currencies brought wider general awareness of cryptography to the masses, and showcased its practical usefulness outside military applications. Increased interest brought more researchers and investors to the field, and previously niche problems and concerns became more widely-discussed. Today most governments understand that crypto-platforms can change many aspects of our daily lives and are forced to take a stance, be it for or against them.

Nowadays many Internet connections are encrypted in some capacity. Be it web-sites using HTTPS, SSH connections, or VPN services, most users make use of some sort of cryptographic protection every day, and blockchain platforms use the same tools and algorithms. While privacy and data security is important for individual user, it is much more so for corporate entities with much more to lose in case of a security breach.

But crypto-currencies, while being the most widely known, are far from the only use-case for blockchain technology and cryptography in general. Blockchain is a relatively new technology, but it already has found many uses in various fields. Since the rise of Bitcoin, which showed the potential of blockchain,

© Springer Nature Switzerland AG 2019
S. Misra et al. (Eds.): ICCSA 2019, LNCS 11620, pp. 495–508, 2019.
https://doi.org/10.1007/978-3-030-24296-1_39

several platforms emerged, offering to provide easy-to-use and well-developed frameworks for creating and using blockchain-based enterprise-level services. The most popular and successful among them are Ethereum, Hyperledger Fabric, R3 Corda, Ripple and Quorum [1]. Among them, Ethereum and Hyperledger Fabric are the biggest general-purpose platforms, have the widest cross-industry reach and are designed to support almost any use-case imaginable. Ethereum is known for its smart-contract functionality, but it is primarily a crypto-currency platform, while Hyperledger Fabric does not have an in-built currency, and is designed for creation of any number of private networks. R3 Corda and Ripple are designed and used for financial sector operations, which require faster transaction processing, and Quorum is a modification of Ethereum, also aimed at financial services. In this paper we will review cryptographic tools used by each platform and compare them in terms of reliability and security.

1.2 Importance of Choice

A user of a blockchain platform may wonder - why do I need to bother with cryptographic algorithms other than provided by the developers? This is, unfortunately often, a question born of necessity. It is no secret that different algorithms have different cryptographic properties, strength and weaknesses, but they also differ greatly in speed and resources required to execute them. This, coupled with other aspects of the blockchain platform, can make it unsuitable for some types of services. For example, one of the biggest complains about Bitcoin platform is the long transaction confirmation time (an average of 10–20 min, on some occasions rising all the way to 2 h [2]), making it unfit for quick everyday purchases. Many solutions were proposed and created to combat this issue, one being the Ripple platform, which only takes a couple seconds per transaction. All prominent blockchain platforms are general-purpose services, to greater or lesser extent, offering application developers their infrastructure and technology. But each type of service demands different things from the platform, so to accommodate all of them it has to offer deep customization of its infrastructure.

There are also unfortunate cases when the choice of any particular algorithm is forced upon develops by third parties. This is usually the case in projects developed for or with government departments. For example, Russian Government requires some personal information to be encrypted exclusively by approved cipher algorithms, all of which were developed in-house relatively recently and are not supported out-of-the-box by any blockchain systems. By providing the ability to customize encryption algorithms, blockchain platforms can ease the pain of developers in similar situations.

1.3 Basics of Blockchain

Before we begin comparing algorithms, we need to understand where they are used and why. In the core of all blockchain technologies lies the eponymous Blockchain, which is a set of ordered blocks of data. Each block contains a number of verified transactions and usually contains a pointer to the previous block in the chain. This, together with the fact that copies of each block are stored on multiple nodes in the network, ensures that no one user can modify the contents of any block without other users detecting it. In most cases, to have any chance to successfully make a malicious transaction, one user has to control more than 50% of the network. This creates a trusted environment where the architecture of the system itself plays the role of a trusted medium.

When a transaction is performed, before it is written into the block, it is validated by other nodes and users of the platform. The exact validation mechanism differs for each platform, and they all require different amount of time and computational resources. If and when a transaction is considered valid, it is written to the current block. A block has a set size, and when it is filled with transactions, it is also verified and is considered written into the blockchain.

The second important part for the reliable system are so-called Smart Contracts, which are essentially small programs that can interface with the blockchain platform, detect and perform certain actions, like transfer of funds, shares and other assets. This allows users to avoid middlemen and costs/risks associated with them.

1.4 Hashes and Keys

There are many different cryptographic algorithms used in different blockchain platforms, but most of them fall into one of two categories - hashing algorithms and asymmetric algorithms. Before we begin comparing them, we need to define what they are, when they are used, and what issues they have.

Hashing Algorithms (or Hash Functions) are designed to generate a "hash value" (or just "hash") from a piece of data. Hash is a bit sequence, frequently presented in character string form. Its length is usually fixed for any given function. The original data can usually be of any size, it will be mapped to a hash of specific length. Changing even one bit in the original data will result in an entirely different hash value for it. This property is used, for example, to verify the integrity of any piece of transferred data. The sender sends the hash value of the message together with it, and receiver can calculate the hash value of the received message and compare it to the one provided by the sender. Any inconsistencies will mean corruption of the message during transfer.

Unfortunately, it is impossible to ideally map a set of values of variable length to a set of values of fixed length, as the first set has higher magnitude. This means that there inevitably will occur situations where multiple different input data packages are mapped to the same hash value. This is called a "collision". Developers do everything they can to make their algorithms stronger, but there is no way to create an ideal function, which would have to fully satisfy the following criteria:

- *Pre-image Resistance.* Knowing a hash value, it should be impossible (or too difficult to be worth) to find a message that produces the same hash value [3].

- *Second Pre-image Resistance.* Knowing a message, it should be impossible (or too difficult to be worth) to find a different message that produces the same hash value [3].
- *Collision Resistance.* It should be impossible (or too difficult to be worth) to find two different messages that produce the same hash value [3].

Collision Resistance implies Second Pre-image Resistance, but does not necessary mean Pre-image Resistance. A hash function which is only Second Pre-image Resistant is considered too weak for practical applications. Together, these criteria mean that an attacker cannot modify the message, without also changing the hash. Thus, if two strings have the same hash, one can be very confident that they are identical. Second Pre-image Resistance prevents an attacker from creating a document with the same hash as a document the attacker cannot control. Collision resistance prevents an attacker from creating two distinct documents with the same hash [3].

In blockchains hashing is used extensively and can be considered essential for their operation. For example, the strength of links between blocks is usually ensured by writing the hash of the previous block into the new one. This way if anyone attempts to change anything in a block, they would also need to change all blocks after it, and do this on a large number of nodes at the same time.

Asymmetric Algorithms (or Public-Key Cryptography) use a pair of keys to create a secure communication channel between two peers. Each peer has its own set of keys. One key is chosen to be a Public Key, and is sent openly to the other peer, another is a Private Key and is kept secret. There are two common uses for Public-Key Cryptography are:

- *Public Key Encryption*, is used when a peer wants to send a secret message to another peer. They use target peer Public Key to encrypt the message and send it through the (potentially compromised) channel. Upon receiving the message, target peer can use their own Private Key to decrypt the message. The message is impossible (or too difficult to be worth) to decrypt without possessing the recipient Private Key.
- *Digital Signatures* are very similar to Public Key Encryption, but the message is also signed with the senders Private Key, and can be verified by anyone who possesses sender's Public Key. This helps ensure that the source of the message is likely to the sender, and that the message was not tampered with.

It is also important to enforce the authenticity of any particular key and its link to the user. There are several ways to do it:

- *Public Key Infrastructure (PKI)*, where one or more parties are designated as *Certificate Authorities* and are responsible for key ownership certification.
- *Web of Trust*, where individual users endorse the ownership in a decentralised system.
- *Domain Name System (DNS)* can be used to look up and verify the signed message.

Public-Key Cryptography is extensively used in blockchain platforms, especially in crypto-currency ones, like Bitcoin. It also underpins such widely-used technologies as Secure Shell (SSH) and Transport Layer Security (TLS).

2   Usage in Blockchain Platforms

That that we know what to look for, we can look at each blockchain platform in-depth and determine which algorithms are in use in each part of the infrastructure. This information is surprisingly hard to find in open sources, and some of it may be outdated.

2.1   Ethereum

Ethereum, arguably the most mature platform currently available, launched in 2015 with intent to provide a platform with robust decentralised application scripting tools. It has a built-in crypto-currency called Ether (ETH) which can be used for both direct transactions and as "fuel" for applications, to compensate mining nodes for performed computations. Like Bitcoin it has "wallets" (or accounts) which consist of a public-private key pair, but Ethereum generates them using Elliptic Curve Digital Signature Algorithm (ECDSA) and secp256k1 [4] constants to define the curve. Message signing process requires both public and private keys and is analogous to DSA [5], but uses KECCAK-256 as a hash function. It is note-worthy that it is referred to as SHA-3 on multiple occasions in code and documentation, but does not follow the FIPS-202 based standard, and generates different hash values. The same hash function is used throughout the platform, and developers are aware of the confusion it causes are are working on fixing it [6].

For inter-node communications Ethereum uses RLPx (not an acronym) transport protocol [7]. It is a TCP-based protocol using Elliptic Curve Integrated Encryption Scheme (ECIES) in its handshake. It also includes the following in its cryptosystem:

- The elliptic curve secp256k1 with generator G.
- NIST SP 800-56 Concatenation Key Derivation Function.
- Hash-based Message Authentication Code (HMAC) using the SHA-256 hash function.
- AES-128 encryption function in CTR mode.

According to publicly available information, Ethereum does not currently support any customization of its cryptosystem, and any tweaking would require changes to the codebase. There are projects looking to find a work-around or fix to this problem [8], but it will not be an easy task.

2.2 Hyperledger Fabric

In contrast to Ethereum, Hyperledger Fabric doesn't have the main blockchain, but instead focuses on providing developers with a framework to create their own blockchains. It does not have an in-built crypto-currency, instead focusing more on the Distributed Ledger side of the blockchain technology, and sports fee-free transactions. Fabric supports both public and private blockchains and has extensive tools for identity and permission management.

Hyperledger is designed to be highly modular and supports BlockChain Cryptographic Service Provider (BCCSP) modules, which can theoretically implement any algorithm. Unfortunately, at this time this feature is not fully-implemented yet as the choice of SHA2-256 hash function is hard-coded in several places [9] and is the only working option in the configuration file. Some evidence also suggests use of SHA3 family of functions as default in early development [10].

User accounts are handled by Certificate Authority (CA) servers, which can be configured to generate X.509 certificates and ECDSA keys [11]. ECDSA has the following options:

– prime256v1 constants with SHA256 hash.
– secp384r1 constants with SHA384 hash.
– secp521r1 constants with SHA512 hash.

We were unable to find information on what exact hash function is used in X.509 certificates created by Fabric, but current standard requirements forbid issuance of certificates using MD2, MD5 and SHA-1 functions.

The platform also allows for encryption (full or partial) of the smart-contract (locally referred to as Chaincode) data. It is handled by the BCCSP wrapper, which allows to perform the same cryptographic operations [12].

Communication between nodes is secured using Transport Layer Security (TLS) protocol. TLS supports a wide range of algorithms, but only some variations of Advanced Encryption Standard (AES), ChaCha20, Rivest–Shamir–Adleman (RSA) and ECDSA are currently considered to be secure.

2.3 R3 Corda

R3 Corda is an interesting platform, in many ways different to others. It was originally developed as closed-source and only went open source in November 2018. It does not actually use blockchain or distributed ledger technology, but rather what is being described as a "shared ledger", and it does not have an built-in currency. By default, information about transactions is only shared with those who are parties to that transaction. This provides increased privacy to users, but eliminates the concept of the block chain itself from the system. Instead Corda links "States" containing references to contract code written in computer code, a hash of a legal document backing the state written in legalese, and a snapshot of various data. User accounts are represented by Identities, which are attested to by X.509 certificate signed by a well known identity.

Corda has been designed to be cryptographically agile, but still restricts user's choice to a set of pre-selected signature schemes [13]:

- Pure EdDSA using the ed25519 curve and SHA-512.
- ECDSA using the NIST P-256 curve (secp256r1) and SHA-256.
- ECDSA using the Koblitz k1 curve (secp256k1) and SHA-256.
- RSA (3072bit) PKCS#1 and SHA-256.
- SPHINCS-256 and SHA-512 (experimental).

There also exists a proposed Blockchained Post-Quantum Signatures (BPQS) algorithm, which has not yet been implemented [14].

Corda uses Advanced Message Queuing Protocol (AMQP) 1.0 over TLS between nodes which is currently implemented using Apache Artemis [15].

2.4 Ripple

Ripple was initially founded in 2012 under a name OpenCoin, and it aims to connect different banks and payment systems through it's crypto-currency called Ripples (or XRP). User account is represented by a Master key pair, and supports the ability to authorize a secondary, Regular key pair, to sign future transactions, while keeping the Master key pair offline. If the regular keys are compromised, they can be replaced by new ones. Master keys cannot be replaced, only disabled.

Instead of one singular ledger, Ripple has a series of ledger versions. At any given time, a node instance has a "current" open ledger, some number of closed ledgers that have not yet been approved by consensus, and any number of historical ledgers that have been validated by consensus. Only validated ledgers are certain to be correct and immutable. Each ledger version consists of the following parts:

- Header, containing the Ledger Index, hashes of its other contents, and other metadata.
- Transaction tree, with transactions that were applied to the previous ledger to make this one.
- State tree, with all the ledger objects that contain the settings, balances, and objects in the ledger as of this version.

Ripple uses SHA256 and SHA512 for all its hashing operations and supports the following cryptographic signing algorithms [16]:

- ECDSA using the elliptic curve secp256k1.
- EdDSA using the elliptic curve Ed25519.

Servers in Ripple communicate to each other using the XRP Ledger peer protocol (RTXP). To establish a connection, a peer makes an outgoing TLS-encrypted connection to a remote peer, then sends a HTTP request with no message body.

2.5   Quorum

Quorum is an enterprise-focused version of Ethereum, and therefore uses much of the same algorithms. It provides level2 service on top of Ethereum which enables it to perform private transactions, and speeds them up using a different consensus algorithm. Public transactions are executed as on standard Ethereum, but private transactions use a different system. Before propagating such transaction, its payload is replaced by a hash. After receiving the transaction, only authorised parties will be able to replace the hash with the actual payload. Quorum uses KECCAK and SHA3 hash functions, ECDSA with secp256k1 constants and Elliptic Curve Integrated Encryption Scheme (ECIES) with AES ciphers.

Each peer in Quorum consists of several semi-independent modules, each communicating using several technologies. It includes Pretty Good Privacy (PGP), mutually-authenticated TLS (in some cases over HTTPS) and NaCl (Networking and Cryptography library).

3   Cryptanalysis

Now that we have a more-or-less complete list of algorithms, let us look into their known strengths and weaknesses. One way to describe the strength of a cryptographic primitive is in terms of a "security level" or "security claim". It can be measured in "bits", with N-bit security level meaning that attacker would have to process at least N^2 operations to break it, or in terms time and memory required. There are other models that better represent true costs for the attacker, but security level offers a convenient way to compare different algorithms and is especially useful in hybrid cryptosystems. Public-key algorithm security is highly dependent on the security of the associated hash function but we will look at them separately from hash functions and ciphers.

3.1   Hash Functions

Cryptographic hash functions can be divided into two categories - "provably secure" ones, based on mathematical problems and proven to be secure, and "ad hoc" functions, where the bits of the message are mixed to produce the hash. Provable functions, while secure, are not unbreakable, and usually too inefficient for practical purposes. Ad hoc functions, on other hand, are much faster, but have no hard guarantees of security, and are subject of rigorous cryptanalysis from researchers around the world. Experts seek vulnerabilities which would allow an attacker to break the function faster than its security claim would indicate.

If such an attack is found, it does not automatically mean that the function no longer secure. An attack can only break a reduced version of the hash or have other issues. We will label such attack as "partial". If an attack does indeed break all rounds of a function, but has not been successfully performed in practice, despite having a substantial theoretical base, we will call it a "theoretical" attack. In an attack was successfully demonstrated in practice it is labeled as a "practical" attack. The summary of currently known attacks on aforementioned hash functions is presented in Table 1. We also include a Streebog hash function in the comparison as its use is required by the Russian Government.

Table 1. Hash function resistance.

Function	Security claim (collision, preimage)	Best collision attack	Best preimage attack
MD2	2^{64}, 2^{128}	practical, $2^{63.3}$ time, 2^{52} memory [17]	practical, 2^{73} time, 2^{73} memory [18]
MD5	2^{64}, 2^{128}	practical, 2^{18} time [19]	theoretical, $2^{123.4}$ time [20]
SHA-1	2^{80}, 2^{80}	practical, $2^{63.1}$ time [21]	partial, 45 of 80 rounds [22]
SHA-256	2^{128}, 2^{256}	partial, 31 of 64 rounds, $2^{65.5}$ time [23]	partial, 43 of 64 rounds, $2^{254.9}$ time, 2^6 memory [24]
SHA-512	2^{256}, 2^{512}	partial, 24 of 80 rounds $2^{32.5}$ time [25]	partial, 46 of 80 rounds $2^{511.5}$ time, 2^6 memory [24]
SHA-3	Up to 2^{512}	partial, 6 of 24 rounds, 2^{50} time [26]	none
RIPEMD-160	2^{80}, 2^{160}	partial, 48 of 80 rounds 2^{51} time [27]	partial, 31 of 80 rounds [28]
BLAKE2s	2^{128}, 2^{256}	partial, 7.5 rounds, 2^{184} time [29]	partial, 6.75 rounds, $2^{253.8}$ time [30]
Streebog	2^{256}, 2^{512}	partial, 9.5 rounds of 12, 2^{176} time, 2^{128} memory [31]	theoretical, 2^{266} time, 2^{259} memory [32]

3.2   Public-Key Algorithms

Public-key cryptography (or asymmetric cryptography) generally makes use of algorithms based on mathematical problems to produce one-way functions. This is what allows users to freely distribute their public keys without compromising security. However, different algorithms are based on different mathematical problems and have different security levels. For practical use, it is important to understand ratios of security-to-size each algorithm provides in regards to their public keys. The summary is presented in Table 2. We also include GOST R 34.10-2012 digital signature standard, required by Russian government in the comparison.

Table 2. Public key algorithm security comparison.

Algorithm	Security level (bits)	Public key size (bits)	Largest broken key (bits)
RSA PKCS#1	128	3072	768
DSA	128	3072	530
ECDSA (secp256k1)	128	256	114
ECDSA (secp256r1)	128	256	114
ECDSA (secp384r1)	192	384	114
ECDSA (secp521r1)	256	521	114
EdDSA (ed25519)	128	256	unknown
ECIES	128	256–283	unknown
ElGamal	128	3072	768
SPHINCS-256	128	1024	unknown
GOST R 34.10-2012	256	512	114

3.3 Ciphers

Comparing cipher security is harder, because it depends heavily on the specific attack used and if the cipher is vulnerable to it in the first place. Thankfully, only a few cipher families are widely-used, so we can take a detailed look into each of them.

AES-128 or Advanced Encryption Standard is a subset of of the Rijndael block cipher family, each with a block size of 128 bits and key lengths of 128, 192 and 256 bits. It is the first (and only) publicly accessible cipher approved by the National Security Agency (NSA) of United States for top secret information. AES is based on a design principle known as a substitution–permutation network, and has in-built support in many hardware systems and devices [33].

Until 2009, the only known successful attacks against AES were side-channel attacks on some specific implementations [33]. Such attacks seek to exploit weaknesses in incorrect or partial algorithm implementation, which usually significantly lowers its security level. In that year, a related-key attack was discovered which makes use of AES's key schedule. This attack requires several different known keys and some knowledge of their mathematical relationship. Its complexity was soon brought down to $2^{99.5}$, however such attacks only work in improperly-designed protocols. Subsequent versions of this attack were published later, but none works against a full 14-round version of AES-256.

In November 2009, the first known-key distinguishing attack was published, but it only worked against 8-round version of AES-128, while full version uses 10 rounds. Only in 2011 the first key-recovery attacks on full AES were discovered [33]. However, their workloads are infeasible on current hardware, with current records being 2^{126} for AES-128, $2^{189.9}$ for AES-192 and $2^{254.3}$ for AES-256 [34].

At present, there are no practical attacks on full and correct AES implementations themselves, but there are multiple side-channel attacks, which target specific hardware. One of the fastest allows to recover the complete 128-bit AES key in just 6–7 blocks of plaintext/ciphertext [35].

ChaCha20 is a family of ciphers closely related to Salsa20. Both ciphers use pseudorandom function based on ARX (add-rotate-xor) operations. Supported key lengths are 128-bit and 256-bit, with 8, 12 and 20-round versions. The only currently known attack can only break 256-bit ChaCha6 with complexity 2^{139} and ChaCha7 with complexity 2^{248}. 128-bit ChaCha6 within 2^{107}, but fails to break 128-bit ChaCha7 [36].

CAST5 or (CAST-128) is a symmetric-key block cipher, approved for Government of Canada use by the Communications Security Establishment, with a 64-bit block size and a key size of between 40 and 128 bits (in 8-bit increments) [37]. Best currently known attack on it is a theoretical one on 6 of 16 rounds ($2^{88.51}$ time, $2^{53.96}$ memory) [38].

3DES - Triple DES (TDES) or Triple Data Encryption Algorithm (TDEA or Triple DEA), is a symmetric-key block cipher, which applies DES three times to each block [39]. In general, Triple DES with three independent keys has a key length of 168 bits (three 56-bit DES keys), but due to the meet-in-the-middle attack, the effective security it provides is only 112 bits. Practical Sweet32 attack on 3DES-based cipher-suites in TLS required $2^{36.6}$ blocks for a full attack, but it is possible to get a collision after around 2^{20} blocks which takes 25 min. OpenSSL does not include 3DES by default since version 1.1.0, and considers it a "weak cipher".

IDEA or International Data Encryption Algorithm is a symmetric-key block cipher intended as a replacement for the Data Encryption Standard (DES) [40]. In 2012, full 8.5-round IDEA was broken using a narrow-bicliques attack (($2^{126.1}$ time), however this attack does not threaten the security of IDEA in practice. The very simple key schedule makes IDEA subject to a class of weak keys containing a large number of 0 bits produce weak encryption [40].

Twofish is a symmetric key block cipher with a block size of 128 bits and key sizes up to 256 bits [41]. Twofish's distinctive features are the use of pre-computed key-dependent S-boxes, and a relatively complex key schedule. Best attack is an Impossible differential attack on 6 of 16 rounds (2^{256} time).

Blowfish is a symmetric-key block cipher, which provides a good encryption rate in software and no effective cryptanalysis of it has been found to date [42]. Its use of a 64-bit block size makes it vulnerable to birthday attacks, particularly in contexts like HTTPS, and the SWEET32 attack demonstrated how to perform plaintext recovery against it.

Camellia is a symmetric key block cipher developed by Mitsubishi Electric and NTT of Japan [43]. It has a block size of 128 bits and key sizes of 128, 192 and 256 bits. There are no known successful attacks that weaken the cipher considerably.

Kuznyechik ("grasshopper") is a symmetric block cipher with a block size of 128 bits and key length of 256 bits, defined in the National Standard of the Russian Federation GOST R 34.12-2015 and also in RFC 7801. Kuznyechik is based on a substitution-permutation network, though the key schedule employs a Feistel network. Currently there are only two known attacks on the cipher. One is a meet-in-the-middle attack on the 5-round version, allowing to recover the key with 2^{140} time and 2^{153} memory [44]. The second is a side-channel attack [45].

3.4 Cryptosystems

Most blockchain platform make use of third-party cryptographic solutions, which provide multi-level protection and include several cryptographic primitives. It is almost impossible to judge the security of the overall system, especially considering all the possible combinations.

PGP - Pretty Good Privacy is an encryption program that provides cryptographic privacy and authentication for data communication. It can be used for signing, encrypting, and decrypting texts, e-mails, files, directories, and whole disk partitions and to increase the security of e-mail communications [46].

Symmetric cryptography is performed using AES, CAST5, 3DES, IDEA, Twofish, Blowfish or Camellia with a session key, which is encrypted using the public key provided by RSA or Elgamal (key length 1024–4096 bits). Signing is done using RSA or DSA, combined with MD5, SHA-1, RIPEMD-160, SHA-2 hash functions.

NaCl - abbreviation of "Networking and Cryptography library" is a public domain library for network communication, encryption, decryption and signatures.

Public-key cryptography uses EdDSA (Ed25519) for signatures, while private-key is done with Salsa20 and AES. Hashing is performed using SHA-2 or BLAKE2.

4 Conclusion

In this paper we presented an overview of cryptographic algorithms used in prominent enterprise-oriented blockchain platforms and compared their security level. As expected, only secure algorithms see any wide use and all platforms provide an acceptable security, but show very low agility in terms of range of supported algorithms, frequently only using a single one for all parts of the system.

This choice of a particular algorithm may be dictated by parameters other than security. For example, Ethereum developers justify their choice of hash function by its inability to be optimized for Application-specific Integrated Circuits, and therefore requirement to use relatively-expensive GPU/CPU mining farms. This is expected to prevent consolidation of mining resources in the hands of any specific group. This can also be viewed from the users perspective - if the only available algorithm does not have the required qualities, user has no choice but to look for another platform. This lack of choice can create problems on the part of the user, especially if they are under pressure from a third party.

Additionally, the security claim of any algorithm can be viewed as proportional to the length of time before it is eventually broken. This is especially concerning considering the developments in quantum computing. Very few blockchain platforms provide any sort of post-quantum secure algorithm, and without ability to choose, the user's security is at mercy of developers. If the currently used algorithm becomes compromised, it would require developer action to change it.

References

1. Fersht, P.: The top 5 enterprise blockchain platforms you need to know about. https://www.horsesforsources.com/top-5-blockchain-platforms_031618. Accessed 20 Mar 2019
2. Average Confirmation Time. https://www.blockchain.com/ru/charts/avg-confirmation-time
3. Cryptographic hash function. https://en.wikipedia.org/wiki/Cryptographic_hash_function
4. SEC 2: Recommended Elliptic Curve Domain Parameters. http://www.secg.org/sec2-v2.pdf
5. Digital Signature Algorithm Patent. https://patents.google.com/patent/US5231668
6. Issue about SHA-3/KECCAK confusion. https://github.com/ethereum/EIPs/issues/59
7. The RLPx Transport Protocol. https://github.com/ethereum/devp2p/blob/master/rlpx.md
8. Multihashing in Ethereum 2.0. https://ethresear.ch/t/multihashing-in-ethereum-2-0/4745/8
9. Peer node configuration file, line 275–277. https://github.com/hyperledger/fabric/blob/release-1.4/sampleconfig/core.yaml
10. "Use SHA-2 as the default hash in all Hyperledger fabric components". https://jira.hyperledger.org/browse/FAB-887
11. Fabric CA User's Guide. https://hyperledger-fabric-ca.readthedocs.io/en/release-1.4/users-guide.html
12. Chaincode for Developers. https://hyperledger-fabric.readthedocs.io/en/release-1.4/chaincode4ade.html
13. Cipher suites supported by Corda. https://docs.corda.net/cipher-suites.html
14. Blockchained Post-Quantum Signatures. https://eprint.iacr.org/2018/658.pdf
15. Networking and messaging. https://docs.corda.net/messaging.html

16. Ripple Cryptographic Keys. https://developers.ripple.com/cryptographic-keys.html
17. Cryptanalysis of MD2. https://link.springer.com/article/10.1007
18. An improved preimage attack on MD2. https://eprint.iacr.org/2008/089.pdf
19. Fast Collision Attack on MD5. https://eprint.iacr.org/2013/170
20. Finding Preimages in Full MD5 Faster Than Exhaustive Search. https://link.springer.com/chapter/10.1007
21. The first collision for full SHA-1. https://shattered.it/static/shattered.pdf
22. Preimages for Reduced SHA-0 and SHA-1. https://online.tugraz.at/tug_online/voe_main2.getvolltext?pCurrPk=36848
23. Improving Local Collisions: New Attacks on Reduced SHA-256. https://online.tugraz.at/tug_online/voe_main2.getvolltext?pCurrPk=69018
24. Preimages for Step-Reduced SHA-2. https://link.springer.com/chapter/10.1007
25. New Collision Attacks against Up to 24-Step SHA-2. https://link.springer.com/chapter/10.1007
26. Song, L., Liao, G., Guo, J.: Non-full sbox linearization: applications to collision attacks on round-reduced KECCAK. In: Katz, J., Shacham, H. (eds.) CRYPTO 2017. LNCS, vol. 10402, pp. 428–451. Springer, Cham (2017). https://doi.org/10.1007/978-3-319-63715-0_15
27. On the Collision Resistance of RIPEMD-160. https://online.tugraz.at/tug_online/voe_main2.getvolltext?pCurrPk=17675
28. Preimage Attacks on Step-Reduced RIPEMD-128 and RIPEMD-160. https://link.springer.com/chapter/10.1007
29. The Boomerang Attacks on BLAKE and BLAKE2. https://eprint.iacr.org/2014/1012.pdf
30. Higher-Order Differential Meet-in-The-MiddlePreimage Attacks on SHA-1 and BLAKE. https://eprint.iacr.org/2015/515.pdf
31. Cryptanalysis of GOST R Hash Function. https://eprint.iacr.org/2013/584
32. The Usage of Counter Revisited: Second-Preimage Attack on New Russian Standardized Hash Function. https://eprint.iacr.org/2014/675
33. Advanced Encryption Standard. https://en.wikipedia.org/wiki/Advanced_Encryption_Standard
34. Improving the Biclique Cryptanalysis of AES. https://link.springer.com/chapter/10.1007
35. Highly Efficient Algorithms for AES Key Retrieval in Cache Access Attacks. https://ieeexplore.ieee.org/document/7467359
36. New Features of Latin Dances: Analysis of Salsa, ChaCha, and Rumba. https://eprint.iacr.org/2007/472.pdf
37. CAST-128. https://en.wikipedia.org/wiki/CAST-128
38. New Linear Cryptanalytic Results of Reduced-Round of CAST-128 and CAST-256. https://link.springer.com/chapter/10.1007
39. Triple DES https://en.wikipedia.org/wiki/Triple_DES
40. International Data Encryption Algorithm. https://en.wikipedia.org/wiki/International_Data_Encryption_Algorithm
41. Twofish. https://en.wikipedia.org/wiki/Twofish
42. Blowfish. https://en.wikipedia.org/wiki/Blowfish_(cipher)
43. Camellia. https://en.wikipedia.org/wiki/Camellia_(cipher)
44. A Meet in the Middle Attack on ReducedRound Kuznyechik. https://eprint.iacr.org/2015/096.pdf
45. Fault Analysis of Kuznyechik. https://eprint.iacr.org/2015/347.pdf
46. Pretty Good Privacy. https://en.wikipedia.org/wiki/Pretty_Good_Privacy

Implementation of an E-Voting Scheme Using Hyperledger Fabric Permissioned Blockchain

Denis Kirillov$^{(\boxtimes)}$, Vladimir Korkhov, Vadim Petrunin, Mikhail Makarov, Ildar M. Khamitov, and Victor Dostov

Saint-Petersburg State University, St. Petersburg, Russia
kirillovdenand@gmail.com, {v.korkhov,v.petrunin}@spbu.ru,
makarovmma@gmail.com, CryptoVoter@gmail.com, greygato@gmail.com

Abstract. Since the issue of using e-voting in both corporate and government voting has not yet been fully resolved, there remains a wide scope for improving existing approaches and proposing new protocols enabling the voting system to be resistant to various kinds of attacks. Due to the rapid development of distributed ledger technologies and their potential for solving existing problems we propose a modified protocol of the published earlier voting scheme which is complemented by blockchain technology to increase trust between participants. This approach allows carrying out combined voting of both traditional paper voting and e-voting. In this paper we describe the architecture of our solution, discuss its implementation based on Hyperledger Fabric platform and demonstrate its functionality.

Keywords: E-voting · Blockchain · Hyperledger fabric · Distributed ledger technologies

1 Introduction

In many countries paper ballots are still used for elections. Nevertheless, technologies are developing rapidly and it has already become commonplace not to use cash and not to deal with paper media anywhere. Paper ballots are used to increase the level of reliability of the voting system since the stakes are high. At the same time attempts to implement existing e-voting protocols in some countries (Estonia [1], Australia [2]) showed that not all security problems were solved [3,4] thereby the skepticism of state agencies towards new solutions increased. An ideal system should satisfy the following principles [5]:

- Eligibility,
- Un-reusability,
- Un-traceability,
- Verifiability,
- Receipt-freeness.

© Springer Nature Switzerland AG 2019
S. Misra et al. (Eds.): ICCSA 2019, LNCS 11620, pp. 509–521, 2019.
https://doi.org/10.1007/978-3-030-24296-1_40

In traditional approaches not all of these properties are held. However, the number of covered ones can be increased by transferring voting to a digital space building more convenience for people. It can also enhance the usage by young people. What is more important, it significantly reduces the election costs and decreases inspectors' efforts.

Voting, in particular elections, is a procedure whose members don't trust each other. Thus, the basic postulate is that the system to be attacked not only by an outside entity but also by the system participants themselves – both the voters and the organizers (juggling the results, disrupting the process itself, etc.). In such circumstances approaches based only on cryptographic technology may not always demonstrate an acceptable result. Some additional tools are required. Recently, distributed ledger technologies have been rapidly developing. These technologies were created specifically to make it possible to come to an agreement even in a non-trusted environment. In this paper, we extend one of the existing approaches to conduct electronic voting with the opportunities provided by the blockchain. The basic concepts of distributed ledger technologies are as follows:

- A copy of the ledger is on each node,
- No single point of failure,
- Changing the ledger only if most nodes agree,
- Possibility to reach an agreement even if some nodes are disconnected during network operation.

Blockchain platforms are usually divided into permissionless (anyone can become a member of the network) and permissioned (only known members are allowed to interact with the network). The first group includes, for example, Ethereum and Bitcoin, and the second one—Hyperledger Fabric, Exonum. Blockchains of the second type are suitable for our purposes, since voting participants usually incorporate organizers, voters, and observers who are known in advance and have different rights. Thereby, Hyperledger Fabric platform has been chosen for our project.

The rest of this paper is organized as follows. Section 2 describes existing approaches to e-voting. The review of the used technologies is presented in Sect. 3. The main description of the protocol is presented in Sect. 4. Security and privacy analysis is conducted in Sect. 5. The final Sect. 6 summarizes obtained results, points out directions of future work and concludes the paper.

2   Related Work

The problem of electronic voting is quite complicated due to a large number of requirements. Therefore there are many works devoted to this topic which propose different approaches in varying degrees covering the necessary restrictions. Completely different cryptographic techniques are used in different approaches: blind signature, ring signature, zero-knowledge proof, homomorphic encryption,

Paillier cryptosystem etc. In this section for the sake of brevity we designate the body that organizes the voting procedure as Certificate Authority (CA).

The paper [6] proposes using CA's blind signature over the public key and digital commitment (it allows one to commit to a chosen value while keeping it hidden to others, with the ability to reveal the committed value later; at the same time a party cannot change the value after they have committed to it) of a voice to gain the right to vote. After that a ballot (public key, digital commitment, CA signature) is broadcasted to all blockchain nodes. Each node verifies the signature, records the given vote to the ledger and the voter receives the id of his vote. If any changes need to be made, voter forms a new ballot containing the vote id which needs to be replaced and data similar to the previous one. After the voting phase is over the voter sends the data to open a digital commitment of his vote, a choice id, and a CA signature over them. Then votes are counted and the results are recorded to the ledger.

Since the blockchain technology is used, every voter at any step can verify that his vote is taken into account, as it is present in the network. A certain degree of un-traceability is achieved by using blind-signed public keys. A vote will not be counted more than once as there is only one choice not replaced by another one belonging to the same public key at each instant of time in the ledger. Receipt-freeness is missing.

A slightly different method is proposed in paper [7]. Voters must have an ID and PIN to enter the system that creates a "wallet" for each user (using NIZKP is possible) whereby it becomes possible to interact with a smart contract which records all voices to the blockchain network. In order to cast a vote, the voter has to call the function of smart contracts (e.g. corresponding to the electoral district) and pass the candidate's number as an argument. The id of the transaction which contains the choice is returned as a result. Smart contracts throughout the elections keep the current progress of the elections (that is, there is a variable that contains the number of votes for a candidate).

In order to achieve un-traceability, a special transaction structure with no "sender" field is used. A voter cannot change his vote. In order to check that the vote is counted elector has to come to the CA and reveal his identity. Moreover, even in this case there is no guarantee that votes are counted correctly.

In the article [8] the e-voting system is implemented on the Ethereum platform. Voting organizer merely creates the smart contract for election and adds addresses of the wallets which are allowed to vote. After that, voters call the function of this smart contract, passing the number of the candidate as a parameter (you cannot change your decision). At the end of the election process, the organizer calls the function that returns the number of the winning candidate number.

This approach has several disadvantages. For example, the following requirements are not met: un-traceability, receipt-freeness. This is due to the fact that the authors do not assume any cryptographic techniques and the network structure of the Ethereum blockchain is transparent and any participant can see the contents of transactions. In addition, the voter must pay a commission for each call to a smart contract. Also, the proposed approach does not scale well due to the small number of transactions processed per minute.

Liu and Wang [9] propose to introduce a certain number of inspectors who take part in the voting phase. Initially, the voter generates a pair of keys one of which (public) sends to the CA along with the data for authentication. The CA checks the voter and publishes a list of registered public keys whose owners are allowed to vote. Then voters form ballots and send them to the CA to blindly sign using a transaction which contains their public key as a value of the sender field. The CA verifies that the voter has the right to vote and has not yet cast a vote and returns the signed data. The voter sends it to all inspectors for signature. After successfully completing this stage the vote is signed by all the controlling participants. The voter generates a new key pair and sends the signed voice to the CA indicating the new public key as the value of the sender field in the transaction. After the end of the voting, CA publishes the results. This approach generally satisfies all restrictions except receipt-freeness.

The approach proposed in the article [10] uses the Paillier cryptosystem and the short linked ring signature (SLRS) as cryptographic techniques. The voting protocol is the following. The smart contract is initialized, and then parameters of Paillier cryptosystem and ring signatures are loaded to the blockchain. After that, admin data is used to enter the system and download the ring signature parameters and the public key of Paillier cryptosystem. To complete registration in the system user generates keys with SLRS and sends the public key to the smart contract. During the voting phase the voter forms the voice and encrypts it using a cryptosystem. Then he calls a function that provides data to confirm that the encrypted voice contains the number of the existing candidate. This data along with the choice is sent to the smart contract. After validation the smart contract adds an encrypted zero to the vote (to ensure receipt-freeness), signs and returns it to the voter. The voter checks the signature on the received message, imposes his ring signature and sends it back to the smart contract. The smart contract verifies the voter has not yet voted and then reports the selected option to the blockchain. When the counting phase comes, the smart contract signs the amount of the encrypted votes and sends it to the administrator who decrypts the amount using the cryptosystem private key and generates data used to verify that the received amount is correct; this information is sent back to the smart contract which calculates the number of votes scored by each candidate and reports these results to the blockchain.

This approach satisfies all the requirements for a voting system. However, receipt-freeness can be bypassed by collecting the private keys of all users from one pool (a pool of encrypted zeros that are added to the encrypted voter's voice to bring some randomness). Increasing the pool size can become a solution, which makes the attack more complicated.

3   Used Technologies

This section provides brief information about the technologies used in the proposed solution.

Blind Signature. This technology is a digital signature mechanism with the additional property that doesn't allow the one who is providing the signature to check what exactly should be signed. This concept was proposed in [11,12]. In our project we use an implementation based on RSA [13].

Secret Sharing Scheme. This approach allows distributing some secret information among several participants so that it can only be recovered by obtaining separate parts of each secretary. Many schemes are a special case of more general theoretical approach [14].

Identity Mixer (Idemix). This technology was developed by IBM and based on cryptographic techniques the development of which was presented at top conferences and carefully checked by the community. The practical implementation is based on the scheme described in [15–17]. Brief description of this technology is provided below.

Suppose there are three parties: the user, the issuer (producing a certificate and confirming the user's identity) and the verifier who wants to make sure that the user gets all attributes that are necessary to perform an action. In this scheme the main issue solved by Idemix is providing the verifier not all the information about the user but only certain attributes or even just a proof that the requested attribute falls within a certain range. In addition, it is possible to provide unlinkability which makes associating two different requests with the same user impossible. Thus Idemix allows users to ensure anonymity and privacy.

Hyperledger Fabric. Aforementioned Hyperledger Fabric is the permissioned blockchain being developed by Hyperledger consortium, in particular by IBM. A distinctive feature of Fabric compared to public blockchains is the way of processing transactions in the following order:

$$endorse \Rightarrow order \Rightarrow validate$$

The first stage includes checking transactions for the possibility of execution. Once they were executed without changing the state of the ledger they should be ordered based on a consensus algorithm. If the agreement is reached, transactions are sent to all nodes that update their copy of the ledger. Thus there are three types of nodes: Endorsing Peer which executes transactions (logic is executed on them), Ordering Nodes which produce ranking, and Committing Peer to maintain a copy of the registry, write transactions to it; Endorsing Peer is also a committing peer.

4   Approach and System Architecture

The proposed approach is based on the article of He and Su [18] who described an e-voting scheme without using the distributed ledger technology. Our current research aims to implement last-mentioned approach as a way to automate the electoral process using distributed ledger technologies.

According to the proposed scenario there is a possibility of electronic voting while some electors cast a vote using traditional paper-based ballots.

Firstly, we need to consider the high-level description of the voting scheme. A certain organizer wants to carry out a voting which provides the possibility of electronic voting. A deadline for registration is announced. Up to this point any voter who is allowed to vote can indicate one's willingness to do it electronically. After entering the system with credentials, received from the voting organizer (for example, x.509 certificates) a notification about using the system needs to be done (decision can be changed later in case if registration time is not over). After the registration deadline, the lists of those who decide to vote electronically is transferred to the structures responsible for conducting the voting in the traditional way. It is done in order to avoid the situation when a participant votes both in person and using the electronic system. When the voting period begins the participants who are voting electronically log into the system and make their decision before the voting has finished. There is a potential opportunity to change the decision before the voting deadline. At the end of this procedure, the results are published and everyone can verify those using the system. Consider the structure of the process.

Participants:

1. *Org* – the central voting authority (it is an organization in terms of Hyperledger Fabric, has one or more physical nodes).
2. *Dep* – is a subdivision (e.g. a territorial election commission) that is responsible for conducting voting in its district (for example, it starts the voting process at certain times, this can be useful if there are several time zones involved). It is either a separate organization or a subdivision of the central agency. It has one or several physical nodes.
3. *CC* – chaincode (smart contract) in terms of Hyperledger Fabric which is responsible for the logic of the voting.
4. *V* – voter, system user (member of one of the divisions).
5. *Ins* – an observer (maybe more than one) has one or several nodes and monitors compliance with voting rules.

The Fig. 1 contains the architecture of our solution. First of all participants (organizer, department, inspector) are connected to the same channel. They have got at least one ordering node that is required to reach consensus. However, inspector nodes are "committing peers" (don't execute any logic, get transactions after ordering). By comparison, organizer and department nodes are "endorsing peers" (approve transactions before they will be accepted by other organizations). In addition, each participant has got several client applications that can interact with Fabric network. In general admin apps initialize voting, user apps cast vote and inspect the voting process. It is worthy of note that each of *Dep*, *Org*, *Ins* is several nodes, as well as participant peers, may have got more than two ones.

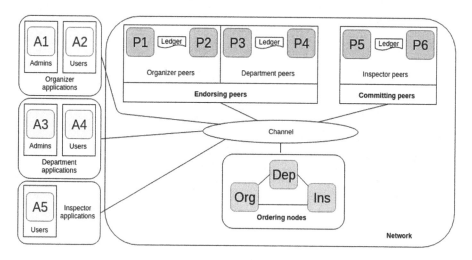

Fig. 1. Architecture of the network.

Now consider the following phases more precisely:

1. Network configuration,
2. Voting configuration,
3. User registration,
4. Voting,
5. Result counting.

4.1   Network Configuration

In the first phase, the main admin determines the rights (read, write) and the number of nodes which every organization has (Fig. 2). Then it extends the network, adds necessary nodes for each organization on which CAs are located, loads logic (chaincode), determines ordering nodes that will be involved in reaching consensus on including transactions into the ledger.

4.2   Voting Configuration

During this phase, the Org administrator generates a list of questions, determines the list of Dep that can participate in this voting (Fig. 3). This data is loaded into the ledger. Then each of the Dep administrators forms an additional data (start/end of voting and registration, list of voters) necessary for holding the voting among voters who belong to this department. This data has to be loaded into the ledger as it is needed for the local voting. Also at this stage, two key pairs are generated $(E_{dep,i}, D_{dep,i})$ for each unit. The public one is recorded to the ledger and the private one is saved in the *private data collection*—a special mechanism in the Hyperledger Fabric, which allows to restrict access to data. After the data is downloaded for each user the list of available polls is updated.

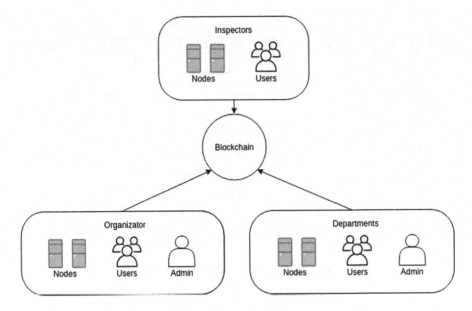

Fig. 2. Participants of the network.

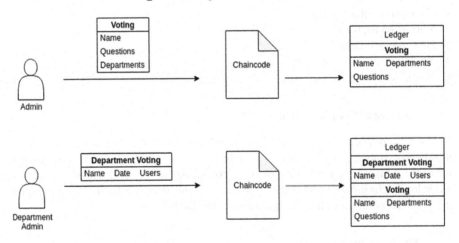

Fig. 3. Initialization voting.

4.3   User Registration

This phase (Fig. 4) is crucial for several purposes:

- To preserve the possibility of a voter to vote using paper-based ballots (if the user has not been registered he is able to vote only in traditional way);
- To ensure the choice privacy and maintain eligibility.

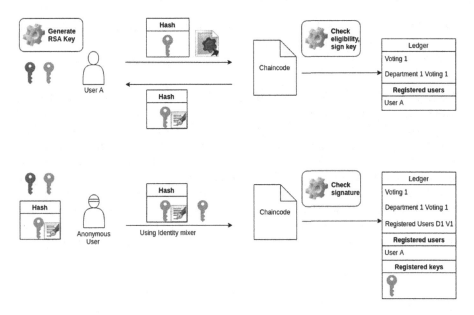

Fig. 4. User registration for electronic voting.

The Sub-step of Obtaining a Blind Signature. During the registration each user generates a pair of keys E_v (public), D_v (private) and a random number R. Then $E_{dep,i}(R) * h(E_v)$ is calculated, here $E_{dep,i}(R)$ is R encrypted with the public key $E_{dep,i}$ of the user department, and $h(E_v)$ is the hash function over the public key of the voter. The result of this expression and the data about elections the voter wants register to are sent to the CC which is in charge of the registration logic. It checks that the current user is allowed to participate in this voting based on data from the CA (user name, department). If it is valid $E_{dep,i}(R) * h(E_v)$ is signed with the private key $D_{dep,i}$ of the department. The received data $D_{dep,i}(E_{dep,i}(R) * h(E_v)) = R * D_{dep,i}(h(E_v))$ (the equality is true since the keys are of the RSA type) is sent back to the user. Then CC records data about that the current user has received a blind signature to the ledger. At the end of the registration phase the list of voters (if it is provided) can be used to avoid revoting. The voter excludes R from $R * D_{dep,i}(h(E_v))$ by multiplying it by R_{inv}, where R_{inv} is the inverse modulo of the department's public key. Then he checks if the hash is signed by its subdivision by comparing $h(E_v)$ and $E_{dep,i}(D_{dep,i}(h(E_v)))$.

The Sub-step of Registering a Public Key that Corresponds to a Person Is Known only by the Voter. At this moment the user has a signed public key $D_{dep,i}(h(E_v))$ which he sends it to the CC along with E_v anonymously using the Identity mixer or idemix (more detail in the next section). There $h(E_v)$ and $E_{dep,i}(D_{dep,i}(h(E_v)))$ are checked. If they are correct, the public key E_v is recorded to the ledger. During the voting phase requests from voters are anonymous (idemix), therefore user's eligibility can be verified using published keys.

Ability to Cancel Registration and Vote Using the Paper-Based Method. In order to provide user an opportunity to vote by the traditional method he needs to be excluded from the list of those who received a blind signature during the first sub-step of registration. This phase is not anonymous. The voter sends to the CC a request to remove the registration key E_v from the list. The CC does not completely delete the E_v key but marks it as revoked. This is necessary as if the user changes his mind and wants to register again he has to register a new key. In addition, he is removed from the list of signed users (again marking him as revoked). If the voter wants to take part in the electronic elections again he moves to the first sub-step and forms a new pair of keys.

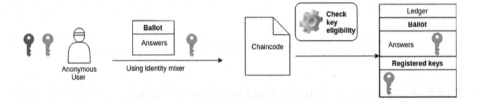

Fig. 5. Voting.

4.4   Voting

During this phase, users who have registered their private keys for voting can send encrypted ballots to chaincode (Fig. 5). Until the end of voting process the voter can change his decision and only the final one is counted. The original article [18] offers to use a symmetric key for encryption. By the end of the voting users have to submit their keys to the system for decrypting ballots and counting votes. However the voter may not provide this data (e.g., network problems). In this case, the bulletin may be considered as spoiled. Therefore it is suggested to form a pair of keys and a private part is divided between organizations and observers. Thus, the results cannot be decrypted until all participants provide their private key parts. And users will encrypt their newsletters using the above public key.

4.5   Result Counting

After the voting is completed participants with private key parts upload them to the CC. Thus, it is possible to decrypt the ballots and to get the results that are published on the ledger.

4.6   Inspectors

In order to increase the voting procedure credibility observers have been introduced into the system which are assumed to be independent and incorruptible. They have physical nodes that store a copy of the ledger. However, since these nodes are committing peers observers are not able to influence on the decision to accept or reject the transaction but they can detect cases of cheating by the other participants. Such situations can take place in the state elections.

5   Security Analysis

Eligibility. This feature assumes that a certificate (e.g., x509), provided to all users, is applied to interaction with the network and registration mechanism that was mentioned above. Note that using the Hyperledger Fabric allows users to avoid creating new certificates and work with those which are used for a particular organization. In the considered scenario it is possible to vote both electronically and on paper. That may cause the problem of defining the user in one of these two groups. In order to do that, we need to exclude those who are in the lists of voters at the first stage of user registration. This is achieved by forming a list of those who need to be deleted from the list of persons allowed to vote at the first stage of user registration. However, this approach has both advantages and disadvantages. The registration stage in the electronic voting includes two steps which should both be completed before the voting has started. Those who apply for registration are excluded from the list of voters allowed for paper voting. There is a possibility that a user does not complete the second phase and therefore he is not able to participate in the voting either through the system or in the traditional way.

Un-Reusability. An elector can vote only if the identifier (public key) is presented in the list of registered keys for the elections. The user cannot register two keys as each key must have a signature of the corresponding department. When the signature on the first key received the user is inserted into the list and no longer able to get a signature for another key.

Un-Traceability. During voting the user's rights are determined based on anonymous identifier (only the voter knows the specific id). And since all requests are sent via idemix there is no linking id (and therefore vote) with a real voter.

Verifiability. Since all voices are recorded in the ledger with reference to id the user can check the results considering his voice (using specific id) thereby making sure that voice was counted.

Receipt-Freeness. This property is not fulfilled in the present implementation since the voter can prove that a certain public key (id that is associated with the choice) belongs to him thereby approving his vote. The problem can be solved by using a ring signature. The core idea is that the ballot is signed by one participant from a certain group and after that, it is impossible to determine who is responsible. It is impossible to prove ownership of a signature even for the person who signed it.

6   Conclusion

The paper is dedicated to a modification of the e-voting protocol proposed in [18] and its implementation using a permissioned blockchain namely the Hyperledger Fabric. That leads to additional benefits:

- Increased transparency and trust,
- Possibility of cancellation of registration,
- Added observers who can detect the presence of fraud or its attempts,
- Immutable ledger history.

As a further improvement of the system, we can suggest applying ring signatures to ensure receipt-freeness as well as finding a solution to a problem when a user is not eligible to vote either electronically or in traditional way because the second stage of registration is not completed.

References

1. Madise, U., Martens, T.: E-voting in Estonia 2005. The first practice of country-wide binding internet voting in the world. In: Krimmer, R. (ed.): Electronic Voting 2006: 2nd International Workshop, Co-organized by Council of Europe, ESF TED, IFIP WG 8.6 and E-Voting.CC, August, 2nd - 4th, 2006 in Castle Hofen, Bregenz, Austria. LNI., GI, vol. 86, pp. 15–26 (2006)
2. Brightwell, I., Cucurull, J., Galindo, D., Guasch, S.: An overview of the ivote 2015 voting system (2015)
3. Springall, D., et al.: Security analysis of the estonian internet voting system. In: Ahn, G., Yung, M., Li, N. (eds.) Proceedings of the 2014 ACM SIGSAC Conference on Computer and Communications Security, Scottsdale, AZ, USA, November 3–7, 2014, pp. 703–715. ACM (2014)
4. Halderman, J.A., Teague, V.: The new south wales ivote system: security failures and verification flaws in a live online election. In: Haenni, R., Koenig, R.E., Wikström, D. (eds.) VOTELID 2015. LNCS, vol. 9269, pp. 35–53. Springer, Cham (2015). https://doi.org/10.1007/978-3-319-22270-7_3
5. Schneier, B.: Applied Cryptography - Protocols, Algorithms, and Source Code in C, 2nd edn. Wiley, New York (1996)
6. Sheer, H., Freya, G., Apostolos, A., Raja, N., Markantonakis, K.: E-Voting with blockchain: an E-voting protocol with decentralisation and voter privacy (2018)

7. Hjálmarsson, F., Hreiðarsson, G., Hamdaqa, M., Hjálmtýsson, G.: Blockchain-based e-voting system. In: 11th International Conference on Cloud Computing (CLOUD), San Francisco, CA, 2018, pp. 983–986. IEEE (2018). https://doi.org/10.1109/CLOUD.2018.00151

8. Koç, A.K., Yavuz, E., Çabuk, U.C., Dalkılıç, G.: Towards Secure e-voting using ethereum blockchain. In: 6th International Symposium on Digital Forensic and Security (ISDFS), Antalya, 22–25 March 2018. https://doi.org/10.1109/ISDFS.2018.8355340

9. Liu, Y., Wang, Q.: An E-voting Protocol Based on Blockchain. IACR Cryptology ePrint Archive (2017)

10. Yu, B., Liu, J.K., Sakzad, A., Nepal, S., Steinfeld, R., Rimba, P., Au, M.H.: Platform-independent secure blockchain-based voting system. In: Chen, L., Manulis, M., Schneider, S. (eds.) ISC 2018. LNCS, vol. 11060, pp. 369–386. Springer, Cham (2018). https://doi.org/10.1007/978-3-319-99136-8_20

11. Chaum, D.: Blind signatures for untraceable payments. In: Chaum, D., Rivest, R.L., Sherman, A.T. (eds.) Advances in Cryptology, pp. 199–203. Springer, Boston (1983). https://doi.org/10.1007/978-1-4757-0602-4_18

12. Chaum, D.: Security without identification: transaction systems to make big brother obsolete. Commun. ACM **28**, 1030–1044 (1985)

13. Rivest, R., Shamir, A., Adleman, L.: A method for obtaining digital signatures and public-key cryptosystems. Commun. ACM **21**, 120–126 (1978). https://doi.org/10.1145/357980.358017

14. Blakley, G.R., Chaum, D. (eds.): CRYPTO 1984. LNCS, vol. 196. Springer, Heidelberg (1985). https://doi.org/10.1007/3-540-39568-7

15. Camenisch, J., Lysyanskaya, A.: Signature schemes and anonymous credentials from bilinear maps. In: Franklin, M. (ed.) CRYPTO 2004. LNCS, vol. 3152, pp. 56–72. Springer, Heidelberg (2004). https://doi.org/10.1007/978-3-540-28628-8_4

16. Au, M.H., Susilo, W., Mu, Y.: Constant-size dynamic k-TAA. In: De Prisco, R., Yung, M. (eds.) SCN 2006. LNCS, vol. 4116, pp. 111–125. Springer, Heidelberg (2006). https://doi.org/10.1007/11832072_8

17. Camenisch, J., Drijvers, M., Lehmann, A.: Anonymous Attestation Using the Strong Diffie Hellman Assumption Revisited. Cryptology ePrint Archive, IACR (2016)

18. He, Q., Su, Z.: A new practical secure e-voting scheme. In: 14th International Information Security Conference (SEC 1998), IFIP/SEC (1998)

Evaluation of Tools for Analyzing Smart Contracts in Distributed Ledger Technologies

Denis Kirillov[✉], Oleg Iakushkin, Vladimir Korkhov, and Vadim Petrunin

Saint-Petersburg State University, St. Petersburg, Russia
kirillovdenand@gmail.com, {o.yakushkin,v.korkhov,v.petrunin}@spbu.ru

Abstract. Despite the fact that the extent of interest in distributed ledger technologies has slightly decreased after the peak of Bitcoin popularity this area continues to evolve. One of the popular areas is the development of smart contracts which introduces a new paradigm of writing programs. This inflicts additional difficulties associated primarily with the high costs of error. This paper reviews the typical vulnerabilities that are widespread during development in the Solidity language. It also presents an analysis of existing tools to help identify software bugs. It is shown that there is no universal technique at the moment and if the risks are high, one should not solely check the code with available instruments but also conduct a manual audit with help of an expert.

Keywords: Smart contracts · Blockchain · Ethereum · Distributed ledger technologies

1 Introduction

The smart contract is a protocol designed for conclusion and performance of commercial contracts inside the blockchain technology. Its verification is necessary in order to ensure that it is correct before installing the contract into the network. This is a crucial point because the code logic of the work operates mainly with financial data and an error can lead to the loss of a huge amount of money. Furthermore, after finding an error it cannot be eliminated because smart contracts are immutable after they are loaded to the network[1]. This approach is very different from the common idea of companies to release a product as soon as possible even if it is still "not ready", to not miss profits. In this case, updates and bug fixes are delivered during a support period. Despite the fact that the risks in the traditional approach can be high as well, smart contracts often store money directly and thus are bug bounty themselves. This means, if an error is found in the code of the smart contract an attacker can immediately exploit it and get the funds.

---

[1] There was a well known incident with The DAO when about $ 50 million was stolen due to a program error.

© Springer Nature Switzerland AG 2019
S. Misra et al. (Eds.): ICCSA 2019, LNCS 11620, pp. 522–536, 2019.
https://doi.org/10.1007/978-3-030-24296-1_41

Next, we will consider contracts written in the Solidity language for the Ethereum platform since it has the most extensive infrastructure for development. Also this language is most popular among new users. We want to provide an analysis of existing tools that can help check smart contracts for vulnerabilities.

The rest of this paper is organized as follows. Section 2 describes existing approaches to verify smart contracts. Classification of possible problems with smart contracts is given in Sect. 3. The detailed analysis of existing tools is presented in Sect. 4. Section 5 concludes the paper and points out directions of future work.

2   Related Work

The security of smart contracts is a fairly popular area that is actively developed. One possibility is to perform an extensive analysis of smart contracts to detect errors and unsafe patterns of source code as well as propose some classification [1]. Other researchers provide own tools (based on different approaches) for identifying such vulnerabilities.

One approach is to use a static analyzers [2]. An intermediate representation is generated from Solidity code as an XML tree. Afterwards, previously known vulnerability patterns can be found using XPath. The advantage of this approach is full code coverage, which is provided.

Furthermore, in [3] it was suggested that correct-by-design contracts should be developed using a finite-state machine. The authors present the framework FSolidM [4] which allows constructing contracts in terms of finite automata and then generate Solidity code that is based on it.

In [5] an opposite approach is suggested. Here, a framework is presented that allows converting the Solidity code (a restricted subset) or the EVM bytecode to F* code (f star is a functional language that is intended for formal verification using the SMT and manual proofs combination).

NUS[2] researchers also propose their approach based on symbolic execution and using Z3 as solver [6]. They also introduced their open source framework Oyente [7].

In opposition to this, scientists from IBM released ZEUS [8] and showed that their approach is better than the NUS solution (significantly fewer false positives, more vulnerable smart contracts were found by the solution). This tool gets the source code and the specification (that this code must comply with) as input. Then it performs static analysis atop the smart contract code and inserts the policy predicates as assert statements at correct program points. After this, the received data is transferred to LLVM bitcode for subsequent verification of violation of assert policies. However, their solution is commercial.

3   Problem Classification

Before proceeding to the classification of vulnerabilities it is necessary to describe some architectural features of code execution for Solidity. First of all, a smart

---

[2] National University of Singapore.

contract is a regular computer program that is executed by a virtual machine and is executed on all network nodes. To accomplish this, the user first has to write contract code and then send a transaction that establishes it to the network at a specific address. There is one more limitation: since the contract will run on every node in order to reduce network load each virtual machine operation carries a price which is expressed in Gas. Therefore, for installing a smart contract and also for subsequent calls of it, the author of the transaction is forced to pay a certain number of ethers for each unit of Gas that will be spent. Also, the transaction contains the number of maximum Gas that is allowed to spend. This is done to ensure the absence of some infinite loop in the function of a smart contract which could spend all the funds of the user calling this function.

Two approaches for classification are considered now. It should be kept in mind that the classification is rather conditional and there might be other views that will also be consistent.

1. The first approach is based on the levels that are available from the Ethereum blockchain.
   (a) Solidity – code level.
       i. Call to unknown. During implementation, a bug can occur which calls a contract function, which does not exist. In this case, the fallback function (the function that is called when money comes to the address) will be called which can lead to unpredictable behavior.
       ii. Gasless send. Let you not have enough money to call someone's fallback function by sending money. Then, if you do not check what the send function returns before continuing with the execution of the code, someone will be deprived of the according reward.
       iii. Exception disorder. The appearance of an exception does not always roll back the states of all participants in the call chain. Therefore as in the previous case, it is necessary to check return values of functions before continuing.
       iv. Type cast. There is no exception when wrong type casts are made, thus the calling code is not aware of any of these errors which could occur.
       v. Reentrancy. Details are discussed below.
       vi. Keeping secrets. In contracts some fields should be set private but their values are changed through a public transaction. Here, everyone can find out the new value of the private field.
   (b) EVM – Ethereum Virtual Machine Level.
       i. Immutable Bugs. These bugs are related to the fact that contracts that are loaded into the blockchain cannot be changed if it turns out that it contains errors.
       ii. Ether lost in the transfer. It is possible to send money to an address that does not belong to anyone, hence it will be irretrievably lost.
       iii. Stack size limit. After exceeding the call limit an exception is thrown.

(c) Blockchain technology level.

    i. Unpredictable state. It is impossible to be sure the contract which has got the transaction is in the same state as at the moment when this transaction was initiated.

    ii. Time constraints. The miner which broadcasts a block with transactions to the network has possibility of slightly changing the timestamp on this block. It can lead to vulnerabilities in contracts that use that timestamp.

2. Another approach is based on common, blockchain-specific and networking errors.

    (a) Common errors.

        i. Integer overflow. We work with money, we don't want a person who has a lot of money to be left with nothing because of an overflow.

        ii. Array length underflow. Details are discussed below.

    (b) Blockchain-specific.

        i. Reentrancy. Details are discussed below.

        ii. Timestamp dependency. Similar to time constraints in the previous classification.

    (c) Networking.

        i. Reachable exception. Similar to exception disorder in the previous classification.

        ii. Failed send. It is possible to constantly reject the transfer of money.

        iii. Transaction ordering. Similar to unpredictable state in the previous classification.

3.1 More Detailed Description of the Problems

Below is a fairly detailed description of the main vulnerabilities that are widespread in smart contracts at various levels. It also provides examples of code that contains an error and code that exploits this vulnerability.

Array Length Underflow. Since Solidity uses positive integers in the range $[0; 2^{256})$, then subtracting one from zero we get is $2^{256} - 1$. It can be used to change any value in the memory of the contract. This is possible due to the fact that the amount of memory allocated for the contract is 2^{256} slots in which information can be stored. And the addresses of these slots can loop (writing something to the address 2^{256} we change the 0 slot). Thus if we have got a dynamic array that contains 2^{256} elements it will cover the entire memory of the contract. By making a record at a specific index in this array we can change an arbitrary value in the contract. It remains to obtain such an array. This is possible to by subtracting 1 from the length of an empty array. Example of a vulnerable contract:

```
1  contract Pwnable {
2    address public owner;
3    address[] a1;
4
5    function Pwnable() public {
6        owner = msg.sender;
7        a1.length -= 1;
8    }
9    modifier onlyOwner() {
10        require(msg.sender == owner);
11        _;
12    }
13    function fun(uint offset, address addr) public
          returns (uint) {
14            a1[offset] = addr;
15    }
16    function transferOwnership(address newOwner) public
          onlyOwner {
17        require(newOwner != address(0));
18        owner = newOwner;
19    }
20 }
```

Reachable Exception. Suppose we have field A in a contract that contains someone's address A_{old}. Now we want to change this address to another address A_{new} after sending A_{old} some money. But if an exception is thrown in the fallback function of the A_{old} the state will be rolled back (the money will not be recorded on its balance). However, the caller will not get an exception but the value false will be returned. If it is not checked, address A_{new} is assigned to A immediately. A_{old} will not receive the money and will lose the position in the contract and thus the preferred treatment. Contract sample (Fig. 1):

```
1  contract King {
2  address public king;
3      uint public prize;
4
5      function King() public payable {
6          king = msg.sender;
7          prize = msg.value;
8      }
9      function() payable {
10          require(msg.value > prize || msg.sender == owner)
            ;
11          uint compensation = calculateCompensation();
12          king.send(compensation);
13          king = msg.sender;
14          prize = msg.value;
15      }
16 }
```

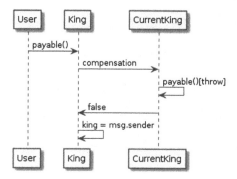

Fig. 1. Reachable exception flow.

Transaction Ordering. Suppose a smart contract which rewards clients if they solve a difficult task. The owner of this contract still has the opportunity to change the compensation of the work. Now, while someone solves the puzzle and agrees to the current reward, the owner changes the amount of the compensation. The transaction of the reward change could reach the contract before the solution of the task is submitted. Then, because of the ordering of the incoming transactions, the resources and time which were needed to solve the puzzle are not rewarded according to the appointed amount (Fig. 2).

```
1  contract Puzzle {
2      address public owner;
3      bool public locked;
4      uint public reward;
5      bytes32 public diff;
6      bytes public solution;
7
8      constructor() public payable {
9          owner = msg.sender;
10         reward = msg.value;
11         locked = false;
12         diff = bytes32 (11111);
13     }
14     function solve(bytes sol) public {
15         require (!locked);
16         if ( sha256(sol) < diff ) {
17             solution = sol;
18             locked = true;
19             msg.sender.transfer(reward);
20         }
21     }
22     function update_reward() public payable {
23         require (msg.sender == owner);
24         require (!locked);
25         owner.transfer(reward);
```

```
26                reward = msg.value;
27        }
28 }
```

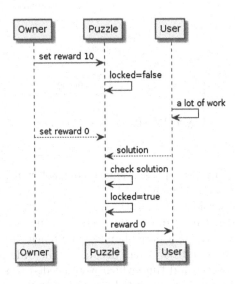

Fig. 2. Transaction ordering flow.

Reentrancy. Let a certain contract keep the money of users and allow them to withdraw their money. This function:

1. Checks the availability of the requested amount of money on the balance,
2. Sends the required amount to the calling user,
3. Reduces the balance.

When receiving money a fallback function is called which may contain some code. So if the withdrawal is called again in this function (even if the first call withdraws all the money) the balance has not decreased. That gives the possibility to receive money until subtraction from the balance occurs at the very end. This will continue until the user removes all the money or reaches the stack size limit (Fig. 3).

Vulnerable contract:

```
1  contract Wallet {
2      mapping (address => uint) private userBalances;
3      address private owner = address(0);
4
5      constructor() public payable {owner = msg.sender;}
6      function deposit(address to, uint val) public {
7          require (msg.sender == owner);
8          userBalances[to] += val;
```

```
 9          }
10          function withdrawBalance() public {
11              uint amountToWithdraw = userBalances[msg.sender];
12              if (amountToWithdraw > 0) {
13                  msg.sender.call.value(amountToWithdraw)();
14                  userBalances[msg.sender] = 0;
15              }
16          }
17  }
```

Attacking contract:

```
1  contract User {
2      function () public payable {
3          if (address(wallet).balance >= msg.value){
4              wallet.withdrawBalance();
5          }
6      }
7  }
```

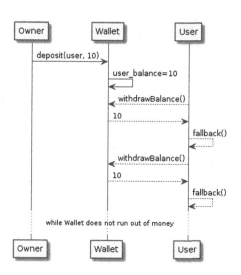

Fig. 3. Reentrancy flow.

Access Control. Often during implementation of smart contract logic you need to verify the sender of a transaction in order to grant certain privileges. However if the *tx.origin* property is used it can lead to issues since this property contains the address of the initiator of the call chain. So if a withdrawal is called that is available only to the contract owner it will not be successful because *tx.origin* will contain our address, not the owner. But by making the same call in the fallback function which will start to be executed if the contract owner transfers some money to us *tx.origin* will contain the owner's address. In such a way we will receive other people's money.

Vulnerable contract:

```
1  contract Wallet{
2    address public owner;
3
4      constructor (address  _owner) { owner = _owner; }
5      function () public payable {}
6      function withdrawAll(address _luckyAddress) public {
7          require(tx.origin == owner);
8          _luckyAddress.transfer(this.balance);
9      }
10 }
```

Attacking contract:

```
1  contract User{
2    Wallet poorWallet;
3      address attacker;
4
5      constructor (Wallet _poorWallet, address
              _attackerAddress) {
6        poorWallet = _poorWallet;
7          attacker = _attackerAddress;
8      }
9      function () payable {
10         poorWallet.withdrawAll(attacker);
11     }
12 }
```

Timestamp Dependency. In many business applications it is necessary to operate with precise time. For these purposes one should not use the timestamp on the block. Miners put this mark and in some cases they are free to change the time value up to a few minutes. It is better to use block numbers as timestamps. Therefore, constructions like ($now\%2 == 0$) should be avoided since an attacker can adjust the time so that this condition will always be fulfilled.

4 Tools

For carrying out a formal verification a corresponding specification is required whereby the validation should be conducted. However, the preparation of such a specification is a laborious and expensive process which may not be justified with frequent changes in requirements. Therefore most of the tools below do not use this approach. We present a list of tools with a brief description and then describe some of them in more detail (Fig. 4).

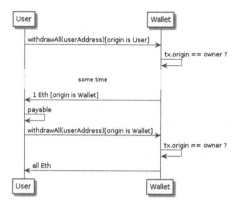

Fig. 4. Access control flow.

- Mythril Classic – uses symbolic execution, taint analysis and control flow checking in order to find security holes.
- Slither – framework for static analysis, allows taint and value tracking.
- Echidna – testing by entering unexpected or incorrect data.
- Manticore – symbolic execution over smart contract bytecode.
- Oyente – symbolic execution over control flow graph.
- Securify – decompiling EVM bytecode and automatic inferencing semantic facts. And using the previously obtained data is looking for patterns of vulnerabilities.
- SmartCheck – static code analyzer using an XML parse tree as an intermediate representation.
- Octopus - using symbolic execution.
- Zeus – using LLVM with policies which is analysed using Seahorn [9].
- Truffle Security – extension for Truffle is based on MythX.
- Mythos – instrument for MythX api.

These tools can be categorized by their kind of approach as followed:

Symbolic Execution. In symbolic execution, the data is replaced by symbolic values with a set of expressions, one expression per output variable. Thus it is possible to receive not just the output of the program depending on certain input but information about the reachable ways of program execution. Also, there is an opportunity for getting the input data which lead to these execution paths. However, there are a number of issues that face symbolic calculations:

1. Unable to handle infinite loops,
2. Problem with handling an external code call,
3. The problem with the rapidly increasing number of possible paths in real applications.

In our case, the following tools fall into this category:

- Mythril,
- Oyente,
- Manticore,
- Octopus.

Using Specification. The use of specifications moves a tool closer to formal verification. So these systems receive some set of conditions (policies) which the code being checked must correspond to. There are some obvious disadvantages of this approach:

1. Check only those conditions that have been set,
2. The need to change policies when changing the code,
3. The difficulty and high development costs.

Tools:

- Zeus,
- Echidna.

Fuzzing. Fuzzing is based on the analysis of the behavior of the program depending on the input data. It involves to use massive amounts of random data as input, called fuzz, in an attempt to make the program crash.
  Tools:

- Echidna.

Automatic Inference. This technique allows the use of certain rules to obtain additional facts about the available data automatically.
  Tools:

- Securify.

Lexical and Syntactic Analysis. Such programs parse the code received at the input. They transform it into so-called lexemes using some formal language and grammar. Then a certain data structure is formed. It contains syntactic information about the source data with which it is convenient to work in the future.
  Tools:

- SmartCheck.

Hybrid Approach. It can use incorporation of symbolic execution, static analysis and dynamic analysis.
  Tools:

- Truffle Security,
- Mythos.

4.1   Comparing Tools

Several of the aforementioned tools are open source and were chosen by us for conducting a comparative analysis based on various indicators. Below is a table (Table 1) that contains information whether these systems can determine if a particular type of smart contract vulnerability exists or not.

Table 1. Tools and their efficiency for vulnerability detection. "+" – is detected, "–" – is not detected, "+/–" – it depends, "?" – the vulnerability is detected but it cannot be mapped with the expected type.

	Underflow	Reentrancy	Ordering	Control access	Reachable exception	Timestamp
Mythril	+	+/–	–	+	+	–
SmartCheck	+	?	–	+	+	–
Oyente	–	+	–	–	+	–
Slither	–	+	–	+	–	–
Manticore	–	+	–	+	+	+
Securify	–	+	+	+	–	–

Based on obtained results some conclusions can be drawn. First, it is clear that no tool could detect all vulnerabilities. This is quite obvious since different approaches have their own advantages that have to be paid. In general, this is reflected in limited functionality (the ability to detect only certain types of vulnerabilities). Further, it can be noted that despite the use of identical approaches (for example, symbolic execution) the results may be quite different. This is probably due to the fact that each team of researchers that develops an analyzer tries to solve an individual task and adds specific functionality without trying to make the tool universal. In addition, you can see that the most difficult vulnerability to determine is the dependence on the order of transactions and the dependence on time. In the first case, it is quite clear: there is a dependence on time that adds additional complexity to the analysis. Regarding the use of the timestamp, it can be assumed that a simple pattern that depends on time (for example, $now\%2 == 0$) will give a large number of false positives and thus such patterns are not added. However it is worth noting that false positives are not so terrible since the developer will simply have to manually double-check the code. And even then just time is lost in this case. The presence of false negatives has a more harmful impact. Actually, the presence of such situations is indeed equivalent to the absence of verification. This happens if we do not include patterns with false positive in the verification rules. Thus, it is an indirect argument for that in some cases the developers of analysis tools are trying to achieve certain indicators that in general may not depend on reliability and security of smart contracts. It is an indirect argument for some cases, when developers of analysis tools are trying to achieve certain indicators that in general may not be associated with reliability and security of smart contracts. However, in matters of money security, it is better to be on the safe side.

Table 2 contains data that shows the analysis tools comparison for other criteria. In particular, it is shown that almost all the presented analysis systems are currently maintained and under active development. This indicates that the tools will improve and soon the previous indicators (Table 1) can be extended. It is also worth noting the most popular approach is to use symbolic execution. Teams following this approach, more often choose Z3 as the SMT solver [6]. Almost all tools were presented in academic papers. This may indicate that there is a fairly strong relationship between the academic environment and business. It is an emphatic success for the area of the distributed ledger technologies since it allows a decreased time period from appearance of a theoretical result to its implementation and active deployment in the industrial sector. The most popular language for implementation is Python.

Table 2. Tools and their common properties.

	Maintain	Type	Paper	Language	Using components
Mythril	Yes	Symbolic execution	Yes	Python	Z3
SmartCheck	Yes	Static analysis	Yes	Java	XML parse tree
Oyente	No	Symbolic execution	Yes	JavaScript	Z3
Slither	Yes	Taint and value tracking	No	Python	LLVM
Manticore	Yes	Symbolic execution	No	Python	Z3
Securify	Yes	Automatic inference	Yes	Java	Z3

As mentioned above many tools using symbolic execution contain some theorem provers or SMT solver for internal computations.

Some of these tools are:

1. Coq is a cross-platform interactive tool for theorem proving that uses its own functional language.
2. CVC3 is an automatic theorem prover. It can process first-order formulas.
3. Z3 is an SMT solver presented by the Microsoft researchers. It is the most popular tool.
4. F* (f star) is a functional language that combines proof assistant and SMT solver. It was also introduced by the Microsoft researchers.
5. Isabelle is a general-purpose proof assistance that enables process a high-order logic.

The comparative Table 3 displays some of the characteristics of these tools. The "extraction" and "code generation" columns should be explained. The first one is responsible for the possibility of translating code written using the presented tools into any other language. The last one is responsible for the ability to generate code from any languages. Why3 is a platform for program verification that allows using third-party provers. The language for writing code is WhyML.

Table 3. Tools for theorem proving and their common properties. "?" – no data. "-" – no extraction.

	IDE	Extraction	OS	Language	API	Code generation
Z3	No	?	L/M/W	C/C++	C/C++, .NET, OCaml, Python, Java	Why3
Coq	Yes	Haskell, Scheme, OCaml	L/M/W	OCaml	?	Why3
CVC3	No	-	L	C/C++	C/C++	Why3
F*	No	OCaml, F#, C	L/M/W	F*	?	Solidity*
Isabelle	Yes	SML, Scala, OCaml, Haskell	L/M/W	Standard ML, Scala	?	Why3

5   Conclusion and Future Work

In this paper we review the existing problems and vulnerabilities which are quite common in smart contracts on the Ethereum platform, in particular for the Solidity language. This topic is important because a growing number of people are coming to this area and they need to start thinking in a somewhat different paradigm in order to avoid losing a lot of money and reputation. Formal verification of programs is a rather complicated and expensive process which is why most of the existing tools do not use this approach. We analyzed several of the most popular tools for searching for vulnerabilities and came to the conclusion that, at the moment, there is no completely versatile and balanced tool. Therefore if there is a need to ensure the reliability and security of a smart contract you should either use all available tools or approach a specialized company that examines smart contracts. And it is better to do both.

As the blockchain technology field evolves and new projects appear that allow smart contracts to be written in general purpose languages (Java, Go, Javascript, Python), it is planned to consider formal verification tools that are suitable for these languages and determine the specifics arising from such analysis.

References

1. Atzei, N., Bartoletti, M., Cimoli, T.: A survey of attacks on ethereum smart contracts (SoK). In: Maffei, M., Ryan, M. (eds.) POST 2017. LNCS, vol. 10204, pp. 164–186. Springer, Heidelberg (2017). https://doi.org/10.1007/978-3-662-54455-6_8

2. Tikhomirov, S., Voskresenskaya, E., Ivanitskiy, I., Takhaviev, R., Marchenko, E., Alexandrov, Y.: SmartCheck: static analysis of ethereum smart contracts. In: Proceedings of the 1st International Workshop on Emerging Trends in Software Engineering for Blockchain, pp. 9–16. ACM, Gothenburg (2018). https://doi.org/10.1145/3194113.3194115

3. Mavridou, A., Laszka, A.: Designing secure ethereum smart contracts: a finite state machine based approach. In: 22nd International Conference on Financial Cryptography and Data Security (2018)

4. Mavridou, A., Laszka, A.: Tool demonstration: FSolidM for designing secure ethereum smart contracts. In: Bauer, L., Küsters, R. (eds.) POST 2018. LNCS, vol. 10804, pp. 270–277. Springer, Cham (2018). https://doi.org/10.1007/978-3-319-89722-6_11

5. Bhargavan, K., et al.: Formal verification of smart contracts: short paper. In: Proceedings of the 2016 ACM Workshop on Programming Languages and Analysis for Security, Vienna, Austria, 24 October 2016, pp. 91–96 (2016). https://doi.org/10.1145/2993600.2993611

6. de Moura, L., Bjørner, N.: Z3: an efficient SMT solver. In: Ramakrishnan, C.R., Rehof, J. (eds.) TACAS 2008. LNCS, vol. 4963, pp. 337–340. Springer, Heidelberg (2008). https://doi.org/10.1007/978-3-540-78800-3_24

7. Luu, L., Chu, D., Olickel, H., Saxena, P., Hobor, A.: Making smart contracts smarter. In: Proceedings of the 2016 ACM SIGSAC Conference on Computer and Communications Security, Vienna, Austria, 24–28 October 2016, pp. 254–269 (2016). https://doi.org/10.1145/2976749.2978309

8. Kalra, S., Goel, S., Dhawan, M., Sharma, S.: Zeus: analyzing safety of smart contracts. In: 25th ISOC Symposium on Network and Distributed System Security (NDSS 2018), San Diego, CA (2018). https://doi.org/10.14722/ndss.2018.23092

9. Urban, C., Gurfinkel, A., Kahsai, T.: Synthesizing ranking functions from bits and pieces. In: Chechik, M., Raskin, J.-F. (eds.) TACAS 2016. LNCS, vol. 9636, pp. 54–70. Springer, Heidelberg (2016). https://doi.org/10.1007/978-3-662-49674-9_4

10. Barrett, C., Tinelli, C.: CVC3. In: Damm, W., Hermanns, H. (eds.) CAV 2007. LNCS, vol. 4590, pp. 298–302. Springer, Heidelberg (2007). https://doi.org/10.1007/978-3-540-73368-3_34

11. Paulson, L.C.: Isabelle: the next 700 theorem provers. In: Odifreddi, P. (ed.) Logic and Computer Science, pp. 361–386. Academic Press, London (1990)

Architecture of a Smart Container Using Blockchain Technology

Oleg Iakushkin$^{(\boxtimes)}$, Dmitry Selivanov, Ekaterina Pavlova,
and Vladimir Korkhov

Saint-Petersburg State University, St. Petersburg, Russia
o.yakishkin@spbu.ru

Abstract. The use of blockchain technology introduces the possibility
to decentralize logistic systems. These are more efficient and the information inside is easy accessible and verifiable. Additionally, data security
is preserved at this time. This paper presents the architecture of a smart
container that uses blockchain technology. It stores its location and status data in a distributed ledger. In addition, users and suppliers can use
the mobile application to access this data. As the information about the
container movements is available in realtime, the relevant parties will be
able to take action quickly when a problem occurs in the supply chain.
Sensitive and private documents will require a permissioned blockchain
infrastructure such as Hyperledger Iroha. Blockchain technologies allow
users to abandon the idea of a central server or a regulatory authority
that support the operation of the system and be responsible for safety
and storage of data. Such a decentralized network does not have a central
point of failure and is better able to withstand malicious attacks.

Keywords: Smart container · Distributed ledger · Blockchain ·
Iroha · Raspberry Pi

1 Introduction

For the management of logistic chain organizing the delivery of goods by unrelated intermediaries it is necessary to form an ecosystem of trust. To realize the possibility of secure information exchange during shipments based on
blockchain [1] technology, there are several main components:

- a "smart container" hardware-software - a system being implemented in the
  field to monitor the current situation
- a software logistic system that allows carriers to exchange orders and optimize
  costs
- an API for building end-user applications

This article describes a smart container that can be transferred between
owners and that will be able to use blockchain technology to store data about
its location, membership status, and other information. Such a container makes

© Springer Nature Switzerland AG 2019
S. Misra et al. (Eds.): ICCSA 2019, LNCS 11620, pp. 537–545, 2019.
https://doi.org/10.1007/978-3-030-24296-1_42

logistic processes more convenient and transparent not only for the end user, but also for suppliers.

Blockchain technologies allow users to abandon the idea of a central server or a regulatory authority that support the operation of the system and be responsible for safety and storage of data. Such a decentralized network does not have a central point of failure and is better able to withstand malicious attacks. In addition, changes in public blocks of the chain are publicly accessible to all parties, which creates transparency of information. It is important to ensure that all information on movements and the final destination point is visible only to the supplier, which is the last destination in the sequence of movements of the container. This distinction is designed to preserve anonymity and prevents the intentional disruption of deliveries. To accomplish this, distribution of access rights in the blockchain framework is used, which will be described in more detail below.

This paper presents two software platforms. The first is for suppliers, providing access to the location and status of all containers that currently belong to them. At the same time it is possible to view information about the previous owner and the next destination. The second platform is for users, providing access to the status and movement history of the container enclosing their order. These platforms are implemented in the form of two mobile clients.

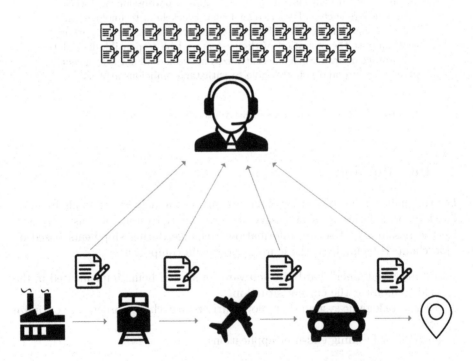

Fig. 1. Centralized logistic system.

Figure 1 is a schematic representation of a centralized logistic process. In this process, some goods were manufactured at the factory, and then sent to the destination using three consecutive movements: by train, by plane and by car. At the same time, a document was generated for each movement. Verification and creating of documents, as well as the administration of movements is performed using some central node. However, to organize the effective work of each of the units, time and money is required.

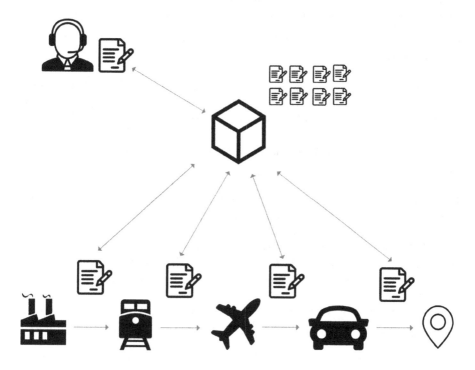

Fig. 2. Decentralized logistic system.

Figure 2 shows a schematic representation of a decentralized logistic process using blockchain technology. In such a system, the organization of the delivery of goods occurs in presence of unrelated intermediaries in a certain ecosystem of trust. The ability to safely exchange information during the course is carried out using the blockchain technology. The number of paper documents or emails will be significantly lower in these ecosystems than in the case of a centralized one. Documents about movements will be stored electronically in a distributed ledger.

2   Current Situation

The existing solution in the market of logistic systems is the "Smart Containers" company [5] and their products SkyCell or FoodGuardian. They provide smart containers for delivering medicine and food.

Until today, their containers are tracked using data that goes to a centralized database. In addition, the administration is done manually. This means that one of the operators checks the location of the containers by contacting the client in specific cases. This creates financial and time costs.

3   Hardware

The compact single board computer Raspberry Pi 3b is used as the main module of the smart container. A GPS module with an external antenna is used to determine the location. In addition, a 3g modem is connected to the Raspberry Pi 3b. Connection devices which are based on 3g technology are preferred because modems using LTE technology have increased power consumption. The RC522 module is used to read RFID [3] tags.

In addition, a Real Time Clock module is connected to the Raspberry PI 3b, since this single board computer does not have a built-in module and resets the local time after a reboot. Several ultrasonic distance sensors are installed to detect the opening and breaking status of the container. They connect to the GPIO connections of the Raspberry PI 3b. Also, the servo drive is used to control the mechanical lock, and the LED RGB module acts for debugging purposes. Further additional components are a microSD memory card module and a battery.

For convenience of connecting modules and sensors, a GPIO expansion board is used. A full description of the hardware architecture of the smart container is presented in Fig. 3.

4   Software

The software consists of the following main parts:

- container software
- c platform for suppliers that provides information on the location of all containers owned by the supplier, delivery dates, and the status of all containers (burglary signals, open/closed state signal, etc.)
- A user platform that provides location and order status information

4.1   Container Software

The operating system for the Raspberry PI is Raspbian. The software for the interactions with the sensors and modules is written in Python 3. Most sensors

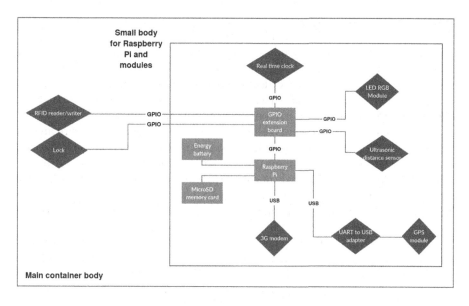

Fig. 3. Hardware architecture of a smart container.

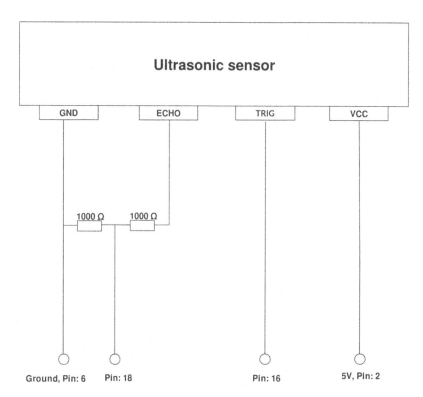

Fig. 4. Schematic representation of the distance sensor connection.

connect to a general purpose input/output (GPIO) interface. The RPi.GPIO library [6] is used to work with this interface.

Interaction with distance sensors occurs through interrupts. As soon as an electrical signal is sent to a certain pin, an interruption is called for data processing. In our case, this data is recorded and compared with previous records. This is done in order to understand whether the container is open at the moment and whether authorized access to its content has been accomplished.

Figure 3 shows the hardware architecture of a smart container. There are two metal bodies. The first body contains Raspberry Pi and main modules/sensors connected to it. The second (main) body contains the RFID reader/writer, the lock and the first body. The ratio of the sizes of metal cases in the figure does not correspond to the real. In reality, a small metal case takes up little space, while the main space remains for storing the contents of orders. The more detailed image of the connection of the distance sensor is presented in Fig. 4

Interaction with the GPS module occurs through reading data from the corresponding tty port on the Raspberry PI. As shown in Fig. 3, The GPS module is connected to a single board computer using a USB connection. However, data is exchanged using the UART interface, which, in the Raspbian operating system, is provided by default with the /dev/ttyAMA0 device. After the module establishes a connection with the satellites, it begins to send data on the latitude, longitude and height to the corresponding tty port at some intervals.

Figure 4 shows a schematic representation of the ultrasonic distance sensor connection. This sensor has 4 connection pins. First pin is called "GND" which means the ground connection that completes electrical pathway of the power. Second pin is called "ECHO". The echo sends a signal back if an object has been detected or not. If a signal is returned, an object has been detected. If not, no object has been detected. Third pin is called "TRIG". A pulse is sent here for the sensor to go into ranging mode for object detection. And last pin is called "VCC". It connects to 5 V of positive voltage for power. Pins 6,8,16 and 18 at the bottom of the figure mean corresponding GPIO pins on the Raspberry Pi. We put two 1000 Ω resistors because the GPIO pins only tolerate maximal 3.3 V.

For reading and writing RFID [3] tags, the RC522 module and the MFRC522 software library [7] in Python is used, which is distributed under the GNU Lesser General Public License.

4.2 Iroha Network

The blockchain framework Hyperledger Iroha [8–10] was chosen for this project. It is designed to be easily embedded in infrastructure projects. In addition, the framework is written in C++ and has a high performance. To join the network, read data and execute commands specific privileges are needed. In Hyperledger Iroha there is a permission distribution system. In addition, targeting mobile platforms and portability of this framework is a strong advantage.

Accounts on the Iroha network are grouped into domains. Here, the "customers" domain for user accounts, the "containers" domain for containers and

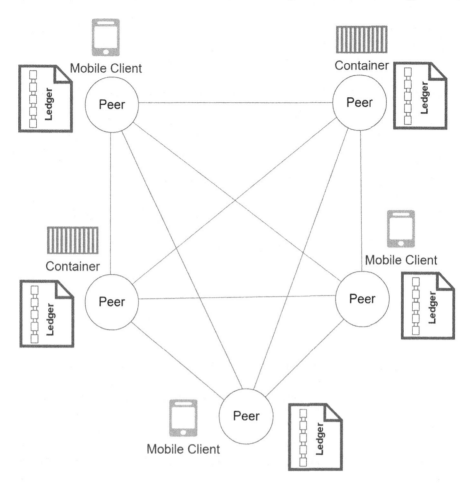

Fig. 5. Schematic representation of a blockchain infrastructure.

the names of the other domains coincide with the names of the supplier companies registered in the network are used. Each physical smart container has a registered account in the "containers" domain with a full history of movements and owners. Each record, for example data about the current location, is safely and securely stored in the account as JSON format. Additional, information also stored there:

- data about the current status: values open/closed;
- order status: values waiting to be sent/in transit/delivered/error/ unauthorized access

Rules in the user domain are adjusted in a way so only the user who is the author of the order can read the data from the account of the corresponding container. In this case, the system of distribution of privileges in the supplier's

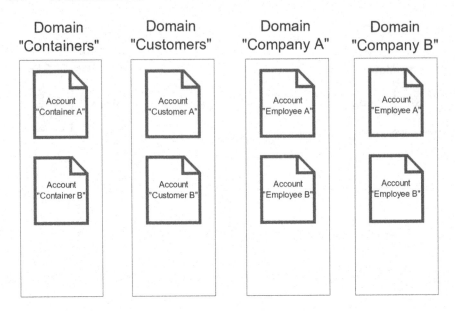

Fig. 6. Domains and accounts structure.

domain is designed that only the supplier who currently owns the container can transfer the ownership status to the next supplier or user. At the same time, information about the previous owner, next destination, as well as the history of movements and container statuses (only during the period of ownership) is available to him.

Figure 5 shows a schematic representation of a blockchain infrastructure. Containers and mobile applications are peers in Iroha network. As it is described above, each smart container has an account in the "containers" domain. Mobile applications also use accounts in the respective domains, depending on whether the account belongs to the customer or employee of the transport campaign. As it is shown in the Fig. 5, every peer keeps a copy of a ledger.

A user with an appropriate level of access can go to the container and open it through a mobile application using NFC [2]. This is made possible by using a set of predefined smart contracts, called teams, that are used to perform key transactions or to obtain information in the blockchain. In addition, mobile clients for users and suppliers use the MapD [4] tool and provide visual information about the history of container movements.

Containers, mobile apps providers and users act as peers on the Iroha Network (Fig. 6).

5   Conclusion

Blockchain technology is an innovation with capability to transform many existing traditional systems into more secure, distributed, transparent, collaborative systems. The described architecture of the smart container allows blockchain technologies to be used in logistic systems to improve safety and efficiency. In this paper, the hardware and software components of the proposed solution are described in detail, as well as their interaction with the Iroha network.

The possibilities of using the system by users and suppliers are also described. At the same time, components such as the container body and mechanical lock can be changed depending on the wishes of customers, which allows to change the level of safety of the contents of the container for individual requirements. As the information about the container movemenents is available in realtime, the relevant parties will be able to take action quickly when a problem occurs in the supply chain [11].

References

1. Crosby, M., Pattanayak, P., Verma, S., Kalyanaraman, V.: Blockchain technology: beyond bitcoin. Appl. Innov. **2**(6–10), 71 (2016)
2. Patel, J., Kothari, B.: Near field communication-the future technology for an interactive world. Int. J. Eng. Res. Sci. Technol. **2**(2), 55–59 (2013)
3. Want, R.: An introduction to RFID technology. IEEE Pervasive Comput. **1**, 25–33 (2006)
4. Root, C., Mostak, T.: MapD: a GPU-powered big data analytics and visualization platform. In: ACM SIGGRAPH 2016 Talks, p. 73. ACM. July 2016
5. SmartContainers, whitepaper. https://smartcontainers.ch/en/assets/20180502_smartcontainers_whitepaper_v2.pdf. Accessed 20 Mar 2019
6. A python 3 module to control Raspberry Pi GPIO channels. https://pypi.org/project/RPi.GPIO/. Accessed 20 Mar 2019
7. A python 3 library to interact with RC522 module. https://github.com/mxgxw/MFRC522-python/. Accessed 20 Mar 2019
8. An introduction to Hyperledger, whitepaper. https://www.hyperledger.org/wp-content/uploads/2018/08/HL_Whitepaper_IntroductiontoHyperledger.pdf. Accessed 20 Mar 2019
9. Hyperledger Blockchain Performance Metrics, whitepaper. https://www.hyperledger.org/wp-content/uploads/2018/10/HL_Whitepaper_Metrics_PDF_V1.01.pdf. Accessed 20 Mar 2019
10. Cachin, C., Vukolić, M.: Blockchain consensus protocols in the wild. arXiv preprint arXiv:1707.01873 (2017)
11. Dolinskaya, I.S., Shi, Z.E., Smilowitz, K.R., Ross, M.: Decentralized approaches to logistics coordination in humanitarian relief. In: IIE Annual Conference. Proceedings, p. 1. Institute of Industrial and Systems Engineers (IISE), January 2011

Methods of Formal Software Verification in the Context of Distributed Systems

Anna Fatkina, Oleg Iakushkin$^{(\boxtimes)}$, Dmitry Selivanov, and Vladimir Korkhov

Saint-Petersburg State University, St. Petersburg, Russia
o.yakushkin@spbu.ru

Abstract. This paper discusses several formal verification instruments and compares them. These tools are Isabelle/HOL, Coq, Verdi, and TLA+. All of them are developed for automatic verification of distributed systems. However, there are a number of differences in implementation and application. Verdi provides an effortless way of implementation to verify some distributed systems. Isabelle/HOL and Coq, on the other hand, can solve a wider range of tasks. These provide a low-level interface and require programming skills. TLA+ allows the user to communicate in pseudocode-like language as well as per algorithm implementation in TLA+/PlusCal. It is the most versatile tool for formal verification which is considered in this paper.

Keywords: Formal verification · Proof assistant · TLA+ ·
Isabelle/HOL · Coq · Verdi · Distributed systems

1 Introduction

In the research area of distributed ledger technologies, the inevitable question is the formalization and verification of developed systems. Any inaccuracy could be exploited as a vulnerability. Therefore, the formal verification of such systems requires special treatment. There are a number of tools for automatic software verification and formal description of models. In this work, a subset of these instruments are considered, that show effectiveness in the formalization of consensus algorithms, such as Casper in Isabelle and Coq, Paxos in TLA+ and Raft in Verdi [12,13,17–19].

This paper briefly describes how to use the considered tools and shows and shows several examples. It also presents a comparison of various tools and describes their suitable use-cases.

© Springer Nature Switzerland AG 2019
S. Misra et al. (Eds.): ICCSA 2019, LNCS 11620, pp. 546–555, 2019.
https://doi.org/10.1007/978-3-030-24296-1_43

2   Formal Verification Tools

The following tools for formal proofs of mathematical statements are considered
in this paper:

- Isabelle/HOL,
- Coq,
- Coq-based Verdi, and
- TLA+.

For Isabelle and Coq an Emacs interface called Proof General [1] is provided,
which is distributed under GNU General Public License. The system TLA+ is
delivered with the IDE called TLA+ Toolbox [2]. Both IDEs have user-friendly

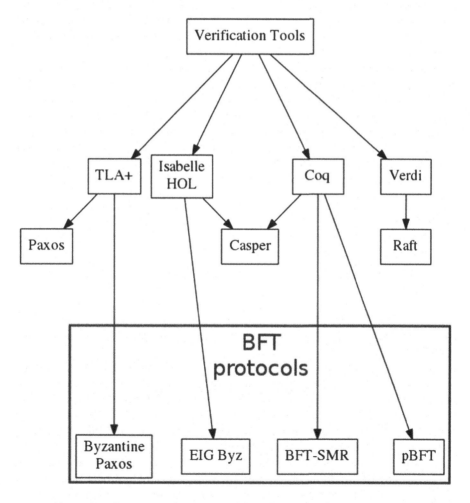

Fig. 1. Verification tools usage for verification of consensus algorithms.

GUIs and user guides. Verdi is a library for modeling distributed systems [3]. It has a command line interface.

Some cases of usage of considered tools for consensus algorithm verification are presented in Fig. 1.

For the Casper protocol there is implementation in both Isabelle/HOL and Coq. Verdi was used for Raft protocol only. To get more information about verification Byzantine Fault-Tolerant protocols, see [22,23].

2.1 Isabelle/HOL

Isabelle/HOL is a proof assistant, which itself is part of the generic system for logical formalism implementation Isabelle [8,9]. HOL stands for Higher-Order Logic. It is a language for theorem descriptions, their according proofs as well as formulas and other mathematical constructions. It also includes various automated proof tools. Basic data types such as **natural**, **real** and **complex** numbers, **bool** and **integer** are supported out of box. The user can also extend existing data types or create new individual types.

There are also more complex data types. For example, **pair**, which is an ordered pair of two elements. Access to the single elements is provided by the **fst()** and **snd()** methods, which return the first and second part of the pair, respectively. **Tuple** is a generalization of pair and contains one to seven ordered elements. A tuple can also be interpreted as a set of nested pairs, from right to left. The degenerated version of the container of ordered numbers called **unit** contains a single element. New data types can also be defined by the user. Listing 1.1 provides an example of this for data using the **record** keyword. Here, a **point** type with two integer fields, **Xcoord** and **Ycoord**, is defined.

```
record  point =
    Xcoord :: int
    Ycoord :: int
```

Listing 1.1. Isabelle/HOL definition of **point**

The Isabelle/HOL notation includes a predefined data structure called **list**. It is a sequence of values of the same type or might be empty. For a **list**, concatenation operations are defined as well as append, reverse and many other instructions.

Isabelle/HOL operates on the concept of **theory**. It is described in a separate file and may include other theories previously described. Mathematical statements are defined inside the **theory**, e.g. **terms** and **formula**. Here, **formula** is a specific **term** with **bool** return value. Isabelle/HOL also supports lambda expressions. If **theory** B is included in **theory** A, then one could use statements in **theory** A which were proven in **theory** B.

Theorems and lemmas are described by the keywords **theorem** and **lemma** and are interchangeable. They indicate just the importance of approval. The content of the theorem is described in quotes, and its proof ends with the keyword **done**. Listing 1.2 presents an example of a simple lemma.

```
lemma app_Nil2 [simp]:  ''xs @ []  =  xs''
    apply(induct_tac xs)
    apply(auto)
done
```

Listing 1.2. Isabelle/HOL lemma example

It says that if adding a blank `list` to another one, it does not change the content of the first. This lemma is proved by the use of built-in automatic methods.

Isabelle/HOL has a number of automatic proof methods. The `simp` method tries to solve a problem by simplification, `arithm` tries to solve a problem as an arithmetic formula and the `auto` method looks for suitable resolve methods automatically. More complex theorems need step-by-step proofs of intermediate expressions. The general scheme of any proof consists of two steps: breaking a global goal into simple subgoals and then proving them according to predefined expressions or previously proved ones. For proofs of intermediate subgoals, one can use different introduction, elimination, destruction, and forward rules. Conjunction, disjunction, implication, modus ponens can act as rules. Isabelle/HOL's most effective and fast proof method is `blast`. It can even resolve complex expressions by consistently applying the rules automatically. For HOL there is a set of freely available theories. Anyone can submit their own theories to a public theory base [10].

2.2   Coq

The formal verification tool Coq [4,5] is similar to Isabelle/HOL. It also contains methods for describing mathematical statements but differs in syntax as well as in a wider range of predefined types and containers. The Coq proof assistant supports basic data types, such as `natural` and `bool`. There is also an extended type which is described by using the `option` keyword. However, unlike Isabelle/HOL, Coq also has types

- `sum(A, B)` and `prod(A, B)`, disjoint sum and product respectively,
- comparison types, (less, equal, greater),
- `ascii` is an eight-bit character
- `string` is a set of eight-bit characters.

More complex data types, e.g. real and rational numbers, are described in separate libraries, `Reals` and `QArith`, respectively. For those, there are also separate libraries of functions that act on these numbers like integration, trigonometry, the theory of series and sequences for real numbers.

As in Isabelle/HOL, in Coq it is possible to define your own data types using the `Record` keyword. In Coq, also classes are supported for which methods are defined for the according instances.

The `list` and `stream` containers defined in Coq are similar. Their description is in the `Coq.Lists` library. List is the limited sequence of items. Concatenation methods are defined as well as methods that return the length of the list and pointers to the first and last elements. `Stream` contains an infinite sequence of elements.

The keyword `Function` specifies the function. An example is shown in Listing 1.3. Here a function called `sum` is created, which adds two numbers of the `nat`(natural) type.

```
Function sum (m n : nat) {struct n} : nat := match n with
    | 0 => m
    | S p => S (plus m p)
end.
```

Listing 1.3. Coq example: addition of two natural numbers.

`Theorem` is used to describe the theorem. An example of a description with according proof is shown in Listing 1.4. The body of it is limited to the keywords `Proof` and `Qeq`.

```
Theorem my_first_proof : (forall A : Prop, A -> A).
Proof.
    intros A.
    intros proof_of_A.
    exact proof_of_A.
Qed.
```

Listing 1.4. Coq theorem example.

To perform the proof, it is necessary to include in the consideration of the hypothesis and the variables that are used. This is done using the `intros` keyword. For automatic proof, a number of different tactics can be used. This example presents the `exact` tactic. If T is our goal, let p be an expression for U. Exact p applies if T and U are converted into each other.

The choice of proof tactics depends on the complexity of the expression which is to be proved. For example, `reflexivity`, `trivial` and `auto` tactics can be used for trivial proofs. A detailed description of tactics and cases of their use are described in the Coq documentation [6]. A broad set of examples is also provided to demonstrate use [7].

2.3   Verdi

Verdi is a Coq-based framework for verification of distributed systems. It allows to search for errors and check the fault tolerance and correctness of building distributed systems. The user describes the specification and behavior. Verdi then simulates various system failures. The library includes a set of templates, i.e. lock server with proof of safety or liveness. In addition, Verdi provides free access to the implementation of the Raft distributed consensus protocol [14,15].

Nevertheless, the development of Verdi has very little progress now. Such a conclusion can be made on the basis of GitHub statistics [20,21] and the official site Verdi. The latest release was submitted in January 2017. The statistics from Verdi and Verdi Runtime repositories are presented in Tables 1 and 2.

Table 1. Verdi GitHub statistics.

Last commit	January 2017
Active pull requests	0
Merged pull requests	0
Open issues	0
Closed issues	0
Contributors (last 6 months)	1
Commits (last 6 months)	2

Table 2. Verdi Runtime library GitHub statistics.

Last commit	January 2017
Active pull requests	0
Merged pull requests	0
Open issues	0
Closed issues	0
Contributors (last 6 months)	2
Commits (last 6 months)	7

2.4   TLA+

TLA+ operates with modules. Modules are described in files using the `MODULE` keyword [16]. These can be nested, that is, another one can be described inside the body of a module. One can also include modules in each other using the `EXTENDS` keyword.

In TLA+ logical, string type and basic numeric data types are available. However, to access operations on numeric types, it is necessary to connect the corresponding modules.

In addition to single elements, TLA+ also provides more complex types - `tuple` and `structure`. A `tuple` is an ordered set of values and is indicated by double triangular brackets. Several functions are defined in order to work with these: combining tuples, retrieving the first and last elements, determining the length of the tuple, adding one element. The `structure` contains key-value pairs of elements. An example of the structure is shown in Listing 1.5. Here, a structure with two fields a and b defined. Accessing an element is done by key.

```
x == [a |-> 1, b |-> {2, 3}];
x.a = 1;
x[``b"] ==_{2,_3};
```

Listing 1.5. TLA+ structure type

Set is one more type. It is denoted by curly brackets and can be of any degree of nesting. Basic set operations are available, such as filtering, fetching a sample, and applying a function to all its elements. Mathematical operators such as union, intersection, the set difference are also available. Functions are defined over sets. An example of the definition of a function that adds elements to a set is given in Listing 1.6.

```
Sum == [x, y \in S |-> x + y]
```

Listing 1.6. TLA+ function that adds elements of set S

Here, one first indicates the name by which the function is accessed, and then the inputs and function body in square brackets.

If necessary, a detailed and consistent description of any algorithm for the model in TLA+ is provided using PlusCal. It is a programming language that is translated into TLA+.

TLAPS (TLA Proof System) is a system that allows users to prove mathematical statements. To describe the theorem, the keyword THEOREM is used. The schema for describing it is shown in Listing 1.7.

```
THEOREM Name == <theorem text>
    BY e1 ,... , em
    DEF d1 ,... , dn
```

Listing 1.7. TLA+ description of theorem

Here $e1, ..., em$ are assumptions and $d1, ..., dn$ are definitions. Assumptions are described using the ASSUME keyword.

For the proof, the keyword BY is needed. If the proof is obvious and does not require consideration of additional assumptions, then the BY OBVIOUS construct can be used.

Also in TLA+ it is possible to use external packages for proving theorems. The corresponding tools that can be used are described in Table 3.

For each of the tactics presented in the Table 3, it is possible to set a time limit by adding to the name tactics T(time in sec). For proof verification using Isabelle with a time limit of 30 s, BY IsaT(30) must be specified. The time limit here is the time after which TLA+ either allows the statement to be proved or gives the message that this cannot be done within the framework of the assumptions under consideration.

Table 3. TLA+ tactics.

Command	What does it do
BY Zenon	Calling Zenon with default timeout of 10 s
BY Isa	Calling directly Isabelle with default tactic and timeout
BY IsaM("blast")	Calling directly Isabelle with modified tactic
BY SMT	Call baseline SMT solver with default timeout of 5 s
BY CVC3	Call CVC3 backend with default timeout of 5 s

3   Summary

This paper discusses several systems of automatic verification and proofs of theorems. All of them are similar in functionality, but there are some differences in terms of interface and application.

TLA+ has the simplest interface for proving theorems and its syntax is close to the mathematical description method. Here, the user operates mainly with the terms of sequences, sets, and other mathematical concepts. TLA+ also provides a set of external tools that verify proofs. Among them is Isabelle which discussed in this article as well as other tools. In addition to the high-level interface, TLA+ also includes PlusCal as a detailed description of the algorithms. Thus, TLA+ is the most versatile tool with a simple interface.

Isabelle/HOL is a programming language that allows the user to describe mathematical statements and how they are proved step-by-step. Compared to TLA+, it is a lower level tool. Isabelle/HOL has a wider functionality for describing mathematical problems. Moreover, it is used in TLA+ as one way to prove out of the box. Coq is very similar to Isabelle/HOL. It has the same basic differences in functionality from TLA+ as Isabelle. Nevertheless, there exist also a number of differences in logic and predefined axioms. For a more detailed comparison of Coq and Isabelle/HOL, see [11].

Verdi is a tool for describing and verifying distributed systems and is based on Coq. The tool provides a simple interface for building systems but has a narrow scope. Although this framework is suitable for verification of consensus algorithms, it is not actively developed at the moment.

Table 4. Verification tools comparison.

	High-level interface	Low-level interface	Easy-to-use	Active community
Isabelle/HOL	No	Yes	No	Yes
Coq	No	Yes	No	Yes
Verdi	Yes	Inherit from Coq	Yes	No
TLA+	Yes	Yes	Yes	Yes

A short brief of compared tools is presented in Table 4. Note that all these instruments are suitable for distributed systems description.

4 Conclusion

Verdi is suitable for a generalized description of distributed ledger systems. There is an implementation of verification of the Raft consensus algorithm using Verdi. However, at the moment, the development of the framework is significantly slowing down.

Both Coq and Isabelle/HOL are used to verify the algorithms of the largest distributed ledger platforms. They are powerful tools for working with both mathematical statements and the formal approach to distributed systems. TLA+ is the most versatile tool presented. It combines both an easy-to-use high-level TLA+ language and the strict algorithmic language PlusCal.

Acknowledgements. We are grateful to Dr. Martin Reinhardt for the help to prepare the text of this paper.

References

1. Proof General. A generic Emacs interface for proof assistants. https://proofgeneral. github.io/. Accessed 20 Mar 2019
2. Leslie Lamport: The TLA+ Toolbox. https://lamport.azurewebsites.net/tla/ toolbox.html. Accessed 20 Mar 2019
3. Verdi. Formally Verifying Distributed Systems. http://verdi.uwplse.org/. Accessed 20 Mar 2019
4. Chlipala, A.: Certified Programming With Dependent Types: A Pragmatic Introduction to the Coq Proof Assistant. MIT Press, Cambridge (2013)
5. The Coq Proof Assistant. https://coq.inria.fr/. Accessed 20 Mar 2019
6. Coq Tactics Cheatsheet. https://www.cs.cornell.edu/courses/cs3110/2017fa/a5/ coq-tactics-cheatsheet.html. Accessed 20 Mar 2019
7. Coq Tactic Index. https://coq.inria.fr/distrib/current/refman/coq-tacindex.html. Accessed 20 Mar 2019
8. The Isabelle development team. Isabelle. https://isabelle.in.tum.de/. Accessed 20 Mar 2019
9. Paulson, T.N.L.C., Wenzel, M.: A Proof Assistant for Higher-Order Logic (2013). http://isabelle.in.tum.de
10. Isabelle Archive of Formal Proofs. https://www.isa-afp.org/. Accessed 20 Mar 2019
11. Yushkovskiy, A., Tripakis, S.: Comparison of Two Theorem Provers: Isabelle/HOL and Coq (2018)
12. Palmskog, K., Gligoric, M., Peña, L., Moore, B., Rosu, G.: Verification of Casper in the Coq Proof Assistant (2018)
13. PoS related formal methods. https://github.com/palmskog/pos. Accessed 20 Mar 2019
14. Woos, D., Wilcox, J.R., Anton, S., Tatlock, Z., Ernst, M.D., Anderson, T.: Planning for change in a formal verification of the raft consensus protocol. In: Proceedings of the 5th ACM SIGPLAN Conference on Certified Programs and Proofs, pp. 154–165. ACM (2016)

15. Ongaro, D., Ousterhout, J.: In search of an understandable consensus algorithm. In: 2014 USENIX Annual Technical Conference (USENIXATC 2014), pp. 305–319 (2014)
16. TLA+ User Guide. https://learntla.com/tla/. Accessed 20 Mar 2019
17. Pîrlea, G., Sergey, I.: Mechanising blockchain consensus. In: Proceedings of the 7th ACM SIGPLAN International Conference on Certified Programs and Proofs, pp. 78–90. ACM (2018)
18. Charapko, A., Ailijiang, A., Demirbas, M.: Bridging Paxos and Blockchain Consensus (2018)
19. Amani, S., Bégel, M., Bortin, M., Staples, M.: Towards verifying ethereum smart contract bytecode in Isabelle/HOL. In: Proceedings of the 7th ACM SIGPLAN International Conference on Certified Programs and Proofs (CPP 2018), pp. 66–77. ACM, New York (2018). https://doi.org/10.1145/3167084
20. Verdi GitHub repository. https://github.com/uwplse/verdi. Accessed 20 Mar 2019
21. Verdi Runtime library repository. https://github.com/DistributedComponents/verdi-runtime. Accessed 20 Mar 2019
22. Rahli, V., Vukotic, I., Völp, M., Esteves-Verissimo, P.: Velisarios: Byzantine fault-tolerant protocols powered by Coq. In: Ahmed, A. (ed.) ESOP 2018. LNCS, vol. 10801, pp. 619–650. Springer, Cham (2018). https://doi.org/10.1007/978-3-319-89884-1_22
23. Vukotic, I.: An Ecosystem for Verifying Implementations of BFT Protocols (2018)

Analytical Comparison of DLT Platforms Activity

Oleg Iakushkin[✉], Anna Fatkina, Dmitry Selivanov, and Vladimir Korkhov

Saint-Petersburg State University, St. Petersburg, Russia
o.yakushkin@spbu.ru

Abstract. This paper describes a method for analyzing and comparing the activity of various distributed ledger platforms. The presented topics are the criteria for evaluating platforms, the method of their ranking and methods for automated collection information about them. A system that allows automatic assessment and ranking of distributed ledger technologies (DLT) with an open GitHub repository has been developed. Visualization of the collected information by means of Elasticsearch and Kibana is described.

Keywords: Analytics · GitHub · Distributed ledger

1 Introduction

There are a number of studies aimed at comparing technologies of distributed ledger and aggregation information about them [1,3,4]. Nevertheless, the distributed ledger field is dynamic, and the information that was relevant yesterday will not be true tomorrow. In this regard, we want to create a system that allows getting the most relevant, systematically updated information. The collection of information and its visualization are carried out automatically. Automation allows not only to provide up-to-date data but also to scale the system to any number of technologies under consideration.

Also, our aim is to present the collected information in a visual and applicable form. A system that makes it possible to automatically evaluate each technology according to several criteria has been developed. The according criteria were designed to provide versatile and objective information within the framework of data that can be obtained from open-access GitHub repositories.

Figure 1 shows the field of distributed ledger analysis. The financial assets area is covered by exchanges. To analyze private blockchains there is a framework called Blockbench [9]. Consensus protocols are considered and described by KPMG, see [2]. Smart contracts field is analyzed in [5,10].

The system described in this paper covers the area of community activity. For a more detailed study of technologies, we provide a visualized comparison of repositories for a number of parameters. On the basis of the chosen parameters, these technologies are estimated.

© Springer Nature Switzerland AG 2019
S. Misra et al. (Eds.): ICCSA 2019, LNCS 11620, pp. 556–566, 2019.
https://doi.org/10.1007/978-3-030-24296-1_44

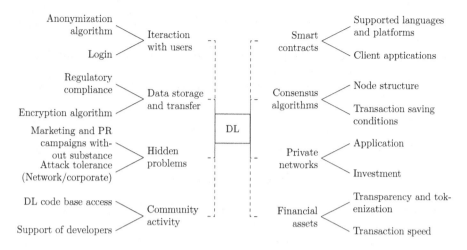

Fig. 1. Distributed ledger analysis. DL—distributed ledger.

2   Criteria and Rating Scale

To evaluate and compare distributed ledger platforms a system of criteria has been developed. According to these criteria, the activity of developing and supporting open source projects is evaluated, based on the corresponding GitHub repositories. The ranking is made on the following grounds:

1. *Developers Activity.* The assessment considers data of 3 months preceding the time of assessment.
   - The average number of code additions per week,
   - The average number of commits per week,
   - Last release date. An inverted scale is used for this item, that is, repositories with older releases are considered less active.
2. *Feedback activity* is shown by the rate of issue closure.
   For each issue i that has at least one comment feedback activity FA reads

$$\mathtt{FA} = \frac{1}{n} \sum_{n} (\mathtt{closed\_at}(i) - \mathtt{created\_at}(i)),$$

   where n is a number of commented issues, $\mathtt{closed\_at}(i)$ and $\mathtt{created\_at}(i)$ are dates of closing and creating of issue i.
   In this criterion, we consider only those issues in which there is at least one comment. Such a condition is imposed in order to avoid counting those issues that developers put for themselves or for those that are closed beyond prescription and non-relevance.
3. *User interest* is made up of
   - Number of forks,

- The number of developing forks. By developing forks, we mean those that do not have the same date of creation and the date of the update. This item shows the interest of users in the development of the product or creating their own based on it.
- Number of issues created in the last 3 months (including open issues),
- The number of stars.

4. *Progress* consists of
    - The growth or decline ratio of the development activity is calculated by the formula

$$D_1 = \frac{\frac{1}{n_3}\sum_{j_3=1}^{n_3} \texttt{commits\_per\_week}(j_3)}{\frac{1}{n_1}\sum_{j_1=1}^{n_1} \texttt{commits\_per\_week}(j_1)},$$

where n_1 and n_3 are numbers of weeks in one and three months, respectively, $\texttt{commits\_per\_week}(j)$ is a number of commits in a week j.
    - Growth or decline ratio of the development team

$$D_2 = \frac{\frac{1}{n_3}\sum_{j_3=1}^{n_3} \texttt{committers\_per\_week}(j_3)}{\frac{1}{n_1}\sum_{j_1=1}^{n_1} \texttt{committers\_per\_week}(j_1)},$$

where n_1 and n_3 are numbers of weeks in one and three months respectively, $\texttt{committers\_per\_week}(j)$ is a number of contributors who made any commit in a week j.

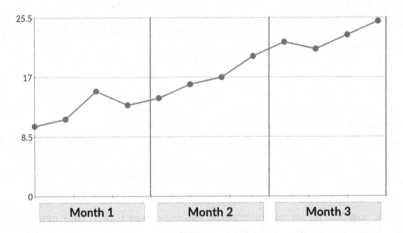

Fig. 2. An Example of growth ratio of activity or number of developers. Avarage for 3 months is 17.25, for the last month is 22.75. Growth ratio is 1.3.

Note that the first two subclauses of criterion 1 are similar. We take both of these points into account because we want to get a measure that does not depend on the work style of developers with GitHub. For example, the presence of a significant number of commits with smaller code changes in the repository will not lead to a high estimate. Also, on the contrary, in the case of active work of developers who rarely make commits, the rating will not be underestimated. To obtain a high or low estimate of developer activity, both of these values have to be considered.

The fourth criterion shows the dynamics of the repository. It compares the data of the last three months with those of the last month. Figure 2 clearly demonstrates how their attitude reflects the growth or decline of the indicator. The value of the coefficient depends on the trend of the corresponding indicator.

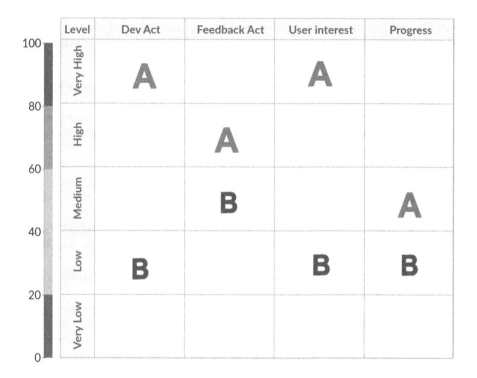

Fig. 3. Scale of ranking criteria values. *A* and *B* are projects to be evaluated.

The rating scale for each of the criteria is presented in Fig. 3. It is dynamic, depending on the values in the database. Thus, the ledger score shows the rank of a specific repository among those considered.

The scale has five levels, from *very low* to *very high*. To determine which level the value of a particular criterion belongs to, it is first scaled 100%, where 100% is the maximum value among all available data and 0% is the minimum. The 100% scale is divided into 5 intervals, each of which includes the upper limit, and the first one also includes 0%.

The ranking takes place automatically via an implemented scoring algorithm. For each considered GitHub repository, a database query is made and the values corresponding to each criterion are calculated. The value of the combined criteria is considered equal to the average of the values of all sub-items of the corresponding criteria. After counting the values of all repositories, they are sorted in ascending order by each of the categories. The rating for the exact repository is set depending on the level to which the scale corresponds to.

3   Automated Information Collection System

We developed an automated information collection system. It obtains public data from repositories of distributed ledger platforms from GitHub using the Github REST API v3. The content and type of the collected data depend on whether the repository is the main project or a satellite project, e.g. for major projects, the following information is collected:

1. Repositories Name, owner, number of stars and subscribers, creation date, last modified date, wiki availability;
2. The branches of the project and their number. Some of the data obtained for each branch are: name, SHA of the last commit, URL of the last commit, whether the branch is protected (protected true/false);
3. Releases, including name, tag, author and date of each release, the total number of project releases;
4. Forked projects, their total. And also for each of the forks: name, owner, creation date, last commit date, number of stars/subscribers, etc .;
5. Closed and open pull requests, their number. Including for each of the pull requests: name, author, date of creation, date of last change, number of requested reviewers, current status;
6. Issues, their number. For each of the issues: name, author, creation date, last modified date, current status, a number of comments;
7. Commit activity. Represents data on the number of commits per day, for all days in the last year;
8. The code frequency of the project. It represents the data of the number of additions and deletions per week, for all weeks over the last year.
9. Contributors, their number, number of contributions for each contributor;
10. The frequency of changes in the project for the top 100 contributors. It represents the data of the number of additions and deletions per week for each of the contributors included in the top 100 by the number of commits for all weeks in the last year;
11. Commits, total in all branches, for a certain period of time (by default for the last 90 days). Including for each of the commits: sha, description, author, date of creation, branch of development, sha of parent commit, number of comments;
12. Commits in the master branch, for all the time. Individual information about each commit is the same as described above;
13. The status of CI builds for all commits for a certain period (default for the last 90 days). For each build: status (failed/successful/pending), title, author, creation date, last modified date.

For satellite projects, the following items are collected:

- Information about commit activity for the last year;
- The number of contributors, as well as the number of contributors for each of them;
- Information about the frequency of changes of the project (code frequency), i.e. the number of additions and deletions per week, for each week for the last year;
- The number of forks, as well as the number of stars/subscribers for each of the forks.

Because information collection about repositories of distributed ledger technologies from the GitHub platform is limited to the maximum allowable number of requests to the GitHub REST API v3 (by default, 60 requests per hour), a proxy server system is used. Therefore, receiving data about repositories occurs in multi-threaded mode. When one of the threads exhausts the allowable amount of requests, it starts using a new proxy server.

In addition, the proxy server is individual for each stream and, according to the GitHub API v3 documentation, performs no more than 60 requests per hour [6]. The software implementation of this uses *request* and *multithreading* libraries. The first of them allows you to create session objects that can use proxy server settings. URL requests are then made through these sessions. The second library is used to implement the multithreading approach.

4   Visualization

4.1   Kibana Visualize and Dashboard

For more convenient monitoring of the project activity, the collected data is arranged in charts. Some charts are presented in Fig. 4

Graphs are built using the Kibana [7] data visualization tool (Visualize & Dashboard). They show values for all downloaded data at the time of viewing. In other words, the data in the graphs are updated automatically.

For various repositories, graphs of compared values are presented, such as:

- The number of contributors and stars in the repository,
- Number of commits per year
- The number of open issues
- Number of forks and releases,
- The dynamics of the creation of pull requests (the total number and the number of those which were merged into the master branch)
- Dynamics of adding commits and closing issues,
- Dynamics of additions and deletions of lines of code.

The Kibana Dashboard provides interactive graphics. By clicking on the value of the repository or on its name in the legend of charts, the corresponding data

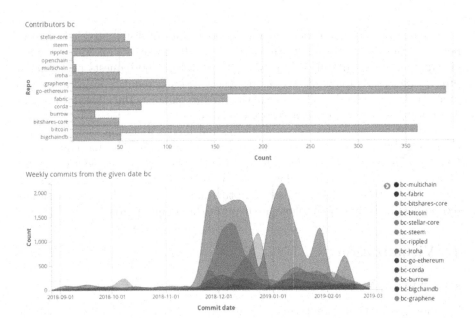

Fig. 4. Charts of comparison repositories. The top chart shows the total number of contributors. The bottom chart shows a weekly commit statistics. Tag cloud shows all repositories presented in database.

on all graphs will be shown exclusively. We have added a tag cloud with the names of all repositories for more convenient filtering.

The ability to filter the names of repositories of platforms of distributed ledgers in the tag cloud by the consensus algorithm has been added. Furthermore, one more cloud of names of consensus algorithms and an additional table of correspondences of algorithms and distributed ledger platforms has been added.

4.2   Kibana Graph

The Kibana Graph tool provides the opportunity to visualize dependencies between data in the elasticsearch database [8]. Unlike Kibana Visualization charts graphs cannot be loaded dynamically. Therefore, when updating the database, one needs to update the graph manually. Nevertheless, in this way it is possible to present the information about dependencies between distributed ledger platforms in a simple and understandable form. Are some examples of the graph.

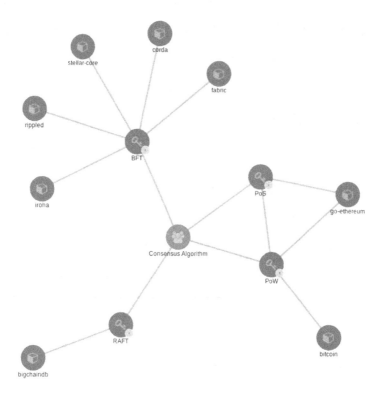

Fig. 5. Kibana Graph: consensus protocols and platforms which use them.

Figure 5 shows a graph with relations between consensus algorithms and the distributed ledger that are in use. In this figure, only four protocols are presented as an example for readability.

Figure 6 shows the dependencies between satellite repositories and their owners. Note that both, organization and user, can be an owner. If the repository is a fork of another one presented in the database, then the owner is referred to a specific user and not to an organization. In Fig. 6, such a relation is shown between the **tangaroa** repository and some users. Some of them made a fork of **juno** project as well.

In Fig. 7 the graph of top contributors for hyperledger satellite repositories is presented. Here, only those contributors have indicated the whose number of commits of the last 3 months in the corresponding repository exceeds 50.

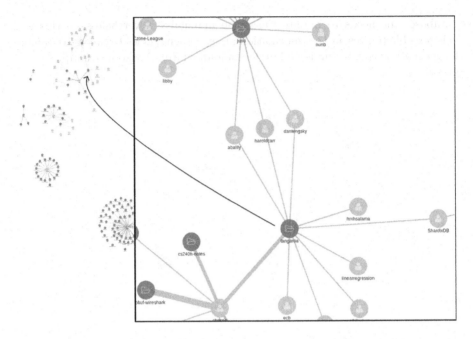

Fig. 6. Kibana Graph: satellite repositories and their owners.

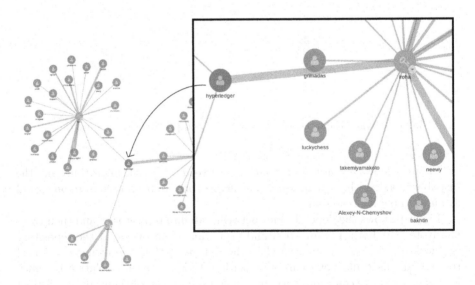

Fig. 7. Kibana Graph: top contributors of Hyperledger satellites.

5   Summary and Future Work

The system presented in this paper allows us to collect, update, visualize data on various distributed ledger technologies automatically, based on their open GitHub repositories. We also provide the opportunity to automatically evaluate and rank technologies according to the developed criteria. These criteria allow considering the activity of technology development, as well as the interaction of developers with users, interest in this technology and the dynamics of product development. Ledger evaluation occurs automatically. Note that this system can be generalized to the repositories of any subject.

Nevertheless, the developed system has a number of disadvantages. It is possible to evaluate only those repositories that are publicly available on GitHub. In addition, the construction of graphs is not automated and in the current implementation, it requires manual updating when updating the database.

When plotting, Kibana needs to run the database queries again. On the one hand, this allows seeing the actual data at any moment. However, on the other hand, it leads to a decrease in performance when the database grows. In the future, we plan to abandon Kibana Graph in favor of Neo4j, which has free community license or free-to-use GraphDB.

6   Conclusion

The presented system allows us to visually get up to date information on the development of projects based on their GitHub repositories, as well as to rank and evaluate them. The paper proposes criteria for evaluating repositories, developed on the basis of open data obtained using the GitHub API. It also describes the possibilities of visualization of this data. Most of the system works in automatic mode, which allows the system to scale to a much larger number of projects to be considered.

Acknowledgements. We are grateful to Dr. Martin Reinhardt for the help to prepare the text of this paper.

References

1. Salimitari, M., Chatterjee, M.: An overview of blockchain and consensus protocols for IoT networks. arXiv preprint arXiv:1809.05613 (2018)
2. Seibold, S., & Samman, G.: Consensus: immutable agreement for the internet of value. https://assets.kpmg.com/content/dam/kpmg/pdf/2016/06/kpmgblockchain-consensus-mechanism.pdf. Accessed 20 Mar 2019
3. Valenta, M., Sandner, P.: Comparison of ethereum, hyperledger fabric and corda. In: FSBC Working Paper, June 2017. Frankfurt School Blockchain Center (2017)
4. Macdonald, M., Liu-Thorrold, L., Julien, R.: The blockchain: a comparison of platforms and their uses beyond bitcoin. Working Paper, pp. 1–18 (2017)
5. Xu, X., et al.: A taxonomy of blockchain-based systems for architecture design. In: 2017 IEEE International Conference on Software Architecture (ICSA), pp. 243–252. IEEE (2017)

6. GitHub Rest API v3, Rate limiting. https://developer.github.com/v3/. Accessed 20 Mar 2019
7. Elastic. Kibana. https://www.elastic.co/products/kibana. Accessed 20 Mar 2019
8. Elastic. ElasticSearch. https://www.elastic.co/products/elasticsearch. Accessed 20 Mar 2019
9. Dinh, T.T.A., Wang, J., Chen, G., Liu, R., Ooi, B.C., Tan, K.L.: Blockbench: a framework for analyzing private blockchains. In: Proceedings of the 2017 ACM International Conference on Management of Data, pp. 1085–1100. ACM (2017)
10. Dinh, T.T.A., Liu, R., Zhang, M., Chen, G., Ooi, B.C., Wang, J.: Untangling blockchain: a data processing view of blockchain systems. IEEE Trans. Knowl. Data Eng. **30**(7), 1366–1385 (2018)

Electronic Expertise Using Distributed Ledger Technology

Oleg Iakushkin[✉], Alexey Pismerov, Vladislav Popov, Anastasia Berlina, and Vladimir Korkhov

Saint-Petersburg University,
7/9 Universitetskaya nab., St. Petersburg 199034, Russia
o.yakushkin@spbu.ru

Abstract. This paper examines how to implement electronic expertise based on the Corda platform. The paper aims to implement such a system, taking as an example the organization of the online contest. A draft solution is created for this task, which demonstrates the necessary tools to solve it and key capabilities that will be required from the platform for the implementation of the electronic expertise system. It justifies the choice of the Corda platform and describes the solution with its use. The main advantages and disadvantages of this approach to the implementation of electronic expertise when using Blockchain are highlighted.

Keywords: Distributed ledger · Corda · Expertise · Grading system

1 Introduction

Systems using peer review have application in many areas of activity, but so far a significant part of them is somehow not computerized and difficult to control. The reasons for this are both attempts at external interference in the rating process (hacker attacks [4], the substitution of evaluated works) and the presence of compromised system participants (for example, the opinion of one or more members of the expert commission cannot be considered independent). There is a growing need for an electronic system to neutralize these potentially dangerous factors. The project, which is the object of this research study, aims to introduce transparency and manageability into the examination process by using technologies based on distributed registries, such as Blockchain.

A blockchain is essentially a distributed record base or publicly accessible transaction ledger [3]. Each transaction in the ledger is confirmed by the consensus [5] of most of the participants in the system, and besides the added information cannot be deleted. The blockchain contains a defined and confirmed record for each transaction ever completed. The essence of the blockchain is that it creates a system of distributed consensus in the digital world. By creating an irrefutable ledger record, it allows participating actors to know for sure that some digital event has occurred, thereby establishing a reliable communication and interaction system.

© Springer Nature Switzerland AG 2019
S. Misra et al. (Eds.): ICCSA 2019, LNCS 11620, pp. 567–576, 2019.
https://doi.org/10.1007/978-3-030-24296-1_45

After having studied the requirements put forward for the peer review system and the possibilities offered by the blockchain, it can be assumed that blockchain or distributed ledger technologies may serve as a suitable basis for the technological stack for development of an electronic examination system.

2 Motivation

We are presented with the challenge of implementing an electronic examination system. As an example of the usage of this system, it is considered the checking of contest tasks performed by students of educational institutions. In this way, it must have interfaces for downloading tasks, solving them, evaluating and viewing results. The assessment will be carried out by averaging the marks obtained from three unrelated auditors. Further, it is necessary to have an integrated authentication and authorization service to ensure secure access to the system and regulate the rights of various users. Among other things, the purpose of the work is to confirm the suitability of applying Blockchain to the provided task as well as uncover the advantages of this technology.

3 Related Work

As of now, expertise systems are attracting considerable interest and thus there are several studies covering different approaches to creating such. Each one of them is implementing distributed ledger technology to achieve its goals. Blockchain [2] is widely used in the design of secure and distributed education systems, as shown in [6] and [7]. Their core principles are akin to ones our system follows: independent and reliable participants of the network safely exchange data, albeit [7] relies more on conventional data-storing such as cloud database instead of distributing portions of data to each party. The similar concept is employed in [8], where Blockchain is used for conducting and evaluating tests in a peer-to-peer manner and creating a self-sustained education ecosystem. Some of the works pay great attention to encrypting the transactions and ensuring the security of the overall communication process.

One of the differences of this work is that here the Corda framework [1] is used to manage low-level Blockchain interactions as opposed to some papers' approach where the basic network structures are implemented manually, which, in turn, may lead to unexpected errors. And, in contrast to more specific software in the field, this system is meant to function as a template to be configured for solving varied tasks.

4 Architecture

The system for conducting online contests consists of three types of participants. The first one forms the tasks that must be performed by the participants of the second type. Furthermore, a competent member of the system will check the solution and rate it. To ensure the impartiality of the assessment, several experts must evaluate the work. The result is calculated as the arithmetic average of all grades. The differentiation of tasks for participants generates the separation of their access rights to different parts of the system. To divide the participants into groups, it is necessary to implement registration, with the further allocation of rights for users from the administrator, who can be the first registered member of the system. It can be seen that the first registered participant has the role of the administrator, but maintaining its existence is unfeasible after the task has been loaded and the roles of the other users are defined. The superuser in the system constitutes its vulnerable part since anyone having access to the administrator account will be able to influence other participants by altering their rights or deleting them from the system. In this way, it is necessary to implement an opportunity to get rid of the user with such broad rights. Each contest naturally has its own deadline. Therefore, one of the necessary parts of the project should be the implementation of time periods during which users will have an opportunity to solve tasks. The same restrictions can be set for work verification. Further, it must be provided an ability to view the results of the contest after its completion. Figures 1, 2, 3, 4, 5, 6 and 7 schematically show the organization of the electronic review system.

4.1 First Block

First, we consider Fig. 1, which shows the scheme of interaction between the administrator and users with the first node of the system.

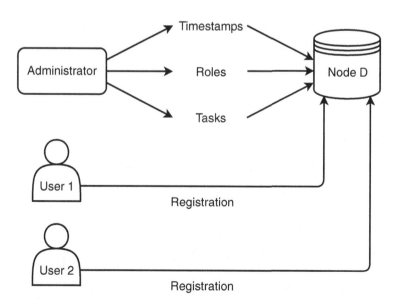

Fig. 1. Administrator and user interaction with the authentication node.

The first block is a node of the blockchain platform for the administrator and users who can register in the system. At this step user interaction with the site is limited. The administrator has a wider range of features; he is given the opportunity to give each registered user the necessary rights. In addition, the administrator is responsible for uploading tasks and determining the time intervals during which they will be available for downloading and performing, and their solutions will be available for checking. First, we consider Fig. 1, which shows the scheme of interaction between the administrator and users with the first node of the system.

4.2 Second Block

In the second block interaction of the contest participant with the task is provided. To confirm the access rights to the assignments, it is necessary to pass authentication, after which participants are given an opportunity to download tasks, write a solution and send it for verification. Only users defined as participants of the contest have access to this part of the system.

Fig. 2. User interaction with the solution node.

4.3 Third Block

The third blocks' structure is similar to the second, but they possess different functions. The third block is intended for users who, upon authentication, have rights to verify the solutions of other participants of the contest. To perform the functions for which the inspectors are registered, they are provided with an interface that allows loading the solution of tasks along with their conditions.

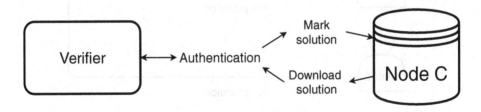

Fig. 3. User interaction with the marking node.

After evaluating the work, the reviewer has an ability to rate it on a 100 point scale and send it further along with the blockchain.

4.4   Fourth Block

The final block of the system is designed to derive the results, which, as mentioned above, are obtained by averaging the estimates received from different inspectors. Viewing of the results is available only to authorized users. At the moment, it remains unclear how nodes interact with each other and what functions they should perform. Further, we consider the pairwise interaction of nodes and what tasks they solve.

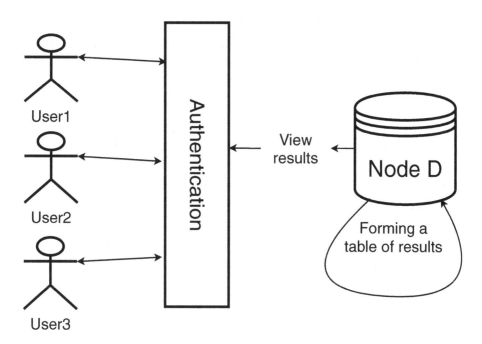

Fig. 4. User interaction with the end result node.

4.5   Task Transfer

Figure 5 shows the administration node and the node for users to interact with. In this case, each participant must have copies of the task loaded by the administrator and solutions should be provided in a predetermined time window. To solve this problem, the node A, up to a certain point, gives only the headers of the tasks without their contents. To control the second time limit, a restriction is implemented on sending a solution to the node B and receiving it at the node C. Also node B provides the ability to download the task to your computer, fill in the fields with the solution and send it to the verifier.

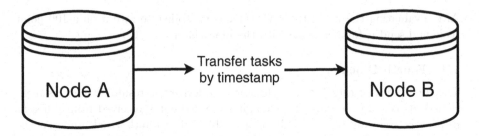

Fig. 5. Interaction between task upload node and solution node.

4.6   Solved Task Distribution

After the competitor has written the solution of the assignment and sent it
further along the chain, it is received at the nodes of the inspectors. These nodes
are used for checking the time window, grading, downloading the task itself and
its solutions for checking and sending the score.

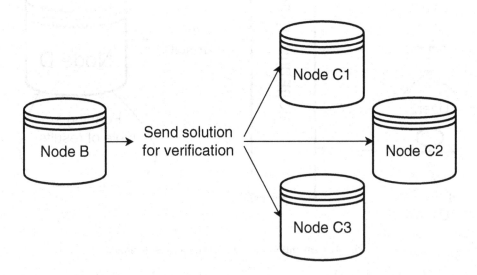

Fig. 6. Interaction between solution node and marking nodes.

4.7   Aggregation of Marks

Afterward, the marks are collected at the node D, and when all the experts
submit the scores for the provided solution, the result is aggregated and displayed in the table. To access all the functions provided by the nodes, the user
must authenticate at each node. Node A functions as the authentication server,
handling all the requests for login and checking user rights and identities.

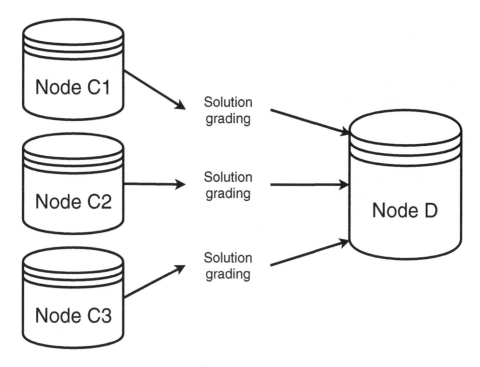

Fig. 7. Interaction between marking nodes and the end result node.

5   Implementation

To accomplish this task, we apply the technology related to the blockchain and in many aspects identical with it - the distributed ledger. As in the blockchain, the distributed ledger contains entries that are not stored or confirmed by a single central site. But in fact, the one who organizes the ledger can manage the structure of the distributed network, its purpose and the form of the transmitted data. Thus, the reliability and security that the blockchain provides are combined with flexibility and the ability to relatively fine-tune the system.

In relation to this task, the use of distributed registries allows increasing the number of users without a threat of system failure by adding new nodes, as well as altering the network structure as the task conditions change. The distribution also means high reliability of the system as a whole - if one of the nodes fails, all other users will be able to continue their activities. This project was implemented using the Corda framework, which provides the most extensive possibilities for working with distributed registries. Its another advantage is the possibility of programming both in Java and in Kotlin [9]. Kotlin was chosen for this work because of the better readability of the code and the large base of programs and examples using Corda.

5.1   Project Structure

The system consists of two layers - a network of nodes, which store and exchange information with each other; and web interfaces that provide user interaction with the corresponding nodes.

To implement the network structure, the following types of nodes are required:

- The notary who oversees transactions
- Node for uploading tasks to the vault
- Node for storing tasks and sending solutions
- Node for grading solutions
- Node for storing results
- Authentication node controlling access rights to other nodes.

The Corda platform operates on several key concepts:

- Flows are sequences of steps used by the node to update the status of the ledger. They determine the behavior of nodes when they receive or send a transaction that changes data on the node. For the download node, there exists only the transaction sending flow, for the view node there is only the flow that accepts the transaction. The remaining nodes can either accept transactions from the previous one in the chain or update the data on the next one.
- Data is presented in the form of states - immutable objects corresponding to facts that are known to one or several nodes. Their immutability is an important feature of the system. States describing the available data consist of: UploadState - contains the hash of the attachment file, SendState - in addition to the hash, contains the name of the student who sends task and its solution, MarkState - the state that stores the name of the completed task, its hash and its mark.
- Also, contracts are used to verify the correctness of transactions - they are classes that contain transaction verification functions.

Web interfaces are implemented for interacting with all nodes except the notary since its existence must remain hidden to users. Each interface provides a user login form to prevent illegal actions against the system. To distribute the application to individual machines, nodes and the corresponding interfaces were assembled into portable executable files using Portable Java. Every application has the form of a built-in browser displaying the web interface, which was implemented using the Electron [10] service.

6   Benchmark

When the system is running, there are additional costs for connecting to the nodes, transferring messages and files from the user's computer to the node as well as between nodes, and the interaction of the nodes among themselves requires the intervention of a notary who checks every transaction and makes entries in the ledger. In order to find out how much these architectural features of the interaction of the nodes between themselves and the user influence the execution time of the typical 6 types of operations, a speed test of the pipeline constructed from nodes connected in the chain was carried out. A pipeline is a sequence of nodes where a file of a certain size is first loaded, and then the file is transferred along the chain to the last node. For testing, we used files of various sizes from two hundred bytes to ten megabytes ([200 bytes, 128 KB, 512 KB, 1–10 MB]). A total of 32 nodes was used, the time was measured using 2-step increments in node count.

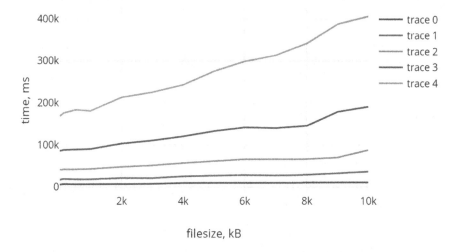

Fig. 8. Chart showing relation of the program run time to the transmitted file size.

In Fig. 8 the steady increase in time delay can be seen, and it is especially noticeable when there are at least eight nodes in the network. Other conclusions that can be made from the graph are that there is a linear relation between running time and node count for example, it takes twice the time for system with 32 nodes to run as opposed to the one with 16 nodes, as well as better than linear relation between running time and filesize it takes about twice the time to transmit 10 MB file through the chain compared to transmission of the 1 MB file. Tests show that the costs of distributed registries for actions as initiating a connection, checking transactions and writing to the ledger are initially large, but the more messages we send, the lower the percentage of work time is spent on expenses caused by the distributed ledger architecture. Even with a relatively large message size, we still experience a slowdown due to the use of distributed registries. Thus, given the fact that in a specific project, nodes can perform secondary functions that will introduce additional delays, it can be concluded that optimizing the system based on distributed registries is one of the key areas of work in developing such a system. The key to optimization can be reducing the number of connections to various nodes initiated by the user, getting rid of redundant checks by contracts and minimizing the number of participants in the transaction, therefore avoiding long waiting for signatures by other participants.

7 Conclusion

The Corda platform allows implementing an electronic expertise system which solves the task at hand and satisfies the specified requirements - the ability to easily change the network structure, to increase the number of users without system failure, and work with node failures. Among the advantages of the used technology is the ability to tune the type of the data received at each node - each participant knows only the information that he must have in order to make a decision. These characteristics were achieved because of the usage of distributed ledger technology, and although it has disadvantages such as low data processing speed and it requires a large amount of memory to store local information, the opportunities provided by it greatly simplify the designing of complex systems.

References

1. Brown, C., Grigg, H.: Corda: an introduction (2016). http://r3cev.com/s/corda-introductory-whitepaper-final.pdf
2. Yli-Huumo, J., Ko, D., Choi, S., Park, S., Smolander, K.: Where is current research on blockchain technology?—A systematic review. PLoS ONE **11**(10), e0163477 (2016). https://doi.org/10.1371/journal.pone.0163477
3. Mike, H.: Corda: A distributed ledger (2016). https://block.academy/researches/corda-technical-whitepaper.pdf
4. Das, D.: Hacking into the Indian Education System. https://deedy.quora.com/Hacking-into-the-Indian-Education-System
5. Watanabe, H., Fujimura, S., Nakadaira, A., Miyazaki, Y., Akutsu, A., Kishigami, J.J.: Blockchain contract: a complete consensus using blockchain. In: 2015 IEEE 4th Global Conference on Consumer Electronics (GCCE), pp. 577–578 (2015). https://doi.org/10.1109/GCCE.2015.7398721
6. Turkanovic, M., Holbl, M., Kosic, K., Hericko, M., Kamisalic, A.: EduCTX: a blockchain-based higher education credit platform. IEEE Access Multidiscip. Open Access J. **6**, 5112–5127 (2018). https://doi.org/10.1109/ACCESS.2018.2789929
7. Islama, I., Md. Kaderb, F., Shina, S.Y.: BSSSQS: a blockchain based smart and secured scheme for question sharing in the smart education system. Preprint submitted to Journal of Parallel and Distributed Computing arXiv:1812.03917v1 (2018)
8. Acharya, R., Binu, S.: Blockchain based examination system for effective evaluation and maintenance of examination records. Int. J. Eng. Technol. **7**(2.6), 269–274 (2018). https://doi.org/10.14419/ijet.v7i2.6.10781
9. "kotlin-stdlib". kotlinlang.org. JetBrains. https://github.com/JetBrains/kotlin/releases/latest
10. "From native to JavaScript in Electron — Electron Blog". electronjs.org. https://github.com/electron/electron/releases/latest

Secret Voting: Knowledge vs Trust

Ildar M. Khamitov[1](✉) ⓘ, Victor Dostov[2] ⓘ, and Pavel Shoust[2] ⓘ

[1] Saint-Petersburg State University,
7-9 Universitetskaya Emb., St Petersburg 199034, Russia
CryptoVoter@gmail.com
[2] Russian Electronic Money and Remittance Association,
5/2 Orlikov per, Moscow 107078, Russia
{dostov,shoust}@npaed.ru

Abstract. In this paper we discuss on the general level the issue of trust the voters put in the secret voting system used in political elections. We promote the point of view that the voters' recognition and acceptance of a particular voting system should be based not on trust, but on knowledge—on the knowledge of what is really happening during the voting, not presumed. The starting point of knowledge is mistrust. We formulate a postulate of mistrust (of an election commission) and keeping it in mind look closely at several deployed voting systems including the Estonian one. We find all of them unacceptable. Then we formulate three criteria for an Internet voting system to be acceptable to the voters (civil society). These are (1) openness, (2) acceptance of the system by an uncertain and broad set of qualified examiners and (3) a verifiable access of unsophisticated voters to the voter's software approved by the aforementioned set of examiners. Finally, we explain only the modest role of the official (government) certification of the voting system in its recognition by the voters (civil society).

Keywords: Secret voting · Internet voting · Mistrust ·
Estonian Internet voting system · Civil society

1 Introduction

When discussing the practical use of a secret voting system in political elections, the issue of trust the voters put in the system under discussion inevitably arises. The issue of trust is particularly acute with regard to technically equipped voting systems, in particular Internet voting systems (which we are most interested in). Usually it is not very clear why the voting system inspires trust in the electorate, what extent this trust should reach to make the voting system acceptable, and so on. And these are not idle questions, because, although it may not be so yet, in the end it is the civil society that has to accept or reject a particular voting system. In this article, we advocate the following view: Russian citizens' recognition and acceptance of a particular voting system should be based not on trust, but on knowledge—on the knowledge of what is really happening during the voting, not presumed. Part of that knowledge is mistrust. In this case, the word "mistrust" doesn't mean having vague doubts, but a certain approach to the analysis/development of the voting system, as well as knowledge on

© Springer Nature Switzerland AG 2019
S. Misra et al. (Eds.): ICCSA 2019, LNCS 11620, pp. 577–586, 2019.
https://doi.org/10.1007/978-3-030-24296-1_46

the basis of which a bad voting system is rejected. The role of trust (whose trust, trust in what and to whom) we will discuss in one of the following sections.

There has been extensive literature on electronic voting. For example, Gritzalis formulated the basic principles and requirements towards secure e-voting [1]. Cloud computing has been proposed in this domain as well [2]. The importance of transparency and audit were underlined in the work by Samra, Hafez, Assassa and Mursi [3]. However, methodological assumptions about the trust issues are still beyond the academic purview.

We will begin by clarifying an approach based on mistrust that forces us to assume the worst. We will formulate the worst in the form of a postulate.

2   The Basic Postulate of Mistrust

The concept of trust is a matter of concern in election systems since the time of Ancient Greeks [4]. Here we look at general trust issues and start with formulating the postulate of mistrust.

Postulate of Mistrust
The main goal of the election commission is to solve the following two tasks:

1. *the election commission shall imperceptibly and unprovably falsify the results of voting,*
2. *the election commission shall imperceptibly and unprovably violate the secrecy of each voter's choice.*

Certainly, there are many villains who pursue the same goal, but the election commission (hereinafter EC) is obviously in the favorable position in terms of achieving this goal, as it is less limited in actions than other villains, as it has access to and influence on data in the process of preparation and voting.

It should be noted that in the context of this essay, the EC is composed not only of those who are formally members of the commission's staff, but also of those who can influence the EC during the preparation, voting and result compilation processes, without being its employees. For example, voting system developers, programmers, contractors, equipment suppliers, system administrators of the EC servers, etc. are among the suspects.

Not all threats to the integrity of the vote are formulated in this postulate, but this is enough for our purposes. We will note only that the secrecy of voting (secrecy of voter's choice) means the right of the voter to keep his/her vote in secret from all and availability of technical means to exercise this right.

Thus, we adhere to a paranoid approach to the analysis of various voting systems.

3   Conventional System of Secret Voting

The secret voting system that uses tangible (usually paper) impersonal ballots, which are collected in ballot boxes at polling stations, we will call a conventional system of secret voting.

The ways to falsify the voting results of the conventional secret voting are too diverse to be discussed here. We will only mention the modern version of falsification by means of abusing new absentee ballots, introduced in 2018 and called "Voting at the place of stay" or "Mobile voter" [5].

The idea is that the EC's accomplice first registers via the Internet as a voter at several polling stations (with a little help from the malicious EC according to our "postulate of mistrust"). At the day of voting this accomplice can cast more than one vote visiting all the polling stations with which he or she has registered.

The protocol of the conventional secret voting was designed to meet the afore-mentioned requirement of the secrecy of voter's choice. However, this protocol is vulnerable. Taking into account a significant progress in printing and other technologies, the conventional voting system should be considered as the open (non-secret) one for the EC. Any operations with tangible objects during personal voting at the polling station makes it impossible to preserve the secrecy of the voter's choice. Firstly, a paper (more generally tangible) ballot is a very complex physical object. The voter cannot check whether the ballot he received is impersonal and does not carry individualizing marks in the form of microtext, micro-punctures, small distortions of the security marks and ornaments, certain displacements of the design elements, invisible chemical marks, RFIDs, etc. Secondly, the EC can install a lot of hidden video cameras at the polling station to reliably record each and every movement of the voter from all view angles.

Conventional voting systems have another significant fault in ensuring the secrecy of choice, associated exclusively with their organizational form. After the end of voting time the votes cast are counted separately at each polling station. In Russia, around 750 people vote at each polling station on average. If all the voters voted unanimously at a given polling station, then, for obvious reasons, there is no secrecy of choice at this polling station. In case of the Internet voting, the "Internet polling station" includes millions of voters—ideally all 110 million Russian voters. A unanimous vote at such a large "polling station" is much less likely than at a small physical one.

4   Voting Using "Black Boxes"

If technical devices (scanners) are used to process and count the tangible (paper) ballots cast at polling stations, we will call such a system a conventional automated system of secret voting. In the terminology of the Central Election Commission of the Russian Federation (CECRF) automated voting is implemented through the Ballot Processing Devices (BPD) [5] with optical scanners. After filling out a paper ballot, the voter inserts it into the BPD's scanner, which draws the ballot into the inside and stores it there.

If voters vote without tangible ballots by pressing buttons or touching touch screens of terminals installed at polling stations, we will call such a system a conventional electronic system of secret voting. Again, in the terminology of the CECRF electronic voting is implemented through the Electronic Voting Devices (EVD). The EVD includes a touch screen, so that the voter makes his choice by touching virtual buttons. In addition to the image on the screen, the voter's choice is printed on a control paper tape and shown to the voter through a small window.

From the point of view of civil society both BPDs and EVDs are "black boxes", that is, devices, which construction and operation algorithm are unknown. The "black box" receives the real choice of the voters as input, and outputs some "result". The way this "result" relates to the choice of voters is unknown to the civil society, but not because its representatives are lazy to examine the construction and software of the "black boxes". Of course, one can study the technical documentation of the "black box", and a small group of experts (certification body) can dig into a couple of "black boxes". What will that prove? On the one hand, there is a need to trust a small group of experts exposed to harmful influences, which is unacceptable in our paranoid approach. On the other hand, the voter will never be able to establish what relation this "black box" at this polling station has to the publicly available technical documentation of the "black box", as well as to those "black boxes" that were presented to the experts. Unfortunately, the copy of a "black box" cannot be digitally signed! Due to the inherent closeness of the "black boxes", voting with their help provides the EC with ample opportunities for falsifying the results of such voting.

BPDs add new methods of fraud in the conventional voting. The voter cannot know what the BPD does with the ballot. A voter sees how the BPD is drawing the ballot into the inside so that the ballot disappears from the sight for some time. So the voter cannot understand what then falls into the translucent receiving ballot box. For example, if the voter's ballot contains a "wrong" choice, the BPD may place it in its secret compartment and drop a pre-prepared ballot with the "right" choice into the receiving ballot box. In this way, the BPD can replace several hundred ballots. Another way of the falsification lies in the fact that the BPD can make the "unwanted" ballot invalid by marking an extra field in the ballot in the process of drawing it into the inside.

Falsification of voting results with the help of the EVDs does not have borders at all. One should not have illusions about the control tape, which is supposedly printed by the EVD. At the end of the voting, a tape bearing the falsified results will be extracted from the EVD, while during the voting, a fragment of a completely different piece of tape with a short list of all options could be shown to the voter via the EVD's window.

In the conventional electronic system of secret voting, when voters vote with the help of EVDs, there is no secrecy of choice at all. In this case, the EC has to exert even less effort than in the case of the conventional voting system to get the name, fingerprints, photograph and the choice of the voter as soon as he or she finishes the voting procedure. In the case of the conventional automated system of secret voting, where voters insert ballots into the BPD's scanner, the only thing the EC will not be able to easily obtain are the voters' fingerprints.

Despite the obvious defectiveness of conventional automated and conventional electronic voting, politicians and officials, as well as some human rights activists, support the deployment of these systems and they are trying to form a positive image of the "black boxes". Often this is done under the slogan of increasing transparency (!?) of the voting process, as well as under the guise of caring for the employees of the EC.

If we reject with indignation the understandable desire to control the voting results, it is difficult to rationally explain why a part of civil society supports the introduction of "black boxes" into the practice of voting. Apparently, the magic words "computerization", "information technology", "high-tech", "innovation" outweigh the arguments of reason. Moreover, many people consider computers and other hardware as independent and impartial creatures who can be entrusted with the sensitive things like an objective vote count. Of course, hardware is devoid of passions, but it is also devoid of mind and conscience so that it thoughtlessly executes the program installed in it. Therefore, the "black box" will falsify the results of the vote, with no remorse, if it is designed and programmed to do so.

5 Estonian Internet Voting System

Early voting via the Internet is allowed in Estonia[1]. The Estonian Internet voting system uses cryptography to imitate the voting by the snail mail with the help of two envelopes.

Leaving the technical and bureaucratic details aside, one of the procedures for the two-envelopes voting goes as follows. The voter receives, either in person, by mail or any other way, the following:

1. paper ballot,
2. impersonal (blank) and non-transparent envelope,
3. personalized (that is, bearing identifying data of the voter) envelope addressed to the EC.

At the appropriate time, the voter fills in the ballot and seals it in the first, impersonal, envelope. Then the voter seals the sealed impersonal envelope in the second, personalized envelope and sends this nested letter to the destination (to the EC). At the post office the voter can further identify himself/herself by presenting his/her passport. It is assumed that the EC has two employees (or departments): Verifier and Teller (Ballot Box Keeper). The nested letter from the voter first gets to the Verifier, which according to the information specified on the outer envelope, checks that the sender is on the list of voters, that is, has the right to vote, and notes the fact of voting in this list. Then the Verifier extracts the impersonal envelope from the outer envelope and passes it to the Teller. The Teller extracts the ballot from the impersonal envelope and unorderly drops it into the ballot box.

The Verifier knows who took part in the vote but doesn't know the voter's choice. The Teller doesn't know who took part in the vote but knows the voter's choice. Communication between the Verifier and the Teller is prohibited. Therefore, the link between the voter's identification data and his or her vote in the current voting is severed.

It is easy to transform this scheme from the mail voting to the Internet voting. The asymmetric encryption with the Teller's public key is used as an impersonal envelope, the voter's digital signature and asymmetric encryption with the Verifier's public key are used as a personalized envelope.

---

[1] The Internet voting has been used in Estonia nine times since 2005. For example, during parliamentary elections in 2007, 2011 and 2015 share of voters who voted over the Internet was 5.5%, 24.3% and 30.5% [6].

However, voting by mail and its Internet counterpart are as bad as possible. These systems are much worse than the conventional voting system. The voter cannot know and cannot check whether the EC follows the declared procedure of processing the nested letter sent by the voter. That's why according to our basic postulate of mistrust, the Verifier and the Teller can (should) collude and find out the choice of the voter. In addition, the joint Verifier-Teller may replace the voter's ballot with any other ballot at their discretion. Moreover, this can be done by the Verifier alone. Thus, in the Estonian Internet voting system, the EC can imperceptibly and unprovable falsify the results of voting, as well as violate the secrecy of each voter's choice.

6 Requirement of Openness

The example of Estonia shows that a simple system of secret Internet voting can be absolutely unacceptable to civil society. At the same time correct system of the secret Internet voting will be technically complex, since it, for example, inevitably has to make abundant use of sophisticated cryptography. For this reason, it seems that civil society will not be able to come to a consensus on any complex voting system, since it does not consist only of doctors of mathematics, cryptography, electronics and IT sciences who understand the issue. Moreover, such professionals form a smaller part of the civil society. Nevertheless, the situation is not hopeless.

For convenience, let's call the mentioned doctor of science a qualified examiner. Thus, the examiner can professionally analyze, if not the entire voting system, but at least its part or level (protocol, software implementation, etc.). The examiner may have nothing to do with voting and even be, for example, a foreigner. If the examiner himself/herself takes part in the voting, in this case we will call him a qualified voter. The voter who is not a qualified one will be called an unsophisticated voter.

It is impossible to have an opinion about the voting system based on knowledge without the full and continuous openness of the system. Thus, we will put forward the requirement of openness.

Requirement of Openness

1. *The protocol of the secret Internet voting,*
2. *the specifications of the protocol,*
3. *the source code of the software (in the voter's computing device), which, interacting with the EC server, executes the protocol in behalf of the voter,*
4. *the executable code of this software, and*
5. *some data (specified by the protocol)*
   must be public, that is, they must be published and available without restriction to all interested persons for study and critical analysis and must be certified and protected from changes by the digital signature of an authorized agency. The fact that the executable code of the voter's software is derived from the presented source code should allow simple verification.

The authorized agency mentioned here may be the EC, but there is no need for the EC to be the publisher of protocols, specifications, etc. This agency cannot be trusted and such trust is not required. The signature is necessary to prevent the authorized agency from disavowing the voting system published, or using something unpublished and not agreed upon with civil society. This signature protects the protocol and the rest of the voting system from unauthorized changes.

Generally speaking, the source code of the voter's software (hereinafter referred to as VSW) can be used to restore both the specifications and the protocol of the voting system, that is, there is no need to publish them. However, the openness of the Protocol expands the range of potential examiners, adding to them, for example, mathematicians and cryptographers who are not engaged in programming. For the convenience of analysis, the description of the protocol is usually made minimal (cleared of details), but complete. The latter means that further detailing of the protocol does not add anything significant to it in terms of the way in which the stated result is achieved. Moreover, the protocol is the starting point for constructing the voting system.

By analyzing the source code, the examiners can make sure that the executable code fully and accurately implements the declared protocol of secret voting, and that it does not contain anything superfluous and harmful to the voter.

In general, the executable code is obtained from the source code by a compilation process, which is carried out by a special compiler program. Unfortunately, depending on the manufacturer, version, and compiler settings, many different versions of executable code can be obtained from the same source code, which executables will be the same in terms of their functionality. This means that looking at the executable code, it is not easy to understand that it corresponds to the given source code, and this is critical for the voters and examiners, because only the source code is analyzed for compliance with the protocol. This explains why the above-mentioned requirement includes the simplicity of verification that the executable code is actually derived from the source code.

The requirement of openness has a couple of side effects. First, the development of the voting system can be entrusted to anyone: it's only important that he had the right talents and was skillful enough in coding. Secondly, a large number of voluntary reviewers makes it possible to find errors and vulnerabilities in the system more quickly and, accordingly, to correct them faster, as well as to improve the system without connection with errors.

It's not necessary to require the openness of the source code of the EC's software, since all the properties of the voting system must be ensured by the protocol.

7   Conditions for the Acceptability of the Voting System

The developers of the system of secret Internet voting try to meet the pre-formulated requirements for such a system. We will not go into the discussion of a possible set of requirements for the voting system and its variations here. Instead, we will formulate the general conditions for the voting system to be acceptable both to qualified examiners and separately to unsophisticated voters.

Conditions of Recognition by the Qualified Examiners

The system of secret Internet voting shall be deemed acceptable if

1. *qualified examiners confirm that the declared properties of the voting system reflect the views of civil society about the correct voting system,*
2. *qualified examiners confirm that the declared properties of the voting system are actually implemented in the VSW, and*
3. *no one (yet) can show such a scenario of the voting participants' behavior, which leads to a significant violation of any important declared property of the voting system (for example, the secrecy of choice).*

Tens of millions of Russian citizens can understand the requirements for the correct secret Internet voting system. Millions of citizens are able to understand the protocol of the correct voting system (subject to the acceptance of the properties of certain cryptographic operations), and tens of thousands will be able to professionally analyze it, as well as to influence its development. Hundreds of thousands of Russian citizens, if not more, can also scrutinize the source code of the VSW and make sure that the VSW fully and accurately implements the declared protocol of secret Internet voting, and does not contain anything superfluous and harmful to the voter[2]. They can also influence the creation of the source code of the VSW at the development stage, and can also check that the EC distributes the version of the executable code of the VSW, which was verified and accepted by civil society and bears the signature of the authorized agency. Numerous tech-savvy foreigners can participate as well.

Such a multi-million team of independent examiners, which team has no formal membership, cannot be bribed, intimidated or misled by various paid certificates. A huge number of people who understand why it is impossible to falsify the result of voting and violate the secrecy of choice, will help an unsophisticated voter (and hence the society as a whole) to develop the trust in the system through developing the trust in independent examiners, some of whom such a voter may know even personally.

Condition of Protection of an Unsophisticated Voter

The voter should be able to obtain the VSW for their computing device and make sure that he or her has at their disposal exactly the version of the VSW approved by the qualified examiners, that is, by the civil society.

The meaning of this condition is that an unsophisticated voter must reliably merge with the crowd and be indistinguishable from a qualified voter. From behind the "wall" of the approved VSW, all voters look as qualified ones. It is therefore important that no villains can deceive the unsophisticated voter into obtaining a malicious VSW. To get the VSW, the voter must follow the approved instructions and, in particular, make sure that he or she has obtained the version of the VSW approved by the civil society. The digital signature of the authorized agency and the publication of this signature on the

---

[2] According to Microsoft, there were 350 thousand professional software developers at the end of 2010, and this figure grows by 20 thousand annually. This estimation is based on the number of licenses for developer's software sold in Russia. Microsoft also estimated number of non-professional software developers at 850 thousand people [7].

websites of parties and public organizations will help him in this. Fortunately for unsophisticated voters, using the right system of secret Internet voting is not much more difficult than, for example, Estonian system, because all the complexity is hidden inside the VSW.

8   Certification, Attestation, Audit and All That

A certificate is a document confirming the compliance of a certain object, such as a voting system, with certain requirements, standards, regulatory documents, etc. Such certificates are issued by an authorized certification organization, by the process of certification.

The main problem with certification is that the group of experts conducting the certification is fixed and small. And a fixed and small group of people (among whom can be stupid, and greedy, and cowardly, and "their own" members) is prone to various outside influences (deception, bribery, intimidation, instruction, etc.). As the result it is not possible to trust such certificates.

In fact, due to the openness, the correct protocol of the secret Internet voting, its specifications and implementation on the voter's side do not require any certification or other approval from the state bodies. More precisely, for the civil society, any official certificate does not provide a decisive reason for accepting a given voting system, and the absence of a certificate does not provide a decisive reason for rejecting the system. A certificate represents only one view in the public debate within the civil society on the acceptability of a particular system of secret Internet voting. If the authorities want someone (some entity) to be engaged in analysis and participate in public discussion of a given system of secret Internet voting on duty, and not only on their own, then they can entrust this care to any of their controlled structures or suitable external organizations. If desired, these structures or organizations can be called the authorized certification organizations.

From the voter's (civil society) perspective, certification, attestation, audit and other similar activities on the side of the EC are of no interest, since they do not play any role in ensuring the integrity of voting and the secrecy of choice. In addition, the results of these activities cannot be verified and determined as to what they relate, as there is no way for all civil society to monitor day and night every action of the staff of the certification organization.

From the government point of view certification, attestation, audit and other similar activities on the side of the EC are still needed, but for other purpose. The purpose is simple. Voting should take place under any conditions, that is, it should be provided with appropriate technical support. This means that the EC staff must be qualified, the equipment must be productive and reliable, the software must be tested, the data must be backed up remotely in real time, the power supply must be uninterrupted, access to the server must be limited, fire safety must be in good condition, etc., etc. All this should be confirmed by certifications, attestations, audits and other similar activities on the side of the EC.

9 Conclusions

Using a paranoid approach to the analysis of several deployed voting systems including the Estonian one, we found all of them unacceptable. So we put forward three criteria for an Internet voting system to be acceptable to the voters (civil society). These are (1) openness, (2) acceptance of the system by an uncertain and broad set of qualified examiners and (3) a verifiable access of unsophisticated voters to the voter's software approved by the aforementioned set of examiners. We believe that the recognition and acceptance of a particular voting system should be based not on trust, but on knowledge—on the knowledge of what is really happening during the voting, not presumed.

References

1. Gritzalis, D.A.: Principles and requirements for a secure e-voting. Comput. Secur. **21**(6), 539–556 (2002)
2. Zissis, D., Lekkas, D.: Securing e-Government and e-Voting with an open cloud computing architecture. Gov. Inf. Querterly **28**(2), 239–251 (2011)
3. Samra, K.M., Hafez, A.A., Assassa, G.M., Mursi, M.F.: A practical, secure, and auditable e-voting system. J. Inf. Secur. Appl. **36**, 69–89 (2017)
4. Randell, B., Ryan, P.Y.: Voting technologies and trust. IEEE Secur. Priv. **4**, 50–56 (2006)
5. http://cikrf.ru/eng/activity/relevant/detail/39450/. Accessed 31 Mar 2019
6. https://www.valimised.ee/en/archive/statistics-about-internet-voting-estonia. Accessed 31 Mar 2019
7. http://cloud.cnews.ru/news/top/index.shtml?2010/04/12/386342. Accessed 31 Mar 2019

Simulation of Distributed Applications Based on Containerization Technology

Daniil Malevanniy[✉], Oleg Iakushkin, and Vladimir Korkhov

Saint-Petersburg State University,
7/9 Universitetskaya nab., St. Petersburg 199034, Russia
rukmarr@gmail.com, o.yakushkin@spbu.ru

Abstract. The logical structure of the underlying network is often neglected in the design and deployment of new distributed systems and sometimes can come into play only after the system reach the production state. This can lead to the vulnerability of the system against intruders controlling the properties of the network. This paper describes a simulation system designed to analyze the influence of the logical structure and quality of the network service on a distributed systems workflow and their general testing during unstable network operation. This system allows developers to detect network vulnerabilities of distributed systems in advance and simplifies further development with regard to new findings.

Keywords: Modeling · Distributed computing · Containerization

1 Introduction

The slowdown in the rate of increase in the performance of computing resources makes developers look for new ways to improve the performance of their products [1]. One of the ways that can provide the desired effect, is the distribution of the workload on several machines. Systems based on this principle are called distributed. As the performance and reliability of the global network increases, distributed systems are becoming more common [2,9,14].

Regardless of how the load is partitioned in such systems, individual machines, or "nodes", of which the system consists, will use network connections to organize work. However, often the development of such systems does not take into account the logical structure of the network on top of which they operate: all nodes are assumed to be directly connected. This approach simplifies development process but can guarantee the correct operation of the application only under normal network conditions and does not allow assessing the impact of networking on the application.

For decentralized services built on the Ethereum platform, it was shown that changing networks between nodes can affect the ratio of their performances in the Ethereum network [3]. And for another distributed system, Bitcoin cryptocurrency, there is already evidence of the successful attacks based on manipulations with the logical structure of the global network in which the system operates [4].

© Springer Nature Switzerland AG 2019
S. Misra et al. (Eds.): ICCSA 2019, LNCS 11620, pp. 587–595, 2019.
https://doi.org/10.1007/978-3-030-24296-1_47

In order to test the operation of distributed systems in case of violations in the functioning of the network and to analyze the influence of the network structure on such systems, we developed a simulation system based on containerization technology. It simulates the operation of the system nodes and network, over which it is deployed, and allows you to dynamically manipulate the quality of the network. To allow access to information obtained during testing, we implemented a monitoring system that visualizes the data generated by the model in real time, taking into account the network structure and allowing to correlate changes in the network with changes in system behavior and immediately plan through the future direction of testing.

As a demonstration of the work of the created simulation system, we analyzed the behavior of DHT Kademlia nodes during network disruption, during which we discovered a temporary slowdown of the entire network operation after one node disconnection and the inability to reconnect the node after a brief interruption of its connection with the rest of the network.

2   Related Works

There are a large number of specialized simulation frameworks for p2p networks, such as NS-3 [5] and PeerSim [6], providing users with ample opportunities for modeling distributed systems, but requiring users to carefully study the documentation and conduct complex adaptation of the tested systems for use in the model. This significantly complicates the comparative testing of several technologies.

Other p2p network simulation systems, such as PeerfactSim.KOM [7] and BLOCKBENCH [8], are focused on benchmarking different solutions and do not allow the model parameters to be dynamically changed, and therefore not suitable for testing the stability of distributed systems.

The VIBES project is the closest in terms of methods and objectives [10], but it is aimed solely at simulating the operation of systems based on blockchain technology and cannot be used to study the operation of other distributed systems, for example, DHT or computing cluster managers.

3   Approach

The purpose of this work is to implement a system that provides users with the opportunity to study the behavior of realistic simulation of a distributed system nodes operation and the network interactions between them.

To build realistic simulations of distributed systems, it may be necessary to simultaneously simulate the operation of a large number of nodes. The simulation system must take this into account and minimize the resources overhead required to simulate the operation of individual node.

Virtual networks connecting the individual nodes of the system in their behavior and logical structure should be close to real networks. For this, system should simulate the operation of dynamic routing protocols that ensure the operation of a real global network [11] and provide tools for describing the logical structure of virtual networks.

In addition to observing the stable operation of simulated distributed systems, it is of interest to study the influence of networks outages on them. The system should provide this capability, allowing users to dynamically change the quality of individual network parts.

However, dynamic changes in the state of network make little sense if the user does not have the opportunity to inspect their impact on the operation of the simulated system. Therefore, a monitoring system is needed that displays the state of the system in real time.

Besides that, modeling the behavior of real large-scale networks may require the creation of highly complex virtual networks. In order to ensure the visibility of the influence of the structure and state of the network at the same time, the monitoring system should take into account the structure of the network when visualizing the state of the system.

Finally, to demonstrate the capabilities of the created modeling system, an example of its work is needed, which uses a widespread and easy-to-understand technology as a simulated application.

4 Results

4.1 Simulation

Network Simulation. For a complete simulation of a distributed application, it is crucial to simultaneously simulate all its components and their network interactions. To build such a model, Kathara framework and Docker containerization platform were used. Based on the description of the network structure, Kathara creates its logical structure, launches docker containers corresponding to the network nodes, creates virtual networks and performs their initial configuration. Thus, based on the description of its structure, a minimally functional network model is built.

In this form, however, this model has few applications, since the networks created by Kathara represent only the physical structure of the network and do not define the logic of packet routing. For the final configuration of the network model, standard Linux utilities, such as ifconfig and route, was used in combination with Quagga suite, which provides a set of implementations of various dynamic routing protocols. Configuring routing logic creates a single logical network model.

To complete the functionality of the model, it is necessary to include nodes with the simulated application in the overall network structure. The only Kathara requirements for using containers as such nodes are the availability of the bash command shell and ifconfig and route commands. These requirements are not always met in basic docker images, but this is easily fixed since all the necessary packages are widely available in package managers.

Network Management. For a more in-depth study of simulated applications, the ability to flexibly adjust the quality of the simulated network is required. For this, the tcconfig package was used, which controls the quality of operation of virtual network interfaces using the Linux tc (transport control) utility. To provide a convenient user interface to console commands from this package, a web form was developed for setting network quality parameters. It allows users to limit the bandwidth and latency of the network interfaces of the container and the percentage of damage, loss, rearrangement or duplication of packets passing through them.

Additional Instruments. Despite the possible usefulness of such models of distributed applications, the format for describing the network structure accepted by Kathara has a drawback—to describe networks even with the simplest dynamic routing, the user must manually configure all the details of the dynamic routing protocol and distribute the IP addresses of subnets and nodes. This makes the change of the network topology of the model extremely time-consuming, which is unacceptable when studying the influence of topology on the operation of the simulated application. To solve this problem, a software interface was created that allows you to describe the network in terms of nodes, connections between groups of nodes and zones of dynamic routing, and then save it in the Kathara lab format. At the moment, the interface supports RIP, OSPF, and BGP protocols, and allows you to select a docker image running on a host, open access to the outside world, and publish ports to the host machine. In this way, access is provided to the main docker container options necessary for the operation of the model and its monitoring.

The selected combination of software allows you to create detailed network topologies from abstract descriptions, model the networks built with these topologies, deploy distributed applications on top of them and change the quality of the network service.

4.2 Monitoring

Monitoring System API. A running model, isolated from the outside world, can hardly be of any benefit when developing or testing an application. Obviously, to obtain useful conclusions from the model, you need to somehow monitor its condition. For this purpose, a web-based model monitoring interface with a software interface for the nodes of the tested application to report their state was developed.

The programming interface is based on the ZMQ messaging library. Each host creates a ZMQ PUSH socket and assigns it to the address "ipc: /// hostsockets / \$ {HOSTNAME}", where \$ {HOSTNAME} is the value of the environment variable HOSTNAME, which is set by Kathara when the container is started. The message format is defined as a JSON object consisting of three fields:

- status—operation status, valid values - an integer from 0 to 3

– traffic—the amount of data processed, any positive integer is valid
– log—output when performing an operation, any string is valid.

It is assumed that the components of the application under test will send messages after each completed logical iteration of their work with the rest of the network. An example of such an iteration is the attempt of the DHT Kademlia client to save and then load a file. Each iteration must check the performance of the application in some way.

Monitoring System User Interface. The messages transmitted through the above-described API contain a large amount of useful information, but they can hardly be called visual. To facilitate the task of analyzing the data obtained, a web interface was implemented to display the structure of the simulated application and visualize the messages received from its components. It is based on the jgraph, a minimalistic JavaScript library designed to demonstrate three-dimensional graphs in a browser. Jgraph was adapted to the needs of the monitoring system, support various shapes of the graph nodes and change in the color or size of the nodes. The structure of the displayed graph is based on the Kathara network configuration. Each message received from the network node is

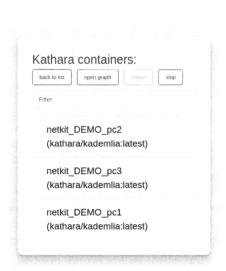

Fig. 1. The initial screen of the monitoring system lists the containers operating within the model and allows you to start and stop the simulation.

Fig. 2. The container network connection status control panel displays the status of the container and the virtual networks to which it is connected.

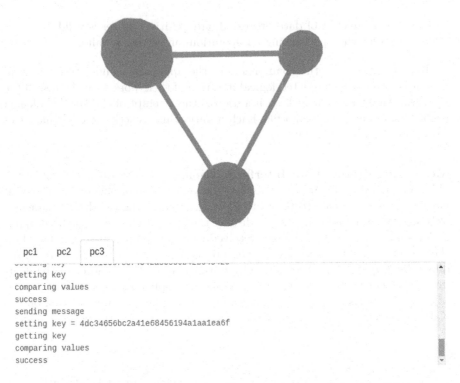

pc1   pc2   pc3

getting key
comparing values
success
sending message
setting key = 4dc34656bc2a41e68456194a1aa1ea6f
getting key
comparing values
success

Fig. 3. Monitoring system interface, visualising simulated underlay network structure as a three-dimensional graph. Each node corresponds to a network node, and the edges between them indicate the presence of a physical connection. The green color of the nodes indicates normal operation, and the size corresponds to the proportion of system traffic passing through it. The depicted network consists of three nodes connected with a common collision domain. (Color figure online)

immediately visualized on the graph: the node color corresponds to the status, and the size corresponds to the amount of data transferred. The text part of the message falls into the log window of the corresponding node. Thus, the entire completeness of the information received from the application components finds one or another visualization in the web-interface of the model monitoring.

The web-based monitoring of the model operation allows users to simultaneously monitor the general state of the network and examine in detail the work process of its individual nodes. The use of the ZMQ library, sharpened for high performance, allows you to quickly visualize network changes, even with a large number of nodes in it.

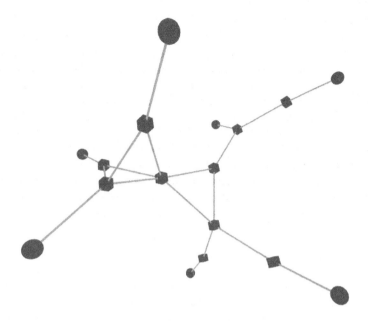

Fig. 4. Visualization of the structure of a more complex network. The round nodes of the graph correspond to the nodes of the distributed system, the square ones - to the routers of the virtual network, which support the work of dynamic routing protocols.

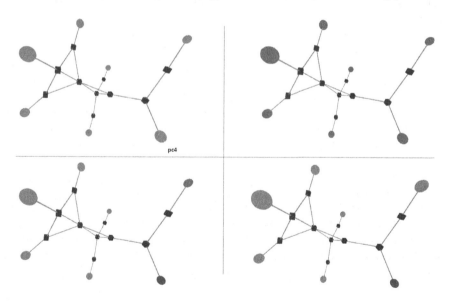

Fig. 5. Visualization of the reaction of Kademlia DHT nodes to the loss of communication with one of them (pc4) in the monitoring system. Consistently: normal network operation, short outage of the whole network, recovery of most nodes, whole network recovery. It should be noted that after the connection of the node to the network was restored, the picture did not change and pc4 could not reconnect to the Kademlia DHT network.

5   Analysis

To demonstrate the capabilities of the created simulation system, an application based on the Python implementation of the Kademlia distributed hash table protocol [13] was deployed. The demo application at the same time provides the network operability and conducts tests of its functionality, storing data in the DHT and then downloading it for comparison. It was wrapped in a docker image and launched on model nodes with different network topologies. During the observation of the model, it was discovered that the server side of this implementation of the Kademlia protocol cannot independently reconnect to the rest of the network after a short of network outage. This example demonstrates how a distributed application simulation system can detect unexpected behavior in the operation of low-level libraries (Figs. 1, 2, 3, 4 and 5).

6   Conclusions

The described modeling system allows a simulation of the operation of distributed applications on different network topologies and with different quality of network operation. This allows developers of such systems to test their work in different conditions, in particular under high loads and poor or unstable network operation. The ability to use dynamic routing increases the realism of the models regarding the operation of distributed applications on top of the real Internet.

The use of containerization technology increases the efficiency of resource utilization relative to virtual machines [12] and allows flexible control over the quality of work of simulated networks using Linux kernel tools. However, the Kathara framework, which is used to configure these networks, was developed at an early stage of technology development and may not fully utilize its potential. It may be wise to consider replacing it with Docker native capabilities.

In addition, despite the completeness of the data presented in the web interface, it is not suitable for in-depth analysis or benchmarking of applications. For the possible implementation of such functionality, it is necessary to think about the organization of storage and access to the data transmitted by the application to the monitoring system.

Simulating the work of a distributed application in a variety of conditions simplifies the life of its developers, and on the other hand, testing different solutions on a real network model can simplify the choice for end users. In addition, the possibility of dynamic changes in the model allows us to study the stability of distributed applications with respect to network attacks.

References

1. Etiemble, D.: 45-year CPU Evolution: one law and two equations. arXiv preprint arXiv:1803.00254 (2018)
2. Skala, K., Davidović, D., Lipić, T., Sović, I.: G-Phenomena as a base of scalable distributed computing —G-Phenomena in Moore's Law. Int. J. Internet Distrib. Syst. **2**(1), 1–4 (2014). https://doi.org/10.4236/ijids.2014.21001
3. Shurov, A., Malevanniy, D., Iakushkin, O., Korkhov, V.: Blockchain network threats: the case of PoW and ethereum. In: Misra, S., et al. (eds.) ICCSA 2019. LNCS, vol. 11620, pp. 606–617. Springer, Cham (2019)
4. Apostolaki, M., Zohar, A., Vanbever, L.: Hijacking bitcoin: routing attacks on cryptocurrencies. In: 2017 IEEE Symposium on Security and Privacy (SP). IEEE (2017)
5. Henderson, T.R., et al.: Network simulations with the ns-3 simulator. SIGCOMM Demonstration **14**(14), 527 (2008)
6. Montresor, A., Jelasity, M.: PeerSim: a scalable P2P simulator. In: Proceedings of the 9th International Conference on Peer-to-Peer (P2P 2009), Seattle, WA, September 2009, pp. 99–100 (2009)
7. Feldotto, M., Graffi, K.: Comparative evaluation of peer-to-peer systems using PeerfactSim.KOM. In: Proceedings of IEEE International Conference on High Performance Computing and Simulation (IEEE HPCS 2013) (2013)
8. Dinh, T.T.A., et al.: Blockbench: a framework for analyzing private blockchains. In: Proceedings of the 2017 ACM International Conference on Management of Data. ACM (2017)
9. Iakushkin, O., Shichkina, Y., Sedova, O.: Petri Nets for modelling of message passing middleware in cloud computing environments. In: Gervasi, O., et al. (eds.) ICCSA 2016. LNCS, vol. 9787, pp. 390–402. Springer, Cham (2016). https://doi.org/10.1007/978-3-319-42108-7_30
10. Stoykov, L., Zhang, K., Jacobsen, H.-A.: VIBES: fast blockchain simulations for large-scale peer-to-peer networks: demo. In: Proceedings of the 18th ACM/IFIP/USENIX Middleware Conference: Posters and Demos (Middleware 2017), pp. 19–20. ACM, New York (2017). https://doi.org/10.1145/3155016.3155020
11. Rekhter, Y., et al.: Application of the border gateway protocol in the internet (1990)
12. Felter, W., et al.: An updated performance comparison of virtual machines and linux containers. In: 2015 IEEE International Symposium on Performance Analysis of Systems and Software (ISPASS). IEEE (2015)
13. Maymounkov, P., Mazières, D.: Kademlia: a peer-to-peer information system based on the XOR metric. In: Druschel, P., Kaashoek, F., Rowstron, A. (eds.) IPTPS 2002. LNCS, vol. 2429, pp. 53–65. Springer, Heidelberg (2002). https://doi.org/10.1007/3-540-45748-8_5
14. Iakushkin, O., Malevanniy, D., Bogdanov, A., Sedova, O.: Adaptation and deployment of PanDA task management system for a private cloud infrastructure. In: Gervasi, O., et al. (eds.) ICCSA 2017. LNCS, vol. 10408, pp. 438–447. Springer, Cham (2017). https://doi.org/10.1007/978-3-319-62404-4_32

Blockchain as a Platform for Fog Computing

Ivan Podsevalov[✉], Oleg Iakushkin, Ruslan Kurbangaliev,
and Vladimir Korkhov

Saint-Petersburg State University, St. Petersburg, Russia
`podsevalov.ivan@yandex.ru, o.yakushkin@spbu.ru`

Abstract. In this article, we observe the prospective approaches and techniques in the modern system of automatic control of a group of robots based on distributed ledger technology, using modern methods and development tools. The architecture of this solution is based on the junction of two rapidly developing technologies, such as the Internet of Things (IoT) and distributed ledgers technologies (DLT). We focused on the advantages of the built-in architecture, chose the platforms on which each step will work properly, and looked up at the problems that may arise when implementing individual module of this architecture.

Keywords: Corda · Distributed ledger · Blockchain · Fog

1 Introduction

Modern people, surrounded by an abundance of technology, strive to assign more and more tasks to machines or smart devices, due to their cost and increasing capabilities. The financial advantage is that people do not need to pay to the machine for the work done; we only purchase and periodically maintain it. If we consider the issue in perspective, then over time the costs pay off. Machines do not have a human factor, which would affect the result of the work. We can be sure that the work will be completed properly within the time frame we have specified.

No system can boast about the stable uninterrupted operation so this is why we would like to have some kind of trusted person who is able to guarantee the authenticity of a particular event. The approach to solving this problem can be implemented by means of distributed ledger technology integrated into the system.

It should be noted the observed forms of interaction are built up in a "person-person" or "person-device" manner. But thanks to the concept of the Internet of Things (IoT) we get another type of device-to-device communication. Based on this, we can create some kind of infrastructure that will allow us not only to manage the devices but also to provide information about their condition.

To this day, the cleaning of large premises is a routine and labor-intensive process that requires the involvement of a group of people to achieve a faster

© Springer Nature Switzerland AG 2019
S. Misra et al. (Eds.): ICCSA 2019, LNCS 11620, pp. 596–605, 2019.
https://doi.org/10.1007/978-3-030-24296-1_48

accomplishment of the task. Similarly with robots: the larger the area, the more machines are needed for fairly fast work. But vacuum cleaning robots are more economically advantageous if we consider this project with a future perspective. What if we could to create a system that would optimally and logically work in a group of vacuum cleaning robots and between groups?

In this article, we will look at and talk about the synergy of the two current technologies - the Internet of Things and distributed ledgers - with a projection on the problem described above. In the process, we will form a methodology, which will be a key component in managing a swarm of vacuum cleaners. We set the task as follows: to solve the problem of consistency, security, and optimal operation of groups of robots on the basis of distributed ledgers and using a simple and intuitive interface to enable the user to control this system. Of course, using the provided client interface, the user will be able to monitor the status and status of the machines. The architecture of the solution and the implementation of the prototype will be covered in the following paragraphs.

We emphasize that our project aims to create a software package for managing a swarm of robots using the blockchain. As a supporting task, we dwelt on the problem of cleaning large facilities with the help of robotic vacuum cleaners, where it is advisable to use a group or even several groups. The number of groups can vary from the area of the room, and the user-defined restrictions. Thus, we would like to implement a system that could automatically manage groups of robots and at the same time maintain some kind of real-time report on past events and current status.

2   Architecture

In this chapter, we observe the architecture of our system (see Fig. 1). The central component of our implementation is the cloud, which provides communication to nodes with the end user. This node is the point of contact of the user with the

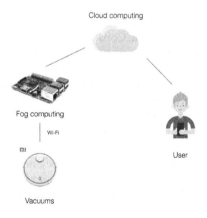

Fig. 1. System architecture

system. In addition, the cloud provides a reliable and secure connection to the microcomputer(s) of the system - Raspberry Pi (RPi). Further, by means of the Wi-Fi wireless LAN technology, secure transfer of data from the RPi to robot vacuum cleaners of a separate group and in the opposite direction is carried out.

Reliability and security at appropriate levels are achieved through the use of distributed ledger technology integrated into our project. Due to its flexibility and technical features, Corda was chosen as the distributed ledger platform. The key factors that have influenced the choice of this platform are limited access, scalability and the presence of more declarative smart contracts, for example, unlike the Ethereum. In addition, not every node can see most of the transaction graph, hence it will not waste resources on processing them. That is, the nodes are obtained only those transactions in which they are involved. Secondly, since there is no single blockchain network, it becomes possible to connect two independent networks through two-way communication between special nodes. Thirdly, an arbitrary ZIP containing geo-information can be included in the transaction. Which can be used in smart-contract code, therefore simplify the development of this system.

3   System Components

As a smart vacuum cleaner, we use Xiaomi Mi Robot Vacuum Cleaner with the Ubuntu 14.04.3 LTS operating system over which the Java Runtime Environment (JRE) is installed and the Corda node is deployed. Note that the robot vacuum cleaner has limited computing power, so the system needs to store and process the minimum necessary data for coordinating the operation of the device.

Raspberry Pi runs on the Raspbian operating system on which the Corda node is deployed using a virtual machine. After receiving data from each member of the group - vacuum cleaning robots, the computer sticks together maps of the area using the software package developed by us and sends further instructions to the robots. The main task the RPi is responsible is work coordination and optimization of vacuum cleaners.

Group of robots led by Raspberry Pi are controlled and coordinated by the cloud server application, based on Corda node software as well. Control of the entire system and monitoring its current state are available through the web API, based on Spring web-server software.

Now we focus on the distributed ledger technology that we use in the project. In a nutshell, we have three types of nodes in our system: for the cloud, for the RPi, and for the robot vacuum cleaner. Let's imagine a network with fifteen nodes - Fig. 2. This diagram clearly shows the interaction areas of individual pairs. For each device, the circle (s) of communication is strictly and clearly defined. For example, a robot from one circle does not have the ability to communicate with the cloud or RPi of another circle and vice versa. In turn, the RPi cannot communicate with the robot cleaner or the RPi of another circle. And, of course, the central node is the Cloud, which does not have access to vacuum cleaners at all.

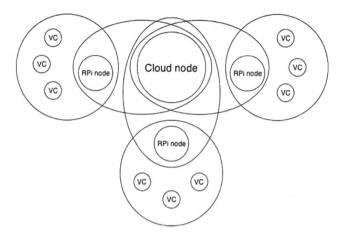

Fig. 2. Interconnection circles

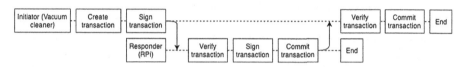

Fig. 3. Flows

The nodes of our system communicate with each other by means of a strictly defined format - Fig. 3. The diagram shows a block of the chain - the State, that is, the data set that is transmitted from one node to another is stored and clearly detected by the system. The state contains a link to the contract, participants (nodes that exchanged information) and some transaction metadata. Thanks to the Corda distributed ledger platform, we can transfer ZIP files from one node to another hashing an attachment, which ensures that we can reliably and securely transfer a map of the area with accompanying data.

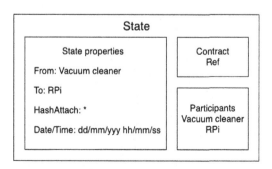

Fig. 4. State

Instead of global translation, Corda uses the node-to-node communication format. This means that in order to coordinate the updates of our ledger, it is necessary to specify the contractors and the necessary information to be transmitted. Corda automates a similar process with the help of flows - Fig. 4.

4   Implementation

One of the important issues in the development of the project is the algorithm (see Fig. 5) for connecting or gluing and synchronizing maps. It is fundamental - without it, the work of the entire system is impossible, since it will not be possible to distribute the task of cleaning between all vacuum cleaners and each robot will start to complete cleaning of the same large area. The process of combining maps can be represented as follows: before starting work, all vacuum cleaners in the same room are set sequentially in one line with a given initial distance of one meter. The first one to go is the cleaner with RPi, then from left to right, the others are turned on. When vacuum cleaners are turned on, each of them draws up a primary map using a LIDAR sensor. Possible variation of this solution - the user is given the opportunity through a special web form to put vacuum cleaners in the order he needs with the distance set by the user.

For further work of groups of vacuum cleaners, these maps must be synchronized both in groups and between groups. Inside the groups, each vacuum cleaner transmits its map and on-time to the RPi. At RPi, data is processed

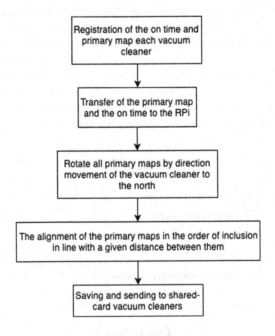

Fig. 5. Algorithm

— the maps from all vacuum cleaners are turned northward by the direction of movement of the robot, then overlapped with each other with a given initial distance in the order that the vacuum cleaners are turned on.

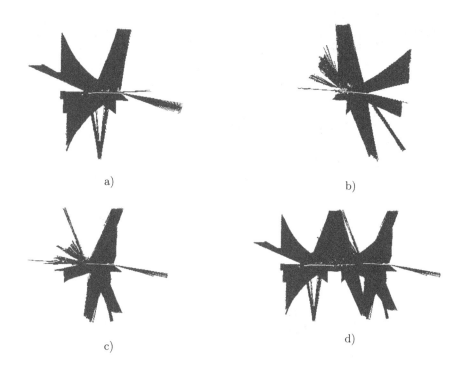

a)

b)

c)

d)

Fig. 6. Map pooling

Thus, knowing the turn-on time and, accordingly, the order, using the data from the compass, you can uniquely glue the maps from different vacuum cleaners into one (see Fig. 6).

Synchronization of maps from different vacuum cleaners within a group occurs through RPi - each vacuum cleaner sends a map to RPi every few seconds from which it is sent to the rest of the robots. In turn, RPi sends the group map to the cloud server, which sends it for synchronization to other RPi, and they to the robots of their group (see Fig. 7). All operations for storing and synchronizing maps are implemented via the blockchain.

There may be situations when the cleaning area is large and requires more than one group. In this case, with known limits of the cleaning area in the cloud, the area is divided into an amount equal to the number of necessary groups and then its cleaning zone is sent to each group and then RPi divides it into equal zones for each vacuum cleaner. The process of separating the harvesting area can be described as follows: the harvesting selection area is a rectangle, it is divided into equal parts on the larger side.

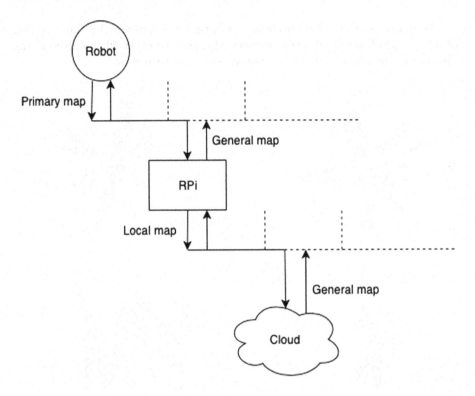

Fig. 7. Communication map

5   Corda Performance Evaluation

For our task the main issue is the speed of data transmission, so we estimated the time cost for data transmission between nodes within the circle. Figures 8 and 10 shows the architectures of the tests produced. For the first test, the ZIP file was uploaded to the central node of the group, after that the data was transferred sequentially from node to node, referring to the hash of the downloaded file. For the second test, the ZIP file was uploaded to the central node of the main group (group 3) and whistles to the nodes within its group, after which similar actions occurred within groups 1 and 2. A series of tests were produced: the file size and the number of nodes in the group changed (see Figs. 9 and 11).

In Fig. 10, the ZIP is uploaded to the Cloud node, after that this node whistled to the nodes in his group (group 3), that is, both RPi. RPi's in turn whistle to the nodes in their groups (groups 1 and 2), that is, all devices. The message will be considered to be distributed when all nodes in the groups have received it. The number of nodes in groups 1 and 2 ranged from 2 to 5, for which tests were performed (see Fig. 11).

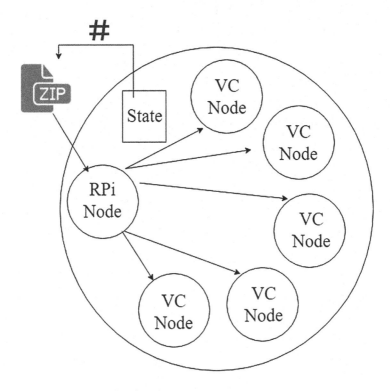

Fig. 8. Group architecture

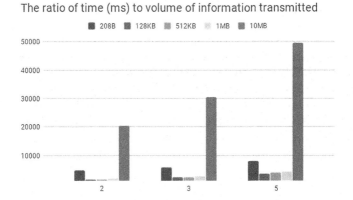

Fig. 9. Test results

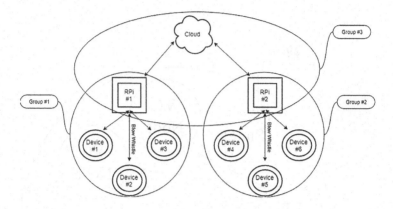

Fig. 10. Groups architecture

The ratio of time (ms) to volume of information transmitted to the groups

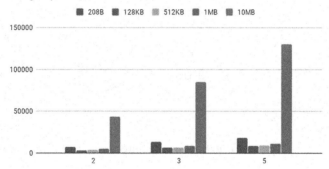

Fig. 11. Test results

6   Conclusion

In the course of creating a control and monitoring system for groups of vacuum cleaning robots, an architecture was created and prototyping of its main components was made. An algorithm for combining maps of several vacuum cleaners is presented and tested, an algorithm for the interaction of system nodes using distributed ledgers to solve key problems of security, stability, and scalability has been compiled. In the future, it is planned to optimize the work of the existing algorithms and will aim at providing user convenience.

References

1. Giese, D.: Having fun with IoT: reverse engineering and hacking of xiaomi IoT devices. DEFCON 26 (2018)
2. Atlam, H.F., Wills, G.B.: Intersections between IoT and distributed ledger. In: Advances in Computers, Chap. 3. Elsevier (2019)

3. Zhang, K., Vitenberg, R., Jacobsen, H.: Deconstructing blockchains: concepts, systems, and insights. In: Proceedings of the 12th ACM International Conference. ACM (2018)
4. Kshetri, N.: Can blockchain strengthen the Internet of Things? IEEE IT Prof. **19**(4), 68–72 (2017)
5. Zyskind, G., Nathan, O., Pentland, A.S.: Decentralizing privacy: using blockchain to protect personal data. In: 2015 Proceedings of the IEEE Security and Privacy Workshops. SPW 2015, pp. 180–184. IEEE (2015)
6. Lyu, X., et al.: Optimal schedule of mobile edge computing for Internet of Things using partial information. IEEE J. Sel. Areas Commun. **35**(11), 2606–2615 (2017)
7. Corda. https://github.com/corda/corda. Accessed 21 Mar 2019
8. Corda Documentation. https://docs.corda.net. Accessed 21 Mar 2019
9. Dustcloud. https://github.com/dgiese/dustcloud. Accessed 21 Mar 2019
10. Dustcloud. https://github.com/Hypfer/Valetudo. Accessed 21 Mar 2019

Blockchain Network Threats:
The Case of PoW and Ethereum

Artem Shurov, Daniil Malevanniy$^{(\boxtimes)}$, Oleg Iakushkin, and Vladimir Korkhov

Saint-Petersburg State University,
7/9 Universitetskaya nab., St. Petersburg 199034, Russia
rukmarr@gmail.com, o.yakushkin@spbu.ru

Abstract. Developers do not properly take into account possible problems on the Internet. This fact can cause problems in the operation of blockchain systems. The subject of our analysis was Ethereum due to its short block creation time and, as a result, a strong reaction to faults in the network. We checked the possible threats from the miners during the unreliable work of the Internet.

For the study, we conducted many simulations of the work of Ethereum with different delays in the propagation of blocks and various mining power allocations. The results showed that if the duration of the troubles is more than 10 h, a miner with 26% can capture the entire Ethereum network, but this requires the intervention of people controlling other nodes. This is possible because it will be more cost-effective for them.

Keywords: Ethereum · Propagation delay

1 Introduction

A blockchain is a distributed database whose nodes store copies of it independently of each other. Information in such a database is presented in the form of an ever-growing list of ordered records, called blocks. The blocks are in a continuous sequential chain, built according to certain rules. Each block contains a set of different transactions, a link to the previous block and other supporting information [1]. Any node (miner) can create a new block by solving a cryptographic puzzle and receiving an award for it. Because of the distributed nature of finding new blocks, several nodes can add different blocks with the same number before they learn about the existence of other blocks, which leads to branching of the chain [2]. In order for all nodes to agree on a single-chain condition, they use a single strategy that selects the only chain of blocks that is correct for all. This strategy is called a consensus algorithm, and different blockchains use different consensus algorithms [3].

There are many researches aimed at analysing the network attacks against blockchains with PoW, but they are aimed at obtaining benefits through double

© Springer Nature Switzerland AG 2019
S. Misra et al. (Eds.): ICCSA 2019, LNCS 11620, pp. 606–617, 2019.
https://doi.org/10.1007/978-3-030-24296-1_49

spending or rewriting transaction history [4–7]. Researches also show that Internet parameters affect the state of blockchain systems [8]. We investigated the possible behavior of miners (more precisely, mining pools) when problems occur on the Internet, if one of them also wants to benefit from the situation.

Our investigation reveals that large mining pools in the Ethereum can capture the entire network (as if they have 50% + power) using the arising delays in the propagation of new blocks between several large parts of the network. But this requires decision-making by a person, otherwise the honest mining of all nodes merely decreases the reliability of the network.

2   Why Ethereum

The complexity of solving a cryptographic puzzle is different for various implementations of the blockchain and is chosen in such a way that the block is created at certain intervals [9]. For example, for the popular blockchain platforms, the time intervals are as follows:

1. Bitcoin - 10 min
2. Litecoin - 2.5 min
3. Dogecoin - 1 min
4. Ethereum - about 15 s.

The data above show that the Ethereum blockchain has a small block finding time and most often faces the concept of forking - when several blocks are located at the same chain height. To reduce the negative impact of this factor, it implements a modified GHOST algorithm [10], the main idea of which is the inclusion of so-called uncle-blocks in the chain.

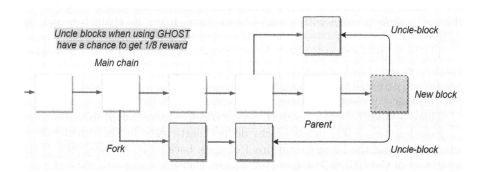

Fig. 1. Modified GHOST implementation.

Uncle-block is a block that is not part of the main chain, but is taken into account by it (Fig. 1). If uncle-block is included in the new block, miners get rewarded for work: 1/32 of the regular award for the miner of the new block and

1/8–7/8 to the miner of the uncle-block (depends on how many generations back the uncle forked). A miner can include up to 2 uncle-blocks, and they must be up to 7 generations back in the main chain.

Different consensus algorithms implemented in various blockchains choose the main chain differently. In bitcoin, the longest branch is selected. This strategy, however, has its drawbacks, since it simply wastes all the blocks that are not present in the main chain [11]. If an attacker can find new blocks quickly enough to create his local chain faster than the rest of the network, then ultimately the entire network accepts its chain as the main one. In particular, by increasing the time propagation of blocks in the network, you can increase the number of orphan blocks and, consequently, slow down the growth of the longest chain of the network. Such a possibility poses a serious risk for the blockchain, since the attacker does not even need to own most of the computing power of the network to be able to control the network [12].

In Ethereum, the chain is selected on the basis of the total complexity of the chain—the sum of the complexities of all the blocks in this chain. The GHOST protocol should solve the problem of delays in the propagation of a new block in the network. In the description of its implementation in Ethereum it is said that uncle-blocks participate in the calculation of the total complexity [13]. But in the client's geth code, when calculating the total complexity, only the block itself is taken into account and the uncle-blocks that he added are uncounted, but uncle-blocks are nonetheless awarded. This is also confirmed by a simple check of the numbers in the blocks created. Perhaps this is done for security reasons: the inclusion of uncle-blocks in the calculation of the total complexity complicate the process of choosing a main chain and possibly creates conditions for micro-attacks (sometimes add an attacker block, although it was found later) [14]. For example, the miner honestly found the block could not get data about the possible uncle-block and spread its block, another miner who found the block a few seconds later and already knew about the uncle-block, adds it to his block, thereby making a chain with his new block more, hence its chain becomes the main.

The difficulty of finding a new block in the network of Ethereum is recalculated every new block according to the formula [15]:

$$diff = (parentDiff + (parentDiff/2048 * max(2 \ if \ len \ parent.uncles \ else \ 1 - ((timestamp - parent.timestamp) \ // \ 9), -99))) + 2^{periodCount-2}$$

where $periodCount = (numberCurrentBlock - bomdDelay)/100,000$

But despite all this, uncle-blocks do not participate in the calculation of which block has the largest total proof of work backing it, although this is the main part of the GHOST protocol. Of course, they are taken into account when calculating the new complexity of finding a block, but this contribution does not compare with the calculation that should be.

Because of the fact that the Ethereum needs a small amount of time to find the block and also considering that the GHOST protocol does not use uncle-blocks in calculating the total chain complexity, delays in the propagation of the blocks can adversely affect the reliability of the created chain.

3   Simulation of Ethereum Network

To analyze the effect of network latency on the Ethereum, a python script was created that simulates Ethereum network operation. The parameters of this simulation are:

1. List of all miners (part of them in total network)
2. New block propagation time.

Also, the mining process is simplified: a number is chosen at random, and it is determined whether it is small enough to find a new block (according to its complexity).

Implemented algorithm:

Listing 1.1. The simulation algorithm

```
miners = create miners with network power percentage

for 1 to the simulation time:
    for each miner in miners:
        r = random number
        if r is small enough to find a block:
            block = creates a new block
            adds this block to miners chain
            t = current time + delay
            add this block to the queue with t

    for all blocks in the queue with the current time:
        for each miner in miners:
            if block can be added:
                adds a block to its chain
```

The limitations of this simulation are:

1. Time step = 1 s
2. The block propagation delay is the same for all miners.

The simulation starts with block number 7,360,216 and the rest of the data corresponds to this point in time: the mining rewards, the difficulty of finding the block, the average block propagation time, and the average network hashrate [16].

Comparison of the results of the simulation and this network can be found in Table 1:

Errors are most likely caused by the simplified concept of mining and the constant power of the network and mining pools.

These graphs show the results of simulations of 24 h of Ethereum network with miners, whose power are related to the power of pools in the real network. Pool - miner association for finding blocks, motivated by the receipt of a constant small profit of a relatively large rare win.

Table 1. Reality vs Simulation

Data for 24 h	Reality	Simulation
Number of all blocks	6400	6350
Number of uncle-blocks	450	500
Uncle-rate	7%	8%
Propagation time	0.5 s	1 s

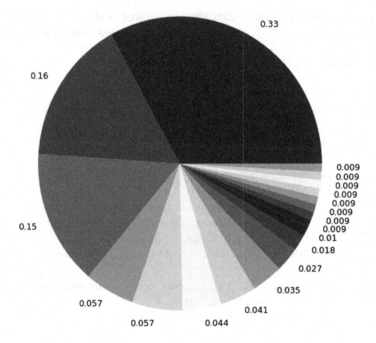

Fig. 2. Percentage distribution of mining pools.

The first graph (Fig. 2) shows the distribution of power miners in the network. The second graph (Fig. 3) shows the general condition of the chain:

1. How many blocks does the chain take into account
2. How many blocks in main chain
3. The number of uncle-blocks in the chain = (1. - 2.).

The third graph (Fig. 4) shows the results of work for each miner separately:

1. How many blocks did he find
2. How many of these blocks are included in the main chain
3. How many blocks are not taken into account at all (orphan)
4. The number of uncle-blocks is (1. - 2. - 3.).

The fourth graph (Fig. 5) shows the number of uncle-blocks and the number of orphan blocks (valid block, but not taken into account in the chain). The graph shows that the number of orphan blocks grows linearly relative to the propagation delays.

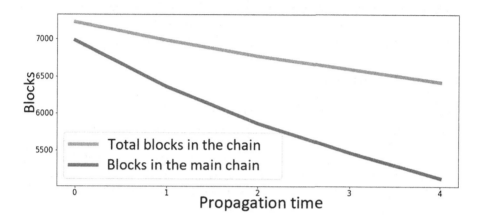

Fig. 3. Main chain.

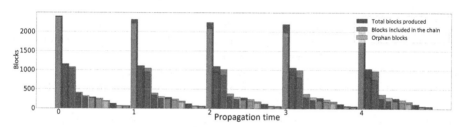

Fig. 4. Blocks created by mining pools.

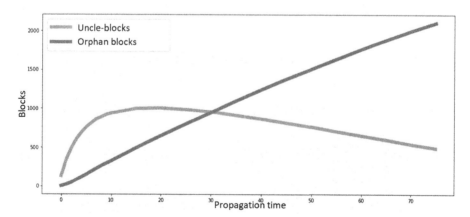

Fig. 5. Loss of Ethereum network.

Already in the second graph (Fig. 3), you can see how strongly the delays affect the Ethereum network: an increase in the block propagation time from 1 s to 3 reduces the number of blocks in the main chain by 14% and increases the number of uncle-blocks by almost 2 times.

The simulation is quite accurate, so using this simulation, we research the operation of the network with different propagation time and network power distributions.Based on the information obtained earlier, it can be concluded that delays can affect the Ethereum network quite a lot.

4   Possible Attack

Suppose that an attacker have the opportunity to influence the operation of the Internet Network: a break in communication, delays and various noises. Possible attack version:

The entire Ethereum network divided into two parts: 51% and 49% of capacity (51% - A part, 49% - B part). The propagation time of blocks between these parts rises to a critical value that must be calculated (hereinafter, we consider delays from 0 to 200 s). The attacking side has 26% (C-part) of the total power in the A part, that is, within the A part, the attackers have 51%, the remaining 25% belong to the D part. The network diagram during the attack is depicted in Fig. 6.

This threat variant is slightly different from the 51% attack [17]: which is that, having 50% + power, you can create a chain of blocks of greater complexity than the other part of the network. In the Ethereum consensus algorithm, like many other blockchain implementations, a chain of greater complexity is always selected (the creation of which used more power). Most complexity in different algorithms is understood in its own way, for example, for Bitcoin it is a chain of greater length, and for Ethereum it is a chain with a greater total complexity of blocks in it.

The network attack is based on the fact that part of the created valid blocks will not have time for propagating across the blockchain network and will not

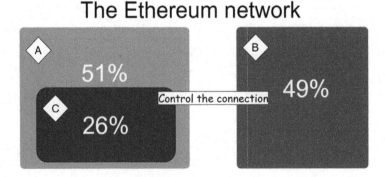

Fig. 6. Network partitioning.

be included in the main chain, despite the fact that the blocks are absolutely correct and can be included in the chain. The meaning of a possible attack is that attackers can control the entire Ethereum network by having far from 51% power, and even if there are mining pools larger than them. The goal is to earn more ETH when mining than usual, as well as impose their fees and manage the execution of transactions.

Firstly, attackers must force the remaining players in part A (D part) to follow their rules. Secondly, together they must get a chain of greater complexity than a chain of the B part. To do this, it is necessary to consider a number of cases and show that these requirements can be met.

Obviously, if A part will be mine without taking into account the chain created by B part, its chain will be the main one, since it has more power. But attackers own only part C (26%), and they need to convince the D part to mine together, without working on the chain B part. For this, the economic benefit for D to work on the chain together with C must be higher than together with B. In this case, we do not consider the bribing option.

5   Analysis

To find out the economic benefits of the D part, two cases were simulated with propagation delays from 0 to 200 s:

1. 25% and 49%
2. 25% and 26%.

Next, we take a closer look at the first situation at 25% and 49% of the power of each part, considering them as pools with corresponding powers. Figure 7 shows the characteristic of the chain relative to each pool:

1. How many blocks each pool produced
2. How many blocks were included in the main chain
3. The number of orphan blocks
4. The number of uncle-blocks is not specified, but it is (1. - 2. - 3.).

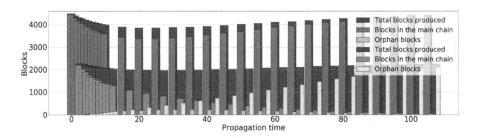

Fig. 7. Mining pools: 25% and 49%.

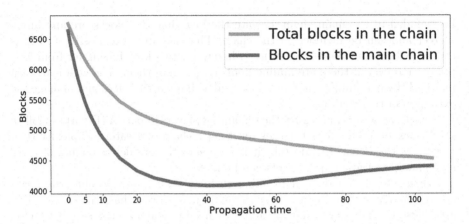

Fig. 8. Mining pools: 25% and 49%.

Figure 8 shows the general condition of the chain:

1. How many blocks does the chain take into account
2. How many blocks in the main chain.

Delays between two parts of the network can be controlled, but delays within each part of the network remain the same. Therefore, we can consider in more detail what will happen to the D part during mining only inside the A part, and mining with the B part (then we control the delay between them).

Below is a graph for the D part (Fig. 9), with its two decisions:

1. Mine with 26% in A parts (brown)
2. Mine with 49% in the B part (blue).

The graph shows that the first solution is most beneficial for the miner (D part), even during normal network operation. As a result: either he creates about 2700 blocks for a chain, or less than 1000 already with a delay of 20 s (1700 blocks is about $ 230,000). The difference almost three times should represent a weighty argument for making a decision of the D part in favour of the attackers.

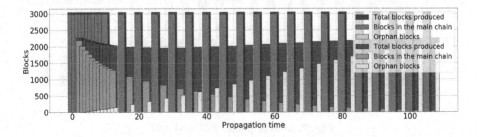

Fig. 9. Two decisions for 25%.

It should also be noted that in the presented simulation there were miners with powers of 49% and 25% represented by a single pool, which cannot be in reality. And their power will be a little less, which should not affect the results in any way. To prove this, another option was researched: 40% and 25%. As a result, the graphics coincided qualitatively, differing only in a slightly smaller number of blocks in all indicators.

It remains to be determined whether the chain made by A part (51%) is larger than that of B (49%). This is not entirely obvious because of the fact that the complexity of finding a new block is constantly recalculated and it is worth checking what happens if the power of the entire network drops twice (since both parts will start mining different chains independently of each other).

Several cases were considered, and all of them are presented in Table 2. The data was collected for the network operation within 24 h, the first column shows the data of the A part, which is taken as the basis for comparison. The first line shows the number of blocks in the main chain, and the second - how many blocks you need to create in order to achieve the same chain complexity as the A part. Because of the fact that the complexity of finding a new block is constantly recalculated, it is impossible to draw conclusions about the power of the chain simply by the number of blocks in it. The difference in blocks is calculated as the difference in the total chain difficulty divided by the complexity of the last block created.

Table 2. Chain comparison

Data for 24 h	$25 + 26$	49	$10 \times 4 + 9$	$32 + 10 + 7$	$32 + 17$	7×7	1×49
Blocks in the chain	5786	6127	5518	5732	5769	5468	5380
Blocks up to 25% + 26%	0	−40	428	228	200	448	541

In a situation where in the B part there is only one miner, who owns the entire power of this part, the attack fails. But having such large pool is unlikely and threatens the entire network due to the 51% attack that was mentioned earlier. In the real situation, when the B part consists of several miners, the network attack is successful. Of course, the 25% D parts also consist of several miners, but in the general distribution of forces is maintained as 51% and 49%, respectively, and makes the chain A parts more powerful than the other chain.

After it has been shown that the fulfillment of all the conditions for an attack can be fulfilled, it is necessary to know how long it takes to carry out an attack. That is, how much minimum time there should be delays between the two parts of the network. For this, simulations of two parts were performed:

1. 26%, 10%, 8%, 5%, 2% (A)
2. 32%, 10%, 7% (B).

As a result, we compared the total complexities of the chains created by parts A and B and counted the number of blocks for which both chains differ. A significant difference in blocks for a successful attack is achieved with 10 h of work of both parts separately from each other and is equal to about 80 blocks. The attack for more than 10 h always becomes successful.

6   Conclusions

In this paper, we show that large mining pools can take over the network, provided that the entire blockchain network is divided into two or more parts between which the delays will be more than regular. But it all depends on the distribution of power during the separation. Not necessarily the most powerful pool can take control of the entire network. There are several main conditions for network capture during network attacks:

1. The attacker needs to be in the most powerful part of the network
2. They need to have there more than 50% + power
3. It is desirable to have not much more than half the power
4. Delays between the two parts of the network should be such that it becomes more cost-effective for each part to work independently of each other
5. Necessary intervention in the normal operation of independent network nodes (to eliminate interaction with another part of the network).

Also, the simulation results show that even the slightest malfunction in the global Internet network leads to a deterioration in network reliability. This may mean that when creating Ethereum, it was assumed that the Internet connection will work stably all the time.

One of the main disadvantages of our simulation is that we do not take into account the behavior of the network operation within each part of the Internet Network when global problems occur. We also consider miners as absolutely identical entities, in reality, the network of Ethereum consists of nodes that use a huge number of different clients to work in the network [18].

In further work on this problem, it is necessary to conduct modeling with uneven delays between parts of the network [19] and various clients for the operation of the Ethereum nodes.

References

1. Pilkington, M.: Blockchain Technology: Principles and Applications. Research Handbook on Digital Transformations, pp. 225–253. Edward Elgar Publishing, Northampton (2017)
2. Decker, C., Wattenhofer, R.: Information propagation in the Bitcoin network. In: IEEE P2P 2013 Proceedings
3. Zheng, Z., Xie, S., Dai, H., Chen, X., Wang, H.: An overview of blockchain technology: architecture, consensus, and future trends. In: 2017 IEEE International Congress on Big Data

4. Natoli, C., Gramoli, V.: The Balance Attack Against Proof-Of-Work Blockchains: The R3 Testbed as an Example (2016)
5. Apostolaki, M., Zohar, A., Vanbever, L.: Hijacking Bitcoin: Routing Attacks on Cryptocurrencies (2017)
6. Heilman, E., Kendler, A., Zohar, A., Goldberg, S.: Eclipse Attacks on Bitcoin's Peer-to-Peer Network (2015)
7. Nayak, K., Kumar, S., Miller, A., Shi, E.: Stubborn Mining: Generalizing Selfish Mining and Combining with an Eclipse Attack (2015)
8. Gervais, A., Karame, G.O., Wüst, K., Glykantzis, V., Ritzdorf, H., Capkun, S.: On the Security and Performance of Proof of Work Blockchains (2016)
9. Kraft, D.: Difficulty control for blockchain-based consensus systems. Peer-To-Peer Netw. Appl. **9**(2), 397–413 (2015)
10. Sompolinsky, Y., Zohar, A.: Secure High-Rate Transaction Processing in Bitcoin (2015)
11. Sapirshtein, A., Sompolinsky, Y., Zohar, A.: Optimal selfish mining strategies in bitcoin. In: Grossklags, J., Preneel, B. (eds.) FC 2016. LNCS, vol. 9603, pp. 515–532. Springer, Heidelberg (2017). https://doi.org/10.1007/978-3-662-54970-4_30
12. Eyal, I., Sirer, E.G.: Majority is not enough: bitcoin mining is vulnerable. In: Christin, N., Safavi-Naini, R. (eds.) FC 2014. LNCS, vol. 8437, pp. 436–454. Springer, Heidelberg (2014). https://doi.org/10.1007/978-3-662-45472-5_28
13. Ritz, F., Zugenmaier, A.: The impact of uncle rewards on selfish mining in Ethereum. In: 2018 IEEE European Symposium on Security and Privacy Workshops
14. Werner, S.M., Pritz, P.J., Zamyatin, A., Knottenbelt, W.J.: Uncle traps: harvesting rewards in a queue-based Ethereum mining pool (2019)
15. A Next-Generation Smart Contract and Decentralized Application Platform. https://github.com/Ethereum/wiki/wiki/White-Paper
16. "blockchain". https://www.blockchain.com/en/
17. Beikverdi, A., Song, J.: Trend of centralization in Bitcoin's distributed network. In: 2015 IEEE/ACIS 16th International Conference on Software Engineering, Artificial Intelligence, Networking and Parallel/Distributed Computing (SNPD)
18. Kim, S.K., Ma, Z., Murali, S., Mason, J., Miller, A., Bailey, M.: Measuring Ethereum Network Peers (2018)
19. Malevanniy, D., Iakushkin, O., Korkhov, V.: Simulation of distributed applications based on containerization technology. In: Misra, S., et al. (eds.) ICCSA 2019. LNCS, vol. 11620, pp. 587–595. Springer, Cham (2019)

Distributed Ledger Technology and Cyber-Physical Systems. Multi-agent Systems. Concepts and Trends

Dmitry Arsenjev(✉), Dmitry Baskakov, and Vyacheslav Shkodyrev

Peter the Great St. Petersburg Polytechnic University, Saint Petersburg, Russia
{vicerector.int, baskakov.de, shkodyrev}@spbstu.ru

Abstract. This paper describes how Distributed Ledger Technologies can be used to enforce smart contracts and to organize the behavior of multi-agents trying to access a different resource. The first part of the paper analyses the advantages and disadvantages of using Distributed Ledger Technologies architectures to implement certain Cyber-Physical and Control Systems. The second part propose perspective applications of Distributed Ledger Technologies in Cyber-Physical Systems.

Keywords: Directed acyclic graph · Distributed Ledger ·
Cyber-physical systems · Robotics · Multi-agent systems · Smart contracts ·
Virtual Power Plant

1 Introduction

Modern society is undergoing a profound transformation of all processes and spheres of human activity. The main trends are focused, in our opinion, in the following major areas:

1. Digital production.
2. The widespread exclusion of man from the contours of decision-making.
3. Increase data processing speed while increasing security.
4. Deep transformation of business models.

The authors suggest that Distributed Ledger Technology has every chance of becoming a new paradigm that will affect the entire landscape of human life. From the point of view of the theory Distributed Ledger Technology has all the signs of a paradigm, namely [1]:

- Paradigm is rarely a copy.
- The use of this technology allows you to achieve success rather than the use of competing ways to solve some problems.
- The use of this technology allows you to solve promising problems, while it is not fully known in advance what these problems will be.

It is important to note that the Distributed Ledger paradigm has already been used one way or another.

S. Misra et al. (Eds.): ICCSA 2019, LNCS 11620, pp. 618–630, 2019.
https://doi.org/10.1007/978-3-030-24296-1_50

Robots that do not interact with humans, that is, autonomous robots, are becoming more common. Autonomous robots perform their tasks without human control. At the same time, the fact that such robots can interact with each other becomes increasingly important and critical. In this case, the first place goes mathematical algorithms that allow you to build models of interaction between such robots. At the same time, according to the authors, the development of this concept in the framework of the algorithms of System 1 and System 2 [2]. More information about these systems of thinking and decision making can be found here [3].

It should be noted that the task of learning robots or other cyber-physical agents is very nontrivial. In addition to learning already on tagged data, it is important to use robots' self-learning algorithms, as well as the ability to transfer this knowledge to other robots or agents. In this case, we get some kind of closed knowledge system, where system agents extract and formalize knowledge from the interaction environment, transfer knowledge to other system participants via secure communication channels, and also control such transfer using the central arbiter. In fact, we get intelligent machines that are able to communicate with each other and transmit knowledge first of all, that is, learn from each other [4]. And here we come to the next stage in the development of artificial intelligence systems, which we call Machine Reasoning (MR) [5].

2 Hierarchical Control

2.1 Objective Function

Modern control systems for complex objects are characterized by a large number of hierarchies and control loops, which makes it necessary to rethink modern concepts of managing complex systems and data processing [6]. The interaction between management levels occurs through a variety of objective functions for each hierarchy. The objective function is a real or integer function of several variables that is to be optimized (minimized or maximized) in order to solve some optimization problem. In addition to the objective function in the optimization problem for variables, constraints in the form of a system of equalities and inequalities can be specified. Thus, the objective function is the concept of achieving in the process of managing one of the particular goals included in the vector of goals. It is important to understand that if the signals about the state of objects are continuous functions of time, then such control systems are called continuous control systems. In the case of the formation of signals in discrete time, we already get control systems discrete. Consider the control function of the hierarchical system in the general case (Fig. 1):

$$\begin{cases} F_1(x_1, x_2, x_3, \ldots, x_m) = 0, \\ F_2(x_1, x_2, x_3, \ldots, x_m) = 0, \\ F_3(x_1, x_2, x_3, \ldots, x_m) = 0 \\ \quad \cdots \\ F_{N-1}(x_1, x_2, x_3, \ldots, x_m) = 0, \\ F_N(x_1, x_2, x_3, \ldots, x_m) = 0. \end{cases} \tag{1}$$

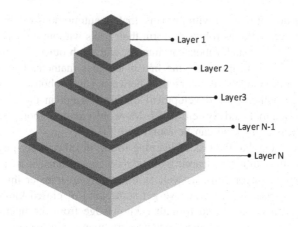

Fig. 1. Hierarchical system.

In this case, the task of managing the entire system will be reduced in the simplest case to minimizing the objective function:

$$S = \sum\nolimits_{j=1}^{N} F_j^2(x_1, x_2, \ldots, x_m) \tag{2}$$

The task of control such a hierarchical system can be reduced to solving a multicriteria optimization problem, namely:

$$\min(F_1(x), F_2(x), \ldots F_N(x)), x \in X \tag{3}$$

In this case, a valid solution $\widetilde{X} \in X$, called effective Pareto or Pareto optimal, if there is no other solution $x \in X$ such, that $F_k(x) \leq F_k(\widetilde{x})$ for all $k = 1, \ldots p$ and $F_i(x) < F_i(\widetilde{x})$ at least one $i = 1, \ldots p$.

Modern control systems are hierarchical structures with many possible vertices, as shown in the figure below [7] (Fig. 2):

2.2   Hypergraph Systems Modeling

A hypergraph is a generalization of a graph in which not only two vertices, but also any subsets can be connected with each edge.

In this formulation, a complex hierarchical system turns into a hypergraph in the mathematical sense H_n, which consists of many vertices $V_n(H_n)$ и hyper scraper $E_n(H_n)$ [8]. An example of a hypergraph is shown in the figure below (Fig. 3):

Directed hypergraph H or Dihypergraph is a hypergraph wit oriented hyperedges (hyperarcs). The extremities of a hyperedge have a very specific sense. A directed hyperedge is defined as a couple $E_j = (A, B)$, where A and B two disjoint set of vertices (Fig. 4).

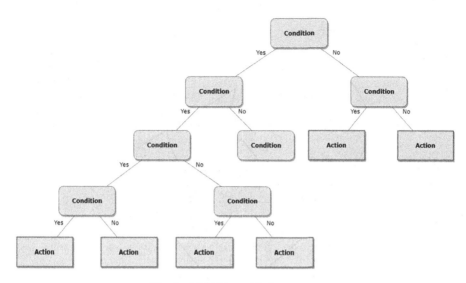

Fig. 2. Multi-hierarchical structure.

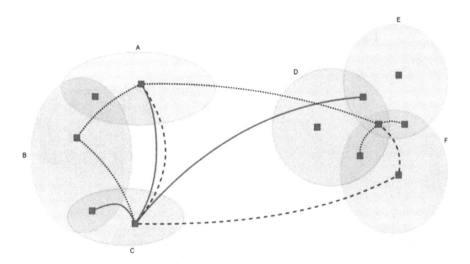

Fig. 3. Hypergraph.

Hypergraphs of various types are becoming increasingly common in systems for managing complex hierarchical structures, which makes it possible to use this mathematical apparatus as applied to Distributed Ledger Technologies [9]. The set of possible solutions is the overlapping sets of optimization functions at each of the levels of the management hierarchy that were presented above (Fig. 5):

A key factor in decision making in such complex control systems is time t, which significantly limits the use of traditional blockchain paradigms [10].

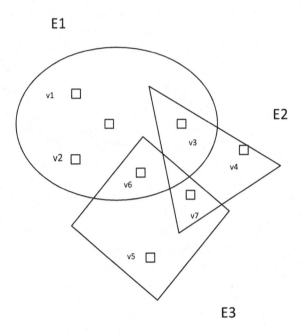

Fig. 4. Hypergraph composed of three hyperedges E_1, E_2, E_3.

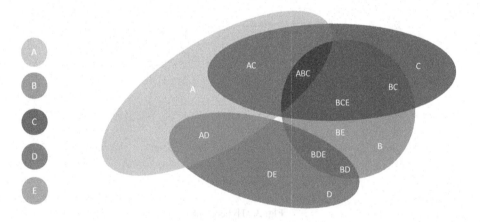

Fig. 5. Sets possible solutions.

2.3 Directed Acyclic Graph (DAG)

According to the authors, the use of a Directed Acyclic Graph (DAG) seems to be one of the promising areas for using the technology of a Distributed Ledger. In this type of graphs, there are no directed cycles, but there may be parallel paths that can lead to the end node, but in different ways. It should be noted that directed acyclic graphs are widely used, including in the tasks of artificial intelligence, together with, for example,

Neural Networks (NN), as well as in statistics and machine learning. The key factor in the use of direct acyclic graphs is precisely the speed of transactions, which is extremely important in real-time control systems with the use of a Distributed Ledger [11]. An example of a directed acyclic graph is shown below (Fig. 6):

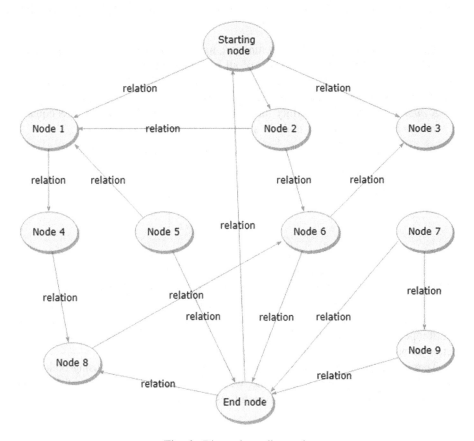

Fig. 6. Directed acyclic graph.

The use of the Directed Acyclic Graph as a mathematical tool is justified, in our opinion, especially in problems of multi-critical optimization. It should also be remembered that the DAG is a co-generalization of trees, that is, forests. Every acyclic digraph has an acyclic ordering of vertices [12].

3 Optimization

The control problem using the mathematical apparatus of graph theory is a complex multi-level optimization problem, which consists of several subtasks, namely:

– Construction of the graph and its nodes.

- Writing for each of the nodes its own objective function, the solution of which will determine the further direction.
- Solution of the optimization problem of finding the shortest path on a graph [13].

To achieve a sufficient level of generality, the utility of a path is defined by a global utility function built as the normalized weighted sum of the following partial utility functions [13]:

- A *topology*-oriented partial utility function, for which the utility of a path is equal to the opposite of the sum of the cost of all nodes belonging to a path.
- A *cost*-related partial utility function, for which the utility of a path is the opposite of the sum of the cost all nodes belonging to path.
- A *quality*-oriented partial utility function, for which the utility of a path is equal to the minimum quality of a node in a path.

Setting the control task will be as follows. We write the matrix of this form:

$$D_J = \begin{bmatrix} F_{1,1} & \cdots & F_{1,N} \\ \vdots & \ddots & \vdots \\ F_{M,1} & \cdots & F_{M,N} \end{bmatrix} \tag{4}$$

$F_{1,1}, \ldots, F_{1,N}$- control objectives function at the $1-$ level of the hierarchy and $F_{M,1}, \ldots, F_{M,N}$ - control objectives function at the $M-$ level of the hierarchy.

The solution of this problem, we can reduce, in fact, to the problem of optimizing Neural Networks or to the problem of optimizing deep models. In fact, in management and control tasks, often, there can be no single solution, and we thus arrive at a possible set of input data. $D_1, \ldots, D_J$. This set of control input matrices is mapped into a certain set of output data, for example, using Neural Networks [14].

That is, we can consider the task of finding the optimal solution using both DAG and Neural Networks. At the same time, we believe that it is the sharing of these two concepts that can bring a significant useful result [15].

4   Smart Systems

The authors see their use in various intellectual systems, where human participation is minimized, as an extremely promising direction for the development of Distributed Ledger Technologies. The use of this technology in the activities of energy companies in the following areas looks promising.

4.1   Energy

The energy sphere of using Distributed Ledger seems to us extremely promising for a number of reasons. Here are the main ones:

- Integrated Process Automation [16]. Distributer Ledger allows you to transform the landscape of traditional business with well-established markets and relationships. We also assume a significant reduction in the risks of certain transactions within the framework of traditional business processes.

- Intellectual billing. Using Distributed Ledger along with Smart Contracts allows you to automate calculations and measurements in Distributed Energy Systems [17].
- Sales and marketing. The key success factor here is the use of Distributed Ledger in conjunction with artificial intelligence systems (Machine Learning and Deep Learning). This symbiosis allows to ensure the construction of an individual consumer profile with the transfer of all data via secure communication channels.
- Communication with intelligent devices via secure channels significantly changes data transfer algorithms, as well as processes in energy companies.
- Security. The use of cryptography significantly increases the security of transactions and provides an unsurpassed level of trust between the participants of the system. Also, the use of Distributed Ledger technology allows better control of data privacy and identity management.
- Transparency achieved using Distributed Ledger.
- Competition. The use of DL technology makes it possible to qualitatively simplify the task of switching between energy suppliers, thereby increasing the flexibility of choice of suppliers for the consumer. There are few works on this subject, but from the point of view of game theory, in any case, the consumer has flexibility, which increases competition [18].
- Algorithms and business models. Automation of processes in the energy sector using the technology Distributed Ledger allows you to qualitatively change the traditional management paradigms. In fact, with the advent of Distributed Ledger, we will observe a breakdown of established development trends and business models. Traditional companies will become Decentralized Autonomous Corporation (DAC), which operate under completely different business laws [19]. This paradigm is quite new, the number of publications on this subject is extremely small [20] (Figs. 7, 8).

4.2   Robotics

The use of Distributed Ledger in cyber-physical systems, such as robotics, is a very promising direction, especially in the field of interaction and intellectual training of elements of such systems. Consider briefly the main directions and prospects for the possible use of Distributed Ledger in such systems:

- Intellectual interaction between robots. In this context, refers to the ability to share information, participate in training and decision-making without human intervention [21].
- Distributed solution of the problem. In this case, we use Distributed Ledger to collect distributed control robots and control the overall goal.
- Distributed Ledger for voting [22].
- Task optimization. In this case, Distributed Ledger is used to optimize the problem being solved from the point of view of controlling the interaction between each other intelligent agents and robots.
- Control of integrity, access, confidentiality and integrity.

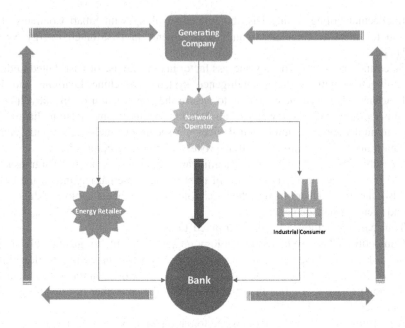

Fig. 7. Traditional market.

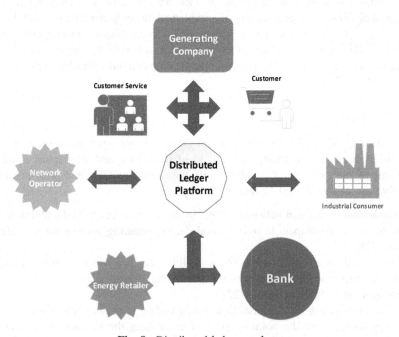

Fig. 8. Distributed ledger market.

The main problem of describing these advantages now is that all solutions are more prototypical in nature without any introduction into real activity. But all this is also explained by the innovation of the Distributed Ledger technology, the development of which is fraught with certain risks and nuances.

4.3   Virtual Power Plants (VPP). Definition

Recently, the concept of a Smart Grid (SG) of power supply has become very popular. A much more impressive continuation of this concept, according to the authors, is the concept of Virtual Power Plants. By introducing the Artificial Intelligence (AI) function into this concept, we are able to generate and sell energy in more flexible realities, taking into account possible supply and demand, which should allow the theory to maximize profits to energy suppliers not through high prices, but rather by reducing generation losses. At the same time, from the point of development of this direction, the authors do not yet have an established terminology. Different authors define this promising direction in their own way. In fact, VPP is defined as a combination of several players, namely, generating companies, consumers of different levels, other players who both produce and generate energy on demand or demand in accordance with requests or demand with minimal human participation [23]. There are alternative definitions, which, under VPP, understand a certain system that is capable in one way or another to generate and accumulate energy demand and supply [24] (Fig. 9).

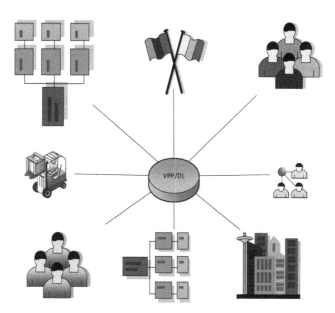

Fig. 9. Virtual power plants.

5   Algorithmic, Management and Technological Limitations

In the process of developing Distributed Ledger, a number of obstacles and limitations must be overcome. The key factor here will be the human factor, since this paradigm substantially rebuilds the landscape of traditional thinking and current business processes, for example [25]. Many authors completely do not take into account the human factor, which can be a significant constraint on the way of implementing these solutions. The next factor that can have a serious impact on the implementation of technologies in the near future may be legislative and legal restrictions that will not allow Distributed Ledger to develop quite rapidly. Various industry standards and regulations will not allow in this case to see rapid and explosive growth in the near future. The authors positively look at this paradigm. In this case, of course, we are aware that the development of this concept will require serious time and effort. An important, in our opinion, restriction may be the algorithmic and mathematical apparatus of this concept. Classical algorithms are not always applicable to real industrial automation solutions [26]. Many algorithms and approaches require more detailed study in the process of implementation in real smart devices, which hinders the development of automation processes based on a Distributed Ledger. Requires serious engineering adaptation of solutions in terms of process automation [27]. At the same time, the authors prudently do not consider open and closed platforms in this case, since the use of the latter will require serious improvement taking into account the features of each specific implementation. Well, an extremely important factor from the point of view of automation of management processes in real cyber-physical systems is the need to build target functions and their multi-criteria optimization [28]. All this will require extremely serious efforts both from the point of view of mathematics and of the engineering final implementation [29].

Nevertheless, the authors believe that the development of Distributed Ledger technologies will continue, which will lead to a profound transformation of all existing and future business processes.

6   Conclusion

In our opinion, Distributed Ledger is a unique technology of the future. Its peculiarity lies in the complex influence on the processes taking place in society. The breadth of future solutions is truly impressive. At the same time, most of the works focus on the technological nuances of technology, going into the field of classical Computer Science, which, in our opinion, is not very true [30]. In fact, it seems to us that the problem lies not so much in technology, but in the management and changing paradigms of doing business [31].

References

1. Kuhn, T.: The Structure of Scientific Revolutions. The University of Chicago Press, Chicago (2012)
2. Peysakhovich, A.: Reinforcement Learning and Inverse Reinforcement Learning with System 1 and System 2 (2019)
3. Kahneman, D.: Thinking, Fast and Slow, Farrar, Straus and Giroux, New York (2013)
4. Lazaridou, A., Peysakhovich, A., Baroni, M.: Multi-agent cooperation. In: ICLR (2017)
5. Bottou, L. (2011). https://arxiv.org/ftp/arxiv/papers/1102/1102.1808.pdf
6. De Domenico, M., et al.: Mathematical formulation of multilayer networks. Phys. Rev. X **3**, 041022 (2013)
7. Boccaletti, S., et al.: The structure and dynamics of multilayer networks. Phys. Rep. **544**, 1–122 (2014)
8. Fong, B., Spivak, D.I.: Hypergraph Categories. J. Pure Appl. Algebr. (2019)
9. Di Francesco Maesa, D., Marino, A., Ricci, L.: Detecting artificial behaviours in the bitcoin users graph. Online Soc. Netw. Media **3–4**, 63–74 (2017)
10. Kotilevets, I.D., et al.: Implementation of directed acyclic graph in blockhain network to improve security and speed of transactions. IFAC **51**, 693–696 (2018)
11. Quiterio, T.M., Lorena, A.C.: Using complexity measures to determine the structure. Appl. Soft Comput. **65**, 428–442 (2018)
12. Bang-Jensen, Jørgen, Gutin, Gregory (eds.): Classes of Directed Graphs. SMM. Springer, Cham (2018). https://doi.org/10.1007/978-3-319-71840-8
13. Comuzzi, M.: Optimal directed hypergraph traversal with ant-colony optimisation. Inf. Sci. **471**, 132–148 (2018)
14. Zhanga, Z., Chen, D., Wang, J., Bai, L., Hancock, E.R.: Quantum-based subgraph convolutional neural networks. Pattern Recognit. **88**, 38–49 (2019)
15. Narayan, A., O'N Roe, P.H.: Learning graph dynamics using deep neural networks. IFAC **51**, 433–438 (2018)
16. Blockchain in energy and utilities use cases, vendor activity. Indigo Advisory Group (2019). https://www.indigoadvisorygroup.com/blockchain
17. Why the energy sector must embrace blockchain now. Ernst & Young Global Limited (2019). https://www.ey.com/en_gl/digital/blockchain-s-potential-win-for-the-energy-sector. Accessed 09 Apr 2019
18. Mengelkamp, E., Gärttner, J., Rock, K., Kessler, S., Orsini, L., Weinhardt, C.: Designing microgrid energy markets. A case study: The Brooklyn Microgrid. Appl. Energy **210**, 870–880 (2018)
19. Hsieh, Y.-Y.: The Rise of Decentralized Autonomous Organizations: Coordination and Growth within Cryptocurrencies. https://ir.lib.uwo.ca/cgi/viewcontent.cgi?article=7386&context=etd. Accessed 10 Apr 2019
20. Kypriotaki, K.N., Zamani, E.D., Giaglis, G.M.: From bitcoin to decentralized autonomous corporations. In: Proceedings of the 17th International Conference on Enterprise Information Systems (ICEIS-2015) (2015)
21. Afanasyev, I., Kolotov, A., Rezin, R., Danilov, K., Kashevnik, A.: Blockchain solutions for multi-agent robotic systems: related work and open questions (2019). https://arxiv.org/pdf/1903.11041.pdf. Accessed 10 Apr 2019
22. Pawlak, M., Poniszewska-Maranda, A., Kryvinska, N.: Towards the intelligent agents for blockchain e-voting system. In: The 9th International Conference on Emerging Ubiquitous Systems and Pervasive Networks (EUSPN 2018), Leuven, Belgium (2018)

23. Ramos, S.: Demand response programs definition supported by clustering and classification techniques. In: 16th International Conference on Intelligent System Applications to Power Systems, Hersonissos, Greece (2011)
24. Pereira, F., Faria, P., Vale, Z.: The influence of the consumer modelling approach in demand response programs implementation. In: 2015 IEEE Eindhoven PowerTech, Eindhoven, Netherlands, 03 September 2015
25. Turk, Ž., Klinc, R.: Potentials of blockchain technology for construction management. In: Creative Construction Conference, CCC 2017, Primosten, Croatia (2017)
26. Rubio, M., Alba, A., Mendez, M., Arce-Santana, E., Rodriguez-Kessler, M.: A consensus algorithm for approximate string matching. In 2013 Iberoamerican Conference on Electronics Engineering and Computer Science, San Luis Potosí, S.L.P., México (2013)
27. Mathias, S.B.B.R.P., Rosset, V., Nascimento, M.C.V.: Community detection by consensus genetic-based algorithm for directed networks. In: 20th International Conference on Knowledge Based and Intelligent Information and Engineering Systems (2016)
28. Liua, Songsong, Papageorgiou, Lazaros G.: Multi-objective optimisation for biopharmaceutical manufacturing under uncertainty. Comput. Chem. Eng. **119**, 383–393 (2018)
29. Xu, C.: A big-data oriented recommendation method based on multi-objective. Knowl.-Based Syst. **177**, 11–21 (2019)
30. Viriyasitavat, W., Hoonsopon, D.: Blockchain characteristics and consensus in modern business. J. Ind. Inf. Integr. (2018)
31. Angelis, J., da Silvac, E.R.: Blockchain adoption: a value driver perspective. Bus. Horiz. (2018)

Deep Learning Approach for Prognoses of Long-Term Options Behavior

A. V. Bogdanov[1,2(✉)], S. A. Bogdanov[1,2], V. P. Rukovchuk[1,2] ⓘ,
and D. S. Khmel[1,2] ⓘ

[1] Plekhanov Russian University of Economics,
Stremyanny lane, 36, Moscow 117997, Russia
bogdanov@csa.ru
[2] Springer Heidelberg, Tiergartenstr. 17, 69121 Heidelberg, Germany

Abstract. Since the inception of asset pricing models, starting as far back as beginning of XX century, and moreover after the fundamental work of Black and Scholes (1973), there has been considerable interest in analytical research of stock exchange equities behavior. Still up to nowadays it remains a critical task for participants engaged in the field of "financial mathematics". The reason of such an undying interest is that to adequately assess investments risks the stock exchange actors (brokers, investors, traders, et. al) need still more and more accurate prediction results obtained as fast as possible. It is a matter of fact proven by numerous researchers that assets derivatives behave differently being observed in small, medium, and long-term frames.

Algorithms for predicting the dynamics of stock options and other assets derivatives for both small times (where one plays on market fluctuations), and medium ones (where trade is stressed at the beginning and closing moments) are well developed, and trading robots are actively used for these purposes. Analysis of the dynamics of assets for very long time-frames (of order of several months and years) is still beyond the scope of analysts as it is expensively prohibited, although this issue is extremely important for hedging the investments portfolios.

The present paper focuses on construction of an effective and resource-intensive model for predicting the behavior of financial instruments, trends and price movements based upon the principles of deep learning. The forecasts obtained by the model showed an almost acceptable compliance with the true prices of the S&P500.

Keywords: Deep learning · S&P500 · Recurrent neural networks · LSTM · TensorFlow

1 Introduction

Many scientists investigating the forecasting of stock and financial markets are trying to introduce machine learning. So, Robert P. Schumaker and Xinchun Chen from the University of Arizona conducted a textual analysis of the stock market forecast using the latest financial news [1]. Their study examines the method of machine learning on financial news using several different textual representations: Bag of Words [2], nominal groups (IG) and named entities. They examined 9,216 financial news articles

S. Misra et al. (Eds.): ICCSA 2019, LNCS 11620, pp. 631–640, 2019.
https://doi.org/10.1007/978-3-030-24296-1_51

and 10,259,042 stock quotes covering the S & P 500 for five weeks. The resulting model was used to estimate a discrete stock price twenty minutes after the publication of a news article. The forecast accuracy was 57%, and profit growth was 2%.

Raj Thakur, Sanchita Badkas, Minakumari Pade and Pallavi Hude. Patila Technical College [3] built a hybrid system on neural networks that tries to predict the price of opening the stock market for several specific companies based on the company's past activity and information from various news sources, combining elements of funda-mental and technical analysis and confirming the viability of this approach.

Felix Min Fai Wong, Zhenmin Liu, Mung Chang from Princeton [4] built a system that predicts price movements only from Wall Street Journal news using Text Mining and sparse matrix factorization. Unlike many existing approaches, the new model can simultaneously use correlations: (a) between stock prices, (b) among news articles, and (c) between stock prices and news articles. Thus, this model is able to predict more than 500 stocks daily with an accuracy of 55.7%.

There are now many open source tools and libraries for creating deep learning models. Most frameworks present a model in the form of a computational graph, static or dynamic:

- The frameworks that declare calculation graphs statically, such as TensorFlow, allow you to first define the architecture of the graph, and then you can run it many times, running some amount of data through it. This makes it easy to distribute tasks for execution on different machines. In addition to this, frameworks can optimize the graph for you in advance. They also allow users to serialize a schedule after it has been created and execute it without requiring the code that built it.
- Frameworks that declare calculation graphs dynamically, such as PyTorch, allow you to implicitly define a computational graph. Dynamic graph structures are usually less invasive and deeply integrated with the programming language used. This leads to a cleaner and more easily debugged code and allows the use of conditional operators and cycles to build more complex graph structures, such as recurrent neural networks. The construction and execution of the graph are inter-twined, which leaves little time for its optimization.

Stating ultimately, the recurrent neural network (RNN) architecture [5], built on the elements of long-time short-term memory (LSTM) [6], was chosen for providing learning procedure. Since the historical process of price movements is a time series, we need to regularly refer to it and to take into account the long-term context for which implementation, in fact, RNN with LSTM is intended.

To implement the selected model, the choice fell on TensorFlow. The popularity of this framework is well deserved: we get support from a large number of developers, extensive documentation choices, open source code, distributed execution of our models, various architectural optimizations, visualization at runtime (which makes it easier to debug the model), and portability to the extent that we can run the model on smartphones with Android.

Next, we will discuss how to build a RNN model with LSTM cells for predicting the S & P500 index.

2 Data Preparation

In this paper, we used data from the S & P 500 from January 3, 1950 (the earliest date that Yahoo! Finance can track) until April 22, 2019. The dataset provides several price points per day. For simplicity, we will use only daily closing prices for forecasting.

A recurrent neural network (RNN) is a type of artificial neural network with recurrent transitions in hidden layers, which allows it to use the previous state of hidden neurons to obtain a new result with new input. RNN can handle sequential data. Long Short-Term Memory (LSTM) is a specially designed cell that helps the RNN better remember the long-term context. Stock prices are time series with lengths N, defined as $p_0, p_1, ..., p_{N-1}$, where p_i – is a closing price at date i, $0 \leq i < N$. Imagine that we have a fixed-size sliding window w (hereinafter referred to as *input_size*), and we move it to the right by w so that there is no overlap between the data in all sliding windows (Fig. 1).

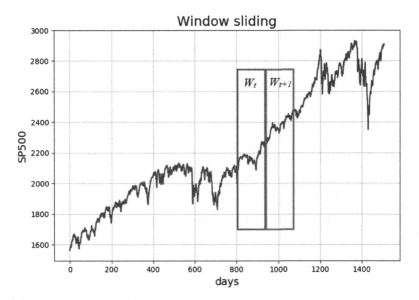

Fig. 1. S & P 500 prices in time. We use data in one sliding window to make a prediction for the next, while there is no overlap between two consecutive windows.

The RNN model we are building has LSTM cells as major hidden elements. We use values from the very beginning of training in the first sliding window W_0 till window at the moment t:

$$W_0 = (p_0, p_1, ..., p_{w-1})$$
$$W_1 = (p_w, p_{w+1}, ..., p_{2w-1})$$
$$...$$
$$W_t = (p_{tw}, p_{tw+1}, ..., p_{(t+1)w-1})$$

to predict prices in the next window W_{t+1}:

$$W_{t+1} = \left(p_{(t+1)w}, p_{(t+1)w+1}, \ldots, p_{(t+2)w-1} \right)$$

Essentially, we are trying to find an approximation function:

$$f(W_0, W_1, \ldots, W_1) \approx \sim W_{t+1}$$

The sequence of prices is first divided into small non-overlapping windows. Each one contains *input_size* numbers, each of which is considered as one independent input element. Then any consecutive input elements *num_steps* grouped into one input for learning, forming a "non-twisted" version of the RNN for training in TensorFlow. The corresponding label is an input element immediately after them

E.g. if *input_size = 3* and *num_steps = 2*, then the first few examples of training will look like this:

$$\text{Input}_1 = [[p_0, p_1, p_2], [p_3, p_4, p_5]], \ Label_1 = [p_6, p_7, p_8]$$
$$\text{Input}_2 = [[p_3, p_4, p_5], [p_6, p_7, p_8]], \ Label_2 = [p_9, p_{10}, p_{11}]$$
$$\text{Input}_3 = [[p_6, p_7, p_8], [p_9, p_{10}, p_{11}]], \ Label_3 = [p_{12}, p_{13}, p_{14}]$$

Since we always want to predict future values, we take the last 10% of the data as test values.

3   Data Normalization

The S & P500 index increases with time, which leads to the fact that most of the values in the test set are out of tolerance, and thus the model must predict values that it has never seen before. It is not surprising that sooner or later the model ceases to behave adequately (Fig. 2).

To solve the problem with the scale, it is necessary to normalize prices in each sliding window. Now the task is to predict the relative levels of change instead of absolute values. In normalized sliding window W_t' at the moment t all values are divided by the last unknown price - the last price in W_{t-1}. Thus, the deviation from the fixed last value of the previous window is taken as the normalization factor:

$$W_t' \left(\frac{p_{tw}}{p_{tw-1}} - 1, \frac{p_{tw+1}}{p_{tw-1}} - 1, \ldots, \frac{p_{(t+1)w-1}}{p_{tw-1}} - 1 \right)$$

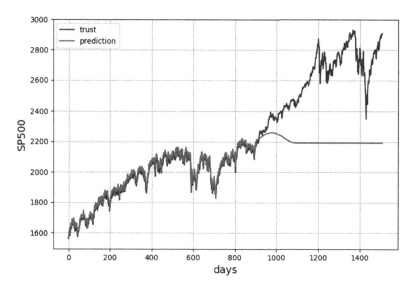

Fig. 2. An example when RNN tries to predict values that lie outside the training data.

4 Building the Model

Definitions to be used in the model (Table 1)

Table 1. Model Definitions in TensorFlow

Константа	Описание
lstm_size	The number of elements in one LSTM layer
num_layers	The number of LSTM-layers
keep_prob	The percentage of items to save in the exception operation
init_learning_rate	Initial learning rate
learning_rate_decay	Rate of learning attenuation in finite epochs of learning
init_epoch	The number of epochs using constant init_learning_rate
max_epoch	Total number of learning epochs
input_size	Sliding window size/one tutorial data point
batch_size	Number of data points for use in one mini-batch
embedding_size	Controls the size of each embedding vector
stock_count	The number of unique stocks in the data set

LSTM-model has *num_layers* of combined LSTM layers, and each layer contains *lstm_size* of LSTM-elements. Then, an exception mask is applied to the output of each LSTM element with the probability of saving *keep_prob*. The goal of the exception is to eliminate the potential strong dependence on a single dimension in order to prevent overtraining [7].

The learning requires *max_epoch* of epochs overall, an epoch is one complete pass through all training data. For one epoch, the training data is divided into mini-batch size *batch_size*. The learning rate if fixed as an *init_learning_rate* for the first epochs *init_epoch*, and then gets decreased by *learn_rate_decay* for each consecutive one.

It is expected that the model will study the price sequence in time of different companies. Because of the different patterns, I would like the model to clearly speak with what stocks it works. Investing is profitable compared to one-hot encoding [8], because:

- Given that N shares are included in the training data, one-hot encoding will result in additional sparse N (or N-1) parameters. As each share is mapped to a much smaller embedding vector of length k, $k \ll N$, we get a much more concise view and a smaller data set.
- Since investment vectors are learning variables, similar actions can be associated with similar investments and help predict each other, such as «GOOG» and «GOOGL».

In a recurrent neural network at one time step t, the input vector contains *input_size* (marked as W) daily price values of i-share, $(p_{i,tw}, p_{i,tw+1}, ..., p_{i,(t+1)w-1})$. The share is uniquely displayed on the length vector *embedding_size* (marked as k), $(e_{i,0}, e_{i,1}, ..., e_{i,k})$. As shown in Fig. 3, the price vector is concatenated with the attachment vector, and then fed to the LSTM cell.

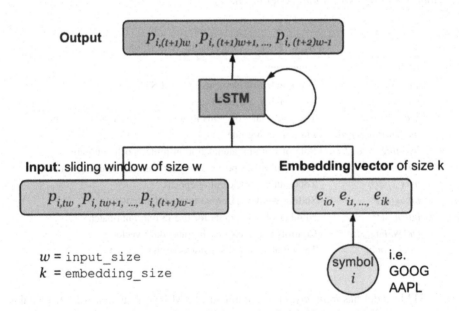

Fig. 3. RNN model for predicting stock prices with an investment.

Another alternative is to concatenate the attachment vectors with the last state of the LSTM cell and obtain new weights W and offset b in the output layer. However, in this way, an LSTM element cannot distinguish the prices of one stock from another, and its power will be largely held back.

5   Experiments

For the first one, the following configuration was used (Table 2):

Table 2. Experiment 1.

Parameter	Value
num_layers	1
keep_prob	0.8
batch_size	64
init_learning_rate	0.001
learning_rate_decay	0.99
init_epoch	5
max_epoch	50
num_steps	30

In general, predicting stock prices is not an easy task. Especially after normalization, price trends look very noisy (Figs. 4a, 4b, 4c).

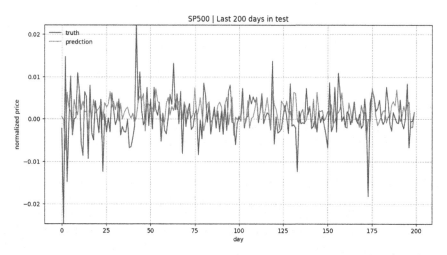

Fig. 4a. The results of the forecast for the last 200 days in the test data. The model learns with *input_size* = 1 and *lstm_size* = 32.

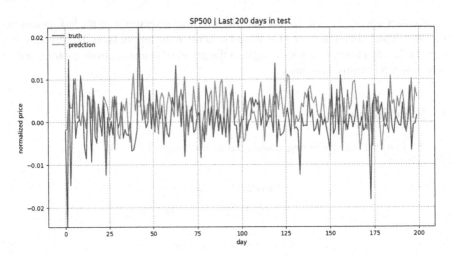

Fig. 4b. The results of the forecast for the last 200 days in the test data. The model learns with *input_size* = 1 and *lstm_size* = 128.

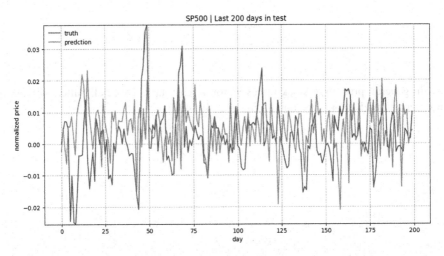

Fig. 4c. The results of the forecast for the last 200 days in the test data. The model learns with *input_size* = 5, *lstm_size* = 128 and *max_epoch* = 75 (instead of 50).

For the second experiment, the following configuration was used (Table 3):

For a brief overview of the quality of prediction in Fig. 5 presents the forecast for the test data "IBM". General trends coincide between true values and forecasts. Considering how the forecasting task is designed, the model relies on all historical data points to predict only the next 5 days (*input_size*). At low value of *input_size* model, there's no need to worry about a long-term growth curve. But as soon as we increase *input_size*, prediction will get way more complicated.

Table 3. Experiment 2.

Parameter	Value
num_layers	1
keep_prob	0.8
batch_size	64
init_learning_rate	0.05
learning_rate_decay	0.99
init_epoch	5
max_epoch	150
num_steps	30
stock_count	100
input_size	5
embed_size	3
lstm_size	256

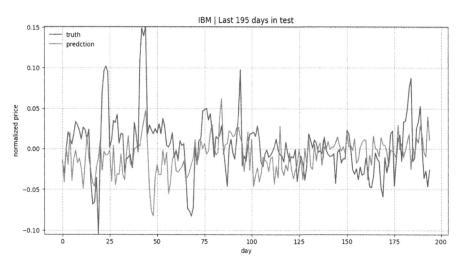

Fig. 5. The true and predicted prices of IBM stocks on a test dataset. Prices are normalized in sliding windows. Y-axis values are multiplied by 2 for a better comparison between true and predicted trends.

Predictive decrease and smooth quite often as you go through the training. Therefore, it is necessary to multiply the absolute values by a constant in order to make the trend more noticeable as in Fig. 5, because we need to know whether the direction of price movement is predicted correctly: up or down. However, there must be a reason for reducing the prediction value. Theoretically, instead of using simple MSE as a loss function, we can choose another method so that if the direction is incorrectly predicted, the penalty will be stronger.

The loss function quickly decreases at the very beginning, but it suffers from an accidental explosion (a sudden peak occurs and then immediately returns). Most likely this is due to its shape. An updated and more adequate loss function can solve the problem.

6 Conclusion

In this paper, we analyzed the various methods of in-depth training, libraries and tools that are in the public domain for the task of forecasting price movements in financial markets. Search, preprocessing and normalization of historical price data S & P500 for training and model testing.

In the process, a software package was obtained for predicting the direction of price movement that implements the recurrent neural network architecture (RNN) built on the elements of long short-term memory (LSTM). The choice was made in favor of just such an architecture, since the price movement history is a time series and it is necessary to regularly refer to it and take into account the long-term context, and the RNN with LSTM is intended for this.

There are many ways to improve the result: design of layers and neurons, different initialization and activation schemes, combination with other models (for example, with intelligent text analysis), etc. It is worth mentioning the presence of a whole class of microprocessors and coprocessors (AI accelerators) that can apply to accelerate the work of existing models due to the highest level of parallelism.

References

1. Schumaker, R.P., Chen, H.: Textual Analysis of Stock Market Prediction Using Breaking Financial News: The AZFinText System. Artificial Intelligence Lab, Department of Management Information Systems, The University of Arizona (2006)
2. Obogashchenie modeli Bag of words semanticheskimi svyazyami dlya povysheniya kachestva klassifikacii tekstov predmetnoj oblasti [Enrichment of the Bag of words model with semantic links to improve the quality of text classification in the subject domain]. http://swsys.ru/index.php?page=article&id=4153. Accessed 04 Apr 2019
3. Thakur, R., Badkas, S., Pade, M., Khude, P.: Stock market prediction using Neural Networks and sentiment analysis of News Articles. D.Y. Patil College of Engineering, Akurdi, Pune (2017). http://dx.doi.org/10.21474/IJAR01/3749. Accessed 04 Apr 2019
4. Ming, F., Wong, F., Liu, Z., Chiang, M.: Stock market prediction from WSJ: text mining via sparse matrix factorization. Princeton University. arXiv:1406.7330v1 [cs.LG] 27 Jun 2014
5. Vvedenie v rekurrentnye nejroseti: RNN, dvunapravlennaya RNN, LSTM, GRU [Introduction to recurrent neural networks: RNN, bidirectional RNN, LSTM, GRU]. https://trainmydata.com/article/vviedieniie-v-riekurrientnyie-nieirosieti-rnn-dvunapravliennaia-rnn-lstm-gru. Accessed 04 Apr 2019
6. Understanding LSTM Networks http://colah.github.io/posts/2015–08-Understanding-LSTMs. Accessed 04 Apr 2019
7. Srivastava, N., Hinton, G., Krizhevsky, A., Sutskever, L., Salakhutdinov, R.: Dropout: a simple way to prevent neural networks from overfitting. J. Mach. Learn. Res. **15** (2014). https://www.cs.toronto.edu/~ hinton/absps/JMLRdropout.pdf. Accessed 04 Apr 2019
8. How to One Hot Encode Sequence Data in Python. https://machinelearningmastery.com/how-to-one-hot-encode-sequence-data-in-python. Accessed 04 Apr 2019. Author, F.: Article title. Journal **2**(5), 99–110 (2016)

Bio and Neuro inspired Computing and Applications (BIONCA 2019)

Using Neural Networks and Hough Transform for Leukocytes Differentiation in Blood Count Images

Yuri Marchetti Tavares[1], Nadia Nedjah[2(✉)], and Luiza de Macedo Mourelle[3]

[1] Naval Weapon Systems Department, Brazilian Navy, Brasilia, Brazil
[2] Department of Electronics Engineering and Telecommunications,
Engineering Faculty, State University of Rio de Janeiro, Rio de Janeiro, Brazil
nadia@eng.uerj.br
[3] Department of System Engineering and Computation, Engineering Faculty,
State University of Rio de Janeiro, Rio de Janeiro, Brazil

Abstract. Automated equipments for blood count have facilitated the clinical routines in medical laboratories. However, when grave anomalies are identified, some samples still need to be analyzed in a traditional way using a microscope. This paper proposes a method to classify the five most common types of leukocytes, present in the human blood using blood smear images. This allows reducing the amount of work, the time spent in the blood test as well as cost of such a test. The results are satisfactory and should contribute positively to the development of an automatic system and/or a smart electronic device, which would come handy for this kind of applications.

1 Introduction

The blood count is a medical routine for blood test to evaluate peripherical blood. It is one of the most requested blood test, and it is used for obtaining diagnostics, clinical evaluations and the evolution process of several diseases [1]. Basically, the blood count provides qualitative and quantitative informations about the blood cells.

The Practical Manual of Hematology [2] states that the human blood consists of plasma (55%) and cells (45%). The formed elements, which are made up of the blood cells and platelets, also called cellular portion presents three types of cells in suspension in the plasm: red corpuscles (erythrocytes), white corpuscles (leukocytes) and platelets. The white corpuscles have also other subdivisions: lymphocytes, basophils, monocytes, eosinophils and neutrophils.

Initially, the blood tests were done through microscopes, where the erythrocytes, leukocytes and platelets are observed and counted using a Neubauer's camera and colored glass slide. With electronics development and automation, several equipments were designed to provide these informations in a fast and precise way.

ⓒ Springer Nature Switzerland AG 2019
S. Misra et al. (Eds.): ICCSA 2019, LNCS 11620, pp. 643–653, 2019.
https://doi.org/10.1007/978-3-030-24296-1_52

The automate analysis has facilitated the performance of the routine in clinics laboratories. The equipments usually allow analysis of 30 to 120 blood counts per hour. The most simple appliances have the impedance principle as reference, with the change of electric current between two electrodes. When a cell transverse the system, there is a change in this impedance and a electrical impulse is generated, according to the diameter of each cell (erythrocytes, leukocytes or platelets). These equipments allow present clinics laboratories to deal with high volume of samples received daily.

However, some samples analyzed by the automate cell counters still require manual evaluation of the blood smear for anomalies observation. Every time a blood test result has to be confirmed, the technician prepares the blood smear of the patient and analyses it with a microscope. This procedure is precise, but also very slow and demands a laborious process. A specific amount of blood is required to put on a glass slide, to color it and to wait until it dries. Afterwards, the technician must check the glass slide and count cell after cell with the microscope. On the other hand, the informations obtained through images and videos have become an important area of research, especially with the development and refinement of sensors and intelligent equipments capable of capturing, storing, editing and transmitting images.

This paper proposes the development of a method that can automate the process of identification and counting of blood cells, that contributes to the decrease of work, of the time to provide the analysis result and even of the cost for the blood exam in hematology laboratories. The objective is to develop a classifier, based on artificial neural networks, capable of identifying blood cells and differ the leukocytes in exams performed with blood on glass slides. The classifier uses the Hough transform, mathematical morphology and segmentation, also based on neural networks, to automate the process of cell counting.

Section 2 presents some related works. First, in Sect. 3 some blood cell components are introduced. Then, in Sect. 4, we describe the methodology and the structure of the proposed method, including segmentation and characteristics extractions. Subsequently, in Sect. 5, we present some results. Finally, in Sect. 6, we draw some conclusions.

2   Related Work

In [3], the authors use the concept of Hough transform showing a methodology for segmenting and counting red cells in images of blood cells. Only the erythrocytes were considered, taking into account their size and shape.

In [4], a system based on neural networks is proposed for classifying blood cells. The aim of the work is the extraction of characteristics only for classifying the three main groups: red cells, white cells and platelets. Aspects of detection and segmentation of cells are not considered, as well as the differentiation of leukocytes.

In [5], a method for segmentation, identification and classification of white cells is proposed, based on the equalization of histogram, thresholding and edge detection. However, the proposed method classifies only three of five subclasses of leukocytes: neutrophils, lymphocytes and basophils.

The present work extends the concept of Hough transform to leukocytes too. One segmentation, based on neural networks, is proposed in order to separate the images in four distinct classes: erythrocytes, cytoplasm, nucleus and background. As part of the segmentation, mathematical morphology and edge detection are used to separate the leukocytes from the rest of the image. These leukocytes are differentiated in five classes (neutrophils, lymphocytes, monocytes, eosinophils and basophils) through the use of another neural network.

3   Blood Cells

The blood consists of a fluid, in which there are cells in suspension, molecules and ions dissolved in water. An important characteristic of the blood is its steady chemical composition and physical properties, assuring physical conditions for the cell function. The cell part consists of 45% of the whole volume.

To perform the exams with microscope, the blood is spread on a glass slide and, then, colored. Coloring is an important step, since it facilitates the microscopic observation of the cells, differentiating them according to their characteristics. Typical dyes used are: methyl blue, which gives a blue color to DNA, RNA, nucleoproteins, basophil granules and, weakly, eosinophil granules, and violet eusinate, which gives an orange color to hemoglobin [1].

Erythrocytes, or red globules, are small circular cells with 7.5 mm of diameter. They do not have a nucleus, but only plasmatic membrane and cytoplasm. They are the most numerous cells of the blood, with 4.5 to 6.5 millions of cells per mm^3. The normal erythrocytes, cells number 1 in Fig. 1, have the shape of a biconcave disk.

Platelets are small cells in the shape of a disk, with a diameter of 2 to $3\,\mu m$, corresponding to cells number 2 in Fig. 1. They are formed of fragments of cytoplasm of the megakaryocyte, original cell, and are responsible for hemostasis and blood clotting.

Leukocytes, or white blood cells, form the most heterogeneous group of blood cells, both from the morphological and physiological point of view. Although they perform the role of organism defense, each subtype holds very specific and distinct functions among themselves, which together, define the immune system [1]. The leukocytes are present in the blood in a very lower number than the erythrocytes, with around 4000 to 10000 leukocytes per mm^3 of blood.

Neutrophils are the leukocytes found in higher quantity in the human blood and are known for presenting a neutral tonality in blood coloring. They have small cytoplasmatic granules, weakly colored in purple-reddish. The mature neutrophil, cell number 3 in Fig. 1, have 12 to 15 μm of diameter. The core is divided in 2 to 5 distinct lobes. The precursor cell of the segmented neutrophil is a band neutrophil. They are so called because their core does not present segmentation.

Eosinophils are slightly bigger than neutrophils, measuring from 12 to 17 μm. The cores have usually two lobes, connected through on filament. The cytoplasm is covered by spherical granules, that are colored in orange-reddish, corresponding to cell number 5 in Fig. 1.

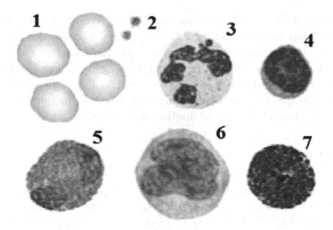

Fig. 1. Different kind of blood Cells (Color figure online)

Basophils have almost the same size as neutrophils, measuring from 10 to 14 μm of diameter. Their central core have two or three lobes, that are usually obscured by cytoplamatic granules colored in black-blueish, as shown by cell number 7 in Fig. 1.

Monocytes are the biggest leukocytes, measuring from 12 to 20 μm of diameter. They are cells of irregular form, with a big and unic core, centrally located. The cytoplasm have a blue-grayish color, as shown by cell number 6 in Fig. 1.

Lynfocytes, corresponding to cell number 4 in Fig. 1, are the second most abundant of leukocytes in the circulation. The are small mononucleus cells, without granules in the cytoplasm, slightly bigger than erythrocytes, measuring from 10 to 16 μm of diameter. Their core is big and homogeneous, showing an intense blueish color.

4   Methodology

For the execution of the proposed method, the procedure is divided into five steps: image acquisition, preprocessing, characteristics extraction, Differential Artificial Neural Network (DANN) training and DANN utilization. The evaluation of the proposed method is also planned.

For the acquisition step, images available from Hemosurf [6] were used as data base. They consist of blood cells obtained from a Zeiss Axioskop microscope and Sony DXC-3000A 3CCD video camera, freely available by Bern University. For this work, images with 1000x zoom were used from the set "Normal White Blood Cells", the set "Examine and Compare Normal Leukocytes", the normal leukocytes set "Blood Film 4" and the basophils and eosinophils set "Chronic Myelocytic Leukemia".

The preprocessing step includes the identification and segmentation of the leukocytes from the acquired images of the previous step. After this step, smaller images were obtained, having isolatedly each white globule. These images were separated by class, so that 70% of the segmented images were used for the DANN and 30% were used for the generalization evaluation.

The next step is the attributes extraction of each isolated white globule. These attributes are inserted as inputs of the DANN.

With the training data base having the characteristics of each cell, the DANN can be trained. Once trained, this net can be used for classifying the five classes of interest, implementing the differentiation of the leukocytes. For the evaluation of the model and of the DANN, a test of the generalization is implemented, with those 30% of the data separated in the preprocessing step.

4.1 Preprocessing

Image segmentation is the main part of the preprocessing step, where leukocytes are identified and separated. For this function, another neural network is used, called Segmentation Artificial Neural Network (SANN). This neural network is of type Multilayer Perceptron, with a hidden layer, a hyperbolic tangent function as transfer function of the hidden layer and a linear function as output transfer function. Cross validation i used with anticipated stop and the error is estimated using the quadratic medium error.

Pixels of the four areas, that we wished to separate, were used as input data of the RANN: red blood cells, leukocytes core and cytoplasm, and background. RGB values of each pixel were considered as inputs. In order to form the training set, small samples of each segmentation class in two images of the data base were selected. Figure 2 shows the segmentation result obtained for one of the images. The pink elements refer to the red blood cells, the green elements are the cytoplasm, the blue elements are the core and the white areas are the background. This is the best achieved result. Three neurons in the hidden layer were used. In order to deal with the fact that part of some red blood cells were wrongly

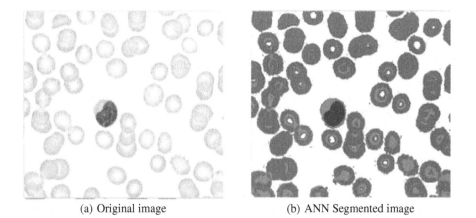

(a) Original image   (b) ANN Segmented image

Fig. 2. Blood cells image before and after segmentation (Color figure online)

marked as cytoplasm, mathematical morphology is inserted into the preprocessing step.

Mathematical morphology consisted, first, of opening and closing operations with a disk type morphological element of 3×3. The aim is thus to fully fill the leukocyte cytoplasm. Afterwards, erosion and dilation operations were implemented to eliminate the red blood cells marked as cytoplasm. The result obtained for Fig. 2 is shown in Fig. 3.

At this processing step, the only thing missing is the identification of the leukocyte. For this function, the Hough transform is used. This transform was proposed by Hough [7] for detecting subatomic particles path, popularized by Rosenfeld [8] and largely used for detecting geometric forms, such as lines, circles and ellipses [9]. This method converts the problem of curve detection in an efficient search for peaks in the parameters space.

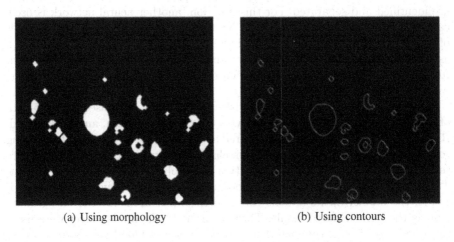

(a) Using morphology   (b) Using contours

Fig. 3. Blood cells image of Fig. 2 digitalized using morphology *vs.* contours

The Hough transform fits perfectly in the detection of the circle center, which represents the leukocyte in the digitalized image. The search parameters were adjusted such that only circles of diameter very close to the leukocytes diameter were found. We also observed that the Hough transform is more efficient when only the objects perimeter were considered. Therefore, before implementing the search, the image is submitted to the Sobel filter for board detection. The resulting image can be seen in Fig. 3. Finally, the leukocyte is extracted independently from the rest of the image, as shown in Fig. 4.

4.2   Characteristics Extraction

The chosen characteristics for the DANN input were selected such that they were able to separate the classes in the best and clearer way possible. The size of the cells, the size of the core and the rate of the red color in the cytoplasm,

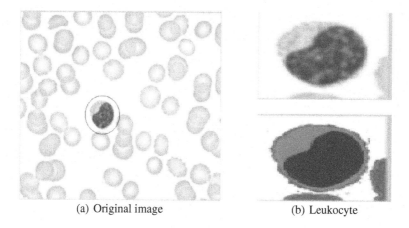

(a) Original image   (b) Leukocyte

Fig. 4. Leukocyte found in the blood cells image of Fig. 2

as indicated by rate R were considered. For each of the chosen cells, these characteristics were calculated using Eqs. (1), (2) and (3):

$$T_T = P_N + P_C \tag{1}$$

$$T_N = \frac{P_N}{T_T} \tag{2}$$

$$R = \frac{\sum R_i}{P_C}, \tag{3}$$

where T_T is the total size of the cell, P_N is the number of pixels corresponding to the core, P_C is the number of pixels corresponding to the cytoplasm, T_N is the size of the cell core, R is the red rate of the cytoplasm and R_i is the value of pixel i red component of the cytoplasm. We observe that the segmentation precision of SANN is of fundamental importance for the calculation of these parameters.

Sometimes, besides the leukocytes, some of the red blood cells are also selected. In order to eliminate these undesirable data, a threshold is defined, when calculating the characteristics: if the size of the core is less than 25% of the cell total size, the datum is eliminated. This way, we can guarantee that only the leukocytes that have core are considered in the construction of the data base.

Figure 5 shows the leukocytes distribution, used in the DANN training, in the characteristics space. The red circles represent the neutrophils, the blue circles are the lymphocytes and the gray circles are the monocytes. The black crosses represent the basophils and the magenta crosses are the eosinophils.

4.3   Differentiation Artificial Neural Network

In order to classify the five classes of leukocytes, an artificial neural network of type Multilayer Perceptron is used, considered an universal approximator [10]. The used topology consists of an input layer, with each input related to

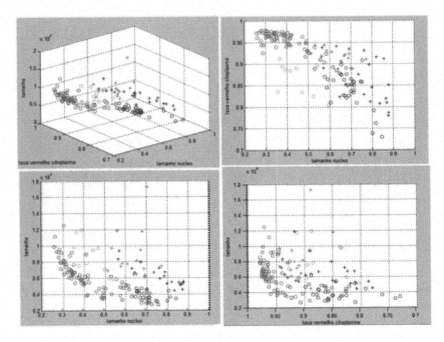

Fig. 5. Representation of the training leukocytes in the feature space (Color figure online)

each characteristic defined in the previous section, and one output, with linear function. Only one hidden layer is used, with hyperbolic tangent as activation function.

During the supervised training, with crossed validation and anticipated stop, the network parameters were adjusted so that its output assumed the pre-established value for each class, according to Table 1. Limited values were established at the output, so that the classificator output showed only discrete values between 1 and 5.

5   Results

In order to implement all the proposed procedure, tha MATLAB 8.3.0532 (R2014a) software is used, running on an ASUS computer, with Intel Core i7-2630 QM 2GHz, 6GB RAM and 64 bits Windows 7 Home Premium operating system. Images processing and artificial neural networks were implemented using the MATLAB toolbox. A independent script is used for the Hough transform. The DANN is then trained with data from the preprocessing step, using the medium squared error as stop criteria, with crossed validation (30%) and anticipated stop.

The best network is identified empirically and has eight neurons in the hidden layer. The training is repeated for 15 times, resulting in a medium squared error

Table 1. Expected values of the DANN output

Blood cell	Class	DANN output
Neutrophil	1	[0.5, 1.5]
Lymphocytes	2	[1.5, 2.5]
Monocyte	3	[2.5, 3.5]
Eosinophil	4	[3.5, 4.5]
Basophil	5	[4.5, 5.5]

of 16.18%. After the training, the network is used for classifying the training data and the confusion matrix showed in Table 2 shows the collected results. We can observe that the network has learned well how to classify the neutrophils with a hit rate of 100% and that the hit rate of the other classes is higher than 54%.

Table 2. Confusion matrix obtained with the training data

Found class	Real class				
	Neutrophil	Lymphocytes	Monocyte	Eosinophil	Bashophil
Neutrophil	66	2	0	0	0
Lymphocytes	0	29	4	0	0
Monocyte	0	6	6	2	0
Eosinophil	0	1	1	12	0
Basophil	0	0	0	2	12

In order to evaluate the generalization of DANN and validate the method, the test set is used. The overall error is 25.35%. To evaluate the error rate, the false positive and the false negative rates for each class, the confusion matrix of Tables 3 and 4 are exploited.

Table 3. Confusion matrix obtained during generalization

Found class	Real class				
	Neutrophil	Lymphocytes	Monocyte	Eosinophil	Bashophil
Neutrophil	30	1	1	0	0
Lymphocytes	2	11	1	1	0
Monocyte	0	4	4	1	1
Eosinophil	0	1	0	4	3
Basophil	0	0	0	2	4

Table 4. Hit rate, false positive rate and false negative rate for each considered class

	Neutrophil	Linfocyte	Monocyte	Eosinophil	Bashophil
Hit	93,75%	64,7%	66,7%	50%	50%
False positive	6,25%	26,7%	60%	50%	33,33%
False negative	6,25%	35,29%	33,3%	50%	50%

We can observe that the network displays the same pattern shown during the training, proving the generalization. Again, the neutrophils hit rate is very high. These results are due to the fact that the neutrophils are the kind of leukocytes that are most abundant in the blood, presenting greater number of data.

It is noteworthy to point out that the result is also influenced by the low quantity of data available. Compared to the red blood cells and platelets, the amount of leukocytes present per mm^3 is very low. This fact hinders the generation of a rich and consistent data base. In order to train the network correctly, it is necessary to have statistical information about the samples. For instance, in the case of the monocytes, the network exploited 11 samples and the generalization test is implemented with 8 samples only. It is noteworthy to emphasize that the difference in contrast and brightness during the images acquisition can influence the results, if there is not enough data.

6 Conclusion

The proposed method was considered promising, showing a satisfactory result and generalization capacity. We can also say that it is applicable to real world systems, in which the resolution conditions, size and brightness of the microscope images can be controlled, providing even also the increase in the results performance.

For future work, we foresee the inclusion of characteristics related to the shape of the blood cell to provide a differentiation of stick neutrophils and segmented neutrophils, and also the identification of abnormal cells. In this last case, it is of great importance when elaborating the evaluation manual of blood smears.

Acknowledgement. We are grateful to the State of Rio de Janeiro funding agency FAPERJ (http://www.faperj.br) for supporting this research.

References

1. Monteiro, F.G.: Comparação dos Resultados de Hemogramas do Contador Eletrónico ABX Pentra 60 com a Microscopia, M.Sc. Dissertation, Federal University of Rio Grande do Sul, Brazil (2005)
2. Vivas, W.L.P.: Manual Prático de Hematologia. http://docente.ifsc.edu. br/rosane.aquino/MaterialDidatico/AnalisesClinicas/hemato/Manual%20de %20Hematologia.pdf. Accessed June 2019

3. Maitra, M., Gupta, R.K., Mukherjee, M.: Detection and couting of red blood cells in blood cell images using hough transform. Int. J. Comput. Appl. **53**(16) (2007)
4. Khashman, A.: Blood cell identification using a simple neural network. Int. J. Neural Syst. **18**(5), 453–458 (2008)
5. Hiremath, P.S., Bannigidad, P., Geeta, S.: Automated identification and classification of white blood cells (Leukocytes) in digital microscopic images. IJCA Special Issue Recent Trends Image Process. Pattern Recogn. (2010)
6. Hemosurf (2014). http://hemosurf.ehb.be/Data/Data_E/wbc.htm
7. Hough, P.V.C.: A Method and Means for Recognizing Complex Patterns, U.S. Patent 3,069,654, December (1962)
8. Rosenfeld, A.: Picture processing by computer. ACM Comput. Surv. **1**, 147–176 (1969)
9. Mukhopadhyay, P., Chaudhuri, B.B.: A survey of hough transform. Pattern Recogn. **48**, 87–116 (2015)
10. Hornik, K., Stinchcombe, M., White, H.: Multilayer feedforward networks are universal approximators. Neural Networks **2**, 359–366 (1989)

Efficient Application Mapping onto Three-Dimensional Network-on-Chips Using Multi-Objective Particle Swarm Optimization

Maamar Bougherara[1,3], Nadia Nedjah[2(✉)], Djamel Bennouar[3],
Rebiha Kemcha[3,4], and Luiza de Macedo Mourelle[5]

[1] LIMPAF Laboratory, Bouira University, Bouira, Algeria
[2] Department of Electronics Engineering and Telecommunications,
State University of Rio de Janeiro, Rio de Janeiro, Brazil
nadia@eng.uerj.br
[3] Département d'Informatique, Ecole Normale Supérieure Kouba, Algiers, Algeria
[4] LIMOSE Laboratory, Boumerdes University, Boumerdes, Algeria
[5] Department of Systems Engineering and Computation,
State University of Rio de Janeiro, Rio de Janeiro, Brazil

Abstract. Network-on-chip (NoC) is considered the next generation of communication in embedded system. In this case, an application is implemented by a set of collaborative intellectual propriety blocks (IPs). The selection of the most suited block from a library of IPs as well as their physical mapping onto the three-dimensional Network on-chip infrastructure to implement efficiently the application are two NP-complete problems. In this paper, we propose to use Multi-Objective Particle Swarm Optimization (MOPSO) to yield the best selection of IP and there physical mapping of a given application on three-dimensional topologies. In this purpose, MOPSO is exploited to obtain the personalized result for the application at hand. Only the used resources, switches and channels by the application mapping are part of the customized implementation platform. The optimization is driven by the minimization of required hardware area, the imposed execution time and the necessary power consumption of the final implementation.

Keywords: 3D NoCs · IP mapping · Multi-objective optimization · MOPSO

1 Introduction

Systems-on-Chip (SoC) integrate a complete system into a single chip. The number of integrated components continues to increase to meet the requirements of today's applications. Thereby, the design of SoCs focuses in communications more than computations [1]. Network-on-Chip (NoC) emerged as a viable

© Springer Nature Switzerland AG 2019
S. Misra et al. (Eds.): ICCSA 2019, LNCS 11620, pp. 654–670, 2019.
https://doi.org/10.1007/978-3-030-24296-1_53

solution to on-chip communication bottlenecks. It's similar to a general network but with limited resources such as area, bandwidth and power.

A NoC consists of set of *resources* (*R*) and *switches* (*S*). Each resource of the NoC is an Intellectual Property (IP) block that can be a general or special purpose such as a processor, memory and DSP [1]. A NoC is designed to run a specific application. This kind of applications is generally limited by the number of the tasks that are implemented in IP block. An IP block can implement many tasks and execute them as a general-purpose processor does. In contrast, an IP block is conditioned to execute some types of tasks. Therefore, it is necessary to choose the adequate IP block before designing an efficient NoC-based system for any application. The choice becomes harder when the number of tasks increases. It is also necessary to map these blocks onto the NoC available infrastructure. The latter consists of a set of cores communicating using switches.

Resources and switches are connected by *links*. The pair (*R, S*) forms a *tile*. The simplest way to connect the available resources and switches is arranging them using topologies, the two-dimensional mesh topology is the most popular used in NoC due to its simplicity however the two dimensional Noc has not been thought to meet the requirement of System-on-Chip in many aspects. Three-dimensional network on chip (3D NoC) is an effective solution to the problem of interconnection complexity of large-scale SoC. 3D NoC breaks the limitations on performance and size of two-dimensional Network on Chip (2D NoC) by using integrated circuit stacking technology.

A three-dimensional (3D) mesh is implemented by stacking several layers of 2D mesh on top of each other and providing vertical links for interlayer communication. The vertical interconnections, Through-SiliconVia (TSV) [18] can be a potential candidate. A switch is able to buffer and route messages between resources. Each switch is connected to up to six other neighboring switches through input and output channels. While a channel is sending data another channel can buffer incoming data. Figure 1 shows the architecture of a 3D mesh-based NoC, where each resource contains one or more IP blocks. In this figure, RNI stands for Resource Network Interface, D for DSP, M for Memory, C for Cache, P for Processor, FP for Floating-Point unit and Re for a Reconfigurable block.

Different optimization criteria can be pursued depending on the detailed information of the application and IP blocks. The application is viewed as a graph of task called Task Graph (TG). The features of an IP block can be determined from its companion library [2]. The objectives involved in task assignment and IP block mapping are multiple and have to be optimized simultaneously. Some of these objectives are conflicting because of their nature. So, IP assignment and IP mapping are classified as NP-hard problems [3]. Thus, it is mandatory to use Multi-Objective Evolutionary Algorithms (MOEAs) with specific objective functions.

In this paper, we propose a multi-objective evolutionary based decision to help NoC designers to select the most suited IP blocks used during the assignment step and their physical mapping in network on chip in three-dimensional topology.

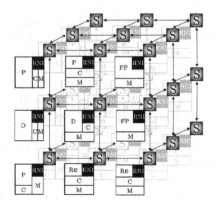

Fig. 1. 3D Mesh-based NoC with 27 resources

For this aim, we use the structure representation of TG in [4] and IP repository data from the Embedded Systems Synthesis benchmarks Suite (E3S) [5] as an IP library for the proposed tool. We use Multi-objective Particle Swarm Optimization (MOPSO) algorithm [6], which was modified to suit the specificities of the assignment and Mapping problems and also to guarantee the NoC designer's constraints.

The rest of the paper is organized as follows: First, in Sect. 2, we present the related work. Subsequently, in Sect. 3, we present the model used for the application structure and IP repository. After that, in Sect. 4 we provide an overview of the assignment and mapping problems. Then, in Sect. 5, we present the for multi-objective approach using MOPSO algorithm used in this work. After that, in Sect. 6, we define the objective functions to be optimized. Later, in Sect. 7, we show some experimental results. Finally, in Sect. 8, we conclude the work and discuss new directions for future work.

2   Related Work

The problems of mapping IP blocks into a 3D mesh-based NoC have been addressed in some previous works. A Branch and Bound algorithm for smart energy aware mapping of tasks have been proposed in [12], the energy model in 2D in [1] was extended for 3D mesh-based NoC topology. In [11] suggest thermal and power task mapping on the platform of 3D mesh-based NoC based on fuzzy logic. A genetic algorithm to build 3D mesh NoC with reduced power consumption from a given application in [17]. The algorithm was tested and validated in an architecture of 32 microprocessors. In [10]. Quantum-behaved particle swarm optimization algorithm is applied to reduce the power consumption, the Simulation results show that this algorithm has faster convergence speed with much better optimization performance compared with particle swarm algorithm. In [9] other varient of particle swarm optimization is used, based on diversity-controlled quantum-behaved particle swarm optimization (DCQPSO).

the results show that this algorithm is able to maintain a stable power optimization efficiency and converges faster. For the first time, a novel meta-heuristic algorithm mimicking hunting behaviors of bats is applied in low power mapping methods in [8]. In [7], the author combines a genetic algorithm with simulated annealing, the Experiments show that ISAGA has a good effect in solving 3D NoC low-power mapping.

All the aforementioned works adopted one single objective. In the following, we describe some works wherein the mapping problem is handled via multi-objective optimization. Thermal and communication aware mapping for 3D NoCs can be performed using genetic algorithms in [13]. A multi-objective rank-based genetic algorithm (RMGA) for 3D NoCs is proposed in [14]. In this paper, two different models have been used for packet latency under no congestion and congestion situations respectively. A multi-objective immune algorithm (MIA) used in [15], Latency and power consumption are adopted as the target multi-objective functions constrained by the heating function. The author in [16] propose a centralized 3D mapping (C3Map) using a new octahedral traversal technology and realized the H-C3Map which is formed from C3Map and attractive and repulsive particle swarm optimization (ARPSO) which reduced energy and latency.

3   Application and IP Repository Models

In order to formulate the IP assignment and mapping problems, it is necessary to define the application internal model that will be used. An application can be represented by a set of tasks that can be executed sequentially or in parallel. It is represented by a directed acyclic graph, called Task Graph (TG) [20].

Definition 1 [19]: A task graph $G = (T, D)$ is a directed graph, wherein a node represents a task $t_i \in T$ and a directed arc $d_{ij} \in D$ between tasks t_i and t_j represents the data dependency between these tasks. The arc label $v(d_{ij})$ characterizes the volume of bits exchanged in communication between tasks t_i and t_j.

Definition 2 [21]: An application characterization graph $G = G(C, A)$ is a directed acyclic graph, wherein each vertex $c_i \in C$ represents a selected IP block and each directed arc $a_{ij} \in A$ characterizes the communication process between c_i and c_j.

In order to help NoC designers and standardize the proposed solution, we structured the used application repository, which is the E3S benchmark suite [22] using XML. XML schema provide a neat and well-accepted model for the task graph and IP repository.

A TG is divided into three major elements: The task graph element is the TG itself, which contains tasks and edges. A task element includes a task element for each task of the TG while an edge element includes an edge element for each arc in the TG. Each task has two main attributes: an unique identifier (*code*) and a task type (*type*), chosen among the 46 different types of tasks included in the E3S library [22]. Each edge has four main attributes: an unique identifier (*id*), an identifier of its source node (*src*), another of its target node (*tgt*) and an attribute representing the communication cost imposed (*cost*). Figure 2 shows the XML representation of a simple TG of E3S.

```
<?xml version="1.0" encoding="ISO-8859-1"?>
<task_graph>
  <tasks>
    <task code ="0" name="src"    type="45" />
    <task code ="1" name="text"   type="44" />
    <task code ="2" name="sink"   type="45" />
    <task code ="3" name="rotate" type="43"/>
    <task code ="4" name="dith"   type="42" />
  </tasks>
  <EDGES>
    <edge name="a0_0" from="0" to="1" cost="1000"/>
    <edge name="a0_1" from="0" to="3" cost="7070"/>
    <edge name="a0_2" from="3" to="4" cost="7070"/>
    <edge name="a0_3" from="4" to="2" cost="7070"/>
    <edge name="a0_4" from="1" to="2" cost="1000"/>
  </edges>
</task_graph>
```

Fig. 2. XML code used to describe tasks

The IP repository is divided into two major elements: the repository and the IPs elements. The repository is the IP repository itself. It is noteworthy to point out that the repository contains different non-general purpose embedded processors and each processor implements up to 46 different types of operations. Not all 46 different types of operations are available in all processors. Each type of operation available to be run in each processor is represented by an IP element. Each IP is identified by its unique identifier. It also includes other attributes such as taskType, taskName, taskPower, taskTime, processorID, processorName, processorWidth, processorHeight, processorClock, processorIdle, Area, Power and cost. The common element in TG and IP repository representations is the type attribute. Therefore, this element will be used to link an IP to a node. Figure 3 shows a simplified XML structure representing an IP repository. The repository contains IPs for digital signal processing, matrix operations, text processing and image manipulation.

4   IP Assignment and Mapping

The platform-based design methodology for SoC encourages the reuse of components to reduce costs and to reduce the time-to market of new designs. The designer of NoC-based systems faces two main problems: selecting the adequate set of IPs and finding the best physical mapping of these IPs into the NoC structure. On a platform-based design, the selection of IPs is called IP assignment stage and the physical mapping is called IP mapping stage.

```xml
<?xml version="1.0" encoding="ISO-8859-1"?>
<repository>
  <ips>
    <ip procName="AMD_ElanSC520-133_MHz--square"
    price="33.0" taskTime="9e-06" taskPower="1.6"
    area="9.61E-6" taskName="Angle2Time Conversion"
    type="0" procID="0" id="0"
    />
    <ip procName="AMD_ElanSC520-133_MHz--square"
    price="33.0" taskTime="2.3e-05" taskPower="1.6"
    area="9.61E-6" taskName="Basic floating point"
    type="1" procID="0" id="1"
    />
    <ip procName="AMD_ElanSC520-133_MHz--square"
    price="33.0" taskTime="0.00049"taskPower="1.6"
    area="9.61E-6" taskName="Bit Manipulation"
    type="2" procID="0"id="2"
    />
      . . .
  </ips>
</repository>
```

Fig. 3. XML code used to represent the repository

IP Assignment is the first step before mapping the application onto NoC [19]. The objective of IP Assignment is to select, from an IP library (IP repository), a set of IPs that exploit re-usability and optimize the implementation of a given application in terms of time, power and area requirements. During this step, no information about physical location of IPs onto NoC is given. The optimization process must be done based on TG and IP features only. The result of this step is a set of IPs that should maximize the NoC performance, *i.e.* minimize power consumption, hardware resources as well as the total time execution of the application. Recall that the result of the assignment step is produced in the form of an ACG for the application's task graph, wherein each task has an IP associated with it. The dynamics of this assignment step is illustrated in Fig. 4(a).

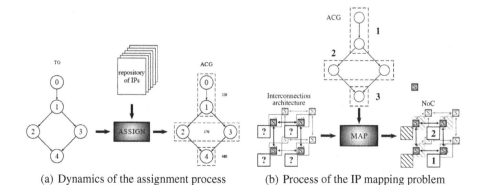

(a) Dynamics of the assignment process   (b) Process of the IP mapping problem

Fig. 4. IP assignment and mapping problems

Given an application, the problem that we are concerned with here is to determine how to topologically map the selected IPs onto the network structure, such that the objectives of interest are optimized. At this stage, a more accurate evaluation can be done taking into account the distance between resources and the number of switches and channels crossed by a data package during a communication session. The result of this process should be an optimal allocation of the prescribed IP assignment to execute the application on the NoC.

5   IP Mapping with Multi-objective Particle Swarm Algorithm

The successful application of PSO in many single objective optimization problems reflects the effectiveness and robustness of PSO. The PSO algorithm for single objective as proposed in [23] is a population-based search algorithm that simulates the social behavior of birds within a flock: the particle simulates the bird's movement while the particle swarm mimics that of the flock. In PSO, each particle position represents a potential solution of the problem.

The particle position x_i, which is a vector of as many coordinates as the dimensions of the search space. It is updated every iteration t using the velocity information as described in Eq. 1:

$$x_i(t+1) = x_i(t) + v_i(t+1). \tag{1}$$

The velocity drives the optimization process to the next position. It is computed as described in Eq. 2:

$$v_i(t+1) = w.v_i(t) + c_1 \times r_1(t)(Pbest(t) - x_i(t)) + c_2 \times r_2(t)(Gbest(t) - x_i(t)). \tag{2}$$

Three terms that are needed to compute the velocity: (i) the inertia, which is based on the previous velocity $w.v_i(t)$. In this term w is the inertia coefficient; (ii) the cognitive term $c_1.r_1(t)(Pbest(t) - x_i(t))$, which quantifies the performance of particle i with respect its previous performance. This component is also known as the "nostalgia" of the particle. In this term, c_1 is the cognitive coefficient and $Pbest(t)$ is the best position founded by particle i so far; (iii) the social component, $c_2.r_2(t)(Gbest(t) - x_i(t))$ which quantifies the performance of particle i with respect to the performance of the swarm of particles. The effect of this term is to attract the particle to the best position found by the particles swarm $Gbest(t)$. In this term, coefficient c_2 is the social coefficient. The cognitive coefficient c_1 and the social coefficient c_2 yield a better performance when they are balanced [24]. Note that $r_1(t)$ And $r_2(t)$ are random numbers selected in the range of $[0, 1]$ at each iteration t.

The PSO algorithm cannot be immediately applied to multi-objective optimization problem. In single-objective optimization, the best solution that each particle uses to update its position is completely determined. However, in multi-objective optimization problems, each particle might have a set of different best, also known as leader, from which just one has be selected in order to update the particle's position. Such set of leaders is usually stored in a different memory, which is distinct of that of the swarm. This memory is identified as the external archive. This is a repository in which the non-dominated solutions found so far are stored. The solutions contained in the external archive are used as leaders when the positions of the particles of the swarm have to be updated. Furthermore, the contents of the external archive are also usually reported as the final results of the algorithm.

In this paper, we improved the PSO method to multi-objective approach. The important part in multi-objective particle swarm optimization (MOPSO) is to determine the best global particle for each particle i of the swarm. To facilitate the selection of best and local best, two archives are maintained in addition to the current state of the swarm. One archive stores the global best individuals found so far by the search process and the other bookkeep the set of local best positions for each member of the swarm. in our approach, the selection is random. The main steps of the algorithm of the applied MOPSO are shown in Algorithm 1.

Algorithm 1. The main steps of modified MOPSO

Initialize the particle of the swarm
Evaluate all the particles of the swarm
Initialize best solutions in archive of leaders
Initialize the archive p_Leader
Initialize the velocity for each particle.
iteration := 0
while iteration < max_iteration **do**
  for each particle **do**
    Select a p_leader
    Update Position using Eqs 1 and 2
    Evaluate particle fitness
    Update p_Leader
  end for
  Update the leaders archive
  iteration := iteration + 1
end while
Return result from the archive of leaders

The PSO is usually used for the optimization of continuous function. However, in this work we use a discrete version of the multi-objective PSO.

6   Objective Functions

Different objective may be considered in the IP assignment and mapping problems. The objectives can be concurrent or collaborative [4]. Concurrent objective should not be grouped, and considered separately during optimization process. Thus, the process can be treated as a multi-objective optimization.

The best solution for multi-objective optimization is the solution with the adequate trade-off between all concurrent objectives. In this paper, we adopt a multi-objective optimization minimizing three objectives: area, power consumption and execution time. These objectives must be computed.

6.1   Area

In order to compute the area required by a given mapping, it is necessary to know the area needed for the selected processors and that required by the used links and switches. As a processor can be responsible for more than one task, each APG node must be visited in order to check the processor identification in the appropriate XML element. Grouping the nodes with the same *processorID* attribute allows us to implement this verification. The total number of links and switches can be obtained through the consideration of all communication paths between exploited tiles. Note that a given IP mapping may not use all the available tiles, links and switches. Also, observe that a portion of a path may be re-used in several communication paths.

Among the routing strategy exists in the literature [25], in this work we adopted a XYZ fixed routing strategy, wherein data emanating from tile i is sent first to the West or East side of the corresponding switch, depending on the target tile position, say j, with respect to i in the NoC 3D mesh, until it reaches the column of tile j. Then, it is sent to the south or North side, also depending on the position of tile j with respect to tile i. Finally, it is sent to the Top or Bottom side until it reaches the target tile. Each communication path between tiles is stored in the routing table. The number of links in the aforementioned route can be computed as described in Eq. 3. This also represents the distance between tiles i and j and it is called the *Manhattan distance* [25].

$$nLinks(i, j) = |x_i - x_j| + |y_i - y_j| + |z_i - z_j| \tag{3}$$

wherein (x_i, y_i, z_i) and (x_j, y_j, z_j) are the 3-dimensional coordinate of tiles i and j respectively.

In the purpose of computing efficiently the area required by all used links and switches, an APG can be associated with a so-called *routing table* whose entries describe appropriately the links and switches necessary to reach a tile from another. The number of hops between tiles along a given path leads to the number of links between those tiles, and incrementing that number by 1 yields the number of traversed switches. The area is computed summing up the areas required by the implementation of all distinct processors, switches and links.

Equation 4 describes the computation involved to obtain the total area for the implementation a given IP mapping M:

$$Area(M) = \sum_{p \in Proc(APG_M)} area_p + (A_l + A_s) \times Links(APG_M) + A_s$$

$$\tag{4}$$

wherein function $Proc(.)$ provides the set of distinct processors used in APG_M and $area_p$ is the required area for processor p, Function $Links(.)$ gives the number of distinct links used in APG_M and A_l is the area of any given link and A_s is the area of any given switch.

6.2 Power Consumption

The total power consumption of an application NoC-based implementation consists of the power consumption of the processors while processing the computation performed by each IP and that due to the data transportation between the tiles is presented in Eq. 5:

$$Power(M) = Power_p(M) + Power_c(M) \tag{5}$$

wherein $Power_p(M)$ and $Power_c(M)$ are the processing and communication power consumption, respectively.

The former can be computed summing up attribute *taskPower* of all nodes of the APG and the latter is the power consumption due to communication between the application tasks through links and switches. The power consumption due to the computational activity is simply obtained summing up attribute *taskPower* of all nodes in the APG and is as described in Eq. 6:

$$Power_p(S) = \sum_{t \in APG_S} power_t \tag{6}$$

The power consumed due communication is an important feature to be considered on a NoC power model in order to get an accurate evaluation. This feature depends on the application communication pattern and the NoC platform. The communication pattern is given by the assignment and mapping, while the NoC platform is defined by the network topology, switching strategy and routing algorithm. The total power consumption of sending one bit of data from tile i to tile j can be calculated considering the number of switches and links the bit passes through on its way along the path. It can be estimated as shown in Eq. 11:

$$E_{bit}^{i,j} = nLinks(i,j) \times E_{L_{bit}} + (nLinks(i,j) + 1) \times E_{S_{bit}} \tag{7}$$

wherein $E_{S_{bit}}$ and $E_{L_{bit}}$ represent the energy consumed by the switch and link tying the two neighboring tiles, respectively [1]. Function $nLinks(.)$ provides the number of traversed links (and switches too) considering the routing strategy used in this work and described earlier in this section. The function is defined in Eq. 3.

Recall that the application TG gives the communication volume $(V(d_{t,t'}))$ in terms of number of bits sent from the task t to task t' passing through a direct arc $d_{t,t'}$. Assuming that the tasks t and t' have been mapped onto tiles i and j respectively. The total network communication power consumption for a given mapping M is given in Eq. 8, wherein $Targets_t$ provides all tasks that have a direct dependency on data resulted from task t and $Tile_t$ yields the tile number into which task t is mapped.

$$Power_c(M) = \sum_{\substack{t \in APG_M, \\ \forall t' \in Targets_t}} V(d_{t,t'}) \times E_{bit}^{Tile_t, Tile_{t'}} \tag{8}$$

6.3 Execution Time

To compute the execution time of a given mapping, we consider the execution time of each task, their schedule and the additional time due to data transportation through links and switches along the communication path. The execution time of each task is defined by the *taskTime* attribute in TG. It is necessary to visit all the tasks of the its TG and schedule them into the own cycle. Thus, a scheduling algorithm ought to be applied.

This paper presents two kinds of scheduling algorithm [26]: one based on the As-Soon-As-Possible (ASAP) scheduling strategy and the As-Late-As-Possible (ALAP) scheduling strategy. The first algorithm schedules tasks in the earliest possible control step. The second algorithm schedules tasks in the latest possible control step.

Links and switches can be counted using the routing table. We identified two situations that can degrade the implementation performance, increasing the execution time of the application:

1. *Parallel tasks with partially shared communication path:*
   When a task in a tile must send data to supposedly parallel tasks in different tiles through the same *initial* link, data to both tiles cannot be sent at the same time.
2. *Parallel tasks with common target using the same communication path:*
   When several tasks need to send data to a common target task, one or more shared links along the partially shared path would be needed simultaneously. The data from both tasks must then be pipelined and so will not arrive at the same time to the target task.

Equation 9 gives the execution time considering the computation and communication for a given mapping solution M:

$$Time(M) = Time_S + Time_c + t_L \times (F_1 + F_2) \tag{9}$$

where $Time_S$ returns the time necessary to processes the tasks of The TG and $Time_c$ the time spent due communication among tasks. It is necessary to add the delay concerning the last two aforementioned situations. Delay caused by the first situation is computed by function F_1 and delay caused the second situation is computed by function F_2.

Function F_1 computes the additional time due to parallel tasks that have data dependencies on tasks mapped in the same source tile and yet these share a common initial link in the communication path. Function F_2 computes the additional time due to the fact that parallel tasks producing data for the same target task need to use simultaneously at least a common link along the communication path.

The time spent due communication between tasks is computed as shown in Eq. 10, which is a extension of the time model presented in [27]:

$$Time_c = \sum_{\substack{t \in APG_M, \\ \forall t' \in Targets_t}} \left\lceil \frac{V(d_{t,t'})}{phit} \right\rceil * T_{phit}^{t,} \tag{10}$$

wherein $V(d_{t,t'})$ is the volume of bits transmitted from task t to task t' and the time required to transfer a *phit* is defined as in Eq. 11:

$$T_{phit}^{t,t'} = nLinks(t,t') \times T_{L_{phit}} + (nLinks(t,t') + 1) \times T_{S_{phit}} \tag{11}$$

where $T_{L_{phit}}$ is the link transmission time and $T_{S_{phit}}$ is the switch processing time used to transfer one phit between two neighboring tiles.

7 Performance Results

The E3S benchmarks suite is used to evaluate the proposed approach. The suite contains the characteristic of 17 embedded processors. These processors are characterized by the measured execution times of 16 different types of tasks, power consumption derived from processor data-sheets, die size required, price and clock frequency. These applications are described by the corresponding TGs. Each one of the nodes in these TGs is associated with a task type. A task type is a processor instruction or a set of instructions. If a given processor is able to execute a given type of instruction, so that processor is a candidate to be mapped onto a resource in the NoC structure and would be responsible for the execution of one or more tasks of the TG. We use 5 random task graphs, generated by the TGFF [5] to perform experiments and evaluate the performance. The generated applications have the characteristics given in Table 1, and they task graphs illustrated in Fig. 5.

Several tentative simulations were performed to find out the set of parameters setting to be in the proposed algorithm. We exploit a population size of

Table 1. Characteristics of the applications

App Id	#Tasks	#Arcs
TG 0	12	16
TG 1	16	22
TG 2	18	23
TG 3	20	27
TG 4	24	32

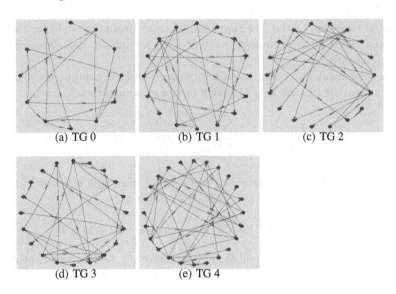

Fig. 5. The task graphs of the mapped applications as generated by the TGFF

500 with w set to 0.8 and c_1 and c_2 both set to 1.49. The algorithm was run for 1000 iterations. Moreover, two scheduling algorithms are used in the simulation: ASAP, whereby a given task is scheduled As Soon As Possible and ALAP whereby a given task is scheduled As Late As Possible.

We provide different results for these applications when using ASAP and ALAP scheduling algorithm. Tables 2 and 3 show the characteristics of the found Mappings for the ASAP scheduling strategy, while Tables 4 and 5 show the same characteristics of the found Mappings for the ALAP scheduling strategy. For each of these applications, we show the total number of non-dominated mapping, the best and the average of power consumption, the hardware area and the execution time. These values are not necessarily extracted from the same solution. Note that the power figures are $Watts$, time is 10^{-3} s and area is 10^{-6} m^2.

Table 2. Results regarding IP mapping in 5×5 NoC with ASAP

App ID	#Mapping	Best			Average		
		Power	Time	Area	Power	Time	Area
0	24	522.66	5.69	59.68	623.83	32.20	129.22
1	20	957.94	49.51	98.32	1107.86	116.17	233.77
2	34	819.11	9.56	134.97	960.25	247.58	204.30
3	34	1159.09	42.06	135.62	1390.71	64.43	229.94
4	34	1149.61	24.96	218.76	1379.34	34.86	415.20

Table 3. Results regarding IP mapping in $3 \times 3 \times 3$ NoC with ASAP

App ID	#Mapping	Best			Average		
		Power	Time	Area	Power	Time	Area
0	43	403.25	5.27	45.11	479.44	6.37	113.48
1	58	757.64	47.95	77.16	855.37	135.07	161.62
2	66	687.44	8.57	116.74	819.26	202.03	213.46
3	47	953.52	40.88	123.21	1124.44	49.48	214.21
4	88	1017.02	24.19	147.50	1149.18	129.50	338.37

Table 4. Results regarding IP mapping in 5×5 NoC with ALAP

App ID	#Mapping	Best			Average		
		Power	Time	Area	Power	Time	Area
0	12	581.90	5.86	64.96	644.48	7.18	179.56
1	28	853.76	51.44	106.57	1001.96	117.29	207.70
2	32	898.65	10.21	135.79	995.52	38.90	220.25
3	25	1103.91	41.70	125.89	1288.34	159.33	221.51
4	41	1189.49	25.55	191.10	1397.00	47.75	347.90

Besides comparing the scheduling algorithm, two topologies are used in the test 2D and 3D mesh. Tables 2 and 4 show the results obtained using 2D mesh, while Tables 3 and 5 show the results obtained using 3D mesh. When we compare the two scheduling strategies in 2D mesh, the comparison between Tables 2 and 4 shows that the results achieved by ASAP scheduling are a better than those evolved by ALAP scheduling. Also, the results achieved by ASAP scheduling are superiors to those evolved by ALAP scheduling in 3D mesh, as shown in Table 5. On the hand, when we compare the two NoCs topologies, it is safe to conclude that mapping in 3D mesh achieves better results than 2D mesh because of the vast number of non-dominated solutions discovered by 3D mesh when compared to those yield by 2D mesh.

Table 5. Results regarding IP mapping in $3 \times 3 \times 3$ NoC with ALAP

App ID	#Mapping	Best			Average		
		Power	Time	Area	Power	Time	Area
0	59	451.18	5.44	50.79	526.68	49.08	137.10
1	53	742.42	51.38	83.74	833.68	335.12	194.59
2	121	691.89	9.34	112.14	846.44	156.93	248.33
3	80	976.84	41.68	127.94	1146.13	163.81	231.15
4	101	1021.83	25.72	219.17	1189.82	49.99	391.36

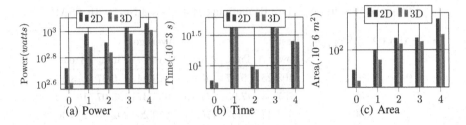

Fig. 6. IP mapping comparison using ASAP scheduling

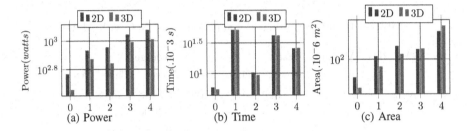

Fig. 7. IP mapping comparison using ALAP scheduling

Besides comparing the solutions obtained, the charts of Figs. 6(a) and 7(a) allow a visual comparison of the power consumption for the mapping yield by the compared topology, regarding the best results. Also, the charts of Figs. 6(b) and 7(b) give a better visual comparison of results regarding the time characteristic considering the best. Finally, the charts of Figs. 6(c) and 7(c) facilitate the comparison of the required hardware area that would be due to the mapping obtained by the compared topologies.

8   Conclusions

The problem of assigning and mapping IPs are NP-hard problems in the NoC design. In this paper, we propose a multi-objective algorithm based on Particle Swarm Optimization to help NoC designers to select a set of appropriate IP addresses from the IP repository and mapping a prescribed set of IPs into an NoC physical structure. We use TGFF [5] to generate randomly the task graphs, and we adopt the E3S benchmark as the IPs benchmark. We use the same objectives used in [4]. Two scheduling algorithm has been tested in our tool. The obtained results show that using 3D mesh topology perform better result than using 2D mesh, The obtained results show also that ASAP scheduling strategy is better then ALAP scheduling. For future work, we intend to use more routing strategies. We also intend to apply other new evolutionary techniques.

References

1. Hu, J., Marculescu, R.: Energy-aware mapping for tile-based NoC architectures under performance constraints. In: Proceedings of the 2003 Asia and South Pacific Design Automation Conference, pp. 233–239. ACM (2003)
2. Ogras, U.Y., Hu, J., Marculescu, R.: Key research problems in NoC design: a holistic perspective. In: Proceedings of the 3rd IEEE/ACM/IFIP International Conference on Hardware/Software Codesign and System Synthesis, pp. 69–74. ACM (2005)
3. Gary, M.R., Johnson, D.S.: Computers and Intractability: A Guide to the Theory of NP-Completeness. W. H. Freeman & Co., New York (1979)
4. Da Silva, M.V.C., Nedjah, N., de Macedo Mourelle, L.: Evolutionary IP assignment for efficient NoC-based system design using multi-objective optimization. In: 2009 IEEE Congress on Evolutionary Computation, pp. 2257–2264. IEEE (2009)
5. Dick, R.P., Rhodes, D.L., Wolf, W.: TGFF: task graphs for free. In: Proceedings of the Sixth International Workshop on Hardware/Software Codesign (CODES/CASHE 1998), pp. 97–101. IEEE (1998)
6. Reyes-Sierra, M., Coello Coello, C.A., et al.: Multi-objective particle swarm optimizers: a survey of the state of-the-art. Int. J. Comput. Intell. Res. **2**(3), 287–308 (2006)
7. He, H., Fang, F., Wang, W.: Improved simulated annealing genetic algorithm based low power mapping for 3d NoC. In: MATEC Web of Conferences, vol. 232, p. 02022. EDP Sciences (2018)
8. Li, J., et al.: Bat algorithm based low power mapping methods for 3D network-on-chips. In: Du, D., Li, L., Zhu, E., He, K. (eds.) NCTCS 2017. CCIS, vol. 768, pp. 277–295. Springer, Singapore (2017). https://doi.org/10.1007/978-981-10-6893-5_21
9. Huang, C., Zhang, D., Song, G.: A novel mapping algorithm for three-dimensional network on chip based on quantum-behaved particle swarm optimization. Front. Comput. Sci. **11**(4), 622–631 (2017)
10. Huang, C., Zhang, D., Song, G.: Low-power mapping algorithm for three-dimensional network-on-chip based on diversity-controlled quantum-behaved particle swarm optimization. J. Algorithms Comput. Technol. **10**(3), 176–186 (2016)
11. Mosayyebzadeh, A., Amiraski, M.M., Hessabi, S.: Thermal and power aware task mapping on 3d network on chip. Comput. Electr. Eng. **51**, 157–167 (2016)
12. Wadhwani, P., Choudhary, N., Singh, D.: Energy efficient mapping in 3d mesh communication architecture for NoC. Glob. J. Comput. Sci. Technol. (2013)
13. Addo-Quaye, C.: Thermal-aware mapping and placement for 3-d NoC designs. In: Proceedings 2005 IEEE International SOC Conference, pp. 25–28. IEEE (2005)
14. Wang, J., Li, L., Pan, H., He, S., Zhang, R.: Latency-aware mapping for 3d NoC using rank-based multi-objective genetic algorithm. In: 2011 9th IEEE International Conference on ASIC, pp. 413–416. IEEE (2011)
15. Sepulveda, J., Gogniat, G., Pires, R., Chau, W., Strum, M.: An evolutive approach for designing thermal and performance-aware heterogeneous 3D-NoCs. In: 2013 26th Symposium on Integrated Circuits and Systems Design (SBCCI), pp. 1–6. IEEE (2013)
16. Bhardwaj, K., Mane, P.S.: C3Map and ARPSO based mapping algorithms for energy-efficient regular 3-D NoC architectures. In: Technical papers of 2014 International Symposium on VLSI Design, Automation and Test, pp. 1–4. IEEE (2014)

17. Elmiligi, H., Gebali, F., El-Kharashi, M.W.: Power-aware mapping for 3D-NoC designs using genetic algorithms. Procedia Comput. Sci. **34**, 538–543 (2014)

18. Davis, W.R., et al.: Demystifying 3D ICS: the pros and cons of going vertical. IEEE Des. Test Comput. **22**(6), 498–510 (2005)

19. Bougherara, M., Nedjah, N., De Macedo, L., Mourelle, R.R., Sadok, A., Bennouar, D.: IP assignment for efficient NoC-based system design using multi-objective particle swarm optimisation. Int. J. Bio-Inspired Comput. **12**(4), 203–213 (2018)

20. Bougherara, M., Nedjah, N., Bennouar, D., Rahmoun, R., Sadok, A., de macedo Mourelle, L.: Core/task associations for efficient application implementation on network-on-chip. In: 2018 International Conference on Computer and Applications (ICCA), pp. 18–22. IEEE (2018)

21. Bougherara, M., Kemcha, R., Nedjah, N., Bennouar, D., de macedo Mourelle, L.: IP assignment optimization for an efficient NoC-based system using multi-objective differential evolution. In: International Conference on Metaheuristics and Nature Inspired Computing (META), pp. 435–444 (2018)

22. Dick, R.P.: Embedded System Synthesis Benchmarks Suite (E3S). http://ziyang.eecs.northwestern.edu/dickrp/e3s/

23. Zhang, L.-B., Zhou, C.-G., Liu, X.H., Ma, Z.Q., Ma, M., Liang. Y.C.: Solving multi objective optimization problems using particle swarm optimization. In: The 2003 Congress on Evolutionary Computation, CEC 2003, vol. 4, pp. 2400–2405. IEEE (2003)

24. Nedjah, N., de Macedo Mourelle, L.: Evolutionary multi-objective optimisation: a survey. Int. J. Bio-Inspired Comput. **7**(1), 1–25 (2015)

25. Liu, S., et al.: Freerider: non-local adaptive network-on-chip routing with packet-carried propagation of congestion information. IEEE Trans. Parallel Distrib. Syst. **26**(8), 2272–2285 (2015)

26. Gruian, F., Kuchcinski, K.: LEneS: task scheduling for low-energy systems using variable supply voltage processors. In: Proceedings of the 2001 Asia and South Pacific Design Automation Conference, pp. 449–455. ACM (2001)

27. Kreutz, M., Marcon, C.A., Carro, L., Wagner, F., Susin, A.A.: Design space exploration comparing homogeneous and heterogeneous network-on-chip architectures. In: Proceedings of the 18th Annual Symposium on Integrated Circuits and System Design, pp. 190–195. ACM (2005)

Evolutionary Design of Approximate Sequential Circuits at RTL Using Particle Swarm Optimization

Rebiha Kemcha[1,2]([✉]), Nadia Nedjah[3], Amin Riad Maouche[2], and Maamar Bougherara[1,4]

[1] Ecole Normale Superieure - Kouba, Algiers, Algeria
rebiha.kemcha@gmail.com
[2] LIMOSE Laboratory, University of Boumerdes, Boumerdes, Algeria
[3] Department of Electronics Engineering and Telecommunications,
State University of Rio de Janeiro, Rio de Janeiro, Brazil
[4] LIMPAF Laboratory, University of Bouira, Bouira, Algeria

Abstract. Evolutionary circuit design has the ability to explore a wide part of the design space and can lead to satisfactory circuits without human experience and knowledge. In this work, we use Multi-Objective Particle Swarm Optimization to evolve approximate sequential circuits at Register-Transfer Level. A circuit is represented by a two-dimensional array. We aim to produce functional approximate circuits having good trade-off between accuracy, delay and area. The results show the efficiency of the proposed approach.

Keywords: Evolutionary design · Sequential circuit ·
Swarm intelligence · Approximate circuit · Integer divider

1 Introduction

Data-rich applications, such as document/image search, image and signal processing, machine learning classifiers, etc., are computationally intensive while achieving their tasks, making their systems more complex and very expensive in terms of resources (delay, power, etc.). Quantum computing, accelerated-based computing and a plenty of other techniques and technologies are used to overcome this problem.

Another promising paradigm, to reduce required resources in such applications, is *Approximate computing*. This paradigm is based on the inherent error resiliency of some applications. An inherent error resilient application tolerates some kinds of errors or loss of certain accuracy in computations, due mostly to the nature of processed data that can be redundant, large and hence noisy. This laxity results from: (i) the limited perceptual ability of human brains and (ii) the "perfect" solution does not exist for some applications.

In this context, approximate circuits represent an attractive solution to replace accurate circuits. They can give the opportunity for such applications

© Springer Nature Switzerland AG 2019
S. Misra et al. (Eds.): ICCSA 2019, LNCS 11620, pp. 671–684, 2019.
https://doi.org/10.1007/978-3-030-24296-1_54

to take full advantage of their error resiliency by relaxing the "correctness" of outputs and trading it against improvements in energy efficiency, area, speed or other parameters [16].

On the other hand, *Evolutionary Circuit Design* is the use of evolutionary algorithms (EA) to evolve electronic circuits instead of conventional design methods such as Karnaugh map or Quine-McCluskey method. The problem of these traditional methods is that they could not lead efficiently to satisfactory results, especially, in case of complex and large circuits. Furthermore, they depend largely on human knowledge and experience. In contrast, the evolutionary design can explore a wide portion of the design space; hence, it can propose newer and/or more performant implementations than those generated with conventional methods. This approach allows a potential evolution of circuits which have known behavioral requirement and a partial even unknown specification.

Thus, evolutionary computation techniques are proving to be useful for design approximate circuits. In fact, the latter can be treated as a multi-objective optimization problem with several conflicting objectives.

The aim of this work is to use multi-objective optimization algorithms to design approximate sequential circuits at Register-Transfer Level (RTL). In RTL, sequential circuits are composed from arithmetic elements, memories, interconnections and clocking. It is known that sequential circuits are cheaper in term of area than combinatorial circuits.

An evolutionary design of an approximate sequential integer divider is proposed herein. Integer division is used in many applications like signal processing, communications, etc., and has a huge complexity when implemented in hardware [13] leading to an excessive consumption of resources. An approximation of such circuit is therefore a good compromise between complexity and accuracy. For this purpose, we use Multi-Objective Particle Swarm Optimization as a method of design by considering error metric, delay and area as objectives to approximate a sequential accurate integer divider.

After the introduction, the paper is organized as follows. Section 2 gives some related researches. Section 3 provides details on MOPSO. Section 4 describes our approach to design approximate sequential circuits as well as the fitness function. In Sect. 5, experiments and results are described. Finally, Sect. 6 concludes the paper.

2   Related Work

Approximate circuits are circuits which meet the needs of error resilient applications while providing a trade-off between accuracy and performance. They constitute an eventual "better" solution than accurate circuits for related domains like: clustering/filtering data, image/signal processing, computer vision algorithms, document search, etc., where it is possible to trade result accuracy against an improvement in power consumption, area, delay or other measures.

Concerning the design of approximate circuits, two techniques are described in this area: over-scaling and functional approximation [17]. In the *over-scaling* technique, approximations are introduced: (i) by creating timing errors to decrease the energy consumption without changing the clock frequency, called "voltage over-scaling" or (ii) by increasing frequency to gain performance without changing the voltage, called "over-clocking" [17].

In the *functional approximation* technique, the logic function computed by the circuit is modified so that it tolerates acceptable errors. For arithmetic circuits, approximations are introduced into building blocks (e.g. adders, multipliers, etc.) for reducing power consumption and design area [16]. These two techniques can be combined.

Circuit approximations are *manually* or *automatically* performed. Manual re-design is the subject of a large number of research works proposing re-design of common arithmetic building blocks such as adders [20], multipliers [21] and dividers [19]. Jiang et al. in [18] survey the design of a plethora of approximate arithmetic circuits and propose others.

However, manual re-design is not efficient to design large and complex circuits. Hence, automated methods as SASIMI [23], SALSA [22] and ABACUS [24] were proposed. These methods use heuristics to approximate circuits and verification engines to check quality of the resulting circuits [25]. They start with a fully functional circuit then apply an iterative stochastic method to approximate it and evaluate it in terms of accuracy and power and/or area [25].

On the other hand, several works address the *evolutionary circuit design*. They exploit the features of evolutionary computation to propose either novel implementations of circuits or more performant ones. Manovit et al. in [1] use Genetic Algorithms (GA) to evolve sequential circuits at Register-Transfer Level (RTL) from partial input/output sequence. They succeed to evolve 2-inputs serial adder, frequency divider, odd parity and modulo-5 detector.

Soliman and Abbas [2] consider a sequential circuit as a grid and separate the combinatorial part from memories. They split the circuit into several subcircuits and evolve them separately at gate level using GA. The authors propose the evolution of 3-bit up-counter with perfect functionality and minimum of logic gates as objectives.

Liang et al. [3] propose a three-step decomposition method and (μ, λ) Evolution Strategy (ES) to evolve Finite State Machines of large sequential circuits. They test their approach on the MCNC benchmark library.

Tao et al. in [4] evolve auto-defined sequence detector, modulo-6 counter, modulo-16 counter and ISCAS089 "lion" circuit. They compare different variants of Genetic Programming (GP) and GA. According to the authors, CGP provides higher results than the other variants of GP, but their GA-based approach was least complex. In [5], the authors combine their first approach with a Lookup-Table (LUT)-based circuit evolution (LCE) to tackle the problem of the evolutionary design of sequential circuit.

After presenting functional approximation and evolutionary design of circuits, we can see clearly that they are closely related [25]. Evolutionary design aims to produce circuits in response to multiple expectations, which can be translated in conflicting objectives among others. Accuracy, power, delay, area, which can be considered as objectives in an approximate circuit design, are naturally conflicting. For this reason, several works addressed the *evolutionary design of approximate circuits* [26,27]. All of these works use a CGP-based approach to design and optimize proposed circuits. Vasicek et al. in [26] evolved approximate 4-bit multipliers, 9-median and 25-median circuits at gate level.

Vasicek and Sekanina in [27] propose a multi-objective evolution of various combinatorial circuits from different libraries as LGSynth or ISCAS. In order to evaluate candidate circuits, the authors use a two-stage approach: (i) the first stage is to evaluate the approximation (an error metric based on Hamming Distance), and (ii) the second stage, which begins after obtaining a set of "accepted" circuits, consists of fitness function with three weighted terms (error, area and delay).

As far as we know, there is no work dealing with the design of approximate sequential circuits at RTL. Hence, our aim is to use Multi-Objective Particle Swarm Optimization to produce approximate sequential circuits with accuracy, delay and area as objectives.

3   Multi-objective Particle Swarm Optimization

Particle Swarm Optimization (PSO) is an evolutionary computation approach proposed by Kennedy and Eberhart [11]. In this technique, an individual, called particle, simulates the bird's movement through the space while the swarm mimics the social behavior of the flock in the search of food. Thus, PSO is a population-based optimization algorithm considering each particle position as a potential solution of the problem [8].

Every particle tries to "fly" toward the best performing particle at that moment and therefore it is given a position and a velocity. The particle position $\vec{x}_i$ is a vector of as many coordinates as the dimensions of the search space. Every iteration t, the position is dynamically adjusted according to values of particle parameters, its previous best position (called *local best*) and the swarm's best known position (called *best particle*). The position is updated using the velocity information as described in Eq. 1:

$$\vec{x}_i(t) = \vec{x}_i(t-1) + \vec{v}_i(t) \tag{1}$$

where $\vec{v}_i(t)$ is the velocity. It is computed as described in Eq. 2:

$$\vec{v}_i(t) = w.\vec{v}_i(t-1) + c_1.r_1.(\vec{x}_{pi} - \vec{x}_i) + c_2.r_2.(\vec{x}_{gi} - \vec{x}_i), \tag{2}$$

where, the term $w.\vec{v}_i(t-1)$, which is based on the previous velocity, is the inertia. It is used to control the trade-off between the exploitation and exploration of the search space [8]. c_1 and c_2 are arbitrary positive constants called *cognitive* and *social coefficient* respectively, and r_1 and $r2$ are random variables $\in [0,1]$ of uniform distribution.

The cognitive term $c_1.r_1.(\vec{x}_{pi} - \vec{x}_i)$ controls the effect of the local best $\vec{x}_{pi}$ on the next position of the particle i. The social term, $c_2.r_2.(\vec{x}_{gi} - \vec{x}_i)$ attracts the particle i to the global best position $\vec{x}_{gi}$ found by the particles of the swarm.

Multi-Objective Particle Swarm Optimization (MOPSO) is the extention of PSO to solve multiobjective problems. The main idea to do this, is to adapt the basic algorithm by adding [9]: (i) an external archive to store non-dominated solutions, (ii) a selection mechanism of leaders and (iii) an archiving method to prune repository of non-dominated solutions once full. The first proposed MOPSO algorithm was developed in [12] by Moore and Chapman in 1999. Algorithm 1 shows the main steps of a basic MOPSO process. Since the first version of MOPSO, a plurality of variants have been proposed. For evolving circuits in this work, we used a variant of MOPSO algorithms namely SMPSO.

Algorithm 1. Pseudocode of a basic Multi-objective PSO

Create the initial swarm
Evaluate all the particles of the swarm
Initialize the velocity for each particle
Initialize the particles memory
Initialize the leaders
iteration ← 0
while iteration < max_iteration **do**
    Compute velocity of particles
    Update position of particles using Eqs 1 and 2
    Mutate particles
    Evaluate particles fitness
    Update Leaders archive
    Update the particles memory
    iteration ← iteration + 1
end while
Return result from the archive of leaders

Speed-constrained Multi-objective PSO (SMPSO) is a multiobjective particle swarm optimization algorithm proposed by Nebro et al. in [7]. It is based on Optimized Multi-Objective Particle Sswarm Optimizer (OMOPSO) [14] features, which include: (i) the use of the crowding distance to filter out the list of leaders (ii) the combination of two mutation operators acting on different subsets of the swarm to accelerate the convergence and (ii) the use of a clustering technique, which is ϵ-dominance to limit the number of solutions in the external archive.

SMPSO incorporates a mechanism for *velocity constriction* and introduces a polynomial mutation operator for $\frac{1}{6}$ of the swarm.

The authors of SMPSO propose to control the accumulated velocity of each variable j in each particle i with *velocity constriction* as described in Eq. 3:

$$v_{i,j}(t) = \begin{cases} delta_j & \text{if } v_{i,j}(t) > delta_j, \\ -delta_j & \text{if } v_{i,j}(t) \leq -delta_j, \\ v_{i,j}(t) & \text{otherwise.} \end{cases} \tag{3}$$

where

$$delta_j = \frac{upper\,Limit_j - lower\,Limit_j}{2} \tag{4}$$

where $upper\,Limit_j$ and $lower\,Limit_j$ are limits of the variable j of the particle position in the search space. These limits prevent the swarm explosion when the velocity of particles become too high. Nebro et al. used the constriction coefficient χ defined firstly by Clerc and Kennedy in [10], based on the values of cognitive and social coefficients c_1 and c_2.

4   Proposed Approach

In RTL, a sequential circuit contains arithmetic components such as adders, multipliers, etc., storage elements such as registers, flip flops, etc. and interconnection elements such as buses, multiplexers, etc. A circuit is controlled by a system clock.

4.1   Circuit Representation

A circuit is represented by a matrix $\mathcal{M}$ of m rows and n columns. It has α primary inputs and β primary outputs. The matrix is composed of cells. A cell represents a component, a list of inputs and a list of outputs. A component can be selected from a list of X components enumerated in Table 1.

Table 1. List of components

Component	Code	#Inputs	#Bits	Area (GE)	Time (ns)
Adder	1	2	16	384	345
Subtractor	2	2	16	384	345
Multiplier	3	2	16	384	380
Register	4	1	16	82	15
Counter	5	0	16	82	2.11
Multiplexer	6	3	16	113	5.25
Equal-to	7	2	16	104	31.5
Greater-than	8	2	16	252	40
Less-than	9	2	16	252	40
And	10	1	1	2	3.5
Or	11	1	1	3	4.7
Not	12	1	1	1	3.8
Buffer	13	1	1	2	3.5

A cell of a column c, where $0 < c \leq n - 1$, draws its inputs from outputs of λ previous columns and outputs of μ next columns except those of the column which contains the cell in question. In addition, inputs of a cell in the first column, $c = 0$, may be the primary inputs. The outputs of circuit cells are labeled from $\alpha + 1, \alpha + 2, \ldots$ to $\alpha + \delta$, where:

$$\delta = \sum_{i=0}^{m-1} \sum_{j=0}^{n-1} \delta_{i,j}, \qquad (5)$$

where $\delta_{i,j}$ is the number of outputs of a cell in the ith row and the jth column. Figure 1 shows an example of a sequential circuit and its corresponding representation. Clock is assumed for registers and counters.

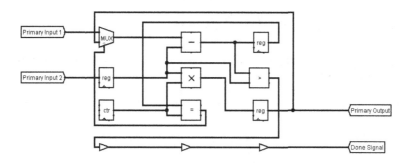

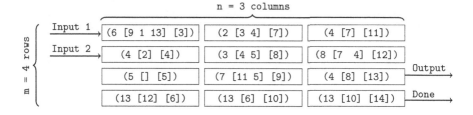

Fig. 1. Circuit representation.

In a circuit designed in this way, the component of each column perform its operation in parallel manner with other column components. Each column is a stage of operations and is executed sequentially with other columns.

4.2 Objectives

The fitness function takes into account three objectives of the evolved circuit $\mathcal{M}$ as defined in Eq. 6.

$$F(\mathcal{M}) = \begin{bmatrix} Error(\mathcal{M}) \\ Area(\mathcal{M}) \\ Time(\mathcal{M}) \end{bmatrix}, \qquad (6)$$

where $Error(\mathcal{M})$ is the error metric measuring the results accuracy of the circuit, $Time(\mathcal{M})$ is the execution time and finally $Area(\mathcal{M})$ is the components area.

Accuracy. The Error metric of an approximate circuit is estimated by comparing the resulting output of the evolved circuit with the outputs produced by an exact solution. To evaluate this objective, we use an universal function proposed by De Oliveira et al. [15]. This function is defined as follows:

$$Error(\mathcal{M}) = log\left(1 + \frac{T_1 + T_2 + T_3}{\rho^2}\right) \tag{7}$$

where term T_1 is the sum of squared errors, which is able to indicate similarities between the measured value $\widehat{y}$ and the expected value y. N is the length of the sequence of inputs/outputs. T_1 is described as follows:

$$T_1 = \sum_{i=1}^{N}(\widehat{y} - y)^2. \tag{8}$$

Term T_2 is the sum of squared Fourier Transform magnitudes of measured and expected values. This term gives extent of the difference between a result computed by the evolved circuit and the one given by the target circuit. Equation 9 shows the formula of T_2.

$$T_2 = \sum_{i=1}^{N}(|\mathcal{F}(\widehat{y}) - \mathcal{F}(y)|)^2, \tag{9}$$

Term T_3 is the sum of squared Fourier Transform phases of measured and expected values. The phase indicates how many results are different from the evolved circuit to the target one. It is computed as follows:

$$T_3 = \sum_{i=1}^{N}\left(\angle\mathcal{F}(\widehat{y}) - \angle\mathcal{F}(y)\right)^2, \tag{10}$$

The last term is ρ^2 which is the square of the Correlation of Pearson ρ. The term $\frac{1}{\rho^2}$ tends to infinity if the measured result $\widehat{y}$ and the expected result y are unrelated and it is close to 1 if $\widehat{y}$ and y are positively or negatively correlated.

$$\rho^2 = \left(\frac{Cov(\widehat{y}, y)}{\sqrt{Var(\widehat{y}).Var(y)}}\right)^2 \tag{11}$$

Area. The total area of the circuit $Area(\mathcal{M})$ (Eq. 12) is an estimation of the area occupied by all involved components $x \in \mathcal{M}$. For simplicity, we do not compute the area of buses and other interconnections except multiplexers. The area is measured using Gate Equivalent (GE). GE represents an estimation of a component area based upon the number of interconnected logic gates used to implement the same functionality of the related component [6]. The area $Area_x$ of each component x is estimated using 2-inputs NAND gate.

$$Area(\mathcal{M}) = \sum_{x \in \mathcal{M}} Area_x. \tag{12}$$

Delay. The performance is, herein, considered as delay taken by the circuit to deliver the first intermediate result. All operations in the same matrix column j are executed in parallel manner. In addition, a column is a stage of operations. t_j is the largest component time among all components of this column. The total time $Time(\mathcal{M})$ is the sum of columns times.

$$Time(\mathcal{M}) = \sum_{j=0}^{n-1} t_j, \tag{13}$$

where t_j is the maximum time of column j.

4.3   Search Methodology

The initial population is seeded with an accurate circuit using a single-objective PSO algorithm (SPSO2011). The tolerated error is a parameter defined by the user as well as the size of the seed. This population is then taken by the multi-objective particle swarm optimization algorithm to start the evolutionary approximation of the accurate circuit. The outline of our approach's steps is as follows:

1. Seed the population with accurate circuit to produce the initial population
2. Initialize all cells with a component x picked from the list of components
3. Update outputs of all cells
4. Interconnect components between them
5. Designate the primary outputs and enable signal of the output register
6. Evaluate the fitness of the circuit
7. Apply the multi-objective optimization algorithm

5   Experiments and Results

This section presents the results of experiments to show the capability of particle swarm optimization to evolve approximate circuits.

In this work, we used jMetal framework [28], which contains several evolutionary algorithms. SMPSO and SPSO2011 are adapted to deal with our problem configuration. Several simulations were performed to find out how to set up the required parameters. For SPSO2011, we kept same setting of parameters implemented in jMetal: $w = 0.721$, $c = 1.193$, $\#iter = 10000$, $swarm\ size = 100$ and number of particles to inform is set to 10. For SMPSO, c_1 and c_2 coefficients are randomly generated from $[1.5, 2.5]$ and weight w is also randomly generated from $[0.1, 0.5]$.

We consider evolving a sequential integer divider shown in Fig. 2a. The accurate circuit has 2 integer inputs (dividend and divisor), 1 integer output (quotient), 3 rows and 4 columns of components. The last column of circuits contains registers to store intermediate results of division. Clock is assumed for components like registers and counters. In this circuit, sequential integer division is performed by successive subtractions of dividend and divisor (for the first clock cycle) or intermediate remainder (for the rest). This operation takes a number of cycles equals to the value of quotient. We evaluate the area of the circuit by summing all components area. The delay is estimated as the maximum time taken to deliver the first intermediate result. The number of clock cycles depends on the operands' values.

We inject the accurate circuit as a gravity center in SPSO2011 algorithm. This technique allows to define the neighborhood of the accurate circuit leading to the generation of some different versions of the concerned circuit.

The representation of an approximate circuits produced by SPSO2011-SMPSO is shown in Fig. 2b. Our algorithm found this solution after 5859 iterations. This circuit has an error of 5.66, which means that it is ±1 from the

Table 2. Accurate and approximate divider performances

	Accurate	Approximate	First circuit found	Best area and time
Error	0	±1	±1	±3
Area	1083	972	970	889
Time	415	400	438.5	395.5

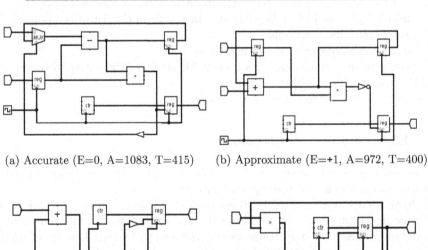

(a) Accurate (E=0, A=1083, T=415)   (b) Approximate (E=+1, A=972, T=400)

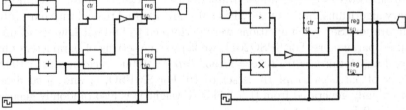

(c) Approximate (E=+2, A=1191, T=400) (d) Approximate (E=+3, A=889, T=395.5)

Fig. 2. Accurate and evolved approximate integer dividers (E = error, A = area, T = time)

accurate result. The first approximation presented in Fig. 2c, was found after 461 iterations, and in terms of time and area, the best circuit shown in Fig. 2d, was found after 14069 iterations. Table 2 presents performances of these circuits.

In matrix representation, the accurate circuit has 3 rows and 4 columns. For its part, the first approximate circuit has 3 rows and only 3 columns, which led to a reduction of area and time. In fact, the time is reduced by 4.7%, but the largest improvement is that of area, which is reduced by 22.5%.

It has been noted that circuits having smaller area than the accurate divider have fewer columns, that is, the components of some columns are not connected to the rest of circuit components. The cells of such components are not involved in the computation of the results and thus they are not taken into account in the performances of the overall circuit.

Table 2 shows the performances of the accurate circuit, an approximate one, first circuit found and best circuit in terms of area and time. The second circuit (approximate) has better area and time than the accurate circuit. The reduction of the area is about 10.2% and that of time is 3.75%.

It has been observed that the error metric $Error(\mathcal{M})$ gives 5.66 for circuits with ±1 from accurate results for a 32-input/output sequence. Each circuit is run 32 times to form the results sequence which is compared with the accurate results in order to define the circuit error metric. In addition, it is noteworthy to mention that circuits with an error metric less than or equal to 7.80 are valid which means that they are sequential and give harmonious results. The value of the error metric depends, obviously, on the results sequence but also largely on the length of the input/output sequence. The circuit that has an error metric of 5.66 gave 4.23 with a 8-input/output sequence. The fitness function has to be normalized to give values independently from the length of test sequences.

The resulting Pareto front is presented in Fig. 3. During the 25000 iterations, only 37 circuits were sequential, which 56.75% circuits gave results with ±4 from the accurate result and the rest were invalid. Note that all circuits of the Pareto front have an error metric less or equal than ±3. Circuits with a ±4 were expensive in terms of area and time comparing to the accurate circuit (e.g., $Area = 1273\ GE$ and $Time = 437.11$ ns).

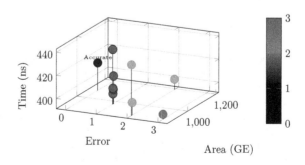

Fig. 3. Pareto Front

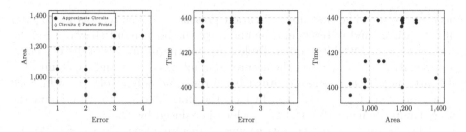

Fig. 4. Performances of 21 valid circuits

Figure 4 presents the performances of some obtained valid sequential circuits considering only two objectives at the same time. Circuits of the pareto front are also plotted. According to the middle plot, more than half of the circuits have more than 420 ns which means that they are worse than the accurate circuit in term of time. Otherwise, according to the plot on the right of Fig. 4, over half of the circuits have less than 1080 *GE*, i.e., they are better than the accurate circuit in term of area.

6   Conclusion

The functional approximation of arithmetic circuits presents a solution for error resilient applications by providing good compromises between accuracy and performance. This work aims to explore the use of MOPSO to design sequential approximate integer dividers at Register-Transfer Level. Two algorithms were used for this purpose, namely SPSO2011 and SMPSO. We evaluate error metric, area and time for each evolved circuit. The obtained results show that an improvment of 22.5% was achieved in term of area. The proposed method shows the possibility to use particle swarm in the design of approximate sequential circuits. In our future research, we will work on producing more results and increasing the scalability of our method and its extension to design accurate sequential circuits.

References

1. Manovit, C., Aporntewan, C., Chongstitvatana, P.: Synthesis of synchronous sequential logic circuits from partial input/output sequences. In: Sipper, M., Mange, D., Pérez-Uribe, A. (eds.) ICES 1998. LNCS, vol. 1478, pp. 98–105. Springer, Heidelberg (1998). https://doi.org/10.1007/BFb0057611
2. Soliman, A., Abbas, H.: Synchronous sequential circuits design using evolutionary algorithms. In: Canadian Conference on Electrical and Computer Engineering 2004 (IEEE Cat. No. 04CH37513), pp. 2013–2016. IEEE (2004)
3. Liang, H., Luo, W., Wang, X.: A three-step decomposition method for the evolutionary design of sequential logic circuits. Genet. Program. Evolvable Mach. **10**(3), 231–262 (2009)

4. Tao, Y., Cao, J., Zhang, Y., Lin, J., Li, M.: Using module-level evolvable hardware approach in design of sequential logic circuits. In: 2012 IEEE Congress on Evolutionary Computation, pp. 1–8. IEEE (2012)
5. Tao, Y., Zhang, Y.: An extrinsic EHW system for the evolutionary optimization and design of sequential circuit. In: Proceedings of the 2018 Artificial Intelligence and Cloud Computing Conference, pp. 174–180. ACM (2018)
6. Nedjah, N., Mourelle, L.D.M.: Encodings and genetic operators for efficient evolutionary design of digital circuits. Int. J. Bio-Inspired Comput. **9**, 197–210 (2017)
7. Nebro, A., Durillo, J., Garcıa-Nieto, J., Coello, C.A.C., Luna, F., Alba, E.: SMPSO: a new PSO metaheuristic for multi-objective optimization. In: Proceedings of the 2009 IEEE Symposium on Computational Intelligence in Multi-criteria Decision-making, pp. 66–73 (2009)
8. Nedjah, N., Mourelle, L.d.M.: Evolutionary multi-objective optimisation: a survey. Int. J. Bio-Inspired Comput. **7**(1), 1–25 (2015)
9. Strickler, A., Pozo, A.: Evolving connection weights of artificial neural network using a multi-objective approach with application to class prediction. In: Nedjah, N., Lopes, H.S., Mourelle, L.M. (eds.) Designing with Computational Intelligence. SCI, vol. 664, pp. 177–197. Springer, Cham (2017). https://doi.org/10.1007/978-3-319-44735-3_10
10. Clerc, M., Kennedy, J.: The particle swarm-explosion, stability, and convergence in a multidimensional complex space. IEEE Trans. Evol. Comput. **6**(1), 58–73 (2002)
11. Kennedy, J., Eberhart, R.: Particle swarm optimization. In: Proceedings of the IEEE International Conference on Neural Networks, vol. 4, pp. 1942–1948, November 1995
12. Moore, J., Chapman, R.: Application of particle swarm to multiobjective optimization, Technical report (1999)
13. Moller, N., Granlund, T.: Improved division by invariant integers. IEEE Trans. Comput. **60**(2), 165–175 (2011)
14. Sierra, M.R., Coello Coello, C.A.: Improving PSO-based multi-objective optimization using crowding, mutation and ε-dominance. In: Coello Coello, C.A., Hernández Aguirre, A., Zitzler, E. (eds.) EMO 2005. LNCS, vol. 3410, pp. 505–519. Springer, Heidelberg (2005). https://doi.org/10.1007/978-3-540-31880-4_35
15. De Oliveira, P.J.A., Nedjah, N., Mourelle, L.D.M.: Uma Heurística Geral Para a Comparação de Sinais. In: Proceedings of XXXVIII Ibero-Latin American Congress on Computational Methods in Engineering (CILAMCE), Florianópolis, SC, Brazil (2017)
16. Venkatesan, R., Agarwal, A., Roy, K., Raghunathan, A.: MACACO: modeling and analysis of circuits for approximate computing. In: 2011 IEEE/ACM International Conference on Computer-Aided Design (ICCAD), pp. 667–673. IEEE (2011)
17. Hashemi, S., Reda, S.: Approximate multipliers and dividers using dynamic bit selection. In: Reda, S., Shafique, M. (eds.) Approximate Circuits, pp. 25–44. Springer, Cham (2019). https://doi.org/10.1007/978-3-319-99322-5_2
18. Jiang, H., Liu, L., Lombardi, F., Han, J.: Approximate arithmetic circuits: design and evaluation. In: Reda, S., Shafique, M. (eds.) Approximate Circuits, pp. 67–98. Springer, Cham (2019). https://doi.org/10.1007/978-3-319-99322-5_4
19. Chen, L., Lombardi, F., Montuschi, P., Han, J., Liu, W.: Design of approximate high-radix dividers by inexact binary signed-digit addition. In: Proceedings of the on Great Lakes Symposium on VLSI 2017, pp. 293–298. ACM (2017)
20. Kahng, A.B., Kang, S.: Accuracy-configurable adder for approximate arithmetic designs. In: Proceedings of the 49th Annual Design Automation Conference, pp. 820–825. ACM (2012)

21. Lin, C.-H., Lin, C.: High accuracy approximate multiplier with error correction. In: 2013 IEEE 31st International Conference on Computer Design (ICCD), pp. 33–38. IEEE (2013)
22. Venkataramani, S., Sabne, A., Kozhikkottu, V., Roy, K., Raghunathan, A.: SALSA: systematic logic synthesis of approximate circuits. In: DAC Design Automation Conference 2012, pp. 796–801. IEEE (2012)
23. Venkataramani, S., Roy, K., Raghunathan, A.: Substitute-and-simplify: a unified design paradigm for approximate and quality configurable circuits. In: 2013 Design, Automation & Test in Europe Conference & Exhibition (DATE), pp. 1367–1372. IEEE (2013)
24. Nepal, K., Li, Y., Bahar, R.I., Reda, S.: ABACUS: a technique for automated behavioral synthesis of approximate computing circuits. In: 2014 Design, Automation & Test in Europe Conference & Exhibition (DATE), pp. 1–6. IEEE (2014)
25. Sekanina, L., Vasicek, Z.: Evolutionary computing in approximate circuit design and optimization. In: 1st Workshop on Approximate Computing (WAPCO 2015), pp. 1–6 (2015)
26. Vasicek, Z., Sekanina, L.: Evolutionary design of approximate multipliers under different error metrics. In: 17th International Symposium on Design and Diagnostics of Electronic Circuits & Systems, pp. 135–140. IEEE (2014)
27. Vasicek, Z., Sekanina, L.: Evolutionary design of complex approximate combinational circuits. Genet. Program. Evolvable Mach. **17**(2), 169–192 (2016)
28. Durillo, J.J., Nebro, A.J., Alba, E.: The jMetal framework for multi-objective optimization: design and architecture. In: IEEE Congress on Evolutionary Computation, pp. 1–8. IEEE (2010)

Machine Learning Models for Depression Patient Classification Using fMRI: A Study

Sanskriti Gupta and Rekha Vig$^{(\boxtimes)}$

The North Cap University, Gurugram, India
sanskritigupta16@gmail.com, rekhavig@ncuindia.edu

Abstract. Depression is a crucial entity of clinical research that imposes challenges to clinicians regarding its diagnosis and correct treatment. Machine learning technologies, are being used successfully for diagnosis of depression, especially using fMRI (functional Magnetic Resonance Imaging). The brain fMRIs are T2* weighted images captured using Blood Oxidation Level Dependent (BOLD) signals and show the functional activity of the brain. BOLD signal maps the activated/functional areas of the brain according the level of oxygen transmitted. Machine Learning and fMRI when taken together provide a tool for clinicians to identify the depressed patients from healthy controls. This paper reviews methodologies of past studies for depression classification using fMRI and machine learning.

Keywords: Depression · fMRI · BOLD · Machine learning

1 Introduction

Functional Magnetic Resonance Imaging (fMRI) has emerged as one of the powerful tools in neuro imaging techniques for studying human brain functions and dysfunctions. It is among the primary techniques for revealing the communication between spatially remote different brain regions and provides a promising way to study interaction between those regions that are engaged simultaneously in a task. fMRI bold signal [1] is temporally coherent between functionally coupled regions forming functional brain networks. To identify the activated brain portions in fMRI data during resting (task-free) state or task instances is crucial neuroscience for planning surgery and diagnosis of psychiatric disease such as Alzheimer, Epilepsy, Dyslexia, Schizophrenia, Depression etc.

Depressive disorder is among the leading causes of functional impairment world-wide. Appropriate diagnosis of depression is a prerequisite for successful medication and to preserve a good health. Tools like brain imaging techniques are very important to researchers for better understanding of brain mechanism implicate in depressive disorder. fMRI is among the popular imaging methods used for studying mental disorders. fMRI measures the variations of oxygenation in blood to form discrete time signals. The signals are known as BOLD signals. fMRI measured using T2* weighted echo-planer imaging techniques are based on bold signals and provide a direct measure of neural activity in the brain. When fMRI data is collected the subject can either be in

© Springer Nature Switzerland AG 2019
S. Misra et al. (Eds.): ICCSA 2019, LNCS 11620, pp. 685–696, 2019.
https://doi.org/10.1007/978-3-030-24296-1_55

the resting state or performing task such as tapping finger, listening music, visualizing facial expression.

Many methods have been used for diagnosing diseases and for classification of normal and diseased subjects. As per the current knowledge, there are no standard automated tools available for disease recognition in the hospitals.

In recent year, owing to increasing success of machine learning methods in the area of image processing these methods are being employed in neuro disorder diagnosis or classification using fMRI. Recent researches using machine learning [2] applied to fMRI neuro-imaging data have been successful in identification of depressed individuals based on their brain activity. Feature selection techniques were developed to filter out a subset of relevant features with an aim of developing robust learning models. In general, these techniques are used as a previous step to classification algorithms for improving prediction accuracy. In addition, they also identify a set of meaningful features that best discriminate classes.

According to Grotegerd, when fMRI data was analyzed using machine learning algorithms, information from fMRI patterns can directly differentiate depressive disorder.

Although much advancement have been made in classifying depressed patients from the healthy ones using in fMRI data, research is still going on in this area to make the system more reliable. This paper presents a review on various techniques for classifying depressed patients. The rest of the paper presents this review in Sect. 2, some performance parameters in Sect. 3 and conclusion in Sect. 4.

2   Literature Survey

The two different approaches for extracting functional connectivity in resting state fMRI are:

1. Model based,
2. Data Driven.

Model based method is the traditional method which utilized seed based voxel method to compute the temporal correlation between time series (BOLD) of a specific brain region and that of other regions. This traditional voxel analysis is widely used for identifying functional brain networks as it is simple, sensitive, and easy to interpret. The networks so formed are however restricted by selection of the seed voxels. The Data Driven method, in contrast to Model based doesn't require assuming a model for exploring functional connectivity. For discovering reliable functionally connected networks (resting state), various methods have been suggested such as principle component analysis, independent component analysis (ICA) [3] and clustering approaches based methods.

Based on these approaches we classify our review into these two broad categories:

2.1 Model Based

Croddock et al. in 2009 [4] proposed a model based method which utilizes Support Vector Classification (SVC) for classification of features obtained by two selection algorithms (one filter method and one wrapper method). Although 95% accuracy was obtained when best feature selection was taken but it also showed an accuracy of 62.5% in the case of no feature selection.

Zeng et al. in 2012 [5] introduced a multivariant pattern analysis method to identify the major brain depression. There is a significant difference in network and region of brain in depressed patient compared to the healthy ones. This strategy was utilized in this method. The fMRI images of each subject after preprocessing were subjected to feature extraction from functional connectivity matrix. The discriminative power of the features was extracted in Eq. 1 using kendall tau rank correlation coefficient, which can be defined for function connectivity feature 'j' as:

$$\tau_j = \frac{n_c - n_d}{m \times n} \tag{1}$$

Where n_d and n_c are the number of discordant and concordant pairs respectively. $m \times n$ are the total number of sample pairs.

Sato et al. in 2015 [6] described a machine learning approach to detect major depression in fMRI data. This model based technique utilized a particular machine learning algorithm for classification, MLDA (Maximum Entropy Linear Discriminant Analysis) with feature selection of voxels having most discriminative features. The results also showed that there was no difference in the classifier decision between patients with no medication and the major depressed patients taking antidepressants.

The traditional Support Vector Machine Learning approach was replaced by Weighted Discriminative Dictionary learning by Zeng et al. in 2016, [7] which depend on the similarity between the dictionary atom and samples to make the representation model more discriminative. In this learning method, an objective function was computed and then the optimization strategy was followed into two sub groups: updating and fixing until all the weights were fixed.

In 2017, Wang et al. [8] proposed a Functional brain network (FBN) based approach for depression disorder classification. The functional connectivity matrix obtained by sparse low rank matrix was first converted into binary matrices by replacing all non-zeros connectivity to 1. Then from this FBN eight graph based features were extracted using Fisher score in Eq. 2. Fisher score for each feature was defined in paper as

$$FS = \frac{p_1(q_1 - q)^2 + p_2(q_2 - q)^2}{p_1 \sigma_1^2 + p_2 \sigma_2^2} \tag{2}$$

Where q is the mean value of features for all the samples, p_1, p_2 are the numbers of samples in the two classes, σ_1, σ_2 is the variance of two classes, and q_1, q_2 is the feature mean value of the two classes.

The larger the fisher score more were the discriminative features. The sparse low rank model and eight graph based features showed promising results for recognition of major depression disorder. The method so proposed was compared on the basis of features and classifier used (Naïve Bayes, k-measure weight, Linear Discriminant analysis and SVM). SVM with eight features was demonstrated as a best in terms of accuracy. The schematic diagram for the proposed method is shown in Fig. 1 below.

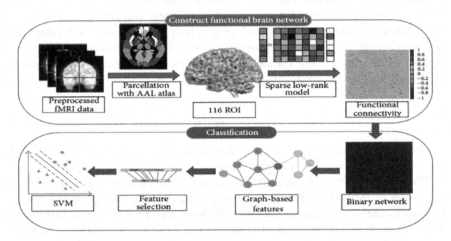

Fig. 1. Classification of depression disorder using functional brain network

2.2 Data Driven

A data driven method has been suggested by Sojoudi et al. in 2010 [9] where spectral clustering was utilized. An individual affinity matrix shows whether the brain region lies in one cluster or other. Network homogeneity as in Eq. 2 measures were used to evaluate the amount of similarity in a network which is derived as

$$Network\ Homogeneity = \frac{\sum_{i=1}^{n}(S_i)^2 - n(\bar{S})^2}{\frac{1}{12}K^2(n^3 - n)} \tag{3}$$

Where S_i is the sum rank of ith time point, $\bar{S}$ is the mean of S_i's, n is the total number of time points, and K is the number of regions within that network.

In 2012, Lu et al. [10] described data driven technique using event related fMRI data as well as resting- state data. On each data set PCA followed by ICA was applied and an absolute correlation coefficient d_{ij} in Eq. 4 was calculated as

$$d_{ij} = \frac{\sum_{t=1}^{T}\left(Se_i(t) - \overline{Se_l}\right)\left(Sr_j(t) - \overline{Sr_j}\right)}{\sqrt{\sum_{t=1}^{T}\left(Se_i(t) - \overline{Se_l}\right)^2 \sum_{t=1}^{T}\left(Sr_j(t) - \overline{Sr_j}\right)^2}} \tag{4}$$

Where Se_i and Sr_j are the event related and resting state components respectively. $i = (1, 2, 3 \ldots M), j = (1, 2, 3, \ldots N)$ Where N is the resting state independent components and M is the number of event related independent component. The spectrum obtained by this was analyzed for top event related component and first feature was selected which showed uneven energy distribution. Then by classification of groups with ROI analysis, the depressed patients were recognized from healthy ones.

Roudina et al. in 2014 [11] proposed a novel feature selection technique to identify the meaningful features that best discriminate the patient classes according to the following equation:

$$\hat{\beta} = \arg \min \beta \in R^p \|Y - X\beta\|_2^2 + \lambda \sum_{k=1}^{p} |\beta_k| \tag{5}$$

Where β is LASSO estimate, $\lambda \in R^+$ is a regularization parameter, p is the number of features, X is data matrix and Y is label vector. On fMRI pre processed data, through LASSO sparse algorithm subset of the relevant features were created. The selection of features was accomplished after several iterations. The selected features which showed non zero coefficients after this whole procedure were subjected to SVM using nested leave one out cross validation scheme.

Jie et al. in 2015 [12] proposed a greedy search algorithm that moves in two directions forward as well as backward. During each iteration, forward selection that starts with empty set added a feature to the current set so as to reduce the loss function. Backward elimination, which starts from the complete set, removes a feature until a loss function exceeds a threshold. Both of these strategies combined with SVM known as SVM-FoBa is an adaptive greedy algorithm. When in forward step a new feature was added, backward step check the new feature subset. The loss function in Eq. 6 can be written as

$$J(w, b) = \frac{1}{2}\|w\|^2 + C \sum_{i=1}^{n} \left[1 - y_i\left(w^T x_i + b\right)\right]_+ \tag{6}$$

Where x_i is the sample with y_i corresponding to its label, w os the weight vector, b is the offset, C is the hyperparameter and $[\cdot]_+$ denotes hinge function. This classification was not just limited to depression disorder from healthy control but it also discriminates bipolar depression from major depression. Hence two data set were used.

Rosa et al. in 2015 [13] describe a sparse network based model for classification of depressed patients and also showed some advantages over whole brain voxel-based approach. The sparse based model shows biologically useful network structures that best discriminates the subjects from controls. In addition to this, this approach was also compared with correlation based metrics models. Here two data sets were taken which were acquired from two different samples. In the first data set, sad faces of different emotions were shown to participants. In second data set, block related designs were

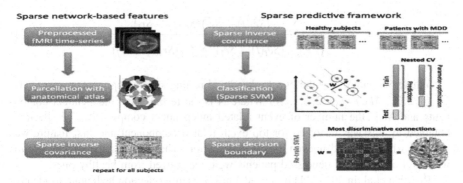

Fig. 2. Flow chart explaining the process of sparse network based model.

utilized where participants were allowed to view different emotions like happy, anxious, neutral and sad faces. The sparse network based proposed model is shown in Fig. 2.

A CCA and ICA based data driven method was proposed by Lin et al. in 2017 [14]. Here for detecting low frequency fluctuations a mixer model of both ICA and CCA was studied. After preprocessing of fMRI data, the cerebrum of each subject was divided into 90 regions using an Automated Anatomical Labeling (AAL). Fisher Discriminant Analysis was done prior to classification for the reduction of dimensionality of feature vector. Only 11 features were selected from these 90 regions. The results obtained from the mixer model were compared with filtered ICA, unfiltered ICA and CCA also.

A novel depression detecting algorithm was proposed by Miholca et al. [15] which utilized Relational Association Rules and Artificial Neural Network for machine learning. Functional connectivity was established based on the relation between different patterns of the activated brain regions. The RAR using fuzzy and crisp has been performed in this paper and the results were presented which shows almost accurate classification of healthy and depressed subjects. Feature selection plays a vital role during the classification.

3 Performance Parameters

To analyze the efficiency of various proposed machine learning approaches used for the classification of major depressive disorder patients from healthy controls, some parameters are studied. These parameters are accuracy, specificity, sensitivity. In regression based models, correlation coefficient is the measurement criteria.

Accuracy: It measures how accurately a test data classified. Mathematically it is defined as:

$$\text{Accuracy} = \frac{\text{PC} + \text{HC}}{\text{PC} + \text{PH} + \text{HC} + \text{HP}} \tag{7}$$

Sensitivity: It is the measurement to accurately identify the subjects. Mathematically it is defined as:

$$\text{Sesitivity} = \frac{PC}{PC + PH} \tag{8}$$

Specificity: It is the measurement to accurately identify the controls. Mathematically it is defined as:

$$\text{Specificity} = \frac{HC}{HC + HP} \tag{9}$$

Where PC, HC, PH, HP represent the number of patients classified as controls, healthy ones classified as controls, patients classified as healthy ones and healthy ones classified as patients respectively.

Correlation Coefficient: It measures how much the model prediction is correlated with associated label value.

Based on these parameters, the reviewed algorithms are compared and depicted in Tables 1 and 2.

Cross-validation is used to estimate the accuracy of an algorithm framed by specific machine learning method [16]. There are various methods for performing cross-validation.

1. Leave-one-out Cross-validation
2. Holdout Cross-validation
3. k-fold cross-validation: the sample.

The first two techniques i.e. Leave-one-out and Hold-out are the variants of k-fold cross-validation with little modification. K-fold cross validation technique splits the data into k sets of same size. After that, it works as follows: (1) classifies one set as test set from its k-set, and combine the other sets to form a training set, (2) training a model on training set by using the learning method, (3) the estimated model is tested on a test set, and (4) at last, computes validation parameter(s) to discover the model's reliability. This procedure is repeated for k-iterations, and at each time a new set classifying as the test set without repetition. The computed validation parameter(s) values are averaged from all the iterations to calculate the overall performance of the machine learning method.

Holdout approach is a k-fold cross-validation approach with k equals to 1. This approach is beneficial when the available data set has a large sample size. On the other hand, leave-one out cross- validation is beneficial when the available data set has considerably too small of a sample size. This approach is also similar to k-fold approach with k equal to the sample size of the data.

Table 1. Model based methods.

Author	Patient sample	Method	Description	Limitations	Result
Craddock et al. [4] (2009)	Subject-20 Control-20	Support Vector Classification (SVC)	Multiple Voxel Analysis using Support vector classification was employed as it produced good prediction accuracy and was less noise sensitive. Four feature selection approaches were compared	Too many iterations were used to remove the lower scoring features that could remove the important features and increase the computational expensive	Accuracy of 95% was achieved using 4 feature selection approaches. Even when no feature selection approach was employed the accuracy comes out to be 62.5%
Zeng et al. [5] (2011)	Subject-24 Control-29	Linear Support-Vector-Machine	To select the relevant features, Kendall tau rank correlation coefficient was utilized for whole brain resting state fMRI	AAL atlas covers the whole brain except the brain system, which can be the major study in depression Too many features can lead to over fitting	Accuracy-94.3% Sensitivity-100% Specificity-89.7%
Sato et al. [6] (2015)	Subject-25 Control-21	Maximum Entropy Linear Discriminate Analysis (MLDA)	A guilt selective change in functional connectivity was used for discrimination	Poor stability	Accuracy-78.26% Sensitivity-72% Specificity-85.71
Wang et al. [7] (2016)	Subject-29 Control-29	Weighted Discriminative Dictionary Learning (WDDL)	Separate dictionaries for patients and controls were formed and then classifier based on the low representation error was calculated for each new sample and hence the classification was done	Dictionary learning method treats all the samples indiscriminately and ignores the valuable relationship between the samples and dictionary atoms	Accuracy-79.31% Sensitivity-75.88% Specificity-82.76%

(*continued*)

Table 1. (*continued*)

Author	Patient sample	Method	Description	Limitations	Result
Wang et al. [8] (2017)	Subject-31 Control-29	Linear Support-Vector-Machine	Functional brain network was created using sparse low rank matrix. And from this functional connectivity matrix the features were extracted	Though it has remarkable accuracy but the construction of sparse low rank matrix was a complex one	Accuracy-95% Sensitivity-96.77% Specificity-93.10%

Table 2. Data driven method

Author	Patient sample	Method	Description	Limitations	Result
Sojoudi et al. [9] (2010)	Subject-16 Control-16	Spectral Clustering Technique	Individual Affinity matrix was constructed for each subject on which spectral clustering was done at group level. The clusters so obtained showed functional network presented in both healthy control and depressed patients	Clusters of data set may contain structures at different scales of density and size using Spectral Clustering	Network homogeneity was decreased in default mode network and visual cortex Network homogeneity was found to be consistent for both regions in patient group
Lu et al. [10] (2012)	Subject-13 Control-13	Pattern Recognition	The resting state as well as task based fMRI was combined for whole brain analysis after PCA and ICA and a correlation coefficient was used to compute the accuracy of the proposed lu algorithm	Whole brain analysis is difficult to interpret	Accuracy-81.82% Sensitivity-84.62% Specificity-77.78%
Roudina et al. [11] (2014)	Subject-30 Control-30	SVM linear kernel	Survival Count on random Subsamples feature selection approach was proposed which selects the stable features. The fMRI data was collected during visualization of happy faces	Limited to specific brain regions and ignores the useful information from whole brain analysis	Accuracy-72% Sensitivity-77% Specificity-67%

(*continued*)

Table 2. (*continued*)

Author	Patient sample	Method	Description	Limitations	Result
Jie et al. [12] (2015)	Subject-21 (BD), 25 (MDD) Control-20	Support Vector Machine-forward Backward elimination (SVM-FoBa)	In order to find the relevant features loss function was computed. In forward selection, the features were selected in order to minimize the loss function and in backward elimination, those features were selected by which the loss function threshold exceeds	Elimination of Voxel-wise analysis may discard the essential information for discrimination	Dataset 1 –Accuracy: 78.95% Sensitivity: 68.42% Specificity: 89.47% Dataset 2 –Accuracy: 85.00% Sensitivity: 83.33% Specificity: 86.67% Dataset 3 –Accuracy: 85.00% Sensitivity: 83.33% Specificity: 86.67%
Rosa et al. [13] (2015)	Subject-30 Control-30	–Sparse L1-norm support vector machines –Non-sparse L2-norm support vector machines	Two fMRI datasets of were taken, one was event based and another one was block based	Sparse models can be highly unstable in facilitating interpretations. Hence hinders their main aim	Dataset 1 –Accuracy: 78.95% Sensitivity: 68.42% Specificity: 89.47% Dataset 2 –Accuracy: 85.00% Sensitivity: 83.33% Specificity: 86.67%
Lin et al. [14] (2017)	Subject-20 Control-20	Linear Support-Vector-Machine (SVM)	Mixture model ICA and CCA was created and hence no need to filter data	Filtering may cause the loss of some useful information and the low frequency noises may ruin the results in the follow-up analysis	Accuracy-91.53% Sensitivity-90% Specificity-93.10%
Miholca et al. [15] (2017)	Subject-19 Control-20	RAR RBFN	fMRI dataset was collected during listening music	Low sample size. As with larger sample size, power of the classification model generalized well	Accuracy-100% Sensitivity-100% Specificity-100%

4   Conclusion

Depressive disorder is a common mental disorder which should be diagnosed in the early stages and accurately for better treatment. Various techniques based on machine learning have been developed so far and were discussed in this paper for the classification of depressed patients from healthy controls. These techniques were compared on the basis of accuracy, specificity and sensitivity. Support vector machine with leave one out cross validation and other machine learning algorithms were currently used and showed promising results. One more approach other than SVM is Rational Association Rules (RAR) and Artificial Neural Network (ANN) [15] which shows most accurate result with 100% accuracy. This paper showed some of the supervised as well as unsupervised machine learning approach for patient identification using fMRI and the review of these techniques was presented here.

Every technique has its own advantages and disadvantages. It is hard to state which technique is better as only accuracy is not sufficient for calculating the performance of a method, other parameters such as sample size is also a main consideration. As we have seen in the literature RAR shows 100% accuracy but the sample size is too small and may show poor accuracy with larger sample size that may not be acceptable.

References

1. Hongna, Z., et al.: The dynamic characteristics of the anterior cingulate cortex in resting-state fMRI of patients with depression. J. Affect. Disord. **227**, 391–397 (2017). https://doi.org/10.1016/j.jad.2017.11.026
2. Patel, M.J., Carmen, A., Julie, C.P., Kathryn, L.E., Reynolds III, C.F., Howard, J.A.: Machine learning approaches for integrating clinical and imaging features in late-life depression classification and response prediction. Int. J. Geriatr. Psychiatry **30**(10), 1056–1067 (2015). https://doi.org/10.1002/gps.4262
3. Ilya, M.V., et al.: Whole brain resting-state analysis reveals decreased functional connectivity in major depression. Front. Syst. Neurosci. **4**(41), 1–10 (2010). https://doi.org/10.3389/fnsys.2010.00041
4. Craddock, R.C., Holtzheimer III, P.E., Hu, X.P., Mayberg, H.S.: Disease state prediction from resting state functional connectivity. Magn. Reson. Med. **62**(6), 1619–1628 (2009). https://doi.org/10.1002/mrm.22159
5. Zeng, L.L., et al.: Identifying major depression using whole-brain functional connectivity: a multivariate pattern analysis. J. Neurol. **135**, 1498–1507 (2012). https://doi.org/10.1093/brain/aws059
6. Sato, J.R., Moll, J., Green, S., Deakin, J.F.W., Thomaz, C.E., Zahn, R.: Machine learning algorithm accurately detects fMRI signature of vulnerability to major depression. Neuroimage **233**, 289–291 (2015). https://doi.org/10.1016/j.pscychresns.2015.07.001
7. Wang, X., Ren, Y., Yang, Y., Zhang, W., Xiong, N.N.: A weighted discriminative dictionary learning method for depression disorder classification using fMRI data. In: Proceedings of the IEEE International Conference on Big Data and Cloud Computing and Networking, Sustainable Computing and Communication, pp. 618–622 (2016). https://doi.org/10.1109/bdcloud-socialcom-sustaincom2016.97

8. Wang, X., Ren, Y., Wensheng, Z.: Depression disorder classification of fMRI data using sparse low-rank functional brain network and graph-based features. Hindwai J. Comput. Math. Methods Med. 1–12 (2017). https://doi.org/10.1155/2017/3609821

9. Sojoudi, A., Seyed, M.S., Gholam, A.H.Z., Hamid, S.Z.: Spectral clustering of resting state fMRI reveals default mode network with specifically reduced network homogeneity in major depression. In: Proceedings of 17th Iranian Conference of Biomedical Engineering (2010). https://doi.org/10.1109/icbme.2010.5704952

10. Lu, Q., Liu, G., Zhao, J., Luo, G., Yao, Z.: Depression recognition using resting-state and event-related fMRI signals. Magn. Reson. Imaging **30**, 347–355 (2012). https://doi.org/10.1016/j.mri.2011.12.016

11. Rondina, J.M., et al.: SCoRS- a method based on stability for feature selection and mapping in neuroimaging. IEEE Trans. Med. Imaging **33**(1), 85–98 (2014). https://doi.org/10.1109/tmi.2013.2281398

12. Jie, N.F., et al.: Discriminating Bipolar Disorder from major depression based on SVM-FoBa: efficient feature selection with multimodal brain imaging data. IEEE Trans. Auton. Ment. Dev. **7**(4), 320–330 (2015). https://doi.org/10.1109/tamd.2015.2440298

13. Maria, J.R., et al.: Sparse network-based models for patient classification using fMRI. Neuroimage **105**, 493–506 (2015). https://doi.org/10.1016/j.neuroimage.2014.11.021

14. Lin, W., Wu, H., Liu, Y., Lv, D., Yang, L.: A CCA and ICA-based mixture model for identifying major depression disorder. IEEE Trans. Med. Imaging **36**(3), 745–756 (2017). https://doi.org/10.1109/tmi.2016.2631001

15. Miholca, D.L., Adrian, O.: Detecting depression from fMRI using relational association rules and artificial neural networks. In: Proceedings of IEEE Conference on Intelligent Computer Communication and Processing, pp. 85–92 (2017). https://doi.org/10.1109/iccp.2017.8116987

16. Patel, M.J., Alexander, K., Howard, J.A.: Studying depression using imaging and machine learning methods. Neuroimage **10**, 115–123 (2016). https://doi.org/10.1016/j.nicl.2015.11.003

Computer Aided Modeling, Simulation, and Analysis (CAMSA 2018)

Detection of Faults in an Osmotic Dehydration Process Through State Estimation and Interval Analysis

C. A. Collazos[1(✉)], Fredy Sanz[1], I. A. Monroy[2],
Adriana Maldonado-Franco[3], Emiro De-la-Hoz-Franco[4],
Farid Meléndez-Pertuz[4], and César Mora[5]

[1] Vicerrectoría de Investigaciones, Universidad Manuela Beltrán,
Bogotá, D.C, Colombia
cacollazos@gmail.com
[2] Licenciatura en Física, Universidad Distrital, Bogotá, D.C, Colombia
[3] Doctorado en Biociencias, Universidad de la Sabana, Bogotá, D.C, Colombia
[4] Departamento de Ciencias de la Computación y Electrónica,
Universidad de la Costa, Barranquilla, Colombia
[5] Centro de Investigación en Ciencia Aplicada y Tecnología Avanzada del
Instituto Politécnico Nacional, México DF, Mexico

Abstract. This article shows the results obtained in the application of State Estimation to a case of fault detection and diagnosis in an osmotic dehydration process. The disturbances that affect the measurements on the system are unknown but it is known that they are bounded. The tools used for the development of this work were the EMV (Extended Mean Value) and SIVIA (Set Inversion Via Interval Analysis) algorithms, which allow obtaining the necessary boundaries for the fault detection and diagnosis algorithm. The paper presents simulations and validations.

Keywords: Physics model · Osmotic dehydration · State estimation · Interval analysis · Faults

1 Introduction

Complex systems are subject to stochastic perturbations, which make the process of modeling them difficult to perform. In most cases, the model obtained does not correctly describe the dynamics of the system. Therefore, not having successful models makes it unreliable to carry out a fault detection study and, later, their diagnosis. This paper presents a methodology for state estimation, where the state equations for the process are known and the disturbances are limited through intervals. Interval algebra has diverse applications as shown in [1] and [2].

Currently, Guaranteed State Estimation Methods have been proposed as an alternative to the Stochastic Model Based Estimation, assuming that the disturbances are bounded. This means that the problem is limited to estimating the various states of the system, which makes it is possible to use these results to perform fault detection. State estimation is fundamental for analysis, design, control and supervision of processes in

© Springer Nature Switzerland AG 2019
S. Misra et al. (Eds.): ICCSA 2019, LNCS 11620, pp. 699–712, 2019.
https://doi.org/10.1007/978-3-030-24296-1_56

engineering [3–6]. Specifically, state estimation methodology based on intervals has received a lot of attention in the last few years and literature about this subject shows a growing progress [7–13]. This document presents a review of the existing theory on the technique of guaranteed state estimation, making use of algebra of intervals to implement it in an osmotic dehydration process. The work is structured as follows: Sect. 2 presents the theoretical basis for the guaranteed state estimation and the physical model of the process, on which the technique was applied, Sect. 3 addresses the methodology and the envelope-based fault detection algorithm for each sampling time, Sect. 4 presents the results obtained on the osmotic dehydration process, and finally Sect. 5 collects the conclusions of the work.

2   Theoretical Framework

2.1   Problem Statement

The unknown state x for a dynamic system is defined by:

$$\dot{x}(t) = f(x(t)), y(t) = g(x(t)), \ x(0) \in [X_0] \tag{1}$$

where $x(t) \in R^n$ and $y(t) \in R^n$, and they denote, respectively, the state variables and the outputs of the system. Initial conditions $x(0)$ are supposed to belong to an initial "box" $[X_0]$. The concept of "box" will be described in Sect. 3. Time is $t \in [0, t_{max}]$. The functions f and g are real and can be differentiable in M, where M is an open set of Rn, such as $x(t) \in M$ for each $t \in [0, t_{max}]$. Besides, function f is at least k-times differentiable in the M domain. The output error is defined by:

$$v(t_i) = y(t_i) - y_m(t_i), i = 1, 2, \ldots, N. \tag{2}$$

We assume that $\underline{v(t)}$ and $\overline{v(t)}$ represent the lower and upper limit of acceptable output error, respectively. These limits correspond to a bounded noise. The integer number N is the total number of records. The interval arithmetic are used to calculate the guaranteed limits for the solution of Eq. 1 in the sampling times $\{t_1, t_2, \ldots, t_N\}$. Even though the studied process is a continuous dynamic system, Eq. 2 indicates that the problem statement is applicable for a discrete system, which is governed by difference equations [4].

2.2   Studied Process (Osmotic Dehydration of Pineapple)

The osmotic dehydration process has highly complex dynamics, which implies that there are a great variety of models and experimental procedures for different kinds of fruits and foods [14–16] and [17]. Independent of the chosen model, some authors coincide that the most significant variables of the process are identified with the food concentration and the concentration of the solution where the food is immersed in [18] and [19]. Pineapple is a completely heterogeneous, highly watery and porous food, that when immersed in solutions with high concentration of soluble solids (sugar), provokes two simultaneous upstream main flows. The first flow corresponds to a transfer of soluble solids (sugar) from the solution to the food. The second one is flow of water from the food that goes highly concentrated to the solution. A third secondary and negligible flow of aroma, vitamins and minerals happens, which is less intense, and occurs from the fruit to the solution. The mass transfer mechanisms that are present in the osmotic dehydration at atmosferic pressure and room temperature are mainly diffusion (Fick's laws of diffusion). These mechanisms are originated by the concentration differences between the food and the osmotic solution where the fruit is immersed in [18, 19] and [20]. Figure 1 shows the previously described flows that occur during the osmotic dehydration.

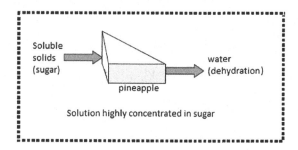

Fig. 1. Mass transfer process between solution and fruit

The sugar concentrations found in the osmotic solution and the fruit are registered by refractometers and reported in refraction indexes or Degrees Brix.

Degrees Brix can be understood as a percentage from 0 to 1 or a mass fraction, that provides the sugar mass contained in the mass of each analyzed component (solution and fruit). The model that was studied in this paper was extracted from [18] and it considers three state variables: concentration in fruit, concentration in tank 1 solution and volume that enters tank 1 from tank 2. The dehydration plant and its operation is described in [18, 19] and [20]. Figure 2 shows the process.

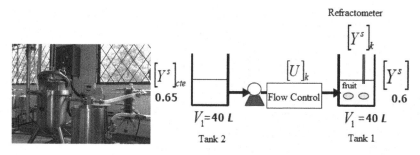

Fig. 2. Pineapple osmotic dehydration process diagram, (Unitary Operations Laboratory - Unisabana)

The model of [18] assumes that there is a perfect mix in tank 1, where the flow is perfectly controlled and the values for concentration in fruit and in tank 1 obey ideally to mass balances. The process is modeled in a discrete manner with a sample time of ΔT. The model is represented by difference equations, as indicated below:

Variation of Sugar Concentration for the Solution:

$$[Y^s]_{k+1}= [Y^s]_k-B[C]_k[X^s]_k\Delta T + ([Y^s]_{cte}-[Y^s]_k)[U]_k\Delta T/[V]_k \qquad (3)$$

Variation of Sugar Concentration for the Food:

$$[X^s]_{k+1}= [X^s]_k + [C]_k[X^s]_k\Delta T + [U]_k[X^s]_k\Delta T/[V]_k \qquad (4)$$

Where:
$[V]_k$ is the variation of thank 1 volume:

$$[V]_{k+1}= [V]_k + [U]_k\Delta T \qquad (5)$$

$[C]_k$ is the variation of thank 1 volume:

$$[C]_k= \mu\frac{[Y^s]_k}{K_{Y^s} + [Y^s]_k} \qquad (6)$$

B is a dimensionless proportion factor between the concentration variation of the solution and that of the food. This parameter is calculated using the final (subindex f) and initial (subindex o) values of the concentrations in solution and food during an experimental process:

$$B = \frac{[Y^s]_f-[Y^s]_o}{[X^s]_f-[X^s]_o} \qquad (7)$$

μ is the maximum change rate in sugar growth for the food. It is represented by:

$$\mu = \frac{ln\left(\frac{[Y^s]_f}{[X^s]_o}\right)}{\left(t_f - t_i\right)} \qquad (8)$$

$K_{Y^s} = 0.65$ (gr. of sugar/gr. of osmotic solution in tank (1) is the saturation constant for sugar concentration in tank 1. The raw material associated to the presented model is pineapple (*ananas comosus* in the cayena lisa variety) in a geometric shape (eighths of slice of 1 cm of thickness without any previous treatment).

The attributes of the osmotic solution for each tank were:

Tank 2: Constant. $[Y^S]_{cte}$ = 0.65° Brix.

Tank 1: Reference. $[Y^S]_{ref}$ = 0.6° Brix.

The process was simulated for a constant lineal entry flow: $[U2]_k$: (0 to 2.09) L/min for 180 min. The calculation of the kinetic parameter $[C]_k$ and the kinetic constants $\mu = 0.0007$ L/min and $B = 0.27$ are assumed as known.

3   Methodology

3.1   Interval Analysis Fundamentals

At first, interval analysis was a response to explain quantification errors that occurred when real numbers were represented rationally in computers and the technique was extended to validated numerics [30]. According to [30], an interval [u] = $[\underline{u}, \bar{u}]$, is a closed and connected subset of R, denoted by IR. Two intervals $[u]$ and $[v]$ are equal, if and only if their inferior and superior limits are the same. Arithmetic operations between two intervals $[u]$ and $[v]$, can be defined by:

$$o \in \{+, -, *, \div\}, [u]o[v] = \{xoy/[u], y \in [v]\} \tag{9}$$

The interval vector (or box) $[X]$ is a vector with interval components and it is equivalent to the cartesian product of scalar intervals:

$$[X] = [x_1] \times [x_2] \ldots \times [x_n]. \tag{10}$$

The vector set of real n-dimensional intervals is denoted by IR^n. A matrix interval is a matrix where its components are intervals. The set of $n \times m$ real interval matrices is denoted by IR^{n*m}. The classic operations for interval vectors or interval matrices are direct extensions of the same operations of point vectors [30].

The operations for punctual vectors can be extended to become classical operations for interval vectors [22]. This way, if: $f : R^n \rightarrow R^m$, the range of function f in an interval vector $[u]$, is given by:

$$f([u]) = \{f(x)/x \in [u]\} \tag{11}$$

The interval function $[f]$ of IR^n to IR^m is a function of the inclusion of f if:

$$\forall [u] \in IR^n, f([u]) \subseteq [f]([u]) \tag{12}$$

An inclusion function of f can be obtained through the substitution of each occurrence of a real variable for its corresponding interval. Said function is called natural inclusion function. In practice, the inclusion function is not unique, and it depends on the syntax of f [30].

3.2   Inversion Set

Consider the problem of determining a solution set for the unknowns u, defined by:

$$S = \{u \in U / \Phi(u) \in [y]\} = \Phi^{-1}([y]) \cap U \qquad (13)$$

where $[y]$ is known a priori, U is a search set for u and Φ of an invertible nonlinear function, which is not necessarily in the classical sense. [9] includes the calculation of the reciprocal image of Φ and that is known as a set inversion problem that can be solved using the SIVIA (Set Inversion Via Interval Analysis) algorithm. SIVIA as proposed in [9] is a recursive algorithm that goes through all the searching space so it does not lose any solution. This algorithm makes it possible to derive a guaranteed enclosure of the solution of set S, that meets: S is factible, enough to prove that $\Phi([u]) \subseteq [y]$. Conversely, if it can be proven that $\Phi([u]) \cap [y] = 0$, then the box $[u]$ is non-viable. On the contrary, there is no conclusion and the box $[u]$ is said to be undetermined. If the box is undetermined, the box is bisected and tried again until its size reaches a threshold precision, specified for $\varepsilon > 0$. This criterion assures that SIVIA finishes after a limited number of iterations.

3.3   State Estimation

State estimation refers to the integration of Eq. 1. Thus, the goal is to estimate the state of vector x in the sampling times $\{t_1, t_2, \ldots, t_N\}$, which correspond to the times of output measurements. The box $[x(t_j)]$ is denoted as $[x_j]$, where t_j represents the sampling time, $j = 1, 2, \ldots, N$ and x_j represents the solution of 1 at t_j. For models like the one presented in 1, the sets are characterized by not being convex and there could even be several disconnected components. Interval analysis consists of enclosing said sets in interval vectors that do not overlap and the usual inconvenient is obtaining wider solution interval vectors each time. This in known as the Wrapping Effect. This way, the wrapping effect yields poor results. The poverty brought by the big width of the set can be reduced through the use of a higher-order k for the Taylor expansion and through the use of mean value forms and matrices of pre-conditioning [13] and [23].

3.4   Prediction and Correction

Prediction aims at calculating the accessibility fixed for the state vector, while the correction stage keeps only the parts of the accessibility set that are consistent with the measurements and the error limits defined by Eq. 2. It is assumed that $[X_j]$ is a box that is guaranteed to contain x_j at t_j. The exterior aproximation of the predicted set $[X_{j+1}^+]$ is defined as the validated solution of the difference equation at t_{j+1}. The set $[X_{j+1}^+]$. is calculated using the EMV algorithm (extenden mean value), defined in [23]. The set is guaranteed to contain the state at t_{j+1}. At t_{j+1}, a "measurement vector", $[y_{j+1}]$, is obtained and it corresponds to the upper and lower limits for measurement noise.

$$\left[y_{j+1}\right] = \left[y_{j+1} - \underline{v_{j+1}}, -\overline{v_{j+1}}\right] \tag{14}$$

Then, the set $[g]^{-1}\left([y_{j+1}]\right)$. is calculated. This evaluation is obtained by the SIVIA algorithm. The expected solution at the sampling time t_{j+1} is finally given by $[x_{j+1}] = \left[X_{j+1}^+\right] \cap [g]^{-1}\left([y_{j+1}]\right)$. The procedure for the state estimation is summarized in the following algorithm: For $j = 0$ to $j = N - 1$ do:

Prediction step: compute $[X_{j+1}^+]$ using EMV algorithm.

Correction step: calculate $[x_{j+1}]$ so that

$$[x_{j+1}] = \left[X_{j+1}^+\right] \cap [g]^{-1}\left([y_{j+1}]\right),$$

3.5   Extended Mean Value (EMV)

The most efficient methods to solve state estimation for dynamic systems are based on Taylor's expansions [23]. These methods consist of two parts: the first part verifies the existence and uniqueness of the solution, using the fixed point theorem and the Picard-Lindelf operator. At a time t_{j+1}, a box, a priori $[\tilde{x}_j]$, that contains all the solutions that correspond to all the possible trajectories between tj and t_{j+1} is obtained. In the second part, the solution at t_{j+1} is calculated using Taylor's expansion, in the term that remains is $[\tilde{x}_j]$. However, in practice, the set $[\tilde{x}_j]$ often doesn't contain the true solution [24]. Therefore, the used technique consists of inflating this set until the next inclusion is verified with the following expression:

$$[x_j] + hf\left([\tilde{x}_j]\right) \subseteq [\tilde{x}_j] \tag{15}$$

where h indicates the integration stage and $[X_j]$ is the first solution. This method is summarized in the Enclosure algorithm, which was developed by [25]. The inputs are $[x_j]$ and $\alpha > 0$ and the output is $[\tilde{x}_j]$:

$$[x_j] = [\tilde{x}_j]$$

While $\left([x_j] + hf\left([\tilde{x}_j]\right)\right) \sim \subseteq [\tilde{x}_j]$ do :

$$[\tilde{x}_j] = inflate\left([\tilde{x}_j], \alpha\right).$$

The function inflate for an interval vector $[u] = [\underline{u_1}, \overline{u_1}], \ldots, [\underline{u_n}, \overline{u_n}]$, operates as follows:

$$\left[(1 - \alpha)\underline{u_1}, (1 + \alpha)\overline{u_1}\right], \ldots, \left(\left[(1 - \alpha)\underline{u_n}, (1 + \alpha)\overline{u_n}\right]\right).$$

Precision depends of the α coefficient. If the set $[\tilde{x}_j]$ satisfies the inclusion presented in Eq. 15, then the inclusion $x(t) \in [\tilde{x}_j]$ is maintained for all $t \in [t_j, t_{j+1}]$. The solution

x_{j+1} of the differential equation given in Eq. 1 at t_{j+1} is guaranteed, in the interval vector $[x_{j+1}]$ and it is given by the Taylor expansion [30]:

$$[x_{j+1}] = [x_j] + \sum_{i=1}^{k-1} h^i f^{[i]}([x_j]) + h^k f^{[k]}([\tilde{x}_j]),\qquad(16)$$

where k denotes the end of the Taylor expansion and the $f^{[i]}$ coefficients are the Taylor coefficients of the $x(t)$ solution, which are obtained in a recursive form by:

$$f^{[1]} = f, f^{[i]} = \frac{1}{i}\frac{\partial f^{[i-1]}}{\partial x} f, i \geq 2 \qquad(17)$$

The application of the inflate function in the set $[\tilde{x}_j]$ leads to increase of its width. The poor quality introduced by the wider set can be reduced through the use of a higher order k for the Taylor expansion in Eq. 17. But the width of the solution always increases, even for higher orders. To sort this obstacle, Rihm [26] proposes evaluating 17 through the extended mean value algorithm, based on mean value forms and preconditioning matrices. This algorithm is used to solve the differential equation given in 1. The inputs for this algorithm are $[\tilde{x}_j], [x_j], \hat{x}_j, [v_j], p_j, A_j, h$ and the outputs are $[\tilde{x}_{j+1}], \hat{x}_{j+1}, [v_{j+1}], [p_{j+1}], A_{j+1}$. The variable $\hat{x}_j$ is the mean point of a certain interval v_j. The initial conditions may be provided by $p_0 = 0, q_0 = 0$ and $v_0 = x_0$. Up next, the secuence of the algorithm is presented:

a. $[v_{j+1}] = \hat{x}_j + \sum_{i=1}^{k-1} h^i f^{[i]}(\hat{x}_j) + h^k f^{[k]}([\tilde{x}_j])$,

b. $[S_j] = I + \sum_{i=1}^{k-1} J(f^{[i]}; [x_j])h^i$,

c. $[q_{j+1}] = ([S_j]A_j)[P_j] + [S_j]([v_j]) - \hat{x}_j)$,

d. $[x_{j+1}] = [v_{j+1}] + [x_{j+1}]$

e. $A_{j+1} = m([S_j]A_j)$,

f. $p_{j+1}] = A_{j+1}^{-1}([S_j]A_j)[p_j] + (A_{j+1}^{-1}[S_j])([v_j] - \hat{x}_j)$,

g. $\hat{x}_{j+1} = m([v_{j+1}])$

In the previous algorithm, I represents the identity matrix (with the same dimension of the state vector). $J(f^{[i]}; [x_j])$ is the Jacobian matrix of the Taylor coefficient, $f^{[i]}$, which is evaluated over $[x_j]$. The variables $\hat{x}_j$ and $[v_j]$ are calculated in the state $(t_j - 1)$.

3.6   Envelope-Based Fault Detection and Diagnosis Algorithm

The detection of a fault, in practice, is a difficult task to perform due to the imprecision presented by the mathematical models that are available for a given process. Generally, a failure is detected when the measured value Y_M does not correspond to the reference value, Y_R, which is provided by the model, as indicated by the Eq. 18.

$$Y_M \bigcap Y_R = 0 \qquad (18)$$

When having interval models of the process, it is feasible to estimate its state, considering the variations of its parameters and the perturbations obtained due the presence of noise in the measurement. This allows determining if a system is:

a. Functioning normally

b. Has a fault that has not been detected, or a false alarm was generated

c. Failing

The envelope-based fault detection algorithm proposes the assignment of three regions:

a. The external region, which corresponds to values that are outside the interval limits of the worst case evaluated for the system, where it has a particularly large amount of noise.

b. The intermediate region, which corresponds to values that are between the worst case and the best case evaluated.

c. The internal region, which corresponds to values that are located within the interval range of the best case, where it displays little presence of noise and a smaller interval width than the worst case.

To determine the envelopes and assign the three regions, the state estimation for nonlinear systems presented in the previous section is used. Once the regions have been determined, we proceed with the evaluation of the type of system operation (Normal, Failure not detected or measurement error, Failed).

The fault detection algorithm is shown below:

h. *Inputs* : Y_M, R_S, W_S.

i. *Outputs* : $[Faults]$

j. *If* $[Y_M > Up\_W_S] \vee [Y_M < Low\_W_S]$

k. *then Fault* (-1)

l. *If* $[Y_M < Up\_W_S]^\wedge [Y_M > Up\_B_S]$

m. *Then Fault* that has not been detected, or a false alarm (1)

n. *If* $[Y_M > Low\_W_S]^\wedge [Y_M < low\_B_S]$

o. *Then Fault* that has not been detected, or a false alarm (1)

p. *If* $[Y_M < Up\_B_S]^\wedge [Y_M > low\_B_S]$

q. *Then Normal* (0)

Where:

Y_M: It is the measured response of the system.

B_S: It is the envelope for the best case scenario.

W_S: It is the envelope for the worst case scenario.

4   Results and Analysis

The state estimation algorithm is applied to the pineapple dehydration model. The analysis is taken to simulation level. Noise R is delimited for the state $[Y^s], [X^s]$ and $[V]$ respectively, as follows:

$$R = \begin{bmatrix} -0.05 & 0.05 \\ -0.05 & 0.05 \\ -0.05 & 0.05 \end{bmatrix} \quad (18)$$

The initial conditions for the state variables $[Y^s], [X^s]$ and $[V]$, are given by:

$$x(0) = \begin{bmatrix} 0.135 & 0.145 \\ 0.600 & 0.610 \\ 40.45 & 40.55 \end{bmatrix} \quad (19)$$

Figures 3, 4 and 5 show the prediction envelope, starting with the estimation envelope (lower and upper EMV), then determining the solution set of the state by means of (lower and upper SIVIA). This way, we obtain the two envelopes that guarantee the status for each sampling time, in each of the output variables. The reference concentration of the process under normal conditions corresponded to 0.65 degrees brix for tank 1 and the data are shown in solid black line for each of the state variables.

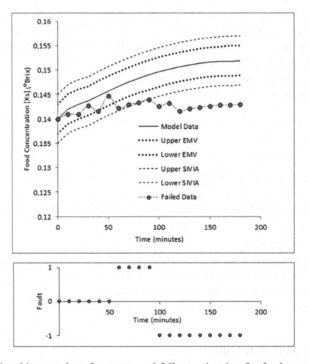

Fig. 3. Resulting envelope from state and failure estimation for food concentration

Figures 3, 4 and 5 also indicate the results obtained for the detection of faults on the system, which correspond to the presence of an inflow of less than $[U2]_k$: (0 to 1.09) L/min with a sampling time of 10 min. This modifies the response of the system in

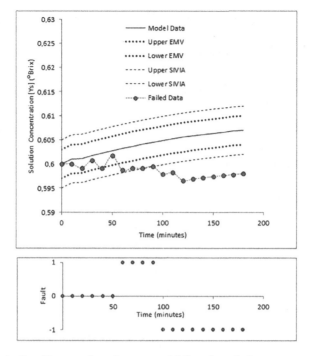

Fig. 4. Resulting envelope for state and failure for solution concentration.

each of the state variables compared to the reference model. The data of the output variables for the new input are shown in continuous red line. The reference concentration for the new input was 0.6° brix for tank 1. The diagnosis of the faults is indicated in the lower part of each of the graphs under the following convention:

(−1): System Failure

(1): The system presents an undetected failure or a false alarm is present, which may be triggered by measurement noise.

(0): System is functioning correctly

Figures 3, 4 and 5 show the response of the system under normal operating conditions, in a time interval of 0 to 50 min. It is shown how the alarm signal (1) is maintained when the system output is located between the interval corresponding to [EMV-lower, SIVIA lower], in a time interval between 60 and 90 min. A failure occurs at t = 100 min, which is shown as the food concentration, solution concentration and food concentration rate begin to decrease at this moment and keep this trend.

From the previous graphs, it can be seen how the envelopes generated by the estimation of states allow to evaluate the behavior of a system and thus determine whether or not it has faults. The purpose of this proposed solution is to perform efficient monitoring of the output of a system at a low computational cost and considering the measurement variability as a result of the disturbances.

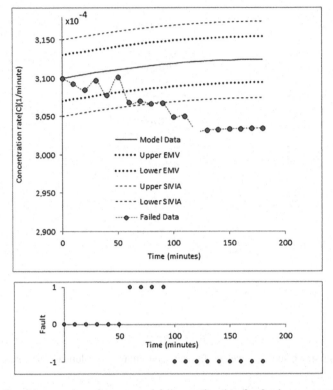

Fig. 5. Resulting envelope for state and failure estimation for food concentration rate.

5 Conclusions

When implementing and applying the estimation technique by the EMV algorithm, it was found that this guarantees the inclusion of the real state within the obtained prediction, as well as the decrease of the wrapping effect, since it makes use of the concept of midpoint interval to calculate an optimal estimate.

The SIVIA algorithm yielded a solution set coherent to the response of the system, which is based on the process model, meaning that the model adequately represents the dynamics of the system. Using the regions for the detection and diagnosis of faults, it is feasible to determine reliable intervals for the correct functioning of the system.

Likewise, the precision of the regions is directly related to the level of uncertainty that is considered for the generation of the envelopes, which varies from process to process and depends on the accuracy of the taken measurements.

By using the classic prediction-correction scheme through the use of the EMV and SIVIA algorithms, it is possible to propose ON-LINE detection and diagnosis techniques given the low computational cost involved in these methods.

As future work, existing control techniques applied in intervals can be used, which allow to control processes within ranges, which contrasts with the classic techniques of automatic control.

The methodology used in this work is applicable to real processes such as those shown in [28, 29] and [30] and may be used for failure detection and diagnostics.

References

1. Burgos, M., González, A., Vallejo, M., Izquierdo, C.: Selección económica de equipo utilizando matemáticas de intervalos. Información Tecnológica **9**(5), 311–316 (1998)
2. Campos, P., Valdés, H.: Optimización Global por Intervalos: Aplicación a Problemas con Parámetros Inciertos. Información Tecnológica **17**(5), 67–74 (2006)
3. Zapata, G., Cardillo, J., Chacón, E.: Aportes Metodológicos para el Diseño de Sistemas de Supervisión de Procesos Continuos. Información tecnológica **22**(3), 97–114 (2011)
4. Jauberthie, C. and Chanthery, E., Optimal input design for a nonlinear dynamical uncertain aerospace system. In: IFAC Symposium on Nonlinear Control Systems, Toulouse-France (2013)
5. Li, Q., Jauberthie, C., Denis, L., Cher, Z.: Guaranteed State and Parameter Estimation for Nonlinear Dynamical Aerospace Models, Informatics in Control, Automation and Robotics (ICINCO), Vienna, Austria (2014)
6. Ortega, F., Pérez, O., López, E.: Comparación del desempeño de estimadores de estado no lineales para determinar la concentración de biomasa y sustrato en un bioproceso. Información tecnológica **26**(5), 35–44 (2015)
7. Kieffer, M., Jaulin, L., Walter, E.: Guaranteed recursive nonlinear state bounding using interval analysis. Int. J. Adaptative Control Sig. Process. **16**(3), 193–218 (2002)
8. Jaulin, L.: A nonlinear set membership approach for the localization and map building of underwater robots. IEEE Trans. Rob. **25**(1), 88–98 (2009)
9. Jaulin, L., Walter, E.: Set inversion via interval analysis for nonlinear bounded-error estimation. Automatica **29**(4), 1053–1064 (1993)
10. Paşca, I.: Formally verified conditions for regularity of interval matrices. In: 10th International Conference, AISC 2010, 17th Symposium, Calculemus 2010, and 9th International Conference, MKM 2010, Paris- France (2010)
11. Rauh, A., Auer, E.: Modeling, Design and Simulation of Systems with Uncertaintites. Springer, Berlin (2011). https://doi.org/10.1007/978-3-642-15956-
12. Jauberthie, C., Verdiere, N., Trave, L.: Fault detection and identification relying on set-membership identifiability. Ann. Rev. Control **37**(1), 129–136 (2013)
13. Nedialkov, N.: Vnode-lp a validated solver for initial value problems in ordinary differential equations. Technical report, Department of Computing and Software (2006)
14. Arreola, S., Rosas, M.: Aplicación de vacío en la deshidratación osmótica de higos (ficus carica). Información tecnológica **18**(2), 43–48 (2007)
15. Arballo, J.: Modelado y simulación de la deshidratación combinada osmótica de frutihortícolas. Ph.D. Thesis in Engineering, Universidad de La Plata, Argentina (2013)
16. García, A. y otros cuatros autores, Análisis comparativo de la cinética de deshidratación Osmótica y por Flujo de Aire Caliente de la Piña (Ananas Comosus, variedad Cayena lisa). Rev Cie Téc Agr **22**(1), 62–69 (2013)
17. García, M., Alvis, A., García, C.: Evaluación de los pretratamientos de deshidratación osmótica y microondas en la obtención de hojuelas de mango (Tommy Atkins). Información tecnológica **26**(5), 63–70 (2015)

18. Jaller, S., Vargas, S.: Comparación de la Transferencia de materia en los procesos de Deshidratación Osmótica a presión atmosférica y con impregnación de vacío en la piña cayena lisa (ananás comosus l. meer) a través de un modelo matemático, Tesis de Pregrado en Ingeniería de Producción Agroindustrial, UniSabana, Chía, Colombia (2000)

19. Gonzalez, G.: Viabilidad de la Piña colombiana var. Cayena Lisa, para su industrialización combinando las operaciones de Impregnación a vacío, deshidratación cayena lisa (ananás comosus meer), Tesis de Doctorado, Universidad Politécnica de Valencia, Valencia, España (2000)

20. Wullner, B.: Instrumentación y Control de un deshidratador Osmótico a Vacío, Tesis de Pregrado en Ingeniería de Producción Agroindustrial, UniSabana, Chía, Colombia (1998)

21. Moore, R.: Automatic error analysis in digital computation, Technical report LMSD-48421, Lockheed Missiles and Space Co, Palo Alto, CA (1959)

22. Moore, R.E.: Interval Analysis. Prentice Hall, New Jersey (1966)

23. Nedialkov, N., Jackson, K., Pryce, J.: An effective high-order interval method for validating existence and uniqueness of the solution of an IVP for an ode. Reliable Comput. 7, 449–465 (2001)

24. Milanese, M., Norton, J., Piet-Lahanier, H., Walter, W.: Bounding Approaches to System Identification. Springer, Boston (1996). https://doi.org/10.1007/978-1-4757-9545-5

25. Lohner, R.: Enclosing the Solutions of Ordinary Initial and Boundary Value Problems, pp. 255–286. Wiley-Teubner, Stuttgart (1987)

26. Rihm, R.: Interval methods for initial value problems in ODEs. In: Herzberger, J. (ed.) Topics in Validated Computations: Proceedings of the IMACS-GAMM International Workshop on Validated Computations, University of Oldenburg, Elsevier Studies in Computational Mathematics. Elsevier, Amsterdam (1994)

27. Walter, É., Pronzato, L.: Identification de mod`eles parametriques à partir de donnees experimentales. Masson (1994)

28. Castellanos, H.E., Collazos, C.A., Farfán, J.C., Meléndez-Pertuz, F.: Diseño y Construcción de un Canal Hidráulico de Pendiente Variable. Información tecnológica 28(6), 103–114 (2017). https://dx.doi.org/10.4067/S0718-07642017000600012. Accessed 20 July 2018

29. Collazos, C.A., Castellanos, H.E., Burbano, A.M., Cardona, J.A., Cuervo, J.A., Maldonado-Franco, A.: Semi-mechanistic modelling of an osmotic dehydration process. WSEAS Trans. Syst. 16, 27–35 (2017). E-ISSN: 2224-2678, Bulgary

30. Duarte, J., Garcia, J., Jimenez, J., Sanjuan, M.E., Bula, A., Gonzalez, J.: Autoignition control in spark-ignition engines using internal model control structure. J. Energy Resour. Technol. 139(2), 022201 (2016)

Security-State Estimation of Electrical Power Systems: A Methodological Proposal

Fredy A. Sanz[1(✉)], C. A. Collazos[1], Iván Ruiz[1],
and Farid Meléndez-Pertuz[2]

[1] Vicerrectoría de Investigaciones,
Universidad Manuela Beltrán, Bogotá, Colombia
fredy.sanz@umb.edu.co
[2] Departamento de Ciencias de la Computación y Electrónica,
Universidad de la Costa, Barranquilla, Colombia

Abstract. Security assessment techniques are a tool that allows the operational personnel of electrical systems to categorize operating conditions in different labels. Nowadays, the large size of power grids and the operating conditions close to their operating limits require efficient, safe and fast procedures to assess the overall grid security, being one of the challenges posed by smart grids conception. In this paper, a supervised learning approach that allows to integrate all the concepts of safety of the electrical network: voltage, angle, frequency, etc., to give an overall assessment of the system in terms of security which may be applied according to the regulations and geographical contexts of each country.

Keywords: Power system security · Power system stability · State estimation · Smart grids

1 Introduction

In the context of Security Analysis (SA), the study of systems behavior depends on a set of contingencies, identifying if the system has necessary security conditions and is capable of surviving after an event or contingency. The power systems behavior and operating restrictions (transformers tabs limits, line power flows limits, etc.), depend on their nature and configuration (power grid topology). Therefore, risks derived from contingencies can affect power system security in different ways, some common faults are: tripping lines, transformers outages, and generators outages, or a combinations of the above, etc. [1, 2].

For on-line SA, different methods have been proposed. In [3] an application using artificial neural network (ANN) models was proposed, considering load changes, and ranking them in the order of severity based on composite security index. Some heuristic and statistical techniques to obtain a power grid diagnosis are used [4–6], although previous works assume that specific contingencies are known, i.e. admittance matrix was assumed known. In [7] the estimation of the equivalent dynamic model through the PMU's (Power Measurement Units) measurements was considered. However, contingencies were not considered, implying an unrealistic case of the power grid due to

© Springer Nature Switzerland AG 2019
S. Misra et al. (Eds.): ICCSA 2019, LNCS 11620, pp. 713–730, 2019.
https://doi.org/10.1007/978-3-030-24296-1_57

topological flexibility and variability that experiment the power grid as a result of failures. On the other hand, in [8] an on-line dynamic security assessment is proposed using the terms of the transient energy function as input features to a machine learning algorithm.

Therefore, in this paper a flexible methodology based on machine learning techniques for on-line security state estimation is proposed, which brings integrally: the concept of security assessment, fast power system security status estimation, flexibility in metrics selection (stability indices), and a reliable estimation of security state under different load scenarios, contingencies and failures. Our proposal consists of the following stages: measurements preparation, stability indices calculation, security state assessment, model building based on machine learning techniques.

This paper is organized as follows. Section 2 presents a brief overview of machine learning approach for power system security-state estimation. The snapshot of methodology proposal is presented in Sect. 3. The IEEE 39-bus test system is used to apply the methodological proposal; implementation and results are shown in Sects. 4 and 5 respectively. Finally discussions and conclusions are presented.

2 Machine Learning in Power System Security-State Estimation

Under the smart grids conception, it is important to note that power systems must integrate new measurement technologies, controls, renewable energies, etc., allowing to have an on-line estimation of the security status. The increasingly inclusion of phasor measurement units (PMUs), permits quickly and accurately measurements of the electrical variables, which are usually stored in a set of instantaneous measurements x_{PMUs}, as shown Eq. 1, including: voltage $V_{i,j}$, currents $I_{i,j}$, active powers $P_{i,j}$, reactive powers $Q_{i,j}$, etc., (where the subscripts i indicate the time when measurement is taken and j involve the bus where a measure is made), serving as input to computational models that support a quick estimation of security status.

$$x_{PMUs} = [V_{i,1}\ldots V_{i,j}\ \ I_{i,1}\ldots I_{i,j}\ \ P_{i,1}\ldots P_{i,j}\ \ Q_{i,1}\ldots Q_{i,j}\ldots] \tag{1}$$

Generally power flows calculation provide data about angles, voltages, active and reactive power, line power flows, switching devices and transformers. In short, a small change in the system load or its configuration involves changes in electrical variables (voltages, currents, power, etc.), i.e. for every change there is a security state of the power grid (normal, alert, emergency, etc.). In this way, as it is shown in Eq. 2, the power grid measurements x_{PMUs} is used to obtain an estimate of the security state y, by means of a function f obtained through machine learning techniques for better time responses. Therefore, the main objective of the methodological proposal is to find a model f, reliable and safe, to predict the security status of the power grid from PMU's measurements.

$$x_{PMUs} \xrightarrow{f} y = \{normal, alert, emergency, \ldots, etc.\} \qquad (2)$$

The security state definition depends on particular issues of the power system. In light of smart grids, a flexible methodology that can be made as robust as required will be proposed, which allows the user to define model requirements, according to the on-line measurable variables and limitations of the power system, i.e. it is possible to decide assess: the static security, the dynamic security, or both.

The security state estimation process include two main phases: *(i)* modeling phase, *(ii)* security state estimation phase, as shown Fig. 1. The second phase is the model implementation in the power grid to security status monitoring. The objective of this paper is a methodological proposal for the modeling phase, which includes the measurement preparation, indices calculation, security state assignment, and model building. Details on each components of the methodology are presented in Sect. 3.

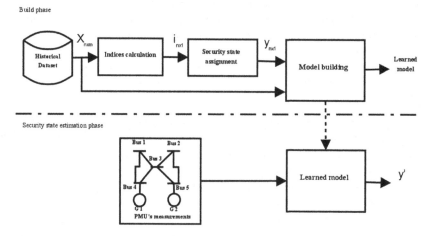

Fig. 1. Security state estimation process for one stability condition (voltage stability, angle stability, frequency stability, etc.)

3 Machine Learning in Power System Security-State Estimation

The methodological proposal is composed of four stages: measurements, indices calculation, security state assignment, and model building. The methodology procedure was schematized previously as modeling phase through Fig. 1, stages are described below. Notice that the procedure described in Fig. 1 includes only one stability condition (e.g. voltage stability, angle stability, frequency stability, etc.). In case that several stability problems are require to analyze, several instances of the procedure must be applied, one for each stability condition.

3.1   Measurements

When a real power system is studied, measurements recorded with PMUs can be considered within a real-time context. However, the power grid contingencies and faults can involve topological changes due to outages in lines, transformers and generators. Which generally cannot be determined immediately, requiring previous analysis for topological changes identification (many authors considers that configuration changes are known after the faults are analyzed and identified [4–7]).

These historical set of measurements X_{PMUs}, is presented in extended form in Eq. 3. where I, V, P and Q are the currents, voltages, active powers, and reactive power respectively. The subscripts: i indicates the measurement of each variable in a moment of time, and j involves the bus where a measure is taken. Security assessment is a combination of system monitoring and contingency analysis [9], from the practical point of view these processes are made online and offline respectively, to identify risky situations and to plan remedial actions. Strictly, if a power system requires static and dynamic security evaluation, the following safety criteria may be considered [10]: angle stability, frequency stability, transient stability, voltage stability, small-signal stability, thermal overloading of electrical network equipment, etc.

$$X_{PMUs} = \begin{bmatrix} V_{1,1} \cdots V_{1,j} & I_{1,1} \cdots I_{1,j} & P_{1,1} \cdots P_{1,j} & Q_{1,1} & \cdots & Q_{1,j} \cdots \\ \vdots \ddots \vdots & \vdots \ddots \vdots & \vdots \ddots \vdots & & \ddots & \vdots \\ V_{i,1} \cdots V_{i,j} & I_{i,1} \cdots I_{i,j} & P_{i,1} \cdots P_{i,j} & Q_{i,1} & \cdots & Q_{i,j} \cdots \end{bmatrix} \tag{3}$$

The goal of this stage is to obtain a dataset adapted to the security requirements of a particular power system, this procedure includes: *(i)* taking measurements from the power grid, *(ii)* recording of electrical variables as historical dataset, *(iii)* security assessment according to the anomalies observed in the historical dataset, and *(iv)* dataset refinement taking into account the observed instabilities. The measurements set preparation is illustrated in Fig. 2.

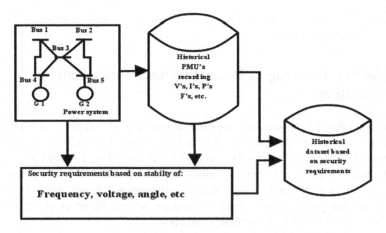

Fig. 2. Measurements set. Using historical dataset, the power grid configuration and their contingencies is possible to determine the existing instabilities and therefore the variables required to estimate the security state.

3.2   Indices Calculation

After deciding which are the stability conditions to consider, appropriate metrics must be selected in order to measure the security degree associated with each stability condition. For example, typical indicators of voltage stability are: Voltage Collapse Proximity Index (VCPI) [11], Fast Voltage Stability index (FVSI) [12], Voltage Stability Index [13], Voltage Margin (Kv) [2], Area of the Voltage Stability Region (AVSR) [14] etc. The stability indicators selected must be subjected to: (i) Knowledge a portion or all of the variables which are used to calculate it, which can be known through PMU's measurements, *(ii)* a familiarity criterion with the index, which regards to operational conditions, efficiency studies, current regulations, etc., providing flexibility to the user's needs.

For stability angle, the following indicators can be used amount others [15]: Expected Stability Margin (EASM), Weighted Probability Index (WPI), and Integral Square Bus Angle (ISBA). In frequency stability analysis some commonly used indices are [16]: Frequency Deviation Assessment (FDSA), Phase Stability Index (PSI), and Constant Frequency Limiter (CFL). On the other hand, considering small-signal stability the following indices may be considered [17]: Single Mode Index (SMI), All Modes Index (AMI), Global Modes Index (GMI), etc. Therefore, the dataset selected must be include the required measurable variables according to the metrics selected for stability evaluation.

According to the types of stability condition selected for the power system, the respective indices are calculated using the measurements contained in Eq. 3. The calculation is performed for each observation (for each instant of time).

3.3   Security State Assignment

Generally, the security states are assigned to measurements groups that fall within a degree of security which are called classes (normal, alert, emergency, ...). They must obey to: the security analysis procedures proposed in the literature [2, 4, 18, 19].

The metrics were previously selected considering measurable parameters with PMUs. After this, security conditions of the power system should be selected and classified in ranges for each index, in detail, the security state ranking process these stages *(i)* electrical variables are measured on-line, *(ii)* a parallel estimator for each stability type is calculated separately, *(iii)* a concept of system security is issued, considering the kind of stability with higher risk. This procedure is shown in Fig. 3, considering different security states and a ranking processor which must select the more severe stability condition and thus emit a security state concept.

The security states assignment described in Fig. 1 includes only one stability condition, however if power system have multiple stability risks, the security state assignment will be obtained through the ranking process described about and shown in Fig. 3.

3.4   Model Building

The goal in this phase is to learn a model f that maps the measurements from PMUs to a security state. The model building includes two stages: *(i)* selection of the most discriminative variables, and *(ii)* learning a classifier that discriminates (separate) observed variables into different classes. The basis of these stages are explained bellow.

Variables Selection. The goal in the variables selection stage is to obtain a lower dimension representation of an original dataset with many samples while maintaining the discriminability between different classes, i.e., security states in the context of this work.

Given the dataset $\{X, y\}$, where $X \in R^{N,M}$ is the matrix containing measured variables from the power system, $y \in R^N$ is a vector of discrete values containing the security state $y \in \{1, 2, \ldots, K\}$ assigned to each sample, M is the total number of variables recorded from the PMUs, K is the total number of security states and N is the total number of observed samples; the variable selection aims to obtain a new dataset $\{X', y\}$, where $X' \in R^{N,P}$ is the matrix containing P selected variables and $P < M$. If the least significant buses to estimate the security status are identified, then the buses that govern the power grid stability are also known. [20]. Generally, variables selection techniques can be chosen through the modeler experience or by benchmarking, some useful techniques are: Square Correlation coefficient (R^2) [21], Fisher's score (f_{score}) [22], Correlation-based Feature Selection (CFS) [23].

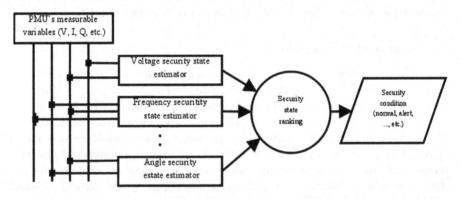

Fig. 3. Security state ranking for two or more stability condition

Classifier. The classifier is responsible for estimating the security state, i.e. it is the model that can take as input the selected PMU's measurements and infers the security state of the power system. The classifier takes an input data x_{PMUs} representing the observations from the PMUs in a given time and assigns it to one of K discrete classes.

$C = \{C_1, C_2, \ldots, C_K\}$, representing the security states of the power system [24]. The classification model has to be learned from a training dataset $\{X, y\}$, where $X \in R^{N,M}$ is matrix with N samples of the M variables measured from the PMUs, $y \in R^N$ is a vector of the security state labels assigned to each sample, $y \in \{1, 2, \ldots, K\}$ and K is the number of security states or classes. To do so, the classifier divides the space of the input vector into decision regions separated by decision boundaries or hyperplanes [24]. Different techniques have been documented as Naive Bayes (NB) [25], Support Vector Machines (SVM) [26], Feed Forward Neural Networks (NN) [27] and Linear Discriminant Analysis (LDA) [28]. Considering the flexibility and future effectiveness of the proposed methodology, we recommend to review the most prominent existing learning algorithms techniques.

4   Methodology Implementation

In order to demonstrate and validate the usability of the proposed methodology, the IEEE 39-bus test system (New England) was used [29]. This test power systems is shown in Fig. 4. This power system was assumed to be vulnerable to voltage stability, leaving aside other stability types. Therefore, the power grid security is modeled and evaluated to be robust respect to voltage stability.

Measurements. As the selected power system is vulnerable respect to voltage stability, voltage measurements and the configuration of the power grid defined in the admittance matrix Y are needed to compute the security state [30].

The New England system was simulated under different conditions to obtain a dataset. The system was subjected to outage-line contingencies on each line, and also to generator-outage contingency in each generator. Therefore the dataset includes the New England voltages obtained by simulation using power flows under different load profiles, lines and generators outages in each devices.

As a result, the measurement matrix is $X_{VS} \in R^{N,M}$, where $M = 39$ is the number of voltage buses and $N = 18764$ is the total number of observations in the different scenarios.

Indices Calculation. There are several alternatives to select a metric to compute the voltage stability [2, 11–14]. In this work the Voltage Collapse Proximity Index (VCPI) was adopted as suggested in [11]. The VCPI for each bus is computed as:

$$VCPI_J = \left| 1 - \frac{\sum_{m=1 m \neq j}^{M} V'_m}{V_j} \right| \tag{4}$$

Where V'_m is defined as:

$$V'_m = \frac{Y_{jm}}{\sum_{l=1 l \neq j}^{M} Y_{jl}} \tag{5}$$

Where, V_j is the voltage phasor at bus j, V_m is the voltage phasor at bus m, Y_{jm} is the admittance between bus j and bus m, Y_{jl} is the admittance between bus i and bus l, j is any monitored bus, m is other bus connected to bus j, M is the number of buses. The term V'_m indicates the current flow participation of bus m. The $VCPI_j$ value ranges between 0 and 1. If the value of this metric is close to 0, it is assumed that the node is stable; however, if the value of the index is close to 1, the node is unstable and a voltage collapse in the power systems is expected. Using historical data to build a model is advantageous, since post-contingency analysis can be performed, to learn more about the power grid as configuration and fault types, i.e. the admittance matrix Y is known, and the voltage stability index may be calculated. Note that if the historical dataset includes voltages measurements, each voltage pattern corresponds to an stability state.

Security State Assignment. Four security states were considered *(K = 4): (i)* normal, all system variables are within the nominal range, the system operates in a secure manner; *(ii)* alert, if security levels fall below a certain limit of adequacy; *(iii)* emergency, when the system has been weakened to a level where a contingency may cause an overloading of equipment that places the system in a hazardous state; and *(iv)* in extremis, occurs if the disturbance is very severe, this state may result after the alert state occurs.. In this work, the VCPI ranges associated with each security level are presented in Table 1. These ranges were applied to the security state of each sample recorded from the selected power system.

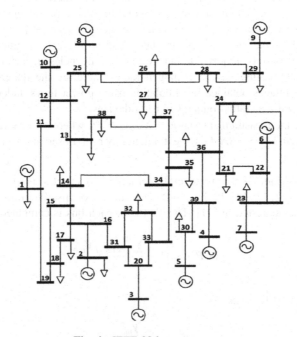

Fig. 4. IEEE 39-bus test system

Table 1. Security-state ranges for New England system

Normal	Alert	Emergency	In extremis
$0 \leq VCPI < 0.25$	$0.25 \leq VCPI < 0.5$	$0.5 \leq VCPI < 0.75$	$VCPI \geq 0.75$

This criterion is applied to each previously calculated VCPI. As a result, each measurement contained in the dataset is associated to a security state or equivalently to one discrete value of $\{1, 2, 3, 4\}$ for normal, alert, emergency and in extremis, respectively.

Model Building. Given the measurement matrix and the security state, we can construct the dataset $\{X, y\}$, where $X \in R^{N,M}$ is the matrix containing voltages measured from the power system, y is a vector of discrete values containing the security state $y \in \{1, 2, 3, 4\}$ assigned to each sample, N is the number of samples and M is the number of bus voltages or variables recorded from the PMUs. This dataset is:

$$
X_{PMUs} = \begin{bmatrix} V_{1,1} & \cdots & V_{1,M} \\ \vdots & \ddots & \vdots \\ V_{N,1} & \cdots & V_{N,M} \end{bmatrix}, y = \begin{matrix} y_1 \\ \vdots \\ y_N \end{matrix} \tag{6}
$$

As a result of the simulation process $N = 18764$ measurements were obtained, of which 3858 belongs to normal, 1286 to alertness, 1336 to emergency state, and 12284 to in extremis. In the case of in extreme state a greater number of observations are included because the system was subjected to multiple contingencies, forcing it to severe conditions that affect security, and in the case of normal state there is a smaller number of observations because this state is only one of the studied cases.

Variables Selection. The variables selection techniques used in this implementation are: square correlation coefficient, Fisher's score, and Correlation-based features selection. These techniques are described below.

Squared correlation coefficient (R^2): This technique computes the squared correlation coefficient for every variable measured from the power system and the vector of security state values or class labels [21], and then selects the P variables with higher R^2 values. The square value of the correlation coefficient R^2 is computed independently for each variable as:

$$
R_j^2 = \frac{\sum_{i=1}^{N}(x_{i,j} - \bar{x}_j)(y_i - \bar{y})}{\sqrt{\sum_{i=1}^{N}(x_{i,j} - \bar{x}_2)^2 \sum_{i=1}^{N}(y_i - \bar{y})^2}} \tag{7}
$$

Where $x_{j,i}$ is the *i-th* sample of the *j-th* variable measured from the PMUs, y_i is the security state or class label associated with the *i-th* sample (measurement at time i) and the bar notation represents the average value across all observed samples. After the R^2 values of all variables are computed, the $P < M$ variables presenting the highest R^2 are selected, but, no specific criterion exists to choose P. Although the R^2 method is simple and easy to understand, it presents some limitations: *(i)* the R^2 value is computed independently for each variable, thus, correlated or redundant variables cannot be identified, *(ii)* the method could discharge variables with low individual R^2 value, but with very high R^2 value when combined with other variables and *(iii)* the number of P selected variable has to be manually defined. These limitations may occur in the security state estimation in power systems using voltage measurements, since neighbor buses may have similar behavior, i.e. they are correlated [20].

Fisher's score (f_{score}): This technique also selects a lower dimension dataset where each variable is chosen according to a score computed under the Fisher criterion [31]. The score is computed independently for each variable considering the distance between samples for the same class (expected to be small) and the distance between samples in different classes (expected to be large). Thus, the Fisher score for each variable is given by [32]:

$$f_{score} = \frac{\sum_{k=1}^{K} n^k (\mu_j^k - \mu_j)^2}{(\sigma_j)^2} \tag{8}$$

Where $(\sigma_j)^2 = \sum_{k=1}^{K} n^k (\sigma_j^k)^2$, μ_j and σ_j is the mean and the standard deviation of the j-th variable, μ_j^k and σ_j^k is the mean and the standard deviation of the j-th variable only for samples in the k-th security state, and n^k is the number of samples in the k-th security state.

Then, the P variables with larger scores are selected, but no specific criterion exits to choose P. Similarly to R^2, the f_{score} technique cannot detect and discharge redundant variables, it could discharge variables with low individual scores but with high scores when combined with other variables, and the number of selected variables P is not automatically determined.

Correlation-based filter selection (CFS): This technique simultaneously assesses correlations between variables with the class labels, as well as correlations between variables, and automatically selects the P variables with the highest discriminative power. CFS is based on symmetrical uncertainty (SU), which is defined as [23]:

$$SU(X, Y) = 2 \left[\frac{H(X) - H(X|Y)}{H(X)H(Y)} \right] \tag{9}$$

Where SU(X, Y) is the SU between the random variables X and Y, $H(x) = -\sum_i P(x_i) log_2(P(x_i))$ is the entropy of X and $H(X|Y) = -\sum_i P(y_i) \sum_i P(x_i|y_i)$ $log_2(P(x_i|y_i))$ is the conditional entropy of variable X given variable Y [33]. However, SU assumes that the random variables X and Y are categorical (i.e., qualitative variables or attribute variables), but the variables that represent the measurements from PMU are continuous.

This problem can be solved by applying the multi-interval discretization method [34]. Then, the automatic selection of variables is performed in two steps. First, a subset of relevant features (i.e., features that are correlated to the class) is selected by choosing all features for which SU(X, Y) > δ, where δ is determined the minimum required relevance to be analyzed for redundancy and is heuristically chosen (in this study, $\delta = 0$ was chosen). Second, redundant variables are detected and discarded if they form a Markov blanket with any other variable, i.e., variable x_i is an approximate Markov blanket for variable x_j, with respect to class label y, if SU(x_i, y) $\geq$ SU(x_j, y) and SU(x_i, x_j) $\geq$ SU(x_j, y) [35]. The advantage of CFS over R^2 and f_{score} is that it automatically selects the P relevant and non-redundant variables.

Classifier. In the present methodology implementation was evaluated using two classification methods with different characteristics. Naive Bayes (NB): Naive Bayes is a probabilistic classifier based on the Bayes theorem which selects the class with the highest probability, assuming that the variables in the dataset are independent [25, 36], Hence the name *naive*. Given the vector of variables $x = [x_1, x_2, \ldots, x_M]$ and the complete set of classes or security states $C = \{C_1, C_2, \ldots, C_K\}$, the posterior probability of each class given the observed variables $p(C_k|x), k = 1, 2, \ldots, K$ according to the Bayes theorem is [24]:

$$p(C_k|x) = \frac{p(x|C_k)p(C_k)}{p(x)} \tag{10}$$

Notice that to compute the posterior probability $p(C_k|x)$, the probability of the variables given the class $p(x|C_k)$ is needed. However, if the dimension of the variable vector x is high, it is necessary to have an extremely large amount of data samples. In consequence, the computation of $p(x|C_k)$ is highly expensive. In order to simplify the computation of this join probability, NB assumes that all variables in x are independent. Thus, the joint probability reduces to:

$$p(x_1, x_2, \ldots, x_M|C_k) = \prod_{j=1}^{M} p(x_j|C_k) \tag{11}$$

Thus, the NB output is simply computed as:

$$y = \mathop{argmax}_{C_k \in C} p(C_k) \prod_{j=1}^{M} p(x_j|C_k) \tag{12}$$

Where y is the security state or class label that presents the maximum probability among all classes. The advantage provided by the NB classifier is its simplicity. Given a training dataset $(X; y); i = 1, \ldots, N$ we only need to estimate the parameters of the probability distribution for each variable in each class (i.e., the mean and standard deviation of a normal distribution), then, when a new sample x is available, the posterior probabilities for each class is computed and subsequently the class with the highest posterior probability is selected.

Support Vector Machine (SVM): The goal in this classifier is to obtain a separation hyperplane, possibly in a higher dimensional and non-linear representation of the variables, which discriminates data into different classes. To do so, the method maximizes the separating margins between the hyperplane and the so-called support vectors i.e., the nearest data points in each class [37]. Thus, the hyperplane is computed through the solution of the following optimization problem:

$$\min_{W,\xi} \frac{1}{2} \left\| w^T w \right\|^2 + C \sum_{i=1}^{N} \xi_i \tag{13}$$

Subject to,

$$y_i\left(w^T X_i + b\right) \geq 1 - \xi_i, \xi_i \geq 0, \forall i = 1,\ldots,N \tag{14}$$

Where w and b are the weight vector and the bias term of the hyperplane, respectively, ξ_i are slack variables introduced because an optimal separating hyperplane might not exist when there is overlap between classes, N is the number of training samples and C is a penalty term for misclassification that determines a trade o between margin width and training error [38].

In this case, the separating hyperplane is linear. However, non-linear decision boundaries can be created through a kernel function applied to the observed data $K(x, x_i)$ [39]. Here, we used as kernel the radial basis function (RBF) which is given by:

$$K(x, x_i) = e^{-\frac{\|x - x_i\|^2}{2\sigma^2}} \tag{15}$$

Where σ determines width of the kernel. In the SVM with RBF as kernel, the parameters C and σ need to be defined. In this work, they were optimized through 5-fold cross validation using exclusively training data [39].

5   Simulations and Results

The dataset generated from the IEEE 39-bus test system shown in Fig. 4 that is presented in Eq. 6 has $N = 18764$ samples, $M = 39$ voltage variables and $K = 4$ security states. For this dataset, 13858 samples belong to normal, 1286 to alertness, 1336 to emergency state, and 12284 to in extremis. In this case problems may arise when a classification algorithm is trained. To examine the effect of the balanced samples, a balanced dataset was randomly selected from the original one, where the number of samples for each class is 1286 or total number of samples is $N = 5144$.

Different experiments are performed, combining the use of each variables selection technique with each classifier. This procedure was applied to both dataset, balanced and unbalanced. In order to measure the classification ability of each classifier accompanied by each variables selection technique a 10-fold cross validation process was carried out [40]. Considering the variable analysis techniques used, different variables were selected in each case, Table 2(A) and (B) show the selected variables for unbalanced and balanced dataset respectively. Classification accuracy results are presented in Table 3(A) and (B) for balanced and unbalanced dataset respectively, where the accuracy is defined as the percentage of correct classification.

In these results, the number of variables selected by the R^2 and F_{scores} methods is $P = 10$. Note that this number was imposed prior to simply accept of 25% of the $M = 39$ variables. However, the number of variables selected by the CFS methods is $P = 6$, which was automatically and is less than 10 selected for other methods.

Comparing box plots in Fig. 5, which explain different classifiers accuracy, the median in the box plot shows better predictability when CFS and all features are used independently of the classifier. However, if all features are used in classification process prediction the time is longer, and comparatively the accuracy between CFS and all features have the same order.

In these results, the number of variables selected by the R^2 and F_{scores} methods is $P = 10$. Note that this number was imposed prior to simply accept of 25% of the $M = 39$ variables. However, the number of variables selected by the CFS methods is $P = 6$, which was automatically and is less than 10 selected for other methods. Comparing box plots in Fig. 5, which explain different classifiers accuracy, the median in the box plot shows better predictability when CFS and all features are used independently of the classifier. Observing Table 3 and in contrast with Fig. 5, it can be concluded that the classifier with better accuracy is SVM. The confusion matrices shown in Tables 4 and 5 explain the percentage of classification achieved by each class respect to all classes. From the confusion matrices, it is evident that balanced datasets allow better prediction between classes than unbalanced datasets. Moreover, if the CFS

Table 2. Variables selection results using 10-fold cross validation

(a) Unbalanced data

Feature selection algorithm	# of selected nodes	Selected nodes
R^2	10	5, 11, 12, 19, 20, 22, 23, 25, 29, 13
Fisher score	10	1, 2, 3, 6, 9, 16, 21, 24, 26, 28
CFE	6	6, 7, 9, 10, 20, 25

(b) Balanced data

Feature selection algorithm	# of selected nodes	Selected nodes
R^2	10	4, 17, 19, 20, 22, 23, 25, 29, 2, 12
Fisher score	10	1, 3, 6, 7, 8, 9, 13, 26, 28, 24
CFE	6	5, 6, 7, 9, 14, 25

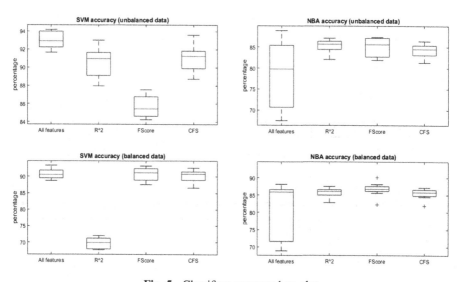

Fig. 5. Classifiers accuracy box plot

Table 3. Classification results using 10-fold cross validation

(a) Unbalanced data

Feature selection algorithm	# of selected features	Naïve Bayes accuracy	SVM accuracy
None	39	78.91%	92.96%
R^2	10	85.30%	90.85%
Fisher score	10	85.09%	85.61%
CFS	6	84.29%	91.10%

(b) Balanced data

Feature selection algorithm	# of selected features	Naïve Bayes accuracy	SVM accuracy
None	39	81.76%	90.79%
R^2	10	85.65%	69.83%
Fisher score	10	86.72%	90.73%
CFS	6	85.46%	91.16%

Table 4. Cconfusion matrix of svm classification (unbalanced data). the entry at the i-th row and the j-th column represents the probability of classifying an state from ci as an state in cj. one of the benefits of the confusion matrices is that allow to find if the model is confusing two classes.

(a) All Features

	C_1	C_2	C_3	C_4
C_1	0.997	0	0.003	0
C_2	1	0	0	0
C_3	0	0	1	0
C_4	0	0	0	1

(b) R2

	C_1	C_2	C_3	C_4
C_1	1	0	0	0
C_2	1	0	0	0
C_3	0.313	0	0.687	0
C_4	0	0	0	1

(c) Fisher Score

	C_1	C_2	C_3	C_4
C_1	1	0	0	0
C_2	1	0	0	0
C_3	1	0	0	0
C_4	0	0	0	1

(d) CFS

	C_1	C_2	C_3	C_4
C_1	1	0	0	0
C_2	1	0	0	0
C_3	0.246	0	0.754	0
C_4	0	0	0	1

Table 5. Confusion matrix of SVM classification (balanced data)

(a) All Features

	C_1	C_2	C_3	C_4
C_1	0.668	0.325	0.006	0
C_2	0.037	0.963	0	0
C_3	0	0	1	0
C_4	0	0	0	1

(b) R2

	C_1	C_2	C_3	C_4
C_1	0.496	0.496	0.008	0
C_2	0.500	0.500	0	0
C_3	0.052	0.013	0.935	0
C_4	0.020	0	0.066	0.914

(c) Fisher Score

	C_1	C_2	C_3	C_4
C_1	0.693	0.289	0.018	0
C_2	0.059	0.941	0	0
C_3	0	0	0	0
C_4	0	0	0	1

(d) CFS

	C_1	C_2	C_3	C_4
C_1	1	0	0	0
C_2	1	0	0	0
C_3	0.246	0	0.754	0
C_4	0	0	0	1

technique is selected then (Figs. 4(d) and 5(d)) the 64.7% and 96.3% of normal and alert states are successfully predicted, while 100% of states of emergency and in extremis can be successfully predicted. Even if the first two classes were not accurately classified, the most risk situations were classified with the 100% of accuracy, which is an important advance in security state estimation.

5.1 Conclusions

An alternative approach to achieve dimension reduction in the original set of variables is to perform feature extraction based on linear or non-linear transformations [41]. Based on this theory the complete m-dimensional set of independent variables is transformed to a q-dimensional reduced set of independent variables [41]. However, with this new data it is very difficult to find a physical meaning of the new variables. This is undesirable in power systems because some voltage buses in a power grid are more vulnerable or unstable due to important loads or generators attached to it. Therefore, if bus voltage data is combined or transformed, the distinctive patterns that show abnormal behaviors may disappear.

In this paper a supervised learning framework for power systems security-state estimation was proposed. The contribution suggests an open methodology to build security status models of the power grid, considering the stability problems, where other stability issues can be included to increase the estimation robustness. The methodology is proposed to be applied using historical measures of power systems, which must be structured in a dataset that allows the metrics calculation for each stability condition, and then building a model that operates with online measurable signals through the PMUs, to estimate security status of the power grid. To explain the methodology application, the IEEE 39-bus test system was used, detailing each steps required to find a reliable model for security state estimation. The dataset was obtained through power flows simulation taking into account multiple load conditions and contingencies. Two datasets were taken into account, balanced and unbalanced, for which models were constructed, tested and validated, showing that balanced dataset is more promise for each assigned class (normal, alert, emergency, in extremis). The obtained models conformed great predictability especially in emergency or in extreme conditions, which is priority for power system monitoring. The obtained results show that machine learning techniques may be successful for power system security on-line monitoring. Further research is required to improve the robustness of the security models to be applied in a real power grid. The methodology used in this work is applicable to real processes such as those shown in [42] and may be used for state estimation.

References

1. Avalos, J.: Analysis and application of optimization techniques to power system security and electricity markets, Ph.D. thesis, University of Waterloo (2008)
2. Jian-Hua, Z., Guohua, Z., Manyin, D., Jingyan, Y.: Indices system and methods for urban power grid security assessment. In: Proceedings of APPEEC 2009, pp. 1–5 (2009)

3. Sunitha, R., Kumar, S.K., Mathew, A.T.: Online static security assessment module using artificial neural networks. IEEE Trans. Power Syst. **28**(4), 4328–4335 (2013). https://doi.org/10.1109/tpwrs.2013.2267557

4. Zhao, F., Guo, Q., Sun, H., Wang, M., Wang, B.: Power system online security operational trend analysis and simulation results. In: 2013 IEEE Power and Energy Society General Meeting (PES), pp. 1–15 (2013). https://doi.org/10.1109/pesmg.2013.6672773

5. Sun, H., et al.: Automatic learning of fine operating rules for online power system security control. IEEE Trans. Neural Netw. Learn. Syst. **PP**(99) (2015). https://doi.org/10.1109/tnnls.2015.2390621

6. Wang, J., et al.: Online probabilistic security risk assessment implementation at china southern power grid towards smart control center. In: 2015 Seventh Annual IEEE Green Technologies Conference (GreenTech), pp. 74–81. https://doi.org/10.1109/greentech.2015.18

7. Beiraghi, M., Ranjbar, A.M.: Online voltage security assessment based on wide-area measurements. IEEE Trans. Power Deliv. **28**(2), 989–997 (2013). https://doi.org/10.1109/TPWRD.2013.2247426

8. Geeganage, J., Annakkage, U.D., Weekes, T., Archer, B.A.: Application of energy-based power system features for dynamic security assessment. IEEE Trans. Power Syst. **30**(4), 1957–1965 (2015). https://doi.org/10.1109/TPWRS.2014.2353048

9. Chakrabarti, A., Kothari, D., de Abhinandan, Mukhopadhyay, A.: An Introduction to Reactive Power Control and Voltage Stability in Power Transmission Systems. PHI Learning Private Limited (2010)

10. Chychykina, I., Styczynski, Z.A., Heyde, C.O., Krebs, R.: Power system instability prevention and remedial measures with online dynamic security assessment. In: 2015 IEEE Eindhoven PowerTech, pp. 1–5 (2015). https://doi.org/10.1109/ptc.2015.7232303

11. Perez Londono, S., Rodriguez Garcia, L., Lopez, Y.U.: Effects of doubly fed wind generators on voltage stability of power systems. In: Proceedings of the Sixth IEEE/PES Transmission and Distribution: Latin America Conference and Exposition (T&D-LA), pp. 1–6 (2012)

12. Taylor, C.: Power System Voltage Stability. McGraw-Hill, New York (1993)

13. Haque, M.: On-line monitoring of maximum permissible loading of a power system within voltage stability limits. IEE Proc. Gener. Transm. Distrib. **150**(1), 107–112 (2003)

14. Lee, C.Y., Tsai, S.-H., Wu, Y.-K.: A new approach to the assessment of steady-state voltage stability margins using the p-q-v curve. Int. J. Electr. Power Energy Syst. **32**(10), 1091–1098 (2010)

15. Momoh, J.A., Makarov, Y.V., Elfayoumy, M.: Expected angle stability margin. In: 1998 IEEE International Conference on Systems, Man, and Cybernetics, vol. 4, pp. 3753–3758 (1998). https://doi.org/10.1109/icsmc.1998.726671

16. Zhang, H., Liu, Y.: New index for frequency deviation security assessment. In: IPEC, 2010 Conference Proceedings, pp. 1031–1034 (2010). https://doi.org/10.1109/ipecon.2010.5696966

17. Sevilla, F.R.S., Vanfretti, L.: A small-signal stability index for power system dynamic impact assessment using time-domain simulations. In: 2014 IEEE PES General Meeting | Conference Exposition, pp. 1–5 (2014). https://doi.org/10.1109/pesgm.2014.6938842

18. Nguyen, T.B.: Dynamic security assessment of power systems using trajectory sensitivity approach, Ph.D. thesis, University of Illinois at Urbana-Champaign (2002)

19. Li, W.: Risk Assessment of power systems. In: IEEE Press Series on Power Engineering (2005)

20. Sanz, F.A., Ramirez, J.M., Correa, R.E.: Experimental design for a large power system vulnerability estimation. Electr. Power Syst. Res. **121**, 20–27 (2015). https://doi.org/10. 1016/j.epsr.2014.11.026
21. Guyon, I.: An introduction to variable and feature selection. J. Mach. Learn. Res. **3**, 1157–1182 (2003)
22. Gu, W., Wan, Q.: Linearized voltage stability index for wide-area voltage monitoring and control. Int. J. Electr. Power Energy Syst. **32**(4), 333–336 (2010)
23. Hall, M.A.: Correlation-based feature selection for machine learning, Ph.D. thesis, University of Waikato (1999)
24. Bishop, C.M.: Pattern Recognition and Machine Learning. Information Science and Statistics. Springer, New York (2006)
25. Morash, V., Bai, O., Furlani, S., Lin, P., Hallett, M.: Classifying fEEGg signals preceding right hand, left hand, tongue, and right foot movements and motor imageries. Clin. Neurophysiol. **119**(11), 2570–2578 (2008). https://doi.org/10.1016/j.clinph.2008.08.013
26. Guyon, I., Gunn, S., Nikravesh, M., Zadeh, L.A.: Feature Extraction: Foundations and Applications. Studies in Fuzziness and Soft Computing. Springer, New York (2006). https:// doi.org/10.1007/978-3-540-35488-8
27. Jensen, C.A., et al.: Inversion of feedforward neural networks: algorithms and applications. Proc. IEEE **87**(9), 1536–1549 (1999). https://doi.org/10.1109/5.784232
28. Innah, H., Asfani, D.A., Hiyama, T.: Voltage stability assessment based on discrimination principle. In: 2012 22nd Australasian Universities Power Engineering Conference (AUPEC), pp. 1–6 (2012)
29. Lakkireddy, J., Rastgoufard, R., Leevongwat, I., Rastgoufard, P.: Steady state voltage stability enhancement using shunt and series facts devices. In: 2015 Clemson University Power Systems Conference (PSC), pp. 1–5 (2015). https://doi.org/10.1109/psc.2015. 7101706
30. Kundur, P., Balu, N., Lauby, M.: Power System Stability and Control, EPRI Power System Engineering Series. McGraw-Hill, New York (1994)
31. Shi, Z., Huang, Y., Zhang, S.: Fisher score based naive Bayesian classifier. In: 2005 International Conference on Neural Networks and Brain, vol. 3, pp. 1616–1621 (2005)
32. Singh, B., Sankhwar, J.S., Vyas, O.P.: Optimization of feature selection method for high dimensional data using Fisher score and minimum spanning tree. In: 2014 Annual IEEE India Conference (INDICON), pp. 1–6 (2014)
33. Yu, L., Liu, H.: Efficient feature selection via analysis of relevance and redundancy. J. Mach. Learn. Res. **5**, 1205–1224 (2004)
34. Fayyad, U.M., Irani, K.B.: Multi-interval discretization of continuous-valued attributes for classification learning. In: IJCAI, pp. 1022–1029 (1993)
35. Chidlovskii, B., Lecerf, L.: Scalable feature selection for multi-class problems. In: Daelemans, W., Goethals, B., Morik, K. (eds.) ECML PKDD 2008. LNCS, vol. 5211, pp. 227–240. Springer, Heidelberg (2008). https://doi.org/10.1007/978-3-540-87479-9_33
36. Fukunaga, K.: Introduction to Statistical Pattern Recognition. Computer Science and Scientific Computing. Elsevier Science (2013)
37. Vapnik, V.N.: The Nature of Statistical Learning Theory. Springer, New York (1995). https://doi.org/10.1007/978-1-4757-2440-0
38. Scholkopf, B., Smola, A.J.: Learning with Kernels: Support Vector Machines, Regularization, Optimization, and Beyond, Adaptive Computation and Machine Learning. MIT Press, Cambridge (2002)
39. Burges, C.J.: A tutorial on support vector machines for pattern recognition. Data Min. Knowl. Discov. **2**, 121–167 (1998)

40. Bengio, Y., Grandvalet, Y.: Bias in estimating the variance of K-fold cross-validation. In: Duchesne, P., RÉMillard, B. (eds.) Statistical Modeling and Analysis for Complex Data Problems, pp. 75–95. Springer, Boston (2005). https://doi.org/10.1007/0-387-24555-3_5
41. Li, J., et al.: Feature selection: a data perspective. CoRR abs/1601
42. Duarte, J., Garcia, J., Jimenez, J., Sanjuan, M.E., Bula, A., Gonzalez, J.: Autoignition control in spark-ignition engines using internal model control structure. J. Energy Resour. Technol. **139**(2) (2016). http://energyresources.asmedigitalcollection.asme.org/article.aspx?articleid=2532521

Robust Control of an Evaporator Through Algebraic Riccati Equations and D-K Iteration

Javier Jiménez-Cabas[1], Farid Meléndez-Pertuz[1(✉)],
David Ovallos-Gazabon[2], Jaime Vélez-Zapata[1],
Hermes E. Castellanos[3], César A. Cárdenas[3], Joaquín F. Sánchez[3],
Gonzalo Jimenez[3], César Mora[4], Fredy A. Sanz[3], and C. A. Collazos[3]

[1] Departamento de Ciencias de la Computación y Electrónica,
Universidad de la Costa, Barranquilla, Colombia
fmelende1@cuc.edu.co
[2] Departamento de Ingeniería de procesos Industriales,
Institución Universitaria ITSA, Barranquilla, Colombia
[3] Vicerrectoría de Investigaciones, Universidad Manuela Beltrán,
Bogotá, Colombia
[4] Centro de Investigación en Ciencia Aplicada y Tecnología Avanzada del
Instituto Politécnico Nacional, México DF, Mexico

Abstract. Evaporation is a process that is widely used in the chemical industry and aims to concentrate a solution consisting of a non-volatile solute and a volatile solvent. In this paper the design of robust control systems for a simple effect evaporation system is presented. Two controllers were designed, the first was based on the Algebraic Riccati Equations (ARE) solutions technique and the second was derived from the D-K iteration method. To show the potentiality of the control system proposed, we present the results of some tests carried out in simulation.

Keywords: Robust control · Single effect evaporator ·
Algebraic Riccati equations · D-K iteration

1 Introduction

Evaporation is a technique widely used in industrial chemical processes and aims to concentrate a solution consisting of a non-volatile solute and a volatile solvent. Water is normally used as a solvent and the process consists in evaporating some of it in order to achieve the concentrated solution. Despite frequent use the various applications of evaporation processes in industry, it has been found that the control strategies currently used on these systems do not offer the best performance [1–3]. For this reason, it is essential to design a system that improves both performance and process control, making it increasingly efficient and secure.

Robust control theory has experienced rapid development with the emergence of powerful tools for the design of control systems. Making possible the control of uncertain systems, and to develope controlled systems with ever better performances. A particular example is the techniques based on Riccati's Algebraic Equations and the

S. Misra et al. (Eds.): ICCSA 2019, LNCS 11620, pp. 731–742, 2019.
https://doi.org/10.1007/978-3-030-24296-1_58

method known as D-K Iteration, which have proved to be very useful in the synthesis of robust controllers H∞ [2, 4–9].

Given the need for improvement in the evaporation systems, this work proposes the design of robust controllers for a system of evaporation of simple effect [2, 6, 10–12]. The modeling and linearization of the study system with respect to a point of operation was performed, additionally, both input and output uncertainties were considered in order to carry out the synthesis of robust controllers. With the design of a control system we tried to keep the system as close as possible to a certain point of operation, mainly we wanted to avoid variations in the density of the product since these affect downstream processes [3, 13, 14].

The paper is organized as follows. Section 2 presents the model of the evaporation process considered. Section 3 presents a controllability analysis of the evaporation process and the controllers synthetized. Section 4 presents some simulation results and Sect. 5 presents the corresponding conclusions.

2   Considered Evaporation Process

The objective of the evaporation system to be controlled is to remove the organic impurities present in the caustic soda (NaOH), the result of its use in previous processes, in order to ensure its reuse in subsequent processes. The first stage of the system consists of a simple effect evaporator where the liquid is processed to achieve a product with a specific density. A simplified diagram of the process is shown in Fig. 1.

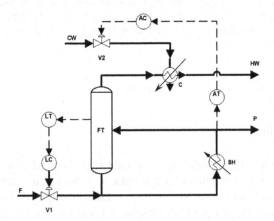

Fig. 1. Simple effect evaporator diagram.

Initially it has the source liquid (SL) to which it is wanted to vary the concentration, later it is passed through steam heaters (SH) in order to achieve a partial evaporation, then part of the liquid coming from the heaters, i.e. the product (P), is used in downstream processes while the rest is sent back to the Flash tank (FT) to be reprocessed. Water vapor escapes through the top of the Flash tank and is condensed (C).

The density of the product and the level of the Flash tank are each controlled by SISO feedback control loops. To control the density of the product ρ_P, the flow of cooling water F_{CW} is manipulated, while the flow of the source liquid F_F is ajusted to maintain a desired level in the Flash tank [1, 13]. The purpose of the control system is to keep the process as close as possible to the selected operating point. It is mainly intended to avoid variations in the density of the product since these affect downstream processes, which in turn constitutes the main source of disturbances in the product flow rate F_P.

2.1 Modeling Considerations

The equations used to describe the system model were obtained from the mass and energy balances in the diagram of Fig. 1. In addition, the following assumptions were made [1, 15]:

- The total volume of liquid in the steam heaters and in the pipe is equivalent to a 23.12 m^2 area tank and 2.21 m height. This volume must be added to the Flash tank.
- The value at which the boiling point of the liquid exceeds that of the water is assumed constant. T_e = 16 °C.
- The difference between the temperature of the hot water and that of the steam to be condensed is assumed to be constant. T_a = 5 °C.
- The temperature of the cooling water is assumed constant T_{RW} = 40 °C.
- The heat capacity of the liquid is assumed constant c_P = 3142 J/kg°C.
- The product density is considered equal to the discharge liquid of the Flash tank $\rho_P = \rho_D$.
- The process is adiabatic and evaporation rates are calculated on the basis of liquid water.
- The volume and mass in the pipes and heaters is kept constant, $F_{FH} = F_{DH}$ and $\rho_{FH} = \rho_{DH}$.
- The heat capacity of the source of the heaters and of the discharge is equal to that of the discharge of the Flash tank, $c_{P,FH} = c_{P,DH} = c_P$.
- The set-point is assumed to be constant at the corresponding steady-state value.
- Flow ranges are: Source liquid flow $F_F = 0 - 50$ m^3/h And Coolant Water Flow $F_{RW} = 0 - 700$ m^3/h.
- Initial conditions at steady state: Flow of the source liquid F_F = 25.0147 m^3/h, Coolant water flow F_{WR} = 313.087 m^3/h, Flash tank level h = 2.71 m, Flash tank discharge liquid density ρ_D = 1762 kg/m^3, Flash tank discharge fluid temperature T_D = 88.431 °C.
- The enthalpy of the vapor escaping from the Flash tank is assumed to be constant H_V = 2660000 J/kg.
- Product Flow $F_P = 10$ m^3/h, Heating flow of heaters F_{FH} = 1000 m^3/h and Density of the liquid source $\rho_F = 1300$ kg/m^3.
- The heat capacity of cooling water and hot water are assumed to be constant and equal $c_{P,RW} = c_{P,AH}$ = 4160 J/kg °C.

2.2 Model Equations

The dynamics of the model are described by the state equations shown below. Details on obtaining this model can be found in [1, 10, 15].

Flash tank level.

$$\frac{dh}{dt} = \frac{1}{A}(F_F - F_P - \dot{m}_v) \tag{1}$$

Density of the flash tank discharge liquid.

$$\frac{d\rho_D}{dt} = \frac{1}{Ah}\left[\left(\frac{F_{FC} - F_P}{F_{FH}}\right)\rho_F F_F - \dot{m}_v\left((F_{FH} - F_P - \dot{m}_v) - \left(\frac{F_{FC} - F_P}{F_{FH}}\right)(F_{FH} - F_F)\rho_D\right)\right] \tag{2}$$

Flash tank discharge liquid temperature.

$$\frac{dT_D}{dt} = \frac{1}{c_P Ah\rho_D}\left[\frac{(F_{FH} - F_P)(\rho_F F_F + (F_{FH} - F_F)\rho_D)}{F_{FH}}c_P T_{DC} - \dot{m}_v H_v \right.$$
$$\left. -c_P T_D\left(\frac{(F_{FH} - F_P)(\rho_F F_F + (F_{FH} - F_F)\rho_D)}{F_{FH}} - \dot{m}_v\right)\right] \tag{3}$$

Evaporation rate.

$$\dot{m}_v = \frac{c_{PRW}(T_D - T_{RW} - (T_e + T_a))}{(H_v - c_{PRW}(T_D - (T_e + T_a)))}F_{RW} \tag{4}$$

3 Control System Design

This section starts with an analysis procedure named input-output controllability analysis [16], this procedure let us to known if an acceptable control performance can be achieved given a plant. Next, the close loop structure considered in the design and the obtained controllers are presented.

3.1 Model Equations

We present the scaled models for the nominal plant and the representation of the effects of perturbations, according to the procedure developed in [16].

$$\dot{x} = \begin{pmatrix} -0.11677 & 0.070084 & -0.0006847 \\ 17.269 & -45.546 & 0.44493 \\ -38.219 & 0.011099 & -15.798 \end{pmatrix} x + \begin{pmatrix} 0.025032 & -0.017466 & 0 \\ -4.2248 & 11.350 & 0 \\ -0.015751 & -0.0027733 & 315.96 \end{pmatrix} u$$

$$y = \begin{pmatrix} 2 & 0 & 0 \\ 0 & 0.0017794 & 0 \\ 0 & 0 & 0.05 \end{pmatrix} x$$

$$(5)$$

$$\dot{x}_p = \begin{pmatrix} -0.11677 & 0.070084 & -0.0006847 \\ 17.269 & -45.546 & 0.44493 \\ -38.219 & 0.011099 & -15.798 \end{pmatrix} x_p + \begin{pmatrix} -0.086505 \\ 0.010181 \\ -0.20965 \end{pmatrix} p$$

$$y = \begin{pmatrix} 2 & 0 & 0 \\ 0 & 0.0017794 & 0 \\ 0 & 0 & 0.05 \end{pmatrix} x$$

$$(6)$$

The input - output controllability analysis of the plant based on the model $y = G(s)u + G_P(s)p$ is performed. Initially, the functional controllability of the G (s) plant is verified, proving that the plant has the same number of inputs and outputs, and that the normal range of G (s) is equal to the number of outputs. It is considered as normal range of G (s) to the range of the matrix G (s) for all values of s, except in a finite number of singularities.

The analysis shows that the first condition is satisfied; the condition of the normal range is equivalent to stating that the minimum singular value of $G(jw)$, $\underline{\sigma}(G)$, must be different from zero (except for those values of jw corresponding to imaginary zeroes).

For the analysis it is required that $\underline{\sigma}(G)$ be as large as possible in the interest frequencies. At frequencies where $\underline{\sigma}(G) < 1$, it is not possible to make changes of magnitude 1 at the outputs using inputs of unit magnitude. It should be noted that since we are working with a scaled model, the maximum variations in the state, input and output variables are of magnitude 1.

Figure 2 shows the singular values of the plant as a function of frequency. The lowest observed singular value is between 1 and 0 (functional controllability) for the frequency range shown. Notwithstanding the fact that the plant has so many inputs and outputs to control, it could lead to difficulties in controlling the nominal plant.

The Relative Gain Arrangement or RGA of a non-singular matrix G is given by $RGA(G) = \Lambda(G) = G \times (G^{-1})^T$. Although this concept was initially introduced as a measure of the interaction of the decentralized control at steady state ($\omega = 0$), the value of the RGA at frequencies close to the cut-off frequency is much more important because it is a good indicator of sensitivity to uncertainty. Therefore, it is difficult to control plants with large elements in the RGA at frequencies close to the cut due to their high sensitivity to uncertainties in the entrances. For the case study when plotting the RGA as a function of frequency it is observed that large values (10^0) are present in the elements of said arrangement which is indicative that the plant is quite sensitive to uncertainties in the inputs (Fig. 3).

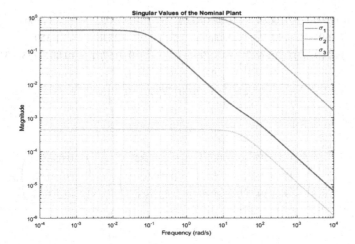

Fig. 2. Singular values of the nominal plant.

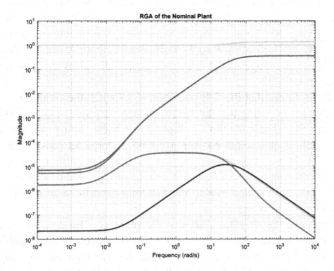

Fig. 3. RGA of the nominal plant

Limitations on system performance are now considered due to restrictions on entries. This is to verify the possibility of achieving a perfect rejection of disturbances by maintaining $|u| \leq 1$. The study system has the form $y = G(s)u + G_P(s)p$; So that to achieve a perfect rejection of disturbances is necessary to do $u = -G^{-1}(s)G_p(s)p$, for the system under study has a single disturbance, so $G_P(s)$ it is a vector. The worst case of the perturbations occurs when $|p(w)| = 1$ and to avoid saturation in the actuators it is necessary to maintain $|u|_{max}$, for which $|u|_{max}$ is required.

Figure 4 shows that for the system being studied, at frequencies lower than 0.1 rad/s a significant control action is necessary. Considering initially the case of

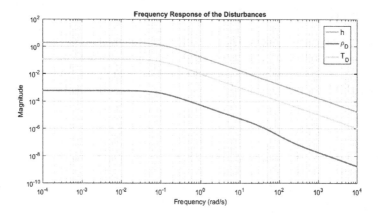

Fig. 4. Frequency response of $G_P(s)$.

control with perfect rejection of disturbances, it is $\left|-G^{-1}(s)G_P(s)\right|_{max}$, therefore it is not possible a total rejection of the perturbations with maximum control inputs unitary as it would cause saturation of the actuators.

Since a perfect rejection of the disturbances is not possible, we consider the problem of verifying if it is possible to achieve an $|e| \leq 1$ error for any $|p| \leq 1$ using $|u| \leq 1$ entries. Each singular value of G, $\sigma_i(G)$ must meet $\sigma_i(G) + 1 \geq \left|u_i^H G_p\right|$ at frequencies where $\left|u_i^H G_p\right| > 1$. Figure 5 shows that the above condition is satisfied at all frequencies.

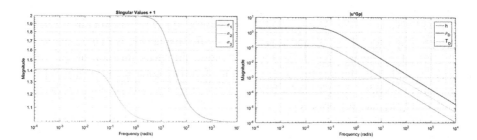

Fig. 5. $\sigma_i(G) + 1$ and $\left|u_i^H G_P\right|$ in frequency

The input - output controllability analysis shows that the system has the following characteristics:

- Although the nominal plant, G (s) is functionally controllable, its minimum singular value is less than 1, which is an indication of possible saturation of the actuators when trying to achieve higher levels of performance.
- The nominal plant presents high sensitivity to input uncertainties (large RGA).
- Although it is not possible to achieve total rejection of disturbances (perfect control), if a steady-state error | e | $\leq$ 1 can be achieved without actuator saturation (acceptable control).

3.2   Controllers

In order to obtain an H_∞ controller, unstructured uncertainties of multiplicative type were considered both in the input and output [16]. Figure 6 shows the block diagram of the system in which, in addition to the uncertainties, both the performance and control signal weights have been included.

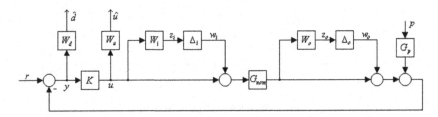

Fig. 6. Block diagram for the closed loop system.

The different weights used for the development of the analysis were:

$$w_i(s) = \frac{0.5077s^2 + 17.46s + 0.6537}{s^2 + 21.36s + 1.354} \quad w_o(s) = \frac{0.4778s^2 + 7.68s + 0.3835}{s^2 + 11.14s + 0.6792}$$

$$w_d(s) = \frac{0.2s + 1 \times 10^{-5}}{s + 5 \times 10^{-7}} \quad w_u(s) = \frac{10s + 0.5236}{s + 0.5236}$$

(7)

The w_d performance objectives were: achieve a steady-state error of less than 5%, a high frequency amplification of less than 5 dB and a closed loop bandwidth of 1×10–5 rad/s. Considering that the rise time of the valves is 60 s, with a minimum attenuation at high frequency of 20 dB and a gain of 1 at low frequency, we chose the weight function of the control signal w_u. Figure 7 shows the block diagram of the system under the M-Δ configuration for the design of robust controllers [4, 16–19]. The controllers obtained are presented below, highlighting that all met the conditions of robust stability and performance.

Controller Obtained by the Riccati Algebraic Equation Solution Method [2, 4, 16–19].

$$K_R(s) = \left[\begin{array}{ccc|ccc} -5e-7 & -3.1e-11 & -3.8e-12 & 2.8e-3 & 4.8e-7 & -1.6e-4 \\ 0 & -5e-7 & 4.6e-14 & 1.6e-4 & 9.6e-7 & 2.7e-3 \\ 0 & 0 & -5e-7 & -4.4e-6 & 2.7e-4 & 5.8e-3 \\ \hline 2.8e-3 & 1.2e-4 & -4.4e-6 & 4e-5 & 9.9e-8 & 2.2e-4 \\ 1.7e-7 & -1.6e-10 & 2.7e-4 & -3.9e-8 & -9.5e-11 & -2.1e-7 \\ -1.1e-4 & 2.7e-3 & 7.4e-8 & -6.9e-4 & -1.7e-6 & -3.7e-3 \end{array}\right]$$

(8)

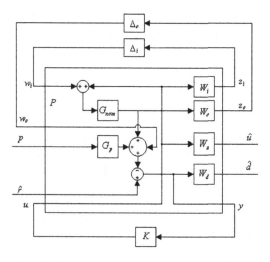

Fig. 7. Configuration for robust controller design

Controller Obtained by the D-K Iteration Method [4, 6, 12, 16]

$$K_{DK}(s) = \left[\begin{array}{ccc|ccc} -5e-7 & 4.9e-10 & 5.7e-12 & 2.6e-3 & 2.2e-7 & -1.5e-4 \\ 0 & -5e-7 & -4.4e-13 & 1.6e-4 & 8.6e-7 & 2.5e-3 \\ 0 & 0 & -7.6e-7 & -2.8e-8 & 2.8e-4 & -7.4e-8 \\ 2.6e-3 & 1.2e-4 & 1e-8 & -2.8e-2 & -3.7e-6 & 9e-5 \\ -2.3e-7 & -3.7e-8 & 2.8e-4 & 2.5e-6 & 3.3e-10 & -7.8e-9 \\ -1e-4 & 2.5e-3 & 2.6e-8 & 4.7e-5 & 6.3e-9 & -1.5e-7 \end{array}\right] \qquad (9)$$

4   Results and Analysis

4.1   Results of the Nominal Closed Loop Simulation

The closed-loop gains and the perturbation transfer function were calculated; this is H_∞ norms of the de $[r] \rightarrow \begin{bmatrix} \hat{d} \\ \hat{u} \end{bmatrix}$ and y $[r] \rightarrow \begin{bmatrix} \hat{d} \\ \hat{u} \end{bmatrix}$ transfer functions respectively, in order to compare the performance obtained with the different controllers. See Table 1.

Table 1. Gain of closed loop and disturbances.

Controller	Loop closed	Disturbances
KR	28.285	6.89
KDK	28.28	7.37

Table 2. Value and errors in stationary state of closed loop system outputs

Outputs	KR	KDK
H	1.9–30%	1.96–27.7%
ρD	1779.8–1.01%	1770.3–0.5%
TD	96.4–7.9%	95–7.4%

With both controllers the same gain of closed loop is obtained, however the smaller amplification of the perturbations is obtained with the KR. Table 2 shows the parameters of the steady-state response of the closed-loop system for each controller.

For both cases a large error was obtained in the first output *(h)* (this is because the original system was stable except for the level of the flash tank), achieving the minimum (27.7%) with the K_{DK} controller. With the ρ_D output, an error of less than 5% was achieved in both cases, the minimum (0.5%) was obtained with the K_{DK} controller. For T_D output the smallest error (7.4%) was obtained with the K_{DK} controller.

4.2   Results of Simulation Considering Perturbations in Inputs

We considered a 10% increase in each of the inputs at different time points according to the following data, for *h* the increase occurs at time *t* = *6* s, for *ρD* at *t* = *7* s and for T_D at *t* = *8* s. The results obtained for each case were as follows (Table 3).

Table 3. Value and errors in stationary state of closed loop system outputs with input disturbances.

Outputs	KR	KDK
H	1.96–27.7%	2.02–25.5%
ρD	1761–0.06%	1761–0.06%
TD	105–18.7%	104.5–18.2%

The minimum error (25.5%) is obtained on the first output with the K_{DK} controller. For the output *ρD*, an error of 0.06% was achieved in all cases. For the T_D output a small improvement in the result is obtained with the K_{DK} controller.

4.3   Results of the Simulation Considering Uncertainties in the Parameters of the System

In this case, changes were made in some of the internal parameters of the system such as the feed flow density (ρF of 1300 kg/m^3 to 1250 kg/m^3), the hot water temperature (T_w of 5 °C to 14 °C) of the valves (*R* from 50 to 100) (Table 4).

For the first output the minimum error (27.7%) is obtained with the K_{DK} controller. While for the output *ρD* an error of less than 5% was achieved in all cases, the lowest one being obtained with the K_{DK} controller. At T_D output the smallest error (7.4%) was obtained with the K_{DK} controller.

Table 4. Value and errors in stationary state of the uncertainty closed loop system outputs.

Outputs	KR	KDK
H	1.88–30.6%	1.96–27.7%
ρD	1776.6–0.83%	1771.7–0.55%
TD	95.4–7.9%	95–7.4%

5   Conclusion

In this paper, we have presented the design of robust control system for a evaporation process. Two techniques were considered, the first is based in the solution of algebraic Riccati equations and the second is known as D-K iteration method. The performance of the synthetized control systems were verified through simulations. The simulations were implemented using MATLAB®, tool used in this type of work [20], and simulation results show that the controller based on D-K iteration method offers a better performance. The methodology used in this work is applicable to real processes such as shown in [21, 22]. The control systems performance validation through experimental tests will be part of future developments.

References

1. To, L., Tadé, M., Kraetzl, M.: Robust Nonlinear Control of Industrial Evaporation System. World Scientific, Singapore (1999)
2. Lutskaya, N.N., Ladanyuk, A.P.: Problems features of the robust control of process plants. Part II. Examples of modeling of robust control systems. J. Autom. Inf. Sci. **48**(12), 62–69 (2016)
3. Wang, T.-C., Lan, W.-W., Chen, C.-L.: An LMI and fuzzy model approach to H∞ PI controller design. J. Chinese Inst. Eng. Trans. Chinese Inst. Eng. A/Chung-kuo K Ch'eng Hsuch K'an **29**(2), 263–277 (2006)
4. Zhou, K., Doyle, J.C.: Essentials of Robust Control, vol. 104. Prentice Hall, Upper Saddle River (1998)
5. Song, H.K., Shah, S.L., Fisher, D.G.: A self-tuning robust controller. Automatica **22**(5), 521–531 (1986)
6. Huo, L., Qu, C., Li, H.: Robust control of civil structures with parametric uncertainties through D-K iteration. Struct. Des. Tall Spec. Build. **25**(3), 158–176 (2016)
7. Salim, S.N.S., Rahmat, M.F., Faudzi, A.A.M., Ismail, Z.H., Sunar, N.H., Samsudin, S.A.: Robust control strategy for pneumatic drive system via enhanced nonlinear PID controller. Int. J. Electr. Comput. Eng. **4**(5), 658–667 (2014)
8. Bejarano, G., Alfaya, J.A., Ortega, M.G., Rubio, F.R.: Multivariable analysis and H∞ control of a one-stage refrigeration cycle. Appl. Therm. Eng. **91**, 1156–1167 (2015)
9. Darwish, M.K., Al-Gobaisi, Barakzai, A.S., El-Nashar, A.M.: An overview of modern control strategies for optimizing thermal desalination plants. Desalination **84**(1–3), 3–43 (1991)
10. Warren, M., Julian, S., Peter, H.: Operaciones unitarias en ingeniería química, 1199 p (1998)

11. Figueroa, J.L., Agamennoni, O.E., Desages, A.C., Romagnoli, J.A.: Robust multivariable controller design methodology: stability and performance requirements. Chem. Eng. Sci. **46**(5–6), 1299–1310 (1991)
12. Azizi, S.M., Khajehoddin, S.A.: Robust load frequency control in islanded microgrid systems using μ-synthesis and D-K iteration. In: 10th Annual International Systems Conference, SysCon 2016 - Proceedings. School of Technology, Michigan Technological University, Houghton, MI, United States (2016)
13. Stephanopoulos, G.: Chemical Process Control, vol. 2. Prentice Hall, New Jersey (1984)
14. Agamennoni, O., Rotstein, H., Desages, A., Romagnoli, J.A.: Robust controller design methodology for multivariable chemical processes: structured perturbations. Chem. Eng. Sci. **44**(11), 2597–2605 (1989)
15. Holland, C.D.: Fundamentals and modeling of separation processes: absorption, distillation, evaporation and extraction (1975)
16. Skogestad, S., Postlethwaite, I.: Multivariable Feedback Control: Analysis and Design, vol. 2. Wiley, New York (2007)
17. Scherer, C.: Theory of robust control. Delft Univ Technol. (2001)
18. Green, M., Limebeer, D.J.N.: Robust Linear Control. Prentice Hall, Upper Saddle River (1994)
19. Dullerud, G.E., Paganini, F.: A Course in Robust Control Theory: A Convex Approach, vol. 36. Springer, New York (2013)
20. Muñoz, Y., Ospino Castro, A.J., Robles, C., Arizmendi, C.: Implementation of a frequency control in a biomass gasifier system. Int. J. Electr. Comput. Eng. (IJECE) **9**(1), 66–67 (2018)
21. Duarte, J., García, J., Jiménez, J., Sanjuan, M.E., Bula, A., González, J.: Autoignition control in spark-ignition engines using internal model control structure. J. Energy Resour. Technol. **139**(2), 66–77 (2017)
22. Castellanos, H.E., Collazos, C.A., Farfán, J.C., Meléndez-Pertuz, F.: Diseño y Construcción de un Canal Hidráulico de Pendiente Variable. Información Tecnológica **28**(6), 103–114 (2017). https://doi.org/10.4067/S0718-07642017000600012. Accessed 20 July 2018

On the Feasibility of Probabilistic Model Checking to Analyze Battery Sustained Power Supply Systems

Marina Dioto[1]([✉]), Eduardo Rohde Eras[2],
and Valdivino Alexandre de Santiago Júnior[2]

[1] Instituto Edson Mororó de Moura (ITEMM), Parque Tecnológico
São José dos Campos, São José dos Campos, SP, Brazil
marina.dioto@itemm.org.br
[2] Instituto Nacional de Pesquisas Espaciais (INPE), Av. dos Astronautas, 1758,
São José dos Campos, São Paulo, SP, Brazil
eduardorohdeeras@gmail.com, valdivino.santiago@inpe.br

Abstract. Probabilistic Model Checking is a Formal Verification method which is able to guarantee, according to a specified probability, the correctness of a system that presents stochastic behavior. It is an approach which has been applied to several different application domains such as biology, communication and network protocols, security, dependability, just to name a few. In this paper, we realize about the feasibility of Probabilistic Model Checking to analyze power supply systems. We modelled and evaluated two types of systems: a solar power system and batteries of artificial satellites. Our findings show that Probabilistic Model Checking provides accurate results and can be used as a complementary approach to traditional simulation tools for Model-Driven Development of complex industrial applications.

1 Introduction

Power supply systems are a set of elements combined together in order to feed an electrical scheme. They are essential because they guarantee the full operation of the hardware during the time that the system was projected to perform. They must be developed with quality due to losses that can happen on their lack or malfunctioning. On this second scenario, they can also represent a risk to the people and the environment around, since they are based on power electronics. Although power supply systems comprise a wide range of source types, on this paper we will focus on battery sustained organizations. These are important to structures that do not have access to an energy generation source all the time, like photovoltaic panels. On these, the battery represents a power accumulator, bringing flexibility to the energy usage distributed along time. However, batteries are intrinsically unstable and reactive components. So, they must operate within a specific window of safety and reliability. This window is determined by

S. Misra et al. (Eds.): ICCSA 2019, LNCS 11620, pp. 743–757, 2019.
https://doi.org/10.1007/978-3-030-24296-1_59

a combination of parameters that, if overreached, could lead the battery to enter on thermal runaway. This reinforces the need for a robustness system.

To achieve this robustness, a strategy is to use Model Driven Development (MDD), which is a methodology that focuses on graphical representations and pre-built application components to enable visually construction of complex applications. This approach is meant (i) to increase productivity and design speed by maximizing compatibility between systems through reuse of standardized models; (ii) to simplify the design process due to models of recurring design patterns in the application domain; (iii) to reduce cost as a result of the replacement of real objects to computational models; (iv) to improve communication between individuals and teams due to patterned and visual language; and (v) to increase reliability as it enables several methods of validation and verification.

The main techniques used in MDD are Unified Model Language (UML), simulation, model transformation, code automatic generation and formal methods. Formal verification is a formal method approach defined as a mathematical analysis to prove or not the correctness of a system in relation to a certain specification or property. The methods for formal verification are basically divided in theorem proving and model checking. The latter is an automated technique that, given a finite state model of a system and a formal property, systematically verifies whether this property is satisfied by a certain state in the model [1].

A branch of this technique is the probabilistic model checking, which considers probabilistic temporal logic and models. It is important to complex systems, since these are subject to various phenomena of a stochastic nature, making it difficult to guarantee its absolute correctness.

In this context, the objective of this work is to study the feasibility of probabilistic model checking to analyse battery sustained power supply systems. We believe that it is relevant to perceive the benefits of a mathematical MDD-based approach to improve the quality of such systems which may be components of applications such as satellites, aircrafts, and mobile phones.

This paper is structured as follows. Section 2 presents an overview of Probabilistic Model Checking. Section 3 shows the case studies we considered in this research. In Sect. 4, we provide details on how we modelled both systems under the stochastic/probabilistic perspective. The evaluation of results is provided in Sects. 5, and 6 contains the information of related work and discussion. In Sect. 7, conclusions and future directions are described.

2   Probabilistic Model Checking

A given stochastic process $\{X_0, X_1, ..., X_n + 1, ...\}$ at the consecutive points of observation $0, 1, ..., n + 1$ constitutes a Discrete-Time Markov Chain (DTMC) if the following relation on the conditional probability mass function (pmf), that is the Markov property, holds for all $n \in \mathbb{N}_0$ and all $s_i \in S$: [2]

$$P(X_{n+1} = s_{n+1}|X_n = s_n, X_{n-1} = s_{n-1}, ..., X_0 = s_0) = P(X_{n+1} = s_{n+1}|X_n = s_n) \tag{1}$$

On DTMC it is used Probabilistic Computation Tree Logic (PCTL), a branching-time temporal logic, based on the Computational Tree Logic (CTL).

Continuous-Time Markov Chains (CTMCs), on the other hand, are distinct from DTMCs as state transitions may occur at arbitrary instants of time and not merely at fixed, discrete time points. A given stochastic process $\{X_t : t \in T\}$ constitutes a CTMC if for arbitrary $t_i \in \mathbb{R}_0^+$, with $0 = t_0 < t_1 < ... < t_n < t_n + 1, \forall n \in \mathbb{N}$, and $\forall s_i \in S = \mathbb{N}_0$ for the conditional probability density function (pdf), the following relation holds: [2]

$$P(X_{t_{n+1}} = s_{n+1}|X_{t_n} = s_n, X_{t_{n-1}} = s_{n-1}, .., X_{t_0=s_0}) = P(X_{t_{n+1}} = s_{n+1}|X_{t_n} = s_n) \tag{2}$$

On CTMC it is used Continuous Stochastic Logic (CSL), which also extends CTL.

The probabilistic model checker used in this paper is PRISM [2], which comports both PCTL and CSL.

3   Power Supply Systems

3.1   Solar Power System

The probabilistic model of a solar photovoltaic power system described in [3] is based on Markov Chain Theory, modeling a stochastic insolation and load demands. The main goal of the original paper is to present a new approach to simulate a standalone photovoltaic system considering the probabilistic characteristics not explored by other computer simulations at the time.

Figure 1 is based on an original illustration from the paper, where we can see the basic structure of the photovoltaic system. The energy captured by the solar array is sent to the electrical demand or to the batteries, if the load demand is less then the array output. When the array output is not enough to supply the load demand, the batteries are used to do it. This flow is guaranteed by the controllers.

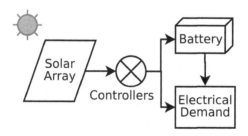

Fig. 1. Standalone photovoltaic power system

According to [3], "the insolation and the load demand are both random and accordingly the battery will behave in some stochastic fashion". The paper also suggest to use discrete time to evaluate the system, which leads us to use a Discrete Time Markov Chain (DTMC) to create the model. So, considering a stochastic process $[X_t : t \geq 0]$, at each moment t in time, we have a state space W composed by the battery charging state S, the insulation level I and the load demand L:

$$W = \{S, I, L\} \tag{3}$$

where:

$$s = S_1, ..., S_m$$

$$i = I_1, ..., I_n$$

$$l = L_1, ..., L_y$$

so:

$$W = [w = (S_i, I_j, L_k) : i = 1, ..., m; j = 1, ..., n; k = 1, ..., y]$$

The insolation I value is generated in a stochastic way. The next insolation level depends only upon the current state, which creates a Markov behavior. The load demand is also unpredictable, but the paper suggests an average daytime L_d and nighttime L_n load demands given by the formulas:

$$L_d = \frac{L * H_d}{24}$$

$$L_n = \frac{L * H_n}{24}$$

where L is the total load demand, H_d is the average daytime hours and H_n is the average nighttime hours. The next battery State of Charge is given by a serie of equations called the energy flow equations. They predict two cases:

Case 1: $S_{min} < S_1 < S_{max}$. If the current battery charging state is between the minimum and the maximum levels of charge, the next state S_2 is given by the systems of equations:

$$A_O \geq L_d \begin{cases} S_2 = S_1 + A_O - L_d - \frac{L_n}{b} \\ b = 1 + f * (r - 1) \\ f = \frac{L_n}{L} \end{cases} \tag{4}$$

$$A_O < L_d \begin{cases} S_2 = S_1 + \frac{A_O - L}{b} \\ b = 1 + f * (r - 1) \\ f = \frac{L - A_O}{L} \end{cases} \tag{5}$$

Where A_O is the array output, b is the battery efficiency, r is the battery round trip efficiency and f is the fraction of the load met by the battery.

Case 2: $S_1 = S_{min}$. If the current state is the minimum charging state of the battery, the next state when the array output is greater than or equal to the load demand is given by the exactly same Equation System 4 shown in case 1, but if we have a greater load demand then the array output, we don't leave the minimum charging state of the battery:

$$S_2 = S_1 = S_{min}$$

In both cases 1 and 2, if the next charging state predicted by the equation overflows the limits established by the constants s_{min} and s_{max}, there is a set of cutoff equations to follow:

$$S_2 < s_{min} \Rightarrow S_2 = S_{min}$$
$$S_2 > s_{max} \Rightarrow S_2 = S_{max}$$

3.2 Batteries of Artificial Satellites

A block diagram model for a battery charging and discharging system in artificial satellites is developed in [4], based on macroscopic principles which can be generalized to a wide variety of topologies and technologies of power supply and batteries. The main goal of the original paper is to discuss the causes and effects of thermal avalanches in these applications.

Figure 2 is based on the paper, in which it is possible to see the basic structure of a satellite power supply system. Its operation can be divided in two periods. The first one, during sunlight exposure, is refereed as "solar". In this case the satellite is fed by a Solar Array Generator (SAG), which is also responsible to recharge the battery (BAT) through a Battery Charge and Heating Controller (BCHC), also responsible to control a heater to maintain the optimum temperature of the batteries. The other phase is during the absence of solar exposition, referenced as "eclipse". In this, the BAT is responsible to supply the satellite while connected through a Battery Discharging Regulator (BDR), which regulates the voltages.

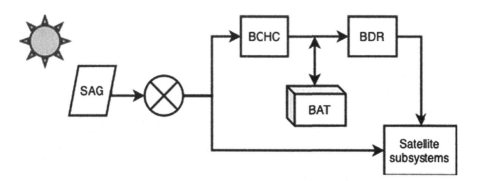

Fig. 2. Satellite power supply system block diagram

The orbital condition of the satellite, which alternates between the solar and the eclipse stages, creates a periodic excitation to the BAT. During the solar period, the input current seen by the battery is positive, which comes from the BCHC (i_{BCHC}) performing its charge. During the eclipse, it becomes negative, causing its discharge to the BDR input (i_{BDR}).

To consider this situation, the author defines the following Boolean variable:

$$s = \begin{cases} 1, & \text{if } 0 < t < T_s \\ 0, & \text{if } T_s < t < T \end{cases} \tag{6}$$

in which t is the time, the interval $(0, T_s)$ represents the solar period and the interval (T_s, T), the eclipse period. This Boolean variable is therefore periodic with period equal to T.

Due to the endothermic and exothermic characteristics of the battery charging and discharging processes, the aforementioned excitation, in turn, causes a heat exchange defined by $q(t)$. This varies in time accordingly to the state that the model is: during charge $q(t) = q_c$ and during discharge $q(t) = q_d$, forcing it to warm up and cool down alternatively.

Regarding the thermal representation of the battery, the author defines a model in which the input is the heat $q(t)$, from the periodic excitation of the logic model, and the output is the battery temperature. The dynamics of the thermal model is therefore described as Eq. (7).

$$dx = \frac{1}{C_{bat}} f(x) + \frac{1}{C_{bat}} q(t) \tag{7}$$

in which x is the battery temperature, C_{bat} is the thermal capacitance, and $f(t)$ is the heat and cooling source function, defined as

$$f(x) = \begin{cases} P_M - k_2(x + 273)^4, & \text{if } x < 0 \\ k_1(x - 10)^2 - k_2(x + 273)^4, & \text{if } 0 \le x \le 10 \\ -k_2(x + 273)^4, & \text{if } x > 0 \end{cases} \tag{8}$$

in which P_M is power, k_1 is the coefficient of the heating source and k_2 is the coefficient of the radiator.

4   Modeling and Properties Formalization

4.1   Solar Power System Modeling and Properties Formalization

In order to model the suggested scenario from the original paper [3], the first approach is to recreate the state structure based on a 3-tuple $W = (S, I, L)$ seen at 3. Using the Prism syntax to model a Discrete Time Markov Chain (DTMC), one module was created for each element of the tuple:

DTMC

```
module battery_state
    \\Module contents
endmodule

module insolation
    \\Module contents
endmodule

module load
    \\Module contents
endmodule
```

Using this approach, there is no W variable: its existence is implied by the state of each module. But, as suggest by the paper, a single 24 h day will be simulated, so a time module was created to control the battery state through the hours:

```
module time
    t : [0..24] init 0;
    [c]t < 24 -> (t' = t + 1);
endmodule
```

The t time variable runs in the $0, ..., 24$ integer range, beginning at 0. The next state is achieved by the sum of 1 at the time variable until this reaches 24 h. Note a c synchronization variable at the front of the step guard condition: this variable also appears at the battery_state module to guarantee a synchronous transition of the charging state within the hours of the day.

The insolation module runs a binary variable to simulate the stochastic behavior of the sun condition: if the state is equal to 0 (no sun at all) it has 50% chance to turn into 1 (sunny) or stay at the same state. The same unpredictable approach is used if the current state equals 0.

```
module insolation
    i : [0..1] init 1;
    []i = 0 -> 0.5:(i' = 1) + 0.5:(i' = i);
    []i = 1 -> 0.5:(i' = 0) + 0.5:(i' = i);
endmodule
```

The paper originally considers a constant insolation in their simulations, but here we decided to test this feature to verify the versatility of the Prism model checker.

The load demand was also suggested to be constant in the paper. Here, however, we created a stochastic behavior of the load in the `load` module:

```
const int L = 3; //Maximum load
module load
    l : [0..L] init 1;
    []l > 0 & l < L -> 0.5:(l' = l + 1) + 0.5:(l' = l - 1);
    []l = 0 -> 0.5:(l' = l + 1) + 0.5:(l' = l);
    []l = L -> 0.5:(l' = l - 1) + 0.5:(l' = l);
endmodule
```

The daily load provided was 240 *amp-hrs* in the paper, but the use of a big integer as a constant would create a state explosion. So, this value was simplified by a factor of 100 and rounded. The maximum load L was empirically rounded up from $2, 4$ to 3 to provide stability to the model, considering the inclusion of a stochastic insolation and load demand, both absent in the original simulation. The load l variable runs in the $0, ..., 3$ range in a probabilistic motion, in which the next state is given by the three conditions seen in the module.

The battery charging state is simulated in the `battery_state` module. Here, all the guard conditions have the synchronous variable c found in the `time` module. This is meant to create a state time-slice each hour.

```
module battery_state
    s : [s_min..s_max] init ceil((3 * s_max) / 4);

    //case a: AO >= Ld
    [c](s > s_min & s < s_max) & s < s2 & (i * AO) >= Ld-> (s' = s + 1); //a1
    [c](s > s_min & s < s_max) & s > s2 & (i * AO) >= Ld -> (s' = s - 1); //a1
    [c](s > s_min & s < s_max) & s = s2 & (i * AO) >= Ld -> (s' = s); //a1
    [c](s = s_min & (i * AO) >= Ld) -> (s' = s + 1); //a2

    //case b: AO < Ld
    [c](s > s_min & s < s_max) & (i * AO) < Ld -> (s' = s - 1); //b1
    [c](s = s_min  & Ld > (i * AO)) -> (s' = s); //b2

    [c]s = s_max -> (s' = s);
endmodule
```

In this module, the state s variable runs in a range limited by two constants: the maximum and the minimum battery load found in the paper:

```
const int  s_max = 42; //Ampere hour
const int  s_min = ceil(s_max * 0.5); //Maximum DoD = 50%
```

The maximum DoD (Depth of Discharge) was limited to 50%, as suggested by the paper. The 4200 Ah (Ampere hour) was shrunken to 42, using the 100 reduction factor to avoid state explosion. The initial state of the s variable was a value in the middle of the maximum and minimum charging state.

The energy flow equations provided in the Eqs. 4 and 5 were used to find the next battery charging state. Cases "a" and "b" were predicted considering an array output greater or smaller than the load demand. The increment or decrement in the battery level is given by comparing the current value of s with the next state s_2 value, given by the equations:

```
//Load
formula Ld = 1 * Hd/24; //Daytime Load
formula Ln = 1 * Hn/24; //Nighttime Load

//Case a
formula f = Ln/1;
formula b = 1 + f * (r - 1);
formula s2 = s + (i * AO) - Ld - Ln/b;
```

Given the fact that when the array output A_O is less than the load demand the battery charge always decreases, the "Case b" equations were not used. The value of the s variable was decreased by 1 instead. When the battery is in its minimum level, it can only rises in "Case a" or remain in "Case b". Once reached the maximum level of charge, the battery will stay there and the simulation is finished.

In order to verify the model, four properties were proposed to check the probability that the battery will get full or empty at the end of the day:

$$P_{>0.1}[t = 24 \wedge s = 42]$$

This property verifies if the state s is maximum (42) at the end of 24 h, with a probability grater than 10%. In the Prism notation, we have P>0.1[F(t=24&s=42)].

$$P_{<0.1}[t = 24 \wedge s = 21]$$

Similar to the anterior, this property verifies if the state s is minimum (21) at the end of 24 h, with a probability less than 10%. In the Prism notation, we have P<0.1[F(t=24&s=21)].

The next two properties state the actual probability of the given scenarios to happen:

$$P_{\bowtie}[t = 24 \wedge s = 42] \tag{9}$$

$$P_{\bowtie}[t = 24 \wedge s = 21] \tag{10}$$

The property shown in the Eq. 9 verifies the actual probability to end the day at full charge while the property in the Eq. 10 verifies the probability of running out of battery in one day. In the Prism notation, the properties are, respectively, P=?[F(t=24&s=42)] and P=?[F(t=24&s=21)].

4.2   Batteries of Artificial Satellites Modeling and Properties Formalization

To model the proposed scheme from the original paper [4], it was used CTMC, as the central variable of interest, the temperature, is defined by the a rate dx. All the elements that have influence on this variation were identified and one module was created for each, using Prism syntax:

```
module time
    \\Module contents
endmodule

module orbital_logic
    \\Module contents
endmodule

module temperature
    \\Module contents
endmodule

module heat_cooling_source
    \\Module contents
endmodule
```

The t variable on the time module runs in the $0, ..., T$ integer range, beginning at 0. It represents the satellite orbit and behaves as a clock to the other modules. Its next state is given by the sum of 1 at the variable until it reaches T, when it returns to 0, characterizing its cyclic nature.

```
module time
    t : [0..T] init 0;
    [] t < T -> (t' = t + 1);
    [orbit_end] t >= T -> (t' = 0);
endmodule
```

The orbital_logic module represents the system's output response from the clock excitation. It runs the state variable s, which is a binary, and the heat variable $q(t)$. When $t < T_s$ (solar period), $s = 1$, and when $t \geq T_s$ (eclipse period), $s = 0$, as stated on Eq. (6). The heat variable $q(t)$ is also a two state element, with a constant value q_c during charge (solar period) and a constant value q_d during discharge (eclipse period).

```
module orbital_logic
    s : [0..1] init 1;
    q: [Qmin..Qmax];
    [solar] t < Ts -> 1:(s' = 1) + 1:(q' = qc);
    [eclipse] t >= Ts -> 1:(s' = 0) + 1:(q' = qd);
endmodule
```

The temperature flow distribution provided in Eq. (7) is expressed as the function for dx.

```
formula dx = ((invCbat)*(f + q));
```

This is used to estimate the battery temperature on module `temperature`, which runs the variable x. The rate of which the temperature is modified is determined by dx. As Prism do not understand negative rates, it was necessary to break the command into three different situations: $dx < 0$ (dx is negative), $dx > 0$ (dx is positive) and $dx = 0$ (dx is zero). The last one does not impact in change on x. Also, it is detected if the temperature is bellow the absolute zero ($Xmin$), evidencing an error in the code; and if the temperature is higher then the maximum accepted before the battery enters thermal runaway ($Xmax$).

```
module temperature
            x: [Xmin..Xmax];
            [dx_negative] dx < 0 & x>Xmin -> (-dx):(x'=x-1);
            [dx_positive] dx > 0 & x<Xmax -> (dx):(x'=x+1);
            [dx_zero] dx = 0 -> 1:(x'=x);
            [alert] x>=Xmax -> 1:(x'=x);
            [error] x<=Xmin -> 1:(x'=x);
        endmodule
```

The `heat_cooling_source` module basically transcripts Eq. (8). It runs a variable f that substitutes $f(t)$, which assumes different functions at three temperature sections.

```
module heat_cooling_source
     f : [fmin..fmax];
     [temperature_range1] x < 0 ->
         1:(f' = ceil(Pm - (k2*pow((x+273.0), 4))));
     [temperature_range2] x >= 0 & x <= 10 ->
         1:(f' = ceil(k1*pow((x-10.0), 2) - k2*pow((x+273), 4)));
     [temperature_range3] x > 10 ->
         1:(f' = ceil(-k2*pow((x+273.0), 4)));
endmodule
```

It was used cost and rewards to reason about quantitative measures relating to model behaviour: to count the number of cycles, checking how many times it passed through `orbit_end`; and to compute the `alerts` and `errors`.

```
rewards "cycles"
     [orbit_end] true : 1;
endrewards

rewards "alert"
     [alert] true : 1;
endrewards
```

```
rewards "error"
    [error] true : 1;
endrewards
```

With the aim of verifying the model, four properties were developed using the patterns presented on [5].

$$P_{<0.1}[\lozenge[T,T]x = X_{max}]$$

Being a Transient State Probability pattern, this property checks if the probability of having a thermal runway before $t < T$ is less than 10%. In the Prism notation, we have `P>0.1[F(T,T) x=Xmax]`.

$$P_{\geq 0.9}[\square[0,100]x > X_{min}]$$

As a Probabilistic Invariant, this property certifies if no error will occur in the next 100 units of time, with a probability of at least 90%. In Prism, it becomes `P>=0.9[[0, 100] x > Xmin]`.

$$P_{\geq 0.95}[\lozenge[0,6015]s = 0]$$

This property was created using the Probabilistic Existence pattern. It certifies if a transition to the eclipse state should occur within 6015 seconds in 95% of the cases. In Prism, it is `P>=0.95[F[0, 6015] s = 0]`.

$$R_{\text{``cycles''}} =?[C \leq 100000]$$

This is a Cumulative Rewards pattern and it sums the number of cycles performed. In Prism, the same property is written as `R{"cycles"}=? [C<=100000]`.

5   Results Evaluation

5.1   Solar Power System Results

In this section, we present the results of our approach applied to the solar power system. The original values were simplified by the factor of 100 to avoid state explosion and were rounded to fit the discrete nature of the state model.

By verifying the four properties, we achieved the following results (Table 1):

Table 1. Results of the properties for the Solar Power System

Property	Result
$P_{>0.1}[t = 24 \wedge s = 42]$	True
$P_{<0.1}[t = 24 \wedge s = 21]$	True
$P_{\bowtie}[t = 24 \wedge s = 42]$	0.17649027
$P_{\bowtie}[t = 24 \wedge s = 21]$	0.08091588

The simulation in the original paper predicted a scenario in which the system is supplied for $98,3\%$ of the time. With $\sim 8,09\%$ of probability to run out of battery at the end of the day, a 92% of system reliability is a very close result to the original one. The author of the paper achieved 13.32% of maximum battery in his simulations, while we got $\sim 17,64\%$ of full charge at the end of the day, another close result.

5.2 Batteries of Artificial Satellites Results

Verifying the four properties stated on Sect. 4 for the satellite model, the following results were achieved (Table 2):

Table 2. Result of the properties for the Satellite Power System

Property	Result
$P_{<0.1}[\lozenge[T,T]x = X_{max}]$	True
$P_{\geq 0.9}[\square[0,100]x > X_{min}]$	True
$P_{\geq 0.95}[\lozenge[0,6015]s = 0]$	True
$R_{\text{“cycles”}} = ?[C \leq 100000]$	1.0

Making a simulation on Prism, it was obtained the two curves bellow. On the first one, it is possible to see the interaction between all variables, mainly the periodic ones. On the second one, the temperature element was isolated in order to have a closer look in its behavior (Figs. 3, 4).

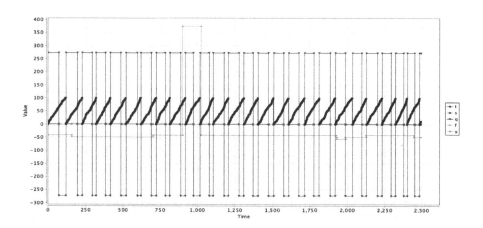

Fig. 3. Satellite Power System Simulation: variables interaction.

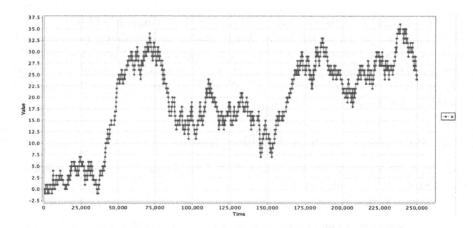

Fig. 4. Satellite Power System Simulation: temperature variation.

6   Discussion of Related Work

In this section, we focus on some relevant studies addressing the analysis of power supply systems.

In [6] the author introduces a battery power supply model based on discrete-time VDHL. It is done an event-driven simulation at a very high level of abstraction. The objective is to estimate battery life-time during design optimization. Different than the strategy used in this paper, the battery is represented only as an electrical circuit.

A mathematical simulation is done in [7] using experimental data to calculate parameters used on the model. The aim is to predict the battery state of charge of a hybrid solar-wind power supply system.

Another simulation method explored for the analysis of satellite power supply subsystem in [8] is the subspace identification. In this paper it is used n4sid together with control techniques to improve fidelity of CBERS-4 operational simulator.

A satellite power supply subsystem is also modeled in [9], but using Simulink. In this case, it was analysed the different performances for each configuration of the solar arrays.

Also in the space application, [10] uses Virtual Test Bed (VTB), an interdisciplinary computational environment, to model, simulate and virtual-prototype the battery power supply system. The author uses the results obtained to compare different chemicals.

It is possible to perceive the plurality of techniques in the literature to model and simulate battery sustained power supply systems. However, all of them have in common the deterministic approach. In other words, it is used past data or mathematical equations to predict the system's exact behavior. Probabilistic Model Checking, on the other hand, considers the stochastic characteristic of the battery. In this way, the objective is not to reproduce a past scenario as it happened once, but to infer patterns and probabilities about that system.

7   Conclusions

In this paper, it is discussed the use of Probabilistic Model Checking on battery sustained power supply systems. We considered two systems in our analysis: a solar power supply system based on DTMC and a satellite power supply system based on CTMC. The results achieved show a behavior similar to the expected, proving the feasibility of the method. Besides, it is obtained a series of probabilistic assumptions to help on the development and maintenance of projects using the studied subsystems. Since batteries are passive and unstable elements, it is difficult to predict its behavior, even through past data comparison. Thus, Probabilistic Model Checking turned out to be a more realistic estimation in this case than other methods based on reproduction of scenarios. Future directions include the investigation of other probabilistic models such as Markov Decision Processes (MDPs) and Probabilistic Timed Automata (PTA) as well as the application of probabilistic model checking to analyze other power supply systems.

Acknowledgments. The authors would like to thank ITEMM for the help in carrying out this work and CNPq for the financial support on the process number 130878/2018-9.

References

1. Baier, C., Katoen, J.P.: Principles of Model Checking. MIT Press, Cambridge (2008)
2. Kwiatkowska, M., Norman, G., Parker, D.: Stochastic model checking. In: Bernardo, M., Hillston, J. (eds.) SFM 2007. LNCS, vol. 4486, pp. 220–270. Springer, Heidelberg (2007). https://doi.org/10.1007/978-3-540-72522-0_6
3. Safie, F.M.: Probabilistic modeling of solar power systems. In: Annual Reliability and Maintainability Symposium, 1989. Proceedings, pp. 425–430. IEEE (1989)
4. de Magalhães, R.O.: Esudo de avalanche térmica em um sistema de carga e descarga de baterias em satélites artificiais. Ph.D. thesis, INPE (2012)
5. Grunske, L.: Specification patterns for probabilistic quality properties. In: ACM/IEEE 30th International Conference on Software Engineering, ICSE 2008, pp. 31–40. IEEE (2008)
6. Benini, L., Castelli, G., Macii, A., Macii, E., Poncino, M., Scarsi, R.: A discrete-time battery model for high-level power estimation. In: Proceedings of the Conference on Design, Automation and Test in Europe, pp. 35–41. ACM (2000)
7. Zhou, W., Yang, H., Fang, Z.: Battery behavior prediction and battery working states analysis of a hybrid solar–wind power generation system. Renew. Energy **33**(6), 1413–1423 (2008)
8. Rodrigues, I.P., Rego, L.F.M., Coimbra, T.d.S., Gruppelli, G.P., Ambrósio, A.M.: Identification and control techniques applied to an operational satellite simulator. Congresso Brasileiro de Automática, 22. (CBA) (2018)
9. Farid, H., El-Koosy, M., El-Shater, T., El-Koshairy, A., Mahmoud, A.: Simulation of a LEO satellite electrical power supply subsystem in-orbit operation. In: Proceedings of the 23rd European Photovoltaic Solar Energy Conference and Exhibition, Valencia, Spain (2008)
10. Jiang, Z., Dougal, R.A., Liu, S.: Application of VTB in design and testing of satellite electrical power systems. J. Power Sources **122**(1), 95–108 (2003)

A Telemedicine System Using Petri Nets

Iván Ruiz[1]([⊠]), C. A. Collazos[1], Fredy A. Sanz[1], José García[2],
Emiro De-la-Hoz-Franco[3], Farid Meléndez-Pertuz[3], and César Mora[4]

[1] Vicerrectoría de Investigaciones, Universidad Manuela Beltrán,
Bogotá, Colombia
ivanruizhidalgo@gmail.com
[2] Programa de Ingeniería Mecánica, Universidad del Valle, Cali, Colombia
[3] Departamento de Ciencias de la Computación y Electrónica,
Universidad de la Costa, Barranquilla, Colombia
[4] Centro de Investigación en Ciencia Aplicada y Tecnología Avanzada del
Instituto Politécnico Nacional, México DF, Mexico

Abstract. Several technologies in electronics and informatics have been
merged into medicine field. It is commonly called telemedicine. Specifically,
this work proposes to scenario and an environment which a specific protocol of
physical rehabilitation process can be executed and applied to a patient by a
healthcare specialist who are geographically distant one another. In this sense, a
Service Oriented Architecture (SOA) was designed and analyzed, trying to
ensure the right communication process. Colored Petri Nets was used as a
formal modelling tool. Finally, a brief mathematical approach is shown aiming
to validate the architecture specifications.

Keywords: SOA · Telemedicine · Physical rehab · Petri nets ·
Mathematical approach

1 Introduction

The health care system and the way they are being provided are involved in several
changes according to the constants technology advances [1]. The inclusion of the
electronic and information technologies into health care system is commonly called
telemedicine. It is possible to ensure that the evolution of mobile communications and
the integration of information and communication technologies within the field of
health have great potential to offer patients convincing alternatives as a replacement for
conventional medical care through synchronous interaction with devices of medical
assistance [2].

This scenario, which makes possible to provide timely attention to patients in a
dispersed geographic location, offers, among other advantages: decentralization of
rehabilitation centers, increased coverage and prevention of infection. Based on the
information presented above, it can be affirmed that telemedicine is an effective way to
assure an adequate health care service [3].

In developing countries, using telemedicine may be an effective way to assure the
right to health care service that must be provided by government [4]. With this aim,
several countries as Colombia, has begun to incorporate many electronic and

© Springer Nature Switzerland AG 2019
S. Misra et al. (Eds.): ICCSA 2019, LNCS 11620, pp. 758–766, 2019.
https://doi.org/10.1007/978-3-030-24296-1_60

information technologies into health care system. For example, authors like [5], the development of a platform to support low-income and geographically isolated hospitals located in the department of Valle del Cauca (Colombia) is presented. This platform is mainly tele-education (in physical rehabilitation). The platform developed in this project, aims to filter the consultations to determine if the patient needs to move to a specialized medical center.

Lozano and Romero [4] carried out a study in the Universidad Nacional de Colombia, focused on providing telemedicine service in radiology (Tele-radiology) is presented. The objective of this architecture is to facilitate to upload information in images of the X-rays of patients so that later they can be analyzed by radiologists. In other studies as [6] deals with the problem of telemedicine applied to psychiatric consultations, which is a work developed by the Universidad CES de Medellín (Colombia). In this work, what the authors propose is a structuring of a teleconsultation protocol for patients with problems framed in psychiatry. For this purpose, a web application through which the services of diagnosis and control of patients were developed.

In other countries, telemedicine is already working. Countries such as Mongolia, telemedicine has been carried out focused on neonatal care in rural regions of that country. In total, 598 patients were treated between 2007 and 2009, of which only 36 were referred to a health center in a main city [7]. This shows that telemedicine is an effective tool to avoid trips to health centers, which could put the integrity and health of the patient at risk.

Woong and Cheol [8] understand telemedicine as an effective tool to prevent and diagnose diseases on time by continuously monitoring the vital signs of the patient. In this sense, Bradley *et al.* [9, 10] presents a device called NeXOS, which help the physiotherapist in the rehabilitation process in patients with physical injuries. Additionally, it has a system capable of connecting to the internet to interact with another specialist (who is geographically distant) in the process of patient rehabilitation. It should be noted that this work does not have an architecture with orientation to services and neither a modeling of it.

Another example of the telemedicine service is the one shown by Ferriol *et al.* [11] where the development of a virtual rehabilitation platform is presented, aimed at elderly people (3rd age) with knee replacement, which is a very frequent surgery in this population. The platform has dynamic material in the form of text, images or video in order to support the rehabilitation process. It also performs a monitoring of the movements of the person with the use of sensors that are able to capture the movements of the patient. Later these data are transmitted to a specialist to be analyzed.

Finally, telemedicine and telehealth are two concepts widely studied because there are many medical specialties. As mentioned, telemedicine has been applied in several areas such as cardiology, pediatrics, radiology, psychiatry, neonatal care and physiotherapy. Hence, this work is focused on making use of information technologies and adapting them to physiotherapy and thus be able to provide the tele-physiotherapy service. To assure an adequate system behavior, a modeling in Petri Nets was developed and studied for both the definitions of the services and the communication among them.

2 Definitions

2.1 Service Oriented Architecture (SOA)

An architecture SOA establish a list of guidelines to design the interaction among independent applications to be access to form internet to its functions which are offered like services. It is a common way to implement an SOA using Web Service technology [12].

There are several principles that an SOA architecture could have. Some principles are given by [13], and they are: reusability, interoperability, auto-content, scalability, modularity, easy to discover and others. From this point of view, SOA allows the creation of services and applications which can exist and be consumed by several users and other applications through network [12].

2.2 Petri Net

A Petri Net (PN) can be defined as a matrix given by $PN = \{P, T, A, M\}$. Next is presented the principal components of a Petri Net [14, 15]:

- Places (P): represented by circumferences and denoted by $P = \{P_1, P_2, P_3, ..., P_n\}$, where $n \geq 0$ is a positive integer.
- Transitions (T): represents by rectangles or vertical lines (see Figs. 1 and 4) and denoted by $T = \{T_1, T_2, T_3..., T_m\}$, where $m \geq 0$ is a positive integer.
- Directed arc (A): represented by arrows. It defines the inputs and outputs from transition to places and vice versa.
- Marks (M): also called as "token", is represented by points in the places; the transitions consume marks from an input and generate marks to output places. M_0 is a vector which contains all tokens at initial system state.

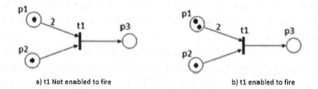

a) t1 Not enabled to fire   b) t1 enabled to fire

Fig. 1. Petri net: firing condition [15]

A transition is enabled if each inlet has as minimum one quantity of marks equally to the arc weight than has associated, past is shown outlined next:

3 General Architecture Proposal

In Fig. 2 is presented the general architecture to allow the attention and therapy process from a Specialist doctor to a patient located in an isolated hospital.

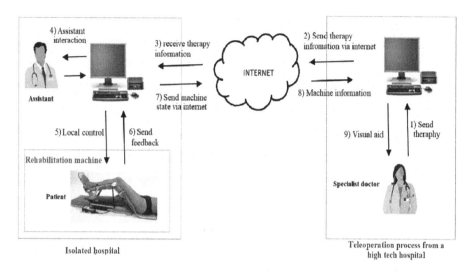

Fig. 2. Proposed architecture for the tele-physiotherapy service

The therapy and attention process have several steps described by Fig. 2. The general process is: a specialist doctor (located in a high-tech hospital) send a therapy process through internet, the information is received by an assistant and a patient (located in an isolated hospital) where the therapy process is executed.

Next, a feedback is sent to the Specialist with the aim to monitor the entire process. Here, it is important to note three persons involved in the process: Specialist Doctor, Assistant and Patient. On the other hand, there are three general process to provide the tele-physiotherapy process (based on [15]):

– *Teleoperation Service:* this service set the telecommands instructions and the Specialist have his feedback
– *Isolated Hospital Service*: Receive the telecommands, also send the feedback information to the specialist and assistant.
– *Physical Rehabilitation Machine Service*: It executes the therapy and have a direct interaction with the patient.

All this persons and process are involved into the tele-physiotherapy process. The operations involved in the process is shown in Fig. 3.

Figure 3 shows the general functions that must be carried out in two hospitals where the therapy process take place: Isolated Hospital and High-Tech Hospital. This allows that the doctor can perform a physical rehabilitation session for a geographically distant patient.

It is important to clarify that the Isolated Hospital must generate a continuous feedback in form of an "echo" to the High-Tech Hospital aiming to continuously inform the current state of the therapy. However, this detail of modelling specification was not taking into account in the present study.

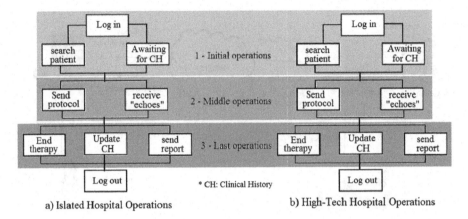

a) Islated Hospital Operations   b) High-Tech Hospital Operations

Fig. 3. Proposed architecture for the tele-physiotherapy service

4 Model in Colored Petri Nets

In order to model the general architecture proposed on Fig. 2, an extension of the ordinary Petri Nets was used. This extension is named Colored Petri Nets (CPN) and CPNtools 4.0 was used to model the system dynamics. The tele-physiotherapy service be seen in Fig. 4.

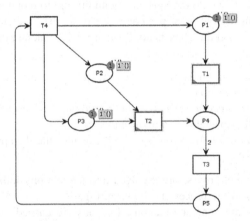

Fig. 4. Tele-physiotherapy service net

The places and the transitions in Fig. 4, are described in Table 1.

Nevertheless, Fig. 4 shows only one tele-physiotherapy service. Given that a service orientation is being used, all services can be called as many times as needed. Thus, the general architecture is showed in Fig. 5:

Table 1. Transitions and places definitions

Place		Transition	
P_1	Doctor available	T_1	Teleoperation Service process
P_2	Patient ready	T_2	Isolated Hospital Service process
P_3	Assistant available	T_3	Physical rehabilitation machine service
P_4	Information through internet	T_4	Save data and set as available the doctor, patient and assistant
P_5	Therapy concluded		

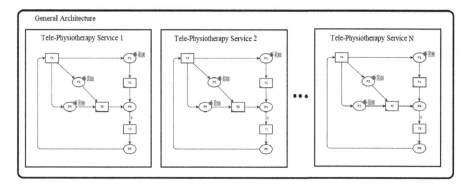

Fig. 5. General architecture

Given the information for both the Fig. 4 and Table 1, an incidence matrix is expressed as follows [14]:

$$a_{ij} = a_{ij}^+ - a_{ij}^- \tag{1}$$

Where, a_{ij}^+ is the post-incidence matrix and a_{ij}^- is the pre-incidence matrix. The difference among both matrices is that a_{ij}^+ specified the weight of the arcs directed from the transition to places and a_{ij}^- from the places to transitions. In this way, we can write those matrices as follows:

$$a_{ij}^+ = \begin{pmatrix} 0 & 0 & 0 & 1 \\ 0 & 0 & 0 & 1 \\ 0 & 0 & 0 & 1 \\ 1 & 1 & 0 & 0 \\ 0 & 0 & 1 & 0 \end{pmatrix} \text{ and } a_{ij}^- = \begin{pmatrix} 1 & 0 & 0 & 0 \\ 0 & 1 & 0 & 0 \\ 0 & 1 & 0 & 0 \\ 0 & 0 & 2 & 0 \\ 0 & 0 & 0 & 1 \end{pmatrix},$$

thus

$$a_{ij} = \begin{pmatrix} -1 & 0 & 0 & 1 \\ 0 & -1 & 0 & 1 \\ 0 & -1 & 0 & 1 \\ 1 & 1 & -2 & 0 \\ 0 & 0 & 1 & -1 \end{pmatrix}$$

A state for a PN shows a change in a tokens distribution as a result as a firing condition execution. The general equation that describes this performance is given by [14]:

$$M_k = M_{k-1} + A^T \mu_k; \quad K = 1, 2, 3 \ldots \tag{2}$$

Where, M_k is the state to calculate, M_{k-1} is the system current state, A^T is the incidence matrix equal to a_{ij} described by Eq. 1, and μ_k is the vector which allows the marks firing through the PN to achieve the state M_k. In order to know the final state, an evaluation on Eq. (2) was done, so $M_{k-1} = M_0 = (1, 1, 1, 0, 0)$ is the initial mark and $\mu_k = (1, 1, 1, 1)$ is the all transitions fire condition to get the PN final state. The result be follows:

$$M_{final} = \begin{pmatrix} 1 \\ 1 \\ 1 \\ 0 \\ 0 \end{pmatrix} + \begin{pmatrix} -1 & 0 & 0 & 1 \\ 0 & -1 & 0 & 1 \\ 0 & -1 & 0 & 1 \\ 1 & 1 & -2 & 0 \\ 0 & 0 & 1 & -1 \end{pmatrix} \cdot \begin{pmatrix} 1 \\ 1 \\ 1 \\ 1 \end{pmatrix} = \begin{pmatrix} 1 \\ 1 \\ 1 \\ 0 \\ 0 \end{pmatrix}$$

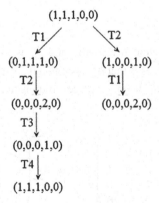

Fig. 6. Reachability tree

It is an important result because it means that the final state is equal to initial state, which is a goal in these kinds of PNs that represent a service available once it be consumed. In Fig. 6, the reachability tree is shown, based on Fig. 4.

In a Petri Net, a reachability tree consists of a finite graph in the form of a tree in which each node is an achievable mark of the network and the nodes are connected by arcs labeled with the transition that is firing to change from one marking to another. It begins form an initial marking M_0 aiming to generate all possible states through firing process.

5 Conclusion

A service orientated architecture was proposed following the guidelines of an SOA architecture for teleoperation of physiotherapy rehabilitation process. In order to assure the correct definition of the services, a modelling in Colored Petri Nets was developed. Therefore, a brief matrix analysis was done to determinate and corroborate if the initial state is equal to final state, which is an important goal in a service request.

The modeling of this architecture was made taking into account the basic principles of SOA, such as interoperability, reusability, low coupling, and self-containment, among others. All these principles are important and make the architecture become service-oriented.

In the model process (see Fig. 4), it is important to note that each transition represents each service involved. Thus, in the future, transition must be a macro-transition using hierarchies which is very important advantage from Colored Petri nets to Ordinary Petri Nets.

In further works, the technological objective of the project is to design an SOA that allows tele-operated human rehabilitation via technical aids; understanding technical aids as specialized machines of a physical rehabilitation therapy session. These technical aids must be provided with sensors (angular position, speed, strength, etc.) that allow monitoring both the state of the machine as well as the evolution of therapy. Then, the development of these machines and a complex tele-physiotherapy architecture will be studied in the future. The methodology used in this work is applicable to real processes and may be used for different fields of application [16].

References

1. Rodríguez, E.: Telesalud en Colombia. Ministerio de la proteccion social (2012). http://www.acreditacionensalud.org.co/catalogo/docs/Revista%20Normas%20y%20Calidad%20N%C2%B0%2090.pdf. Accessed 15 febrero 2013
2. Heinzelmann, P., Lugn, N., Kyedar, J.: Telemedicine in the future. J. Telemed. Telecare **11**, 384–390 (2005)
3. Kopec, A., Rodriguez, G.: Aplicaciones de telecomunicaciones en salud en la subregion Andina. Organismo Andino de Salud-Convenio Hipolito Unanue, Bogota DC (2006)
4. Lozano, A., Romero, E.: Telemedicina y telerradiología. La experiencia en la Universidad Nacional. Revista Colombiana de Radiologia, pp. 2435–2439 (2008)
5. Yunda, L., Gomez, L., Rodriguez, S., Millán, R., Tobar, M.: Plataforma Web para un nuevo modelo de tele-rehabilitación, de base comunal, en areas rurales. Revista S&T **9**(19), 55–67 (2011)

6. Londoño, N., Castaño, P., Montoya, D., Ruiz, C.: Protocolo de telemedicina para la consulta psiquiátrica. Revista Ingeniería Biomédica **3**(5), 43–49 (2009)
7. Global Observatory for eHealth: Telemedicine Opportunities and Developments in Member States. World Health Organization, Geneva (2010)
8. Woong, T., Cheol, H.: A healthcare system as a service in the context of vital signs: proposing a framework for realizing a model. Comput. Math Appl. **64**, 1324–1332 (2012)
9. Bradley, D., Acosta, C., Hawley, M., Brownsell, S., Enderby, P., Mawson, P.: NeXOS – the design, development and evaluation of a rehabilitation system for the lower limbs. Mechatronics **19**, 247–257 (2009)
10. Bradley, D., Acosta, C., Hawley, M., Brownsell, S., Enderby, P., Mawson, P.: Remote rehabilitation - the NeXOS project: lessons learnt and questions raised. In: IEEE 11th International Conference on Rehabilitation Robotics, Kyoto, Japan (2009)
11. Ferriol, P., Beatle, M., Arrivi, E., de Alarcon, P., Farreny, M.: TeleRHB: Telerehabilitación en personas mayores. XXVII CASEIB - Sociedad Española de Ingeniería Biomédica, vol. 1 (2009)
12. Microsoft Corporation, La arquitectura orientada a servicios (SOA) de Microsoft aplicada al mundo real, Estados Unidos (2006)
13. Josuttis, M.: SOA in Practice the Art of Distributed System Design. O'Reilly, Sebastopol (2007)
14. Zurawski, R., Zhou, M.: Petri nets and industrial application: a tutorial. IEEE Trans. Ind. Electron. **41**(6), 567–583 (1994)
15. Ruiz, J.G., Collazos, C.: Modeling in petri nets of a dispersed system in a physical rehab. Revista Ingeniería Biomédica **11**(21), 49–55 (2017)
16. Campuzano, J., Melendez, F., Nuñez, B., Simancas, J.: Sistema de Monitoreo Electrónico de Desplazamiento de Tubos de Extensión para Junta Expansiva. Revista Iberoamericana de Automática e Informática Industrial **14**(3), 268–278 (2017)

Particle Charging Using Ultra-Short Pulse Laser in the Ideal Maxwellian Cold Plasma for Cancer Treatment Based on Hadron Therapy

Vala Mehryar Alviri[1], Sheida Asad Soleimani[2], Sasan Soudi[3],
and Morteza Modarresi Asem[1(✉)]

[1] Department of Clinical Biomedical Engineering,
Tehran Medical Sciences Branch, Islamic Azad University, Tehran, Iran
`mehryarvala@gmail.com`, `Modaresi.bme@gmail.com`
[2] Department of Biomedical Engineering, South Tehran Branch,
Islamic Azad University, Tehran, Iran
`Sheidasoleimani95@gmail.com`
[3] Student Research Committee of Biomedical Engineering,
Tehran Medical Sciences Branch, Islamic Azad University, Tehran, Iran
`sasan.soudi.1@city.ac.uk`

Abstract. In biomedicine the utilization of accelerators, enables the arrangements of mixes to be utilized in cancer treatment. Accelerators are the standout among the most imperative uses of the electric and attractive fields manage the movement of charged particles. Additionally, the investigation of the plasma requires the examination of the charged particle movements in an electromagnetic field. The laser driven acceleration of particles is a standout among the most critical utilization of the laser plasma interaction. This plan depends on the alteration of the laser electromagnetic field into the plasma wave. These high stage velocity plasma waves can trap and quicken plasma electrons to exceptionally high energies. The plasma condition of issue might be characterized as a blend of decidedly charged ions, electrons and impartial atoms which comprises a perceptible electrically unbiased medium which reacts to the electric and attractive fields in an aggregate mode. In ideal Maxwellian plasma, the energy distribution function of charged particles is Maxwellian and subordinates from Maxwell-Boltzmann distribution. Cold plasma spoke to extremely helpful apparatuses empowering interaction with organic tissue without the warm harm and this innovation improvement brought about the quick formation of another field of plasma medication. Consequently, Hadron therapy is a high-precision procedure in cancer radiation therapy, which permits getting a better conformal treatment with deference than conventional radiation therapy strategies which depends on particle accelerating. This paper surveys on ions importance as charged particles with ultra-short pulse laser in an ideal Maxwellian cold plasma due to cancer treatment via Hadron therapy.

Keywords: Charged particle · Electromagnetic field · Ponderomotive force ·
Ultra-short pulse laser accelerator · Ideal Maxwellian cold plasma ·
Cancer treatment · Hadron therapy

© Springer Nature Switzerland AG 2019
S. Misra et al. (Eds.): ICCSA 2019, LNCS 11620, pp. 767–784, 2019.
https://doi.org/10.1007/978-3-030-24296-1_61

1 Introduction

Amid the most recent two decades, the hypothetical and connected research on vortex electromagnetic wave beam conveying photon orbital angular momentum has an extraordinary improvement. The azimuth phase distribution of vortex wave beam prompts a Helicity wave front and can exchange angular momentum from photon to issue particles. Many cutting-edge innovations depend on this impact [1]. The issue of particle motion in electromagnetic fields is principal and permeates both research facility and plasma material science. The electromagnetic interaction administers numerous parts of our day by day lives. In spite of the fact that the solidarity of the electric and the phenomenon is built up through Physics hypotheses. The motion of charged particles in an electromagnetic field is of incredible functional significance. It is utilized in observation instruments, accelerators, mass spectroscopy, and the consideration of particle reactions [2]. In the sequence of cancer look into, the laser is connected as a kind of smaller scale careful instrument of incredible precision for use in investigation in science, cytology, cytogenetics, spectroscopy, and in the cancer treatment [3]. For some scientists and physicists, laser innovation opens an altogether new, net and even brilliant field [4]. The laser beam is monochromatic, coherent and has direction since the light can be engaged by any focal point framework lastly, it has huge high energy and high power [3]. The vitality of the laser at that point is basically a framework which optically rams a mass and energizes the atoms to a higher energy and as the energy drops there is stimulated emission of radiation [5]. The steady propagation of ultra-short pulse laser in plasma is basic to the realization of particle accelerators. For the plasma oscillation to effectively quicken an electron pack it must have a high-level of cognizance [6]. With ultra-short and high exceptional laser beats the physical lead of the medium changes profoundly in a period equal or shorter than the beat span. This ultra-quick change in the physical traits of the medium starts spatial and ghostly adjustments in the multiplying laser beats. Examination of these changes could redesign the perception of how extreme optical heartbeats incite in plasma [7].

The ideal Maxwellian cold plasma is widely used to describe biomedical approaches. For plasma that is in positional thermodynamic harmony and non-balance, an assortment of hypothetical approximations and physical models have been created to manage the conduct of particles and the related photon emission forms in cold plasma with ion temperatures nigh room temperature [8]. Ideal Maxwellian cold plasma is utilized for medical aims for treatment of cancer, explicitly, in Hadron therapy and productive particle acceleration. Hadron therapy is a particular sort of oncological radiotherapy, which makes utilization of quick Hadrons to get better dose depositions when contrasted and the ones of X-rays utilized in usual radiotherapy [9]. This technique is a settled way to deal with treat cancer because of the positive ballistic properties of ion beams which advance the solution of one of the primary issues of radiation therapy, in particular, the radiance of a cancerous tumor with an adequately powerful and homogeneous portion, guaranteeing that the radiance of the encompassing healthy tissues and organs is insignificant. The approach depends on the productive particle acceleration [10].

1.1 Motivation

Charged particle beams fill two segregated aims in biomedical research: (i) They might be used for examination and diagnosing aims from one viewpoint (ii) and for fitting material properties and for therapy on the other. Various applications of high-energy electron beams incorporate radiation sterilization of medical instruments, radiation science, and radiation treatment [11]. Hadron therapy is a powerful approach for cancer treatment. Compelling particle charging in ultra-fast laser, can intensify the acceleration energy. Moreover, utilizing ideal Maxwellian cold plasma in therapeutic manners, causes remarkable outcomes. As an important consequence, surveying on the ion properties, obtains better results in cancer treatment through Hadron therapy. This paper investigates multiple procedures around the benefits of cancer treatment with ions in comparison to other conventional particles in Hadron therapy and demonstrates the superiority of ions as dose carrier particles. This paper is organized as follows. Section 2 gives an explanation about the Contribution. Section 3 presents Hadron Therapy Procedure Based on Charged Particles. In Sect. 4 Simulations and Experimental Results is expounded. Section 5 is devoted to Conclusion and Prospective Works.

2 Contribution

2.1 Charged Particle Specifications in Applied Fields

The motion of a charged particle in the concurrent attendance of both electric and magnetic fields has an assortment of manifestations such as straight line motion to the cycloid and other wrapped motion. Both electric and magnetic fields confer acceleration of the charged particle. However, there is a qualification for magnetic field as acceleration because of magnetic field relates just to the alteration of the path of motion. Magnetic force being constantly ordinary to the velocity of the particle will in general move the particle about a circular direction. Then again, electric force is along electric field and is able to realize alter in both path and greatness relying on the underlying direction of the velocity of the charged particle of regard to electric field. On the off chance that velocity and electric vectors are at an angle that the particle pursues a parabolic way.

It can understand the origin of electromagnetic field in heavy-ion collisions by considering collision of two ions of radius "R" with electric charge Ze ("e" is the magnitude of electron charge) at impact parameter "b". According to the Biot and Savart law, the electromagnetic field in the center-of-mass frame has magnitude [12]:

$$\overline{EM} \sim \gamma Ze \frac{b}{R^3} \qquad (1)$$

and points in the direction perpendicular to the reaction plane (span by the momenta of ions). Here, $\gamma = \sqrt{S_{NN}}/sm_N$, is the Lorentz factor.

2.2   Ultra-Short Pulse Laser Propagation in the Plasma Channel

Lasers are a standout among the hugest inventions of the twentieth century. At the point when laser made its presentation in 1960, it was known as a solution searching for an issue. Around then, unique gatherings over the world were attempting to comprehend the conduct of issue, especially atom, within the sight of an external field. Lasers gave an amazing source of high field to help up these examinations to better dimension. The invention of pulsed lasers opened energizing exploration openings in the field of laser-matter interaction. Laser plasma interaction physics is one of the most superb, innovative and entrenched tributary in physics. The inclusion of ultra-short lasers is, in any case, moderately quiet later. This section is about the physics and innovation concerned with the generation of ultra-short laser pulses that was activated by the invention of laser mode-locking, a standout among the most striking interference phenomena in nature. Synchronous oscillation of an expansive number of exceedingly coherent, phase-locked longitudinal modes a laser yield a resultant field equivalent to zero more often than not with the exception of short interim. Because of productive interference between the wavering waves, the whole energy of the radiation field is thought inside these brief periods. As an outcome, laser mode-locking prompts the formation of a short light pulse circling in the resonator. Each time the pulse hits a halfway reflecting mirror, a little portion of its energy is coupled out of the oscillator, bringing about a train of ultra-short beats at the output of the mode-locked laser [7].

To comprehend the stimulation of electron plasma waves (Langmuir) in plasma utilizing lasers, one needs to comprehend the idea of ponderomotive force. "F" is free electrons, for example, the ones extant in plasma, can shudder in the electric field related to the electromagnetic wave. The motion of the electron within the sight of electric field is represented by the Lorentz force. In the case of higher, non-uniform electromagnetic (or purely electric) field, the expression for the Lorentz force has a second order term known as the ponderomotive force (F_P), which is proportional to the gradient of the second power of electric field [7]:

$$F_P \propto \nabla E^2 \tag{2}$$

or in terms of laser intensity [7]:

$$F_P \propto \nabla I \tag{3}$$

where, "E" is the electric field and "I" is the intensity of the laser pulse. In this way, one can see from the above equation that any spatial variation in the laser intensity profile will act to push the electrons/ions from the region of higher force to the region of lower intensity through the ponderomotive force, which is proportional to the slope (gradient) of the light intensity.

2.3   Maxwell-Boltzmann Distribution

The Maxwell–Boltzmann distribution is broadly used to portray astrophysical, fusion, and other research facility plasma. In ion, the charge particles may experience collisions with one another, and sometimes with alternate species (ions, electrons, and/or neutrals) in the plasma. In this manner, it is impossible to investigate the motion of every particle to get a naturally visible image of the plasma forms that is valuable for evaluating the execution and life of the devices. Luckily, much of the time it is not important to follow singular particles to comprehend the plasma elements. The impact of collisions is to build up a distribution of the speeds for every species. In the normal, and without different forces, every particle will at that point move with a speed that is exclusively a function of the naturally visible temperature and mass of that species. The charged particles in the thruster, hence, can more often be described by different velocity distribution functions, and the arbitrary motions can be determined by taking the moments of those distributions [13].

2.4 Cold Plasma

Ongoing advancement in plasma types prompted the production of the cold plasma with ion temperatures near room temperature. This makes these plasma not the same as run of the generic low-temperature plasma of a run of the generic electrical release. Such plasma speaks to helpful tools empowering interaction with natural tissue without the thermal harm. Cold plasma innovation and improvement brought about fast formation of another field of plasma medication [14]. A normal cold plasma source appears in Fig. 1. The plasma source is outfitted with a couple of High-Voltage (HV) electrodes- a focal terminal (which is disconnected from the immediate contact with the plasma by ceramics) and an external ring anode as appeared in Fig. 1.

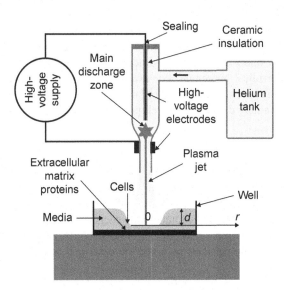

Fig. 1. Schematic view of the plasma gun [15].

Electrodes are associated with an auxiliary twisting of a HV resonant transformer which makes a voltage "V" of up to 10 kV at a frequency of approximately 30 kHz [15]. Each charged particle in a plasma has an electric charge. Any alternative motion of plasma can be disjointed into a superposition of sinusoidal oscillations with frequency "ω", and wavelength "λ". Here, we will consider that any quantities (density "n", velocity "v", and electric field "E") have a sinusoidal waveform. Thus, the plasma density is represented as [15]:

$$n = \bar{n} Exp(j[\mathbf{k}.\mathbf{r} - \omega t]) \tag{4}$$

where, $\bar{n}$ is the density amplitude, "$\mathbf{k}.\mathbf{r}$" is the wave propagation, and "t" is the time.

While the impacts of an electric field on cells have been known for quite a while, cold plasma offers a lot bigger exhibition of conceivable pathways because of the nearness of different chemically active species and charged particles. Cold non-thermal atmospheric plasma can have enormous applications in biomedical instruments. Specifically, plasma treatment can conceivably offer a minimum-invasive medical procedure that permits specific cell expulsion without affecting the entire tissue. Conventional laser medical procedure depends on thermal interaction and prompts unintentional cell passing, i.e., corruption, and may cause changeless tissue harm. Conversely, non-thermal plasma interaction with tissue may permit explicit cell evacuation without necrosis. These interactions incorporate cell separation without influencing cell suitability, and controllable cell death. It can be also additionally utilized for corrective strategies for recovering the reticular engineering of the dermis. The point of plasma interaction with tissue is not to denature the tissue yet rather to work under the limit of thermal damage and to instigate a chemically explicit reaction or modification. The presence of the plasma can advance a substantial reaction that would prompt the ideal impact. The synthetic reaction can be advanced by turning the pressure, gas composition, and energy. In this manner, the essential issues are to discover conditions that produce impact on tissue without thermal treatment. Overall, plasma treatment offers favorable position that could have never been thought of even with the most exceptional laser medical procedure. For example, cold plasma has exhibited extraordinary guarantee in cancer treatment. As of late, cold plasma interaction with tissues has turned into an extremely dynamic research point because of its potential [15].

2.5   Plasma Particle Phenomena

Plasma particles change their momentum, energy, and states of excitation or charge through particle collisions. Two sorts of collisions in plasma can be recognized, specifically, elastic and non-elastic. Elastic collisions can be comprehensively characterized as occasions in which the total kinetic energy of the particles is monitored and the particles hold their original charges [16]. Elastic collisions in which momentum is redistributed between the particles involved are described as follows [15]:

$$A_{fast} + B_{slow} \rightarrow A_{slow} + B_{fast} \tag{5}$$

Non-elastic collisions are those in which the kinetic energy is redistributed between the particles and is moved into some inside mode of at least one impacting particles or into the creation of another particle(s). Non-elastic collisions lead to immediate and invert forms, which incorporate particle excitation and de-excitation, ionization and recombination, charge exchange, dissociation, and charge neutralization. These elementary processes are described by Eq. 6 [15]:

$$A_{fast} + B \leftrightarrow A_{slow} + B^* \tag{6}$$

Several major ionization pathways can be recognized in the typical plasma systems which are depicted in Table 1.

Table 1. Types of collisions in the typical plasma system [15–18].

Types of collisions	Definitions	Equations
Direct ionization	By electron impact is the ionization of neutrals from the ground state by electrons having a high enough energy to cause ionization in a single act. The reverse process is the recombination by which ions capture the free electrons to neutralize the ion into an atom	$A + e \leftrightarrow A^+ + 2e$ or $A + e \leftrightarrow A^+ + e + e(h\nu)$
Stepwise ionization	By electron impact is the ionization of a previously excited neutral species	$A + e \rightarrow A^* + e$ and then $A^* + e \rightarrow A^+ + 2e$
Ionization by collisions of heavy atoms	In which the particle's kinetic energy can lead to the ionization process	$A_{fast} + B \rightarrow A_{slow} + B^+ + e(ionization)$
The photoionization	Process in which the ionization is caused by the photons' interaction with neutral atoms	$A + h\nu \leftrightarrow A^+ + e$
Charge exchange collisions	Positive ions can collide with atoms and capture a valence electron, resulting in charge transfer from the atom to the ion	$A^+ + B \rightarrow A + B^+$
Associative ionization	It is a gas phase chemical reaction in which two atoms/molecules collide and form an ion via interaction. The energy that is released as a result of the chemical reaction is transferred into the electron's energy	$A + B \rightarrow AB^+ + e$
Penning ionization	Involves a reaction between neutral atoms/molecules	$A^* + B \rightarrow B^+ + e + A$
Coulomb collisions	They are elastic collisions between charge particles, such as Electron-electron, electron-ion, and ion-ion collisions	–

3 Hadron Therapy Procedure Based on Charged Particles

3.1 Definition

The cells in the body duplicate and pass on. While recreating, they pass their deoxyribonucleic corrosive (DNA) to daughter cells. DNA encodes the hereditary instructions utilized in the advancement and functioning of all known living creatures. This hereditary information is encoded as a grouping of nucleotides to be specific adenine, thymine, cytosine and guanine. DNA has a twofold helix structure comprising of two strands of nucleotides that are associated by hydrogen bonds. The DNA spine is impervious to cleavage and the twofold stranded structure gives atoms an implicit copy of the encoded information. DNA is composed into long structures called chromosomes. The DNA figures out which proteins the cells can create. Cells with functional DNA harm don't deliver suitable daughter cells. Radiation treatment works by harming the DNA. It can be realized that the DNA in presence 3.5 billion years prior needed to manage cosmic rays and other antagonistic elements. In this manner, it was exposed to common selection. When one of the strands of DNA is harmed, another strand can fix it. At times the DNA can be utilized from another chromosome. Siege with substantial ions is considerably more successful in harming the two strands of DNA than X-rays since they hit the objective all the more accurately and produce progressively predictable harm [19]. For the treatment of tumors that are found all the more profoundly in body tissue, the particle accelerator must create beams with higher energy communicated in electron volts (eV). Tumors closer to the body surface are dealt with utilizing low-energy particles. The accelerators utilized in Hadron treatment commonly produce particles with energies in the range 70–250 MeV. Tumor cell damage can be expanded by altering the energy of the particles amid treatment. Tissues closer the body surface (outside the tumor volume) experience-less radiation harm and profound tissues inside the body is presented to a low number of particles; subsequently, their radiation portion presentation is less. The characteristic precision of a Hadron beam as far as the portion conveyed to tumor tissue is the primary favorable position of Hadron treatment, as contrasted and traditional treatment including photons and electrons [19].

Exactly when a charged molecule goes through a medium, it ionizes particles in its way and passes on a portion of radiation. As referenced in advance, while plotting the vitality of this ionizing radiation as the molecule experiences issue, there is a sharp apex called Bragg crest, which is seen with particles, alpha-particles and particles going before they stop. Therefore, the vitality crest occurs in light of the fact that the cooperation cross segment of the molecule increases with reducing vitality. This wonder is used in the Hadron treatment to center the effect of the pillar on the tumor being managed, while constraining the unfavorable ramifications for the including solid tissue. Figure 2 demonstrates our implementation on how X-ray and particle beams infiltrate human tissue [19]. For particles and heavy ions, the radiation dose increments as the particles enter through tissue and consistently lose energy (i.e., the dose increments with expanding tissue thickness until the Bragg peak is achieved), which happens close as far as possible of the movement scope of the particle. Note that past the Bragg peak the dose goes to zero for particles and about zero for heavy ions. Figure 2 likewise demonstrates that X-rays infiltrate further. However the radiation portion consumed by the tissue demonstrates an exponential decay with increasing thickness [19]. For this propose, we used the Bethe-Bloch equation that describes an energy loss. For a particle with charge "z" (in products of the electron charge), and the energy "E", voyaging a separation "x" into an objective of an electron with a number density "n" and the mean excitation potential "I", the relativistic rendition of the equation peruses in SI units, and the Bethe-Bloch equation is as follows [18]:

$$-\left\langle \frac{dE}{dx} \right\rangle = \frac{4\pi}{m_e c^2} \cdot \frac{nz^2}{\beta^2} \cdot \left(\frac{e^2}{4\pi\varepsilon_0} \right)^2 \cdot \left[ln\left(\frac{2m_e c^2 \beta^2}{I.\left(1 - \beta^2\right)} \right) - \beta^2 \right] \qquad (7)$$

where "c" is the speed of light and, "ε_0" is the vacuum permittivity, $\beta = \frac{u}{c}$, "e" and "m_e" are the electron charge and rest mass, respectively.

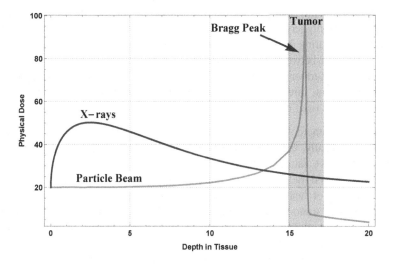

Fig. 2. Proposed simulation of the Bragg peak.

3.2 Hadron Therapy Methods

(A) Fast Neutrons Therapy: This approach is a particular and exceptionally powerful type of outside beam radiation treatment. Usually used to treat certain tumors that are radio-resistant, which means they are exceptionally hard to kill utilizing conventional X-ray radiation treatment. It has ended up being viable at treating salivary organ tumors and certain types of cancer, for example, adenoid cystic carcinoma [20].

(B) Proton Therapy: This technique is a developing treatment approach for cancer that may have particular points of interest over conventional radiotherapy. This identifies with its capacity to limit the high-dose treatment zone to the tumor volume and subsequently limiting radiation portion to encompassing ordinary tissue [21].

(C) Negative Pions Therapy: Negative pions with energies of 60–90 MeV (expand 12–23 cm in tissue) are the energy for radiotherapy. The organic adequacy for about monoenergetic negative pions at the pinnacle of the profundity portion dispersion was seen to be essentially higher than at the entry. For pion light emissions force spread that are remedially significant, the qualifications in natural feasibility are diminished widely [22].

(D) Ion Therapy: This is a type of outer beam radiotherapy utilizing beams of energetic ions for cancer treatment. Carbon-ion radiotherapy has progressively earned logical attention as mechanical conveyance options have improved and clinical examinations have shown its treatment focal points for some cancers, for example, prostate, head and neck, lung, and liver cancers, bone and delicate tissue sarcomas, locally intermittent rectal cancer, and pancreatic cancer, including privately propelled infection. This technique utilizes particles more monstrous than protons or neutrons. Carbon ions have potential focal points over protons: They give a superior physical portion distribution since sidelong dispersing is reduced; and they have higher relative organic adequacy and a lower oxygen improvement proportion; alluring highlights for eradication of radio-resistant, hypoxic tumors. The distinction between thickly ionizing cores and scantily ionizing X-rays and protons offers further potential radiological points of interest, for example, diminished fix a limit, diminished cell-cycle reliance, and conceivably more grounded immunological reactions [23].

Neon ion radiotherapy has natural and physical points of interest over mega-voltage X-beams. Organically, the neon shaft diminishes the oxygen improvement proportion and expands relative natural viability. Cells irradiated by neon ions show-less variation in cell-cycle related radiosensitivity and diminished fix of radiation damage. The physical conduct of heavy charged particles permits the exact conveyance of high radiation doses to tumors while limiting irradiation of typical tissues [24]. In radiotherapy, oxygen particles have more natural points of interest than light columns. Oxygen particles have a higher Linear Energy Transfer (LET) and greater Relative Biological Effectiveness (RBE) than lighter ones. High vitality ionizing radiation, through passing on portion to issue, and making Bragg tops in a particular zone in the goal, is an appropriate alternative for radiation treatment. What's more, the portion of the oxygen shaft toward the completion of the Bragg crest prompts a generous inclination that keeps the assimilation of unwanted doses to delicate organs [9].

Cancer treatment with ions is favored in correlation with different strategies for Hadron treatment, on account of some physical properties. Ions, store their greatest energy thickness in the Bragg peak toward the end of their range. Ions infiltrate the patient for all intents and purposes without diffusion. Being charged, they can without much of a stretch be framed as barely engaged 'pencil beams' penetration profundity, so any piece of a tumor can be precisely and quickly eliminated. In this way ions, permits exceedingly conformal treatment of profound situated tumors with millimeter exactness, giving a negligible dose to the encompassing tissues. The physical and radiological contentions can be abridged as pursues. In a cell, an ion leaves around multiple times more energy than a proton having a similar range. This creates a thick section of ionization, particularly close to the Bragg peak region of the track, causing many 'Double Strand Breaks' and 'Different Damaged Sites', when crossing the DNA contained in the cell core. Thus, the consequences for the cell are subjectively not quite the same as the ones delivered by meagerly ionizing radiations, for example, X-beams and protons. Truth be told, these radiations connect chiefly by implication with the DNA through the production of dynamic radicals that, achieving the DNA, produce for the most part repairable 'Single Strand Breaks'. Consequently, high ionizing ions demonstrate their viability against hypoxic and other shrewd radio-resistant tumors, for example, tumors that need to keep portions of 2–3 multiple times higher in the event that they are to be controlled with either photons or protons [23].

Because of the much larger proportion of direct impact, ions have at the Bragg peak, or many endpoints and conveyed doses, a Radio Biological Effectiveness (RBE) which is around multiple times bigger than the one for X-rays and protons. In the backing off of an ion in tissue this impact winds up essentially when the Linear Energy Transfer (LET), the 'stopping power' in physicist speech, ends up bigger than $\approx 20\,\mathrm{keV/\mu m}$. Because of this generally high 'threshold', protons carry on along their full range– with the exclusion of the last tenth of a millimeter– for all intents and purposes as the electrons which are placed in motion by the high-energy photons created with therapeutic linacs (linear accelerator) and have a LET in the range $0.2–0.5\,\mathrm{keV/\mu m}$. Therefore, the broad radiological and clinical involvement with photon radiation treatment can be connected to proton treatment [25]. The presence or absence of oxygen in cells has a strong impact in the biological effects of radiation and hypoxic tissues are known to be less radiosensitive. This impact– which is communicated regarding Oxygen Enhancement Ratio (OER) – is especially subject to LET. For low LET radiation, for example, X-rays or protons, hypoxia speaks to a genuine limitation factor to the viability of the treatment. For high LET this impact is restricted and carbon ions speak to a powerful apparatus for the treatment of hypoxic radio-resistant tumors [26].

4 Simulations and Experimental Results

4.1 Particles in the Plasma Channel with Electromagnetic Field

To afford a quantitative estimate of magnetic field, we need to take into account a realistic distribution of protons in a nucleus. The magnetic field at point "r" created by two heavy ions moving in the positive or negative z-direction can be calculated using the Lienard-Wiechert potentials as follows [12]:

$$eE(t,r) = \alpha_{em} \sum_a \frac{\left(1 - v_a^2\right)R_a}{R_a^3 \left[1 - \frac{(R_a \times v_a)^2}{R_a^2}\right]^{3/2}} \tag{8}$$

$$eB(t,r) = \alpha_{em} \sum_a \frac{\left(1 - v_a^2\right)(v_a \times R_a)}{R_a^3 \left[1 - \frac{(R_a \times v_a)^2}{R_a^2}\right]^{3/2}} \tag{9}$$

with $R_a = r - r_a(t)$, where sums run over all Z particles in each nucleus, their positions and velocities being r_a and v_a. The magnitude of velocity v_a is determined by the collision energy $\sqrt{S_{NN}}$ as mentioned in Eq. 1 and the particle mass m_p, $v_a^2 = 1 - \left(2m_p/\sqrt{S_{NN}}\right)^2$. These equations are derived in the eikonal approximation, assuming that particles travel in straight lines before and after the scattering. This is a good approximation since baryon stopping is a small effect at high energies [12]. It should be noted that in theoretical physics, the eikonal approximation is an approximate method useful in wave scattering equations which occur in optics, seismology, quantum mechanics, quantum electrodynamics, and partial wave expansion.

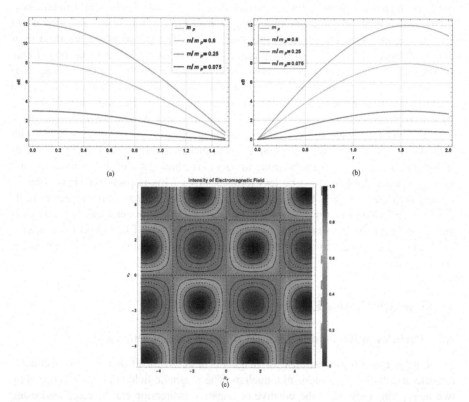

(a)   (b)

(c)

Fig. 3. Proposed Simulations of the absolute value of (a) electric field, (b) magnetic field at $t = 0$, as a function of r, for collision at $\sqrt{S_{NN}} = 100$ GeV, for m_p, $m/m_p = 0.6$, $m/m_p = 0.25$, and $m/m_p = 0.075$, and (c) The intensity Plot of electromagnetic field based on $R_a \times v_a$ variatons.

Figure 3 shows our simulation on the electric and magnetic field components at $t = 0$, at the origin in a collision at $\sqrt{S_{NN}} = 100$ GeV for m_p, $m/m_p = 0.6$, $m/m_p = 0.25$, and $m/m_p = 0.075$. Based on Fig. 3, the actual distribution in a given event shows that there is not only magnetic field along the axes directions, but also other components of electric and magnetic fields. This leads to event-by-event fluctuations of the electromagnetic field. According to Eqs. 8 and 9, the manner of electric and magnetic field for a charged particle is proportional to the particle mass. Hence, Fig. 3 illustrated the electric (Fig. 3(a)) and magnetic (Fig. 3(b)) field for different masses of particle toward proton mass. Based on the results of Fig. 4, as the particle mass, decreases, the electric and magnetic fields decrease and by increasing of particle mass, the electric (Fig. 3(a)) and magnetic (Fig. 3(b)) fields, increase too. Figure 3(c), also demonstrates the Intensity plot of electromagnetic field in terms of R_a and v_a. Based on mentioned plot, the intensity of the electromagnetic field is alternatively as a function of the position and velocity vectors. Therefore, for suitable angle between fore-said vectors the intensity of electromagnetic field is maximum. As mentioned, ions are heavier particles in comparison with Neutrons, Protons, and Pions. So, using ions for cancer treatment in Hadron therapy can strengthen the electromagnetic fields and cause effective and better results in the treatment of cancerous tissues. Also, in amplified electromagnetic field, the particle will be accelerated more, then, the initial gained energy increases, so the energy loss through the matter decreases and the received dose in cancerous target, which, carried by accelerated ion, increases. Also, based on Eq. 2, the ponderomotive force gained by the particle, in an ultra-short laser pulse, is proportional to gradient of the second power of electric field. As a result, heavy ions will get more ponderomotive energy, which causes better acceleration. Further, as shown in Eq. 4, by increasing in an electromagnetic wave, the wave propagation, increases, which causes an increase in plasma density. Finally, this section shows that using heavy ions, can cause better results in Hadron therapy. Energy loss due to the particle accelerator and shoot through patient body, is inversely proportional to X^2 paramiter. The X^2 parameter defined as [12]:

$$X^2 = \frac{h^2 (eB)^2}{4\pi^2 m^6} P^2 \left(Sinh^2 \eta + Cos^2 \varphi\right) \tag{10}$$

where, "h" is the Planck constant, "e" is the electron charge, "m" is the particle mass, "p" is the particle momentum, also, "η" and "φ" are azimuth angles. Figure 4 shows the X^2 parameter in terms of particle mass and azimuth angles, based on Eq. 10. As shown in Fig. 4(a), the variations of X^2 parameter is precipitate for different values of particle mass. Also, as the particle mass increases, the intensity of mentioned parameter decreases. Accordingly, by particle mass increasing, the energy loss decreases. So, using heavy ions will decrease the energy loss in Hadron therapy. Figure 4(b), also shows the front view of mentioned plot for better conception. On the other hand, the initial energy of charged particles, origins from ponderomotive force, and as defined in Eq. 3, the ponderomotive force is proportional to the gradient of laser intensity. So, by decreasing of the energy loss, the secondary energy increases and the effective laser intensity increase too. Therefore, based on obtaining results from fore-said Fig. 4, using heavy ions can decrease the energy loss through matter, in cold plasma perimeter, which is an important approach in Hadron therapy, that means receiving a maximum dose in cancerous target.

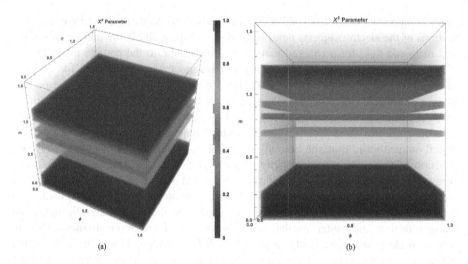

Fig. 4. Proposed Simulations of the X^2 parameter. (a) in terms of particle mass and azimuthal angles, and (b) in the front view of plot.

4.2 Ideal Maxwellian Energy Distribution for Charged Particles

The system of interest (which is ideal cold plasma in this paper) contains a large number of particles (ideal cold plasma constitutive particles), have a Maxwellian velocity distribution, which is the most probable distribution of velocities for a group of particles (plasma constitutive particles) in thermal equilibrium. In one dimension, the Maxwellian velocity distribution function is [13]:

$$f(v)dv = \left(\frac{m}{2\pi kT}\right)^{\frac{3}{2}} 4\pi v^2 e^{\frac{-mv^2}{2kT}} \, dv \tag{11}$$

and, molar mass is defined as:

$$M = mN_a \tag{12}$$

where "m" is the mass of plasma constitutive particles, "k" is Boltzmann's constant, and the width of the distribution is characterized by the temperature "T". Moreover, "v" is the velocity of perimeter particle and "N_a" is Avogadro number. It should be noted that in this section, the purpose of "particles", is the "perimeter constitutive particles". Figure 5, shows the proposed implementation of Maxwell-Boltzmann particle velocity distributions for Helium, Neon, Argon, Xenon, and Ideal Cold Plasma, respectively, based on Eqs. 11 and 12. According to Fig. 5(a), the probability of particle density in higher velocities is major. Also, plasma density strongly dependent on the degree of ionization and collision mean free path of electron- atom impact, voltage which are applying for discharge is another fact. Particles in unit volume is increased (atoms, ions electrons). It means that the mass density is not changed. Plasma density is not combined density of species, but it is density of any species (either electron or ion).

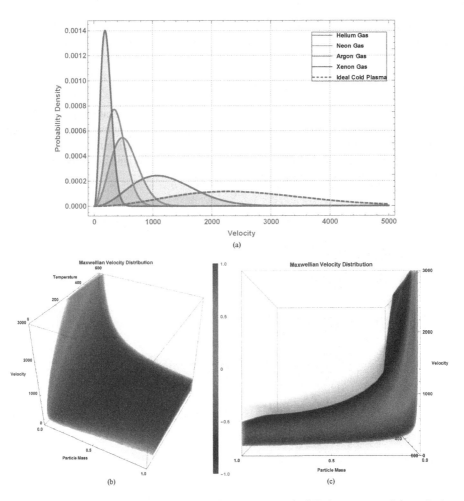

Fig. 5. Proposed Maxwellian Implementations. (a) Maxwell-Boltzmann particle velocity distributions. (b), and (c) Maxwellian velocity distribution in terms of particle mass, velocity, and temperature, respectively.

Therefore, the plasma density is less than the gas density in contents of ion and accordingly it is lighter than gas. Hence, in ideal cold plasma, gaining major values of velocity is probable and according to Eq. 6 and Table 1, the collisions of a fast particle (ion) and ideal cold plasma may cause ionization. Effective ionization during the interaction of an ultra-short laser pulse with matter is one of the most important procedures for accelerating particles [27]. Therefore, ideal Maxwellian cold plasma can cause better particle acceleration in Hadron therapy. According to Fig. 5(b) and (c), the Maxwell–Boltzmann distribution is the chi distribution with a scale parameter estimating speeds in units proportional to the square root of the proportion of temperature and particle mass, respectively. Also, it can be concluded that, however, the density is more probable in light particles, but high-speed values only occur for heavy particles.

Additionally, the thermal equilibrium distribution function for a particle defined as Eq. 13 [27]:

$$f = \frac{\rho}{4\pi m^4 T \beta} e^{-\beta P v} \tag{13}$$

where, "ρ" is the mass density, "m" is particle mass, "T" is temperature; $\beta = 1/T$, "P" is particle momentum, and "v" is the velocity. Figure 6, demonstrates the thermal equilibrium distribution for a particle with mass "m" and velocity "v". As can be concluded from mentioned figure, incretion in particle mass and velocity, can cause reduction in thermal equilibrium distribution.

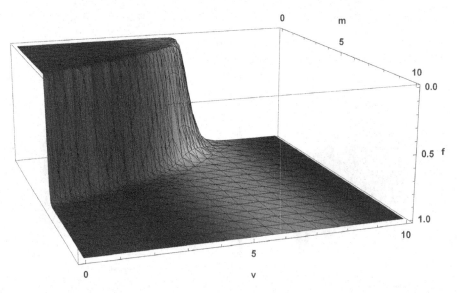

Fig. 6. Proposed Simulation of thermal equilibrium distribution in room temperature, in terms of particle mass and velocity.

5   Conclusion and Prospective Works

The motion of charged particles in an electromagnetic field is of incredible functional significance. The investigation of particle motion in electromagnetic fields is essential and pervades plasma physics. For some biologists and physicists, laser innovation opens an altogether new, special and even great field. Additionally, an ultra-short pulse laser is a powerful instrument for accelerating Hadrons in cancer treatment. The ideal Maxwellian cold plasma is utilized to improve biomedical thoughts for accelerating particles in Hadron treatment. Mentioned approaches are on the transfer of Hadron treatment for treatment of wide range cancer types. Hadron treatment speaks to the significant contribution to the fix of patients and many intriguing advancements, at the front line of science and innovation, are in advancement. Thus, the creators give this paper the point of better cancer treatment by means of Hadron treatment. Based on surveys on Hadron therapy methods done in this paper, ions can provide acceptable results in Hadron therapy because of their amazing properties.

This paper demonstrates that using ions, as heavy particles, can strengthen the electromagnetic fields and causes effective and better results in the treatment of cancerous tissues. Also, in the amplified electromagnetic field, the particle will be accelerated more, then, the initial gained energy increases, so the energy loss through the matter decreases and the received dose in cancerous target, which, carried by accelerating ion, increases. In addition, heavy ions will get more ponderomotive energy, which causes better acceleration. Further, by increasing in electromagnetic wave, the wave propagation, increases, which causes an increase in plasma density. Besides, using heavy ions can decrease the energy loss through matter, in cold plasma perimeter, which is an important approach in Hadron therapy, that means receiving a maximum dose in cancerous target. Moreover, this paper demonstrates the collisions of the ion, as a fast particle and ideal cold plasma may cause ionization, and effective ionization during the interaction of an Ultra-Short Laser Pulse with matter is one of the most important procedures for accelerating particles. Therefore, ideal Maxwellian cold plasma can cause better particle acceleration in Hadron therapy.

The advancement of Hadron treatment methods over late years drives directly to a quickly expanding number of working frameworks which may result in saturation of the quantity of particle facility installations in creating nations in certain years. Nevertheless, there are as yet progressing necessities of ideal techniques for precise cancer treatment. Forthcoming, authors have decided to investigate other parameters which improve the quality of Hadron therapy procedures.

References

1. Chen, Q., et al.: Secular simulation for dynamics of charged particles in the vortex electromagnetic wave beam. In: 2016 IEEE MTT-S International Conference on Numerical Electromagnetic and Multiphysics Modeling and Optimization (NEMO) (2016). https://doi.org/10.1109/nemo.2016.7561609
2. Kählert, H., et al.: Magnetic field effects and waves in complex plasmas. Eur. Phys. J. D (2018). https://doi.org/10.1140/epjd/e2017-80409-x
3. Goldman, L.: Recent Results in Cancer Research. Springer (1966). https://doi.org/10.1007/978-3-642-87268-6
4. Wang, C., et al.: Study of a high-energy proton beam produced by ultra-intense pulse laser. J. Russ. Laser Res. (2017). https://doi.org/10.1007/s10946-017-9653-5
5. Gao, Y., et al.: Design of ultra large normal dispersion ZBLAN photonic crystal fiber and its application in mid-IR ultra short fiber lasers. IEEE Photonics J. (2018). https://doi.org/10.1109/jphot.2018.2872985
6. Shvets, G., et al.: Instabilities of short-pulse laser propagation through plasma channels. Phys. Rev. Lett. (1994). https://doi.org/10.1103/physrevlett.73.3540
7. Pathak, N.C.: Laser Pulse Propagation in Plasmas and its implication on frequency up-shift and electron acceleration (2011)

8. Tanaka, H.: Plasma medical science for cancer therapy: toward cancer therapy using nonthermal atmospheric pressure plasma. IEEE Plasma Sci. Soc. (2014). https://doi.org/10.1109/tps.2014.2353659

9. Rezaee, L.: Design of spread-out Bragg peaks in Hadron therapy with oxygen ions. Rep. Pract. Oncol. Radiother. Elsevier J. (2018). https://doi.org/10.1016/j.rpor.2018.08.004

10. Bulanov, S.V.: Laser ion acceleration for Hadron therapy. In: International Conference Laser Optics. IEEE (2014). https://doi.org/10.3367/ufnr.0184.201412a.1265

11. Sigmund, P.: Particle Penetration and Radiation Effects. Springer, Heidelberg (2006). https://doi.org/10.1007/3-540-31718-x

12. Tuchin, K.: Particle production in strong electromagnetic fields in relativistic heavy-ion collisions. Adv. High Energy Phys. (2013). https://doi.org/10.1155/2013/490495

13. Tu, B.S., et al.: Simulating a low-temperature Maxwellian plasma using SH-HtscEBIT. Phys. Lett. A (2018). https://doi.org/10.1016/j.physleta.2018.06.049

14. Booker, H.G.: Cold Plasma Waves. Springer, Dordrecht (1984). https://doi.org/10.1007/978-94-009-6170-8

15. Keidar, M., et al.: Plasma Engineering. Springer (2018). https://doi.org/10.1016/c2017-0-00107-6

16. Morse, E.: Fusion. Springer (2018). https://doi.org/10.1007/978-3-319-98171-0

17. Belkić, D.: Advances in Quantum Chemistry. Springer, New York (2013). https://doi.org/10.1016/b978-0-12-396455-7.00001-7

18. Abbas, S.A.: Group Theory in Particle, and Hadron Physics. CRS Press, London (2016). ISBN 9781498704663

19. D'Avila Nunes, M.: Hadron Therapy Physics and Simulations. Springer, New York (2013). ISBN 978-1461488989

20. McFarlin, W.A.: Fast Neutron Cancer Therapy with the TAMVEC. IEEE Plasma Sciences Society (1971). https://doi.org/10.1109/tns.1971.4326183

21. Olsen, D.R.: Proton therapy– a systematic review of clinical effectiveness. Radiother. Oncol. (2007). https://doi.org/10.1016/j.radonc.2007.03.001

22. Raju, M.R.: Negative pions in radiotherapy: a brief review. Eur. J. Cancer (1974). https://doi.org/10.1016/0014-2964(74)90177-7

23. Enferadi, M., et al.: "Radiation therapy in the early 21st century: technological advances. Curr. Cancer Ther. Rev. J. (2011). https://doi.org/10.2174/157339411797642614

24. Linstadt, D.E., et al.: Neon ion radiotherapy: results of the phase I/II clinical trial. Int. J. Radiat. Oncol. Biol. Phys. (1991). https://doi.org/10.1016/0360-3016(91)90020-5

25. Amaldi, U., et al.: Accelerators for Hadron Therapy: from Lawrence cyclotrons to linacs. Instrum. Methods Phys. Res. Sect. A Accel. Spectrometers Detect. Assoc. Equip. (2010). https://doi.org/10.1016/j.nima.2010.03.130

26. Tikhonchuk, V.T.: Physics of laser-assisted ion acceleration. Instrum. Methods Phys. Res. Sect. A Accel. Spectrometers Detect. Assoc. Equip. (2010). https://doi.org/10.1016/j.nima.2010.01.051

27. Palmer, C.A.J., et al.: Rayleigh-Taylor instability of an ultrathin foil accelerated by the radiation pressure of an intense laser. J. Phys. Rev. Lett. (2012). https://doi.org/10.1103/physrevlett.108.225002

Author Index

Printed in the United States
By Bookmasters